# The Handbook of Body Psychotherapy & Somatic Psychology

# The Handbook of Body Psychotherapy & Somatic Psychology

Edited by
Gustl Marlock and Halko Weiss
with Courtenay Young and Michael Soth

Foreword by Bessel A. van der Kolk, MD

North Atlantic Books
Berkeley, California

Copyright © 2015 by Gustl Marlock, Halko Weiss, Courtenay Young, and Michael Soth. All rights reserved. No portion of this book, except for brief review, may be reproduced, stored in a retrieval system, or transmitted in any form or by any means—electronic, mechanical, photocopying, recording, or otherwise—without the written permission of the publisher. For information contact North Atlantic Books.

Published by
North Atlantic Books
Berkeley, California

Cover and book design by Suzanne Albertson
Printed in the United States of America

*The Handbook of Body Psychotherapy and Somatic Psychology* is sponsored and published by the Society for the Study of Native Arts and Sciences (dba North Atlantic Books), an educational nonprofit based in Berkeley, California, that collaborates with partners to develop cross-cultural perspectives, nurture holistic views of art, science, the humanities, and healing, and seed personal and global transformation by publishing work on the relationship of body, spirit, and nature.

North Atlantic Books' publications are available through most bookstores. For further information, visit our website at www.northatlanticbooks.com or call 800-733-3000.

Library of Congress Cataloging-in-Publication Data

Handbuch der Körperpsychotherapie. English
  *The handbook of body psychotherapy and somatic psychology* / edited by Gustl Marlock, Halko Weiss, Courtenay Young, Michael Soth.
    p. ; cm.
Includes bibliographical references and index.
ISBN 978-1-58394-841-5 (hard cover)—ISBN 978-1-58394-842-2 (e-book)
I. Marlock, Gustl, editor. II. Weiss, Halko, 1947–, editor. III. Young, Courtenay, editor. IV. Soth, Michael, editor. V. Society for the Study of Native Arts and Sciences, sponsoring body. VI. Title.
  [DNLM: 1. Psychotherapy—methods. 2. Mind-Body Therapies. 3. Psychiatric Somatic Therapies. WM 420]
RC480.5
616.89'14—dc23                                                              2014026736

3  4  5  6  7  8  9   SHERIDAN   20  19  18  17

North Atlantic Books is committed to the protection of our environment. We partner with FSC-certified printers using soy-based inks and print on recycled paper whenever possible.

# CONTENTS

Foreword: Bessel A. van der Kolk    x

Introduction to the American-English Edition    xv
Michael Soth and Courtenay Young

1  Preface: The Field of Body Psychotherapy    1
Gustl Marlock and Halko Weiss

## SECTION I:
## A Historical Overview of Body Psychotherapy

2  Introduction to Section I    20
Gustl Marlock and Halko Weiss

3  The History and Scope of Body Psychotherapy    22
Ulfried Geuter

4  The Influence of Elsa Gindler    40
Judyth O. Weaver

5  The Work of Wilhelm Reich, Part 1: Reich, Freud, and Character    47
Wolf E. Büntig

6  The Norwegian Tradition of Body Psychotherapy: A Golden Age in Oslo    62
Nicholas Bassal with Michael Coster Heller

7  The Work of Wilhelm Reich, Part 2: Reich in Norway and America    71
Courtenay Young with additional material from Wolf Büntig

8  Body Psychotherapy as a Major Tradition of Modern Depth Psychology    83
Gustl Marlock

9  Genealogy of Body Psychotherapy: A Graphic Depiction    102
Heike Langfeld and Dagmar Rellensmann

## SECTION II:
## Fundamental Perspectives of Body Psychotherapy

10  Introduction to Section II    114
Gustl Marlock and Halko Weiss

11  The Primacy of Experiential Practices in Body Psychotherapy    117
Don Hanlon Johnson

12  Neurobiological Perspectives on Body Psychotherapy    126
Christian Gottwald

13  Body Psychotherapy as a Revitalization of the Self: A Depth-Psychological and Phenomenological-Existential Perspective    148
Gustl Marlock

14  The Concept of Energy in Body Psychotherapy    163
Andreas Wehowsky

15  The Organization of Experience: A Systems Perspective on the Relation of Body Psychotherapies to the Wider Field of Psychotherapy    176
Gregory J. Johanson

## SECTION III:
## Psyche and Soma

16  Introduction to Section III    194
Gustl Marlock and Halko Weiss

17  Soma Semantics: Meanings of the Body    197
David Boadella

18  The Neurotic Character Structure and the Self-Conscious Ego    205
Alexander Lowen

19  The Embodied Unconscious    209
Ian J. Grand

20  The Body Unconscious: The Process of Making Conscious: Psychodynamic and Neuroscience Perspectives  219
Marilyn Morgan

21  The Maturation of the Somatic Self  230
Stanley Keleman

22  "Body Schema," "Body Image," and Bodily Experience: Concept Formation, Definitions, and Clinical Relevance in Diagnostics and Therapy  237
Frank Röhricht

23  The Bodily "Felt Sense" as a Ground for Body Psychotherapies  248
Eugene T. Gendlin and Marion N. Hendricks-Gendlin

24  The Body and the Truth  255
Halko Weiss and Michael Harrer

25  Body, Culture, and Body-Oriented Psychotherapies  264
Ian J. Grand

## SECTION IV:
## Somatic Dimensions of Developmental Psychology

26  Introduction to Section IV  274
Gustl Marlock and Halko Weiss

27  Shapes of Experience: Neuroscience, Developmental Psychology, and Somatic Character Formation  277
Marianne Bentzen

28  The Main Variants of Character Theory in the Field of Body Psychotherapy  301
Andreas Sartory with Gustl Marlock and Halko Weiss

29  Early Interaction and the Body: Clinical Implications  305
George Downing

30  Affective-Motor Schemata  322
Andreas Wehowsky

31  Prenatal and Perinatal Psychology: Vital Foundations of Body Psychotherapy  332
Marti Glenn

32  Multiple Levels of Meaning-Making: The First Principles of Changing Meanings in Development and Therapy  345
Ed Tronick and Bruce Perry

33  Pattern and Plasticity: Utilizing Early Motor Development as a Tool for Therapeutic Change  356
Susan Aposhyan

34  Attachment Theory and Body Psychotherapy: Embodiment and Motivation  366
Mark Ludwig

35  The Development of Autonomy from a Body Psychotherapy Perspective  380
Ute-Christiane Bräuer

## SECTION V:
## Methodological Foundations

36  Introduction to Section V  390
Gustl Marlock and Halko Weiss

37  Sensory Self-Reflexivity: Therapeutic Action in Body Psychotherapy  392
Gustl Marlock

38  Consciousness, Awareness, Mindfulness  402
Halko Weiss

39  Bodily Expression and Experience in Body Psychotherapy  411
Ron Kurtz

40  The Experiencing Body  419
Halko Weiss

41  Movement As and In Psychotherapy  426
Christine Caldwell

42  "When Is Now? When Is Now?": Corrective Experiences: With Whom? When? And Where?  436
Albert Pesso

43  On Vitality  444
Michael Randolph

## SECTION VI:
## The Therapeutic Relationship in Body Psychotherapy

44 Introduction to Section VI — 454
Gustl Marlock and Halko Weiss (with Michael Soth)

45 Entering the Relational Field in Body Psychotherapy — 461
William F. Cornell

46 Enhancing the Immediacy and Intimacy of the Therapeutic Relationship through the Somatic Dimension — 471
Richard A. Heckler and Gregory J. Johanson

47 Transference, Countertransference, and Supervision in the Body Psychotherapeutic Tradition — 479
Michael Soth

48 Touch in Body Psychotherapy — 494
Gill Westland

49 The Somatics of Touch — 509
Lisbeth Marcher with Erik Jarlnaes and Kirstine Münster

50 The Empty Voice of the Empty Self: On the Link between Traumatic Experience and Artificiality — 518
Tilmann Moser

## SECTION VII:
## Clinical Aspects of the Therapeutic Process

51 Introduction to Section VII — 530
Gustl Marlock and Halko Weiss

52 The Relevance of Body-Related Features and Processes for Diagnostics and Clinical Formulation in Body Psychotherapy — 532
Frank Röhricht

53 The Role of the Body in Emotional Defense Processes: Body Psychotherapy and Emotional Theory — 543
Ulfried Geuter and Norbert Schrauth

54 The Spectrum of Body Psychotherapeutic Practices and Interventions — 553
Ilse Schmidt-Zimmermann

55 Regression in Body Psychotherapy — 571
Peter Geissler

56 The Unfolding of Libidinous Forces in Body Psychotherapy — 580
Ebba Boyesen and Peter Freudl

57 Risks within Body Psychotherapy — 587
Courtenay Young

## SECTION VIII:
## Functional Perspectives of Body Psychotherapy

58 Introduction to Section VIII — 596
Gustl Marlock and Halko Weiss

59 Energy and the Nervous System in Embodied Experience — 600
James Kepner

60 The Role of the Autonomic Nervous System — 615
Dawn Bhat and Jacqueline Carleton

61 The Role of the Breath in Mind-Body Psychotherapy — 633
Ian Macnaughton with Peter A. Levine

62 Heart, Heart Feelings, and Heart Symptoms — 644
Courtenay Young

63 Dreams and the Body — 652
Stanley Keleman

64 Visual Contact, Facing, Presence, and Expression: The Ocular Segment in Body Psychotherapy — 658
Narelle McKenzie

65 Segmental Holding Patterns of the Body-Mind — 666
Jack Lee Rosenberg and Beverly Kitaen Morse

66 Horizontal Grounding — 675
Angela Belz-Knöferl

67 Vertical Grounding: The Body in the World and the Self in the Body  684
Lily Anagnostopoulou

68 Entering the Erotic Field: Sexuality in Body-Centered Psychotherapy  692
William F. Cornell

## SECTION IX:
## Body Psychotherapeutic Treatment of Specific Disorders

69 Introduction to Section IX  702
Gustl Marlock and Halko Weiss

70 Body Psychotherapy for Severe Mental Disorders  704
Frank Röhricht

71 Body Psychotherapy and Psychosis  717
Guy Tonella

72 Body Psychotherapeutic Treatments for Eating Disorders  724
Sasha Dmochowski, Asaf Rolef Ben-Shahar, and Jacqueline A. Carleton

73 Body Psychotherapy with Narcissistic Personality Disorders  737
Manfred Thielen

74 Vegetotherapy with Psychosomatic Disorders: Functionalism in Practice  748
Xavier Serrano Hortelano

75 Oral Depression  756
Guy Tonella

76 Sensory-Motor Processing for Trauma Recovery  763
Pat Ogden and Kekuni Minton

## SECTION X:
## Some Areas of Application of Body Psychotherapy

77 Introduction to Section X  774
Gustl Marlock and Halko Weiss

78 Body Psychotherapy with Parents, Babies, and Infants  776
Thomas Harms

79 A Return to the "Close Body": Child Somatic Psychotherapy  787
Nicole Gäbler

80 Subsymbolic Processing with an Alexithymic Client  794
John May

81 A Somatic Approach to Couples Therapy  802
Rob Fisher

82 Emotional First Aid  811
Eva R. Reich and Judyth O. Weaver

83 The Use of Body Psychotherapy in the Context of Group Therapy  816
Michael Soth

84 Research in Body Psychotherapy  834
Barnaby B. Barratt

## SECTION XI:
## Interfaces with Other Modalities of Psychotherapy

85 Introduction to Section XI  846
Gustl Marlock and Halko Weiss

86 Dance Therapy  849
Sabine Trautmann-Voigt

87 The Significance of the Body in Gestalt Therapy  863
Wiltrud Krauss-Kogan

88 Somatic Emotional Release Work among Hands-on Practitioners  872
Ilana Rubenfeld with Camilla Griggers

89 Cognitive Behavioral Therapists Discover the Body  883
Serge K. D. Sulz

90 The Positive Management of the Body: A Salutogenic and Transcultural Perspective  891
Nossrat Peseschkian

**SECTION XII:**
**Existential and Spiritual Dimensions of Body-Oriented Psychotherapy**

91 Introduction to Section XII 900
Gustl Marlock and Halko Weiss

92 The Awakened Body: The Role of the Body in Spiritual Development 903
Linda H. Krier and Jessica Moore Britt

93 Existential Dimensions of the Fundamental Character Themes 912
Halko Weiss

94 Body Meditation in the Tibetan Buddhist and Bön Traditions 921
Daniel P. Brown

Index of Names 929
Subject Index 939

# FOREWORD

Bessel van der Kolk, United States

**Bessel A. van der Kolk** is an internationally respected authority on post-traumatic stress and related phenomena, due to his activities as a clinician, researcher, and teacher. His work integrates developmental, biological, psychodynamic, and interpersonal aspects into the treatment of the effects of trauma, and his book *Psychological Trauma* offered the first integral perspective on this topic. Beyond that, he and his colleagues have published extensively on this research subject, particularly in the areas of clinical manifestations, cognition, memory, and psycho-biology.

Dr. van der Kolk is a former president of the International Society for Traumatic Stress, a professor of psychiatry at the Boston University Medical School, and the head physician of the Trauma Center at the Justice Resource Institute in Brookline, Massachusetts. He has taught at universities around the world, including Harvard University, and has been a main presenter at several Body Psychotherapy conferences.

Our relationship to our own body determines how we make our way in the world (Damasio, 1999; Panksepp, 1996; Llinas, 2001)—our physical sensations and body movements are the foundations of our sense of who we are. With all other animal species, we share built-in physical mechanisms for survival: "fight or flight" strategies are universal and primitive defensive behaviors. These responses are not thought out; they are instinctually orchestrated by the reptilian brain and initiated even before we become aware of them. When neither fight nor flight is able to ensure safety, animals become immobilized. Under extreme conditions of threat, similar behaviors can be observed in people, as well.

Biological measures of the effects of stress in lower animals, whose behavior can be studied in extensive detail in the laboratory, are traditionally focused on survival. However, humans are different from either snakes or rats: together with other primates we are intensely social creatures who depend for our survival and sustenance on our relation with the "troop," our social network—a network that changes in shape and configuration throughout the course of the human life cycle. One of the most important effects of stress in humans is how it is affected by the position of the individual within the group.

The quality of life, for human beings, depends on our capacity to engage effectively and collaborate with other members of our species. Humans, like other primates, fundamentally barely exist as individuals—from the cradle to the grave we live in troops, and all our actions (and thoughts) are defined by the social context within which we live.

The essence of our lives—what is dangerous, safe, or satisfying—is all fundamentally defined by our relationships within the social realm, the quality of our connections with other members of our species. These connections, while experienced as belonging to the realm of "self and other," have a deep physical foundation: we have little to say over whether our organisms will perceive a particular sensory stimulus as safe, dangerous, or exciting, and we have little conscious control over whether, in response to those stimuli, our bodies freeze, tense up, space out, or mobilize for a fight, or whether we open up and engage. These decisions are automatically made by our subcortical brain, which immediately transforms sensory input into physical reactions.

One of the fundamental tasks of our brains is to create a map of the world in order to guide us in how to go about finding food, mates, shelters, and companionship. This map is constructed entirely on the basis of prior experience. Routinely following these internal road maps allows us to deal with any new situations in old remembered ways. Experience, particularly in the first few years of life, profoundly shapes what this map looks like, including our relationship to ourselves. Feeling loved and secure leaves us with a harmonious relationship toward our body, its needs, and its capacities—free to explore the world. In contrast, encounters with abuse, neglect, and domination render us physically powerless, frozen, constricted, immobilized, or activated and offensive—trauma and disrupted attachment patterns cause people to lose their way in the world.

Being totally dependent on interactive caregiving systems, particularly early in the life cycle, forces humans to develop far-reaching capacities to adapt to their caregiving environment. These adaptations fulfill a useful function in the context of dysfunctional caregiving systems, but they often persist well after they cease to be useful. In fact, in new environments, these old patterns often interfere with achieving personal fulfillment.

This handbook explores the variety of those adaptations and their long-term consequences. Whatever the adaptation, early confrontations with fear, threat, and abandonment leave people with boundary problems: trying to determine what is safe inside and outside, and what needs to be avoided or attacked. The legacy of having been physically trapped, unable to protect oneself, or caught in conflicting expectations is expressed in bodily reactions such as chronic physical discomfort and illness, unmodulated emotions, and failure to fully, *physically and mentally,* engage with the present moment.

Disconnections from caregivers and other overwhelming experiences alter people's relationship to their bodies in ways that make them constricted, uptight, helpless, disconnected, hurt, on edge, frantic, and at odds with themselves and their environment. In order to regain a sense of control over one's physical reactions and to focus on whatever needs to be done, it is necessary to mobilize the body. Unless we *physically* come to grips with the remnants of fear and defensiveness lodged in our physical reality, the imprints of the past may permanently alter whether we feel at home in our bodies and may interfere with our openness to engage in new experiences, and learn from them.

The exploding interest in working with these bodily states has occurred simultaneously with three major scientific developments that support how fundamental bodily function is for effective operation of the human organism: (1) the explosion of research on the effects of trauma upon the formation of the human psyche; (2) the evolution in the neurosciences that made it possible to visualize and track what happens in the brain when people feel, think, and sense; and (3) attachment research—which has discovered how the quality of attunement between people in general, and between mothers and babies in particular, determines how people exist in and move through the world in the long term—has had a major impact on our understanding of how brains develop.

All together these developments point to three fundamental tenets:

1. Physical sensations and action patterns are the very foundation of consciousness and the sense of self.
2. Humans, like all primates, are first and foremost social animals whose biology constantly interacts—as illustrated by how mothers regulate the physiological states of their babies (and vice versa); how lovers profoundly affect the physical (and thereby emotional) states of their partners; and the physiological comfort we feel when we see the face, or hear the voice, of someone we love and trust.
3. Experiences of trauma, including helplessness and physical paralysis, interfere with the subsequent capacity to take focused action. This is accompanied by physiological shifts in the brain and body and results in people losing touch with their internal workings and their sense of physical purpose.

These advances in understanding about the makeup of the personality have helped to start integrating the various treatments that utilize physical sensations and muscular actions to let go of patterns of fear, helplessness, and numbing that were once established to foster survival and maintenance of the attachment bond.

Mainstream psychotherapy helps people by providing a helpful presence ("relationship") as an alternative to the original formative relationships that may contain previous experiences of unbearable terror and helplessness, and can provide insight into the origins of a client's misery, while the client is feeling understood and supported. When done right, such understanding and support can give people the courage to face realities that are intolerable when faced alone or as a child, and help give voice to the unspeakable. However, although talking and figuring out why one feels bad can be a helpful first step to understand what is going on, it is unlikely to change fundamentally how one physically experiences oneself.

Mainstream medicine tries to help people feel better by prescribing medications that alter the sensitivity of various brain structures. However, our research has demonstrated that familiarizing oneself with one's internal sensations and experimenting with changing them provide vastly greater relief and positive therapeutic outcome than either medicines or understanding alone (van der Kolk et al., 2007).

Many cultures have ancient and elaborate traditions, such as Yoga, Tai Chi, meditation, and Qigong, that emphasize working with bodily states to affect mental function. All around the world, people have always dealt with stress and misery by singing, drumming, and engaging in rhythmic physical activities. In Western psychology, paying attention to and working with bodily states is a relatively recent phenomenon. Little systematic attention was paid to this issue prior to the work of Wilhelm Reich, less than a century ago.

Confrontation with physical dysfunctions and the possibility of healing through movement, touch, and sensory integration are so obvious that various principles keep being rediscovered by different individuals, often individuals with backgrounds in dance and massage, more than in academic psychology or medicine, often with no training, and sometimes little interest in the scientific method. Because of a lack of a common language, and an absence of valid ways of measuring outcome, there has been too little communication or cross validation between various schools of Body Psychotherapy.

Many of these creative individuals are represented in this handbook, which constitutes a critical attempt to begin the creation of some unified concepts and elements of a common language, issues that are essential for this field to emerge from its prescientific phase. There is an urgent need to determine systematically which method is most effective for what population; what the critical therapeutic ingredients are; and what modifications would be most useful for different clients.

This handbook promises to be an important step toward helping to integrate the fragmentation of this field that consists of numerous different methods that are in need of a greater appreciation of commonalities and differences. It attempts to give voice (a left-brain activity) to the sensations, emotions, and impulses that are essentially beyond words (right-brain issues), and that, until now, have largely eluded analysis with conventional methods. What unites these various methods is the common notion that, in order to change, people need to have *physical* experiences that directly contradict or replace past feelings of helplessness, frustration, and terror.

The rational mind is vulnerable and goes "offline" when people are terrified. It tends to stop functioning properly when someone is reminded of terrifying stimuli related to the past. This process automatically triggers emotions and behaviors that were originally utilized to cope with threat. Psychotherapy has historically relied on analyzing the source of the problem in order to produce psychological change, or has set up programs to help to alter people's behavior by encouraging them to behave differently.

There has been a presumption of a close, if not causal, relationship between insight and change. However, there is little relation between *knowing* and changing: having insight into the source of a problem does not in any way guarantee being able to fix it. Neuroscience research shows that there is little connection between the various brain centers involved in understanding, planning, and emotion—we simply are not capable of understanding our way out of our feelings—whether they are feelings of love, fear, deprivation, or hate. In fact, our logical selves tend to run behind our emotional urges and may primarily function to rationalize our loves and hates—our minds are much like talk shows on television, trying to explain the day's events after the sun is down.

Other people can point out to us how useless or irrational it is to continue to behave in a certain way, or feel strongly about something that happened long ago. With the "best of intentions" they urge us to let bygones be bygones (unless they are members of the same injured ethnic group or family faction). The net result is just that we feel stupid and learn to keep our feelings to ourselves. Insight and understanding frequently build only strong upper lips.

In contrast to this understanding, paying close attention to one's internal life, to the flow of physical sensations, feelings, internal images, and patterns of thought, in short, working with the "felt sense" (Gendlin, 1976)—the ebb and flow of inner experience—can make an enormous difference to the way we feel and act. This is particularly relevant when people need to free themselves from the repetitive emotions of rage, terror, helplessness, and despair that are often the leftovers from past insults and injuries.

The rational brain is geared to the outside world, and not inward. The only pathway in the brain from the conscious self to the emotional brain, i.e., the only way that people can effectively influence how they feel, runs from areas in the conscious mind that convey the sense of being in touch with oneself and one's bodily states (the medial prefrontal cortex and insula) to the emotional centers of the brain (centering on the amygdala), then to the arousal centers, and finally to the hormonal and muscular output centers. This means that working with deep sensations and feelings has the potential of attaining a sense of internal equilibrium and balance. This appears to be the only pathway toward gaining a sense of being the master of one's own psyche—of being in charge of one's life.

Most "psychological" problems are rooted within our relationship to ourselves, to our internal sensations that have become blunted, exaggerated, or "stuck." Hence, the process of psychological change is fundamentally concerned with regaining a healthy relationship to our *internal* feeling states. Whereas feelings of panic, constriction, and uptightness usually start when our organism is unable to cope with overwhelming realities—and when there is nobody who can take over for us when we no longer are able to cope—the persistence of the associated urges and sensations often results in illness. People are naturally more vulnerable when they are young and when they are developing any such disorganized relations with themselves and they are most dependent on well-attuned inputs being received from others when making their way in the world.

When something is threatening and disorganizing enough, such as being assaulted or witnessing some horrendous scene (or even simply being chronically ignored or mistreated), people can become so disorganized that it can dramatically alter their biology and their sense of themselves. When that happens, the way that they learned to cope in childhood with threats to safety and abandonment may become a chronic pattern as an adult that no longer serves any useful function—they become *physically* stuck in the past, and they are unable to mobilize their *physical* organisms to fully engage in the present.

When people give up on being in charge of their lives by ignoring what they feel, they become internally frozen and start expecting others to tell them what they feel (or should be feeling) and what to do. Unfortunately, friends, and even therapists, may fall into the trap and start to give advice to such "helpless" people about what they could or should do. This, of course, rarely works, because frozen "bodies" not only cannot generate their own action patterns, they also have trouble following the suggestions of others. These "helpful" interventions usually end up in "irrational" explosions of frustration—by the advisee, or from the, now helpless, "guiding lights" of the friends or therapists.

With the recent stunning advances in medical technology, there has been a correspondingly profound impoverishment of traditional medical practice. One manifestation of this is the increasingly almost exclusive reliance upon invasive procedures and chemicals to alleviate so-called "illness." There has been a "medicalization" of normal "life" problems, which can disempower us and take us away from our selves.

However, without being able to relate to one's body as the container of one's self-experience, true integration, empowerment, and thus healing is not possible. Only when we are able to quiet down, get in touch with ourselves, and master our inner physical experiences, can we regain the capacity to use our normal resources, as well as speech and language, to convey to others what we feel, know, and "remember." After regaining a physical sense of one's self and befriending one's inner experience, some people may choose to tell the story of what got them in trouble, while others decide to just go on with their lives. Body Psychotherapy helps with both these processes. I can therefore strongly recommend this handbook.

## Acknowledgment

I wish to acknowledge the many contributions of Peter Levine, PhD, to the concepts expressed in this foreword.

## References

Damasio, A. (1999). *The feeling of what happens.* New York: Harcourt Brace.

Gendlin, E. (1976). *Focusing.* New York: Guilford Press.

Llinas, R. R. (2001). *The I of the vortex: From neurons to self.* Cambridge, MA: MIT Press.

Panksepp, J. (1996). *Affective neuroscience.* New York: Oxford University Press.

van der Kolk, B., Spinazzola, J., Blaustein, M., Hopper, J., Hopper, E., Korn, D., & Simpson, W. (2007). A randomized clinical trial of EMDR, fluoxetine and pill placebo in the treatment of PTSD: Treatment effects and long-term maintenance. *Journal of Clinical Psychiatry, 68,* 37–46.

# Introduction to the American-English Edition

**Michael Soth and Courtenay Young,
United Kingdom**

This handbook was envisaged and originally commissioned in 2003, and approximately half the chapters were originally written in German, with the other half being written in English, these being the main operative languages of most of the contributors. The English chapters were then all translated into German, and the result was a massive 100 chapters and about 1,000 pages, which was eventually published as *Handbuch der Körperpsychotherapie* by Schattauer in 2006, for the German-speaking market. This handbook has sold exceptionally well (the first two printings sold out), and it was also received very well throughout the profession, prompting efforts toward completing the corresponding English version that had always been intended: with many of the original German chapters now being translated into English.

With Body Psychotherapy increasingly constituting an international—if not global—community of practitioners, an English-language (and updated) edition was also sorely needed, as no other book exists that is as comprehensive and as inclusive of the multitude of approaches and schools within Body Psychotherapy. However, putting all of this together has taken a lot longer than we would have liked or imagined.

We, the additional editors, Courtenay Young and Michael Soth, were invited to join the original two editors, Gustl Marlock and Halko Weiss, specifically for this edition. Courtenay has exceptional editorial skills and a flair for the English language, and Michael is fluent in both English and German: both are also very well-established and published Body Psychotherapists. Working as a group, we have cut out some chapters, updated lots of references, and included some new chapters, drawn particularly from the United States, so that this handbook is now definitively a "proper" second edition, and is therefore *not* just a simple translation of the original German edition.

We have also been given a wonderful opportunity to revise and polish the resulting manuscript. What you have now—finally, in your hands—is the end result of overcoming considerable challenges and of an intercontinental collaboration, especially between many people, mainly in North America, in many different European countries, and in South Africa, Australia, and New Zealand. We thank everyone for their contributions and for their trust and enthusiasm.

We also hope that this handbook will spark a deepened understanding and cross-fertilization, not only between the different, sometimes very distinct, branches of Body Psychotherapy itself, but also with the rest of the field of psychotherapy and its community of practitioners, and that it will help to address (and lay to rest) some of the lingering misconceptions and misunderstandings that have historically existed about Body Psychotherapy.

One clarification is needed "up front" with regard to terminology: "Body Psychotherapy" is professionally well defined and accepted in Europe, via its European association (the EABP), in existence since 1988, and also through its scientific validation as a mainstream within psychotherapy by the European Association for Psychotherapy (EAP). The equivalent terminology used in the United States is both "Body Psychotherapy," via the US association (USABP), and, more academically, "Somatic Psychology": and so we have expanded the title of this handbook accordingly. The two main Body Psychotherapeutic associations (EABP and

USABP), while being entirely separate, also cooperate together very well, and now co-produce the *International Body Psychotherapy Journal* (www.ibpj.org), in which further peer-reviewed articles, research, and more recent material on this particular type of psychotherapy can be found.

There are also some transatlantic differences. In Europe, through the work of the EAP, there are now quite long-standing attempts to establish psychotherapy as an independent profession in its own right: separate from, but parallel to, Clinical Psychology. In this context, Body Psychotherapy can therefore be seen as a significant "mainstream" within this emerging profession. However, this concept is relatively "alien" in America, where psychotherapy is seen much more as an "activity" practiced by certain mental health professionals: psychiatrists, psychologists, licensed social workers, family therapists, etc. Indeed, in many US states, the actual practice of psychotherapy is statutorily restricted to these professions.

There is also a much greater emphasis in the United States on the study of psychology (an academic qualification) being "almost" sufficient for the practice of psychotherapy, whereas in Europe most of the psychotherapeutic trainings are much more experientially oriented and modality based, and not necessarily linked to a university degree. So, when reading this handbook, please see the concept of "psychotherapy," and thus the field (study and practice) of Body Psychotherapy, as an entity, reasonably separate from the statutory politics, academic distinctions, and professional requirements of (particularly) psychology, psychotherapy, and also psychiatry. Interestingly, in this context, the USABP is now starting the process toward establishing a Somatic Psychology division of the American Psychological Association (APA), in order to help clarify what is different and unique about Body Psychotherapy in relation to other psychotherapies.

The whole field of Body Psychotherapy itself is also changing—quite rapidly. So, it may also be significant to note what has happened in the field of Body Psychotherapy over the last ten years or so, particularly since the first edition of this handbook was originally conceived and written.

## Neuroscience

The expanding field of neuroscience has confirmed many of the basic assumptions that have underpinned Body Psychotherapeutic theory and practice for decades, lending the discipline a much-deserved boost of credibility and interest. Although some of this development was under way at the turn of the millennium, and was reflected in the German edition, since then we have seen much stronger and even more far-reaching corroborations. These have been taken up enthusiastically by the discipline: most recent conferences have been replete with presentations involving neuroscience (especially as it relates to early bonding and development attachment theory, but also in relation to trauma and other areas).

Based as it used to be more on holistic intuition, rather than scientific research, and grounded in experiential knowledge as distilled from our own therapeutic processes (both as clients and as therapists), the field of Body Psychotherapy has benefited from this unexpected "scientific" impetus toward its coming-of-age. We are now actually being able to see (literally) some of the massive and subtle complexity of the links between the mind and the body: the psyche and the soma. This—of course—still does not properly or completely "evidence" the practice of Body Psychotherapy, but it provides a very solid basis upon which we now need to demonstrate—as perhaps no other psychotherapy really can—the efficacy and effectiveness of psychotherapeutic work, with a distinctive orientation toward the body.

Although there are problems arising from too eagerly importing the underlying paradigms of neuroscience into a practice that hinges on subjectivity and intersubjectivity, there has been an extraordinary shift throughout the field of the "talking therapies" toward recognizing the significance of the concept of (at least) embodiment, but also of many other body-oriented concepts, like the "storing" of trauma within the body and the importance of mindfulness practice. We can only welcome these developments.

As can be expected, however, while translation of these insights into practice has been slow and awkward—

amorphous notions regarding the "quality of relationship" and "implicit relational knowing" abound throughout the field, so the actual "engagement with the body" has been somewhat haphazard—frequently it has been grafted onto an existing approach, rather incongruously, as an additional "body-oriented technique"—like EMDR and "mindfulness practice" suddenly becoming "acceptable" within Cognitive Behavioral Therapy (CBT).

It is in this historical watershed situation that Body Psychotherapy and Somatic Psychology—and this handbook—can make a very significant contribution. As a community of experienced practitioners, we have a well-established canon of both theoretical models and effective techniques, grounded in decades of accumulated practice as embodied, self-reflective practitioners—and it is this track record of practice, training, and teaching from generation to generation that has built up a wealth of skills and ways of working that, we believe, are now both available and also urgently needed by the rest of the field of psychotherapy.

## Relationality

Relationality has been one of the growing edges of the field of psychotherapy, and has now become something of a "buzzword," although, upon closer inspection, the apparently growing consensus that "it's the *relationship* that matters" breaks down into the same traditional schisms and dogmatisms that have characterized the field for a century, with each tradition within psychotherapy tending to claim its form of relationality for itself. The implicit assumption is that the particular "relational" style within that modality—which they have been pursuing all along—is the quintessence of therapeutic relating.

However, this stance fails to acknowledge that there are an established (if we take an unbiased, phenomenological look at the field as it is) multiplicity of relational modalities and therefore many different kinds of therapeutic relatedness. There is not just *one* kind of therapeutic relating, but a pluralistic diversity of different—and sometimes contradictory—ways of relating that all seem to "work" at different times, in different situations, and with different therapists and clients, and *all* these therefore need to be acknowledged as valid, at least in principle.

Like other humanistic and integrative traditions, Body Psychotherapy has taken on board these challenges and opportunities in varying degrees—a discourse that is steadily evolving, especially fairly recently—and this trend has therefore been mentioned, but has not been fully reflected on, in this handbook.

## Mindfulness

As Body Psychotherapists, we have long been practicing something very similar to mindfulness—mindful awareness of bodily dynamics, and also encouraging this in our clients—certainly since the mid-1960s. However, early Body Psychotherapists never properly addressed the component of the client's mental capacities, but this emphasis is now changing. We have also been using mindfulness and present-moment awareness as essential tools in therapy, as therapists, to "resonate" somatically with our clients and to reflect inwardly on what might be happening in their bodies, using our own mindful awareness of our bodies. Three significant examples of this are: that (i) Ron Kurtz built mindfulness practice into the essence of Hakomi; (ii) David Boadella has long been writing about and incorporating "somatic resonance" into Biosynthesis; and (iii) Ilana Rubenfeld practices a form of "mindful touch." Many other Body Psychotherapists—as you will discover—also use various aspects of their own forms of mindfulness practice, both personally and therapeutically.

However, especially over the last ten years, we have also seen the growth of more traditional mindfulness practice spread out from its several long-standing Buddhist traditions to forms that have recently become "adopted" (or even "claimed") by CBT: it is now much more widespread, as it also happens to be a very effective non-pharmaceutical technique (or treatment) for the reduction of anxiety.

Body Psychotherapy lends itself particularly well to various forms of mindfulness practice (as there is a focus on the body from the beginning), plus there is a certain degree of skepticism about relying only on one's cognitive capabilities, like reflection. However, mindfulness practice goes way beyond being very aware of, and alert toward, the present moment and bodily experience, as—beyond that—it subtly trains the mind (psyche) to develop new states of consciousness and different levels of awareness. It is an ongoing practice, both to develop these specific capacities, and also to apply them and their qualities to a greater awareness of self.

## Globalization

The global discourse within the field of Body Psychotherapy over recent decades—restricted as it has been, of course, by language barriers—has been somewhat haphazard, and has been based largely on the personal connections between international trainers and in certain countries through a series of international conferences (mainly on both sides of the Atlantic), or through students training abroad and bringing their learning back home. This has had a somewhat limiting effect such that the geographic spread of Body Psychotherapy has remained restricted to particular schools being known and favored in particular countries. The integration *between* the different schools has happened mainly at the various international Body Psychotherapeutic conferences, particularly those biannual ones organized by the EABP, and the triannual International Scientific Committee (ISC) Body Psychotherapeutic conferences, alternating on each side of the Atlantic. These developments, integrations, and amalgamations between the concepts, ideas, and practices of the various schools of Body Psychotherapy are also helping to consolidate the field and to create more of a "collective" view about Body Psychotherapy: epitomized in a "forum" of different Body Psychotherapeutic training organizations within the structure of EABP.

The field of Body Psychotherapy—to judge by such recent conferences—seems determined to maintain its diversity, even at the price of a fairly low overall coherence, and thus its consequent lack of a well-defined, recognizable profile in the public domain.

Although it still struggles a bit to differentiate itself clearly and publicly from "bodywork" and other allied complementary therapies, the field of Body Psychotherapy and Somatic Psychology has not yet made any great efforts to develop a common "brand" or image, with the public seeing the different schools and orientations of Body Psychotherapy as somewhat distinct and unrelated therapeutic approaches, rather than as all operating under an identifiable shared umbrella. This has had both advantages and disadvantages, but we hope that this handbook will help to set the tone for the future.

Notwithstanding these issues, limitations, and challenges, we can say overall that Body Psychotherapy—in its rich and somewhat-fragmented diversity—is increasingly well established, is becoming much more recognized, and is also—as can be seen—steadily expanding its scientific basis with studies in both efficacy and effectiveness.

Owing to Body Psychotherapy's theoretical and therapeutic successes and its enhanced profile, the paradigmatic boost by neuroscience, and a general cultural shift toward holistic and systemic perspectives across all kinds of disciplines, attention to the complexities of the mind-body connection is becoming increasingly fashionable, and all kinds of different therapies and therapists are now attempting to jump on this particular bandwagon.

Recent initiatives by the USABP to collate an international database of body-oriented approaches have seen a rush by many trainers and practitioners to become included. Having struggled for recognition by the mainstream professions, and, for many years, having operated with an attitude that welcomes and includes "all comers," the question is now shifting toward defining what might be the "proper" boundaries of the field or discipline of Body Psychotherapy: i.e., what is (or should be) included in a body-oriented type of psychotherapy (whatever its origins)? Is it enough simply to graft a few body-oriented techniques onto a traditional "talking therapy," or to include a psychological (possibly Gestalt) perspective in what is essentially a bodywork practice? The answer is a definitive "No!" Body Psychotherapy is—as we hope you will discover—something much more profound, and it also contains a meta-level of both theoretical and practical concepts and orientations.

Nowadays, we also find that the various overlaps between, say, Body Psychotherapy and other psychotherapies are becoming much less extraordinary and more frequent and (hopefully) much more cooperative. We can learn much from each other—if we are all open and willing to do so.

We have not quite yet reached the point of being able to run "conversion courses," so that (for example) a Gestalt Psychotherapist, or a Psychodynamic Psychotherapist can successfully "add on" the necessary competencies of a Body Psychotherapist—but we are possibly not that far away from this point.

In the face of all these challenges that might cause the wealth and the wisdom of the Body Psychotherapeutic tradition to become dispersed and diluted, this handbook is also a milestone. Nothing else exists like this global, fairly comprehensive collection of writings—managing to integrate and include the multitude of different schools and thus delineating the underlying basics of the different approaches; nothing else even resembling it has so far been attempted. We hope that it will make a productive and lasting contribution to the further development of the field.

Maybe the feedback from our readers, not just (we hope) Body Psychotherapists, but anyone interested in this fascinating field, will also help us to move forward. We are exposing ourselves to external comment and reflection, which we welcome. We therefore hope that you really enjoy this new edition, that it benefits your understanding of both our world and your world—as you also have bodies—and that you can use the extensive references to further your reading in, and deepen your understanding of, this very interesting field.

In conclusion, the original editors of the German edition must also be congratulated for several significant achievements: to draw together such a wide variety of approaches and practitioners, and to both embrace and to select from their diversity, requires a deep and nonpartisan immersion in the field. It depends mostly on long-standing personal connections with the representatives of the various schools and with both the "elders" and the current practitioners in the field. And not just *any* connection will do: a "good-enough" connection is needed to make such collaboration workable. In view of the traditional fragmentation of the field, this is a remarkable achievement.

Associated with this was the challenge of negotiating with some contributors to avoid using some of their personal predilections so as to prevent them from using this opportunity to profile their own particular approach. The original editors selected the authors, not only for their recognized specialties, but also for their wider contributions to the field, and then insisted that they address the various topics and themes fairly comprehensively, and in as nonpartisan a fashion as possible, to do justice to the overall tenor of the handbook. Arguably, they have succeeded in extracting the best from the large number of contributors, in terms of each author's expertise in the field. Sadly, in the intervening decade between the first and second editions, we regret that some of these original authors have since passed away.

Some readers might also wonder why there are still so many German authors in this edition. This is partly because Body Psychotherapy has had a longer and deeper tradition (including in the academic realm) in German-speaking countries than anywhere else, and partly because body-oriented therapies have been included in most hospital-based treatments for many years; there are also uniquely many "psycho-somatic" hospitals in Germany.

In retrospect, the structure of the handbook was also very well thought out and comprehensive, and has stood the test of time well, since the plans were formulated for the original German edition. Although some chapters have been dropped and several new ones written, the overall shape of the handbook has remained largely unchanged. The sections and chapters read well in sequence—although realistically, most readers will probably use this handbook more as a reference manual, but hopefully also as a treasure trove with which to engage selectively, and with which to learn and delight from.

## Acknowledgments

We would like to extend our great appreciation to the Deutsche Gesellschaft für Körperpsychotherapie (DGK)

[German Association for Body Psychotherapy] for their very generous and unstinting financial support, particularly for the translation of nearly half the chapters from German into English. This edition would just not have been possible without that support.

We have also received some financial support—but also particularly help with advertising and publicity, contacts, and encouragement—from the European Association for Body Psychotherapy (EABP).[1] The EABP and the United States Association for Body Psychotherapy (USABP)[2] form the two main pillars—the essential basis—of our professional "family"; there is a really good collegial feeling, and many of the chapters' authors are members of one or the other of these two great professional associations.

A lot of encouragement (and some advertising space) has also been extended from the *International Body Psychotherapy Journal*:[3] Therefore, we would like to thank its editor, Jacqueline Carleton, and her staff, as well as the USABP's *Somatic Psychotherapy Today*[4] and its editor, Nancy Eichhorn, for their enthusiasm for this edition of the handbook. We also look forward to their forthcoming reviews.

Finally, our main contact and editor at North Atlantic Books, Erin Wiegand, has been very generous with her advice, support, and especially her flexibility with deadlines. Working with her (albeit via transatlantic emails) has been a great pleasure, and we would like to thank her and all the other folks at North Atlantic Books[5] who have made the eventual publication of this edition possible.

---

1 www.eabp.org
2 www.usabp.org
3 www.ibpj.org
4 www.usabp.org/somatic-psychotherapy-today-2
5 www.northatlanticbooks.com

# 1
## Preface: The Field of Body Psychotherapy

Gustl Marlock, Germany, and Halko Weiss, United States

Translation by Warren Miller

**Gustl Marlock,** MA Educational Science (Paedagogy), is a fully licensed Psychological Psychotherapist and Child and Adolescent Psychotherapist. He has completed a range of trainings in Biodynamic and Unitive Body Psychotherapy, Group Analysis, Gestalt, Psychodynamic, and Positive Psychotherapy. He draws on more than thirty-five years of experience and an extensive knowledge of a wide variety of therapeutic traditions, cultures, languages, and methods.

He is the director of the German training program in Unitive and Integrative Body Psychotherapy, an approach founded by Jacob Stattman that systematically integrates Body Psychotherapy with Psychodynamic and Existential Psychotherapy. He also is a lecturer, training therapist, and supervisor for Psychodynamic Psychotherapy and an advisory board member at various academies for Psychodynamic Psychotherapy. He has contributed numerous publications to the discourse on the history, metatheory, and methodology of Body Psychotherapy and Psychodynamic Psychotherapy.

**Halko Weiss,** PhD, is a clinical psychologist and a lecturer for the Bavarian Licensing Board for Psychotherapists and for ZIST Academy, a licensing school for psychotherapists. He is a co-founder of the Hakomi Institute in Boulder, Colorado, working closely with Ron Kurtz for many years and playing an important role in the development of the Hakomi Method and its educational materials. He also founded the Hakomi Institute of Europe and continues to provide new directions for the Hakomi Institute by developing new programs, such as a training course in interpersonal skills, called HEART (Hakomi Embodied and Aware Relationships Training).

Halko teaches Body Psychotherapy at the University of Marburg, and couples therapy in association with the University Hospital in Tübingen, Germany. He is the initiator of and a researcher for the largest multicenter scientific research project to date on the efficacy of outpatient Body Psychotherapy that was conducted in cooperation with the University of Tübingen. Halko is also the author of numerous scientific publications contributing to the discourse on contemporary Body Psychotherapy.

Among the list of his publications are five books: *To the Core of Your Experience*, with D. Benz (Luminas Press); *Handbuch der Körperpsychotherapie* [Handbook of Body Psychotherapy], with G. Marlock (Schattauer, Stuttgart); *Das Achtsamkeitsbuch* [The Mindfulness Book], with M. Harrer and T. Dietz (Klett-Cotta, Stuttgart); the best-selling *Das Achtsamkeitsübungsbuch* [The Mindfulness Practice Book], with M. Harrer and T. Dietz (Klett-Cotta, Stuttgart); and *Slowing Down and Waking Up: The Hakomi Method of Mindfulness-Centered Somatic Psychotherapy,* with G. Johanson and L. Monda (Norton, New York). A book on Common Factors in Mindfulness is planned for publication by Schattauer in 2015.

Aside from his work as a teacher of Body Psychotherapy and as a couples therapist, he is a frequent trainer and coach for corporate executives. He was originally trained as a Rogerian and Behavioral Psychotherapist and began his career in private practice, as well as a lecturer at the University of Hamburg and as a consultant to social service providers.

Body Psychotherapy has recently emerged from its somewhat shadowy existence at the exotic margins of psychotherapy in the post-war era to become a respected movement well-established within the mainstream of modern psychotherapy. Despite skepticism that was leveled against it in the past, the psychotherapeutic field of today cannot be properly imagined without it. Interest in the body within the context of psychotherapy is now increasingly obvious. If one, for example, recalls the topics and highlights of recent depth-psychological, psychoanalytic, or cognitive behavioral conferences, an interesting trend can be discerned: along with neurobiology and mindfulness, the topic of the body in psychotherapy is one that is now receiving particular attention. This growing presence in the clinical field and its increasing reflection in the academic literature are two more indicators that help consolidate the growing status of Body Psychotherapy. Even if recognition by scientific and professional policymakers lags somewhat behind this development, it is highly likely that the current interest in the reintegration of the body into psychotherapy will continue to grow.

## The Growing Significance of the Body

Expansion of knowledge in a variety of areas has furthered and supported this change: in the field of neurobiology, for instance, we have witnessed, over the last two to three decades, a vast expansion of knowledge about the workings of the body. Research findings from this field have convincingly established that a contemporary understanding needs to transcend traditional dualistic notions of the body-mind relationship. Top-down, mind-over-body notions of control have been replaced by ideas of self-organization and mutually reciprocal feedback loops between the body and mind, to the point where we can say, "There is no such thing as a mind without a body."

Traditional references to a dichotomy between mind and body, or between consciousness and unconscious processes, do not support, and frequently impede, the theory and practice of our discipline, especially if they do not incorporate the bodily dimension of experience, for example, in the form of "somatic markers" (Damasio, 1994).

Insights from contemporary research on infant development, attachment theory, and prenatal and perinatal psychology also challenge some of the basic tenets of psychoanalytic theory and emphasize the pre-verbal domains of experience in their significance for the development of neuronal pathways, as well as the foundational structures and the mood dispositions of the psyche. The roots of the symbolic representations (that psychoanalytic theory refers to as "object relations") can also be found in early pre-verbal forms of relational events. Daniel Stern describes these events as a "dance," and the medium of this dance is the body, whereas speech plays much more of a secondary role. Here, we are in the realm of what neurobiologists call "implicit" or "procedural" memory (see Chapter 12, "Neurobiological Perspectives on Body Psychotherapy" by Christian Gottwald).

In the future, we might well expect that body-oriented topics such as "affect motor schemas" (see Chapter 30, "Affective-Motor Schemata" by Andreas Wehowsky) and "bodily micro-practices" (see Chapter 29, "Early Interaction and the Body: Clinical Implications" by George Downing) will also come to be viewed as essential—in all relevant disciplines—for a thorough understanding of formative relational experiences.

An increasing number of substantive indicators from neuropsychological research also suggests that traumatic experiences reach deeply into the affective and vegetative domains and are stored in the limbic system. Psychotherapeutic methods that are primarily cognitive and verbally oriented are thus not particularly well equipped to meet the demands of this somatic reality at the root of subjective experience. The depth and the degree of "autonomy" of the associated neurovegetative arousal processes (van der Kolk, 1987) call for approaches that include, and are rooted in, close attention to the regulation of the bodily aspects of affective and vegetative arousal (see Chapter 76, "Sensory-Motor Processing for Trauma Recovery" by Pat Ogden and Kekuni Minton).

In response to this growing interest in the body in psychotherapy, the established field of Body Psychotherapy *is* well equipped in these domains, and can offer a broad array of methods and clinical knowledge that can help to balance psychotherapy's lopsided orientation toward an ideal of rational enlightenment that—with its seeming disregard for the somatic and affective dimension of subjectivity and experience—has dominated the psychotherapeutic field for far too long.

In this regard, Body Psychotherapy, along with Gestalt Therapy and Psychodrama for example, belongs to a group of psychotherapeutic approaches that have rehabilitated the active and emotional aspects of therapeutic self-exploration and change by utilizing movement, intentional action, emotional expression, and the completion of emotional cycles (see Chapter 53, "The Role of the Body in Emotional Defense Processes: Body Psychotherapy and Emotional Theory" by Ulfried Geuter and Norbert Schrauth).

The body plays a central role in another important evolution taking place in all major branches of the field: the ongoing and substantial research on mindfulness, which is recognized as having a bearing on the work of all psychotherapeutic modalities. The key principles of mindfulness have long been supported by various approaches of Humanistic Psychology and Body Psychotherapy, although not with this exact term, but through similar and associated concepts (Rogerian "empathy," for instance, or the concept of "awareness" in Gestalt Therapy), or implicit in psychotherapeutic attitudes. What is becoming increasingly accepted is that mindfulness stands and falls with embodiment—its primary focus is the body. Practicing mindfulness means paying close attention to the somatic realm and becoming ever more finely attuned to the myriad of events, cues, and nuances that constitute our moment-to-moment state of being—with ourselves and with others. Who we are—as clients or therapists, i.e., our self—is a flow of self-states in the context of embodied self-organization. This is managed mostly prereflexively, subliminally, by implicit relational knowing and implicit memory. Being mindful of these processes thus also forms the professional foundation of the therapeutic position and presence that a practitioner is able to generate and sustain (see Chapter 38, "Consciousness, Awareness, Mindfulness" by Halko Weiss).

The progressive growth over recent decades of such body-oriented approaches—i.e., ways of working that emphasize and intensify both awareness of and engagement with lived, felt, embodied, here-and-now subjective experience—can be viewed as a historical "stretching exercise": a reaction against the rigid setting of classical psychoanalysis, based as it was on a somewhat phobic notion that equated "action" with "acting out," and which has paralyzed much of the psychodynamic field for decades. These experientially oriented approaches have succeeded in opening up far-reaching and creative "therapeutic playing fields" and are recently finding substantial backing from the field of neuropsychology (see Chapter 12, "Neurobiological Perspectives on Body Psychotherapy" by Christian Gottwald; Chapter 20, "The Body Unconscious: The Process of Making Conscious: Psychodynamic and Neuroscience Perspectives" by Marilyn Morgan; and others in this Handbook). While it has to be acknowledged that Cognitive Behavioral Therapy also has an action-focused and experience-activating orientation, its traditional origins tend toward a more mechanistic understanding of the body and its affects, rather than the creative exploration of subjective experience and its psychodynamic foundations.

## A Hidden Tradition

It is not very well known that in the origins of modern psychotherapy—i.e., the point in history when Depth Psychology ceased to be framed in purely metaphysical or religious terms—a reasonably strong body-oriented current of psychological practice already existed. This tradition has subsequently been repressed by the established research community—or at least significantly underestimated—and has largely been forgotten by the field of psychological therapy as a whole. It is only now, about a century later, that this work (a form of somatic, educational, and therapeutic bodywork, initiated at the beginning of the twentieth century by a few courageous pioneers, predominantly women) is beginning to be properly recognized, certainly in its significant influence on the later development of Body Psychotherapy. Elsa Gindler can be considered an exemplary representative of this tradition (see Chapter 4, "The Influence of Elsa Gindler" by Judyth Weaver; and Chapter 6, "The Norwegian Tradition of Body Psychotherapy: A Golden Age in Oslo" by Nicholas Bassal and Michael Coster Heller).

This lack of recognition and exclusion from mainstream psychotherapy has not only overshadowed the origins of body-oriented practice, but has been a historical feature of Body Psychotherapy ever since. To some extent, this is due to a lack of theoretical elaboration and formulation of their work by body-oriented theoreticians and practitioners—a flaw that should not be overlooked and that has characterized the Body Psychotherapy tradition throughout most of its existence.

Even Wilhelm Reich, whose theoretical brilliance and clinical competence would have enabled him to carry forward a productive, if controversial, discourse with the rest of the field, ended up detaching himself from the mainstream, following his exclusion from the International Psychoanalytical Association in 1934. Feeling justifiably slighted, he withdrew and developed a conceptual framework and formulation that no longer aimed at exchange or dialogue with the increasingly established psychoanalytic field. This historical development has affected—with the exception of some parts of Gestalt Therapy—nearly all body-oriented psychotherapeutic approaches since Reich for decades. Arguably, both sides of the divide, and the psychotherapeutic field as a whole, continue to suffer from the legacy of these splits. The movement toward psychotherapy integration has—over the last twenty years—significantly lessened the fragmentation of the field and enhanced the cross-fertilization between, and interchange across, diverse therapeutic modalities. But the polarization between a verbal-reflective-cognitive notion of mind and an embodied, holistic understanding still pervades the field, to the detriment of effective practice everywhere.

Body Psychotherapy's traditional aversion toward intellectual discourse has certainly been a significant factor in perpetuating these splits, for a variety of historical reasons, as well as other factors inherent in its practice. Many pioneers of Body Psychotherapy were simply much more focused on creating experientially oriented and efficacious practices, than in formulating these conceptually and explaining them theoretically.

To a large extent, they were not at all interested in finding and developing any links with psychoanalytic concepts and categories. While some of this disinterest can be seen as a manifestation of a methodological principle, its main thrust was almost certainly a one-sided reactivity, on all kinds of levels (including the transferential). The early pioneers of "somatic work" at the beginning of the twentieth century, who did not explicitly define their work as psychotherapeutic, were predominantly focused on bodily experiences, and were reluctant to interrupt this experience through interpretations and theoretical reflections that might have had a distancing or distorting effect on their somatic experiences.

To some extent, therefore, the lack of theoretical elaboration might be seen to be inherent in the subject of body-oriented practice itself. Through their uncanny capacity to penetrate into an otherwise neglected phenomenological domain of experience, body-oriented approaches have—going back all the way to their early somato-educational origins—been able to develop extensive knowledge that is primarily practical, i.e., knowledge that cannot be captured or explained by theoretical (psychoanalytic) concepts, and even less so by academic descriptions of the body from within the culturally predominant paradigm of natural science. Ultimately, this practical knowledge can be accessed and developed only through one's own experiential self-exploration. Practitioners rooted in this kind of "embodied knowing" may successfully apply this to the healing and self-development processes of others, by being able to reach the sensory-motoric "roots" of both arrested personal development and illness via the avenue of—largely prereflexive, unconscious—bodily experience. Instead of grasping for those aspects of a person's suffering and well-being that can be scientifically categorized and objectified from a third-person perspective, the focus of inquiry is more on the person's immediate experience, as mediated and manifested also—alongside emotional, imaginal, and mental processes—through the person's somatic organization and its subjective relevance and meanings.

This kind of intersubjective knowing, rooted in self-exploration and awareness of one's own body-mind experience, was still accessible to some of the great physicians and psychologists of the nineteenth century, like Carl Gustav Carus. Their practice was influenced by the nature philosophy of romanticism, and contained significant elements that prefigured psychoanalysis and its theory of the unconscious. They were still capable of thinking and speaking about the body as a manifestation of subjectivity, as a felt and lived experience of embodied meaningfulness (as in Winnicott's famous phrase: "the psyche indwelling in the soma")—a capacity and perspective that became increasingly marginalized and lost, in contrast to the paradigm of modern natural science that has acquired its almost absolute dominance. The only remnants that have survived within academic circles can be traced in little-known aspects of anthropology (like the work of Buytendijk and Plessner) or in philosophy (like the work of Merleau-Ponty and Marcel).

Other areas where somatic experience and a language of subjective embodiment were cultivated were in the late nineteenth- and early twentieth-century German-Swiss "back-to-nature" Lebensreform [Life Reform] Movement, and later in the various disciplines—often belittled or denigrated in health, bodywork, and body-oriented therapies—that emerged in the late twentieth century.

However, this way of embodied speaking and relating does not lend itself to scientific abstraction; on the contrary, it always was, and possibly will remain, tied to the specific context of a distinctive helping relationship, to the subjective particularities of the work with individual patients, as it expresses unique, intuitive, creative, and situationally contingent psyche-soma relationships. It is of necessity a "first- and second-person" language, closer to poetic expression than to traditional (more objective and impersonal) scientific and intellectual generalizations.

Unlike other "talking therapies," therefore, the meta-psychology, theory, and practice of Body Psychotherapy cannot exclusively be structured according to linguistic principles and abstract categories of thought; pre-verbal and nonverbal kinesthetic channels of perception—sensing, feeling, somatic exploration of gesture, posture, and movement—are necessarily included among its essential working modes (see Chapter 37, "Sensory Self-Reflexivity: Therapeutic Action in Body Psychotherapy" by Gustl Marlock). A common consequence of such exploration is the discovery that speech as well as thought appear to arise naturally *out* of "sensing" (what Gendlin [1998] calls the "felt sense"), and that meaningful connections emerge on the experiential basis of "vital and felt evidence" (Petzold, 1977). Making sense and meaning, or developing a narrative—i.e., aspects of therapy considered crucial in modern talking therapies—can be subjectively experienced as arising *within* and *through* somatic awareness—without needing to be imparted from the outside in the form of interpretations, by one's own or somebody else's mind. This view of the body, as something considerably more than nonconscious matter, implies that "meaning" can be arrived at via a totally different process that does not rely upon mental reflection.

As Robert Bly describes in *News of the Universe: Poems of Twofold Consciousness,* the assumption of a single form of consciousness contained only in the human mind is an "insult to matter": the body is the foundation of our being and any grounded, tangible sense of self, fundamental to all other psychological processes—emotional, imaginal, mental (and inextricably interwoven with them)—can then be seen as a source of subjective meaning, without which the therapeutic endeavor loses conviction, impact, and connection to everyday reality. The somatic ground of existence is an essential pillar of the healing process—but remains largely inaccessible, is unavailable, and effectively gets dissociated and lost in purely verbal "talking therapies."

## Autonomy and Discourse

In retrospect, it could be considered an advantage that the historical tradition of Body Psychotherapy developed largely outside the established and official routes, especially as the discourses of academically established psychology and psychotherapy education became increasingly scientific, rigidly cognitive, or narrowly psychoanalytic. Not being as bound by these established orthodoxies, dogmas, and taboos, Body Psychotherapy was able—particularly since the 1960s—to develop in a burst of creativity, which may be comparable to the inspirations of the early psychoanalytic movement at the beginning of the twentieth century. Not being controlled or recognized by official institutions, the spread of Body Psychotherapy—apart from its experiential appeal and clinical effectiveness—relied instead upon important societal trends, such as feminism, Humanistic Psychology, and the ecological movement, which share many essential values with Body Psychotherapy.

The lack of any unified theory or theoretical cohesion, as well as the wide variety of paradigms and theoretical models that characterize the field of Body Psychotherapy—factors that mitigate the recognition of the approach as a coherent, circumscribed, and clearly identifiable influential social entity—is redeemed by a vibrant diversity and creativity in terms of clinical practice, a fact that is cherished and appreciated across the multitude of branches and schools of Body Psychotherapy, despite an undeniable degree of original competition between them.

A surprisingly high degree of unspoken and implicit agreement can now be found among Body Psychotherapists regarding the basic principles of their work, with earlier misunderstandings, distortions, and overinflated claims of supremacy (by some of the approaches) having either softened over time or even been eliminated altogether. This maturing of the profession has occurred in a natural self-regulatory fashion, and through the growth and activities of professional associations of Body Psychotherapists, rather than through implementation of any rigid theoretical doctrine: so it seems that a major unifying revisioning (like a "Vatican Council") was not needed in the field of Body Psychotherapy.

For example, some approaches of the 1960s and 1970s (that were probably influenced by primal therapy) are being viewed today as both having frequently exaggerated their efficacy, and also sometimes—by emphasizing catharsis over containment—forced the expression of emotions. Furthermore, the way that generalizations about character types and schemas have been used in the past is now being viewed as somewhat too mechanistic and relationally insensitive. The former practice of "body reading," then quite common in some areas of the Body Psychotherapeutic field, often served merely to give an aura of "quasi-scientific" mystique (or pseudo-objectivity) to the therapeutic procedure. The last fifteen years have seen increasing attempts at a self-reflective working-through of Body Psychotherapy's own psychic "wounds" and "shadow" aspects as a tradition, especially the "hidden 'medical model' assumptions" that have pervaded the field since Reich and led to objectifying ways of working in spite of "humanistic" principles to the contrary (Soth, 2005).

## Important Pioneers of the Second Generation

Not until the second half of the twentieth century, and after its acceptance within the context of the developing Human Potential Movement, did the field of traditional Body Psychotherapy slowly open itself toward a discourse with the larger world of established psychotherapy.

The following is an incomplete list of some of the important pioneers who were instrumental in the development of Body Psychotherapy as a distinct psychotherapeutic modality: in the United States there was, first of all, Alexander Lowen, the grand seigneur of Bioenergetics, who (initially with John Pierrakos) reconnected the Reichian perspective with psychoanalytic theory and psychodynamic thinking. With Lowen's work and through his oeuvre of books, he transcended the hermetic and sectarian language barriers that had begun to surround Reichian circles, as well as their partial disinterest in the psychodynamic aspect inherent in character-analytic work; Stanley Keleman is also recognized as the main person who worked most constructively toward a somatically grounded theory conceptualizing the influence of emotional experience on body structure. His contribution has had a significant impact on the field, and his book

*Emotional Anatomy* (1985) is now considered among the classics of Body Psychotherapy.

With his psycho-motor approach, Al Pesso developed a method, rooted in body language and similar to Psychodrama, where internalized and conflictual object relations are reenacted on a therapeutic "stage" and thus become available to be worked through emotionally, by providing corrective therapeutic experiences that facilitate the belated maturation of traumatically aborted early development. His work has significantly contributed to the rapprochement between the Body Psychotherapeutic and psychoanalytic traditions.

In Europe, the lifework of Helmuth Stolze cannot be underestimated—at least within the German-speaking countries—as he was the first person to develop the phenomenology of the body and its symbolic functions within the context of Psychodynamic and Depth Psychology. He played a critical role in making Body Psychotherapy an acceptable modality in many psychosomatic hospitals, which are a cherished particularity, especially in Germany.

Two other names need to be cited in the context of this obviously incomplete tribute: Eugene Gendlin has made an important contribution by creating a conceptual framework for the important phenomenon, recognized through clinical experience by Body Psychotherapists from across all the various schools: the indisputable observation that the body engenders a prereflexive form of "knowing," accessible only through the channels of sensing, feeling, and kinesthetic awareness, rather than through objective interpretation, which constitutes its own kind of intelligence and evidence. To do justice to this form of "knowing," Gendlin originated the term "felt sense" and elaborated its theoretical and clinical implications.

Last, but not least, into the picture comes David Boadella, based in England and later in Switzerland, at a time when Reich's work was surrounded by prejudice and seen as a mixture of madness, communism, and sexual chaos (in the late 1950s and early 1960s). He, and a few other free-spirited activists (such as A. S. Neill and Paul Ritter), kept both the psychotherapeutic, as well as the educational, tradition of Reich's legacy alive (Boadella, 1973). His contributions to the field of Body Psychotherapy have been enormous, and include the founding (in 1971) and continuous editing of his journal, *Energy & Character,* which—throughout the last forty years—has been the most important international forum for discussion across the widely different schools of Body Psychotherapy, as well as the development of his own particular way of working, Biosynthesis. His theoretical contributions and diverse, nuanced, and clear writings, as well as his gentle, behind-the-scenes, political presence, have helped immensely in putting the field of Body Psychotherapy onto some solid ground.

The above outline and recognition of some of the significant contributions to the field give some indications of the central motive for the development of this Handbook. The currently increasing interest in Body Psychotherapy, or at least in aspects of its methodology, frequently leads to superficial misunderstandings and misappropriations of its principles, models, and techniques. In the fashionable rush to translate neuroscientific insights into effective psychotherapeutic practice, and the long-overdue attempt to reintegrate the body into the "talking therapies," the recent success of Body Psychotherapy has created its own problems (Soth, 2010; Young, 2011).

Without a clear understanding of the distinctions between "bodywork" and Body Psychotherapy, there is a proliferation of supposedly theory-free "body techniques," which are being applied pragmatically, and sometimes successfully, without any awareness of the historical depth and clinical breadth of the field of Body Psychotherapy. Frequently this lack of awareness and knowledge, regarding the antecedents and the tradition of somatic work, along with its substantial philosophical, theoretical, and clinical wealth, creates the impression that the "wheel" of therapeutic work with the body has only just been invented.

Furthermore, without a reasonably clear understanding of the organic evolution of the Body Psychotherapeutic approach over the last century or more, its historical origins and sources, the mutual interweaving of embodied theory and technique, the philosophical underpinnings, and how these are embedded in paradigm shifts that were well ahead of their time, plus the rich diversity of this complex, differentiated, multifaceted field (which nevertheless constitutes a recognizable whole), current well-meaning and well-intentioned attempts to graft the "body" onto the practice of established "talking therapies" are bound to remain relatively superficial and incoherent.

If the current interest in and recognized "promise" of the body in psychotherapy is to fulfill its potential in actual therapeutic practice, we need to ground these attempts in the fertile, accumulated soil of the mature and accomplished tradition of Body Psychotherapy, which has been dedicated to developing an embodied, somatic psychotherapeutic practice.

Therefore, our intention in preparing this—admittedly rather voluminous—Handbook is to remedy the relative dearth or obscurity of some of the published material on Body Psychotherapy and the concomitant lack of recognition of the tradition by the rest of the professional field, as well as by the general public.

In making available a more comprehensive and non-partisan account of the field of Body Psychotherapy than is currently available, we thought it appropriate to let many of its most important pioneers and practitioners speak for themselves. Their persistence, inspiration, and visionary power have sustained Body Psychotherapy through difficult and unfavorable times to its current emergence. Among other things, this Handbook is therefore dedicated to their historical endeavors and their considerable merit.

## Heterogeneity and Spectrum

The significant pioneers of Body Psychotherapy have passed onto us the legacy of a range of diverse traditions. Having repeatedly pointed to the fact that the "field" of Body Psychotherapy is characterized by its heterogeneity, we can now enunciate the following paradox: Body Psychotherapy *in itself*—as a theoretically and clinically unified field—does not actually exist. Rather, there is a plurality of different presumptions and positions that, in some cases, are quite difficult to reconcile with each other. Both in metatheoretical as well as in clinical-methodological terms, the various schools and approaches are actually widely divergent. However, there does exist an implicit set of essential parameters that allows these disparate branches to recognize their links with each other as relatively diverse "members" of a common "species."

In this respect, the situation in the "field" of Body Psychotherapy does not differ significantly from that of psychoanalysis, a point that critics sometimes lose sight of: as we simply can no longer speak of "psychoanalysis" as an entity in itself. Rather, what we find is, in the words of the psychoanalyst Wolfgang Mertens, "a sometimes peaceful, sometimes contentious coexistence of many theories and schools" (Koukkou, Leuzinger-Bohleber, and Mertens, 1998, p. 15). The various schools of Freudian, Alderian, Jungian, Lacanian, Kleinian, Object Relations, Ego Psychology, Interpersonal, Feminist, Culturalist, Relational, and other forms of psychoanalysis share as little "common ground" between them as the many diverse forms, orientations, and theories of Body Psychotherapy.

The difference with Body Psychotherapy is to be found in its historical development. Whereas psychoanalysis developed from one relatively unified and established point—after getting rid of some early dissidents—and, over time, became more differentiated, the development of the Body Psychotherapy movement followed rather the opposite trajectory. Whereas Freudian theories and writings were the cornerstone for the many different schools of psychoanalysis, there was not really a central point of reference to agree with, or diverge from, in Body Psychotherapy.

Cognitive Behavioral Therapy also developed from the central ideas of learning theory and expanded its conceptual framework from there. Body Psychotherapy, in contrast, had different points of origination and lineages of tradition, some of which then further differentiated themselves internally, such as the post-Reichian tradition, for example. The many "fathers" and "mothers" of Body Psychotherapy hardly knew each other, or about each other, and consequently had little mutual exchange, and their basic assumptions and concepts differed widely—until relatively recently. After having existed independently for a long time, sometimes even without knowledge of one another, these various diverse schools have begun to connect through associations, at conferences, and via discourses over the last two decades. This book celebrates that consolidation.

We would be very pleased if this Handbook could, as we hope that it will, play a useful role in promoting this process of convergence and contact, and this particular interest has been a guiding principle in the organization of this Handbook. We have tried to consolidate the structure of this Handbook according to important general questions and essential focal areas, rather than according to the particular schools, their founders, histories, proponents, or their specialties, which are quite divergent.

Although in-depth dialogue between the different schools of Body Psychotherapy has remained somewhat limited, we consider the historically evolved lack of a unified "body" of theory and practice not only as a handicap, but also as an asset and a gift. In compiling this Handbook, we have, therefore, at no point tried to diminish the contradictory diversity by prematurely asserting any one particular perspective among the multitude as in any way definitive for the whole discipline. Rather than promoting a partial and limited perspective—i.e., ultimately that of the editors—in the supposed interest of clarity and coherence, we have striven to let the selection of the authors reflect the wide spectrum that exists within the field, even if our appreciation of its colorful diversity might not appeal to proponents of oversimplifying, quasi-scientific methodologies or typologies, or those representatives of therapeutic monocultures who are caught in vested, hegemonic interests.

Our hope is that this "general assembly" of disparate authors, representing a wide range of Body Psychotherapeutic perspectives and dialects, will stimulate far-reaching exchange and dialogue and engender mutual connections, and also—where necessary—respectful and necessary debates and disputes.

On the other hand, we also did not want this Handbook to serve simply as a forum for the self-presentation of the various schools. We evolved the structure of this Handbook strictly from the inherent demands of the subject matter, trying to do justice to the major themes and topics that arise from therapeutic work and that need to be comprehensively addressed by any community of practitioners that claims to constitute a recognizable therapeutic approach. Our selection of authors—insofar as they are representatives of specific schools of Body Psychotherapy—has been guided by their established expertise in certain areas of the field. The primary criterion for inviting an author to submit a chapter on a certain topic was whether their work (or the school they founded or represent) is recognized as having made important theoretical and technical contributions and, therefore, whether they seem to be particularly competent and qualified to represent the larger field as well.

We recognize and acknowledge that, for readers from outside the field, this array of divergent contributions must come across at times as somewhat confusing. The underlying reasons, both historical and substantive, for this confusion of names of methodologies within Body Psychotherapy will become transparent—and hopefully more accessible and acceptable—throughout the Handbook.

As has been the case across the therapeutic field throughout its history, the various schools of Body Psychotherapy organized themselves around a founding "father" or "mother" (originating frequently in a separation or split from their own teachers or therapists). This has led to a high degree of fragmentation within the field and an insularity between the different approaches, often resulting in self-aggrandizement and a somewhat sectarian overvaluation of their chosen orientation by the respective students, adherents, and (dare we say) disciples.

This tendency, which was more commonplace in the past, occasionally still continues, mainly at the margins of the Body Psychotherapeutic field and, in these days of economic difficulty, fueled by market pressures. Some new schools can be seen to emerge, centered around charismatic individuals, who have found ways of repackaging frequently very "old" wine into supposedly new bottles, without these schools necessarily contributing anything special, or anything really new; typically, these fashionable newcomers avoid the challenges of wider professional discourse.

Meanwhile, the much larger "core" of the field of Body Psychotherapy has matured and consolidated itself, containing a variety of different, recognized schools that are now solid and well established, and are continuing to develop and evolve throughout the recent decades. Some of these try to maintain an independent position, such as Integrative Somatic Therapy [Integrative Leibtherapie], or Paul Boyesen's Psycho-Organic Analysis, but most of them are associated with, and are represented in, the two large professional organizations, the European Association for Body Psychotherapy (EABP) and the United States Association for Body Psychotherapy (USABP), and these therefore constitute much of the current "mainstream" of Body Psychotherapy.

In preparing this Handbook, we have been oriented predominantly toward this mainstream, and have—as much as possible—tried to allow eminent writers and practitioners of most of these schools and traditions to express and represent their different perspectives. Beyond that, a large and growing number of colleagues identify themselves as "Body Psychotherapists" in a wider, more collective sense, rather than as members of specific schools. The lively exchange and debates that characterize the biannual conferences in Body Psychotherapy, on both sides of the Atlantic, substantiate and consolidate this trend toward a significant faction of therapists transcending the boundaries of their particular schools. Recent years have also seen a significant leap in the number of books published about Body Psychotherapy, emerging from within this central mainstream, as well as particular schools within this field. At the time of publication, there are now also at least three regular peer-reviewed professional journals: *Body, Movement and Dance in Psychotherapy,* and its German-language equivalent, *körper–tanz–bewegung* [Body–Dance–Movement], and the development of the *USABP Journal* into the *International Body Psychotherapy Journal,* along with an ever-expanding *EABP Bibliography of Body Psychotherapy,* with currently well over four thousand entries, available online (www.eabp.org/bibliography).

## Body Therapy and Body Psychotherapy

In this context, another peculiarity of Body Psychotherapy, as a field of practice, calls for some clarification, and that is its connection with, as well as differentiation from, various forms of "bodywork" or "body-oriented complementary therapies." As the chapters on the history of Body Psychotherapy will demonstrate, therapeutic work with the body acquired prominence in the early twentieth century, through a collective avant-garde movement that came to be known in Europe as the Life Reform Movement [Lebensreformbewegung]. This movement was to inform sociocultural notions of individuation and health throughout the twentieth century, and has had an unrecognized influence on modernity's ideas of what it means to express one's subjectivity and to become a fulfilled individual. The philosophy of this movement viewed the relationship to one's body as a core issue within the wider project of human self-development. This view emphatically heralded a new understanding of the self, and the body acquired a "center stage," not only with regards to the more obvious body-related areas such as diet, exercise, and sexuality, but also through a subcultural bursting forth of all kinds of pedagogic, therapeutic, and artistic work with and through the body and "bodywork." Methods ranged from gymnastic approaches to forms of modern expressive dance (see Chapter 3, "The History and Scope of Body Psychotherapy" by Ulfried Geuter; and Chapter 8, "Body Psychotherapy as a Major Tradition of Modern Depth Psychology" by Gustl Marlock).

The Life Reform Movement spawned a wide range of disciplines that implicitly recognized the interconnectedness of body, mind, and psyche, and used the body as one avenue into working with the whole interconnected system. Although their self-definition was inherently "therapeutic," there was wide variation as to how directly and explicitly the psychological dimension was included and addressed in these different approaches. Precisely because they were all underpinned by a paradigm shift toward holistic intentions that refused to perpetuate the traditional divisions between body, mind, and psyche, the scope of these disciplines and the boundaries between them were incredibly fluid.

A large number of somatic educational and bodywork methods, such as the Feldenkrais Method, Alexander Technique, Sensory Awareness, Hellerwork, various forms of Breath Therapy and Breath Education, and similar body-oriented "therapies," certainly intend to stimulate growth and healing within the psyche and are unquestionably effective in this respect; they also have shaped and enriched Body Psychotherapy in many significant ways (see particularly: Chapter 4, "The Influence of Elsa Gindler" by Judyth Weaver; and Chapter 86, "Dance Therapy" by Sabine Trautmann-Voigt).

However, as many of these methods do not specifically and systematically address and integrate the psyche in their various approaches, do not directly make psychological experience the focus of their therapeutic work, and do not highlight the client-therapist relationship, they cannot properly be classified as "Body *Psycho*therapies." The same applies to the various massage traditions, which predominantly need to be considered as "body therapeutic," rather than "Body *Psycho*therapeutic."

Out of this fluid multitude of therapeutic methods, some eventually did develop beyond purely somatic work into psychosomatic, and then into explicitly psychotherapeutic approaches, such as the German approaches of "Funktionelle Entspannung" [Functional Relaxation], "Konzentrative Bewegungstherapie" [Focused Movement Therapy], and Postural Integrative Psychotherapy; together with some of the Reichian, Neo-Reichian, and Gestalt Therapy traditions, as well as parts of the Dance Movement Therapy tradition. For us to classify a therapeutic approach as *psycho*therapy (however much that may need to include the body) requires—as a minimum—that the attention and awareness of both client and therapist are oriented toward *psychological* experience, i.e., how the various processes of the body-mind, reaching across the spectrum from sensation and emotion to imagination and mind, are perceived, interpreted, processed, represented, and translated into intention, behavior, and meaning, both *subjectively* and *intersubjectively*.

Psychic experiences arise in the interaction between self-awareness and awareness, and we understand *psycho*therapy as attending to the structures, processes, and developments of that subjective experience, and how it translates into a person's being, doing, and relating in life. It is precisely because Body Psychotherapy does not restrict its notion of psyche, subjectivity, and identity just to the verbal-reflective mind, but sees—following Reich and others—psychology as indistinguishable and mutually constitutive with biology (including anatomy, physiology, neurology, etc.), that these confusions between "bodywork," "body therapy," and "Body Psychotherapy" necessarily arise. If anything, these overlaps and confusions have increased since the hippie and New Age movements in the 1960s, as a proliferation of hybrid forms has occurred, including many new "body therapies" that in their overall therapeutic intention, effect, and modus operandi are often recognizable as somewhat "*psycho*therapeutic."

But according to the definition and understanding above, we can draw some sort of dividing lines, albeit somewhat fuzzy, between body-therapy work and Body Psychotherapy on the one hand, and between Body Psychotherapy and the "talking therapies" on the other. Naturally, there are syntheses, combinations, overlaps, and crossovers that can be very creative in the border areas of these respective domains. This is one of the reasons why we have asked some of their representatives, such as Don Johnson and Ilana Rubenfeld, for their contributions. From their particular perspectives, they may be in a particularly advantageous position to shed light on some topics that are relevant to the field of Body Psychotherapy as a whole.

## The Common Ground

Despite all their heterogeneity, the Body Psychotherapeutic approaches clearly share some common ground that differentiates them from the other modalities of psychotherapy. What unites them is their holistic perspective, oriented toward the systemic wholeness of subjective experience, in which the psychic dimension of human experience and the bodily dimension of lived experience are equally appreciated.

> [Body Psychotherapy] involves a different and explicit theory of mind-body functioning, which takes into

account the complexity of the intersections and interactions between the body and the mind. The common underlying assumption is that the body is the whole person and there is a functional unity between mind and body. The body does not merely mean the "soma" and that this is separate from the mind, the "psyche." (*EABP Introductory Handbook*, 1994)

The premodern philosophical notion of "soma" actually integrates these two dimensions as the animate or "ensouled" body. One of the principal axioms of Body Psychotherapy is that human subjectivity and experience—psyche—is *embodied*. With reference to the work of Merleau-Ponty, we could also speak of the necessarily embodied nature of human "situatedness" in the world: human experience is mediated through the body, and the human self is constituted by bodily experience, or—in other words—the sense of self emerges out of a—however indirectly, dimly, or clearly perceived—body-based consciousness. These issues are also addressed when we consider the concept of the "proto-self" (Damasio, 1994) or in studies of artificial intelligence, where those designing robots struggle with the "requirement" of a sense of "embodiment" for their creation.

Formative experiences not only shape the brain and psychic structure, but also leave scars, marks, and traces somatically, in the way they are processed, stored, carried, and remembered in bodily experience, regardless of what language different approaches use to describe the resulting, clearly identifiable patterns: "character structures" (Reich, 1933/1970), "affect motor schemas" (Downing, 1996), "entanglements" (Uexküll, 1997), "insults to form" (Keleman, 1985), etc.

In order to do justice to the complexity of these phenomena, and the concomitant splits, dissociations, and polarizations within the body-mind experience, Body Psychotherapy strives to move fluidly between the somatic pole and the psychic pole, weaving back and forth in order to integrate these two dimensions. Sometimes the therapeutic process leads from a psychic starting point into a deeper affective or somatic experience of self; at other times, sensing and body awareness lead toward clearer insights into psychic reality.

The same is true in regard to the therapeutic relationship that—as a dynamic body-mind system—is seen and understood to comprise the same poles: body and psyche. Body Psychotherapists attend to the shifting interpersonal dynamics on both somatic and psychic levels, as well as between these two poles in each person. The conflicts, oscillations, and polarizations between body and psyche, and the various configurations and constellations between them, are understood as central to the therapeutic process. Whether they conceive of the therapeutic relationship in psychoanalytic terms of transference and countertransference, or in more existential-dialogic terms, like somatic resonance; whether they include, allow, or invite physical contact, or whether they use therapeutic touch or not—regardless of style, technique, or relational modality—Body Psychotherapists will invariably place high value and significance on their intricate and attuned perception, monitoring, reflecting, and engaging with the two bodies in the consulting room—the client's and the therapist's—and how integrated, conflicted, or dissociated the somatic and psychic poles are in each person's experience from moment to moment.

Lastly, we find one more common denominator of the Body Psychotherapeutic field in its anthropological foundations: it is part of its historical legacy to tend toward conceiving human nature as essentially positive and good. This perspective distinguishes it from Cognitive Behavioral Therapy, which tends toward a neutral stance in this regard, and classical psychoanalysis, with its rather misanthropic and pessimistic perspective. Body Psychotherapy's view of human nature, as essentially positive at its core, can be historically situated as emerging in the middle of the last century, through the work of Abraham Maslow and the spirit of Humanistic Psychotherapy, which resonates with some of the increasingly influential Eastern religious and philosophical views.

So, we can summarize the common foundations of Body Psychotherapy in four basic premises:

1. It is necessary to view the psychic dimension of human experience, human development, and human relating as inseparable from the somatic dimensions—body, mind, and psyche are a functional unity, an interconnected, dynamic system, which may or may not be experienced as a subjective whole. The human ability to differentiate and discriminate leads to illusions of dichotomies and dualities that separate phenomena into distinct and often antagonistic parts and that are, in reality, mutually constitutive as different, but interconnected and inseparable aspects of the whole.

2. A specific implication that follows from this principle is that formative experiences in human development have lasting structural effects on both psychic and somatic levels and dimensions of being.

3. The psychic dimension can be accessed, touched, and affected via the bodily dimension, and vice versa.

4. There is a basic tendency to trust the inherent potential of "human nature"—admittedly a dubious term that has often been misused ideologically—for self-regulation, for self-organization, and for an organic unfolding type of maturational growth and development (Jung called this "individuation").

## Polarities within the Field

To facilitate an initial overview and orientation in this diverse and potentially confusing field of Body Psychotherapy, we want to describe briefly some polarities that pervade the spectrum of approaches and generate some of its key features and dynamics. We lay no claim for this to constitute a generally applicable matrix. It is true that the various methods often emphasize one or another of these various polarities, which will be discussed; but many take a middle or synthesizing position, and some explicitly strive to span the whole width of the field. Our intention in outlining the following polarities is to capture the main differences and disputes between the various schools and to show the range of different positions and perspectives that exist in relation to key theoretical and methodological questions.

### Treatment versus Phenomenological Orientation or Learning

Some methods, such as the orthodox Reichian approach, classical Bioenergetics, or some massage-oriented approaches, strongly define themselves, or operate implicitly, within the traditional "medical model" conceptualization of psychotherapy, applying standard "medical" notions such as "pathology," "patient," "assessment," "diagnosis," "intervention," and other terminologies consistent with a "treatment" approach. Typically, such a third-person, objectifying stance would be associated with what Martha Stark calls a "one-person psychology," where the therapist's focus is on the patient and the patient's pathology, applying generally validated theories in a quasi-scientific fashion to the particularities of the specific individual "case."

On the other hand, many other Body Psychotherapeutic approaches (for example, Gendlin's "Focusing," Mindell's "Process Oriented Psychotherapy," or Kurtz's "Hakomi Method") emphasize the phenomenological, explorative, and investigative "process," oriented toward the "client's" self-regulation and self-determination. A "treatment" orientation on the therapist's part is not conducive to facilitating this kind of exploratory process, which is why it is usually associated with a relational stance of collaboration between client and therapist. Here, the starting point cannot be a diagnosis by an "expert" of a "patient." Instead, a shared attitude of curiosity may draw attention to an experiential phenomenon (for example, a tight neck) that currently affects the "client." Explorative suggestions (such as adding or relieving tension in this area, inviting somatic imagery, or even using touch or pressure) are designed to remain experience-based, and engage both client and therapist in a process of investigation, or even play, which may engender new experiences or insights into correlations between psyche and soma, functions and meanings, as well as discovering the possible origins.

### Energetic Body versus Knowing Body

Some significant approaches within the field, such as the work of Lowen, Pierrakos, or some of the Scandinavian

Body Psychotherapy schools, have built on Reich's model of "bioenergy." They proceed from the assumption of an energetic flow within the body that determines the psychosomatic condition of an individual. By observing and "reading" the body, this energy flow can be studied, diagnosed, monitored, and (some would even say) quantified, and thus—on the basis of the therapist's accurate perception and understanding—can be influenced via appropriate therapeutic interventions. The energized, freely pulsating body, unencumbered by chronic blockages and armoring, is viewed as psychologically and physically healthy. Therefore, these approaches look for energetic "blockages"—for example, a lack of flow toward the body's periphery. Therapists aim to identify and release these "blocks" in order to help reestablish the client/patient's healthy energetic flow. In this way of working, the therapist can draw upon a wide spectrum of techniques, developed and refined over decades and appropriate to a wide range of physical tensions, symptoms, and conditions. Examples of such techniques include physical massage, stress positions, or the liberation of motoric aspects of inhibited or repressed affects, via expressive movements.

Other Body Psychotherapists are reluctant to apply such quantitative concepts, borrowed from the natural sciences, to the client's own subjective body-mind experience. They may subscribe to qualitative perceptions and descriptions that are also part of the energy concept, like vitality and spontaneity, especially when they emerge from the client's own experience and their "felt sense."

At the other end of the polarity, the use of the energy model is relinquished altogether (see, for example, Chapter 39, "Bodily Expression and Experience in Body Psychotherapy" by Ron Kurtz). Instead, information theory is used to describe somatic patterns and the experiential structures of embodiment. Here, the interest turns toward the body's experientially gained "knowing"—what neuroscience is now calling "implicit and procedural" knowledge, or as Bollas (1987) terms it, the "unthought known." According to this perspective, the therapeutic process is understood as follows: embodied knowledge that is limiting and therefore psychotherapeutically relevant, acquired by the body-self under stressful and adverse circumstances and operating outside awareness below the threshold of consciousness, is to become revealed, experienced in more depth or detail, and then processed and worked through, with all of the inherent implications. Experiences that expand this kind of knowledge and inform the soma in novel ways—what psychoanalysis calls "corrective emotional experience" and Clarkson (2003) would classify as "reparative" and "developmentally needed"—are thought to play a significant and fundamental role in therapeutic change.

**Analytic and Insight-Oriented versus Functional-Developmental**

We consider this particular polarity as fundamental to the understanding of the spectrum of Body Psychotherapy. One of the poles derives from the historical origins of part of Body Psychotherapy from within the tradition of psychoanalysis. As a result of this influence, the discovery of the unconscious background of present experiences and symptoms, and therapeutic work with unconscious relational dynamics, constitute essential elements in most approaches to Body Psychotherapy, focusing on interpretation and insight, and on the client's developing an understanding of the inner world of their psyche and their self-organization by making unconscious material conscious. What Body Psychotherapy adds to this standard psychoanalytic perspective is—as outlined above—the holistic-systemic understanding of the intricate interconnections between body, mind, and psyche and their functional identity, in Reich's terminology. The organization of the body is understood to reflect the inner landscape of the psyche, which can therefore be discovered through an analysis of the person's somatic experiences. The body is therefore considered part and parcel of the processes of discovery, as well as the processes of "working through."

At the same time, Body Psychotherapy has also developed the other pole—a way of working that we want to call "functional-developmental." In this polarity, therapeutic work is focused on detailed experiential engagement with body-mind processes that are essential for the client's development as *psychosomatic* functional systems—for example, respiration, muscle tone, the balance of the autonomic nervous system, and bodily flexibility, as well as specific functions such as vision or sexual sensitivity and potency.

At this end of the spectrum, rather than addressing the conflictual or traumatic history embodied in characterological patterns, Body Psychotherapy directly engages with the unfolding of body-mind resources, which may be unavailable due to psychodynamically arrested development, but without becoming overly concerned with insight into such history. Instead, the aim is to expand the client's functional capacities, through educating subjective awareness in the present, thus encouraging the client to "inhabit" their experience fully and to be in contact with the psychosomatic functional systems that constitute their being and are always already understood to consist of psychic, as well as bodily, micropractices and macropractices. The development and expansion of functional capacities that are facilitated in the therapeutic process can emphasize spontaneous recovery or—depending on the method—rely more on mindful practicing.

### Focus on Nonverbal Processes versus Focus on Dialogic Relating

Most Body Psychotherapy approaches forgo verbal exchange in some phases of the therapeutic process, or (at times) limit themselves to giving simple instructions (e.g., in Biodynamic Massage Psychotherapy, Dance Movement Psychotherapy, Character-Analytic Vegetotherapy, etc.). At these moments, the aim is for the client to rediscover their bodily sensations and somatic expressions: nonverbal methods like lingering, "being," sensing, expanding, stretching, etc., are therefore supported. The emphasis is on movement, self-expression, or—as in Vegetotherapy—the surrender to autonomic or interior somatic processes. The body is assumed to be able to recover its ability to experience itself and to function better—there is a built-in self-healing process. The therapeutic assumption is that this process goes hand in hand with the opening and liberation of the psyche.

On the other hand, some methods value highly intimate and ongoing dialogue about the experiences of the client (e.g., Pesso's work, Unitive Psychology, Analytic Body Psychotherapy, etc.). Even as virtually all methods include at least some moments of sensing and lingering in the therapeutic process, methods at this end of the spectrum value highly the interweaving of somatic experience with symbolic representation. Through the verbal exchange, meanings can be distilled and formed from the somatic experience.

### Touch versus No Touch

For a number of widely different Body Psychotherapeutic methods (e.g., Biodynamic Psychotherapy, postural or structural work, Rubenfeld Synergy, etc.), touch is almost indispensable, as many of their techniques depend on it—though in very different ways. Because bodywork is often based on massage techniques, this is quite easy to comprehend. Beyond that, touch can initiate several somatic processes directly, attention is directed by touch, and this can trigger important experiences. For example, a therapist whose client/patient is in a regressive state might consider holding her (or him) for a while (and giving their body an experience of being held in supportive intimacy) as the strongest and most transformative intervention available.

In other methods, touch plays much less of a central role, or can be waived altogether, depending on personal style and presenting issues. Sensing, awareness, increasing sensitivity, breathing, etc., is sufficient for some psychotherapists to work with the bodily dimension.

### Regression versus Working in the Here and Now

Because body-based work intrinsically is emotionally highly evocative, and because traumatic experiences are also "stored" somatically, regressions can easily be triggered. Some approaches utilize this option to a high degree (for example, Primal Therapy and Daniel Casriel's "New Identity Process") or aim to make systematic use of it. The primary therapeutic significance of regression is that it allows access to otherwise repressed and unavailable formative childhood or earlier experiences. Here, the significance of affect discharge or catharsis is considered just as important as bodily "enacted" forms of corrective emotional experiences.

At the other end of the spectrum, there are approaches such as Gestalt Therapy and associated methods that emphasize working very much in the here and now, and—similar to classic analysis—bring those more obvious aspects of regression into consciousness that function as a defense. The focus is less on catharsis and corrective experiences and more on therapeutic "working through" and "maturing."

Some of these methods, and some of the authors in this Handbook (e.g., Downing, Geissler, Marlock, etc.), have striven for a critical and differentiated synthesis of these poles. The explicitly trauma-oriented methods of Body Psychotherapy (e.g., Levine, Ogden, Marcher) also tend to take a complex and well-substantiated center position in this polarity.

## Organization of the Handbook

This Handbook attempts to convey a contemporary overview of Body Psychotherapy, as a whole. However, due to the previously mentioned complexity of the field, the picture cannot be complete, due to all of its diverse specificities. In addition, the field of Body Psychotherapy shows significant geographic variances between several large communities, some east of the Atlantic, especially in the German-speaking countries, in Scandinavia, in the more Latin-speaking parts of Europe, and in Russia, as well as those west of the Atlantic, in the United States and in Canada. There are also significantly growing communities of Body Psychotherapists in Japan, in South America, and in Australia.

The reader will notice stylistic and methodological differences that are in part due to historical and cultural factors. Whereas, for example, the theoretical approach of our North American colleagues is commonly more pragmatic, our colleagues in the German and French language areas generally strive more toward epistemological rigor.

Considering the complexity and diversity of the field of Body Psychotherapy, this Handbook primarily aims to examine the large and formative themes within the field. Its history, metatheory, characteristic individual theories, methods, as well as applications and clinical practice will be discussed in the subsequent sections and chapters, in order to form a reasonably comprehensive overall picture. Each section begins with a short introduction, which is intended to provide an overview and to show links among the different contributions that follow.

Rather than to present particular schools or their representatives, the focus of the contributions is to characterize important thematic aspects of Body Psychotherapy. It is easy to see how such an organization can lead to redundancies and overlaps in the bigger picture, as many themes are intimately connected, or closely related. In the different introductions, the reader will also occasionally find references to other relevant authors who have made essential contributions to the topics at hand, and who can be referred to for further inquiry into respective questions.

As mentioned previously, we have striven to let authors speak on topics for which they hold a specific authority. This relationship is elucidated in short biographical introductions at the beginning of each chapter. There, as well as in the introductions to the different sections, we have attempted to clarify the author's particular perspective, theoretical orientation, and approach. It was often not possible for the authors (with exception of some of our pioneers) to present their current and favorite topics: instead, they were asked to address a particular topic that needed a competent author to complete the overarching task.

The reader will also notice the choice of a wide variety of approaches with respect to content and in linguistic style. Different levels of craftsmanship point to the diversity among schools, and differences in backgrounds and orientations of the authors. The spectrum of chapters ranges from concrete, descriptive, even poetic contributions, through Reichian and analytic dialects, to rigorous and sober "scientific" contributions.

Finally, despite the title, it is very important to us to emphasize that this Handbook is not an attempt to present

Body Psychotherapy in the form of a psychotherapeutic instruction manual. Good therapeutic interventions always have two prerequisites: the therapist needs a comprehensive understanding of what he is doing, one that reaches deep into metatheory and anthropology, and is paralleled by substantial self-exploration. Specifically, because of the depth and dynamic of the emotional processes that largely characterize Body Psychotherapy, as well as in regard to the subtlety of sensory perception and communication, intensive personal experience of Body Psychotherapy is considered absolutely indispensable. This requires comprehensive training, as well as concrete guidance (clinical supervision) with regard to the practical, emotional, and professional challenges of the work.

## Body and Soma

In conclusion, we want to point out that we have decided to use the term "Body Psychotherapy" for this Handbook, as its use has become established in the large international and national organizations. It must be noted, however, that this name is still open to debate. For many colleagues (for example, Judyth Weaver), the term "body" holds a limiting connotation that goes against our intentions. The critique is epistemologically substantiated and holds that this term does not specifically convey the animatedness of the body, and that it distorts the understanding of a subjectively experienced body through an objectifying perspective. Although one of the German words for "body," "Leib," does convey this meaning, there is really no English equivalent term. In English-speaking countries, like the United States and Australia, the term "Somatic Psychology" is frequently being used as an alternative. So, we have added this to the title of this edition. We hope that readers can keep all these points in mind.

## References

Boadella, D. (Ed.). (1973). *In the wake of Reich.* London: Coventure.

Bollas, C. (1987). *The shadow of the object: Psychoanalysis of the unthought known.* New York: Columbia University Press.

Clarkson, P. (2003). *The therapeutic relationship.* London: Whurr.

Damasio, A. (1994). *Descartes' error: Emotion, reason and the human brain.* New York: Penguin Putnam.

Downing, G. (1996). *Körper und Wort in der Psychotherapie [The body and word in psychotherapy].* Munich, Germany: Kösel.

*EABP Introductory Booklet.* (1994). Available at www.eabp.org.

Gendlin, E. (1998). *Focusing-oriented psychotherapy: A manual of the experiential method.* New York: Guilford Press.

Keleman, S. (1985). *Emotional anatomy.* Berkeley, CA: Center Press.

Koukkou, M., Leuzinger-Bohleber, M., & Mertens, W. (Eds.). (1998). *Erinnerung von Wirklichkeiten: Psychoanalyse und Neurowissenschaften im Dialog, Vol. 1: Bestandsaufnahme* [Reminders of reality: Psychoanalysis and neuroscience in dialogue, Vol. 1: Inventory]. Stuttgart, Germany: Internationale Psychoanalyse.

Petzold, H. (1977). *Die neuen Körpertherapien [The new body therapy].* Paderborn, Germany: Junfermann.

Reich, W. (1933/1970). *Character Analysis, 3rd ed.* New York: Farrar, Straus & Giroux.

Soth, M. (2005). Embodied countertransference. In N. Totton (Ed.), *New Directions in Body Psychotherapy* (pp. 40–55). Berkshire, UK: Open University Press.

Soth, M. (2010, Autumn). The return of the repressed body—not a smooth affair. *The Psychotherapist (UKCP journal),* 19–21.

Uexküll, T. (1997). *Psychosomatic medicine.* Munich, Germany: Urban & Schwarzenberg.

van der Kolk, B. A. (1987). *Psychological trauma.* Washington, DC: American Psychiatric Press.

Young, C. (Ed.). (2011). *The historical basis of Body Psychotherapy.* Galashiels, Scotland: Body Psychotherapy Publications.

# SECTION I

A Historical Overview of Body Psychotherapy

# 2
## Introduction to Section I

**Gustl Marlock, Germany, and Halko Weiss, United States**

**Translation by Warren Miller**

The history of Body Psychotherapy is a significant part of the history of psychotherapy (as a whole), and, additionally, the history of psychotherapy can only be understood comprehensively if the "fate" of the body within psychotherapy is reflected upon. Upon closer examination of Body Psychotherapy's history, and its relation to the larger field of psychotherapy, it becomes apparent that, in psychotherapy's general efforts to lessen or heal psychic suffering, the manifestation of people's problems in their bodily aspects (which were largely ignored) have been largely integrated over time, to quite a large degree by the field of Body Psychotherapy.

In the Preface to this Handbook, we outlined how it can be shown that many of the dialectics between body and speech, feeling experience and cognition, psyche and soma, have been prevalent throughout the history of Body Psychotherapy. There are different phases of synthesis, fragmentation, and reintegration between the body and the psyche that characterize this development. The fate of the work of Pierre Janet and Wilhelm Reich (as well as that of Franz Anton Mesmer) is particularly illustrative in showing how much the history of this discourse was permeated and determined by historical constellations, by politics, and by trends and movements according to the particular *zeitgeist* of the time, and also by issues of power and dogmatic exclusion.

In retrospect, as we can also see from his contribution of Chapter 3, "The History and Scope of Body Psychotherapy," Ulfried Geuter outlines the development of the European Lebensreform (Life Reform) Movement and its preoccupation with the body (particularly in the late nineteenth century and early twentieth century), which has been an important source of inspiration for a variety of body therapies and somatic educational methods, as well as for the whole of Body Psychotherapy itself. Beginning with this movement, Geuter traces the branches and ramifications of Body Psychotherapy into the present day. He shows that, in order to more deeply understand the differences between the various approaches and methods, it must be assumed that specific approaches develop and emphasize particular perspectives in regard to theory, metatheory, and methodology. If the particularities of specific approaches are seen as reflecting relevant and important issues for the larger field of Body Psychotherapy, Geuter's overview offers valuable information for a comprehensive understanding of body psychotherapy as a whole.

Two pioneers of body therapy and Body Psychotherapy are each commemorated with individual, biographically oriented chapters: Judyth Weaver writes about "The Influence of Elsa Gindler" in Chapter 4, and Wolf Büntig writes about the early work of Wilhelm Reich in Chapter 5. Elsa Gindler was a central figure in somatic education in the early twentieth century in Germany, and her work has had an immense influence, both directly and indirectly, on somatic education, body therapy, and Body Psychotherapeutic methods thereafter. Her contribution can also be seen as exemplary and representative of other influences from the Life Reform Movement, but the significance of Elsa Gindler's work has nearly been forgotten at times. Weaver illuminates Gindler's subtle yet formative inspiration to the whole field.

The fact that there are a couple of chapters about Wilhelm Reich hardly needs any explanation. Despite all the criticism that was (and still is) leveled against some aspects of his work, Reich was a central figure within Body Psychotherapy for the first half of the twentieth century. Many approaches and schools of Body Psychotherapy can trace their source back to Reich. Büntig displays, as much as it is possible in this brief format, the manifold aspects of Reich's work and shows how Reich's fate was connected with the political and professional controversies and dramas of the twentieth century. Those more interested in delving deeply into the width of Reich's work and its significance are referred to the comprehensive biographies of Myron Sharaf (1983) and David Boadella (1973/1987).

This theme is picked up again in Chapter 7 by Courtenay Young in his development of the later part of Büntig's (original German) chapter; he focuses on Reich's later work after about 1935, and particularly focuses on Reich's work in America. In between these two chapters, Chapter 6 is an interlude from Nicholas Bassal and Michael Heller that explores "The Norwegian Tradition of Body Psychotherapy: A Golden Age in Oslo."

Gustl Marlock, in Chapter 8 on "Body Psychotherapy as a Major Tradition of Modern Depth Psychology," writes first about the historical relationship between Body Psychotherapy and Psychodynamic Psychotherapy. He demonstrates that Body Psychotherapy has made essential contributions to the development of the psychodynamic paradigm, and continues still to do so today.

What then follows are a number of short but comprehensively graphic illustrations that are intended to help the reader gain an overview of the multifaceted and differentiated (at times quite confusing) relationships between the rest of psychotherapy and the various forms of Body Psychotherapy. These illustrate some of the various relationships, influences, and historical connections that characterize this complex field. They further clarify how closely the history of Body Psychotherapy is related to the history of Humanistic and Psychodynamic Psychology.

Then, Heike Langfeld and Dagmar Rellensmann write about the "Genealogy of Body Psychotherapy" in Chapter 9 and illustrate this with a number of quite complex diagrams and schemas by Hans-Jürgen Buch. In regard to these illustrations, it is noteworthy to discover how many influences there have been in the development of Body Psychotherapy. Many colleagues have participated in the effort to draft these graphics, so as to make these illustrations as representative as possible. Nonetheless, some degree of relativity and bias are unavoidable in creating such a depiction.

If any further general reading on this topic in Section I is desired (besides the references mentioned by the various authors), we can recommend that you read Don H. Johnson's *Bone, Breath, and Gesture* (1995) for an overview of the spectrum and history of somatic educational methods, and David Boadella's comprehensive understanding of the roots and traditions of Body Psychotherapy (Boadella, 1990). There is also a recent book, *The Historical Basis of Body Psychotherapy, edited by Courtenay Young (2011).*

## References

Boadella, D. (1973/1987). *Wilhelm Reich: The evolution of his work*. London: Vision; London: Routledge & Kegan Paul.

Boadella, D. (1990). Somatic Psychotherapy: Its roots and traditions. *Energy & Character, 21(1), 2–26*.

Johnson, D. H. (1995). *Bone, breath, and gesture*. Berkeley, CA: North Atlantic Books.

Sharaf, M. (1983). *Fury on earth: A biography of Wilhelm Reich*. London: Andre Deutsch.

Young, C. (Ed.). (2011). *The historical basis of Body Psychotherapy*. Galashiels, Scotland: Body Psychotherapy Publications.

# 3

## The History and Scope of Body Psychotherapy

**Ulfried Geuter, Germany**

**Translation by Christine M. Grimm**

**Ulfried Geuter** has worked for many years at the Free University of Berlin, researching the history of psychology. He has taught Body Psychotherapy at universities in Berlin, Innsbruck, and Marburg. Dr. Geuter has published extensively. In 2015, he will publish a book on the theoretical foundation of Body Psychotherapy and a second one on the principles of treatment. One of his important scientific contributions to Body Psychotherapy has been presenting historical outlines of the development, fundamental starting points, and thought processes of Body Psychotherapy in an understandable way. He is considered an expert on the history of Body Psychotherapy. In his own practice, he combines psychoanalysis and Body Psychotherapy and has also examined the relationship between psychodynamic affect research and Body Psychotherapeutic concepts and interventions. Dr. Geuter is co-editor of the German-language journal *körper–tanz–bewegung* [Body–Dance–Movement] and has been co-editor of *Psychoanalyse und Körper* [Psychoanalysis and the Body]. He has been strongly involved in the efforts to develop Body Psychotherapy theory more academically. He is also a founding member of the German Association for Body Psychotherapy. Geuter is a Doctor of Philosophy and a licensed psychologist, and teaches Body Psychotherapy as a professor at the University of Marburg. In addition to his education in Biodynamic Body Psychotherapy, he has also had advanced training in client-centered psychotherapy and psychoanalysis. He works as a Body Psychotherapist and psychoanalyst in his own private practice in Berlin. In addition, he is a psychotherapy teacher and lecturer at several licensed schools for advanced training in psychotherapy.

Body Psychotherapy has its origins in psychoanalysis and the reform movements in gymnastics and dance at the beginning of the twentieth century (Geuter, 2000a, 2000b). In the beginning, Freud massaged his patients or placed his hand on their forehead in order to stimulate associations (Breuer and Freud, 1895). Later, he attempted to direct all motoric impulses toward the psychological realm (Freud, 1914) and restricted his therapeutic communication to listening. The abstinence from physical contact made sense for patients who had suffered from the (so-called) transference neuroses, and for whom the goal of the treatment was to raise their repressed undesired ideas into consciousness: these, in many cases, had a sexual nature.

On the other hand, at this time, the German physician Georg Groddeck (from whom Freud adopted the concept of the Id [1990]) treated patients who probably tended to suffer more from functional and psychosomatic complaints by combining a type of deep connective-tissue massage with the therapeutic conversation. Groddeck communicated with words, and with his hands, wanting to relax the tensions and expand the breathing (Downing, 1996, pp. 346ff.). He also treated Freud's Hungarian student Sándor Ferenczi, with whom he was close in the 1920s (Will, 1987, p. 66).

Ferenczi, who frequently worked with patients who had been traumatized at an early age, had experimented since the 1920s with an "active technique" in which he used facial expressions and gestures as the language of the unconscious. He later offered patients a form of bodily contact, in ways such as holding them (especially in cases of affective shocks), during the therapy hour (Polenz, 1994). Ferenczi also searched for a psychoanalytic treatment for borderline patients and psychotics, reaching beyond the taboo of touch. Together with Otto Rank, in the 1920s, he already emphasized the healing effect of activating the experience in contrast to the "working-through" that Freud favored. However, under pressure from the associational politics of Freudian psychoanalysis, he recanted his experience-oriented, body-oriented, and relationship-oriented approaches for a period of time (Nagler, 2003). After his death, Ferenczi's ideas were thoroughly suppressed by psychoanalysts, so that they were not able to develop in any significant way.

However, the greatest influence on the development of Body Psychotherapy was exerted by Wilhelm Reich, who was also originally a student of Freud (see Chapter 5, "The Work of Wilhelm Reich, Part 1: Reich, Freud, and Character" by Wolf Büntig). Reich was the first psychoanalyst to deal extensively with the borderline disorder, which he called the "instinctual character" (Reich, 1975). He searched for a new treatment technique to help patients who did not have a stable ego structure and were therefore not capable of the predominant verbal-associative work. Similar to later Ego Psychology, he assumed that there were basic "instinct-defense" configurations in the therapeutic work and he therefore granted a very central and important role to the analysis of character defense (Geuter and Schrauth, 1997). From his early clinical work, he was also very interested in the psychological and physiological effects of sexual repression (Reich, 1927/1986).

In contrast to the immediate interpretation of unconscious conflicts, customary at that time, Reich gave priority to the analysis of the patient's resistance. According to his observations, the consequences of "chronic" (long-term) defense processes are character patterns or attitudes, which are often accompanied by characteristic bodily postures. He believed that the reason for this is that the emotional processes of repression are connected with physical processes of repression: the muscular prevention of impulses toward actions and drives. These repressions therefore become associated with muscle tensions that can lead to the development of chronic defense structures (Reich, 1933). This is why he also began working with the physical defense in therapy, such as with the tensed muscles, or the restrained breathing pattern: the resultant physical expression of the patients' repressed emotions should help to raise awareness of their unconscious into consciousness. Whereas Freud wanted to push ahead with the memory to the original affect, Reich took the opposite path by relaxing the physical defenses to the affect and, therefore, as a result, to the memory. To describe his method, Reich created the term "*Vegetotherapy*" in the mid-1930s. Reich had moved from Vienna to Berlin in 1930. Here, he received additional impulses that assisted his change from psychoanalysis toward what would later become Body Psychotherapy. This is also where he met his second life-companion, Elsa Lindenberg, who worked as a dancer at the Berlin State Opera under Rudolf Laban and who had attended courses taught by the body awareness educator Elsa Gindler (Geuter, Heller, and Weaver, 2010).

## The Reform of Gymnastics and Body Culture and the Experience of the Body-Self

In that 1920–1930s era in Europe, Laban was the most important theoretician of expressionist dance, which was free from any fixed steps and forms, and in which the dancers could express their inner movement or, as Laban formulated it, should "open the floodgates of inner motion" (Laban, 1926, p. 132). Isadora Duncan and Mary Wigman had created this style of dance at the beginning of the twentieth century in Berlin.

The reformation of dance was part of a number of various contemporary reforms of the "Victorian" lifestyle, such as the new youth movement, body-culture movement, the Life Reform Movement, and a reformation in gymnastics, which also had one of its centers in Berlin, where Elsa Gindler's "Seminar for Harmonizing Body Formation" was located.

This "school" was the one most closely connected with the beginnings of Body Psychotherapy, although Gindler represented a somato-educational approach without any psychotherapeutic claims. Through experiencing their own bodies, people were more able to find idiosyncratic movements within themselves that made it possible for them to let changes occur from within their body, so that it could better execute its natural functions (see Ludwig, 2002). Gindler did not develop any particular theory, although Heinrich Jacoby (1983), a musician who worked together with her, recorded some of her teachings that allow us to recognize a concept of learning about one's biologically suitable behavior patterns. However, Gindler's work had profound emotional effects, despite its intentions. Charlotte Selver writes that "the degree to which the individual becomes more capable of feeling and learns to make friends with what is gradually uncovered" opens the path to more extensive experience and deeper relationship (Selver, 1988, p. 61).

In addition to Elsa Lindenberg, the participants in Gindler's courses included Laura Perls (the wife of Fritz Perls), as well as Charlotte Selver, Lily Ehrenfried, Clare Fenichel, and Gertrud Heller. The latter were movement teachers who later passed their knowledge on to psychotherapists, such as Ehrenfried to Hilarion Petzold, and Selver to Erich Fromm. The principle of awareness in Perls's Gestalt Therapy can also be traced back to Selver, who called her method of bodywork "Sensory Awareness" in the United States. Ruth Cohn studied Gindler's work and possibly adopted from it the principle of the movable equilibrium for her theme-centered interactions (Cohn, 1975). Clare Fenichel, the wife of the famous psychoanalyst Otto Fenichel, worked to a ripe old age in the United States as a Gindler teacher. George Downing (1996) studied with Magda Proskauer, a student of Heinrich Jacoby. Impulses from Gindler's work have also gone into movement therapy with children who are disabled or have developmental disorders (i.e., the work of Emmi Pikler, Elfriede Hengstenberg, and Miriam Goldberg). Via Carola Speads, and her pupil Berta Bobath, Gindler's approach also passed to Bonnie Bainbridge Cohen (1993), founder of Body-Mind Centering (see Aposhyan, 2004).

Some of the Body Psychotherapeutic approaches that focus on the experience of the body-self have thus been strongly influenced by the work of Elsa Gindler. One of the far-reaching developments for the German-language region was the development of "Concentrative Movement Therapy" by psychoanalyst Helmuth Stolze (1984). He had learned about Gindler's work through Gertrud Heller, a dancer and movement therapist who worked at a psychiatric hospital in Scotland as a relaxation teacher.

Stolze was additionally influenced by the psychotherapist Gustav Heyer. In a lecture on "The Treatment of the Psyche Starting from the Body" in 1931, at the Sixth Congress of the General Medical Society for Psychotherapy in Dresden, Heyer had argued that analytical work must be supplemented by a "physiological theory and therapy" (Heyer, 1931). Furthermore, the body must be included in the treatment of neurosis through gymnastics, massage, or breathwork. In the 1940s, Heyer offered courses in breathing therapy within the scope of the psychotherapeutic training at the German Institute for Psychological Research and Psychotherapy in Berlin. He also spoke of the Gestalt symbolism of physical movement, a thought that was found in the Gestalt circle theory by Viktor von Weizsäcker. This concept entered into the Concentrative Movement Therapy method, which has become widespread in Austria and Germany. It utilizes offerings of conscious personal experience, and makes use of equipment like balls, ropes, or sticks. What is experienced in the movement or action is then worked through on the basis of the person's psychodynamic background. However, it can also develop its own effects without verbal clarification. This method has the goal of equally making possible experience and learning, as well as uncovering the unconscious material (Pokorny et al., 1996).

Marianne Fuchs founded "Functional Relaxation," which is another specialty within the German-language region. Fuchs was influenced by the Life Reform Movement and had studied at the Günther School for Gymnastics, Music, and Dance in Munich with the musician Carl Orff, among others. She continued her studies in breathwork and later worked at Ernst Kretschmer's psychiatric clinic at the

University of Marburg teaching rhythmic body formation to the patients.

When she treated her ailing one-year-old son, who suffered from spastic bronchitis, with a fine touching of the rib cage and with tones that followed his hampered breathing rhythm, she was able to influence his breathing rhythm and intercept the asthmatic attacks (Arnim, 1993, 1994). On the basis of her experiences, Fuchs developed a method that attempts to achieve a relaxation of the organism by releasing muscular tensions through exhaling (Fuchs, 1989). As in the Gindler work, Functional Relaxation involves training the person's "proprioceptive" sense, which means promoting the perception of one's own body with the goal of letting the autonomous body processes achieve equilibrium. The method has subsequently proved to be especially effective for the treatment of asthma, but is also used clinically for many functional diseases, pain disorders, and somatizing disorders (Loew et al., 1996).

By exploring these subsequent developments, it is easy to show that the evolution of Body Psychotherapy came from within a widely based interest in body awareness, movement, and expression that flowered (particularly in Germany before the Nazi era, but that also had strong effects overseas). In the United States, Body Psychotherapy—to a large extent—followed Selver's experience-based concepts (see Chapter 11, "The Primacy of Experiential Practices in Body Psychotherapy" by Don Johnson).

## Libido, Conflict, and Liberation: The Aftermath of Wilhelm Reich

The focus of the previously mentioned approaches can be described as organismic relaxation and the self-regulation of psycho-physical functions. In contrast, the Body Psychotherapy approaches, based on Reich, focused on loosening the character defenses and uncovering the resisted, conflict-laden, mental contents, impulses, or instinctual needs, and these approaches later became widespread. Reich adhered to Freud's earlier view, which was that suppressed sexual energy is the energetic source of neurosis. He was concerned with releasing the drive from the repression, leading to self-regulation; others in the field considered it to be the result of an organismic self-perception (see Geuter, 2000a, pp. 68–70).

This means that there were two different ideological positions in the beginnings of Body Psychotherapy. The body-educational work had its background in the conservative cultural criticism of the modern world. This contrasted the "nature" of the "body" with the "decadence" of "civilization," and the organic "rhythm" of the body with the "beat" of the machine. In contrast, Reich was both a Freudian and a Marxist who had assumed the causes of the plight of humanity were socially generated. His understanding was that society shaped people's character structures (Reich, 1933). He wanted to liberate what had been suppressed, so he became heavily involved with Marxist-oriented sexual politics.

However, Reich—like others who thought in terms of the organism—in his later work, assumed the primacy of biology and thus subordinated psychological work to working with "bio-energy." Thus, both starting positions in Body Psychotherapy had something in common, which could be called the rebellion of the subjective nature against objectification.

Reich had to leave Germany in 1933 and eventually settled in Oslo, Norway, living there from 1934 to 1939. This was the "Golden Age" of Body Psychotherapy in Norway (see Chapter 6, "The Norwegian Tradition of Body Psychotherapy: A Golden Age in Oslo" by Nicholas Bassal and Michael Coster Heller [also Heller, 2007]). After he had emigrated to the United States in 1939, and after the ravages of the Second World War, Oslo became a center for the development of Body Psychotherapy that continued working with the character-analytical vegetotherapeutic approach, mainly through Reich's student Ola Raknes (1970). Various Neo-Reichians, like Gerda Boyesen, David Boadella, Federico Navarro, and Malcolm Brown, all studied with Raknes in the post-war years.

In Scandinavia, Vegetotherapy developed in close connection to physiotherapy. In addition to working with Raknes, Gerda Boyesen studied with the renowned physiotherapist Aadel Bülow-Hansen, who had worked with the psychiatrist Trygve Braatøy. Boyesen learned the techniques of deep-tissue massage from her, developing the concept that the energy of repressed affects can become congested not only in the muscles, thus forming "character armor," but also in the person's connective tissue and their intestines (see Chapter 56, "The Unfolding of Libidinous Forces in Body Psychotherapy" by Ebba Boyesen and Peter Freudl).

Boyesen (1987), as the founder of Biodynamic Psychology, became known for one particular form of massage in which the patient's bowel sounds are listened to with the stethoscope, giving a form of biofeedback that indicates the changing-over from the sympathetic to the parasympathetic nervous function. In her concept of the "vasomotoric" circle, there are similarities with the theory of the functional circles in Functional Relaxation (see Geuter, 2000a, as well as Chapter 53, "The Role of the Body in Emotional Defense Processes: Body Psychotherapy and Emotional Theory" by Ulfried Geuter and Norbert Schrauth). In the 1970s and 1980s, Boyesen, with help from David Boadella and others, turned the London Center for Biodynamic Psychology into a leading center for Body Psychotherapy in Europe.

Boadella (1987) later founded his own school of Biosynthesis, in Switzerland, which, following the embryological model's example of three germ layers (endoderm, mesoderm, and ectoderm), teaches special techniques for working with the vegetative level (centering), the muscular level (grounding), and the cognitive level (looking).

Federico Navarro (1986) continued to elaborate on Reich's theory of segmental armoring. He initially spread Vegetotherapy into Italy, and then later into Brazil. Another student of Raknes, Malcolm Brown (1985), in his Organismic Psychotherapy, introduced the differentiation between catalytic and nourishing touch. Whereas catalytic touch serves the liberation of repressed affects, nourishing touch—similar to the "safe holding environment" of Winnicott—assists in bringing the body into a state from which an inner reorganization can take place according to its inherent wisdom.

Body Psychotherapy is strong in Norway, Sweden, and Denmark to this day. In Oslo, Norway, Nic Waal developed a test for measuring muscle tension, and Lillemor Johnsen studied the relationships between childhood history, breathing, and muscle tone (Boadella, 1990, p. 20). From the 1950s onward, psycho-motor physiotherapy was developed in Norwegian psychiatry (Ekerholt, 2010; Thornquist and Bunkan, 1991). More recently, Kirsti Monsen (1989) connected self-psychological and affect-theoretical concepts with Body Psychotherapy and, together with Jon Monsen (Monsen and Monsen, 2000), proved the effectiveness of psychodynamic Body Psychotherapy in the treatment of pain. In Sweden, several people combined Reichian Body-Oriented Psychotherapy and Eastern body awareness traditions into psychiatric physiotherapy (Mattson, 1998). And, in Denmark, Lisbeth Marcher has founded Bodynamics, in which she closely connects physical and psychological development in the emergence of psychomotor patterns. She tries to ascertain how and when specific muscles become activated in human development, and each muscle is related to a certain psychological meaning (Macnaughton, 2004).

Reich also left his mark during his American exile. His later concepts were that psychotherapeutic work was possible to a large extent without any psychodynamic work and solely by dissolving blockages of the basic life "orgone" energy—the existence of which he assumed. Orgone therapists, like Elsworth Baker (1967), continue in this work, primarily in America.

Another American student of Reich, Charles Kelley (1970), in his Radix Emotional Work, developed techniques for dissolving tension patterns that block certain feelings and became known for the development of special eye exercises. However, he understood his work to be more educative, rather than as a form of psychotherapy.

The greatest development of Reich's work was found in Bioenergetic Analysis, which his students Alexander Lowen and John Pierrakos developed in the 1950s. Pierrakos (1987) later went his own way and developed Core Energetics, as he wanted to focus less on the consequences of earlier injuries and more on the essential core of a human being's natural vital energy, which is their fundamental potential filled with love. Lowen became well known for some confrontational work on the consequences of earlier deficits and conflicts. He further elaborated on Reich's theory of character structures and added the "oral character" (Lowen, 1958) to those Reich had already described. According to Lowen, character structures are reaction patterns that live in the present, but were created in childhood as an early set of responses to the refusal to meet a child's needs. Lowen was also the first to introduce Body Psychotherapeutic work when the client is standing. This paved the way out of the more regressive (supine, lying-down) work into the more here-and-now reality where a person is standing and becoming more "grounded" (see Chapter 67, "Vertical Grounding: The Body in the World and the Self in the Body" by Lily Anagnostopoulou).

In Bioenergetics, many exercises have been developed in which the chronically tensed muscles are placed under stress until they release the tension that they hold (Lowen and Lowen, 1977). Their goal was to help the inhibited affects express themselves in a physical way. Whereas Reich saw the liberation of sexuality as central, Lowen speaks of freeing an inhibited life energy or vitality. The goal of the treatment is not orgiastic potency, but to increase the general joy in life.

Jack Lee Rosenberg, Marjorie Rand, and Diana Asay (1985) also represent the energetic model. However, in the arena of self-psychology, they see the development of the sense of self as the central goal of psychotherapy. In this understanding, discharging blocked energy is a technique that helps their clients to examine the origin of their blockages and comprehend their function on the basis of their life story. According to this approach, the trapped self can appear when these blockages are successfully cleared away.

The cathartic approach in psychotherapy, which can be traced back to Breuer, Freud, and Reich, has spread to other therapeutic methods since the 1970s. For example, in Primal Therapy, Arthur Janov (1970) emphasized the importance of physical mobilization in order to reestablish access to the "primal" early childhood experiences that have been split off from the body and feelings. Another body-oriented therapy (but not a psychotherapy), Rebirthing (Orr and Ray, 1983), attempts to produce cathartic release by means of altered states brought about by hyperventilation. Both methods have been subjected to criticism as patients quickly fell into distressed body-emotion states. In Bonding Therapy, which was called the New Identity Group Process in earlier times, developed by Daniel Casriel (1969), the inadequate early attachment experiences were addressed through strong physical interactive experiences in therapeutic groups, and the feelings that had been suppressed or split off at an earlier time were then able to be released. The early Encounter Group movement provided some of the background experiences of this and other cathartic group approaches.

Catharsis has suffered a bad reputation in psychotherapy for a long time. However, Harald Traue (1998) points out that—from the perspective of empirical health research—catharsis contributes to dissolving emotional repression where patients do not subjectively experience emotions, which can be established in the form of physiological reactions and behavior. But, according to the empirical studies, it seems important that the expressed feelings are conflict-charged or unconscious for a therapeutically fruitful catharsis to occur. Moreover, these feelings should be cognitively linked and the patient should become more emotionally expressive (Traue, 1998, p. 376; see also Traue and Pennebaker, 1993).

As a result of Freud's taboo on touching the patient, touch in psychotherapy has been quite controversial for a long while. The conflict about physical touch within psychoanalysis, as it took place in the beginning, particularly between Freud and Ferenczi, came to a standstill in the 1930s for various reasons (Mintz, 1969). One of the major reasons was that Ferenczi was ostracized by the official psychoanalysts, and was even declared mentally ill by Freud's biographer, Ernest Jones. In Britain, the psychoanalysts Michael Balint (1952), a student of Ferenczi, and Donald Winnicott (1965), however, considered physical touch to be helpful in states of deep regression. Winnicott offered patients his hand in order to give them support. Recently, in the United States, and partly in England, there has emerged a broader discussion about the value of touch in the treatment of physical illnesses and in the promotion of healthy development in general (Field, 2001; Barnard and Brazelton, 1990) and its benefits for psychotherapy in particular (Field, 1998; Fosshage, 1994; Horton et al., 1995; Hunter and Struve, 1998; Smith et al., 1998; Tune, 2005). This has been conducted possibly as an attempt to overcome the social "phobia" about touch in psychotherapy, especially in America. In this process, touch in psychotherapy is considered partially as a means for imparting empathy and support, partially to strengthen the therapeutic bond, and as a restorative agent for touch "deficits" in the patient's process. However, catalytic touch is barely considered.

The current debate is far less characterized by the rigid psychoanalytic rules of abstinence from touch and the fear of psychotherapists' abuse, and more by an open search for helpful psychotherapeutic contact, in contrast to debates within European psychoanalysis (for example, Holder, 2000). Also, modern Anglo-American Body Psychotherapy has now begun to explicitly address the issue of touch in psychotherapy (Young, 2005, 2009; Zur, 2007) (see also Chapter 48, "Touch in Body Psychotherapy" by Gill Westland).

## Expression and Movement

### The Beginnings of Dance Therapy in the United States

Starting as early as the 1940s, dance, or dance-movement, therapy developed into another branch of Body Psychotherapy in the United States. Dance therapy uses the expressive movement as an essential medium of the treatment. The founders of this direction were dancers who brought the elements of expressionist dance into their psychotherapeutic work. Above all, this occurred in the psychiatric clinics (Chaiklin, 1975; McNeely, 1987). One of these women was Marian Chace, who began to dance with psychiatric patients for whom there was no medication at that time at a hospital in Washington, DC, at the beginning of the 1940s (Chace et al., 1993). Chace had learned Psychodrama, which uses the body techniques of the theater, from Jacob Moreno (1964). In the clinic she worked together with the neo-psychoanalysts Frieda Fromm-Reichmann and Harry S. Sullivan. She understood physical postural, tension, or breathing patterns and coordination difficulties as an expression of inner conflicts (Duggan, 1983; Siegel et al., 1999, pp. 11ff.).

One of the other pioneers of dance therapy was Trudi Schoop (1981), a Swiss expressionist dancer who worked in a psychiatric clinic in California after the Second World War. Liljan Espenak (1972, 1981) was an Adlerian psychotherapist and a student of Mary Wigman, the expressionist dancer, and made use of the conscious coordination of body parts and rhythmic improvisations in her method called Psychomotor Espenak. Mary Whitehouse (1979), who was also a student of Wigman and in analysis with C. G. Jung, applied Jung's method of active imagination to dancing; the patients should express images, ideas, and sensations in movement.

In 1965, the above-mentioned dancers founded the American Dance Therapy Association. Dance therapy not only was able to establish itself in American psychiatric clinics, but also became an academic subject of study at several American universities over the course of the next few decades (see also Chapter 86, "Dance Therapy" by Sabine Trautmann-Voigt).

## Experience, Relationship, Mindfulness: The Humanistic Paradigm

A new major impulse for the development of Body Psychotherapy came from the social movements of the 1960s, which championed the causes of sexual liberation, creativity, new life-forms, and the emancipation of the individual. These impulses also included the encounter groups, the Human Potential Movement, and the growth of humanistic psychotherapy. Reich's books (having been burned in 1933 in Germany, and in America in the 1950s) were being read once again, especially in the student movements. His thinking seemed to fit with the idea of freeing people from their inner authoritarian conditioning in order to be able to change their outer circumstances more effectively. A multitude of new psychotherapeutic directions blossomed, which had as a center the Esalen Institute in California.

These new psychotherapies were characterized by the humanistic paradigm of self-actualizing the potentials inherent to the human being and put a new focus on waking up a person's resources. They also included several of the Neo-Reichian schools of therapy, and these approaches also brought psychotherapy together with creative arts and with Asian body and martial arts techniques. One of the leading representatives of humanistic psychology, Charlotte Bühler, wrote the preface to one of the first anthologies on the new methods of movement and body therapy in 1973 (Petzold, 1974). At that time, these methods were based upon the understanding of offering alternatives to the established or "ruling" paradigms of traditional psychotherapy and psychiatry. This meant that they flourished initially at the fringes of these institutional disciplines. At the same time, their theories reflected new social demands for more individual flexibility, creativity, and personal responsibility.

With them came a renaissance of the experience concept (Gendlin, 1961; see also Chapter 23, "The Bodily 'Felt Sense' as a Ground for Body Psychotherapies" by Eugene Gendlin and Marion Hendricks-Gendlin), which had imprinted the beginnings of the Body Psychotherapeutic approaches that dated back to Gindler's tradition (Geuter, 2004). At that time, many people became involved in personal-growth, therapy, and encounter groups as a way to expand their inner possibilities and to seek an identity that they believed they had lost. The body became a very significant reference point in this search for the self.

Humanistic psychotherapy has had a very strong influence on the understanding of the psychotherapist's role in the new Body Psychotherapies. Whereas Reich espoused the traditional analytical model of a "one-person psychology" (Kirman, 1998), even if he was one of the first psychoanalysts to demonstrate approaches toward a two-person psychology, and whereas Lowen mainly followed a traditional image of the therapist as the knowing physician (Heisterkamp, 1993, pp. 28ff.), most Body Psychotherapists since the 1970s have followed Carl Rogers's idea that the psychotherapist should be available as a helpful person in an interaction where "there are just two people in the room." The idea of the human, "I-Thou" encounter by the philosopher Martin Buber (1979) also became influential. Therapy came to be understood as an existential encounter between two human beings in which the therapist is present as authentically as possible—which was represented by Gestalt Therapy in particular. As a result, the therapeutic attitudes within Body Psychotherapy became less reserved and, as with Rogers, more empathetic, supportive, and loving. Rogers's approach, of supportively working with the person's resources, was explicitly combined with work on muscular armoring by Malcolm Brown (1985).

Today, within Body Psychotherapy, elaborated psychoanalytical approaches are being integrated into an interactional work with the transference (Moser, 2001; Heisterkamp, 2002; Soth, 2009). Geissler and Heisterkamp (2007) see the psychotherapist as co-moving to the life movement of the patient. Stanley Keleman (1987) has presented a body-related concept of transference and countertransference processes that understands this as a pattern of a psychological and somatic pulsatoric bond. In this understanding, the patient also connects with the therapist through resonating muscular reaction patterns, which trigger somatic reactions in the countertransference: this is now known as "somatic resonance" or "somatic attunement" and, as a concept, has extended far beyond Body Psychotherapy. Fritz Perls, who had completed a part of his analysis with Reich in Berlin in the early 1930s, included thoughts and techniques from Body Psychotherapy in Gestalt Therapy and also from the "body staging" of Psychodrama (Paul Goodman, the theoretician of Gestalt Therapy, was also in analysis with Reich) (Perls, Hefferline, and Goodman, 1973). What both directions have in common is the concept of clearing away blocks that limit the person's emotional experience (Revenstorf, 2000, p. 208). Perls—like Reich in his resistance analysis—gave priority in therapy to observations of the process and the analysis of the "how" of a message over its content. And similar to how Reich had written about the analysis of the "instinctual character" that the transference must be discussed "daily" (compare with Geuter and Schrauth, 1997), Perls emphasized the work in the here-and-now. Both approaches also have the mutual aspect of confronting the person's defenses (Bock, 2000). These three ways of thinking were later integrated within psychoanalysis, especially in Otto Kernberg's (1989) concept on the treatment of borderline disorders.

However, Perls was critical of Reich's attempts at physically confronting resistance. In contrast to the Body Psychotherapists, Perls never really worked with direct interventions on the body, but with the awareness of processes in the body and their affective meanings, especially when he worked in conjunction with Ilana Rubenfeld (2001). Various other Gestalt therapists have come to form a closer connection between Gestalt Therapy and bodywork (above all, see Kepner, 1987; Ginger, 2007).

Also characteristic of that time, as for all of Humanistic Psychotherapy, was the process of integrating the thoughts of C. G. Jung and existentialism, as well as the connection with the ideas and practices of various spiritual traditions. Most of the Body Psychotherapeutic schools tend toward Jung's understanding of seeing general life energy within the libido, instead of the Freudian instinctual theory of drives. They tended to adopt Jung's concept of both subject and object interpretation of the dream, or his work with imagination. Furthermore, Malcolm Brown (1985) has also taken up the theory of the archetypes.

Like Jung, Jay Stattman (1989; Stattman et al., 1989, 1991), the founder of Unitive Psychology, emphasized, with his active imagination, work with inner images during the state of waking consciousness in a "creative trance." Like many others, he took up the statements by the existential philosophers Gabriel Marcel (1935) and Maurice Merleau-Ponty (1945) that the human being does not *have* a body but *is* his or her body (Marlock, 1993, p. 10).

The concept of the subjective, experienced body (which in German is referred to as "Leib" instead of "Körper," both can be translated as "body") is also central for Hilarion Petzold (2003), who has founded Integrative Body and Movement Therapy as one psychotherapeutic method within a broader integrative theory of psychotherapy in general. This method has been decisively influenced by the French existential philosophers and has combined elements of Reichian Body Psychotherapy, Gestalt Therapy, Psychomotor Movement Therapy, and Ferenczian psychoanalysis into a synthesizing approach that has been broadly substantiated through scientific and clinical research. Petzold, as well as Yvonne Maurer (1999), represents a bio-psychosocial model of disease and treatment, whereby Maurer with Uexküll and colleagues (1994) combines systemic theoretic concepts with body-related approaches.

Psychiatrists Christian Scharfetter and Wolfgang Blankenburg also adopted the body-philosophical tradition of Marcel, Merleau-Ponty, and others to describe the disturbed physical nature of psychotic patients. According to Scharfetter, the body assumes a central importance in the "therapeutic reconstruction of the ego" (1998, p. 26). The experience of being "my body" is understood, within the phenomenological concept of the body, as essential for a cognitive-affective consciousness and identity.

The idea of attaining a psychotherapeutic effect through inner mindfulness, which is foremost directed at the body, was also stimulated through the reception of Eastern meditation and mindfulness techniques. Ron Kurtz, the founder of Hakomi Therapy, describes Buddhism and Taoism as sources of his thinking. In terms of theory, Hakomi is based upon the Neo-Reichian character structure model and on system-theoretical concepts (Kurtz, 1983, 1990). However, unlike the Neo-Reichians, the treatment philosophy has a radically noninvasive approach as its foreground. The patient can be guided into a state of "inner mindfulness." Once in this state, she should observe how she habitually organizes herself and how she initially perceives the world and relates to it from unconscious outlooks. As in all the therapeutic methods based on self-experience in Humanistic and Body-Oriented Psychotherapy, Hakomi assumes that only what has been deeply experienced can really cause change.

The practice of spiritual traditions to produce healing in changed states of consciousness, such as shamanistic trances, became a possible means of psychotherapeutic work for Stanislav Grof (1985, 1987). However, Grof came to this conclusion on the basis of his scientific research as a psychiatrist. Within this framework, he studied altered states of consciousness that had been produced by psycholytic substances such as LSD. When this was banned, he developed his Holotropic Breathwork as a method through which people can attain such states of consciousness without drugs. According to Grof, people can do this through specific breathing techniques quite similar to hyperventilation and other audible and rhythmic stimulations with the help of music. Once they are in these states, they can encounter significant natal, prenatal, and even transpersonal experiences.

With the method called Focusing, Eugene Gendlin (1998), out of client-centered psychotherapy and on the basis of a Process-Oriented theory of experience, developed a body-oriented method of psychotherapy. Focusing involves an exploration of the emotional assessment of cognitions from the body outward. In six established steps, the patient explores the feelings that arise from within the body as a response to a situation or to a question. Gendlin calls this feeling the "felt sense."

So far, the history of Body Psychotherapy has focused mainly on developments in Germany, England, and the United States, which have also been described by Eiden, Goodrich-Dunn and Greene, Young, and others (in Young, 2010), but Body Psychotherapy has found its way into other countries, too.

## Further Developments in Other Countries

Similar to the spread of psychoanalysis, Body Psychotherapy has spread primarily within most European countries, North America (the United States and Canada), Australia, Israel, Mexico, and Brazil. The beginnings of its expansion also exist in Japan, South Africa, and Russia. At the same time, special characteristics of the individual countries that are related to local traditions can be identified. This provides a particularly unique flavor that is sometimes exported back and adds to the richness of the field.

Some of the special characteristics in the German-language regions, and in Norway and Denmark, have already been mentioned. In Russia, Lev Vygotsky introduced movement work to child therapy quite early in its development (Petzold, 2003, pp. 443f.). Some of the more recent developments in Russia resulted from David Boadella's teaching groups there in the 1980s and early 1990s, and these have added a particular slant toward a restoration of the upset balance of biological processes in the human body (Baskakov et al., 2004).

In France, we find a major tradition based on the theory of psycho-motoric development, as well as a psycho-motoric education that is already given a special place in the kindergartens and brings a greater social acceptance of expressionist body techniques with this (Calza, 1994; LeCamus, 1983, 1988). Richard Meyer (1982) has argued for using the body as an expressionist organ in psychoanalysis (which he calls "Somato-Analysis"). Meyer does not work with prescribed physical exercises but with the spontaneous and autonomous expressions of the patients with the intention of bringing the current experience to its complete gestalt.

In Italy, Neo-Reichian Body Psychotherapy has developed since the 1960s. This was initially because Ola Raknes taught Vegetotherapy in Italy as a visiting therapist until a ripe old age; his student Federico Navarro lived there until he moved to Brazil. Luciano Rispoli and Barbara Andriello continued vegetotherapeutic work in Naples under the name Functional Body Psychotherapy, because they understood posture, movement, dreams, cognitions, emotions, and neurovegetative reactions as psycho-physical functions of the self that are thought to work in a dynamic parallel manner, and not in a hierarchical form or structure (Rispoli, 1993, 2008). Psychotherapy should diagnose dysfunctions and help restore natural functions such as natural breathing, with the goal of integrating the functions for the harmonization of the self. Another development was when Rome-based American psychiatrist Jerome Liss developed his theory of Biosystemics, in which he mainly integrates Bioenergetic Analysis with systemic theory (Liss and Stupiggia, 2000).

Bioenergetics, Biosynthesis, and Biodynamics, as well as dance therapy, are also very widespread in Brazil. A special approach, the method of "Toques Sutis"—the fine touching—can be traced back to the Hungarian physician Pethö Sándor (1974). In 1949, he came to Brazil and taught body-therapeutic techniques in combination with Jungian analysis at the Papal University of São Paulo. In this method, a subtle touching is performed on established body points, which leads to deep relaxation. The concept is similar to that of Biodynamic Psychotherapy—that very deep relaxation has a special mobilizing dynamic on unconscious material.

## Psychoanalysis, Developmental Psychology, and Body Psychotherapy: New Connections

In addition to the directions of the investigative and functional bodywork and the uncovering energetic-expressive Reichian work, a third line of development in Body Psychotherapy has been able to establish itself: this follows a model of the "dialogic body" (Geuter, 1996), which means studying the body in relationship to others through its affective-motoric messages and working therapeutically with the body-to-body dialogue in the therapeutic relationship. This line was only recently taken up again, in the course of the new Ferenczi debates, and under the influence of findings in infant research.

In the German-language region, it has produced developments in the establishment of Analytical Body Psychotherapy (Geissler, 1998, 2001; Geissler and Heisterkamp, 2007; Maaz and Krüger, 2001). Since the late 1980s, the psychoanalyst Tilmann Moser (1989, 1993, 1994) has argued for including the body in work with severely disturbed patients, who do not have the necessary intact ego function for a verbal-associative, psychoanalytic therapy. A central feature of Moser's work is that the patient can explore the physical "engram" of the early parent-child dialogue and therefore the deeply buried emotions and wishes in a body-language dialogue with the therapist. The therapist offers this dialogue and gives the patient the necessary support. In this process, Moser does not just see the therapist as a transferential object, but also as a director who stages the unconscious. Günter Heisterkamp (1993) sees opportunities in "bodily types of treatments" for the psychoanalytic process by reenacting early childhood relationship patterns and thereby enriching the perception and understanding with an "embodied certainty."

There are also approaches in dance therapy for linking Body Psychotherapy with psychoanalytic methods and developmental-psychological findings. Albert Pesso (1973; see also Chapter 42, "'*When* Is Now? When Is *Now*?': Corrective Experiences: With Whom? When? And Where?"), who was originally a dancer with Martha Graham, uses his Psychomotor Therapy to work in groups with the method of having the members embody a patient's internalized object concept or help act out a significant experience from their past. These are then explored and changed in a bodily dialogue. In this process, the "others" may not only represent real objects, but also embody ideal parent figures with whom the patient can then enter into an inner dialogue. Elaine Siegel (1984) in the United States and Sabine Trautmann-Voigt and Bernd Voigt in Germany (Siegel et al., 1999) represent an Analytical Dance and Movement Therapy that works with the "moving action dialogues." Siegel sees motility as an indicator for developmental levels, as an expression of inner conflicts, as a carrier of life experiences, and as a medium for interventions. The analytical dance therapy works with movement associations that are equivalent to the associations of thoughts and words in psychoanalysis on the basis of a psychodynamic understanding.

There has also been increased discussion in more recent times about the value of body-related methods for the treatment of prenatal and perinatal traumatization. In England, an early initiative had been launched in this direction by Frank Lake (1966), a psychotherapist from the tradition of the object-relationship theory. Similar initiatives are now coming from the United States, above all from William Emerson (1999), who has been responsible for a multitude of techniques for working with the consequences of such traumatization.

Stanislav Grof (1985) also understands his work as an attempt to gain access to the formative experiences from the various phases of birth. He has summarized these experiences into a system of birth matrices. A completely new field of Body Psychotherapy is the work with corresponding disorders in babies and children (Harms, 2008;

see also Chapter 78, "Body Psychotherapy with Parents, Babies, and Infants"). George Downing also works with disturbed or dysfunctional mothers by using split-screen videos of the mothers' and babies' bodily actions (Downing et al., 2008). Downing (1996) has proposed an elaborated concept for placing Body Psychotherapy on the basis of the developmental-psychological research and the object-relationship theory. Downing assumes that children learn the "body micropractices" of affect-regulation in their very early body-to-body interactions with adults (see Chapter 29, "Early Interaction and the Body: Clinical Implications" by George Downing). In these interactions, the child develops "motoric convictions" that connect with affective tones and cognitive assessments into "affect-motoric schemes." Such schemes can be recognized in adults as bodily action strategies in relationships with other people. According to Downing, they structure the interpersonal field. Bodily techniques can contribute toward exploring and understanding these schemes. Within the psychodynamic model of Downing, the physical dimension of psychotherapy is also helpful for directly changing dysfunctional schemes. Bodywork can help to develop missing schemes, stimulate the inhibiting ones, or overcome the obstructive ones.

## From the Different Schools to a Unified Clinical Body Psychotherapy

For decades, the development of different schools and systems was in the foreground of Body Psychotherapeutic theory formation. As Petzold had already determined at an early point in time, this field suffered under a "method inflation in which every little technique was elevated into the status of its own method" (Petzold, 1977, p. 13). At that time, Petzold called the concepts of Reich, Perls, and Lowen the "common basic positions" of the various directions. This has radically changed since then. On the one hand, a more broadly differentiated psychodynamic reflection has been added that integrates the concepts of self-psychology, object-relationship theory, and developmental-psychological research. Very fruitful additional theoretical impulses are currently coming from research on cognition and emotion, embodiment research, and neuroscience that, for example, emphasize the meaning of the implicit memory that is bound to the body (Carroll, 2006; Geuter, 2006; Koch, 2006; Storch, 2006).

A second factor is the increased efforts of placing Body Psychotherapy on a solid basis of research into its clinical practice (for example, Röhricht, 2000, 2009). A third factor appears to be emerging through the increasing discussion regarding the usefulness of Body Psychotherapeutic concepts and interventions in terms of specific disorders. This has been fruitful, for example, in trauma therapy (Levine, 2010; Ogden, Minton, and Pain, 2006; Rothschild, 2002) and in the treatment of psychoses (Röhricht and Priebe, 2006). The inclusion of the body is also being discussed more and more for the treatment of disorders in which verbal work alone often does not help, such as in trauma treatment and somatoform disorders (Joraschky et al., 2002; Röhricht, 2011) or eating disorders (Forster, 2002; Vandereycken et al., 1987). These developments suggest that the various body-related approaches can be integrated into a comprehensive "General Psychotherapy." Going into this direction, as a theory and as a treatment technique, Body Psychotherapy should profit from further theoretical, empirical, and clinical elaboration as an independent psychotherapeutic approach (see Geuter, in press; Barratt, 2010; also Chapter 84, "Research in Body Psychotherapy" by Barnaby Barratt).

## References

Aposhyan, S. (2004). *Body-Mind Psychotherapy: Principles, techniques, and practical application.* New York: W. W. Norton.

Arnim, A. v. (1993). Die Entstehungsgeschichte der subjektiven Anatomie [The History of the Origins of Subjective Anatomy]. *Fundamenta Psychiatrica, 7,* 64–71.

Arnim, A. v. (1994). Funktionelle Entspannung [Functional Relaxation]. *Fundamenta Psychiatrica, 8,* 196–203.

Bainbridge Cohen, B. (1993). *Sensing, feeling, and action.* Northampton, MA: Contact.

Baker, E. F. (1967). *Man in the trap.* New York: Macmillan.

Balint, M. (1952). *Primary love and psycho-analytic technique.* London: Tavistock.

Barnard, K. E., & Brazelton, T. B. (Eds.). (1990). *Touch: The foundation of experience.* Madison, CT: International Universities Press.

Barratt, B. B. (2010). *The emergence of Somatic Psychology and BodyMind Therapy.* Basingstoke, UK: Palgrave Macmillan.

Baskakov, V. Y., Berezkina-Orlova, V., Vorobyova, E., Svetlana, G., et al. (2004). *The Russian Body-Oriented Psychotherapy in personalities.* Moscow: Russian Association for Body-Oriented Psychotherapy.

Boadella, D. (1987). *Lifestreams: An introduction to Biosynthesis.* London: Routledge & Kegan Paul.

Boadella, D. (1990). Die somatische Psychotherapie: Ihre Wurzeln und Traditionen [Somatic Psychotherapy: Its roots and traditions]. *Energie und Charakter* [Energy & Character], *21*(1), 3–41.

Bock, W. (2000). Der Glanz in den Augen: Wilhelm Reich, ein Wegbereiter der Gestalttherapie [The sparkle in the eyes: Wilhelm Reich, a pioneer of Gestalt Therapy]. In B. Bocian & F.-M. Staemmler (Eds.), *Gestalttherapie und Psychoanalyse: Berührungspunkte–Grenzen–Verknüpfungen* [Gestalt Therapy and psychoanalysis: Points of contact–boundaries–connections] (pp. 109–141). Göttingen, Germany: Vandenhoeck & Ruprecht.

Boyesen, G. (1987). *Über den Körper die Seele heilen: Biodynamische Psychologie und Psychotherapie. Eine Einführung* [Healing the body through the soul: Biodynamic Psychology and Psychotherapy. An introduction]. Munich, Germany: Kösel.

Breuer, J., & Freud, S. (1895/2000). *Studies on hysteria.* New York: Basic Books.

Brown, M. (1985). *The healing touch: An introduction to Organismic Psychotherapy.* Mendocino, CA: LifeRhythm.

Buber, M. (1979). *Das dialogische Prinzip* [The dialogic principle]. Heidelberg, Germany: Lambert Schneider.

Calza, A. (1994). *Psychomotricité* [Psychomotoricity]. Paris: Masson.

Carroll, R. (2006). A new era for psychotherapy: Panksepp's affect model in the context of neuroscience and its implications for contemporary psychotherapy practice. In J. Corrigall, H. Payne, & H. Wilkinson (Eds.), *About a body: Working with the embodied mind in psychotherapy* (pp. 50–62). London: Routledge.

Casriel, D. (1969). *A scream away from happiness.* New York: Grosset & Dunlap.

Chace, M., Sandel, S. L., Chaiklin, S., & Ohn, A. L. (1993). *Foundations of Dance/Movement Therapy: The life and work of Marian Chace.* Columbia, MD: American Dance Therapy Association.

Chaiklin, S. (1975). Dance Therapy. In D. X. Edman & J. E. Dyrud (Eds.), *American handbook of psychiatry* (pp. 701–720). New York: Basic Books.

Cohn, R. (1975). *Von der Psychoanalyse zur Themenzentrierten Interaktion* [From psychoanalysis to theme centered interaction]. Stuttgart, Germany: Klett-Cotta.

Downing, G. (1996). *Körper und Wort in der Psychotherapie* [Body and word in psychotherapy]. Munich, Germany: Kösel.

Downing, G., Bürgin, D., Reck, C., & Ziegenhain, U. (2008). Interfaces between intersubjectivity and attachment: Three perspectives on a mother-infant inpatient case. *Infant Mental Health Journal, 29,* 278–295.

Duggan, D. (1983). Tanztherapie [Dance Therapy]. In R. Corsini (Ed.), *Handbuch der Psychotherapie* [Handbook of psychotherapy] (pp. 1256–1269). Weinheim, Germany: Beltz.

Ekerholt, K. (Ed.). (2010). *Aspects of psychiatric and psychosomatic physiotherapy.* Oslo: Oslo University College.

Emerson, W. (1999). *Origins of adversity: The treatment of prenatal and perinatal shock.* Petaluma, CA: Emerson Training Seminars.

Espenak, L. (1972). *Bodynamics and dance in individual psychotherapy.* Columbia, MD: American Dance Therapy Association.

Espenak, L. (1981). *Dance Therapy: Theory and application.* Springfield, IL: Charles C. Thomas.

Field, T. (1998). Massage therapy effects. *American Psychologist, 53,* 1270–1281.

Field, T. (2001). *Touch.* Cambridge, MA: MIT Press.

Forster, J. (2002). *Körperzufriedenheit und Körpertherapie bei essgestörten Frauen* [Contentment with the body and body therapy in women with eating disorders]. Herbolzheim, Germany: Centaurus.

Fosshage, J. L. (1994). The meanings of touch in psychoanalysis: A time for reassessment. *Psychoanalytic Inquiry, 20,* 21–43.

Freud, S. (1914). Remembering, repeating, and working-through. In J. Strachey (Ed.), *The standard edition of the complete psychological works of Sigmund Freud, Vol. 12* (pp. 145–150). London: Hogarth.

Freud, S. (1990). *The ego and the id.* New York: W. W. Norton.

Fuchs, M. (1989). *Funktionelle Entspannung: Theorie und Praxis einer organismischen Entspannung über den rhythmisierten Atem* [Functional Relaxation: Theory and practice of an organismic relaxation through rhythmizing breath]. Stuttgart, Germany: Hippokrates.

Geissler, P. (Ed.). (1998). *Analytische Körperpsychotherapie in der Praxis* [Analytic Body Psychotherapy in the practice]. Munich, Germany: Pfeiffer.

Geissler, P & Heisterkamp, G. (2007). *Psychoanalyse der Lebensbewegungen: Zum körperlichen Geschehen in der psychoanalytischen Therapie. Ein Lehrbuch.* [Psychoanalysis of life movements: For physical events in psychoanalytic therapy. A textbook.] Wien: Springer.

Geissler, P. (Ed.). (2001). *Psychoanalyse und Körper* [Psychoanalysis and the body]. Giessen, Germany: Psychosozial.

Gendlin, E. (1961). Experiencing: A variable in the process of psychotherapeutic change. *American Journal of Psychotherapy, 15,* 233–245.

Gendlin, E. (1998). *Focusing-oriented psychotherapy: A manual of the experiential method.* New York: Guilford Press.

Geuter, U. (1996). Körperbilder und Körpertechniken in der Psychotherapie [Body images and body techniques in psychotherapy]. *Psychotherapeut* [Psychotherapist], *41,* 99 106.

Geuter, U. (2000a). Historischer Abriss zur Entwicklung der körperorientierten Psychotherapie [Historical outline of the development of Body-Centered Psychotherapy]. In F. Röhricht (Ed.), *Körperorientierte Psychotherapie psychischer Störungen* [Body-Centered Psychotherapy of psychological disorders] (pp. 53–74). Göttingen, Germany: Hogrefe.

Geuter, U. (2000b). Wege zum Körper: Zur Geschichte und Theorie des körperbezogenen Ansatzes in der Psychotherapie [Paths to the body: The history and theory of the body-centered approach in psychotherapy]. *Energie und Charakter* [Energy & Character], *31*(22), 103–126.

Geuter, U. (2004). Körperpsychotherapie und Erfahrung: Zur Geschichte, wissenschaftlichen Fundierung und Anerkennung einer psychotherapeutischen Methode [Body Psychotherapy and experience: The history, scientific foundation, and recognition of a psychotherapeutic method]. *Report Psychologie* [Report on psychology], *29*(2), 98–111.

Geuter, U. (2006). Körperpsychotherapie: Der körperbezogene Ansatz im neueren wissenschaftlichen Diskurs der Psychotherapie [Body Psychotherapy: The body oriented approach within the recent scientific discourse of psychotherapy]. *Psychotherapeutenjournal, 5*(2), 116–122 and *5*(3), 258–264.

Geuter, U. (in press). *Körperpsychotherapie: Grundriss einer Theorie für die Klinische Praxis* [Body Psychotherapy: Outline of a theory for clinical practice]. Heidelberg, Germany: Springer.

Geuter, U., Heller, M. C., & Weaver, J. O. (2010). Elsa Gindler and her influence on Wilhelm Reich and Body Psychotherapy. *Body, Movement and Dance in Psychotherapy, 5,* 59–73.

Geuter, U., & Schrauth, N. (1997). Wilhelm Reich, der Körper und die Psychotherapie [Wilhelm Reich, the body, and psychotherapy]. In K. Fallend & B. Nitzschke (Eds.), *Der "Fall" Wilhelm Reich: Beiträge zum Verhältnis von Psychoanalyse und Politik* [The "case" of Wilhelm Reich: Articles on the relationship between psychoanalysis and politics] (pp. 190–222). Frankfurt, Germany: Suhrkamp.

Ginger, S. (2007). *Gestalt Therapy: The art of contact.* London: Karnac Books.

Grof, S. (1985). *Beyond the brain: Birth, death and transcendence in psychiatry.* Albany, NY: State University of New York Press.

Grof, S. (1987). *The adventure of self-discovery.* Albany, NY: State University of New York Press.

Harms, T. (2008). *Emotionelle Erste Hilfe* [Emotional First Aid]. Berlin: Leutner.

Heisterkamp, G. (1993). *Heilsame Berührungen: Praxis leibfundierter analytischer Psychotherapie* [Healing touch: The practice of body-based analytical psychotherapy]. Stuttgart, Germany: Pfeiffer.

Heisterkamp, G. (2002). *Basales Verstehen: Handlungsdialoge in der Psychotherapie* [Basalunderstanding: Action dialogues in psychotherapy]. Stuttgart, Germany: Pfeiffer.

Heller, M. (2007). The Golden Age of Body Psychotherapy in Oslo I: From gymnastics to psychoanalysis. *Body, Movement and Dance in Psychotherapy, 2,* 5–16.

Heyer, G. R. (1931). Die Behandlung des Seelischen vom Körper aus [The treatment of the psychological from the body]. In E. Kretschmer & W. Cimbal (Eds.), *Bericht über den VI. Allgemeinen Ärztlichen Kongress für Psychotherapie in Dresden* [Report on the 6th General Medical Congress for Psychotherapy in Dresden] (pp. 1–9). Leipzig, Germany: Hirzel.

Holder, A. (2000). To touch or not to touch: That is the question. *Psychoanalytic Inquiry, 20,* 44–64.

Horton, J., Clance, P., Sterk-Elifson, E. J., & Emshoff, J. (1995). Touch in psychotherapy: A survey of patients' experience. *Psychotherapy, 32,* 443–457.

Hunter, M., & Struve, J. (1998). *The ethical use of touch in psychotherapy.* Thousand Oaks, CA: Sage.

Jacoby, H. (1983). *Jenseits von "Begabt" und "Unbegabt": Zweckmässige Fragestellung und zweckmässiges Verhalten: Schlüssel für die Entfaltung des Menschen* [Beyond "gifted" and "ungifted": Expedient questions and expedient behavior: A key for the development of the human being]. Hamburg, Germany: Christians.

Janov, A. (1970). *The primal scream.* New York: Dell.

Joraschky, P., Arnim, A. von, Loew, T., & Tritt, K. (2002). Körperpsychotherapie bei somatoformen Störungen [Body Psychotherapy in somatoform disorders]. In B. Strauss (Ed.), *Psychotherapie bei körperlichen Erkrankungen: Jahrbuch der medizinischen Psychologie* [Psychotherapy in bodily illnesses: Yearbook of medical psychology] (pp. 81–95). Göttingen, Germany: Hogrefe.

Keleman, S. (1987). *Bonding: A somatic-emotional approach to transference.* Berkeley, CA: Center Press.

Kelley, C. R. (1970). *Education in feeling and purpose.* Santa Monica, CA: Interscience Workshop.

Kepner, J. I. (1987). *Body process: A Gestalt approach to working with the body in psychotherapy.* Cleveland, OH: Gestalt Institute of Cleveland Press.

Kernberg, O., et al. (1989). *Psychodynamic Psychotherapy of borderline patients.* New York: Basic Books.

Kirman, J. H. (1998). One-person or two-person psychology? *Modern Psychoanalysis, 23,* 3–22.

Koch, S. C. (2006). Interdisciplinary embodiment approaches: Implications for the creative arts therapies. In S. C. Koch & I. Bräuninger (Eds.), *Advances in Dance/Movement Therapy: Theoretical perspectives and empirical findings* (pp. 17–28). Berlin: Logos.

Kurtz, R. (1983). *Hakomi Therapy.* Boulder, CO: Hakomi Institute.

Kurtz, R. (1990). *Body-Centered Psychotherapy: The Hakomi Method.* Mendocino, CA: LifeRhythm.

Laban, R. v. (1926). *Gymnastik und Tanz* [Gymnastics and dance]. Oldenburg, Germany: Gerhard Stalling.

Lake, F. (1966). *Clinical theology: A theological and psychiatric basis to clinical pastoral care.* London: Darton, Longman & Todd.

LeCamus, J. (1983). Praxis der Psychomotorik in Frankreich: Geburt, Wiedergeburt und differenzierte Auseinandersetzung mit dem Körper [The practice of Psycho-motorics in France: Birth, rebirth, and a differentiated confrontation with the body]. *Motorik* [Motorics], *6,* 1–10.

LeCamus, J. (1988). *Les Origines de la motricité chez l'enfant* [The origins of motricity in children]. Paris: P.U.F.

Levine, P. (2010). *In an unspoken voice: How the body releases trauma and restores goodness.* Berkeley, CA: North Atlantic Books.

Liss, J., & Stupiggia, M. (Eds.). (2000). *La Terapia Biosistemica: Un approccio originale al trattamento psicocorporeo della sofferenza emotiva* [Biosystemic Therapy: A special approach to mind-body treatment of emotional harm] (3rd ed.). Milan, Italy: Franco Angeli.

Loew, T., Siegfried, W., Martus, P., et al. (1996). Functional Relaxation reduces acute airway obstruction in asthmatics as effectively as inhaled terbutaline. *Psychotherapy and Psychosomatics, 65,* 124–128.

Lowen, A. (1958). *The language of the body.* New York: Grune & Stratton.

Lowen, A., & Lowen, L. (1977). *The way to vibrant health.* New York: Harper & Row.

Ludwig, S. (2002). Elsa Gindler—von ihrem Leben und Wirken: wahrnehmen was wir empfinden [Elsa

Gindler—Her life and work: Perceiving what we feel]. Hamburg, Germany: Christians.

Maaz, H.-J., & Krüger, A. H. (Eds.). (2001). *Integration des Körpers in die analytische Psychotherapie: Materialien zur analytischen Körperpsychotherapie* [Integration of the body into analytical psychotherapy: Materials on Analytical Body Psychotherapy]. Lengerich, Germany: Pabst Science Publishers.

Macnaughton, I. (Ed.). (2004). *Body, breath and consciousness: A Somatics anthology.* Berkeley, CA: North Atlantic Books.

Marcel, G. (1935). *Être et avoir* [Being and having]. Paris: Aubier.

Marlock, G. (Ed.). (1993). *Weder Körper noch Geist: Einführung in die Unitive Körperpsychotherapie* [Neither the body nor the mind: Introduction to Unitive Body Psychotherapy]. Oldenburg, Germany: Transform.

Mattson, M. (1998). *Body awareness: Applications in physiotherapy.* Umea, Sweden: Umea University Medical Dissertations, Department of Psychiatry and Family Medicine.

Maurer, Y. (1999). *Der ganzheitliche Ansatz in der Psychotherapie* [The holistic approach in psychotherapy]. Vienna: Springer.

McNeely, D. A. (1987). *Touching: Body therapy and Depth Psychology.* Toronto, Canada: Inner City Books.

Merleau-Ponty, M. (1945). *Phénoménologie de la Perception* [Phenomenology of perception]. Paris: Gallimard.

Meyer, R. (1982). *Le Corps Aussi: De la psychoanalyse à la somatoanalyse* [Also the body: From psychoanalysis to somatoanalysis]. Paris: Maloine.

Mintz, E. (1969). Touch and the psychoanalytic tradition. *The Psychoanalytic Review, 56,* 365–376.

Monsen, K. (1989). *Psykodynamisk kroppsterapi* [Psychodynamic body therapy]. Oslo. Tano forlag.

Monsen, K., & Monsen, J. T. (2000). Chronic pain and psychodynamic body therapy: A controlled outcome study. *Psychotherapy, 37,* 257–269.

Moreno, J. L. (1964). *Psychodrama* (Vol. 1). New York: Beacon House.

Moser, T. (1989). *Körpertherapeutische Phantasien: Psychoanalytische Fallgeschichten neu betrachtet* [Body-therapeutic fantasies: Psychoanalytic case histories reconsidered]. Frankfurt, Germany: Suhrkamp.

Moser, T. (1993). *Der Erlöser der Mutter auf dem Weg zu sich selbst: Eine Körperpsychotherapie* [The rescuer of the mother on the path to herself: A Body Psychotherapy]. Frankfurt, Germany: Suhrkamp.

Moser, T. (1994). *Ödipus in Panik und Triumph: Eine Körperpsychotherapie* [Oedipus in panic and triumph: A Body Psychotherapy]. Frankfurt, Germany: Suhrkamp.

Moser, T. (2001). *Berührung auf der Couch: Formen der analytischen Körperpsychotherapie* [Touch on the couch: Forms of Analytical Body Psychotherapy]. Frankfurt, Germany: Suhrkamp.

Nagler, N. (2003). Auf der Suche nach einem soziokulturellen Ferenczi-Bild jenseits von Demontage und Hagiographie [In search of a sociocultural Ferenczi image beyond dismantling and hagiography]. *Integrative Therapie* [Integrative Therapy], No. 3–4, 250–280.

Navarro, F. (1986). *Die sieben Stufen der Gesundheit: Eine psychosomatische Sicht der Krankheit* [The seven steps of health: A psychosomatic view of illness]. Frankfurt, Germany: Nexus.

Ogden, P., Minton, K., & Pain, C. (2006). *Trauma and the body: A sensorimotor approach to psychotherapy.* New York: W. W. Norton.

Orr, L., & Ray, S. (1983). *Rebirthing in the New Age.* Berkeley, CA: Celestial Arts.

Perls, F. S., Hefferline, R. H., & Goodman, P. (1973). *Gestalt Therapy: Excitement and growth in the human personality.* New York: Penguin.

Pesso, A. (1973). *Experience in action.* New York: New York University Press.

Petzold, H. (Ed.). (1974/1988). *Psychotherapie und Körperdynamik: Verfahren psycho-physischer Bewegungs- und Körpertherapie* [Psychotherapy and body dynamics: Methods of psycho-physical movement and body therapy]. Paderborn, Germany: Junfermann.

Petzold, H. (1977). *Die neuen Körpertherapien* [The new body therapies]. Paderborn, Germany: Junfermann.

Petzold, H. (2003). *Integrative Therapie* [Integrative Therapy] (2nd rev. ed.) (Vol. 3). Paderborn, Germany: Junfermann.

Pierrakos, J. (1987). *Core energetics.* Mendocino, CA: LifeRhythm.

Pokorny, V., Hochgerner, M., & Cserny, S. (1996). *Konzentrative Bewegungstherapie: Von der körperorientierten*

*Methode zum psychotherapeutischen Verfahren* [Concentrative Movement Therapy: From the body-oriented method to the psychotherapeutic approach]. Vienna: Facultas.

Polenz, S. v. (1994). *Und er bewegt sich doch: Ketzerisches zur Körperabstinenz der Psychoanalyse* [And it moves after all: Heretical thoughts about the physical abstinence of psychoanalysis]. Frankfurt, Germany: Suhrkamp.

Raknes, O. (1970). *Wilhelm Reich and Orgonomy.* Harmondsworth, UK: Penguin.

Reich, W. (1933/1970). *Character Analysis.* New York: Farrar, Straus & Giroux.

Reich, W. (1975). *The instinctual character: In early writings.* New York: Farrar, Straus & Giroux.

Reich, W. (1927/1986). *The function of the orgasm: The discovery of orgone, Vol. 1.* New York: Farrar, Straus & Giroux.

Revenstorf, D. (2000). Nutzung des Affekts in der Psychotherapie [Use of the affect in psychotherapy]. In S. Sulz & G. Lenz (Eds.), *Von der Kognition zur Emotion: Psychotherapie mit Gefühlen* [From cognition to emotion: Psychotherapy with feelings], pp. 191–215. Munich, Germany: CIP-Medien.

Rispoli, L. (1993). *Psicologia Funzionale del Sé* [Functional psychology of the self]. Rome: Astrolabio.

Rispoli, L. (2008). *The basic experience and the development of the self: Development from the point of view of functional psychotherapy.* New York: Peter Lang.

Röhricht, F. (2000). *Körperorientierte Psychotherapie psychischer Störungen* [Body-Oriented Psychotherapy of psychological disorders]. Göttingen, Germany: Hogrefe.

Röhricht, F. (2009). Body Oriented Psychotherapy. The state of the art in empirical research and evidence-based practice: A clinical perspective. *Body, Movement, and Dance in Psychotherapy, 4,* 135–156.

Röhricht, F. (2011). Das theoretische Modell und die therapeutischen Prinzipien/Mechanismen einer integrativen Körperpsychotherapie (KPT) bei somatoformen Störungen [The theoretical model and the therapeutic principles/mechanisms of Integrative Body Psychotherapy]. *Psychotherapie-Wissenschaft, 1,* 41–49.

Röhricht, F., & Priebe, S. (2006). Effect of Body-Oriented Psychological therapy on negative symptoms in schizophrenia: A randomized controlled trial. *Psychological Medicine, 36,* 669–678.

Rosenberg, J. L., Rand, M. L., & Asay, D. (1985). *Body, self and soul: Sustaining integration.* Atlanta, GA: Humanics.

Rothschild, B. (2002). *The body remembers: The psychophysiology of trauma and trauma treatment.* New York: W. W. Norton.

Rubenfeld, I. (2001). *The listening hand: How to combine bodywork, intuition and psychotherapy to release emotions and heal the pain.* London: Piatkus.

Sándor, P. (1974). *Técnicas de Relaxamento* [Techniques of relaxation]. São Paulo: Vozes.

Scharfetter, C. (1998). Ich-Psychopathologie und Leiberleben [Ego psychopathology and body experience]. In F. Röhricht & S. Priebe (Eds.), *Körpererleben in der Schizophrenie* [Body experience in schizophrenia] (pp. 25–39). Göttingen, Germany: Hogrefe.

Schoop, T. (1981). *. . . . komm und tanz mit mir! Ein Versuch, dem psychotischen Menschen durch die Elemente des Tanzes zu helfen* [. . . Come and dance with me! An attempt to help the psychotic person through the elements of dance]. Zurich, Switzerland: Verlag Musikhaus Pan.

Selver, C. (1988). Sensory Awareness. In H. Petzold (Ed.), *Psychotherapie und Körperdynamik: Verfahren psychophysischer Bewegungs- und Körpertherapie* [Psychotherapy and body dynamics: Methods of psycho-physical movement and body therapy] (pp. 59–78). Paderborn, Germany: Junfermann.

Siegel, E. V. (1984). *Dance-Movement Therapy: Mirror of our selves: The psychoanalytic approach.* New York: Human Sciences Press.

Siegel, E. V., Trautmann-Voigt, S., & Voigt, B. (1999). *Analytische Bewegungs- und Tanztherapie* [Analytic movement and Dance Therapy]. Munich, Germany: Reinhardt.

Smith, E. W. L., Clance, P. R., & Imes, S. (Eds.). (1998). *Touch in psychotherapy: Theory, research, and practice.* New York: Guilford Press.

Soth, M. (2009). From humanistic holism via the "integrative project" towards integral-relational Body Psychotherapy. In L. Hartley (Ed.), *Contemporary*

*Body Psychotherapy: The Chiron approach* (pp. 64–88). London: Routledge.

Stattman, J. (1989). *Creative trance.* Amsterdam: International Academy for Bodytherapy.

Stattman, J., Aalberse, M., Brauer, U. C., Marlock, G., Grohmann, P., & Richter, A. (1991). *Unitive Body-Psychotherapy: Collected papers, Vol. II.* Frankfurt, Germany: AFRA.

Stattman, J., Jansen, E. M., Marlock, G., Aalberse, M., & Stubenrauch, H. (1989). *Unitive Body-Psychotherapy: Collected papers, Vol. I.* Frankfurt, Germany: AFRA.

Stolze, H. (Ed.). (1984/2002). *Die Konzentrative Bewegungstherapie: Grundlagen und Erfahrungen* [Concentrative Movement Therapy: Fundamentals and experiences] (2nd ed.). Berlin: Springer.

Storch, M. (2006). Wie Embodiment in der Psychologie erforscht wurde [How embodiment has been studied in psychology]. In M. Storch, B. Cantieni, G. Hüther, & W. Tschacher (Eds.), *Embodiment: Die Wechselwirkung von Körper und Psyche verstehen und nutzen* [Embodiment: Understanding and using the relation between body and psyche] (pp. 35–72). Bern: Huber.

Thornquist, E., & Bunkan, B. H. (1991). *What is Psychomotor Therapy?* Oslo: Norwegian University Press.

Traue, H. C. (1998). *Emotion und Gesundheit: Die psychobiologische Regulation durch Hemmungen* [Emotion and health: The psychobiological regulation by inhibition]. Heidelberg, Germany: Spektrum Akademischer.

Traue, H. C., & Pennebaker, J. (Eds.). (1993). *Emotion, inhibition and health.* Cambridge, MA: Hogrefe & Huber.

Tune, D. (2005). Dilemmas concerning the ethical use of touch in psychotherapy. In N. Totton (Ed.), *New dimensions in Body Psychotherapy* (pp. 70–83). Maidenhead, UK: Open University Press.

Uexküll, T. v., Fuchs, M., Müller-Braunschweig, H., & Johnen, R. (Eds.). (1994). *Subjektive Anatomie: Theorie und Praxis körperbezogener Psychotherapie* [Subjective anatomy: The theory and practice of Body-Centered Psychotherapy]. Stuttgart, Germany: Schattauer.

Vandereycken, W., Depreitere, L., & Probst, M. (1987). Body-Oriented Therapy for anorexia nervosa patients. *American Journal of Psychotherapy, 61,* 252–258.

Whitehouse, M. (1979). C. G. Jung and Dance Therapy. In P. L. Bernstein (Ed.), *Eight theoretical approaches in Dance-Movement Therapy* (pp. 51–70). Dubuque, IA: Kendall Hunt.

Will, H. (1987). *Georg Groddeck: Die Geburt der Psychosomatik* [Georg Groddeck: The birth of psychosomatics]. Munich, Germany: Deutscher Taschenbuch.

Winnicott, D. W. (1965). *The maturational processes and the facilitating environment.* New York: International Universities Press.

Young, C. (2005). "To touch or not to touch: That is the question": Doing effective Body Psychotherapy without touch. *Energy & Character, 34,* 50–64.

Young, C. (2009). Doing effective Body Psychotherapy without touch: Part II: The process of embodiment. *Energy & Character, 37,* 36–46.

Young, C. (Ed.). (2010). *The historical basis of Body Psychotherapy.* Galashiels, Scotland: Body Psychotherapy Publications.

Zur, O. (2007). Touch in therapy and the standard of care in psychotherapy and counselling: Bringing clarity to illusive relationships. *USABP Journal, 6*(2), 61–94.

# 4

## The Influence of Elsa Gindler

Judyth O. Weaver, United States

**Judyth O. Weaver** has a PhD in Reichian Psychology, was a professor at the California Institute of Integral Studies for twenty-five years, and was a co-founder of the Santa Barbara Graduate Institute, where she created the Somatic Psychology program. As chairperson of that department, she contributed to the development of curriculum for MA and PhD degrees in Somatic Psychology. In the 1970s, she was a founding faculty member at Naropa University, Boulder, Colorado.

Dr. Weaver has developed her own integrated manner of working, which she calls "Somatic Reclaiming," and frequently presents her work at conferences and teaches at workshops and trainings at Esalen Institute in California, and in Japan, Russia, India, Taiwan, and Canada. She has written a wide variety of publications and also has a private psychotherapy practice in Seattle, Washington.

Her background in somatic work and Body Psychotherapy includes a range of trainings. She began studying after returning from three years in Asia, most of these spent in a Zen Buddhist monastery in Japan, and she later integrated this practice with Tai Chi and Sensory Awareness, which she studied with Charlotte Selver and Charles Brooks beginning in 1968. She was certified by Selver to teach in 1983. She is also certified as a Somatic Experiencing Practitioner, in Biodynamic Craniosacral Therapy, and in Prenatal and Birth Therapy. She is a Rosen Method practitioner and senior teacher; and a master teacher in Tai Chi Chuan, which she has been practicing since 1968. She also trained with, and had a deep friendship with, Eva Reich from 1984 until her passing in 2008.

## Introduction

Elsa Gindler (1885–1961) might today be considered as a grandmother of Somatic Psychology and Body Psychotherapy, despite never being a psychologist or psychotherapist. As a young woman diagnosed with a severe illness, she had worked by herself to try to heal, and in order to explore possibilities for her regeneration and health, she began to give her complete attention to what was happening within herself at every moment in every activity during the entire day. A devoted student, colleague, and friend, Elfriede Hengstenberg explained, "She found that in this practice she came into a state where she was no longer disturbed by her own thoughts and worries. And she came to experience—consciously experience—that calm in the physical field [Gelassenheit] is equivalent to trust in the psychic field. This was her discovery, and it became basic to all subsequent research" (Hengstenberg, 1985, p. 12).

Gindler had studied "Harmonische Gymnastik" originally with Hedwig Kallmeyer, but in teaching it she eventually felt that the fixed set of common movements for everyone was a narrow approach. She wanted freedom for people to explore independently and to develop individually—a way to experience and learn from one's own somatic behavior in all of life's situations. Her work developed, offering opportunities for each person to become more aware of what was happening in their own organism. In her classes, she did not teach "techniques," and eventually she changed from using the word "exercise" [Übung] to "experiment" [Versuch]. The natural activities of everyday life were the material for her classes. Gindler's focus was *tasten;* in English, we would say, "sensing our way."

By 1913, Gindler had developed her way of working with relaxation. Attention to the breath was basic: "For her breathing was a teacher: simply being attentive to it is a way of learning how things are with one, of learning what needs to change for fuller functioning—for more reactivity in breathing and thus in the whole person. She did not teach others what they 'ought' to be, but only to find out how they were" (Roche, 1978, p. 4). About her work of being present, Gindler wrote only one article: "Die Gymnastik des Berufsmenschen" [Gymnastics for Working People], which appeared in the journal of the Deutschen Gymnastik-Bund [German Gymnastik Federation] (Gindler, 1926). She never gave a name to the simple, deep processes in which she led her students. Charlotte Selver, one of several disciples who brought Gindler's work to the United States, says that the closest Gindler got to a name was "Arbeit am Menschen"—"working with the human being," though others think that was just a phrase that was used about her work. Gindler lived her entire life in Berlin. She never advertised her classes, yet over the years her work spread and has had a far-ranging influence in many fields, in particular that of psychotherapy.

In 1925, Elsa Gindler met the experimental musician and educator Heinrich Jacoby. After studying with each other, they collaborated in the development of what is now sometimes termed the "Jacoby-Gindler work." Jacoby had a great interest in psychoanalysis, and through him Gindler became interested and referred her students to the work.

## Influence on Psychotherapy in Europe

Gindler herself had many students who were involved in the psychotherapeutic field. Clare Nathansohn began studying with her in 1915, and when Otto Fenichel, a student of Freud, married Clare, he also began studying with Gindler. Clare Fenichel said of her experience, "I got my husband to go, too, and he was very interested. Later on he would have me talk to his psychoanalytic groups about the Gindler work, and then we would all discuss it" (Fenichel, 1981, p. 6).

With reference to Gindler's interest in psychotherapy, Clare Fenichel said, "Psychoanalysis spread at that time and some of her pupils were into it. One of them was my husband, and there were others. Gindler was interested to see what was going on and she learned. From then on she said things in class that she could have said only if she considered mental activity as an important matter much involved with movement." Fenichel goes on to say, "She knew more and more about human beings. And this is the important thing; she became more and more interested not just in the body but the whole being. She said, 'If you don't want to get over the rope, don't be surprised that you can't make it.' She noticed that something that is not 'body' gets the body going. And that 'something' effects the function of this body" (Ibid., p. 8).

Wilhelm Reich never studied with Gindler, but it seems he was influenced by her approach in several ways. After the Reichs left Vienna and moved to Berlin, Annie, Reich's first wife, studied with Clare Fenichel. Reich's daughter Eva remembers the many Sunday picnics of the close friends, the Reichs and the Fenichels, where her father would assiduously question Clare about Gindler's work. "Now, tell me, what is it that you do?" he would ask (Reich, 1984).

Elsa Lindenberg, Reich's second "wife" and long-term companion, studied with Gindler both before and after the Second World War. She also studied with Clare Fenichel while she was living in Norway with Reich. Eva Reich felt that the vicarious knowledge of Gindler's work and the direct influence of Lindenberg definitely had an effect on her father's becoming much more aware of his psychoanalytic clients' breathing and body state, movement and positions while working with them (Reich, 2001).

## Influence in Other Fields

Gindler's work also gave many other people the depth and connection for which they were looking. Ruth Nörenberg, who came to Gindler after she had studied gymnastics at the Loheland School, said, "It soon became clear to me, however, that the Gindler work was not just 'Gymnastik' in the usual sense, but was an education of the whole human being, a 'Lebens-Schule' (school of life) as she [Gindler] called it" (Nörenberg, 1981, p. 20).

She wrote about her work with Gindler:

> Through our experimentation I managed, slowly and painfully, to work myself out of a number of holes, by gradually coming to a fuller understanding of the deep sense of Elsa Gindler's teaching—until I found the path to myself. This process was not unlike a psychological "depth analysis" (of which, however, nothing was known at that time) even with respect to the subsequent "catharsis," the clearing up of inner disorders. I gradually learned to be more in charge of myself, to understand myself better—without falling into those unproductive and crippling feelings of inferiority that so easily deteriorate into depressions.
>
> The unity of mind, body and spirit was much discussed at that time. There, in Gindler's classes, we experienced it in practice. And a clear consciousness of this has never left me. (Ibid.)

After the war, Nörenberg became a physical therapist and felt she was able to work in the spirit of Gindler.

For others, the Gindler work fulfilled a different need. Else Henschke-Durham had many physical problems when she came to study with Gindler at the age of eighteen. She had been working with small children and difficult or disturbed older ones of working parents. Durham relates, "Under Elsa Gindler's guidance I became aware that the organism was not just a machine to be used, that there was a way for me to become familiar with it, to relate to it, to allow it to function according to its own needs. What a revelation! . . . With incredible persistence, Elsa Gindler made me aware that unneeded contractions . . . were brought on by my mental attitude. My holding was a defense" (Durham, 1981, p. 17).

Durham was encouraged by Gindler to go to the United States, and, in 1934, opened a studio in New York. Like so many other Gindler students, she received referrals of medical and psychoanalytic patients and worked with them very successfully. In 1941, she married a European psychiatrist and psychoanalyst. Durham wrote of the times: "Interest in psychoanalysis was just spreading but often even deep psychoanalysis did not free a person from the physical tensions that had developed through repressions and negative resistances; here was an area left out. So we worked together. Analysts came with their personal needs, and then sent their analysands" (Ibid., p. 18).

Many others developed their understandings and enhanced their careers from Gindler's work. Lily Pincus, author of *Death and the Family* (1974) and co-author of *Secrets in the Family* (1978), among other books, studied with Gindler from 1928 to 1939. First a social worker, and then a family therapist at the Institute for Marital Studies in the Tavistock Institute for Human Relations in London, Pincus describes Gindler's work as helping her students to "harmonize body, intellect and feeling through self-awareness" (Pincus, 1981, p. 32).

In her article "From Dance to Psychotherapy" (Heller, 1983, pp. 3–8), Gertrud Falke-Heller describes how Gindler influenced her transformation from a famous dancer and dance teacher to an occupational therapist who was able to work with both neurotic and psychotic patients. After leaving Germany, she worked with the Kurt Jooss dance company in England and as "Teacher of Relaxation" at the Crichton Royal Hospital, with shell-shocked soldiers and others suffering from neuroses, psychoses, schizophrenia, and asthma. She eventually taught at Freiburg University and later at the Lindauer Psychotherapy Conference.

Heller's student Dr. med Helmuth Stolze, developed his psychotherapeutic process based on movement as inner experience and called it "Konzentrative Bewegungstherapie" [Concentrative Movement Therapy]. Stolze eventually taught with Heller and later with Miriam Goldberg. Stolze's description of KBT (CMT) sounds very reminiscent of Gindler when he says that it "cannot be systematized into exercises. Its application is, rather, of an intuitive character, obedient to the moment . . ." He goes on to say,

> In the inquiry into what a man is in his very self, the therapist must be able to experience himself and, over and over again, make himself ready for the experi-

ence. A therapist who is "insensitive," who is too "deaf" and "dumb" as to what is going on, who has "no taste of" and cannot "smell out" his patients is not capable of working . . . only a therapist who is entirely "present" in "readiness for experiencing" can be effective in this therapy. (Stolze, 1983, p. 15)

Many of Gindler's students throughout Europe have had a profound influence on other modes of working with people. Gindler's longtime friend and colleague Elfriede Hengstenberg had been certified to teach "Bode Gymnastik"; in 1920 she also received a teaching certificate from Gindler. Hengstenberg worked with children, preferring to work together with their parents when possible. She preferred to begin work with the mothers prenatally, and afterward to continue working with the children's parents and teachers as the child developed. She also gave workshops for the Hungarian pediatrician Emmi Pikler, who after the Second World War established an orphanage. There, at Lóczy, Pikler showed how supporting natural development in the child's own time—and on his or her own initiative and independent experimentation—also facilitates mental and emotional development (Pikler, 1994).

Moshe Feldenkrais, developer of "Awareness through Movement" and "Functional Integration," now more commonly known around the world as the "Feldenkrais Method," was also influenced by Gindler's work through his studies with her close colleague Heinrich Jacoby (Feldenkrais, 1981).

## Influence in the United States

One of the most important inspirations for Somatic Psychotherapists of many persuasions has been that from Charlotte Selver (1901–2003). Selver was a graduate of the Bode Gymnastik school in Munich, and had done graduate work with Mary Wigman, a pupil of Laban, in Dresden, before she came to study with Elsa Gindler in Berlin in 1923. Following her studies with Gindler, she emigrated to the United States in 1938, and settled in New York City, where she offered classes and private sessions in the "Gindler work." Selver coined the name "Sensory Awareness," "to single out the awareness of direct perception, as distinguished from the intellectual or conventional awareness—the verbalized knowledge—that is still the almost exclusive aim of education . . ." (Brooks, 1974, p. 232). In 1958, Charles Van Wyck Brooks began studying with Selver. They eventually married, and in 1963 he began teaching with her.

During her early days of teaching, one of Selver's most ardent students was the prominent psychoanalyst Erich Fromm. In 1955, Fromm and Selver gave a joint lecture at the New School for Social Research, entitled "On Being in Touch with Oneself" (Roche, 1999, 2000).

Clara Thompson, who co-founded the William Alanson White Institute of Psychiatry (with Erich Fromm and Harry Stack Sullivan), was also one of Selver's students, as were many other of her colleagues at the institute. Betty Winkler Keane was a very successful actress when her psychiatrist, Thompson, recommended that she take classes with Selver. Keane, who eventually collaborated with Jungian analyst Edward Whitmont (he worked at the verbal level and she at the nonverbal level), was one of the first of Selver's students to begin teaching. Keane worked in New York City, weaving together Jungian analysis with acting out dream sequences and the work of sensing.

Fritz Perls, one of the twentieth century's most influential innovators in psychotherapy, was deeply influenced by Gindler's work. In the early 1930s, Perls was a patient of Wilhelm Reich, and Perls's wife, Laura, was a student of Gindler. Both Fritz and Laura, the developers of Gestalt Therapy, later studied with Selver in New York—Fritz very extensively and also privately. In 1947, Perls gave a talk at the William Alanson White Institute entitled "Planned Psychotherapy," in which he said, "I recommend as necessary complementary aspects of the study of the human personality at least three subjects: Gestalt psychology, semantics, and last but not least, the approach of the Gindler School" (Gregory, 2001, pp. 14–17).

Alan Watts, the popular proponent of Zen Buddhism in the West, studied with Charlotte Selver, and they presented many workshops together in New York and California. He introduced her to the Esalen Institute, the newly founded center for the study of human potential in California, and in 1963, Selver presented Esalen's very first experiential workshop. Over time, her teaching there brought about a great breadth of contact and influence within the psychotherapeutic community in the United States.

Many have been influenced by the work of Gindler and Selver and have incorporated it into their own modes of psychotherapy. At Esalen, Seymour Carter studied Sensory Awareness with Selver and Brooks, and Gestalt Therapy with Perls. He taught there and in Europe for years. Marjorie Rand, an international trainer of Integrated Body Psychotherapy (IBP), also acknowledges the influence of Sensory Awareness on her work (Rand, 2001). I began intensive studies with Charlotte Selver and Charles Brooks in 1968, eventually integrating Sensory Awareness into my form of Somatic Psychotherapy that I call "Somatic Reclaiming."

## Other Influences

Gindler's work has also traveled to the East and influenced therapists and counselors there. In 1972, at the Esalen Institute, Professor Hiroshi Ito, the first Japanese counseling psychology graduate from the United States (1948), participated in workshop sessions in Sensory Awareness with me. Returning to Japan, Ito reformed his teaching and created "New Counseling," which included the practice of Sensory Awareness and eventually the Alexander Technique.

Peter Levine, creator of "Somatic Experiencing," who uses fine somatic tracking in his Body Psychotherapy work to resolve shock and trauma affect, cites a workshop taken with Charlotte Selver in 1968 that had great influence on his work. Doris Breyer, a student of Mary Wigman and a professional dancer, studied with Gindler before coming to New York in 1942, where she worked and trained with Alexander Lowen. When she moved to California, Stanley Keleman studied with her and also referred many of his clients to her (see Chapter 21, "The Maturation of the Somatic Self" by Stanley Keleman).

Other Gindler students came to the United States to live and teach and had significant influence on different modes of work with children and adults in both creative and therapeutic processes. Carola Speads was Gindler's teaching assistant from 1925 to 1938. Speads brought her work to New York and, for a time, shared a studio with Charlotte Selver. Speads called her work "Physical Re-education" and had a very successful practice until her death in 1999. Susan Gregory, a Gestalt therapist, recital artist, and former opera singer, was Speads's student from 1963 to 1995 and calls the Gindler work "an essential part of Gestalt therapy's historical ground" (Gregory, 2001).

Other areas of expression and creativity have also been influenced by the work of Elsa Gindler. Mary Whitehouse, creator of "Movement in Depth," also known as "Authentic Movement," studied briefly with Selver and Brooks, as did Mary's students Joan Chodorow and Janet Adler. Aligned with Jungian Depth Analysis, Chodorow's work is focused in the context of analytic work, and Adler's is developing with particular interest in mystical experience.

Although the "Rosen Method" is not considered a psychotherapy, or even a Body Psychotherapy, its founder Marion Rosen felt she was influenced by Gindler's work through her teacher Lucy Heyer. Even though there is no record of Heyer studying with Gindler, Rosen felt she had been strongly influenced by Gindler and has carried that into her own work. Lucy's husband, Gustaf, was a psychoanalyst; the Heyers were part of a group in Munich that was using somatic methods in conjunction with psychoanalysis. Rosen studied with Heyer for two years before leaving Germany. She relates:

> During this time I became very familiar with the body and truly admired how it was put together. That knowledge complemented what I was seeing in the work that Mrs. Heyer's husband was doing with psychiatry; I began to see how they worked together. The Heyers used massage and breathing to open people up and make it easier for them to get in touch with their problems in psychotherapy. They found that this way of treatment was much shorter and more effective. (Rosen, 2003, p. 3.)

Here again, the Gindler work was used as an adjunct to psychotherapy. Eclectic psychotherapist Claudio Naranjo says:

> Psychotherapy as a healing modality has changed and evolved . . . Despite not fitting the description of psychotherapy, Marion Rosen's approach suggests ways of meditation-in-relationship using skillful touch. It is clearly related to earlier approaches to emotional healing—notably Reichian work—that allow the person's deeper self to emerge by assisting in the dissolution of "character armor." (Naranjo, 2003, p. ix)

All of Gindler's students worked in their own individual ways. Mary Alice Roche was a director of The Lifwynn Foundation for Laboratory Research, which promotes the work of Trigant Burrow, the first American-born psychoanalyst and founder and onetime president of the American Psychoanalytic Association. A longtime student of Sensory Awareness, researcher and editor of many bulletins of the Charlotte Selver Foundation (later named the Sensory Awareness Foundation), Roche says:

> . . . [Gindler] offered them the possibility of being responsible to themselves in simply finding out how it is, and how it wants to change. This is one way her work was, and still is, different from all "systems." In that early article she was already saying, "Each student is working in his own fashion. That means that each one in the class is working differently . . . The student begins to feel that he is in charge of himself . . . His consciousness of self is heightened." (Roche, 1978, p. 4)

Roche also suggests that:

> . . . it was the genius of Elsa Gindler that the path she opened led, not to some preconceived ideal she had set for her students, but to a continually unfolding discovery of their own unique way of being. Since no one can really copy another's way of being, no student could copy Gindler in any other manner than by becoming ever more himself or herself. Teacher and student worked together, growing in their own ways, toward their own innate power, their own creativity. (Roche, 1983, p. 1)

## Implications for Psychotherapy

Elsa Gindler's process of attending fully and exploring all the basic, natural activities of life has had a profound influence on a wide variety of people and applications. Without being a method or a technique, Gindler's approach has made a huge impact among many psychotherapeutic disciplines.

The uniqueness Gindler looked for in her students is just what we hope and work for with our clients in psychotherapy—to help them uncover their connection to and faith in their own innate beings. Without a sense of this in their own organisms, physical and sensorial as well as mental and emotional, the wholeness of the human being we are working with will not feel complete. Focusing on the experiences in their bodies, their senses, the somatic elements of a person's consciousness supports them to stay in the present and work with the reality of what is happening—to work with the actuality of the affects. To be grounded in and support them to experience and work from their inside out allows the organic processes to return to their natural balances.

Somatic inquiry, essential to so many integrated psychotherapeutic approaches, especially when working with pre-verbal and other deep issues, instructs the practitioner how to work at depths and with delicacies without projecting or interfering. The clarity of Sensory Awareness leads both the therapist and client in working with all aspects of the client's direct experience. The Somatic Psychotherapist is thereby supported to be less directive, as the client is allowed to discover and claim his or her autonomy.

Used within therapeutic sessions as well as integrated in psychotherapy, the simple, basic work of sensing, derived from Elsa Gindler, is one of the essential and vital foundations of the field of Somatic Psychology or Body-Oriented Psychotherapy.

## References

Brooks, C. V. W. (1974). *Sensory Awareness: The rediscovery of experiencing.* New York: Viking Press.

Durham, E. H. (1981). The nineteen twenties and thirties. *The Charlotte Selver Foundation Bulletin: Elsa Gindler, 1885–1961, 10*(II), 17.

Feldenkrais, M. (1981). *The elusive obvious.* Capitola, CA: Meta.

Fenichel, C. N. (1981). From the early years of the Gindler work. *The Charlotte Selver Foundation Bulletin: Elsa Gindler, 1885–1961, 10*(II), 4–9.

Gindler, E. (1926). Die Gymnastik des Berufsmenschen [Gymnastics for working people]. *The Journal of the Deutschen Gymnastik-Bund* [German Gymnastics Federation].

Gregory, S. (2001). Elsa Gindler: Lost Gestalt ancestor. *British Gestalt Journal, 10*(2), 114–117.

Heller, G. F. (1983). From dance to psychotherapy. *The Charlotte Selver Foundation Bulletin: The work after Elsa Gindler, 11,* 3–8.

Hengstenberg, E. (1985). Her teacher—Elsa Gindler. *The Charlotte Selver Foundation Bulletin: Elfriede Hengstenberg—Her Life and Work, 12,* 12.

Naranjo, C. (2003). Foreword. *Rosen Method Bodywork.* Berkeley, CA: North Atlantic Books.

Nörenberg, R. (1981). Letter to Charlotte Selver. *The Charlotte Selver Foundation Bulletin: Elsa Gindler, 1885–1961, 10*(II), 20–21.

Pikler, E. (1994). Excerpt from Peaceful babies—Contented mothers. *Sensory Awareness Foundation Bulletin: Emmi Pikler, 1902–1984, 14,* 5–37.

Pincus, L. (1974). *Death and the Family.* New York: Random House.

Pincus, L. & Dare, C. (1978). *Secrets in the Family.* New York: Pantheon.

Pincus, L. (1981). On Elsa Gindler. *The Charlotte Selver Foundation Bulletin: Elsa Gindler, 1885–1961, 10* (II), 32.

Rand, M. (2001). Personal communication with author.

Reich, E. (1984). Personal communication with author.

Reich, E. (2001). Personal communication with author.

Roche, M. A. (1978). Foreword. *The Charlotte Selver Foundation Bulletin: Elsa Gindler, 1885–1961, 10*(I), 4.

Roche, M. A. (1983). Foreword. *The Charlotte Selver Foundation Bulletin: The work after Elsa Gindler, 11,* 1.

Roche, M. A. (1999). Sensory Awareness. In N. Allison (Ed.), *The illustrated encyclopedia of body-mind disciplines* (pp. 231–235). New York: Rosen.

Roche, M. A. (2000). Sensory Awareness: Conscious relationship. *Somatics, XII*(4), 4–54.

Rosen, M., with Brenner, S. (2003). *Rosen Method bodywork.* Berkeley, CA: North Atlantic Books.

Stolze, H. (1983). Concentrative Movement Therapy. *The Charlotte Selver Foundation Bulletin: The work after Elsa Gindler, 11,* 9–15.

# 5

## The Work of Wilhelm Reich, Part 1

*Reich, Freud, and Character*

**Wolf E. Büntig, Germany**

**Translation by Christine M. Grimm**

**Wolf Büntig** played a guiding and inspiring role for Humanistic Psychology in Germany: As a physician and psychodynamic therapist, he had already recognized its significance at an early point in time and rendered service to its spread. Since the beginning of the 1970s, his seminar center ZIST, near Munich, has become a meeting place for psychotherapy teachers from around the world, including many Body Psychotherapists.

Dr. Büntig is a medical psychotherapist and teacher therapist for psychotherapy based on Depth Psychology, Gestalt Therapy, Bioenergetics, and for the Balint Groups. In addition, he has been trained in hypnotherapy according to Erickson, Family Constellations, and encounter groups. His trainers from Gestalt Therapy, as well as the Body Psychotherapists Alexander Lowen, Stanley Keleman, and Malcolm Brown, have heavily influenced his work. Spiritually oriented teachers, such as Karlfried Graf Dürckheim and Ali Hameed Almaas, have also had a major influence upon him.

Among other areas, the emphasis of his own work lies in the field of psycho-oncology and the advanced training of psychotherapists. He has published numerous articles on Body Psychotherapy, Gestalt Therapy, and psychosomatics.

**Editors' Note:** *Some of the post-1934 developments of Reich's work are now dealt with in Chapter 7, "The Work of Wilhelm Reich, Part 2: Reich in Norway and America" by Courtenay Young (with translated excerpts from Wolf E. Büntig's original German chapter).*

There is no doubt that Wilhelm Reich was one of the most controversial figures in the history of psychoanalysis. At the same time, Reich was one of the individuals responsible for making the therapeutic technique of psychoanalysis into a systematically teachable and learnable method. He was initially one of Freud's most creative, most highly scientifically trained, and most resolute students. He took up Freud's ideas at a point in time when Freud himself had, in many ways, resigned from being revolutionary and such ideas had (in fact) become highly inopportune for the psychoanalytic movement. Reich, tenacious and spirited, was a very gifted clinician and passionate scientist. He belonged to the closest circle around Freud and was one of the most important functionaries of the Psychoanalytical Association in Vienna.

Yet, after his move to Berlin in 1930, and definitely by 1934, his relationship with psychoanalysis had become so uncomfortable that he was "disposed of" through a process of expulsion that was not official, nor even proclaimed. At the same time, the Norwegian, Swedish, and Danish groups of analysts were instructed not to include Reich, who had by then emigrated to Scandinavia.

Despite everything that we have learned from psychoanalysis about the power of repression, the process of Reich's expulsion from psychoanalysis appears virtually unbelievable when we also consider his fundamental contributions to this field, which will become clear in this chapter. He later became one of the most outstanding innovators of twentieth-century psychotherapy.

## Reich Becomes a Psychoanalyst

Reich, born in 1897 in Galicia, lost both his parents quite tragically: his mother by suicide when he was fourteen and, three years later, his father to pneumonia. Very shortly afterward, he became an officer in the Austrian army in 1915, and, at the end of World War I, settled in Vienna. He attended lectures on law for a while, and then decided to study medicine.

Reich discovered Freud's work by coincidence. In January 1919, interested medical students established a seminar on sexology. Reich, who had read extensively on a variety of topics, joined it, enhanced it, and later led it. During this time, he came across *Three Essays on the Theory of Sexuality* (Freud, 1905). He wrote the following about it: "One must know the atmosphere described in sexology and psychiatry before Freud in order to understand the enthusiasm and relief that came over me when I encountered him. . . . The sex drive suffered a special existence in science. . . . Freud had built a street to the clinical understanding of sexuality" (Reich, 1942/1969, p. 38).

In the summer of 1919, Reich gave a presentation in a student seminar on the concept of the libido, which was later published (Reich, 1922). He succeeded in creating a connection between known sexual theories. Authors before Freud had simply used the term "libido" to describe the conscious desire for sexual actions: it was a word from Consciousness Psychology. It was not clear what "libido" was, or what it should be. Freud believed that the drive could not be grasped in words. He thought that what we experience are just the "derivatives of the drives": sexual images and affects. Reich interpreted Freud in the following way: "We cannot become conscious of the drive itself because it is what rules and controls us. It can only be recognized through the expression of the affect, just as electricity only becomes measurable through its energy expressions, without our knowing the actual nature of the electricity."

Whereas the "libido" of the pre-Freudian research meant the tangible, conscious sexual desire, Reich understood the "libido" of Freud to be nothing other than the energy of the sexual drive itself (Reich, 1942/1969, p. 39). Captivated by the resolute, scientific-energetic thinking of Freud, and influenced by the *zeitgeist* at the turn of the century, like with the major scientific discoveries of magnetism, electricity, and the steam engine, Reich believed that it could one day be possible to measure this energy. Fifteen years later, he thought that he had proved the identity of bioelectrical and sexual energy (Reich, 1934).

The encounter with Freud determined Reich's choice of a career: he thereafter devoted himself completely to psychoanalysis. Subsequently, he essentially dedicated himself to the following four topics: the completion of the Freudian theory of the cause of neuroses; the deepening of the Freudian instinct theory; the development of a scientific theory of the therapeutic technique; and studying the causes of sexual suppression.

Toward the end of 1919, Reich, who had just turned twenty-two years of age, established himself as a psychoanalyst: a training analysis was not yet required at that time. Reich participated in all the sessions of the Vienna Psychoanalytical Association, and his colleagues, most of whom were much older, were impressed by the alert interest and clear intellectual capacity of the young student. After a lecture on the libido conflict in Ibsen's *Peer Gynt* in October 1920, Reich was accepted as a member of the Vienna Psychoanalytical Association.

Perhaps it should be mentioned here that, for all his fervent "adoption" of psychoanalysis as the method of prevention (or reduction of symptoms) of neuroses, Reich's own psychoanalysis was probably not complete, nor completely successful. There is some clear evidence that his attitude toward women (namely, his mother) was always very ambivalent. There are strong suggestions that his mother had been unfaithful with his tutor when Reich was in his early teens, and that he discovered this, and possibly told his father, thus being (in some way) complicit in his mother's suicide. Three years later, his father (effectively) also committed suicide, though making it look like pneumonia to ensure that Reich got his health insurance money (Sharaf, 1983, pp. 42–49). If there was any truth to any of this, it could explain quite a lot (among other things) about his attitude toward women, his psychosomatic skin condition, and also his attitude toward various "father" figures (Freud, Einstein, etc.).

## Libido and the Function of the Orgasm

The theory and technique of psychoanalysis were created mainly as a response to the problems in treating hysterical patients. From a very early point, Freud saw that his patients' hysterical symptoms mostly disappeared when their childhood memories, which were thought to be the basis of hysteria, could be remembered with emotional affect. As a result, Freud formulated the hypothesis that the therapeutic effect was based upon the emotional discharge associated with the memory, and that the hysterical symptoms depicted an abnormal form of releasing quantities of energetic arousal that could not be dissipated in any other way.

Consequently, Freud found a connection between psychological illness and emotional energy at a relatively early point in time. He thought that psychic illness did not occur if the primary energy connected to it could be discharged. Already in 1894, he had spoken of quantities of arousal that decrease, increase, and can be shifted and discharged, and how they spread through the memory traces of images over the surface of the body like an electrical charge (Freud, 1894, p. 74). Careful analysis of the hysterical symptoms brought Freud to the insight that this arousal had a sexual nature. Sexual arousal—which Freud called "libido" from that time on—could also spread to or accumulate in the nongenital parts of the body, especially in the so-called erogenous zones. He later wrote, "Anyone who sees a child sinking back satisfied from the breast, falling into sleep with reddened cheeks and a blissful smile, will have to say to himself that this picture also remains definitive as the expression of the sexual gratification in later life" (Freud, 1905, p. 82).

For Reich, Freud's libido theory was the *élan vital* of psychoanalysis. Reich dedicated himself with great zeal to the theoretical and empirical underpinning of the "economic factors" of this theory. Reich did not yet foresee how much he would alienate himself from Freud and his colleagues, because, during the time in which Reich was expanding on Freud's libido theory, they were concentrating less and less on the dynamics of instinctual drives, and more and more on the content and structure of psychic life, i.e., the development of Ego Psychology.

In 1905, Freud listed three problems that did not appear to him to be solvable through the libido theory, as it existed at that time: the antithesis of tension and lust in sexuality; the knowledge that was lacking about the nature of healthy sexuality; and the energy dynamics of fear. Reich's responses to these three (to date) unanswerable questions formed the foundation of his "sex-economic" theory.

## Tension and Lust

Freud was the first to point out the peculiar phenomenon that sexual tension has a pleasurable aspect. According to the then-prevailing school of thought, tension and lust were incompatible. In the development of his theory, Reich (1942/1969, pp. 55ff.) drew upon new psychological research that had broken with the concept that our perceptions are just passive experiences, without any personal activity of the ego. He showed that every perception is supported by an active "adjustment" to the respective stimulus (see Büntig, 1977).

Now it became possible to explain that the same stimuli that tend to trigger a pleasurable sensation are not perceived as such, or are even perceived as unpleasurable in some cases, or with a different inner attitude.

So, the pleasure of sexual tension was in the expected relaxation after orgasm, and the experience of pleasure depended upon the satisfying discharge of arousal in the movements of the orgasm. This is where Reich began to overcome the duality of drive and lust, and that of arousal quantity and pleasure quality. Instead, he came to see the sexual drive as nothing other than the motoric aspect of lust. He differentiated between a motoric-active and a sensory-passive part of the lust, both of which merge into one. Pleasurable sensation and motoric activity in the sexual act are two different forms of expressing one and the same arousal process. Reich thought the preventive subsiding of sexual arousal (as in *coitus interruptus*) was responsible for the unpleasurable tensions that, in his opinion, ultimately lead to neurasthenic and anxiety-neurotic symptoms (Reich, 1923).

Reich presented these thoughts to the Vienna Psychoanalytical Association in June 1921. But he was not properly understood, and so he decided to limit himself in his lectures, for a while, to purely clinical observations.

## Healthy Sexuality: Orgiastic Potency

At that time, no one had any clear concepts about healthy, undisturbed, nonperverted sexuality. "Victorian" morality and ignorance about sexual issues were widespread in Europe, and Vienna was particularly puritan. In a clear contradiction to Freud's original assumption, that neurosis and a healthy sexual life are irreconcilable, various psychoanalysts believed that many neurotics had a normal sex life.

In November 1923, Reich presented his first formulation of the "sex-economic" theory of neuroses (Reich, 1924b). He had developed this during three years of meticulous research on this topic using the large population of largely working-class people coming to the free psychoanalytical and sexual clinics. At his presentation at the association meeting, he encountered an icy silence and a disapproving discussion, but he did not let himself become discouraged. Instead, he continued his detailed studies of his patients' sexuality, as well as their fantasies and guilty feelings. He began to understand that the inability of his patients to surrender fully to their sexual arousal, and to abandon voluntary control of their muscle movements during the sexual act, was the main cause for their lacking any real gratification from their sexual activities. Essentially, their physical (and cultural) tensions basically inhibited their enjoyment.

One year later, he introduced the term "orgiastic potency" in a lecture to the 1924 Psychoanalytical Congress in Salzburg and defined it as: "the ability to surrender to the flow of biological energy without any type of inhibition and the ability to completely discharge all of the accumulated sexual arousal through the involuntary, pleasurable contractions of the body" (Reich, 1924a). Reich proposed the so-called "tension-charge" formula with which he described the general process of sexual and, in later studies, the general processes of vegetative, orgiastic, and energetic arousal as follows: tension–charge–discharge–relaxation.

Reich's book *The Function of the Orgasm* conveys a thorough definition of orgiastic potency, supported by an impressive wealth of clinical observations, and a detailed description of the qualitative features during the course of arousal in both healthy and unsatisfying sexual experiences (Reich, 1927).

## Fear and the Theory of Sex Economy

Freud had already postulated that pent-up sexual energy was a source of some forms of neurotic fear (Freud, 1895). Freud spoke of an actual neurosis, only when the fear appeared to have no psychic content and was simply based on frustrated arousal. He contrasted this to "psycho-neurotic fear," which can be traced back to traumatic childhood experiences. Reich's orgasm theory overcame this sharp division and solved the problem (which Freud thought was very difficult to resolve) of how sexual arousal can be transformed into fear. His clinical observations clearly showed that (1) every psycho-neurosis had an actual-neurotic core, and (2) every actual neurosis had a psycho-neurotic superstructure. Reich was convinced of Freud's original assumption that the energy from physical sexual arousal is transformed into fear when the path to its discharge remains blocked. But it was still not clear how this could happen, as it was thought that sexual arousal was a distinct physical process, whereas the conflicts of the neurosis had a purely emotional nature. Reich wrote:

> It cannot be any other way than that a minor conflict produces a small disturbance of the sexual-energy

balance. This minor stasis intensifies the conflict, and this in turn increases the stasis. This is how the psychic conflict and the physical arousal stasis intensify each other. The central psychic conflict is the parent–child relationship. It is never lacking in a neurosis. It is the historical experience material from which the neurosis feeds itself in terms of content. . . . However, the child-parent conflict alone could not produce a lasting disruption of the emotional equilibrium if it was not constantly fed through the actual arousal stasis. . . . The arousal stasis is therefore the continually existing illness factor that does not feed the neurosis in terms of content but energetically. (Reich, 1942/1969, p. 102)

From that time on, Reich gave the name of "stasis anxiety" to the actual neurosis. In 1924, he treated two women with cardiac neurosis and observed that their cardiac neuralgia diminished as soon as they got to the point where they could experience genital arousal. Conversely, every slowing down of excitation and arousal produced immediate feelings of oppression and anxiety in the heart area.

This meant that the congested sexual arousal and fear were related to the functions of the autonomic nervous system. Reich drew the conclusion that sexual arousal is not transformed into anxiety, as Freud had assumed, but that the same arousal that appears in the genitals as a pleasurable sensation is registered as anxiety when it is felt in the heart area. These thoughts led him to the development of the provisional hypothesis that anxiety is the emotional counterpart of the vasomotoric neurosis (Reich, 1925b), forming the initial approach for his later studies regarding the antithetical functions of psychosomatic diseases.

## Reactions to Reich's Orgasm Theory

Reich's orgasm theory can therefore be seen as the natural continuation of Freud's libido theory, and it became the theoretical basis for most of Reich's further psychotherapy work. However, very few people really understood it, or possibly (because of the title) didn't want to understand it. After the Salzburg lecture, "Karl Abraham congratulated him on the successful formulation of the economic factor of the neurosis" (Boadella, 1973, p. 19). Arthur Kronfeld described Reich's book *The Function of the Orgasm* as the most important contribution since Freud's *The Ego and the Id* (Kronfeld, 1927; see also Boadella, 1973, p. 21, for a quotation from this review). Valuable support also came from Eduard Hitschmann, the director of the psychoanalytic outpatient clinic in Vienna. However, the reactions of most psychoanalysts were uncomprehending, ambivalent, or even disapproving. When Reich presented his manuscript to Freud, the latter said, "So thick?" in a disappointingly cool voice, though he wrote to Reich, saying it was "valuable, rich in observation and thought." But Freud later mocked the orgasm theory as Reich's "hobbyhorse" (Boadella, 1973, p. 21).

A rift then became apparent in the Vienna Psychoanalytical Association. Reich had succeeded in a decisive further development of Freud's libido theory, exactly at the point in time when Freud had let go of it: "Anxiety never arises from the repressed libido. If it had been enough for me in earlier times to say that after the repression an amount of anxiety appears in place of the expected expression of libido, I would have nothing to retract today" (Freud, 1926, p. 138).

Few people attacked Reich's concept directly; most of them ignored it or—even worse—adopted it as if it were analytical general knowledge, without acknowledging Reich's authorship. The list of plagiarists made by Boadella (1973), in which illustrious names such as Fenichel and Erikson are included, is shamefully extensive.

Reich's observations have also never been seriously refuted. The studies on sexuality by Kinsey (Kinsey et al., 1948; Kinsey, 1953) and by Masters and Johnson (1966) are difficult to compare with Reich's studies, because they lump together every climax in the genital embrace as an orgasm, independent of the wholeness of the partners' relationship, including both orgasmically "potent" and "impotent" reactions. A more precise discussion of this, and similar work, can be found in Boadella's (1973) writings.

Tage Philipson (quoted in Boadella, 1973) and Alexander Lowen (1965) deepened the understanding of Reich's studies of the relationship between sexuality and overall personality. For Theodore Wolfe—one of the pioneers of psychosomatic medicine in America—Reich's book *The Function of the Orgasm* contains the key to the psychosomatic problem (Foreword in Reich, 1942).

## The Therapeutic Technique

Freud had recognized early on that the symptoms of his hysterical patients improved when an energetic reaction could be produced in the form of an emotional discharge. Today, we understand this to mean all of the arbitrary and involuntary reflexes through which the affects can be released—from bursting into tears, to an actual act of revenge (as shown by experience)—and are thus therapeutic. When this reaction occurs with sufficient intensity, a good portion of the affect disappears; in colloquial language, these everyday observations are expressed through phrases like "having a good cry" or "blowing off steam."

In using the "free association" technique, Freud soon discovered the phenomenon of resistance. During therapy, the patients vehemently defended themselves against certain memories and thoughts. From this observation, Freud concluded that "forgetting" is the result of an active process, which he initially called "defense" and later "repression." The function of the repression was to weaken the emotionally charged ideas and therefore to protect the patients against the painful experiences of their emotions (and their memories).

The doctrine of repression became—just like the teaching of the so-called transference theory—one of the two mainstays of the theoretical edifice of psychoanalysis. However, at least and not at first, psychoanalysis did not succeed in developing a practical, systematic method of resistance analysis. This task was left to Reich to accomplish.

## From the Interpretation of Resistance to Character Analysis

In September 1922, at the International Psychoanalytical Congress in Berlin, Freud gave a lecture on "The Ego and the Id." This lecture clearly illustrated the shifting of his interest away from the suppressed instincts, more toward the defense mechanisms of the ego. These powers of defense themselves—even though parts of the ego—were unconscious for the most part. In the same lecture, Freud discussed the so-called "negative" therapeutic reaction that was supposedly responsible when the condition of many patients got worse, instead of better, through the analysis. Freud later identified this with the hypothetical "death wish" that he had postulated in 1920.

Going in a radically different direction, a proposal by Reich helped to establish the Vienna Seminar for Psychoanalytical Therapy. Although it was initially under the direction of Hermann Nunberg, Reich himself directed the seminar from 1924 to 1930. In addition to systematic research on the resistance of patients and their typical defense patterns, the seminar, especially under Reich, saw its mission as being the careful analysis of the therapy process. It became increasingly obvious from this that the resistance intensified with the increasing depth of the analysis and the closer that it came to the memory of the traumatic situation.

The seminar succeeded, over time, in revealing the patients' typical defense patterns. Through clinical examples, it was increasingly possible for Reich to show that all of these resistance patterns in the transference occurred as latent doubt, mistrust, and hostility toward the analyst. Reich considered the uncovering of this latent negativity in the therapy to be one of the most important tasks of the therapeutic process.

Even if the analysis appeared to be occurring in a disorderly manner, a more precise study of it showed that the patient defended himself systematically, and in a characteristic way, against the analysis and the related uncovering of his concealed emotions. As a result, Reich and the colleagues in the technical seminar shifted the emphasis of their attention away from the individual forms of resistance toward examining the specific patterns of resistance, or what came to be called "character structures." On the basis of these studies, and his experiences in the psychoanalytical clinic with impulsive and psychopathic patients,

Reich supported the transition from symptom analysis to the therapy of character (Reich, 1925a).

At the Tenth Psychoanalytical Congress in Innsbruck in 1927, Reich introduced the concept of the "character armor" for the first time. This consists of many layers of defense reactions built up over time into a solid structure against the suppressed drives and any reactive hostility triggered by the suppression of the drives. Reich recognized that the function of the character armor was to exist as a form of "frozen history." Every unresolved conflict in the development of the individual left behind a trace in his character development, which takes the form of a rigid posture, behavior, or expression that serves in the defense of unreleased emotions. Reich had now found a clear relationship between the sex-economic theory of pent-up emotion and the concept of the character structure: The emotion was bound in the character armor, and emotional discharge and psychoanalytical healing were not possible as long as the character armor protected the patient against their intense repressed feelings.

Reich's major work, *Character Analysis* (1933a)—which is still considered a classic long after his death—points out three areas of emphasis: (1) developing a systematic technique for interpreting the patients' characteristic postures and attitudes in order to free their suppressed emotionality from its armoring; (2) developing a clear concept for the goal of the analytical therapy, namely a sex-economic change from neurotic to healthy behavior; and (3) systematically describing the various character structures and the typical conflict situations that produced them in childhood.

## The Genital Character and the Neurotic Character Structures

When looking at the personality structure of his patients, Reich saw three main layers: The surface layer is a social facade of withheld feelings, compulsive politeness, false friendliness, and compliance. Most (if not all) attempts at analysis failed when this facade was not penetrated. Beneath it is the layer of secondary drives and needs with, as Freud saw it, all of the hidden negativity of the repressed unconscious. Through the persistent, structured character-analytical work, Reich often succeeded in penetrating this layer and advancing into the layer of "primary needs"—the third layer. Reich called the individual, whose actions were motivated by these primary impulses that are "moral by nature," the "genital" character. While the genital character also achieved an identification with his core in his consciousness, the "impulsive" characters and "psychopaths" were identified with the secondary hostility that arises through suppressing the drives, and the neurotic character structures with their respective characteristic facade.

By systematically classifying characteristic behavior and defense patterns with the typical situations of frustration that occur in childhood, Reich differentiated the various character structures that he had noted at that time: the phallic-narcissistic and the passive-feminine man, the masculine-aggressive woman, the hysterical woman, as well as the compulsive characters of both genders (Reich, 1933a).

Reich's improvement of the analytical technique, and the psychoanalytical understanding of the characteristic resistance patterns in relationship to the primary conflicts that had produced them, was—despite the resistance of the conservative analysts—largely seen as a substantial enrichment of psychoanalysis. However, his trailblazing clarification of the problems around masochism brought him into a sharp opposition to Freud, and also with a large portion of the German-speaking psychoanalytical movement. By this time, Reich had left Vienna (in 1930) and settled in Berlin. However, things began to get worse.

In 1932, Reich's work on the "masochistic character" succeeded in providing a detailed description of this structure and the dynamics upon which it is based. This was the clinical refutation of the "death wish," as postulated by Freud (Reich, 1932b). Masochism is the prototype of a "secondary" drive: "[It] does not correspond with any biological drive. It is the result of a gratification disorder and an always unsuccessful attempt to correct this disorder. It is the result and not the cause of the neurosis" (Reich, 1942/1969, pp. 220ff.). This contradiction of Freud by Reich did not go down at all well.

## The Character of Society

After the libido theory and the therapeutic technique, the psychoanalytical criticism of society was the third approach of Freud's that Reich had adopted, clinically substantiated, and theoretically advanced—at a time when Freud had already resigned from interest in it.

Because of the growing influence of National Socialism (fascism), the pressure on psychoanalysis had increased considerably, but Freud not only gave up on the social-critical demands of psychoanalysis that had been implicit in his early writings, he also abandoned the man, Reich, whom he had repeatedly encouraged to translate his psychoanalytical ideas into practice.

As the first assistant of the Vienna Psychoanalytical Outpatients Clinic, Reich had the opportunity of convincing himself, over the years, that neuroses were not just the strange quirks of the unsatisfied socialites—as the opponents of psychoanalysis had claimed—but were endemically included in all layers of society. The clinic was open for two hours every day to advise and treat people who could not afford the fees of the analysts. Here, Reich was confronted every day with the sexual and material miseries of the working people. What gradually emerged for him were three essential complexes of issues: first, the change in neuroses as a result of reforming the care and education of children; second, overcoming society's opposition to physical (carnal) pleasures through sexual reform; and third, overcoming the authoritarian suppression in society through social reforms.

Reich did not study sociology at his desk, nor in a university, but in his clinical practice, and on the street. He had already been deeply affected by his clinical experience with working-class people. After being an eyewitness to a massacre during a political rally in Vienna in 1927, he became a member of the "Arbeiterhilfe" [Worker's Aid], a subgroup of the Austrian Communist Party. Originally, he had hoped to be able to place psychoanalysis and Marxism on a mutually equal basis, as both seemed destined to change the world for the better.

In 1928, Reich spoke for the first time at a large student gathering about the relationship of psychoanalysis to Marxist sociology (Reich et al., 1929). Encouraged by Freud, in January 1929, Reich founded the "Socialist Association for Sex Counseling and Sex Research" and opened a total of six sex-counseling centers for workers and employees, with four young medical psychoanalysts and three obstetricians. The clinics were free and open to anyone who needed help, support, advice, and information on questions about raising children, marriage problems, birth control, sexual problems, and sex education. This was new, radical, and also extremely popular.

In addition, lectures and discussions took place at the clinic on a regular basis. Reich continued in this work for about three years in Vienna and another three years when in Berlin. Hundreds, even thousands, of people came to these clinics. Later, he also published sexual education pamphlets that were distributed by the Communist Party. This was radical, particularly for these times: in the late 1920s and early 1930s, Reich made countless enemies, and not only risked his reputation, but also his medical livelihood, by propagating concepts like free access to contraceptives for young people and the right of women to have an abortion (Boadella, 1980).

Yet five years were to pass before he noticed that he had fallen between two stools. The theoreticians and functionaries of both of these two large movements, which both came into being around the start of the twentieth century, did not want to hear about any possible synthesis between psychoanalysis and Marxism. Reich's ideas were therefore controversial and not really welcome in either camp.

## Cultural Debate with Freud

In those early days in Vienna, meetings in which the functionaries of the Psychoanalytical Association came together were held at Freud's house every four weeks. They discussed the relationships between civilization and neurosis. Above all, the issue of whether sexual repression and the frustration of drives were necessary in order for culture to develop was talked about. These discussions were the background for Freud's book *Civilization and Its Discontents* (1930), which appeared a short time later. On December 12, 1929, Reich had given a lecture on the prophylaxis (treatment) of neuroses. He took the clear standpoint that neuroses can be prevented—but only when upbringing, family life, and the forms within society are changed. Freud's response (then) was that it was not the task of psychoanalysis to save the world. In addition, culture—which was built upon the abstention from drives—has priority in any case, and rightfully so, because it is its task to protect people from their primary hostility toward each other. Consequently, Freud also contradicted Reich on this point because the latter had interpreted this hostility and hatred as secondary reactions to the frustration of the natural drive (need) for love in childhood.

Despite this dispute, at the end of his book *Civilization and Its Discontents,* Freud took up Reich's question as to whether the diagnosis is justified that many manifestations of civilization—or even all of humanity—had become neurotic under the pressure of these "civilizing" influences.

Reich had decided to leave Vienna, and moved to Berlin in 1930, with his wife and two young daughters, where the circle of psychoanalysts seemed more open to his character-analytical ideas, and which had a more politically progressive attitude than Vienna, in general. Ultimately, he hoped for an improvement both in the work atmosphere there and also to the reception of his ideas. In the course of 1930, he compiled the theoretical conclusions emanating from his work as a sex counselor in the book *Geschlechtsreife, Enthaltsamkeit, Ehemoral* [*Sexual Maturity, Abstinence, Marriage Morals*] (Reich, 1930). In it, he developed a comprehensive criticism of the authoritarian family and compulsive marriage, and described the contradictions in which conservative attempts for sexual reform must inevitably become entangled when they do not want to let go of the traditional concepts of morality.

In his last visit with Freud, he discussed the book with him, and once again attempted to explain the differences between natural morality and compulsive morals, as well as between the typical forms of the patriarchal family and a natural family life that is based upon love, mutual respect, and sexual tenderness. Freud apparently reacted in a heated way: "Your views have nothing to do with the 'middle' course [mainstream] of psychoanalysis" (Higgins and Raphael, 1967).

Once in Berlin, Reich found a much better climate for the development of his sex-economic and sociopolitical interest. His orgasm theory was better understood; many analysts came to him in order to learn the technique of character analysis; and he was very busy with lectures about the social origins of neuroses. There were already quite a few Marxist analysts in the Berlin Psychoanalytical Association, such as Siegfried Bernfeld, who had already been interested in the relationship between psychoanalysis and Marxism since 1925. Otto Fenichel, whom Reich had known from Vienna, was also present and supported his ideas: Fenichel and his wife Clare became good friends with Reich and Annie and their children.

## Berlin: 1930–1933: The Sexual-Political Movement

A fortunate coincidence had brought Reich another substantial confirmation of his theory regarding the connection between sexual repression and economic conditions. The famous anthropologist Bronislaw Malinowski had sent him a copy of an ethnographic study on the sex life of the Trobriand islanders (1929) for review, which deeply influenced his thoughts. In an earlier book, Malinowski had already rejected the psychoanalytic view that the parent-child conflict leading to the formation of neurotic character structures was a biological fact, and had postulated that the Oedipus complex must be understood only as a product of the (neurotic) society in which it existed. The Trobriand islanders, a matrilineal society, supposedly raised their children free of any societal pressure based on violence or morality, and also affirmed their sexuality. Reich studied other ethnographic sources—above all, Friedrich Engels's work on the origin of the family—and showed the correlation between the development of patriarchy and a morality hostile toward sexuality in his next book, *The Invasion of Compulsory Sex-Morality* (Reich, 1932a).

At that time, there were about eighty splinter groups in Germany striving for reforms in the area of sexuality. Reich suggested that these scattered groups join together in an umbrella organization, independent of all their different party affiliations, and founded the German Unified Association for Proletarian Sexual Reform, with the blessing of the German Communist Party. The association soon had forty thousand members, and Reich traveled frequently, helping to establish clinics, speaking to youth groups, and leading discussions (Boadella, 1973, p. 83). Reich's events were very popular with young people from all political parties. However, his program of reform was far ahead of its time in terms of the demands it made; a few examples of these proposals are: the protection of children and adolescents against seduction by adults; equality for married and unmarried couples; and the prevention of neuroses through a more life-affirming upbringing. In the Western world, some of them are only now just being politically and legally implemented. His basic ideas of a society that is more free and oriented toward the needs of the people were diametrically opposed to the interests of the two major totalitarian systems, fascism and communism (now becoming Stalinism), which were just beginning to become really powerful and to establish themselves in these "masses" (in Reich's words).

Reich had recognized that much of what he fought for was incompatible with conventional social structures and traditional capitalism. Soon thereafter, Reich had to accept that his sexual politics were also incompatible with state capitalism, when many of the progressive laws related to sexual politics had had to be repealed during the course of an increasing bureaucratization in Soviet Russia. Sexual "science" had become a "bourgeois heresy" that distracted from the economic class struggle for the communists, while the psychoanalysts called Reich's sexual politics a "communist red herring" or Reich's "Bolshevist error."

Reich, who had spent years struggling to achieve a synthesis of psychoanalysis and Marxism, and had once proudly said that psychoanalysis was the mother and Marxism the father of his sex-economic work, received little love in return from the "parents" of his favorite child. A short reprise of his own tragic relationship with his parents (mentioned above) is therefore perhaps appropriate here.

Finally, despite all of Reich's efforts to demonstrate the apparent common grounds of both directions, he was later excluded, both from the German Communist Party in 1933, and from the German and the International Psychoanalytical Associations in 1934. By this time, he had also had to leave Germany after the National Socialist "takeover" in 1933, and especially after his publication of *The Mass Psychology of Fascism* (1933b). He moved to Copenhagen, Denmark, on a six-months' visitor's visa.

## Crisis and Emigration

The years 1933 and 1934 were a very "interesting" period for Reich. He became uprooted in almost every relationship that he had: his marriage to Annie was at an end; he was *persona non grata* in Germany; he was "on the way out" both with the communists and with the psychoanalysts. After the Reichstag fire and the "takeover" in Germany by the National Socialists, Reich—like many other intellectual and political leftist personalities—was threatened with immediate arrest. With Hitler's seizure of power, it became apparent that the Socialist Revolution had failed and the sexual-political movement collapsed. He fled, initially back to Austria: his wife, Annie, and the two children had moved back there, as Reich's marriage had started to fall apart in 1932–1933 as a result of his affair with Elsa Lindenberg, and he had begun to lose contact with his two children, Eva and Lore (both of whom he adored), as a result.

Reich was not welcomed back in Vienna in 1933, as he was regarded as a disruptive influence. In March 1933, the head of the International Psychoanalytic Verlag (International Psychoanalytical Publishing Company) informed Reich that his contract for the publication of *Character Analysis* had been terminated "for political reasons." As a result, Reich thereafter had to publish his most orthodox psychoanalytical work—which later became a classic—with his own funds in Denmark.

Just at this time, a young physician, Tage Philipson, from Copenhagen, visited Reich in Vienna, as he had wanted to train in character-analytical therapy with him. The young man had been warned by the Viennese analysts not to work with Reich because he was purportedly a Marxist. But Philipson invited Reich to go to Copenhagen with him to set up a training course with others interested in this work. So, Reich emigrated for the second time in two months. He moved the "Verlag für Sexualpolitik" (Publishing Company for Sexual Politics) to Copenhagen, started living there with Elsa Lindenberg (his second "wife"), and also published *The Mass Psychology of Fascism* (Reich, 1933b) there as well. This is a very telling statement about fascism, written just as it was on the rise: so, again, Reich was way ahead of his time.

Whether it was this publication, connected with his open hostility toward National Socialism (and theirs toward him), or whether it had to do with his differentiation from Freud—it was in the following year, at the Thirteenth International Congress of Psychoanalysis in Lucerne in August 1934, that Reich was expelled from the German, and therefore also from the International, Association for Psychoanalysis: this was a bitter blow.

A special session had been called, under the chairmanship of Anna Freud, at which Reich was urged to resign his membership. He refused, and defended his work as a consistent development of further psychoanalytical research and theory. As a conclusion, in case he was to be expelled, he also demanded publication by the International Psychoanalytical Association of the reasons for his expulsion. A board meeting (which Reich was not permitted to attend) followed this special session. He was therefore not able to respond to the various personal attacks made against him in this board meeting (according to information by the attending Norwegian analysts) (Boadella, 1973, pp. 111–115). Reich's exclusion was never publicly recognized as such. Boadella wrote the following about it: "Through the myth of resignation, the analysts succeeded in shaking off the responsibility for having excluded from their ranks the man who Freud had called the founder of the modern psychoanalytical technique" (Ibid., p. 114).

Ernest Jones has reinforced the myth of "resignation" in his Freud biography (Jones, 1955), while Anna Freud reportedly said, "A great injustice has happened here." However, expelling their "black sheep," Reich, as a political embarrassment, did not really help the German Psychoanalytical Association. Just a short time later, the majority of the board itself was scattered throughout the entire world and the negligible remainder was "brought into line" under the iron rod of National Socialism.

Reich's enforced emigration and these expulsions effectively ended his career as a significant psychoanalyst. It is eerie to see how he disappeared from psychoanalytical circles, hardly leaving a trace. Although his technique of resistance interpretation and character analysis is still practiced throughout the world, in one form or another, no one really appears to know the originator of the method. Erich Fromm and Karen Horney adopted Reich's characterological and social ideas (Fromm, 1945, 1947; Horney, 1939), but they ignored his authorship and, in some cases, even appeared clearly to deny it (Boadella, 1973, pp. 79, 91–94).

Reich was simply forgotten (or ignored) by the psychoanalysts, but he celebrated a strange and surprising comeback decades later, after his death, in Europe and America, when he was "discovered" by the young leftists, the humanistic psychologists, and the hippie movement in the 1960s. A large portion of these were very mistrustful of the Freudian style of psychoanalysis that placed the preservation of culture above the gratification of individual needs, and Reich's ideas consequently offered a therapy in the direction of adaptation. One of the most outstanding intellectual leaders of the young leftists was Herbert Marcuse. In his book, *Eros and Civilization* (1956), he recognized that "the most serious attempt" to develop the critical social theory, implied by Freud, could be found in the early writings of Wilhelm Reich.

## Muscle Armor and Character-Analytical Vegetotherapy

At that "fatal" 1934 congress in Lucerne, Reich had presented a paper about "Psychic Contact and Vegetative Streaming" (1935).

He presented his concepts of the uniform, and simultaneously opposing, nature of the physical and the psychic, postulating that the human organism—despite its tremendous differentiation—behaves like an amoeba, in principle, and should be seen as a whole. It reacts with contraction to unpleasurable situations, and with expansion to pleasurable ones. Reich was clearly not understood.

In the same lecture, he introduced the term of "muscular armoring" for the first time and spoke of the functional identity between muscular and character-related armoring. This was based on years of minutely observing clinical patients, which had resulted in the finding that resistance in the analysis, and the suppression of strong emotions such as anger, fear, grief, or lust, was always associated with a corresponding muscular tenseness. It was clear to him:

> that the muscular tension, wherever it occurs, is not something like a "consequence," an "expression," or a "side effect" of the repression mechanism . . . [but] represents the most essential part of the repression process. Without exception, our patients report that they had experienced periods in childhood during which they had learned certain practices of vegetative behavior (breathing, pressing the belly, etc.) in order to suppress their impulses of hatred, fear, and love. Up to now, analytical psychology had just paid attention to what the children suppress and which reasons cause them to learn to control their affects. The way in which the children tended to fight against the stirrings of the affects remained unheeded . . . *Every muscular tenseness contains the story and the meaning of its origin* . . . The neurosis is not just the expression of a disturbance in the psychic equilibrium but it is . . . *the expression of a chronic disturbance of the vegetative equilibrium and the natural mobility* . . . The psychic structure is therefore simultaneously a specific biophysical structure; it represents a certain state of the individual's vegetative play of the forces . . . *The tenseness of the musculature is the physical side of the repression process and the basis of its lasting maintenance.* It is never the individual muscles that become tense but muscle complexes belonging to a vegetative *functional unit.* If, for example, an impulse to cry is to be suppressed, not only the lower lip is tensed but also the entire mouth and jaw musculature, as well as the corresponding neck musculature; so these are basically those organs that become active as a functional unit in crying. (Reich, 1942/1969, pp. 258–260; emphasis in the original)

Reich's character-analytical observations, of typical types of behavior that can be classified with specific character structures, were now supplemented by his study of the typically associated body postures. Reich deciphered these postures, which had become the patient's "second nature," as a series of constructions (or constrictions) whose function it was to control emotions and feelings through controlling tension, movement, and breathing. Later, Reich described typical tensions of entire muscle groups, from head to foot, that served to suppress the person's emotions. Reich called the most effective among these types of affect blocks the "breath block," which even infants use when they become frustrated for too long. It consists of contracting the diaphragm and hardening the stomach muscles. Not only does it protect against the undesired expression of feelings—it also diminishes their formation.

Reich finally tended, more and more in therapy, toward provoking cathartic reactions—through direct work on the patient's body. He had developed this aspect of his work in the first months of exile from Germany, in 1933 and 1934, while he was first living with Elsa Lindenberg. She had been trained with Elsa Gindler and there is some strong evidence that this "body-oriented" connection led Reich into working directly with the patient's body (Geuter et al., 2010; Young, 2010).

He called this further development of his therapeutic method "Character-Analytic Vegetotherapy." He was now not only releasing the patient's affects bound into their armor by means of the character-analytical work, but also through the direct manipulation of contracted musculature, by means of pressure points and massage.

The resolution of muscular tension in the therapy session sometimes led to the most vehement emotional discharges, with involuntary clonic muscle convulsions that were occasionally preceded by increased tenseness. The resolution of this tenseness—through muscle convulsions—was always perceived as a relief by the patients, and usually had a feeling of relaxation throughout the entire organism as a result, which corresponded with the more objective reason of a loosening up of the patient's organism. A fine wavelike movement, that could affect the entire body, accompanied free, unhindered breathing: Reich called it the "breathing wave." This often led to a spasm of discharge affecting the whole body. Because of its similarity to the movements during orgasm, Reich called this the "orgasm reflex" (Reich, 1937b). The therapeutic goal of the character-analytical technique—restoration of the orgiastic potency and self-regulation in love and work—was now supplemented by the goal of Vegetotherapy, which Reich called "vegetative liveliness." One of the outstanding characteristics of vegetative liveliness was the willingness of the patients to allow and accept (even come to enjoy) the vegetative streamings that were produced through the liberation of the energy from muscular tensions. In the therapy, the various types of sensations of warmth, tingling in the skin, and light trembling in the limbs and trunk became a pulsating reflexive movement that extended over the entire body.

## The Physiological Body in Psychotherapy

In Copenhagen, Reich once again resumed his studies of the direct therapeutic work, and continued with his advance into the area of psychosomatics. His research on the character-related armoring of patients confirmed studies by Friedrich Kraus (1919), a Berlin internist, on the electrophysiology of the bodily fluids. According to Kraus, all body tissue is electrically charged, due to the ionization of the bodily fluids. The movement of the ionized bodily fluids causes electrical currents, and an increasing charge in the tissue, especially in cases of swelling or excitation. Conversely, there is a decreased charge when the swelling of tissue subsides, or the excitation reduces.

Reich understood this to mean that the feelings of tingling, shivering, and melting that his patients experienced were the occasional intense manifestations of these "vegetative currents." Reich related the contrary directions of flow taken by the bodily fluids—on the one hand, in the direction of an expansion and increasing swelling, and then in the direction of a contraction and reduction in the swelling of the tissue—to his theory of the antithesis of sexuality and fear, of lust and retreat.

In the following period, Reich thoroughly dedicated himself to studying all of the literature that seemed important within this context in order to place his analytical theory on a sound physiological basis. He occupied himself with the physiology of the autonomous nervous systems, with the chemistry of fear, and with plasma movements in protozoa. He finally integrated a series of apparently unrelated findings, from various areas of research that appeared to be unconnected, into his comprehensive "theory of the fundamental antithesis of vegetative life."

In the state of fear, the arousal of a human being emphasizes the sympathetic nervous system (adrenaline reaction), whereas the vagus nerve in the autonomic nervous system (choline reaction) predominates in a state of pleasurable arousal. The research of Kraus reinforced Reich in his assumption that the direction in which the ionized fluids move is the decisive factor for the effect of the sympathetic nervous system and vagus nerve in the arousal balance.

## Conclusion

Reich had succeeded in creating an integrated theory regarding the functional unity of psychic behavior and the physical postures of the character structures. He also substantially improved the therapeutic technique for overcoming the abnormal attitudes that inhibit sexuality. In addition, during the following period, he examined the role of sympathicotonia[7] in the development of various psycho-

---

6 Sympathicotonia: a stimulated condition of the sympathetic nervous system, marked by vascular spasms, heightened blood pressure, "goosebumps," a heightened sensitivity to adrenaline, and the dominance of other sympathetic functions.

somatic diseases, such as hypotension of the cardiovascular system, muscular rheumatism, bronchial asthma, peptic ulcers, and general spasms of all types of the ring muscles (Reich, 1942/1969, pp. 311ff.). However, even this did not satisfy Reich—it drove him on to search for the nature of "bioenergy"—the stuff from which, as Freud once said, fear is made.

## References

Boadella, D. (1973). *Wilhelm Reich: The evolution of his work.* London: Vision Press.

Boadella, D. (1980). *Leben und Werk des Mannes, der in der Sexualität das Problem der modernen Gesellschaft erkannte und der Psychologie neue Wege wies* [The life and work of the man who recognized the problem of modern society in sexuality and showed psychology new paths]. Stuttgart, Germany: Scherz.

Büntig, W. E. (1977). Die Gestalttherapie Fritz Perls' [The Gestalt Therapy of Fritz Perls]. In *Die Psychologie des 20. Jahrhunderts* [The psychology of the twentieth century], Vol. IV. Zurich, Switzerland: Kindler.

Freud, S. (1894). *The defense-psychoses: The standard edition of the complete psychological works of Sigmund Freud, I.* London: Hogarth Press.

Freud, S. (1895). *Studies on hysteria.* London: Hogarth Press.

Freud, S. (1905). *Three essays on the theory of sexuality: The standard edition of the complete psychological works of Sigmund Freud, V.* London: Hogarth Press.

Freud, S. (1926). *Inhibition, symptoms and anxiety: The standard edition of the complete psychological works of Sigmund Freud, XIV.* London: Hogarth Press.

Freud, S. (1930). *Civilization and its discontents: The standard edition of the complete psychological works of Sigmund Freud, XIV.* London: Hogarth Press.

Fromm, E. (1945). *Escape from freedom.* New York: Owl Books.

Fromm, E. (1947). *Man for himself.* New York: Rinehart.

Geuter, U., Heller, M., & Weaver, J. O. (2010). The significance of Elsa Gindler. *Journal of Body, Movement & Dance in Psychotherapy, 5*(1), 59–74.

Higgins, M., & Raphael, C. (1967/1972). *Reich speaks of Freud.* London: Souvenir Press.

Horney, K. (1939). *New ways in psychoanalysis.* New York: W. W. Norton.

Jones, E. (1955). *The life and work of Sigmund Freud (Vol. III).* London: Hogarth Press.

Kinsey, A. (1953). *Sexual behavior in the human female.* Philadelphia: W. B. Saunders.

Kinsey, A., et al. (1948). *Sexual behavior in the human male.* Philadelphia: W. B. Saunders.

Kraus, F. (1919/1926). *Allgemeine und spezielle Pathologie der Person* [General and special pathology of the individual]. Leipzig, Germany: Klinische Syzygiologie.

Kronfeld, A. (1927). Book review of "The function of the orgasm." *Arch. für Frauenkunde* [Archive for Gynecology], 14.

Lowen, A. (1965). *Love and orgasm.* New York: Macmillan.

Marcuse, H. (1956). *Eros and civilization.* New York: Vintage Books.

Masters, W. H., & Johnson, V. E. (1966). *Human sexual response.* Boston: Little, Brown.

Reich, W. (1922). Trieb und Libido: Begriffe von Forel bis Jung [Drive and libido: Concepts from Forel to Jung]. *Zeitschrift für Sexualwissenschaften* [Journal for Sexology], 9, 17–19, 44–50, 75–85.

Reich, W. (1923). Zur Triebgenetik [Drive genetics]. *Zeitschrift für Sexualwissenschaften* [Journal for Sexology], 10, 99–106.

Reich, W. (1924a). Die therapeutische Bedeutung der genitalen Libido [The therapeutic meaning of the genital libido]. *International Zeitschrift für Psychoanalyse* [International Journal for Psychoanalysis], 10.

Reich, W. (1924b). Über Genitalität vom Standpunkt der psychoanalytischen Prognose und Therapien [Genitality from the standpoint of psychoanalytical prognosis and therapies]. *International Zeitschrift für Psychoanalyse* [International Journal for Psychoanalysis], 10.

Reich, W. (1925a/1975). The instinctual character. In *Early writings.* New York: Farrar, Straus & Giroux.

Reich, W. (1925b). Die Rolle der Genitalität in der Neurosentherapie [The role of genitality in neuroses therapy]. *Zeitschrift Ärztliche Psychotherapie* [Journal for Medical Psychotherapy].

Reich, W. (1927/1986). *The discovery of orgone, Vol. 1: The function of the orgasm.* New York: Farrar, Straus & Giroux.

Reich, W. (1930). *Geschlechtsreife, Enthaltsamkeit, Ehemoral: Kritik der bürgerlichen Sexualreform [Sexual maturity, abstinence, marriage morals: Criticism of the middle-class sex reform].* Vienna: Münster.

Reich, W. (1932a/1971). *The invasion of compulsory sex-morality.* New York: Farrar, Straus & Giroux.

Reich, W. (1932b). Der masochistische Charakter: Eine sexualökonomische Widerlegung des Todestriebes und des Wiederholungszwanges [The masochistic character: A sex-economic refutation of the death-wish and recidivism]. *Internationale Zeitschrift für Psychoanalyse [International Journal for Psychoanalysis], 18,* expanded in W. Reich (1933a/1980). *Character Analysis.* New York: Farrar, Straus & Giroux.

Reich, W. (1933a/1980). *Character Analysis.* New York: Farrar, Straus & Giroux.

Reich, W. (1933b/1980). *The mass psychology of fascism.* New York: Farrar, Straus & Giroux.

Reich, W. (1934). Der Orgasmus als elektrophysiologische Entladung [The orgasm as an electrophysiological discharge]. *Zeitschrift für Politische Psychologie und Sexualökonomie [Journal for Political Psychology and Sex Economy], I.*

Reich, W. (1935/1980). Psychic contact and vegetative streaming. In W. Reich, *Character Analysis.* New York: Farrar, Straus & Giroux.

Reich, W. (1937a). *Experimentelle Ergebnisse über die elektrische Funktion von Sexualität und Angst [Experimental findings on the electrical function of sexuality and anxiety].* Copenhagen: Sexpol.

Reich, W. (1937b). *Orgasmusreflex, Muskelhaltung und Körperausdruck [Orgasm reflex, muscle posture, and bodily expression].* Oslo: Sexpol.

Reich, W. (1942/1969). *The function of the orgasm.* New York: Orgone Institute Press.

Reich, W., Fromm, E., & Bernfeld, S. (1929/1966). Dialektischer Materialismus und Psychoanalyse [Dialectical materialism and psychoanalysis]. *Studies on the Left, 6.*

Sharaf, M. (1983). *Fury on earth: A biography of Wilhelm Reich.* London: Andre Deutsch.

Young, C. (2010). On Elsa Lindenberg and Reich. In C. Young (Ed.), *The historical basis of Body Psychotherapy* (pp. 207–238). Galashiels, Scotland: Body Psychotherapy Publications.

# 6

## The Norwegian Tradition of Body Psychotherapy

*A Golden Age in Oslo*

Nicholas Bassal, Australia,

with Michael Coster Heller, Switzerland[7]

**Dr. Nicholas Bassal** completed his medical degree in 1976 and then began studying nutritional medicine, massage therapy, herbal medicine, homeopathy, and Shiatsu. In the following year, he established Australia's first Holistic Medical Centre, which now has a team of practitioners and integrates complementary and alternative health care systems with mainstream medicine. In the last ten years, Nick has studied Hakomi Therapy and become a Certified Hakomi Therapist, using that mindfulness-based, body-oriented form of psychotherapy for both psychological and medical presentations. This has now become his passion and the main modality of his practice.

**Michael C. Heller** is a Doctor in Psychology, and is the author of an encyclopedic work on Body Psychotherapy, published in French by De Boeck, and in 2012 in English by W. W. Norton & Co. He is a specialist in body-mind issues, non-verbal communication, and Body Psychotherapy. He lives and works in Lausanne as a private psychotherapist, also giving supervision.

[7] This chapter summarizes (and completes) Michael Coster Heller's two 2007 articles on "The Golden Age of Body Psychotherapy in Oslo," published in the *Journal of Body, Movement and Dance in Psychotherapy*, *2*(1), 5–16; & *2*(2), 81–94.

## Introduction

In the period just before the Second World War, Oslo, Norway became a crucial center for those interested in what eventually became the start of Body Psychotherapy. There, for a relatively short while (1934–1939), psychiatrists, psychoanalysts, psychologists, physiotherapists, dance therapists, and vegetotherapists passionately discussed with each other how the body could be used within a psychotherapeutic setting. The catalyst of these discussions was Wilhelm Reich. His energy mobilized the traditional interest in the arts of the body in Scandinavia, as well as created a fertile intellectual environment. The result was an era of competence that was perhaps never found again in the field of Body Psychotherapy. It is sadly largely unknown, because most of the relevant literature exists only in Norwegian. Today, Norway is still one of the few European countries in which science and body techniques can associate in a way that can be utilized by health and academic institutions. This historical debate delineated some of the discussions that have dominated the field since these days, with the hope that in the future, these topics will again be approached with as much passion and thoroughness.

## Themes That Weaved into the Golden Age of Body Psychotherapy in Oslo

Before we study the Golden Age of Body Psychotherapy in pre-war Oslo in any further depth, we will begin our journey in nineteenth-century France. One of the most famous French biologists was Claude Bernard, who was profoundly influenced by Lamarck's theory of evolution and Darwin's subsequent developments. Bernard showed, in 1878, that plants and animals share a certain number of central features that can be considered as the basic properties of life. One of them is that all living organisms have membranes that mostly contain a form of water that acquires a certain number of properties regulated by physiological systems. This biologically regulated fluid forms the "internal milieu of an organism" (Bernard, 1865, II.I, pp. ii–iii). Some of these properties are vital and must vary as little as possible. Survival requires that the envelope containing the internal milieu has the means to protect the inner biological fluids from varying, even when the external environment imposes vast changes on the organism. The laws of the internal milieu are roughly the same for all living organisms. Evolution has mostly influenced the means that an organism has to regulate these crucial biological properties.

Now, we can cross over to the United States to appreciate the contribution of Walter Bradford Cannon (1871–1945). He was professor and chairman of the Department of Physiology at Harvard Medical School. Cannon (1932) is hardly ever mentioned nowadays, but his influence is omnipresent. He was such an authority in the realm of psycho-physiology that his ideas were widespread and his models were considered as standard knowledge in most university courses of physiology between 1920 and 1950. During the First World War, he was a medical doctor in the US Army. This is how he arrived in Paris, where he was able to get a more detailed vision of Claude Bernard's theories. It was after this enlightening experience that Cannon developed his notion of homeostasis. Homeostasis organizes all the regulation systems that coordinate the requirements of the internal milieu and environmental variations. They form the crucial ecological environment of the mind for all the scientists who assume that psychological dynamics form a powerful adaptive dimension. This vision influenced Jean Piaget's theory on intelligence (e.g., 1945, p. 356f.; 1947, p. 179f.), Gregory Bateson's models of human interaction (e.g., 1949), Lev Vygotsky's ideas (1934) on thought and language, and Wilhelm Reich's notion of self-regulation, followed later by Eva Reich's work (1980) and Gerda and Mona Lisa Boyesen (1974a; 1974b; 1980). This general trend was supported by the development of cybernetics in the field of artificial intelligence, which Piaget, Bateson, and Laborit rapidly incorporated.

Now, we can cross the Atlantic again, over to Sweden toward the end of the eighteenth century, where another character in our story was born. Pehr Henrik Ling (1776–1839) was a gymnast and teacher. He developed a system of medical gymnastics, exercises, and maneuvers to promote better health. He drew on techniques from the Turkish Empire and from China. Perh Henrik Ling distinguished basic forms of touch, such as effleurage, petrissage, friction, tapotement, compression, and vibration. The result became, and is still known as, "Swedish Massage" and forms a broad set of techniques that began to place Scandinavia as a new reference for physical bodywork in the world.

The final protagonist in this prelude was born in Austria. Here lived the neurologist Sigmund Freud (1856–1939), who began his psychoanalytic research in the 1890s by showing that problematic relations between mind and somatic dynamics are at the root of most hysterical symptoms.

Now, our story can begin properly: In the 1920s, Otto Fenichel (1897–1946) had created a sexology seminar in the Viennese faculty of medicine. There, he talked of how sexology had been transformed, by youth movements that wanted greater sexual freedom, and by Freud's psychoanalysis, which showed how the repression of sexuality had propagated neuroses for centuries. Fenichel also presented new findings on the physiological dimension of sexual behavior. One of the members of this seminar was Wilhelm Reich (1897–1957), who was still a medical student. They became friends and comrades in leftist political movements, and they joined the psychoanalytical association together. At first, Reich mostly studied the sexual behavior of Viennese citizens, and the impact of their sexual fantasies on their behavior. When he became one of Freud's trainers, he developed a theory of character structure, and a theory about the relationship between orgasm and mental health. In his correspondence, Freud expressed his doubts about the relevance of Reich's idealistic model of orgastic potency, but he personally wrote to Reich to congratulate him on his theory of character.

At the beginning of the 1920s, Otto Fenichel moved to Berlin to join the local Psychoanalytic Society and clinic. "Many came to Berlin because the Berlin Policlinic offered the most rigorous and structured education in psychoanalysis in the world" (Makari, 2008, p. 372). This structured formation quickly attracted candidates, not only from Germany (Erich Fromm, Karen Horney, and Edith Jacobson) but also from Austria (Melanie Klein and Helen Deutsch), England (Edward and James Glover), Hungary (Michael Balint, Sándor Radó, and Franz Gabriel Alexander[8]), Norway (Nic Waal and Ola Raknes), and from the United States (Trygve Braatøy). All these therapists, as well as many others, are still discussed today.

One of the important shifts in psychoanalytic theory proposed by this Berlin group was the emphasis on basic regulation systems. They seldom used the term, as their notions on the subject were still implicit; however, the notion and the term were floating in the air. The Berlin movement gave less importance to "unconscious internal objects," and initiated a form of thinking that focused on unconscious repair systems.

Otto Fenichel met Clare Nathansohn, a pupil of a famous gymnast named Elsa Gindler (1885–1961). She soon became Mrs. Clare Fenichel. According to Clare, a mutual friend introduced them to each other: "I thought, 'Poor guy, he does not know it is the body!' And he, of course, thought, 'She does not know it is the mind!'" (C. Fenichel, 1981, p. 6). Otto Fenichel regularly began to follow Gindler's course for men, to try to rid himself of the terrible migraines that no physician had been able to cure. The Psychoanalytic Institute and Gindler's school were only a ten-minute walk from each other.[9] Gindler's courses treated Fenichel's migraines so well that he became even more interested in her method. He asked Clare to come to the Psychoanalytic Institute to present Gindler's work. These presentations were followed with open discussions. In 1927, Otto gave a presentation at the institute on how to integrate certain aspects of Gindler's (Gindler, 1926) work into psychoanalytical thought.[10] This presentation became an article (Fenichel, 1928) in which he showed how Freud's "motoric ego" interacts with muscle tone (hypertonia and hypotonia) and with breathing.

Wilhelm Reich, his wife Annie, and their two children left Vienna in 1930 when Reich went to join the famous Berlin Institute. There, Fenichel presented Reich to everyone as a friend and as an eminent psychoanalyst who had worked with Freud for ten years. The two families became very close: Annie and her daughters (Eva and Lore) took gymnastics courses with Clare, and maybe with Gindler also. Reich did not learn this method, but later used some of the techniques that were described to him on his patients. Reich had not done much thinking about the body itself in therapy before he met the Fenichels in Berlin. His tendency to integrate body awareness into psychoanalytic sessions started when he met Elsa Lindenberg, an acquaintance of the Fenichels. She was a dancer who had worked with the dancer and choreographer Rudolf Laban (1950). Laban's "Movement Analysis" had an immense impact on the development of dance therapy (Payne, 2008). Lindenberg had also followed courses with Elsa Gindler. About this time, Reich left Annie, who remained a close friend of the Fenichels, for Elsa Lindenberg, who became Reich's second "wife" (Young, 2010).

Fenichel's association with Gindler in Berlin played an important role in the development of Body Psychotherapy (Geuter, Heller, and Weaver, 2010). Gindler influenced post-war developments in psychoanalytical psychosomatics, Gestalt Therapy, and Vegetotherapy in the United States, where most of the therapists of the Berlin Institute had emigrated, even though she never left Germany. For example, among her ex-students were Laura and Fritz Perls, who had trained with Otto Fenichel and later lived at the Esalen Institute in Big Sur, California. They had known Wilhelm Reich, Kurt Goldstein, and Elsa Gindler in pre-war Germany, before they created, with other colleagues,

---

8   Radó and Alexander created psychoanalytic psychosomatic theories when they emigrated to the United States.
9   Information furnished by Ulf Geuter by phone (August 2010).

10  See Mühlleitner (2008) for more details on the content of this paragraph.

Gestalt Therapy in the 1940s and 1950s (Clarkson and Mackewn, 1993). Gindler also inspired Charlotte Selver, then Charlotte Silber, the founder of Sensory Awareness, with whom Fritz Perls and Erich Fromm improved their knowledge of Gindler's work.

After a few years in Berlin, and after the takeover of the National Socialists in 1933, and after his separation from Annie, Wilhelm Reich and Elsa Lindenberg went first to Copenhagen, then Malmö, both for six months each on visitor's visas. They finally settled in Oslo. Reich and Lindenberg lived and worked together there from 1934 until Reich's departure to the United States in 1939. During the year of temporary exile, 1933–1934, he developed a new approach in therapy that focused more on the global organismic system of the body. He used this method with patients, trained colleagues, and later called it "Character-Analytic Vegetotherapy." The focus of this work was explicitly developed, not as a psychotherapy, but more as a way of treating the vegetative roots of psychopathology. It is highly probable that most of Reich's bodywork was influenced by Elsa Lindenberg, who also became a famous vegetotherapist in Norway. Reich had asked her to continue courses with Clare Fenichel to improve her knowledge of Gindler's work (C. Fenichel, 1981). Elsa Lindenberg was thus a significant catalyst in this body-oriented development.

## The Golden Age of Body Psychotherapy

So, it was then in Oslo that the influence of the body and movement on psychotherapy deepened and matured. Being a talented dancer, Lindenberg had been trained to acquire a broad knowledge of what could be done with breathing, posture, and movement. In Oslo, she worked as a choreographer, participated in the development of Reich's Vegetotherapy, and created her own form of dance psychotherapy, which is still taught in Norway. Reich and Lindenberg were also joined by many non-psychotherapeutic people who were fascinated by the work they were doing, and the spirit in which they were doing it: A. S. Neill from Scotland (Placzek, 1983), who created the progressive school, Summerhill; Ola Raknes (1970), whose influence mostly spread within the realm of Reichian psychotherapists; as well as Gerda Geddes, an early dance-movement (psycho)therapist, who, much later, brought Tai Chi to Britain (Woods, 2008).

The Vegetotherapy that Reich had created and developed in Oslo was a powerful way of putting the whole homeostatic system of an organism into movement and sensations, so as to support an in-depth transformation of its dynamics. Although some Norwegian vegetotherapists integrated Reich's energy theory, most of Reich's colleagues remained close to a modernized version of a holistic psycho-physiology, which was originally inspired by Walter Bradford Cannon, and by Kurt Goldstein for neurology, as well as by Edmund Jacobson's bodywork on progressive relaxation.[11]

Imagine how rich the discussions on body and mind, on psychotherapy, physiotherapy, and dance must have been in Oslo in that mid-1930s period. Meetings were intense, rich, and passionate. Rivalries, competition, and admiration moved within informed, imaginative, and creative minds. This new trend was influenced by debates between Otto Fenichel and Wilhelm Reich, which had a strong impact on the professional development of Nic Waal (Waal et al., 1976), Trygve Braatøy (1954), and Aadel Bülow-Hansen (Thornquist and Bunkan, 1991).

Trygve Braatøy (1904–1953) was born in the United States to Norwegian parents. He studied neurology in Paris and trained as a psychoanalyst with Otto Fenichel in Berlin. He then went to Norway, where he worked in Oslo's hospitals, and later (in 1935) became professor of psychiatry and head of Oslo's psychiatric institutions. Braatøy remained, first of all, a physician who was deeply interested in Reich's attempt to include bodily phenomena into psychotherapy.

When Reich arrived in Oslo, he became involved with the physiotherapists of the psychiatric hospital, and the

---

11  Goldstein (1939) is, for example, mentioned as a central influence by Gerda Boyesen (2001). Jacobson (1934/1962) was a pupil of Cannon and William James, who developed relaxation using psycho-physiological techniques. Goldstein's technique was often used in Oslo at that time.

quasi-folkloric passion of Scandinavians for body-oriented methods. Given the many discussions in Berlin by Fenichel and Reich on ways of including bodily dynamics during psychoanalytic sessions, Braatøy began to explore ways of using the bodily knowledge that was available around him. For example, he analyzed the biomechanical implications of having patients lying on a couch, its influence on the mind of patients, and on their way of communicating with a psychotherapist. He would discuss certain motor patterns displayed by patients with them, and sometimes he would touch a patient who needed comfort. He also included the analysis of the breathing patterns of his patients in his psychoanalytic work. His humanistic stance was manifestly influenced by Reich's work with Character Analysis. However, Fenichel and Braatøy both found Reich's bodywork somewhat simplistic and inadequate. They did not believe that one could acquire good body techniques without a complete training in physiotherapy (like with Bülow-Hansen), or bodily awareness methods such as Elsa Gindler's.

Braatøy had managed to interest a famous orthopedic physiotherapist in Oslo, named Aadel Bülow-Hansen, to develop forms of massage that could be used in a complementary way with a psychoanalytically oriented psychotherapy. With this meeting, the theme of this chapter finds its place, namely the association of the Scandinavian traditions of body techniques and psychoanalysis.

Bülow-Hansen and her colleagues developed an incredibly refined set of massage methods, which coordinated postural dynamics, muscle tone, breathing, relaxation, and emotional release. This form of combined treatment helped patients to become more aware of their emotions and their breathing, and to feel what emerged once their muscle tone became more flexible. They could then feel less anxious, and learn to trust that they could experience and contain their emotions. This often helped the patients to become more creative in their psychotherapy. And when psychotherapy helps patients to accept their needs and their identity, they can more easily appreciate what the massage inevitably activates in them. This positive therapeutic feedback was aimed at a relatively narrow set of patients who were diagnosed as neurotic and rigid, rather than psychotic. Today, a wider population is still being approached in this way.

Gradually Braatøy and Bülow-Hansen began to incorporate each other's points of view. For example, Braatøy had found that taking the startle reflex into account during psychotherapy could become very useful. Bülow-Hansen then developed ways of working on how the startle reflex influenced breathing that could induce deep emotional discharge. This way of combining professional physiotherapy and psychotherapy influenced (and trained) a new generation of body-oriented psychotherapists, such as Berit Bunkan (2003), Gerda Boyesen (1985), and Lillemor Johnsen (1981). It also became a central strategy in many institutions, like the Esalen Institute in California and the center for sexology of the Geneva psychiatric institutions. There, psychoanalysts like Willy Pasini collaborated with psycho-motoricians like Veronique Haynal (Pasini, 1997; Pasini and Andreoli, 1993).

Lillemor Johnsen's "Integrated Respiration Therapy" directly influenced Lisbeth Marcher in Denmark (Marcher and Fich, 2010), who later developed her own Body Psychotherapy method of "Bodynamics." Gerda Boyesen, who had completed a psychology degree, then trained with both Ola Raknes and Bülow-Hansen, and later developed the method she called "Biodynamic Psychology and Psychotherapy."

Ebba Boyesen (1985), Gerda's eldest daughter, also had the impression that the startle reflex, the orgastic reflex, and the birth reflex may have the same sensory-motor organization that accomplishes different functions in different contexts. This may explain why problems in one of these sensory-motor systems seems to influence the other two, and why, in psychotherapy, one often needs to consider the other two patterns when focusing on one of them.[12]

This period of the history of Body Psychotherapy in Oslo can indeed be called a "Golden Age," as a very high degree of refinement between physiotherapy and psychotherapy was achieved, due mainly to the cooperation of

---

12  Fright and pleasure are also associated in the brain's thalamus.

Braatøy and Bülow-Hansen. When Braatøy left the hospital, Aadel Bülow-Hansen created her own institute, which exists today as the Psychomotoric Institute of Oslo. Members of this institute, like Berit Heir Bunkan (2003), who was also a psychologist, managed to incorporate this method, and its new developments, as a part of the Norwegian health system, and an active third generation is developing the work of Bülow-Hansen in the larger Norwegian towns (Thornquist and Bunkan, 1991).

The various actors of the Oslo "Golden Age" generally avoided Reich's later theories on energy, and kept a position close to Cannon's, which assumes that emotions are connected to different psychological and neurological functions, global physiological regulation systems, and interindividual regulation. This position has recently been reintroduced and developed in academic research programs (e.g., Trevarthen, 2005, p. 67; Panksepp and Smith Pasqualini, 2005), and is still being defended by several Body Psychotherapy movements (Caldwell, 2012; Totton, 2003; Downing, 1996).

## Gerda Boyesen and Biodynamic Psychology

One of the children of Oslo's "Golden Age" was Gerda Boyesen. As mentioned, she had studied clinical psychology, and had been to psychotherapy (training analysis) sessions with Ola Raknes. When she expressed her desire to become a vegetotherapist, Raknes told her that Reich had asked all his trainees to become medical doctors, but that in Norway becoming a physiotherapist was good enough. So Gerda Boyesen then trained in physiotherapy, specializing at the Bülow-Hansen Institute.

She later developed useful ways of using the association between the digestive system's peristaltic movements and the discharge of emotions in psychotherapy. She coined the term "psycho-peristalsis" to designate the psychological functions of the gastrointestinal system. She also used Cannon's homeostatic vision of the organism, associating emotions with global organismal regulation systems. Cannon and his followers (e.g., Jacobson, 1967, p. 131) focused on how negative affects could block peristaltic mobility. Gerda Boyesen showed that by freeing up the digestive system, one may not only induce relaxation, but also manifest expressions of repressed emotions (M-L. Boyesen, 1974a; 1974b).

When Gerda Boyesen arrived in London in the 1970s, her training background was much more sophisticated than that of most of her colleagues in Body Psychotherapy at that time. When she worked with a patient, or made a public demonstration, she could achieve things that were astounding to most of her colleagues. She had a particularly gentle way of helping a person to get in contact with their deep vegetative flows, to open the person's breathing and emotions, and to support their deep relaxation. For most Body Psychotherapists whom she met, her methods and technique were phenomenal. She had gone to London in 1970 because Ola Raknes was feeling too old to travel much at the time, and had asked her to take over his practice there.

In Oslo, it was mainly psychotherapists who had teams up with physiotherapists who were practicing Body Psychotherapy (influenced by Fenichel and Braatøy). That was no longer possible in London, so Gerda Boyesen had to combine the physiotherapeutic and psychotherapeutic techniques that she had learned on one patient, at one time, somewhat as Reich and Raknes had done. This change in her practice forced her to innovate by introducing the refinements of Scandinavian bodywork within a Reichian characterological framework. She introduced Reichian therapists in London to her way of combining Scandinavian massage, breathing exercises, analysis of hypertonia and hypotonia, how emotions and physiological fluids combine, and so on. This new approach, which combined the ideas of Fenichel and Reich, as well as the work of several other Scandinavian colleagues, became known as Biodynamic Psychology (Boyesen and Boyesen, 1980; Nunneley, 2000; Boyesen, 2001). One of the main characteristics of this method was to focus on how the organism manages to regulate itself, both emotionally and physiologically: this is a core feature of the method. Issues more related to interpersonal interactions (transference, family systems) were recognized, but were not considered as issues so centrally.

Following a rationale that remains close to Cannon's theory on the homeostatic regulation system and on the viscera, Gerda Boyesen formed the impression that peristaltic movements played a central role in the regulation of the bodily fluids and therefore the energetic systems, which also influenced the person's sexual and emotional regulation systems. She began to use a stethoscope (anesthescope) during massage sessions, and found that certain forms of touch (and appropriate verbal interventions) released certain peristaltic noises. Like Cannon, she observed that these associations were complex. For example, it seems that when a person is intensely aroused (sympathetic autonomic nervous system reaction), or when they experience a nonemotional form of relaxation, little or no peristaltic noise can be heard in their abdomen. Conversely, when there was an emotional discharge or a release of tension in relaxation (parasympathetic autonomic nervous system reaction), peristaltic noises (gurgles and flowing sounds) could easily be heard and then encouraged and built up. However, she also noticed that Cannon's model could not explain all the clinical phenomena she observed, and that an energetic model close to Reich's was needed as well to explain the powers of organismic self-regulation, and its capacity to repair old psychological and somatic wounds. Her energetic model was perhaps closer to alchemy and spiritual models, than Reich's; and this was a road that was also followed by one of her close colleagues, David Boadella (1987).

## Conclusion

Even to this day, Norway has a wealth of experience and information in Body Psychotherapy and continues to explore the connections between the psyche and the soma: for example, research by Berit Heir Bunkan (2003) in her doctoral thesis on the relation between body structure and psychosis. Her work is based on a coding system, which allows a reliable transcription of most of the items that physiotherapists tend to scan when they look at a person's body. As the notation system is digitized, it can be analyzed with computer programs for research and diagnostic purposes. This opens the door for even deeper research and refinement. Norwegian colleagues might be sitting on a goldmine of practical knowledge that is still growing and could become useful to the world. In Oslo today, vegetotherapists, still inspired by Reich and Raknes, motoric therapists inspired by Bülow-Hansen, dance therapists trained by Elsa Lindenberg, pupils trained by Gerda Boyesen, pupils of Nic Waal, and the Bodynamic school from Denmark are still in constant interaction, discussing openly with each other. Their work and their critical assessments of each other are now gently spreading and being incorporated throughout Europe. Marcher's Bodynamic work is also quite well known in North America.

## References

Bateson, G. (1949/1972). Bali: The value system of steady state. In G. Bateson (Ed.), *Steps to an ecology of mind* (pp. 107–127). New York: Ballantine Books.

Bernard, C. (1865/1984). *L'introduction à l'étude de la médecine expérimentale [Introduction to the study of experimental medicine]*. Paris: Flammarion.

Bernard, C. (1878/1966). *Leçons sur les phénomènes de la vie communs aux animaux et aux végétaux [Lessons on the phenomena of life common to animals and plants]*. Paris: Librairie philosophique J. Vrin.

Boadella, D. (1987). *Lifestreams: An introduction to Biosynthesis*. London: Routledge.

Boyesen, E. (1985). De la naissance à l'orgasme [From birth to orgasm]. Interview by Michael Coster Heller. *Adire, 1,* 45–48.

Boyesen, G. (1985). *Entre psyché et soma: Introduction à la psychologie biodynamique [Between psyche and soma: An introduction to Biodynamic Psychotherapy]*. Paris: Payot.

Boyesen, G. (2001). Body Psychotherapy is a psychotherapy. In M. Heller (Ed.), *The flesh of the soul: The body we work with* (pp. 33–44). Bern: Peter Lang.

Boyesen, G., & Boyesen, M-L. (Eds.). (1980). *The collected papers of Biodynamic Psychology* (Vols. 1 & 2). London: Biodynamic Psychology Publications.

Boyesen, M-L. (1974a). Psycho-peristaltis. *Energy & Character, 5*(1), 5–16.

Boyesen, M-L. (1974b). Psycho-peristaltis, Part II. *Energy & Character, 5*(2), 9–20.

Braatøy, T. (1954). *Fundamentals of psychoanalytic technique: A fresh appraisal of the methods of psychotherapy.* New York: John Wiley & Sons.

Bunkan, B. H. (2003). *The Comprehensive Body Examination (CBE): A psychometric evaluation.* Oslo: Faculty of Medicine, University of Oslo.

Caldwell, C. (2012). Sensation, movement, and emotion: Explicit procedures for implicit memories. In S. C. Koch, T. Fuchs, M. Summa, and C. Müller (Eds.), *Body memory, metaphor and movement* (pp. 255–265). Amsterdam: John Benjamins.

Cannon, W. B. (1932). *The wisdom of the body.* New York: W. W. Norton.

Clarkson, P. & Mackewn, J. (1993). *Fritz Perls.* London: Sage.

Downing, G. (1996). *Körper und Wort in der Psychotherapie: Leitlinien für der Praxis* [Body and word in psychotherapy: Guidelines for practice]. Munich, Germany: Kösel.

Fenichel, C. N. (1981). From the early years of the Gindler work. *The Charlotte Selver Foundation Bulletin: Elsa Gindler, 1885–1961, 10*(2), 4–9.

Fenichel, O. (1928). Organ libidinization accompanying the defense against drives. In H. Fenichel (Ed.), *O. Fenichel: The collected papers of Otto Fenichel, 1st Series* (pp. 128–146). New York: W. W. Norton.

Geuter, U., Heller, M. C., & Weaver, J. O. (2010). Elsa Gindler and her influence on Wilhelm Reich and Body Psychotherapy. *Journal of Body, Movement & Dance in Psychotherapy, 5*(1), 59–74.

Gindler, E. (1926/1995). Gymnastik for people whose lives are full of activity. In D. Johnson (Ed.), *Bone, breath and gesture: Practices of embodiment* (pp. 5–14). Berkeley, CA. North Atlantic Books.

Goldstein, K. (1939). *The organism.* New York: Zone Books.

Jacobson, E. (1934/1962). *You must relax.* Columbus, OH: McGraw-Hill.

Jacobson, E. (1967). *Biology of emotions.* Springfield, IL: Charles C. Thomas.

Johnsen, L. (1981). *Integrated respiration theory/therapy: The breathing me: Birth and rebirth in the fullness of time.* Author.

Laban, R. (1950/1988). *The mastery of movement.* Rev. by Lisa Ullmann. Tavistock, UK: Northcote House.

Makari, G. (2008). *Revolution in mind: The creation of psychoanalysis.* New York: Harper.

Marcher, L., & Fich, S. (2010). *Body encyclopedia: A guide to the physiological functions of the muscular system.* Berkeley, CA: North Atlantic Books.

Mühlleitner, E. (2008). *Ich—Fenichel: Das Leben eines Psychoanalytikers im 20. Jahrhundert* [I—Fenichel: The life of a psychoanalyst in the twentieth century]. Vienna: Zsolnay.

Nunneley, P. (2000). *The Biodynamic philosophy and treatment of psychosomatic conditions: Vol. 1 & 2.* Zurich: Peter Lang.

Panksepp, J., & Smith Pasqualini, M. (2005). The search for the fundamental brain/mind sources of affective experience. In J. Nadel and D. Muir (Eds.), *Emotional development* (pp. 5–30). Oxford, UK: Oxford University Press.

Pasini, W. (1997). Metapsychology of experience. In J. Guimon (Ed.), *The body in psychotherapy* (pp. 127–131). Basel, Switzerland: S. Karger AG.

Pasini, W., and Andreoli, A. (1993). *Le Corps en psychothérapie* [The body in psychotherapy]. Lausanne, Switzerland: Editions payot.

Payne, H. (2008). *Dance Movement Therapy: Theory, research and practice.* Oxon, UK: Routledge.

Piaget, J. (1945/1970). *La naissance de l'intelligence chez l'enfant* [The origins of intelligence in the child]. Neuchâtel, Switzerland: Delachaux et Niestlé.

Piaget, J. (1947/1967). *La psychologie de l'intelligence* [The psychology of intelligence]. Paris: Armand Colin.

Placzek, B. R. (Ed.) (1983) *Record of a Friendship: The correspondence of Wilhelm Reich and A.S. Neill, 1936-1957.* New York: Farrar, Strauss & Giroux.

Raknes, O. (1970). *Wilhelm Reich and Orgonomy.* London: Pelican.

Reich, E. (1980). Prevention of neurosis: Self-regulation from birth on. *Journal of Biodynamic Psychology, 1,* 18–49.

Reich, W. (1933/1945/1987). *Character Analysis.* New York: Farrar, Straus & Giroux.

Reich, W. (1947). *The function of the orgasm.* New York: Bantam Books.

Thornquist, E., & Bunkan, B. H. (1991). *What is Psychomotor Therapy?* Oslo: Norwegian University Press.

Totton, N. (2003). *Body Psychotherapy: An introduction.* London: Open University Press.

Trevarthen, C. (2005). Action and emotion in development of cultural intelligence: Why infants have feelings like ours. In J. Nadel & D. Muir (Eds.), *Emotional development* (pp. 61–91). Oxford, UK: Oxford University Press.

Vygotsky, L. S. (1934/1978). *Thought and language.* Cambridge, MA: MIT Press.

Waal, N., Grieg, A., & Rasmussen, M. (1976). The psychodiagnosis of the body. In D. Boadella (Ed.), *In the wake of Reich* (pp. 266–281). London: Conventure.

Woods, F. (2008). *Dancer in the light: The life of Gerda "Pytt" Geddes.* Aberdeen, Scotland: Psi Books.

Young, C. (2010). On Elsa Lindenberg and Reich. In C. Young (Ed.), *The historical basis of Body Psychotherapy* (pp. 207–238). Galashiels, Scotland: Body Psychotherapy Publications.

# 7

## The Work of Wilhelm Reich, Part 2

*Reich in Norway and America*

Courtenay Young, Scotland, UK

with additional material from Wolf Büntig, Germany

**Courtenay Young** is one of the editors of this American-English edition of *The Handbook of Body Psychotherapy and Somatic Psychology* and is also a well-known European Body Psychotherapist, is an Honorary Member of EABP, and is still very active in the politics of psychotherapy, helping to ensure that Body Psychotherapy, as a significant mainstream, has its rightful place in the field of European psychotherapy.

He is also a founding member of USABP and was recently elected to the International Scientific Committee (ISC) of Body Psychotherapy. He is the editor of the *International Journal of Psychotherapy*, and has been on the editorial board of other journals (such as the International journal *Body, Movement and Dance in Psychotherapy*). He has written numerous published articles and two books, and is editing and publishing a series of books on Body Psychotherapy. He lives and works in the Scottish Borders, near Edinburgh.

*Editors' Note: Some elements of this chapter have been abstracted from a much longer chapter in the original 2006 German edition, and some important themes in Reich's life in America were added. Translations of all of Wolf Büntig's original contributions have been respected and are included.*

### Reich in Norway (1934–1939): The Biological Era

Much has been written about the pre-war "Golden Age" of Body Psychotherapy in Norway (Heller, 2007a, 2007b; Heller, 2012, pp. 464–486; and see also Chapter 6, "The Norwegian Tradition of Body Psychotherapy: A Golden Age in Oslo" by Nicholas Bassal and Michael Coster Heller); however, Bassal and Heller did not mention some aspects of Reich's "scientific" work in this Norwegian period.

This "Golden Age," while being incredibly social and productive on the surface and which heralded the development of Reich's actual "Body Psychotherapy" work that he had started a couple of years earlier, had its shadow side as well, for his relationship with Elsa Lindenberg was increasingly fraught, and this period was also characterized by a virulent newspaper campaign in Norway against him. However, Reich considered his "real" work then to be in the field of microbiology: the discovery of the origin of "life energy"—which he later called the "orgone."

Reich involved himself, somewhat obsessively, in an amazingly detailed level of brand-new scientific research when he moved to Oslo. David Boadella, in his meticulous fashion, has detailed much of the "bion" research work that Reich conducted in these years (Boadella, 1973, pp. 130–156). In 1934, Reich published a fairly seminal paper (and his first "scientific" paper) on "The Orgasm as an Electrophysiological Discharge."

In this period, he was on the point of a "breakthrough" into a whole new field of research that could potentially have formed a biological basis of Body Psychotherapy: in this sense, he was (perhaps) one of the first neuroscientists. However, he was—perhaps unconsciously—also nearly at a point of having a "mental breakdown."

Reich had started off by trying to measure the electrical charges of the skin, on the hypothesis that—if the bodily tensions described in Character Analysis (Reich, 1933; 1937) were not just figments of the imagination—then they should be "measurable": "It was only 10 years previously that Hans Berger had designed the earliest electro-encephalograph for recording brain waves. Reich's idea was construct an electro-dermograph that would record the electrical activity of the skin" (Boadella, 1973, p. 131). This was a prototype of similar machines available today.

> A professor of clinical psychology in Oslo had opened his laboratory to him as Reich wanted to find out how the electrical potential of the skin reacts to lust and fear, as well as how the erogenous zones behave in comparison to the rest of the body's skin. The device required for this purpose is now standard. (Büntig, 2006)

What Reich wanted to record was whether the skin responded differently in states of pleasure or anxiety, and (particularly) whether the electrical properties of the skin in the erogenous zones were different from electrical properties in other areas. In this respect, he was possibly more than thirty years ahead of his time.

> There was an increase [in charge] when the stimulation was pleasurable, and a decrease of the charge when the stimulus was perceived as unpleasurable. Mechanistic swelling of the erogenous zones was not always connected with a change of the charge, an analogy to the "cold erection." Fear, anger, or terror led to a sharp decrease. Pleasant arousal led to a strong increase of the charge (Reich, 1937a). (Büntig, 2006)

In the first two years of this period of biological research, he felt that he had confirmed his "tension-charge" formula and "that the clinical formulation of the sex-economic antithesis of sexual pleasure and anxiety, vegetative expansion and contraction, was supported by these experiments" (Boadella, 1973, p. 134). In this respect, he had built on to his study of the early work of Friedrich Kraus (another Austrian) on the autonomic nervous system, whose work on bioelectrics is now considered as a forerunner to Reich's work.

As he continued working in this brand-new field, into the bioelectrical studies of sex and aversion, he needed a lot of emotional and financial support and help, as well as new state-of-the-art equipment.

> Thanks to the generous financial support from friends, [his laboratory] was equipped in a first-rate way for the circumstances of those times. Above all, Reich needed an extremely strong microscope with a magnification of up to 6000 times. Although the details of the [biological] structures were lost with this, the finest movements could be studied. These high demands on the magnification possibilities of the microscopes have still made it impossible, even today, for most laboratories to check Reich's experiments. The electron microscope has little use here since Reich was concerned with the study of living organisms.
>
> All of these observations confirmed Reich's assumption that the human organism in its basic enormous differentiation actually acts like the amoeba on the whole: It responds to pleasure with expansion, peripheral swelling, and an increasing electrical charge of the periphery and to aversion with a shrinking and withdrawal of the energy into the interior. Reich published the results of his studies of literature and the subsequent electro-physiological experiments in various places (Reich, 1934a, 1934b, 1935, 1942) (Boadella, 1973).

Uniquely, for the time, Reich had begun to bridge the gap between biology and psychology, illustrating the proposition that the whole complex human organism responds similarly to the basic pulsation that he felt he had identified:

> In the last chapter of the third edition of his book *Character Analysis,* we find a brilliant application

of this principle to an understanding of the schizophrenic character structure: On the basis of his experiences in early childhood, the schizophrenic expects nothing other than rejection, lack of love, and terror. As a result, all of the energy is withdrawn into the center while the surface appears dull and without charisma (1933).

Reich studied the literature on the flow of plasma in amoebas. The stretching out and retracting of their pseudopodiums was accompanied by the dilution or thickening of the plasma surrounding them. They appeared to react to pleasure with expansion, and unpleasure with retreat. Reich summarized his conclusions from all of these observations in the article "Der Urgegensatz des vegetativen Lebens" (The Fundamental Antithesis of Vegetative Life) (Reich, 1934a). (Büntig, 2006)

At the same time, Reich was also developing his new techniques in Character-Analytic Vegetotherapy in his clinical work with his patients. He was building up a substantial clinical practice, as well as doing his laboratory work. He was also extending his social life and his relationship with Elsa Lindenberg, although serious tensions were already starting to develop (see Young, 2010). He had written the first draft of *People in Trouble* (Reich, 1953c), and the first principles of what he later called "work democracy" were being formulated. It was indeed an incredible "Golden Age," but—as mentioned—much of this has been ignored, except by Heller (as above), Boadella (1973) as mentioned, and perhaps also Sharaf (1983).

This side of his work in Norway has been, sadly, even more neglected: his work on what he called the "bions." Well-known researchers and laboratories, both in Paris and in Nice, eventually confirmed Reich's studies into these fundamental particles of biological life (Reich et al., 1938), but these have been largely ignored by everyone else—especially after his "exile" from the world of psychoanalysis.

This area of (what would now be called "crossover") research involving these "bion" experiments led—almost inevitably—to practical research (with mice) into the biological origins of cancer, which is what he saw as the antithesis of healthy life (Boadella, 1973, pp. 149–151). This "bion" research work started in about 1936 and developed until he left for America in 1939, by which time he had sent many of his samples on ahead; however, "Reich was to spend the next ten years confirming and amplifying them" (Ibid., p. 155).

> In 1939, a psychosomaticist, Theodore Wolfe, came to Oslo in order to study with Reich and, with the increasingly obvious signs about the onset of a war with Germany, convinced him to go to America where he would find a more suitable atmosphere for his work. For the sixth time within a relatively short period, Reich moved to another country and started over again. (Büntig, 2006)

However, there seems to have been few new developments of this aspect of his "bion" work once he arrived in America, as he became much more involved with his therapy work, his attempt to "establish" his orgone box as a fundamental reconceptualization of physics, and (later) in his atmospheric (weather control) work. While these topics seem (almost alarmingly) diverse, Boadella (1973) manages to draw these together into a very coherent whole.

Before we consider Reich's work in America more fully, it is somewhat perplexing why this biological aspect of his work was not more widely disseminated and accepted. Partially, it was due to his "style" of writing, as some of his word use and syntax were beginning to become quite "distinctive," eccentric, and marginalized. As mentioned, in reaction to his published work, there had also been an incredibly virulent newspaper campaign in Oslo against him and his research work, which was also extended to his psychoanalytic work. It felt (to him) as if this might well have been orchestrated, which either could or would have added justification to his increasing paranoia, but it was still exceptionally unpleasant. However, it is significant that this vitriolic outpouring was paralleled a decade or so later in the United States; so it is also worth considering how much of this was possibly self-generated. Whereas some people seemingly just didn't want to know about someone (a radical; a foreigner?) who was actually exploring the origins of life, or the possible causes of cancer, some people also (obviously) didn't like being told how "neurotic" they were: the (later) publication of *Listen, Little Man!* epitomizes something of Reich's potential dictatorial and condemnational attitude. But it is too easy to dismiss Reich as being his own worst enemy: he also had a lot of good things to say about other people's both positive and negative reactions in *The Murder of Christ* (Reich, 1953b).

## Life in America (1939–1957): The "Orgone" Era

Having left Elsa Lindenberg behind in Norway (by all accounts, at her choice), and also being emotionally quite devastated at their separation, Reich was in a very difficult "life" situation. He was (again) an émigré: and he came across to America with essentially only what was in his pockets, and in his head. On arrival in America, Reich rented a spacious house on Long Island, in the state of New York. Quite soon after his arrival, he met Ilse Ollendorf—who later became his second (legal) wife and—after an initial miscarriage in 1940—the mother of his son, Peter (born 1944). She has described some of his work and their life together in a very lively way (Ollendorf-Reich, 1969), but she also states that she could not "follow" his work, so perhaps she was more of a "mate" than a full partner.

In the introduction to Ilse's biography of Reich, Paul Goodman writes: ". . . [it] is a frank and reasonable account of how it is to be near, day in day out, a great and problematic person" (Ibid., p. xiv); and she writes: "What kind of man was Reich? To some he was a hero who could do no wrong and who was above human faults and weaknesses; to others he was 'that mad scientist'; but to all, without a doubt, he was a genius" (Ibid., p. xviii). Both authors comment on his vitality, his drive, and also refer to his (relative) intolerance toward others who were less driven. So, it seems, nothing would really stop him working:

> Reich had an appointment as a Professor of Medical Psychology at the New School for Social Research in New York, and started lecturing on the "Biological Aspects of Character Development." He also started training therapists, doctors, and teachers in a series of study seminars that met at his house on a regular basis and later became the core group of the new institute that Reich established in New York. (Büntig, 2006)

As well as all this, Reich continued with the biological studies that he had begun in Norway: above all, he was fascinated by the "cancer process" and the (negative) radiating properties of the "bions" that he had discovered (see his later [1948a] publication *The Cancer Biopathy*). For Reich, these biological experiments continued to correlate seamlessly with his formula of organismic and sexual pulsation and his form of Body Psychotherapy: tension–electrical charge–electrical discharge–relaxation.

At the same time, he was (apparently) under surveillance by the FBI: "A 1940 security investigation was begun to determine the extent of Reich's communist commitments" (US Government, 2006; Bennett, 2014).

> Soon after his arrival in the United States from Oslo, radical psychoanalyst Wilhelm Reich became the subject of intensive inquiry by the Federal Bureau of Investigation. Part of what motivated the FBI's case against Reich was an anonymous claim that he had been a member of the Norwegian Communist Party. The initial investigation led to Reich's arrest and detention for nearly a month after the United States declared war on Germany in December, 1941. Some years later, after Reich became a naturalized citizen of the United States, a more extensive investigation occurred, this time by the Immigration and Naturalization Service. The INS looked to strip Reich of his citizenship, and central to its efforts was the very same anonymous claim about his membership in the Norwegian Communist Party. (Bennett, 2014, Abstract)

An entire series of additional experiments finally helped him come to the conclusion that the "radiation" properties that he had observed microscopically were not actually limited to the "bion" cultures. Instead, he was observing, particularly in the hills of upstate Maine, the results of a previously unknown form of energy that appeared to have a universal effect—everywhere. This is what he called "orgone" energy (Reich, 1942).

So convinced was Reich of this revolutionary discovery that he wrote to Albert Einstein in December 1940, and went and demonstrated a prototype of the orgone energy accumulator to Einstein in Princeton in (about) January or February 1941. However, although Einstein confirmed Reich's actual findings, he put a different interpretation on them. In a lengthy, well-documented scientific paper with demonstrational experiments (see Reich, 1953a), Reich refuted this, but Einstein never replied. Reich was baffled and bitterly disappointed by this (lack of) response from this "authority" figure that Einstein represented (at that time).

> Unfortunately, from this time on Reich no longer distinguished as carefully between the observed facts and his interpretations of them. This is one of the significant reasons why his work has been emphatically rejected. It also made it easy for his critics and opponents to dismiss both the facts and his interpretations as wild fantasies. (Büntig, 2006)

Many of Reich's observations and experimental findings throughout the following years of his life in America could actually be called "fantastic," insofar as they often go well beyond the scope of what can be easily explained through conventional physics and by mainstream science. They also have very little to do with Body Psychotherapy, per se.

There seemed to be no immediately clear connection between his diverse work in the fields of psychiatry, psychology and psychotherapy, microbiology, cancer research, neuroscience, the physics of radiation, and meteorology—to name just a few. Boadella (1973), however, does a very good job of developing the "red thread" of Reich's thinking and drawing logical connections between the developments in his clinical work and in his scientific work. But Reich's own writings, in these "scientific" areas, become increasingly difficult to read as he develops his own terminology, with little reference to any of the scientific findings of other researchers; and he seemed to be on an increasingly divergent path of his own.

The fact that many of his "experiments" have since been replicated by others, albeit mostly followers of Reich, and most of these experiments have been published in various issues of the little-known *Journal of Orgonomy,* means that virtually nothing of this later scientific work has ever been widely accepted. To him, this was tragic: his perception of himself as a revolutionary, an activist, and a groundbreaking "scientist" was never externally substantiated, and was ultimately condemned.

In essence, Reich believed that there was an ever-present form of benign radiation that was fundamentally connected to the "life force," and he called this "orgone energy"; his experiments demonstrated—almost irrevocably—that organic materials absorbed this energy and inorganic materials (metals) reflected it. On this basis, he built his "orgone energy accumulators."

> [Reich's] various attempts to explain it are too provisional, partly too bizarre, and occasionally too colored by delusional wishful thinking to be described here in detail. However, the phenomenon cannot be doubted. Many of his experiments were repeated and confirmed. Especially in recent times, we hear from very different directions about energy phenomena that are very similar to the observations made by Reich. Examples of these are Chinese *chi* or *ki* energy, the energy system of acupuncture, and the aura of all living organisms that can be [demonstrated] with Kirlian photography and whose energy basis is unknown to us. (Büntig, 2006)

The reason that this is still significant within Body Psychotherapy is that, based on his "bion" work and on his laboratory experiments with mice, this "orgone energy" seems to affect the development of basic human health, and thus cancer cells. When mice with cancer cells were subjected to orgone energy, the tumors significantly diminished. However, as Boadella points out, this "conclusion" was based on a whole series of experiments and tests over several years on what are now called "mycoplasmas," but what Reich called "T-bacilli" (Boadella, 1973, pp. 186–211).

In Reich's studies of the cancer problem, his capability and propensity for functional thinking [was] especially clear. He never became entangled in the details but always saw the larger functional correlations. He dedicated himself to the cancer problem in three ways: He studied cell formation and cell decomposition in the tumors and blood of cancer patients, developing three diagnostic tests; he researched the bioenergetic background of the cancer disease; and finally, he experimented with a combination of vegetotherapy and orgone radiation in his orgone accumulators for the treatment of patients suffering from cancer. All of his data, hypotheses, and speculations are summarized into a unified overview of the problem in Reich's book *The Cancer Biopathy* (1948). (Büntig, 2006)

If this worked on mice, then—he thought—it might also work for humans. Reich's understanding of the "cancer process"—what he called the "cancer biopathy"—was based on:

> . . . his studies of the origin of the cancer cell, based on microscopic observations during the last two years in Norway; the clinical accounts of the cancer process, based on a number of patients suffering from the disease, whom Reich accepted for observation and treatment free of charge; and the actual treatment process that he initiated, at first with mice and later with patients. (Boadella, 1973, p. 186)

The fundamental origins of cancer are, as yet, still basically unknown: what we do know is that certain physical, chemical, or biological agents, and some environments, can "turn on" (or mutate) inactive but potentially cancer-causing genes and processes in the body—proto-oncogenes—and due to this altered activity, normal healthy control mechanisms are suppressed and abnormal (cancerous) growth or development processes take place. Reich was trying—way ahead of his time—to move toward a better understanding of these basic life and health processes. From his clinical work, he had made a significant observation:

> Every one of the cancer patients he dealt with was deficient in libido. All suffered from [what he identified as] chronic sexual stasis, in many cases of a severe form involving abstinence over a decade or more . . . (Ibid., p. 194)

Now, whether this was an accurate observation, or whether (because of his earlier studies in the sex clinics in Vienna) he saw everyone in this way, is very difficult to say. However, he was remarkably observant, and he was also an excellent clinician, so we should perhaps give him some benefit of the doubt. And, this leads directly to his next observation.

Reich . . . came to the conclusion that there are basically two fundamental biological reactions to sexual stasis or every suppression of emotional life: either the expression of strong emotions to the outside world is prevented, which is still experienced internally in the form of anxiety attacks or stress, or the emotions are deprived of their power through a process of inner withdrawal. In the cancer personality, strong sexual stasis is united with characteristic resignation and devitalization. Reich depicted the cancer process as a major central disruption of the entire organism since it strikes the center of the life process, the metabolism of the cell. (Büntig, 2006)

> Cancer revealed itself [to Reich] to be such a severe disturbance [of the basic biological process] that it manifested at the core of the life process, in the very metabolism of the cells. (Boadella, 1973, p. 194)

This connected up with his scientific observations of the "bions" through the microscope, and with his scientific experiments with laboratory mice. The cancer "process" was one of both psychological and physiological contraction, followed by a shrinking, which produced the characteristic weakening on a cellular level, followed by the development of tumors, and this led to the dying phase, as the organism became increasingly weakened by the toxicity of the tumors.

Seeing cancer as a functional psychosomatic disease was quite revolutionary, but (whether or not, or to what extent, it is accurate) it led to a couple of unfortunate developments. One was the way in which he fundamentally pathologized everything: cancer was a biological development of a fundamentally psychological problem; so there was therefore something "wrong" with the patient; and thus it needed a "doctor" to "cure" the "sick" patient. This was a vision of those times, but it also caused people to look more at the problems, rather than for ways in which to help.

In all fairness, Reich's solution—equally revolutionary, but ultimately disastrous—was to promote his "orgone energy accumulator," which, he believed, helped to concentrate the cosmic, life "orgone" energy into the subject (when they were seated in the accumulator) and thus help them to reinforce their life energy and stimulate their natural healing processes.

However, as the cancerous tumors softened and broke down, this produced additional toxic effects on an already weakened organism, and especially put strain on the kidneys trying to excrete too much toxicity too rapidly. A secondary problem came when the subject's organismic energy began to "expand" and so came into conflict with the basic (restrictive) fear processes that had initiated the (originally psychological) contraction.

From 1941 onward, he started to work on the treatment of people with cancer. Initially, his results were very positive and were written up in great detail. Most of these people were in the terminal stages of their cancer and had come to Reich as a last resort. However, he was able to show that, if the cancer was caught in time, the treatment was reasonably effective and that the cancer was possibly reversible. Reich published the results of his experimental Orgone Therapy on a total of fifteen patients, of which thirteen had been "given up" by orthodox medicine (Reich, 1943).

> Every one of these experienced relief from pain, so that dependence on drugs could be cut down or dispensed with altogether. In every case, the tumors reduced in size and breast tumors disappeared altogether. Four patients showed ossification in previously damaged bones on X-ray plates. Six patients who had previously been unable to work resumed their occupation. Five patients who had been dismissed by their physicians as hopeless, with inoperable cancers, responded so well that their life was prolonged by at least two years and they were still active and in good condition at the time Reich published his report. (Boadella, 1973)

In the following period, there was further developmental work with the "orgone energy accumulator," and it was shown to be reasonably effective with other conditions like angina, arteriosclerotic heart disease, myo-degeneratio cordis, hypertensive states, coronary occlusion, rheumatic heart disease, etc. Accumulators with an increasingly stronger effect were also developed, above all by Dr. Walter Hoppe in Israel (1950, 1968a, 1968b). There was—at no time—any claim that these accumulators could "cure"— only potentially "benefit" an existing deleterious condition.

> The reactions to Reich's experimental cancer therapy with the orgone accumulator were and are very diverse. They range from blind faith through thoughtful interest to blind hostility. Many of Reich's observations from that time have been confirmed today by a great variety of researchers in the fields of biology, physics, and medicine who often have never even heard his name. Only in recent times, has the interest of even official medical organizations awakened to Reich's work. Above all, this is true in Italy where the work of Wilhelm Reich was also discussed in a number of seminars on cancer prophylaxis at the suggestion of Professor Chiurco, an internationally known cancer researcher. (Büntig, 2006)

However, in the 1940s and early 1950s, the reaction of the official world of medical "experts" in the United States to this weird "German" (and possibly communist) doctor heralded the beginning of the end of Reich's activities.

Possibly stimulated by the covert, misguided, and improper FBI investigation (Bennett, 2014), in 1945, the

Food and Drug Administration (FDA) started to prosecute him for "fraud" for promoting an unproven cancer cure and for shipping "orgone energy accumulators" over a state line: "fraudulent" because orgone energy (supposedly) doesn't exist. They also chose to include all his written works in this prohibition, on the grounds that these promoted the accumulator. His reaction was ultimately disastrous: he chose not to appear in court. Reich did not challenge the legitimacy of the injunction on scientific, factual grounds (as he was convinced that a court of law was not the appropriate place to do this); nor did he choose to withdraw the accumulator and continue with his other work; nor did he contest the legality of the injunction, and fight it on constitutional grounds; instead, he appealed to the presiding judge and set out his reasons for not appearing in court. However, the injunction was (not surprisingly) granted, and he was eventually prosecuted and imprisoned for "contempt of court" based on this first nonappearance. Others chose to try to challenge the injunction on all of the above grounds, but without success. Reich's reaction was to attack the FDA investigators in quite an unbalanced way. And he lost, tragically and fatally.

## Free Self-Realization and the Emotional Plague

What Reich was increasingly promoting, perhaps without fully realizing it initially, and through the organic pathology of the cancer biopathy, was actually a sense of "freedom" and "self-realization" or "self-actualization"—and (in this) he was a decade in advance of the Humanistic Psychology movement: "Reich had once again arrived at the fundamental social problem of how to fight the general functional disorder that occurs everywhere in the society. In his opinion, this problem was what caused the shrinkage of the organism" (Büntig, 2006). And again:

> Reich soon saw the limits of therapeutic possibilities in treating what he had diagnosed as the general subservience of human beings and their fear of freedom and personal responsibility. He believed that the only lasting solution for the prevention of neuroses that can be effected is by raising children in a way that affirms their freedom and their sexuality. (Ibid.)

Within this context, the encounters he had with Vera Schmidt (1927) and A. S. Neill (of Summerhill School fame) were very encouraging for him, because these people practiced almost exactly the principles that Reich had described as essential for the development of free personalities, in a free kindergarten (in Russia), or a free school (in England).

For the first time, Reich's close colleague Tage Philipson explicitly formulated the principles of self-regulation. He demanded that (even, or especially) the infant in society be treated as an individual, with its own rights, and that its organismic rhythms must be respected in order for it to develop healthily, which was also quite revolutionary for the culture of that time.

> The task of researching the properties of emotional health in the newborn and small children and the conditions for an optimal upbringing was so important for Reich that he founded the Orgonomic Infant Research Center. Later, he left almost his entire inheritance to a foundation established for this purpose. The main task of the foundation was caring for expectant mothers, looking after the mother and child during the birth and the first weeks thereafter, recognizing and possibly preventing armoring during the early years, and follow-up checks of juveniles whose development had been observed during childhood. (Büntig, 2006)

## The Emotional Plague

However, this perspective extended much further. According to Reich, the "organized" repression of free self-realization, which has permeated throughout the entire human society over (at least) the last six thousand years, was attributed to what he called the "emotional plague." He used this term to describe any group irrationality and destructiveness that had been rationalized through ideologies or morality. This included the "murder of Christ," the suppression of women, the idealization of "heroes," politicians, and generals, and the destructive potential of gossip, backbiters, self-haters, critics, and anyone with an essentially "fixed" opinion.

The word "plague" was intended to portray the contagious nature of this social hysteria, as well as the difficulties in resisting it. Reich found that all groups with mutual goals, even rational goals like his own, were susceptible to this sort of contagion (Reich, 1933).

In his last and possibly most significant books, he did not treat the problems of self-regulation and the emotional plague scientifically, but polemically in one case, and allegorically in the other. His book *Listen, Little Man!* (1948b; 1972) is an emotionally charged lecture to everyone who shirks acknowledging any responsibility for himself or herself. In *The Murder of Christ* (1953b), Reich used "Christ" as a symbol of the natural "organic" human being. He describes him as an example of a free, warm, loving, self-regulating, and unarmored human being who was in contact with his own feelings, as well as the subtle energies of the cosmos; who had natural powers of healing; and who had something to say to his fellow human beings about how to live more healthily. In an exemplary way (for the emotional plague), Christ was "murdered" by an unfeeling and hardened "power group" that was able to manipulate and count on the support of adverse public opinion. And, to emphasize this, there were a couple of virulently antagonistic and erroneous newspaper articles (Brady, 1947a, 1947b) against him and his work that started public antipathy prior to his trial and conviction.

However, Reich also continued doggedly: to hold annual "scientific" seminars at his home base in "Orgonon," in Rangeley, Maine; to start experimenting with weather control, through the use of "cloud busters" that "drew down" the orgone energy in clouds and weather systems into running water and into the earth (a little like Benjamin Franklin's experiments with a lightning conductor); to continuing with his "orgone energy" experiments—including the disastrous attempt to "neutralize" nuclear (isotopic) radiation with an orgone energy accumulator, which just created what he called "deadly orgone radiation" (DOR) that seriously affected him (emotionally, psychologically, and psychosomatically) and also many of his "followers"; and to theorize about how alien spaceships were propelled (at a time when UFO mania was just starting). All this had a varied impact, especially when combined with other negative inputs:

> In the years 1950 and 1951, Reich performed an experiment on the interaction of orgone energy and radioactive energy that escalated into a small catastrophe. Most of the colleagues—and Reich himself—became physically and/or emotionally ill following the experiments. (Büntig, 2006)

As mentioned earlier, none of this later work, significant or not as it might be, had very much to do with the actual practice of Body Psychotherapy itself, except (possibly) to provide a "scientific" and/or energetic theoretical basis.

## The End

During his entire life, Reich had been a vehement fighter against what he later called (toward the end of his life) the "Emotional Plague"—and he also became a victim of it himself. It is difficult to say when this process of Reich's "estrangement" from others began. But it is certain that Reich differentiated, less precisely, between neutral "scientific" observations and his "assumptions" about these observations; and he increasingly tended to force all of his observations into a coherent (for him) worldview, especially after his move to the United States.

The many involuntary "new beginnings"—from Austrian soldier (1914–1918), to doctor (1919–1926), to psychiatrist and psychoanalyst (1920–1934); to social activist (1929–1933); and to body-oriented psychotherapist and experimental scientist (1934–1939); from Austria to Germany (in 1930), then to Denmark (in 1933), then to Sweden (in 1933–1934), then to Norway (in 1934), and then to the United States (in 1939); etc.—may well have contributed to Reich's psychological uprooting.

In 1942, he moved one last time—this time voluntarily—to Rangeley, Maine. Together with the help of colleagues, he bought a piece of land there and built a home and a research institute that he called "Orgonon." It is still in existence.

After the DOR experiments (1951–1952), Reich's scientific writings were permeated with defensive passages that show increasing evidence of a seriously deficient (or inflated) self-image, and a real and increasing fear of persecution (Ollendorf-Reich, 1969).

Until 1954, Reich's "orgone energy accumulators" had been sold very successfully. However, the American Food and Drug Administration (FDA), which had already led a campaign against the accumulators since 1945—claiming they were promoted as an untested "cure" for cancer—put a final end to everything. In view of the overall approach of this campaign against Reich, as well as the (again) increasingly virulent newspaper campaign (Brady, 1947a, 1947b), his feelings of being politically and publicly persecuted appear almost rational.

In March 1954, he was eventually put on trial, having first refused to attend an initial court hearing, as he claimed that a "legal court" had no business trying to decide what was properly scientific or not. This "motion to dismiss" was (improperly) ignored and dismissed and became his ultimate downfall: he then became officially in "contempt of court" and was successfully prosecuted—on that basis alone.

What seems extraordinary is that (at that time) the FDA also obtained an injunction to destroy, by incinerator burning, all of his then-published articles and other writings, including any descriptions related to the construction and use of the orgone-energy accumulators. The distribution and sale of all his other writings was also prohibited.[13] Even if we assume that the (so-called) beneficial effect of the accumulators was not adequately proved, it may well appear to be justifiable that their sale was stopped. However, the destruction and burning (banishment) of Reich's books can be understood, not only as a political reaction of the McCarthy era, with the goal of preventing the spread of Reich's "radical" or "revolutionary" ideas—after all, he was once a communist (in Nazi Germany) and had been investigated (somewhat incompetently) by the FBI—but also as an unconscious reaction of the "emotional plague" against a force "for" life energy.

Some of Reich's research has subsequently been replicated, published, and properly peer-reviewed. James DeMeo replicated Reich's technology for "cloudbusting" (drawing down rain with the power of orgone energy), as a graduate thesis at the University of Kansas in 1977. Researchers Stefan Müschenich and Rainer Gebauer at the University of Marburg demonstrated some of the effects of the orgone accumulator in 1987, and Günter Hebenstreit at the University of Vienna replicated their findings in 1995. There have been other research experiments and findings (naturally) supprting his work that have been published in the *Journal of Orgonomy*.

Reich was sentenced to two years in prison—just for contempt of court—and his foundation was fined $10,000. All of his books were taken from the marketplace and burned, together with all his published journals and all the stock of orgone energy accumulators, in the presence of two FBI agents. After he had been declared mentally sound, according to law, Reich was incarcerated in the federal prison of Lewisburg, Pennsylvania, in March 1957. He died there eight months later (two weeks before his potential release on parole) on November 3, 1957.

The burning of his books continued into the 1960s and 1970s; "No scientific or professional organizations,

---

13  By order of the court (Case #1056, March 19, 1954, US District Court, Portland, Maine; Judge John D. Clifford Jr.), the following books were "BANNED, until expunged of all references to the orgone energy: The Discovery of the Orgone: Vol.I, The Function of the Orgasm Vol.II, The Cancer Biopathy; The Sexual Revolution; Ether, God and Devil; Cosmic Superimposition; Listen, Little Man; The Mass Psychology of Fascism; Character Analysis; The Murder of Christ; People in Trouble." And the following publications were "BANNED and ORDERED DESTROYED: The Orgone Energy Accumulator: Its Scientific and Medical Use; The Oranur Experiment; The Orgone Energy Bulletin; The Orgone Energy Emergency Bulletin; International Journal of Sex-Economy and Orgone Research; Internationale Zeitschrift fur Orgonomie; Annals of the Orgone Institute." Accessed online: dirtworship.wordpress.com/tag/wilhelm-reich/.

nor journalist's, writer's or 'civil liberties' unions publicly objected to the book burning, or acted to help Reich in any manner" (DeMeo, 2010).

## Epitaph

There has been a steadily increasing interest in Reich, since his death, with several books being written, films being made (even recently), and new evidence being "released" (under the 1967 US Freedom of Information Act). The Wilhelm Reich Archives also "opened up" in 2007 and were made publicly available, fifty years after his death. But, unless some brave souls take up his former scientific research, or unless a US president repeals Reich's conviction (and there have been requests for this to be done), it is likely that this is the end of the story of the originator, the "source," and much of the dynamic energy of modern Body Psychotherapy. Reich was either a genius, or a delusional paranoid, or (perhaps) one of those very few people who "actually" changed the world, or (maybe) a bit of all of these. What is still valid (irrespective of the above) is the potential "strength" of Body Psychotherapy in supporting the basic "energies" of psychotherapeutic life; what is still valid is that (at least 50 years after his death) there is still a strong interest in his work, and what is also occasionally significant is the "strength" of societal counterreaction to any realistic chance of fully achieving the potential of the implications of his work.

## References

Bennett, P. W. (2014). Wilhelm Reich, the FBI and the Norwegian Communist Party: The consequences of an unsubstantiated rumor. *Psychoanalysis and History, 16*, 95–114.

Boadella, D. (1973). *Wilhelm Reich: The evolution of his work*. London: Vision Press.

Brady, M. E. (1947a). The new cult of sex and anarchy. *Harper's Magazine*.

Brady, M. E. (1947b). The strange case of Wilhelm Reich. *New Republic*.

Büntig, W. E. (2006). (Trans. from) Das Werk der Wilhelm Reich [The work of Wilhelm Reich]. In G. Marlock & H. Weiss, *Hanbuch der Körperpsychotherapie [Handbook of Body Psychotherapy]* (pp. 41–61). Stuttgart, Germany: Schattauer.

DeMeo, J. (2010). *New Evidence on the Persecution and Death of Wilhelm Reich*. Retrieved from www.orgonelab.org/ReichPersecution.htm

Heller, M. C. (2007a). The Golden Age of Body Psychotherapy in Oslo I: From gymnastics to psychoanalysis. *Journal of Body, Movement & Dance in Psychotherapy, 2(2)*, 81–94.

Heller, M. C. (2007b). The Golden Age of Body Psychotherapy in Oslo II: From vegetotherapy to non-verbal communication. *Journal of Body, Movement & Dance in Psychotherapy, 2(2)*, 81–94.

Heller, M. C. (2012). *Body Psychotherapy: History, concepts, and methods*. New York: W. W. Norton.

Hoppe, W. (1950). Further experiences with the orgone accumulator. *Orgone Energy Bulletin, 2*.

Hoppe, W. (1968a). *Die Behandlung eines malignen Melanomas mit Orgonenergie* [The treatment of a malign melanoma with orgone energy]. Proc. II. Int. Seminar on Cancer Prophylaxis and Prevention, Rome.

Hoppe, W. (1968b). *Biopsychische und biophysische Krebsentstehung im Lichte der Orgonomie* [Biopsychic and biophysical cancer formation in the light of orgonomy]. Proc. II. Int. Seminar on Cancer Prophylaxis and Prevention, Rome.

Ollendorf-Reich, I. (1969). *Wilhelm Reich: A personal biography*. New York: St. Martin's Press.

Reich, W. (1933/1980). *Character Analysis*. New York: Farrar, Straus & Giroux.

Reich, W. (1934a). Der Orgasmus als elektrophysiologische Entladung [The orgasm as an electrophysiological discharge]. *Zeitschrift für Politische Psychologie und Sexualökonomie [Journal for Political Psychology and Sex Economy], I*.

Reich, W. (1934b). Der Urgegensatz des vegetativen Lebens [The fundamental antithesis of vegetative life]. *Zeitschrift für Politische Psychologie und Sexualökonomie [Journal for Political Psychology and Sex Economy], I*.

Reich, W. (1935/1980). Psychic contact and vegetative streaming. In W. Reich, *Character Analysis*. New York: Farrar, Straus & Giroux.

Reich, W. (1937). *Experimentelle Ergebnisse über die elektrische Funktion von Sexualität und Angst* [Experimental findings on the electrical function of sexuality and anxiety]. Copenhagen: Sexpol.

Reich, W. (1942/1969). *The function of the orgasm.* New York: Orgone Institute Press.

Reich, W. (1943). Experimental orgone therapy of the cancer biopathy. *International Journal of Sex-Economic and Orgone Research, 2.*

Reich, W. (1948a). *The cancer biopathy.* In *The discovery of the orgone, Vol. II.* New York: Orgone Institute Press.

Reich, W. (1948b/1972). *Listen, Little Man!* Rangeley, MN: Orgone Institute Press; London: Souvenir Press.

Reich, W. (1953a/1999). *The Einstein Affair. In:* Higgins, M. B. (ed.) *American Odyssey: Letters and journals 1940-1947.* New York: Farrar, Strauss & Giroux.

Reich, W. (1953b). *The Murder of Christ.* New York: Farrar, Straus & Giroux.

Reich, W. (1953c/1976). *People in trouble: The emotional plague of mankind, Vol. 2.* Rangely, ME: Orgone Institute Press; New York: Farrar, Straus & Giroux.

Reich, W., du Teil, R., & Hans, O. (1938). *Die Bione: zur Entstehung des vegetatives Lebens.* Oslo: Sexpolverlag.

Reich, W., du Teil, R., & Hans, O. (1979). *The bion experiments on the origin of life* (D. Jordan & I. Jordan, Trans.). New York: Farrar, Straus & Giroux.

Schmidt, V. (1927). *Psychoanalytical education in Soviet Russia.* Leipzig, Germany: International Psychoanalytical Publishing House.

Sharaf, M. (1983). *Fury on earth: A biography of Wilhelm Reich.* London: Andre Deutsch.

US Government. (2006). *21st Century Secret Documents Wilhelm Reich: FBI Declassified Documents, Orgone Biological Energy, Orgone Accumulator* [CD-ROM]. Progressive Management.

Young, C. (2010). On Elsa Lindenberg and Reich. In C. Young (Ed.), *The historical basis of Body Psychotherapy (pp. 207–238).* Galashiels, Scotland: Body Psychotherapy Publications.

# 8
## Body Psychotherapy as a Major Tradition of Modern Depth Psychology

**Gustl Marlock**, Germany

**Translation by Michael Soth**

**Gustl Marlock's** biographical information can be found at the beginning of Chapter 1, the Preface to this handbook.

## From Mesmer to Freud

When considering the position of Body Psychotherapy within the context of modern Depth Psychology, two essential aspects stand out. First, we encounter a fundamental difficulty that exists in Western philosophy, epistemology, and science: the various aspects of what it is to be human—body, mind, and soul—have been abstracted and separated theoretically and practically for such a long time that it becomes both intellectually and linguistically hard to grasp and formulate them as interdependent aspects of a unified, functioning whole. Instead, the dynamic complexity of the body-mind relationship invariably disintegrates into its disparate components or polarities. If the connections between these fragmented and split components are then attended to at all, they are seen primarily in mechanical or reductionistic terms. Unfortunately, the few exceptional "body-philosophical" or embodied approaches that have been formulated, such as those by Plessner (1975), Merleau-Ponty (1945), and Marcel (1963), have largely been ignored and have not had any significant impact on Western philosophical and academic (though this may now be changing—see Gallagher, 2005).

The fundamental problem at issue here—the question of how knowledge is acquired, conceptualized, and languaged, and the underlying body-mind problem—which Schopenhauer called the "world knot"—does not originate, as is often thought, with Descartes and his *res cogitans* and *res extensa*; and we can safely assume that it will not be settled with the neuropsychologically substantiated objections by Damasio (1995).

Second, the therapeutic discourse itself is profoundly conditioned by its historical and social context. What was and is judged to be therapeutically meaningful and correct—and even the practical success of particular approaches—depends upon the respective social and cultural contexts within which therapy is practiced and understood, as well as misunderstood.

The struggle for knowledge and truth—in the field of psychology, as elsewhere—does not take place in a sphere of dialogue free from vested interests, power, and domination. What Foucault (1998) has called "strategies of power" is directly relevant to the position of Body Psychotherapy within the larger tradition of Psychodynamic and Depth Psychology. The fact that some sectors of the psychotherapeutic field still contest the credibility of Body Psychotherapy and see it as an approach that has not proved its validity (scientific and otherwise) reflects the long-term effects and impact that particular interest groups and their established position, bias, and power strategies have on the field and its dynamics of status, division, and exclusion (see Chapter 5, "The Work of Wilhelm Reich, Part 1: Reich, Freud, and Character" by Wolf E. Büntig; also Fallend and Nitzschke, 1997).

Unless one subscribes to the widespread romantic genius myth that surrounds Sigmund Freud, the birth of modern Depth Psychology should actually be dated about one century earlier, long before Freud first developed psychoanalysis.

In his comprehensive and fundamental study, Ellenberger (1973) located the German physician and "magnetizer" Franz Anton Mesmer (1734–1815) at the beginning of a "modern" attitude toward the human unconscious and an understanding of, and an approach to, the phenomena of psychosomatic disorders or disease.[14] Mesmer appears as the first person to have broken with the previously taken-for-granted religious concepts that attributed the unconscious causes of mental illness and its bizarre and unintelligible manifestations to demonic forces or diabolical obsession.

But it is interesting to note that already in these early origins of Psychodynamic Psychology we find a polarization between primarily energetic-physical understandings of and approaches to the unified whole of body-mind-psyche versus those that focus on the mental level and on language. This dichotomy has structured and overshadowed the development of the field ever since, and its dominating influence can be traced until the late twentieth century. The fact that George Downing entitled his work on the synthesis of these two poles *Körper und Wort in der Psychotherapie* [Body and Word in Psychotherapy] reflects the historically continuing relevance of this dichotomy within the field (Downing, 1996).

Mesmer himself was inspired by fluidistic ideas deriving from ancient Greece, as well as the discovery of electricity and gaseous substances, which was generating a fascination in the popular science of his day (Sarasin and Tanner, 1998; Darnton, 1983). His theory proposed a subtle, vitalistic fluid pervading every aspect of the universe, which, when unevenly distributed throughout the human body, would lead to disease. Such theoretical ideas prefigure some of Reich's work and resonate with the more energetically oriented schools and factions of Body Psychotherapy. These parallels extend also to the treatment process (if one can use a term implying such scientific rigor to describe Mesmer's practice): his patients' reactions—whether they can be ascribed to his various kinds of technical apparatuses or to the immediate effect of his personal presence (called "rapport" and later interpreted as hypnotic effect)—would be called vegetative and motoric abreactions in the Reichian tradition and be seen as cathartic discharges of blocked psycho-vegetative arousal.

Only a short time after Mesmer, one of his students, the Comte de Puységur, took the rapidly spreading therapeutic art of "animalistic magnetism" in another direction. He put his patients into a hypnotic sleep or "artificial somnambulism" that did not result in the kind of physical crises or abreactions that Mesmer's fluidistically oriented practice did; instead, a strange form of "lucid wakefulness" occurred, during which Puységur's patients began to speak: they formulated what seemed to be spontaneous insights into the causes of their disease. Free from the inhibitions of their characteristic normal waking state, they spoke about their worries, burdens, and conflicts; they also described steps they considered necessary for their healing process.

This change from Mesmer to Puységur represents a historic blueprint that became replicated in the way that psychoanalysis later changed from a cathartic method into a language-oriented approach. During the last decade of the nineteenth century, Freud experimented with a variety of methods to gain access to his patients' unconscious—hypnosis and touch as well as dreams—that frequently

---

14  Editor's Note: Mesmer's (somewhat revolutionary) understanding of health as the free flow of living energy through thousands of channels in our bodies has obvious resonances with modern Body Psychotherapy. According to him, illness was caused by obstacles or obstructions in this flow (we might call these "blocks," or "tensions," or "chronic character patterns"). However, the process of overcoming these obstacles and restoring the flow of health often produced a temporary "crisis" of disruption before health could ultimately be restored. Mesmer claimed to be able to aid or stimulate the efforts of Nature with his techniques of "animal magnetism," and if this healing crisis did not happen (or had not happened) naturally and spontaneously, then his interventions could help to restore health, albeit by provoking the crisis. Unfortunately, a royal commission to examine the efficacy of his methods chose to examine whether he had "discovered" a new physical fluid, which he had never claimed. He became discredited and was driven into exile.

led to expressions of intense feelings. For some years, Freud considered such cathartic abreactions crucial to the treatment, but once psychoanalysis began to gain social recognition, these vegetative and affective-motor components gradually disappeared from the practice. They were increasingly replaced with predominantly mental rather than energetic "insights" gained from Freud's innovative version of Puységur's "lucid conversation": free association.

Ellenberger's fundamental research work indicates that, even in these early phases of the depth-psychological modern era, the polarization between energetic-physical and verbal-mental approaches, as exemplified by Mesmer and Puységur, made little sense, especially when reduced to questions of "correct" or "incorrect" practice. Ellenberger explicates that the intermittent successes of both approaches cannot be comprehended in terms of the effectiveness of their practice or their respective theoretical underpinnings. Rather, the success story of both approaches is more appropriately understood against the background of specific psycho-social contexts and their shifting fashions and preferences.

This is not just a question of "fashionable trends," although this is indeed always a factor in the popularity of a therapeutic approach. Mesmer became a medical celebrity in Paris during the last years of the "Ancien Régime" of Royalist France, primarily treating upper-class women suffering from so-called "vapors."[15] At the time, this was the most widespread form of "social neurosis" (Ellenberger, 1973). Mesmer's patients suffered from various types of nervous fits and frequently fainted. His approach suited his clientele's inclination toward vegetative-motoric discharge of psycho-nervous excitation. Puységur, on the other hand, belonged to the philanthropic wing of the aristocracy and primarily treated people from a completely different level of society—i.e., farmers and the lower classes. A more detailed discussion might explicate in some detail how—with the help of "artificial somnambulism"—lower-class patients, on the eve of the French Revolution, were capable of transforming their otherwise-limited linguistic abilities into a surprisingly lucid and insightful faculty of speech. It was precisely the contrast between the normal speech habits of these servants and farm girls and their astonishing new-found verbal capabilities when hypnotized—affecting their vocabulary as well as style and grammar—that appeared extraordinary and notable to the commentators of the time.

Approximately one century later, early psychoanalysis would open up a similar space for "lucid speech" to a clientele consisting primarily of young, sensitive, middle and upper class women and their suffering. Having been severely restricted into a tight corset of social roles that denied them development of their talents, social self-determination, and their sexuality, these women made it possible for a young psychoanalysis to develop into a new type of "talking cure" that would decisively imprint itself upon the twentieth century. By these women engaging in what at first was probably more of a dialogic, conversational encounter than a treatment, their sensitivity, their intelligence, and—above all—their repressed libido could be articulated and find acknowledgment; they thus helped their ambitious doctors to attain insights into the "unconscious" meaning of hysterical symptoms.

But before discussing psychoanalysis more extensively, it needs to be noted that this historical account of Body Psychotherapy would not be complete without addressing other significant antecedents to modern Depth Psychology.[16] According to our current state of knowledge, a major figure, long before Wilhelm Reich, was the French physician and scholar of humanities Pierre Janet.

## Janet's Legacy

It is primarily thanks to modern trauma research (van der Kolk et al., 1996, p. 47f.) that Janet is being recognized, having all but disappeared into footnotes on the history of

---

15  The vapors is an archaic term for certain mental or physical states, such as melancholia, hysteria, mania, clinical depression, bipolar disorder, fainting, withdrawal syndrome, mood swings, or PMS, ascribed primarily to women and thought to be caused by internal emanations.

16  It would obviously also be justified to speak of a third, hypnotherapeutic line. However, that would greatly exceed the scope of this chapter.

psychoanalysis. Subsequent to van der Kolk's initial paper, David Boadella has worked to appropriately depict Janet as one of the great founding figures of Body Psychotherapy (Boadella, 1997).

During the second half of the nineteenth century, Janet, who practiced at the Pitié-Salpêtrière Hospital in Paris under Charcot, developed a therapeutic system that he called "psychological analysis." His medical thesis, *L'état mental des hystériques,* was published in 1892. Although downplayed (or disowned) in its significance by Freud and his circle, it can be considered one of the most important sources of psychoanalysis.[17]

In an early case study, Janet sketched the basic principles of the cathartic method, which would soon became a core concept of early psychoanalysis and later played a central role in Reich's vegetotherapeutic approach (Ibid.). In addition, Janet studied the correlations between neurotic symptoms and patterns of breathing. He described, in detail, the distortions and restrictions in the breathing patterns and rhythms of neurotic patients. In his descriptions, he anticipated many later insights into the manifestations of dysfunctional breathing patterns. These include, for example, the horizontal splitting of the breathing pattern along the diaphragm, and an antagonistic breathing pattern that is known in Body Psychotherapeutic circles today as "paradoxical" breathing.

David Boadella has pointed out that Janet thus formulated early insights into a phenomenon that, about forty years later, Reich would call "diaphragm block," viewing it as a central mechanism of neurotic defense against emotions and emotional contact.

Reich later also described the splitting of the body into two halves as an essential factor of schizophrenic processes (Reich, 1945). This insight harks back to an intuition of Greek antiquity that appeared in Janet's work, and can also be found again in the work of Paul Eugen Bleuler, a pioneer in the therapeutic treatment of schizophrenia. The Greek word *schizophrenia* means "to be split or divided at the diaphragm."

Janet also investigated the correlations between neurotic structure and the contractions of the muscular system. He not only emphasized the importance of massage for treatment, but also utilized touch and massage as somatic nonverbal dialogue with patients. In this pioneering work, he aimed to direct the attention of the hysterical patient to her physical sensations, attempting to restore essential bodily functions, such as breathing or mobility. "Through massage," he writes, "the majority of the people who I described have been healed insofar as the freedom of movement was restored in the chest, waist, and abdomen" (Janet, in Boadella, 1997).

David Boadella has drawn attention to the immense complexity of Janet's work, which also contained early indications regarding the importance of reconstructing and reeducating the client's capacity for emotional-motoric actions and/or movements. However, in order to do justice to the far-reaching significance of Janet's research, we must emphasize the fact that he already grasped and described—about one century before trauma research achieved a scientific breakthrough by recognizing its significance in the context of trauma—the essential phenomenon of "dissociation." He thus anticipated one of the fundamental principles of modern trauma theory: overpowering traumatic experiences cannot be integrated under unfavorable circumstances. "The memory traces of trauma continue as unconscious 'fixed ideas.' These cannot become fluid as long as they cannot be translated into a personal narrative. Instead, they continue to burst out as threatening perceptions, obsessions, flash-backs and somatic re-experiencing, e.g. in anxiety reactions" (according to van der Kolk et al., 1996). Even before Reich expanded his character-analytical understanding to include bodily aspects of characterological habits, Janet had formulated basic principles of Body Psychotherapy in 1929:

> A new physiological psychology replaces the earlier idea of personality as a metaphysical (disembodied) soul. Personality cannot be found in such a notion of

---

[17] Whereas Adler and, above all, Jung acknowledge the influence of Janet on their work, Freud downplayed Janet's influence, even though Janet was obviously the author of many decisive concepts. This applies particularly to early psychoanalysis.

soul but in the body. By becoming aware of the body, personality is discovered . . . We feel our body, we feel our skin, we feel the warmth of the body, we feel the inner organs; and this organization of sensations in relation to our body gives us our personality. The characteristic features of personality—unity, identity, and differentiation—are rooted in the characteristics of the body . . . It is not possible to progress with the study of personality without first understanding what it means to possess a body. (Janet, in Boadella, 1997)

Ironically, Janet's work was accepted in France and in America more so than in the rest of Europe. The Austrian, German, and British psychoanalysts, who initially dominated Freudian psychoanalysis, seemed to be following a different track, and there may have been some cultural bias (against the French) as well. Janet's achievements were beyond reproach. In 1898, he was appointed lecturer in psychology at the Sorbonne, and by 1902 he had attained the chair of experimental and comparative psychology at the Collège de France, a position he held until 1936. He became a member of the Institut de France in 1913; there are few more prestigious positions. In 1919, he wrote a book on dissociation and psychological healing (Janet, 1919/1976), which C. G. Jung used as a basis for his work on the topic. In 1923, Janet wrote a definitive text, *La Médecine Psychologique,* about suggestion, and between 1928 and 1932, he published several seminal papers on memory. In all, his output was prodigious, more than fourteen thousand published pages, mostly in French and in a rather dry style. However, the fifteen lectures he gave at Harvard Medical School in 1906 were well received and were published as *The Major Symptoms of Hysteria* (Janet, 1907), and he received an honorary doctorate from Harvard in 1936.

## Early Psychoanalysis and the Body

Even as Janet formulated his ideas, Freudian psychoanalysis had surpassed him—by far—in popularity. It is one of the curiosities of modern Psychodynamic Psychology that the pioneering work of Janet, who predated Freud's fundamentals of psychoanalysis, was almost completely forgotten or ignored during the twentieth century, and psychoanalysis became the absolute dominating force in the field of depth-psychological therapy, at least until the last decades of the century. Historically, if Janet's approach had prevailed, all the subsequent efforts at reintegrating the body into psychotherapy would have been superfluous. Instead, the body was lost—at least from the mainstream of Psychodynamic Psychology.

One reason for this was certainly Freud's tendency to emphasize the psychological dimension at the expense of the somatic, dismissing the body or giving it a background role at most; this can be illustrated, for example, by how he approaches the concept of "repression" in purely mental terms. In this tendency, Freud was not alone—he was part of a larger movement at that time that was attempting to emancipate psychology as a separate science, independent from the materialistic reductionism of medicine.

However, the success of psychoanalysis can best be explained by the central position that it gave to sexuality. At the time of the "Belle Époque,"[18] Freud was at the absolute peak of the *zeitgeist*—the spirit of the times. The intellectual and artistic avant-garde throughout the European metropoles were gripped—both in theory and in their daily lives—by an anti-Victorian discourse and sexuality. These were *the* central motifs of the literature, the visual arts, and cultural criticism at the beginning of the twentieth century, and a young and incipient psychoanalysis reflected and intensified this *zeitgeist* (Marlock, 2001).

In the early years of psychoanalysis, the body still retained a significant role, in three respects:

> First, Freud had originally worked directly on the client's body, in the form of touch and massage. However, in contrast to others like Groddeck, for Freud the meaning and function of pressure and touch were primarily oriented toward confronting his patients' resistance. This was the entrée for Reich's later work in Character-Analytic Vegetotherapy.

18  Belle Époque (French for "Beautiful Era") was a period in European social history that started during the late nineteenth century and lasted until 1914.

Second, Freud's "cathartic method" was based on recognizing the significance of the patient's affects and their expression for the therapeutic process, understanding that both expression and inhibition were inseparable from bodily processes. Although steeped in reductionist assumptions and simplistic expectations of a liberating "cure," the "cathartic method"—both in early psychoanalysis, as well as in manifold later forms throughout the history of Body Psychotherapy—was nevertheless groundbreaking in giving central importance to emotion, as well as lending substance to the notion of "working through." Reich held onto and continued to build on these intuitions of early psychoanalysis.

Third, psychoanalysis, in its early stages, was very aware of the significant role that traumatic experiences and emotional injuries play, in the broadest sense, in the development of neurotic symptoms. It also recognized—then—that these symptoms were largely embodied, and that direct access to those embodiments could play a significant role in the healing process.

All three aspects were relegated to the background or lost in psychoanalysis as it increasingly established itself throughout the first half of the twentieth century, with the practice of interpretation, based on insight, taking center stage and remaining unchallenged for a long time as the exclusive theory of therapeutic action.

The tradition of Body Psychotherapy, however, kept all three aspects alive and continually developed them further, albeit in relative obscurity on the fringes of the psychotherapeutic field. Reichian, Neo-Reichian, and Gestalt traditions maintained a focus on the essential significance of emotions to the therapeutic process, which was reflected in training curricula, assessment criteria, and the values of these communities of practitioners for decades.

During the last decade of the past century, then, the trend reversed, partly with the help of paradigm shifts in neuroscience: the larger field of psychotherapy began to pay attention to the body-mind, emotion, and embodiment and can now benefit in turn from this "preserved" knowledge that had been "cultivated" in Body Psychotherapy, although it is debatable how deep recent attempts at reincluding the body in psychotherapy really go (Soth, 2010) A shift from cognitive to affective neuroscience is paralleled throughout the psychotherapeutic field, which is recently beginning to accept again the centrality of emotion to therapeutic practice (Sulz, 2000). This topic will be addressed in some detail later in this book (see Chapter 53, "The Role of the Body in Emotional Defense Processes: Body Psychotherapy and Emotional Theory" by Ulfried Geuter and Norbert Schrauth); suffice it to say that there is a growing consensus throughout the current depth-psychological field that emotional states (including what Stern calls "vitality affects"), emotional attunement and responsiveness, and emotional regulation and expressiveness are of crucial and fundamental significance in *all* therapy, but especially when dealing with so-called "early, pre-Oedipal" or "structural" disorders (Rudolf, 2004) that reach back into pre-verbal phases of child development.

## Traumatic Experiences and Emotional Injuries

In 1895, influenced by Charcot (and possibly Janet), Freud and Breuer worked on the basis of a shared understanding that all their hysterical patients remained fixated on the traumatic experiences at the root of their symptoms, because the overwhelming affect intensity of the trauma had become dissociated and repressed (Breuer and Freud, 1895). Some years later, however, Freud rejected the dissociation theory and the significance of traumatic experiences for the etiology of neuroses and instead described the neurotic dynamic as the result of *intrapsychic conflict* between instinctual drives and ego defenses. This shift was decisive for the further development of psychoanalysis. Jeffrey Masson (1984), who initially in his role as one of the historians of psychoanalysis had privileged access to sensitive archival material including Freud's correspondence, then presented a well-founded, highly critical, and provocative study of what he called the Freudian "betrayal of truth," based upon Freud's repudiation of the "seduction theory." In Freud's letters, it becomes clear that he moved away from believing his female patients' stories of seduction and sexual abuse by family members in order to make psychoanalysis more acceptable to the medical-psychiatric establishment. The young discipline of psychoanalysis, encountering hostility from all social quarters and thus in a beleaguered outsider position, was unlikely to succeed by insisting on a socially explosive and thus inconvenient truth. As Masson shows, a theory of neuroses that explained these stories as disturbed neurotic fantasies and wish fulfillments created by suppressed sexual feelings proved preferable to the "seduction theory," which was abandoned in spite of abundant clinical evidence. Although Freud's later essays contain many subtle contradictions regarding the phenomena of traumatic experiences, and show that this revision of his theory was by no means as categorical and comprehensive as it appears, in practice it constituted a momentous shift with far-reaching and tragic consequences for the further development of psychoanalysis from then on. As Masson and others have described, the patients' real experiences of emotional injury and traumatization as the main focus of therapeutic inquiry into the unconscious were relegated in favor of hypothetical reconstructions of the child's fantasy life as determined by suppressed sexual desires and instinctual drives (however, see Juliet Mitchell, 1983).

Bessel van der Kolk, in his study of the history of trauma in psychotherapy, corroborates this historical analysis and describes how Freud's early insights into the nature of traumatic damage lost their significance almost entirely. Advances in the field of neuropsychology since the 1970s have made a fundamental "rehabilitation" possible, not only of the early theories, but also of the thousands of traumatized patients who have been "misunderstood" and "misinterpreted" for decades and whose traumatic damage has thus remained untreated (van der Kolk et al., 1996).

Changes in social climate have also played a large role here: confrontation with the consequences of the Holocaust; the traumatic aftermath of the Vietnam War (as it has become apparent in its veterans); the growing women's movement; the increased awareness of racial and social repression; and public exposure and discussion of the massive extent of sexual abuse throughout all strata of society— all have fostered a strong sensitivity toward the effects of emotional and physical traumatization.

As van der Kolk traces the history of trauma, there were dissident voices from within psychoanalysis, starting with Ferenczi, who—in his own tenacious way—did hold onto the significance of emotional-physical injuries and experiences of abuse (Ibid., p. 56). But over many decades—and through the use of outright denunciatory politics—the mainstream of psychoanalysis managed to hold onto its hegemonial and exclusionary power position. Toward the end of his long and creative work life, Ferenczi fell victim to these same tendencies within the psychoanalytical associations that Reich had experienced before him (Nagler, 2003; Cremerius, 1997). Alice Miller—who was perhaps the most radical person within psychoanalysis to revive the position of Ferenczi—also saw herself forced to break with psychoanalysis at the beginning of the 1980s. Her work and writing challenged the established and engrained psychoanalytic assumptions that—in her view, damagingly and erroneously—attributed the causes of neurosis to the "child" and its "drives." By blaming the child's psyche and conferring a status of guilt upon innate instincts at odds with civilized and reality-adjusted behavior, she saw psychoanalysis effectively scapegoating the child and thus concealing the far-reaching social facts of emotional injury and abuse perpetrated by adults on innocent children (Miller, 1981a, 1981b; Miller and Jenkins, 2004). Turning away from and against classical psychoanalysis, it is not surprising that Miller then oriented herself toward primal therapy, a derivative of the Body Psychotherapeutic tradition. Ferenczi's legacy—apart from his influence on the psychoanalysts, Enid and Michael Balint, and Cremerius in Germany—is probably most comprehensively carried and continued *outside* psychoanalysis, by body-oriented approaches such as Hilarion Petzold's Integrative Body Therapy.

In contrast to historical developments within the mainstream of psychoanalysis, the diverse field of Body Psychotherapy has always preserved an inherent knowledge about the consequences of traumatization and emotional injury. Although Janet's work was historically largely ignored and forgotten, its influence lived on, augmented by Freud's early work as discussed above, via Ferenczi and more explicitly Reich, who formulated the energetic dynamic component of therapeutic transformation (catharsis affect associated with trauma).

But Body Psychotherapy did not only manage to preserve an etiological focus on emotional and traumatic developmental injury as underpinning *all* adult psychological suffering, whether this manifests as common neurosis or—in more explicitly pathologizing terms—as personality disorders. More importantly, the tradition developed, in a myriad of ways, through independent efforts across the variety of schools, an embodied practice that is now capable of inspiring and reinvigorating the rest of the psychotherapeutic field at the beginning of the twenty-first century.

Such embodied practice can be recognized as providing a space for—and attuned attention to—not only the psychic and mental manifestations of suppressed, lost, split-off, or unintegrated emotions and feelings, but also—in terms of the phenomenology of the therapeutic encounter—the equally present and experientially impactful manifestations on embodied, nonverbal, subliminal, relational levels (what modern relational practice likes to call "implicit relational knowing"; Lyons-Ruth et al., 1998). Through being attuned to and resonating with both the denied intensities of emotion as well as the habitual psychological and somatic mechanisms that defend against these unbearable experiences, a therapist practicing in this orientation is always already identifying the felt reality of emotional injury and cannot help but perceive and acknowledge the significance of past relational trauma and the interpersonal origins of intrapsychic suffering, across the whole spectrum of emotionally overwhelming experience, from misattunement to outright violence.

This manifests in all aspects of the Body Psychotherapy tradition, including its various trainings, which emphasize experiential work, both in terms of students' own emotional process as well as their perceptive skills, oriented to therapeutic work that explores, discovers, and uncovers emotional nuance and depth rather than "cognitive" insight or understanding. This does not mean, as some critics still believe, that thinking and self-reflection become irrelevant nor is there a conceptual vacuum. There is, however, a prioritizing of embodied and relationally embedded thinking (or, as some schools call it, "organic thinking" that is rooted in a "felt" sense of self) over abstract and academic knowledge, i.e., process thinking rather than static conceptual thought.

It is, therefore, not surprising that the emergence of modern approaches to post-traumatic symptoms and disorders, which have seen such widespread acceptance and success in recent years, originated in the field of Body Psychotherapy.

Apart from the more clinically framed approach of EMDR (Eye Movement Desensitization and Reprocessing) developed by Shapiro (2001), which rather accidentally acquired body-oriented features, all other serious contenders of modern trauma therapy came straight out of the stable of Body Psychotherapy and were directly linked to Reich. His understanding that trauma symptoms affect all aspects and levels of somatic functioning, reach right down into the vegetative-physiological level, and are anchored in the autonomic nervous system provides the foundation for therapeutic approaches developed by Lisbeth Marcher (Marcher and Fich, 2010), Peter Levine (1997), Babette Rothschild (2000), and later Pat Ogden (Ogden, Minton, and Pain, 2006). Reich's theories and the implicit intuitions on the basis of which Body Psychotherapists have been working for decades are now being comprehensively confirmed and substantiated by the findings of modern trauma research (van der Kolk et al., 1996).

## Object Relationships and the Significance of Real Experiences

Acknowledging, validating, and prioritizing the reality of traumatic emotional experience is not the only foundational principle that Body Psychotherapy has kept alive over the last century. Associated with this is another, equally important principle, regarding the interpersonal reality of relational experiences in childhood development, especially in the formation of psychological "dis-ease," disturbance, and disorders.

Reich's *Character Analysis* is all about "real" developmental injury between "real" people: traumatic interactions between caregivers and children that have *systematic* emotionally wounding consequences. Character structure theory, as developed by Lowen and culminating through Stephen Johnson's work[19] in a method that reintegrates a wide spectrum of developmental theories (including psychoanalytic ones), explicates the psychological and body-mind adaptations to relational trauma (what Boadella calls "transmarginal stress"). The Reichian tradition is, therefore, firmly committed to the interpersonal and social reality of childhood trauma, manifesting in internalizations of external conflictual relationships in the child's "primary scenario" (Rosenberg et al., 1989); and modern trauma theory and therapy as well as interdisciplinary research into early attachment is increasingly acknowledging the social epidemic of developmental trauma, not only through explicit abuse, but through parental failures in attunement, mirroring, and intersubjective engagement.

Its relative obscurity and independence from the rest of the psychodynamic field has allowed Body Psychotherapy to bring about in this respect a probably even more fundamental revision of the classical analytic perspective: rather than seeing mental processes as underpinned by unconscious fantasies derived from conflicts about instinctual drives, intrapsychic conflict is seen as an internalized reflection of actual interpersonal experiences—an internalization of emotionally wounding relationships that were not—using Winnicott's phrase—"good enough" responses to the child's object-seeking needs.

This shift of emphasis in psychodynamic thinking—which is frequently underestimated in its paradigmatic significance—culminated in the 1980s in Greenberg and Mitchell's *Object Relations in Psychoanalytic Theory*, which precipitated a sea change in psychoanalysis. But this historical watershed can be considered as only the end point of struggles that can be traced back to Ferenczi and Otto Rank. They formed a thread of thought focused on the here and now psychotherapy, an undercurrent within psychoanalysis that eventually led to the development of Carl Rogers's "person-centered" therapy and Reichs Characteranalysis (Kramer, 1995). However, two students of Ferenczi, Balint and Winnicott, were instrumental in forming the British "Object Relations" school, and developing an "independent" position between the bitterly polarized schools of Anna Freud and Melanie Klein that dominated psychoanalysis in the United Kingdom in the 1940s and 1950s. This has become a recognized and influential tradition worldwide (Cashdan, 1988), building on the early work of Fairbairn and his student Guntrip, and significantly influencing psychoanalysis in South America and the United States (Kernberg, 1976). It informs most modern developments in psychoanalysis—including Self Psychology (Kohut, 1971), intersubjectivity (Brandchaft, 1986), relational psychoanalysis (Mitchell, 1988), as well as infant development theory (Stewart, 2003; Stern, 1985) and the theory of motivational systems by Lichtenberg (Geissler, 2002).

Although less drastic in the tradition of Body Psychotherapy, as it was never as committed to drive theory in the first place, the paradigm shift toward Object Relations becomes clearest in the theory of subjective anatomy (Fuchs et al., 1994). And although it has been rightfully criticized for its mechanistic and objectifying implications in both theory but more importantly in practice (Soth, 2006; and the characterology of Alexander Lowen 1958)—which has such fundamental importance across all post-Reichian schools—it is much more aligned with an interpersonal and Object Relations perspective than with Freud's drive theory.

Although Lowen saw himself as firmly on psychoanalytic ground, especially as his character structure theory was a clear elaboration of psycho-sexual stages of development (at the time considered to be well-established clinical categories within psychoanalytic discourse), the trajectory of Lowen's work was much more consistent with a humanistic and Object Relations perspective.

This is very apparent in Lowen's foundational assumption that the child has fundamental requirements and basic

---

19  S. Johnson (2010). *Stars into stone: A clinician's guide to masochism.* Available online: stephenjohnsonphd.com/?id=papers#stars.

"rights," including the right to exist (safety), the right to need (support and nurture), the right to be independent (freedom), the right to be loved and respected as a sexual and gendered being, and, of course throughout it all, the inherent right not to be violated or abused.

The whole edifice of character structure theory is built upon an assumption of these basic human "rights." Lowen explained the formation of psychic disturbances and disorders as a function of how these needs and rights had been responded to in the child's development. His theory was a consequent elaboration of Reich's Character Analysis; Reich had clearly located the origins of defensive character formations in real interpersonal conflict between the child's needs and the family and social environment (Reich, 1933/1980, pp. 373ff.). Rather than following Freud in conceiving intrapsychic conflict as an inherent given of the human situation, Reich and then Lowen and later Pierrakos understood character as an existential compromise, due to the child's needs and rights being neglected, inadequately met, burdened with conflict, or otherwise invaded or violated. In distinguishing the specific inner conflicts of each respective character structure corresponding to different developmental windows, Lowen is implying an actual pathogenic relationship with significant others that has become internalized, structured into the child's body-mind organization, and thus maintained in an embodied way at the price of restricted self-actualization. There is no trace here of Freudian or Kleinian versions of drive theory nor inherent death wishes or ego-psychological formulations. Although Lowen did not conceptualize subjective experience in terms of internal object relations, as Kernberg (1976) does, and Lowen's theory of mind is rather undifferentiated, it is nevertheless firmly oriented toward real experiences of deficient and wounding early object relations, and needs to be seen as belonging to that tradition.

Lowen's theory constitutes a historical leap in the development of Body Psychotherapy, reconnecting theory and practice with the psychodynamic origins that marked Reich's Character Analysis at a time—1950s and 1960s—when these were in danger of becoming entirely lost, not only because of Reich's death in 1957, but also because the emphasis of Reich's work had already shifted away from psychoanalysis years before

Reich's theories have had a profound, though largely unacknowledged, influence on psychoanalysis, by shifting the focus from the rather arbitrary presentation of haphazard symptoms to a systematic engagement with the client's whole life history as manifested in their character, understood as a protective layering of impulses, anxieties, and defenses (Malan, 1995). The frequently used metaphor of these defensive layers unfolding in the therapeutic process like onion skins, being peeled away successively in reverse chronological order to how they were laid down, is beautifully illustrated in some of Reich's own exquisite case studies.

Otto Kernberg is the renowned psychoanalyst best known for having explicitly built his theories on the basis of Reich's Character Analysis theory, applying it especially to narcissistic and borderline pathologies, and going much further than Lowen and others in elaborating the internalization process: he speaks of pathogenic relational units consisting of the parent as well as the child position, which both become internally frozen as fixed and static objects, locked into an internal replication of the original outer relationship with each other. However, having absorbed Reich's theory, Kernberg stops short of integrating Reich's "functionalism" and his way of working with the body; in terms of technique and therapeutic frame, Kernberg remains entirely within a classical psychoanalytic paradigm.

As a result, there are major differences between established psychoanalytic ways of addressing character and the Body Psychotherapy perspective, which understands all aspects of character formation as embodied, affecting *all* levels of body-mind. Although on the whole, Body Psychotherapy used to somewhat conflate cognitive processes with the defensive operations of the mind, thus neglecting to develop a differentiated appreciation of the mental unconscious, some schools have arrived at a much more balanced position through the integration of psychoanalytic principles. This allows an understanding of internal objects as embodied flesh-and-blood realities, in contrast to the Object Relations tradition, which still conceives of internal objects as mental representations.

We do not necessarily need to subscribe to the more literal, objectifying, and causalistic aspects of Lowen's approach and formulations, but can instead view his basic attitudinal and character types as dynamic patterns, encompassing both psychological and somatic dimensions, and fulfilling both protective and adaptive functions. It is one of the essential strengths of the Body Psychotherapy tradition, following Reich, to approach character as embodied, not only theoretically, but in every aspect of practice: every step of character formation (Johnson, 1983)—from the original impulse to the organismic response and the turning against the self (internalization) as well as the adaptive formation of the compromise—is best understood as a neuro-bio-psychosomatic process, encompassing all levels of body-mind, from the physiological to the muscular, from the breath to *all* mental processes, including fantasies and conscious thought.

Whatever the original wounding at the root of character formation, the main purpose of the various chronic types of character defenses is to prevent the repetition of that same wounding—i.e., character is designed to protect against the reexperiencing and the reoccurrence of emotional injury and relational trauma, based on real interpersonal events that did occur. Unlike Anna Freud's psychoanalytic conception of defense mechanisms against fantasy derivatives of instinctual drives, the defenses of character are designed to protect the integrity of both the child's organism and the child's subjective sense of self.

All character types—e.g., the "frozenness" of the schizoid withdrawal and dissociative "flight from the body"; the resignation of the oral-depressive position devoid of impetus and aggression; or the various other forms of bodily, emotional, and psychological rigidity—are essentially fixed survival patterns, rooted in vegetative processes well below the threshold of consciousness, as well as in neurological fixations in the emotional and motoric regions of the brain. Their primary purpose is to protect the integrity of the organism as well as the sense of personhood.

It follows from this understanding that whatever our therapeutic approach toward accessing and bringing these protective mechanisms into awareness, a special sensitivity and respect are required as to the inherent traumatic and survival quality that they literally "contain." This is especially the case when considering the kind of spectacular and cathartic physical interventions for which the tradition of Body Psychotherapy is famous. But it applies to *any* intervention intended to confront the client's character traits: transferential entanglements and the reenactment of the original wounding via the therapeutic interaction are likely, and retraumatization is possible.

Day-to-day clinical observations in the Body Psychotherapeutic field have corroborated the basic principles of defensive-protective character patterns over and over again; these basic principles have been substantiated repeatedly. Invariably, confronting such characterological patterns and bringing awareness to their inherent defensive mechanisms will—and, in many cases, needs to—lead to the restimulation of buried fears and anxieties and sometimes regression; frequently, affectively charged memories will surface, at times condensed into "primal scenes" that tend to contain the originally wounding relationship experiences in various degrees of explicitness.

At this point, another decisive difference between the Body Psychotherapy tradition and classical psychoanalysis becomes apparent: the latter sees the mechanism of therapeutic action as inherent in the therapist's interpretations, based on the notion that the client's ego will be strengthened by insight into the roots of the transference. According to the theory, this is supposed to result in a lessening of internal conflict and the need to maintain symptom-forming defenses, thus leading to an overall reduction of anxiety (Stark, 1999, p. 9).

Body Psychotherapy, in contrast, approaches embodied psychic defenses in order to loosen—both literally and psychologically—biographical fixations that, in terms of self-psychology, are best described as "developmental arrest," leading to the embodied and subjectively felt reassimilation of split-off experiences, feelings, and parts of the personality that had to remain suppressed due to characterological compromises. It was in this context that

Hilarion Petzold—in an early publication on the therapeutic relationship—reinterpreted the transference through the language of Gestalt as an unfinished situation waiting to be completed (Petzold, 1980).

We can say in conclusion that all the aspects discussed above incline the field of Body Psychotherapy toward a paradigm shift that asserts and emphasizes the meaning and importance of "real" relational experiences, both at the etiological root of psychological wounding and as a central feature of how therapy needs to address those wounds. This paradigm shift toward the embodied realities of intersubjective relating—in terms of both the past and the present—is illustrated by the way in which a group of analytical Body Psychotherapists, especially within the German-language regions (Moser, 1986; Geissler, 2003b), has gone far beyond the frame of the traditional analytical setting. In their work, originally inspired by Al Pesso, psychoanalytic interpretations of early biography become reanimated through the use of strongly body-oriented "enactments" in which wounding formative relational experiences are "worked through" and completed through corrective experiences (Pesso, 1986). These enactments focus on the communicative aspects of bodily expression and experience rather than on the bodily defenses of character; they constitute a proactive reparative technique at odds with and transcending traditional psychoanalytic practice, while at the same time being entirely consistent with a psychodynamic understanding of early wounding and its consequences.

## Convergences between Body Psychotherapy and the Wider Field of Psychodynamic Psychology

Such convergences between Body Psychotherapy and the wider field of Psychodynamic Psychology can be seen to have occurred increasingly during recent decades. In order to complete this brief historical overview, some of these developments need to be mentioned.

One of these convergences is between Body Psychotherapy and Prenatal and Perinatal Psychology, a branch of developmental psychology originated by the psychoanalyst Otto Rank and others. The connection and overlap between these traditions is obvious, considering their shared emphasis on pre-verbal levels of experience and the possibilities of bodily regression and reenactments (Boadella, 1987; Janus, 2000; Verny, 1987).

Pre-verbal experience also plays a decisive role in modern infant research. For a number of reasons, it has been enthusiastically received and assimilated by the Body Psychotherapy community (compare with Trautmann-Voigt and Voigt, 1997; Geissler, 2003b; May, 2004; Thielen, 2003). Daniel Stern's (2004) theory of RIGs (Representations of Interactions that have been Generalized) emerged from the observation of real interactions—rather than hypotheses of "clinically reconstructed infants"—and emphasized the quality of the actual parent-child relationship. He thus extended and substantiated a theoretical position—as Winnicott had done previously—that does not locate the etiology of psychic disorders in the inherently conflictual psyche of the child, supposedly possessed by asocial drives. Stern's theory corresponds well with the established notions and models of the Body Psychotherapy tradition, as the shared focus on pre-verbal experience reveals the importance of the body in establishing the quality of the parent-child relationship, which can then be also thought of as somatic emotional co-regulation.

The bodily dimension has been developed even more strongly by George Downing, whose theory of affect-motor schemata was also formulated on the basis of mother-infant research (Downing, 1996) and is equivalent to Stern's RIGs. Unlike traditional character-analytical theories, Downing's dynamic model escapes the dangers of rigid concretization, and thus generates an understanding that therapeutic access to those areas of experience that are called implicit or procedural memory is most appropriately possible through a combination of bodily awareness and attunement to the atmospheric feeling quality of the body.

Lichtenberg's theory of motivational systems must also be mentioned in this context (Lichtenberg et al., 1992), as it has been taken up strongly by the Body Psychotherapeutic community in recent years. The developmental-psychological components that he designated correspond readily with the basic motifs of developmental psychology, as established by Lowen, Pierrakos, Boadella, and others.

One last point of convergence should at least be touched upon: what we are currently observing in the field of Psychodynamic Psychology is increasing attention to the so-called "structural disorders." The structural deficits indicated by the term refer to the impaired regulatory ability essentially of prereflexive emotional experience. It is therefore not surprising that nonverbal and Body Psychotherapeutic methods are widespread in clinical contexts dedicated to structural disorders, e.g., psychosomatic clinics, and often become an integrated component of such treatment. Like no other tradition, Body Psychotherapy has accumulated immense knowledge about accessing and engaging the deepest layers of human experience, including a clear perspective on the psychosomatic nature of affects. The connection between psyche and soma is as essential in healthy self-regulation as it is decisive in the treatment of psychosomatic diseases. The dissociative tendency of psychosomatic patients to defensively construe their complaints as exclusively bodily dysfunctions can be more suitably and successfully addressed with a Body Psychotherapeutic approach, rather than other verbal or interpretive methods.

In this context, Helmuth Stolze has described the feedback loops of perception, which are rooted in body sensation, movement, and feeling, upon which thinking and language are built; this is a much more elegant formulation than the otherwise amorphously defined "bottom-up processes," as they are called by the modern schools of neuropsychology.

Clinical experience impressively substantiates the important contribution that the Body Psychotherapeutic tradition can make in responding to the challenge that structural and psychosomatic disorders are posing to psychotherapy.

## Body, Eros, and Narcissism

To conclude this historical overview of the depth-psychological field and the place of Body Psychotherapy within it, we need to put these developments into their wider sociological and political context.

Freud's retreat from the body, and the increasing disembodiment of psychoanalysis, are certainly also related to his orientation toward the middle-class enlightenment ideals and ideology at the beginning of the twentieth century, as well as the social constraints of middle-class (Victorian) Vienna. Although Freud's theories still conceive the human subject as anchored in nature (or—we might say—effectively reanchor it there), human identity, morality, and freedom were firmly located in reason and rational understanding, as envisaged by the enlightenment and exemplified by the writings of Immanuel Kant (1781) and his notion of the "transcendental subject." As a result, the human body disappeared almost completely from philosophy and cognitive theory.

It is in this crucial respect that Freud's orientation differs, despite many areas of overlap and common interest, from the main currents that constituted the *zeitgeist* of the avant-garde at the beginning of the twentieth century. Historical research has found a common denominator for these currents as the Life Reform Movement—the source of a paradigm shift that continues to send its ripples in many different directions, even into the twenty-first century.

The German philosopher Gernoth Böhme has pointed out that a preoccupation with the human body was at the center of the Life Reform Movement (Böhme, 2001), propagating a new relationship to ourselves as human beings through a variety of forms—such as the gymnastics movement, nudist culture, forms of creative self-expression in dance, clothing, and sexual reform, as well as diet and nutritional programs—primarily engendered via a new way of relating to our own bodies. Historically, the Life Reform Movement can be seen as a reaction to the shadow aspects of modernity and modernization, raising critical objections to the consequences of both industrialization and urbanization, as well as—and this applies primarily both to the middle classes and to the intelligentsia—to puritanical Victorian morals. The progressive spirit of this epoch focused its protest on *Civilization and Its Discontents* (Freud, 1930).

In contrast to Freud, who was inclined to respond to this discontent in a rather conservative and pessimistic way, the Life Reform Movement—in terms of both the practical aspects of life as well as in its artistic expressions—created utopian visions in which the body was of central relevance, in two respects: (1) Although not always articulated explicitly, the Life Reform Movement propagated the value of the natural world and a reconnection and reconciliation with nature, based on a critique of the increasing mechanization and instrumentalization of the body in the context of industrialization, and a recognition of alienation as a fundamental concomitant of modernity. It thus presaged a threat to resources and principles that—as the following century would show—would increasingly disappear; and (2) At the same time, the traditional Christian view of the body as inherently sinful became the focus of sociocritical discourse.

It was in this historical and sociopolitical context that utopian visions of a "liberated body" arose, through activities as diverse as expressionist dance, nudity, or the far-reaching potential of human sexuality. All strands of the Body Psychotherapy tradition owe their original inspiration to this spirit. Reich was an outstanding child of this time, which may explain the central, sometimes "fetishized," position that sexuality acquired in his work.

Freud's theoretical development, on the other hand, and the disappearance of the body from psychoanalysis, was based on his fear that the young "science" of psychoanalysis might be inundated by the forces of Eros that it had summoned up. The "taboo" against physical closeness, established via the stepping-stones of transference and the principles of neutrality and abstinence, is directly related to Freud's early clinical experiences, which we might call—with a slight touch of irony—the "primal scenes" of a young psychoanalysis (Marlock, 2001). Among the best known of these are: Breuer's entanglement with his patient Anna O.; Freud's own distress vis-à-vis several of his female patients physically displaying their love for him; and the affair between Sabina Spielrein and the then "crown prince" of psychoanalysis, Carl Gustav Jung. After her separation from Jung in 1912, she went into analysis with Freud in Vienna, and Freud split with Jung in 1913. She was probably the first analyst to formulate the hypothesis of the death instinct, as her conception of the sexual drive contained both an instinct of destruction and an instinct of transformation, which she presented to the Vienna Psychoanalytic Society in 1912; her hypothesis anticipated both Freud's "death wish" and Jung's views on "transformation." She may have thus been very inspirational for both men.

The Austrian author Norbert Nagler, one of the most knowledgeable experts regarding the social and political situation in which the development of Psychodynamic Psychology took its course at the beginning of the twentieth century, has associated the disappearance of the body from psychoanalysis with a basic conservative disposition on Freud's part (Nagler, 1987). Nagler sees the specific disembodied form that psychoanalytic "togetherness" was allowed to take as rooted in Freud's obeisance to middle-class mores and values: their socially sanctioned code of conduct prized abstinence and renunciation. The class snobbery of distinguished ladies, their lifestyle and orientation toward linguistic forms of symbolization, have contributed decisively to shaping the "talking cure," emphasizing a mode of speaking that places great emphasis upon the well-mannered representation of the instinctual drives, via the spoken word.

A more phenomenological approach to the prevalent hysterical symptoms presented by these ladies—full of uncontrolled bodily expressiveness, precisely and bizarrely cutting across civilized and cultivated conduct—would have suggested a much more dialectical approach to the body-mind or body-psyche relationship (Ibid.; Marlock, 2001).

Reich took a very different path, engaging with working-class people and championing sexuality (and what Georges Bataille [1976/1991] has called its "transgressive" dimensions), which Reich initially thought of as sociological, political, and revolutionary, and later as "oceanic" and "transcendental."

In the changed (and charged) historical context of the 1960s, when for the period of about a decade sexuality once again became the great metaphor of happiness and liberation, history rehabilitated the almost-forgotten Body Psychotherapeutic tradition of modern Psychodynamic Psychology. In an environment of youthful rebellion that revived almost all of the motifs and practices of the then-forgotten Life Reform Movement, Gestalt and Body Psychotherapy were accepted with an enthusiasm similar to the response to psychoanalysis at the beginning of the twentieth century, especially in avant-garde circles. The mixture of Body Psychotherapy, Gestalt, and Humanistic Psychology affected the exploding Human Potential Movement like an alchemical substance, resulting in lasting changes throughout the entire field of psychotherapy, even informing later developments in psychoanalysis: Rogerian empathy can be detected in the formulations of self-psychology; the Gestalt principle of "here and now" can be traced in Stern's concept of the "present moment" (Stern, 2004).

Sexuality was not the only area that the *zeitgeist* of the 1960s resonated with in Body Psychotherapeutic theory and practice: emancipation of the senses and greater self-expression played a central role, as well as the "modern" wish for self-determination and greater freedom from authoritarian constraints.

Since then, with the advent of postmodernism, the social parameters have changed again, to some extent reversing these earlier developments. Deep structural changes can be seen manifesting in shifting dynamics between the "pleasure" and "reality" principles, in the far-ranging sexualization of everyday life, in narcissistic preoccupation with images and the fetishization of "surfaces," and the corresponding disappearance of the depth dimension that used to be considered equivalent with the *psyche* in earlier times. The problems and disorders of postmodern identity also manifest in relationship to the bodily dimensions of self, reflected in clinical conceptualizations that describe the increasing prevalence of narcissistic disorders, eating disorders, body dysmorphic disorders (dysmorphobia), and other disturbances of body image, body schemas, and embodiment in general. Interestingly, Freud's patient the Wolf Man would probably be diagnosed nowadays with body dysmorphic disorder (Freud, 1918).

Thus, postmodern civilization creates serious challenges for current Body Psychotherapy, not only on clinical but also on metatheoretical levels.

## In Retrospect

Wilhelm Reich's exclusion from psychoanalysis in 1934 had left the field of Psychodynamic Psychology with a detrimental legacy of splits: separate therapeutic traditions evolved in isolation from each other, building theories and professional identities based upon divisions, ignorance, and historic falsehoods that have lasted for decades.

As a result, the wider field still does not fully appreciate that the psychoanalytic theory of character is essentially based on Reich's work, and that—as the head of the Technical Seminar in Vienna—he made major contributions to a modern understanding of defense mechanisms and their manifestations as resistances in the therapeutic context. This is why very few psychoanalysts appreciate the extent to which Anna Freud's systematic description of defense mechanisms is largely "borrowed" from Reich. Only fairly recently has the significance of Reich's approach been acknowledged by the psychoanalyst Otto Kernberg (1976), as the notion of "character" plays a central role in Kernberg's theory and practice.

In this historical perspective, Reich is definitely due some sort of "apology," mainly because he was the first to draw attention to the "formal" aspects of personality. His character-analytical practice emphasized that the way in which a patient communicates—the "how" of the process—is just as significant as the content of the communication—the "what"—and the meaning—the "why." How to use this insight therapeutically constitutes one of the areas in which Depth Psychology can learn much from the Body Psychotherapeutic tradition. Attention to such formal aspects of character and expression has been cultivated in many branches of Body Psychotherapy—in this context, Stanley Keleman's (1985) approach deserves to be mentioned in particular.

Because of the paucity of historical awareness throughout the field, it is important to underscore that Wilhelm

Reich's exclusion from psychoanalysis did not occur on the basis of theoretical conflicts or divergences—for example, with regard to the role and significance of the body in Reich's work. The essential reason for the break was almost certainly entirely political in nature. Reich was already a controversial figure in many respects, and that applied to his work with the bodily aspects of sexuality and character. However, at the time of his 1934 exclusion from the Psychoanalytical Association, these developments of his work were in their very early stages, and insufficient to cause the rupture, which therefore needs to be seen politically, in terms of both the politics of the profession, as well as the politics of the times.

It took about half a century until two young analysts investigated Reich's "case" in the context of the history of psychoanalysis and the rise of fascism (Fallend and Nitzschke, 1997; see also Lothane, 2001; Frosh, 2003). Their well-founded research shows that Reich's exclusion (in 1934) was driven by less than praiseworthy motives, as it constituted a core element in a complex strategic attempt to adapt psychoanalysis to the prevailing desire to "cooperate" with German fascism in that era. Reich's previous flirtation with communism was also probably significant. Whereas one part of the psychoanalytic movement accommodated itself to fascism, and even cooperated with it (this part was quietly allowed to rejoin the psychotherapeutic establishment with relative ease after the war), the Austrian and German analysts directly relevant to the Body Psychotherapeutic tradition (Reich, Annie Reich, Otto Fenichel, and Fritz Perls) all went into exile, as did Max Eitingon, president of the German Psychoanalytic Society (DPG), Erich Fromm, Ernst Simmel, Siegfried Bernfeld, and Edith Jacobson (who escaped after arrest in 1938). Viktor Frankl ended up in a concentration camp along with at least fifteen other German-Jewish psychoanalysts: fortunately he survived, though the others did not. For these and various other reasons, neither Annie nor Wilhelm Reich, nor Perls, nor Fenichel, sought any connection with the European psychoanalytic mainstream after their exile.

Reich, in particular, developed in very different directions, as we have seen, e.g., his orgone research, and formulated theories that from his point of view far transcended the realm of psychology, and were way beyond being recognized by the rest of the field. Yet, in spite of this, both Body Psychotherapy and its younger cousin, Gestalt Therapy, can clearly be seen as neoanalytic approaches. Their lack of recognition as great traditions in the developmental line of Psychodynamic Depth Psychology has nothing to do with their lack of validity or substance, and everything to do with the political trauma of German history, and the ongoing power struggles throughout the therapeutic professions. An acknowledgment and appreciation in recognition of these facts is probably long overdue.

## References

Bataille, G. (1976/1991). *The accursed share (Vols. II & III).* New York: Zone Books.

Boadella, D. (1987). *Lifestreams.* London: Routledge & Kegan Paul.

Boadella, D. (1997). Awakening sensibility, recovering motility: Psycho-physical synthesis at the foundations of Body Psychotherapy: The 100-year legacy of Pierre Janet (1859–1947). *International Journal of Psychotherapy, 2(1), 45–56.*

Böhme, G. (2001). Anfänge der Leibphilosophie im 19. Jahrhundert [The beginnings of the somatic philosophy]. In L. Bucholz, R. Lotacha, H. Peckmann, & K. Wolbert (Eds.), *Die Lebensreform [Life Reform].* Darmstadt, Germany: Häuser.

Brandchaft, B. (1986). British object relations theory and Self Psychology. *Progress in Self Psychology, 2, 245–272.*

Breuer, J., & Freud, S. (1895/2000). *Studies on hysteria.* New York: Basic Books.

Cashdan, S. (1988). *Object Relations Therapy: Using the relationship.* New York: W. W. Norton.

Cremerius, J. (1997). Der Fall Reich: Ein Beispiel für Freuds Umgang mit abweichenden Standpunkten eines besonderen Schülertypus [The case of Reich: An example of Freud's approach to the deviating standpoints of a special type of student]. In K. Fallend & B. Nitzschke (Eds.), *Der "Fall" Wilhelm Reich: Beiträge zum Verhältnis von Psychoanalyse und Politik [The case of Wilhelm*

Reich: Contributions to the relationship of politics and psychoanalysis]. Frankfurt, Germany: Suhrkamp.

Damasio, A. (1995). *Descartes' error.* New York: Penguin.

Darnton, R. (1983). *Mesmerism.* Cambridge, MA: Harvard University Press.

Downing, G. (1996). *Körper und Wort in der Psychotherapie [Body and word in psychotherapy].* Munich, Germany: Kösel.

Ellenberger, H. (1973). *The discovery of the unconscious.* New York: Basic Books.

Fallend, K., & Nitzschke, B. (1997). *Der "Fall" Wilhelm Reich* [The case of Wilhelm Reich]. Frankfurt, Germany: Suhrkamp.

Foucault, M. (1998) *The History of Sexuality: The Will to Knowledge,* London: Penguin.

Freud, S. (1918/1995). From the history of an infantile neurosis. Republished in P. Gay, *The Freud reader.* London: Vintage.

Freud, S. (1930/2010). *Civilization and its discontents.* New York: W. W. Norton.

Frosh, S. (2003). Psychoanalysis, Nazism and "Jewish science": A ferocious silence. *International Journal of Psychoanalysis, 84, 1315–1332.*

Fuchs, M., Uexküll, T. v., Müller-Braunschweig, H., & Johnen, R. (1994). *Subjektive Anatomie [Subjective anatomy].* Stuttgart, Germany: Schattauer.

Gallagher, S. (2005). *How the Body Shapes the Mind.* New York: Oxford University Press

Geissler, P. (2002). Following in the footsteps of Ferenczi, Balint and Winnicott: Love and hate in a setting open to body- and action-related interventions. In D. Mann (Ed.), *Love and hate: Psychoanalytical perspectives* (pp. 267–283). Hove, UK: Brunner-Routledge.

Geissler, P. (2003a). *Körperbilder* [Body images]. Giessen, Germany: Psychosozial.

Geissler, P. (2003b). Psychoanalyse und Körper: Überlegungen zum gegenwärtigen Stand analytischer Körperpsychotherapie [Psychoanalysis and the body: Considerations on the current status of Analytical Body Psychotherapy]. In P. Geissler (Ed.), *Psychoanalyse und Körper [Psychoanalysis and the body], Vol. 1.* Giessen, Germany: Psychosozial.

Janet, P. (1907). *The major symptoms of hysteria.* New York: Macmillan.

Janet, P. (1919/1925/1976). *Psychological healing: A historical and clinical study (2 vols.)* (E. Paul & C. Paul, Trans.). London: Allen & Unwin.

Janet, P. (1997). Quoted in Boadella, Awakening sensibility, recovering motility. *International Journal of Psychotherapy, 2*(1), 45–56.

Janus, L. (2000). *Die Psychoanalyse der vorgeburtlichen Lebenszeit und der Geburt [The psychoanalysis of embryonic life and the newborn].* Giessen, Germany: Psychosozial.

Johnson, D. H. (1983). *Body: Recovering our sensual wisdom.* Boston: Beacon Press.

Kant, I. (1781/2008). *Critique of pure reason.* London: Penguin Classics.

Keleman, S. (1985). *Emotional Anatomy.* Berkeley, CA: Center Press.

Kernberg, O. F. (1976). *Object relations theory and clinical psychoanalysis.* New York: Jason Aronson.

Kohut, H. (1971). *The analysis of the self: A systematic approach to the psychoanalytic treatment of narcissistic personality disorders.* Chicago: University of Chicago Press.

Kramer, R. (1995). The birth of client-centered therapy: Carl Rogers, Otto Rank, and "the beyond." *Journal of Humanistic Psychology, 35*(4), 54–110.

Levine, P. (1997). *Waking the tiger: Healing trauma: The innate capacity to transform overwhelming experiences.* Berkeley, CA: North Atlantic Books.

Lichtenberg, J. D., Lachmann, F., & Fosshage, J. (1992). *Self and motivational systems.* New York: Analytic Press.

Lothane, Z. (2001). The deal with the devil to "save" psychoanalysis in Nazi Germany. *Psychoanalytic Review, 88*(2), 195–224.

Lowen, A. (1958). *The language of the body (originally published as Physical dynamics of character structure).* New York: Grune & Stratton.

Lyons-Ruth, K., et al. (1998). Implicit relational knowing: Its role in development and psychoanalytic treatment. *Infant Mental Health Journal, 19*(3), 282–289.

Malan, D. (1995). *Individual psychotherapy and the science of psychodynamics (2nd ed.).* London: Butterworth Heinemann.

Marcel, G. (1963). *The existential background of human dignity.* Cambridge, MA: Harvard University Press.

Marcher, L., & Fich, S. (2010). *Body encyclopedia: A guide to the psychological functions of the muscular system.* Berkeley, CA: North Atlantic Books.

Marlock, G. (2001). Zwischen Verheissung und Verflüchtigung [Between promise and disappearance]. In P. Geissler (ed.), *Über den Körper zur Sexualität finden [Finding the way to sexuality through the body].* Giessen, Germany: Psychosozial.

Masson, J. (1984). *The assault on truth: Freud's suppression of the seduction theory.* New York: Farrar, Straus & Giroux.

May, M. (2004). *Selbstregulierung [Self-regulation].* Giessen, Germany: Psychosozial.

Merleau-Ponty, M. (1945). *Phénoménologie de la perception [The phenomenology of perception].* Paris: Gallimard.

Miller, A. (1981a/1991). *Thou shalt not be aware: Society's betrayal of the child.* New York: Farrar, Straus & Giroux.

Miller, A. (1981b/2002). *The truth will set you free.* New York: Basic Books.

Miller, A., & Jenkins, A. (2004/2005). *The body never lies: The lingering effects of cruel parenting.* New York: Norton.

Mitchell, J. (1983). Narcissus and Oedipus: The children of psychoanalysis. *New Left Review,* no. 140, 92–96.

Mitchell, S. A. (1988). *Relational concepts in psychoanalysis: An integration.* Cambridge, MA: Harvard University Press.

Moser, T. (1986). Die Anschaulichkeit des Unbewussten [The graphic nature of the unconscious]. In A. Pesso (Ed.), *Dramaturgie des Unbewussten [Dramaturgy of the unconscious].* Stuttgart, Germany: Klett-Cotta.

Nagler, N. (1987). Einige Vorbemerkungen zum Leib-Seele Problem in der Psychoanalyse Freuds [Some preliminary remarks on the body-soul problem in Freud's psychoanalysis]. In H. Petzold (Ed.), *Integrative Therapie [Integrative therapy].* Paderborn, Germany: Junfermann.

Nagler, N. (2003). *Die paranoide Rufmordcampagne gegen Sándor Ferenczi und seinen Entwurf zu einer ganzheitlichen Psychoanalyse [The paranoid smear campaign against Sándor Ferenczi and his draft of a holistic psychoanalysis].* Unpublished manuscript.

Ogden, P., Minton, K., & Pain, C. (2006). *Trauma and the body: A sensorimotor approach to psychotherapy.* New York: W. W. Norton.

Pesso, A. (1986). *Dramaturgie des Unbewussten [Dramaturgy of the unconscious].* Stuttgart, Germany: Klett-Cotta.

Petzold, H. (1980). *Die Rolle des Therapeuten und die therapeutische Beziehung [The role of the therapist and the therapeutic relationship].* Paderborn, Germany: Junfermann.

Plessner, H. (1975). *Die Stufen des Organischen und der Mensch: Einleitung in die philosophische Anthropologie [The levels of the organic and man: Introduction to philosophical anthropology].* Berlin: Walter de Gruyter.

Reich, W. (1933/1980). *Character Analysis.* New York: Farrar, Straus & Giroux.

Reich, W. (1945). *Character Analysis (3rd Ed.).* New York: Simon & Schuster.

Rosenberg, J. L., Rand, M. L., & Asay, D. (1989). *Body, self, and soul: Sustaining integration.* Atlanta, GA: Humanics.

Rothschild, B. (2000). *The body remembers: The psychophysiology of trauma and trauma treatment.* New York: W. W. Norton.

Rudolf, G. (2004). *Strukturbezogene Psychotherapie [Structure-oriented psychotherapy].* Stuttgart, Germany: Schattauer.

Sarasin, P., & Tanner, J. (1998). *Physiologie und industrielle Gesellschaft [Physiology and industrial society].* Frankfurt, Germany: Suhrkamp.

Shapiro, F. (2001). *Eye movement desensitization and reprocessing: Basic principles, protocols, and procedures.* New York: Guilford Press.

Soth, M. (2006). The potential and pathology of character structure theory. *Presentation at EABP Congress, Askov, Denmark.*

Soth, M. (2010). The Return of the Repressed Body—Not a Smooth Affair. *UKCP Journal 'The Psychotherapist', Autumn 2010*

Stark, M. (1999). *Modes of therapeutic action.* Northvale, NJ: Jason Aronson.

Stern, D. (1985). *The interpersonal world of the infant: A view from psychoanalysis and Developmental Psychology.* New York: Basic Books.

Stern, D. (2004). *The present moment*. New York: W. W. Norton.

Stewart, H. (2003). Winnicott, Balint and the independent tradition. *American Journal of Psychoanalysis, 63(3)*, 207–217.

Sulz, S. (2000). *Von der Kognition zur Emotion [From cognition to emotion]*. Munich, Germany: CIP-Medien.

Thielen, M. (2003). *Körperpsychotherapie und Säuglingsforschung [Body Psychotherapy and infant research]*. Lecture at the 2nd Congress of the German Association for Body Psychotherapy in Berlin. Unpublished manuscript.

Trautmann-Voigt, S., & Voigt, B. (1997). *Freud lernt laufen [Freud learns to walk]*. Frankfurt, Germany: Brandes & Apsel.

van der Kolk, B., McFarlane, A., & Weisaeth, L. (1996). *Traumatic stress*. New York: Guilford Press.

Verny, T. R. (Ed.). (1987). *Pre- and Perinatal Psychology: An introduction*. New York: Human Sciences Press.

# 9

## Genealogy of Body Psychotherapy

*A Graphic Depiction*

Heike Langfeld and Dagmar Rellensmann, Germany,

with assistance from Ulfried Geuter, Gustl Marlock, and Halko Weiss

Graphic Design: Hans-Jürgen Buch, Germany

Translation by Christine M. Grimm

**Heike Langfeld** is qualified in Business Administration, is a Body Psychotherapist, and is an organizational and management consultant. She was trained in systemic organizational consulting through CONECTA, Vienna, and elsewhere, and is trained in Unitive/Integrative Body Psychotherapy. Heike Langfeld has been working in the field of management training and organizational consulting for the German postal service for more than a decade and is a consultant for businesses and organizations in the nonprofit sector. She is a member of the German Association for Body Psychotherapy (DGK) and the European Association for Body Psychotherapy (EABP), and is doing research on the history of Body Psychotherapy.

**Dagmar Rellensmann**, MD, is a specialist in psychosomatic medicine and psychotherapy. She is trained in Psychodynamic Therapy, Self Psychology, Biodynamic Psychology, and Unitive/Integrative Body Psychotherapy. In her research, she explores the historical and philosophical foundations of psychotherapy, and those of Body Psychotherapy in particular.

The following pages and diagrams attempt to document—graphically—the variety of the origins of and influences on the various directions and modalities of Body Psychotherapy, as well as something of its historical context and the complexity of its relationships. The surveys, overviews, and charts were compiled from accessible information, which is sometimes quite contradictory, depending on its source. Because of the limited space, a subjective selection was often made as to which people and methods are depicted in the graphs and charts. Among other things, those chosen were the ones who have had, or continue to have, an essential influence in the field of Body Psychotherapy in this historical sense.

The graphical survey about the developmental history of the Body Psychotherapeutic tradition (Figure 9.1) is divided into various fields to ensure a better overview. In the graphics, because of the different perspectives, some of the names appear more than once in the different contexts. Where it has been (graphically) possible, we have tried to summarize as many influences as possible under the important founders of the different individual modalities of Body Psychotherapy. To ensure better clarity, the arrows that mark the connections within the field and from the respective fields are printed thicker than the arrows from the outside to the inside of the field.

However, for the sake of clarity, we have not marked the different types of connections or influences between the persons listed, such as teacher-student relationships, collegial exchanges, influences through significant works, and even those that ended later with an abandonment or a turning away from the original direction. The birth years and probable death years were added to the names when we were able to identify them.

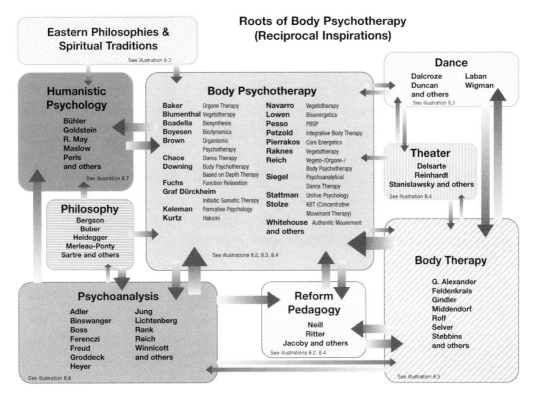

Figure 9.1. Influences on Body Psychotherapy: An Overview

The roots of Body Psychotherapy in philosophy, from which psychology separated in the course of the nineteenth century, were not depicted on a special page but divided among the various fields. Individuals were usually not named, but primarily the basic directions (for example, body philosophy, existentialism) were given (Geuter, 2000).

The Body Psychotherapeutic field was divided—and also just for the sake of clarity—into those who have essentially been influenced by Wilhelm Reich, his theories, and/or his methods or by one of his successors—in Norway on the one hand, and in the United States (after 1939) on the other (Figure 9.2). This is followed later by the portrayal of the dance-therapeutic directions (Figure 9.3) and other developments that were independent of Reich, such as procedures and methods inspired by theater, for example (Figure 9.4).

The time axis begins with the forerunners of Body Psychotherapy: the Body Culture [Körperkultur] Movement that emerged as part of the Life Reform Movement at the turn of the century from the nineteenth to the twentieth century, and oriented itself upon the "liberation of the body" with all its varied practices, in the areas of breath, movement, voice, rhythm, dance, and theater. These had a particular impact, especially in European German-language countries, resulting from German romanticism and the youth movement.

The worldwide spread of these methods was accelerated after a blossoming in the 1920s, ironically as a consequence of fascism—as well as of psychoanalysis. The majority of the Body Culture Movement, and nearly all of the significant analysts, either had to, or wanted to, emigrate. These included Mary Wigman (originally, Marie Wiegmann), Charlotte Selver, Carola Speads (originally, Spitz), Lily Ehrenfried, Clara Fenichel—and the psychoanalysts Freud, Ferenczi, Rank, Adler, Otto Fenichel, and Wilhelm Reich.

104 | A HISTORICAL OVERVIEW OF BODY PSYCHOTHERAPY

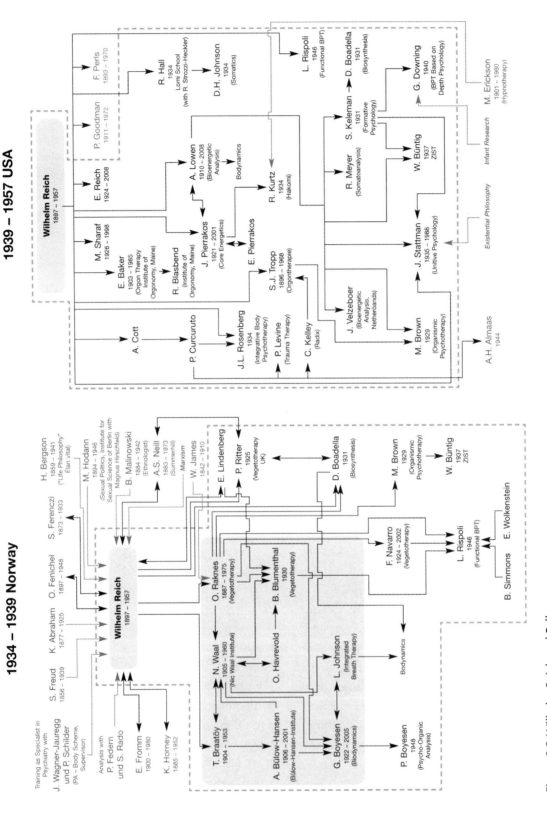

Figure 9.2. Wilhelm Reich and Followers

## The Roots of the Dance-Therapeutic Branch of Body Psychotherapy

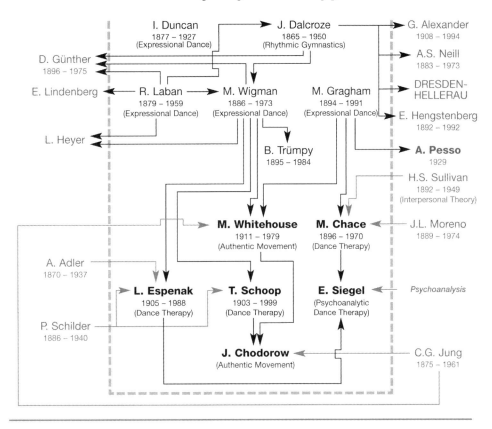

## Eastern Philosophies – Spiritual Traditions

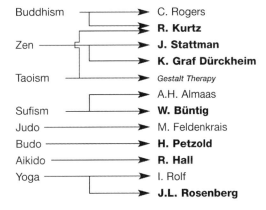

Figure 9.3. Development of Dance Therapy and Spiritual Traditions

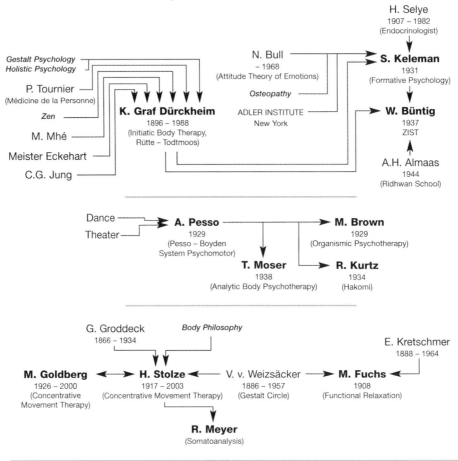

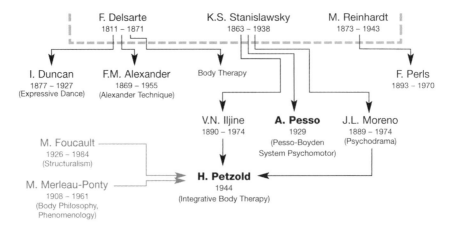

Figure 9.4. Other Influences on Body Psychotherapy

Very few (primarily breath therapists and some psychoanalysts) remained in Germany. They were more or less forcibly united into the German Institute for Psychological Research and Psychotherapy, in which the National Socialists (such as J. H. Schultz, who developed Autogenic Training) worked next to convinced anti-fascists (such as the psychoanalyst John Rittmeister, who was executed in 1943 as a member of the Roten Kapelle [The Red Chapel]) and with those who attempted to preserve their way of working in Germany. G. R. Heyer (see Figure 9.5) joined the institute in 1938 (at the request of his friend C. G. Jung, the intermittent or temporary president of the international association that had been initiated by the National Socialists), and Heyer became a member of the NSDAP[20] in 1940.

We have ended the graphics—in terms of time—with those who were born before the end of the Second World War (with very few exceptions), which means the teachers of the current generation of Body Psychotherapists. Because of this, only the beginnings of important Body Psychotherapeutic movements in recent years that have arisen outside of Europe and the United States are contained in these historical diagrams.

Graphics suggest a beginning and an end, a limited scope, and a clear classification from here to there, from teachers to students, from one field to another. However, this does not correspond with the life course of developmental processes and their complexity. For example, there appears to be a clear separation (in Figure 9.1) between Body Psychotherapists, such as Dürckheim and Petzold (2005), and the multitude of body therapies. But this is not really the case—the borders become blurred in many areas. Whether the work can be called "body therapy" or "Body Psychotherapy" depends on perspective, as well as the setting and the basic profession.

In their origins, most of the mentioned Body Psychotherapies have come either from psychoanalysis or from an integration of body therapies with a psychoanalytic or humanistic therapy. The bodily interventions that have mainly been developed from the work by Janet, Groddeck, Schilder, Ferenczi, and Reich are often combined with other work (see Figure 9.6).

From the beginning, these were mostly forms of treatment developed in the work of doctors and psychologists for emotional disorders. Reich is generally recognized among them as a pioneer of Body Psychotherapy, even though significant early concepts of his—such as how to deal with negative transference—have received little acceptance in Body Psychotherapy circles.

Most Body (Psycho)therapeutic methods that were developed outside of the Reichian tradition, and its long history, tend to take a more background position. At the end of the nineteenth century, Janet had already begun to use body interventions in his work with traumatically caused diseases or disorders. The same applied to Ferenczi around 1920. Marianne Fuchs also was already working with the breath and the body at the end of the 1920s in the psychiatric clinic at the University of Marburg under Kretschmer, and later in the area of anthropologically based psychosomatics in Heidelberg under Viktor von Weizsäcker.

The Body Therapeutic procedures were developed from gymnastics, medical massage, breath techniques, and dance, often as a self-healing method for bodily illnesses or the consequences of accidents of the founders (such as Kofler, F. M. Alexander, Gindler, Feldenkrais, and G. Alexander). Some of them worked out or developed their approach to working with the body in a completely new way and adopted hardly any of the existing body or psychological and philosophical traditions. They built their approach upon exact observation and persistent practice of the resulting experience of body functions.

F. M. Alexander, who developed his practice in Australia, should be particularly mentioned within this context. But this also largely applies to others named within the body-therapy diagram (Figure 9.5): G. Groddeck, M. Fuchs, I. Middendorf, and E. Gindler experimented a great deal with their own body, as well as with those of others. This is also how the practice of S. Keleman's Formative Psychology was developed. The resulting procedures were

---

20 NSDAP: National Sozialistische Deutsche Arbeiter Partei: the German Nazi Party.

108 | A HISTORICAL OVERVIEW OF BODY PSYCHOTHERAPY

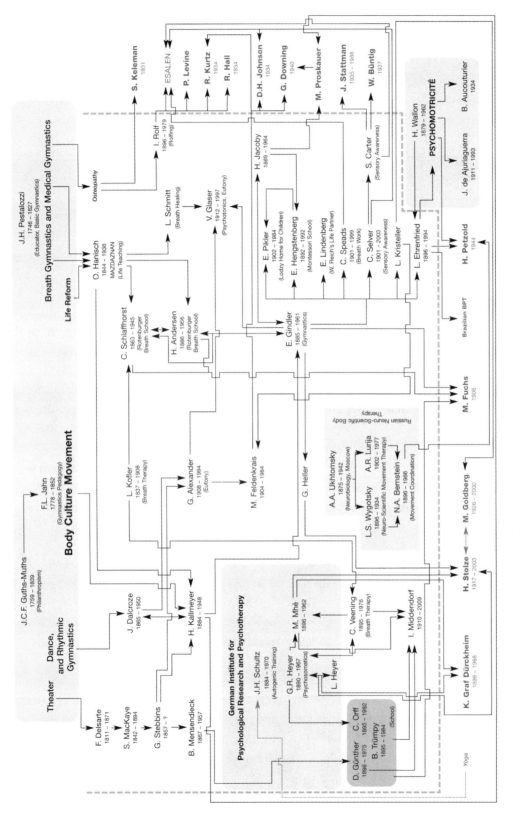

Figure 9.5. Body Culture Movement and Body Psychotherapy

Genealogy of Body Psychotherapy | 109

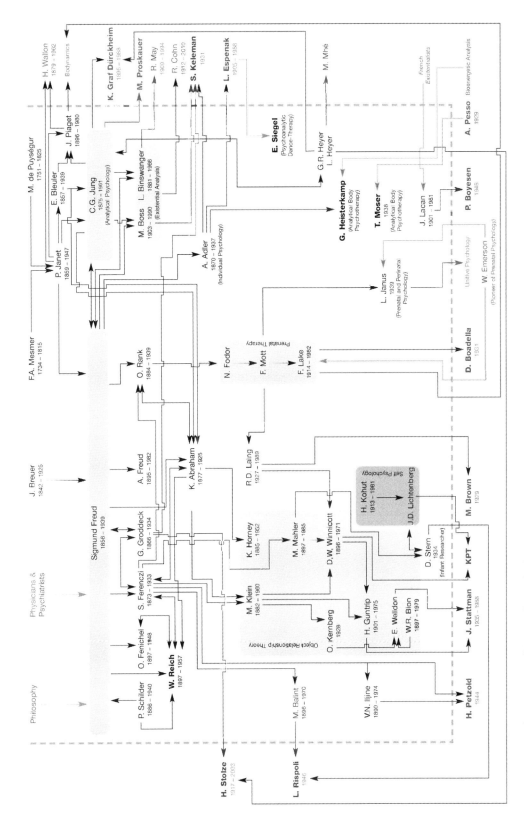

Figure 9.6. Developments within Psychoanalysis

often applied later in psychiatric and psychotherapeutic clinics (such as by G. Heller in England) or in cooperation with psychotherapists and psychiatrists (such as Bülow-Hansen with Braatöy, or Lucie Heyer-Grothe with G. R. Heyer).

Above all, during the heyday of the Body Therapy Movement in Germany between 1920 and 1932, there were many acquaintances and friendships between the analytic community, which was still quite small at that time, and the body therapists who were enlarging their practices into the realms of emotional experience. Some psychoanalysts trained with Elsa Gindler or her female students (for example, Otto Fenichel—his wife, Clara, was one of Gindler's students; Fritz and Laura Perls both studied Gindler's work; and Reich's new partner, Elsa Lindenberg, had deepened her knowledge with Laban and Gindler). By the same token, the body therapists were often involved in analytic treatment. Carola Speads and Charlotte Selver left Germany in 1938, and later had many contacts with representatives of Humanistic Psychology in the United States (see Figure 9.7).

The methods of the various body therapies changed the practice of Body Psychotherapy, above all in the direction of developing more subtle approaches. On the other hand, Reich, Ferenczi, and their colleagues and successors—who had usually had a strong academic training—contributed more strongly to the theoretical aspects of Body Psychotherapy, as did the French "Psychomotricité" (Wallon, Ajuriaguerra, and Aucouturier) that was developed within universities and the field of child psychiatry.

This makes clear that the directional arrows in the diagrams frequently do not signify an explicit teacher-student relationship, or the assumption of a teaching. Instead, they indicate contacts, relationships, inspirations, and even (occasionally) rejected influences. These were often related to geographic locations in which the artists, philosophers, writers, educators, psychoanalysts, and body therapists met, became acquainted, and shared views with each other—such as in Vienna, Berlin, Dresden-Hellerau, and Ascona (Monte Verità). These exchanges lasted up until the era of National Socialism and were reestablished at the beginning of the 1960s, during the time of the development of the Humanistic Psychology movement that started at the Esalen Institute in Big Sur, California (Figure 9.7).

Some Body Psychotherapists have adopted the methods of their teachers and made very few changes to them: examples of this are Raknes and Blumenthal with Reich's Character-Analytic Vegetotherapy, and Baker and the other "Orgonomists" with Reich's later Orgone Therapy. On the other hand, Lowen and Pierrakos, from a basis in Reich's work, developed methods of what they called "Bioenergetic Analysis" that were totally their own. In the massage treatments that supplement their psychotherapy, Bülow-Hansen and Nic Waal have used different and divergent methods. Gerda Boyesen initially adopted the Bülow-Hansen procedure, and then added to it the hypotonia concepts of Lillemor Johnsen, who had studied with Waal. For many Body Psychotherapists, the work of Reich was a significant source of inspirations, even if they had never met him personally (for example, Boadella [1990] and Rispoli).

As a result, the graphics provide a selected overview of the contacts within the community of people working with the body. Because this is also a historical depiction, it does not contain any indications of the influences, or the confirmation of the body-oriented methods, by the modern natural sciences, like neuroscience and neuro-psycho-immunology.

### References

Boadella, D. (1990). Die somatische Psychotherapie: ihre Wurzeln und Traditionen [Somatic Psychotherapy: Its roots and traditions]. *Energie und Charakter: Zeitschrift für Biosynthese und Somatische Psychotherapie* [Energy & Character: Journal for Biosynthesis and Somatic Psychotherapy], *21*(1).

Geuter, U. (2000). Wege zum Körper: Zur Geschichte und Theorie des körperbezogenen Ansatzes in der Psychotherapie [Paths to the body: The history and theory of the body-centered approach in psychotherapy]. *Krankengymnastik: Zeitschrift für Physiotherapeuten* [Physiotherapy: Journal for Physiotherapists], no. 7, 1175ff. & no. 8, 1346ff.

Petzold, H. (2005). Materialien zur Geschichte der Körperpsychotherapie [Materials on the history of Body Psychotherapy]. *Krankengymnastik: Zeitschrift für Physiotherapeuten* [Physiotherapy: Journal for Physiotherapists], no. 2, 332–337.

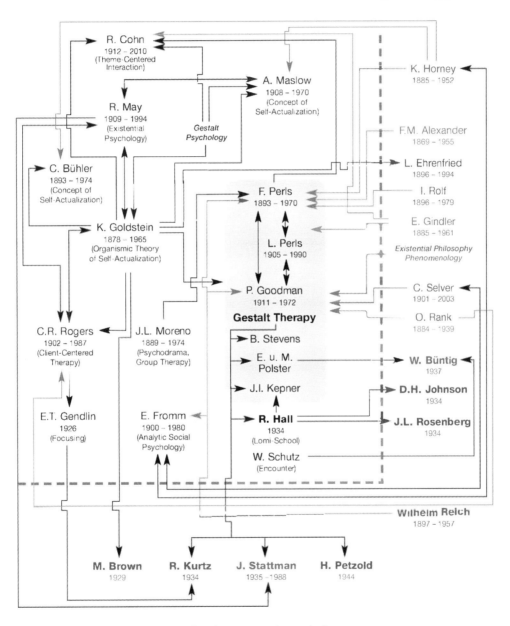

Figure 9.7. Connections within and with Humanistic Psychology

# SECTION II

# Fundamental Perspectives of Body Psychotherapy

# 10
## Introduction to Section II

Gustl Marlock, Germany, and Halko Weiss, United States

Translation by Warren Miller

As we have already noted in the Preface, there was never an intention at any time during this handbook's development to present *the* definitive theory of Body Psychotherapy. There are a number of reasons why such an undertaking is just not feasible.

First, the field of Body Psychotherapy is characterized by far-reaching divergences and differences among the various therapeutic approaches; and, as yet, it lacks a proper culture of in-depth dialogue and constructive controversy. However, in this context, a more fundamental issue (that applies not just to psychotherapy) needs to be raised: In previous times, before any experience of the modern urban world, people lived in small ethnic groups, clans, and secluded cultures and could spend a large part of their life without ever meeting someone who believed in a different god, or who had a different perspective on the world, or who cherished other myths, rites, and customs, or who revered other fetishes: these days are almost definitely over: multiculturalism is here to stay, whether we like it or not. Considering also the fatal consequences of universal claims made particularly in the nineteenth and twentieth centuries for singular worldviews and theories, no one perspective today can claim any supremacy or universal applicability with any degree of good conscience, or with any clarity, or with any real degree of success.

Instead, we have a stance with many postmodern characteristics that comes to the fore: fluid, multiple, and even sometimes incongruent perspectives are given preference over monolithic hegemonies. A tolerance of different, even contradictory, theories begins to emerge that respects these diverse perspectives, even if they emerge from within a similar context. The growing understanding of the cultural relativity of knowledge, and the contributions from constructivist philosophy, have driven this growth forward, and this increasing maturity has given the "science" of psychotherapy the liberty to develop these different perspectives virtually simultaneously. Parallel theories can thereby be tested, applied, compared, and criticized; and integration can be searched for on a higher level, without having to succumb to hasty eclecticism. In the same sense, and for many of these reasons, the multitude of post-Freudian psychotherapies have become increasingly sophisticated.

So, the trend toward an increasing permeability of the boundaries of psychotherapeutic traditions and their ideological identity can perhaps be better understood. Cognitive Behavioral Therapy is moving away from just thoughts and actions, toward the emotions and the unconscious, as well as toward the body; psychoanalysis is moving—albeit somewhat reluctantly—toward the body, and toward the nuances in the actual present-moment content of the dialogue, rather than just an interpretation of it; Gestalt and Body Psychotherapies are more clearly recalling their psychoanalytic roots and incorporating psychodynamic perspectives, as well as somatic developments; and, collectively, all psychotherapies are currently being challenged or inspired by the recent multitude of discoveries in neuropsychology, affect regulation, and infant research. All psychotherapies are also increasingly being required to "prove" their efficacy and effectiveness.

Hence, without deducing any particular propaganda out of this jigsaw, the *zeitgeist* is nevertheless becoming fairly obvious, as it leans toward psychotherapeutic approaches that are increasingly integrative. Interestingly, some schools of Body Psychotherapy have long actualized this development toward the integration of fundamentally different psychotherapeutic perspectives, while avoiding the already-mentioned dangers of eclecticism, or promoting reductionist standardization through the back door. Some examples of these integrative Body Psychotherapeutic schools include: Biosynthesis (Boadella); Functionalism (Rispoli); Integrative Leibtherapie [Integrative Body and Movement Therapy] (Petzold); Integrative Body Psychotherapy (Rosenberg); the Hakomi Method (Kurtz); and Unitive Psychology (Stattman). Rather than having people talk about their various methods, in Section II, the different authors have been asked to present a range of fundamental perspectives on Body Psychotherapy.

Don Hanlon Johnson, in Chapter 11, "The Primacy of Experiential Practices in Body Psychotherapy," presents the tradition of somatic educational methods, illustrating the primacy of direct bodily experience as an essential element that belongs to most Body Psychotherapeutic approaches, perhaps not always in theory, but certainly in practice. Johnson formulates several principles of "somatic learning" and "somatic intelligence" that, as expressed here, are more essentially and existentially meaningful than analytic interpretation or cognitively oriented interventions.

In Chapter 12, "Neurobiological Perspectives on Body Psychotherapy," Christian Gottwald develops a neuropsychologically grounded perspective on Body Psychotherapy that illustrates the significance of integrating the body into the therapeutic process.

Coming from the psychodynamic background of Body Psychotherapy, Gustl Marlock, in Chapter 13, "Body Psychotherapy as a Revitalization of the Self: A Depth-Psychological and Phenomenological-Existential Perspective," presents a view of multidimensional understanding that integrates both phenomenological-hermeneutical and existential perspectives. This is an understanding that does not remain rigidly attached to classic psychodynamic dogmas of instinctual (drive) theory, nor to Reich's concept of energy.

In contrast, as is evident in many chapters in this handbook, the concept of bodily energy coined by Reich, either explicitly (e.g., Buhl, Lowen, and Boyesen) or implicitly, continues to be a central reference point in the field of Body Psychotherapy. Therefore, Andreas Wehowsky, in Chapter 14, "The Concept of Energy in Body Psychotherapy," presents a differentiated discussion of the energy concept and its importance to this subject. Whereas Wehowsky's critical debate attempts to salvage the energy concept for Body Psychotherapy, Marlock treats it as secondary or marginal. So, Chapters 13 and 14 simultaneously reflect both the ongoing and dramatic, as well as the underlying, controversy within the field of Body Psychotherapy regarding this concept, which many therapists see as a fundamental issue. (Incidentally, a very different perspective on energy in the body is explored later in Chapter 59, "Energy and the Nervous System in Embodied Experience" by James Kepner.)

In Chapter 15, "The Organization of Experience: A Systems Perspective on the Relation of Body Psychotherapies to the Wider Field of Psychotherapy," Gregory Johanson strives to describe core elements of Body Psychotherapy, in both theory and practice, that are applicable to all its schools from a systemic perspective. He draws upon concepts of the self-organization of living systems, especially those of Gregory Bateson and Ken Wilber, as well as the theory of complex adaptive systems. It becomes clear not only that the interplay between the individual and his or her environment can be understood in such a systemic fashion, but also how this perspective can be applied toward an understanding of both the psychic and somatic inner worlds. These inner worlds are self-organizing, and can be understood and therapeutically treated in the light of principles that characterize all self-organizing systems: that their quality depends on the degree of internal communication; that their response to the world necessitates levels of adaptation; that they form internal models of reality; and that they are able to integrate informational elements into, or expel them from, their organization. It is this last point of understanding that we see increasingly permeating modern Body Psychotherapeutic modalities.

# 11

## The Primacy of Experiential Practices in Body Psychotherapy

Don Hanlon Johnson, United States

**Don Hanlon Johnson** is perhaps best known for writing some of the first reputable modern books about Body Psychotherapy: *Body: Recovering Our Sensual Wisdom* (1983), *The Body in Psychotherapy: Inquiries in Somatic Psychology* (edited with Ian Grand, 1998), as well as *Bone, Breath, and Gesture: Practices of Embodiment* (1995) and *Groundworks: Narratives of Embodiment (1997)*. He is the founder of the first fully accredited graduate program for somatic psychology at the California Institute of Integral Studies (CIIS) in San Francisco, where he continues working as a professor. He received his PhD in Philosophy from Yale University, with his doctoral dissertation on relations between changes in the body and changes in consciousness, and he was one of the first long-term students of Ida Rolf, whom he supported in the founding of the Rolf Institute. As the director of the Somatic Education and Research Project at Esalen Institute, and in similar functions throughout his career, he engaged himself to facilitate dialogue among the schools of Somatic Psychology in order to promote Somatic Psychology's influence in the Western culture of healing. The following contribution is an expression of this commitment to embodiment, and its significance for human well-being. His numerous and significant publications have contributed to the founding of a historiography of Body Psychotherapy.

Body Psychotherapy (or Body-Oriented Psychology) is formed by the confluence of two currents moving in opposite directions. The more well-known current developed as a branch of the depth-analytic therapies, developed by Wilhelm Reich, who was originally inspired by Freud's early recognition of the specific bodily roots of mental disorders.[21] The innovators in this movement created technical practices of breathing, touch, sensory awareness, and movement that were conceptualized and taught within pre-existing psychoanalytic theory, with articulated language constructs and sometimes bewildering dictionaries of character types. Another robust current of development moved in an opposite direction—from sustained, deliberate, and reflective bodily practices toward new theory-building.

This second current, whose origins go back to the late nineteenth century, is not as widely known as the psychoanalytic community, because its originators typically developed their approaches in private institutes, informal schools, or clinics, outside of universities, and have written very little. They include: Eutony, Focusing, Sensory Awareness, Feldenkrais, Rolfing, the F. M. Alexander Technique, Continuum, Body-Mind Centering, Authentic Movement, Middendorf Breath Work, and many others. The nature and effects of these practices are not easy to articulate. They are not taught within a psychological framework, even though they have psychological implications. Nor

---

21 For example, Sigmund Freud, "Some Points for a Comparative Study of Organic and Hysterical Paralyses" and "Observations of a Severe Case of Hemi-Anaesthesia in a Hysterical Male" in *The Standard Edition of the Complete Psychological Works of Sigmund Freud, Vol. I* (James Strachey, Trans.) (pp. 169ff., 30ff.). London: Hogarth Press, 1966

are they just "physical," like physical therapy or classical Swedish massage. Because of their primarily experiential nature, they exist in a realm whose meanings are not easily captured within the dominant intellectual categories. What follows are three illustrations of this bottom-up movement: Focusing, Authentic Movement, and Body-Mind Centering.

## Focusing

Eugene Gendlin (1962, 1998), the creator of Focusing, gives a paradigmatic example of this countercurrent from Isadora Duncan's autobiography:

> For hours I would stand quite still, my two hands folded between my breasts, covering the solar plexus. My mother often became alarmed to see me remain for such long intervals quite motionless as if in a trance—but I was seeking and I finally discovered the central spring of all movements, the crater of motor power, the unity from which all diversities of movements are born . . . (Isadora Duncan, 1927, p. 75)

Gendlin comments on this text:

> Isadora Duncan stands still, sometimes for a long period. She senses dance steps she could move into, but they don't feel right. What would feel right is not sure yet. She is "seeking," she says above, "looking for," "waiting for" the right "feel" to come, "willing to let" it come. This seeking, waiting for, looking, and letting is a kind of action. It is a way of relating to, "interacting with" . . . What? Where? It is interaction with a right feel, a new kind of feel which "will come" in a new place.
>
> This feel, and this new space, are both made in this very interaction.
>
> Her new looking, waiting for, letting . . . These change what comes, but it is still not right. She responds to its changed way of feeling by being differently toward it in some way. She *points to* a facet of the feel of what she would dance, *pursues it*. In response to the *pointing* and the *pursuing*, the feel itself becomes more distinct, like something there, a datum, an object, something in a space that wasn't there before.
>
> As it forms, the "feel" understands itself, so to speak. It carries its own "yes, yes . . ." with it. She is "in touch with herself" in a new way—not just a self that was there before, waiting. Rather, a new, changed, more right "feel" is there, and is the "being in touch with." Then she dances what she could not have danced before. (Gendlin, 1998)

"Then she dances what she could not have danced before." Here is the heart of this reverse movement in the development of new approaches to psychotherapy, whose source lies in methodically cultivated bodily experience, and language emerging from that experience. During the past century, tens, perhaps hundreds, or thousands of people in Europe and the Americas have been engaging in this family of bodily practices. They attend to their experiences of moving, breathing, being touched; they wait; new movements arise along with old memories, long forgotten, and new solutions to life problems, with new strengths to confront old wounds, loosening the bonds of an outdated sense of self. These new movements and solutions emerge not from the side of already-made psychological notions, but from an experiential realm that carries an intelligence that has not yet been formulated in language and concept. These discoveries come not from already-crafted depth-psychoanalytic theory, but from quiet systematic and communal reflections on bodily experience in specific kinds of ways, created by a very large number of Somatics innovators, often working largely in silence.

Gendlin has been a major voice of this countermovement, showing how our bodies are the carriers of meanings not yet put into concept nor word, and that attending to bodily experiences is the key to creative thought-forms that can carry us forward into new worlds of activity (Gendlin, 1962). Both his psychotherapeutic method and his considerable body of theoretical texts have at their core the righting of a historical imbalance in which theoretical constructs are given more value than not-yet-conceived experiential processes. His theories are derived from decades of observing and documenting the results of human growth processes, paying careful and sustained attention to the bodily "felt sense" and how attention to that sense slowly emerges into new verbal, conceptual expressions. His methods are designed to help people turn their attention toward the bodily "felt sense" as the source of fresh language and concepts in response to needs that are not met by the old. As in the work of his early partner Carl Rogers, there is a freshness in his spare conceptual frameworks, redolent of characteristically American pragmatism, without a hint of psychoanalytic seasoning.

This turn toward experience, learning to wait attentively until fresh notions emerge before speaking, is characteristic of many practices. It is not easy to do this; as in the cultivation of a spiritual life, one needs methods of slowing down, paying attention, and savoring silence. Especially for the well educated, it is much easier to rush into analytical thought and vocabularies. So the vast number of highly skillful practices are also methods of allowing practitioners to gain a greater access to this nonverbal realm, and to remain in it for a longer period of time, especially in comparison to the time one usually spends in the realms of talk, thought, and entertainment.

It is in this context of methods of settling into not-yet-verbalized bodily experiences that one can understand various methods of bodily practices, and their impact on the understanding of psychotherapy and the education of psychotherapists.

## Authentic Movement

Focusing, as described above, typically involves two people sitting quietly, learning to pay attention to the ebbs and flows of experience, waiting for words to emerge that truly express those experiences. Authentic Movement is another widespread bodily discipline that involves a similar attitude, but in the context of movement. Its origins are in the work of Mary Starks Whitehouse (1911–1979), one of the founders of Dance Therapy, though Janet Adler (2002) developed it in its present form and name.

The emphasis is on the long and sustained practice of quiet movement, usually in pairs or groups. One person in the pair or group adopts the role of noncritical witness, eyes open, present to what is happening, creating an atmosphere of containment, so that the mover is free to allow new, and possibly fearful, experiences to emerge in movement. The mover moves with eyes closed. At the end of a period of movement, which may last from a few minutes to an hour or more, there is a disciplined period of discourse whose aim is to allow words to emerge—in much the same way that movements emerged, not talking about the experience, but allowing words and thoughts to come from it.

This practiced discourse within a nonjudgmental atmosphere of safety is what makes Authentic Movement unique among body-movement practices and brings it into the arena of being a psychotherapy. The moving and the speaking, and sometimes writing, allow the mover to claim forgotten or rejected dimensions of the self. Mary Whitehouse writes of how she came to develop this practice, which she called "Moving in Depth":

> What I began to understand during the beginning of my work in movement in depth was that in order to release a movement that is instinctive (i.e., not the "idea" of the person doing that movement nor my idea of what I want them to do), I found that I had to go back toward not moving. In that way I found out where movement actually started. It was when I learned to see what was authentic about movement, and what was not, and when people were cheating, and when I interfered, and when they were starting to move from within themselves, and when they were compelled to move because they had an image in their heads of what they wanted to do; it was then that I learned to say "Go ahead and do your image, never mind if you are thinking of it," and when to say "Oh, wait longer. Wait until you feel it from within." (Whitehouse, 1999a, p. 23)

The practice involves teaching people how to wait, as Isadora Duncan did, for movement to arise and evolve as one gives oneself to it within an atmosphere of quiet attention. It is a sustained, tutored, disciplined waiting for movement—and words—to come from the self, instead of from habitual movements—or words—or moving and speaking as others would have us do, or as we think they would have us do.

> A word about what this way of working with the body requires. There is necessary an attitude of inner openness, a kind of capacity for listening to one's self that I would call honesty. It is made possible only by concentration and patience. In allowing the body to move in its way, not in a way that would look nice, or that one thinks it should, in waiting patiently for the inner impulsive, in letting the reactions come up exactly as they occur on any given evening—new capacities appear, new modes of behavior are possible, and the awareness gained in the specialized situation goes over into a new sense of one's self . . . (Whitehouse, 1995, p. 250)

These teachers do not use words like "instinctive" and "natural" in the technical, academically charged senses, but in a more ordinary street-usage, used to describe commonplace experiences of the difference between posed, predictable, habitual, or stereotypical movements, and those that surprise us as being fresh and spontaneous.

> Authentic Movement is movement that is natural to a particular person, not learned like ballet or calisthenics, not purposeful or intellectualized as "this is the way I should move"—to be pleasing, to be powerful, to be beautiful or graceful. Authentic Movement is an immediate expression of how the client feels at any given moment. The spontaneous urge to move or not to move is not checked, judged, criticized or weighed by the conscious mind. (Adler, 1999, p. 122)

Janet Adler uses "authenticity" in the same sense as Heidegger does in *Being and Time,* returning to the Greek roots of the word "self-posited."

> My core being is mine to be in one way or another. That core being has always made some sort of decision as to the way in which it is in each case mine . . . And because core being is in each case essentially its own possibility, it *can*, in its very Being, "choose" itself and win itself; it can also lose itself and never win itself; or only "seem" to do so. But only in so far as it is essentially something which can be *authentic*—that is, something of its own—can it have lost itself and not yet won itself. (Heidegger, 1962, p. 68)[22]

And:

> "Inauthenticity" . . . amounts rather to a quite distinctive kind of Being-in-the-world—the kind which is completely fascinated by the "world" and by the Dasein—with of Others in the "they." (Ibid., p. 220)

Just as we are our "own," to dispose of within the "they" world of gossip, trivia, and opinion, so too our movements, our speaking, and our thinking are ours to give over to preconceived notions about how we should move, speak, or think; or, we can wait in silence until movements and words come from within ourselves.

> When movement was simple and inevitable, not to be changed no matter how limited or partial, it became what I called "authentic"—it could be recognized as genuine, belonging to that person. (Whitehouse, 1999b, p. 81)

Adler's account (1999) transforms Wilhelm Reich's distinction between voluntary and involuntary movements. For Reich, the paradigm of the involuntary is the tremulous shaking or "streamings," associated with orgasmic

---

22  I have taken the great liberty of translating "Dasein," untranslated in the English texts, as "core being." There are thousands of pages of argument published about the proper translation of this central concept of Heidegger's work.

release, evoked in the various exercises of bioenergetic therapies, and mirrored in other kinds of energy discharge. Whitehouse, Adler, and their associates have been exploring a much wider realm of different kinds of nondeliberate movements, opening up different realms of feeling, memory, and image. And unlike Reich, Adler extends this direction of movement into language and thought itself.[23] This breadth of bodily exploration, seeking primal roots of movement and words in many new areas, has made the practice more congenial to non-Reichian analysts and psychologists who feel the Reichian paradigm is too constricted. Practice is in the foreground, constantly being the norm against which words and theory are being reshaped.

## Body-Mind Centering

The school of Body-Mind Centering, founded by Bonnie Bainbridge Cohen (1993), is a particularly important practice for identifying which regions of bodily experience are missing or deficient in any particular bodily approach to the roots of personality. For that reason, it might be called a systems approach to Body Psychotherapy.

Like Isadora Duncan, Cohen began her career as a dancer. With Erick Hawkins, Cohen worked out experiences similar to the ones that Gendlin describes: moving, stopping, waiting, listening, allowing new movements, energized by new bodily impulses, images, memories, feelings. At the same time, her university education (as a physical and occupational therapist) prompted her to find ways to make that process more nuanced and articulate by engaging in a lifelong systematic investigation of the relationships between experienced realities and biomedical maps of the body. Experimenting on her own over many years, she discovered that each region of the lived body has its characteristic state of consciousness: images, feelings, sensations, intuitions about the world, perceptions of other people, words and ideas—in short, its own "mind" (Stark Smith, 1993, p. 64). As with Gendlin and Adler, the interface with psychology emerges when one methodically situates oneself in one of these regions, or *minds*, and patiently waits for new words and ideas to emerge from the experience itself.

Cohen went about her experiments in this way: She would pose to herself the question "What is the *mind* of the bones [or lungs, heart, thymus gland, . . .]?" For as long as it takes—sometimes, she says, a year or more for a particular system—she would spend hours a day working with movement and guided awareness to explore the regions mapped out by anatomical drawings of the bones of the body: the large and obvious bones of the legs and arms, as well as normally obscure bones, such as the metatarsals in the center of the foot, the tiny carpals in the hand, and the cranial bones. Over the months, she familiarized herself with the distinct qualities of this skeletal hinterland, its associated images, memories, emotions, thoughts, tones of voice, qualities of movement, words, and concepts rooted in that "mind." After satisfying herself that she had gained enough information for the moment, she might then shift her work to the "mind" of the nervous system, spending months focusing on the contours and weather patterns in that realm. She has thus transformed biomedical maps from descriptions of an objectified body to maps of how to gain different experiences of the self.

> [I find these things] through the sensory feedback system. If you move your pelvis with your bones in your sensation, it registers one way; if you move your pelvis with your muscles in your sensation, it registers another way; if you move with your organs in mind then it registers differently. (Stark Smith, 1981, p. 7)

Cohen's experiments led her to find specific experiential practices for entry into a particular region—methodically directed breathing, movements, and attention. In the case of the glands, for example:

> [I open the glands] through breathing into that area. Through sounding into that area. Through a hissing breath. And then through moving. Once you've located a place it is easy to initiate movement from there. We watch for what mind comes out of that place;

---

23 Janet Adler's book details this process.

what actions come out of it; what are the efforts; what are the dynamics of that movement; what are the feelings and forms of that movement; what is the sound. All of that information comes out of that place . . . With the glands we went into automatic movement and watched what emerged. (Stark Smith, 1993, p. 57)

Over these years of work, she reached the ability to discern with clarity the experiential characteristics of one system of the body as contrasted with another:

From the gland work, I went into the nervous system more carefully, contrasting the control of the nervous system and the brain with the control of the glands. Working with the brain as a major control system after working with the glands was moving from a very hot, emotional, volatile, chaotic system of energy and process to a cool system of organization, clarity and crystallization. There's a wildness to the glands and a sense of control in the nervous system. (Ibid.)

As that quotation implies, her mapping is not confined to specific regions, but extends to relationships among regions: "If you are going to move one bone, another bone has to countersupport it. In the same way, if you are working with the nervous system, you balance it with the endocrine system and if you're in the endocrine, you support it with the nervous system" (Stark Smith, 1993, p. 64).

By exploring the layers of experience rooted in different regions of the body, Cohen has woven an intricate system for touching other people and giving them movement instructions that will lead them into unfamiliar regions of experience. She can focus so intently on her bones, as distinct from her muscles, as distinct from her organs, that her touch and movement instructions can help others find those same areas.

If I'm working with any area of someone else's body, I will go into that area of my own body to see. In the process I become more open also. It becomes like two bells ringing on the same pitch. We can resonate each other. (Ibid., p. 5)

Like the Jungian framework that provides a useful map for understanding limitations of the individual psyche to thinking, sensing, feeling, or imagining (Holifield, 1998), Cohen's practices reveal how a particular emphasis in Body Psychotherapy might be too confined to a particular class of bodily experiences. For example, some methods dwell exclusively on peristaltic and orgasmic movements; others, solely on sensing; others, on kinesthesia; and so forth. The Cohen framework constantly challenges practitioners to expand the repertoire of their experiences, so as to become familiar with other aspects of their "minds."

From these investigations, Cohen has derived a wide range of methods of touch and body-movement direction. Even though she makes no claims that her work is any form of psychotherapy (Aposhyan, 2004),[24] the practice has profound implications for bodily based refinements of familiar concepts of attunement, presence, projective identification, and empathy. In the education of therapists, there is always the perplexing question of how to educate novices in these essential aspects of the clinical relationship. The practices of Body-Mind Centering add a rich complexity of detail to what can otherwise be an empty idea. Gaining the facility to enter a variety of discrete bodily states can give the therapist an identifiable, teachable repertoire of possibilities for perceiving the experiential world of one's client and entering that world with him or her. This is a different form of Rogerian listening, methodically rooted in bodily experience, lifted to the most subtle nuances of intricate experiential contact between therapist and client: fluid to fluid, lungs to lungs, bone to bone, thymus to thymus.

## The Primacy of Experiential Practice over Conceptual Systems

One tangible difference that appears institutionally between European and American notions of theory and practice is that Body-Oriented or Somatic Psychology in the United States is an academic discipline offered in the psychology

---

24 Susan Aposhyan has shown how Bonnie Bainbridge Cohen's work can form the basis for an approach to Body Psychotherapy (see Aposhyan, 2004).

departments of many universities, whereas in Europe, even though there are some academic professorships in this field, it is pursued principally within private groups offering practical training outside of academia.

Eugene Gendlin, Bonnie Bainbridge Cohen, and Janet Adler embody a characteristically American approach to theory construction, representative of the robust intellectual pragmatist tradition articulated by William James, C. S. Peirce, and John Dewey. Knowledge, in this tradition, gets its validation in experiential action, which, upon reflection, reshapes preexisting words and theories.[25]

Bodily practices are not simply, or even primarily, techniques for therapists to use with clients; they are also considered essential in the very education and continuous cultivation of the therapist. A particular clinical session may even look—to the outsider—like any other kind of psychotherapy, with both therapist and client sitting in chairs discoursing. But the experiential world is very different, with the therapist having cultivated a highly skilled sensitivity to nuances in the client's nonverbal expressions, hints in his or her discourse of bodily references, distortions of body image, and many other aspects that reveal themselves only to one who has become richly situated within his or her own bodily reality by sustained practices of bodily exploration. This educated sensibility creates a different kind of attunement and empathy unique to Body Psychotherapy, a deeply embodied connection absent in exclusively verbal modes of therapy.

To understand this difference between a European and a North American tradition, it is helpful to situate both with reference to Asian notions of mind and body. Yasuo Yuasa is a Japanese scholar of the relation between bodily practices—martial arts, meditation, theater, music, writing practices—and theory development on the part of practitioners. He argues that the most profound difference between Asian and European intellectual traditions lies in the priority given to theory or practice:

> What might we discover to be the philosophical uniqueness of Eastern thought? One revealing characteristic is that personal "cultivation" is presupposed in the philosophical foundation of Eastern theories. To put it simply, true knowledge cannot be obtained simply by means of theoretical thinking, but only through "bodily recognition or realization," that is, through the utilization of one's total mind and body. Simply stated, this is to "learn with the body," not the brain. Cultivation is a practice that attempts, so to speak, to achieve true knowledge by means of one's total mind and body. (Yuasa, 1987, p. 25)[26]

The break, he argues, between theory and practice is an exact mirror of the Cartesian gap between mind and body, where theory is the principle of order. Practice is merely the shaping of so-called "chaotic" experience by the mind, having no intrinsic intelligibility apart from the theories that shape it.

The Japanese view is helpful in mitigating a tendency of Europeans to mistake a North American emphasis on practice and experience for a trivial anti-intellectualism. America lies between the two great intellectual traditions of Asia and Europe; it has been a place where experimental practices occurring within a reflective communal atmosphere have taken precedence over preexisting theories imported whole cloth from the Old Worlds, East and West. The populist current of Body Psychotherapy or Somatic Psychology has its unique flavor from the fact that psychotherapists identified with this field are involved in the

---

25 Two books that give a very important picture of the relationships between American philosophy and Somatics are: Thomas Hanna's *Bodies in Revolt: A Primer in Somatic Thinking* (San Francisco: Holt, Rinehart, and Winston, 1970); and Bruce W. Wilshire's *The Primal Roots of American Philosophy: Pragmatism, Phenomenology, and Native American Thought* (Harrisburg: University of Pennsylvania Press, 2000). Wilshire has been particularly important in articulating the implications of the well-known fact that John Dewey studied with F. M. Alexander for more than twenty years. Dewey's crafting of the enormously important system of progressive education is a direct application of the Alexander Technique to the structures of teacher-training and curriculum development.

26 See also Y. Yuasa, *The Body, Self-Cultivation, and Ki-Energy* (Shigenori Nagatomo & Monte Hull, Trans.). New York: SUNY Press, 1993.

methodical investigation of many regions of bodily experience through long-term skillful practices outside the clinical relationship itself. Therapists bring to the clinical relationship the results of such practice—juice, contact, and a readier access to intrapsychic material. They also continually reshape their thinking about the nature of therapy in light of these practices.

Righting the imbalance of theory over practice within the field of Body Psychotherapy or Somatic Psychology might be helpful in creating a more communal dialogue where participants and practitioners might join in shared reflections on the specific intricacies of the practices themselves. This is a basis for a grounded collaborative, field-generating discourse, and for appropriate research models. I have made a very modest foray into advancing such a model (Johnson, 2000). Most of the approaches to Body-Oriented Psychology and Psychotherapy share practices of breathing, touching, and sensing. But there is little common development of the descriptions of how these practices are used in any particular school of work and their results. What are the experiential differences, for example, between different styles and rhythms of touch? Or between working with clients clothed, or in their underwear? Or between moving with eyes open, or eyes closed? Or between giving specific kinds of guided imagery to explore body regions? Or between allowing clients or directing them in certain postures, movements, and sensations?

Such a shift of focus away from already-formed theories of how the body impacts psychology into the less verbose world of experiential practices might help foster the embodied sense of community that Wilhelm Reich (1933/1970, p. xxiii) called a "work democracy," a badly needed model of sane collaboration in an increasingly insane world.

## References

Adler, J. (1999). Integrity of body and psyche. In P. Pallardo (Ed.), *Authentic Movement: Essays by Mary Starks Whitehouse, Janet Adler and Joan Chodorow.* London: Jessica Kingsley.

Aposhyan, S. (2004). *Body-Mind Psychotherapy: Principles, techniques and practical applications.* New York: W. W. Norton.

Cohen, B. B. (1993). *Sensing, feeling and action.* Berkeley, CA: North Atlantic Books.

Duncan, I. (1927). *My life.* New York: Liveright.

Gendlin, E. T. (1962). *Experiencing and the creation of meaning: A philosophical and psychological approach to the subjective.* Evanston, IL: Northwestern University Press.

Gendlin, E. T. (1998). *The Focusing handbook.* Chapter VIII-A: The direct referent, a) Introduction: www.focusing.org/process.html

Heidegger, M. (1962). *Being and time (J. Macquarrie & E. Robinson, Trans.).* New York: Harper & Row.

Holifield, B. (1998). Against the wall/her beating heart: Working with the somatic aspects of transference, countertransference, and dissociation. In D. H. Johnson & I. Grand (Eds.), *The body in psychotherapy* (pp. 59–84). Berkeley, CA: North Atlantic Books.

*Johnson, D. H. (1983). Body: Recovering Our Sensual Wisdom.* Boston: Beacon Press.

Johnson, D. H. (1995). *Bone, Breath and Gesture: Practices of embodiment: Vol. 1.* Berkeley, CA: North Atlantic Books.

Johnson, D. H. (1997). *Groundworks: Narratives of Embodiment.* Berkeley, CA: North Atlantic Books.

Johnson, D. H. (2000). Intricate tactile sensitivity: A key variable in Western integrative bodywork. In C. Saper & E. Mayer (Eds.), *The biological basis for mind body interactions.* Amsterdam: Elsevier.

Johnson, D. H., & Grand, I. J. (Eds.). (1998). *The body in psychotherapy: Inquiries in Somatic Psychology.* Berkeley, CA: North Atlantic Books.

Reich, W. (1933/1970). *The mass psychology of fascism (Vincent Carfagno, Trans.).* New York: Farrar, Straus & Giroux.

Stark Smith, N. (1981). Interview with Bonnie Bainbridge Cohen. *Contact Quarterly, no. 1.*

Stark Smith, N. (Ed.). (1993). *Sensing, feeling, and action: The experiential anatomy of Body-Mind Centering.* Northampton, MA: Contact Editions.

Whitehouse, M. S. (1995). The Tao of the body. In D. H. Johnson (Ed.), *Bone, breath, and gesture.* Berkeley, CA: North Atlantic Books.

Whitehouse, M. S. (1999a). An approach to the center. In P. Pallardo (Ed.), *Authentic Movement: Essays by Mary Starks Whitehouse, Janet Adler and Joan Chodorow.* London: Jessica Kingsley.

Whitehouse, M. S. (1999b). C. G. Jung and Dance Therapy. In P. Pallardo (Ed.), *Authentic Movement: Essays by Mary Starks Whitehouse, Janet Adler and Joan Chodorow.* London: Jessica Kingsley.

Yuasa, Y. (1987). *The body: Toward an Eastern mind-body theory* (Nagatomo Shigenori & T. P. Kasulis, Trans.). New York: SUNY Press.

# 12
## Neurobiological Perspectives on Body Psychotherapy

**Christian Gottwald, Germany**

**Translation by Warren Miller**

**Christian Gottwald** is particularly qualified to delineate a shared neuropsychological/Body Psychotherapeutic perspective, given his extraordinarily broad and multifaceted training and wide range of clinical experience. As neurologist, psychiatrist, medical psychotherapist, former scientific assistant and later director of the outpatient psychotherapy clinic at the University of Mainz, he is very familiar with the medical model. At the same time, he went through a number of psychotherapy trainings, aside from his work as psychoanalyst and teaching analyst, including in Organismic Psychotherapy (Malcolm Brown), Pesso-Boyden System Psychomotor, and Hakomi Experiential Psychology. Additionally, he was trained in Gestalt Therapy and has participated in other trainings in the tradition of Humanistic Psychology. Aside from his work in private practice in Munich since 1980, he works as lecturer, trainer, and supervisor.

Dr. Gottwald is a member of the Hakomi faculty in Germany, and in numerous publications and presentations he has expressed his view on how neuropsychological research might inform psychotherapeutic perspectives. His area of specialization is "Awareness-Centered Body Psychotherapy."

Neurobiology is devoted to the investigation of the brain and nervous system. Particularly since the turn of the century, new research technologies have generated an ever-expanding number of research findings. As a field of knowledge, neurobiology is still very young and in the process of formulation. From the perspective of neurobiological research, reality currently seems as if one were looking at a world through a series of small holes. Depending on the hole that one looks through, different aspects present themselves. Many different facets of findings that, at times, seem to contradict one another emerge from different levels of research (for example, molecular, cellular, structural, and anatomical levels). Some neurobiologists, such as Joachim Bauer, Gerald Hüther, Josef LeDoux, Allan Schore, Stephen Porges, Bessel van der Kolk, and Gerhard Roth, actively support Body Psychotherapy in retaining an overview in this vast research area. From the psychotherapeutic point of view, preliminary conclusions have also been drawn by Beutel (Beutel et al., 2003; Beutel, 2008), Cozolino (2003), Grawe (2004), Levin (2003), and Solms (Solms and Turnbull, 2002).

This brief description of some aspects of the research findings from the field of neurobiology that are relevant, and perhaps stimulating, to Body Psychotherapists is given from the perspective of a neurologist, psychiatrist, and psychodynamically oriented Body Psychotherapist. Beginning with Wilhelm Reich, Body Psychotherapy has a very long tradition and a broad empirical basis.

A consistent picture is also built up from neurobiological research, which has a greater value for practical work. An expanded understanding of numerous psychosomatic and psychic phenomena is now possible. Research findings now confirm much of the empirical work, and show how effective psychotherapy actually changes the brain. These results imply that new impulses lead to changed priority assessments and altered points of emphasis. From this perspective, some speculations, hypotheses, and perspectives for Body Psychotherapy can be developed. Although somewhat premature and not yet scientifically validated, such speculations and hypotheses can actually have a heuristic value, but conclusive results and established theses for both psychotherapy and Body Psychotherapy have not yet been properly established, and any firm conclusions are therefore premature.

## Endorsement of Psychotherapy

Some of the central postulations and original theories of Sigmund Freud, along with those of psychodynamically oriented Body Psychotherapy, are now supported by neurobiological research findings—in particular, the premise of the predominance of the unconscious and the origin of neurosis in early childhood (Roth, 2001, p. 454).

## Limitations of Talk and Cognition

That there are limitations of cognition and talk (in regards to their efficacy in psychotherapy) is also becoming increasingly clear (see Damasio, 2001; Spitzer, 2001; Roth, 2001; LeDoux, 2003). Gazzaniga (2000) also did some trials with patients who had had the connection between their right and left brain hemispheres severed and was able to show that, when they were to give verbal explanations for right hemispherically generated behaviors, their conscious, speech-generating left hemispheres made up fictitious accounts. Interestingly, there are no direct pathways between the speech areas and the motor and sensory areas of the cortex. Gerhard Roth states:

> Speech . . . serves . . . to legitimize our predominantly unconsciously regulated behaviors for ourselves and for others. . . . Verbal communication only then effects a change in our partners, when they are already in a state of consonance with us, be it due to internal processes of making meaning or through non-verbal communication. (Roth, 2001, p. 452)

People aren't guided by their egos, nor informed by their verbalizations, but operate mainly through the unconscious, via affects and emotions from deeper-seated brain structures, in particular from those of the brainstem and limbic system. These are (basically) devoid of language. The fundamental significance of the deep body in the field of affects and emotions is finally becoming recognized in more detail (Niedenthal et al., 2005; Damasio and Kober, 1999; Damasio, 2001).

Human experience is always a combination of the whole unity of the sensory-motor-affective systems. Body Psychotherapy offers a therapeutic setting that goes beyond the normal conscious and verbal conceptualizations to help integrate information from all of the person's sense organs, their affects, their motor behavior, as well as information from their subconscious and unconscious ("implicit memory"). Therefore, Body Psychotherapy, in particular, can consider itself as relevant to, and possibly validated by, these neurobiological findings, even if neurobiology has not yet addressed Body Psychotherapy specifically. Conversely, within the scope of an embodied relationship, this allows a conscious shaping of the therapeutic situation with inclusion of all sensual organs, the affects, and the motoric system.

## Ego and Self

The ego and the self don't occupy specific locations in the brain. In the neurobiological sense, the self can be conceived of as an organizing principle. Damasio (2001) describes the self as a recurrently reconstructed biological status that enriches experience with a sense of subjectivity. Many modules within the network that structures the brain contribute to the generation of such self-experiences. As for the ego, the prefrontal cortex is a central region contributing to the generation of ego states. It plays a central role, alongside the anterior cingulate cortex for the working memory, especially in the processes of awareness and in the self-regulation of affective states, which are generated mainly in the limbic system (LeDoux, 2003). Rüegg (2001, p. 83) cites numerous studies that demonstrate the importance of the influence that the ego can have in the appraisal of situations—for example, in determining the stress response of the human organism.

People can significantly influence how they assess and evaluate situations. Accordingly, adequate self-regulation and self-awareness are considered important goals of therapy. One way in which Body Psychotherapy pursues these goals is to support the client's bodily self-confidence; for example, through (Lowen's Bioenergetic) "grounding" techniques, or through generative foundational practices similar to those in martial arts, where participants learn to be present in their center, in the lower abdomen (called the *hara* or *dan tien* in Eastern disciplines), or in the contact of their feet with the floor, i.e., to be there "internally present" (Gottwald, 2008).

## Body-Mind-Spirit Unity

The view that both Humanistic Psychotherapy, and most Body Psychotherapists, have long held—that body, mind, and spirit are a unity—is increasingly becoming substantiated by neurobiological findings. The traditional (Descartian) body-mind split is now no longer tenable from the perspective of the natural sciences. Not only the neocortex, but, in particular, some of the inner circuits among the brainstem, midbrain, basal nuclei, thalamus, and the limbic system (probably with contributions from nerve cells in the intestine, the so-called "gut-brain"), and also neurotransmitter substances that are found, not only in the brain, but throughout the body and in the blood, together determine the consciousness that is generated in the associative areas of the neocortex, along with behavior, perception, emotions, cognition, and experience. The previous separation between organically based and mentally conditioned suffering essentially no longer exists and cannot be substantiated.

## The Experience of the World as a Constructed Reality

Every individual regularly reconstructs their experience of the world on the basis of a great number of signals (electrical and chemical, possibly in connection with quantum physical phenomena). The outer realities, and the person's inner reality, are two totally different systems, with significant differences in essence and quality. The physical and chemical properties of the outer reality, and the processes of the brain utilizing both the inner and outer experiences, are fundamentally different, in both the physical and the chemical sense, just as the external physical and concrete reality, when captured by a camera, is translated into digital "pixels" that can then be "processed" and even "altered."

Chemical and physical signals that are already transformed by the sense organs are "constructed" by the brain into a subjective reality, which many people naively believe to be "real." However, that phenomenological reality doesn't exist outside in the environment, but instead is generated in a multilevel process of transformation and interpretation *within* the organism. Even perceptions—just like memories—are in no way equal to an objective reality: perception can't happen without the body and brain, and further necessitates interaction of these with the exterior and interior environment. Perceptual schemas are acquired and built up in the early learning environment. At the same time, a unity of perception and action has now been demonstrated to operate on a neural level (Roth, 2001). The importance of the fact that experienced reality and perception are continuously and unconsciously constructed can hardly be overstated. The range of possibilities that Body Psychotherapy can draw upon in attending to different states can enable clients to gain a more direct experience of their unconscious processes of reality construction. As clients notice these phenomena, they can take a more active and conscious part in this process, and their mood and self-image change.

## Brain Development and Neuroplasticity

As a living system, the brain needs to, and has the ability to, continuously adapt to its environment. The social environment especially plays a very significant role in structuring the brain. Although the essential network of brain cells is originally determined by genetics, its further developmental processes develop in a highly individualized fashion that is almost totally dependent on growth experiences. Genetic factors have their biggest influence perhaps only in the very earliest stages of brain development. As we grow up, the experiences that are encountered in respective environments play the most important role. The infant's brain is still developing and growing, and our early (and then also later) experiences definitely "shape" the brain. Although the adult brain is less plastic, early experiences—and structures—that are well "laid down" or "built into" our brains can also be changed or reversed later in life, as there is an ongoing development of organic linkages in the brain, and even the creation of new neurons out of neuronal stem cells remains a possibility throughout life (Gage, 2000). With advanced age, the so-called "neuroplasticity" then decreases, but still exists to a degree.

The experiences of the infant and toddler are stored in different centers of the associative neocortex and limbic system in what Damasio calls "dispositional representations" (Damasio and Kober, 1999, pp. 151ff.). Naturally, these dispositional representations also need to be understood as dynamic and environmentally co determined patterns. In this regard, psychoanalysis speaks of self- and object-representations. Daniel Stern (1998) refers to the same idea when he speaks of "implicit relational knowledge." This knowledge contains the early impressions that the child has of him- or herself and his or her early caretakers (objects), along with associated affective tones and perceptions that result in the variety of worldviews that can emerge from the whole of a particular experience.

Future research will need to clarify how these affective tones are also associated with, and stored by, the distribution of neurotransmitters and hormones in the blood, and tension states in the muscles and tissues of the body and the intestine. Candace Pert (1997, 1999), for example, has shown how receptors for neuropeptides can be found not just in the brain but also throughout the whole body.

It is clear that the brain develops in an intersubjective field. From this field, dynamic *internal models of realities* emerge that are closely linked with respective bodily conditions. The biographical sediments, with their organic residue, can be thought of as a form of "software," carrying the possibility of being reprogrammed. This potential of the organic structure of the brain for change is called "neuroplasticity," which forms one of the most essential concepts of neurobiology. Although in the past it was assumed that the potential of the neurons and brain metabolism to adapt and change was unlikely, there are now numerous and definite indications to the contrary (Damasio, 1996). It could therefore be said that the brain is like a lifelong construction site. Throughout the course of our lives, neurons form new linkages on the basis of respective experiences with the environment and how they are used: this is a process of "reinforcement." The neurobiologist Joachim Bauer (2002) describes how both positive and negative experiences can lead even to the so-called "expression" or "suppression" of genetic potentials. During our lifetime, it is believed that we draw on only 20 percent of our genetic potential. It is conceivable that, with greater consciousness, we could come to express more of this potential in the future.

The prefrontal cortex is usually viewed as the seat of consciousness and ego functions. It lies beside the anterior cingulate cortex, which is also the center regulating processes of attention, working memory, and self-regulation. The hippocampus in the temporal lobe organizes the storage and retrieval of memories. Because the fastest changes in the neural network occur in these areas, quick changes (that are effected through psychotherapy) are likely to be correlated with changes in these areas. The role and the importance of the prefrontal cortex and of the anterior cingulate cortex have been repeatedly confirmed (LeDoux, 2003; Roth, 2009). Similar neuroplastic potentials also appear to exist in the hippocampus.

In the neuroplastic process, the strength of the neural connections (synapses) changes with usage. Whereas the synchronicity of excitation of neurons and their connections strengthens the corresponding neural cell assemblies, along with their connections, the neural connections that are not used tend to lose synapses and may ultimately disassemble altogether in a process called "pruning." The survival of neurons, and the quality of their synaptic connections, is dependent on regular excitation ("Neurons that fire together, wire together") (Siegel, 2000; LeDoux, 2003).

Recurring stimulation and the synchronicity of experiences lead to a strengthened connection among cell assemblies, which corresponds with the basic tenets of learning. Recurrent stimulations from experience lead to increasingly focused and differentiated responses (Spitzer, 2000). In the end, we can think of the brain and its neural connections by using the motto of Hebb's Axiom: "Use it or lose it!"

The significance of this discovery cannot be underestimated. Hüther (2003) discusses how we can limit our potentials if we use our brains one-sidedly. This causes increasingly inflexible routines and automatisms. In particular, our body image, our self-image, and our sense of self are in need of continuous validation through our senses, and through an uninterrupted stream of up-to-date sensory information (Ramachandran, 2001). Experiments with sensory deprivation prove this point. Using simple experiments, Ramachandran was able to show how the body image can change within minutes in response to deceptively altered touch (Ibid.). The body image is continuously being re-created. Psychic structure is much more dynamic and dependent on bodily states and interactions than previously suggested by the comparably static psychoanalytic term of "structure."

There is a lifelong process by which we can learn and modify the structure of our brain (see Damasio, 2001; Hüther, 2001; LeDoux, 1996, 2001; Merzenich et al., 1990; Roth, 1997, 1999, 2001; Spitzer, 2000, 2001, 2002). It seems probable that, with many patterns of experience and skill, it will be similar to the acquisition of language: learning one's native language during childhood is relatively effortless. But later, even into old age, we still retain the ability to learn new languages, including phonemes, but it takes more effort. Roth (2001) summarizes: ". . . early childhood influences and experiences are of particular importance in shaping our character and building a frame through which we process later experiences. The later the influence, the stronger it needs to be in order to produce sustainable effects."

## Memory and Recollection

Memory and learned patterns fundamentally organize our experience and behavior from moment to moment, as well as throughout our lives. Psychotherapy always touches upon these associated memory patterns, be it consciously or unconsciously. The German title of one of Daniel Schacter's books (1997, 2001) fittingly reads, *Wir sind Erinnerung* [We Are Memory]. Every significant experience that the infant and toddler has is stored somehow in its neural networks—specifically, in a variety of sensory maps that serve for multiple and parallel storage. Given certain experiences at a later age, earlier memories are often recalled and simultaneously reinforced and/or changed at the same time (Nader et al., 2000; Loftus, 2001). Every current experience therefore is, albeit unconsciously, highly conditioned by memories.

Today's predominant view of the brain is still heavily influenced by Aristotle's metaphor for memory. Aristotle had compared the process of memory storage with writing on an originally blank tablet of wax. Today, we know that external (including not consciously accessible, but so-called subliminal) stimuli evoke the brain to search its established neural networks for similar memories, or biographic-contextual patterns (structural analogies). Current experience and behavior are determined by these spontaneously recalled patterns. Memory is always a creative and dynamic, reconstructive and intersubjective, set of processes.

Drawing upon the research of Daniel Schacter, we can differentiate two fundamentally different forms of memory. Memory, as it is commonly thought of, is the equivalent of the so-called "explicit," "declarative," or "conceptual" memory. This form of memory includes words as well as images. Explicit memories are easily recalled. For activation of such a memory, only one aspect of the respective memory content is needed. This form of memory is often used in the "normal" psychotherapeutic process: by associations, by free association, by prompting and interpretations, and by guesswork (often based on experience). So-called autobiographical memory works similarly. Its content can be verbally communicated. Explicit memories are predominantly stored in the prefrontal cortex.

Then there is the "implicit," "procedural," or "perceptual" memory (see also Kandel, 1995, p. 672). Although implicit memory is much more extensive than explicit memory, and it has a much stronger impact on our current experience and behavior, it is not directly consciously accessible. Implicit memory can be thought of as the "substratum of the unconscious." As such, it contains contents that are crucial to the psychotherapeutic process. This memory system is not as easily accessible through conscious, attentional processes. It does not contain linguistic or image contents, but instead is structured by sensory and motor memories (Schacter, 2001, p. 92). It can be thought of as an affective-sensory-motor unit that is inseparably connected with the body. Implicit memories are stored predominantly in the limbic system, rather than the prefrontal cortex, and (as such) are "subconscious." Traumatic memories, in particular, are stored in these forms of implicit memory. Such memories—and the attendant fear and anger—are associated with patterns of excitation in a particularly important part of the limbic system—namely, the amygdala. The amygdala plays a central role in the emotional appraisal of events. Additionally, the amygdala plays an important role in learning processes that link reward and punishment with respective events.

Sigmund Freud, in his letters to Wilhelm Fliess, described how memories can be changed. Just as any experience is shaped by memory, any experience can also lead to the retrieval of memories. Psychotherapy, but also any other significant encounter, can change such memories. In any form of psychotherapy that aims for personality change, the conscious involvement of memories is therefore almost inevitable. Psychotherapy can effect a progressively focused reorganization and expansion of memory, conditioned by more recent (psychotherapeutic) experiences.

Body Psychotherapy is very conducive to gaining access to implicit memories, and therefore to the subconscious, and even sometimes to the unconscious. Using such an approach, implicit, bodily oriented, and limbic-system-based traumatic memories in particular can be more easily actualized, brought into consciousness, and then linked with different words and associations, understood in their historical context, and then extended with new salutary reembodied experiences. Novel experiences that are holistic and include bodily experience can thus potentially clear traumatic memories, rewriting the traumatic "program" (van der Kolk et al., 2000; Ogden et al., 2006). In any case, they can offer a positive exploration and differential expansion of the traumatic memory patterns and the underlying neural networks. The "demasking" (an expression of Bach-y-Rita) of older neuronal networks, and the recourse to potentials that had been established prior to traumatizing, or to new potentials, also plays a very important role here (Hüther, personal communication, 2002).

## State-Dependent Memory and Learning

Bower (1981) noted that, when a significant mood was evoked in test subjects, this led to the expansion of their explicit memory of emotional events. For example, there seems to be a unanimous agreement that, in a happy mood, it is easier to recall events that were previously experienced in this mood, whereas, in a depressed mood, it is easier to recall different instances in which one felt depressed. Memory contents are linked with the sensory impressions from the respective sense organs that originally contributed to the basic experience. Memory recall, then, is facilitated through renewed stimulation of such sensory impressions.

The neurobiologist LeDoux now proposes that the probability of memory recall increases as the number of cues that are present during the memory recall approaches that of the original learning event (2001, p. 228).

Accordingly, Body Psychotherapeutic techniques offer a progressively focused recall of memories, through conscious interactive stimulation of respective sense impressions or movements. On the basis of his extensive literature review of the neurobiological research findings, the psychotherapy researcher and cognitive behavioral therapist Klaus Grawe (2000) supports the notion that emotionally significant memories are most directly and effectively recalled when sensory and motor aspects are drawn upon and when earlier contexts are represented. He finds that memory recall is far less effective through words and concepts, and that the change process happens only with what can be holistically recalled, and with what can be linked with other resources and memories. Existing cell assemblies thereby might be integrated into more complex and higher-order schemas. The mere recall of old memory patterns, on the other hand, would merely strengthen these patterns, which could even lead toward retraumatization. The discrepancy between the former, problematic contents of the implicit memory system and a corrective emotional experience could then be viewed as meaningful learning. In either case, such a process goes hand in hand with organic changes in the brain, which include genetic expression.

## Learning and the Expansion of Memory

Psychotherapy can therefore be viewed as an expansion or modification of existing, neurally anchored patterns. It can further be said that corrective emotional experiences (in the sense of Alexander and French, 1946, 1980) promote learning, which expands memory and therefore experience and behavior. In this context, here is a brief list of some of the central, neuroscientific findings on learning. Learning is facilitated under the following conditions:

- The right blend of familiarity and novelty, the absence of which inhibits learning
- Presentation of an issue that invites the use of many different sense modalities
- Simultaneous support through positive emotions and rewards
- Stronger emotions and sensory intensity that lead to stronger memory storage
- An adequate level of challenge and simultaneous avoidance of sensory overstimulation
- A sufficient level of repetition

Body Psychotherapy can easily take these conditions into consideration. Old, well-worn patterns are examined and then expanded upon with novel experiences, which can be enriched by drawing upon all the present-day senses and their qualities, affects, and movement. The subsequent anchorage of new experiences is equivalent to the level of storage of the expanded memory in multiple sensory and motor maps (a little like the redrawing or updating of the maps of a country with new developments, new highways, expansion of cities and airports, etc.).

## Here and Now

Neurobiologists emphasize the significance of the "present moment" as the only window of opportunity in which to effect real change (for example, see Pöppel, 2000; Henningsen, 2000). As Body Psychotherapy facilitates the realization of memories in the present, it can be thought of as supporting the re-presentation, and re-minding, of the past. Memories are significantly affected by the context in which they are recalled. Every recalled memory is re-stored in a more or less changed fashion (Nader et al., 2000; Loftus, 2001). In the present, we constantly construct a subjective reality. With the help of suitable forms of attention, we can gain awareness of this process and then learn to become increasingly conscious and effective in co-creating this reality with new, embodied experiences.

Therefore, and possibly beginning with Fritz Perls (1973), awareness of present-time experience and its structure (rather than recollection of the past) stands at the center of the modern Body Psychotherapeutic endeavor.

Contemporary Body Psychotherapy supports the intentional expansion of awareness, both of the "now" and of the "old story," as it is embedded in the present-time experience of the self and the environment. Over time, this leads to an increasing differentiation of present circumstances from the background of the past, and from the subjectively experienced reality of the present. Awakening from the "trance" of memory thus leads to conscious disidentification from early neurotic patterns.

## Perception, Consciousness, and Attention

Consciousness also arises when the brain is confronted with cognitive or motor tasks for which it has not yet established appropriate neural networks. Furthermore, consciousness arises when what is happening within the body or the environment is sufficiently interesting: the brain needs alertness, consciousness, and attention, particularly for problem solving and new learning. Alertness increases as the reticular formation in the brainstem is stimulated (LeDoux, 2003); all new sensory impressions and movements can offer such stimulation. This is an important mechanism that can be utilized in the context of Body Psychotherapy.

Without this sort of attention, our functioning lacks flexibility. We become entrapped by learned automatic and rigid patterns that are represented in the brain, as mentioned above, as having become habitual and unconscious. Attention leads to an excitation of neural cell assemblies in the respective parts of the brain that are associated with focusing attention, to a synchronicity of brain waves in these regions of the brain, and to an interconnected neuronal network of excitation (Spitzer, 2001, p. 156; Singer, 2004). Attention is linked significantly with increased activity in the orbitofrontal cortex and the anterior cingulate cortex, areas that support the functions of the ego and working memory. Excitation of these areas is a fundamental precondition for influencing the process of change and for learning new patterns, as Ahissar and colleagues (1992) have been able to show in impressive experiments with monkeys (see also LeDoux, 2003). Without attention to the stimuli of learning, no change in cortical representation occurred (see also Spitzer, 2001, p. 159; Jenkins et al., 1990).

The activation of cell assemblies associated with a specific learning task then is a precondition for change. Attention also serves to decrease the activity of inhibitory neurons, which thus leads to an increase in activation. The bodily oriented mental state of "mindfulness" in psychotherapy therefore supports such activation and provides a condition conducive to change. It strengthens the working memory and the influence of the prefrontal lobe and anterior cingulate cortex on deeper parts of the brain and opens the door to "implicit memories" that can help to restructure our personality.

In relation to external stimuli, the brain utilizes two sets of criteria to determine if attention and consciousness will be activated: Is the event known or unknown, important or unimportant? Is it interesting or uninteresting? These criteria also are important in maintaining a stable and meaningful perception. At the same time, a level of familiarity is important as well. A certain challenge and optimal stress level are seen as conducive to learning. Sufficient motivation and stimulation are helpful (for example, see Roth, 1997, pp. 180ff.).

On the basis of neurobiological findings, attention, by which we mean the attentive experiencing of the present, must be seen as a very central element of change. Just learning to be "mindful" by itself strengthens the reflective ego functions. Various approaches of Body Psychotherapy take these attentional processes into account in different ways. Many Body Psychotherapy approaches have been influenced by the theories and methods of Humanistic Psychology and Gestalt Therapy in particular. "Awareness," as emphasized by Gestalt Therapy; also particularly the state of "mindfulness," as developed by Ron Kurtz; and the "pilot function," as described by Al Pesso—all are examples of working with attentional processes.

In 1985, Jon Kabat-Zinn and colleagues (1985), working from a cognitive behavioral perspective, were able to show that eight weeks of mindfulness training in itself could lead to significant improvements in all sorts of psychosomatic illnesses. *This state of increased attention or mindfulness is a "whole body" state, not just a "mental" state.* It seems very possible that other Body Psychotherapy techniques might only gain their full effectiveness when used with degrees of mindfulness.

In a mindful state, new experiences lead to a transformation of experience and behavior. As an aside, regressive processes remain containable through the use of mindfulness, helping clients to feel safe within themselves. Strengthening the connection between the "felt" experience and the "speaking about" experience facilitates a distance from the regressive experience that is neither too immersed nor dissociative. Speaking about the inner experience while in a state of mindfulness is an opportunity that is particularly cultivated in the Hakomi Method, and allows the therapists to share in the inner processes of their clients. In this way, affects and emotions arising from the limbic system can be identified and linked with the speech areas and the brainstem. Psychodynamically, this increases the probability that previously implicit or procedural memories can be consciously experienced, then be stored as explicit memories.

An important additional point: A confrontation with too many simultaneous stimuli, or stimuli occurring in rapid succession, in the same area of the brain, potentially has a negative effect. It can create the chaotic input quoted by Spitzer (2000, p. 219). That's why it is advisable not only to support the increased awareness of psychotherapeutic processes but also to slow them down, in order to reduce the level of arousal and allow for their proper integration into a "mindful" presence (Ogden et al., 2006). This allows a clearer perception of effective factors and facilitates a more efficient integration of the experience.

Michael Posner also describes different neurobiological modules of "attentional networks" (Posner and Raichle, 1996). For example, the superior colliculus in the midbrain seems to make it easier to shift focus from one thing to the next. It is likely that, in EMDR (Eye Movement Desensitization and Reprocessing), the ongoing alternation between directions of view seems to activate the superior colliculus, helping the person to shift attention and thus loosen established traumatic patterns.

Alternatively, it seems that the pulvinar in the midbrain is more associated with the ability to sustain attention. Crick (1994) emphasizes the role of the nucleus reticularis thalami in directing attention, rather like a spotlight working in conjunction with the cortex. The prefrontal cortex, for example, in conjunction with the anterior cingulate cortex, generates controlled and focused attention. The anterior aspect of the cingulate additionally makes important contributions in the emotional appraisal of the contents of attention (see Roth, 2001; Etkin et al., 2005).

Neurobiology thereby gives indications for an increasingly differentiated manner of guiding attention and consciousness processes. Currently, this effort is reflected in Body Psychotherapy practice, particularly in the Hakomi Method.

It is likely that the work with attentional processes will become increasingly refined in the future. The different possibilities for influencing attention that are provided by the different modules of attentional networks in the brain (for example, the ability to focus the attentional "spotlight") appear to be accessible to conscious guidance and to be available for training. Neurobiological research will most likely shed increasing light on these clinical possibilities. Similar and respective processes of both increased awareness (consciousness) and attention are also described by the psychoanalyst and neurobiologist Beutel (2008), when he emphasizes that psychotherapeutic processes should be conducted with mutual "insightfulness."

## Emotion, Affect, and Feeling: Foundations

Emotions and feelings are particularly easy to access in Body Psychotherapy. For this reason, the following points are of special interest in this context. Among others, Izard (1991, 1992), Damasio (2001), and LeDoux (1996, 2001) have all done important research on emotions and feelings; recent studies also include those by Niedenthal and colleagues (2005).

The qualities of our experience, our perceptions, our behavior, and in particular our thinking, our memories, our volition, and the choices we make are critically informed by our emotions. As mentioned previously, people seem to be changed less through just cognitional changes, talking, or even insights, but more so through different emotional experiences. Additionally, the emotional condition is significantly correlated with general health and the condition of the immune system. Damasio views this as the unconscious and primary foundation of experience. Nonetheless, emotional signs can be externally perceived by others ("e-motion"); and in the focused perceptual training of Body Psychotherapists, this skill can be practiced in highly differentiated ways—for example, in Al Pesso's MicroTracking (Pesso and Perquin, 2008). In contrast to emotions, Damasio defines feelings as those emotions that are experienced within, and that we become conscious of.

This differentiation also seems quite useful from a Body Psychotherapeutic perspective. Accordingly, what others call "affects" are closest to Damasio's understanding of emotions. They provide an orientation to the highly complex interrelations between the world and subjective reality. The emotional content of information is an essential determinant in decision-making processes. Emotions further serve to differentiate between relevant and irrelevant stimuli.

Affects, emotions, and feelings in turn are indivisibly integrated with the body, in particular with mimic and posture (again, see Niedenthal et al., 2005). Carroll Izard's 1991 description captures the essence of the reciprocal feedback between these different systems. Damasio terms the affective reactions of the body that are triggered by internal or external stimulation as "somatic markers" (Damasio and Kober, 1999, pp. 168ff.). They are the end products of signals from various receptors in the organs or joints and of complex control circuits. Hormones from the reward system and the stress system, the sexual system (testosterone and estrogen), the thyroid, and numerous neuropeptides (see also Pert, 1997) make further contributions to the shaping of experiences and their processing in the prefrontal cortex and the anterior cingulate cortex.

Neurobiology confirms that any sort of psychotherapeutic work that does not take people's "somatic markers" and emotions into account is rather questionable. As Body Psychotherapists, we can draw on a long history of clinical experience about how to recall and utilize this kind of experience and emotions in a focused fashion, and how the general emotional mood can be influenced in a variety of ways.

Seeing the body, the affects, and the emotions as all intimately interrelated, and as playing such a central role in conditioning our experience, gives us the obvious possibility to contact all the person's affective, sensory, and motor channels for the expansion of their emotional experience in a number of increasingly differentiated ways.

Affects, for example, are always embodied. They are composed of physiological aspects, but also of emotions and impulses. Such impulses can come into consciousness more easily when they are brought into awareness in an embodied therapeutic relationship; then possible actions can be implemented through a state of mindfulness. Generally, it can be said that abiding mindfully with sensations and affects leads to contact with the emotions and opens up their context in the present. This leads to the rise of feelings, and, as these feelings come into consciousness, they quite naturally lead to underlying associated memories and childhood emotional states, which then can be worked with in a psychotherapeutic or healing fashion.

## Conscious Formation of Emotions: Correlations with the Body

Initially, vague affects and emotions, as well as unclear fragments of memory, can be intensified, not only by means of mindfulness, but also through interventions that are energizing—for example, through the utilization of breath and voice interventions. The focused observation and articulation of breathing and voice, as well as the modulation of the tonus in the voluntary and involuntary muscles, are common practice in all schools of Body Psychotherapy that go back to Wilhelm Reich.

Neurobiology is now doing research on a wide range of reciprocal relationships between bodily states, affects, feelings, and ideas. Antonio Damasio (Damasio and Kober, 1999, p. 204) referred to the well-known studies by Ekman and Friesen (1974). They had instructed normal test subjects to move their facial muscles in a particular way. The subjects didn't know that, in doing so, the researchers "constructed" an emotional expression. A happy facial expression, for example, led subjects to feel happy; an angry expression led to an experience of anger. Izard also noted these correlations (Izard, 1991). Damasio goes on to illustrate that our ideas also can generate particular experiences that are otherwise created by real bodily states (Damasio and Kober, 1999, pp. 204ff.). He terms this way of generating experiences as offline and top-down, as opposed to most experiences, which are generated through direct stimulation of the body (online and bottom-up). Ramachandran (2001) noted that laughter leads to relaxation, a correlation that recently has come to be utilized in so-called laughter seminars. Rüegg (2001) noted that a strong voluntary or involuntary contraction of the arm musculature during strong grasps (for example, when activating the brakes of a bicycle or clenching fists) leads to a marked activation of the sympathetic nervous system and the release of noradrenaline. Rüegg goes on to report that the Danish researchers Vissing and Hjortso (1996) found that this activation occurs even when strong grasps are merely intended or imagined in thoughts. Recently, it was reconfirmed how even a sustained holding of a pen between one's lips or teeth can influence the emotional state (Glenberg et al., 2005; Niedenthal, 2005).

For a long time, Body Psychotherapists have been utilizing the analogous relationships between bodily reactions on the one hand, and affects, feelings, and ideas on the other: helping their clients to change gestures, postures, and tension patterns of voluntary and involuntary muscles, or the state of tissues and joints, breath, and vocal expression when one wishes intentionally to modulate the emotional state. To bare one's teeth and push the lower jaw forward (a Bioenergetic exercise), for example, can facilitate contact with one's unexpressed anger and rage.

"Centering," "grounding," vertical alignment, and breathing techniques from martial arts, using the breath energy *chi*, or *ki*, can also work as well to change the basic mood, overcome fear, gain a sense of strength and peace, and increase one's sense of safety in the world. Body-Oriented Psychotherapy techniques with individuals include ways such as these to deepen the felt sense and good feelings about oneself: different kinds of body contact; certain touch techniques that trigger an increased release of oxytocin; the careful handling of emotional states; the restructuring of bodily gestures; the differentiated use of voice; conscious modification of muscle tone; the informed handling of ideas; and the conscious modification of spatial experience—all of which cannot be described in detail within the scope of this chapter. This also applies to the anchoring of new experiences and behavioral possibilities via the use of different sense modalities.

Considering the potency of strong emotions to effect neuroplastic changes in the brain, Body Psychotherapists should ask themselves a critical question: Does a too-frequent or undifferentiated provocation of aggressive or painful feelings, as well as unreflective regressive body-work, lead to a phenomenon known as "kindling," which is an inappropriate facilitation of such predominantly reactive feelings? Kindling is generated by intensive, recurrent stimulations similar to those stimulants that help to cause epileptic seizures (Dennison and Teskey, 1995). For this reason, any therapy, but especially body-oriented therapies, should make every effort to avoid unnecessary repetitions of extreme emotional states triggered by chronic failures, despair, or past traumas. The intentional recall of traumatic material is useful only when a new healing experience can be offered in its place; otherwise, this recall can lead to a consolidation of established patterns of trauma and distress and no new expansion of their affected neural pathways (van der Kolk et al., 2000; Ogden et al., 2006). More is written about this in Chapter 57, "Risks within Body Psychotherapy" by Courtenay Young; and about working with people in trauma in Chapter 76, "Sensory-Motor Processing for Trauma Recovery" by Pat Ogden and Kekuni Minton.

## The Gut-Brain

The role of the so-called "gut-brain" receives some more explicit attention in its relationship to our fundamental sense of aliveness, affects, and emotions. The "gut-brain" is an aspect of the parasympathetic nervous system and is connected to the (main) brain, via the vagus nerve. It is also sometimes referred to as the "enteric nervous system." According to Schore (2003), William James, Wenger, and Gasanov all emphasized the role of sensations from the intestines as significant in the creation of emotions, as early as 1922.

The enteric nervous system comprises more than a hundred million neurons—which makes it more extensive than the spinal cord, but only one-tenth the size of the main brain—all embedded in the lining of the gastrointestinal system. Ninety percent of its neural connection with the brain is composed of afferent fibers (leading to the brain), and only 10 percent of efferent fibers (leading from the brain to the intestines), but it also has numerous sets of interneurons, all of which makes it capable of carrying reflexes and acting as an integrating center in the absence of any input from the central nervous system.

The enteric nervous system basically regulates gastro-intestinal motility and digestion, and is also assumed to provide essential messages for the immune system. It synthesizes 90 percent of the neurotransmitter serotonin and utilizes more than thirty neurotransmitters, most of which are identical to those found in the central nervous system. Via the vagus nerve, the brain is updated not only on the situation within the intestines, but also on the state of other organs and the immune system.

Rüegg (2001) refers to this system as our "sixth sense," colloquially known as "gut feelings." It is assumed that information from the enteric nervous system, in the form of somatic markers, plays a constitutive role in the formation of our moods. Following this rationale, stimulation of the vagus nerve, as a treatment intervention for patients with particular kinds of depression, has recently found acceptance within the standard medical practice community. Before this, forms of touch linked to the abdominal organs have been used as a treatment approach in the context of Body Psychotherapy. Gerda Boyesen's "Biodynamic Psychotherapy" approach is particularly focused on working with the enteric nervous system; on forms of massage that help affect the enteric nervous system; and also on the concept of the "digestion of emotions" as a day-to-day emotional regulator (Boyesen and Boyesen, 1980).

## Rating Systems: Reward System and Stress System

The emotional system and the related rating systems are of great importance for our existence in this world. The brain needs to decide, from moment to moment, which tasks are to be addressed at any particular moment in time. This is determined by memory, as well as by the limbic system's emotional appraisal of the situation. Bauer (2006a) speaks about different types of motivation. The emotional rating also determines what is saved in the memory. Roth states, "In the end the rating systems are dependent upon the action in the sensoric and motoric centres, and *in toto* from the complete history of the brain, in which these cyclic connections between perception, rating, memorization, attention, realization and behavior happened numerous times" (Roth, 1997, p. 241). Successful psychotherapy should be able to influence these rating systems and thereby the person's motivation.

### Reward System

Sufficient motivation is fundamental to facilitate any new experience or behavior. It results from positive experiences, which cause a stimulation of the so-called "reward" system. This is located in the midbrain. Essential parts are the ventral tegmental area, the ventral striatum, and the nucleus accumbens. Central messenger substances of this system are dopamine, endogenous opiates (such as encephalins and endorphins), as well as oxytocin, vasopressin, and (in the male) adiuretin. The reward system is connected with many other brain regions, especially with the emotional centers and the prefrontal cortex. It decides whether the environment presents "targets" for which it is rewarding to mobilize. In principle, the activation of the reward system causes well-being and a readiness to concentrate and to act.

There is a pronounced effect on the activation of certain genes and on pain sensitivity, and the reward system also strengthens the immune system: "Motivation systems turn off if there is no chance of social benefit and they turn on in the contrary case, i.e. if there is appreciation and love" (Bauer, 2006a, p. 35).

The transmitting agent oxytocin is of special importance, as it has a cause and effect of binding powerful relationship experiences. Most forms of friendly interaction cause its release, especially caresses or tender massages, stimulation of the erogenous zones, and during orgasm; but also even when persons are encountered from whom the respective tenderness might be expected or wished for (Ibid., p. 49). Oxytocin, and the endogenous opiates, reduce stress and fear by calming the stress and fear center of the amygdala and of the upper emotional center of the anterior cingulate cortex (Bauer, 2006a). The reward system was discovered almost by accident by the Canadian scientist James Olds (1995) in 1954.

In experiments with rats, he had stimulated a part of the hypothalamus with an electrode; this obviously caused pleasure in the rats. In another experiment, the rats could give themselves an electric impulse of the electrode located in their hypothalamus with a lever. The rats were obviously so fascinated by the effect of this stimulation that they used the lever more and more often to stimulate themselves. Finally, they even forgot to eat and drink. This process can be looked upon as equivalent to a dependence or an addiction. In 2001, John Reynolds showed that, some minutes after use of the lever, the synaptic strength between neurons in the midbrain had become altered. From these experiments we can recognize how effective stimulation of the reward system seems to be.

In this context, studies in monkeys are also of interest, in which higher-ranking monkeys showed a higher dopamine level and were also less at risk to become cocaine dependent. Bauer emphasizes that the base of all motivation is to find and to give interhuman acknowledgment, appraisal, attention, or affection. From the neurobiological point of view, we are creatures in search of social resonance and cooperation (Bauer, 2006a).

Thomas Insel therefore created the term "social brain" in 2004. Hence, we should strive for the inclusion of the reward system in therapy at any moment and ask ourselves: "How can we support our patients in well-being and acting more efficiently, and how can we create the respective experiences together?" "What strengthens their immune system and helps them to get healthy again?" "At the same time the question is important: What concerns the patient emotionally?" "What impulses are necessary to motivate and prepare them for a change?"

Holistic, embodied, and positive new experiences within therapy seem to contribute directly to the individual's well-being and motivation. Such experiences lead some patients, perhaps for the first time, to the awareness of how a particular behavior or a contact can make reward a possibility. Contact itself is motivating for most people, physical contact probably much more so.

**The Stress or Fear System**

The stress or fear system works to a certain degree contrarily to the reward system. This large cybernetic system comprises the amygdala, the hypothalamus, and aspects of the brainstem, as well as the pituitary and the suprarenal or adrenal glands. Stress leads to an activation of the noradrenergic and dopaminergic systems, through the release of noradrenaline, dopamine, corticotropin-releasing factor, and cortisol.

This release in the sympathetic branch of the autonomous nervous system results in several distinct cardiovascular, gastrointestinal, renal, and endocrine changes as the whole body adapts, almost instantaneously, to being able to implement the "fight or flight" behaviors. This is mentioned in other parts of this chapter, and in other chapters. What I would like to focus on here are the more positive aspects of stress.

Hüther (1997, 2001, 2003) noted that some level of stress is both necessary and sufficient to effect an optimal level of activation of the brain. A meaningful level of healthy stress, or "eu-stress," is dependent on the respective individual's appraisal of a situation, seeing the situation not as distressful but more as a potential for success, fulfillment, exploration, or development. This kind of eu-stress, with its respective hormonal side effects, can be generated in psychotherapy through techniques such as helping the client change by a "skillful frustration" (as it is commonly known in Gestalt Therapy) of the person's games, familiar distress patterns, or their "aliveness-avoiding" techniques. This helps the person to find benefits within a so-called stressful situation.

When a stimulus causing stress cannot be met with a new coping strategy, anger, helplessness, fear, or sadness can ensue. Overwhelming stress of this sort leads to a massive release of cortisol. Perception is narrowed, and the possibility of any creative openness disappears. However, this can be ameliorated, as Hüther (2003) noted in an experiment in which a monkey, isolated in a cage, was confronted with a dog. The monkey's cortisol level instantaneously increased massively, but when the monkey was in the cage not with a dog but with a friendly monkey, its cortisol level rose very little.

In contrast to such animal experiments, it has been shown that breast-feeding, intimate contact, and even mutual orgasm raise the level of oxytocin, which in turn strengthens the bonding experience and behavior of partners (Uvnäs Moberg, 2003). Besides that, oxytocin appears to be the foundation of monogamous and parental care behaviors. Oxytocin generally increases a sense of well-being. Furthermore, this substance also seems to lead to the noteworthy reciprocal care behaviors in groups of chimpanzees that can be observed after volatile arguments. Afterward, they embrace one another, shake hands, and pet and kiss each other, even on their lips.

Harry Harlow's famous experiments with rhesus monkeys had previously illustrated the significance of touch (Harlow and Harlow, 1962). For therapy, and particularly Body Psychotherapy, this means that adequate and, as far as possible, embodied positive bonding experiences, often using touch, can prevent an unnecessary increase in cortisol levels and the senseless repetitions of stress. Corrective healing experiences that have come to be internalized over the course of therapy should have a similar effect—in particular, if they are repeatedly embodied, as well as being remembered. Such reinforcement would correspond with Damasio's (1996) notion of "top-down" activation of experiences.

Raleigh and colleagues (1991) reported on experiments with monkeys that showed that dominant and submissive behaviors in male animals are determined by experiences of victory and defeat. Among other effects, these experiences determined the concentration of the neuromodulator serotonin in their brains. A higher serotonin level leads to more effective dominance behaviors. A conscious regulation of stress levels in the therapeutic situation can therefore be possible through modulating confrontation with friendly care, or even touch. This was initially the essence of the German "Behandlung" (applying a hand) treatments. In Body Psychotherapy, so-called "grounding," "facing" (instead of confrontation), and even basic practices from the martial arts can provide a better foundation for more sensible dominance behavior, and help produce a respectively higher level of serotonin, while touch and massage in the context of Body Psychotherapy can most probably influence oxytocin metabolism, and thereby the client's sense of well-being. In these ways, neurobiology can give us a better understanding of the mechanisms of the body in therapy.

## Post-Traumatic Stress Disorders

Active control of the stress system is of particular importance in the context of post-traumatic stress disorders. Secondary changes in the control loops between the amygdala, hypothalamus, pituitary gland, and adrenal cortex (HPA axis) play a central role in these disorders that some people experience because of trauma. Traumatized people can have great difficulties verbalizing their traumatic affects. Imaging methods can show that, during activation of implicit traumatic memories, the speech center (Broca's area) is not co-activated through trauma-associated stimuli (van der Kolk et al., 2000). From the side of the frontal lobe, it can be seen that initially it is hardly possible at all to influence the activation of the traumatic emotions mediated by the amygdala. Respective trauma-associated stimuli essentially correlate with fragments of implicit memory. In particular, the fear and anger components of such experiences seem to be mediated by the amygdala.

Imaging methods can show, for example, that visual stimuli that are associated with trauma can activate the amygdala, without activating the cognitive structures of the associative cortex (LeDoux, 1996). Body Psychotherapy seems to be in a particularly suitable position to help to transform implicit and traumatic memories into explicit memories that can then be verbalized so that a degree of conscious control can be exercised.

However, as mentioned, those Body Psychotherapeutic methods that are essentially nonverbal interventions can also be very emotionally evocative. Particularly, in regard to post-traumatic stress disorders, such methods must be used with great care to prevent any "flooding" of traumatic memories and "kindling" or retraumatizing levels of stress activation of the amygdala. Influenced by the insights of research into neurobiology today, we—as Body Psychotherapists—try first to help patients with their post-traumatic stress disorder symptoms in order to help stabilize them in their life, and to train their mindful awareness. Our orientation is toward enabling patients to preserve the connection to the present and to stay in contact, to slow down their traumatic processes, and only then, in connection with all embodied possibilities, intentionally to remember memories with traumatic content, and then to reorganize these to overcome their disability (van der Kolk et al., 2000; Ogden et al., 2006).

## Mirror Neurons

In another neurobiological discovery, in 1996, Rizzolatti and colleagues found neurons in the premotor cortex of monkeys that they came to refer to as "mirror neurons" (Gallese et al., 1996; Rizzolatti et al., 2002). These neurons were activated when other monkeys were observed executing certain movement patterns. The authors proposed that these neurons constitute the neural foundation of learning through imitation, but also affect resonance behaviors and empathy. They view this facility as an "inner repetition" of the behaviors of others. We recognize other individuals and their emotional state by generating somato-sensory representations. We simulate, in our brain, how the other individual might feel in similar states (summary in Bauer, 2006a, 2006b; Gallese, 2003; Adolphs, 2003). This means inevitably that our brain is activated in those parts that are being activated in the person observed. Meanwhile, there are numerous other studies that show that mirror neurons not only exist in the premotor cortex, but that the sensory and affective maps of the brain seem to contain mirror neurons as well. They become activated when sensory or affective experiences, such as disgust, are observed in the environment. Bauer (2002) has offered a good summary of these studies. Although it could be premature to evaluate the significance within psychotherapy and Body Psychotherapy of mirror neurons at this time, they might constitute the neural foundation of general curative factors that become active in every psychotherapeutic encounter with a significantly experienced other.

## Summary of Clinical Implications for Body Psychotherapy

Psychotherapeutic research demonstrates that only up to 15 percent of the results of the overall outcome of psychotherapy depend on the method of treatment. About 30 percent depend on the quality of the therapeutic relationship, 15 percent are effects of stimulated hope (the "placebo effect"), and 40 percent result from individual and specific factors in the life of patients (Asey and Lambert, 2001). We can pick up important hints from neurobiology as to how and why we should focus our complete attention more and more on this 85 percent of effective factors. Therefore, some of the central aspects regarding how neurobiological research findings could find reflection in the practice of psychotherapy and Body Psychotherapy are summarized below.

Neurobiology shows us how our current experience is unconsciously and continuously re-created by correlating new stimulations with past experiences. Body Psychotherapy can inspire patients (or clients) to develop the awareness of their perception and experience in this creative, and initially unconscious, act so that they become increasingly able to attend to and consciously co-create this process.

However, we can now be certain that body, soul, and spirit are always a psycho-social-biological unity, interwoven inseparably with the environment. Humans are a self-organizing, living, so-called "distributive" system with many parallel pathways of signals and distinctive levels, which are always in flux. Affects, emotions, and feelings are an essential element and an expression of this unity. This basis of processes of change still has a long road to go before arriving in the general consciousness. But we are also interested in the consequences for practical psychotherapeutic work.

Manfred Spitzer, a psychiatrist and neurobiologist from Ulm, Germany, emphasizes the relevance of play for learning and growth (Spitzer, 2000). A therapeutic "playing field," devoid of threatening consequences, could offer a space to learn and practice any desired new behaviors. In the practice of Body Psychotherapy, such a playing field should be arranged to have the quality of openness toward creative development in many different forms. To give one example, Al Pesso has always viewed the therapeutic situation as a "possibility sphere" (Turnbull and Collins, 2008; Pesso and Perquin, 2008). Obviously, the possibilities within such a playing field are much more open and plentiful than in the orthodox "talking" cure. The patient can naturally assimilate a scenery of possibilities into the frame of his current worldview, structure, range of experience, behavior, and history. He projects himself, and his worldview, into the scene and then acts accordingly, being able to experience the changes. Aside from individual Body Psychotherapy, Body Psychotherapeutic group therapy presents a particularly rich playing field with many additional figures that can serve to carry a person's projections. Of course, it is possible for the therapist to influence and mold this scenery as well.

In all of this work, it is considered essential that patients participate in the unfolding events with a mental state of self-awareness or *mindfulness*. While they may follow their impulses and act upon them, they are also invited to observe themselves and all their reactions mindfully all the time. All sensory channels can be drawn upon to allow for a fresh perception of the current environment. Particularly with adults, mindful action ("acting in") is often necessary for this kind of perception to gain enough weight to lead to the recognition of hitherto established experiences, especially those imprinted in social contexts according to a dysfunctional model of the world and the self.

Understanding one's background gives better access to the self, part of the implicit relationship knowledge, thus allowing new healing experiences for one's expansion and development. A differentiation of the model of the expanded, or new, reality from the past experiences that shaped the older model can, as a first step, lead to a *disidentification* from the neurotic experience or the now-dysfunctional or inappropriate survival technique. At this point, the patient often gets in touch with his original childhood feelings and related experiences of deprivation and traumatization. Novel experiences can then link themselves meaningfully with the older experiences of deprivation and trauma, and the previously rigid patterning can then start to change.

In therapy, if patients learn to utilize this state of awareness, they will have this ability increasingly available and will be able to participate in life in a more and more aware or "present" manner. They will also be able to distinguish more clearly the neuronally wired implicit knowledge of relationships and the shadows of their past. Thus, they can learn to realize the present better, and recognize the signals of the sensual impressions and their somatic markers, becoming aware of their present-day options and discerning between these two levels. Basically, they learn qualities of consciousness by which they can gradually and increasingly influence what is happening in their day-to-day life.

The quality of a positive relationship with a significant "other" contributes to a large degree toward the success of any psychotherapy, so such a relationship is therefore the foundation of any form of Body Psychotherapy. As mentioned above, the range of someone's possibilities with regards to experience is initially determined by the wiring of their brain. This wiring is determined by a combination of genetic factors, social contexts, past events, and the person's resulting habits that have been practiced up to the present moment. The neurobiological findings about the inevitability of the established neural wiring make certain demands on the therapist to approach the client's experience with an attitude of respectful acceptance. Any ideas about how the client "should" become different (in personality, behavior, etc.), particularly in the beginning phases of therapy, are completely out of place and, most often, stem from the therapist's lack of understanding.

Methods of how to work with the transference and countertransference in differentiated ways, how to discern self- and object-representations, i.e., the patient's models of reality, and how to work with their core beliefs are addressed in other chapters in this handbook. Nonetheless, something needs to be emphasized here in this context: many patients have so few sufficiently positive object-representations that their inner experience is like a desert that doesn't allow for sufficient positive experiences in the present. Just as the child's brain is originally shaped through its experiences in early childhood with its mother, neurobiological healing must take place in the intersubjective field between the patient and the therapist. Fundamental experiences that are missing can then be re-created in concrete and embodied ways. Holistic experiences, which may include bodily encounters with the therapist or—in group settings—with other group members, thicken the so-called "corrective experiences" as described by Alexander and French (1946, 1980). Just as the radiant gaze of the mother, as well as her touch and vocalizations, hold a great significance for the infant, the visual, auditory, and other sensory sense channels continue to have a much stronger effect on the client's experience than mere words. From this perspective, even an empathic "hmm" contains much more nuanced and multidimensional information on how the therapist relates to a client's expression than any long, verbal explanation. Appropriate embodied contact and novel healing experiences support the expansion and internalization of more adequate "dispositional representations" of new and helpful object-experiences, as Damasio says. Established, repetitively used, one-sided, often dysfunctional, coping strategies contain the danger of becoming fixed, in a neurological sense, due to the strengthening of neural connections through repetition.

If encounters with the therapist, or other group members, are offered in such a way that all sense channels, movement, and touch are used simultaneously, so as to make a new experience sufficiently impressive, organic changes in the brain, in the form of neuroplastic processes, can be facilitated; these advance psychological growth in later stages of life, making expansion upon previously stored memories eminently possible for people in therapy. It is therefore my contention that Body Psychotherapy experiences are more likely to assist the patient to develop new neurological pathways, as these are experienced within more sensory and supportive channels than just the verbal and cognitive.

One characteristic of health is the ability to respond flexibly and to regenerate oneself: this is the concept of "resilience" (Antonovski, 1987). By offering a range of new experiences from within a supportive environment, Body Psychotherapy can assist the building of resilience. New models, patterns, and possibilities of how to interact with the environment in less dysfunctional ways can be offered, tried out, and experienced; then a new pattern is laid down.

The recovery of otherwise initially inaccessible "resources" and "novel holistic" experiences that can potentially be recalled obviously comes to the center of the healing process once again, and not only when working with trauma. Additionally, resources, and a wide range of coping strategies that the patients are unfamiliar with, can be offered to them over the course of therapy. Resuscitating existing neuronal patterns of experiencing and behavior (resources) and connecting them to other patterns is easier than generating totally new experiences with these new patterns and their neuronal connections. Therefore, it makes sense to call upon existing resources as frequently as possible, especially those existing prior to traumatization or states of deficiency in the patients. Paul Bach-y-Rita (1990) described this process as "de-masking of fundamental older neuronal stimulation patterns."

This can happen, for example, in mindful bodywork done in a warm-water (95°F) shallow pool, in which patients in the group can feel. According to Gerald Hüther (personal communication, 2008), existing positive experiences from earliest childhood (or even from intrauterine experiences in the amniotic fluid) can be called up from the deeper (more unconscious) areas of the brain and thus become accessible and worked with.

So-called "reconstructive bodywork" (like this kind of work in the water) or grounding, balance, expansion of breath and voice (as in Yoga), or elements from martial arts techniques can be very useful, but space does not allow for their further discussion here. However, the psychoanalyst and neurobiologist Manfred Beutel (2008) believes that changes of implicit procedures are possible by nonverbal communication below the threshold of conscious perception.

When such regenerative additional possibilities are just practiced, but can't seem to be properly experienced, or learned by the patients, the therapist is often faced with the ramifications and implications of an old, probably complex, story. This then indicates that it is necessary both to attend to the present structure of experience "mindfully," and also to explore important old, associated feelings and the historical background so as to enrich the patient within a deeper emotional framework, which can then be worked with to create new healing experiences. This approach could be referred to as "revealing bodywork."

In the unfolding of these old feelings, therapists should probably begin to give more consideration to a particular set of neurobiologically substantiated facts: every experience that has an emotional impact conditions the brain. Any reexperiencing of old suffering or deprivation—without a concomitant restorative or healing experience—can destabilize the patient's present equilibrium and potentially retraumatizes them. The neural connections correlating with these negative experiences are then strengthened further; this is not therapeutic. To recall old pain, and experiences of deprivation and/or trauma, is therefore useful only when therapy can offer the experience of a better "ending" to these old, painful stories.

An actualization of the person's problems, in a mental state of awareness or mindfulness, displays the contemporary structure of the experience and then leads it back into the past experience. This procedure allows for a differentiation of the old story from the new possibilities that are available in the present. In this therapeutic process, the patients should be made to feel as safe as possible. This condition makes it easier for them to relax, which makes access to their emotions and feelings easier, creates a more positive and supportive environment, and—on occasion—even leads to a spontaneous recollection of the original conditions of deficit.

There is also a psycho-biological presumption (or impulse coming from the patient) of "wanting" to heal. There are many different reasons why patients need novel and clearly embodied present-time experiences in which they find that sufficient support is available, and missing experiences are provided in the here and now. Pesso (Pesso and Perquin, 2008) refers to this type of intervention as the "antidote." It seems reasonable to strive toward improvement of the patient's situation from the very beginning of therapy through offers of such positive experiences. At the same time, this might represent an activation of their reward system and an improvement of the state of their immune system (Bauer, 2006b).

Embodied experiences, in a good therapeutic relationship, in connection with all the senses (especially touch) and movement, are direct and intensive. The qualities of these new experiences (and their respective neurobiological connections regarding the possible neuroplastic changes) demonstrate, in a very impressive manner, that patients can have a justified hope for an improvement in their situation. This results in a direct influence on the effects of the therapeutic process (i.e., on the 15 percent placebo effect). This in turn improves the working relationship, even when uncomfortable experiences cannot be avoided.

A sufficient degree of emotional involvement and activation, or challenge and temporary destabilization of the patient, might be considered necessary to allow for new learning to occur (Hüther, 2003). But as patients usually experience a significant level of psychological strain as it is, they commonly do not need an additional challenge from the therapist. Additionally, the reactivation of the old story also generates a lot of stress and distress. In individual cases, the therapist must consider the right mixture of safety and relaxation, as opposed to challenge, on an ongoing basis, as his part of the co-creation of the therapeutic process.

Proper therapy results in increased ego strength. Subsequently, "internalization" allows for improved self-regulation and self-awareness. This leads to a stronger inclusion of and co-regulation from the prefrontal lobe and the anterior cingulate cortex, which is likely to form a stronger connection with the amygdala, the center that regulates traumatic memory.

Old memories can be reexperienced and be changed and expanded with novel and healing elements; the person's memories thus become recategorized. As the reconstruction of the brain needs time and repetition, in the Hakomi Method, we repeatedly invite our patients to remember positive new experiences, in between sessions, as vividly as they can, using gestures and concrete substitute symbols that the patients choose. Clinically, we have the strong impression that the repeated recollection of new experiences strengthens their internalization. This also implies a transformation and a novel synaptic connection of control loops in the brain—for example, in the sensory and motor maps of the parietal and prefrontal cortex.

Given that a stable therapeutic alliance has been properly established, and these safeguards are considered, some of the findings of neurobiology can offer very helpful information about the reframing of experiences for patients. Occasional relapses into older ways of behavior and experience, particularly under stress, are a natural part of the psychotherapeutic process, considering the extent of much more deeply engrained and habitual neural connections. It is good and relieving for both therapists and clients to know that. Here, the image of a deeply worn rut in an age-old paved road, or an old phonograph record that had been scratched, can be helpful. It takes practice, repetition, and time to make—and reinforce—new pathways outside of the old rut.

## Future Prospects

To date, Body Psychotherapeutic methods have not been evaluated neurobiologically. A huge amount of research is evidently called for to examine and clarify some of the Body Psychotherapeutic possibilities, questions, and speculations, as presented in this chapter. In the future, the short- and long-term effects of touch, movement, and gesture, as well as the inclusion of the senses in Body Psychotherapy, are likely to be shown and substantiated in detail through techniques like functional Magnetic Resonance Imaging (fMRI) and other methods. There are very strong indications suggesting that integrative, multimodal treatment models that include psychotherapy, as well as psycho-pharmacological treatment, among other things used when or as necessary, offer the best approach for most chronic disorders. In dealing with such chronic disorders, an integrative understanding of psychotherapy, and Body Psychotherapy, can offer essential and effective help. The value of Body Psychotherapy—and other body therapeutic methods such as Feldenkrais, Rolfing, etc.—in multimodal and integrative treatment models is likely to become increasingly evident. The dialogue between different schools of psychotherapy and Body Psychotherapy can also be enriched by neurobiological understandings. The various different models of healing could (and should) be discussed, and researched, taking neurobiological findings into consideration. Modern psychotherapy and Body Psychotherapy could (and should) become grounded, not only in Depth Psychology, but also in neurobiology. Similarly, these disciplines could benefit from adopting more of a Body Psychotherapy perspective.

## References

Adolphs, R. (2003). Cognitive neuroscience of human social behaviour. *Nature Reviews Neuroscience, 4,* 165–177.

Ahissar, E., Vaadia, E., Ahissar, M., Bergman, H., Arieli, A., & Abeles, M. (1992). Dependence of cortical plasticity on correlated activity of single neurons and on behavioral context. *Science, 257(5075),* 1412–1415.

Alexander, F., & French, T. M. (1946). *Psychoanalytic therapy: Principles and application.* New York: Ronald Press.

Alexander, F., & French, T. M. (1980). *Psychoanalytic therapy: Principles and application.* Lincoln, NE: University of Nebraska Press.

Antonovski, A. (1987). *Unraveling the mystery of health: How people manage stress and stay well.* San Francisco: Jossey-Bass.

Asey, T. P., & Lambert, M. J. (2001). Empirische Ergebnisse für die allen Therapien gemeinsamen Faktoren: Quantitative Ergebnisse [Empirical results for all common factors in therapies: Quantitative results]. In M. A. Hubble, B. L. Duncan, & S. D. Miller (Eds.), *So wirkt Psychotherapie: Empirische Ergebnisse und praktische Folgerungen [How psychotherapy works: Empirical results and practical implications]* (pp. 41–81). Dortmund, Germany: Modernes Leben.

Bach-y-Rita, P. (1990). Brain plasticity as a basis for recovery of function in humans. *Neuropsychologia, 28,* 547–554.

Bauer, J. (2002). *Das Gedächtnis des Körpers: Wie Beziehungen und Lebensstile unsere Gene steuern [The memory of the body: How relationships and lifestyles control our genes].* Frankfurt, Germany: Eichborn.

Bauer, J. (2006a). *Prinzip Menschlichkeit: warum wir von Natur aus kooperieren [Principles of humanity: Why we cooperate naturally].* Hamburg, Germany: Hoffmann & Campe.

Bauer, J. (2006b). *Warum ich fühle was du fühlst? Intuitive Kommunikation und das Geheimnis der Spiegelneurone [Why do I feel what you feel? Intuitive communication and the mystery of mirror neurons].* Hamburg, Germany: Hoffmann & Campe.

Beutel, M. E. (2008). Vom Nutzen der bisherigen neurobiologischen Forschung für die Praxis der Psychotherapie [The benefits of recent neurobiological research to the practice of psychotherapy]. *Psychotherapeutenjournal, 8,* 384–392.

Beutel, M. E., Stern, E., & Silberzweig, D. A. (2003). The emerging dialogue between psychoanalysis and neuroscience. *Neuroimaging Perspectives: Journal of the American Psychoanalytic Association, 51,* 773–801.

Bower, G. H. (1981). Mood and memory. *American Psychologist, 36,* 129–148.

Boyesen, G., & Boyesen, M-L. (1980). *The collected papers of Biodynamic Psychology* (Vols. 1 & 2). London: Biodynamic Psychology Publications.

Brody, A. L., Saxena, S., Schwartz, J. M., et al. (1998). FDG-PET predictors of response to behavioral therapy and pharmacotherapy in obsessive-compulsive disorder. *Psychiatry Research, 84(1),* 1–6.

Cozolino, L. (2003). *The neuroscience of psychotherapy: Building and rebuilding the human brain.* New York: Norton.

Crick, E. (1994). *Wie die Seele wirklich ist [As the soul is real].* Munich, Germany: Artemis & Winkler.

Damasio, A. R. (1996). The somatic marker hypothesis and the possible functions of the prefrontal cortex. *Philosophical Transactions of the Royal Society, B: Biological Sciences, 351,* 1413–1420.

Damasio, A. (2001). *Descartes Irrtum [Descartes' error].* Stuttgart, Germany: Schattauer.

Damasio, A., & Kober, H. (1999). *Ich fühle, also bin ich: Die Entschlüsselung des Bewusstseins [I feel, therefore I am: The decoding of consciousness].* Munich, Germany: List.

Dennison, Z., & Teskey, G. C. (1995). Persistence of kindling: Effect of partial kindling, retention interval, kindling site, and stimulation parameters. *Epilepsy Resume, 21(3),* 171–182.

Ekman, P., & Friesen, W. V. (1974). Detecting deception from the body and face. *Journal of Personality and Social Psychology, 29,* 288–298.

Etkin, A., Phil, M., Pittenger, C., Polan, H. P., & Kandel, E. R. (2005). Toward a neurobiology of psychotherapy: Basic science and clinical applications. *Journal of Neuropsychiatry & Clinical Neurosciences, 17,* 145–158.

Gage, F. (2000). Mammalian neural stem-cells. *Science, 287,* 1433–1438.

Gallese, V. (2003). The roots of empathy: The shared manifold hypothesis and the neural basis of intersubjectivity. *Psychopathology, 36,* 171–180.

Gallese, V., Fadiga, L., Fogassi, L., & Rizzolatti, G. (1996). Action recognition in the premotor cortex. *Brain, 119,* 593–609.

Gazzaniga, M. S. (Ed.). (2000). *The new cognitive neurosciences.* Cambridge, MA: MIT Press.

Glenberg, A. M., Havas, D., Becker, R., & Rinck, M. (2005). Grounding language in bodily states. In R. Zwaan & D. Pecher, *The grounding of cognition: The role of perception and action in memory, language and thinking.* Cambridge, UK: Cambridge University Press.

Gottwald, C. (2008). Körpertherapie auf dem Boden von potenzialentfaltender Gestalttherapie [Grounded Bodytherapy from developmental Gestalt Therapy]. In L. Hartmann-Kottek & U. Strümpfel (Eds.), *Gestalttherapie [Gestalt Therapy]*. Berlin: Springer.

Grawe, K. (2000). *Psychologische Therapie [Psychological therapy]*. Göttingen, Germany: Hogrefe.

Grawe, K. (2004). *Neuropsychotherapie [Neuropsychotherapy]*. Göttingen, Germany: Hogrefe.

Harlow, H. F., & Harlow, M. K. (1962). The effect of rearing conditions on behavior. *Bulletin of the Menninger Clinic, 26,* 213–224.

Henningsen, P. (2000). Vom Gehirn lernen? Zur Neurobiologie von psychischer Struktur und innerer Repräsentanz [Learning from the brain? On the neurobiology of psychological structure and internal representation]. *Forum der Psychoanalyse [Psychoanalysis Forum], 16,* 99–115.

Hüther, G. (1997). *Biologie der Angst [Biology of fear]*. Göttingen, Germany: Vandenhoeck & Ruprecht.

Hüther, G. (2001). *Bedienungsanleitung für ein menschliches Gehirn [Operating instructions for a human brain]*. Göttingen, Germany: Vandenhoeck & Ruprecht.

Hüther, G. (2003). Die nutzungsabhängige Reorganisation neuronaler Verschaltungsmuster [The use-dependent reorganization of neuronal wiring patterns]. In G. Schiepek (Ed.), *Neurobiologie der Psychotherapie [Neurobiology of psychotherapy]*. Stuttgart, Germany: Schattauer.

Izard, C. (1991). *The psychology of emotions.* New York: Plenum Press.

Izard, C. (1992). Four systems for emotion activation. *Psychological Review, 99,* 561–565.

Jenkins, W. M., Merzenich, M. M., & Recanzone, G. (1990). Neocortical representational dynamics in adult primates. *Neuropsychologia, 28,* 573–584.

Kabat-Zinn, J., Lipworth, L., & Burney, R. (1985). The clinical use of mindfulness meditation for the self-regulation of chronic pain. *Journal of Behavioral Medicine, 8(2),* 163–190.

Kandel, E. (1995). *Neurowissenschaften [Neuroscience]*. Heidelberg, Germany: Spektrum Akademischer.

LeDoux, J. (1996). *The emotional brain: The mysterious underpinnings of emotional life.* New York: Simon & Schuster.

LeDoux, J. (2001). *Das Gehirn und seine Wirklichkeit [The brain and its reality]*. Munich, Germany: dtv.

LeDoux, J. (2003). *Das Netz der Persönlichkeit: wie unser Selbst entsteht [The power of personality: How our self is created]*. Düsseldorf: Walter. (Orig.). *The synaptic self: How our brains become who we are.* New York: Penguin.

Levin, F. (2003). *Psyche and brain: The biology of talking cures.* Madison, CT: International Universities Press.

Loftus, E. F. (2001). Falsche Erinnerungen [False memories]. In Rätsel Gehirn [Puzzle Brain]. *Digest 2: Spektrum der Wissenschaft,* 62–67.

Merzenich, M. M., et al. (1990). How the brain functionally rewires itself. In M. Arbid (Ed.), *Natural and artificial parallel computation.* Cambridge, MA: MIT Press.

Nader, K., Schafe, G. E., & LeDoux, J. E. (2000). Fear memories require protein synthesis in the amygdala for reconciliation after retrieval. *Nature, 406,* 722–726.

Niedenthal, P. M., et al. (2005). Embodiment in attitudes, social perception and emotion. *Personality and Social Psychology Review, 9(3),* 184–211.

Ogden, P., Minton, K., & Pain, C. (2006). *Trauma and the body: A sensorimotor approach to psychotherapy.* New York: W. W. Norton.

Olds, J. (1995). Self-stimulation of the brain. *Science, 127,* 315–324.

Perls, F. S. (1973/1976). Gestalttherapie in Aktion [Gestalt Therapy in action]. Stuttgart, Germany: Klett-Cotta.

Pert, C. (1997). *The molecules of emotion: Why you feel the way you feel.* New York: Scribner.

Pert, C. (1999). Moleküle der Gefühle [Molecules of emotion]. Reinbek, Germany: Rowohlt.

Pesso, A., & Perquin, L. (2008). *Die Bühnen des Bewusstseins oder: werden wer wir wirklich sind [The stages of consciousness or: to be who we really are]*. Munich, Germany: CIP-Medien.

Pöppel, E. (2000). *Grenzen des Bewusstseins [Boundaries of consciousness]*. Frankfurt, Germany: Inselverlag.

Raleigh, M. J. McGuire, M. T., Brammer, G. L., Pollack, D. B. & Yuwiler, A. (1991). Serotonergic mechanisms promote dominance acquisition in adult male vervet monkeys. *Brain Research.* 559 (2), 181-190.

Ramachandran, V. (2001). Die blinde Frau, die sehen kann: Rätselhafte Phänomene unseres Bewußtseins [The blind woman, who can see: Puzzling phenomena of our consciousness]. Hamburg, Germany: Rowohlt.

Rizzolatti, G., Fadiga, L., Fogassi, L., & Gallese, V. (2002). From mirror neurons to imitation: Facts and speculations. In A. N. Meltzoff & W. Prinz (Eds.), *The imitative mind: Development, evolution, and brain bases* (pp. 247–266). Cambridge, UK: Cambridge University Press.

Roth, G. (1997). *Das Gehirn und seine Wirklichkeit [The brain and its reality]*. Frankfurt, Germany: Suhrkamp Taschenbuchverlag.

Roth, G. (1999). Entstehen und Funktionen von Bewusstsein [The origin and function of consciousness]. *Deutsches Ärzteblatt, 96*(30), A-1957 / B-1686 / C-1567.

Roth, G. (2001). *Fühlen, Denken, Handeln [Feeling, thinking, touching]*. Frankfurt, Germany: Suhrkamp.

Roth, G. (2009). *Aus der Sicht des Gehirns [From the view of the brain]*. Frankfurt, Germany: Suhrkamp.

Rüegg, J. C. (2001). *Psychosomatik, Psychotherapie und Gehirn [Psychosomatics, psychotherapy and the brain]*. Stuttgart, Germany: Schattauer.

Schacter, D. (1997). *Searching for memory: The brain, the mind and the past*. New York: Basic Books.

Schacter, D. (2001). *Wir sind Erinnerung [We are memory]*. Reinbek, Germany: Rowohlt Taschenbuchverlag.

Schore, A. N. (2003). *Affect regulation and the repair of the self*. New York: W. W. Norton.

Siegel, D. L. (2000). *The developing mind: Towards a neurobiology of interpersonal experience*. London: Guilford Press.

Singer, W. (2004). Ein Spiel von Spiegeln [A game of mirrors]. *Spektrum der Wissenschaft (Spezial), 1*, 20–25.

Solms, M., & Turnbull, O. (2002). *The brain and the inner world: An introduction to the neuroscience of subjective experience*. London: Karnac Books.

Spitzer, M. (2000). *Geist im Netz [Ghost in the network]*. Heidelberg, Germany: Spektrum Akademischer.

Spitzer, M. (2001). Ketchup und das kollektive Unbewusste [Ketchup and the collective unconscious]. Heidelberg, Germany: Spektrum Akademischer.

Spitzer, M. (2002). *Lernen [Learning]*. Heidelberg, Germany: Spektrum Akademischer.

Stern, D. N. (1998). *Die Lebenserfahrung des Säuglings [The lived experience of the infant]*. Stuttgart, Germany: Klett-Cotta.

Turnbull, J. K., & Collins, J. (Eds.). (2008). *Leadership learning*. Basingstoke, UK: Palgrave Macmillan.

Uvnäs Moberg, K. (2003). *The oxytocin factor: Tapping the hormone of calm, love and healing*. Cambridge, MA: De Capo Press, Perseus Books.

van der Kolk, B. A., McFarlane, A. C., & Weisaeth, L. (2000). *Traumatic stress: The effects of overwhelming experience on mind, body and society*. New York: Guilford.

Vissing, S. F., & Hjortso, E. M. (1996). Central motor command activates sympathetic outflow to the cutaneous circulation in humans. *Journal of Physiology, 492*, 931–939.

# 13

## Body Psychotherapy as a Revitalization of the Self

*A Depth-Psychological and Phenomenological-Existential Perspective*

**Gustl Marlock, Germany**

**Translation by Regina Mirvis, Elizabeth Marshall, and Michael Soth**

**Gustl Marlock's** biographical information can be found at the beginning of Chapter 1, "Preface: The Field of Body Psychotherapy."

When we speak of the body—colloquially as well as scientifically—our general conditioning presupposes a quantifiable, measurable, and influenceable object. Since the advent of modern science, this view of the body has become fundamentally anchored in our thinking and in the bodily self-awareness of most modern individuals. Due to this "objectification" of the body, the discipline of Body Psychotherapy, more so than other therapeutic approaches in the field of Depth Psychology, runs the risk of falling into the trap of a *scientistic self-misunderstanding*. Jürgen Habermas (1968) coined this phrase in an attempt to establish the scientific status of psychoanalysis by means of fundamental epistemological thought. He pointed out a problematic and misleading self-comprehension of psychoanalysis, which similarly applies to Body Psychotherapy.

Habermas traced this *"scientistic self-misunderstanding"* in psychoanalysis back to Freud's original work, which was pervaded by a paradigm clash between the natural sciences and the humanities. Habermas showed that Freud was attempting to couch the foundations of what he wanted to be a new science in terms, categories, and metaphors borrowed from the natural sciences. However, in exploring the realm of subjectivity, especially unconscious subjectivity, Freud struggled with the objectifying assumptions and methodologies of biology, neurology, and medicine, which were at odds with a process basically designed to discover and uncover the meaning of incomprehensible symptoms: i.e., more of a humanistic 'science'. Freud tried to formulate connections between symptoms and formative relational constellations, as well as to design a therapeutic process in which these correlations could be discerned and reconstructed, but he tried to do so in categories that were not appropriate to intersubjective relating, but were couched in the language of inanimate objects and homeostatic biological systems.

Considering that the objectification of the body has been taken for granted in Western culture, by attempting to address and include the body in psychotherapy, Body Psychotherapy is liable to import some of these cultural assumptions. As a discipline, therefore, Body Psychotherapy is even more strongly susceptible than the psychoanalytic *interpretive* reconstruction of the early relational background to the fundamental scientific fallacy that Habermas is challenging: the assumption that we are dealing with quasi-scientific laws concerning therapeutic theory and practice, as if we could achieve—through working with the body—the same instrumental mastery regarding mental suffering as, for example, physics affords us when dealing with gravity.

This exists, not only in the prevalent objectifying stance toward the body, but also in the actual techniques that Body Psychotherapy has developed, designed to influence bodily affect, muscle tone, and regulation processes, that invite instrumentalist attitudes. Another factor is Freud's "energy" concept—adopted by Reich and developed significantly by him—which is rooted in physics and the thermodynamics of inanimate systems, and thus lends itself to being applied in objectifying therapeutic attempts at manipulating the client's energetic state.

In his early theorizing, Freud had pursued an energy-distribution model that subordinated the task of exposing unconscious fixations and their corresponding relational background to a seemingly objective scientific model of energetic activation. In this early model of Freud's work, aversion and fear were the result of an overaccumulation of excitement, whereby the intensity of excitement was assumed to be proportional to the amount of accumulated energy, which—when discharged—was proportional to feelings of pleasure.

Whereas Freud later concentrated increasingly on the dynamics of psychological processes, Reich continued to pursue Freud's scientific dream of discovering the material substrate of the basic "drive" energy. Reich's conceptualizations of energy took over and became center stage in his thinking and increasingly concrete and literal. Having abandoned any metaphoric connotations of how the term "energy" is customarily used, Reich bequeathed later generations a "strained" and "overloaded" concept of energy that indiscriminately combines different levels of explanatory categories and power by incorporating diverse therapeutic phenomena into a convenient "catch-all" term (see Chapter 14, "The Concept of Energy in Body Psychotherapy" by Andreas Wehowsky).

Ever since that time, there have been attempts throughout the field of Body Psychotherapy to resurrect and reinstate the energy concept, to describe and explain various phenomena, leading to diverse and disparate meanings and connotations that are at times being subsumed under the term "energy," including, for example:

- The *quantitative* aspects of affective and psychodynamic processes, which, in early psychoanalysis, were considered to be the third "economic" aspect of metapsychology, alongside the topical model of psychic spaces (conscious, unconscious, and preconscious) and the dynamic aspect (as a result of internal conflict)

- The neurophysiological, vegetative basis of all human emotional processes
- The subjective experience of the intensity of desires, feelings, or impulses
- A basic principle of the human soul responsible for movement (which psychoanalysis conceptualized as psychic energy, and which Reich—during different phases of his work—variously called libido, vegetative energy, and later "orgone" energy)
- Some people have included certain metaphysical variables in the notion of "energy," such as fundamental, cosmic forces, ethers, or the ground of being (in Chinese, the *Tao* [natural energy] or *chi* [personal energy]).

Despite countless arguments and references exposing the inadequacy of the attempt to reduce the multidimensionality and complexity of body-mind existence to just *one* concept of energy (which furthermore is misconstrued in a pseudo-scientific manner as quantifiable and manageable, by applying the laws of physics equivalent to the manipulation of other natural forces), the notion of "energy" still holds sway as the dominant explanatory model in some parts of the Body Psychotherapeutic field. This has remained unchanged, although it has been conclusively shown that the origins of this energy concept go back to the physiological theories of the nineteenth century, which described the body as merely a thermodynamic machine (Sarasin and Tanner, 1998), and there has been some comprehensive criticism of Reich's attempts (later on in his work) to subsume even the divine versus the devil in his formulation of antagonistic energetic states, which he called "Orgone" and its obverse, "deadly orgone energy" (DOR).

But, perhaps the persistence of the "energy" metaphor cannot be explained solely through its reductionist qualities, nor through the dubious fact that it appears to simplify, in a kind of linguistic regression, the difficult articulation of highly complex, dynamic body-soul experiences. Perhaps the value of the "energy" metaphor for the field of Body Psychotherapy, albeit originating historically in its medico-scientific self-definition, lies in the fact that it fulfilled an important function by helping to put into words and to assert some central dimensions of personal experience that, for example, differentiate Body Psychotherapy from more analytic practice. These dimensions need to be languaged and include intensity of emotions, feelings, and passions; vital and powerful self-expressions; flowing pleasurable sensations; and even ego-transcending orgasmic experiences, sometimes referred to as cosmic or oceanic. It is this emphasis on and cultivation of the experience of "vitality" (see also Chapter 45, "Entering the Relational Field in Body Psychotherapy" by William Cornell) that characterizes Body Psychotherapy, in contrast to the purely "talking therapies" like Cognitive Behavioral Therapy and psychoanalysis.

Reich's attempts to grasp this vitality more comprehensively than Freud can be understood historically in the context of a central theme preoccupying the German educated classes throughout the eighteenth and nineteenth centuries: "What *is* life, and what constitutes being alive?" Beginning with Kant, and reemphasized by Herder, Schelling, and Goethe, it is a theme that moved thinkers during the Enlightenment period, and especially within the romantic natural philosophy movement. The concept of a life force or life energy—which Kant described as a substance that differs from, yet is connected to, matter; and which Goethe described as an "activity"—can be found everywhere, including in Hahnemann's homeopathy, as well as in the philosopher Henri Bergson's *élan vital,* to which Reich often referred[27]

Reich's legacy is, however, somewhat problematic in its attempt to reduce the vitality of the body-self—its complexity and the movement of emotional experience and human action—to a positivistic and materialistic construction of the term "energy." To describe significant elements of Body Psychotherapeutic theory and practice as "energetic processes" is, of course, not entirely misguided: as mentioned above, emotion and its blockage or its expression into movement does have quantitative aspects that involve the use and transformation of "energy" and can legitimately be described by the term. The same applies to the neurovegetative level of excitement that constitutes an essential facet of human emotions. Even the most subtle thoughts, as well as the most audacious or bizarre human dreams, involve neurophysiological excitement and therefore biological energetic processes.

However, the attempt to explain all these phenomena in a reductionist manner is problematic, as if they all hinged on one kind of energetic force understood as physically moving through the body like through a hydraulic system of pipes that can be in a state of "healthy" flow versus "unhealthy" blockage. Such simplistic energy concepts—borrowed from the world of physics, chemistry, or biology—tend to take on a life of their own and become reified in a therapeutic context.

A similar point has been made for psychoanalysis by Rudolf (1976), who described how Freud's spatial-physical vocabulary, originating from classical mechanics, developed into an oversimplifying description of the *psyche* and interpersonal relations in terms of a mechanistic apparatus, especially in Ego Psychology. Suddenly these terms are no longer understood as metaphors, but appear as definite and fixed realities in an objectified world. Energetic terms such as "charge," "discharge," "distribution," and "flow" are all strongly suggestive of mechanical contraptions: they create the impression that psychotherapy is equivalent to natural processes that can be controlled and harnessed, like the conversion of electricity into heat, light, kinetic movement, or sound energy[28]

Regarding this confusion between natural sciences and the humanities, and the differing methodologies required

---

[27] The question of whether the Reichian concept of vital energy can find a more adequate context of explanation in the frame of a complex systems theory (Bateson) or a "postmaterialist science" (Beckmann) will not be further discussed here. The question of scientific access and disposition of vital energy probably belongs less to the domain of psychotherapy than to a much more general art of healing

[28] To this extent, Reich's avoidance of differentiated psychodynamic work was consistent in his later phase of work, at least in respect to the fundamental axioms of his thought at that time. His later practice cannot therefore really be characterized as psychotherapeutic

to approach their respective fields of study, the challenge by Habermas and others in relation to psychoanalysis (Habermas, 1968; Lorenzer, 1973) remains valid—namely, that therapy is a *human* activity, which *cannot* be studied or understood by the attempt to exclude the subjective dimension, as the natural sciences quite validly attempt to do in their study of objects or processes. There is no therapy to be studied once we have—supposedly—removed the subjective dimension: the therapeutic process depends on the perspectival interpretation of reality, via the human subject. Therapy essentially is an activity of *self-reflection* and *self-exploration.*

This self-reflective process may take very different forms in Body Psychotherapy and in psychoanalysis—with emphasis on a sensory-emotional bodily experience, rather than on a cognitive, rational approach. But the more that we can understand Body Psychotherapy, as a depth-psychological-existential form of psychotherapy, the more we can appreciate the self-reflective nature of therapy as a human process of learning and development, rather than a mechanical process of rearranging the distribution of energy, or the conversion of energy, within the body. It is actually the conscious reassimilation of repressed (or dissociated) parts of one's biography that resolves unconscious fixations; this may well result in actual energetic changes and improved regulation, which will also affect body processes, such as excitation patterns, emotional expression, muscle tone, breath, posture, etc. However, this should be understood primarily as an existential-psychological evolution of human awareness, rather than as a process of literal energetic transformation with some psychological benefits.

The crux of the epistemological contextualization of psychoanalysis and Depth Psychology, initiated by Habermas (1968), Ricoeur (1969), and others, is that—if we can think in terms of causalities at all—psychotherapy does not deal with causalities of a material, scientific nature, but engages with *causalities of fate.* These do not have the same scientific status as the laws governing the earth's orbit around the sun, for example. Thus, they cannot be described by the scientific formulas of cause and effect, but follow a different logic altogether: as biographical "causality correlations" that are best grasped as having a narrative or dramatic nature. These dramas revolve around successful (or failed) socialization processes of the past, and their effects in the present.

The revolutionary paradigm shift precipitated by Freud's theory consisted precisely of challenging classical medical psychiatry and its explanations of psychological suffering on the basis of organic and neurological dysfunction, and postulating instead a historical, narrative dimension. Since then, Depth Psychology has succeeded in demonstrating the significance of subjective biography as a meaningful story that can be translated for therapeutic purposes into techniques that reconstruct each individual's biography through interpretation of infantile development and its unconscious impact on the present. Materialistic-mechanical models, and their cause-and-effect constructions of therapy, systematically fail to grasp the impact and power of such a narrative, explanatory foil of socialization theory.

## Body, History, and Meaning

The notion of therapeutic "reconstruction" circumscribes the attempt to see through (and past) the superficial manifestations of ostensible symptoms and acute suffering, and grasp their origins and roots in early socialization and learning processes that have become almost second nature, that surface in the present, and that burden the person with unresolved conflicts, deficient self-development, and restricted ego functions.

Psychodynamic approaches address these connections between the past and the present traditionally through interpretation, or, in recent years, increasingly through dialogue focused on their manifestations on the level of transference and countertransference. Psychoanalytic tradition is well aware of the vicissitudes that surround the differentiated exploration of the deep structure of the *psyche* and its biographical origins. Although not entirely free from its own technological distortions in the self-definition and understanding of its practice, psychoanalysis, as a tradition, has accumulated a deeper appreciation than Body

Psychotherapy has of the significant role that *insight, understanding,* and *meaning* play in the reconstructive phase of therapy. As such, analysis involves the struggle to gradually come to *understand* the symptoms and the often fateful and inscrutable context of psychic pain. Habermas, Lorenzer, Ricoeur, and others have suggested that such a process is best characterized as *hermeneutical.*

The German philosopher Wilhelm Dilthey (Dilthey et al., 1991) originated and proposed hermeneutics as a general principle of human self-understanding.[29] His concern was to establish a proper foundation for the humanities and to clearly distinguish these from the natural sciences. He contrasts the kinds of *explanations* pursued by natural science with the *comprehension* sought by the humanities. Such comprehension is engendered by methodical reconstructions of primal correlations of meaning, which are the result of a hermeneutical process, striving to understand historical rather than objective realities. A singular phenomenon, such as a symptom, can be understood only in correlation to the context of a whole that lends it meaning. In the case of a symptom, this involves deciphering its *meaning,* within its relational context, in which mingle both past and present, early and current dimensions of experience. Similar to the way in which literary critique approaches the "meaning" of written texts, analysts can be seen to orient toward a meaningful narrative, whereby initial fragments, such as inexplicable distress or a current difficulty, become rounded out into a coherent story.

Reich's early character-analytical case studies are artful illustrations of this process: pieces of initially fragmented information (for example, his patients' exaggerated politeness, compulsive behavior, or affected mannerisms) gradually coalesce into a significant shape and story that, eventually, reveals explicitly the dramatic beginnings of a burdened personal biography. In practice, the art and craft of facilitating this kind of unfolding toward meaning is a well-recognized and established competence throughout the Body Psychotherapeutic field, although some elements—e.g., the communication of subtle linguistic and relational symbolic meanings—are not as differentiated as in the analytic tradition. However, Body Psychotherapy generally excels in understanding the character-forming impact of early experiences, as they are embodied and as they manifest throughout the many levels of the client's body-mind system (Lowen, 1981; Johnson, 1988).

### The Implications of Energetic Monism[30]

Following Reich, who had repeatedly warned of the dangers inherent in mechanistic conceptualizations when dealing both with the dynamic processes of the *psyche* and with those of the body, David Boadella, among others, has frequently critiqued the tendency toward reification and mechanistic attitudes (Boadella, 1987). In discussing Reich's character-analytical perspective, Boadella advocates referring to character processes rather than character structures. In spite of this, it is precisely with regard to energy-technological ideas and models that misunderstandings with far-reaching consequences have become engrained throughout the field of Body Psychotherapy. One of these is the notion that it is possible to instrumentalize bodily interventions in order to move, redistribute, or change the aggregate state of an actual "energy" (e.g., charge, blockage, or flow) present in the client's system.

The concepts of charge and discharge—connected to the economic understanding of the function and nature of affects, emotions, and feelings—tend to promote mechanical, reifying, and often regressively self-referential attitudes. These terms are used and understood in ways that distort the essential fact that human emotion is always *relational,* has the quintessential function of making contact, and serves to orient the self in relation to others

---

29  Dilthey, representing the school of Romantic Hermeneutics, stressed that a historically situated interpreter—a "living" (rather than a Cartesian or "theoretical") subject—uses "understanding" and "interpretation," which combine individual-psychological and sociohistorical description and analysis to gain a greater knowledge of various texts and authors in their contexts

30  Monism is a philosophical theory reducing reality to just one single entity or category—like idealism, materialism, or energy theory: i.e., "Everything is energy."

(objects) and the world. This fact is not at all mitigated by the recognition—highly relevant for psychotherapy—that such relatedness and orientation do not always find a healthy and functional expression, but may be disturbed, dysfunctional, and impaired by wounding past experiences.

Another danger inherent in such a monistic and absolutizing conception of "energy" is its reductionist oversimplification of the complexity of human development and maturation processes, which—among other things—rely on a deeper level of contact and resonance with one's own emotions, as well as their differentiated regulation. For example, a particularly "high" level of energy—in and of itself—is not necessarily conducive to human development and maturation. Rather, the therapeutic revival of the self depends upon the extensive recovery of the complexity of sensing and feeling, through the restoration and development of a vital, emotional ability for resonance, both inwardly and outwardly, and through the maturational skills of a flexible and intelligent regulation of one's own emotions and feelings. Regulatory capacity implies a spectrum of abilities, from holding and containing one's emotions on the one hand, to translating them into expression, communication, and action. Representatives of energetic monism tend to bypass this recognition, instead turning the expression and discharge of emotions into an obsession. Such a dogmatic bias toward an energetic "discharge" misses the reality that catharsis is often motivated by the wish to evacuate and get rid of feelings, rather than surrendering and "having" them. Emotional expression may then function as a resistance, and the therapist may be colluding in a narcissistic transference, veiled in energy ideology.

Similarly, in relation to the hyperaffective states of post-traumatic stress disorder (PTSD), the therapeutic usefulness of energetic monism is questionable. Although there is therapeutic validity in helping clients to learn ways of deconditioning the arousal patterns entrenched in the limbic system and the brainstem, below the level of purely verbal exchanges, it is important to remember that it is people—not "energies"—who are learning to calm down.

It is indisputable that Body Psychotherapy is capable—more than many other therapeutic approaches—of helping clients to tap back into their vitality and the wealth of human feelings, sensations, and actions that have become barricaded behind, or buried under, psychological and body defense mechanisms. Undoubtedly there are linguistic problems in describing these vitalizing and dynamic aspects without falling into the trap of assigning a central role to the ideas of energetic monism. When attempting to describe the vital relationship qualities of mother-child interactions, Daniel Stern drew upon a term stemming from music: *vitality contours.* And Gregory Bateson (1979)—in his effort to bring a holistic conception to the mind-nature relationship—accorded ancillary significance to energetic aspects. However, while acknowledging that a certain degree of energy is necessary to conserve self-organizing systems, his primary point was to show that it is not decisive for the *quality* of the organization.

We can conclude that Body Psychotherapy has no need to cling to a "hypothetical energy" of which even Lowen says—slightly incongruously—that it is not that important to understand "the ultimate nature of this fundamental energy" (Lowen, 1981). As Fritz Perls (1973) demonstrated early on, the concept of excitation is perfectly sufficient for the field of psychotherapy, especially because it can be further differentiated into the terms "*excitement*" and "*arousal.*" On that basis, connections between emotional, neurovegetative, and motor processes can be described within the framework of conventional theory and nomenclature. This leaves the term "energy" to be used metaphorically, as it is in common parlance, in describing attributes and qualities of movement in bodily psychological processes, such as dynamics, intensity, strength or weakness, voluntary or involuntary movement, vitality, balance, and also rest.

## On the Status of Character-Analytical Theory

By formulating the "functional identity" of mental and somatic processes, what nowadays we would call a holistic perspective, Reich (1971) established the biological roots and the embodied nature of what were previously considered purely psychological notions like personality and character. It is understandable, therefore, that occasionally a degree of materiality can be seen to slip into the discourse of Body Psychotherapy, which can mislead therapists into assuming that they are dealing primarily with physical, objective bodies and realities. Mechanical-objectivist notions have been—and continue to be—widespread and entrenched throughout those branches of Body Psychotherapy that are strongly focused on characterology.

Returning to the hermeneutical perspective of social embeddedness favored by the humanities, especially regarding the formation of character patterns during early developmental experiences, several authors, notably Hilarion Petzold (1996), have brought a philosophically based concept of embodiment ("*Leib*" in German) into this discussion, in order to insist that we are dealing not with a physical object, but rather with an experiencing, embodied, environment-oriented somatic *subjectivity*. Some critics then went overboard, "threw the baby out with the bathwater," and dismissed the idea of characterological patterns altogether.

In between these historically long-standing and polarized disputes, some fundamental considerations should be noted. Embodied character typologies do not describe any objective, quantifiable realities; neither do they deliver explanations of causal connections. Character-analytical categories are not much more than possible templates or tendencies, which we could also refer to as "prototypes." They serve as generalizing shorthand indicators for mutual understanding among therapists, and are thus similar to the literary stereotypes, or prototypes, in philology that are helpful in capturing and articulating succinctly the idiosyncratic characteristics of a person and their thinking, feeling, and actions within their historical situatedness. The significant characteristics of speech are referred to as "idiomatic," which is why idiom and character coincide in some psychoanalytic personality theories in which verbal communication constitutes the primary level of reconstruction (Bollas, 1992; Cornell, 2005).

The humanities do not operate with explanations, as do the natural sciences, but rather attempt to understand the meaning and significance of phenomena (Habermas, 1968). The same is true in regard to the bodily level of character-analytical reconstructions: a depth-psychological approach does not primarily view the body in a quasi-scientific fashion as a system of energy, but pays attention first and foremost to the messages that it conveys. One of the most fundamental principles of Body Psychotherapy is that the body does indeed "speak," express, and communicate the person's inner, psychic realities. The origins of this paradigm in modern times can be traced back historically: to the expressive concepts of the human self during the period of romanticism (Taylor, 1994); to the important work of Charles Darwin regarding the physical expression of emotions and affects (Darwin, 2000); and to the ideas of an expressive, feeling body found in the arts and in the Life Reform Movement (Buchholz et al., 2001). Especially in its expression of suffering, the body became a fundamental element in modern psychosomatic thought.

Although we can recognize a cross-cultural human ability to "read" and understand the emotional expressions of the body (as Darwin had already pointed out), we must not lose sight of an underlying principle formulated by Lorenzer (1973) in terms of verbal communications within psychoanalysis, but equally valid in terms of the communications of the body: every interpretation by the therapist is of a hypothetical nature. Any assignment of *meaning* is to be approached as an experimental trial. We need to be aware of this, not only because the language of the body consists of ambiguous messages with multiple meanings, but also because a bodily configuration, such as a certain character stance, for example, can only reveal its full meaning relationally, through *dialogic* exploration. At the beginning of any therapeutic process—regardless of previous knowledge and the validity of theoretical generalizations—the therapist's phenomenological perceptions offer only a limited and one-dimensional window on the client's reality, for example, their physical rigidity. The complex meaning, significance, and function of such rigidity—both internally as well as interpersonally—can only be discovered step-by-step. In speaking of the "rigidification" of character, Body Psychotherapists circumscribe the dynamic interplay of unconscious muscular operations and their defensive functions. These somatic structures and dynamics constitute the foundation of particular self-representations, maintained through a "somatic loop" (Damasio, 1994). They influence thought, feeling, and, above all, nonfeeling, and are historically connected to partially unconscious inner convictions and fears. Because such complex patterns are automatic identity-forming processes, operating unconsciously like reflexes, triggered through emotional stress and activated or reinforced via the autonomic nervous system, they need to be comprehensively raised into awareness in order to be worked through.

Here, a further decisive point becomes clear with regard to the objectified or "reified" forms of character-analytical practice. Ultimately, it is not the therapist who should be deciphering the codes of body language, as the expert who then administers appropriate interventions, but the clients themselves who—with the help of the therapist—investigate the unconscious aspects of their own life story, through their own bodily sensations, and thus begin to reaccess those repressed, lost, dissociated, or underdeveloped parts of themselves. However, at this point, the Body Psychotherapeutic process differs fundamentally from the psychoanalytic method, in that it does not rely on insight as its primary therapeutic vehicle. When the bodily defenses against emotion are loosened, other forms of self-recognition become possible that can "touch" and "move" the client, much more deeply and comprehensively than any mental insight. In contrast to other methods relying on more mental reconstructions, Petzold has elucidated how such embodied experiences, which can rightly be described as deep and moving, provide the client with "vital evidence" (Petzold, 1996, p. 375). In describing these intense, condensed experiential processes—typical and constitutive of Body Psychotherapy—he explicates how an integrated experiencing of the person's body, emotions, and their correlative meanings can lead—literally—to very vital and significant realizations. Fritz Perls—in his somewhat Californian "Zen" manner—called such evidential experiences "mini-satori." However they manifest themselves, they are considered indispensable to any process of fundamental change and transformation.

## Character, Emotion, and Scenarios

Alongside and on top of the psychodynamic work of biographical insight and narrative, Body Psychotherapy strives to facilitate direct bodily experiences of developmentally acquired character attitudes that will impact on the lives of the patients and on their relationships. From an existential point of view, one might speak of body-soul patterns or configurations of "being in the world." In terms of technique and methods, there are a multitude of ways in which a therapist might facilitate such processes: in principle, any fragment of body-mind experience and relational context may provide a window into an in-depth awareness. However, what is always involved are different forms of self-exploration through feeling and sensing. These can be initiated through movement, or by focusing on a particular facial expression, or on a certain posture; if they do indeed hold charge and significance, they will be accompanied by specific corresponding sets of emotion that are evoked through deepened awareness. Paying attention to the breath and sensing the qualities of the breathing cycle can lead to an intensified level of self-perception of the body. Is the breath subdued, heavy, held in (due to fear or dread), shallow, or rather accelerated? Or is there a feeling of joy or happiness evolving from a full and gentle breath, reaching up from the belly into the top of the rib cage?

Our relationship with gravity is another possible area of exploration. How do we experience the fact that, as humans, we are capable of counteracting gravity? Does a person experience their erectness as being graceful, or as an effort? Perhaps, during moments of self-exploration, we may become aware that the person's posture has collapsed, or buckled at the mid-torso. Is this perception of the body's physical collapse connected to the person's corresponding general feeling in life: that it is "all too much"; that they are "not up for it"; or that—for some mysterious, fateful reason—they lack the strength to sustain their position in life?

Countless further examples can be cited from the technical repertoire of Body Psychotherapy. The point here is to indicate how the detailed perception of one's own body, and its sensations and emotional tone, opens up directions and possibilities for the therapeutic journey—and its process of opening, unfolding and deepening. Through sensory reflexivity, people can find a deeper and more conscious access to their body-mind states and vitality affects that often operate outside general awareness and that, from behind the scenes, influence and determine moods, feelings, and thought processes that reflect these underlying somatic configurations.

The "felt sense" of the body therefore becomes a gateway, especially when given appropriate time, space, and attention, that opens to an immediacy and intensity of perception that can only rarely be achieved through any form of verbal exploration. Talking therapies tend to take for granted the "distance" that modern individuals seem to have from their own bodies, and also from their feelings, and therefore effectively collude with this separation as "normal"; but, from the perspective of Body Psychotherapy, we regard the reduced perception of one's own body—the toning down and minimization of somatic cues—as one of the most fundamental defense mechanisms. A general constriction of bodily self-perception fends off the majority of the unpleasant aspects of one's own psychological-emotional reality, prior to and more effectively than any more-specific psychic defense mechanisms.

If therapeutic attention and intention can stay long enough with the perception of the body—"long enough" meaning both within the framework of an individual therapy session, as well as across the entire therapeutic process—fundamental patterns of being and perception usually emerge from behind the client's current mood and psychological state. Typical examples include: a feeling of distance or disconnection; or a hypotonic resignation; or a depressive heaviness, immobility, and joylessness; or, alternatively, a level of vegetative excitement and hypertonicity in the muscular system, which signals a permanent readiness to fight or defend oneself; or a distrustful reservation, from behind which (upon more extensive exploration) a fear of being injured or hurt emerges; or degrees of callousness and insensitivity are contacted that cover a deeper potential compassion.

These are examples of basic character attitudes, or personality traits, that normally remain preconscious or unconscious. This means that they largely go unnoticed, or remain ambiguous, and manifest only in fragmentary and symptomatic self-perceptions—they do not fully emerge into awareness, nor do they have any degree of comprehensive significance. They are accompanied by moods that can pervade long phases in one's life as vague, but familiar, background feelings. In order for these personality traits, or—to quote Bourdieu (1994)—a person's "habitus," to become conscious, and thus to become available to reflexive self-awareness, it is often necessary for a therapist to confront them, gently and compassionately. An introspective procedure of self-perception or self-examination, just by itself, is not always sufficient.

The character-analytical tradition conceptualized these basic personality traits as character "structures" and fixed attitudes. Lowen (1981) described corresponding postural "holding" patterns, such as "holding oneself together," "holding oneself up," and "holding oneself back." These patterns can be understood as survival compromises, developed to cope with unbearably conflicted, deficient, or traumatizing experiences, as well as chronic defensive operations, directed toward both the inside and the outside. Such holding patterns usually arise as a result of developmental wounding, in relation to needs or motivations in early life, and they are maintained against the possibility of ever being exposed again to a similar, intensely painful, or life-threatening experience of neglect, hurt, rejection, suppression, or hostility. (A discussion of "patterns of holding" can be found in Chapter 53, "The Role of the Body in Emotional Defense Processes: Body Psychotherapy and Emotional Theory" by Ulfried Geuter and Norbert Schrauth, and also in Chapter 54, "The Spectrum of Body Psychotherapeutic Practices and Interventions" by Ilse Schmidt-Zimmermann.)

George Downing (1996) has gone beyond the rigidity of traditional character-analytical theory with his more fluid and dynamic theory of "affective-motor schemas." He states that the reactions to the wounding experiences of misregulation in early life can be understood in terms of either underdeveloped, or overdeveloped, affective-motor schemas. Hypotonic listlessness could be an example of an underdeveloped schema; a phallic-aggressive habitus could be an example of an overdeveloped schema. Such affective-motor schemas can either activate, or deactivate, certain muscle groups, muscle tone, and breathing patterns, and have a profound effect on the person's vegetative system and their body's metabolic processes. Affective-motor schemas can also illustrate the physical side of "pathological" conditions of the self. What Kohut's (1977) Self Psychology describes as a consequence of bad mirroring and resonance can also be seen to correlate with deeply rooted physical conditions: for example, the understimulated or overstimulated self; and the overstrained and fragmented self.

Emotional character traits differ from actual emotions in that they are not actually "felt" as an emotion in the present, but are "old feelings" effectively frozen into the body—they are historical emotions that have become chronically blocked and somatized, and are therefore not accompanied by any acute, episodic processes of excitement or awareness. They formulate themselves as basic, acquired defensive schemas that are used, then learned, and can be seen to have, and be experienced as having, a regulatory "survival" function in an adverse situation. Embodied defense mechanisms are rooted in natural, intrinsic capacities, designed to regulate emotions and their motor components: for example, holding one's breath, due to fear; constricting the throat and clenching the teeth, in order to keep in strong emotions; restraining the desire to attack or flee, through the immobilization of the relevant musculature; hardening oneself, in order not to show any feelings of vulnerability; or to inhibit tender affection or love; or collapsing in order to evade excessive strain or exertion. These regulatory capacities were developed as necessary tools for adaptability and survival, and—as such—are basically functional and make sense (in the context that they were developed). When they become chronic, due to systematically unresolved or unresolvable wounding experiences, they subsequently operate unconsciously, as automatic processes, and—as such—they lead to character fixations, whose restricted

facilities we later find within the spectrum of clinical personality theory.

Such character traits, constituted by specific defensive operations, contain within them certain affective-motor convictions (Downing, 1996) that then become expressed, on the psychological level, as basic relational attitudes: for example, "the world is an insecure and dangerous place"; "being in a relationship and having freedom cannot go together"; etc. These schemas illustrate a central point in Damasio's (1994) theory: that, through our bodies, we are implicitly always, in some way, emotionally related to our environment (or perceived environment). When the therapeutic process brings greater attention and more conscious awareness to these character attitudes and affective-motor schemas, which can then become intensified and revitalized, so this *relatedness* becomes a central aspect of experience. Character attitudes and affective-motor schemas therefore imply, contain, and convey old relationship constellations that, from a psychoanalytic perspective, can be seen as internalized object-relations, with a small proviso regarding the prenatal and perinatal dimensions of experience: in these very early phases of development, we cannot really speak of "object" relationships; rather, these fall into the category that the German philosopher Thomas Macho creatively identified as an "object-relationship."

The Body Psychotherapeutic approach—to becoming conscious of dysfunctional and limiting object-relationships (or character patterns) and then to engage in a process of working through them—contrasts with the psychoanalytic approach in several respects: first and foremost, Body Psychotherapy is much less reliant on interpretation and the development of the so-called "transference neurosis." From the more holistic point of view of Body Psychotherapy, transference processes are only one of the dimensions in which fixations from the past manifest themselves. Through focusing on the somatic and spontaneously experienced dimensions of embodied defense mechanisms, the therapeutically relevant emotions (implicit in the constellated object-relations) can be accessed and released with a degree of immediacy and intensity, which can otherwise be found only in psychodramatic methods (Uexküll et al., 1994).

Whereas the analytic tradition speaks of the internalization of object-relations—though no substantial conclusion has ever emerged about how and where these processes are actually stored—the Body Psychotherapeutic perspective assumes that the so-called psychic self- and object-representations are clearly rooted in a variety of somatic anchors, configurations, and affective-motor schemas. Experientially, they simply manifest as a particular "felt sense"—e.g., of desire, or of the sensation of fear, or as an attraction, or an aversion; and when therapeutic exploration facilitates a more differentiated and unfolded experience, these schemas reveal themselves as connected to relational scenarios in which these feelings arose and from which they originate.

Herein lies an essential objection against the exclusively energetic understanding of emotions: although emotions and feelings are indeed grounded in bodily processes of excitement, and rooted in visceral, muscular, and vegetative systems, their primary significance does not lie in their homeostatic regulation of the body-mind through repressing or discharging them, but in their relatedness to "others," imagined or real. Emotions are always related to others—in psychoanalytic parlance: to objects, whether these are external or internal objects (i.e., aspects of our own self) or even of an impersonal nature.

At the core of all Depth Psychology, we encounter the recognition, confirmed by clinical experience, that we only rarely find ourselves fully in the here-and-now. Rather, our experiencing—our emotional reactions and our behavioral actions—is usually refracted through unconscious scenarios of our past history to which we are fixated, and that therefore shape our "presence." We know from the clinical experience of Body Psychotherapy that strong emotional processes often accompany this fixation. Neuropsychological research has impressively documented this as a *limbic* fixation, especially in the case of traumatic experiences. Recently, neuropsychology has become much more interested in observing how emotional fixations are mediated, mostly through the brainstem and the vegetative system, thus taking up a thread of research that Reich originally initiated in his work on "bions" in the 1930s and 1940s, albeit within the limitations of scientific knowledge at the time.

Body Psychotherapists also know that early wounding scenarios will possibly be transferred onto the therapist, and can thus readily reveal themselves and also intensify in the therapeutic encounter. Accordingly, they also understand that these transferences must be sustained and must survive, be held up in contrast against the reality of the current relationship, and be worked through. They appreciate and include the psychoanalytic recognition that the royal road toward change is via interpretation, as well as the dialogic, intersubjective work on the relationship. However, while Body Psychotherapy includes these ways of working, it also often transcends them: it has its own techniques and methods for working through emotional fixations to internalized object-relationships and past scenarios.

Fritz Perls characterized such biographical fixations as being manifested in the transference as *"unfinished gestalten,"* or, as he casually called them, "unfinished business." He developed an impressive and effective technique for Gestalt Therapy, whereby a staged, dramatic orchestration in the here-and-now attempts to create a new dialogue with the old "objects"—a dialogue that is vibrant and expressive on affective, emotional, and motoric levels, and that goes beyond old, compromised forms, finding new possibilities for contact and resolution. The expression, integration, and assimilation of warded-off emotions and parts of the self are part of such a process, which addresses the dramatic structure of formative relationships, corrective experiences, and affective-motor potential in one coherent method.

Habermas (1968) referred to the fact that, from an analytic or depth-psychological perspective, the formative relationship constellations can be interpreted along the lines of a theatrical model—in other words, like acts of a drama. Apart from Gestalt dialogues, via two-chair or empty-chair work, or in Psychodrama, rarely has this been as consequently transposed into a therapeutic method as in Al Pesso's Psychomotor Therapy. In staged work—also called *"enactments"*—old scenarios, affective-motor schemas, and their psychodynamic equivalents are re-created, emotionally acted out, and then worked through, and—speaking in terms of Pesso's approach—"completed" through corrective emotional experiences that enact ideal and/or reconciliatory scenarios (Pesso, 1986: foreword by Tilmann Moser).

Even in therapeutic approaches such as Bioenergetics, focused on working with bodily emotional defenses and on the expressive completion of emotional cycles, scenic thinking is present in the background. It is really only against this historic backdrop that an assessment and valuation of emotional processes can be made. This is essential, as the crucially important question (concerning strong, regressive emotional episodes) is whether one is dealing with defensive or chronic regressions, instead of regressive processes that are functional and that promote integration (compare with Marlock, 1992; Geissler, 2001). An exclusively energetic model of simple charge and discharge is rarely sufficient in making these kinds of assessments.

More recently, various modalities of psychoanalytic approach have been distinguished, especially in the United States (Stark, 1999), reflecting an actual shift in analytic practice, away from the classical position relying on insight through interpretation, and toward a paradigm focusing on "corrective emotional experiences" (Ibid.). This perspective, deriving from Alexander and Balint, that attempts to counterbalance structural deficits with empathic closeness and corrective experiences in the therapeutic relationship, is actually quite widespread within the field of Body Psychotherapy. It can be seen most clearly in the work of Ron Kurtz, and also, as mentioned, of Al Pesso. One of the well-recognized dangers of providing corrective experiences is a regressive fixation to an idealized object; Al Pesso explicitly avoids this transferential danger by remaining in the background as the director of the process and allowing various members of the therapy group to embody the ideal parental figure as actors in the drama.

The bodily aspects of such experiences seem to be extremely important (Roth, 2003; Grawe, 2000). A direct somatic experience—for instance, being held in a relationship—can profoundly promote vegetative soothing and the digestion of an emotional cycle (for more on "emotional cycles," see Chapter 53, "The Role of the Body in Emotional Defense Processes: Body Psychotherapy and Emotional Theory" by Ulfried Geuter and Norbert Schrauth). As long as the potential for such corrective experiences does not restrict or prematurely foreclose the necessary space for negative transference processes, such techniques can make an exceedingly important contribution to the resolution of the embodied fixations of past wounding scenarios.

However, the potential of Body Psychotherapy extends far beyond corrective experiences: following Fritz Perls and Paul Goodman, we can characterize this potential as the "revival" or the "revitalization" of the self. In working in an embodied way with clients' emotional defenses, and by extending their expressive, emotional, and behavioral capabilities, Body Psychotherapy helps to resolve the emotional immobility, numbness, and dysregulation that are part and parcel of biographically embodied patterns of compromise.

Through reclaiming capacities of feeling that reawaken passionate engagement with both inner and outer worlds, a vibrant and powerful feeling of "self" begins to reemerge. These kinds of therapeutic effects cannot possibly result from techniques that are focused merely on rearranging the body energetically; for they require an intersubjective engagement; they evolve within a relational container that depends on therapeutic dialogue and relationship, in which the therapist, who has (hopefully) explored his own emotional and existential depths, can share these, and can also hold those of the client. When emotional reintegration takes place, carefully and respectfully within a benign relational space that is contained—as trauma therapy has shown—within a "window of tolerance" between numbness and overwhelm, then emotional vitality, differentiation, and maturity can often result. A typical sign of such therapeutic progress in Body Psychotherapy is that clients in more advanced stages of therapy are quite clear and explicit that—in spite of the risks of vulnerability and pain associated with their rediscovered joy as well as with their experiencing of difficult feelings—they would never want to go back to the numb, dissociated states of contactlessness that they remember bringing into therapy at the outset.

In working like this, Body Psychotherapy has accumulated sufficient evidence over the years to allow us to make one essentially optimistic statement: when the distorted, over- or underdeveloped, rigid or inhibited affective-motor schemas of neurosis, or personality disorder, do loosen up, become more fluid, and lose their dominance, then spaces for new development open up in psychic areas that until then have only been "innate potentials," as George Downing would say. His impression is that—even when inaccessible and immobilized for a long time—these undeveloped schemas inherently want to grow and develop:

> They are unlike growing bones, which lose their capacity to reach their full size once a particular developmental window has been missed. On the contrary, such schemas have a strong tendency to right themselves, an easily stimulated, innate readiness to develop and refine themselves further. (Downing, 1996, p. 192)

How such schemas and subtle psychological capabilities, resources, and potentials, coupled with affective-motor schemas and bodily micropractices, awaken and unfold is a phenomenon that we observe frequently in Body Psychotherapy. They manifest, for example, in qualities of emotional serenity, power, or strength; in abilities to assert oneself, to open up and surrender emotionally, as well as to disconnect and separate oneself. This includes the unique human feature of upright locomotion—the unstable (yet for our species essential) psychological and affective-motor capacity to stand and walk upright, as well as simultaneously being solid and "grounded."

## Body Psychotherapy as Maieutics[31]

In conclusion, an essential aspect for a comprehensive understanding of Body Psychotherapy should not go unmentioned: even though the structuralist terminology of character-analytical theory forms part of the conceptual framework of Body Psychotherapy, as discussed above, it is essential that the therapeutic process itself is not misunderstood in fixed, structuralist terms. Otherwise, reified and objectifying thinking, which—as we have seen—pervades the kind of energetic monism commonly found in some parts of the Body Psychotherapeutic field, is likely to cut across the dynamic and relational processes essential to therapy.

On the metapsychological level, thinking and speaking in terms of structure is just one entirely valid and helpful perspective that contributes to therapeutic competence. We must not, however, imagine that the therapeutic process can be instrumentalized and reduced to this level, or be subsumed under such structuralist, objectifying principles that are fundamentally incapable of doing it justice. This conclusion is inescapable when we recognize that the therapeutic process is of a categorically quite different nature—namely, phenomenological and developmental. As such, it demands of the participants an open and unbiased attitude, without prior fixed assumptions about what will happen and what will emerge. Ideally, the therapist, as well as the client, will both follow and approach one another in a language of *exploration,* rather than *explanation,* of experience as it is, and as it presents or reveals itself (Boadella, 1987). This more dynamic perspective is becoming increasingly common in psychotherapy. The significance of such an open, phenomenologically inspired stance for the practice of Body Psychotherapy can be demonstrated most clearly with regard to the following two points: Body Psychotherapists pay particular attention to a multitude of spontaneously arising, subconscious, *subsymbolic,* and *protosymbolic* body postures, movements, and gesticulations that, at times, may emerge via disturbing waves of arousal and excitation. Such spontaneous expressions can appear, unfold, and reveal themselves in their full and true *meaning, if and* only if they are not interfered with by preestablished interpretations, assumptions, and structures; they require—ideally, from both parties—a relatively impartial space, regardless of whether they emerge via attention to the content of the interaction (what is being spoken about), via the process (how it is being spoken about), or via the relational dynamics, including the transference and countertransference.

---

31 Maieutics: relating to the Socratic method.

The value of phenomenological openness can be seen even more clearly when one observes the deepest level of therapeutic interactions. Body Psychotherapy is fairly exceptional in the way that it can allow access to, and insight into, what Hilarion Petzold calls the level of *autonomous bodily reaction*. He has described this level with precision, taking into consideration its possible fetishization (Petzold, 1996): he refers to phases in the therapeutic process when previously unrealized parts of the self are discovered or reclaimed. This can manifest in a multitude of ways: at times, with the energetic intensity of a thunderstorm; at other times, as fierce pain and convulsions; or as infectious laughter; or as sheer, unbearable joy. What is revealed during these experiences can cast a spell on the present, like the birth of a new being, or the emergence of a new citizen of the earth.

In such moments, when psychological and body defenses are loosened and the rational control of the ego is suspended, autonomous body processes can bring repressed, dissociated, or unrealized parts of the self up to awareness and expression. Because many Body Psychotherapists have themselves experienced the power of such spontaneous, uncontrolled processes—by surrendering to them without knowing at the outset where they would end up—they have a tendency to be less afraid of these processes than the rest of those in the therapeutic field. It is essential to realize that—especially on this level of therapeutic work—Body Psychotherapy and Gestalt Therapy are imbued with a kind of knowledge akin to that of *midwives*. This is an area of knowledge traditionally outside the male, patriarchal domain, but we can recognize it as indispensable, especially when it comes to new beginnings and to the birthing of human subjectivity.

## References

Bateson, G. (1979). *Mind and nature.* New York: Bantam.

Boadella, D. (1987). *Lifestreams.* London: Routledge & Kegan Paul.

Bollas, C. (1992). *Being a character: Psychoanalysis and self-experience.* New York: Hill & Wang.

Bourdieu, P. (1994). Structures, habitus, power: Basis for a theory of symbolic power. In: N. B. Dirks, G. Eley, & S. B. Ortner (Eds.), *Culture/power/history: A reader in contemporary social theory*, (pp. 155–199). Princeton, NJ: Princeton University Press.

Buchholz, K., Latocha, R., Peckmann, H., & Wolbert, K. (2001). *Die Lebensreform: Bd. 1, Bd. 2 [Life Reform (Vols. 1 & 2)].* Darmstadt: Häusser Media.

Cornell, W. F. (2005). *In the terrain of the unconscious: The evolution of a transactional analysis therapist. Transactional Analysis Journal, 35,* 119–131.

Damasio, A. (1994). *Descartes' irrtum [Descartes' error].* Munich: List.

Darwin, C. (2000). *Der Ausdruck der Gemütsbewegungen bei dem Menschen und den Tieren [Emotional expression in man and animals].* Frankfurt: Eichborn.

Dilthey, W., Makkreel, R. A., & Rodi, F. (Eds.). (1991). *Wilhelm Dilthey, selected works: Introduction to the human sciences* (Vol. 1). Princeton, NJ: Princeton University Press.

Downing, G. (1996). *Körper und Wort in der Psychotherapie [Body and word in psychotherapy].* Munich: Kösel.

Geissler, P. (2001). *Mythos Regression [Myth regression].* Giessen: Psychosozial.

Grawe, K. (2000). *Psychologische Therapie [Psychological therapy].* Göttingen: Hogrefe.

Habermas, J. (1968). *Erkenntnis und Interesse [Knowledge and interest].* Frankfurt: Suhrkamp.

Johnson, S. (1988/2000). *Der narzisstische Persönlichkeitsstil [Narcissistic personality style].* Cologne: Edition Humanistische Psychologie.

Kohut, H. (1977). *The restoration of the self.* Chicago: University of Chicago Press.

Lorenzer, A. (1973). *Sprachzerstörung und Rekonstruktion [Voice destruction and reconstruction].* Frankfurt: Suhrkamp.

Lowen, A. (1981). *Körperausdruck und Persönlichkeit [Bodily expression and personality].* Munich: Kösel.

Marlock, G. (1992). Notizen über Regression [Notes on regression]. In: G. Marlock (Ed.), *Weder Körper noch Geist [Neither body nor spirit]*, (pp. 147–166). Oldenburg: Transform.

Perls, F. (1973). *The Gestalt approach & eye witness to therapy.* Ben Lomond, CA: Science & Behavior Books.

Pesso, A. (1986). *Dramaturgie des Unbewussten [Dramaturgy of the unconscious]*. Stuttgart: Klett-Cotta.

Petzold, H. (1996). *Integrative Bewegungs und Leibtherapie: Bd. 1 & 2 [Integrative movement and body therapy (Vols. 1 & 2)]*. Paderborn: Junfermann.

Reich, W. (1971). *Charakteranalyse [Character Analysis]*. Cologne: Kiepenheuer & Witsch.

Ricoeur, P. (1969). *Die Interpretation: Ein Versuch über Freud [Interpretation: An essay on Freud]*. Frankfurt: Suhrkamp.

Roth, G. (2003). *Fühlen, Denken, Handeln [Feeling, thinking, action]*. Frankfurt: Suhrkamp.

Rudolf, G. (1976). *Über die Schwierigkeiten zwischen menschliche Beziehungen mit Hilfe psychoanalytischer Beschreibungsmodelle zu erfassen: Eine Kritik der Ich-Psychologie. Zeitschrift für Psychosomatische Medizin und Psychoanalyse Nr. 2 [Difficulties of describing human relationships with the help of psychoanalytic descriptive models: A critique of Ego Psychology. Journal of Psychosomatic Medicine and Psychoanalysis No. 2]*. Göttingen: Verlag für Medizinische Psychologie im Verlag Vandenhoeck und Ruprecht.

Sarasin, P., & Tanner, J. (1998). *Physiologie und industrielle Gesellschaft [Physiology and industrial society]*. Frankfurt: Suhrkamp.

Stark, M. (1999). *Modes of therapeutic action*. Northvale, NJ: Jason Aronson.

Taylor, C. (1994). *Quellen des Selbst: Die Entstehung der neuzeitlichen Identität [Sources of the self: The emergence of modern identity]*. Frankfurt: Suhrkamp.

Uexküll, T., Fuchs, M., Müller-Braunschweig, H., & Johnen, R. (1994). *Subjektive Anatomie [Subjective anatomy]*. Stuttgart: Schattauer.

# 14
## The Concept of Energy in Body Psychotherapy

**Andreas Wehowsky, Germany**

**Translation by Warren Miller**

**Andreas Wehowsky** had a Diploma in Sociology, was a fully accredited psychotherapist in private practice, and was an internationally active senior trainer, teaching supervisor, and teaching therapist. From 1987 to 1998, he worked closely with David Boadella, and for many years he was a co-editor of the journal *Energy & Character*. As a trainer in Biosynthesis, he made many personal contributions to the development of this method. He was an acting partner of a consulting company and also worked in the areas of coaching, organizational consulting, and management training. He was trained in Neo-Reichian bodywork (Helen Davies and Will Davis), Biosynthesis, Core Energetics (John Pierrakos), the EOS method (Julius Kuhl), Psychodynamic Psychotherapy, as well as systemic supervision and organizational consulting. Since 1994, he also explored Bön Buddhism intensively.

Andreas Wehowsky participated in the discourse on Body Psychotherapy through numerous scientific publications. In particular, his long-term study and exploration of Ken Wilber's Integral Psychology strengthened his desire to advance the integration of Body Psychotherapy into broader interdisciplinary discourses. Sadly, Andreas died suddenly in 2010.

In recent years, Body Psychotherapy has been wrestling with the concept of energy and its practical applications. Although "energy" has informed Body Psychotherapy from its earliest historical roots, lately there's been so much controversy about this concept, and its uses, that some of the leading voices in Body Psychotherapy would prefer to discard it altogether. What at one time was a pioneering accomplishment of Body Psychotherapy is now at risk of being thrown overboard. Without the concept of "energy," however, Body Psychotherapy risks losing contact with groundbreaking developments in biophysics, energy medicine, neuroscience, psychology, and the rapidly growing field of energy psychology. Discussions of energy seem more common in any of these fields at this time than in Body Psychotherapy. To understand why this is the case, it is useful to reflect on the history of the concept of energy.

### From Libido to Orgone Energy

If we look far back into history, it is easy to see that many cultures have associated healing with a variety of experiences and concepts of life energy for thousands of years. Freud introduced the concept of libido into modern psychology to refer to quantifiable drive energies having to do with love in the widest sense (Laplanche and Pontalis, 1975). But, by that time, there had already been outstanding pioneers of psychotherapy—for example, Franz Anton Mesmer (eighteenth century) and Gustav Fechner (nineteenth century), who had worked with energetic phenomena. Pierre Janet (1859–1947), from the French school of Dynamic Psychiatry, worked with concepts of energy and was an important early influence on Freud (Boadella, 1997).

The origin of modern Body Psychotherapy is generally associated with Reich. Whereas Freud's "libido" remained a metaphorical concept, as it seemed impossible to measure such energy at the time, Reich pursued finding measurable correlates of energy. He built on developments in medicine and biology, which had demonstrated the functional division of the autonomous nervous system into a sympathetic and a parasympathetic branch (Ludwig R. Müller), a similar functional polarity between directions of energy flow toward the world and away from it (Max Hartmann and Ludwig Rhumbler), and polarities of charging and discharging processes in vegetative bioelectric flows (Friedrich Kraus). Reich linked the expansion of organismic energy toward the periphery of the body with the experience of genital lust, and chronic contraction with experiences of fear and anger. His theory of the orgasm described processes of tension, charge, discharge, and relaxation, as well as processes of energetic congestion and stasis. Discovery of such energetic blockages led to fundamental insights into the coherence of psychic defense structures and body armoring, which he elaborated in *Character Analysis*. The concept of armoring referred to the sum of all repressed defensive forces, the blockage of plasmatic motility, and the resulting restrictions in contact capability.

These developments led to the expansion of the practice of his psychotherapeutic work: the exploration of the unconscious was no longer restricted to the analysis of the psyche but could now include work with chronic tensions in the body. Vegetotherapy, named in reference to the autonomic nervous system, discovered typical muscular tension patterns in different segments of the body, and concerned itself with their resolution and the restoration of unhampered breathing.

In his further theoretical work, Reich enunciated the functional identity and antithesis of psyche and soma, both governed by a common functional principle that Reich came to call orgone energy. The discovery of orgone energy, derived from "organism," was an outcome of Reich's research on the radiation properties of SAPA bions and eventually expanded to research on the interactions between organisms, the atmosphere, and cosmic phenomena. In numerous experiments, he attempted to measure the effects of orgone, using optical, thermal, electroscopic, and fluorescent research designs (Boadella, 1995). This research led Reich to an exploration of plasma streams and energetic processes in the borderline area between organic and inorganic matter, a more fundamental level than that of the autonomic nervous system, which he subsequently viewed as the mediator between orgone energy and the organism (Lassek, 1997a). Reich developed the idea of a basic level of regulation below the cellular level.

Today this is referred to with different concepts such as the "living matrix," a network of mechanical, vibratory, energetic, electrical, and informational phenomena (Oschman, 2001, 2003). The concept of orgone energy, also called bioenergy, referred to a general creative life energy underlying all phenomena. This conceptualization led to another modification to the practice of psychotherapy. Work with the energetic system moved to the front and center of Reich's research, at times at the expense of his therapeutic work in Character Analysis and Vegetotherapy. The goal was to restore an unhindered flow of pulsation through the body and to free the expression of suppressed impulses, as well as to work with highly charged (blocked) processes (Lassek, 1997b). Will Davis has shown specific ways to target the plasma, a substance that constitutes the basis of the different kinds of connective tissue and their respective organ systems, such as the muscular system, and how the work of restoring pulsation must support not only the expressive "outstroke," but often also the energy-collecting and energy-restoring "instroke" (Davis, 1997). Today, there is wide agreement that the energy in different kinds of connective tissue has a close relationship with the meridian system of acupuncture (Curtis and Hurtak, 2004; Oschman, 2003).

The critical step that Reich took in his transition from Vegetotherapy to Orgone Therapy is a change in paradigm from a neurophysiologically oriented view of energy as mainly pertaining to the nervous system, to a more basic form of life energy. This step has since been repeated in different ways, independently from Reich. A prominent example is Albert Szent-Györgyi's electronic biology, which is one of the foundations of contemporary research into the living matrix (Oschman, 2003). The reason that Reich's work on orgone energy isn't cited in this research is due to the speculative overloading of the concept. In the end, orgone energy remained an empirically unverifiable postulate, and as such couldn't be used to explain specific measurable phenomena.

## The Difficult Inheritance of an Overstretched Concept of Energy

After Reich's death in 1957, several of his students founded their own schools. Only some of them continued to use the concept of orgone energy. At the same time, the concept of "bioenergy" gained in popularity. Bioenergy was generally associated with the life force and, beyond that, was largely undefined. One of the reasons why the idea of orgone energy lost popularity is the somewhat ambiguous way it was conceptualized. On the one hand, Reich made efforts to measure its effects directly; and on the other hand, he assigned it the status of a fundamental, cosmic force, which Boadella interprets as a source or ground of being (Boadella, 1994, appendices). If this holds true, we could acknowledge Reich's philosophical and spiritual intuition, but then, paradoxically, we would also have to admit that such an essential source would elude any attempts at definition, making measurability impossible. Orgone energy can't claim to be both. It seems that Reich was possibly too rash in extrapolating from his research on energy. This resulted in an inflated and overgeneralized conceptualization of energy in which experimental and cosmological meanings were all mixed up with one another. It is the concept's overgeneralized definition that made it untenable. Contemporary energy medicine has replaced the generic conceptualization of energy with multiple, specific, and measurable energies (Oschman, 2001).

## From Energy-Monism to the Complementarity of Energy and Consciousness

The positioning of energy as the primordial ground and functional principle unifying soma and psyche creates a second problem: it introduces a reductionist trait into the model. It implies that consciousness is a secondary phenomenon deriving from the primordial energy. Ken Wilber considers this a subtle form of materialism (Wilber, 2003). Orgone energy, when thought of as Reich's concept of universal energy, is rather like the *Tao;* but it is more commonly likened to the life force, when in the body, similar to the Chinese concept of *chi,* the Indian concept of *prana,* or the Japanese *ki* energy, to name just a few examples. But *chi, prana,* or *ki* represent only one kind of energy among numerous energies that are distinguished in today's research (Jobst, 2004). They certainly do not represent the primordial ground, or the *Tao*. In other words, Reich's conceptualization is due for a thorough revision. The task at hand is to describe the relationship between energy and consciousness in the light of contemporary science. This immediately evokes the old philosophical question of the relationship between matter and consciousness. There are several basic and unreconciled stances that developed in relation to this question (Wehowsky, 1997a), which makes it impossible to comment on this issue without taking a position among them. I find it useful to consider matter and consciousness as two givens that are not reducible to each other. Wilber, likewise, interprets matter and consciousness as the exterior and interior manifestations of phenomena (Wilber, 2003). The exterior manifestation is thereby considered as categorically measurable, whereas the interior manifestation refers to a subjectively experienced reality. The elementary building blocks of matter, such as quarks, electrons, protons, atoms, and molecules, are in interaction with the four correlating fundamental forces of gravity, electromagnetism, weak nuclear force, and strong nuclear force. Wilber hypothesizes that, as matter evolves into ever more complexity, correlating energies become progressively subtle. A spectrum emerges, ranging from gross energies (the four basic forces of matter) to subtle energies (more in the body) to causal energies. This spectrum of exterior forms of matter and energy, with increasing complexity, corresponds to progressively complex forms of interior consciousness. In other words, instead of using a generic concept of energy, we are now not only talking about different kinds of energies, but also about different *levels* of energy that are in correlation with the complexity of material forms and the levels of consciousness.

The Dutch researcher Johannes J. Poortman did extensive research on this subject in different cultures and eras, which was published as *Vehicles of Consciousness,* and his findings lend support to Wilber's model. Poortman uses the concept of psycho-hylism to refer to a belief found in many cultures: that a subtle body or matter always accompanies the soul. This basic idea is developed in the concept of hylic pluralism, in which different levels of subtle matter are differentiated (Poortman, 1978; Wehowsky, 1997a). The above deliberations can be summarized in four postulates:

1. A generic concept of energy is currently neither useful nor tenable, as associated fundamental scientific problems haven't been resolved yet (Oschman, 2002). The use of a multilevel model circumvents this problem.
2. The use of a multilevel model further prevents a mix-up of different levels of energy, with a supposed energetic, cosmic source (*Tao*).
3. The clarification of this mix-up resolves the subtle reduction of consciousness to energy.
4. The multilevel model is applicable to energies as well as to consciousness. Each level of consciousness—in the domain of psychology, this refers to the personality—has a correlating level of energetic organization.

## Conventional and Unconventional Energies

The exploration of increasingly subtle levels of energy brings us nearly to the limits of what we can measure. That's why we make a basic distinction between conventional and variously defined unconventional energies. In physics, the conventional energies consist of the four basic forces of matter, though recent developments in string theory complicate this. A few theories have been developed that propose a unified root to the four forces and multidimensionality beyond the space-time continuum, but such unconventional models are currently not widely accepted (Wehowsky, 1998), nor have they been fully proved.

Biology, biochemistry, and biophysics describe conventional energies that are operative in the metabolic processes of living bodies' organs. Such energies include bioelectricity, biomagnetism, and biophotonic radiation, conceived of as the highly coherent bioelectric radiation of biological matter. These scientific fields also entertain discussions about unconventional energies beyond electromagnetic radiation. Examples include so-called non-Hertzian waves (Benor, 1992) and nonenergy information fields, such as the morphogenetic fields of Alexander Gurwitsch, Rupert Sheldrake, and Peter Gariaev, which can have correlating material and energetic aspects (Curtis and Hurtak, 2004).

These discussions are of great significance for energy medicine. There is basic agreement that today's technology is surprisingly capable of showing and measuring nonmaterial phenomena (Curtis, 2004). The task is no less than to facilitate a paradigm shift from the currently predominant biomolecular medical paradigm to an understanding that conceives of the body as an energetic biocomputer (Curtis and Hurtak, 2004). In the conventional spectrum, it is in particular the measurable biomagnetic fields in the extremely low frequency range (below 100 hertz) that play a central role in healing processes. The information these fields offer not only facilitates tissue regeneration, but also makes traumatic experiences that are imprinted and frozen in the body accessible and resolvable. Medical and psychotherapeutic applications of such fields occur through the use of machines and through fields that experienced therapists and healers are able to generate themselves (Oschman, 2001).

Reich's research into the interactions between cosmic, atmospheric, and organismic energy is being revisited in Oschman's concept of entrainment, referring to the coupling of frequencies. Oschman illustrates how healers, therapists, and clients can tune their brain waves to couple up with the electromagnetic "Schumann" resonance between the earth and the ionosphere in order to create optimal conditions for healing processes to take place (Oschman, 1997). More recently, different forms of light medicine have been emerging that use the bioelectromagnetic and cellular effects of light for the regulation of biochemical and biophysical processes (Jobst, 2004). The utilization of energy as information beyond bioelectromagnetism and the complex world of quantum information and nonlocal interactions are driving research on light therapies and biophotonic intercellular communication. This research reaches into the unconventional realm of nonmaterial light beyond the electromagnetic spectrum (Curtis, 2004).

In the newly forming field of energy psychology, findings from energy medicine are applied primarily to the meridian system. One important historical development in this field can be traced from George Goodheart's Kinesiology (Gin and Green, 1997) to Roger Callahan's (2002) Thought Field Therapy, and its simplification in the Emotional Freedom Techniques of Gary Craig (2010), to the work of Fred Gallo (2005), who developed the Energy Diagnostic and Treatment Methods (EDxTM) and the Negative Affect Erasing Method (NAEM). These methods are now being used to treat the post-traumatic sequelae of traumatic experiences, as well as many affective disorders, such as phobias, anxiety disorders, guilt feelings, and depression. The methods are based on the assumption that the subtle energies in the body function as a regulatory system for emotions and for health in general (Gallo, 2000). Energy psychology also establishes linkages with other important methods, as a look at the program outline of the Association for Comprehensive Energy Psychology's Toronto conference of 2004 clearly illustrates (Feinstein, 2004). Such methods include EMDR, the trauma therapy of Peter Levine—which establishes an important link to the tradition of Body Psychotherapy (Levine, 1997)—and Bessel van der Kolk's (van der Kolk et al., 1996) research on trauma and the brain.

Energy psychology sees itself as a family of methods that address the "human vibrational matrix" that emerges from the interactions among the meridians, the chakras, and the human energy field. Other potential linkages with Body Psychotherapy suggest themselves concerning the connections between the vibrational matrix and the connective tissue system. Glaser had described the interactions between the meridian system, body posture, and emotional states in the 1920s as the foundation upon which he developed Eutony (Glaser, 1993). Maggie Phillips has submitted proposals for the development of integral therapy models that take energetic processes into consideration (Phillips, 2000).

As mentioned previously, in his *Integral Psychology,* Wilber distinguishes three major families of energies. Referencing established traditions, he refers to them as gross energies, subtle energies, and causal energies. He further subdivides the family of subtle energies into four levels, consisting of two bio-fields (etheric and astral) and two psychic fields (psychic-1 and psychic-2). The etheric field permeates the living organism, flows through the meridians, and connects the physical body with the astral field. "Astral" refers to strong instinctive and affective energies that are associated with the brainstem and limbic system. From an evolutionary standpoint, psychic energies arise with the emergence of the cortex. "Psychic" in this case refers to mental activities in general or as pertaining to the thought field (Burr, 1973). The subdivision into psychic-1 and psychic-2 energies refers to a further development of consciousness in the sense of increasing complexity. Wilber describes this progression with reference to meme theory's stages of evolutionary-cultural consciousness. The causal energies refer to a further, higher level of consciousness on a causal-creative plane (Wilber, 2003).

As we can see, Wilber's multilevel model enters the realm of unconventional conceptualizations, which must seem speculative from the standpoint of conventional psychology. However, the research into meditative states and human consciousness and its accompanying energetic states, in the great spiritual traditions, as well as the intersubjective and cross cultural replicability of these experiences, lend support to such conceptualizations.

In conventional psychology, it is difficult to apply a multilevel model of correlation between consciousness and energy as consistently as Wilber conceptualized it. With respect to the spectrum of energy, it wouldn't suffice to correlate neurophysiological findings on the activation and deactivation of hierarchically organized networks of levels and structures in the brain with respective subcortical and cortical processes of consciousness. In addition, it would be necessary to identify how inhibition and facilitation are regulated in the interplay of biomolecular processes (e.g., neurotransmitters, neuropeptides), bioelectrical fields (e.g., brain waves), bioelectromagnetic fields (e.g., biophotons), and more subtle fields (e.g., morphogenetic fields and nonlocal genetic information based on the particle-wave duality of DNA) (Curtis and Hurtak, 2004; Gariaev et al., 2000).

## Energy in Personality Psychology

Even without taking on such a challenging project, there are some noteworthy developments in psychology that continue to advance our understanding of the correlations between energy and consciousness. Traditionally, the concept of energy has commonly been referred to in discussions of temperament when distinctions are drawn between motor activation and sensory excitation (Schimmack and Reisenzein, 2002). Whereas basic tendencies of approach and avoidance can already be observed on this subcortical level (Kuhl, 2001), we speak of motivation, in a narrow sense only, at higher cognitive levels of the personality in reference to reward-driven and goal-oriented behavior. But even at the cognitive level, motivation remains closely linked to energy as the experience of motivation simultaneously activates various mental systems that prepare the body for action (Kuhl, 2000). The problems of a generic concept of energy become evident where energetically strong intentions do not automatically lead to behavior of matching intensity (Ibid.). A distinction between different functional systems of personality and respectively matching energetic states is needed to explain such circumstances. Heckhausen's action-phase model offers such conceptual distinctions between information-processing and behavior-regulating systems of the psyche. Grawe used this model to identify the generic therapeutic factors of different psychotherapeutic approaches: motivational clarification in Depth Psychology, and problem solving in cognitive behavioral psychotherapy (Grawe, 1998). The Personality System Interactions (PSI) theory of Julius Kuhl achieves a high degree of integration between motivational, cognitive, and personality psychologies, and makes an important contribution toward the understanding of the dynamics between energy and cognition.

PSI theory conceptualizes personality as constituted by four central cognitive macrosystems, and describes the interactions among these systems in detail. A balanced interplay between these systems allows for experiences to be processed in a way that facilitates the development of self, and for behavior to be regulated volitionally and effectively. Such functional integration is the result of reciprocal activation and inhibition among the personality systems. Fundamentally, this interplay is based on energetic processes of excitation and inhibition that can be modulated *bottom up* by temperament, affect, cognitive personality style, and motivation, as well as *top down* through volitional self-regulation. Modulation here means that it is always an excitatory or inhibitory flow of energy that either activates or inhibits states of consciousness associated with the four macrosystems, and thus determines the strengths of their connection (Kuhl, 2001; Wehowsky, 2004).

From a PSI theory perspective, Kuhl finds current dynamic/energetic concepts in psychology insufficient. Although addressing such singular issues as excitation, motivation, and memory activation, these concepts fall short of addressing the interconnections (Kuhl, 2000). Given this background, PSI theory takes two important steps forward. First, the generic concept of energy in psychology is differentiated into specific energetic states and their modulation. Their function is to activate respective cognitive macrosystems (we could speak of sensory excitation, motor activation, intentional concentration, and serene relaxation). Second, the model proposes two enervating and two inhibiting flows of energy that establish connections between the systems and stabilize information exchange. This flow of energy between the personality systems creates the conditions that allow even the subtlest cognitive processes to unfold (Ibid.).

Kuhl's model proposes seven functional levels of personality, wherein energies are predominantly associated with the subcognitive and body-based level of temperament. The dynamic conceptualization of motivation at the intersection of somatic and mental levels of function shows that cognitions and energies interact at this level as well. Furthermore, Kuhl proposes that cognitive representations at the mental levels of the personality gain their strength through energetic activation. We could understand this as the modulated interplay between subcognitive (energetic and affective) and cognitive levels of function. Beyond that, we could also speculate whether a multilevel model of energies suggests itself once again. In this case, we would need to ask if cognitive representations aren't simply information linked with subtle energetic processes that correspond with excitations and activations on a basic, organismic level in fractal interactions and resonances via facilitating and inhibiting processes. In short, this model also allows for a hierarchical organization of multiple energies.

Aside from such speculations, Kuhl's theoretical work has a number of implications for Body Psychotherapy, which include the following:

- The model proposes concrete and specific mutual interactions between energetic dynamics and cognitive functions. It preempts the temptation to idealize a generically conceived high level of energy, as the model predicts this would lead to a very unbalanced cognitive state. Instead of a generic high level of energy, what counts is the flexibility with which energetic and cognitive states can be changed and maintained as part of a mature and competent personality.

- Kuhl's elaborations show how subcognitive (energetic and affective) and cognitive levels are linked together. They mutually influence one another in bottom-up and top-down processes. In other words, there is not one right entry point for interventions. Interventions can be effective one way or another, depending on the specific situation, and there is no primacy for either energetic or cognitive interventions.

- If the therapeutic goal of free streaming or flowing is to be meaningful, it can't be narrowly focused on the energetic level. The idea that cognitive themes automatically resolve themselves once the energy has been balanced is basically naive, although this does sometimes happen. The revitalization of encapsulated and stagnant subcognitive and cognitive information processing through energetic means can be viewed as a prerequisite for the subsequent development of self-regulatory competencies on the cognitive level, rather than a magic replacement for work on the personality.

- PSI theory presents an integrative theory of personality. It systematically integrates energetic dynamics and differentiates between somatic and mental levels of personality. As such, it can explain the effectiveness of Body Psychotherapy, can inform Body Psychotherapy on a wide range of issues, and is particularly well positioned to support an energetic approach and point to linkages with cognitive processes.

## Subjective Experience and the Psychology of Vitality

The intent of this chapter up to this point has been to elucidate the concept of energy in Body Psychotherapy differently from an objective, scientific perspective. This perspective needs to be complemented by a description of subjective experiences of energetic phenomena, and how these can be put into language. In clinical practice, the subjective experience of clients and therapists is in the foreground anyhow. It's a given that the verbal expression of these somatic events serves to communicate experiences. The use of metaphors in this context is expected and legitimate. Furthermore, it is no surprise that commonly used metaphors tap into language concepts associated with the four (or five) elements. Water, in particular, seems to have a rich source of associations. Experiences of flowing and streaming are commonly used to communicate experiences of well-being, pleasure, and, in a more objective sense, health. Conversely, images of freezing and flooding often describe states of pain and stress. The hardness of tension and softness of relaxation reflect the earth element; heat, cold, and charge reflect the fire element; and oscillations, vibrations, and resonances primarily reflect the air element. But there are also more complex metaphors and symbols that serve verbally to express bodily sensations, feelings, and inner states, such as a "punch in the stomach" or a "lump in the throat." This is a language of intensities, forms, and states that speaks of a wealth of phenomena beyond verbal thought contents, and is often intuitively associated with energies.

Although, scientifically, it would certainly be interesting to establish correlations between subjective experiences of energies, and objective, measurable findings, currently this seems out of reach for Body Psychotherapy, in particular when considering a multilevel model of energies. More research is needed to that end. Therapeutic and energetic work in the context of a research setting that allows for real-time measurement of specific energies is still rare. But the need to clarify the scientific concept of energy does not call the subjective validity and significance of the perception of energies into question. Many empirical studies have successfully researched energy as a subjective variable, especially using the concept of vitality. In this context, "vitality" is used in a wide sense in which the subjective perception of life force is based not merely on physical health, but more so on the experience of a coherent self as the source of motivation, autonomy, self-realization, and personal well-being (Ryan and Frederick, 1997).

## Between the Paradigms of Energy and Organization

Reich's development of Vegetotherapy and Orgone Therapy established a strong foundation for the Neo-Reichian schools of Body Psychotherapy that followed. Each of the numerous Body Psychotherapeutic schools has also developed its own specific ways of working, and some have made important linkages to other traditions. This means that it is difficult to make general statements about the role of energies in these various schools of Body Psychotherapy. Nonetheless, it seems important to touch upon some important themes.

The significance of energetic and somatic work becomes evident in the names of the early Neo-Reichian schools. The prominent example is "Bioenergetics," developed by Lowen and Pierrakos. Although this name designates the focus of this approach as work with energy, elements of Character Analysis that had also been central to Vegetotherapy were integrated into this approach. The specific work with energy followed the tradition of Vegetotherapy in focusing on pulsating cycles of charge and chronic tension patterns, so-called armoring, in different organ systems. The Neo-Reichian schools developed some areas of specialization—for example, with focus on the muscular system, on contact functions mediated by the sense channels, or on metabolic processes in the inner organs. Meanwhile, breathing processes always remained central in their significance for the general level of energy. Some schools, such as the school of Will Davis, developed an orgone-therapeutic focus on the ground substance of the connective tissue system (Davis, 1997). The exploration of different organ systems led to the development of central therapeutic principles and processes such as grounding, centering, facing, containment, charge, release, bonding, and the intentional direction of affect-motor schemas and fields (Downing, 1996; Boadella, 1993). Different schools emphasized the central concept of pulsation, which refers to rhythmic processes of expansion and contraction, and charge cycles to varying degrees. Based on the interplay of character structures and somatic armoring, the Bioenergetic tradition, in particular, greatly emphasized emotional expression, commonly intensifying energetic charge to a high degree so as to initiate cathartic releases. On the other end of the spectrum, Biodynamics, developed by Gerda Boyesen, for example, focused on developing gentler ways of releasing tensions. More recent developments have led to a deeper understanding of character structures, structural disorders, and traumas that has enabled a better integration of energetic processes. The one-sided overemphasis on catharsis has been balanced with complementary principles and methods to create a more differentiated approach. In particular, the distinction of hyper- and hypoprocesses in breathing, musculature, and digestion enabled more differentiated energetic work to match the differentiations in characterological diagnostics.

As these notes on the correlations between energies and organ systems (musculoskeletal system, breathing, digestion, nerve and sense organs system) suggest, the energetic dimension of somatic work was complemented by considerations of morphological aspects of embryological development early on. Biosynthesis, in particular, traced the development of the organ systems back to the three layers of embryogenesis: endoderm, mesoderm, and ectoderm (Boadella, 1991). The integration of energetic and morphological aspects led to reflections on soma and character, in which the concept of volitional and consciously accessible organization, or formation, gained prominence. This integrative achievement is mainly the work of Stanley Keleman and David Boadella (Keleman, 1985; Boadella, 1991).

These developments have led to a wealth of theoretical and clinical knowledge, which is documented in the extensive literature on this subject (EABP, 2002; Geuter, 2002; Freudl, 2000). But recent developments have also presented problems, particularly in regard to the concept of energy. A controversy on this subject has also led to divisions in Body Psychotherapy. Although this chapter's initial tasks were to illustrate the problems of a generic concept of life energy, which is based on Reich's concept of orgone energy, and to show possible paths forward, I now want to reflect on the clinical implications of the energy concept.

## On the Complementarity of Energy and Relationship

In the past, the premise was that the restoration of the free flow of life energy was the decisive therapeutic intervention leading toward better (psychological and physical) health, and that Body Psychotherapists have the basic knowledge about how to restore this flow, frequently established an implicit expert-patient relationship between therapist and client: a relationship that is also sometimes shaded by narcissistic hues. Along these lines, therapists worked with standardized therapeutic goals and protocols. The caricature of this was captured in the 1970s idea that a therapeutic session must lead to a catharsis, so as to count as: (1) having touched the core issues or humanity of the client; (2) having proved effective and given value for money; and (3) having demonstrated the competence of the therapist.

Since then, the discussion of transference and countertransference phenomena within Body Psychotherapy has become much more widely accepted, and there is less of this "performance art."

Nowadays, the potential of therapeutic relationships to offer corrective experiences is also generally more recognized, and therapists seek to engage in intersubjective and collaborative therapeutic relationships. These changes have led to an increased awareness of the psychotherapeutic relationship as an important therapeutic factor. Beyond critiquing Reich's concept of energy and the one-sidedness of its therapeutic applications, some leading Body Psychotherapists came to reject the use of energy concepts altogether, viewing energy work and relational work as diametrically opposed to one another. But with this, they are throwing the baby out with the bath-water, as such a critique neglects the relational aspects that have been historically associated with the concept of energy by Reich and his followers. Examples of such associations include the principle of vegetative identification, and the knowledge of motivational and object-oriented directions of pulsation. In addition, to construe independent and complementary categories as contradictory and mutually exclusive constitutes a categorical error. Instead of insisting that mutual influences between energetic and relational processes have important implications for Body Psychotherapeutic work that need to be taken into consideration, this critique splits the dimensions of energy and relationship into two mutually exclusive "either-or" categories.

The proposition that energetic patterns have no relational history, and, conversely, that relationships exist devoid of energetic processes, constitutes a relapse into old dualisms. It suggests that although the development of consciousness and the psyche is shaped by relationships, the closely linked formative processes of energetic embodiment are not. In contrast, Allan Schore, for example, describes how the energetic regulation in different kinds of attachment between children and their parents plays a crucial role in the neurobiological development of the children's brains that even manifests in structural morphogenesis (Schore, 2003). Energy and relationship therefore are not mutually exclusive but complementary categories (Wehowsky, 1998). Just like energy and consciousness, they act interdependently at each level of personality and development, as Wilber clearly laid out in his Integral Psychology model. Contemporary research on therapeutic factors in psychotherapy suggests that change processes occur when problems and resources are activated. Although these activations occur in relationships, the choice of words seems to implicitly note the significance of energetic aspects in experientially oriented processes.

## On the Complexity of the Energy Concept in the Multilevel Model

In consideration of Body Psychotherapy's potential to activate states, problems, resources, affects, body perceptions, key scenes, motives, and unconscious or preconscious memories that are not easily accessible by cognitive or verbal means, the concept and process of embodiment has always been one of Body Psychotherapy's specific therapeutic factors. Activation and deactivation, facilitation and inhibition, can serve as central concepts for the description of energetic processes manifesting in the regulation or dysregulation of activation states, or in pattern formations that simultaneously represent information. Complementarity of consciousness and energy means that states are constituted of energetic patterns of activation as well as by consciousness processes, and that these are mutually conditioning each other. The multilevel model proposes that each level is characterized by its respective complementary correlations between energy and consciousness.

One of the most important scientific distinctions being discussed is the distinction between the levels of affects and cognitions. The affective neuroscience of Jaak Panksepp underlines the importance of the distinction between cortical-cognitive and subcortical-affective types of activation and consciousness (Panksepp, 2003a). Affects arise from analog information processing, which reaches deeply into the neurobiological and neurodynamic structures of our embodiment and penetrates our movements, behaviors, and higher cognitive processes (Ibid.). These neurodynamic structures in turn point to an even deeper level of cellular and molecular processes (Panksepp, 2003b). Allan Schore views this lower level as housing the central energetic and metabolic regulators for affective states (Schore, 2003). Oschman takes it another step with his concept of the living matrix. This model describes a continuum of subatomic and quantum physical processes that function as an integrative regulatory communication system that is faster and more fundamental than the nervous system (Oschman, 2003).

These deliberations propose that energetic and consciousness processes correlate at many levels of our bodily, affective, and cognitive organization. In the light of this complexity, a generic concept of energy seems neither useful nor tenable. Rather, it challenges Body Psychotherapy to specify at which level of the energetic spectrum it operates and what specific energy it is addressing. In this pursuit, it can be helpful to recall a basic premise of affective neuroscience that states that neurobiological functions of the body and the brain lead to intrinsically positive or negative affective states of varying types and intensity (Panksepp, 2003a), which in turn influence cognition via the principle of state dependence. This thought is central to Kuhl's PSI theory, as previously mentioned. Following PSI theory, regulation between cognitive systems is effected through energetic facilitation and inhibition, mutually conditioned by affective, motivational, cognitive, and volitional modulators. This spectrum between organismic base-regulation and volitional self-regulation spans the field in which Body Psychotherapy can practically orchestrate its energetic interventions and theoretically specify its domain. In complementarity with cognitive interventions, it can thereby contribute to flexibility and effectiveness of modulation between the systems of the psyche.

## Outlook and Challenges

The central thesis of this chapter is that Body Psychotherapy should definitely not abandon its conception of energy. Instead, previous conceptualizations of energy urgently need to be revised in the light of current research from different disciplines. On the one hand, such a revision will show that many of the theoretical foundations and practical experiences not only stand the test of time, but also can even be counted among the particular strengths of Body Psychotherapy. On the other hand, the differentiation of a generic energy concept into more specific terms, as illustrated by the multilevel model and the interactions between energies and consciousness, is long overdue and would advance the identification of Body Psychotherapy's specific therapeutic factors. The following themes seem relevant in this context:

> Contemporary trauma research and therapy, in particular, recognize the significance of subcognitive information processing and the role energetic interventions can play in this context. Body Psychotherapy has a high degree of expertise in these areas. It has the potential to bring its knowledge into dialogue with more recent developments, such as energy psychology and EMDR, in order to arrive at a higher, and possibly common, level of integration, and present new strategies for intervention. Examples along these lines include the appreciative and critical examination of the methods of energy psychology by Maarten Aalberse (Aalberse, 2001), and Maggie Phillips's integrative model (Phillips, 2000).

> Neurophysiological and neurobiological research by researchers such as Schore, Panksepp, and Kuhl penetrates deeply into energetic and affective foundations of development, contact, and self-regulation (Schore, 2003; Panksepp, 1998; Kuhl, 2001). Here the concepts of energy are rehabilitated rather than abandoned. At the same time, they are brought into different contexts. Even Panksepp, who in the context of his affective neuroscience more frequently speaks of neurodynamics and activation rather than of energy directly, believes that psychology gave up using energy metaphors such as organic "pressure" and "drives" prematurely as the digital information processing paradigm took hold in the context of the cognitive revolution (Panksepp, 2003a). As this research is well received, we are encouraged to creatively develop and further systematize interventions and techniques that address relational dynamics and developmental, formative processes.

Wilber's Integral Psychology places energies in correlation with consciousness processes on an individual level as well as on a collective level. It further integrates scientific models of developmental stages with developments in areas of reality that are central to us—namely, self, nature, and society. The dimensions of this model and the interactions it describes can serve to overcome reductionisms such as the dualism between energy and relationship. It can support the complexity of Body Psychotherapeutic work through an understanding of the complexity of energy in all areas of reality and at all levels of development (Wilber, 2003).

These are only some perspectives that can contribute to the rehabilitation of the concept of energy in Body Psychotherapy by putting it on new foundations. From this new vantage point, we are challenged to make the concept of energy an essential and integral aspect of the theory and practice of Body Psychotherapy.

## References

Aalberse, M. (2001). Intention Movements, meridian rebalancing and choreographic psychotherapy (Manuscript only).

ACEP (Association for Comprehensive Energy Psychology) (2004). *The Energy Field, Vol. 5.*

Benor, D.J. (1992). *Healing Research: Holistic Energy Medicine and Spiritualit.* Vol. 1 & 2. Helix Editions; Deddington, Oxon.

Boadella, D. Appendices: Responses to Critiques of the energy model in body psychotherapy. www.vkdnet.de/website/archiv/downloa.htm

Boadella, D. (1991). Befreite Lebensenergie. Einführung in die Biosynthese. München: Kösel.

Boadella, D. (1993). Shape Flow and Postures of the Soul. *Energy & Character 30, No. 2.*

Boadella, D. (1994). Energetic Healing: The orgone theory of Wilhelm Reich in its scientific and philosophic context (Manuscript).

Boadella, D. (1995). *Wilhelm Reich: Pionier des neuen Denkens [Wilhelm Reich: Pioneer of new thought]*. München: Scherz.

Boadella, D. (1997). Awakening sensibility, recovering motility: Psycho-physical synthesis at the foundations of Body-Psychotherapy: The hundred year legacy of Pierre Janet (1859–1947). *International Journal of Psychotherapy 2, No. 1, pp. 45–56.*

Curtis, B.D. (2004). Energy Medicine: From Knowledge to Practice. *The Journal of Alternative and Complementary Medicine 10, No. 1, pp. 7–8.*

Curtis, B.D. & Hurtak, J.J. (2004). Consciousness and Quantum Information Processing: Uncovering the Foundation for a Medicine of Light. *The Journal of Alternative and Complementary Medicine 10, No. 1, pp. 27–39.*

Davis, W. (1997). Biological Foundations of the Schizoid Process. *Energy & Character 28, No. 1, pp. 57–76.*

Downing, G. (1996). *Körper und Wort in der Psychotherapie [Body and Word in Psychotherapy].* München: Kösel.

EABP (The European Association for Body Psychotherapy) (2002). The EABP Bibliography of Body-Psychotherapy on CD-ROM.

Freudl, P. (2000). *Energie & Charakter: Bibliographische Analyse von 30 Jahrgängen der wichtigsten Zeitschrift (1970–2000) [Energy & Character: A bibliographic analysis of 30 years of the Journal (1970-2000).* Elmshorn: Archiv für Körperpsychotherapie.

Gallo, F.P. (2000). *Energy Diagnostic and Treatment Methods.* New York: W.W. Norton & Co.

Gariaev, P.P., Tertishny, G.G. & Leonova, K.A. (2000). The Wave, Probabilistic and Linguistic representations of Cancer and HIV. *Journal of Non-Locality and remote Mental Interactions 1, No. 2,*

Geuter, U. (2002). *Deutschsprachige Literatur zur Körperpsychotherapie: Eine Bibliografie [German-language literature for Body Psychotherapy: A Bibliography].* Berlin: Ulrich Leutner Verlag.

Glaser, V. (1993). *Eutonie: Das Verhaltensbuch des menschlichen Wohlbefindens [Eutony: The behavior of the book of human well-being].* Heidelberg: Haug.

Grawe, K. (1998). *Psychologische Therapie [Psychological Therapy].* Göttingen: Hogrefe.

Jobst, K.A. (2004). Editorial Part 1. Science and Healing: From Bioelectromagnetics to the Medicine of Light: Implications, Phenomena, and Deep Transformation. *The Journal of Alternative and Complementary Medicine 10, No. 1, pp. 1–3.*

Keleman, S. (1982). *Leibhaftes Leben: Wie wir uns über den Körper wahrnehmen und gestalten können [Body Life: How we perceive ourselves in the body].* München: Kösel.

Keleman, S. (1985). *Emotional Anatomy: The structure of experience.* Berkeley: Center Press.

Kuhl, J. (2000): A Functional-Design Approach to Motivation and Self-Regulation: The Dynamics of Personality Systems Interactions. In: M. Boekaerts, P.R. Pintrich & M. Zeidner (Eds.) *Self-regulation: Directions and challenges for future research*, (pp. 111–169). New York: Academic Press.

Kuhl, J. (2001). *Motivation und Persönlichkeit [Motivation and Personality].* Göttingen: Hogrefe.

Laplanche, J. & Pontalis, J.-B. (1975). *Das Vokabular der Psychoanalyse [The vocabulary of psychoanalysis].* Vol. 1. Frankfurt: Suhrkamp.

Lassek, H. (1997a). *Orgon-Therapie: Heilen mit der reinen Lebensenergie [Orgone Therapy: Healing with the pure life energy].* München: Scherz.

Lassek, H. (Ed.) (1997b). *Lebensenergie-Forschung [Life Energy Research].* Berlin: Simon & Leutner.

Levine, P.A. (1997). *Waking the Tiger: Healing Trauma.* Berkeley: North Atlantic Books.

Oschman, J.L. (1997). Therapeutic Entrainment. *Journal of Bodywork and Movement Therapies, Vol. 18.*

Oschman, J.L. (2001). *Energy Medicine.* New York: Churchill Livingstone.

Oschman, J.L. (2002). Science and the Human Energy Field. *Reiki News Magazine 1, No. 3.*

Oschman, J.L. (2003). *Energy Medicine in Therapeutics and Human Performance.* Edinburgh: Butterworth Heinemann.

Panksepp, J. (1998). *Affective Neuroscience: The Foundations of Human and Animal Emotions.* New York: Oxford University Press.

Panksepp, J. (2003a). At the interface of the affective, behavioral and cognitive neurosciences: Decoding the emotional feelings of the brain. *Brain and Cognition 52, pp. 4–14.*

Panksepp, J. (2003b). Biological Psychiatry Sketched— Past, Present and Future. In: J. Panksepp, (Ed.) (2004). *Textbook of Biological Psychiatry.* New York: John Wiley & Sons.

Phillips, M. (2000). *Finding the Energy to Heal. How EMDR, Hypnosis, TFT, Imagery and Body-Focused Therapy Can Help Restore Mindbody Health.* New York: W.W.Norton & Company.

Poortman, J.J. (1978). *Vehicles of Consciousness: The Concept of Hylic Pluralism (Ochema).Vol. I–IV.* Utrecht: Theosophical Publishing House.

Ryan, R.M. & Frederick, C. (1997). On Energy, Personality and Health: Subjective Vitality as a Dynamic Reflection of Well-Being. *Journal of Personality, 65, 3.*

Schimmack, U. & Reisenzein, R. (2002): Experiencing Activation: Energetic arousal and tense arousal are not mixtures of valence and activation. *Emotion, 2, (4), pp. 412–417.*

Schore, A.N. (2003). *Affect Dysregulation and Disorders of the Self.* New York: W.W. Norton & Co.

Wehowsky, A. (1997a). Entwicklung und Entdeckung [Development and Discovery]. *Energie & Charakter, 14.*

Wehowsky, A. (1997b). Konzepte der Erdung. In: M. Glatzer (Ed.) *Die Psychotonik Glaser im Licht aktueller Entwicklungen [Psychotonic glasses in the light of current developments].* Stuttgart: Hippokrates.

Wehowsky, A. (1998). Energy in Somatic Psychotherapy. *Energy & Character, 29, No. 2.*

Wehowsky, A. (2004). Zum Kompetenzkompass der Selbststeuerung [The compass of competence for self-control]. In: P. Geißler, P. (Ed.) *Was ist Selbstregulation? Eine Standortbestimmung [What is self-regulation? A position of determination].* Gießen: Psychosozial-Verlag.

Wilber, K. (1999). Integral Psychology. In: *The Collected Works of Ken Wilber: Volume Four.* Boston & London: Shambhala, pp. 423–717.

Wilber, K. (2003). *Excerpt G: Toward A Comprehensive Theory of Subtle Energies.* Boston & London: Shambhala

# 15

## The Organization of Experience

*A Systems Perspective on the Relation of Body Psychotherapies to the Wider Field of Psychotherapy*

### Gregory J. Johanson, United States

**Gregory J. Johanson**, PhD, is a Body Psychotherapist as well as a pastoral theologian, and is a member of the American Psychological Association and the American Association of Pastoral Counselors. He is co-founder and senior trainer of the Hakomi Institute; editor and co-editor of professional journals such as the *Hakomi Forum* and the *Journal of Self Leadership*, and on the editorial boards of the *Annals of the American Psychotherapy Association*, the *Journal of Pastoral Care and Counseling*, and the *USA Body Psychotherapy Journal*. He has served as an adjunct faculty member at several universities, including the Marriage and Family Therapy Program, Central Connecticut State University; DMin in Pastoral Counseling, Drew University; a research faculty member at the Santa Barbara Graduate Institute at the Chicago School of Professional Psychology; Loyola University of Chicago Graduate School, Institute for Pastoral Studies; Graduate Department of Counselor Education, Northeastern Illinois University; Columbia College of Chicago Graduate School of Dance/Movement Therapy; George Fox Evangelical Seminary; and Master of Counselling Program, Project Advisor, University of Lethbridge.

Through his wide-ranging clinical and academic experience—Dr. Johanson is a pastoral psychotherapist and a licensed professional counselor—as well as his degrees in psychology, philosophy, and theology, including a postdoctorate at the Center for the Study of Religion at Princeton University, his particular interest lies in the spiritual and metatheoretical aspects of human development. He is one of the founding members of Ken Wilber's Integral Institute and has issued more than 150 publications, among them *Grace Unfolding: Psychotherapy in the Spirit of the Tao Te Ching* (with Ron Kurtz), which has been translated into several languages.

Dr. Johanson currently serves as director of the Grace Counseling Center in Stayton, Oregon, director of Hakomi Educational Resources, and an internationally active trainer of Body Psychotherapy. The following contribution is informed by his multiple therapeutic trainings, including psychoanalysis, Cognitive Behavioral Therapy, and a range of methods of Body Psychotherapy, as well as systemic frames of reference informed by the sciences of complex, adaptive, nonlinear living systems.

## A Living Systems Approach

There are many ways in which one could relate Body Psychotherapies to the realm of psychotherapy in general. This overview is based, in a simplified way, on some basic principles of systems theory widely conceived. The main rationale is that this provides the barest, elementary, underlying structure for understanding psychotherapy in general. One does not have to be familiar with systems theory to follow the ensuing argument. However, it is an approach that has been widely recommended. For the field of psychology in general, Olds (1992, pp. 19–20) noted, "one of systems theory's strengths is that it allows for ever increasing levels of complexity within its explanatory scope, yet also avoids reductionism." From the psychoanalytic world, Peterfreund (1983, p. x) writes that he found an "information-processing and systems frame of reference . . . to be very congenial because it had greater explanatory power than psychoanalytic metapsychology and was far more consistent with contemporary scientific thought." Likewise, Lichtenberg and colleagues (1992, p. 36), in agreement with Rosenblatt (1984), Rosenblatt and Thickstun (1977), and Sameroff (1983), all advocate a systems approach.

Body-centered psychotherapies have brought considerable study to how various aspects of the body reveal mental-emotional issues, and how mental-emotional activity reflects or registers throughout the body (Siegel, 2006). One can study how a mental attitude is simultaneously a "full-body event" that affects sensation, feelings, breathing, posture, and more. Or one can experiment with a slight change in the body, and study what mental-emotional material is evoked thereby. Therapies that explore and employ this functional unity of the mind-body interface in their work have directed much attention to the body itself as a physical entity. This focus has led in turn to considering the body in terms of the sciences of complexity and complex adaptive systems (CAS) (Briggs and Peat, 1989; Gleick, 1987; Johanson, 2009a; Kauffman, 1995; Maturana and Varela, 1992; Prigogine and Stengers, 1984; Waldrop, 1992). Here there are principles that characterize humans as "nonlinear living organic systems."

These are not principles that say everything there is to say about humans with higher consciousness, or the intricacies of psychodynamic or behavioral methods, as LeShan (1990) points out, but they are foundational (Johanson, 2009b). One metaprinciple is that development is by envelopment, as Wilber (1995) has emphasized. This implies that principles that guide our fundamental material, biological, and rational functioning are never superseded, but are included, and added to, in ever more inclusive realms of functioning. These basic, organic principles underlie the work of Body Psychotherapists in the same way that they underlie the work of other more relationship-centered, behaviorally centered, cognitive-centered, or dream-centered psychotherapists.

## Interrelationships and Splits

Looking at the work of one philosopher of science, Bateson (1979), a number of propositions are found that describe living organic systems that can be said to have a "mind" of their own. The first is that such a system is a whole, made up of parts. Koestler (1976) adds that this whole then becomes part of a greater whole, and thus, the most fundamental unit of life can be termed a "holon," or whole-part. Feminist psychologists have emphasized this by saying that the self is always and only a self-in-relation (Jordan et al., 1991; Prozan, 1992). Wilber (1995) expresses this by saying that psychology is always also sociology. That the meaning of something is intimately related to its context is a fundamental point of postmodernism (Carroll, 1992).

Because humans can be seen as holons, composed of subsystems that also participate in suprasystems in increasing levels of complexity, an implication for therapists is that all these levels could be important, and therefore need appropriate attention in a treatment regimen if one is to be holistic and responsible. For example, if a woman presents herself as depressed, it might mean that there are metabolic deficiencies to attend to, developmental-psychological issues as well as family dynamics in play, trauma perhaps, workplace stresses, communal displacement and isolation, and/or oppressive political-economic structures. Because no single practitioner has skills in all these areas, a healing practice of any orientation should ideally be done in conjunction with an interdisciplinary referral network.

As a poor generalization, it might be said that talk therapists traditionally tend to work to find some sort of a balance between pharmacology, psychotherapy, and social-work interventions. Body-centered psychotherapists tend to also embrace the alternatives of complementary medicine such as clinical nutrition, orthomolecular psychiatry (Hoffer and Osmond, 1960), movement therapy (Caldwell, 1996), massage, deep-tissue work, homeopathy, acupuncture, etc. Although there are multicultural sensitivities in both camps, neither has responded in a particularly significant way to the growing literature on cross-cultural counseling, in terms of actual clinical practice (Paniagua and Yamada, 2013).

Wilber (2000), as well as Habermas (1987) clarify what is at stake by noting that a human holon not only has an individual and a communal aspect, but also an internal-subjective and external-objective aspect. Following Wilber in plotting the individual-communal vs. the interior-exterior results in a four part grid, or four quadrants. These suggest that the intentional, cultural, social, and behavior aspects of a holon are inseparably intertwined, with no one quadrant able to reduce the others to itself. Internal-individual consciousness (II quadrant) has a degree of autonomy, but is highly influenced by internal-communal dispositions (IC quadrant), namely the values of the multiple cultures in which one is immersed. These values might or might not have strong support through actual social structures that embody the values in the external-communal (EC) quadrant world of laws, educational systems, housing arrangements, legal systems, economic policies, etc. These three quadrants work in terms of mutual, reciprocal influences with the external-individual (EI) quadrant of one's objective underlying physiology, and observable behavior.

For a therapy to be considered "integral," Wilber (2000) argues that it must acknowledge the validity of all of these quadrants, as well as the development or evolution that holons go through in their various states of consciousness, from the pre-personal to the personal to the transpersonal. Goodrich-Dunn and Greene (2002) report that, in the 1980s and beyond, Body Psychotherapy pioneers, such as Pierrakos, Pesso, Brown, Kurtz, Kelley, and Rubenfeld generally moved to put their mind-body therapies within these larger contexts (Heller, 2012). As Reich (1949) did before him, D. Johnson (1992, 1993, 1995) has also attempted to address cultural aspects of body-centered work, and Murphy (1992) has dealt with the more transpersonal aspects. More traditional therapists in America have increasingly sought to integrate cultural and/or spiritual dimensions into their work (Hearnshaw, 1987; Koch and Leary, 1992). Again, therapies in all schools are still struggling to

Four Quadrants of a Holon (Wilber)

|  | INTERNAL | EXTERNAL |
|---|---|---|
|  | +Dialogical<br>+Hermeneutical<br>+Consciousness | +Monological<br>+Empirical, Positivistic<br>+Form |
| Individual | **(II) Intentional Aspect (I)**<br>Sigmund Freud<br>C. G. Jung<br>Jean Piaget<br>Aurobindo<br>Plotinus<br>Gautama Buddha | **(EI) Behavioral Aspect (It)**<br>B. F. Skinner<br>John Watson<br>Empiricism<br>Behaviorism<br>Biochemistry<br>Neurology |
| Collective | **IC) Cultural Values (We)**<br>Thomas Kuhn<br>Wilhelm Dilthey<br>Jean Gebser<br>Max Weber<br>Hans-Georg Gadamer | **(EC) Social Structures (It)**<br>Systems Theory<br>Talcott Parsons<br>Auguste Comte<br>Karl Marx<br>Gerhard Lenski |

deal with the fullness of the data generated from a four-quadrant, all-levels integral approach (AQAL).

## Self-Organization

Bateson's second proposition is that, for a system to be organic, the parts must communicate within the whole. Body Psychotherapy generally accepts this as a fundamental principle, as in "Your body speaks its mind" (Keleman, 1989), etc. Bateson's third principle is that, if the parts are in fact communicating, the system is self-organizing, self-directing, and self-correcting. The system is characterized by complex, nonlinear determinism, which is a way of saying it has a mind of its own, an inner wisdom that guides it. This has been demonstrated even on the level of an amoeba, which will resist being blocked in a petri dish by seeking to find its way around any obstruction introduced.

It is this principle of self-knowing that has been reflected in the hermeneutical tradition in psychoanalysis (Mitchell, 1988), which emphasizes that there is no correct external interpretation for a patient's presentation. Indeterminate meaning must be examined synthetically through a collaboration (Duncan, 2010) that helps the patients explore how they have organized their experiences from within their unique inner worlds. Similar symptoms may have radically different meanings to a variety of persons. Likewise, Gedo (1979, 1986) emphasizes the inner wisdom of self-organization, whereas Lichtenberg, Lachmann, and Fosshage (1992) emphasize the relevance in human subsystems "of the organizing principles of self-organizing, self-stabilizing, dialectic tension, and hierarchical arrangement for the formation and function of each system" (p. 35). This leads them, in their interventions, to "attempt to understand from within the perspective of the analysand and thereby mitigate (clearly not eliminate) the imposition of our perception of reality onto the analysand" (p. 118).

Together, Bateson's last two principles suggest that one way of understanding therapy in general is as a matter of addressing the splits in or barriers to communication that exist within an organism (Nelson, 1994; Wilber, 1979). Medical therapies seek to make sure internal organs are communicating with each other through the nervous system and endocrine system, and try to repair disruptions caused by external traumas. Depth psychotherapies typically help one part of the mind speak to another, through resolving inner conflicts; this conflict resolution makes unconscious elements conscious. Mind-body therapies bridge splits between mind and body. Family therapists work on communication breaks within a family. Transpersonal therapists address splits between the whole person and the larger environments around them. On the most basic, simplistic, but essential level, coaches teach football teams to "huddle" in order to get them all on the same page. Organizational development specialists make sure that production is not out of touch with sales, or vice versa. Political leaders endeavor to keep governments in touch with each other (Gibb, 1978; Guevara, 1996; Hesselbein et al., 1998).

## Organizing Experience

Bateson's fourth proposition is that although energy, in the right form and quantity, is necessary for a system to function in an optimal way, it is a collateral or secondary matter. What is of primary importance is the way a system processes information. A raging rhinoceros, or a bomb, has a lot of energy, but not much creativity in terms of organizing, directing, or correcting. However, with a relatively minor amount of energy, a human mind can figure out a way to write Shakespearean sonnets, or go to the moon.

In terms of processing information, Bateson's fifth proposition is that incoming information is coded, filtered, or organized: life is a creative act. A person is never simply imprinted with stimuli as a direct representation, but is active in constructing what experience the stimuli evokes, and what expressions are formed in response. Various people react in empirically demonstrable different ways to the same stimuli. Philosophers such as Langer (1962) speak of the symbolic transformation of the "given," which makes the Kantian "thing-in-itself" available only through filters or schemas.

How people organize their experience, and how they might transform themselves through reorganizing their experience, is a common thread that goes through most psychotherapies today. Although there is a considerable debate on the factors affecting how one's experience becomes organized, and the most effective therapies with which to help one reorganize those experiences, it is clear that a central issue is the organization of experience. This is what Stolorow and colleagues (1987) outline for the psychoanalytic world. It is what Mahoney (1991) is saying in the cognitive behavioral world; what Schwartz (1995) says from an experiential family therapy perspective; what Thelen (1989) argues in Developmental Psychology; and what a host of others maintain who hold some variation of the constructivist position. It is what Kurtz (1990) points to for the world of Body-Centered Psychotherapy.

To amplify this from the psychodynamic tradition, Horner (1979) notes, "the newborn infant organizes its world into meaningful patterns" (p. 4). Organizing tendencies and capabilities are intrinsic to the organism. Horner references Piaget's (1936) concepts of assimilation and accommodation as a major way of understanding the basic processes of organization.

## Core Organizers

"The outcome of the processes of organization—assimilation, accommodation, generalization, differentiation, and integration" is "an enduring organization or structure within the mind" (Horner, 1979, pp. 10–11). This structure has been referred to in terms of schema, self-representation, self-object tie, self-narrative, filter, map, introject, script, mind-set, imaginative gestalt, conditioning, memes, and several other terms. Kurtz prefers the term "core organizing belief." By whatever term, this enduring organization functions phenomenologically as the creator that gives rise to the physical creation that people manifest. It does this through imaginatively transforming stimuli into experience, and then constructing expressions in response. These organizational feats are all accomplished outside of conscious awareness in implicit memory (Amini et al., 1996), thus making much of one's admittedly complex behavior essentially automatic and habitual, reflective of a constancy of character.

Postmodernists and narrative theorists (Bruner, 1990; Crites, 1971; Omer and Alon, 1997; Ricoeur, 1984; White and Epston, 1990) note that language is not a passive naming of perceptions in these organizational processes, but functions actively to evoke, shape, and convey the interiority of the speaker to one's self and others. Language meshes with memory, anticipation, and schematic-gestalt structures in forming the core organizing beliefs that become the symbolic transformers that organize one's experience and give it its characterological consistency. Thus, language has been the basis of talk therapies, though they have not always taken account of the limits of language within ordinary consciousness (Johanson, 1996).

From the linguistic perspective, the central task of imaginative transformation and organization through language is to form and use the core organizing beliefs as the basis for a core narrative. Life cannot be lived, or interpreted, piecemeal and chaotically. There must be a story line to provide a human identity that can organize; make sense out of; bring coherence, pattern, connectedness, and meaning to the multiple mini-stories with contexts within contexts—the kaleidoscopic arrays of possible human experiences that William James termed a potential "blooming, buzzing confusion."

A human core narrative must be inherently historical. Intentions, motives, and passions must make sense in terms of temporality: the lived experience of past memories, present experience, and future anticipations, or what Kierkegaard (1954) termed necessity, freedom, and possibility (Garff, 2005). Researchers (like Stern, 1985; and Tronick, 2009) note that children indeed register and begin this crucial process of organizing experiences prior to verbalization, and some (Lake, 1966, 1981; Pesso, 1969, 1973, 1990) say prior to birth. Who the child is and becomes can never be quantified or intuited from lists of facts, roles, functions, or characteristics, but only from learning the story she constructs to weave these things, along with her memories, hopes, fears, sufferings, and enjoyments, into a meaningful whole.

## Organizing In

This overall perspective on the organization of experience does not preclude psychoanalytic notions that narratives somehow restructure the movement of human desire. However, it does go beyond Kris (1982, p. 10) and others who have suggested that possible organizers of experience could be frustrated desires, forgotten fears, rekindled injuries, internal conflicts, memories of relationships, or enduring character traits. The concept of "core organizing narrative belief" suggests that any significant desire, fear, injury, conflict, or memory becomes part of a larger pattern of meaning that organizes life in the present. Organisms are intolerant of not making sense out of individual events: they must be organized into core interpretive themes. This need is so strong that some researchers believe that this is what leads to false memory syndrome (Furtado, 2003).

If one asks what experiences and expressions, in particular, are organized into core narrative beliefs, the answer is virtually *everything*. In addition to the suggestions of Kris above, Burnham (1969) refers to drives, emotions, and cravings; Winnicott's work (1965) points to well- or ill-timed relational empathy and interactions offered by primary caregivers; Horner (1979) notes normal maturational skills related to walking, talking, thinking, sensing, and so forth; and Erikson (1959, 1963) points to a lifetime of developmental issues that impact everyone. Current literature emphasizes the *integration* of all aspects of the mind-body (Johanson, 2011; Siegel, 2009, 2010).

The end result is that one's entire mind-body-spirit and history is organized. This is what has led body therapists to affirm that one's entire being reveals holographically. Although there are certain constants among people—such as having fingers, breathing, standing upright, locomotion, thinking, and relating—no two persons have the same fingerprints, breathe alike, have the same posture, move or walk in the same manner, think exactly the same, or engage in the same quality of relationships. Each person's uniquely characteristic way of being in the world can be revealed in a millisecond through voice, touch, movement, gesture, or any number of other indicators. Thus, any such aspect of one's creation can theoretically provide a royal road back to the unconscious creator level of one's core organizing narrative beliefs.

## Organizing Transference

This overall revelation of one's total personhood is what led psychoanalysts Stolorow and Atwood (1994) to reformulate the concept of transference from "an outdated archeological metaphor to one emphasizing the psychological process of organizing current experience," which is "the expression of a universal psychological striving to organize experience and construct meaning" (p. 37). "Transference, at the most general level of abstraction, is an instance of organizing activity." It is "neither a regression to nor a displacement from the past, but rather an expression of the continuing influence of organizing principles and imagery that crystallized out of the patient's early formative experiences" (Ibid., p. 36). Because this is true for both analyst and patient, therapy must necessarily be intersubjective, with neither party able to claim unprejudiced reality for their perceptions, but hopefully with the analyst having a larger view of possibilities.

"Another advantage of the concept of transference as organizing activity is that it is sufficiently general and inclusive to embrace the multiplicity of its dimensions" (Stolorow, Brandchaft, and Atwood, 1987, p. 37). It is the multiple dimensions of transference, revealed throughout the physical organism, on which body-inclusive therapists have concentrated. For instance, the posture of one whose upper body appears displaced upward and who is not able to breathe into his lower stomach could well be a reflection of what Loevinger (1976) has termed "a self-protective characterological organization." Here there might be a history of the patient having his basic needs and vulnerabilities used against him by those who wanted to gain power and control over him. His body is possibly revealing the belief that the world is organized around power games where one wins or loses; that it is best to become larger, tougher, countermanipulative, and more invulnerable, because people are basically out for themselves and are only as loyal as their self-interests go, etc. Thus, he has difficulty organizing in the possibility of mutual vulnerability in a relationship, because his core organizing beliefs warn that there is danger in again allowing the interpersonal intimacy that previously betrayed and wounded him.

## Organization Revealed

Body-centered psychotherapists are certainly in agreement with psychodynamic therapists that the quality of relationships is organized, and that relational material can be central to therapeutic processes (Fisher, 2002; Rosenberg et al., 1985). Likewise, cognitions are organized (Kurtz, 1990) and dreams are organized (Gendlin, 1986), as is well known in the mainstream therapeutic world; both cognitions and dreams can be addressed in body-centered ways.

Then there is a veritable plethora of other aspects of one's being that body-centered practitioners have explored that are also organized through the influence of core beliefs about the world. The following is a partial listing of such aspects with some representative references: posture (Dychtwald, 1977; Kurtz and Prestera, 1976; Lowen, 1958; Reich, 1949); movement (Caldwell, 1996; Chodorow, 1991; Feldenkrais, 1972; Pesso, 1973); musculature (Macnaughton, 1998; Marcher, 1996); development (Aposhyan, 1999; Frank, 2001); breathing (Braddock, 1995; Hendricks, 1995); sexuality (Keleman, 1975; Rosenberg, 1973); body image (Hutchinson, 1985; Kruger, 1990, Schilder, 1970); expression (Levy, 1996; Polhemus and Benthall, 1975); auras (Pierrakos, 1987); awareness (Bakal, 1999); sensation (Gendlin, 1996; Kurtz, 1990; Ogden, Minton, and Pain, 2006); energy (Brennan, 1998; Joy, 1979); touching (Brazelton, 1990; Brown, 1990; Campbell, 1989; Ford, 1993; McNeely, 1987; Smith, Clance, and Imes, 1998); gestures (D. Johnson, 1995); standing-facing-handling-timing (Hanna, 1980); anatomy (Keleman, 1985; Marrone, 1990; Olsen, 1991; Pesso, 1973); pushing-reaching-pulling (Bainbridge Cohen, 1993); sense of self (Kruger, 1989; Marcher, 1996; Mindell, 1982); embodiment (Conger, 1994; Mazis, 1994); and more (Caldwell, 1997).

As noted above, all these human aspects are examples of creatively organized experience: aspects of individual creation. Each one represents a royal road to the unconscious level of the creator that gave rise to the creation. The length of the above list, which goes far beyond the relationships, cognitions, behaviors, and dreams that most traditional therapists are familiar with, makes a formidable case for why every therapist ought to be body-inclusive of a wide range of human phenomena, regardless of what one's primary area of training might be. There can be little justification for employing just one avenue of therapy alone, and thereby withholding from a patient the efficacy and efficiency of accessing core organizers through numerous available channels.

The issue of touch in psychotherapy arises, of course. It is a valid point that one should have training in the clinical and ethical use of touch, which body-centered psychotherapists have explored for many years (Barstow, 2002; Hunter and Struve, 1998; McNeely, 1987; Peloquin, 1990; Smith, Clance, and Imes, 1998; White, 2002). It should also be noted that traditional psychodynamic and cognitive behavioral researchers have generated a wealth of literature dealing with touch and the mind-body interface, to which this chapter can only allude (refer to the above references on touch). It is as if the body-centered and talk-centered therapists might actually be discovering that they have set up offices across the hall from each other in the same building. It is now well beyond the time when they should start to compare notes, and learn from each other, with the well-being of their clients as their governing concern.

## Organized Out

When any of the creative human expressions listed above are used as an access route to core organizers, the issue is not discovering the normal human capacity to organize that makes sense and meaning of life. That is a given, and reflects normal functioning. Because the organism is only optimally self-organizing, self-directing, and self-correcting when all the parts are connected within the whole, the key therapeutic issue becomes discovering and exploring what has been "organized out." Characterological level therapy (S. Johnson, 1985, 1994) that transforms significant developmental issues (Loevinger, 1976) happens at the barriers, at those points of resistance to including in one's core schemas fundamental human needs for support, autonomy, inclusion, and so forth. What is preventing someone from "organizing in" some significant aspect of life so that there can be better connections and feedback within the whole, as well as a more consistent, flexible overall narrative? What fears, traumas, or experiences maintain those barriers or resistances that keep needful and realistically possible life functions, such as self-assertion or submission, in an "organized out" position?

Kohut (1977) refers to a "cohesive self" when the self has successfully integrated and organized in relevant life factors. Horner (1979) writes that "the mobilization of any sensations, feelings, or impulses (as well as their derivative ideation) that lie outside whatever centers of organization might exist will have a disorganizing impact upon the individual" (p. 12). Bromberg (1998) teaches that the goal of psychoanalytic treatment is the construction of a more inclusive reality that reconnects dissociated psychic functions, so that there is enhanced perception and increased harmony among the multiplicity of ego states. All of this "becomes linguistically symbolized by the consensual construction of new narrative meaning" (Ibid., p. 171). Jungians (for example, Singer, 1972) speak of integrating one's shadow to form a more complete soul. Family therapist Schwartz (1995) talks about bringing the multiplicity of split-off or antagonistic parts within one's inner ecology into the awareness and harmonious leadership of the larger self.

Not every therapist thinks theoretically or precisely in these terms. However, the argument here is that scanning for what is "organized out" is an instructive metaperspective on how practitioners actually work, which is consistent with our CAS model. What is it about this client that makes him radically self-reliant, and unable to organize in the possibility of support? Why is this person able to make contracting movements, but is unable to flow with "organizing in" expansive movements as well? How come this Vietnam vet cannot take in the information that the war is over, and keeps hitting the deck whenever a car backfires? Is it not interesting that the therapist feels like feeding and nurturing this client, who seems to have "organized out" independence and self-sufficiency?

## Therapeutic Reorganization

All of the above questions, in relation to how one is creatively organized, set up the possibility of becoming curious (Johanson, 1988) about the specific observations of both client and therapist. This curiosity can then generate a process for using the observations to provide a royal road back to the level of the "creator" that often includes early memories frozen in time (Kurtz, 1990; Pesso, 1973; Schwartz, 1995). In promoting such a process, body-inclusive psychotherapists are in essential agreement with Stolorow, Brandchaft, and Atwood (1987) when they say:

> We would therefore do away with the rule of abstinence and its corresponding concept of neutrality and replace them with an attitude of sustained empathic inquiry, which seeks understanding of the patient's expressions from within the perspective of the patient's subjective frame of reference. From this vantage point, the reality of the patient's perceptions of the analyst is neither debated nor confirmed. Instead, these perceptions serve as points of departure for an exploration of the meanings and organizing principles that structure the patient's psychic reality. (p. 43)

This stance on the part of body-inclusive therapists reflects a strong view of transference. Because transference reflects unconscious organizing of any and all situations, nothing can short-circuit, interfere with, or do away with it. It is omnipresent. All touch, personal interactions, experiments with gratifying or not gratifying, attempts to move, stand, or breathe in different ways serve as grist for the therapeutic mill, in that all such interventions will evoke a reaction or response based on transference that can then be woven into the process. Offering schizoid-withdrawn persons friendliness might evoke anxiety. Offering them silence and distance might evoke more calmness. Either response reflects the organization of the transference, and can be brought under curious self-reflective observation.

When a Focusing therapist invites a client to get a "felt sense of a situation"; when Kepner (1987) asks, "What are you aware of in your body?"; when Pesso (1973) invites someone to "Notice what happens when . . . [some experiment is performed]"; when Kurtz (1990) instructs someone to stay mindfully with a sense of anxiety in their chest and allow it to say more about itself; when Rand (Rosenberg et al., 1985) asks a client to "reference her experience" as she draws a "boundary" around herself; when Heckler (1984) asks someone to study how they are holding back their grief; when Ogden (Ogden et al., 2006) instructs a person to simply focus on sensation; when Caldwell (1996) invites someone who has been furrowing his brow to do it self-consciously; when Rubenfeld (2000) asks a client to imagine herself as an older woman and give that person a voice; and when Schwartz (1995) asks someone how he feels toward a frightened part of himself—these are all examples of directing awareness toward present, "felt" experience.

They are all examples of promoting experiential knowledge in clients (Barratt, 2010), which Gendlin (1962) has argued for years is the crucial factor in successful therapy (Bernet, 2002). They direct awareness toward right-brain experience itself, as opposed to left-brain theories *about* experience. Reflective awareness is able to be with and to study the experience, without being at the mercy of simply acting it out. This addresses the objection of Watzlawick (Watzlawick et al., 1974) that consciousness is always a central problem, because it is already organized, and therefore paradoxical or hypnotic techniques must be employed. The engagement of experiential awareness makes possible a therapy that gets beyond the limitation of words (Heller, 2012; Johanson, 1996; Wiener, 1999), and is efficiently brief, as well as characterologically deep, as Ecker and Hulley (1996) have outlined.

Body-inclusive therapists are able to employ the possibility of three distinct modes of therapeutic relationship, as outlined by Stark (1999). Clearly, the way of managing consciousness (Kurtz, 1990) described in the paragraph above is what Stark outlines as one-person therapy. It is an intrapsychic intervention that invites clients to have in-depth conversations with themselves, empowering them to mine the wisdom of their own experience. Therapists become safe and wise collaborators who stand beside their clients as they engage in this inner process that produces many of the characteristics that Peterfreund (1971) affirms in a heuristic, process-oriented, productive therapy hour.

Another dimension is typically added in body-inclusive psychotherapies whenever a core organizing belief is accessed that remains stuck in the past because it has not been able to update its "files" in terms accommodating new information about the current situation. When Pesso (1973) suggests reenacting core memory scenes with parents, friends, or neighbors, accommodating what should have ideally happened; when Kurtz (1990) appears as a magical stranger in someone's memory to help them know what they could not have known at the time; when Pierrakos (1987) asks someone who doubts support to fall backward from a chair into his arms; when a number of people in a Psychodrama group say to someone who has accessed a shameful memory that it is all right to cry; when Schwartz (1995) collaborates with a client's self in offering a jealous part what it needs; or when a relational therapist looks at a client in such a way that she realizes she is not being judged like she has always experienced authority figures doing before—another critical element of previously *missed experience* is made available.

Clients are then supported in "organizing in" or introjecting this new experience, which usually consists of new possibilities that were previously "organized out." This is the meaning of transformation, and of working with transference (Feinstein, 1990), as outlined above. Note that transformation here refers to adding in excluded possibilities, but does not require tearing down or discarding the older, self-protective options already in place. It is more the addition of discernment, options, and choice in the place of habitual, automatic reactions. Clients are aided in this transformation in an experiential way that goes far beyond and much deeper than insight. Insight in ordinary consciousness is never enough to foster healing. It takes new experiences to counterbalance old experiences. Watzlawick (Watzlawick, Weakland, and Fisch, 1974) is correct that ordinary consciousness is already organized, which means it is already filtering out evidence contrary to the core beliefs around which it is organized. Introducing new possibilities, previously "organized out," depends on maintaining the altered state of experience near consciousness (Johanson and Kurtz, 1991; Siegel, 2010). Almaas (1988) and Schwartz (1995) also note that positive, essential, healing qualities of the larger self-state can be brought to bear, as well as the more passive aspects of the observing ego.

In providing these new experiences that help connect the person to a wider range of life and energy, the process has turned into what Stark (1999) terms "one-and-a-half-person therapy." The client is still subjectively processing, while the therapist or group contours itself to provide the precise, ideal missing experience that the client could never integrate before. It is important at this therapeutic moment of transformation for the therapists to take their cues from the exact intuitions of the clients, in terms of what the client believes is needed for him or her to heal. Thus, the therapists are considered only half-present, because though authentic and genuine in what they are offering, they are not present as fully mutual, interactive partners.

The next stage for some body-centered psychotherapists might be termed the "integration phase." Here the therapists are fully with the clients as they experiment with taking their transformations into real space and time in terms of actual relationships and situations. At this point, the possibility arises of entering into what Stark terms "two-person therapy," in which both client and therapist seek to be present in their intersubjective fullness.

Because therapists are often highly significant persons in the lives of clients, it is natural that clients would want to try out their newly transformed ways of being with their therapists. For instance, if the issue dealt with in the previous two stages was that the person could indeed "organize in" the possibility of anger in relationships, it should not be a surprise if the client becomes a bit testy in a way that explores whether the therapist can indeed tolerate the client's anger, and whether the therapist will respond in similar ways as the client's primary figures from the past did. This is a crucial therapeutic moment. If the therapist reacts with shaming or blaming toward the client's (possibly unreasonable) anger, it could be a characterological disaster that confirms the client's worst fears, and throws doubt onto the previous stages of the therapy. For the therapist to be real, affected by the anger, but able to maintain the relational connection, could be a powerful repair, and a confirmation for the client's new, enlarged worldview. It strengthens the integration of new self-narratives and metaphors (Weiss, 1995). It meets projective identification with projective redemption, as Barbera (2001) suggests. An authentic interpersonal matrix also overcomes the limitation of a therapist who is "constantly empathic" and thus "may seriously inhibit the patient's own creative powers" (Bromberg, 1998, p. 158) through limiting the possible range of interactions. The skillful balancing of all three of Stark's therapeutic modes can be highly effective.

## Hierarchy and Organizational Failure

If the therapeutic process described above has been potent enough to "organize in" a new range of experience, the system's core organizers, or "memes" (see Dawkins, 1989, p. 186), that implicitly control the structures, schemas, or filters of what Stolorow and Atwood (1994, p. 25) call one's "prereflective unconscious" are altered. This affects the way the system replicates itself. In order to preserve itself, as well as to expand, an organism must have the system memory not only to organize the system's experience and expression, but also to replicate it. What the gene does on the level of biology, the meme does on the level of the compounded individual. From a therapy standpoint, system replication is often too efficient and overly powerful, not allowing the client to recognize something new as new.

Ideally, one's memes, or core organizers, would have semi-permeable boundaries, supporting the balance between continuity and flexibility that would allow the normal informational processes of assimilation and accommodation that Piaget (Piaget and Inhelder, 1969) describes.

Too often, however, there has been enough trauma along the way to rigidify replication. The organism does not accommodate to new information by expanding its memes, but assimilates the new information into old schemas, whether it is a good fit or not.

This limitation in organizational capacity gives rise to the phenomenon that Freud (1911) recognized early on: that people compulsively repeat old patterns of being and relating. The patterns or strategies might have been quite adaptive once, but in new circumstances they can become unhelpful and unhealthy. People literally cannot recognize, accommodate, or organize in a fresh situation as being novel. Every therapy deals functionally with the repetition compulsion (perhaps without the philosophical speculation that Freud attached to it). It can be used as a helpful concept around which the various body-centered and other-centered therapies can share their respective clinical discoveries in attempting to deal with it (Johanson, 2002).

One of the reasons that the repetition compulsion is so rigid in replicating a system, and why S. Johnson (1985) terms characterological change "the hard work miracle," relates to Bateson's sixth proposition, concerning living organic systems—namely, that information is organized into a hierarchy of logical levels of organization. While this is true in general (Lichtenberg, Lachmann, and Fosshage, 1992, pp. 35ff.), body-inclusive psychotherapists have become especially aware of it in the case of trauma (Herman, 1992; Ogden, Minton, and Pain, 2006; Levine, 1997; Porges, 1995, 2011; Rothschild, 2000; and van der Kolk, 2002).

The lesson from trauma is that experiences that go beyond the capacity of the nervous system to assimilate or accommodate activate more primitive levels of the triune brain that initiate fight, flight, freezing, and dissociative responses that are prior to, and not subject to, cortical control. Working on a purely verbal level with trauma may actually serve to retraumatize a person through prematurely loosening helpful dissociations (Bromberg, 1998, pp. 189ff.; van der Kolk, 2002), and/or reinforcing the physiological conditioning in play. Work in this area has led to a deluge of new research in neurophysiology that has shed light on memory, behavior, relational attachment, and more (Lewis et al., 2000; Amini et al., 1996; Llinas, 2001; Panksepp, 1998; Pert, 1999; Schore, 1994; Siegel, 1999; van der Kolk et al., 1996; Vincent, 1990). The good news is that what is being learned about good therapy with trauma victims also constitutes good therapy with developmental issues of clients on a characterological level (Morgan, 2002).

## Systemic Synthesis

In addition to the wide variety of psychotherapies in general, the psychoanalytic-psychodynamic tradition itself has a great many schools that are not easy to reconcile (Buirski, 1994). One constant thread that weaves through all schools of Depth Psychotherapy, however, is working with transference. From a CAS standpoint, the essence of transference is that it functions to organize the experience of individuals based on core beliefs that make sense of the world, and to orient persons within those meanings. The fullness of the "holonic" world (Koestler, 1976) includes all the intentional, cultural, societal, and behavioral dispositions that develop through pre-personal, personal, and transpersonal levels of consciousness.

Core narratives that organize experience and expression automatically, below the level of conscious awareness, affect virtually all aspects of one's being. Psychodynamic therapists have focused on how core narratives organize relationships. Cognitive therapists have concentrated on how worldviews and thoughts affect the person; behaviorists on the responses people typically make; and others on the dreams that the imagination generates.

Body-inclusive therapists acknowledge all these dimensions of transference. They also insist that significant core beliefs are embodied in the total organism, and therefore are revealed in a wide variety of physical manifestations. Any number of physical expressions of transference in sensations, feelings, posture, breathing, movement, gestures, and more could and should be used as royal roads to the unconscious level of core organizers. When more of the mind-body is incorporated, more depth is added to depth therapies. More efficiency and efficacy is likewise added, since it is harder for the body to lie in its revelation of core beliefs, because the musculature and physiology are organized by deeper levels of the triune brain than are thoughts, theories, stories, or interpretations.

For the sake of those seeking healing and growth, it is ethically imperative that therapists who work with various manifestations of transference consult with and learn from each other about the most successful ways to help those in their care reorganize around more inclusive, satisfying ways of being in the world.

# References

Almaas, H. (1988). *The pearl beyond price: Integration of personality into being: An object-relations approach.* Berkeley, CA: Diamond Books.

Amini, F., Lewis, T., Lannon, R., & Louie, A. (1996). Affect, attachment, memory: Contributions towards psychobiologic integration. *Psychiatry, 59,* 213–239.

Aposhyan, S. (1999). *Natural intelligence: Body-mind integration and human development.* Baltimore: Williams & Wilkins.

Bainbridge Cohen, B. (1993). *Sensing, feeling and action.* Northampton, MA: Contact Editions.

Bakal, D. (1999). *Minding the body: Clinical uses of somatic awareness.* New York: Guilford Press.

Barbera, M. R. (2001). Projective redemption in couples therapy: Interrupting projective identification cycles. *Psychoanalysis and Psychotherapy: The Journal of the Psychoanalytic Institute of the Postgraduate Center for Mental Health, 18*(2), 171–192.

Barratt, B. (2010). *The emergence of Somatic Psychology and bodymind therapy.* New York: Palgrave Macmillan.

Barstow, C. (2002). *Right use of power: Ethics for the helping professions: A resource and training manual.* Boulder, CO: Many Realms.

Bateson, G. (1979). *Mind and nature: A necessary unity.* New York: E. P. Dutton.

Bernet, M. (2002). The effectiveness of Body Psychotherapies as a function of effortless awareness of body sensations. In *Emergence and Convergence: Conference proceedings of the Third National Conference of the United States Association for Body Psychotherapy,* 407–422.

Braddock, C. (1995). *Body voices: Using the Power of breath, sound and movement to heal and create new boundaries.* Berkeley, CA: Page Mill Press.

Brazelton, T. (Ed.). (1990). *Touch: The foundation of experience.* Madison, CT: International Universities Press.

Brennan, B. A. (1998). *Hands of light: A guide to healing through the human energy field.* Toronto, Canada: Bantam Books.

Briggs, J., & Peat, F. D. (1989). *Turbulent mirror: An illustrated guide to chaos theory and the science of wholeness.* New York: Harper & Row.

Bromberg, P. M. (1998). *Standing in the spaces: Essays on clinical process,* trauma *and dissociation.* Hillsdale, NJ: Analytic Press.

Brown, M. (1990). *The healing touch.* Mendocino, CA: LifeRhythm.

Bruner, J. (1990). *Acts of meaning.* Cambridge, MA: Harvard University Press.

Buirski, P. (Ed.). (1994). *Comparing schools of analytic therapy.* Northvale, NJ: Jason Aronson.

Burnham, D. (1969). Child-parent relationships which impede differentiation and integration. In D. Burnham, A. Gladstone, & R. Gibson (Eds.), *Schizophrenia and the need-fear dilemma* (pp. 42–66). New York: International Universities Press.

Caldwell, C. (1996). *Getting our bodies back.* Boston: Shambhala.

Caldwell, C. (Ed.). (1997). *Getting in touch: The guide to new body-centered therapies.* Wheaton, IL: Quest Books.

Campbell, D. (1989). *Touching dialogue: A Somatic Psychotherapy for self-realization.* New York: Inhand Books.

Carroll, J. B. (1992). Psychology and linguistics: Detachment and affiliation in the second half-century. In S. Koch & D. E. Leary (Eds.), *A century of psychology as science* (pp. 825–854). Washington, DC: American Psychological Association.

Chodorow, J. (1991). *Dance Therapy and Depth Psychology: The moving imagination.* New York: Routledge.

Conger, J. P. (1994). *The body in recovery: Somatic Psychotherapy and the self.* Berkeley, CA: Frog.

Crites, S. D. (1971). The narrative quality of experience. *Journal of the American Academy of Religion, 39,* 291–311.

Dawkins, R. (1989). *The selfish gene* (2nd ed.). Oxford, UK: Oxford University Press.

Duncan, B. (2010). *On becoming a better therapist.* Washington, DC: American Psychological Association.

Dychtwald, K. (1977). *Bodymind.* New York: Pantheon Books.

Ecker, B., & Hulley, L. (1996). *Depth-oriented brief therapy.* San Francisco: Jossey-Bass.

Erikson, E. (1959). *Identity and the life cycle.* New York: International University Press.

Erikson, E. (1963). *Childhood and society.* New York: W. W. Norton.

Feinstein, D. (1990). Transference and countertransference in the here-and-now therapies. *Hakomi Forum, 8,* 7–13.

Feldenkrais, M. (1972). *Awareness Through Movement.* New York: Harper & Row.

Fisher, R. (2002). *Experiential Psychotherapy with couples: A guide for the creative pragmatist.* Phoenix, AZ: Zeig, Tucker, & Theisen.

Ford, C. W. (1993). *Compassionate touch: The role of human touch in healing and recovery.* New York: Simon & Schuster.

Frank, R. (2001). *Body of awareness: A somatic and developmental approach to psychotherapy.* Hillsdale, NJ: Analytic Press.

Freud, S. (1911). Remembering, repeating, and working-through. In *Standard Edition, Vol. XII.* London: Hogarth Press.

Furtado, T. (2003). Recovered memory revisited: A new research study reopens an old controversy. *Psychotherapy Networker, 27*(2), 13–14.

Garff, J. (2005). *Søren Kierkegaard: A biography.* Princeton, NJ: Princeton University Press.

Gedo, J. (1979). *Beyond interpretation.* New York: International Universities Press.

Gedo, J. (1986). *Conceptual issues in psychoanalysis.* Hillsdale, NJ: Analytic Press.

Gendlin, E. T. (1962). *Experiencing and the creation of meaning: A philosophical and psychological approach to the subjective.* New York: Free Press of Glencoe.

Gendlin, E. T. (1986). *Let your body interpret your dreams.* Wilmette, IL: Chiron.

Gendlin, E. T. (1996). *Focusing-oriented psychotherapy: A manual of the experiential method.* New York: Guilford Press.

Gibb, J. R. (1978). *Trust: A new view of personal and organizational development.* Los Angeles: Guild of Tutors Press.

Gleick, J. (1987). *Chaos: Making a new science.* New York: Viking.

Goodrich-Dunn, B., & Greene, E. (2002). Voices: A history of Body Psychotherapy. *USA Body Psychotherapy Journal, 1*(1), 53–117.

Guevara, K. (1996). Creating organisations fit for the human spirit through Hakomi. *Hakomi Forum, 12,* 9–22.

Habermas, J. (1987). *The philosophical discourse of modernity.* Cambridge, MA: MIT Press.

Hanna, T. (1980). *The body of life.* New York: Knopf.

Hearnshaw, L. S. (1987). *The shaping of modern psychology.* London: Routledge & Kegan Paul.

Heckler, R. S. (1984). *The anatomy of change.* Boston: Shambhala.

Heller, M. C. (2012). *Body Psychotherapy: History, concepts, and methods.* New York: W. W. Norton.

Hendricks, G. (1995). *Conscious breathing.* New York: Bantam.

Herman, J. (1992). *Trauma and recovery.* New York: Basic Books.

Hesselbein, F., et al. (Eds.). (1998). *The community of the future.* San Francisco: Jossey-Bass.

Hoffer, A., & Osmond, H. (1960). *Chemical basis of clinical psychiatry.* Springfield, IL: Thomas.

Horner, A. J. (1979). *Object relations and the developing ego in therapy.* New York: Jason Aronson.

Hunter, M., & Struve, J. (1998). *The ethical use of touch in psychotherapy.* Thousand Oaks, CA: Sage.

Hutchinson, M. G. (1985). *Transforming body image.* Trumansburg, NY: Crossing Press.

Johanson, G. J. (1988). A curious form of therapy: Hakomi. *Hakomi Forum, 6,* 18–31.

Johanson, G. J. (1996). The birth and death of meaning: Selective implications of linguistics for psychotherapy. *Hakomi Forum, 12,* 45–55.

Johanson, G. J. (2002). Far beyond psychoanalysis: Freud's repetition compulsion and the USABP. In *Emergence and Convergence: Conference proceedings of the Third National Conference of the United States Association for Body Psychotherapy,* 446–469.

Johanson, G. J. (2009a). Non-linear science, mindfulness, and the body in Humanistic Psychotherapy. *Humanistic Psychologist, 37,* 159–177.

Johanson, G. J. (2009b). Psychotherapy, science and spirit: Nonlinear systems, Hakomi Therapy, and the Tao. *Journal of Spirituality in Mental Health, 11*(3), 172–212.

Johanson, G. (2011). Mindfulness, emotions, and the organization of experience. *USA Body Psychotherapy Journal, 10*(1), 38–57.

Johanson, G. J., & Kurtz, R. (1991). *Grace unfolding: Psychotherapy in the spirit of the "Tao-te Ching."* New York: Bell Tower.

Johnson, D. H. (1992). *Body: Recovering our sensual wisdom.* Berkeley, CA: North Atlantic Books.

Johnson, D. H. (1993). *Body, spirit, and democracy.* Berkeley, CA: North Atlantic Books.

Johnson, D. H. (Ed.). (1995). *Bone, breath, and gesture: Practices of embodiment.* Berkeley, CA: North Atlantic Books.

Johnson, S. M. (1985). *Characterological transformation: The hard work miracle.* New York: W. W. Norton.

Johnson, S. M. (1994). *Character styles.* New York: W. W. Norton.

Jordan, J. V., Kaplan, A. G., & Miller, J. B. (1991). The role of sisters in women's growth. In *The complexity of connection: Writings from the Stone Center.* New York: Guilford Press.

Joy, W. B. (1979). *Joy's way: A map for the transformational journey: An introduction to the potentials for healing with body energies.* Los Angeles: J. P. Tarcher.

Kauffman, S. (1995). *At home in the universe: The search for laws of self-organization and complexity.* New York: Oxford University Press.

Keleman, S. (1975). *The human ground: Sexuality, self and survival.* Palo Alto, CA: Science and Behavior Books.

Keleman, S. (1985). *Emotional anatomy.* Berkeley, CA: Center Press.

Keleman, S. (1989). *Your body speaks its mind.* Berkeley, CA: Center Press.

Kepner, J. (1987). *Body process: A Gestalt approach to working with the body in psychotherapy.* New York: Gestalt Institute of Cleveland Press.

Kierkegaard, S. (1954). Fear and trembling: The sickness unto death (Walter Lowrie, Trans.). Garden City, NY: Doubleday.

Koch, S., & Leary, D. E. (Eds.). (1992). *A century of psychology as science.* Washington, DC: American Psychological Association.

Koestler, A. (1976). *The ghost in the machine.* New York: Random House.

Kohut, H. (1977). *The restoration of the self.* New York: International Universities Press.

Kris, A. O. (1982). *Free association: Methods and process.* New Haven, CT: Yale University Press.

Kruger, D. W. (1989). *Body self and psychological self: Developmental and clinical integration in disorders of the self.* New York: Brunner/Mazel.

Kruger, D. W. (1990). Developmental and psychodynamic perspectives on body image change. In T. Case & T. Pruzinsky (Eds.), *Body images: Development, deviance, and change* (pp. 255–271). New York: Guilford Press.

Kurtz, R. (1990). *Body-Centered Psychotherapy: The Hakomi Method.* Mendocino, CA: LifeRhythm.

Kurtz, R., & Prestera, H. (1976). *The body reveals.* New York: Harper & Row.

Lake, F. (1966). *Clinical theology: A theological and psychiatric basis to clinical pastoral care.* London: Darton, Longman & Todd.

Lake, F. (1981). *Tight corners in pastoral counseling.* London: Darton, Longman & Todd.

Langer, S. (1962). *Philosophy in a new key* (2nd ed.). New York: Mentor.

LeShan, L. (1990). *The dilemma of psychology: A psychologist looks at his troubled profession.* New York: Dutton.

Levine, P. (1997). *Waking the tiger: Healing trauma through the body.* Berkeley, CA: North Atlantic Books.

Levy, F. (1996). *Dance and other expressive art therapies: When words are not enough.* New York: Routledge.

Lewis, T., Amini, F., & Lannon, R. (2000). *A general theory of love.* New York: Vintage Books.

Lichtenberg, J. D., Lachmann, F.M., & Fosshage, J. L. (1992). *Self and motivational systems: Toward a theory of psychoanalytic technique.* Hillsdale, NJ: Analytic Press.

Llinas, R. R. (2001). *I of the vortex: From neurons to self.* Cambridge, MA: MIT Press.

Loevinger, J. (with Blasi, A.). (1976). *Ego development.* San Francisco: Jossey-Bass.

Lowen, A. (1958). *Physical dynamics of character structure.* New York: Grune & Stratton.

Macnaughton, I. (Ed.). (1998). *Embodying the mind and minding the body.* Vancouver, Canada: Integral Press.

Mahoney, M. J. (1991). *Human change processes: The scientific foundations of psychotherapy.* New York: Basic Books.

Marcher, L. (1996). *The body self in psychotherapy: A psychomotor approach to Self-Psychology.* Novato, CA: Bodynamic Institute.

Marrone, R. (1990). *Body of knowledge: An introduction to Body/Mind Psychology.* Albany, NY: State University of New York Press.

Maturana, H., & Varela, F. (1992). *The tree of knowledge: The biological roots of human understanding.* Boston: Shambhala.

Mazis, G. A. (1994). *Emotion and embodiment: Fragile ontology.* New York: Peter Lang.

McNeely, D. A. (1987). *Touching: Body therapy and Depth Psychology.* Toronto, Canada: Inner City Books.

Mindell, A. (1982). *Dreambody: The body's role in revealing the self.* Santa Monica, CA: Sigo Press.

Mitchell, S. A. (1988). *Relational concepts in psychoanalysis: An integration.* Cambridge, MA: Harvard University Press.

Morgan, M. (2002). *This sacred ground so finely assembled: Neuroscience, trauma, Hakomi Psychotherapy.* Monograph of Hakomi Institute of New Zealand.

Murphy, M. (1992). *The future of the body: Explorations into the further evolution of human nature.* Los Angeles: Jeremy P. Tarcher.

Nelson, J. E. (1994). *Healing the split: Integrating spirit into our understanding of the mentally ill.* Albany, NY: State University of New York Press.

Ogden, P., Minton, K., & Pain, C. (2006). *Trauma and the body: A sensorimotor approach to psychotherapy.* New York: W. W. Norton.

Olds, L. E. (1992). *Metaphors of interrelatedness: Toward a systems theory of psychology.* Albany, NY: State University of New York Press.

Olsen, A. (with McHose, C.). (1991). *Body stories: A guide to experiential anatomy.* Barrytown, NY: Station Hill Press.

Omer, H., & Alon, N. (1997). *Constructing therapeutic narratives.* Northvale, NJ: Jason Aronson.

Paniagua, F., & Yamada, A. (Eds.). (2013). *Handbook of multicultural mental health* (2nd ed.). San Diego, CA: Academic Press.

Panksepp, J. (1998). *Affective neuroscience: The foundations of human and animal emotions.* New York: Oxford University Press.

Peloquin, S. M. (1990). Helping through touch: The embodiment of caring. *Hakomi Forum, 8,* 15–30.

Pert, C. B. (1999). *Molecules of emotion.* New York: Touchstone.

Pesso, A. (1969). *Movement in psychotherapy.* New York: New York University Press.

Pesso, A. (1973). *Experience in action: A psychomotor psychology.* New York: New York University Press.

Pesso, A. (1990). The effects of pre- and peri-natal trauma. *Hakomi Forum, 8,* 35–44.

Peterfreund, E. (1971). *Information, systems, and psychoanalysis* [Psychological Issues, Monograph 25/26]. New York: International Universities Press.

Peterfreund, E. (1983). *The process of psychoanalytic therapy.* Hillsdale, NJ: Analytic Press.

Piaget, J. (1936). *The origins of intelligence in children.* New York: International Universities Press.

Piaget, J., & Inhelder, B. (1969). *The psychology of the child.* New York: Basic Books.

Pierrakos, J. (1987). *Core Energetics.* Mendocino, CA: LifeRhythm.

Polhemus, T., & Benthall, J. (Eds.). (1975). *The body as a medium of expression.* New York: Dutton.

Porges, S. W. (1995). Orienting in a defensive world: Mammalian modifications of our evolutionary heritage. A polyvagal theory. *Psychophysiology, 32,* 301–318.

Porges, S. (2011). *The polyvagal theory: Neurophysiological foundations of emotions, attachment, communication, and self-regulation.* New York: W. W. Norton.

Prigogine, I., & Stengers, I. (1984). *Order out of chaos: Man's new dialogue with nature.* New York: Bantam Books.

Prozan, C. K. (1992). *Feminist psychoanalytic psychotherapy.* Northvale, NJ: Jason Aronson.

Reich, W. (1949). *Character Analysis.* New York: Orgone Institute Press.

Ricoeur, P. (1984). *Time and narrative* (Vol. 1) (K. McLaughlin & D. Pellauer, Trans.). Chicago: University of Chicago Press.

Rosenberg, J. L. (1973). *Total orgasm.* Berkeley, CA: Bookworks, Random House.

Rosenberg, J. L., Rand, M., & Asay, D. (1985). *Body, self and soul: Sustaining integration.* Atlanta, GA: Humanics.

Rosenblatt, A. (1984). The psychoanalytic process: A systems and information processing model. *Psychoanalytic Inquiry, 4,* 59–86.

Rosenblatt, A., & Thickstun, J. (1977). *Modern psychoanalytic concepts in a general psychology (Psychological Issues, Monograph 42/43).* New York: International Universities Press.

Rothschild, B. (2000). *The body remembers: The psychophysiology of trauma and trauma treatment.* New York: W. W. Norton.

Rubenfeld, I. (2000). *The listening hand.* New York: Bantam Books.

Sameroff, A. (1983). Developmental systems: Context and evolution. In W. Kessen (Ed.), *Mussen's handbook of child psychology* (Vol. 1) (pp. 238–294). New York: Wiley.

Schilder, P. (1970). *The image and appearance of the human body: Studies in the constructive energies of the psyche.* New York: International Universities Press.

Schore, A. N. (1994). *Affect regulation and the origin of the self.* Hillsdale, NJ: Lawrence Erlbaum.

Schwartz, R. (1995). *Internal family systems theory.* New York: Guilford Press.

Siegel, D. J. (1999). *The developing mind: Toward a neurobiology of interpersonal experience.* New York: Guilford Press.

Siegel, D. J. (2006). An interpersonal neurobiology approach to psychotherapy: Awareness, mirror neurons, and well-being. *Psychiatric Annals, 36,* 248–256.

Siegel, D. J. (2009). Emotion as integration: A possible answer to the question, What is emotion? In D. Fosha, D. J. Siegel, & M. Solomon (Eds.), *The healing power of emotion: Affective neuroscience, development, and clinical practice* (pp. 145–171). New York: W. W. Norton.

Siegel, D. J. (2010). *The mindful therapist: A clinician's guide to mindsight and neural integration.* New York: W. W. Norton.

Singer, J. (1972). *Boundaries of the soul: The practice of Jung's psychology.* Garden City, NY: Doubleday.

Smith, E., Clance, P., & Imes, S. (1998). *Touch in psychotherapy: Theory, research, and practice.* New York: Guilford Press.

Stark, M. (1999). *Modes of therapeutic action: Enhancement of knowledge, provision of experience, and engagement in relationship.* Northvale, NJ: Jason Aronson.

Stern, D. N. (1985). *The interpersonal world of the infant.* New York: Basic Books.

Stolorow, R., & Atwood, G. (1994). Toward a science of human experience. In R. Stolorow, B. Brandchaft, & G. Atwood (Eds.), *The intersubjective perspective* (pp. 15–30). Northvale, NJ: Jason Aronson.

Stolorow, R., Brandchaft, B., & Atwood, G. (1987). *Psychoanalytic treatment: An intersubjective approach.* Hillsdale, NJ: Analytic Press.

Thelen, E. (1989). Self organization in developmental processes: Can systems approaches work? *Minnesota Symposia on Child Psychology, 22,* 77–117.

Tronick, E. (2009). Multilevel meaning making and dyadic expansion of consciousness theory: The emotional and polymorphic polysemic flow of meaning. In D. Fosha, D. Siegel, & M. Solomon (Eds.), *The healing power of emotion: Affective neuroscience, development, and clinical practice* (pp. 86–111). New York: W. W. Norton.

van der Kolk, B. A. (2002). Beyond the talking cure: Somatic experience, subcortical imprints and the treatment of trauma. In *Emergence and Convergence: Conference proceedings of the Third National Conference of the United States Association for Body Psychotherapy,* 89–112.

van der Kolk, B., McFarlane, A., & Weisaeth, L. (Eds.). (1996). *Traumatic stress: The effects of overwhelming experience on mind, body, and society.* New York: Guilford Press.

Vincent, J-D. (1990). *The biology of emotions.* Cambridge, UK: Basil Blackwell.

Waldrop, M. M. (1992). *Complexity: The emerging science at the edge of order and chaos.* New York: Simon & Schuster.

Watzlawick, P., Weakland, J., & Fisch, R. (1974). *Change: Principles of problem formation and problem resolution.* New York: W. W. Norton.

Weiss, H. (1995). The emergence of the other. *Hakomi Forum, 11,* 70–79.

White, K. E. (2002). A study of ethical and clinical implications for the appropriate use of touch in psychotherapy. *USA Body Psychotherapy Journal, 1*(1), 16–41.

White, M., & Epston, D. (1990). *Narrative means to a therapeutic end.* New York: W. W. Norton.

Wiener, D. J. (1999). *Beyond talk therapy: Using movement and expressive techniques in clinical practice.* Washington, DC: American Psychological Association.

Wilber, K. (1979). *No boundary: Eastern and Western approaches to personal growth.* Los Angeles: Center Publications.

Wilber, K. (1995). *Sex, ecology, spirituality: The spirit of evolution.* Boston: Shambhala.

Wilber, K. (2000). *Integral Psychology: Consciousness, spirit, psychology, therapy.* Boston: Shambhala.

Winnicott, D. W. (1965). *The maturational processes and the facilitating environment.* New York: International Universities Press.

# SECTION III

## Psyche and Soma

# 16

## Introduction to Section III

Gustl Marlock, Germany, and Halko Weiss, United States

Translation by Warren Miller

*Persons suffering from excessive grief . . . remain motionless and passive, or may occasionally rock themselves to and fro. The circulation becomes languid; the face pale; the muscles flaccid; the eyelids droop; the head hangs on the contracted chest; the lips, cheeks, and lower jaw all sink downwards from their own weight. Hence all the features are lengthened; and the face of a person who hears bad news is said to fall.*

These sentences were written in the mid-nineteenth century by the great natural scientist Charles Darwin (1998, p. 176), in his comprehensive and now-classic book on the subject of bodily expressions of emotion. Darwin thereby made a correlation between body language and emotion as the basis of a systematic description that would later play a central role in the field of Body Psychotherapy: namely, the connection between somatic and psychological processes.

Body Psychotherapy has since expanded the Darwinian perspective by questioning how the human ability to be emotionally expressive is shaped and restricted by the processes of civilization and cultivation. Subsequently, the question of emotional expression led to the formation of perspectives on the biographical development of posture and character. Perspectives were also advanced regarding the human ability to symbolize differentiated emotional processes through the body.

Body Psychotherapy—for the most part—does not claim to have solved the mystery of the body-mind relationship, which Schopenhauer referred to as the "knot of the world." It has, however, contributed to a historical change in epistemological, philosophical, and popular thinking that is about fundamentally rehabilitating the body. Today, hardly any scientist or philosopher would presume that the mental and emotional dimensions can exist, or be thought of, independently from the bodily dimension.

This rehabilitation is clearly demonstrated by the enthusiasm with which the fashionable category of "embodiment" is being discussed in circles of avant-garde epistemology, human sciences, and even in the realm of artificial intelligence.

In the history of Western thought, the body was assigned a position of lesser value. Plato gave the body, along with the rest of all matter, the status of an inferior manifestation in contrast to the superior field of pure ideas. The tendency to denounce the body as transitory and impure culminated in the translation of these concepts from Platonism to Christianity. Modernism, if under another title, also carried on the tendency to devalue the body, so that the postulation of the primacy and superiority of the mind can be traced from Descartes to Kant and down to Freud.

The rational mainstream of modernist thinking has been opposed by the traditions of thought that validated the body and viewed rationality critically. But, although romanticist natural philosophy and the somatic philosophical work of Schopenhauer essentially went into Freud's concept of the unconscious, the eventual equation of the body with its basic drives rigidified into a perspective that identified the body as animalistic.

The mixture of "physicalism" and empiricism that shaped modern natural science has not significantly improved the status of the body and has restricted perspectives about the mystery of the body-mind. Whereas the physicalistic viewpoint has the tendency to reduce mental processes to physical processes, the empirical perspective tended to view the body as a passive object whose features and abilities were signified as quantifiable and describable in mechanistic terms.

In the twentieth century, Nietzsche's objection to the traditional Western rejection of the body challenged the dominance of rationalistic and mechanistic thought. With his plea about the power of human existence and creativity as being rooted in the vitality of the body, Nietzsche had a strong influence on the direction of the Life Reform Movement. The Life Reform Movement, in turn, is one of Body Psychotherapy's central historical points of origin. This background is the origin of several decisive figures of thought in the Body Psychotherapeutic tradition. They all have the body-mind-spirit entity as their foundation, and they always attempted to understand existence as *embodied.*

*The body expressing the soul* is also postulated as one of these fundamental figures of thought. It shaped psychosomatic thinking, as well as theories on body language, and the expressive language of the living (Reich, 1971). The body expressing the soul is also at the core of the dance movement therapeutic tradition.

In this context, David Boadella discusses the question of the body's language in Chapter 17, "Soma Semantics: Meanings of the Body."

In Chapter 18, "The Neurotic Character Structure and the Self-Conscious Ego," Alexander Lowen describes once again, with reference to Reich, how the dynamic and dialectic body-mind-spirit relationship is viewed in clinical terms from a "bioenergetic" perspective.

Chapter 19, by Ian Grand, "The Embodied Unconscious," clarifies how the classic concept of the unconscious can be understood in the context of Body Psychotherapy, while Chapter 20, by Marilyn Morgan, "The Body Unconscious: The Process of Making Conscious: Psychodynamic and Neuroscience Perspectives," sketches how, under neuropsychological considerations, unconscious psychic contents can be revealed from the dimension of bodily experience, and how such body-based discoveries can inform the psychotherapy process and advance it forward.

Of all the founders of current Body Psychotherapy methods, Stanley Keleman (1989) is probably the one who most consistently thought out his developmental-psychological models of the body. His conception of "Formative Psychology" emphasizes the significance of the bodily forms that humans create in relation to biographical changes that affect the self. No other Body Psychotherapeutic approach has developed such a clear perspective on the bodily aspects of human maturation. His contribution, Chapter 21, "The Maturation of the Somatic Self," is a clear further development of his 1979 book, *Somatic Reality.* Keleman describes this new perspective in a nearly poetic and sometimes very personal style.

In Chapter 22, "'Body Schema,' 'Body Image,' and Bodily Experience: Concept Formation, Definitions, and Clinical Relevance in Diagnostics and Therapy," Frank Röhricht introduces a concept that is rooted in the work of Piaget and the theories on body image that were developed by the psychoanalyst Paul Schilder in the 1930s. Schilder's preliminary work was underestimated for a long time, and only in the context of Body Psychotherapy has it been thoroughly further developed and advanced.

Eugene Gendlin and Marion Hendricks-Gendlin describe in Chapter 23, "The Bodily 'Felt Sense' as a Ground for Body Psychotherapies," how, during practice of the therapeutic process, sensing into the somatic domain can form a psychic experience. In his approach, which has become known as "Focusing," Eugene Gendlin has described a core element of Body Psychotherapy in a format that has found wide acknowledgment.

Subsequently, in Chapter 24, "The Body and the Truth," Halko Weiss and Michael Harrer describe why Body Psychotherapists presume that a dual perspective on the therapeutic process—both body and psyche at the same time—can open up deeper personal truths and evidence-based experiences for clients.

In conclusion, Ian Grand, in Chapter 25, "Body, Culture, and Body-Oriented Psychotherapies," examines how cultural and social circumstances enlist themselves and are also displayed in the somatic reality of a person. Reich gave decisive impulses for theory development regarding the correlation between psychic-bodily structure and the formative societal conditions in the twentieth century (Reich, 1972). His original inspirations were further developed into some important theories of the twentieth century: the theories of the "authoritarian personality" of the Frankfurt school, the concept of "habitus" by the French sociologist Pierre Bourdieu (1982), as well as Klaus Theweleit's (1977) treatise on the *Bodies and Fantasies of Soldierly Men in Fascism*.

In the last few decades, academic psychology and neurobiology have also produced impressive research findings regarding the relationship between emotional experience and bodily expression, in particular with respect to facial expressions (Ekman, 2004), and how the body participates in the emotional experience.

## References

Bourdieu, P. (1982). *Die Feinen Unterschiede* [The fine differences]. Frankfurt, Germany: Suhrkamp.

Darwin, C. (1998). *Der Ausdruck der Gemüthsbewegungen be idem Menschen und der Thieren* [The expression of emotions in man and animals] (Reprinted from Stuttgarter Ausgabe of 1872). Nördlingen, Germany: Greno.

Ekman, P. (2004). *Emotions Revealed: Understanding Faces and Feelings*. Cheshire, UK: Phoenix Press.

Keleman, S. (1989). *Emotional Anatomy*. Berkeley, CA: Center Press.

Reich, W. (1971). *Charakteranalysyse* [Character Analysis]. Cologne, Germany: Kieperheuer & Witsch.

Reich, W. (1972). *Massenpsychologie des Fascismus* [The mass psychology of fascism]. Cologne, Germany: Kieperheuer & Witsch.

Theweleit, K. (1977). *Männerphantasien* [Male fantasies]. Frankfurt, Germany: Stroemfeld.

# 17

## Soma Semantics: Meanings of the Body

David Boadella, Switzerland

**David Boadella**, DScHon, Psychotherapist SPV, UKCP and ECP, is one of the grand pioneers of Body Psychotherapy, as mentioned in Chapter 1, the Preface to this handbook. He studied pedagogy, literature, and psychology, and was trained in Character-Analytic Vegetotherapy by Ola Raknes. He is the founder of Biosynthesis, a school of Body Psychotherapy that has synthesized insights and methodological assets from a wide variety of scientific and psychotherapeutic fields into a unique Body Psychotherapeutic approach.

David Boadella's work, comprising decades of practice as a psychotherapist, having lectured worldwide, and having written numerous books and papers, has been a vital contribution to the development of a differentiated theory of Body Psychotherapy. He was the first president of, and is an honorary member of, the European Association for Body Psychotherapy (EABP). He founded the journal *Energy & Character* in 1970, and has been its editor ever since; this is a journal that has played a critical role in the development of the field of Body Psychotherapy. In 1995, the Open International University for Complementary Medicine awarded him an honorary doctor of science degree. He is the co-director of the International Institute for Biosynthesis (IIBS), together with his wife, Silvia Specht Boadella, PhD, and they train Biosynthesis therapists from around the world.

The term "language of the body" has been used for nearly a generation (Boadella, 1987). We have not only many languages of the body, but also many bodies of language. Therefore, I prefer to use a term like "soma semantics," which means "meanings of the body." The Greek word *soma* means body in a similar sense to the German word "Leib," meaning the lived-in or alive body, as distinct from the objective body, which can be dissected and analyzed. *Soma* actually means form: we can have many forms, and so we have more than one body. Soma also includes the concept of subtle bodies, or energy fields, and, in the historical tradition of the West, these different somas were carefully distinguished.

Soma can then come to mean something more like a "morphic field," in the sense used by Rupert Sheldrake (1988). In Biosynthesis, we have developed the concept of seven different "life fields" of experience and expression. Semantics relates to levels of meanings. Different bodies, or life fields, speak different languages, and only one of these languages is verbal. Our work in Biosynthesis is therefore a process of multiple translations between information fields associated with a person. I will give examples of these translations later.

In focusing on the theme of soma semantics, I am concentrating on three main aspects: diagnosis, therapeutic praxis, and therapeutic resonance. This threefold division corresponds to sensing, acting, and feeling, which in turn are related to the three embryological organizing principles of the body.

## Diagnosis: Character as Process

We are familiar with the concept of diagnosis, from the ICD-10 and the DSM-IV and other such manualized overviews. Traditional diagnosis has many shortcomings: first, there is the tendency to overemphasize the pathology of the person, and to overlook the healthy tendencies or potentials. Second, there is the tendency to focus on symptoms, and to overlook the pattern underlying the symptoms. Third, there is the naive belief that, if we know the diagnosis, we can be led by some kind of shortcut to the remedy. Fourth, there is the tendency to base a diagnosis primarily on what a client reports, his verbal statements, rather than his total expressiveness. Fifth, there is a tendency to think that once diagnosis is finished, therapy can begin.

A classic example of this last point was in a well-known experiment carried out in the United States (Rosenhan, 1973) where a group of people feigned auditory hallucinations in order to gain admission into twelve different psychiatric hospitals. The admitting psychiatrists dutifully took careful written notes of the statements of the "patients," which were carefully tailored to be inconclusive. The group were nearly all diagnosed with schizophrenia, based on the symptoms they reported, and were duly hospitalized. None of the doctors or hospital staff realized their mistake, but many of the real inpatients realized that these new entrants were imposters. They moved, looked, and behaved like nonpsychotic persons. The schizophrenics were more accurate in their visual perceptions than the psychiatrists, basing their diagnoses on verbal accounts: the schizophrenic inpatients used a natural phenomenological diagnosis, instead of a clinical casebook checklist, which incidentally was either inaccurate or wrong. The end of the story is that some members of the group had some difficulty getting out of the hospitals, as the psychiatrists believed that their later statements that they were students, and not patients, were a typical "delusion" and released them only when they admitted to being mentally ill and taking prescribed antipsychotic medicine (which they flushed away).

Based on reportage, in Body Psychotherapy, "symptom diagnosis" is often extended by what is called "body reading," a form of diagnosis including the detailed appearance, posture, and observation of muscle-tension structures in the main muscles of the body. Unfortunately, in many cases, there persists a naive belief that one can identify a handful of "body types," and that once a person has been allocated to one of these body types, elements of their history can be deduced, according to a theoretical characterological schema. Such body reading runs the risk of excessive "objectification," especially if the body reader is a medical doctor, and especially if the client is partly unclothed, so that one can see the posture and muscle structures better. Such methods of diagnosis run the risk of a "cookbook recipe" approach to therapy, based on such a diagnosis.

So, it seems more appropriate to understand diagnosis to be a function of the sensory system. Diagnosis literally means "knowing further," or "sensing deeper." By the sensory system, I mean that we sense the client through our eyes, through our ears (listening not only to what is being said, but to how it is being said), and through our hands, in situations where therapeutic touch is acceptable to the client. These are "exteroceptive" signals. We also get kinesthetic (proprioceptive) information when the client moves, and sensory information when we are in physical or near-physical contact. We also receive interoceptive messages: sensing how our heart rate, peristalsis, breathing rhythm, and autonomic tonus respond to a client. Wilhelm Reich called this vegetative identification. I will return to this aspect later.

The second aspect is that the way we use diagnosis in Biosynthesis is dynamic, not static. It is not based on standing a client against a wall and "assessing" them. It is based on human feedback after a period of interaction and therapeutic exploration: it is therefore retrospective, as much as prospective.

Third, we embed the client's own self in the diagnostic procedure: the client's own sense of their changing situation, given a different set of parameters, or not, is of immense value, during or after a therapeutic exchange. The client's feedback enables us to evolve and refine our therapeutic approach in the direction of better fine-tuning to the actual unique individual whom we are seeking to help. Diagnosis is thus not that of an expert overseeing a sick individual, but a process of co-responding and mutual sensing. We are building a story together. So, the therapist is not posing as a detective; rather, there is a joint exploration and evolving dialogue.

Another important feature of this understanding of diagnosis is that it never stops, just as the sensory system is never switched off. Diagnosis—in this respect—is there from the beginning of the first session, until the end of the last one. The joint exploration is continuously updated week after week.

In Body Psychotherapy, in general, there has been a strong focus on the character, including the somatic aspects of character. The concept of character is very old, and has come down to us from the ancient Greeks. In the early days of psychoanalysis, Karl Abraham (1921, 1924) again brought in the concept of character more strongly, and Wilhelm Reich developed it even further. When Reich (1933/1972) spoke of "character structure," he meant by this that human character has a complex layering, or internal structure: an individual architecture that can be unfolded as a psychodynamic and somato-dynamic system. Reich focused strongly on the negative and limiting aspects of character, and sought to help people to free themselves from their neurotic character-armoring. But he also recognized that, if the growth forces within and around a person are in balance, there can be healthy character formation.

Some Body Psychotherapy methods, among them Biosynthesis, prefer to speak of character process, rather than character structure. The process is the evolution, in an individual, of tendencies, patterns, directions, beliefs, and so forth: there is a mixture of healthy potentials, and restrictive limitations and blockages. But, even within a blockage, the potential for undoing it lies latent. The term "structure" tends to suggest a rigid entity, which is certainly how some neurotic patterns can appear at first glance. The term "process" suggests that we have a history: we developed our character trends in infancy and consolidated them throughout our childhood and adolescence. I view this process as the best set of defenses that we could develop, in order to survive certain deficits, "insults," or traumas in infancy or childhood. Reich (1933/1972) spoke of character as "frozen history." Therapeutic work tries to unfreeze that history, and help to get the person growing and evolving, so that change becomes possible in the present, and thus "character," or perhaps the underlying personality, can evolve in a more fluid way into the future. In this way, the negative fate of character can gradually transform into the positive destiny of personality.

As a therapist, I am more of an optimist than a pessimist. Deep down, life has created us with tremendous potentials for contact, for enjoyment, and for healing when we have received wounds on the way. Within neuroscience, two opposite viewpoints have emerged, which reflect determinism and liberalism, respectively: on the one hand, we are told that early trauma stunts development "irreparably." If this is true, psychotherapists should pack up and go home. On the other hand, we are told of the enormous plasticity of the brain, and the body, and the ability of the organism to build new structures if it develops new functions (LeDoux, 2002). From this viewpoint, it is never too late to learn something new: emotionally, cognitively, or motorically, or even better, in all three areas.

A similar distinction between a relative emphasis on pathology or on health is found in the approaches of Kernberg on the one hand, and Kohut on the other. Kernberg's (1984) "object relations" theory emphasized the primary nature of what we would call secondary frustrations. Kohut's (1977) "Self Psychology," on the other hand, was much influenced by Winnicott (1965), and his concept of the "potential space" and of the maturational process. Biosynthesis feels much closer to the intersubjective process approach, which grew out of Winnicott and Kohut, than to the more pathologizing diagnostics of Kernberg.

## Morpho-Dynamics: Patterns of Choice and Change in Therapy

I have defined *soma* as "form," in the widest possible sense, and thus as something much more than the physical body. We have many fields of form: sometimes these are called "schemas" (body schemas, motor schemas, etc.); sometimes they are patterns of images (such as archetypes), or patterns of belief (thought modes, etc.). These fields of form, which we call "life fields" in Biosynthesis, can be either relatively incoherent in relation to each other, or relatively coherent. Trauma fragments the person, and creates the incoherence; therapy seeks to integrate him or her and increase coherence.

"Morpho-dynamics" means "patterns of changing form." These changes can be physical, tangible, and measurable—such as changes in muscle tone, vegetative tone, or breathing rates; or the changes can be subtle, more internal, less visible, more something to be sensed in the contact that one person has with the other. I use the word "resonance" to incorporate working with these more subtle bodily influences (Boadella, 1981, 1982).

The most basic and tangible fields are what we call "motoric fields," patterns of movement (Boadella, 2000a). The overt movement patterns are connected to the alpha neurons in the pyramidal nervous system, which regulates all voluntary movement. Beyond this, we have gamma neurons in the extrapyramidal nervous system, which regulates the intention for movement (Bennett, 2006). Just as character patterns have layers, so does muscle tone. So, in working with what we call "shape flow," through fine proprioceptive contact with the major muscle groups of a client, we can help to elicit the underlying tendencies for healthy movement responses. The French psycho-physiologist Henri Laborit (1980) defined neurosis as an inhibition of action. We should qualify this by saying "appropriate action." Research in the field of the psycho-biology of trauma (van der Kolk et al., 1996) has shown that trauma states are coupled with states of motoric imbalance (extreme hypertension or agitation, or collapse and helplessness), both of which block appropriate action. The latent inhibited action pattern is specific to the original invasion or deprivation when it arose, in a particular person's life process. Freeing this pattern is what we mean by "morpho-dynamics," the self-organizing evolution of new action-forms.

This sort of motoric work is one level of soma semantics, the nonverbal language of shape, flow, and creative movement. As therapists, we move between the spoken language and the motoric language, translating up from movements to words, and translating down from words to movements. This principle of translation applies to all the life fields: we find ways to connect fields of imagery and patterns of movement, for example. Other examples are given in the next section. So, we move from fragmentation and disconnection between the multiple languages of the body, toward weaving them back together into an organic web of relatedness, which is how the body and its energy fields and expressive dimensions are organically programmed to be by nature.

For example, a woman in a therapeutic group is dealing with a traumatic background with her grandfather. Typically, she is afraid of anger, afraid of speaking about it, and so forth. The therapeutic work is trying to help her to mobilize her anger. In mobilizing her anger, the more she gets an anger impulse, the more her voice fades away, until her anger impulse turns into anxiety. In working with her, encouraging her to feel her resistance to the anger impulse, it becomes clear that something is not right here: it is so contradictory. And so then it is necessary for her to sense the intentionality in her arms, because it is the arms that are primary for expressing anxiety. Her intentionality simply becomes confused in relation to this action. There is a weakening and restricting effect on her voice. It is necessary to try to sense her kinesthetic language: what are her arms really trying to express? What happens is that her arms are trying to move downward, not forward. So it is important to follow this inner intentionality, without trying to understand why at that particular moment. It is a question of helping the impulses within the latent motoric field to unfold. She is encouraged to follow this movement. And where does this lead her? She is pushing herself down to the ground, and seemingly getting stronger and stronger as she does so. At the same time, her voice is getting stronger. So now we get more coherence and less interference. Then she starts to speak. And the first word she says is "me." Out of the new "soma semantic," she begins to build more ego autonomy. Then, as the process continues, we find out that she is talking to her grandfather. He is in his grave. In her imagination, in her body impulses, she is putting the lid on his coffin, kneeling on it, pushing it down. And she is saying, "You are never coming out of here again. You can never threaten me anymore. Here you stay, here you belong: it is over!" These words complete her action, just as her action completes something that was incomplete in her psyche; something was incomplete in her body language. What she needs was not helped by her initial anger response, which was more a reaction, or an unsatisfactory attempt to repel the invader, whereas her new action pattern—a reenactment of a piece of somatic imagery—works. It is specific to her situation.

Then follows one more aspect of her "soma semantic": the wider symbolic meaning of the word "Kreuz" ("cross") and a connection with "back." For her, the word "Kreuz" is a word of triumph coming from the base of her spine; it is a word of resurrection (becoming upright again), her coming off the "cross" of her trauma with her abusive grandfather. It is also a sense of the horizontal energies running through her arms, and the vertical energy running up her back, meeting at the crossing point between her shoulder blades, which is behind the area of the heart.

The point of this clinical vignette is to emphasize the centrality of the therapeutic focus at the key moment of picking up on her specific intentionality. She does not know what it is about; we do not know what it is about; but there is wisdom in the body, in the soma, which leads to the successful motoric impulse, which unfolds the inhibited action. We can see how the fields of meaning resonate with each other to get the coherence between the movement, the body sense, the affect, the symbol, the insight, the relational context, and then suddenly it all clicks into place and this gives a new sense of inspiration and value to her life.

## Dimensions of Resonance: Energies in Dialogue in Relationship

One of the strange splitting phenomena that has arisen within Body Psychotherapy is that between "working with energy" and "working with relationship." It is interesting to look at this historically: Freud began working energetically—that is, cathartically—and he worked in the early years with touch, and with awareness (at least) of breathing rhythms. Then he became overwhelmed by the transference reactions of his patients and by the high-energy processes of the emotional life that he tapped into. So, he turned against direct touch with the "abstinence principle" and turned against too much overt emotional expression or movement, which he labeled as "acting out."

Later generations of psychodynamic therapists developed much more insight into patterns of what they called "object relations," and of transference and countertransference within the therapeutic relationship.

Wilhelm Reich, as a good character-analyst, worked both energetically, with the principles of early psychoanalysis carried much deeper and further with the transference, as well as with the qualities of contact in the relationship. He warned of the dangers of what he called "muscle-pushing," and emphasized that interventions always needed to be within the field of attunement between client and therapist. He worked with great sensitivity with respect to qualities of eye contact, and to the timing of his interventions. Moreover, Reich (1951) was one of the earliest psychodynamic therapists to explore qualities of contact in the parent-infant relationship.

His writings on what he called "orgonotic" contact through the eyes, and through touch particularly, were published well before the major studies of John Bowlby (1969, 1972, 1980) on attachment, and were a whole generation in advance of later work by Margaret Mahler (Mahler et al., 1975) on mirroring, and of the work of Daniel Stern (1980) on attunement. Some later developments within Body Psychotherapy may have neglected the relational aspects, and were thus in danger of becoming a one-person psychology or, better still, a one-person biology. However, the group who called themselves "Analytical Body Psychotherapists" (Berliner, 1994) took a swing in the opposite direction. Here, classical psychodynamic insights were coupled with "body awareness," but there was a major retreat from the rich insights of the energetic model: thus, "energy" became polarized against "relationship."

The reality is that nearly all our emotions evolve within relationships, and that the "corrective emotional experiences," which we need to work through our long-held stresses and shocks, can take place within the therapeutic relationships. Even a therapist who thinks he "only works energetically" is inevitably in a relationship with the client, for better or worse. And the therapist who thinks he works only with relationship is inevitably having energetic effects on the client, for better or worse (see also Young, 2012).

One of the most integrative understandings of the "energies in relationship" theme has come from the monumental work of Allan Schore (1994). Schore is a psychodynamic psychologist in the tradition of Bowlby and Stern. He is also a neurobiologist with a very rich understanding of the energy-conserving and energy-activating aspects of the vegetative nervous system. He shows how every contact-dance between mother and baby is also an energetic interaction with profound effects on body, breathing, eyes, and brain. Laborit's (1980) work would add on the muscles as well.

So, soma semantics inevitably involves the fields of interaction within human relationships (Boadella, 1997). There are two areas here that I would like to emphasize. First, there is the question of somatic transference, and, second, a widening of our concept of the therapeutic relationship.

The concept of projective identification was introduced by Melanie Klein (1946), who understood it as the projection by the client of negative emotions, onto (and I would add "into") the therapist, who identified with them. This process has something in common with what Reich called "vegetative identification" and with what we call "somatic resonance." If the client is angry, and does not express it, the therapist can "catch" the unexpressed anger, and may begin to feel it as a burning energy in the pit of his stomach. He may begin to rationalize the anger, or he may act out the anger on the client unconsciously as part of his countertransference. The whole point is that in addition to the known dynamics of projective identification, we have a deeper organic layer of interoceptive responses to the emotions of the other.

There are several points to be made about this aspect of the different languages of the body. First, when this process remains unconscious, it can lead to negative therapeutic reactions, but when it becomes conscious, it can become a rich learning area for the therapist: a diagnosis of how the client induces feelings in others, or of how feelings were induced in him by others, or both. As Spinoza pointed out more than three centuries ago, affects have effects.

Second, it is a rich area for therapeutic learning if the client can study in the therapist how the therapist reacts (hopefully differently from the client) to the induced feelings, and can then have an experience of positive mirroring: new paths of emotional possibility can open up.

A further point is that it is not only clients who project, and therapists who identify. Therapists can project, and clients can identify. We must be careful not to get our clients to unconsciously act out our own emotional scripts. Melanie Klein (1946) emphasized the negative transferential aspects of projection and identification. Allan Schore (1994) has also emphasized the positive aspects; so here we should perhaps talk of somatic resonance as a process of fine empathic attunement between therapist and client, and of a possible acceptance of this by the client as the incorporation of new trust in relating. In Biosynthesis, we seek to "fine-tune" the channels of contact through the eyes, the qualities and modes of language, the rich spectrum of the elements of touch, and the finer nuances of intuitive awareness of the other; the relational field then becomes the overall container within which all the other life fields are helped to reintegrate.

There is a danger that the word "transference" becomes itself pathologized. Transference just means to "carry across" (Boadella, 2000b), and this not only means that there is the risk that we overemphasize the negative contents at the expense of other aspects, but it might also mean that we could infantilize the client by reducing the whole of his emotional life to early childhood scenarios. Even positive feelings may then be seen only psychodynamically, even interpreted as "neediness," and resisted, with the belief that the role of the therapist is to offer only "optimal frustration."

It is helpful to look beyond the psychodynamic level of the therapeutic relationship, important as this is, to other dimensions of relationship, and modes of dialogue. There is a range of these, corresponding to the major "life fields."

We can distinguish the developmental relationship, where the therapist offers new skills, and helps the client to unfold new action pathways and motoric-emotional possibilities. We can also recognize the real relationship of two human beings, which transcends the roles of helper and helped: one client is helped when he sees in the therapist's eyes a tear in response to his pain; another is supported when the therapist shows human anger on his behalf, which he had not yet felt for himself.

Beyond these, there is the contractual relationship, with agreements about time, space, money, and other pragmatic aspects. And if the therapist and client dream about each other, there can be an imaginal relationship working to illuminate the therapy.

And beyond all that, there is the silent being-together at an almost meditative level of tuning in, which is no regression to the symbiosis of infancy, but a genuine tuning in of the heart.

The EABP 1999 congress at Travemünde was entitled "The Flesh of the Soul: The Body We Work With" (Heller, 2000), but in our exploration of the deeper levels of soma semantics, we must also remember the resonances of the "soul" of the "flesh," and the spirit and language of the soma (Boadella, 1995).

# References

Abraham, K. (1921). Contributions to the theory of the anal character. In D. J. Stein & M. H. Stone (Eds.), *Essential papers on obsessive-compulsive disorders.* New York: New York University Press, 1997.

Abraham, K. (1924). The influence of oral erotism on character-formation. In S. M. Perzow & M. F. R. Kets de Vries (Eds.), *Handbook of character studies: Psychoanalytic explorations.* Madison, CT: International Universities Press, 1991.

Bennett, M. V. L. (2006). Electrical synapses between neurons synchronize gamma oscillations generated during higher level processing in the nervous system. *Electroneurobiologia, 14(2), 227–250.*

Berliner, J. (1994). Von der Bioenergetischen Analyse zur analytischen Körperpsychotherapie [From Bioenergetic Analysis to Analytic Body Psychotherapy]. In P. Geissler (Ed.), *Psychoanalyse und Bioenergetic Analyse [Psychoanalysis and Bioenergetic Analysis].* Vienna: Peter Lang.

Boadella, D. (1981). Firing zones, muscle tone and the orgasm reflex. *Journal of Biodynamic Psychology, 2, 5–18.*

Boadella, D. (1982). Transference, resonance and interference. *Journal of Biodynamic Psychology, 3, 73–93.*

Boadella, D. (1987). *Lifestreams: An introduction to Biosynthesis.* London: Routledge.

Boadella, D. (1995). Inspiration and embodiment. *Energy & Character, 26(2), 5–20.*

Boadella, D. (1997). Embodiment in the therapeutic relationship. *International Journal of Psychotherapy, 2(1), 31–44.*

Boadella, D. (2000a). Shape flow and postures of the soul. *Energy & Character, 30(2), 7–17.*

Boadella, D. (2000b). Transference, politics and narcissism. *International Journal of Psychotherapy, 4(3), 283–312.*

Bowlby, J. (1969). *Attachment and loss: Attachment* (Vol. 1.). London: Tavistock.

Bowlby, J. (1972). *Attachment and loss: Separation, anxiety and anger* (Vol. 2). London: Tavistock.

Bowlby, J. (1980). *Attachment and loss: Loss, sadness and depression* (Vol. 3). London: Tavistock.

Heller, M. C. (Ed.). (2000). *The flesh of the soul: The body we work with.* Bern: Peter Lang.

Kernberg, O. (1976/1984). *Object relations theory and clinical psychoanalysis.* Northvale, NJ: Jason Aronson.

Klein, M. (1946). Notes on some schizoid mechanisms. *International Journal of Psycho-Analysis, 27, 99–110.*

Kohut, H. (1977). *The restoration of the self.* Madison, WI: International Universities Press.

Laborit, H. (1980). *L'Inhibition de L'Action [The inhibition of action].* Paris: Masson.

LeDoux, J. (2002). *Synaptic self: How our brains become who we are.* London: Macmillan.

Mahler, M., Pine, F., & Bergman, A. (1975). *The psychological birth of the human infant.* New York: Basic Books.

Reich, W. (1933/1972). *Character Analysis* (3rd ed.). New York: Farrar, Straus & Giroux.

Reich, W. (1951). Armouring in human infants. *Orgone Energy Bulletin, 3(3), 121–138.*

Rosenhan, D. L. (1973). On being sane in insane places. *Science, 179(70), 250–258.*

Schore, A. (1994). *Affect regulation and the origin of the self: The neurobiology of emotional development.* Hillsdale, NJ: Lawrence Erlbaum.

Sheldrake, R. (1988). *The presence of the past: Morphic resonance and the habits of nature.* London: Collins.

Stern, D. (1980). *The interpersonal world of the infant.* New York: Basic Books.

van der Kolk, B. A., McFarlane, A. C., & Weisaeth, L. (Eds.). (1996). *Traumatic stress: The effects of overwhelming experience on mind, body, and society.* New York: Guilford Press.

Winnicott, D. (1965). *Maturational process and the facilitating environment: Studies in the theory of emotional development.* London: Hogarth Press.

Young, C. (Ed.). (2012). *About Relational Body Psychotherapy.* Galashiels, Scotland: Body Psychotherapy Publications.

# 18

## The Neurotic Character Structure and the Self-Conscious Ego

### Alexander Lowen, United States

**Alexander Lowen** was a student of Wilhelm Reich and was one of the central and formative people in the history of Body Psychotherapy. Along with John Pierrakos, Lowen founded the approach of Bioenergetic Analysis, a revision of Reich's Character-Analytic Vegetotherapy, and in 1956 established the International Institute for Bioenergetic Analysis in New York. With its various spin-offs, this school continues to be the largest school of Body Psychotherapy today, and has had a lasting influence on various other approaches. In particular, these are: the differentiation and further development of Reich's character-analytical theory; the reintegration of Body Psychotherapeutic methodology and theory into a psychodynamic perspective; the creation of a multitude of body exercises for clinical application; as well as a comprehensive body of writings. In particular, Lowen's numerous books make his contribution an extremely important foundation of Body Psychotherapy.

Alexander Lowen was originally a lawyer. Only after going into therapy with Reich, did he decide to become a physician and psychotherapist. Since the mid-1950s, he promoted his work around the world, establishing Bioenergetic Analysis as an international method of Body Psychotherapy, and—until his death in 2008—he continued to work with individuals and groups well into his nineties. In the following contribution, which Alexander Lowen wrote in 2002 for the German edition of this handbook, he retraces the fundamental tenets of Bioenergetic Analysis, which views the dissolution of the neurotic character structure as resulting from the recollection and revitalization of the somatic dimension. His books are available through Bioenergetics Press: www.bioenergeticspress.com.

Since its inception, Bioenergetic Analysis has been based upon the dialectical understanding of the relationship between the body and the mind. That understanding postulates that, while the body and mind are a unity on a deep level, on a more superficial level, body and mind can be opposite forces within an organism, each of which influences the other. This understanding is portrayed in a diagram that shows the unity and antithesis of these forces. Reich used this diagram (see Figure 18.1) in all his writings about the human condition, and I have made it one of the basic concepts of Bioenergetic Analysis.

Processes that belong to the body or physical side of an organism are movement and feeling. On the mental side, the corresponding functions are thinking and images. In a healthy organism, these functions are fully integrated so that the organism operates from a deep sensing of its being.

Neurosis and, to a greater degree, psychosis is associated with a loss, to some degree, of this integration. Here is a good example: Some years ago, I was consulted by a successful businessman who was involved in a neurotic relationship with a woman. He had a fixed smile on his face and described himself as a very happy man. When he dropped the smile, he looked like a very sad individual. He was like a clown, who wears a big, broad smile, which is a false facade. In the case of a clown, the smile is a mask, which he can remove. The contradiction in my patient represented a split in his personality, between his feeling and his expression. He had cut off his feelings to project an untrue image.

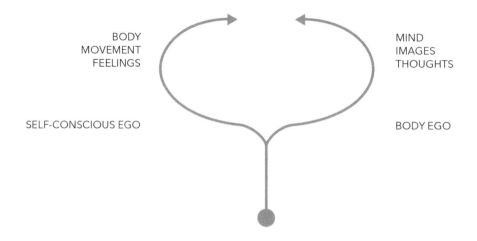

Figure 18.1. Reich's model of the body-mind relationship

This ability to suppress feelings and to project an image is a typically human function. I don't believe it is found in any other creature. In animals, other than humans, the antithesis between mind and body exists, but it does not constitute a split. An animal always functions as a unity. That split is the result of the development in the human personality of a self-conscious ego. In any organism that has a brain, there is a degree of consciousness, an awareness of behavior, and an ability to learn. But no animal is self-conscious, as this represents an ability to see one's self as if from outside of the body.

I believe this development in humans stems from the acquisition of language. Words have become images of objects, and even of feelings and thoughts. Descartes' formulation "I think therefore I am" is an accurate statement of the ego position of modern humans. Thinking is a function that depends on words, or on symbols that can be translated into words. Now, language is a function of the left cerebral hemisphere, which also contains the nerve centers for the right half of the body—the more aggressive side of the body in most people. If we think of the ego as a sense of self, we must realize that young children and even animals have this sense of self that Freud called a "body ego." The rise to dominance of the logical thinking mind created a special type of consciousness, which I call "self-consciousness," and thus gave rise to a self-conscious ego.

People who are self-conscious are constantly judging their behavior and their responses. Consciousness involves judgment, which is related to the need to discriminate. A wild animal needs to discriminate between many different situations and a variety of options for action, some of which would have a negative effect upon its well-being, and some of which are positive. Our senses are necessary for this purpose of discrimination, which is a normal function enabling us to protect our well-being. It is another matter when we examine or judge our feelings, which in effect means judging ourselves. If a child feels sexually excited by a parent of the opposite sex, the child should not be blamed or shamed for such a pleasant feeling. By the same token, the child should not be criticized or punished for expressing a negative feeling toward their parent. In contrast to actions, negative feelings do not injure another person. Every person must be true to his body—and its feelings, because to reject a feeling is to reject the self. This is especially true for children who do not have the strength or self-possession to handle or express their feelings in a socially approved fashion.

Negative criticism of children only forces the child to turn against its self. Children whose feelings are not accepted by their caregivers will turn against themselves in an effort to gain some approval. They will feel ashamed and guilty about themselves, feelings that are both painful and self-destructive. All neurotics suffer from painful feelings of shame and guilt, which they can avoid only by numbing or deadening themselves.

The neurotic character structure is not a conglomeration of injuries and defenses that can be analyzed one by one, nor is it a series of scattered muscular tensions—a tense neck, a rigid jaw, contracted shoulders, etc.—that block the flow of excitation and feeling in the body. True, each tense muscle group is a result of traumatic experiences that block the expression of feelings. But the character structure is an organized system of defenses, aimed to promote the survival and security of the individual. These defenses become organized within the body by a set of muscle tensions, postures, facial expressions, and the like. And these defenses are integrated and coordinated to promote maximum security, which the individual feels to be necessary, and yet also provide an opportunity for that individual to try to find some sort of fulfillment in their life. The person's character structure was not built in a day, but over a period of years—around six usually—within which the child strives to find some positive meaning in its life. It is like being in a walled city or a fortress, depending on the degree of fear. It cannot be analyzed away, nor can it be demolished by force. It is part of the individual's nature—their second nature, to be exact—and therefore beyond the conscious will of the individual to change. In fact, it was the will of the individual, in the form of his self-conscious ego, that constructed the fortress, which will be defended by that ego against any attempt to penetrate it. We must accept that a verbal analysis, either as transference or resistance analysis, is relatively impotent to change it. It cannot be broken down from without. But, although it may be an impregnable defense, it is also a prison for the individual. And so he comes to therapy because he wants to get out.

Because the fortress is his body, and within his body, he must realize that it is only really through his body that a significant change in that fortresslike character structure can be achieved. It isn't a structure of stone, but of frozen life, and the actual treatment is a thawing-out process. The body needs to be unfrozen gently. This process will require both heat (energy) and movement (vibration) in order to mobilize and release that held-in life force. Analysis, in the form of understanding, is necessary, for the liberation of feelings is both a painful and a frightening process, and it must be done very slowly. Still, there is no mystery to the healing process. Heat and movement require energy, and that is provided by a better respiration, a deeper breathing. Breathing exercises help only a little, because their value is limited to the period of the exercise. The deeper breathing has to be involuntary and associated with the person's feelings. Their breathing was frozen in order to block their feelings; it thaws only as their feelings are allowed to flow. One feeling that is blocked is often sadness, which must be expressed by deep sobbing and crying—sometimes by a depth of crying that rocks the patient's body to its core.

The body's spontaneous motility has to be mobilized in order to shake the body free from its state of frozen shock. Stated simply, it has to vibrate from head to toe. This cannot be done quickly. It is a continuous, ongoing process in which the patient's conscious engagement in this process is an important factor. I am writing this chapter because I have found that it works. But it is a slow and long process, and progress in this undertaking depends largely on the degree that the therapist himself has undergone this process of coming alive—of surrendering of their self-conscious ego to the body-based ego.

A Body Psychotherapy training program needs to be acutely aware of grounding its therapeutic work in the reality of the body's energetic processes—primarily, breathing and movement. No individual, conditioned within our culture, breathes fully and deeply, nor does the wave of excitation flow freely through his body, because of the chronic muscular tensions that imprison his body and deaden his spirit. One can say that the person is afraid to break out of his prison, which is true, but it is even truer that he lacks the energy to do so because his breathing and mobility are reduced. What I have learned in my many years of being a bioenergetic therapist is that this disturbance of respiration is due to the fear, and thus to the inability, of the patient to cry deeply or to scream loudly. That fear stems from his experience that crying or screaming would evoke an angry response from his parents, and, in most cases, a threat of rejection or punishment. But, just as the crying of a child is its primary mechanism to release fear and pain, so it is the main mechanism in an adult to release the chronic tensions that decrease one's aliveness and energy. I have not seen any patient coming in to therapy who could cry deeply and freely. The inner tube of the body, which is the respiratory organ, is always severely contracted. In most cases, this contraction also involves the alimentary canal to some degree. The crying that releases pain is a sobbing sound that echoes through this tube and can end in a piercing scream that now discharges the pain and terror that the child experienced early in life, but didn't (or couldn't) allow itself to feel.

If deep breathing charges and energizes the organism, vibration is the discharge function. Because charge and discharge have to be in balance, the stronger the vibration, the deeper the breathing, and vice versa. The key to allowing the vibration is in grounding. Unless a person is grounded, the energy just cannot flow freely through his body.

I have found that really powerful grounding positions have to be used in order to really ground the patient. This occurs only when the energy, or the wave of excitation, flows into the ball of the foot. This point or place in the foot corresponds to the balls of the eyes, the palm of the hands, and the balls in the genitals. Using one leg, rather than two, in the grounding position intensifies the degree and extent of the process if a satisfactory result is really to be achieved. (For further details, see Lowen, 2004, p. 240.) At the same time that a patient works regularly with breathing, crying, and vibration, the therapist must be aware of the specific tensions that are part of the whole defensive structure, and that must be understood and addressed if the breakdown of the defensive character structure is to be achieved. Of course, working this way will evoke feelings of anger, which must also be expressed. But with anger, as with crying, the extent of the release depends on the degree of its spontaneity and the fullness of its expression.

It is understood that Bioenergetics involves a verbal exchange between the therapist and the patient as an essential part of the therapeutic process. But this exchange is meaningful only if it is connected with, and based upon, an understanding of the energetic dynamics of the neurotic character structure. The aim of the therapy is to give the patient a clear and strong feeling of who he or she is. As opposed to the neurotic character structure, a healthy sense of self is not a rigid or fixed image, but a feeling of aliveness and responsiveness, stemming directly from the experience of the body. Because every person is his or her body, the feeling of connectedness is the basis of who he or she is. Health is to be *some*body.

### References

Lowen, A. (2004). *Honoring the body.* Alachua, FL: Bioenergetics Press.

### Bibliography of Lowen's Main Writings

Lowen, A. (1958). *The language of the body.* New York: Macmillan.

Lowen, A. (1965). *Love and orgasm.* New York: Macmillan.

Lowen, A. (1967). *The betrayal of the body.* New York: Macmillan.

Lowen, A. (1970). *Pleasure: A creative approach to life.* New York: Penguin.

Lowen, A. (1975). *Depression and the body.* New York: Penguin.

Lowen, A. (1976). *Bioenergetics.* New York: Penguin.

Lowen, A. (1980). *Fear of life.* New York: Macmillan.

Lowen, A. (1984). *Narcissism: Denial of the true self.* New York: Macmillan.

Lowen, A. (1988). *Love, sex, and your heart.* New York: Macmillan.

Lowen, A. (1989). Bioenergetic Analysis. In R. J. Corsini & D. Wedding (Eds.), *Current psychotherapies* (4th ed.) (pp. 572–583). Itasca, IL: Peacock.

Lowen, A. (1990). *The spirituality of the body.* New York: Macmillan.

Lowen, A. (1995). *Joy: Surrender to the body and to life.* New York: Penguin.

Lowen, A. (2004). *Honoring the body.* Alachua, FL: Bioenergetics Press.

Lowen, A., & Lowen, L. (1977). *The vibrant way to health: A manual of exercises.* New York: Harper & Row.

# 19

## The Embodied Unconscious

Ian J. Grand, United States

**Ian J. Grand**, PhD, is Professor Emeritus and former chair of the Somatic Psychology program at the California Institute of Integral Studies (CIIS) in San Francisco. He was formerly co-director of the Center for the Study of the Body in Psychotherapy at CIIS.

He studied with Fritz Perls and Stanley Keleman, and was the lead organizer of the Extended Growth Program at Esalen Institute, director of the Experimental College at San Francisco State University, director of the Social Physiology Institute in Berkeley, and program chair of the Integral Health Programs at CIIS.

Ian Grand was the editor of the *Journal of Biological Experience: Studies in the Life of the Body*. He has published numerous scientific papers, and with Don Hanlon Johnson co-edited the now-classic *The Body in Psychotherapy: Inquiries in Somatic Psychology*. He is the author of *A Beginner's Palette of Somatic Psychotherapy, and Qualities and Configurations: A Workbook in Somatic Psychology*. The width of perspective that characterizes Ian Grand's work spans from fundamental philosophical discussions of the uniquely human trait of creating meaning, to the relationship between the media, pop culture, and somatic psychological development. His theoretical as well as clinical approach are informed by a multidisciplinary perspective that views the body and psyche as embedded in social and cultural contexts. The question of how psychic representations, symbolizations, and processes of identity formation might be grounded in somatic experience is a particularly interesting area of inquiry for him.

> *When all our latent memories are taken into consideration it becomes totally incomprehensible how the existence of the unconscious can be denied. But here we encounter the objection that these latent recollections can no longer be described as psychical, but they correspond to residues of somatic processes from which what is psychical can once more arise.* (Freud, 1957/1975, p. 60)

Since its beginnings, analytic thought has linked the body and the unconscious—at least conceptually. Freud considered organismic experiences such as sexuality, aggression, sensation, digestion, and elimination as "primary processes" upon which the psyche builds its functioning, and, in his approach, people came to understand how living toward or away from these primary processes leads to health or dysfunction.

In general, psychodynamic thinking about the unconscious begins with the idea that there are forces, drives, images, and motivations of which we are largely unaware that shape our responses to the world and our feelings of self. Some analytical thinkers emphasize children's experience of the first two years of life as the ground of psychic functioning, whereas others note that unconscious structuring of interactions and senses of self continues throughout the person's life span.

Drive theory (Freud, 1961), and its derivatives, see the conflict between organismic drives and the environment as the root of unconscious patterning. From this perspective, the self develops defenses against aspects of itself, such as erotic delight or interpersonal aggression, that are threatening because of the disapproval, or lack of support, from the social surround. To ward off the threat, the self enacts a variety of defensive maneuvers, such as repression, dissociation, projection, and denial, all of which are enacted unconsciously. The juicy emotionality and the desires of the organism become increasingly thwarted.

Object Relations, relational, and other theorists see the relational shaping of the body as primary. Mitchell, for example, states: "Desire is experienced always in the context of relatedness, and it is that context which defines its meaning. Mind is composed of relational configurations . . . Experience is understood as structured through interactions" (1988, pp. 3–4). Excitation, feeling, and expression develop in relational settings. Systems theorists assume that, in the family system, there are embodied roles, rules, and identities that are distributed among the family members without overt discussion or negotiation. Interactions with siblings, grandparents, friends, and teachers also shape patterns of the self.

Other models of the unconscious suggest that there are enhancing unconscious developments, as well as conflictual ones. Early childhood theorists, such as Stern (1985), Tronick (2003), and others note that the child and the caregiver develop greetings, play, and behavioral routines that can be seen as positive to both. Still other theorists hold that the basic structuring of the underlying processes of affect, affect regulation, thought, interaction, and self-identity is part of the unconscious that can be worked into the person's quest for self-understanding and self-development. Neumann (1979) and other Jungians talk about what Neumann calls the "creative unconscious"—which he sees as shaping the experience of persons and creating possibilities for creative becoming. Similarly, Balint (1999), Winnicott (1991), Milner (1957), Loewald (1988), and Bollas (1987) have all talked about the creative aspects of the unconscious. As in dreams, conscious and unconscious materials continually interact and mutually shape each other in creative plays of becoming.

Body-oriented psychotherapists have taken all of these assumptions about unconscious self-formation, and have attempted to understand how the person structures his or her body and body processes, and enacts or physically embodies these different structural modes of unconscious functioning.

## Somatic Analytic Approaches

In Somatic Psychotherapeutic approaches, the questions that are asked are: How, literally, does the psyche affect its development along any of these lines? What are the actual mechanisms of repression? How do we develop particular patterns of being with other people? When children are told to be quiet, or to stop hitting or biting, or to inhibit their curiosity, how do they actually carry that out? How do wonder, curiosity, and creativity get inhibited or enhanced?

In *Civilization and Its Discontents,* Freud talked about the bodily means of identity formation and rejection of unwanted or noxious elements both from within and without:

> One comes to learn a procedure by which, through a deliberate direction of one's sensory activities and through suitable muscular action, one can differentiate between what is internal—what belongs to the ego—and what is external—what emanates from the outer world. . . . This differentiation, of course, serves the practical purpose of enabling one to defend oneself against sensations of unpleasure which one actually feels or with which one is threatened. In order to fend off certain unpleasurable excitations arising from within, the ego can use no other methods than those which it uses against unpleasure coming from without, and this is the starting-point of important pathological disturbances. (Freud, 1961, pp. 14–15)

Body-oriented analytic practices take these notions seriously and work directly with the ways that individuals bodily construct their refusals of the world and their refusals of the upwelling of their own desires, feelings, and emotions. Reich, for example, developed the idea that there is a process he called "muscular armoring"—patterns of muscular holding that inhibit certain expressions, gestures, and feelings—formed in response to conflictual developmental situations (Reich, 1970). Reich also charted organizations of bodily energies and hormonal expressions that promote habitual patterns of feeling. By analyzing and working directly with these bodily formations, he thought, one could directly address and alleviate the conflicts presented by the client.

Marcher (Bentzen, Bernhardt, and Isaacs, 1996) and Aikin (1979) looked at how ego strength could be understood in terms of hyperarousal or hypoarousal of muscular tonicity; and Frank (2001) has explored the way clients enact developmental parameters of differentiation of self and other, reaching out and pushing away, and relationship to the ground and correlated this with early developmental stages of the embodied psyche. Cornell (2003) continues to write about eros and the body in therapy.

Similarly, in a somatic approach outside of psychotherapy, F. M. Alexander (1932/2001) developed the notion of "use" to describe the patterns of bodily habit that a person develops and automates. For Alexander, postural, gestural, and muscular holdings are enacted habitually and are changed through time only with the practice of both awareness and new patterns of use. What is common to these approaches is the idea that there are patterns of bodily functioning, limited vocabularies of emotion and expression, that are formed by persons during their developmental process.

In general, somatic theories of the unconscious look at how senses of self and the world are structured bodily; how the relational history and the historical self-use of the person become their "embodied unconscious." These theories assume that the body is the site of psychic structuring of both possibility and difficulty, and that working directly with aspects of embodiment can affect persons' experience of themselves and the world. Historically built processes of perception, feeling, and expression shape the way in which subjects see and interact with the worlds they encounter.

## Empirical Corroborations

There is a growing literature in a number of fields that seems to lend empirical support to the idea of the role of nonconscious body organization in self-experience, interaction, and judgment of others. This literature also indicates new directions for Body-Oriented Psychotherapies.

In early work, Jacobson (1967) researched the relationship between kinds of thought and muscular activity. In experiments that measured the electrical potentials in muscles, he showed, for example, that when a person imagines throwing a ball, there is actually a higher electromyographic charge in the arm that is imagined to be throwing the ball, than in the other arm. The subject is unaware of this difference.

In social psycho-physiology research, Cacioppo and colleagues (1986) and others have suggested that facial muscle patterns, postural attitudes, and gestural repertoires "interact with, and form units of action with areas of the brain" and that ". . . All this occurs outside of and parallel to conscious experience, shaping it and being in turn shaped by it."

Numerous recent studies have also begun to link body processes and unconscious structuring of neurocognitive processes. Waldstein (2003) reported that hypertension affects cognitive functioning. DePaulo and Friedman (1997) noted that nonverbal behaviors could impact people's perceptions of and reactions to others. Similarly, Lakin and Chartrand (2003) noted that there are nonconscious behavioral imitations that increase feelings of affiliation, and Kolb, Gibb, and Robinson (2003) have shown links between behavior and brain plasticity.

A number of studies of neuronal plasticity have supported the basic claims of Somatic Psychology that use alters tissue state (Kandel, 2006; Kolb, Gibb, and Robinson, 2003). Plasticity refers to the ability of both neurons and areas of the brain to change structure and function. Although it was formerly believed that the neuronal structure was fixed, the current view is that changing behavior results in alteration in the number of neuronal synapses, the structures of neurons, and their biochemical processes. Ebert and colleagues (1995), for example, compared neural images of violinists and cellists with those of non-musicians, and found that the representations of the fingers of the left hand of the string players were larger than those of the non-musicians.

Kandel (2006) and his colleagues did a set of neuroimaging experiments that looked at the responses to emotional expressions as the subjects looked at pictures of people expressing fear (taken from Paul Ekman's library of images). One group of subjects was rapidly shown the pictures, at a speed below the threshold of conscious recognition. In the second group, the images were looked at consciously. The results were astounding. All the volunteers had activation of the amygdala, but the two groups had different patterns of activation. Different areas of the amygdala were activated. It was also found that differential areas outside the amygdala were also activated. There were different pathways for conscious and unconscious apperception. According to Kandel (2006), "... these ideas confirm biologically the importance of the psychoanalytic idea of unconscious emotion."

Currently, the so-called "embodiment" paradigm in academic psychology is looking systematically at ways in which the neural functioning of relationship, affect, cognition, and action are organized in larger body and environmental systems (Niedenthal, Barsalou, Winkielman, Ric, and Krauth-Gruber, (2005); Semin and Smithe, 2008). Arbib and his discussants in an issue of *Behavioral and Brain Sciences* (2005) have proposed extensions of mirror-neuron theory that underscore the complex body/environment organizations in humans involved in advanced processes of imitation.

Although all this research is in its infancy, it does seem to corroborate or indicate earlier Somatic Psychology understandings that hold that there is a complex structuring and automatization of body/brain processes and interactions that unconsciously inform how people enact within themselves and interact with the world.

## Developing the Embodied Unconscious

Somatic theories speculate that, through time, people develop the unconscious patterns of postural use, gesture, excitation, and expression by which they experience themselves and interact with the world. The claim is that, in interaction with their social surround, the person develops tissue organizations that hold back, or exaggerate, feeling or expression, kinds of excitations, ways of acting, postures, and gestures, which the person automates, and which develop particular bodily states through time.

There are several different orders of unconscious body organization, and one way of describing these is as follows. The schema given here is illustrative and is not meant to be definitive.

**Somatic Representations**

There are a number of somatic theorists who build on the concept of representations. In these theories, a person's bodily enactments are seen as representations of the person's history of contact and expression.

First, there is an order of unconscious body organization that results from direct bodily contact. Children are handled in particular ways during feeding, rocking, excitatory play, diaper changing, etc., and develop either an aversion to, or a liking for, the kinds of physical and emotional handling they receive. They repeat these patterns of touch and holding in the kinds of contact that they make with themselves (Spitz, 1964) and later with others.

There are also environments of sensation and excitation of which the children are a part and that also influence the development of bodily responses. Anzieu (1984), for example, talks about what he calls "sensory envelopes," such as heat, sound, and smell as well as touch, presumably—through which the infant organizes his or her experiences and develops unconscious patterns of recognition and repetition.

Unconscious patterns of response to these direct somatic experiences are laid down and continue throughout the life span. They form what Bollas (1987) has called "the unthought known." The person knows something that has not been put into language, but exists in them as organized bodily responses to past somatic experiences.

A second order of unconscious representations occurs in the interaction between children and caregivers. There are mutual patterns of gesture and response, affective plays that are rehearsed, are enacted repeatedly, and become part of a repertoire of engagement by which and through which the child meets the world (Tronick, 2003). On the basis of extensive infant observation, Downing (2000) talks about what he calls "body micropractices" that infants develop as "procedural or implicit knowledge."

Children have a wide range of affective enactment. As Jaffe and colleagues (2001) note, there is a mutually choreographed dance of development in which each involved person develops in response to the other's dynamics. They squeal with laughter, cry and are disorganized, or are angry and loving. There is the arising of their appetites, their demands and frustrations, and their exploration of the world in creative play. All this occurs in an embodied field of caregivers' responses and children's responses to the caregivers' responses.

In these dances of caregivers and recipients, somatic holdings and ranges of feelings are developed that both restrict and make possibilities for the growing child. This kind of process continues throughout childhood and indeed throughout the life span.

As the child grows older, he or she learns to handle various kinds of excitations in the familial field. Libidinal desires, aggressions, needs for holding, and creative play are all developed in a field of interaction, which is then represented as the holding and expressive pattern of the body in interaction with itself or others.

Development can be seen as an ongoing organization of covert and overt bodily states as representations of the past (or, more precisely, a representation of the creative and defensive structurings of the past that the person has formed in response to environmental and self-signals). What is represented bodily is the person's enactments toward, and with, various parties in the person's family of origin, the family process as a whole, and the specific self that the person forms in interaction with these various others. The family is itself nested within various communities of participation and institutional and economic environments. There are great variations in kinds of families and unconscious influences on family life from the social surround. Later representations for the individual are formed in interactions with friends, teachers, partners, and people at school and work. These socially based organizations of self and other representations can be in conflict with each other and in conflict with values of expression, excitation, and feeling in the family.

Socially based representations come from the culture and social structures in which people participate. Evans (2008) has described three aspects of the social unconscious that he calls the "preconscious," the "productive unconscious," and the "repressive unconscious." Hassin and colleagues (2005), in reviewing stereotyping and other unconscious social behaviors, have termed socially based automatic behaviors as the "new unconscious."

In somatic therapies, all this is seen as directly occurring bodily, and both the tissue state of the client, and the interactions of therapist and client, are seen to reflect these histories.

**Somatic Unconscious Identity**

An extension of these ideas about representation is the role of the body in terms of identity. From the somatic perspective, self-experience and enactment are grounded in bodily sensation, posture, and gait. Parameters of self-feeling and self-expression are structured by ranges of movement, muscular usage, and rhythms of action and speech. Different organizations of the body lead to different self-feelings.

In one line of somatic thinking, developing a socioemotional body is seen to be analogous to the training that an athlete does. There is a (nominal) given body; but from this body different bodies are made with different trainings. Weight-lifting repetitions, for example, develop muscle tissue that is significantly different from the muscle tissue developed by swimming or long-distance running. Cardiovascular training develops specific lung and heart functions. Similarly, emotional and feeling use through time develops particular bodily states.

Damasio (1999) suggests that there are "body schemas" that form the ground for what he calls the "proto-self," the "core self," and the "extended self" to emerge. Cognitive function and consciousness are dependent upon these body schemas of perceptual and feeling organization.

As both Downing (2000) and Frank (2001) have noted, there is a forming of self-recognition through the gestures, expressions, and touch of caregivers. The patterning of senses of both self and other begins with the infant's self-exploration in which it tries different movements, feels itself sensorially, and explores the external world, both the mother and the environment. The infant learns about ranges of feeling, in its hungers, defecations, delights, disgruntlements, and how these are received. These interplays with the world continue as the child learns various coordinations having to do with walking, talking, and play. There is a dance of expression, gesture, and feeling possibilities that arise in the interaction with particular others. This process continues throughout the lifetime and forms specific repertoires of interactional possibility that are not known consciously, but exist in the unconscious of the individual.

Gaddini (1980) noted that imitation is another process for developing a sense of self. In imitation, bodily movements, gestures, and rhythms, patterns of speech and walk, kinds of expression and demeanor are all copied by the child, practiced, and automated. These enactments become part of its unconscious sense of self. Meltzoff and Moore (1995) showed that children begin imitating the movements and expressions of adults at six weeks of age; and Gratier (2003) showed that there are cultural rhythms of speech by which East Indian mothers interact differently with their children than do Berkeley or Parisian mothers that are copied, are practiced, and then become part of the person's identity.

Throughout the life span, people are covertly and overtly encouraged to form particular kinds of enactments of self, and the adaptation of these styles of living is done somatically. Forms of differential motor skills, motor attitudes, sensory responses, and relational enactments are formed and automated. There are basic assumptions concerning bodily enactments of self, made in various cultures and social strata, that, together with the person's own creative activity, shape the psyches of individuals and groups (Holland et al., 1998; Rogoff, 2003). These become the basis for the person's lived bodily identity.

## Somatic Defenses, Refusals, Dissociations, and Denials

In another line of somatic analytic explanation, the person's organization of muscular use, excitation, and breath are also seen to both reflect and enact the person's psychic conflicts.

In Reich's and Lowen's character-analytic approaches, for example, the form of the body is seen as resulting from psycho-sexual-social repression and emotional conflicts (Reich, 1970; Lowen, 1975). The organism is seen as a pulsing, excitatory process that develops emotion, feeling, and desire, and responds to the frustration of these with aggression. The body is a source of erotic delight and engagement with the world, as well as the source of destructive impulses. In opposition to these primordial processes, the person enacts muscular rigidities and flaccidities, interferences in their breathing patterns, and inhibited movements that are all structured as introjected familial and societal injunctions against them. Unconsciously, the person represses particular impulses and effects these repressions through somatic means (Cornell, 2003).

There is also a growing current literature from the relational school of psychodynamics that sees the organization of selfness as basically multiple, including a variety of self-organizations, both conscious and nonconscious, integrated and dissociated (Davies, 1996). The development of these selves occurs over the bridge of actual experiences in the person's history and is enacted bodily.

Embodied relational therapies extend relational theory to include the unconscious organization of feeling, breath, movement, and interpersonal enactment (Totton, 2005). Soth (2005) theorizes embodied enactments of transference and countertransference. Similarly, a number of body-oriented clinicians (e.g., Levine, 1997; Ogden et al., 2006), working with trauma, have argued that there are bodily dissociations, lack of feelings and sensations, or hyperarousals that result from emotional, physical, or sexual trauma, and that these can be worked with directly in a bodily fashion.

The defenses described in the analytic literature have been accomplished through somatic means, on either overt or covert levels of organization. In this sense, somatic organization is seen to be the mechanism by which the person's defenses are actually enacted.

An individual may, for example, limit his or her range of movement, or rigidify the musculature, or make it flaccid, so as not to feel a given feeling or to express a particular emotion. Through holding the breath, or making it shallow, or through limiting movements like clenching the abdomen, the person can refuse feeling various kinds of emotional stimulations, or through chronic hypermovements, or hyperventilation, they can overstimulate themselves and move away from less excited, but riskier, feelings.

From a somatic perspective, we seek to avoid conflict or intimacy through somatic displacement and misdirection. A person may, for example, attempt to avoid an underlying depression or meaninglessness through compulsive athletic activity, or avoid tender feelings and vulnerability through an aggressive, critical, or threatening demeanor. Over the abyss of jagged and splintered feelings, we may create bridges of daily "normalcy," organized as routine somatic functions. We may try to avoid the sense of our own death through somatic obsession or pathological overactivity. Again, all of this is embodied, and all of it is constructed, or maintained, largely unconsciously.

**The Bodily Structuring of Creative Unconscious Processes**

Finally, somatic theories draw on a long history of thought concerning what Gustl Marlock (in Chapter 8, "Body Psychotherapy as a Major Tradition of Modern Depth Psychology") has called the vitalistic unconscious of the romantic tradition. As noted above, there are a number of writers in both traditional psychodynamic and Jungian theory who are concerned with what Neumann called the creative unconscious. Winnicott (1991) was concerned with creative possibilities and noted that children's early experiences with caregivers in play set the stage for the person's ability to enter creative transitional space in adulthood. Similarly, in her book *On Not Being Able to Paint,* Joanna Field (Milner, 1957) noted that there are often unconscious strictures on creativity that can be accessed through creative processes such as drawing.

In various somatic approaches, the bodily unconscious is also seen as a place of ongoing creation and curiosity, a place in which both inner and outer worlds are explored and enacted in new and generative ways. As bodies, we play with materials, sounds, colors, gestures, excitations, and ideas with varying feelings and tissue organizations. Dreams are body organizations of figures, qualities of color, density, gestures, rhythms, all of which have veiled, symbolic, somatic significance.

As Winnicott (1991) pointed out, there is an introduction through play to the transitional world, the world of creation, the liminal place of emergence. The way that a child plays and explores the world is also structured bodily, in response to how such play is received by caregivers, other children, teachers, and other adults. In the same way that other feelings and actions are defended against, creative play and participation in the making and forming of possibility can be restricted. Movements, excitations, and creative manipulations of the world are stopped through muscular holding. Play with expression and the following of one's impulses in paint, movement, and sounds are inhibited.

From the standpoint of somatic analytic approaches, creative emergence must be practiced. Somatic approaches such as Authentic Movement (Pallaro, 1999), Keleman's Formative Psychology (Keleman, 1987), and various dance, movement, and play therapies educate the sensitivity of the person to his or her own creative impulses and their ability to follow these impulses to expression and creative enactment (Krantz, 2012). A process of attunement to the somatic processes of unconscious creation can be learned, in which people learn to follow impulses from their inchoate beginnings, through the frustrations of their forming, and finally to their enactment and solidification.

## Gratifications and New Learning

There have been traditional analysts who have incorporated some somatic work in their work with clients. For the most part, however, traditional analysts, unlike their somatic counterparts, have been hesitant to use both touch and movement expression. Different skills and understandings are required.

In somatic work, there is direct somatic intervention. Through physical and psychological exercises, movement, touch, and guided breathwork, clients are invited to experience directly how they bodily enact qualities of feeling and expression. Client and analyst are engaged in an embodied dance of response and counterresponse, resistance and counterresistance.

In this process, aspects of unconscious structuring make themselves known. As clients do various movements, feelings and images occur in both the client and the analyst. Somatic associations occur, radiating directions of feelings and ideas, pulses and rhythms, sensations. All this is followed and worked with. The therapist works with issues of embodied transference, countertransference and co-transference in his or her own embodied psyche, and within the therapist/client field (Dosamentes-Beaudry, 1997). The conflicts, limitations, and enactments (of the past) can now be allowed to be felt.

Somatic work with the unconscious is educative. It is not simply events from the past that are analyzed and worked with. New possibilities for experience are also worked with directly. Although new experiences are part of all psychotherapies, they form an explicit dimension of the various somatic approaches. New experiences of expression, interaction, and self-conduct are explored, practiced bodily, and then automated (Glaser and Kihlstrom, 2005).

Somatic work can also be gratifying. Feeling and moving states are explored that give satisfactions that may not have been experienced in the client's past. Over the bridge of the relationship with the therapist, and with ranges of newly explored enactments, clients can feel and express themselves in different ways. Through the somatic work, they can come to experience kinds of self-enactments that are intrinsically pleasurable, exciting, creative, and empowering.

Somatic theories assume a process that is like that of an art student learning various aspects of technique, experimenting with different ways of drawing, and using various mediums. For example, clients may be asked to explore a range of movement or expression outside of their normal range. They may be asked to move more quickly than is their habit, or move more slowly, or make large gestures or smaller ones.

Through practice, clients' knowledge of their specific bodily structuring increases and the habitual behavior of the client transforms. The range of possibility for creative emergence is extended.

## Residues and Creative Possibilities

All this brings us back to the epigram from Freud with which this chapter began. There are, as Freud noted, somatic residues: structures, unconscious representations, and enactments of the past that have been embodied and automated. These residues form the ground for psychic experience.

As we have seen, somatic theories assume that these residues can be experienced, understood, and worked with directly. A process is envisioned in which, through a creative interplay between organism and social surround, tissue capabilities are developed and then automated.

These automated tissue states are crystallizations of psychic possibility, which in turn continue to produce psychic creations unconsciously. In somatic approaches, the embodied unconscious is seen to develop throughout the life span. The multiple tissue organizations that are developed at different ages, and with various people in diverse social situations, interact both to impede and modify each other and to create new possibilities.

What is taught in Body-Oriented Psychotherapies is a practice of embodied self-engagement in which, like jazz musicians, we work with both somatic residues and future possibilities. A process is established whereby the person can make use of what is emerging "ongoingly" and what is working below the level of consciousness and is to be known only indirectly. A way of bodily working with unconscious processes is established and becomes part of one's living.

Finally, this work is about our embodied aliveness, in ourselves, and in community, life as a continual embodied creation. The unconscious is seen here as both what impedes and what furthers this embodied enterprise.

## References

Aikin, P. A. (1979). The participation of neuromuscular activity in perception, emotion, and thinking. *Journal of Biological Experience, 1(2),* 12–32.

Alexander, F. M. (1932/2001). *The use of the self.* London: Orion Books.

Anzieu, D. (1984). *The skin ego.* New Haven, CT: Yale University Press.

Arbib, M. A. (2005). From monkey-like action recognition to human language: An evolutionary framework for neurolinguistics. *Behavioral and Brain Sciences, 28,* 105–167.

Balint, M. (1979/1999). *The basic fault: Therapeutic aspects of regression.* London: Routledge.

Bentzen, M., Bernhardt, P., & Isaacs, J. (1996). *Waking the body ego, II.* Novato, CA: Bodynamic Institute USA.

Bollas, C. (1987). *The shadow of the object: Psychoanalysis of the unthought known.* New York: Columbia University Press.

Cacioppo, J. T., Petty, R. E., Losch, M. E., & Kim, H. S. (1986). Electromyographic activity over facial muscle regions can differentiate the valence and intensity of affective reactions. *Journal of Personal Social Psychology, 50(2),* 260–268.

Cornell, W. (2003). The impassioned body: Erotic vitality and disturbance in psychotherapy. *British Gestalt Journal, 12(2),* 97–104.

Damasio, A. (1999). *The feeling of what happens: Body and emotion in the making of consciousness.* New York: Harcourt Brace.

Davies, J. M. (1996). Linking the "pre-analytic" with the postclassical: Integration, dissociation and the multiplicity of unconscious process. *Contemporary Psychoanalysis, 32(1),* 553.

DePaulo, B. M., & Friedman, H. S. (1997). Nonverbal communication. In D. T. Gilbert, S. T. Fiske, & G. Linzey (Eds.), *The handbook of Social Psychology (4th ed.).* New York: McGraw-Hill.

Dosamentes-Beaudry, I. (1997). Somatic experience in psychoanalysis. *Psychoanalytic Psychology, 14,* 517–530.

Downing, G. (2000). Emotion theory reconsidered. In M. Wrathall & J. Malpus (Eds.), *Heidegger, coping and cognitive science.* Cambridge, MA: MIT Press.

Ebert, T. C., Pantev, C., Wienbruch, B., & Taub, E. (1995). Increased cortical representation of the fingers of the left hand in string players. *Science, 270,* 305–307.

Evans, F. (2008). *The multivoiced body: Society and communication in the age of diversity.* New York: Columbia University Press.

Frank, R. (2001). *Body of awareness: A somatic and developmental approach to psychotherapy.* Cambridge, MA: Gestalt Press.

Freud, S. (1957/1975). The unconscious. In *Standard Edition of the Complete Psychological Works of Sigmund Freud, Vol. 14* (pp. 159–160). London: Vintage.

Freud, S. (1961). *Civilization and its discontents* (J. Strachey, Ed.). New York: W. W. Norton.

Gaddini, E. (1980). Notes on the mind-body question. In A. Limentani (Ed.), *A psychoanalytic theory of infantile experience: Conceptual and clinical revelations.* London: Routledge.

Glaser, J., & Kihlstrom, J. (2005). Compensatory automaticity: Unconscious volition is not an oxymoron. In R. Hassin, J. Uleman, & J. A. Bargh (Eds.), *The new unconscious.* New York: Oxford University Press.

Gratier, M. (2003). *Protoconversation and the roots of belonging.* Paper presented at Society for Psychological Anthropology annual meeting, San Diego, CA.

Hassin, R., Uleman, J., & Bargh, J. R. (Eds.). (2005). *The new unconscious.* New York: Oxford University Press.

Holland, D., Lachicotte, W., Skinner, D., & Cain, C. (1998). *Identity and agency in cultural worlds.* Cambridge, MA: Harvard University Press.

Jacobson, E. (1967). *Biology of emotions.* Springfield, IL: Charles. C. Thomas.

Jaffe, J., Beebe, B., Feldstein, S., Crown, C., & Jasrow, M. (2001). *Rhythms of dialogue in infancy: Coordinated timing in development.* Boston: Blackwell.

Kandel, E. R. (2006). *In search of memory.* New York: W. W. Norton.

Keleman, S. (1987). *Bonding.* Berkeley, CA: Center Press.

Kolb, B., Gibb, R., & Robinson, T. E. (2003). Brain plasticity and behavior. *Current Directions in Psychological Science, 12(1),* 1–5.

Krantz, A. (2012). Let the body speak. *Psychoanalytic Dialogues, 22*(4), 437–448.

Lakin, J. L., & Chartrand, T. L. (2003). Using nonconscious behavioral mimicry to create affiliation and rapport. *Psychological Science, 14*(4), 334–339.

Levine, P. (1997). *Waking the tiger: Healing trauma.* Berkeley, CA: North Atlantic Books.

Loewald, H. (1988). *Sublimation: Inquiries into theoretical psychoanalysis.* New Haven, CT: Yale University Press.

Lowen, A. (1975). *Bioenergetics.* New York: McCann.

Meltzoff, A., & Moore, M. K. (1995). Infants' understanding of people and things: From body imitation to folk psychology. In J. L. Bermudez, A. Marcel, & N. Eilon (Eds.), *The body and the self.* Cambridge, MA: MIT Press.

Milner, M. (Joanna Field). (1957). *On not being able to paint.* New York: Tarcher/Putnam.

Mitchell, S. (1988). *Relational concepts in psychoanalysis: An integration.* Cambridge, MA: Harvard University Press.

Neumann, E. (1979). *Art and the creative unconscious.* Princeton, NJ: Princeton University Press.

Niedenthal, P. M., Barsalou, L. W., Ric, F., & Krauth-Gruber, S. (2005). Embodiment in the acquisition and use of emotion knowledge. In L. Feldman Barrett, P. M. Niedenthal, & P. Winkielman (Eds.), *Emotion and consciousness* (pp. 21–50). New York: Guilford.

Ogden, P., Minton, K., & Pain, C. (2006). *Trauma and the body: A sensorimotor approach to psychotherapy.* New York: W. W. Norton.

Pallaro, P. (Ed.). (1999). *Authentic movement.* London: Jessica Kinsley.

Reich, W. (1970). *Character Analysis.* New York: Farrar, Straus & Giroux.

Rogoff, B. (2003). *The cultural nature of human development.* New York: Oxford University Press.

Semin, G. R., & Smithe, E. R. (Eds.). (2008). *Embodied grounding: Social, cognitive and neuroscientific approaches.* Cambridge, UK: Cambridge University Press.

Soth, M. (2005). Embodied countertransference. In N. Totton (Ed.), *New directions in Body Psychotherapy* (pp. 40–55). Berkshire, UK: Open University Press.

Spitz, R. A. (1964). The derailment of dialogue: Stimulus overload, action cycles, and the completion gradient. *Journal of the American Psychoanalytic Association, 12*(4), 752–775.

Stern, D. (1985). *The interpersonal world of the infant.* New York: Basic Books.

Totton, N. (Ed.). (2005). *New dimensions in Body Psychotherapy.* Berkshire, UK: Open University Press.

Tronick, E. Z. (2003). "Of course all relationships are unique": How co-creative processes generate unique mother-infant and patient-therapist relationships and change other relationships. *Psychoanalytic Inquiry, 23*(3), 473–491.

Waldstein, S. R. (2003). The relation of hypertension to cognitive function. *Current Directions in Psychological Science, 12*(1), 9–13.

Winnicott, D. W. (1991). *Playing and reality.* New York: W. W. Norton.

# 20

## The Body Unconscious

*The Process of Making Conscious: Psychodynamic and Neuroscience Perspectives*

### Marilyn Morgan, New Zealand

**Marilyn Morgan** was a psychotherapist and counselor in private practice, and a faculty member at the Eastern Institute of Technology, an accredited college in New Zealand, where she taught psychotherapy. As a faculty member, she contributed to the development of the curriculum for training in psychotherapy, and subsequently developed an accredited training program in Body Psychotherapy, which is based on Hakomi Experiential Psychotherapy. Her work was informed by trainings in Process-Oriented Psychotherapy (Arnold Mindell), Bioenergetics, a number of trauma therapy methods, and in particular by the Hakomi Method. She was a registered general and obstetric nurse, and a Hakomi trainer and supervisor. She was formerly a board member of the New Zealand Association of Psychotherapists, and served as adviser to governmental commissions numerous times. She played a vital role in introducing a diversity of psychotherapeutic approaches to New Zealand, and in developing and implementing respective educational material. She drew on her postgraduate work in neuropsychology for the following contribution. Unfortunately, she died in 2008.

Psychotherapists have increasingly come to appreciate the inseparable nature of the body and the unconscious. Tuning in to body sensations and movement is often a speedy route to the unconscious, and involving the body in psychotherapy can be a powerful tool in eliciting awareness and therapeutic change. Clinical observations made by body-oriented psychotherapists are now beginning to be supported by recent discoveries in neuroscience. It is easy to ride this wave of excitement and to assume more scientific evidence than is currently available.

A growing number of scientists and psychotherapists, which include, among many others, Daniel Siegel, Candace Pert, Louis Cozolino, Allan Schore, and Eric Kandel, are anticipating further scientific confirmation of their early tentative hypotheses. Cozolino says, "Psychotherapists are clinical neuroscientists" (Cozolino, 2003 p. 291). In similar words, Susan Vaughan (1997), psychiatrist, psychotherapist, and writer, asserts, "I am a microsurgeon of the mind." Lewis and his colleagues say that when a therapist wants to help, "he wants to alter the microanatomy of another person's brain" (Lewis et al., 2001 p. 176). These are optimistic statements based on research and hypotheses that are, as yet, preliminary in nature. Much of this early research will need to be replicated, and methods found that ascertain whether results from animals can be applied to people.

### The Psychodynamic Unconscious

Freud gave the unconscious a central place in psychological theory and practice, describing the unconscious as the "true psychical reality." Somatic aspects of the unconscious were in the background, generally being seen as "symptoms" of psychic conflict, such as happened in "hysteria." One of the main purposes in psychotherapy, for Freud, was to make the unconscious conscious. Freud, originally a neurologist, started out with the intention of making psychoanalysis a scientific discipline. If he had had the modern technology to view and measure the living brain in action, he might not have given up his scientific project of 1895. In fact, many of Freud's ideas and theories, gained from clinical observation, are now receiving scientific interest, and some tentative support (Cozolino, 2003, p. 6; Vaughan, 1997, p. 5; Tallis, 2002, p. 177; Solms and Turnbull, 2002, p. 294).

The dynamic unconscious of Freud has been described as "the process whereby unacceptable or frightening contents of the mind . . . are banished from conscious awareness, but continue to exert an influence, either by pushing to re-emerge into consciousness or by finding displaced and disguised expression through psychological symptoms, dreams, slips of the tongue or somatic disorders" (Mollon, 2002, p. 27).

In the psychodynamic view, when material that is unacceptable to the ego emerges, anxiety is created, and the thoughts or impulses are pushed out of awareness by defenses. These defenses usually operate automatically. They are deployed to protect against the difficult emotions and knowledge following traumatic and painful life experiences, or infantile desires persisting due to developmental arrest. Maintaining defenses takes psychic energy, and too many may thus weaken the ego (Tallis, 2002, p. 62).

## The Body Unconscious in Neuroscience

The neuroscientist has a somewhat more pragmatic, broad, and biologically focused view of the unconscious. The body, and the brain as part of the body, forms the foreground. For the neurologist, unconscious, or nonconscious, processes control and monitor human functioning on many levels, from physical homeostasis to emotional responses and many behavioral reactions. A great deal of functioning proceeds automatically. The conscious mind, having a minor role in day-to-day regulation, is free to reflect on, and attend to, chosen aspects of experience, and to respond to novel tasks.

For a neuroscientist, the conscious mind involves functions of awareness, attention, and explicit memory, including factual and autobiographical material. When the individual is conscious, there is a subjective sense of remembering, noticing, and thinking. Focal attention, and a functioning hippocampus (part of the limbic system), is needed for the encoding of explicit memory. Memory storage takes place in a variety of cortical areas, and occurs through a consolidation process. On the other hand, the unconscious involves implicit memory, neural networks representing learning that originally occurred out of awareness, or that have become lost to awareness, and now operate in an automatic way. Some learning is inherently inaccessible to consciousness. The brain can be described as "an anticipatory machine" where ingrained prototypical neural links are formed (termed neural "attractors") that influence perception according to past experience. This will lead us, at times, to see what we expect to see, rather than what is actually present. Types of implicit memory, unconscious by definition, include procedural memory (movement and behavioral patterns), emotional memory, and somatic memory, which are held in the body tissues.

## Emerging Parallels between Psychodynamic and Neuroscientific Views

Links are being made that may lead us to a theory of the unconscious that incorporates psychodynamic theory, clinical observations including body phenomena, and neuroscience. Solms and Turnbull have argued for a correspondence between the Freudian perspective and scientific studies of the brain and body as a whole: in their book *The Brain and the Inner World,* they link neuroscience discoveries with psychodynamic concepts of repression, "good and bad" splitting, childhood experience, personality, dreams, and fantasy. They also say, "The visceral body is the bedrock of consciousness" (Solms and Turnbull, 2002, p. 75). Solms and Turnbull also believe it is possible to find the neurological correlates of psychoanalytic concepts and to give them a firm, organic foundation (Ibid., p. 104). Damasio asserts, "I believe we can say that Freud's insights on the nature of consciousness are consonant with the most advanced neuroscience views" (Damasio, 1999,

p. 38). Some concepts seem to already relate across disciplines. According to the neurologists, representations of external objects become "wired" into our nervous system, the development of many neural circuits being creations of the brain, and experience dependent (Ibid., p. 320). Object-relations theorists talk of internalization processes whereby objects in the child's external world become part of the inner landscape. Stern (1985) describes the infant's forming of representations of early interactions with caregivers that shape later relational behavior. Solms and Turnbull link transference phenomena and body memories to procedural memory, and state, "Perhaps future interdisciplinary collaboration between psychotherapists and neuroscientists will help us differentiate more precisely among 'procedural' memory subsystems" (Solms and Turnbull, 2002, p. 160).

As I consider clinical examples from my own psychotherapy practice, I will look at explanations derived from the viewpoints and languages of psychodynamic and neuroscience, and suggesting possible links. To quote Eric Kandel, "I began to think that psychoanalysis is not biological enough. It (research into links between psychotherapy and neuroscience) opens up a fascinating new area" (Matthews, 2004, p. 27).

## Richard: A Clinical Illustration of Body-Unconscious Processes

A client, Richard, is telling me about how a friend has borrowed money. He sighs deeply and sinks in the chair before saying that he could not possibly ask for his money back and doesn't care too much about the loss as he is used to it. I notice Richard's voice develop a whine, and his arms and hands become tense. I ask Richard to pay attention to what is happening in his body. He stops, turns his attention inward, and reports, "My stomach is knotted." His hands form a fist. I suggest he stay with the sensation in his stomach, feeling it. As his face flushes, Richard says firmly, "I'm angry!" Then he sighs as he hears an inner voice warning him that he shouldn't be angry with his friends. As we stay with the emerging experience, an image appears in Richard's awareness. It is his mother's face showing tears and blame when he, as a little boy, tried to express his anger at her. He feels paralyzed and his hands drop passively. Richard was surprised at what was there, hidden away in his unconscious. By paying careful attention to body signals he had uncovered unconscious factors that were influencing his present thoughts, feelings, and behavior.

These phenomena can be variously explained, according to the modality. Psychodynamically, Richard's anger could be seen as unacceptable to his ego, with the inner conflict having activated defenses. The body is therefore background. Using a more cognitive approach, underlying psychological patterns, such as Richard's passivity in relationships, may be called "schema" or "templates," and again the focus is more on the mind than on the body. John Briere (2002), who specializes in trauma recovery, and describes himself as a cognitive behavioral therapist, calls these unconscious patterns "deep cognitive structures."

Process Work, as a psychotherapeutic method, has reclaimed the body: Arnold Mindell, a physicist, and a Jungian by training, developed this modality. Mindell is likely to depict Richard's unconscious anger conflict as the "secondary process," which expresses itself through "signals," including body sensations and symptoms such as the sigh, the whine in the voice, and tension in the arms. In relation to traditional science, Mindell asserts that one can only truly explore the psychological depths by both "using a measuring stick and by using one's own experience" (2000, p. 23).

Hakomi, a body-inclusive psychotherapy developed by Ron Kurtz, emphasizes "core beliefs." Core beliefs drive us and are described as habits, operating outside of awareness. Kurtz said that whatever a person is telling you—that is, whatever he or she is aware of—there is another, deeper layer or organizing material (which the storyteller is presently unaware of), and this layer is organizing the telling, the teller, and the tale. For the client, core beliefs aren't beliefs at all; they are just the way the world is and they are not normally available for doubt (Kurtz, 1990). Core beliefs are unconscious and are as deeply rooted in the body as in the mind. Richard had chronic tension in his muscles, discomfort in his belly, and a feeling of pressure across his shoulders. His "core beliefs," and related body stance, were related to suppressing his anger, due to a fear of being blamed and losing approval.

**Richard: Neuroscientific Explanations**

Richard's somatic, psychological, and relationship patterns could also be seen as a result of neural circuitry, stored as "implicit memory" in deep brain structures. In his early life, nerve endings would have grown at certain synapses, and other alternative connections would have died away. Richard would have developed these patterns of nervous firing when he was a boy, the pattern being developed in response to interactions upon which his survival (both physical and emotional) depended, in any particular environment. Each time this pattern was triggered by a set of stimuli that resembled the early situation, the likelihood of future repetitions would be greater. His emotional response would result from "a collection of neural dispositions in a number of brain regions located largely in subcortical nuclei of the brain stem, hypothalamus, basal forebrain and amygdala" (Damasio, 1999, p. 79).

## Early Developmental Influences

Psychodynamic theory details the influence that early relationships have on unconscious and conscious structures of self. Infant research also emphasizes the importance of early development. Daniel Stern (1985) intensively studied babies and young children. He recognized that the basic sense of self is somatic in nature and is dependent on the degree of attunement in the interactions of the mother and baby. Sensory memories are formed that link with body and emotional experience to form the core self. Many years later, Allan Schore's writing on neurological development research has supported the work of Stern. Schore describes how, through attuned interaction, specific circuits develop in the right hemisphere of the infant's brain that allow the baby to experience and regulate states of excitement and pleasure. The child can control this through eye contact (Schore, 1994). As long ago as 1958, Alexander Lowen was saying, based on his clinical work, ". . . the living organism expresses itself in movement more clearly than in words. But not alone in movement! In pose, in posture, in attitude and in every gesture, the organism speaks a language which antedates and transcends its verbal expression" (Lowen, 1958, p. xi).

Stern describes how the baby develops internal, somatic representations of relationship patterns even before the verbal self develops. Schore details the neural circuits that allow for regulation of negative emotional states such as shame. As the child grows, there are times when the parent interrupts the excited grandiosity. The experience of having a limit set, or seeing disapproval in the parent's facial expression, followed by empathic repair of the distressed state in the child, is the interpersonal experience that allows the neural development. Many clients have not experienced attuned, empathic relationships in their early life, and are subsequently unable to manage, or experience, their emotions. A speculative conclusion would be that they just don't have the requisite neural wiring or somatic substrate to allow emotional regulation and expression. "Body armoring," as described by Reich (1972) and Lowen (1958), can literally cut off body responsiveness.

## Attachment Theory and the Body Unconscious

Attachment theory details the impact of early caregiver relationships, which lead to the development of what is termed a secure or insecure attachment (Bowlby, 1969; Ainsworth et al., 1978; Sroufe, 1996). "The patterning or organization of attachment relationships during infancy is associated with characteristic processes of emotional regulation, social relatedness, access to autobiographical memory, and the development of self-reflection and narrative" (Siegel, 1999, p. 67). It can be extremely useful for the psychotherapist to have an understanding of the client's attachment processes and their somatic correlates. An awareness of the responses that the client engenders in the therapist, and the reparative relationship experiences needed for change, can greatly augment the therapy. "The recognition of the body's messages in the contained holding atmosphere of the therapist's office replicates the original healing touch of the mother in a completed natural protest sequence that helps the patient define, map, create and restore an accurate image of the body-self and its goodness" (Goodwin and Attias, 1999, p. 235).

## Trauma and Neglect

It has always been asserted by psychodynamic theorists that early failures in care lead to disorders of self and neurotic or psychotic states in later life. According to neuroscience, trauma and neglect, causing overwhelming stress, especially in the early years, lead to the laying down of protective and disorganized emotional and procedural memories. There is also a direct imprint on the brain structure and function, sometimes leading to brain damage. For those abused and neglected in childhood, there is evidence of a reduced size in the left hemisphere and the left hippocampal area, fewer connections between the left and right hemispheres, a poorly developed cerebellar vermis (this helps in the sequencing of thought and movement and in calming arousal), and irritable limbic arousal mechanisms. High levels of stress hormones are toxic to certain parts of the brain, and during high arousal explicit memory may not be properly encoded (Teicher, 2002). Results from continuing research in brain plasticity in adult life are giving us hope for repair of this damage. A number of writers believe we can assist our clients literally to grow new connections, expanding possibilities for function, and supporting integration processes (Siegel, 1999; Cozolino, 2003; Vaughan, 1997).

## Unconscious to Conscious

The unconscious is a central concept in psychodynamic psychotherapies. Some trauma therapists lean toward neuroscientific explanations of nonconscious elements of therapeutic change. Whether we understand Richard's discoveries about his anger as implicit memory becoming integrated into awareness, or as conflicted material from the unconscious now entering consciousness as insights, there are some common principles regarding psychotherapeutic healing. The language and framework may be different, but it is the emergence of unconscious material into awareness that is seen to be the essential step. Theodore Blau, in *Psychotherapy Tradecraft,* says, "Traditional psychoanalytic theory proposes that the analysis approaches conclusion when the patient brings unconscious ideas into conscious awareness" (Blau, 1988, p. 114). Bruce Perry, writing as a child psychiatrist from a neurological perspective, puts it this way: "As a rule children exposed to chronic abuse or neglect early in childhood will have little cognitive understanding of how the anxiety, impulsivity and social and emotional distress they suffer are related to the brain's creation of memories during previous traumatic experience" (Perry, 1999, p. 21). With regards to healing, Perry goes on to say, "When an individual becomes self-aware there is the potential for insight. With insight comes the potential for altered behavior" (Ibid., p. 34). Conscious reflection upon distressing or traumatic material, and the creation of a meaningful narrative, act to relieve emotional distress (Cozolino, 2003).

## Accessing the Unconscious Using the Body

Over the years, therapists have used a variety of ways to access unconscious material, including hypnosis, creativity, free association, and working with dreams. Body Psychotherapy maintains that the integration of the body into the therapy facilitates accessing unconscious memory, allows for a deep understanding of emotional experiences, aids the release of stored tension and body armoring, and contributes to integration, behavioral change, and the capacity for pleasure and satisfaction in life. In his therapy explorations, Richard discovered core beliefs about himself. "I must not get angry," "It's no use trying," and "I must please others." He also found core beliefs about the world of others, including, "If I stand up for myself, others will suffer and will not like me." His body was telling him about his holding back, the anger, and the guilt related to it. Sensing his body led him to his core material; somatic, emotional behavioral imprints here translated into words.

## Bringing Together Traditional and Neuroscientific Perspectives in Body Psychotherapy

People come to therapy for a number of reasons. They may feel anxious, upset, depressed, unsatisfied with life. Their intimate relationships may be in trouble, triggering a host of irrational, intense emotional responses. Sometimes feelings are overwhelming, behavior impulsive and destructive, or there is a deadness and inability to feel at all. Old traumatic memories may be intruding as obsessions, flashbacks, or body symptoms. If our clients could resolve these issues by using their willpower, and conscious, rational processes, they would have already done so. They want to change and don't know how. From a neuroscience perspective, we could say that our clients suffer from implicit memory problems. Much learning has occurred without conscious awareness, imprinted in the body-mind through subcortical mechanisms. As Daniel Stern has described, the basic sense of self is somatic and nonverbal in nature. Procedural memory, emotional responses, body structure and function, behavioral patterns, perceptual biases of expectation all contribute to what has been termed a "character style." David Boadella points out that we regularly see, in therapeutic work, how a person who tries to share—through the mind—what is going on in his life, is sometimes speaking just from his character pattern that he is trapped in. Interrupting the verbal communication, in such cases, and encouraging expression of the deeper feelings, elicits the true message hidden within, or underneath, the superficial expressions (Boadella, 1987).

The deep, core roots of self are in the body. Emotional processes are inseparable from the body. As Candace Pert (1999, p. 141) said, "The body is the unconscious mind." It makes sense for therapists to use body interventions as a route to access the unconscious, also to effectively facilitate and consolidate new learning, to allow frozen and incomplete experiences to sequence, and to resource the client during therapy. An understanding of neuroscience has helped us see that for change to occur in the implicit memory system, the relevant neural networks need to be activated (Nader, 2003). Memories from early in life, traumatic or deeply upsetting memories, and complex character patterns are usually not consciously understood, nor are easily accessible through left-brain, linguistic processes.

## Transference, Empathy, and the Therapeutic Relationship

The attuned therapist who can track his or her internal world of mind and body is in a position to provide, in terms of neuroscience language, the "limbic resonance" needed to change deeply rooted attachment patterns. Lewis and his colleagues (2001) assert that therapy is a living embodiment of limbic processes, as "corporeal" (body oriented) as one's digestion or respiration. Empathy has been considered of vital importance for therapeutic change in a number of therapeutic modalities, including Self Psychology and Rogerian client-centered therapy. Neuroscience is starting to show that tuning in to our clients, right brain to right brain, means that we literally affect each other's brain processes. This is not a verbal or logical process, but it is intuitive and felt through the whole body-mind (Ibid.). Many therapists learned in their training that one couldn't feel another's pain. It has to be one's own pain, perhaps triggered by the other person. This was the era when individualism was highly valued, a perspective held by Fritz Perls. Modern neuroscience has shown this assertion to be wrong. We are intricately interconnected (Mindell, 2000 Lewis et al., 2001).

Freud believed that it was good that transference occurred in therapy. It brought an opportunity to increase insight and therapeutic change. Analysts were trained to be acutely aware of transference dynamics, which were seen to manifest through emotions, behavior, and words. Body therapists may notice the relationship dynamics through observing the client's body state and movements, and by tuning in to their own sensations and impulses. From a neuroscience perspective, the limbic resonance, right brain to right brain, allows for empathy, mirroring, and an exchange of emotional and somatic information. The sensitive therapist, who is tuned in to his or her own somatic reality, can empathically monitor the inner world of the client and respond, not automatically and unconsciously, but therapeutically. "Attractors manifest themselves in a radiant aura of limbic tones. If a listener quiets his neocortical chatter and allows limbic sensing to range free, melodies begin to penetrate the static of anonymity" (Lewis et al., 2001, p. 169).

**Paul: Transference and the Body Unconscious**

Paul has lots of confidence. He settles into his chair, casually brushes back his wavy hair, expands his chest, and nonchalantly crosses his legs. His eyes are direct and challenging as he expounds his theory as to why he seems to attract conflict in his life. Paul is sure he can resolve any difficulties he has through his spiritual practice. We could see Paul as having a narcissistic sense of entitlement, or as demonstrating a psychopathic character style. We could look at his avoidant attachment style, and we could wonder what neural templates he has formed from early experience. We could think about his dominant sympathetic nervous system and wonder about neurotransmitters in the brain.

Paul says that he has come to therapy as a piece of personal research for a philosophical assignment. He despises weakness and values confidence and success. Paul describes how his parents left him with a distant relative when he was three years old, and how he never saw them again. The woman who brought him up had been dutiful, but disinterested in having a small child around. Paul says with a small, smug smile that he is a much better person for having had these experiences; they have made him into the successful man he is today. Yet he wonders what goes wrong in his personal relationships. This aspect of his life is driven by unconscious factors. Initially in therapy, Paul had no idea of the deep grief and anger that he still carried in relation to his early abandonment. He did not see how his feeling of superiority and his need to always be in control undermined his relationships and prevented him from having the intimacy he so desperately longed for.

Paul tried hard to always be in control during his early therapy. With compassion and using psychodynamic interventions, I pointed out to him how he devalued therapy, and had tried to undermine me on a number of occasions. After this session, Paul was embarrassed and shocked to find that he was becoming attached to me, even feeling an emotion that he supposed was love. We could describe Paul's feelings in terms of transference. In spite of feeling shame, he did, however, accept the invitation to mindfully tune in to his body while he was feeling the love and vulnerability. An ache developed in his chest, and tears came to his eyes. The pattern of muscular holding and sensation in the body was in that moment, due to focused attention, a trigger to emotional associations, probably mediated by the amygdala (Damasio, 1999). Paul very quietly said, "I'm scared you are going to leave me." After some time of feeling the emotions and allowing thoughts and images to arise, Paul linked his sadness and fear to the small boy who had suffered the loss of his parents. He realized that he was seeing me like a mother, and felt his grief at losing his own mother. Paul's experiences could be explained as the transference becoming conscious, or as Paul finding and feeling the deflation that existed below the inflation, or discovering his "real" self. We could say that focusing on the body allowed implicit memory patterns to be activated. Somatically, this was the beginning of a melting process in Paul that allowed him to both think and feel.

## Windows of Opportunities for Change

Therapies, such as Gestalt and Hakomi, emphasize working with what is manifest in the here and now, being in touch with these bodily sensations, thoughts, emotions, or relationship dynamics. Using an understanding of neuroscience, it would seem that when the neural pattern is "alive" in the present moment, then the memory is fluid, and it can be modified. Exciting new research is being reported on just how fluid memories are, suggesting that permanent memory is a myth (Nader, 2003; McCrone, 2003). For reconsolidation to occur, special, carefully monitored conditions need to be present. Research on teaching Japanese students to differentiate an "r" sound from an "l" sound has shown that controlling the learning conditions allows change that does not occur in everyday life (Lewis et al.,

2001, p. 179). There has to be an optimal level of arousal for attention and nerve growth. Too much arousal tends to lead to dissociation and is toxic to vital parts of the nervous system such as the hippocampus, causing shutdown and even neuronal death. Too little arousal, and protein synthesis in the nerves does not occur. New information and experience that are congruent with the desired change has to enter the system. New procedural memories are also established through mirroring, "a direct absorption of information received from the body-self of the therapist" (Bentzen et al., 1997, p. 45). Interesting neurophysiological research on mirror neurons (Wylie and Simon, 2002, p. 28) may give us a greater understanding of these processes.

**Marianne: Issues from Birth**

Marianne was an adopted child who was parented as a "replacement" child for grieving parents whose three-year-old had died suddenly the year before. The angelic presence of the dead child was always there in Marianne's world. Marianne's mother was aloof, and Marianne was always a good, quiet child. Later in Marianne's childhood, a relative sexually abused her for several years on a regular basis. As an adult, Marianne was intellectually bright, but troubled with persistent anxiety and sleeplessness. When Marianne came for therapy, she had great difficulty in making any eye contact. She would startle at the slightest noise. She couldn't remember much of her childhood, but said, in a flat tone, that her parents had done their best. On one occasion, when I suggested that Marianne notice her body sensations, she said that she was unaware of any body feeling. Her body sense was almost entirely dissociated from consciousness.

Looking back: Marianne, as a newborn baby, unparented in her hospital crib, is forming memory. The billions of neurons in her brain are busy making connections, wiring together according to the kinds of experience she is exposed to. Surplus neurons are "pruned." This early learning prepares the child for a particular world. Within the limits of genetic parameters, the structure and function of her body are literally being shaped. Procedural memories are laid down, forming the basis for future behavioral patterns. The amygdala and related brain structures record emotional experiences, evaluating the world, coding experience according to "good" and "bad" categories (LeDoux, 2002). Somatic and sensory memories, neural attractor patterns, will influence all future perception. The amygdala and right brain are "online"; the hippocampus is as yet immature. Marianne's mother tells her that, even as an infant, her body would tense and pull away.

As she sits in her chair during therapy as an adult woman, Marianne automatically pulls back, her eyes wary, and her head turned a little, away from contact. Body-mind therapists like Lowen, who added somatic understanding to psychodynamics, believe that those early experiences in relationship impact upon the character and body-mind, and they would understand Marianne's way of being in the world from this perspective. We can also speculate from a neuroscientific perspective, using our—as yet tentative, but growing—knowledge to understand what is unfolding. Marianne cannot consciously remember her arrival in the world, yet it's likely that her body remembers. The well-recognized phenomenon of infantile amnesia results partially from the fact that the young child cannot lay down explicit memory, an ability that awaits the maturation of the hippocampi and of the left hemisphere, including the specialist language areas.

Implicit memories from infancy may be accessed during therapy, being experienced in their full emotional and somatic intensity, but without language or narrative. The client may struggle to make cognitive sense of these experiences, yet have an intuitive knowing that is hard for the left brain to trust, or even put words to. Observations of this nature that psychotherapists have made over the years regarding early memory are yet to be validated by quantitative research. Stanislav Grof's early research, using LSD, and (later) special breathing techniques, showed how early emotionally intense, formative experiences could reemerge, be reexperienced vividly, and then be integrated with symptom relief. He described how the manifestations of early experience were somatic in nature (Grof, 1975). Further research, using modern brain-measuring technology, could add immensely to our scientific understanding of these frequently described clinical phenomena.

Once, after Marianne had missed a session, she was astounded to hear that I cared whether she came or not. This could be seen as transference, with her internalized mother being projected onto me, or as her avoidant attachment templates having predisposed her to have certain perceptions and expectations. The tragedy is that these patterns can be self-fulfilling in nature, whether psychodynamically or neuroscientifically understood.

### Sara: A Depressed Mother

Sara was neglected by a depressed mother, and sexually abused for many years by her father. She tells me that she is feeling restless, out of sorts, but doesn't really know why. Her relationship with her own little girl is strained. Sara doesn't really want to be around her. She feels bad about this. I ask Sara to take a moment to feel what is happening in her body. Sara is used to being mindful in her therapy sessions, and she easily turns her attention inward. After a moment, Sara tells me she has a sick feeling in her stomach. As she feels these sensations, her lips curl in an expression of disgust and her face pales.

I have spent time with Sara establishing a safe, supportive therapeutic relationship, which is a foundation of many psychotherapy approaches. For Sara, this is important for a number of reasons. She has had few experiences of being validated, and of having someone there who cares and who is emotionally responsive. Her adult relationships have been abusive. On a cognitive and also on a deep unconscious level, Sara does not know or expect kindness and empathy: it is not familiar. Yet, in her eyes, I see the longing, and, in my chest, I feel the ache that relates to the void in her own heart. In her intuitive, somatic core sense of self (as described by Stern), Sara knows what is needed, even if she doesn't expect it. "If someone's relationships today bear a troubled imprint, they do so because an influential relationship left its mark on a child's mind. When a limbic connection has established a neural pattern, it takes a limbic connection to revise it" (Lewis et al., 2001, p. 177).

The therapeutic work with Sara can be understood from a psychodynamic, trauma therapy, body therapy, and neurological perspective. The relationship, as well as altering attachment patterns, also provides safety that allows optimum arousal for processing and change. When Sara uses her right frontal cortex to remember autobiographical memory, she doesn't find a lot from childhood. This is typical of an avoidant attachment pattern, of a schizoid character style, and of a person who has been traumatized. There are fragments of memory, most of it foggy and ghost-like. She is easily triggered into emotional reactions that overwhelm her. When Sara was a child, her amygdala and related brain structures were, it seems from research so far, faithfully recording emotional memory, and overwhelming traumatic experiences left sensory and procedural imprints (Perry, 1999). These memories have not been integrated into a coherent narrative, but have dominated Sara's life in ways that cause distress and dysfunction.

When Sara stops her words, which tend to tumble forth in a rather disorganized fashion, and slows down, she starts to become aware of emotions and body sensations. These are frightening to Sara, so we need to proceed slowly, keeping part of her awareness as an internal observer. Taking time allows Sara to activate areas in her right cerebral hemisphere that mediate internal attention, especially awareness of the body. These hemispheric areas include the right frontal lobe, the cingulate gyrus, and the right parietal lobe (Austen, 2001, p. 163). There is some evidence that the hippocampus acts like an index, gathering fragments of memory and bringing them together (Schacter, 1996, p. 87). As Sara starts to feel her body sensations, she is scared. It is probable, based on theory from Schore and others (Lewis et al., 2001), that my calm presence then acts, through our limbic connection, as a regulator of her emotions. This is the function that the mother normally provides for the baby, and starts to allow a "wiring" of corticolimbic circuits that will gradually lead to Sara's being able to manage her own strong emotions (Schore, 1994). We also want to keep her left brain and hippocampus "online" so that Sara can begin to integrate her experiences. Even though consolidation processes are not yet fully understood at the physiology level, it is known that utilizing left- and right-brain hemispheres is important (Siegel, 1999; Gazzaniga, 2002).

Staying with the sensations of nausea is uncomfortable for Sara, but she does so, and, after a few moments, she sees an image. It is her father's face. Speculation based on early research would suggest the following understanding, which may, in the future, be validated, enlarged, or revised, depending on the outcome of scientific findings. Implicit memory mediated by the amygdala has activated body sensation, which has proved to be a cue for unintegrated emotional memory to come into Sara's consciousness. Focusing attention on the sensation itself may also have facilitated an upward flow of information, stored in body cells, through neuropeptide release (Pert, 1999). When Sara becomes aware of the image, her left brain starts to make sense of it. Both left-brain and right-brain processes are active. Sara cries, something she would not let herself do as a child. There is release and a sense of completion. Sara talks about how vulnerable she was as a child, now using her adult knowledge to reflect on the memories emerging. She becomes angry, and immediately feels guilty, shutting down the anger through tightening her throat.

I assist Sara by using a technique from Hakomi Psychotherapy called "taking over." Sara's fists are clenched and she wants to strike out. At the same time, she is holding back, guilty and afraid. With her permission, I apply some pressure, pushing against Sara's fists, assisting the holding-back impulses she has, and thus giving Sara some safety and freedom to fully go with the expressive urges. Immediately Sara starts to feel the strength in her arms and begins to push forward with some glee. Sara is able to use the muscles in her arms to express the anger. She adds words, saying what was silenced all those years ago. Later, after the session she writes in her journal, doing further integration as she brings conscious reflection to her experience. In the next session, Sara tells me she understands why her daughter has irritated her. She dared to get angry! Sara was surprised that she felt some warmth and acceptance toward her daughter, the first positive feeling for some time.

## Conclusion

Through bringing the current concepts and language of neuroscience into parallel with traditional psychodynamic understandings, it is possible that we could enrich our knowledge of the often-mysterious field of psychotherapy. We may gain even more respect for the influence of the unconscious, and the playing out of conscious and unconscious information in the body. Scientific explanations add credibility in our society, where left-brain knowledge is highly esteemed. We stand to gain a deeper appreciation of our clients, and more awareness of the unfolding, moment-to-moment processes. Having a deeper, multilayered understanding of what might be happening in psychotherapy, we can make more effective, conscious choices of interventions.

## References

Ainsworth, M. D. S., Blehar, M. C., Waters, E., & Wall, S. (1978). *Patterns of attachment: A psychological study of the Strange Situation.* Hillsdale, NJ: Erlbaum.

Austen, J. H. (2001). *Zen and the brain.* Cambridge, MA: MIT Press.

Bentzen, M., Jarlnaes, E., & Levine, P. (1997). The body self in psychotherapy: A psycho-motoric approach to Developmental Psychology. In I. McNaughton (Ed), *Embodying the mind and minding the body.* Vancouver, Canada: Integral Press.

Blau, T. H. (1988). *Psychotherapy tradecraft: The technique and style of doing therapy.* New York: Brunner/Mazel.

Boadella, D. (1987). *Lifestreams: An introduction to Biosynthesis.* London: Routledge & Kegan Paul.

Bowlby, J. (1969). *Attachment and loss: Attachment* (Vol. 1). New York: Basic Books.

Briere, J. (2002). Treating adult survivors of childhood abuse and neglect: Further development of an integrative model. In J. E. B. Myers, L. Berliner, J. Briere, T. Hendrix, C. Jenny, & T. A. Reid (Eds.), *The APSAC Handbook on Child Maltreatment (*2nd ed.*)* (pp. 21–54). Thousand Oaks, CA: Sage.

Cozolino, L. (2003). *The neuroscience of psychotherapy: Building and rebuilding the human brain.* London: Heinemann.

Damasio, A. (1999). *The feeling of what happens.* New York: Harcourt Brace.

Gazzaniga, M. S. (2002). The split brain revisited. *The hidden mind. Scientific American, 12*(1), 27–31.

Goodwin, J. M., & Attias, R. (Eds.). (1999). *Splintered reflections: Images of the body in trauma.* New York: Basic Books.

Grof, S. (1975). *Realms of the human unconscious: Observations from LSD research.* London: Souvenir Press.

Kurtz, R. (1990). *Body-Centered Psychotherapy: The Hakomi Method.* Mendocino, CA: LifeRhythm.

LeDoux, J. E. (2002). Emotion, memory and the brain. *The hidden mind. Scientific American, 12*(1).

Lewis, T., Amini, F., & Lannon, R. (2001). *A general theory of love.* New York: Vintage.

Lowen, A. (1958). *The language of the body.* New York: Macmillan.

Matthews, P. (2004). Total recall. *New Zealand Listener, 192,* 31–33.

McCrone, J. (2003). Not-so total recall. *New Scientist, 178*(23), 93.

Mindell, A. (2000). *Quantum mind: The edge between physics and psychology.* Oakland, CA: Lao Tse Press.

Mollon, P. (2002). The unconscious. In I. Ward (Ed.), *On a darkling plain: Journeys into the unconscious.* Cambridge, UK: Icon Books.

Nader, K. (2003). Memory traces unbound. *Trends in neuroscience, 26*(2), 65–72.

Perry, B. (1999). Memories in fear. In J. M. Goodman & R. Attias (Eds.), *Splintered reflections: Images of the body in trauma* (pp. 9–18). New York: Basic Books.

Pert, C. B. (1999). *Molecules of emotion.* New York: Touchstone.

Reich, W. (1972). *Character Analysis (3rd ed.).* New York: Farrar, Straus & Giroux.

Schacter, D. L. (1996). *Searching for memory: The brain, the mind, the past.* New York: Basic Books.

Schore, A. N. (1994). *Affect regulation and the origin of the self.* Hillsdale, NJ: Lawrence Erlbaum.

Siegel, D. J. (1999). *The developing mind: Toward a neurobiology of interpersonal experience.* New York: Guilford Press.

Solms, M., & Turnbull, O. (2002). *The brain and the inner world: An introduction to the neuroscience of subjective experience.* London: Karnac.

Sroufe, L. A. (1996). *Emotional development: The organization of emotional life in the early years.* New York: Cambridge University Press.

Stern, D. (1985). *The interpersonal world of the infant: A view from psychoanalysis and Developmental Psychology.* New York: Basic Books.

Tallis, F. (2002). *Hidden minds: A history of the unconscious.* London: Profile Books.

Teicher, E. M. (2002). Scars that won't heal: The neurobiology of child abuse. *Scientific American, 286*(3), 54–61.

Vaughan, S. C. (1997). *The talking cure: The science behind psychotherapy.* New York: Grosset/Putnam.

Wylie, M. S., & Simon, R. (2002). Discoveries from the black box: How the neuroscience revolution can change your practice. *Psychotherapy Networker, 26*(5), 26–37.

# 21
## The Maturation of the Somatic Self

### Stanley Keleman, United States

**Stanley Keleman**, DC, PhDHon, is one of the grand pioneers in the field of Body Psychotherapy. As senior trainer, he was one of the founding members of the Bioenergetic Institute in New York. Later, he developed his own method: Formative Psychology®, and established a teaching institute in Berkeley. Originally educated as a chiropractor, over the course of his career, he has assimilated a wide range of perspectives, including Adlerian psychoanalysis, the existential perspective of Medard Boss, as well as the Initiation (Body) Therapy of Graf Dürckheim, and—over the course of decades—has created a remarkable body of work, as well as a unique therapeutic method. He has also influenced a great number of people, both professionally through his writings and teachings, and personally through his warmth and presence.

Whereas in many Body Psychotherapeutic approaches the body is viewed, for example, from a psychodynamic frame of reference, Stanley Keleman bases his Formative Psychology directly in the body, perhaps more decisively than any other modality of Body Psychotherapy or Somatic Psychology, viewing the therapeutic process and its meanings as emerging out of the formative capacities of the body. His extensive publications, including his classic book, *Emotional Anatomy (1985)*, form a comprehensive theory, which not only addresses clinical and therapeutic questions, but speaks further to fundamental creative processes and existential questions, such as the process of human development, aging, and dying. This chapter is written from the perspective of a master teacher.

He is director of research for the School for Form and Movement in Zurich, Switzerland, and the Institute for Formative Psychology in Solingen, Germany. He was recently honored with Lifetime Achievement Awards from both the European and the American Body Psychotherapy Associations, and he received an honorary PhD from Saybrook University for his contributions to the field of Humanistic Psychology and a Lifetime Achievement Award from the USABP.

### The Mature Body

It was not too long ago that adolescence was first recognized as a phase of life that was neither adult nor child, but rather a separate body shape with its own somatic experience. Similarly, in my work, I have come to find a bodied shape between the full-grown adult and the aged adult, between the filled-out, firm-bodied adult shape that we spend almost five decades to form, and the shrinking, diminishing shape of the aged person. This phase of bodied life I call the "mature somatic self."

Our destined shapes are always a potential within us, and we are always in the process of forming the next stage of our bodied self. From the pantheon of our biological inheritance, we are born and grow from an involuntary, pre-personal program and from our own voluntary effort. The somatic shapes that are established up to and through the full-grown adult set the stage for the mature soma—a newly recognized shape—to emerge. The coming of the mature soma is the body's own hunger for the next stage of its embodiment; and it is each person's opportunity to form another personal body from the ever-present genetic background.

The urge of the soma to form its mature body is, I believe, felt as a longing to be a deep, subjective self—a self we may take a lifetime to know. In this sense, I would speak of the mature soma as a genetic presence wishing to make a personal subjectivity through its own voluntary efforts. Involuntary processes are continually maintaining and changing our body's anatomical structures as it prepares to form the next stage of its development. Having some voluntary influence in these inherited, pre-personal patterns gives us some say in how our future is embodied.

As life moves past the phase of full-bodied alpha adult, many people have difficulty envisioning a desirable future and they are vulnerable to loss, sorrow, and despair. It is all too easy to fall into a pattern of overwhelm and helplessness when faced with a future that is dominated by uncertainty and decline. By learning to voluntarily influence our shapes and form our behavior, we can make maturity a time of empowerment and optimism, a richly layered tapestry of past, present, and future.

## Voluntary Effort and Self-Forming

In speaking of bodying as a process of forming and of the somatic self as the sum of form and function, feeling and expression, I base my approach firmly in the arena of anatomical structure. All human behavior arises from anatomical structure. In my book *Emotional Anatomy*, I illustrate how the body's innate pulsatory function of compressing and expanding, gathering and extending, is an important way the body communicates with itself to make shapes and how body shapes give rise to feeling and expression. Out of this understanding, I have developed a method for voluntary self-management and self-growth. Voluntary self-regulation influences body shape and experience; it reorganizes how a person thinks, feels, and behaves. Through voluntary effort, the body grows its own personal somatic reality.[32]

## Forming an Adult Soma

Using our ability for voluntary influence is important in any stage of life, but it has a particular urgency in the mature stage. If we lack a way to give support to our body's Formative function, it is difficult to form new acts, new experiences, new realities, and new memories. Many people become victims to the trajectory of their lives because they do not know how to influence deep, instinctual patterns of behavior. In my clinical experience, the ability for self-management is an antidote to powerlessness; it offers a way to expand what nature has given us; it is a way to form and deepen a life, not simply be formed by life.

Our soma is a dynamic morphology of evolutionary anatomical events—a complex, organized amalgam of our genetic inheritance combined with the structures and behaviors we develop through experience, both voluntarily and involuntarily. For example, when I was a young adult, I put my efforts into forming a reality-oriented, instinctual, societal, and personal somatic male identity. Instinctually and voluntarily, I organized appropriate shapes and behaviors to manage my excitement to form a personal somatic structure capable of shaping and influencing my emotions and thoughts, my needs for contact and relationship, for power and pleasure. I formed a many-layered "Stanley Keleman," organizing satisfying ways to work, learn, love, and make meaning. This continuing process of forming my adult identity, and now my older, mature, adult identity, still goes on.

We carry within us the memory of the bodies that we formed in response to life's earlier stages. The stages of the adult "Stanley," as I have lived them, are all bodied shapes: the young, the full-grown, and the mature body, the Brooklyn man, the worldly man, the therapist, the teacher, husband, father, and friend. These are more than images or ideas. Each has a distinct somatic shape with its own memories; each has been influenced by my own voluntary effort to form a deep, personal self, as well as to participate in forming the next stage of my embodiment.

As adults, we are many-bodied, and each of our bodied shapes has its special feelings, needs, images, actions,

---

[32] For a fuller discussion of voluntary influence, see S. Keleman (2007), The Methodology and Practice of Formative Psychology. *USA Body Psychotherapy Journal, 6*(1), 20–21.

and worldview. Over a lifetime we live a series of somatic shapes with complex emotions and feelings, desires and expressions. Becoming an adult is a genetic promise; being a personal, mature adult takes work. Being an intellectually or economically successful adult does not mean that a person has a satisfying emotional, psychological, or social life. Sadly, contemporary men and women usually achieve maturity in only a segment of their soma, usually the brain. We, as a society, are overly concerned with intellectual development; we are not encouraged to invest a similar effort to develop and personalize our instinctual and emotional somatic behaviors.

Having some mastery of how we are bodily present—that is, how we voluntarily organize and manage the configuration of head, eyes and mouth, chest, arms and hands, pelvis, legs and feet in the readiness to act—has a lot to say about "Here I am," and self-esteem and satisfaction. If our muscular tonus is underused and our neural management is undeveloped, so is excitement and expression on a personal and instinctual level. All behavior takes practice and management, whether it is a child learning to walk, a young person learning social skills, or a virtuoso mastering their instrument. Similarly, developing a mature somatic emotional life takes practice and self-management.

It takes time and commitment to personalize one's inherited behavior into satisfying and appropriate expression. The ability to express oneself with a developed emotional and somatic sophistication is more than instinctual excitation, assertion, or sexuality. Growing a mature self with multiple shades and gradations of behavior and meaning requires a somatic subjectivity and expressive complexity.

## Somatic Subjectivity and Maturity

Somatic subjectivity is a particular way of knowing oneself, a self-intimacy that enriches the mature soma. The Formative process and its urges for more body, up to and including the full-grown alpha adult, is weighted toward exploring and mastering relationships with the external world. After the alpha adult, there is another stage of forming that is weighted toward an inward exploration, toward deepening and differentiating our internal experiences and pulsations to make meanings that have subjective and personal importance. Make no mistake, this does not mean a retreat from the world or relationships with others, but it does mean a different way of being bodily present.

Recognizing the Formative process and developing the Formative function to grow our maturity help us avoid the common confusion between aging and maturing. Maturing is not simply the normal concomitant of adulthood, nor is it equivalent to aging; it is the forming of a particular stage and style of living with its own kind of vitality and expression. Within an individual life, a personally formed mature body can be a deeply satisfying and fruitful phase of life, with its own process of renewal and sense of future. We can see it in persons such as Georgia O'Keeffe, Albert Einstein, and Eleanor Roosevelt. Access to the Formative function is not limited to the gifted and famous. It is the birthright of every man and woman who wants to participate in growing, forming, and deepening through all the stages of living.

## The Mature Shape

The mature shape differs from both the adult shape and the aged shape. It has a pear-shaped lower center of gravity, and the shoulders are less square. Metabolism slows and the soma becomes more porous and malleable, more inclusive and more receptive. As our bodied shape softens and becomes less hard-muscled, response time becomes slower. As our experience slows, porosity increases. The gift of porosity is the ability to savor experience. We flow more like a meandering stream, rather than excitatory rapids. Being somatically mature is more like being a bass violin than a trumpet: There are more deep tones and layers of resonance. The pattern of the mature-bodied shape, then, carries with it a flow of many currents; we fill ourselves up with feelings from our inner anatomic ocean.

The main somatic statement of maturity is the appearance of a slower heartbeat and a deeper amplitude that expresses a steady presence, rather than a preparation for quick action. This somatic structure has a porous, rigid organization and a presence with softer pulses of longer duration. Its expanding and gathering back is a slower pulsatory pattern of reaching and taking back, giving and receiving.

It is easier to receive and give with a semi-porous emotional presence, and to receive and hold without the density of possessing. Love at this stage is not the exploding excitement and assertive sexuality of the alpha adult. Now it is tender pulses that organize porous intimacy from within oneself and with another. It takes voluntary effort to develop the right amount of structural porosity and rigidity to sustain these deep, sweet, liquid experiences that come from our cellular collective. The process of self-organizing is a way to develop somatic subjectivity and to sustain a quality of vitality that is the foundation of the mature soma.

As we enter the mature-adult phase, our somatic structure needs more voluntary effort to develop a personal form. We learn to support desired behaviors by making small, deliberate changes in our bodied shapes, such as giving a porous, yielding shape more firmness, or decreasing a compact, dense, isolating shape by introducing a soft firmness. When done in small, incremental steps, these changes form a continuum of multiple shapes, shapes that are similar yet different.

Making measured, steplike shifts in our somatic emotional shape organizes a multilayered interior dimension and presence. Knowing how to make these small somatic adjustments expands our library of body shapes and expands the choices we have of how to act; more choice equals more freedom to form and live the life we want.

## The Difference between Maturity and Aging

Unfortunately, many people are unprepared for maturity because they have confused it with the physical declines of aging. They have not been educated to know that even small efforts of self-influence have a big impact. Forming oneself, even in small degrees, is empowering. When we lack the tools for self-forming, life forms us rather than us forming our life.

Many people reach the stage of maturity feeling unfinished or incomplete; there is confusion about what comes next. We all dread the fantasized and real demons of aging; we fear, rightly or wrongly, that aging will bring pain, emotional distress, humiliation, dependency, or loss of status, and most of all we fear the inability to influence our behavior or circumstances. The specter of an aging adult life that is too unpredictable, or of a future that is nothing more than an inevitable decline, drives many people to chase after the illusion of youth or to retreat and cling to memories of a younger self.

When the shapes and behaviors of our alpha adult begin to diminish, it is easy to slip into a process of loss and depression. As our anatomical structure loses muscle mass, strength, and mobility, the body compensates by instinctively organizing a rigidity that is intended to give stability but that actually serves to mute the vitality of the pre-personal, ancient body. The instinctive response to pull in and hunker down limits our ability to organize new form and to respond in novel ways to changing life circumstances.

Instinctively, the body prepares to act by organizing degrees of muscle rigidity or compression. In an aged person, muscular tonus is weakened and breathing is shallow compared to the muscle tone and strong chest exhalation of the adult, so the aged often give up on action because they are expressively diminished.

When our inherited organizing process and its urge to body forth is thwarted, whether through ignorance or by the reflexive muscular compression of trying to hold ourselves together, we inhibit the generation of new experiences. This can lead to more anxiety and depression. Many people live in the body shape of despair because they do not have the tools to disassemble old patterns or to engage the body's innate urge to form its next stage of development. When we commit to empowering ourselves by influencing our somatic shapes, when we learn to disorganize muscular, neural, and emotional patterns that are no longer useful, and when we actively participate in reorganizing shapes and behaviors appropriate for our age, we are growing a future. Voluntary influence, then, becomes the basis of hope and optimism.

If we assume that we cannot influence our somatic organization or experience, we become victim to a narrative of decline rather than of forming. It is my experience that the loss of self-influence is more important than the loss of independence. If we live long enough, there comes a time when we will be dependent on the help of others. Knowing how to use voluntary effort restores a sense of self-empowerment and self-esteem. Even in the late stages of aging, and into the process of dying, I have witnessed voluntary effort as a key influence in forming a kinder, more human fading of existence.

At any stage of human embodiment, using voluntary effort to organize ourselves gives us some say in our destiny. In the later and end stages of life, it transforms the impersonal into the personal. Our life is continually forming and re-forming, and we have many somatic possibilities. We are not just waiting to become old or die; we are living to form ourselves through the many stages of a personal existence.

## Learning to Embody Our Experiences

Whether we are working with ourselves or with others to learn the skills for developing somatic maturity, it is essential to have an understanding of the nature of this stage of life, to have a frame of reference and a language for communicating and sharing our efforts as we strive to give meaning and value to our experiences.

Learning to embody our experience and to make a personal somatic self is important at any age, but it has special meaning for maturity. The mature person gathers years and incorporates experiences differently from the young. The ripening of life that sets the stage for maturity is not an illness, a failing, or a tragedy; it is an opportunity to participate in creating new anatomical shapes and new experiences—often with more porosity and poetry—and new subjective meanings. The important operant is to know how to organize your form in the world and to keep on forming it.

As an example, a client in her mature years told me:

My life is like a stream. It roared, then surged, now it flows gently, but with enough force to make secondary eddies, little whirlpools of life in me. I am pulled down and then back up. Being with you is like a gentle tide. I enjoy this bobbing to and fro with you, between now and yesterday, wondering about tomorrow. My responses make the world fresh and vibrant in contrast to the dawn and twilight of my being here. It is a joy to be so welcomed by the present, even though the shadows give me a fright.

Being an adult is always a collaboration of the body we have and the one we are forming. Every somatic stage and shape is special unto itself, and is in a continual process of renewal and dialogue with what is, what was, and what can be. People who are growing into their mature age and shape have specific concerns. They desire to be part of a circle of contact. They do not want to be isolated or infantilized or treated as if they no longer have an independent existence. What they do not recognize is that sharing oneself, being part of a community, or having a level of competence are not just mental ideas; they are body shapes, postures, anatomic organizations of the soma that can be influenced and altered.

Several years ago a successful therapist came to see me when he was making a transition from his sixties to his seventies. He was a short, powerful, mesomorphic man with a dominating personality. He presented himself in a posture of aloofness and a stiff, ramrod stance that held his head high. In his work and life, he prided himself on taking charge of every situation. However, he had a persistent feeling of never being really good enough. As he aged, he feared becoming physically and emotionally diminished. As we worked with disorganizing the stances that made him successful, he realized that he was slowing down and that he needed more time to respond. He increasingly felt the discrepancy between his body time and the image that he had of himself to be always at the ready. He began to differentiate his stiff, rigid shapes into softer, more porous, receptive shapes and began to have a subjective experience of his own sense of time.

Experiencing his slower time gave him a sense of belonging to himself, of valuing what he experienced and not always having to be better. As he was able to use voluntary effort to change his rigidity, he experienced a different sense of himself and, as he responded to his changed body shapes rather than to his images, he found his work to be more satisfying and he found it easier to relate to his way of functioning. Forming a somatic subjectivity involved reorganizing his posture of pride and rigidity and disassembling it in steps to allow the experience of his visceral pulse. This was a fresh experience that helped him to establish a dialogue with his own quantity and quality of vitality. He learned to use voluntary effort to make layers of self-contact and to relate to the underformed in himself without self-criticism.

Living is one lifelong transition, a continuum of bodies and experiences appearing in the arc of embodied existing. When people experience the value of cultivating somatic maturity and the rewards of voluntary self-influence, they come to understand that they are involved in a pioneering evolutionary process, not only to connect body shape and life experience, and to know that body shapes are the source of lived experience, but also to know that voluntary self-influence is an empowerment that gives each of us the ability to create and live new experiences and new expressions.

An artist in his early seventies came to see me with a sense of depressiveness and defeat. He was a creative and visual person who had experienced much of his vitality through his images. He felt now that his younger indefatigable self was gone, his life was over, and that it had been a failure in spite of his considerable accomplishments. He felt empty, and his reflections on past events were without satisfaction. When I asked him to show me his body shape of defeat and depression, he collapsed his chest and muted his breathing. I asked him to make his collapsed shape more by intensifying the muscular pattern and then slowly, step by step, to disorganize the muscular shape he had organized. As he practiced increasing and decreasing his muscular patterns, his chest spontaneously began to rise and his breathing expanded, giving him more cellular space. He immediately felt the pulsatory experience; and, over time, as he practiced influencing his posture of defeat, he reported that his feelings of loss and emptiness were being replaced by body shapes that gave him different sensations and new images.

He learned to support and sustain these new shapes through voluntary effort. The feelings coming from his chest and heart gave him new, imaginative narratives about how to form his future. He felt empowered by his own efforts and was able to organize his mature man with a renewed sense of creativity and vitality. He took pleasure from his efforts and felt satisfaction in his accomplishments.

As a person accumulates age and seeks to develop somatic maturity, using voluntary effort to shift the body's architecture initiates a cascade of events and experiences. The notion of maturity as a one-directional diminishing is challenged when a personally organized somatic subjectivity is brought into play. Of course, the progression of our somatic shapes as we mature and age includes the fading of shapes to which we have become habituated and may be reluctant to let go. But at the same time, we are capable of growing different shapes, rich with feeling and subjective experience, as well as growing new functions enlivened with experiences from our body's deep, pulsatory patterns.

As we learn to support our Formative function, and as our body and brain generate new experiences and expressions, we no longer waste ourselves in pretending to be a "youthful oldster." We experience the power of life's instinctive urge to form itself combined with our personal, voluntary effort to develop in this vital stage of our existence. Maturity is a form of gestation; like conception and birth, it is a process of development over time.

Another client of around seventy, whom I had known for many years, asked to work with a dream. In the dream, she was at the lakeshore, in the house of her childhood. She stood at the doorway in the early morning and saw her maternal grandmother, elegantly dressed, coming from the lake onto the shore, limping toward her and leaning on a cane. In the dream, she felt transfixed in stillness, waiting to receive the approaching figure.

She felt the dream to be important but that somehow she was missing something. At first, she reported her experience as encountering her grandmother with joy, but as she began to make a muscular model of her grandmother's shapes, she felt that her present body was being approached by her older body, and it frightened her. What could she do to avoid becoming dysfunctional? Could she live with her body changes and still feel functional and graceful? Experiencing her own voluntary efforts to organize the body attitudes of the dream figure of her grandmother, she came to understand that she could choose not to become a victim to her feared image of aging. She had a task, which was to voluntarily participate in her changing shapes, and over time to form behaviors and expressions and an identity that supported her maturity and her grace.

## The Promise of Maturity

The soma, as a Formative process, embodies both the personally formed and the inherited, universal body. William James (1890) spoke of the "transcendent," meaning what one feels oneself connected to. He stated that it is both "bigger than yourself, and . . . more than just your mind." On one side it was inexplicable; on the other, it was a continuation of your conscious life. Similarly, I speak of the Formative Somatic Process. On one side is the body we know, the one that walks and talks and lives its daily life—the known, given, active body. On the other side, we are a living continuum of a universal, animate, forming process largely below awareness, but that has an urge to make itself known and to continually form a personal soma from the inherited body.

Our inherited bodying process is given; we are born, we grow, we age, and then we die. This is not something we decide intellectually or personally. It is pre-personal; it comes from a deep, involuntary place. And it is bigger than the "I."

Understandably, we may be confused or frightened by whatever transcends our ability to control or predict. It is much easier, much safer, to identify ourselves with the body seen in the mirror—to love it, to hate it, to see it as too thin, too fat. Rarely do we understand, or accept, that in the most basic sense, we are our bodies, and more—that our bodies are a suborganization, a microcosm of the creative, organizing principle of the biosphere. We are a complex, organizing pattern of tissue pulsations, concentric rings that radiate inward and outward in waves of expansion and gathering back. Our body is a pulsing organism that is bringing its multiple forms into existence by giving them more body. This primary process of embodiment is an expression of the biological, universal body.

Our ability to engage the primary Formative process voluntarily is also the ability to incarnate our experiences into a personal, somatic world. It is a way to bring what many consider the realm of the sacred into daily life, to form a secular sacred, to engage the deep self to form the somatic soul. In the mature soma, the ability to engage with our inner pulses and tides of excitation gives a depth to our experience and helps to form a subjectivity from which we can create value and meaning. To mature is to voluntarily form ourselves, to be empowered and optimistic, to live a layered and rich personal existence appropriate for our age and to offer the gift of self-forming to others. This is the promise of maturity.

## References

James, W. (1890). *Principles of psychology.* Cambridge, MA: Harvard University Press.

Keleman, S. (1985). *Emotional anatomy.* Berkeley, CA: Center Press.

# 22

## "Body Schema," "Body Image," and Bodily Experience

*Concept Formation, Definitions, and Clinical Relevance in Diagnostics and Therapy*

**Frank Röhricht, United Kingdom**

**Translation by Warren Miller**

**Frank Röhricht** is a consultant psychiatrist, head physician, and clinical director at the Newham Centre for Mental Health in London. He is a Body Psychotherapist and was trained in Neo-Reichian (Integrated Body Psychotherapy) and psychodynamic approaches. His extensive research and publications on the phenomenology of embodiment and Body Psychotherapy strategies of intervention for severe mental disorders are an extraordinary contribution to the field of Body Psychotherapy. His dissertation was on the topic of "Body Schema and Body Image and Their Relationship to Psychopathological Symptoms in Patients with Acute Paranoid Schizophrenia." He is also a member of the EABP Scientific and Research Committee, and he has led randomized controlled trials (RCTs) that demonstrate the efficacy of Body Psychotherapy intervention techniques on patients with chronic and severe mental illness, i.e., in schizophrenia, chronic depression, and somatoform disorders.

Currently, Professor Röhricht continues working in this area of research in association with the Universities of Essex, London, Dresden, and Munich, making him one of the preeminent researchers in the area of body image phenomenology in mental illnesses. His book on Body Psychotherapy (Röhricht, 2000) is the first textbook on the application of Body Psychotherapeutic methods in psychiatry. Additionally, he is a co-founder of the Dresden workgroup "Body Image / Body Psychotherapy," which works to foster dialogue between academic research and clinical practice.

He holds honorary professorships at the University of Essex (Centre for Psychoanalytic Studies) and St. George's Medical School, University of Nicosia/Cyprus; he is a Fellow of the Royal College of Psychiatrists, and a member of the German College of Psychosomatic Medicine, as well as the director of the science and research division of the German Association for Body Psychotherapy. His teaching experiences include teaching courses in psychiatry for postgraduates and numerous presentations at symposiums and conferences, a background that explains his matter-of-fact academic language.

Since the term "body schema" was first introduced to scientific literature more than a hundred years ago, a multitude of body-related phenomena have been gathered under this heading. Increased efforts toward demarcation of the term have begun only since the 1990s. For the German-language area, a consensus paper on terminological definitions and differentiation of distinct aspects of bodily experience was recently worked out (Röhricht et al., 2005). The difficulties in defining these terms can be viewed as stemming from the fact that this endeavor evokes the mind/body problem—the subject of an ongoing philosophical and epistemological debate—and touches on fundamental questions of human existence (Röhricht, 2000). From the perspective of Body Psychotherapy, the engagement with this dimension of self-experience is practically relevant in two ways:

1. An operationalized, descriptive, and content-analytic description of the different aspects of bodily experience lends itself as an intervention-specific criterion of Body Psychotherapeutic evaluation for purposes of diagnostics and psychotherapeutic research.

2. Going with the general trend in psychotherapy practice and research to focus on specific disorders and associated phenomena, Body Psychotherapy can be utilized as an essential tool for orientation in the identification of patterns of disordered bodily experience.

## Survey of the History of Concept Formation and Definitions of Associated Aspects

As early as the beginning of the 1930s, Conrad (1933) identified problems in the inflationary use of terms that aimed to describe the phenomenon of the perception of the body and concluded that clear terminological definitions were to be found only in rare cases. Meermann finds: "In regard to the terms body image, body schema, body perception, -ego, -self, -fantasy, -concept, etc., the scientific literature is characterized by nearly 'Babylonian' terminological confusion" (Meermann, 1985, p. 5).

A neurologist, Sir Henry Head, first described the term "body schema": at the beginning of the last century, Head (1920) used the term to conceptualize a function of the central nervous system—namely, the postural orientation of one's own body. According to Poeck and Orgass (1963, p. 539), the term referred to the neurophysiological phenomenon of a "spatial image of one's own body," developing "on the basis of tactile and kinesthetic sensations that accompany the initially automatic movements of the child in its first months of life." Poeck and Orgass (1963) furthermore cite writings by Bonnier (1905), who, even before the turn of the millennium, supposedly postulated a sense of space ". . . in which all parts of the peripheral and central sensibility jointly contribute to define the objective and subjective orientation." The conceptual images of one's own body that emerge in this way are structured schematically, based on neurologically patterned memories and information from stimuli that are organized by the physiology of perception. This definition of the "body schema" term was expanded upon by Head (1920), who postulated the "existence of organized models of our body" that prescreen, filter, and evaluate incoming sensory impulses, and thereby serve integration. Among these models, the postural scheme forms the basis for the perception of positions, movement directions, and postural tone; and the superficial scheme (body surface scheme) forms the basis for an exact localization and discrimination of stimuli. Poeck and Orgass (1963) summarize this theoretical perspective, emphasizing how the concept is to be understood in a physiological sense, as ". . . a standard that any stimulus can be compared with before entering consciousness"; they cite Head's comment, ". . . the schema contextualizes a sensation in its relationship to the body as a whole, before it reaches consciousness" (Ibid., p. 539).

Subsequently, all developments of the concept of sense perceptions that followed have been contextualized by this schema, while also simultaneously driving an ongoing reorganization of this schema. Paul Schilder (1935/1978) transformed and further developed the body schema concept by adding a psychological-psychoanalytic dimension, emphasizing the term "body image"; the introduction of the body image concept, however, seems to have paved the way for the previously mentioned "Babylonian terminological confusion."

Hartmann and Schilder (1927) drafted the body schema concept as the "image of one's own body, which is alive in us." The introduction of a subjective experiential reality that this alludes to is mirrored by the formation of "body image" as a term. Hartmann and Schilder (Ibid., p. 667) described a "spatial image" and a "representational image that everyone has of themselves." In this context, the authors speculated about the interplay of spinal and cortical centers with images of childhood memories. Drawing on psychoanalytic libido theory, they assume that ". . . affective-libidinal factors influence the body schema. Federn is to be endorsed when he emphasizes that awake people too, depending on their drive-disposition, will experience particular parts of the body schema in particular ways."

Following Hartmann and Schilder, the expansion of the body schema concept, through the addition of the psychological dimension, is carried forward without terminological differentiation from the neurophysiological concepts of Poeck and Head (see above). Among others, Conrad points out the mix-up of the "body as subjectively experienced phenomenon on the one hand, and objective reality on the other." Then he claims to take the concept of body schema another step forward, prefacing his definition by stating that "this consciousness of one's own embodiment must be an expression of a holistic process in the truest sense of the word, and therefore be subject to the laws of Gestalt processes" (Conrad, 1933, p. 367).

Conrad viewed the consciousness of one's own embodiment as a unity as the *a priori* constituent and, via associating of concepts, he comes close to Head's notion of "preconscious schemas" while including the psychological dimension introduced by Schilder. Conrad's definition is as follows: "Consciousness of one's own body as a foreground before the background of the field of awareness and action as a whole, in the wider sense of gestalt psychology" (Ibid.).

With the introduction of the body image concept, Schilder created the possibility of a terminological differentiation between two different dimensions of bodily experiences. Federn picked up on this possibility in the 1950s and—in reference to Freud—introduced another term—namely, "body ego." Following Federn, the body schema represents a ". . . mental knowledge of one's own body; the body image is the changing mental representation of the body; and through all changes the body ego is the ongoing sense from the body" (Federn, 1952, cited by Meermann, 1985, pp. 14–15).

Joraschky (1983) defined "body ego" as the representation of experientially processed bodily experiences. In reference to Federn, Kiener (1974) defined the "body ego" as an agile spatial figure that essentially is characterized by a sense of "me," ". . . belonging directly to my self," and "suffused by me (my soul)."

Kiener published his examinations of body image (*Untersuchungen zum Körperbild* [Studies in Body Image]) in 1974 and differentiated between "body schema," "body image," and "body ego." The interactions among these matrices are sketched out as follows: "Although normally the body ego has the same figure as the body and shows the same expansion as the body schema, body ego and body schema are not identical; the body ego is that part of the body schema that is experienced bodily as 'myself'" (Kiener, 1974, pp. 335–336).

Meermann (1985) operationalized the term "body schema" for his disorder-specific, phenomenological examinations as the ". . . ability to accurately estimate the distance between bodies in reference to one's own body," and in his definition he referred essentially to Shontz (1974) and Kolb (1975). They differentiated four matrices: "body schema," "body self," "body fantasy," and "body concept," which they all subsumed under the general heading of "body image." The body schema matrix here is viewed as a stabile foundation for the other matrices of bodily perception, which in turn have a modulating effect on the body schema.

Baumann (1986) presented the term "body schema" from the perspective of kinesiology and cited the foundations of Ungerer's (1958) movement theory, which posit as prerequisite ". . . that prior to movement execution there must be a representation of the body, that is, of the body in its parts, and their position, organization, and expansion in relation with another."

An example for the psychoanalytic understanding of the term can be found in Torres de Beà's article "Body Schema and Identity" (1987). It becomes apparent that this perspective shuns a terminological differentiation of different aspects of bodily perception, as (for example) Shontz proposed under the heading of "body image," in favor of an understanding that encompasses all experiential domains (cognitive as well as affective). In his definition, he refers to De Ajuriaguerra and his contribution to *The Body Percept*: "He deemed it as the result of the cognitive and affective organization of the person and pointed out the relationship between 'body schema' and the concept of identity, which follows the undifferentiated phase of ego-development" (De Ajuriaguerra, 1965, p. 175, my translation of the original). De Ajuriaguerra goes on to say that the body schema initially represents an undifferentiated body. As development proceeds, it is transformed into the representation of an articulated body, which not only is characterized by boundaries and surfaces, but also envelops "*particular contents,*" organs and differentiated segments with specific functions. The psychoanalytic perspective of the genesis of the body schema significantly differs from the concepts presented earlier; it is shaped by developmental psychology and comes to describe the body schema development in analytic fashion: ". . . the body schema of the child begins as preconception . . . in the mind of its parents. The sources of the body schema lie in these significant processes of development and differentiation" (Ibid., p. 176, my translation of the original).

The body schema is here viewed as a "representation of the body in the mind" and as such meets the psychoanalytic criteria of an "inner object." Plassmann describes the "function of the body as primary object" in a fundamental and guiding way: ". . . there is an accumulation of indications that support a primacy of bodily experience, that is, the function of the body as primary object. Possibly elementary, bodily based perceptions such as the phenomenon of being alive or embodied-being itself, are the very first contents (introjects) of the psychic apparatus, which constitute the very core of a subsequently much more differentiated self concept" (Plassmann, 1993, p. 263).

New impulses for the conceptualization of bodily experiences as constituents of self-(awareness) and interrelatedness are emerging within the field of (embodied) cognitive sciences. Fonagy and Target (2007) summarize from a psychoanalytic perspective: "A second aspect of the embodiment approach in cognitive science is the emphasis on the sense of having an extended self. This connects a perception of self with one's environment, culture, and history. Moving from the physical experience of being in and part of a world, the template extends to incorporate the construction of an autobiography and engagement with historical cultural narrative systems." Implicit memory systems (with their emphasis on procedural learning, nonverbal behavior, and emotional processing) serve as a central nervous substrate for the storage of embodied, biographical narratives. Between the subjective and objective poles of ambiguity, of the body as subject and object ("to be and to have a body"), corporeal memory systems span across all aspects of bodily experience (perceptual, cognitive, affective, psycho-motor, and self-reflective consciousness).

## Bodily Experiencing and Diagnostics

The particular perspective of (psycho)therapists taking note of the bodily experience of their clients has diagnostic relevance. The specific history-taking in pre-therapy pays attention to significant events and facts: current physical complaints, illness, relevant previous physical health problems, operations, accidents and traumas (e.g., sexual/physical abuse or other physically traumatizing incidents), current and previous somatic treatments, important bodily experiences (e.g., processes in puberty, changes following pregnancy, relevant weight changes, etc.), and noticeable behavioral problems during childhood, such as stuttering, bed-wetting, prolonged thumb sucking, etc. Actual bodily realities and habits are also captured systematically: dietary habits, personal bodily hygiene, clothing, bodily activities (sports or gymnastics, exercising, etc.), sexuality, body contact, tics and ritualistic body-related habits, self-harming behavior, drugs and alcohol, and other toxic inputs.

Apart from collecting the biographical data of a client's individual bodily history, a body-oriented anamnesis (patient's history) can explicitly examine various aspects of bodily experience and gather further important information for a comprehensive problem analysis, an assessment of conflict-specific habitual reactions, and treatment planning. Body-related phenomena can be viewed not only as somaticized symptom formations of complex psychic processes but, further, as entry points for related therapeutic efforts. Analogous to the psychoanalytic process that captures information for interpretation from free-floating verbal association, the therapeutic information gathering in Body Psychotherapy often starts with an exploration of feelings, thoughts, and attitudes as expressed through body awareness and movement. Observational categories include preferences, expression of needs, significant observations regarding any mismatch/incongruence between verbal and nonverbal contents, and behavioral coping strategies (such as adaptation or avoidance). Therapists pay attention to significant statements relating to the body such as: "My head is too heavy for my body"; "I found it difficult to relax in that particular situation"; "I felt uncomfortable to say no, and that made me feel tense around the shoulders"; "It was like hitting the wall"; "I feel like being wrapped up."

A brief, cursory overview outlines the disorder-specific peculiarities in the bodily experience of different groups of patients against the background of the currently available literature. These findings from descriptive, phenomenological psycho-pathology research allot Body Psychotherapy a particular methodological advantage, as it can draw upon body-based and/or related nonverbal intervention techniques, and therefore can offer creative therapeutic answers in response to these somatic phenomena. Specific assessments of bodily experience are called for to systematically assess this dimension of the disorder (i.e., questionnaires, self-assessments, projective and perceptive procedures, movement analysis, etc.). A further refinement of such instruments toward the development of practical, short versions for everyday practice is currently still outstanding. Relevant literature references and thoughts on specifically Body Psychotherapy treatment approaches can be found comprehensively in Röhricht (2000, 2009a) and in Chapter 70, "Body Psychotherapy for Severe Mental Disorders" by Frank Röhricht.

**Mood Disorders**

*Depression*

People suffering from depression experience the following range of symptoms, often leading to a significant reduction in their overall quality of life and psycho-social functioning: loss of ability to experience pleasure, inability to initiate and conduct activity, and negative and suicidal thoughts. Bodily vegetative symptoms feature centrally: disorders of vitality feelings, complaints of organ dysfunction, decreased muscle tone, and depressively inhibited—or also, but rarely, agitated—psycho-motor presentation. In addition, psychotically depressed patients suffer from body-related delusions with the following dominant themes: illness/death, contamination/soiling, functional disorders of body parts, and fragmentation; perceptual disorders comprise mainly experiences of "blockages" and "pressure."

Those symptoms are often associated with a corresponding set of bodily symptoms/somatic complaints, including severe fatigue, motor weakness, back and chest pain, headaches, gastrointestinal problems, etc. Phenomenological research identified specific patterns of body image aberration in depressive and anxiety disorders—i.e., patients displayed significantly higher body dissatisfaction scores, negative body images with boundary loss and somatic depersonalization, and a higher number of physical complaints as compared with other groups of patients (e.g., Marsella et al., 1981; Priebe and Röhricht, 2001; Röhricht et al., 2002). In relation to Laban's conceptual analysis of movement framework (North, 1972), anecdotal evidence in the literature suggests that there tends to be either a lack of engagement with the efforts in depression, resulting in passivity in relation to flow, time, weight, and space; or a predominance of the "yielding" efforts (free flow, sustained time, indirect space, and light weight) rather than the "fighting" efforts (bound flow, sudden time, direct space, and strong weight) (Stanton-Jones, 1992). Other research with a specific focus on the analysis of gait pattern and body posture in depressed patients similarly identified reduced gait velocity, increased standing phases, and slumped posture, with reduced vertical movement of the upper body (Wendorff et al., 2002; Michalak et al., 2009).

Physical complaints and body-related phenomena are now regarded as "common presenting features throughout the world" (Bhugra and Mastrogianni, 2003). The link between depressive symptoms and bodily experience suggests that Body Psychotherapy can be particularly effective in improving depressive symptoms (see the results from a recent randomized controlled trial: Röhricht et al., 2013).

*Mania*

There is a relative paucity of research on bodily experiences in mania. Symptom descriptions include somatic phenomena as follows: psycho-motoric hyperactivity; body-size overestimation / expansive body schema, often pertaining to the hands; in psychotic states, patients describe somatic delusions and hallucinations (dominant theme: pregnancy); and abnormal bodily sensations / cenesthesia (flowing, burning, fluctuations in temperature).

**Anxiety Disorders**

Body-related phenomena in anxiety disorders differ little from those of depressive disorders, which leads to the question of a nosological commonality (cothymia concept); anxiety symptoms often manifest as a somatic "anxiety equivalent" (e.g., hyperventilation, thoracic tightness, globus, shaking, sweating, rapid pulse, etc.); also: body-boundary disorders, and de-somatization. Specific results from phenomenological research can be identified as follows: body perception is negatively correlated with anxiety levels (Röhricht and Priebe, 1996), a phobic anxiety-depersonalization syndrome has been identified (Noles et al., 1985), body image satisfaction is low in anxiety patients (Marsella et al., 1981; Löwe and Clement, 1998); from a clinical perspective, therapists often describe a so-called "Bermuda Triangle": anxiety–tension headache–anger.

**Eating Disorders**

Ever since the early work and publication by Bruch (1962), clinicians have been focusing on severe distortions of body-size perception as one of the main diagnostic criteria in anorexia nervosa (this is included as essential diagnostic criteria in ICD and DSM classification systems). Despite partially contradictory results from studies, the finding of disturbed body-size perception has also been identified as a significant prognostic predictor for the course of treatment; patients with significant overestimation of body width—in particular, in the area of the face, the trunk, and the thighs—tend to have more severe and chronic manifestations of the illness and/or relapse more frequently (e.g., Keel et al., 2005; Bachner-Melman et al., 2006).

Furthermore, bodily symptoms include identification with skeletal appearance; panic fear of the state of "being fat"; bizarre bodily perceptions in immediate relation to the taking in of food; and, in regard to the motor domain, hyperactivity with excessive sports/training, lack of the experience of tiredness, and denial of bodily weakness.

A summary of the literature on bodily experience in eating disorders (Röhricht, 2008) as a guiding source of information for the development of specific Body Psychotherapeutic strategies is as follows:

- General dissatisfaction with bodily realities and negative judgments regarding body weight, body proportions, and general appearance, associated with lack of self-esteem, uncertainties in respect of self-evaluation, low mood, and feelings of anger and disgust toward one's own body. A pervasive feeling of failure and bodily incapability (body image and cathexis aspects of bodily experience).

- Anorexia nervosa and bulimia nervosa patients overestimate all body dimensions, despite visual control and external corrections. The body-size estimations are characterized by bizarre and unstable judgments (perceptual aspects of bodily experience).

- The body is perceived often as alien, passive, and at times lacking in vitality, which often results in somato-psychic depersonalization. Patients suffer from obsessional focusing on negative body images, body control, and body weight (affective/cathexis aspects of bodily experience).

- The body is experienced as an unpredictable object and hence is constantly exposed to attempts of regaining control; this is often accompanied by an avoidant and controlling behavior pattern in respect to personal hygiene, clothing, social interaction, sexual behavior, and excessive exercising (psycho-motor aspects of bodily experience).

## Personality Disorders

For these very heterogeneous disorders, no specific patterns of body schema have been described in the literature to date.

## Schizophreniform Disorders

With regard to abnormal bodily sensations in schizophrenia, a variety of psycho-pathological symptoms have been identified in systematic phenomenological research (reviews: e.g., Fisher, 1970, 1986; Kolb, 1975; Röhricht and Priebe, 1997; Priebe and Röhricht, 2001; Jenkins and Röhricht, 2007).

Patients suffering from schizophrenia present with severely impaired reality testing, manifested in a loss of grounding with centralized body schema (perceptual "retreat" from the periphery of the body and underestimation of the size of the lower extremities and correlating body image distortions); aside from this static pattern, the body schema of these patients is frequently characterized by dynamic distortions: shrinking or ballooning, cenesthesias (qualitative abnormal body sensations), bizarre psycho-motor presentation (extreme form: catatonic agitation or immobility), and—less specifically—body-boundary loss and de-somatization, subjectively experienced as fear of body loss/disintegration and resulting in reconstructive behavioral efforts (i.e., mirror exposure, compulsive rituals). Body-related delusions and hallucinations typically include: penetration; the imagination that there is an external control of one's bodily functions; sensations that individual body parts are missing; implantations of metals or other materials in one's body; changes in the brain and thought processes; as well as changes to gender identity. In terms of psycho-motoric abnormalities, patients display a range of stereotypical movements with repetitive self-contact, self-stimulation with clapping hands, and tapping body parts against objects (du Bois, 1990; Joraschky, 1983).

The overall picture can be best described as one of disintegration and disembodiment (Röhricht, 2000; Scharfetter, 1995). Sass and Parnas (2003) described two main facets of self-experience for schizophrenia patients: a ". . . decline in the fundamental sense of existing as a subject of awareness and action (diminished self-affection) and exaggerated, reflexive awareness of aspects of experience that are normally tacit or presupposed (hyper-reflexivity) . . ." This syndrome often results in a range of cognitive and behavioral consequences that seem to be directed toward "rescuing" core aspects of a coherent—even though compromised—self-consciousness.

Patients suffering from negative symptoms of schizophrenia often display features suggestive of an abnormal relationship with their own bodies, in terms of how their bodies move, their actual/phenomenological bodily experiences, and their verbal reflections on this. Movement tends to be slow and lethargic. Eye contact and emotional rapport with other group members, or with the therapist, is often completely lacking or very limited. Röhricht and Priebe (1996) found negative symptoms (BPRS-subscale anergia) to be associated with disturbed body-size perception. However, the evaluation of effects of Body Psychotherapy in chronic schizophrenia with predominant negative symptoms suggests that the "symptoms" of social and emotional withdrawal are better understood as coping mechanisms in response to perceived existential threats. The phenomenon of affective blunting is thereby more of an artifact: patients experience the full range of emotions, but cannot, and/or do not want to, communicate those to the outside as expressive gestures (Röhricht and Priebe, 2006).

## Bodily Experience and Psychotherapy Research

The conception of an intervention strategy that is based upon a disorder-specific, or a phenomenon-oriented, approach allows for a clear definition of outcome criteria. These, in turn, should be plausible in relation to the chosen strategy of intervention, at least in a theoretical-hypothetical sense. Such an approach is particularly relevant for evaluative and comparative psychotherapy research, in which different schools of therapy jointly work toward the identification of strategies that can be generalized, in the spirit of evidence-based medicine. Fiedler (2002) points out that this approach is not antithetical to an individual, client-centered psychotherapy, but that it recognizes the necessity of individual treatment planning. The course of therapy should be informed by a comprehensive analysis of relevant causal factors, disorders, and phenomena, and with reference to foundational knowledge, and should proceed "... between deficit orientation and resource activation ... ; between biographical and present-time exploration; and between client-centeredness and psycho-education" (Ibid., p. 25). To date, a systematic appreciation of phenomenological research has not been done on body-somatic experiences as part of any Body Psychotherapeutic research, but this offers itself up for the design of future evaluation studies; in this regard, Body Psychotherapy has a specific perspective and a specific clinical approach in the sense of a specific therapeutic intervention strategy. While hypothesis-driven Body Psychotherapeutic research can refer to theories, such as those of Developmental Psychology in hypothesizing on the development of body-ego structure, it should simultaneously evaluate explicit concepts for the treatment of specific disorders in regard to the bodily experience, and define the body schema/body image disorders as primary or secondary outcome criteria in the design of the study.

## Conclusions in Regard to the Clinical Practice of Body Psychotherapy

Staunton (2002) offered a description of the model of Body Psychotherapy: "The fundamental premise in body psychotherapy is that our core beliefs are embodied, and that until we begin to experience the pain held in them directly through our bodies, they will continue to run our lives" (p. 4).

Taking into account the centrality of bodily experiences for intervention strategies within Body Psychotherapy, I would like to offer an outline of a model of relational psychodynamically informed Body Psychotherapy:

- The process in Body Psychotherapy is initiated, centering around the immediateness of (bodily, emotional, and perceptive) experiences and through processes of focusing the person's self-experiences, attention, and awareness toward their bodily reality, whereby patients reach a position of basic embodiment.
- This results, via a mobilization of emotional and nonverbal or pre-verbal aspects of underlying conflicts, in some kind of critical (and partially cathartic) destabilization, which paves the path for a process of affect regulation.
- At this point, altering bodily processes is fostered, and an integrative, self-determined reorganization of reactive and solution-focused behaviors emerges; emotionally corrective experiences occur.
- Implicit interaction patterns/enactments will be exemplified and investigated, both verbally and nonverbally. This enables the conscious exploration of the past and present relational meaning-making, in terms of significant narratives.
- The field of Body Psychotherapy is aiming to identify the common ground between the various Body Psychotherapy schools, especially regarding their theoretical underpinnings and intervention techniques. The latter can be identified as follows:
- The body and its experience are viewed as important diagnostic mediums for the identification of (for example) self-potentials or conflict-laden material; the stages of body-ego development hereby serve as a frame of reference.
- Bodily expression, bodily spontaneity, and flow of movements are drawn upon as avenues of communication and are utilized therapeutically.
- The significance of the healthy personality-aspects and resources is emphasized, and an effort is made to identify the bodily experience of these aspects.
- Frequently, tension arcs are employed in which stimulation, charge, discharge, and settlement follow each other.

None of these potentially curative factors is the domain of a specific therapeutic technique or school. Instead, predominant values are ascribed to the quality of the specific embodied therapeutic relationship in Body Psychotherapy, and to the client-centered and resource-oriented perspective of the therapist in regard to problem resolution.

Treatment/technical considerations can be described as follows: For the practice of Body Psychotherapy, and in reference to Scharfetter and Benedetti (1978), we can propose a paradigm for its therapeutic approach: "... somatically oriented therapy is derived from insight-oriented psychopathology holding the experience of the client as its starting point and taking cues to the concrete further proceeding from his 'symptoms.'" The implied necessity of including the body in the psychotherapeutic process can be arrived at from different theoretical perspectives, including anthropology, Developmental Psychology, intervention-technique issues, ethology, (affective) neuroscience, phenomenology, and embodied cognitive sciences.

Referring to the last two of the above, in congruence with the main theme of this chapter, the evaluative perspective is shifted to a disorder-specific, syndrome-oriented view—that is:

- Toward the diagnostically classified dominant symptoms of the respective disease.
- To the specific patterns of disorder in bodily experience in the respective disease, as identified by phenomenological research.
- To the pattern of embodied and environmentally embedded conflict patterns.

This means that the key question is: "Which specific contribution can Body Psychotherapy make in the treatment of patients, with characteristics as described above—that is, in regard to disorder-specific and/or psycho-pathological symptoms that are body-based?" This systematization therefore necessitates a welcome departure from the narrower differentiations of Body Psychotherapy schools by their spectrum of interventions and, instead, emphasizes the overlaps and fundamental commonalities in theory and practice.

## References

Bachner-Melman, R., Zohar, A. H., & Ebstein, R. P. (2006). An examination of cognitive versus behavioral components of recovery from anorexia nervosa. *Journal of Nervous and Mental Disease, 194*, 697–703.

Baumann, S. (1986). Die Orientierung am und im eigenen Körper: Das Körperschema im engeren Sinne [The orientation of and in my own body: The body schema in the strict sense]. In J. Bielefeld, *Körpererfahrung: Grundlage menschlichen Bewegungsverhaltens [Body experience: Basis of human movement behavior]* (pp. 161–185). Göttingen, Germany: Hogrefe.

Bhugra, D., & Mastrogianni, A. (2003). Globalisation and mental disorders: Overview with relation to depression. *British Journal of Psychiatry, 184*, 10–20.

Bonnier, P. (1905). L'Aschématie [Aschematia]. *Revue Neurologique, 13*, 606–609.

Bruch, H. (1962). Perceptual and conceptual disturbances in anorexia nervosa. *Psychosomatic Medicine, 24*, 187–194.

Conrad, K. (1933). Das Körperschema: Eine kritische Studie und der Versuch einer Revision [The body schema: A critical study and an attempt at revision]. *Zeitschrift der gesamten Neurologie und Psychiatrie [Journal of Complete Neurology and Psychiatry], 147*, 346–369.

De Ajuriaguerra, J. (1965). *The body percept.* New York: Random House.

du Bois, R. (1990). *Körper-Erleben und psychische Entwicklung: Phänomenologie, Psychopathologie und Psychodynamik des Körper-Erlebens mit Beobachtungen an gesunden und schizophrenen Jugendlichen [Bodily experience and mental development: Phenomenology, psychopathology and psychodynamics of bodily experience with observations of healthy and schizophrenic adolescents].* Göttingen, Germany: Hogrefe.

Federn, P. (1952/1978). *Ich-Psychologie und die Psychosen [Ego Psychology and the psychoses].* Frankfurt, Germany: Suhrkamp.

Fiedler, P. (2002). Verhaltenstherapie: störungsspezifisch und allgemein [Behavioral therapy: Specific and general disorders]. In D. Mattke, G. Hertel, S. Büsing, et al. (Eds.), *Störungsspezifische Konzepte und Behandlung in der Psychosomatik [Disorder-specific concepts and treatment in psychosomatic medicine]* (pp. 25–37). Frankfurt, Germany: VAS.

Fisher, S. (1970). *Body experience in fantasy and behavior.* New York: Appleton Century.

Fisher, S. (1986). *Development and structure of the body image (Vols. 1 & 2).* Hillsdale, NJ: Lawrence Erlbaum.

Fonagy, P., & Target, M. (2007). The rooting of the mind in the body: New links between attachment theory and psychoanalytic thought. *Journal of the American Psychoanalytic Association, 55,* 411–456.

Hartmann, H., & Schilder, P. (1927). Körperinneres und Körperschema [Body interior and body image]. *Zeitschrift der gesamten Neurologie und Psychiatrie [Journal of Complete Neurology and Psychiatry], 109,* 666–675.

Head, H. (1920). *Studies in neurology (Vol. 2)*. Oxford, UK: Oxford University Press.

Jenkins, G., & Röhricht, F. (2007). From cenesthesias to cenesthopathic schizophrenia: A historical and phenomenological review. *Psychopathology, 40,* 361–368.

Joraschky, P. (1983). *Das Körperschema und das Körper-Selbst als Regulation-sprinzipien der Organismus-Umwelt-Interaktion [The body schema and the body-self as regulatory principles of organism-environment interaction]*. Munich, Germany: Minerva Publikation Sauer GmbH.

Keel, P. K., Dorer, D. J., Franko, D. L., Jackson, S. C., & Herzog, D. B. (2005). Post-remission predictors of relapse in women with eating disorders. *American Journal of Psychiatry, 162(12),* 2263–2268.

Kiener, F. (1974). Untersuchungen zum Körperbild: 1. & 2. Teil [Studies on body image (Parts 1 & 2)]. *Zeitschrift für Klinische Psychologie und Psychotherapie [Journal of Clinical Psychology and Psychotherapy], 21,* 335–351, & 22, 45–66.

Kolb, L. C. (1975). Disturbances of the body image. In M. F. Reiser (Ed.), *American handbook of psychiatry (Vol. 4),* 2nd ed. (pp. 810–837). New York: Basic Books.

Löwe, B., & Clement, U. (1998). Somatoforme Störung und Körperbild: vergleichende Studie [Somatoform disorder and body image: A comparative study]. *Zeitschrift Psychosomatische Medizin, 44,* 268–278.

Marsella, A. J., Shizuru, L., Brennan, J., & Kameoka, V. (1981). Depression and body image satisfaction. *Journal of Cross-Cultural Psychology, 12,* 360–371.

Meermann, R. (1985). Körperschemastörungen [Body image disturbance]. Unpublished habilitation thesis, University of Münster, Germany.

Michalak, J., Burg, J., & Heidenreich, T. (2009). Don't forget your body: Mindfulness, embodiment and the treatment of depression. *Psychosomatic Medicine, 71,* 580–587.

Noles, S. W., Cash, T. F., & Winstead, B. A. (1985). Body image, physical attractiveness and depression. *Journal of Consulting Clinical Psychology, 53,* 88–94.

North, M. (1972). *Personality assessment through movement.* London: MacDonald & Evans.

Plassmann, R. (1993). Organwelten: Grundriss einer analytischen Körperpsychologie [Body worlds: The body plan of an analytic psychology]. *Psyche, 47,* 261–282.

Poeck, K., & Orgass, B. (1963). Über die Entwicklung des Körperschemas [On the development of body image]. *Fortschritte der Neurologie und Psychiatrie [Progress in Neurology and Psychiatry], 32,* 538–555.

Priebe, S., & Röhricht, F. (2001). Specific body image pathology in schizophrenia. *Psychiatry Research, 101,* 289–301.

Röhricht, F. (2000). *Körperorientierte Psychotherapie psychischer Störungen: Ein Leitfaden für Forschung und Praxis [Body Psychotherapy for psychiatric disorders: A guide for research and practice]*. Göttingen, Germany: Hogrefe.

Röhricht, F. (2008). Die multimodale, körperorientierte Psychotherapie (KPT) der Essstörungen: theoretische und erfahrungsbezogene Ansätze für eine Manualisierung [The multimodal, Body-Oriented Psychotherapy (KPT) of eating disorders: Theoretical and experiential approaches to manualization]. In P. Joraschky, H. Lausberg, & K. Pöhlmann (Eds.), *Körperorientierte Diagnostik und Psychotherapie bei Essstörungen [Body-oriented diagnostics and psychotherapy for eating disorders]* (pp. 281–293). Giessen, Germany: Psychosozial.

Röhricht, F. (2009a). Ansätze und Methoden zur Untersuchung des Körpererlebens [Methodology in assessment of bodily experience]. In P. Joraschky, T. Loew, & F. Röhricht (Eds.), *Körpererleben und Körperbild: Ein Handbuch zur Diagnostik [Body experience and body image: A handbook on diagnostics]* (pp. 35–52). Stuttgart, Germany: Schattauer.

Röhricht, F., Beyer, W., & Priebe, S. (2002). Disturbances of body experiences in acute anxiety and depressive disorders—neuroticism or somatization? *Psychotherapie Psychosomatik Medizinische Psychologie, 52,* 205–213.

Röhricht, F., Papadopoulos, N., & Priebe, S. (2013). An exploratory randomized controlled trial of Body Psychotherapy for patients with chronic depression. *Journal of Affective Disorders, 151,* 85–91.

Röhricht, F., & Priebe, S. (1996). Body image in patients with acute paranoid schizophrenia: A longitudinal study. *Nervenarzt, 67,* 602–607.

Röhricht, F., & Priebe, S. (1997). Disturbances of bodily experience in schizophrenic patients: A review. *Fortschritte Neurologie Psychiatrie, 65,* 323–336.

Röhricht, F., & Priebe, S. (2006). Effect of Body Oriented Psychological therapy on negative symptoms in schizophrenia: A randomised controlled trial. *Psychological Medicine, 36,* 669–678.

Röhricht, F., Seidler, K. P., Joraschky, P., Borkenhagen, A., Lausberg, H., Lemche, E., Loew, T., Porsch, U., Schreiber-Willnow, K., & Tritt, K. (2005). Konsenspapier zur terminologischen Abgrenzung von Teilaspekten des Körpererlebens in Forschung und Praxis [Consensus paper on the terminological differentiation of various aspects of bodily experience]. *Psychotherapie Psychosomatik Medizinische Psychologie, 55,* 183–190.

Sass, L. A., & Parnas, J. (2003). Schizophrenia, consciousness, and the self. *Schizophrenia Bulletin, 29,* 427–444.

Scharfetter, C. (1995). *The self-experience of schizophrenics: Empirical studies of the ego/self in schizophrenia, borderline disorders and depression.* Zurich, Switzerland: Private publication.

Scharfetter, C., & Benedetti, G. (1978). Leiborientierte Therapie schizophrener Ich-Störungen: Vorschläge einer zusätzlichen Therapiemöglichkeit und grundsätzliche Überlegungen dazu [Body-Oriented Therapy of schizophrenic ego disturbances: Proposals for additional therapeutic possibility and basic thoughts about this]. *Schweizer Archiv für Neurologie, Neurochirurgie, Psychiatrie [Swiss Archives of Neurology, Neurosurgery and Psychiatry], 123,* 239–255.

Schilder, P. (1935/1978). *The image and appearance of the human body.* New York: International Universities Press.

Shontz, F. C. (1974). Body image and its disorders. *International Journal of Psychiatry in Medicine, 5,* 461–472.

Stanton-Jones, K. (1992). *Dance Movement Therapy in psychiatry.* London: Routledge.

Staunton, T. (2002). Introduction. In T. Staunton (Ed.), *Body Psychotherapy* (pp. 1–6). Hove, UK: Brunner-Routledge.

Torres de Beà, E. (1987). Body schema and identity. *International Journal of Psychoanalysis, 68,* 175–184.

Ungerer, D. (1958). Die Bedeutung des Bewegungsentwurfs für den motorischen Lernprozess [The importance of motion design for the motor learning process]. *Leibeserziehung,* 245–248.

Wendorff, T., Linnemann, M., & Lemke, M. R. (2002). Lokomotion und Depression [Locomotion and depression]. *Fortschritte Neurologie Psychiatrie, 70,* 289–296.

# 23

## The Bodily "Felt Sense" as a Ground for Body Psychotherapies

**Eugene T. Gendlin and Marion N. Hendricks-Gendlin, United States**

**Eugene T. Gendlin**, PhD, born in Vienna, has made a significant contribution to the foundation of Body Psychotherapy with his methodological concepts on implicitly complex experiencing. He was a student of Carl Rogers, received his degree in philosophy at the University of Chicago, and began lecturing there in 1963. His philosophy book *Experiencing and the Creation of Meaning* (1962) brought a whole new approach to concept formation. His second book, *Focusing* (1978), in which he illustrates the practical application of his philosophy in psychotherapy, sold more than four hundred thousand copies in the first year. It has been translated into many languages, and has brought him worldwide acclaim. There are now more than 1,200 Focusing professionals in more than thirty countries, including thousands of Focusing-trained psychotherapists, who practice his approach today. The American Psychological Association has honored Gendlin repeatedly for his development of Experiential Psychotherapy.

This chapter shows how at-first-unnoticed bodily feelings can bring forth new experiences and meanings. Direct reference to what he calls the "felt sense" stands at the center of his theory and practice of Body-Oriented Psychology.

Gendlin is professor emeritus of the University of Chicago. He is the founder, and was for many years the editor of *Psychotherapy: Theory, Research and Practice*, the Clinical Division Journal of the American Psychological Association. He is the author of numerous books, including *Focusing-Oriented Psychotherapy* (1997a), and has published many scientific papers in the areas of psychology and philosophy, most of which have been collected in the Gendlin Online Library (www.focusing.org/gendlin). His "philosophy of the implicit" has been influential in a wide range of disciplines.

**Marion N. Hendricks-Gendlin**, PhD, directs the international Focusing Institute and teaches Focusing worldwide. Beyond that, she has been active in promoting community mental health services by founding the network organization Changes. Dr. Hendricks-Gendlin has more than thirty years of experience as a psychotherapist. She worked as a trainer of psychologists for the New York State hospital system, and for ten years was a core faculty member of the Illinois School of Professional Psychology in Chicago. A main subject of her recent work is defining "felt sense literacy" and how that might become a movement that would make Focusing available to anyone. Dr. Hendricks-Gendlin is the author of numerous scientific papers.

**Editors' Note:** *This chapter is a revised (2014) version of one that originally appeared in the German (Schattauer, 2006) edition of this handbook.*

The client's side of the change process has usually been discussed in relation to the question "Exactly what should the therapist respond to in the client?" The usual answer has been "the feeling," but that term can be confusing. It is not exactly "the feeling." We want to respond to *that*, in the client, from which "change steps" come. What is that, in the client, from which change steps come? They come from an *unclear* "*edge*," a sense of something more than one usually says and knows. We call such an unclear edge a "felt sense." A felt sense is a sense of meaning that is felt in the body. Because it is felt, we need to be precise about how it differs from the usual recognizable feelings.

## A Bodily Felt Sense Is Not an Emotion

The felt sense is unclear and is less intense than emotions. For example, a client may feel angry and be able to say why she is angry. *That* is clear. In an effective therapy process, that expression would help to "open things up," and new, further steps would then arise. But suppose the client says, "I'm angry, I told you why, and that's all. Nothing further comes." Let us say that the therapist has responded appropriately to the anger and its reasons. What exactly is not happening here?

When therapy works, new steps of living would come here. Do they come from the emotions exactly (anger, sadness)? Many therapists think so. If nothing is happening, they assume that the anger must not have been felt sufficiently. But people often have the same feelings over and over, without any change steps coming.

T: From the bodily sense of "that whole situation," what change steps might come?

C: (silence) . . . (breath) . . . It feels sort of heavy . . . Oh, it *wants to* stay angry . . .

T: Something there *wants to* stay angry.

C: Mhm . . . (silence) . . . Oh (breath) . . . Yeah . . . if I stop being angry, I won't do anything about it . . . yes . . . I'd love just to say it's OK and not have to cope with the situation. I've done that so often.

These steps did not come exactly from the feeling of anger. Rather, it is the "heavy" quality that opens into these steps. That heavy quality is the felt sense. Implicitly, it is a feeling of the whole situation.

The felt sense is less intense than the ordinary feelings. *From* a felt sense, very intense feelings can come, but the felt sense itself is less intense. Without quiet concentration, one might not find it. The steps of change come from an unclear, fuzzy, murky "something there," an edge, an odd sort of direct datum. But most often there is at first no such datum. Typically, at first one finds only the already-known feelings without edges, and no felt sense.

## Finding a Bodily Felt Sense

We have developed various little instructions for finding the felt sense. For example, "Put your attention in your right toe . . . Now in your knee . . . Can you find your knee without moving it? . . . Now your pelvis . . . Come up into your stomach. How is it in there—warm and fuzzy, or how?"

Or we ask the client to refer to the stomach and chest to "see if you are comfortable there." The unease that usually comes there can develop into a felt sense. It is less intense and not as rough on the person as the ordinary feelings are. There is even an odd sort of gratitude that comes from this bodily discomfort, as if it were thankful for one's attention.

Many people have difficulty attending directly to the comfort or discomfort in the middle of their bodies. They do not sense the body directly. Many people must first discover this simple human capacity before they can find the felt sense. That seems strange to those who have always done it.

Characteristic of a felt sense is its implicit complexity. It may feel only "heavy" or "tight," but one can sense that it contains a great deal more. Ordinary bodily sensations are, for example, a belt that is too tight, or a muscle pain, or a stomach ache. The uneasy sense of a situation or problem can also come there, in the middle of the body, but it includes the implicit complexities of your whole situation. That (equally physical) heaviness or tightness is the felt sense "of" the situation. In it you can feel more than you know or could think.

The felt sense differs from both the ordinary feelings and from what we call the "emotions." Emotions are well known and usually limit us temporarily to a narrow scope, whereas the felt sense is usually wider than all our already-known feelings.

## The Situational Body

The notion of body in the phrase "bodily felt sense" comes from the "philosophy of the implicit" (Gendlin, 1997a,

1997b). The body is radically redefined. We have not had a theory that accounts for how it is that psychological problems and psychological change can be expressed or arrived at through the physical body. Although it is widely accepted that the organism is one system, there has not been an adequate theory to explain the oneness of mind and body.

We all know that our bodies can be comfortable or uncomfortable about, or in, a particular situation. But how is that actually possible? The body doesn't "know" the situation! However, we don't usually phrase it that way. We say that we know the situation and that our bodies only react to what we know. If we think it's a good situation, the body is supposed to feel comfortable. If we think that the situation is dangerous, the body is then supposed to react with anger or fear. And of course our bodies do react to what we think—*but not only to that*. Our bodies feel a situation directly.

For example, if you see someone whom you know on the street, but you don't remember who it is, this is totally different from seeing a stranger. This person gives you a very familiar feeling. You cannot place the person in your mind, but your body knows who it is (or knows that you know them). What is more, your body knows how you feel about that person. Although you don't remember who it is, your felt sense of that person has a very distinct quality.

If you had to describe your felt sense of the person whom you cannot place, you might say, for example, "It is a sense of something messy, sort of unclean. I feel a little apprehensive, as if I'd rather not have much to do with that person, but there is also mixed in with it some odd curiosity that doesn't feel right, and uhm . . ." If you went further into it, you could probably find out more and more, both about the person and about yourself. You might even then remember who it is, from the felt sense.

But the whole felt sense cannot be put into words. However well you express it, there is always more left in it than what you have said. Even to say some of it, you have to make up new phrases, because it does not easily fit into the usual phrases and categories. This "complex" is uniquely your felt sense of just that person. Any other person would give you a very different bodily felt sense.

Let us say you suddenly remember who the person is. Now you might be surprised. You might say, "I didn't know that I feel this way about that person!"

We have situational bodies: our body senses situations. But how can we explain this? In physiology and current philosophy, the body is—mistakenly—assumed to be able to take in information about the world only through the five senses. It (supposedly) cannot contain information that it has not seen, heard, smelled, tasted, or touched. Some philosophers have said that our minds have innate ideas, but that was always questionable. The most common ancient and modern assumption has been that we cannot really know anything that doesn't come through our five senses. Understanding how our minds and bodies relate has always been a problem. But the body, at any rate, isn't supposed to have any information other than through its five senses. But what about all these instances of a bodily "knowing" of situations? They are all odd and unexplained, especially if one holds to the usual assumption that we can know only through the five senses.

How is it that we have situational bodies? How can we think about this bodily knowing? The bodily knowing of situations precedes human or conscious activity. For example, a plant does not have our five senses. It does not see, hear, or smell. And yet, obviously, the plant contains the information involved in its living. It lives from itself; it organizes the next steps of its own body process, and enacts them if the environment cooperates to supply what it needs. So the plant has the information about its living in and with the soil, the air, the water, and the light. It has the information, or we could say it "is" the information, because the plant body is made up of elements from soil, water, air, and light. It makes itself out of those and so, of course, it contains (it is) information about those. But the information is not about soil and water lying out there by themselves. Rather, it is much more complex information about the plant's living process, an interaction with those, making itself out of them. We notice that the plant doesn't need the five senses in order to *be* this kind of information. The plant organism is an interaction with its relevant environment in its ongoing process of living.

Animal bodies also contain (are) this kind of information. They also make themselves out of the stuff they eat, the water they drink, and the air they breathe. The five senses are not separated bits out of which the world is put together.

A higher animal understands its situation. It may not know what brought it about, but it understands how the situation needs to be different, and it will do what needs to be done as much as it can. An animal can look at you in such a way that you also understand some of its situation.

In fact, there are no already-separated five senses in animals. When we humans separate the five senses, we unintentionally drop out what we now call the "visceral" sense of the whole situation. We consider each sense separately: the visual, the auditory, and each of the other three. But human beings do still have the capacity to sense a whole situation, as animals do. We humans also have language and culture, but we can think of our linguistic and situational knowledge not as separate and floating, but as elaborations of what our already-intricate plant bodies or animal bodies understand.

A human felt sense is a very special human product, but how animal bodies understand their situation is already more like a felt sense than most people currently ever have. The capacity to deliberately form a felt sense is a human capacity, with several hundred thousand words and the whole culture always implicit. It may take a few minutes before the felt sense comes to a person. It is a bodily happening that implicitly includes all of this human elaboration. But it is continuous with the most basic body-environment processes. In this way, we can think of how the living body knows (feels, lives, is) its situation from the body. But what is a situation?

A situation is never just something external. For example, suppose it is an external fact that the door is locked. But a locked door by itself, out there alone, is not a situation. The situation is that I am coming home and find that I've lost my key. Or the situation is that I'm crouching behind that locked door, hoping it will hold, while three guys are trying to break it down. Or perhaps I am locked in, and trying to get out. A situation always involves some living thing that is in the process of organizing its further living.

In a rough way, we can say that the body "knows" our situations because it *is* our living in them. From the body come our next moves, not just inhaling and eating, but also our interactions with others and what we are about to say to them.

How was all this ignored for so long? It was ignored because none of this easily fits into a world constructed entirely of empty space, time, and five separated sense perceptions. The world so constructed has long been considered fundamental to science. Although there has been much philosophical critique of it, we are only now developing the concepts of a viable alternative model and an alternative science.

## A Bodily Felt Sense Is Always "This," Intricate and Particular

A bodily felt sense does not fit the common names or categories of feelings. It is a singular sense of *this* situation. Although such a body sense comes as one feeling, we can sense that it contains an implicit intricacy.

For example, your body sense of a person whom you know contains implicitly all your past history with that person, and all that you hope for with that person. It also contains what that person rouses in you, and some of your own unresolved troubles. It also implicitly contains the exact way in which you do and don't like the person, and much more. Let me roll all that together and call it an "*implicit intricacy.*" You might be able to think about three or four of those things, but most of them are understood implicitly.

An implicit intricacy does not yet have separated strands or parts. Yet later when those appear separately, we say they were already there in the single sense we had at first. We don't usually think of physical feelings as containing a whole complex mesh. Physical sensations are assumed to be simple: a pain or a sensation is just what it seems to be. It seems to be opaque: we don't expect a hidden complexity, for example, in the stabbing pain of a twisted ankle, or in the sensation of red. A complex situation might have led to the twisted ankle, but we don't expect to find the intricacy of the situation inside the pain.

What distinguishes the kind of physical sense that I am discussing is that it does contain an implicit intricacy, "all" about that person, event, or situation. This mesh contains the person's history, as it is functioning in this event. Implicitly it contains characteristic ways of responding, what the person is going to do next in the day, and so on. A whole, vast multiplicity of implicit aspects in the person's functioning and dysfunctioning is always involved.

If the person can attend and refer to this bodily-felt mesh, new possibilities and alternatives can arise. This opens a bodily kind of psychotherapy. In the example below, the therapist (T) invites the client (C) to move from an intense feeling to attend to the implicit intricacy of the whole situation:

C: I feel like no one wants to relate to me. Like something is wrong with me and I don't know what. Like I am a monster [self-attack]. I know what set off the feeling. Last night at church . . . [she then tells of a brief conversation with a friend about babysitters in which she ended up feeling criticized].

T: So, can you just step back a little and get a sense for that whole situation, that whole thing with her? What is your sense of the situation?

C: [She is quiet, getting a felt sense, and then begins to cry.] Oh! I know what it is. I was so excited! [symbolization from felt sense] My daughter wants to babysit so much, and I feel like I spoiled it . . . I felt so excited that I didn't pay attention to what was coming back to me from her. I just kept talking because I was so excited and I wanted it to happen . . . actually, now that I think of it, I did feel sort of like I didn't really agree with some of the way she was thinking about child care. I remember feeling like she seemed sort of overly protective or rigid in her approach.

T: So, in your excitement, you really didn't pay attention to some of your own signals. You actually didn't like what she was saying, but you didn't stop and pay attention to your own feeling.

C: Yeah . . . that's right . . . I feel better now that I have a sense of what happened for me.

If the therapist "reflects" what the client has said, this is done with the expectation that the client will "correct" the reflection. A number of such corrections are usually necessary before a response carries the client forward. Here, the reflection (the second T) was accepted immediately. At the second C, after the therapist invites the client to get her whole sense of the situation, the client is able to step back from the self-attacking, freshly come down into her body, and ask inside, "What is my bodily sense of that whole situation with this person? How was it for me?" She is silent for a few minutes, in order to let an at-first-vague sense of self form in her body. A felt sense usually comes in the middle of the body, in the solar plexus, or chest area. This sense is not yet in words. The client then pays attention to that vague sense with the question inside, "What is this like? What is the quality of it?" As she pays attention to her felt sense, what emerges is the sense of excitement. The emergence of the words "Oh! I know what it is. I was so excited!" is a small "felt shift." The words are new and surprising to the client. The content of "excitement" is quite different from "I am a monster." And the move to words, which carries her forward in her body, is felt as relief and tears: a whole-body response. Change is directly felt in the body. It is an immediate experience.

We speak of "opening and entering" the bodily felt sense. This kind of bodily experience is like entering through a doorway. Any kind of Body Psychotherapy will be more effective if the client can be helped to refer directly to the bodily felt sense level and enter through this "door."

## The Bodily Felt Sense Implies Its Own Next Steps

A felt sense is an "implying" of exact next words or images or body gestures that have not yet come. Only some exact word or action will "carry forward" what is bodily implied. When that happens, there is a change in the body, because what was implied has happened, and now something further is implied. This carrying forward is like water that quenches thirst. Only certain "objects" will carry forward this implying—e.g., water (but not oil), orange juice, and perhaps even some unfamiliar liquid can carry forward what is implied by the thirst. Therefore, we say that what is implied is "neither determined nor arbitrary." Even though only certain exact words or things (including body gestures) carry forward the felt sense, these have not yet happened. Many different things could carry forward. The words, images, gestures, and actions that are implied are not already formed, sitting in some unconscious place. Carrying forward is not a representational process of copying what is already formed but hidden. It is rather a generating of a fresh next step out of the bodily implying.

When what is implied occurs, there is a bodily felt shift. There is a release of tension, and a sense of "Yes, that is right. That is exactly what it is." The unfolding of the felt sense is usually a gradual process of tiny movements until there is this characteristic felt shift.

The body's implying of next steps means that the client can get in touch with her *own* inner blueprint of how to move in an embodied way that carries life forward. For example, Alexander bodywork focuses on change at the level of automatic, spontaneous bodily function. The technique involves inhibiting old physical-response patterns and replacing them with new and better response patterns. This can be very helpful, but these new response patterns are imposed on the organism only from outside. The technique does not address the story of why the habit was there in the first place; it only addresses the fact that the habit is destructive and that the teacher does know a better way. This is brought through a conscious giving of orders to the body as a way of overriding the old response patterns as the teacher adjusts the body to give it a right experience.

With the integration of Focusing, the client gets in touch with her *own* newly arising blueprint of how to be in a very physically alive way. "What Alexander imposed from without can be awakened from within" (McEvenue, 2002).

In *A Process Model* (1997b), Gendlin derives many new concepts of the living body (plants, bacteria, animals, and humans). He also derives a new *kind* of concepts. He develops a new model, an alternative to the familiar model of inanimate particles in supposedly empty space and time.

Bacteria and plants *are,* but do not also *have,* their living. Consciousness is a late product, a "turn" by which animals *have* as well as *are* their earlier stages. The earlier stages always still function, although differently before and after each further development. Therefore, humans still have all their earlier stages even after language has developed, but may overlook them, as if everything begins with language. If we can also *refer directly* to the implicit intricacy, which is always still functioning, we make it possible to *think with the implicit.* We become able to go back and forth between verbal-conceptual and bodily-implicit understandings so as to think with both in turn. A kind of thinking based on both is surely a major human development.

The new philosophical model explains on many levels how it is that the body is involved in psychological change. This new philosophical understanding also makes possible a more effective kind of psychotherapy. Working through the body can bring already-implicit change in situations. It can unite all Body Psychotherapies and guide practice. Knowing that the body can imply exact next steps in a situation enables the clinician to work with the client so that such steps emerge.

Today, people often live at various distances from this bodily source. You have a bodily orienting sense. You know who you are, and how you come to be in this room. To know this, you don't need to think. The knowing is physically sensed in your body and can easily be found. But this bodily knowing can extend much more deeply. You can learn how to let a deeper bodily felt sense come in relation to any specific situation. Your body "knows" the whole of each of your situations, vastly more aspects of them than you can possibly just think. Here, you find an intricate bodily knowledge, and new steps that want to come, and will come if you can wait here and allow them to emerge. You can sense your living body directly under your thoughts and memories, and under your familiar feelings. Focusing happens at a deeper level than your feelings. Under them you can discover a physically sensed "murky zone" that you can enter and open. This is a source from which new steps emerge. What was carried in the body implicitly (the so-called "unconscious") can develop, become explicit, and thereby carry life forward. When found, the bodily felt sense is a palpable presence underneath.

## References

Gendlin, E. T. (1962/1997). *Experiencing and the creation of meaning: A philosophical and psychological approach to the subjective.* Evanston, IL: Northwestern University Press.

Gendlin, E. T. (1978/1981). *Focusing.* Bantam Books.

Gendlin, E. T. (1997a). *Focusing-oriented psychotherapy: A manual of the experiential method.* New York: Guilford Press.

Gendlin, E. T. (1997b). *A process model.* New York: Focusing Institute.

McEvenue, K. (2002). *Dancing the path of the mystic and the story of a man in conflict.* Toronto, Canada: Wholebody Works.

# 24
## The Body and the Truth

Halko Weiss, United States, and
Michael Harrer, Austria

Translation by Regina Mirvis

**Halko Weiss's** biographical information can be found at the beginning of Chapter 1, the Preface to this handbook.

**Michael Harrer**, MD, is a psychiatrist, as well as a psychotherapist, psychotherapy lecturer, and supervisor (ÖVS, ÖBVP). After his training in Psychodynamic Therapy, Catathymic Imaginative Psychotherapy, and hypnotherapy, he turned toward Body Psychotherapy (Hakomi) in recent years, in order to give his integral bio-psycho-socio-spiritual understanding of the human condition a more methodical framework. The focal points of his work are psycho-oncology, terminal care, and grief counseling, as well as medical training in psycho-social/psychosomatic medicine.

Dr. Harrer is in private practice in Innsbruck, as well as co-founder and chairman of the information center "Network for Cancer–Prevention–Aftercare." He is co-author (with Halko Weiss) of three books on mindfulness, and maintains a website on mindfulness (www.achtsamleben.at).

"The body does not lie!" These provocative words are by Alexander Lowen (1988, p. 83), captured quite early on in the development of Body Psychotherapy, and have become one of its basic claims. To this day, most Body Psychotherapists would probably still accept this claim as a rationale for including the body in psychotherapy, albeit probably formulated in a somewhat more differentiated fashion. On closer scrutiny, two messages are implied in Lowen's statement:

- The body allows access to the most meaningful parts of one's personal truth.
- Human consciousness, in its predominantly verbally oriented manifestation, has only a limited access to reality—both in ordinary and in more fundamental terms—and much remains hidden from it, or is accessible only in a censored, distorted form.

## The Dubiousness of Memories and Interpretations

Freud had already emphasized that what a human being is conscious of, and can verbally express, constitutes only a fraction of the "individual reality" that constitutes and defines his existence. It also frequently contradicts, or only loosely relates to, actual behavior.

A well-known neuropsychological experiment with so-called "split-brain" patients bears this out. In such patients, the connection between the two hemispheres of the brain has been cut, usually in order to treat cramping seizures. Consequently, neither hemisphere knows what the other knows or is doing, as they are not receiving any direct information from each other. A clever experimental design ensures that only the nonlinguistic brain hemisphere receives the instruction to carry out a particular task. It is only while the task is already being executed, and by observing the requested activity in action, that the other hemisphere, responsible for language, is receiving any information about the assignment. When the person is questioned about the motives for their activity, the language-producing hemisphere will usually generate and offer a range of very sensible and rational reasons. However, these reasons *typically have no connection whatsoever with the actual assignment* (Singer, 2003a, 2003b; Spitzer, 2004, pp. 331ff.).

In neuropsychology, the ability to invent unconscious reasons for one's own behavior is called "confabulation." Gerhard Roth, a well-known neurobiologist, describes this accomplishment: "The ego confabulates, that is to say, it delivers—what the observer recognizes as—pseudo-explanations, usually ones that are in accordance with self-esteem and the expectations of the social environment" (Roth, 2003, p. 38) (translations by Michael Soth).

Therefore, he concludes,

> Regarding our ability to understand our own actions, we are not very far from such split-brain patients. We are massively influenced by our unconscious, without exactly knowing what is happening to us; we do not understand the language of the unconscious mind. Yet as we have to justify all our feelings, thoughts and actions—in both logical and verbal terms—to ourselves and especially to others, we are constantly fabricating stories. We also tend to believe in them and attempt to convince others of their veracity. (Roth, 2001a, p. 370)

He continues,

> The compulsion to verbally legitimize ourselves—vis-à-vis ourselves and others—can explain the mechanisms of radical distortion and reinterpretation which humans observe each other as capable of, to the point where people deny the obvious in their own behavior. For the most part, this is not a question of "bad faith" or evil intentions, but is based on the simple fact that our conscious existence, which for the main part is verbally mediated, is not a simple extension of the unconscious; on the contrary, it has a different form of existence, namely a social one. (Ibid., p. 370f.)

The phenomenon of confabulation is not the only one that suggests a degree of skepticism toward the human faculty for mental and symbolic representation. For example, research on perception and memory demonstrates that any information entering the brain is immediately both re-formed and re-processed, and this happens again with each recall. The "false memory syndrome" is a particularly extreme variation of this phenomenon. A famous example concerns the great pioneer of Developmental Psychology, Jean Piaget (Tavris, 1993). Piaget consistently alleged, as a child and adolescent, that, at two years of age, he had been the victim of an attempted abduction. He could remember details of sitting in his pram, witnessing the fight between his nurse and the kidnapper, even noticing scratches on the kidnapper's face. He also remembered a policeman, dressed in a short coat, wielding a truncheon, who chased the kidnapper away. This story was substantiated by the nurse and by other family members. Piaget was sure about remembering the incident precisely. But his memory was wrong: the kidnapping attempt never happened. Thirteen years after the "kidnapping," the nurse confessed to his parents in writing that she had contrived the entire story. Piaget later wrote that he must have heard the story and projected it into the past in the form of a visual memory. The memory of a memory, but nevertheless false.

False memories are characterized by fragments of memories that are confused, interchanged, and blended: these memory fragments may stem from different times, yet are sometimes remembered (or put together) simultaneously. Sometimes dreams appear as real experiences. Supposedly, other false memories result from intense questioning and the suggestive conduct of therapists (Schacter, 1995, 1996). Elizabeth Loftus (1994) was even able to show that it is rather easy to implant false memories. And Freud describes "screening memories," which, through the consolidation of many real and fantasized elements, nevertheless contain something essential from childhood (Laplanche and Pontalis, 1986, p. 133f.).

Psychodynamic theories also recognize the human capacity and tendency to cope with internal tension and threats not only by denying and distorting reality, but also by inventing reasons through creative acts of rationalization. Freud showed, early on, how the ego unconsciously employs an array of defense mechanisms to repress, deny, split off, dissociate, project, etc., thus conflicting inner and outer realities.

Narrative approaches to psychotherapy similarly emphasize the human capacity for "story-making," and how people discover or invent their own personal history, to confer meaning and significance to their experience after the event, and to modulate it.

Furthermore, a significant part of perception occurs outside consciousness (subliminally) and becomes either focused or blocked out by means of selective attention. As a result of the fuzziness of neural processes, the absorbed information is not processed and stored with precision, but is constantly being changed and reedited (Goleman, 1985).

In conclusion, it makes sense for therapists to be informed—by a basic awareness of these mechanisms—as to how they approach the stories and explanations that their clients volunteer in therapy. The body can be of immense help in the search for a broadening and deepening understanding of personal truth.

## "Truth" and Its Meaning for Body Psychotherapy

The epistemology of postmodernity gives us a fairly clear answer to the question regarding truth: there is, in and of itself, no such thing as "truth," nor is a human being even capable of recognizing it. On the other hand, there are different types and levels of truth, and these can be validated and developed through scientific methods.

The contemporary philosopher Ken Wilber (1996, 2000) has proposed theories that can be useful toward an understanding of truth, and that function within the framework of psychotherapy. Building on the work of Koestler (1967), Bateson (1979), Jantsch (1980), and other theorists, Wilber (2000) points out that the universe, including humans, is composed as a layered hierarchy (holarchy) of wholes/parts (holons). Each holon includes and integrates all lower holons contained within it, and occupies its particular "worldspace" commensurate with its place, stage, and level, with its own corresponding reality and truth. This understanding creates a vision of multiple, ever more encompassing, and context-dependent truths. This model allows us to draw the following conclusion, especially in regard to the body in psychotherapy: the integration of a larger whole (for instance, a human being operating on a high developmental and functional level) requires all constituent holons to be apprehended, differentiated, and taken into account—each with their respective truths.

From the context of Body Psychotherapy, we are especially concerned to include not only the somatic levels of the whole, but all constituent aspects participating in the "holarchy" of the human being and that contribute their own particular truth to the diversity of the whole. Only by integrating the diverse truths from all the different "lower" levels will a higher, encompassing truth become possible, because higher levels build upon lower ones, and evolve *from* and *through* them. And as long as the foundational truths of the body are undeveloped and unconsidered, potential qualities of higher levels (e.g., mental and spiritual experiences) cannot unfold but remain incomplete.

Furthermore, Wilber's "quadrant model" suggests that the effort to move toward higher truths depends upon the capacity to integrate two—often polarized and considered mutually exclusive, but equally necessary—perspectives from which observations and descriptions can and need to be made: particularly the external-objective view and the internal-subjective view.

### External-Objective (Third-Person) Perspective

In this stance, "facts" are observed or measured from the outside, and described as objectively given in third-person objectifying language ("he," "she," "it")—e.g., skin resistance, metabolic activities in the brain, or nonverbal behavior.

In psychotherapy, these observations by the therapist—offered in a dialogic process of joint hermeneutical exploration—can support the client in uncovering their important subjective "truths," which may not have been conscious before. The "external-objective" view thus constitutes a backdrop to the shared generation of meanings, which are then validated by mutual understandings, intersubjective agreements, and a consensual "social fit."

### Internal-Subjective (First- and Second-Person) Perspective

This is based on introspection and speaking in the first person ("I"), where the client describes his or her subjective experience. Here, significant criteria of truth are "authenticity" and "openness," or candor. One form of subjective truth, which is especially relevant in the context of psychotherapy, is the direct and immediate "experience of evidence." Bühler (1907) coined the term "Aha! effect" to describe such experiences; this has since been acknowledged by many therapists, including Perls (1974), as an essential step in the therapeutic process.

These two perspectives, and their interplay within the context of Body Psychotherapy, inform the rest of this chapter.

### Body Structure, Body Language, and Body Expression

In declaring that "The body does not lie," Lowen referred to those messages and manifestations of the body that are externally visible, asserting that he trusted the expression of a person's body more than anything they would communicate to him in words. Alongside body language, as conveyed through facial expressions, gestures, etc., he was focusing especially on the body's overall structure and posture, the language of somatic self-organization.

Lowen refers to a similarly challenging point of view from Charles Darwin, who wrote, "The movements of expression give our spoken words liveliness and energy. They reveal the thoughts and intentions of others more truthfully than words do, which can be distorted . . ." (Lowen, 1992, p. 9).

A vignette from medical practice may serve to illustrate this contrast between verbal and nonverbal expressions:

> During his rounds, a doctor informed a female patient waiting in her bed that her liver biopsy had returned normal and she would be allowed to go home the following day. When he asked her if she was happy she said, "Yes." Her simultaneous gesture of hopelessness (lifting of her underarms with her palms facing up and then dropping of both arms) did not elude him and coming closer to the bed he asked again, "Yes?" In response, she broke into tears, explaining her fear of going home to an empty house, as her husband had recently left her to move in with his girlfriend. This interaction facilitated a subsequent discussion of the patient's social situation, who was in severe danger of falling back into an earlier pattern of alcohol abuse when faced with her grim life circumstances upon returning to an empty home. (Adler and Hemmeler, 2000, p. 22f.)

Based upon the ubiquity of such experiences, Lowen claims that "there is almost no psychiatrist who does not continuously use this information. Nevertheless, psychiatrists—and also the public—shy away from viewing this information as absolutely dependable, because they cannot immediately verify it objectively" (Lowen, 1988, p. 84).

Body Psychotherapy understands the body as the physical side of human wholeness, mutually corresponding with the mental side as two interrelated aspects of the underlying unity of "embodied mind." Adherents of this point of view—following Reich's theory of "functionalism"—assume that the outer form of physical self-organization reveals corresponding structures on inner psychological levels. In the early years of Body Psychotherapy, this understanding led to quite naive and mechanical forms of "body reading." Based on fixed assumptions regarding simplistic correspondences between physical characteristics (e.g., locked knees) and psychological traits (in this example, orality), it was believed possible to diagnose an individual's character patterns with degrees of certainty, based merely on observations of a few physical characteristics. As the different schools of Body Psychotherapy have accumulated experience over the last decades, such attitudes and approaches are now generally considered to be inadequate.

However, this does not invalidate the basic assumption—which therefore remains largely accepted—that fundamental life themes do manifest and express themselves in, and via, the body, and that these themes can be approached and revealed in their individual particularity through a complex process of therapeutic uncovering. No longer applied in mechanical ways, the translation of this assumption into everyday Body Psychotherapy practice is a subtle and sophisticated affair. It is no longer a question of simplistic correspondences between the physical and the psychological, but more of a complex and intuitive "art" or craft. It is something that has been developed by the tradition of Body Psychotherapy, more as a community of practitioners, passed from generation to generation of therapists, and that is supported by a growing body of knowledge and intuition, rooted in the ongoing experience of therapeutic practice.

By observing the patient's physical organization—both obvious, as well as very subtle—some details of their underlying unconscious psychological processes can be discovered, identified, and worked with. This often allows an unusually direct and immediate access to fundamental and therapeutically significant traces of early imprinting, and the client's subjective truths. In this way, perceiving and working with the client's body allows the therapist to gain some degree of independence, or distance, from the patient's verbal statements and explanations: there is a parallel process of observing and listening and comparing these two inputs. Diversions, confusions, and one-sided blinkeredness can thus be more readily avoided—and these can be significant dangers when therapists rely solely on the verbally communicated contents of the client's conscious mind.

When somatic experience is attended to in the therapeutic relationship and becomes a valid focus of communication and reflection, a dialogic process both between immediate experience and reflective interpretation, as well as between client and therapist, is required. Both cooperate toward a joint construction of meanings and their symbolic comprehension—a process that can be understood, according to the German philosopher Hans-Georg Gadamer (1960), as hermeneutical evolution; that is to say: in the context of dialogic interaction, truth continues to reveal itself in an ongoing process.

To sum up, many Body Psychotherapists share the view that the somatic route toward a person's core, to their organizing beliefs about themselves, their relationships, and their subjective world, is—for the most part—more direct, more efficient, and faster than any method that relies on words alone as its starting point: we get closer to the "truth" of the person.

Petzold (2003, pp. 68, 77) formulated the idea of a "hermeneutic spiral," continuously unfolding within the intersubjective realm of therapy, consisting of four stages: apprehending, comprehending, explaining, and reorienting. Once aspects of somatic self-organization have been apprehended (i.e., brought into awareness), the subsequent steps (comprehending and explaining) may lead to a reorientation that, in turn, will tend to generate a renewed and transformed body awareness. Here, the term "awareness" is meant to indicate the patient's subjective sense of their own body—an internal "view" that allows for novel, moving, enhancing, and therefore transformative experiences. Often, the therapist will support this process with their own external perspective, by guiding the patient's attention along a path that can lead toward therapeutically significant subjective truths, thus allowing these truths to emerge into the client's consciousness.

## Self-Perception and the Experience of Evidence

In the psychoanalytic tradition, Winnicott's contribution was significant in establishing the importance of somatic apperception as a path toward a more authentic self: "Mind becomes the location of False Self, and the development of

False Self is based on a dissociation between intellectual activity and psychosomatic existence" (Winnicott, 1965, pp. 140–152; quoted by Aron, 1998, p. 21).

This resonates with Body Psychotherapy's practice of engaging directly with somatic apperception: when a client's awareness is oriented toward their body and its spontaneous life expressions, an integral component of the self can be seen to emerge as an object of perception and observation.

Damasio corroborates the importance of somatic experience as a foundation of a sense of self, by suggesting, ". . . that the highly constrained ebb and flow of internal organism states, which is innately controlled by the brain, constitutes the background for the mind, and, more specifically, the foundation for the elusive entity we designate as self" (Damasio, 1999, p. 30).

Thus the client's introspection and attention to their somatic experience can indeed be seen to foster a deeper exploratory process. Subjectively, clients often feel surprised, astonished, curious, and fascinated by the phenomena that they encounter during their investigations of their somatic affective internal world. These phenomena are then held in awareness, examined more deeply, and eventually investigated with respect to their deeper meaning. What Petzold calls "hermeneutics from the body ['Leib']" (2003, p. 68) implies a therapeutic practice that allows clients not only to experience scenes of their life as rationally comprehensible and transparent, but to actually experience them emotionally and somatically. For the client, this can generate a sense of "vital evidence" (Ibid., p. 694), engendered by the synergy of bodily and emotional experience as well as rational insight in a context of "relatedness" (i.e., with social significance), thus forming a comprehensive "total event."

Such significant experiences of "vital evidence" are rare events in therapy if the somatic basis of experience is not consistently included. If therapy fails to facilitate the client in learning to listen to their initially obscure states and signals arising from the realm of their body, a foundational aspect of tangible connectedness and attachment is missing. Consequently, the client's sense of subjective truth is compromised in its intensity, as it is not carried by the wholeness and comprehensiveness that are prerequisites for the experience of a "total event." (See also Chapter 23, "The Bodily 'Felt Sense' as a Ground for Body Psychotherapies," by Eugene Gendlin and Marion Hendricks-Gendlin.)

### The "Knowledge" of the Body

The body is molded and shaped by a wide variety of factors during the course of its lifetime. Starting with its basic genetic makeup, there are a myriad of contributing influences: the effects of nutrition, the extent of exercise and muscular training, injuries that may leave structural scars, wrinkles that are formed during a lifetime of facial expressions, its basic anatomical structure, the development of muscular armoring, down to its immunological history and memory.

The "knowledge" of the body refers to all of these levels, and many more, and each can be seen to have its particular kind of "consciousness." The question is: which aspects of this multidimensional tapestry can be accessed in such a way that we can indeed speak of "knowing" or "knowledge"—or the "truth."

Body Psychotherapy assumes that the ensouled body (Leib), or Winnicott's "psyche indwelling in the soma" (being a human being that is in a condition of body-mind integration or wholeness), emerges from within the underlying body-mind unity; the body therefore has access to information that mental processing does not, in some cases not in principle, and in others at least not initially.

There is abundant evidence that the body indeed seems to "know" more, and to know it much earlier, than the conscious mind. Miltner and colleagues (2003, p. 380), for example, studied people with different phobias, and found that even *subliminal* visual presentation of phobic objects, such as spiders or snakes (or of angry or threatening faces in the case of a social phobia), resulted in significantly raised levels of electrodermal reactions, in contrast to nonphobic people. Thus, phobic individuals can be demonstrated as reacting *somatically* to the fear-inducing stimulus, even when it was not perceived consciously at all. Pure body reactions—manifested via a person's "individual physiology" (in this case, the measurable skin reaction)—are thus a reliable indicator of a psychological condition, allowing us to reliably conclude that a particular trigger (e.g., a spider) must have a special, extraordinary meaning for a particular patient.

Damasio (2003, pp. 119ff.) has documented the fact that the body reacts to stimuli *before* a person is aware of any feeling. As an example, he explains (Ibid., pp. 138ff.) how subjects respond to photos of people who are showing strong emotions: certain muscle groups in their own faces, i.e., those they would have used to imitate the emotions exhibited in the photos, are instantly and imperceptibly activated. The subjects were entirely unconscious of the "preconceived" mirroring activity of their muscles. Yet, electrodes, distributed across their faces, registered the correlating electromyographic changes.

These kinds of phenomena indicate, not only a "knowledge" of the body, but also its capacity for dynamic comprehension of others and the world around us. For the purposes of therapy, we cannot afford to ignore or neglect such avenues of knowing, and it makes sense to access and utilize them—an area in which the tradition of Body Psychotherapy has developed rich and diverse expertise.

## The Presymbolic, Pre-verbal Space

Current developments in neuropsychology seem to be on course toward confirming two fundamental recognitions common to all psychodynamic schools of therapy—namely, that the defining structures of the personality develop very early in life, and that the conscious mind finds it difficult, if not impossible, to access these formative experiences. The neurobiologist Gerhard Roth, for example, explains how—within the first three years of life, during the formation of the emotional, "limbic" structures of the brain—a child establishes complex and affective "evaluation systems." These systems (or pathways) effectively ensure that our brains make all of our operative decisions in the light of past experiences. As the brain structures that store explicit, episodic memories are not yet "online" when these prior formative experiences occur, the developmental origins of the principles underpinning and guiding later action precede conscious memory. Roth continues:

> What is called character or personality is formed very early and largely unconsciously, becoming increasingly resistant against learning from later experiences. The ego, which does not begin to evolve in its typical human manifestation until the third or even the fourth year of life, therefore finds itself, so to speak, situated into, and carried by, this [prior] "limbic" personality. (Roth, 2001b, p. 58f.: translation by Regina Mirvis)

Consequently, the memory banks of the conscious mind do not contain symbolic representations of those constituent elements of the developmentally much earlier "limbic personality" that determine a person's character in fundamental ways. It can thus be assumed that what often emerges during therapy as supposedly very early "narrative memories" were actually generated at a later point, possibly as creative, but secondary, renditions of earlier experiences, initially stored quite differently.

Modern Developmental Psychology (Dornes, 1997, p. 14) conceives of mental development as progressing from the storage of sensory-motor-affect schemata, via image representation, to the verbal encoding of psychic experiences (see also Chapter 30, "Affective-Motor Schemata" by Andreas Wehowsky). Many contemporary psychotherapeutic schools assume that reactivation of early sensory-motor-affective patterns is possible. Clients can work through and integrate this level of experience in therapy, supported by their now-existing adult faculties of symbolization that allow them to find additional image and verbal representations for such experiences as well.

The infant researcher George Downing (1996, p. 102f.) writes on this issue, "In certain regressive body states, the preverbal past can be re-traced with a precision unlike anywhere else." He continues:

> Of course we are assuming an important premise here, namely, that these regressive body states are in fact symbolizing real past events, i.e., that—by

incorporating selected motoric elements—they recapitulate experiences that indeed occurred in one form or another, albeit being subject to possible distortions through fantasy. To date, this premise is supported only by unsubstantiated evidence from clinical experience. There is no evidence yet from direct scientific research. (translation by Regina Mirvis)

## Signposts to Truths

In conclusion, the more that we understand about confabulations, defense mechanisms, and the different operational modes of memory, the more good reasons we have to be skeptical when assessing the substance and "truth" of a client's verbal communications. By including the body and its structures, its flow of energy, its armoring, and its movement, in therapy, we gain a therapeutic access to those sensory-motor-affective experiences that have left crucial imprints on a person's internal world (on all levels, including mental), and therefore continue to shape and organize their character. When these imprints and patterns become reactivated within the sheltered space of therapy, they can be experienced in a new way by the client themselves, as well as being observed by the therapist. This reactivation has the potential to become a starting point for an "experience of vital evidence," an experience that brings together many aspects of subjective and intersubjective truths and may engender, for the client, the unfolding of a fundamental reorientation and restructuring. This is—perhaps—as close to the "truth" as anyone can get.

## References

Adler, R., & Hemmeler, W. (2000). Von der Biomedizin zur Infomedizin: Luxus oder Notwendigkeit? [From bio-medicine to informational medicine: A luxury or necessity?]. In R. Adler (Ed.), *Psychosomatik als Wissenschaft [Psychosomatics as science]*. Stuttgart, Germany: Schattauer.

Aron, L. (1998). The clinical body and the reflexive mind. In L. Aron & F. S. Anderson (Eds.), *Relational perspectives on the body*. Hillsdale, NJ: Analytic Press.

Bateson, G. (1979). *Mind and nature: A necessary unity.* New York: E. P. Dutton.

Bühler, K. (1907). Tatsachen und Probleme zu einer Psychologie der Denkvorgänge [Facts and problems of a psychology of the thought processes]. *1. Archiv für die Gesamte Psychologie, 9,* 297–365.

Damasio, A. R. (1999). *The feeling of what happens: Body, emotion and the making of consciousness.* New York: Harcourt Brace.

Damasio, A. (2003). *Looking for Spinoza: Joy, sorrow and the human brain.* London: Heinemann.

Dornes, M. (1997). *Die frühe Kindheit [Early childhood].* Frankfurt, Germany: Fischer.

Downing, G. (1996). *Körper und Wort in der Psychotherapie [The body and word in psychotherapy].* Munich, Germany: Kösel.

Gadamer, H-G. (1960). *Wahrheit und Methode: Grundzüge einer philosophischen Hermeneutik [Truth and method: Outlines of philosophical hermeneutics].* Tübingen, Germany: Mohr.

Goleman, D. (1985). *Vital lies, simple truths: The psychology of self-deception.* New York: Simon & Schuster.

Jantsch, E. (1980). *The self-organizing universe: Scientific and human implications of the emerging paradigm of evolution.* New York: Pergamon Press.

Koestler, A. (1967). *The ghost in the machine.* London: Arkana.

Laplanche, J., & Pontalis, J-B. (1986). *Das Vokabular der Psychoanalyse [The vocabulary of psychoanalysis].* Frankfurt, Germany: Suhrkamp.

Loftus, E. (1994). *The myth of repressed memory.* New York: St. Martin's.

Lowen, A. (1988). *Bioenergetics.* New York: Penguin.

Lowen, A. (1992). *Körperausdruck und Persönlichkeit [Body shape and personality].* Munich, Germany: Goldmann.

Miltner, W. H. R., Krieschel, S., Hecht, H., Trippe, R. H., & Weiss, T. (2003). Angstmotivierte Aufmerksamkeitsanomalie: Psychobiologische Grundlagen und neuronale Aspekte ihrer therapeutischen Modifikation [Fear-motivated anomaly of attention: Psychobiological bases and neural aspects of their therapeutic modification]. In G. Schiepek (Ed.), *Neurobiologie der Psychotherapie [The neurobiology of psychotherapy]*, pp. 378–403. Stuttgart, Germany: Schattauer.

Perls, F. S. (1974). *Gestalt Therapy verbatim.* New York: Bantam Books.

Petzold, H. (2003). Integrative Therapie: Modelle, Theorien und Methoden für eine schülenübergreifende Psychotherapie [Integrative therapy: Models, theories and methods for an education-spreading psychotherapy]. Paderborn, Germany: Junfermann.

Roth, G. (2001a). *Fühlen, Denken, Handeln [Feeling, thinking, touching].* Frankfurt, Germany: Suhrkamp.

Roth, G. (2001b). Das Unbewusste aus der Sicht der Hirnforschung [The unconscious, from the view of brain research]. In M. Cierpka & P. Buchheim (Eds.), *Psychodynamische Konzepte [Psychodynamic concepts].* Berlin: Springer.

Roth, G. (2003). Wie das Gehirn die Seele macht [How the brain makes the soul]. In G. Schiepek (Ed.), *Neurobiologie der Psychotherapie [The neurobiology of psychotherapy].* Stuttgart, Germany: Schattauer.

Schacter, D. C. (Ed.). (1995). *Memory distortion.* Cambridge, MA: Harvard University Press.

Schacter, D. C. (1996). *Searching for memory: The brain, the mind, and the past.* New York: Basic Books.

Singer, W. (2003a). *Bindungsprobleme: Neurobiologische Überlegungen [Linkage problems: Neurobiological considerations]* [CD]. Cologne, Germany: Supposé.

Singer, W. (2003b). *Ein neues Menschenbild? [A new idea of man?].* Frankfurt, Germany: Suhrkamp.

Spitzer, M. (2004). *Selbstbestimmen: Gehirnforschung und die Frage: Was sollen wir tun? [Self-determination: Brain research and the question: What are we to do?].* Heidelberg, Germany: Spektrum Akademischer.

Tavris, C. (1993, Jan. 17). Hysteria and the incest-survivor machine. *Sacramento Bee, Forum section.*

Wilber, K. (1996). *A brief history of everything.* Boston: Shambala.

Wilber, K. (2000). *Sex, ecology and spirituality: The spirit of evolution.* Boston: Shambala.

Winnicott, D. W. (1965). *The maturational process and the facilitating environment.* New York: International Universities Press.

# 25

## Body, Culture, and Body-Oriented Psychotherapies

**Ian J. Grand, United States**

**Ian J. Grand's** biographical information can be found at the beginning of Chapter 19, "The Embodied Unconscious."

*Finally, it must be understood that dancing while embracing is a product of modern European civilization. This should show you that things quite natural for us are historical; they may horrify everyone else in the world.*

—Marcel Mauss (1934)

At least since Rousseau, there has been an explicitly held belief in the West that there is an antagonism between civilization, on the one hand, and body and nature on the other. In this view, the so-called primitive, the natural man, the noble savage, lived close to nature and didn't have the inhibitions of the European.

Psychologies based on this underlying notion assume that cultural repression of primal feelings and bodily enactments is the root of all neurosis. It is held that there is innate, unmediated, and natural sexuality, aggression, and grace; and that there is a universally natural way of mothering and child rearing that, if adopted by everyone, would mitigate against psychic dysfunction. In this view, the liberation of these presumed natural feelings and enactments is the road toward healing; therefore, the role of therapy is, in one respect, to overcome the inhibiting effects of culture.

A contrasting view concerning the complex relationship between culture, desire, and expression sees the body as the "ground" of cultural enactment. In this view, cultural values are made manifest as bodies and it is in culture that bodies are constituted, for both good and bad, with particular ranges of feeling, movement, and gesture. Each stage of development is influenced by the cultural surround, as well as by the family of origin. In this view, neurosis arises as conflict in bodily structured cultural imageries, and therapy becomes the exploration of ranges of embodied values (Farr and Moscovici, 1984; Duveen and Lloyd, 1990; Hassin et al., 2005).

A current view, that synthesizes these positions, holds that there is a double benefit—bodily feelings on the one hand, and cultural learnings, institutions, and constructions, enacted as body, on the other—and that these are seen to shape and form each other. There is a creative shaping of experience that originates simultaneously, and differentially, in both culture and body, and is both rooted in individual bodies and extends beyond them. The person's creative development of bodily enacted expressions and values is influenced by cultures in multiple ways, and interactions with cultural institutions can lead to either empowerment or diminishment of lived possibility (e.g., Kristeva, 2002; Lave, 1991; Rogoff et al., 2005).

In this chapter, I will develop this latter view, presenting research that indicates how the body-psyche is formed through social and cultural means. I will then describe how various practitioners have begun to combine these understandings with the insights of body-based psychotherapies to develop new ways of working with clients.

Throughout our development, we are influenced in our bodily "becoming" by cultural forces beyond the family of origin. To understand behavior and motivation, it is not sufficient simply to look at and judge familial interactions, assumed to be outside of the social structures and beliefs in which the family is embedded. Family members interact with each other using tropes, creatively composed of expressions and behaviors that are often incorporated from the cultural surround. Birthing, infant care, the training of various emotional expressions and character traits, differential treatment of boy and girl children—all are creations, based on various cultural values.

One illustration of these cultural influences is a small pamphlet that new mothers at the Research Hospital in Kansas City, Missouri, were given, in 1949, entitled "Instructions for Mothers." The pamphlet gave a series of instructions that told the mother how to handle her newborn "infant"; these included:

> 10) Handle infant as little as possible. So do not pick [it] up to show to relatives and friends. Keep [it] quiet and free from commotion and infection.

> 13) Do not pick up baby every time it cries. Normal infants cry some every day to obtain exercise. Infant is quickly spoiled by handling.

In contrast to these instructions, current belief holds that infants are not "spoiled" by handling, and, in fact, actually require significant levels of tactile stimulation and the security of clinging, being held, and being rocked. Mutual excitation between the caregiver and the infant is now seen as desirable and necessary, and extended family and social connections and bonding with these are also considered important in the rearing of a child.

Although many of us may now currently be quite disturbed by these 1949 instructions, it is clear that a woman of that time and place, wanting to be a good mother, might well have often followed the hospital's advice. When working with an adult who had been reared in these conditions, it might be important to note that these instructions came from outside the family of origin. Because these reflected ideas of child rearing, that were prevalent in the North American mainstream culture of the time, good or bad mothering practice was, in part, independent of the specific mother or the family.

Similarly, Cho and colleagues (2005) found that Taiwanese and American grandmothers held markedly different views about the virtue of encouraging self-esteem in children. American grandmothers had two views, one skeptical and one more in line with their daughter's valuing of self-esteem. The Taiwanese grandmothers felt that self-esteem was peripheral. The predominant culture tends to ignore other views, or consider them as deviant.

The influence of the social surround continues throughout childhood and during adolescence and adulthood. We are continually influenced, in our sense of self, and in our sense of interaction and emotional expression, by agencies and institutions outside the family of origin, such as schools, religious institutions, peer groups and the media.

Wortham (2006), for example, tells the story of a fourteen-year-old African American ninth-grade student, who became a scapegoat for both students and teachers in her class, changing her embodied sense of self; and Corwin (2012) writes about changes in the attitude of elderly nuns toward their bodies after changes in the teachings of the Catholic Church. D'Andrade and Strauss (1994) and other workers in Cultural Psychology note that the attitudes individuals hold toward romance and relationships derive in part from media and other cultural and community images that are widely held. Abbey and Falmagne (2008) described intrapsychic tensions stemming from the incorporation of complex and diverse social identities and the conflicts between them. Rogoff (2003) talks about "the cultural nature of human development."

A large number of studies since the 1980s have highlighted the significance of social influences on the formation of a sense of embodiment: Delamont and Stephens (2008) wrote about "diasporic capoeira" practice; Hanson about drag-kinging (Hanson, 2007); Eckert (1989) and Grand (1998, 1999, 2006, 2009) showed that schooling, media, advertising, and health practices form specific culturally-based unconscious dynamics; and Aktar (2004) described unconscious aspects of socially-influenced organizations in India.

In all of these examples, a creative (or potential) interaction is described between the growing experiential body-psyche of the person, the influences of the family (which are embedded in social values), and social values that exist outside the family of origin. The pervasive influence of the social surround in psychic development continues to influence people throughout their lives. There are empowerments and enhancements that develop through social roles, sports, movement, and meditation practices; and there can be a variety of socially-based diminishments as well (Coughey, 1984; Eckert, 1989; Shapiro and Shapiro, 2002; Gimlin, 2002; Johnson, 1994).

As with other psychological processes, a good deal of social and cultural influence occurs outside of consciousness. Hopper (2003) suggests that there is a social unconscious, and that the psyche is both organic and social. He notes that, "attempts to understand the social unconscious are met with a mixture of personal and social resistance, because feelings of personal and social powerlessness follow from increased insight into social facts and social forces" (p. 128). He goes on to cite Foulkes (1964), who suggested that, ". . . the individual is as much compelled by these colossal forces as by his own id and defends himself against their recognition without being aware of it."

In looking at the development of the dynamic psyche from a sociocultural viewpoint, we can follow the suggestion by Rogoff and colleagues (2005) that, "A focus on the organization of children's participation in cultural practices offers, indeed requires, attention both to the guiding role of cultural traditions and to the active role of individuals themselves." They go on to note that "investigating the organization of children's participation in everyday activities offers a way to address the dynamic nature of repertoires of cultural practice—the formats of interaction with which individuals have experience and may take up, resist, and transform" (Ibid.).

In the past few decades, developments in Social Psychology have shown how various social stereotypes can be primed and activated (Wyer and Srull, 1994). In this work, words, figures, and images that are found to be associated with a particular stereotype are used as "primes." People are given "tests" in which these primes are embedded. Then, aspects of their behavior are observed and compared with those of people who have not been given the primes.

In one such experiment (Bargh, 1997), subjects were given a scrambled word test that included a number of words that were primes for the stereotype of aging, such as Florida, bingo, walkers, etc. After taking the "test," subjects left and walked down a corridor where, unknown to them, the speed of their walking was timed. The speed of primed subjects was compared to the speed of people given a similar task that did not include the primes. People who had gotten the primes walked more slowly down the corridor. As can be seen in this example, bodily enactment can be affected by social priming.

Similar work has been done related to both racial and gender stereotypes. Steele (1997) showed that both women and African American students at Stanford did less well on exams, when they had been primed by gender or racial stereotypes.

Hall (1990) noted that body postures, gestures, the construction of interpersonal space, and the establishment of personal rhythm, and a sense of proper timing, are all entrained by, and learned in, particular cultural settings. People take offense and are activated by intrusions into what they think of as proper social distance, or what they assume to be the proper time for events to take place. Hall suggests that Latin American time and space constructions, for example, are quite different from those of North American and European white cultures, and from those of various Middle Eastern, or aboriginal cultures.

There are also cultural constructions of proper expression. In some cultures, loud, expressive aggression is considered to be bullying and something to be dismissed; whereas, in others, it may be a show of personhood and strength. Modesty and deference in social manners are considered virtuous in some cultures, and considered as weak and repugnant in others. All of this is constructed bodily through the use of muscular inhibitions, movements, and gestures, and excitatory and inhibitory processes. Individuals in these cultural settings come to identify with, and live from, the body organizations that they develop to enact these cultural modalities. As Connerton (1989) notes:

Every group, then, will entrust to bodily automatisms the values and categories which they are most anxious to conserve. They will know how well the past can be kept in mind by a habitual memory sedimented in the body. (p. 102)

In all cultures, class and ethnic identifications are made. In the United States, for example, there are characteristic white American patterns of looking, talking, gesturing, and acting; Latina American patterns; Asian American patterns; Jewish American patterns; African American patterns; as well as patterns of sexual identities, among many others. All of these are stereotyped, identified with, and also resisted; and each of these categories also has different regional, class, and gender manifestations, roles, and enactments of privilege, power, class, deference, and refusal. All of this is enacted as in posture, gait, breath, closeness and distance, gesture and expression.

It is here that we see the import of what Marcel Mauss was getting at in the epigraph at the beginning of this chapter. Social somatic organizations and activities are historically and culturally situated, and what we see as natural, and teach without question, is not necessarily seen as natural to other people. When people from various cultures and ethnicities come together, there are complex, embodied, culturally derived differences (both conscious and unconscious) that come into play, and that become sources of situational pressures. People respond bodily to each other in complex patterns of emotion, gesture, excitation, and posture. These differences are formed throughout the lifespan (Banerjee, 1997).

There are multiple cultural influences and enacted presences in which our behavior is situated and organized. Different cultures encourage different social bodies, with specific ranges of both personal and interpersonal feeling, expression, and action by employing different behavioral and attitudinal "trainings" that accrue through time. These trainings encourage particular muscular usages, postural and gestural stances, and different levels of excitation.

Ewen (1989), for example, has shown that there are different kinds of bodies that have been valorized in previous centuries and that the basis of this valorization has to do with social values promulgated by those particular cultures. He shows the changes in which women's body types (in particular) have been valued; for example, the Rubenesque look of the seventeenth century, or the skinny, high-fashion-model look of the late twentieth century. For Ewen, writing in the 1980s, the latest version was the so-called "hard body" of women who trained in the gym. We can also consider the modern trends for piercings and tattoos, as well as similar extreme phenomena (like cutting, anorexia and eating disorders), and other body-dysmorphic disturbances in this light.

Cultural attitudes are also created through imitation, in which social images are translated into patterns of muscular and visceral usage. The child plays at being a superhero, derived from a TV show, or a movie, or a book, by adopting postures, speech patterns, and gestures; the young adult is mentored at work by bosses, or by fellow workers, and consciously or unconsciously practices the attitudes that are supposed to bring success—or develops imitated patterns of resistance and rebellion. Adults may also choose to practice meditation and breathing and movement techniques that lead to extended ranges of physiological and social function. In all these cases, body patterns, as social representations, are built, identified with, automated, and held mostly below the level of consciousness. The therapeutic implications of the view I have been developing here are enormous.

According to this view, people enact particular socially derived values as forms of body organization, and these bodily attitudes can become fixed and unchanging. They are one of the means by which self-identity, as well as social interaction, is formulated. In the therapeutic setting, one can explore experientially the socially derived values and attitudes that a client has embodied, and can thus enable the client to experiment with new embodied possibilities. There are also conflicts that occur in the living of the body that have, as their root, social valorizations of kinds of bodies; and working with these is different from working with traditionally framed conflicts derived from interactions in the family alone.

The social somatic approach involves an investigation of socially and culturally-based body attitudes through explorations of movements, gestures, breath, etc.—the whole range of body approaches that are described elsewhere in this handbook. The differentiating alertness here is to the sociocultural roots of experience. Some psychological conflicts experienced by individuals, for example, can be seen as embodied conflicts of attitude, gesture, muscle and tissue state that arise from incorporated and created social values and injunctions. Embodied social values and social injunctions can conflict with each other in a not-often-discussed psychological dynamic.

One client, for example, had a dense, muscular body. He regularly worked out with weights and had developed a strong weightlifter's body. When asked to make soft, languid, large, and extended movements of his arms, he became quite anxious and panicky. These movements were, for him, indications of what he considered to be a form of "femininity" that he did not want to express. As it turned out later, the client was a closeted gay man, who had erected a powerful, "manly" body to misdirect people from assuming that he was gay. The musculature that he built up also misdirected himself away from feelings and movements that were clearly unacceptable to him because of the cultural values toward homosexuality that he had internalized. It should be noted as well that the idea of lifting weights and developing a particular kind of body from this activity is also culturally based.

A session with another client also illustrates how bodily organized social values can affect a person's functioning. In this particular session, we explored the client's feeling of inadequacy in dealing with his employees. He felt awkward, stiff, shy, and clumsy when approaching them, he said.

I asked him to demonstrate how he approached his employees to show me how he enacted this awkwardness bodily. As he did this role-play, we noticed that his shoulders were pulled up; he looked around warily; his breath was held; his feeling was confined in the upper part of his body.

As we continued to explore these bodily feelings, through both movement and sensory reflection, the client began to associate to his early years in school. He could not, he said, recall playing with other children before starting school. Other children did not go to his home, nor he to theirs. He had not learned how to play ball, or to engage in any other athletic activity. As an unexpressive and clumsy child, he was the target of physical and verbal abuse from the other children. He was afraid to go home after school because he was regularly waylaid, called a sissy, taunted, or punched. He never talked about these experiences with anyone, embracing the injunction to "brace up" that he had received from his environment when his mother died.

In high school, this client had developed an intellectual persona that served him well: he became outgoing and charming. This social persona, also enacted bodily, was created on top of the bodily attitude of fear, shame, and inadequacy from his earlier school experiences. In the current situation, in dealing with his employees, whom he felt intimidated by, he again felt the deeper layer of fear, while also trying to maintain his outgoing and charming demeanor. He was afraid of confrontation and afraid of his own anger at his ineptness. He felt (had embodied) the somatic conflict of the social attitudes that he had developed.

These clients' development of conflicting social attitudes is not unusual. In most contemporary societies, there are multiple cultures and subcultures to which one belongs. There can be internalized cultural conflicts expressed as conflicted senses of how to act, move, gesture, and comport oneself. Internalized racism, homophobia, class attitudes, sexism, and anti-Semitism are good examples, as well as valuations of kinds of demeanor and expression.

There are also socially engendered family social myths, stories, and roles that become sources of conflictual embodied representations. Examples are the immigrant and/or class story: a family emigrates from a poor country, or is part of a poor class, lives in penury, and then, through sacrifice and hard work, lays the groundwork for the professional lives and the material well-being of future generations. The subsequent generations that have not had this struggle still retain images of it as somatic representations in their psyche, derived from the imitation and incorporation of their parents and grandparents' attitudes, as well as the somatic images of the world to which they currently belong.

Clients bring stories of suffering from and/or overcoming racism, religious persecutions, or gender discrimination, and the bodily means that family members adopted to attempt to protect themselves. There are stories of coming into one's roles at work, at school, and in spiritual pursuits, and stories about love, grieving, family illness, and parenting. When we approach these stories, from a social and cultural view, we see that, in all these stories, there are social and cultural underpinnings—lived as a form of embodiment. They are enacted as embodied social representations, and these enactments can be empowering or restricting. All of them can be analyzed and worked within a body-oriented psychotherapeutic framework.

In one group, for example, there was a conversation about summer camp as a place where work roles are practiced and developed. One woman talked about going to safety patrol camp. The members of the safety patrol were children stationed at street corners who stopped traffic and told the other children when they could cross the street. The camp they attended taught them how to be good safety patrol persons. The woman then recalled what it was like being a safety patrol member. She particularly remembered the winter. The weather was cold, she said, and all the members got together early in the morning and had cocoa together. Then they went to their posts. She showed us, while standing, the somatic attitude of being the safety patrol person, enacting the directing of the other kids. She adopted what she considered to be a look of pride and control by lifting up her eyebrows, tilting her head, lengthening her neck, puffing her chest, and planting her feet. Getting into the bodily attitude itself gave her a feeling of responsibility and competence, she reported, and she traced current feelings of adequacy and caregiving to this attitude that she had developed in the culture of the safety patrol. In practicing being a safety patrol person, she had developed a body shape and inner feeling that continued into the present day.

In body-oriented approaches, one can, as in this last story, work experientially with people by beginning with their story and then exploring how they embody it. One can also begin with movement or feeling in a particular part of the body and explore the embodied social somatic associations that occur.

In another group, I asked participants to begin to feel the back of their legs while moving and interacting. There were a large number of felt associations to the exercise. One woman noted a recurring concern with what she called her "floppy buttocks," and through that, she realized her preoccupation was generational and was socially embedded. She remembered how her mother and grandmother would wear girdles to overcome their fear of jiggling flesh, and then have to undo some of the hooks at some time in the day in order to become more comfortable: allowing herself to feel the back of her legs had led to these associations.

By contrast, another woman then talked about what a miracle girdles had been for her. She was a pudgy kid, she said, and the girdle gave her a new, sleek look, although there was still, she said, a "roll" on top. In these examples, there are historically based concerns, self-valuations, self-deprecations, and a practice of embodiment (girdle-wearing) that were socially enjoined and had personal ramifications.

After a set of exercises, a student in a different class talked about the "boy" and "man" code of behavior in which one was taught to endure pain, refuse emotion, and eschew intimacy. He managed to verbalize what many, many boys have experienced: the social "conditioning" that is supposed to differentiate a "boy" from a "man": we—men—all needed to learn what would seemingly be acceptable to other men. If we did these things, or behaved in this way, we would become a "man."

The consciousness of the roots of each of these persons' embodiments came with the direct experiential exploration of different tissue states, postures, and movements. The interpretation was not limited to their family of origin but, rather, nested the understanding of family injunctions and valuations within larger social realities.

In these classes, we were able to spend time unpackaging a wide range of self-evaluations and bodily practices that were taken from the culture and enacted in individual people's lives. These senses of self were embodied and automated, and—through social somatic psychological exercises and interpretations—they could be explored.

There are groups and individuals who are now applying social and cultural somatic understandings in a wide variety of settings. My colleagues and I have begun to develop a form of somatic psychodynamics that looked at personal development in embodied social/cultural terms (Grand, 2006, 2009). In this work, we attempt to describe quite precisely the bodily enactments, feelings, and responses that occur as we look together at the social representations of race, ethnicity, class, and gender. Fears, defenses, affirmations, and refusals are analyzed in terms of the cultural learning in which they arose; the emotional structures, postures, and gestures by which we learned senses of "self" and "other" have now been encoded and explored. We have developed embodied explorations of internalized racial, ethnic, and gender representations, and we also look at the creative processes of the organism by which, in interaction with the social materials given by a particular epoch, the individuals and groups shape bodily experience.

A group of African Americans called SASHA (Self Affirming Soul Healing Africans), use a social somatic approach that incorporates breathwork, and other body-oriented approaches to explore what they called the "condition of slavery" (Johns, 2008). This group found that there are various effects within the body-psyche that have emerged from generations of slavery in the United States, which include specific ways in which contemporary African Americans feel themselves, and also how they interact with both other African Americans, white Americans, and other cultures.

In related work, drama therapist Armand Volkas (Volkas, 2009; Leveton and Volkas, 2010) has brought together children of Holocaust survivors and children of German World War II parents and has worked with the bodily emotional structuring that occurs as they come together. He has also done similar work with Arab and Jewish groups, and with blacks and whites.

There are a number of other body-oriented practitioners whose work is indicative of some applications of the perspective we have been talking about. Lori Clarke (2005), in Newfoundland, employs body-based investigations as a tool to help teenagers work to understand, and undo, violence. Ilse Schmidt-Zimmermann (2003) has looked at issues of class as significant factors in the development of anorexia. Aisha Castillo (2013) writes about what she calls "the new face of oppression" in dealing with movement from a multicultural perspective; and Jolene Guilliams (2013) has written about a case in which she brought together somatic learning and multicultural family systems to deal with the psychological conflicts of a biracial woman. Keiko Lane (2010) has been working with how transgenerational cultural trauma is enacted bodily.

What we see in all these approaches is a reorientation of our ideas about the role of social and cultural environments in embodied development. In this emergent view, the development of the psyche occurs throughout the life span, is bodily based, and is continually influenced by, and interacting with, the social surround. The body creatively interacts with social institutions and images to form representations of "self" and "other" and different kinds of feelings and enactments, from which it then lives. Body-based therapies can work with these representations and enactments, thereby extending the ranges and possibilities for living in both individuals and groups.

## References

Abbey, E., & Falmagne, R. J. (2008). Modes of tension work within the complex self. *Culture and Psychology, 14(1),* 95–113.

Aktar, S. (2004). *Freud along the Ganges: Psychoanalytic reflections on the people of India.* New York: Other Press.

Banerjee, M. (1997). Peeling the onion: A multilayered view of children's emotional development. In: S. Hals (Ed.), *The development of social cognition,* (pp. 241–272). Hove, UK: Psychology Press.

Bargh, J. A. (1997). The automaticity of everyday life. In: R. S. Wyer Jr. & T. K. Srull (Eds.), *Handbook of social cognition* (2nd ed.), (pp. 1–61). Mahwah, NJ: Lawrence Erlbaum.

Castillo, A. (2013). *The new face of oppression: A discussion around racial oppression and movement.* Paper presented at Integrative Seminar, California Institute of Integral Studies, San Francisco, Sept. 2013.

Cho, G. E., Miller, P. J., Sandel, T. L., & Wang, S. (2005). What do grandmothers think about self-esteem?: American and Taiwanese folk theories revisited. *Social Development, 14(4), 701–721.*

Clarke, L. (2005). Personal communication.

Connerton, P. (1989). *How societies remember.* Cambridge, UK: Cambridge University Press.

Corwin, A. (2012). Changing God, changing bodies: The impact of new prayer practices on elderly nuns' embodied experience. *Ethos, 40(4), 390–410.*

Coughey, J. (1984). *Imagining social worlds: A cultural approach.* Lincoln: University of Nebraska Press.

D'Andrade, R., & Strauss, C. (Eds.). (1994). *Human motives and cultural models.* Cambridge, UK: Cambridge University Press.

Delamont, S., & Stephens, N. (2008). Up on the roof: The embodied habitus of diasporic capoeira. *Cultural Sociology, 2, 251–274.*

Duveen, G., & Lloyd, B. (1990). *Social representations and the development of knowledge.* Cambridge, UK: Cambridge University Press.

Eckert, P. (1989). *Jocks and burnouts.* New York: Teachers College Press.

Ewen, S. (1989). *All consuming images.* New York: Basic Books.

Farr, R., & Moscovici, S. (1984). *Social representations.* Cambridge, UK: Cambridge University Press.

Foulkes, S. H. (1964). *Therapeutic group analysis.* London: Allen & Unwin.

Gimlin, D. (2002). *Body work.* Berkeley: University of California Press.

Grand, I. J. (1998). Psyche's body: Toward a somatic psychodynamics. In: D. H. Johnson & I. J. Grand (Eds.), *The body in psychotherapy: Inquiries in Somatic Psychology* (pp. 171–194). Berkeley, CA: North Atlantic Books.

Grand, I. J. (1999). Cultural identities and practices of community. *Futures, 31(5), 475–485.*

Grand, I. J. (2006). Body, culture, and psyche: Toward an embodied socio-cultural psychotherapy. *The Journal of Biological Experience: Studies in the Life of the Body, VIII(1).*

Grand, I. J. (2009). *Qualities and configurations.* San Francisco: Author.

Guilliams, J. (2013). Paper presented at Integrative Seminar, California Institute of Integral Studies, San Francisco, Sept. 2013.

Hall, E. T. (1990). *The hidden dimension.* New York: Anchor Books.

Hanson, J. (2007). Drag kinging: Embodied acts and acts of embodiment. *Body and Society, 13(1), 61–106.*

Hassin, R. R., Uleman, J. S., & Bargh, J. A. (2005). *The new unconscious.* New York: Oxford University Press.

Hopper, E. (2003). *The social unconscious.* London: Jessica Kingsley.

Johns, T. A. (2008). *We are Self Affirming Soul Healing Africans.* San Francisco, CA: California Institute of Integral Studies.

Johnson, D. H. (1994). *Body, spirit, and democracy.* Berkeley, CA: North Atlantic Books.

Kristeva, J. (2002). *Revolt, she said* [Interview by P. Petit]. New York: Semiotext(e).

Lane, K. (2010). Personal communication.

Lave, J. (1991). Situating learning in communities of practice. In: L. B. Resnick, J. M. Levine, & S. D. Teasley (Eds.), *Perspectives in socially shared cognition.* Washington, DC: APA.

Leveton, E., & Volkas, A. (2010). Healing the wounds of history: Germans and Jews facing the legacy of the Holocaust. In: E. Leveton (Ed.), *Healing collective trauma using socio-drama and Drama Therapy.* New York: Springer.

Mauss, M. (1934/1979). Body techniques. In: B. Brewster (Trans.), *Sociology and psychology: Essays, (pp. 95–123). London: Routledge.*

Rogoff, B. (2003). *The cultural nature of human development.* New York: Oxford University Press.

Rogoff, B., Moore, L., Najafi, A. D., Correa Chavez, M. C., & Solis, J. (2005). Children's development of cultural repertoires through participation in everyday routines and practices. In: J. Grusec & P. Hasting (Eds.), *Handbook of socialization.* New York: Guilford Press.

Schmidt-Zimmerman, I. (2003). *Image and body: The limits of feasibility.* Paper presented at DGK Conference, Free University, Berlin.

Shapiro, S., & Shapiro, S. (2002). *Body movements.* Cresskill, NJ: Hampton Press.

Steele, C. M. (1997). A threat in the air: How stereotypes shape intellectual identity and performance. *American Psychologist, 52(6), 613–629.*

Volkas, A. (2009). Healing the wounds of history: Drama Therapy in collective trauma and intercultural conflict resolution. In: D. R. Johnson & R. Emunah (Eds.), *Current approaches in Drama Therapy.* Springfield, IL: Charles C. Thomas.

Wortham, S. (2006). *Learning identity: The joint emergence of social identification and academic learning.* Cambridge, UK: Cambridge University Press.

Wyer, R. S., & Srull, T. K. (Eds.). (1994). *Handbook of social cognition* (2nd ed.). Mahwah, NJ: Lawrence Erlbaum

# SECTION IV

Somatic Dimensions of Developmental Psychology

# 26
## Introduction to Section IV

Gustl Marlock, Germany, and Halko Weiss, United States

Translation by Warren Miller and Michael Soth

In their original formulation, the developmental concepts of early Depth Psychology were firmly rooted in the body. Freud's notion of the libido, and the way he described early developmental processes corresponding to the erogenous zones of the body, meant that his early theorizing relied significantly on the body, much more so than the later ego-psychological and—with the exception of Winnicott—object-relational models of psychoanalysis.

Therefore, body-based developmental theories could evolve only outside of the psychoanalytic mainstream: many of these developments happened within different aspects of Body Psychotherapy. These now form part of a pool of different theories—along with other long-underestimated perspectives, such as attachment theory (Schore, 2003a, 2003b)—from which a variety of depth-psychological groupings are striving to build a more comprehensive understanding of childhood developmental processes.

Three theoretical approaches can be considered particularly significant in connection with the Body Psychotherapeutic tradition:

First and foremost, there are the influential character-analytical theories that historically constituted—and continue to do so—the foundation of most Body Psychotherapeutic schools, building on Reich, Elsworth Baker, Lowen, Pierrakos, Kurtz, and Boadella. Stanley Keleman deserves a special mention in this context, as his theory of "emotional anatomy" formulates its particular understanding of developmental and formative processes, based more on the phenomenology of the body than most other approaches. Marianne Bentzen, who played a key role in the development of a more differentiated and complex characterology at the Bodynamic Institute in Denmark, integrates essential aspects of traditional, character-analytical, character-analytic, and somatic developmental psychology with more recent findings from neuropsychology and neuromotor research in Chapter 27, "Shapes of Experience: Neuroscience, Developmental Psychology, and Somatic Character Formation."

Next, we insert a short overview of the common typologies that were developed within this tradition, presented by Andreas Sartory (in collaboration with Gustl Marlock and Halko Weiss), as Chapter 28, "The Main Variants of Character Theory in the Field of Body Psychotherapy." However, given the very brief format in this context," this overview is restricted to fairly abstract schemas and broad outlines.

Second, there is the very complex theory of "subjective anatomy" developed by Thure von Uexküll, Marianne Fuchs, and others in the field of psychosomatic medicine. Although particularly noteworthy, it is unfortunately (so far) known mostly in German-speaking countries, and it has not been translated. It describes infantile development on the basis of functional systems: the intrauterine system, the respiratory system, the symbiotic system, and the "situational" system, which refers to the child's inner landscape. The authors refer to the increasing differentiation and complexity of human maturation as "entanglement." Those wanting to learn more about this particular theory are referred to the comprehensive (German) textbook by Uexküll and colleagues (1994).

Third, it is important to mention the influence of modern infant research, for which—interestingly—there have been forerunners in the field of Body Psychotherapy. Reich, for instance, systematically and clinically described relevant observations of infants as early as the 1940s, although his focus was largely on the bodily manifestations of desire and fear. In contrast, modern infant research is particularly interested in studying interactions within the mother-child relationship. These observations have resulted in the reformulation of theories regarding childhood development and have stimulated the theory of basic motivational systems by Joseph Lichtenberg. Here, the work of George Downing, outlined in Chapter 29, "Early Interaction and the Body: Clinical Implications," is invaluable for Body Psychotherapists. He emphasizes the nonverbal character of the early relationship, speaking of the interaction in terms of a "two-person psychology." His theory of affective-motor schemas and bodily micropractices describes the somatic equivalents of Daniel Stern's "RIGs" (Representations of Interactions that have been Generalized), while also dynamically reformulating the older, more rigid, and crude concepts of character structure. Two chapters are devoted to his contribution: Chapter 29 addresses the transfer of infant research findings into clinical practice; and Chapter 30, "Affective-Motor Schemata" by Andreas Wehowsky, comprehensively discusses and appreciates Downing's theory.

Quite early on, the main Body Psychotherapeutic tradition engaged with those particular branches of modern psychodynamic psychology that—building on work by Otto Rank—explore the significance of the actual birth experience. Such very early experiences can be seen to manifest themselves in regressive, body-based therapy, whether this is conceptualized as "body memory" (as it is commonly called) or as the—clinically observable— capacity to reconstruct the birth experience via association, or to allow its reenactment. Over the last few decades, these two traditions have cross-fertilized and enriched each other theoretically as well as methodically. This is exemplified by David Boadella, who was influenced by Francis Mott (as well as by Reich, Keleman, and Frank Lake): Boadella formulated fundamental therapeutic principles—such as "facing," "grounding," and "centering"—in reference to the embryological germ cell layers (ectoderm, mesoderm, and endoderm) that are the first stages of differentiated fetal development.

Many methods of therapeutic work with prenatal and perinatal experiences, going back to Frank Lake (1966), are based on body processes and reenactments. They are being taught in the context of Body Psychotherapeutic or integrative trainings, more so than in the psychoanalytic tradition. More recently, the philosophical emphasis on "spheres" and birth, developed by the German philosopher Peter Sloterdijk (2011), and echoing contributions by Rank and Graber, had a significant influence on the evolving theory of Unitive Psychology.

In Chapter 31, "Prenatal and Perinatal Psychology: Vital Foundations of Body Psychotherapy," Marti Glenn illuminates how a perspective that reaches back into the fundamental realms of experience can be significant for modern psychodynamic psychotherapy, and especially Body Psychotherapy. Her authority, with regard to this field, is quite paramount in the United States, because she founded and directed the Santa Barbara Graduate Institute that, for a short while, offered master's and PhD courses in this discipline. She further illustrates how prenatal and perinatal therapeutic work, with its respective elemental patternings, is inseparably tied into the development of the body.

In Chapter 32, "Multiple Levels of Meaning-Making: The First Principles of Changing Meanings in Development and Therapy" by Ed Tronick and Bruce Perry, we find that, as Mezirow states: "A defining condition of being human is that we have to understand the meaning of our experience" (Mezirow, 1995, p. 5). Indeed, they state that the failure to make "meaning" becomes a psychic catastrophe: and that meaning-making is a series of psycho-biological processes that involve not only the brain but all the other somatic systems within the body, which go to generate a set of implicit meanings and memories that shape our ways of being—and understanding—in the world.

Susan Aposhyan, previously the director of another academic Body Psychotherapy (Somatic Psychology) program, at Naropa University in Boulder, Colorado, explores the genetic templates of movement, developed from Bonnie Bainbridge Cohen's Body-Mind Centering in Chapter 33, "Pattern and Plasticity: Utilizing Early Motor Development as a Tool for Therapeutic Change."

In Chapter 34, "Attachment Theory and Body Psychotherapy: Embodiment and Motivation," Mark Ludwig, former director of the Somatic Psychology master's program at John F. Kennedy University in Berkeley, California, and now based in the California Institute of Integral Studies in San Francisco, discusses the parallel development of these two traditions, especially regarding the long-standing background controversy between classical psychoanalytic drive theory and object-relations theory—i.e., between theories postulating internal conflict with instinctual drives versus those that emphasize object-seeking attachment needs and relational experiences. Lowen's and Pierrakos's revisions of Reich's developmental theories complement the research on infant attachment and bonding that was initiated by John Bowlby (1999).

Each era of therapeutic thought revolves around central, at times also fashionable, motifs. One that is currently in the foreground is the developmental-psychological significance of early relationships. From a Body Psychotherapeutic perspective, it is important to note that—aside from the communicative competencies that are described by infant researchers—bodily, motor competencies of the infant also play a large role in the development of a sense of agency and autonomy.

Finally, Ute-Christiane Bräuer discusses this topic in Chapter 35, "The Development of Autonomy from a Body Psychotherapy Perspective," in reference to two successful traditions of Body-Oriented Developmental Psychology: the work of Bernard Aucouturier (2005), which influenced the French psycho-motoric tradition; and the almost-forgotten work of the Hungarian psychoanalyst and child therapist Emmi Pikler. Over the course of several decades, Pikler, at the Lóczy orphanage in Budapest, offered children optimal support through an educational approach based primarily on what she called "free motoric development."

## References

Aucouturier, B. (2005). *Le Méthode Aucouturier: Fantasmes d'action et practique psychomotrice* [The Aucouturier Method: Action fantasies and practical Psycho-motorics]. Louvain, Belgium: De Boeck.

Bowlby, J. (1999). *Attachment: Attachment and loss* (Vol. 1) (2nd ed.). New York: Basic Books.

Lake, F. (1966). *Clinical theology: A theological and psychiatric basis for clinical pastoral care.* London: Dartman, Longman & Todd.

Mezirow, J. (1995). Transformation theory of adult learning. In: M. R. Welton (Ed.), *In Defense of the Lifeworld*, (pp. 39–70). New York: SUNY Press.

Schore, A. N. (2003a). *Affect dysregulation and disorders of the self.* New York: W. W. Norton.

Schore, A. N. (2003b). *Affect regulation and the repair of the self.* New York: W. W. Norton.

Sloterdijk, P. (2011). *Bubbles: Spheres: Vol. I: Microspherology* (Wieland Hoban, Trans.). Cambridge, MA: MIT Press.

Uexküll, T., Fuchs, M., Müller-Braunschweig, H., & Johnen, R. (1994). *Subjektive Anatomie* [Subjective anatomy]. Stuttgart: Schattauer.

# 27

## Shapes of Experience

*Neuroscience, Developmental Psychology, and Somatic Character Formation*

**Marianne Bentzen, Denmark**[33]

**Marianne Bentzen** is a co-founder of Bodynamic Analysis and the Bodynamic Institute in Copenhagen, which have gained an international reputation for their specific and differentiated concepts on Somatic Developmental Psychology. She comes from a background as a psycho-motor therapist, with further training in the tradition of Biosynthesis (Boadella), Somatic Experiencing (Levine), Systems-Centered Training (Agazarian), meditation, and interpersonal neurobiology. After retiring from her position in the faculty of the Bodynamic Institute, where she also served as training director for thirteen years, she has co-founded, with psychologist Susan Hart, a developmental neuroaffective approach to psychotherapy. She currently has a private practice and conducts trainings independently in Scandinavia and Europe.

Bentzen has presented her work at numerous European universities and in psychiatric hospitals, has published a series of scientific papers, has written several chapters in books, and has co-authored at least one book in Danish. She is a member of the psychotherapy association of Denmark, and was the chairperson of the ethics committee of the European Association for Body Psychotherapy for several years.

> *I am not saying that the mind is in the body. I am saying that the body contributes more than life support and modulatory effects to the brain. It contributes a content that is part and parcel of the working mind.*
>
> —**Damasio (1994, p. 226)**

This chapter compares findings in developmental neuroscience and infant research, from children from birth to two years old, with five basic somatic character structures derived from the slightly varied descriptions of development in three different somatic character systems: Bioenergetics, Hakomi, and Bodynamics. These comparisons show: (1) a strong correspondence between neuroaffective development, posture, and behavior of misregulated children, and the somatic character structures for which that age is considered a formative stage; and (2) that the developmental stages, traditionally described as oral, anal, and oedipal, are—contrary to current characterological thinking—usually activated before the child is two years old.[34]

---

[33] **Editors' Note:** This chapter is one of the first comprehensive attempts to tie recent findings from neuroaffective and neuromotor child development research into Body Psychotherapy, informed by Developmental Psychology, as developed foremost by Reich and Lowen. Bentzen illustrates how "dysregulation" in early developmental phases may affect the ensuing maturational process. She also relates the neuropsychology of child development to structures of somatic formation and to a theory on behavioral patterns that was conceptualized within the framework of Body Psychotherapeutic characterology.

[34] Although these structures obviously exist in both genders, only the male pronouns are used in this chapter, for simplicity of language: "he" instead of "he or she" or "s/he," "his" instead of "his or her," etc.

## Introduction

Like traditional character-analytical theories, most theories about somatic character rest on Developmental Psychology. They posit that, with the formation of emotional and psychological patterns, there is a formation of motor habits and "energy" patterns in the body that develop according to key interactive patterns throughout childhood. Body Psychotherapists assume that central parts of the personal narrative are accessible only in the inner sensory field, and that they are existentially grounded in the person's motor patterns and habits.

A widespread misunderstanding about somatic character theory is the belief that it claims that body structure creates personality. The true theoretical foundation of somatic character development is that experience shapes the body, as well as the psyche, in coherent and characteristic ways. Put differently, all experience has somatic components that shape neuroaffective habits, whereas experience and affect both shape neuromotor habits.

In Somatic Psychotherapy, the body is considered to be an essential part of the story of the psyche, but definitely not the whole story. In reading the somatic character structure in the adult or in the older child, the therapist is reading stages of affect and affect regulation, visible in the motor system, and is "reasoning backward" from there. If a person is showing postures, movements, and gestures typical of a certain developmental age and interaction, the therapist assumes that corresponding states of neurological activity, self-representations, and affect (psycho-social character) are present to some degree or other (Bernhardt, Bentzen, and Isaacs, 1996). As in the usual psychodynamic approach, the therapist relies on the verbal narrative of the client to flesh out the story of the postural habits he is seeing. Reich said that character is frozen history. Perry and colleagues (1995) state, "*Experience can change the mature brain—but experience during the critical periods of early childhood organizes brain systems!*" (The original was in capitals and italics!)

Somatic character theories view a specific character structure as shaped both at the *age* at which a certain neurological and interactional maturity develops, and also by those earlier and later experiences—including current lifestyle—that resonate with *theme* and *level of processing and interaction* inherent to that maturity. Any individual with normal levels of brain function will thus show elements of all the character structures.

## Formative Factors in Character Formation

In recent decades of developmental research and brain research, there has been a great deal of scientific inquiry into the formative dynamics of the personality. Geneticists and developmental researchers alike agree that virtually all psychological and physiological traits develop out of an intimate interplay between genetic predisposition and environmental influence (Perry, 2002; Ridley, 2003; Rutter, 2006; Cuhna and Heckman, 2010; Tabery and Griffiths, 2010). Inborn temperament can be tested in early infancy, shows stability (Chess and Thomas, 1996; Kagan, Snidman, Kahn, and Towsley, 2007), and is shaped by the quality and availability of the intersubjective field, that sense of shared presence between infant and caregiver (Thelen and Smith, 1994; Aitken and Trevarthen, 1997; Beebe and Lachmann, 2002; Stern, 1995, 2004; Gerhardt, 2004; Hart, 2011). We need the loving attention of another to become a self.

Three mental states (Stern, 1995, 2004) are considered central to good intersubjective attunement: shared attention, shared intention, and the ability to participate in the affective states of another. Attunement is a delicate process consisting of thousands of daily, tiny, interlocking dance movements, in which, in the healthy parent-child relationship, the synchrony of misattunements occurs dozens or hundreds of times each day (Tronick and Gianino, 1986; Tronick and Weinberg, 1997). However, misattunements on average last only two seconds, because both the parent and the child have a biological desire to reattune. Research indicates that it is the repair through somatic resynchronization rather than the absence of misattunement that develops basic trust and healthy maturation (Trevarthen, 1979, 1990, 1993a, 1993b). Pervasive or unrepaired misattunements may be caused simply by lack of sufficient attunement capacity in the caregiver, perhaps caused by underlying stressors, as well as by specific traumatic events. Character defenses develop from ingrained habits, because infants, for better or worse, easily identify and prefer the interaction patterns they are used to (Sander, 1977, 1983, 1987, 1988; Bentzen, Jarlnaes, and Levine, 2004; Hart, 2011). Fortunately, the dance of microattunement through somatic mirroring allows the child to directly absorb and identify positive inner states of the caregiver, as well as negative (Stern, 1995).

The neural mirror systems are a complex brain network of neurons that allow humans to experience the intention movements and feeling states of others as their own. Mirror-system activation is essential to empathic capacity, and is activated by seeing, hearing, or even reading about the movements and feelings of others, or even by experiencing the touch of others (Gallese, Fadiga, Fogassi, and Rizzolatti, 1996; Gallese and Goldman, 1998; Gallese, 2001; Keysers, 2011). Infants are born with a rudimentary capacity to mirror, but it can fail to develop if it is not engaged by the mirroring of the caregiver (Perry and Slavavitz, 2007). In children as well as adults, mirror activity in the brain is weakened or deactivated by stress. Mirroring is also affected by power relationships (Hogeveen, Inzlicht, and Obhi, 2014). In interactions with attention to one person having power over another, the empowered person responds with reduced empathy and mirror activity in the brain, while the weaker person responds with increased mirror activity.

Specific traumatic events are perhaps the most commonly considered reason for personality problems. However, according to developmental research, it is primarily the millions of microinteractions, beginning before birth and continuing throughout life, that create the very experience of our being in the world; and the thousands of microattunements with a caring therapist that can later improve one's self-sense in therapy (Stern, 2004).

Finally, different stages of development offer different themes and challenges to the child and the parent (Hart, 2011; Hart and Bentzen, 2012). The parent-child microinteractions during these different stages will shape somatic character through the interaction and psycho-motor skills that the child is developing at the time. Traditionally, the character structures are seen to develop during the first six years or so of life. However, while writing this chapter, I found to my considerable surprise that in terms of neuroaffective development, the core issues of all five character structures are activated during the first twenty-four months of life.

## Three Systems of Somatic Developmental Character Structure

There are many different systems of somatic character: Reich (1949) began to work with the body in the 1930s, and developed the first systematic method of psychodynamic somatic character structure. All later schools have built on, or been influenced by, his concepts. In the following, I will use just three systems that are organized primarily from a developmental understanding, and that are also currently taught in trainings in Europe and North America. All three systems are still refining and changing their theories (and there are, of course, many more other Body Psychotherapeutic modalities, also in processes of develoment and change):

- **Bioenergetic Analysis** (henceforth called Bioenergetics) is directly descended from Reich's work. Lowen's first popular book about character, *The Language of the Body,* was published in 1958. Most other somatic character systems have been strongly influenced by this system, and (for the reader from a nonsomatic background) the relationship to traditional psychoanalytic character structure is fairly obvious. Over the intervening years, however, this system has abandoned psycho-sexual charge as the central concept and has embraced attachment theory, with flow and muscular blocking seen as a response to developmental thwarting.
- **Hakomi** was developed by Kurtz and his staff in the mid-1970s. It introduces the idea that character traits may be seen as "overdeveloped" skills, as well as traumatic regressions. It focuses on development as the learning processes of a self-organizing

body-mind system, which requires certain healthy experiences to mature optimally. Character formation may then be understood as constructive attempts to cope with unhealthy formative interactions. Hakomi thus emphasizes more positive aspects of character.

- **Bodynamic Analysis** (henceforth called Bodynamics) originally developed out of a northern European tradition of psycho-motor developmental awareness work. During the 1980s, Marcher (Marcher and Fich, 2010) and her colleagues combined psycho-motor development with Bioenergetic character theory and developed a model based on motor and psychological child development, and a corresponding theory of specific muscle activation. "Mutual connection" is seen as the basic drive, rather than sexuality. The response of the environment to this basic drive determines whether healthy or unhealthy character develops.

There is a great deal of overlap between these three character models, and each also has concepts that are unique to themselves. Because this chapter functions as a brief introduction to somatic character, the main focus will be on areas of general agreement and some basic body concepts, rather than on details and differences between the systems. Unfortunately, this means that I will not devote any space to the healthy character, which is a strong focus in both Hakomi and Bodynamics. I will outline five structures described by all three systems:

I. Schizoid (hysteric)
II. Oral
III. Psychopathic
IV. Masochistic
V. Rigid (phallic and hysteric)

Although there is widespread dissatisfaction with these pathological labels, I will use them in this chapter because there are no other universally known "tags" for these somatic character structure types. All three systems present two structures at some or all character levels, such as early and late, or compensated and oral. Bodynamics, inspired by the earlier work of Johnsen (1976) on developmental resources, defenses, and resignation in the body, has two positions at each developmental stage: an early, more resigned, and posturally collapsed one, and a late, more controlled, and posturally tense one. However, all three systems use the general postural concepts of collapse and flaccidity as well as the concepts of muscular tension and character-armoring.

In this chapter, I will outline the following points for each of the five character structures: core elements of neuroaffective development and formative age, clinical descriptions and studies of children, and somatic character structures. Because the formative stages are not mutually exclusive, most people have a mixture of several character structures, though one or two often predominate.

## I. Prenatal and Neonatal Development: The Autonomic Nervous System, Early Infant Contact Disturbances, and Schizoid-Hysteric Traits

Stephen Porges (1997) describes three phylogenetic stages of neural development in the autonomic nervous system and three corresponding levels of emotive and interactive behaviors. The autonomic nervous system is the part of the brain that matures first. The first two aspects of the autonomic nervous system are active at birth, and the third matures during the first six weeks after birth.

The first stage is the primitive, "*unmyelinated vagal parasympathetic*" system, which activates digestion and responds to novelty or threat with a reduction of metabolic output and immobilization (freezing). The second stage is the "*spinal sympathetic*" nervous system, which can increase metabolic output and inhibit the action of the primitive vagal system on the intestine, allowing "fight-or-flight" behaviors to emerge. The third stage is the "*myelinated vagal parasympathetic*" system, uniquely mammalian, which can regulate metabolism to allow fine-tuned engagement and disengagement with the surroundings. It controls facial expressions, sucking, swallowing, breathing, and vocalization. It also inhibits the sympathetic action on the heart, supporting calm behavior and pleasurable interaction.

The myelinated, social vagal system is active under conditions of normal interaction—for instance, when the baby smiles, gurgles, and makes different noises to invite food, sleep, or play. When the child is stressed, this organization gives way to the phylogenetically earlier "fight-or-flight" system. In the infant, this first means crying, and increased startle and gripping reflexes. With more intense activation, the infant screams while flailing and twisting in an increasingly disorganized manner. Finally, if there are no outlets for fight-or-flight responses, the most primitive system and the dissociative parasympathetic coping strategy become dominant: the infant withdraws, becomes passive and quiet or immobile, and shows little or no interest in contact or food.

According to Perry and colleagues (1995), the infant has two separate reaction patterns to severe stress. Perry's descriptions correspond to Porges's levels of activation. The first is a sympathetic arousal state, and the second is a parasympathetic dissociative state. When the infant is frightened, his heart rate and breathing increase, his blood pressure goes up, he becomes alert, and he cries. This is essentially the "fight-or-flight" response, Porges's second phylogenetic stage of arousal. If the arousal state of the infant is not regulated, after a while he will dissociate, withdraw from external stimuli, and become extremely passive. The intense sympathetic activation is still present, but the parasympathetic inhibition overrides it. This is the action of the first phylogenetic stage of the polyvagal system. The infant is in a state of highly activated, frightened helplessness and resignation.

Brodén (2000), director of a treatment facility for disturbed infants in Sweden, describes the traits and attachment styles of infants with ongoing unregulated stress. Following the attachment research of Ainsworth and others, she describes children in three states: "overpassive," "overactive," and "stable." Brodén states that the typical "overpassive" infant in her practice (corresponding to the parasympathetic, dissociative state and the schizoid structure) does not fuss, rarely invites contact, and seems content when left to his own devices. He is disinterested in food and pleasurable activities, but likes to spend time alone in bed. He is slow to engage, and rarely smiles. Even when staff members pick up this child for a cuddle, they usually put him down again quickly because he has no "molding behavior." He doesn't cuddle up to the body of the adult, and this makes him seem to reject the physical contact. He does not have the spontaneous somatic responses that make contact rewarding for others, so they often disengage after attempting a few times to elicit some form of welcome. Brodén emphasizes that she is describing contact-disturbed infants, and not autistic ones.

The "stable" children, in Brodén's practice, are managing conditions of insufficient nurturing very well. Their biological functions and rhythms are simple and stable; they are easy to feed and get to sleep; and they adapt well to changes. They are described as actively "helping" their mothers with their overexpressive signals, frequent smiles, and generally positive response. Deprived of sufficient maternal response, they readily turn to others and greedily absorb contact and nurture. The motor patterns of these infants are staccato and uncoordinated. Deprived of maternal holding, Brodén reasons, they "hold" themselves with strong tensions in their back, shoulders, and neck. The staff has nicknamed them "swan-neck children" because of their long necks and tendency to hold the head stiffly. These "stable" children have trouble relaxing into holding and contact, and instead seem to stay "on alert" and to take an unreasonable amount of responsibility for the contact, particularly for eye contact. In terms of physiological activation, these infants show a fairly high level of sympathetic arousal, but still organized in contact strategies.

Brodén's "overactive" infants have extreme and diffuse movement patterns, and may even seem spastic. Their facial expressions are worried and guarded. They actively resist body contact and eye contact, and their general activity level is very high and avoidant. They seem generally unsatisfied, and often go into incomprehensible states of crying and screaming. They are easily frustrated and upset, and difficult to calm. It is difficult for them to wait for food, and meals are like battlegrounds. When fed, they are often so upset that they have trouble settling into eating, and then quickly tire. Often they gulp their food and then throw up after eating. The infants' biological rhythms are very irregular, and they are easily disturbed and upset. These infants live at the physiological level of disorganized sympathetic activation and fight-or-flight response.

Bioenergetics describes the developmental stages as having a "hierarchy of needs," not unlike Maslow's self-actualization pyramid. The basic need during intrauterine and early postnatal existence is the "right to exist"—which is internalized through being welcomed (Lowen, 1958; MacIntyre and Mullins, 1976; Ingen-Housz, 2003). Because the infant is completely dependent on parental figures for emotional as well as physical nurture, other schools emphasize that this right has meaning only when described as a "right to exist" and "to belong with someone." When this right is threatened, schizoid or hysteric character elements result. Both respond to a "threat of annihilation"; but, whereas the schizoid structure emerges from ongoing hostility, coldness, or abandonment, the hysteric structure is generally understood as an adaptation to sudden, less constant, traumatic events. These distinctions correspond well to Porges's and Perry's assertions that the infant first reacts to stress with sympathetic fight-or-flight arousal, and withdraws into parasympathetic dissociation only when the threat is perceived as being more constant.

The prenatal and neonatal infant has no sense of a separate self, and is completely dependent on his caregiver for basic modulation of arousal. If he is frequently abandoned, or treated with hostility, he habituates to a constant level of fear and distress as his "normal" resting state. This is thought to be the most common formative dynamic of the schizoid character pattern. Isolation impacts the emerging self-regulation, and if the infant's experience is not offset, the later formation of internalized objects of self and others will be hostile and depersonalized. Adults with schizoid traits describe their inner experience of their self as alien, disconnected, fragmented, and deadened. The person is identified primarily with the mind and often distrusts and dislikes the body and its unruly feelings. The social world and other people are felt to be alien, stressful, or innately hostile. As Lake (1966) puts it, "Saying good-bye is like getting a new lease on life." If this person suddenly gets in touch with excitement and feelings, he may not be able to regulate them. These states then become synonymous with intolerable levels of arousal, terror, rage, destruction, and/or pain. Under extreme stress, he may dissociate further into flares of rage or terror.

The schizoid posture is characterized by deep holding patterns in the core of the body, and a habituated parasympathetic dissociative activation that leaves the skin and the extremities cold. Movements are often stiff and clumsy, and there is little spontaneous movement. Even when he is trained in athletics or dance, his movements are outer-directed (which corresponds to later cortical control patterns) rather than inner-directed (corresponding to early neuromotor integration). His breathing is shallow, and the general physical impression is of a person who has withdrawn as far as possible from aliveness. Like Brodén's "overpassive" infant, the schizoid structure does not know how to shape himself to touch and physical contact, and his body seems unresponsive to closeness. He often avoids mutual eye contact. Even when he does meet the eyes of another, his gaze seems unfocused, and the other has no feeling of an emotional or contactful meeting.

Reich viewed the schizoid character structure as having a primary blocking around the eyes and in the suboccipital orienting muscles of the neck. Their body is characterized by deep, "frozen" holding patterns in and around the joints, twists and significant differences of organization between their right and left side, as well as between different parts of the body. The description of this somatic pattern has elements of the disorganized flailing of the infant in severe sympathetic distress frozen in a matrix of dissociated primitive parasympathetic inhibition. Often the basic autonomic rhythms are in disarray: sleep patterns are fragile, digestion may be too rapid, the person is hypersensitive or numb to sensations and external stimuli, and a complaint of constant loose stools or incontinence is often heard.

**Schizoid Somatic Pattern**

*The schizoid structure is shaped by threat of annihilation. (Bioenergetics)*

Formative age: second trimester to three months (Bodynamics). Also called the "tactile" or "ocular" stage of development in other systems. This infant (Figure 27.1) was born five weeks early, and shows some very early neurosomatic organization, governed by the unmyelinated parasympathetic vagus. He has some muscle tone and beginning reflexes, which make him flex his legs and fingers and turn his head, tilting it a bit backward.

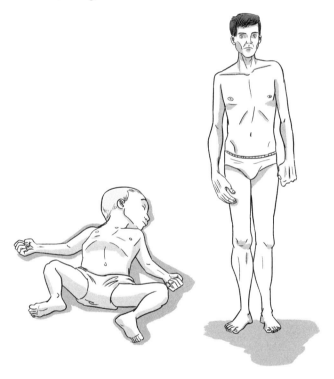

Figures 27.1 and 27.2. Drawings sketched from photos in Bentzen (1963) and Hviid (1992)

This man has been asked to stand straight (Figure 27.2). His posture shows the asymmetry and twists of the schizoid pattern. There is little evenness between the right side and the left side of the body. The arms and legs are stiff and have little charge. His gaze seems unfocused and distant. The main aliveness is deep in the torso and in the head. He seems to have little natural muscle tone. In somatic character reading, this posture translates into: holding together against fragmentation, and contraction toward the body core and into the head. The posture shows strong tension at the base of the skull, corresponding to the activation of the earliest startle and orienting reflexes.

Some character structures are described in similar ways in different systems but assigned to different developmental stages. Most notable is perhaps the *hysteric,* which Bioenergetics and Hakomi describe as a "genital" or "oedipal" structure. Bodynamics sees the hysteric as part of the schizoid or existence structure, a result of the "schizoid-hysteric split" first described by Lake in 1966. Boadella (1986) considered the schizoid versus the oedipal theory of the hysteric structure and pointed out that an infant who feels compelled to fling himself into contact for dear life is quite likely to expand his survival strategies with flirtatious and seductive behavior when he or she reaches the oedipal stage. The two explanations can then be understood as complementary, rather than mutually exclusive.

When deeply frightened, an infant will flail, scream, and "try to grab" his parent with his eyes and intensified gripping reflexes. If this feeling of threat and coping strategy is internalized as a representation of being in the world, the adult is likely to feel threatened by fairly small separations and upsets. He will respond with strong contact-hunger, emotion, and excitement in an attempt to get the interpersonal closeness that will help him feel less threatened. This is the inner landscape of the adult hysteric structure: "Saying good-bye is like dying" (Lake, 1966). The primary identification is with emotions, relationships, and the body. Often the person distrusts the mind and its silent machinations.

According to Lake, it is only when the threat becomes pervasive and seemingly unending, giving a sense of "no way out," that the individual will withdraw into himself and into the state of the schizoid structure described above.

Bodynamics describes the adult hysteric (emotional existence) structure as "looking as if he has a small head," and Hakomi (Ogden, 1985) describes the schizoid as having a long neck. Johnsen and Bodynamics find that the early gripping reflexes in the hands and feet as well as early neck reflexes are often also present. As in the schizoid, the body characteristics of this structure are fragmented, but more symmetrical. Joints are typically overly flexible rather than stiff. There are lots of facial animation, expressive body movements, and lots of emotion.

Several somatic systems warn that this structure can be incorrectly assessed as healthy in traditions that rely heavily on encounter, contact intensity, and emotional catharsis, all central elements of the defense pattern of the hysteric structure.

The "overactive" infant, described by Brodén (2000), has no direct counterpart in the developmental somatic character systems. Lake, however, describes the schizoid-hysteric condition as a split branch, in which a person "flips" between the two stress responses of sympathetic and parasympathetic override. Both the schizoid and the hysteric structures can have elements of the overactive pattern. The hysteric generally lives in a continuum that stretches from a sympathetically charged, survival-motivated socialization to a desperately or chaotically agitated sympathetic fight-or-flight arousal with sudden dissociated pockets. The schizoid generally lives in a continuum that begins in the dissociated parasympathetic state and may be overridden by the chaotically agitated sympathetic fight-or-flight state under extreme stress. If the person has more contact-seeking characteristics, he will generally be assessed as more hysteric, whereas the contact-avoidant individual will be assessed as more schizoid.

## II. The First Year: The Maturation of the Limbic System; "Schemas of Being With"; and the Oral-Depressive and Oral-Paranoid Structures

In terms of neurological development, the first year is characterized by explosive neuronal growth. This growth is intimately shaped by the specific life conditions and interactions in the infant's new social environment. The primitive brainstem structures are already functioning, and the mammalian vagal system will mature during the first several weeks. At around six weeks, the infant is capable of interactive facial and eye expressions, which makes mutual gaze interactions possible. The amygdala, a part of the limbic system that is already active at birth, gives the infant the capacity to have emotional experiences linked to external events. Although the amygdala is known for its function in *aversive* conditioning, this ability only matures some time after birth. This maturational difference permits early attachment, regardless of parental behavior (Schore, 1994). Until the capacity for aversive learning has matured, the infant will continue to turn toward an insufficient or abusive caregiver, but will respond with stress and fear while doing so (Sullivan et al., 2001).

The amygdala is central to forming emotional memories: Damasio (1994) and LeDoux (1989, 1996, 2002) point out that it receives input from many other brain structures. During the first year, the amygdala ripens to be able to process and coordinate sensory and kinesthetic information and emotive response (later in life, it also assesses information from higher cortical areas of the brain, allowing more considered responses).

The brain areas involved in the mirror-neuron network also mature during the first year. In the first two months of life, exact mirroring and simple rhythmic attunement are central to interaction. After two months, the empathic information from the mirror system allows the infant and caregiver to establish complex interactions (Trevarthen, 1993a, 1993b; Tronick and Weinberg, 1997), as the implicit mirroring allows a growing feeling of each other's intentions and inner states (Keysers, 2011). In the process of developing intersubjectivity, sense of self, and belonging, play activities are enormously important. There is a specific brain network involving areas of the limbic brain (Panksepp and Biven, 2012), and play activities begin in the first few months of life with exciting coordinated psycho-motor interaction games with the caregiver, such as playful tickling and "I'm coming to *get* you!" Later, the child graduates to rough-and-tumble play with the caregiver, and later again to peer play and role-play. This has led Panksepp (Ibid.) to wonder why play activity, with its strong anxiety- and depression-reducing properties, is so underutilized in psychotherapy.

The orbitofrontal cortex undergoes rapid maturation from around eight to eighteen months (Schore, 1994), and is central to the ability to form attachments and relate in meaningful sequences. This part of the brain handles emotional evaluation. Positioned between the limbic system and the frontal cortex, it is central to the capacity for self-regulation of affect, and the regulation of the autonomic nervous system, while also forming the basis of cognitive assessments. The inner state of caregiving strongly activates the fronto-limbic cortex in the caregiver. In the infant, the orbitofrontal cortex is strongly involved in the internalization of love and safe caring.

A number of motor skills are central in the development of the infant during the first year. In the earliest months, the coordination of sucking and swallowing is established, as well as that of eyes, neck, and facial expression. These abilities are crucial to the infant's contact with his mother and to his ability to follow her with his eyes. He is also exploring the rest of his visual world, and, as voluntary reaching, gripping, and handling overrides his inborn gripping reflex, he can reach for and handle the things he sees. Letting go is more difficult, and is learned between the fifth and twelfth month. Around six to eight months, after some intensive training sessions of simultaneously lifting arms, legs, and head while belly-down on the floor, the infant's spine strengthens to the point that he can actually sit up straight. This heralds the beginning of rolling, scooting, and creeping, which quickly give way to crawling, standing, and walking with hand support as his legs begin to hold his weight and their coordination improves. He launches into exploring the world, his capacity to handle arousal grows, and his needs differentiate. The loving, regulating, and encouraging caregiver shapes the emotional tone of the sense of self that he develops during these processes.

Stern (1995, 1977/2002) has studied mother-infant interactions during these crucial months. His phrase "schemas of ways of being with" is a term for the internalization of early contact experiences. He describes the following interaction as typical of an infant with a passively depressed mother, not an agitated or anxious one—one who has become so after the infant has some experience of normal behavior and developed some schemas for it.

The infant attempts to engage and "reanimate" the mother, but is unsuccessful. He then responds with resonant affect and motor changes: his posture deflates, his positive feelings drop, and his face falls. Stern describes this as a "microdepression." He makes the point that this microdepression is not only a response to lack of stimulation, but an imitative, resonant, or contagious process. At the neuroaffective level, this is an example of an emotional transmission through neurological mirroring, creating "limbic resonance."

"The two phenomena—being with via identification and imitation, and the experience of depression—become linked in a single moment of subjective experience" (Stern, 1995, p. 101). When this happens repeatedly, the infant establishes a schema of being with Mother, a norm, in which he imitates more and loses self-agency, as well as positive affect and motor competency.

Stern then goes on to describe a condition he has investigated in adults: that once this schema is in place, the desire to be with someone will in itself trigger the microdepression. Stern repeatedly and decisively points out that the infant is not a telepath, and that he cannot know the mother's fantasy world. What he *can* know is how she is responding to him. This he knows intimately and minutely in the delicate dance that they share. Stern here mentions the difficulty of having an observer correct a poorly attuned mother in this attunement process. Corrections make her self-conscious and awkward, and the dance is lost, with mother and child still struggling.

During the first six months of life, the infant is interested primarily in dyadic contact, and develops "schemas" for all his family members, as well as for the recurring events in his life and their variations. In the second half of the first year, the infant's ability to handle excitement grows enormously. His grasp of his inner and outer world is becoming increasingly differentiated and complex. At around six months, his interest turns toward the object world, and the role of his mother changes from primary focus to one point in a triangle: the triangle of mother, infant, and the plaything or the other person currently under investigation; both this triangle and the differentiation require much greater flexibility and maturity from the mother. Her baby needs her to read and care for his differentiating needs and feelings correctly, to be in affective visual contact when needed, and to be both a safe companion and a delighted supporter of his exploration of the outer world.

In the "hierarchy of needs" for the growing child, Bioenergetics suggests that the issue in the first year of life is the right to have needs, to differentiate them, and to be loved as a separate being. The formative dynamic of the "oral" character structure is thought to be lack of early interpersonal nourishment and support or, less commonly, deprivation of physical nourishment. The mother is seen as either unavailable, weak, depressed, ill, or resentful of the differentiating needs of the child. As inchoate inner needs emerge and are not mirrored or responded to, the child collapses into a state of helplessness and resignation. This experience is internalized as a self-representation of being infinitely needy and unfulfilled in a world with no gratification available.

The early, depressed structure is often described as needy, compliant, dependent, overly verbal and helpless. He is seen as sucking others' energy. The dynamic of "trying to get mother to react right" and the microdepression following failure is also described in the oral patterns. With pleasant invitation and compliance, the adult tries to get the desired closeness in his relationship to intimates or to a therapist. However, his attempts are colored with resignation, as if he "expects a no." Sørensen (1996), chief psychologist of a Danish psychiatric ward, describes the early oral structure as always ready to engage, if there is a chance of contact (p. 188) and grateful to get what he can, but without the kinesthetic sense of self needed to discern the quality of the interaction, or whether it matches his needs. This is partly because he fails to recognize what he is getting while he gets it, and partly because his containment and object constancy is poor—he quickly loses the feeling of being full and satisfied.

Bioenergetics, Bodynamics, and Hakomi all describe similar postures in the oral stage. Both early and late "oral" character types have a collapsed "S"-shaped spine, sunken chest, head held forward, and weak legs with locked knees. This description of low energy and motor passivity corresponds well to Stern's description of the infant in microdepression.

The flaccid belly protrudes like a "half-filled sack" (Lowen, 1958). The early oral structure is described as having a weak, longing gaze and soft, inviting lips, whereas the late oral structure is described as having a more aggressive, suspicious expression, and either pouting mouth or clenched jaws. The energy flow is described as weak in the whole body, especially in the arms and legs. The strongest and most contactful energy is in and around the mouth and eyes. These physical characteristics correspond to specific levels of neuromotor maturity. Before six months or so, the baby's deep intrinsic spinal muscles and muscles of the torso cannot yet hold him upright in the sitting position for any length of time. The same muscle groups seem unable to hold the adult oral structure in a wholesome, erect standing or sitting posture. In the infant, the neck muscles and the eye-head coordination have matured in the first couple of months. Correspondingly, the adult in the oral structure uses his neck and head position to compensate for the weak postural capacity of the torso.

The dissatisfaction in the late oral structure is understood to correspond to the infant's unhappiness with having his increasingly differentiated needs and feelings incorrectly "read" and responded to by the caregiver. A dissatisfaction of this rather sophisticated nature is generally predated by a better "match" or "reading" at the earlier, less complex stages of interaction. The adult late oral structure distrusts the authenticity or validity of what is given, and expects it to be withdrawn without notice. This thwarts his deep desire for closeness and exciting interaction. Hakomi (Weiss, 2003) states that this structure had enough determination and strength to erase totally the option of support, and instead rely on itself: "I will not expose myself to that yearning ever again and be in pain forever."

Another effect of incorrect reading by the regulating caregiver is incorrect identification of one's own needs and feelings. The infant develops schemata of "being with" through resonance and interactive response. Schemata based on incorrect mirroring will not satisfy him, nor will they sufficiently regulate or mature his affective state or his interactions.

In the adult interaction, the late oral structure has a set idea of what he needs and should have, complete with the frustration of not getting it right, based on his incorrect schema. This means that attempts to satisfy him usually fail partially or completely. He then either fumes silently, because he does not trust anything that is not spontaneously given, or he impatiently tries to "correct" the other until he gets exactly what he wants. In both these scenarios, sensitive two-way attunement and discovery of how to match the inner state with the "right next action" are lost. As in Stern's corrections to the misattuned mothers, the dance is lost, he cannot find his way to it, and his attempts to find it push it further away.

**Oral Somatic Pattern**

> *The oral structure is shaped by threat of abandonment. (Bioenergetics)*

Formative age: birth through eighteen months (Bodynamics). Called the oral stage of development by most systems. This baby is sitting up (Figure 27.3), but his spine is not yet strong enough to hold him in the upright position. He collapses, and his head angles upward awkwardly to make eye contact. Except for the head position, this is also the posture of the motor collapse of the infant in "microdepression." This early stage of somatic organization is thought to define the oral posture of the man (Figure 27.4).

His spine is collapsed, his head falls forward as he gazes longingly into the world, and his arms and legs are passive. In the standing position, spinal collapse forms an "S" curve, rather than the infant "C" curve. There is a general sense of low tone and little strength in the body, especially in the arms and chest. This posture is read in somatic character systems as "collapsed," but holding on against abandonment.

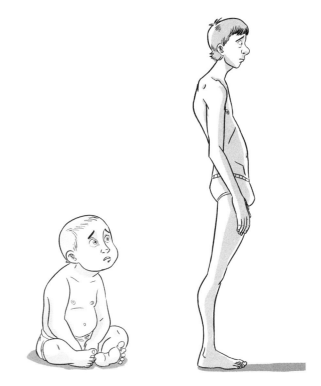

Figures 27.3 and 27.4. Drawings sketched from photos in Bentzen (1963) and Hviid (1992)

## III. Eight to Fifteen Months: Orbitofrontal Elation, Inner Representations, and the Psychopathic Structure

Toward the end of the first year, a great many powerful new cortical developments occur. From eight to fifteen months, the brain undergoes a massive pruning of synaptic connections, in which unused connective possibilities are culled. Such pruning occurs several times during childhood and is probably related to qualitative leaps in affective and cognitive organization.

At around nine months, the infant becomes able to manage much higher levels of pleasure and excitement, particularly in intense dyadic contact with the mother. From about ten months to thirteen and a half months, a strong heightening of positive affect and lowering of negative affect is observed (Schore, 1994, p. 132). Neurologically, this elation reflects the development of dopamine circuits from the limbic system and into the orbitofrontal cortex, which "comes online." The orbitofrontal cortex is central to the linking of externally experienced events with internal states and feelings. The right lobe, related primarily to emotional processing, is larger and has much stronger connections into the limbic system than the left lobe does.

This right-brain maturation allows the toddler to form an inner schema of the different emotional expressions of his mother, linking them to his own inner sensory and emotional response. Also, he begins to have a sense of time, or temporal coherency. This allows him to form an experience-based representation and expectancy of future events, which he uses to guide his actions. In other words, the orbitofrontal cortex is the center of object constancy. However, the maturation of complete inner schemata seems to depend on the development of high levels of dopaminergic excitement in the relationship, and it may be disturbed both by insufficient arousal and by hyperarousal. Burton and Levy (1991; see Schore, 1994, p. 191) suggest that, with insufficient arousal, the toddler's representations remain more primitive and piecemeal. Hyperarousal, on the other hand, is thought to lead to unmodulated rage responses. Gaensbauer and Mrazek (1981; see also Schore, 1994, p. 207) describe a mother teasing her infant from anger into a state of unmodulated rage.

In terms of psycho-motor organization, the infant becomes capable of independent locomotion at about ten months. He begins autonomous explorations of the world, crawling and toddling out into the environment, frequently returning to interact with, touch, or lean against the caregiver. Mahler described this stage as the practicing period, and the behavior is aptly called "psychological refueling" (Mahler, Pine, and Bergman, 1975). At this age, the beginning autonomy of the infant greatly expands the complexity of intrapsychic and interpersonal events, and the somatic character systems focus on somewhat different aspects of this complexity in their personality descriptions.

Bioenergetics describes the basic issue of psychopathic structure as the "right to be free" (from the manipulative needs of others), and the somatic tension pattern as "holding up against falling down." In Hakomi, the psychopathic structure is linked to the long process of the child forming a self-image, and learning honesty in needs, weaknesses, intention, and feeling. In Bodynamics, the (activity directing autonomy) structure is organized around the toddler's excitement with his impulses and ideas, and his insistence on following his own desires. Bodynamics sees the unmodulated excitement of practicing, and the late-practicing-age social and sexual exploration as the basis of this structure.[35]

The early practicing child needs help to modulate some very high states of excitement, and the mother may not be able to do this. Unregulated high arousal becomes disorganized. In the child, this becomes evident as the child's involuntary excitation and entrainment keep him active—perhaps crawling or walking—until he is crying with fatigue, but still can't stop himself.

One formative dynamic of the psychopathic structure is thought to be the relationship to a mother who is extremely manipulating. She induces the child to believe that he can manage by himself. She denies his helplessness or is afraid of it, and ignores his neediness and weakness, focusing only on his strengths. In this stage of basic reality testing and subsequent modification of inner schemata, she does not help him test reality, so he maintains grandiose and unrealistic images of himself and his abilities.

Another theory is that the mother is overly excited by the accomplishments of her child, and is overidentified with him. This means that, instead of being with a containing, sharing, and regulating mother, the child is met with an escalating excitement that overwhelms him, making him lose track of his own feelings and activity in the surge of maternal affect and contact. He then begins to avoid contact with the overstimulating mother, and, in the

---

35 Bodynamics also describes a collapsed psychopathic (activity avoiding autonomy) structure, corresponding to insufficient dopaminergic excitation in the practicing infant. The adult is described as having a wide pelvis and narrow, collapsed chest. Hakomi assigns a similar body type to the oedipal-hysteric structure, and Bioenergetics to the masculine-aggressive and passive-feminine rigid structures. Both the overlap in formative stages and the similar interaction dynamics of having excitement and charge denied or rejected may contribute to the difference in assignment of this posture and body type.

absence of her regulating contact, he forms a more partial schema of his inner states and emotions. Driven by the inner dopamine high, he dives into the sympathetic excitement and intense task-absorption of the practicing child, and denies the vegetative needs that would lead him back to the mother, about whom he is now ambivalent.

In the adult psychopathic structure, this excitation shows up as a constant and passionate drive onward to the next activity, with no time for reflection, completion, or digestion. He is perennially excited and enthusiastic about whatever he happens to be doing at the moment, and his enthusiasm is very catching. He is extremely resistant to negative feelings, and moves on to the next passion as soon as he gets bored, or develops unpleasant or ambivalent feelings with his activity. He immediately forgets or suppresses negative interactions and feeling states. He is extremely hard to "pin down" and correct. If this is attempted, he may respond with extreme rage. This structure corresponds to the high-arousal dopamine-activated hyperactivity seen in the practicing stage.

The psychopathic structure's inner representation of self and world is that he has to do it himself—who else is there? He may help other people, but he doesn't feel that he needs help—he doesn't recognize feelings of inadequacy or neediness, because schemata for them are partial or missing. Underlying this is a fear of being engulfed by the mother.

The somatic holding pattern of the psychopathic structure is: tense legs, a tight pelvis, tends to walk on his toes, and lifts his whole body up by the shoulders. He has a magnetic gaze, and a very engaging manner. He is described as having his energy displaced upward, and tends toward motor and verbal activity.

The practicing-age infant walks on his forefoot. His falling reflexes in his arms and shoulders are just beginning to become active, and he uses his arms and shoulders to keep his balance as well as to handle objects and play with people. He is "up" in his own body, and is also fascinated with getting up on high things—climbing stairs, chairs, kitchen counters, or even refrigerators, to the horror of parents and caregivers. The social charisma, excitement, and varied "language babble" are also typical of the practicing stage.

**Psychopathic Somatic Pattern**

*Formative age: eight months to two and a half years. (Bodynamics)*

Hakomi states that the formative age is before four, while the child is developing its self-image in interaction with the image held by others. This early toddler is flooded with excitement (Figure 27.5). He is passionately focused outward, and is intensely engaged and engaging. He is walking, but his legs are not yet fully up to the task and he is using his shoulders, arms, and hands to keep his balance. His energy is going up in more ways than one. If his legs do not stabilize, he may become a toe-walker and have trouble developing normal walking and push-off.

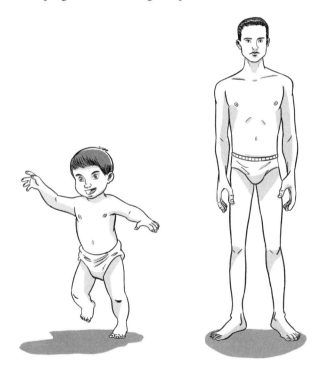

Figures 27.5 and 27.6. Drawings sketched from photos in Bentzen (1963) and Hviid (1992)

The somatic organization of the man in Figure 27.6 is similar to that of the young toddler. He has overdeveloped, square shoulders, a tight pelvis, and tight, thin legs. He is standing on the forefoot, with little or no weight on his heels. Although a drawing does not show it, he probably holds his balance with a lot of subtle movement. His gaze is magnetic and engaging. In a somatic reading, this posture would be interpreted as displaced upward and outward, probably to avoid the fear and ambivalence that this structure associates with a deeper sense of the kinesthetic self and with the supporting floor; the relationship to grounding is often considered a clue to the relationship to the mother, the first environment.

## IV. The Second Year: Inhibitory Regulation and the Masochistic Structure

In the beginning of the second year, the intense pleasurable dynamic and interaction of the previous months changes radically. The earlier general state of pleasurable dopaminergic excitement is now followed by a period of anxious, depressed, shame-responsive hypothalamic-pituitary-adrenocortical (HPA) activity, starting between twelve and fourteen months. We are now at the end of the critical period for practicing, and the beginning of the rapprochement phase.

This development heralds the beginnings of the development of social inhibitory capacities in the child. Great importance is placed on the development of shame. This intense swing from a positive sympathetic to a stress-deflated parasympathetic state is thought to activate further development of the fronto-limbic structure (affect regulation) and the maturation of the orbitofrontal cortex (object constancy and emotional assessment). The fearfulness, depression, sensitivity, and separation anxiety described at this stage of child development fits the descriptions of the emerging adrenocortical function. This affective state is triggered by normal misregulations as well as shaming interactions.

Some authors speak of an actual shift from a nurturing to a socializing relationship. Tulkin and Kagan (1972) note that the interaction with the ten-month-old is 90 percent centered on love and positive interactions, and 5 percent is used to limit the child. At around fourteen months, the child is exploring up to six hours a day, and the percentages of limiting interactions rise dramatically. The mother of the eleven- to seventeen-month-old intervenes to stop her child from some activity about every nine minutes (Power and Chapiesky, 1986; see Schore, 1994, p. 200). This means a great many interactions in which the toddler creatively tries to find ways of doing what he wants, while the parents try to prevent him from doing it. Many authors describe shaming as being a primary way that caregivers regulate the actions of their toddlers. Schore states that the ensuing frustration (in the toddler, not the parent) and internal stress trigger the further maturation of the cortex.

Absent at twelve months, embarrassment and shame are first seen in the toddler at around fourteen months. A shame-inducing reunion scenario might go like the following: In his foray into the world, the toddler has found a lovely, squishy, sweet-tasting thing on the grass, which he is bringing back to his mother. He is very excited and anticipating the intense pleasure of her delight and sharing. Mother looks at him, disgust etched on her features, and shouts, "*No! Bad! Dirty ice-cream!*"

With this strong misattunement, the toddler is abruptly plunged from a state of pleasurable, high-dopaminergic, sympathetic excitement into a sudden, stress-filled, parasympathetic vagal activation. His excitement is sharply inhibited, his heart rate abruptly slows, his body and limbs lose tonus, his head hangs, his face loses tone, and he blushes. His legs may even give way. He feels lost, and his mother seems like an alien being to him. It is now vital that his mother act to regulate him out of this state of intense shame, because his immature nervous system does not yet know how to do this for himself. He will probably try to make contact with her to reestablish the lost regulatory flow and, with it, the good inner feelings. If all goes well, his mother will now reattune and stay in contact with him until he is "back on his feet" again. Through this kind of interaction, the toddler's sense of object constancy deepens as he incorporates that conflict and painful misattunements can be healed.

In a later typical regulatory situation, the toddler is heading toward a nice muddy puddle, and his mother, some distance away, breaks off her conversation with a friend, tenses up, and frowns at him. Because he is strongly sensitized to her nonverbal responses, he picks up this signal, pauses, and changes direction. The injunction has now become part of a more modulated dialogue. The toddler is internalizing his mother's rules, and the socialization process is moving ahead.

Around eighteen months, shame signals are becoming an internal guiding system (Greenspan, 1988). Moving toward a puddle, the child may stop, remember his mother's frown, frown in imitation, struggle a while between desire and inhibition, and finally turn away.

Newer psychoanalytic theory (Schore, 1994) suggests that the socializing function of shaming and shame are at the very heart of the development of a sense of self. It describes the toddler as living in a dreamlike present until the shaming parent and his own emotional response jerk him into full wakefulness. In this context of early ego formation, it is interesting to note that many theoreticians speak of the shame process, with its abrupt plunge into the dissociative vagal activation, as being one of the most intensely kinesthetic feelings that we experience (Ibid.).

Pathological exchanges may occur in this vital process. Unregulated parental expressions of rage and contempt evoke intense and unrelieved shame and humiliation. Shame-humiliation dynamics have been found to consistently accompany child abuse (Kaufman, 1989; Lewis, 1992; see Schore, 1994, p. 207). If the stresses of the child's life are too overwhelming, he may become stuck in a vagally dominated state of diminished movement and interest in the environment, and a general activation of the anxiety-deflation-shame state.

In the somatic character traditions, Bioenergetics focuses on the right to be self-directed and on the somatic tension pattern of holding in against humiliation and shame. Hakomi states that the innate issues of the formative stage of the masochistic structure are responsibility and freedom, and that the structure "clamps down and sticks to the ground." These two systems often see the psychopathic and masochistic structures as complementary. In Bodynamics, the threatened right of the (self-sacrificing will) structure is to make choices and develop one's will. The structure is strongly driven by shame, guilt, and overresponsibility.

Although there have been attempts to distinguish decisively between shame and guilt, current findings indicate that guilt is a later modification of the same neurological processes as shame. As such, guilt is usually more specific and localized, whereas shame is usually more global and pervasive. The formative age of the masochistic structure is traditionally the anal stage (in Bodynamics, two to four years). Because the affective processes of socialization and shaming, and the body postures related to it, emerge around fourteen months, it seems reasonable to set this as the beginning of the formative "window" of this structure.

The masochistic structure is thought to have the following formative dynamic: The primary caregiver overcontrols, nags, rages, or shames the child, and the child responds with shame and guilt. He collapses into anxiety and self-judgment, and draws back from asserting himself in relationships as well as in activities. Fearful of asserting himself, he also turns his anger inward.

The masochistic structure's inner representation of self and world is that he is deficient. He is locked in a struggle to be good, and he fails abjectly. He feels that his failure is the cause of all kinds of calamities—his own accidents, his mother's pain or illness, and nebulous unknowable catastrophes. His representations are much more complex than those described in earlier structures, because this structure spans a later and more diverse range of cognitive development. Because the ability to form object-representations has reached a level of beginning causal and temporal coherence, the masochistic structure can be immobilized by fear of the future as well as fear of the consequences of his actions. He is self-effacing and submissive, and afraid of choices and independent action. He takes on burdens and either fails or is driven by fear of failure. Hakomi and Bioenergetics sum up the central belief of this structure: "Submission is the price for intimacy."

This description corresponds to an ongoing neurological dynamic of anxiety-worry (hypothalamic-pituitary-adrenal activation) and a constant level of inhibitory shame. Accordingly, the masochistic posture is based on a shame- or guilt-based collapse in the spine, and hunches inward like a shamed toddler. The butt is tucked under, and the shoulders are drawn protectively up and forward.

Another aspect of this structure is the sense of burdens. Beginning around the age of two, the child's balance and gross motor control have now improved. He delights in carrying things around, and will test his limits by trying to carry objects that are too heavy for his body. He will also engage in "helping Mother," practicing his entry into the world of responsibility. The masochistic structure typically takes on physical and emotional burdens and is ambivalent about them—wanting to do it right, but feeling overwhelmed and confused by the tasks he has accepted.

**Masochistic Somatic Pattern**

*The masochistic structure is shaped by threat of humiliation. (Bioenergetics)*

Formative age: two to four years (Bodynamics). Hakomi states that the formative age is when the child is becoming autonomous: learning to walk, move freely, and assert itself. This child is in the acute state of shame (Figure 27.7). He is hunching his shoulders, making an unhappy, shameful face, and squeezing down into himself in his seat on the floor. The head and neck are pulled into the torso. His arms and legs are flexed. Because motor control in his legs is still quite immature, he will find it hard to stand or walk in this state, but will tend to collapse to the floor or ground.

The adult is in a similar state of neuromotor organization (Figure 27.8). His back and shoulders are hunched forward, and he is "tucking his tail." His facial expression is apologetic and suffering, and perhaps angry as well. His arms and legs are flexed, and he seems to be weighed down by an invisible yoke on his shoulders, and perhaps also invisible weights in his hands.

A somatic reading would describe him as weighed down by responsibility and tucking his tail in shame, while the solar plexus area, traditionally related to feelings of dignity and personal power, is collapsed.

Bioenergetics and Bodynamics both describe a later development of this structure: the sadistic (in Bodynamics: judgmental will) structure. It is described as having the same basic inner dilemma, but whereas the masochistic

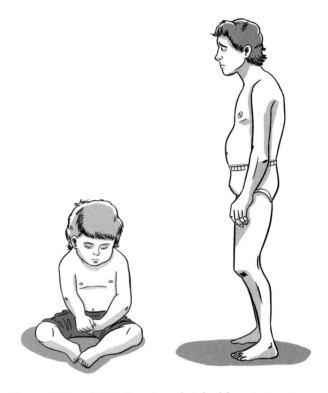

Figures 27.7 and 27.8. Drawings sketched from internet photo and personal photos

structure submits to get intimacy, the sadistic structure rejects intimacy as well as submission and instead chooses self-assertion and loneliness. This structure takes a controlling, judgmental stance. Bodynamics (Bernhardt et al., 1996) describes that the child moves from self-correction to commenting on, correcting, punishing, and shaming the behavior of others. Bioenergetics describes the structure as being mixed with the later rigid structure and the issue of opening the heart. In Hakomi, these phenomena are seen as elements of the psychopathic structure. Bodynamics states that the child's dilemma is that it is not allowed both personal empowerment and intimacy. The early, self-sacrificing structure gives up empowerment, and feels ashamed, dejected, and, under that, angry. The late, judgmental structure gives up intimacy, and is coldly and angrily controlling.

The posture of the sadistic structure is similar to that of the masochistic structure, but expresses anger rather than shame, and the spine behind the solar plexus is held aggressively straight instead of collapsing.

## V. The Second Year: The Impact of Genital Sensory Maturation and Gonadal Steroids on Brain and Interaction, and the Rigid Structures

The most pervasive aspect of gender differentiation is linked to the level of sex hormones, which are very high at birth, and then slowly decrease through childhood, until they rise sharply again when the child approaches sexual maturity. From birth, high levels of sex hormones are circulating in the infant's body. Impressive evidence has linked early gonadal steroids to establishment of sexual dimorphism in the maturing limbic system and cortex, including the orbitofrontal cortex (Schore, 1994). The neurological and psycho-social impact of these sex hormones in infancy seems to place the first beginnings of social gender identification at birth. Gender identification is critically dependent on social interactions. Nurturing contact raises the levels of gonadal steroids circulating in the infant's bloodstream. The sex hormones then unlock genetic potential, and initiate sex-linked differentiation in the cerebral cortex and brain circuits. The sexual differences that develop during prenatal existence and during the first years become a permanent part of the brain. These include differences in the regulation of sexuality, aggression, and emotion as well as spatial coordination. This sexual dimorphism extends to the differentiation and use of the right and left hemispheres, and influences, among other things, the relationship between verbal and emotional processing.

In the middle of the second year, the child can correctly identify boys and girls. At around eighteen months, the gender process in the infant has matured to the point that both his brain and his sense of self have a definite and irreversible gender (Schore, 1994). Working models of maleness and femaleness, as well as personal identification, have already been internalized (Schore, 1994), and parents respond with pleasure to sex-typed play, rewarding boys for exploratory behavior and object play, and girls for quiet, social activities (Fagot, 1975; O'Brien and Huston, 1985).

The motor and sensory connections to the legs, pelvic floor, and genitals mature rapidly during the second year of life, and around the age of eighteen months the toddler becomes much more interested in touching and exhibiting his genitals (Kleeman, 1966, 1975). This development occurs when the shame response has been established for some months, and the two dynamics often become intimately connected (Nathanson, 1987). Parents frequently respond with embarrassment or shaming when the toddler fondles his genitals. According to Reich and Lowen, shame is a basic part of the regulation of the sexual drive.

At this time, the practicing period offsets, and, according to Schore, the imprinting process on the mother offsets too. The toddler is beginning to establish deeper relationships to other people besides the mother, and is developing his first experiences with triangular relationships. This process began with people and objects in the middle of the first year, but now he actively seeks other adult and child contacts, and experiments with them. With his parents, he begins to pull one close while pushing the other away. He may try to keep this triangular balance for minutes or days, but sooner or later he will try the opposite configuration, and "switch intimacies." In this process, he seems motivated partly by a desire to test his power to direct the situation, but he also seems to be "feeling out" the different qualities of claiming an alliance with one parent while holding away the other. Ganging up with his father feels different from ganging up with his mother. Schore (1994, p. 267) also briefly mentions a theory of "father-imprinting" that is thought to onset at this time.

These behaviors, beginning in the middle of the second year, correspond to the dynamic described as "oedipal," commonly held to belong to middle childhood. In light of the above research findings, it seems reasonable instead to set the beginning of the formative age of gender identification and interaction at birth, or at least at eighteen months, at the onset of irreversible gender sense, genital sensory maturation, and interpersonal triangular experimentation.

The somatic systems differ in their views of the posture and personality of the character structures of the oedipal, gender-differentiating period.[36] Bioenergetics, Bodynamics, and Hakomi roughly agree only on the posture and personality dynamics of the rigid-phallic structure. For the other oedipal character structures, there is little agreement, as the three systems focus on different mixtures of oedipal structure with preexisting oral, psychopathic, masochistic, or schizoid-hysteric character traits. The reason for this general confusion might well be that the neuroaffective origins of schizoid-hysteric, oral, psychopathic, masochistic, and oedipal stages are closely knit and even have large developmental overlaps in time. The three systems focus on different clusters of postural and personal characteristics that emerge and intermingle during the first eighteen to twenty-four months, whereas the traditional psychodynamic view is that these patterns develop more sequentially during the first six years!

The rigid-phallic structure is identified with performance, both sexual and task-oriented. Hakomi and Bioenergetics describe it as industrious and overly focused. In Bodynamics, inspired by the works of Erik Erikson, gender issues have been separated from achievement issues, which are placed at Erikson's (1950) "age of industry," around preschool and school age. These later issues will not be described in this chapter.

Bodynamics notes that the key to the gender-differentiating (oedipal) stage is the quality of interaction and assigned identity: if parents define the child as sexual, whether good or bad, this is the identity he will internalize. If the interactions, and the child, are defined as sweet and loving (energy coming from the heart) and not sexual, whether good or bad, that is the identity that he will internalize.

The phallic structure has a lot of energy and excitement, more than any other character structure. He is organized around the internal experience of needing to be grown-up, or to achieve, or to perform. He is afraid of opening his heart to—another—rejection. He is afraid of opening himself, relaxing, and losing control, so despite his very high level of performance, he cannot seem to attain satisfaction and release. Bioenergetics and Hakomi describe both structures for both sexes, but Bioenergetics sees the rigid-phallic as more common in men, and the hysteric as more common in women, although this cultural pattern is changing. Bodynamics' (seductive) position has a high charge in the pelvis and genitals, and a hurt, guarded closure in the chest and heart, corresponding to the Bioenergetic and Hakomi descriptions of the rigid-phallic structure.

In Hakomi, the formative belief of the person with a phallic structure is that he is not good enough to have a place in the adult world. Just "being" is not enough, and not good enough. One central interaction thought to lead to the phallic structure is that the father rejects the child or makes him feel inferior. The child struggles to "grow up fast" and attempts to take adult gender roles and responsibilities. Another dynamic is the parental requirement that the child be a "little man" or "little lady." The love and acceptance of the parent depends on how well the child lives up to this demand.

The phallic structure has internalized the following representations of self and world. He feels fully alive and fully himself only when engaged in a task, or right after finishing it. He feels that he must achieve and strive to be the perfect man/woman/executive/doctor/dancer, etc. Only if he succeeds will others love and recognize him, or alternately: will he be worth loving and recognizing?

### Rigid (Phallic) Somatic Pattern

*The rigid structure is shaped by fear of surrender. (Bioenergetics)*

Formative age: three to six years (Bodynamics). Hakomi states that it occurs when the child is old enough to be aware of sexual differences. (The children shown here are four to five years old, the age traditionally assigned to the oedipal stage.)

---

[36] Because the core issue of the rigid character structure is gender identification, and because family structures and gender roles are culturally set, different formative dynamics must be expected in different cultures. These character descriptions have been developed in the North American and northern European cultures, and may only be fully valid there.

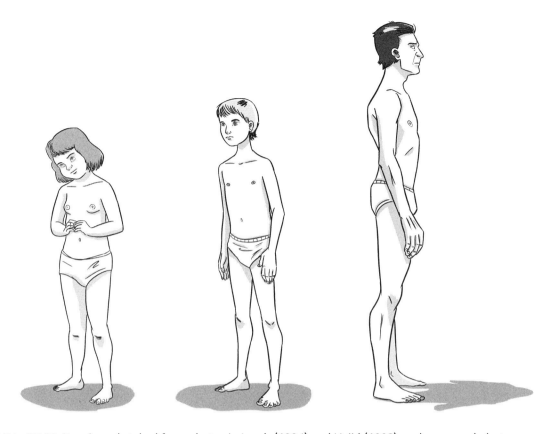

Figures 27.9 to 27.11. Drawings sketched from photos in Leach (1994) and Hviid (1992), and a personal photo

In her posture, this girl shows both openness and innocent flirtation (Figure 27.9). Her head is angled, and her facial expression is playfully inviting. Her shoulders and chest area, traditionally connected to heart feelings, is somewhat collapsed, and her pelvis and genital area show some congestion and fullness. Her chest seems smaller and more fragile. She combines the pelvic characteristics of the Bioenergetics mixed-rigid structures or Hakomi's hysterical structure with some of the characteristics of the Bodynamics romantic structure.

The boy has the typical leggy and straight posture of middle childhood (Figure 27.10). His back is straight and arched, his legs are tense, straight, and muscular, and the general sense is of energy and presence. His shoulders and arms show a neuromuscular "readiness" to do something.

The man has a similar somatic organization (Figure 27.11). His posture is straight and confident, his spine is overarched, his legs are straight and tense, and his shoulders and arms are ready for action. His body is symmetrical, powerful, and controlled. His face shows tension. The whole posture has an upright tense quality.

In a somatic reading, this posture has a lot of "life energy," but uses it to keep control, stay on top of things, and achieve, achieve, achieve. He is holding back against the fear of surrendering to softer feelings and to vulnerability.

Not surprisingly, the postural characteristics of both the phallic and hysteric structures epitomize some of the gender stereotypes of our culture. The phallic structure has a straight posture, with a shapely, tense chest and a tight, charged pelvis. His back is straight or arched, his legs are straight, and the general impression he gives is of a "good soldier" (Hakomi), a "toreador" (Bodynamics), or a "knight"—in either chain mail or plate armor (Bioenergetics).

Hakomi describes the oedipal-hysteric structure as expressive and clinging, like the schizoid-hysteric of Lake

(1966) and Bodynamics. This structure is identified with his feelings, and is very sensitive and easily upset. He exaggerates emotions and is theatrical in his expression. He tends to have trouble focusing, is easily distracted or scattered, and is often inconsistent. Hakomi and Bioenergetics also state that he tends to use sexuality as a form of defense against deeper feelings and commitments. He may be promiscuous, or have his sexual activity with one person while he has his heart and deeper companionship (nonsexual) with another. He is often seductive or flirtatious.

Bodynamics' romantic structure has overactivity or openness in the chest and heart, is wasp-waisted, avoids feelings and sensations from the genital area and the pelvis, and exaggerates ideals and loving feelings. The posture is similar to that of Bioenergetics' hysteric structure.

Hakomi describes the body of the hysteric as being like a child's upper body in a wide pelvis. The shoulders, arms, and chest are all underdeveloped and tense, and in the woman the breasts are often small. The abdomen and pelvis are soft, wide, and round. The posture is straight, and the head is held high.

The three systems describe similar formative dynamics for this structure. The parents reject the child's sexuality, perhaps because they are afraid of their own sexual feelings for him. One commonly described dynamic is that one or both parents are contactful in the first years, but then withdraw and lose interest. The parents may also reject the child's feelings and desire for loving intimacy, or deny the child's growing individuality and personhood.

The hysteric structure has internalized the following sense of world and self. He feels that his love and his feelings are not enough or not good enough, or they are too much, and he is searching desperately for someone who will accept him "as he is," while simultaneously withdrawing from the deeper involvement that would make his heart vulnerable to another wounding. Unlike the phallic structure, he feels his hurt and betrayal, and is identified with it. He therefore sees other people as being potentially wonderful and potentially betraying, as he struggles with his inner yearning and distrust.

The mixture of oedipal and preexisting oral or masochistic characters—the passive-feminine structure for men, and the masculine-aggressive structure for women—have the wide pelvis and narrow chest/shoulders of Hakomi's hysteric and Bodynamics' early psychopathic structure. If we accept that socially formed gender identity begins at birth, it seems likely that "mixed" structures would originally form together.

As earlier mentioned, the sex hormones underlying crucial gender differentiation are all active from birth, and are regulated by the caregiving interactions at the onset of the oral process. Genital sensitivity and genital interest mature in the late practicing period. In the actual life of the toddler, elements of caregiving are interwoven with socialization, excitement, sexuality, shame inhibition, gender learning, differentiation of object-relationships, and social interactions with more people and in more complex situations. The many different views of somatic oedipal character formation reflect this complexity.

These reflections on the oedipal character formation conclude this reflection on neuroaffective development and somatic character. I have focused on neuroaffective and psycho-motor development during the first wave of brain maturation from birth to two years old as a primary window for the formation of adult character. This view conflicts with traditional theories, wherein the masochistic and oedipal structures form largely after the second year. However, looking at neurological maturation and interpersonal interaction, it seems clear that the child has all the basic affective personality components of the traditional five stages of character in place by the end of the second year. In the next section, I have some concluding thoughts about formative character dynamics outside the first wave of brain development and outside the scope of this chapter.

## Other Perspectives on Character Development

Clearly, the whole personality is not developed by age two! The structures described above deepen and differentiate through middle childhood and the teenage years as new cortical, psychological, and somatic competencies mature (Giedd et al., 1999; Giedd, 2002; Shonkoff and Phillips,

2000) and as peer relationships become an important factor in character development (Shonkoff and Phillips, 2000; Cummins, 2006). Beginning around the age of two, a left-hemisphere verbal identity forms along with the development of language and the refinement of mentalizing capacity (Allen, Fonagy, and Bateman, 2008; Hart, 2011), which is the ability to empathically reflect on the feelings and actions of oneself and others, and is closely linked to stress resilience. Curiously, the differences between verbal and nonverbal identity formation have generated little interest in the field of character theory, whether traditional or somatic. The vast impact of peers and group identification processes around the early school age have been considered characterologically only by Erik Erikson (1950) and Bodynamics; and neither contemporary research findings on neurological changes occurring in prepuberty and puberty (Robinson, 2009; Giedd, 2002; Giedd et al., 1999) or the considerable body of child and adult studies on social-dominance motivation (Cummins, 2006; Dunbar, 1998; de Waal, 2006; Hart and Bentzen, 2012) is assimilated in psychodynamic personality theory.

Finally, there is the important issue of correlating somatic character to validated psychological personality tests. To my knowledge, two attempts have been made in the last decade to do this. Fehr (2006) describes strong correlations between the Bioenergetic structures and the generally accepted "big five personality traits": openness to experience, conscientiousness, extraversion, agreeableness, and neuroticism. Glazer and Friedman (2009) report satisfactory correlations between different raters of Bioenergetic character, but low reliability when compared to traditional personality measures. Hopefully, this chapter opens the way for fresh studies of somatic character.

# References

Aitken, K. J., & Trevarthen, C. (1997). Self-other organization in human psychological development. *Development and Psychopathology, 9,* 651–675.

Allen, J. G., Fonagy, P., & Bateman, A. W. (2008). *Mentalizing in clinical practice.* Washington, DC: American Psychiatric Publishing.

Beebe, B., & Lachmann, F. M. (2002). *Infant research and adult treatment: Co-constructing interactions.* Hillsdale, NJ: Analytic Press.

*Bentzen, B. S. (1963). Børnemotorik* [Children's motor skills]. Copenhagen: *Gyldendals pædagogiske bibliotek.*

*Bentzen, M., Jarlnaes, E., & Levine, P. (2004). The body self in psychotherapy: A psychomotoric approach to Developmental Psychology.* In I. MacNaughton (Ed.), *Body, breath and consciousness.* Berkeley, CA: North Atlantic Books.

Bernhardt, P., Bentzen, M., & Isaacs, J. (1996). Waking the body ego II. *Energy & Character, 27(1),* 38–50.

Boadella, D. (1986). *Maps of character.* Weymouth, Dorset, UK: Abbotsbury Publications.

Brodén, M. (2000). *Mor og barn i ingenmandsland* [Mother and child in no-man's-land]. Copenhagen: Hans Reitzels.

Burton, L. A., & Levy, J. (1991). Effects of processing speed on cerebral asymmetry for left- and right-oriented faces. *Brain and Cognition, 15,* 95–105.

Chess, S., & Thomas, A. (1996). *Temperament.* New York: Routledge.

Cuhna, F., & Heckman, J. J. (2010). Investing in our young people. In A. J. Reynolds, A. Rolnick, M. M. Englund, & J. Temple (Eds.), *Cost-effective early childhood programs in the first decade: A human capital integration* (pp. 381–414). New York: Cambridge University Press.

Cummins, D. (2006). Dominance, status, and social hierarchies. In D. M. Buss (Ed.), *The handbook of Evolutionary Psychology* (pp. 676–697). Hoboken, NJ: Wiley.

Damasio, A. (1994). *Descartes' error: Emotion, reason and the human brain.* New York: Grosset, Putnam.

de Waal, F. (2006). *Our inner ape.* New York: Riverhead Trade.

Dunbar, R. (1998). The social brain hypothesis. *Evolutionary Anthropology: Issues, News, and Reviews, 6(5),* 178–190.

Erikson, E. H. (1950/1993). *Childhood and society.* New York: W. W. Norton.

Fagot, B. I. (1975). Sex differences in toddlers' behavior and parental reaction. *Developmental Psychology, 10,* 554–558.

Fehr, T. (2006). Multidimensional Bioenergetic Personality Analysis: A statistical approach. *European Journal of Bioenergetic Analysis and Psychotherapy.*

Gaensbauer, T. J., & Mrazek, D. (1981). Differences in the patterning of affective expressions in infants. *Journal of the American Academy of Child Psychiatry, 20,* 673–691.

Gallese, V. (2001). "Shared manifold" hypothesis: From mirror neurons to empathy. *Journal of Consciousness Studies, 8*(5–7), 33–50.

Gallese, V., Fadiga, L., Fogassi, L., & Rizzolatti, G. (1996). Action recognition in the premotor cortex. *Brain, 119*(2), 593–609.

Gallese, V., & Goldman, A. (1998). Mirror neurons and the simulation theory of mindreading. *Trends in Cognitive Sciences, 2*(12), 493–501.

Gerhardt, S. (2004). *Why love matters: How affection shapes a baby's brain.* New York: Brunner-Routledge.

Giedd, J. N. (2002). *Inside the teenage brain.* Interview. Frontline.

Giedd, J. N., et al. (1999). Brain development during childhood and adolescence: A longitudinal study. *Nature Neuroscience, 2*(10), 861–863.

Glazer, R., & Friedman, H. (2009). The construct validity of the Bio-energetic character typology: A multimethod investigation of a humanistic approach to personality. *Humanistic Psychologist, 27*(1), 24–48.

Greenspan, S. I. (1988). The development of the ego: Insights from clinical work with infants and children. *Journal of the American Psychoanalytical Association, 36*(suppl.), 3–55.

Hart, S. (2011). *The impact of attachment.* New York: W. W. Norton. Trans. from Danish (2006). *Betydningen af Samhørighed [The importance of cohesion].* Copenhagen: Reitzels.

Hart, S., & Bentzen, M. (2012). Jegets fundament: den neuroaffektive udviklings første vækstbølge og de neuroaffektive kompasser [The foundation of the ego: The first wave of neuroaffective development and the neuroaffective compasses]. In S. Hart (Ed.), *Neuroaffektiv psykoterapi med voksne [Neuroaffective Psychotherapy with adults].* Copenhagen: Hans Reitzels.

Hogeveen, J., Inzlicht, M., & Obhi, S. S. (2014). Power changes how the brain responds to others. *Journal of Experimental Psychology, 143,* 755–762.

Hviid, T. (1992). *Kroppens Fortællinger I Billeder* [Body stories in photos]. Aarhus, Denmark: Modtryk.

Ingen-Housz, M. (2003). *Personal* communication.

Johnsen, L. (1976). *En nøgle til livsglædens skjulte kilde [A key to happiness' hidden source].* Copenhagen: Borgen. Danish ed. of Johnsen, L. (1981). *Integrated respiration theory/therapy: Birth and rebirth in the fullness of time.* Tulsa, OK: Private publication.

Kagan, J., Snidman, N., Kahn, V., & Towsley, S. (2007). The preservation of two infant temperaments into adolescence. *Monographs of the Society for Research in Child Development, 72*(2, Serial No. 287), vii.

Kaufman, G. (1989). *The psychology of shame.* New York: Springer.

Keysers, C. (2011). *The empathic brain.* Groningen, Netherlands: Social Brain Press.

Kleeman, J. A. (1966). Genital self-discovery during a boy's second year. *Psychoanalytic Study of the Child, 21,* 358–392.

Kleeman, J. A. (1975). Genital self-stimulation in infant and toddler girls. In I. Marcus & J. Franin (Eds.), *Masturbation* (pp. 77–106). New York: International Universities Press.

Lake, F. (1966). *Clinical theology.* London: Darton, Longman & Todd.

Leach, P. (1994). *Your baby and child.* New York: Alfred A. Knopf.

LeDoux, J. E. (1989). Cognitive-emotional interactions in the brain. *Cognition and Emotion, 3,* 267–289.

LeDoux, J. E. (1996). *The emotional brain: The mysterious underpinnings of emotional life.* New York: Simon & Schuster.

LeDoux, J. E. (2002). *Synaptic self: How our brains become who we are.* New York: Viking Penguin.

Lewis, M. (1992). *Shame: The exposed self.* New York: Free Press.

Lowen, A. (1958). *The language of the body.* New York: Collier Books.

MacIntyre, J., & Mullins, R. (1976). *A "new look" at character: The Bioenergetic Training Manual for the first year in Bioenergetic Analysis,* ed. and self-published by Michael J. Maley.

Mahler, M., Pine, F., & Bergman, A. (1975). *The psychological birth of the human infant.* New York: Basic Books.

Marcher, L., & Fich, S. (2010). *Body encyclopedia: A guide to the psychological functions of the muscular system.* Berkeley, CA: North Atlantic Books.

Nathanson, D. L. (1987). A timetable for shame. In D. L. Nathanson (Ed.), *The many faces of shame* (pp. 1–63). New York: Guilford Press.

O'Brien, M., & Huston, A. C. (1985). Development of sex-typed play behavior in toddlers. *Developmental Psychology, 21,* 866–871.

Ogden, P. (1985). The chart. In R. Kurtz (Ed.), *Hakomi Therapy.* Boulder, CO: Hakomi Institute.

Panksepp, J., & Biven, L. (2012). *The archaeology of mind: Neuroevolutionary origins of human emotions.* New York: W. W. Norton.

Perry, B. (2002). Childhood experience and the expression of genetic potential: What childhood neglect tells us about nature and nurture. *Brain and Mind, 3*(1), 79–100.

Perry, B. D., Pollard, R. A., Blakley, T. L., Baker, W. L., & Vigilante, D. (1995). Childhood trauma, the neurobiology of adaptation, and "use-dependent" development of the brain: How "states" become "traits." *Infant Mental Health Journal, 16*(4), 271–291.

Perry, B. D., & Slavavitz, M. (2007). *The boy who was raised as a dog: And other stories from a child psychiatrist's notebook: What traumatized children can teach us about loss, love and healing.* New York: Basic Books.

Porges, S. W. (1997). Emotion: An evolutionary by-product of the neural regulation of the autonomic nervous system. *Annals of the New York Academy of Sciences, 807,* 62–77.

Power, T. G., & Chapiesky, M. L. (1986). Childrearing and impulse control in toddlers: A naturalistic investigation. *Developmental Psychology, 22,* 271–275.

Reich, W. (1949/1971). *Character Analysis.* Rangeley, ME: Orgone Institute Press; New York: Farrar, Straus & Giroux.

Ridley, M. (2003). *Nature via nurture: Genes, experience, and what makes us human.* New York: HarperCollins.

Robinson, R. (2009). From child to young adult, the brain changes its connections. *PLoS Biology, 7*(7).

Rutter, M. (2006). *Genes and behavior: Nature-nurture interplay explained.* Oxford, UK: Blackwell.

Sander, L. (1977). Regulation of exchange in the infant-caretaker system and some aspects of the context-content relationship. In M. Lewis & L. Rosenblum (Eds.), *Interaction, conversation and the development of language.* New York: Wiley.

Sander, L. (1983). Polarity, paradox and the organizing process in development. In J. D. Call, E. Galenson, & R. L. Tyson (Eds.), *Frontiers of Infant Psychiatry* (Vol. 1). New York: Basic Books.

Sander, L. (1987). Awareness of inner experience: A systems perspective on self-regulatory process in early development. *Child Abuse and Neglect, 11*(3), 339–346.

Sander, L. (1988). Event structure of regulation in the neonate-caregiver system as a biological background for early organization of psychic structure. In A. Goldberg (Ed.), *Frontiers in Self Psychology* (pp. 3–27). Hillsdale, NJ: Lawrence Erlbaum.

Schore, A. (1994). *Affect regulation and the origin of the self: The neurobiology of emotional development.* Hillsdale, NJ: Lawrence Erlbaum.

Shonkoff, J. P., & Phillips, D. (Eds.). (2000). *From neurons to neighborhoods: The science of early childhood development.* Washington, DC: National Academies Press.

Sørensen, L. (1996). *Særpræg, Særhed, Sygdom [Eccentricities, peculiarities, symptoms].* Copenhagen: Hans Reitzels.

Stern, D. N. (1995). *The motherhood constellation.* London: Karnac Books.

Stern, D. N. (1977/2002). *The first relationship.* Cambridge, MA: Harvard University Press.

Stern, D. N. (2004). *The present moment in psychotherapy and everyday life.* New York: W. W. Norton.

Sullivan, R. M., Landers, M., Yeaman, B., & Wilson, D. A. (2001). Neurophysiology: Good memories of bad events in infancy. *Nature, 407,* 38–39 *(quoted by R. Adolphs, The neurobiology of social cognition. Current Opinion in Neurobiology, 2001(11), 231–239).*

Tabery, J., & Griffiths, P. E. (2010). Historical and philosophical perspectives on behavioral genetics and developmental science. In K. T. Hood, C. T. Halpern, G. Greenberg, & R. M. Lerner (Eds.), *Handbook of developmental science, behavior, and genetics* (pp. 41–60). New York: Wiley-Blackwell.

Thelen, E., & Smith, L. (1994). *A dynamic systems approach to the development of cognition and action.* Cambridge, MA: MIT Press.

Trevarthen, C. (1979). Communication and cooperation in early infancy: A description of primary intersubjectivity. In M. Bullowa (Ed.), *Before speech: The beginning of interpersonal communication.* Cambridge, UK: Cambridge University Press.

Trevarthen, C. (1990). Growth and education of the hemispheres. In C. Trevarthen (Ed.), *Brain circuits and functions of the mind* (pp. 334–363). Cambridge, UK: Cambridge University Press.

Trevarthen, C. (1993a). The function of emotions in early infant communication and development. In J. Nadel & L. Camaioni (Eds.), *New perspectives in early communicative development.* London: Routledge.

Trevarthen, C. (1993b). The self born in intersubjectivity: The psychology of an infant communicating. In U. Neisser (Ed.), *The perceived self: Ecological and interpersonal sources of self knowledge* (pp. 121–173). New York: Cambridge University Press.

Tronick, E., & Gianino, A. (1986). Interactive mismatch and repair: Challenges to the coping infant. *Zero to three: Bulletin of the National Center for Clinical Infant Programs, 5,* 1–6.

Tronick, E. Z., & Weinberg, K. (1997). Depressed mothers and infants: The failure to form dyadic states of consciousness. In L. Murray & P. Cooper (Eds.), *Postpartum depression and child development.* New York: Guilford Press.

Tulkin, S. R., & Kagan, J. (1972). Mother-infant interaction in the first year of life. *Child Development, 43,* 31–42.

Weiss, H. (2003). Personal *communication.*

*Acknowledgment:* Marianne Ingen-Housz, international trainer in Bioenergetic Analysis, kindly corrected my statements about Bioenergetic Analysis in this chapter. Any other mistakes are all mine.

# 28
## The Main Variants of Character Theory in the Field of Body Psychotherapy

Andreas Sartory, Austria,

with Gustl Marlock, Germany, and Halko Weiss, United States

Translation by Warren Miller

**Andreas Sartory** was a successful businessman, who, in 1997, after an extensive journey through South America, "converted" to psychotherapy as a better way of supporting other people in their lives. He has trained in Peter Levine's trauma work, Somatic Experiencing, as well as in Hakomi and Psychodrama. His work carries a strong level of spirituality.

This chapter introduces the major variants of Body Psychotherapeutic character typologies, presented purely in a visual and schematic form. Apart from Stanley Keleman's model, they all derive—directly or indirectly—from Reich's theories, as developed further by Lowen (Bioenergetics) and Pierrakos (Core Energetics).

There is considerable variety in how firmly the different schools of Body Psychotherapy hold onto these models (Tables 28.1–28.3), with some viewing them as clearly defined typologies, whereas others conceive of them as basic matrices and prototypes that people tend to gravitate toward from their self-organization processes.

Due to limitations of space, the "character types" are presented only as very simplified sketches. Our main intention is to give an overview as to how the basic principles and character types have been developed, in different ways, by the various schools. To delve deeper into their views on character theory, we recommend the textbooks of the respective schools.

| COMPULSIVE CHARACTER | MASOCHISTIC CHARACTER | PHALLIC-NARCISSISTIC CHARACTER | HYSTERICAL CHARACTER |
|---|---|---|---|
| All muscles of the body—in particular, those of the pelvic floor, the pelvis, the shoulders, and the face—are tense. Masklike, hard physiognomy, disjointed awkwardness. Pedantic sense of order, tendency toward labored, ruminating, obsessive thinking. | Tendency toward lamentation, conveying constant sense of suffering. Unskillful social behavior. "Look how unhappy, lonely, and abandoned I am." Chronic tendency toward submissive self-humiliation and self-deprecating mannerisms. | Athletic bodily structure; facial features characterized by hard, sharp, masculine lines. Appears self-confident, arrogant, strong, often imposing. | Subtle or obvious flirtatiousness in gait, gaze, and voice, particularly in women. Softness, overly polite, feminine facial expression in men. Movements are soft, rocking, and sexually provocative. Behaviorally labile. Strongly suggestible, paired with strong reactions of disappointment. Tendency toward daydreaming. |

Table 28.1. Character theory according to Reich

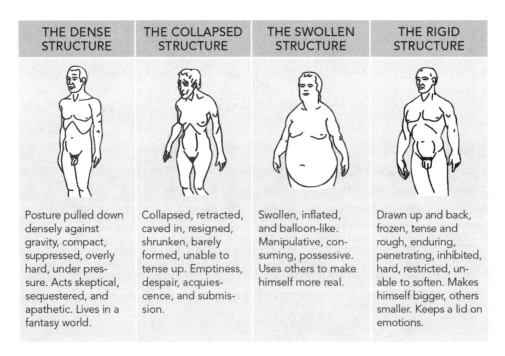

| THE DENSE STRUCTURE | THE COLLAPSED STRUCTURE | THE SWOLLEN STRUCTURE | THE RIGID STRUCTURE |
|---|---|---|---|
| Posture pulled down densely against gravity, compact, suppressed, overly hard, under pressure. Acts skeptical, sequestered, and apathetic. Lives in a fantasy world. | Collapsed, retracted, caved in, resigned, shrunken, barely formed, unable to tense up. Emptiness, despair, acquiescence, and submission. | Swollen, inflated, and balloon-like. Manipulative, consuming, possessive. Uses others to make himself more real. | Drawn up and back, frozen, tense and rough, enduring, penetrating, inhibited, hard, restricted, unable to soften. Makes himself bigger, others smaller. Keeps a lid on emotions. |

Table 28.2. Character theory according to Keleman

| SCHOOL | SCHIZOID | ORAL | ORAL-COMPENSATED | MASOCHISTIC | PSYCHO-PATHIC 1 | PSYCHO-PATHIC 2 | RIGID | |
|---|---|---|---|---|---|---|---|---|
| | | | | | | | HYSTERIC | PHALLIC |
| BIO-ENERGETIC & CORE ENERGETIC | Contracted; frozen, lifeless; stiff, tense; robotic; suspicious (paranoid eyes, sometimes squinting) | Collapsed posture; sunken chest; without energy; yearning, searching for holding | Not described in this schema | Squashed, held in (neck, pelvic floor); passive resistance; shame & guilt; baby face | Energetically pulled up, pumped-up chest; eyes charged and intense; manipulative; capable of performing | Not described in this schema | Well-proportioned physique, hypertonic musculature, expressive eyes, fears and avoids surrender, tense jaw, passivity equated with vulnerability; expects to appear ridiculous and stupid when letting go | |
| HAKOMI | Contracted, uncoordinated; sensitive; withdrawn, shy | Low tonus; collapsed, dependent, compliant; searching for contact | Strong body; active, musculature high tonus; independent | Compacted; center of gravity low; slow, over-loaded, but tenacious | Dominant, controlling, can be generous; physically: high point of gravity | Description of body not possible, as no fixed features, other than hyper-flexible | Is very energetic, chest protected and held, expressive, holding on, emotional; hypertonic; upright, industrious, overly rational and focused | Flexible body, charming, seductive, opportunistic |
| BODY-NAMIC | EXISTENCE: From 4 months Embryo–1 month | NEED: until 1.5 years | AUTONOMY: 8 months–2.5 years | WILL: 2–4 years | LOVE-SEXUALITY: 3–6 years | | FORMING OPINIONS: 5–9 years | SOLIDARITY, ACHIEVEMENT-ORIENTED: 7–12 years |

Table 28.3. Character theory in Bioenergetic, Core Energetic, and Bodynamic Psychotherapy

## References

Bentzen, M., Bernhardt, P., & Isaacs, J. (1996). Waking the body ego II. *Energy & Character, 27(1)*.

Bernhardt, P., Bentzen, M., & Isaacs, J. (1997). *Waking the body ego. Bodynamic Analysis: Lisbeth Marcher's Somatic Developmental Psychology. Part I: Core concepts and principles.* Copenhagen: Bodynamic Institute.

Boadella, D., & Smith, D. L. (1986). *Maps of character.* Abbotsbury, UK: Abbotsbury Publications.

Dietrich, R. (1999). *Das Labyrinth der fünf Charakterstrukturen [The labyrinth of five character structures].* Elixhausen, Österreich, Austria: Verlag Dietrich.

Keleman, S. (1992). *Verkörperte Gefühle [Emotional anatomy].* Munich: Kösel.

Kurtz, R. (1985). *Körperzentrierte Psychotherapie: Die Hakomi Methode [Body-Oriented Psychotherapy: The Hakomi Method].* Essen: Synthesis Verlag.

Lowen, A. (1981). *Körperausdruck und Persönlichkeit [Body language and personality].* Munich: Kösel.

Reich, W. (1945/1970). *Charakteranalyse [Character Analysis].* Cologne: Kiepenheuer & Witsch.

# 29

## Early Interaction and the Body: Clinical Implications

### George Downing, France

**George Downing**, PhD, is a clinical psychologist of American origin, now living in Paris, and is on the teaching faculties of the Pitié-Salpêtrière Hospital and Paris University VIII.

Early interactions between caregivers and infants are fascinating and intricate. The research about it moves steadily forward. What is of value here for the therapist working with adults or with children? Which findings help us best to understand our patients? What might be implied for treatment? These are questions that bedevil many therapists.

If these questions are relevant for most types of therapy, they are especially so for practitioners of body psychotherapy. Much of early adult-infant interaction involves a large body and a small body finding out how to relate to each other.

I will summarize here a few points about the research, and then make some suggestions about psychotherapeutic practice. In addition to the research itself, I will draw upon my personal experience, working in settings involving parent-infant psychiatry.

### Two Familiar Points

One often hears in the psychotherapy world the following two claims:

1. When parents and infants, or parents and small children, interact, there takes place a second-by-second flow of signals and responses. This has been shown by the video-microanalytic research of Beebe (Beebe and Jaffe, 2008; Beebe and Lachmann, 2014), as well as Stern (1985, 2010) and Tronick (2007), among others. What seems to be of a high positive benefit in these exchanges are episodes of response "matching": other names used are "attunement," "mirroring," "echoing," "synchronization," and "contingency."

2. Attachment research highlights another critical type of early interaction. This is the sequence of events taking place when an infant or child communicates a need for calming, consolation, or emotional reassurance. Does the parent give the needed soothing (Ainsworth et al., 1978)? Can the child accept and use what is given? A prevalence of successful exchanges is associated with so-called "secure attachment." When such exchanges appear dysfunctional, this predicts one or another form of "insecure attachment."

Both ideas, so stated, seem clear enough. But if we look more closely, it turns out that a lot more needs to be said.

### The Complexity of Matching

What the research of more recent years demonstrates is that "matching" is not always good. If some kinds of matching help infants to thrive emotionally, other forms have an opposite effect. I will here describe some of these more problematic forms of matching.

305

## Pacing

Imagine an infant is awake, alert, and looking at his parent (or another caregiver). On her (or his) side, the parent is looking at the infant. They interact.

But . . . how rapidly does the parent respond to the infant? How rapidly does the infant respond to the parent? Looking at the bidirectional flow, we can speak about the "pacing," the "tempo," the "rhythm," and also (ultimately) the "coherence" of the interaction.

The interesting, indeed stunning, research finding is that if synchronization between mother and child happens at too fast a rate, this ultimately has negative effects. Evidence from Beatrice Beebe and her team (Beebe and Lachmann, 2013; Jaffe et al., 2001) shows this consequence quite starkly. They observed and measured the precise rhythmic timing of more than sixty parent-infant dyads.

To their surprise, they discovered that infants who, at four months, were caught up in a (comparatively) more rapid coordination turned out, at twelve months, when examined in the Ainsworth "Strange Situation" (Ainsworth et al., 1978), to be insecurely attached. Indeed, those infants for whom the exchange went the fastest were the ones most likely to manifest a "disorganized" attachment, the least-favorable type of insecure attachment. What Beebe calls "mid-range" matching, neither too high nor too low, turned out to be best for child development.

To qualify these remarks, what Beebe actually coded was "contingency," which is a wider concept than "matching." B's response is "contingent" upon A's initial signal as long as it occurs directly after [i.e., within three seconds] A's action. B's response might or might not be one of "matching," in the sense of a display of a similar emotion. If you study videos from Beebe's cohort, however, you soon find that most of the dyads with excessive contingency also have high matching.

## Negative-Negative Matches

Suppose an infant is crying strongly. She is making facial expressions of evident distress. Intuitively, if you think about it, you might expect it to be unhelpful if the mother (or father, or other caregiver) were simply to duplicate the signals of distress.

Suppose a two-year-old is communicating angry protest. Should the adult respond with equivalent signs of anger?

Just as you might guess, it turns out that such negative-negative matches are undesirable, and strongly so. Like excessive matching, this is another bad form of synchronization. Cristina Riva Crugnola (Riva Crugnola et al., 2014; Riva Crugnola et al., 2015) who, like Beebe, combines microanalytic and attachment measures, has looked at such "negative-negative" events in detail. She demonstrated that higher frequencies of these exchanges during the early months are correlated with more negative attachment outcomes for the child at age twelve months.

A special variant of negative-negative matching concerns what has been called "coercive process" (Patterson, 2002). A preschool-age child is misbehaving, or so thinks their parent. The parent attempts to set a boundary; the child refuses to comply.

One or the other then begins to amplify his or her negative tone. The other amplifies likewise. Together they escalate, stimulating each other upward, until the parent (often) finally gives up. Because the child (often) wins, and doesn't have to do what was requested, he or she ends up being "trained" over time to amplify negatively. Of course, this leads to many further problems.

## Selective Tracking

Here is a complexity that doesn't necessarily have negative consequences. But it is of interest to any therapist who gives attention to the bodily components of interactions.

Parents have distinct patterns, statistical prevalences, with regard to exactly what types of signals they respond to (Beebe and Lachmann, 2014). One mother will closely track her infant's vocal sounds. She will react more to these productions than, say, to infant "look–look away" patterns. Another mother may have the opposite tendency.

We are talking here only about tracking. There are a multitude of actions that the infant may be producing: gaze direction, various sounds, facial expression, self-touching, touching of the mother, arching the back, looking away, crying, and so on. But what the parent reacts to in all of this variety is quite selective. Responding to only a part of the infant's expressive package, she unconsciously filters out the rest.

On his side, the infant is equally selective. He picks up on certain elements of the mother's expressive package, and then filters out the other elements. Quite quickly he gets into a "selected" set of responses: this is "selective tracking." It is not negative; it is just selective—and therefore is somewhat limited.

**Selective Responding**

Parents not only track, but also respond selectively. One adult's contingent reactions might consist more of facial expressions; another favors a style of touching; another, vocal expressions; or the like (Beebe and Lachmann, 2014). Some channels of communication are used more, others are used relatively little. (Remember, this involves *contingent* reactions, not affective signals in general.) Infants also respond selectively.

Oddly, these variations of response tendency can be somewhat independent of the tracking tendency. This is true on the side of both the adult and the infant. Two mothers might both closely follow infant facial displays; yet the one matches more using vocalizations, and the other matches using facial expressions.

Stern (1985) once spoke of "cross-modal attunement." We can now say that far more of this goes on than he had ever guessed, and infants, as well as adults, do it. It is a two-way, mutual response mechanism; however, once this has been established, one party can always break the pattern—because of stress or distress—and this may set up stress or distress in the other party.

**Matching with Contradictions**

It is not at all rare, unfortunately, to see a parent providing synchronized responses, but with a double, contradictory quality. Here, at moment *X*, the father gives a warm smile, but it is packaged in almost the same half-second with a "nasty" poking of the finger. Another father might couple a gentle touch with a facial expression of disgust.

Many such combinations are possible. Many are in fact seen. One imagines that this could be seriously disorienting for the infant, who is supposed to be learning how to read the adult's body and facial expressions, long before the acquisition of language. Occasionally, we even find an infant responding with his own "split" or "contradictory" signal-sending.

To the small extent that such mixed signals have been studied, they have been associated with negative outcomes in later childhood (Beebe and Lachmann, 2014; Lyons-Ruth and Jacobvitz, 1999); however, I can add—from personal experience—that these are quite commonly seen in parent-infant psychiatric treatment settings. While the "psychiatric" parent may start to give mixed signals, the child soon starts to respond in a similar fashion, as this is its learning environment. This contradictory response then "confuses" the parent still further, and the spiral escalates.

**Matching with Continuation**

We turn now to a more positive phenomenon. A major limitation of the concept of matching is that it describes only a very brief event, and not what comes afterward. Suppose the parent matches the infant and/or the infant matches the parent. Good enough: but does the process stop here, or does it continue? Is there a repetition and an elaboration of the matching, a mutual response taking it further? Does something develop over several seconds, or longer?

As you might imagine, this kind of thing is easy enough to see in an informal way, but rather elusive when it comes to any form of reliable coding: Beebe (Beebe and Lachmann, 2014) discussed some of this; Feldman's coding system (Feldman, 1998), exceptionally, has a distinct category for continuation; Tronick's (2007) concept of "dyadic expansion" would also seem to be an important subtype; and Fogal's (1993) coding system at least captures nicely, on a microlevel, the length of time the parent and the infant appear to remain in contact (i.e., it captures one aspect, length of time, but not the second aspect, elaboration).

Speaking informally, when—during the treatment of parent-infant dyads—you find something of this type of matching starting to happen, it seems to be a good sign. Typically, it accompanies other positive changes.

### Continuation with Guidance

An important variant of continuation can occur when the infant or child is in a negative state, and the parent steers her out of it, or tries to.

The parent "matches," but in a fairly low-key manner: a kind of semi-matching. Then she steers, she lures the child into a different state, by introducing inflections or interventions that move the child gradually toward a more positive affect zone.

This could sound like mismatching, but it is not, because the inflections come in small steps, and only to the extent that the infant follows along—i.e., he begins to shift his expression as well (Beebe and Lachmann, 2014). In a sense, it is a form of contradictory matching, but a beneficial one, and with a beneficial intent and outcome. Fonagy and Gergely (Fonagy et al., 2002) have spoken of "markers" that an adult can add to her expressions. Perhaps she makes a sad face, but—at times—"marks" it with a hint of a smile, or a little tickle, or something else that helps or leads the child out of his distressed state.

This is a very helpful concept. Marker use is also a type of what could be called "beneficial contradictory matching." In addition, when you see it occurring, it is often in a context of continuation with guidance.

There is almost no research about marker use (Fonagy and Gergely's original description was not based on any data, for example), but a good guess is that it is highly favorable for development. Fonagy and Gergely advance a complicated theoretical account of why this might be so. A more parsimonious explanation would be that, through a kind of imitation learning, the infant or child is acquiring new affect skills. She is learning how to regulate her negative emotions and how to elaborate her positive ones.

### Attachment Transactions

Concerning attachment, I will confine myself to a brief comment about a very large subject. Many therapists have become aware of the invaluable findings of modern attachment research. But two points are worth underlining, especially if we are talking about how the body is brought into play.

First, what we want to see, in determining if an infant or young child has a "secure attachment," is something more than just open communication of a need. An attachment transaction has three parts. Person *A*—an infant (let's say)—openly signals a need for . . . (say) . . . soothing. Person *B*—a parent (let's say)—reacts by giving "adequate enough" soothing: but that is not the end. The third step is that person *A* must then take in, and use, the provided soothing, allowing himself (in this instance) to regulate his distress downward.

Clearly, this third step demands a set of body capabilities, in itself. For example, an infant with a "resistant" attachment, category C, during the second reunion moment of the Ainsworth "Strange Situation" (Ainsworth et al., 1978), will dart across the room to the reentering parent with an open display of distress, just as we might wish to see. It is the third step, the allowing of calming, that often goes awry. One set of abilities, the showing of the need, is available for use. The other set, the allowing of calming, can be essentially underdeveloped. (We could also go on to talk about overdeveloped defensive procedures that one sees in this context.)

The second significant point is that, in development, a child needs to learn the competencies belonging to both sides of an attachment transaction. This means she needs to learn the skills of step 2, the giving of soothing, as well as those of steps 1 and 3. A child begins to acquire this, to the extent that he does, starting usually in the second year of life (Bloom, 2013). Unless she has learnt this, as a child, then she may later find it difficult to give it, as an adult.

The standard coding of the "Strange Situation" looks only at the child's actual behavior. Karlen Lyons-Ruth (Bronfman et al., 2004), however, has created a highly useful coding system for the adult's behavior, as well. It is extraordinary, using this lens, to see—on a micropractices level—the wide range of difficulties that some adults have in giving the child what is needed. One observes not only the missing abilities, but also the complicated defensive ways to utilize the body.

Interestingly, the valuable research of Robert Marvin and Jude Cassidy (Marvin, 1999) demonstrates how some young children have very underdeveloped step 1 skills, yet have excellent step 2 skills. At the age of twelve months, in a "Strange Situation," they manifest a "disorganized" attachment: their actions—especially during the second reunion—become fragmented, or even contradictory in nature.

Yet, during the second and third years of life, they become expert at giving soothing. We find here a "parentified" child, whose solution to his dilemma has been to take control of the child-parent relationship, and to take control specifically by being the one who takes care of the other.

This has obvious negative implications, but we can notice one positive consequence: the child has developed good procedural capacities for emotional giving and nourishing.

## Body Organizing: A Unifying Concept

So, how can we best make sense of this rich array of findings? The concept of *body organizing* provides a useful lens. In the first months of her life, the infant is building up a complex repertoire of body organizing "know-how." She is learning far more than simple motor skills, like reaching and grasping. She is developing intricate modes of using the full range of resources of her body in all her interactions. She is learning, as well, how to use her body for emotional regulation, in general.

As adults, we are constantly organizing our bodies on a second-by-second basis. We adjust posture, movement, breathing, facial expression, muscle tightening, muscle loosening, body language, gestures, etc. But the same is also true for an infant or child. Her capacities will be fewer, and often of a lower complexity, yet many are being exercised from very early on, starting almost immediately after birth.

This is procedural know-how, but—for us adults at least—it is not entirely unconscious. It is a mistake, by the way, to equate procedural know-how with a necessary lack of conscious awareness (Stanley, 2011). Some of it we are aware of, and can consciously influence: we guide and inflect, suppress or allow. Heller (2012), Stern (2010), and Tronick (2007) have expressed similar ideas.

But, for an adult or an older child, an awareness of body organizing is a fundamental component of subjective conscious states. Often, it is minimally present, just as thoughts and emotions are often minimally present, but it can be brought more into greater focus at any time.

This form of proprioceptive awareness overlaps with emotion, when the latter is present: think of what Frijda (1986; c. f. Downing, 2000) has called the "action readiness" of feelings. But, it is far more differentiated than emotion, and often operates independently of the latter.

Body organizing is a form of behavior, strictly speaking, but such a special subtype that it makes sense to have a distinct category for it. What we ordinarily think of as behavior occurs in discrete global chunks. I decide to get a glass of water from the kitchen. I get up, go there, bring the glass of water back, sit down again—chunk ended. In contrast, body organizing never stops (except perhaps during sleep: a question that I put aside for the moment). Body organizing is a steady stream, often done relatively unconsciously. When we consciously access it, and perhaps steer, or adjust, or permit it, we modify something that was already under way.

Harrison (2013) and Tronick (2007, 2013) suggest that body organizing is one form, among others, of "meaning-making," and this makes quite a lot of sense. At a minimum, we can say that the body-organizing stream not only sets the stage for global behavior, but also affects information flow, because it constantly modifies the parameters of the perceptual field (Myin and O'Regan, 2009; Tversky, 2009).

The infant appears to build up a "core repertoire" of body organizing know-how during (approximately) the first two years. How can we further describe this repertoire?

## The Core Repertoire: Characteristics

What one sees as clear as a bell in both clinical—i.e., used for intervention (Downing, 2008)—and research videos is that every infant develops his own idiosyncratic core repertoire. Some of this know-how will be akin to that of other infants, and some will be special—unique—unto himself.

Concerning his interactions, he will develop a good number of variants in how he engages himself in these different contexts. We will see some body organizing tendencies that are used more in interactions with his mother, others with his father, and others with his older sister, or other siblings. Still other tendencies will show up when he engages simultaneously with his mother and his father, or with other groupings (Fivaz-Depeursinge and Corboz-Warnery, 1999). In addition, some organizing know-how will be confined to specific activities—e.g., feeding. Certain of these "micropractices" (Downing, 2005) will be facilitative in nature: they mobilize positive emotional contact, or appropriate boundary setting, or practical cooperation (Tomasello, 2009), for example.

Others are defensive in nature: they protect the infant from some of, for him, the more difficult aspects of a relationship. Consider an infant regularly confronted with excessive physical intrusion: there exist various options for how he might learn to respond. One such "choice," among others, might be to lower his gaze, stiffen his upper body a bit, and focus his attention on physical objects below. Here is a group of micropractices that, in its original setting, makes perfect sense. It was likely happened upon initially by chance, and then reinforced by its successful protective result (Downing et al., 2008). Once ingrained, however, it can have negative effects in later childhood and in adulthood. The adult will of course execute more evolved and subtle versions.

A third critical aspect of any infant's core repertoire concerns what is missing or underdeveloped. Some of the potential positive facilitating abilities may have had little opportunity to emerge, but they have just not received the parental scaffolding or reinforcement that they would have needed.

Some procedural micropractices belong exclusively to interaction—e.g., tracking and response patterns. Some are used both in solo and in interactional contexts—e.g., emotional regulation abilities.

I would add that what body psychotherapists call "grounding" seems to be an important part of the core repertoire. The assumption, developed primarily by Lowen (1958), is that the child's process of learning to stand and walk is highly intertwined with, and affected by, experiences of a relational and emotional kind.

Here again, we lack empirical information, of course. There exist some fine examples of research about the emergence of, successively, sitting, crawling, standing, walking; but exactly how interactional exchanges might shape these capacities has been studied very little.

What I have seen from clinical videos suggests that the slow attainment of vertical modes of body organizing is indeed an area fraught with emotional dynamics. Although I will not go into detail here, I suspect there are a lot more variations than were guessed at by Lowen. In any case, it makes sense to see the procedural capacities involved in "grounding" as significant.

Another area of guesswork concerns the effects of body-to-body contact. By this I mean when an infant's or small child's body is held flush against the adult body. Is there, as one suspects, a complex reciprocal exchange taking place here? Does one body make a minute adjustment, the other body an adjustment in response, and so on? How fine-grained do such exchanges become? What are typical positive and negative variations, and how are these correlated with subsequent developmental outcomes?

Excellent questions, but no one has yet developed the research instruments that we would need to record and quantify such a process. For sure, in the future, this will become an important field of investigation. In the meantime, the reasonable default assumption is that micropractices concerning body-to-body contact—be they facilitating, defensive, or underdeveloped micropractices—also represent another important component of the core repertoire.

Early interaction will of course be affected by whatever neurophysiological factors the infant brings to the table. The role of temperament here has long been known (Kagen, 2010). However, a much more complex picture is starting to emerge thanks to epigenetics research. Though a lively field, research about the relation of epigenetics and behavior is still in its infancy, so it seems premature to draw a lot of conclusions. What exactly is the range of effects that prenatal and postnatal gene expression can have upon the formation of procedural micro/practices? Are such influences for the most part of an indirect nature—e.g., by altering the hypothalamic-pituitary-adrenal (HPA) axis (Lester, 2013)? To what extent will more specific causal variances be found? We can count on learning much of interest along these lines in the coming years.

Bruce Perry (2008, 2013a, 2013b) has suggested persuasively that, for some infants and small children, trauma can have an analogous role. Extreme forms of trauma occurring during the prenatal period, or during birth, or during the first three years of life, as well as extreme neglect, can very likely compromise one or another specific aspects of brain development. And this, in turn, may create constraints on the shaping of the procedural core. Here is yet another significant area where, in the future, we will hopefully profit from more precise empirical investigations.

## Concerning Terminology

As an aside: in the past, speaking and writing about such procedural abilities, I have at times used the term "affective-motor schemas." My thought was to draw an analogy with Piaget's "sensory-motor schemas."

I have been forced to realize that the term does not quite fit. The microfpractices presented in interactions involve much more than just emotional signaling. Multiple purposes are in play. For example, I lean forward, so that I can better see the other's face. Or I move one hand, so as to spatially illustrate something that I am saying with my words. "Joint cooperation procedures" (Tomasello, 2009) represent a more complex example of reciprocal body-organizing, which includes, but is considerably wider than, just an expression of affect.

## Subsequent Childhood Years

Obviously, the core repertoire of interactional and regulatory procedural know-how evolves further as the child grows older. Here again, good research information is harder to come by.

My hypothesis, which is hardly radical, is that "social" bodily microfpractices are developed extensively during the school-age years. Or, rather, they should be: some children will develop them poorly—e.g., a socially isolated child, or a hyperactive child who has poor social perception, or an autistic spectrum child, or a child who has been bullied or abused. These social microfpractices are, as it were, a series of further layers added on to the core repertoire.

Severe trauma, particularly if bodily in nature (e.g., sexual abuse, physical violence, lengthy painful medical procedures, etc.), can also introduce significant changes. New protective and defensive procedural elements may be added. For some traumatized children, a tendency to dissociate easily, and thereby reduce complex body organizing to more simple forms, may emerge. Plus, as mentioned above, very early trauma, occurring before the initial core repertoire is formed, may well have still more pernicious effects, in that brain development may also be significantly affected.

The adolescent years add further layers, it would seem. Partly, this reflects the onset of new sexual feelings, partly more motor finesse, and partly something else, I suspect. It is no small matter for a young person to discover that he or she is now socially perceived in a totally different way. He or she now has more sexual presence in the world, like it or not, and must develop new procedural ways with which to navigate this altered universe of seeing and being seen. Naturally, sexual activity, whenever it eventually becomes part of an adolescent's or adult's life, is a dimension of the body, organizing itself in its own right.

We can only guess how much of the original core repertoire (the bodily microfpractices built up in the first two years) remains intact, at least in some form, during the rest of development. The question is significant, here again.

My strong sense is that probably quite a bit of it remains: the positive facilitating aspects, the defensive aspects, and especially the underdeveloped aspects. An adult's social veneer renders these elements less obvious, but a trained eye can see them.

What we know, from longitudinal attachment research, modestly supports this idea. Attachment patterns tend to have a certain degree of stability (Steele and Steele, 2005). Take a child who, at twelve months, in the "Strange Situation" paradigm, manifests an avoidant attachment to both parents; then follow him over the years; and we are likely to see him as an older child, or as an adult, displaying analogous versions of the same traits. So, what does all of this imply for clinical work? What can it mean for psychotherapy to add in a serious focus on the process of body organizing?

## Two Models of the Purpose of Body Psychotherapy

The principal concern of the early body psychotherapists was with the static body. Reich thought patients suffered chiefly from chronic, enduring muscular tensions. He considered that their bodies were "armored," a state of affairs that inhibited their "energy," or life force. Therapy should therefore aim to reduce the armoring and thereby liberate their life force.

To give a different priority instead to the ongoing process of body organizing is to adopt a quite different perspective. The core procedural repertoire, not the chronic tensions, becomes the main target for change. An emphasis is now placed upon the teasing out, and altering of, specific procedural practices. Underdeveloped positive micropractices are therefore supported and expanded. Overdeveloped defensive practices are (hopefully) reduced and left behind. This is a process view, rather than a static perspective.

Of course it can be argued that a tight, tense, constricted body will have that much less open room to explore and cultivate new modes of body organization. There is some truth in this point, and I will return to it shortly. Nevertheless, to take body organizing as psychologically more primary, and muscular alignment as essentially secondary, is to think in another—a very different—way. It thus leads to a different style of practical (clinical) work.

Most body psychotherapeutic approaches mix the two points of view to some degree. It is helpful to think of this as a spectrum. Reich, in his later years, is representative of one pole. His emphasis predominantly favored the static body, despite some attention given to procedural specifics (e.g., in his work with eye contact, breathing, and pelvic release).

Lowen, who learned from Reich, stayed with very similar theoretical constructs. Therapy (according to him) should concentrate upon muscular "blocks" (Reich's armoring) and the freeing of "energy." Yet, on a practical level, Lowen stood more toward the middle of the spectrum, with a greater interest than Reich in distinct procedural capacities—e.g., emotional reaching (think of attachment needs), and ways to create a body sense of setting boundaries. Especially, his work with "grounding" reflects a concern with the concrete flow of body organization.

A good representative example of the opposite pole is Stanley Keleman (1975). Originally a colleague of Lowen, Keleman migrated, with time, to a quite different therapeutic style, with a lot of slow, precise attention to how—in the session—the patient acted to compose his or her body. The patient is aided to sense these elements from within, and, where appropriate, to explore alternatives.

Some other approaches, quite close to this second polarity, are those of Peter Geissler and his colleagues (Geissler, 2009; Geissler and Heisterkamp, 2013), Ron Kurtz (1990), Pat Ogden (Ogden, Minton, and Pain, 2006), and Al Pesso (1973). My own approach stands somewhere here too, having profited from close acquaintance with both Lowen's and Keleman's perspectives.

Concerning these two diametrically opposed models of purpose, for myself a basic issue has to do with the allocation of resources. When serious work with body organizing is joined with psychotherapy, then there is a lot to do. And there are a good number of new skills a therapist must learn for it. On the other side, first, the right sort of work with body organization will, in itself to some degree, effect static bodily changes. Second, more extensive work with muscular alignment and the like can be done well, if not better, elsewhere, by another kind of professional. Excellent resources exist for this today: Alexander Technique, Hellerwork, Rolfing, the Feldenkrais Method, Tai Chi, deep tissue massage, yoga, and others.

## Clinical Implications: One Possible Answer

My own methodology has evolved over a good many years. I became closely acquainted with early interaction research, and came to see the concept of moment-by-moment body organizing, including reciprocal body organizing in relationships, as fundamental. This raised for me a question that has occupied me ever since: What, on the level of therapeutic technique, will best help a patient to restructure the procedural core?

I was also confronted with a second issue, one reflecting certain personal particulars. In Paris, where I live, I was asked, at one point, to join a child psychiatry team at Pitié-Salpêtrière Hospital. Things evolved, and I became progressively more engaged with psychiatric settings, both with children and with adults. (In Europe, the use of psychotherapy in psychiatric clinics is much more frequent than in the United States.)

Now, if you really believe in including a focus on the body in therapy, how are you going to do it in this particular context? As Röhricht (2000) has nicely described, patients with a serious psychiatric disorder present us with a definite paradox. Many are scared by the idea of deepened contact with their bodies. At the same time, these are patients who are even more in need of such help. What might be a form of good solution here? Fortunately, in recent years, enormous changes have taken place in psychiatric work itself. There has been a proliferation of disorder-specific treatment programs, cognitive behavioral in nature, some of them manualized and researched. They reflect a way of thinking that I at first found tedious, but that, over time, I came to appreciate. Clarity counts for a lot. What I felt more critical about was what seemed to be, in these programs, an insufficient attention to the patient's body. There appeared to be an empty niche here, and I puzzled about what that might imply. Much reflecting and practical probing ensued.

The result—and this is what I now do and teach—I regard as a form of cognitive behavioral therapy, an enhanced version of which I call "Body-Focused Therapy." Today, there exist admirable CBT modalities that—in different ways—put emphasis on the body: e.g., Greenberg's (2002) Emotion-Focused Therapy, Gilbert's (2009) Compassion Focused Therapy, the body-oriented mindfulness approach of Segal, Williams, and Teasdale (2002), and some of the newer CBT work with imagery, such as that of Hackmann, Bennett-Levy, and Holmes (2011). However, systematic work with procedural body organizing, though akin to, is not the same as these. The difference has some significant clinical consequences.

The name "Body-Focused Therapy" is a misnomer, of course. The method is as much centered upon beliefs and global behavior as upon procedural organizing. Mentalization is also regarded. The choice reflects what is arguably a peculiarity of the current mainstream psychotherapeutic landscape, that there is widespread underestimation of the resources of the body itself.

## Attention to Body Organizing: Some First Remarks

Diverse as the cognitive behavioral therapeutic world has become, common to all forms is one or another style of exploration of various states of consciousness.

The patient speaks about, for example, a problem, a recent event, a relationship, or even something happening between himself and the therapist. He (or she) is then asked to make explicit what thought or thoughts are present within. Perhaps additional thoughts, implied by or alongside the first ones, will be asked for as well. It is likely that he or she will also be asked, at some point, about any accompanying emotions. CBT "guided discovery" is probably the single most used technical procedure in psychotherapy today.

Nothing is easier than to make periodic reference to body organizing during such guided discovery. "Show me, with one hand or both (i.e., by making a gesture), what it is like to have this thought." "As you focus on this thought, what does your body start to do: what tiniest something moves or changes?" "Could you find a posture that goes with having this thought?" I mention just a few of the many possibilities.

Some patients immediately manage quite well with these interventions that highlight body organizing. Others fumble around at first, but then gradually pick up the knack, just as often is the case with a focus on thoughts or emotions during guided discovery.

You might think—offhand—that a move toward body organizing would be the same as going toward emotion. However, it doesn't quite work in that way. Even if the therapist asks with regard to an emotion, e.g., "Where in your body do you feel that sadness?," this intervention, though excellent in itself, will not typically elicit any degree of body organizing. Simply to perceive, in my body, a sadness, or a pain, is not yet to sense *what I am doing* with my body with this particular emotion. However minute, however faintly felt, it is the subjective perception of action that is the target here: "What does this feeling make me want to do?"

One can, of course, move from the recognition of emotion toward body organizing, just as one can move from thoughts: "Show me with a hand, or both hands, what this joyful feeling is like," and so on. What we obviously require—in order to conduct guided discovery in this way—is a paradigm much wider than the standard notion of "thoughts and feelings." A more effective paradigm is a sort of triangle: "thoughts and feelings and body organizing." At any time, a therapist can shift from one point of this particular triangle to either of the other two. She (or he) can weave about appropriately, as fits the investigative process with that particular client that day.

## Replays and Body Organizing

A therapist who uses guided discovery will frequently encourage a patient to explore "replays," a staple of numerous CBT approaches. The patient revisits a specific interaction, usually problematic, but sometimes positive, that he (or she) has recently experienced. The therapist and the patient, step-by-step, examine some part, or perhaps all, of the interaction, trying to get a sense of what happened outwardly, as well as what took place inwardly.

Information about body organizing is of course elicited as well. But now its purpose becomes double. Although the immediate information is helpful in itself, its exploration also allows the therapist to introduce a more general theme. Sooner or later, a new kind of question will be regarded during these replays. Instead of just (variants of) "How in the interaction are you step-by-step composing your body?," there will be (variants of) "How in the interaction, step-by-step, are the two of you jointly composing your bodies?" asked at times as well.

The intent is to build up a new concept of how interpersonal body organizing unfolds. Most adults have only a hazy sense, if any, of the bidirectionality of joint body organizing. It is not something they have thought about much, let alone regularly noticed.

A firm grasp of such a concept can, of course, only be acquired gradually. Hence, education about it plays a critical role in the therapy. As she begins to understand better the "body-with-body" co-creation of interaction, the patient will adopt new goals and procedures for herself in this area.

Replays like this are used for other ends as well: for example, work with mentalization—i.e., for work with what we might call "other-mentalization," the capacity to generate productive hypotheses about what the other person is experiencing and thinking. Fonagy (2008) and his colleagues have written extensively about the helpfulness of replays for this particular purpose.

Basically, mentalization is a cognitive process, not something done with the body. Of course this depends on how you define it, a controversy that I will not address here. Nevertheless, if we are talking about mentalizing "in the moment"—i.e., occurring during a particular interaction—what happens with joint body organizing goes hand-in-hand with (good or poor) mentalization thinking.

On the practical level, Fonagy and his colleagues work with mentalization above all when examining the therapeutic relationship. For them this is the main field of investigation; replays of outside interactions (i.e., with persons other than the therapist) are secondary.

With the methodology being described here, the reverse is the case. A spotlight is brought to the therapeutic relationship at times (Gilbert, 2007; Katzow and Safran, 2007; Safran and Muran, 2000). This may well also include, when appropriate, some investigation of how the therapist and the patient are coordinating their particular body organizing: a subject that I have written about elsewhere (Downing, 2011). Issues about mentalization are likely to be raised as well. But, over the course of the therapy, given a cooperative working atmosphere in the sessions, what is taking place in outside relationships is kept just as much in the foreground of the therapy, if not more so. The patient is thereby supported to keep discovering how he (or she) uses their body in diverse settings, with diverse relationships, and in diverse emotional climates.

This emphasis reflects two realities. One is that different settings elicit different procedural processes. The patient becomes an observer across multiple contexts in order to gather the insights she needs. A second reality concerns change. As helpful as an emergence of new ways to relate in the therapeutic relationship can be, generalization is not assured. It makes sense to combine such explorations with a systematic attention to the nuances of body organizing in as wide a range of current relationships as possible.

At times, when exploring the specifics of an interaction, attention is given as well to whatever interpersonal dynamic scenarios (e.g., dominance/submission) may be in play. An overview of the various scenarios being activated in different parts of the patient's life progressively emerges (c.f. Ryle, 1990, 1997; Ryle and Kerr, 2002). By means of detailed investigation of replays, and of on-the-spot patient-therapist exchanges, and perhaps of an occasional video of interaction (see below), the patient becomes acquainted with typical groupings of micropractices that she (or he) tends to mobilize when playing out either side of these scenarios.

### Finding New Beginnings

Sometimes the hardest step in any CBT-based procedure is that of "belief modification." A dysfunctional belief has been clarified. An alternative belief has been formulated, through inquiry, or simply by the therapist proposing it. The patient weighs the two beliefs and (perhaps) can see, abstractly, that the alternative belief might have something to it, or at least might have some pragmatic advantage. Yet, this intellectual insight in itself may bring little real change. The dysfunctional belief still holds the person in its grip.

One of the best merits of the triangle paradigm is how it can assist with this dilemma. A move from the alternative belief toward body organizing can give the former a bit of flesh, so to speak: "So, imagine again what it would be like to believe this other idea, this notion that you in fact are someone worthy of being respected by another person. Imagine really believing that, and show me, with one or both hands, or with your whole body, what it is like."

A patient may or may not succeed in vividly exploring this image, but if she does, she will normally experience the new thought—or feeling—in a very altered manner, however briefly. There will be a heightened openness to the thought, a "trying it on" for size, literally, in a much more than intellectual manner. Usually, this form of embodiment of the change in itself will not tip the scale, but it is a definite and considerable help.

There are a number of related techniques. For example, sometimes the therapist will ask the patient to move back and forth a few times between the different body "anchorings" of these competing beliefs. Typically, the patient will be struck by the contrast, and the alternative belief will hopefully gain in attractiveness.

A similar option is available when motivational work must be undertaken. The patient is considering (say) the advantages and disadvantages of a decision to give up drinking, or heroin. Working from both sides, the therapist first validates what the patient sees as the various disadvantages, while trying to strengthen her representations of the advantages (Miller and Rollnick, 2002). The advantage representations can then be linked to body-organizing experiments: "Imagine again this idea that you had of being able to relate, in new ways, to your baby daughter. Imagine seeing her with this new openness, and feel what your body wants to do with that. See how your body wants to arrange itself; how it wants to position itself; or if it wants to gesture or move in some way."

What in this approach we call "body strategies" provides another contribution. Typically these are elicited when a patient is forming a plan for a new global behavioral step. If it seems warranted, the therapist aids the patient to find one or more cognitive, and one or more body-oriented, strategies that can support the intended behavior.

Example: A school-age girl, with excessive anxiety, and who has been refusing to go to school, agrees to a program of graduated exposure. For the next three days she will get ready on time in the morning and go cooperatively to her mother's car, where she and her mother will sit for a short while. Further steps will be taken on successive days. The therapist asks her what, in the immediate plan, looks or feels like the hardest step. She talks about the moment of reaching the front door of her home. She is next asked to imagine this moment, as if it were happening now, and then to find something helpful that she can say to herself. She comes up with one or more such "self-speech" strategies. The therapist follows this up by moving to what, with the body, might help: "What could you do with your breathing? Or, with a gesture? Or with a way to stand, or move? Or with a way to focus on some particular body part, like your feet, or anywhere else?" and so on. One or more body strategies are then added to the cognitive ones.

Notice that, instead of a standard proposal of deeper breathing, the therapist here elicits the girl's discovery of what might aid with her breathing. What patients sometimes find within themselves is sometimes quite different from what the therapist expects will work. Not only that, but a patient, in finding her own strategy, will be the more motivated to use it.

Such work with belief modification, motivation, and body strategies tends to resonate with almost all patients. With highly disturbed psychiatric patients, it can be especially advantageous. For some patients of this type, to go directly to their emotions can be problematic, evoking fears of losing control. A move instead to "show me with a hand," or "find a posture," or the like, creates less a sense of threat. Because the patient is actively maneuvering their body, and usually doing this quite slowly and consciously, he (or she) feels more in charge. They know that they can stop the action at any point they like.

Another aspect is still more important, for all kinds of patients. A certain number of these elicited procedural doings will feel slightly unfamiliar to the patient, in a good sense. Something she is unaccustomed to is now surfacing, if only for seconds, a "something" that hints at new opportunities. Yet, because it has come out of her, she nevertheless feels it belongs to her. The more such explorations accumulate, the more there emerges a kind of profile, a hazy but motivating sense of what might become a different way to live in the world.

### Short-Term Body-Focused Therapy

The present approach that has been outlined is practiced in both short-term and long-term forms. The short-term version is more used in institutional settings, although at times in private practice too. A therapy of between two and six months is fairly typical. Usually the therapy is individual. In some institutions, it is done in more of a group format. Work with the "thought–feeling–body organizing" triangle, as described above, is central. Other treatment elements are added in accordance with a patient's diagnostic profile. Some of these, not described here, will include additional ways to focus on the body that are specific to a particular disorder or problem.

A psycho-educational component nearly always plays a role in short-term work. Once the patient has experienced some initial tastes of different body organizing alternatives, the therapist introduces the concept of the procedural repertoire (naturally using appropriate language). Over time, key notions are explained and elaborated: that each person functions in the world with a central repertoire of ways in which they utilize their body; that how one organizes oneself on this level is intertwined with how one organizes oneself with thoughts; that this repertoire has roots in their childhood past; and that aspects of these can now change.

Explained too is that the most essential part of the therapy is actually what takes place outside of the sessions. The patient is helped to cultivate new habits of observation: concerning their thought–feeling–body organizing links, and also concerning the details of their specific interactions. These observation skills are often presented as one form of mindfulness (Hayes, Strosahl, and Wilson, 1999; Lineham, 1993; Segal, Williams, and Teasdale, 2002).

Naturally, frequent collaborative plans are made concerning how the patient can implement these new body-organizing alternatives in her life. This takes place in two ways. On the one hand, specific new alternatives often emerge during explorations in the sessions. How such an alternative might be put to use perhaps will then be discussed, and a concrete plan made. On the other hand, the patient is encouraged herself to be explorative, outside the sessions, in discovering potential new bodily resources. She is aided to develop a spirit of adventure about this, allowing "felt" alternatives spontaneously to manifest themselves now and then.

An additional aid, done by some practitioners of Body-Focused Therapy, is occasional work with video. There is no quicker way for patients to grasp the subtleties of interactions than to see themselves on film as others see them (Downing, 2008; Downing et al., 2013; Riva Crugnola, Ieradi, Albizzart, & Downing, 2015, in press; Wortmann-Fleischer, 2012; Wortmann-Fleischer et al., 2005). The patient organizes that a short video (e.g., ten minutes) be filmed: a video of herself interacting with another person (e.g., a partner, her child, a friend; or, if the patient is a child, a parent, a sibling, or a friend).

During a session, she and the therapist then look together at the video, noting and reflecting upon details and specifics of the patient's reciprocal body organizing. Such work requires a certain amount of additional training on the part of the therapist. Some therapists also use such work with video as a group therapy module (Riva Crugnola, Ieradi, Albizzart, & Downing, 2015, in press; Wortmann-Fleisher, Hornstein, & Downing, 2005).

From time to time, if and when a patient seems ready, a brief investigation of his childhood past may take place. This occurs most frequently during an investigation of a core dysfunctional belief. The question of what may have happened in past family dynamics to create this belief is raised and pondered upon: there then needs to be an assessment of how "functional" (or dysfunctional) this belief actually is now.

A second level of questioning is sometimes added. Might the preverbal past be relevant here too? What, on a procedural level, might have laid a base for the later verbal belief? Why did the patient learn to utilize his body in certain ways and not others? What procedural expectations may have been created, and what corresponding micro-practices developed? Naturally, if such questions are posed, the therapist underlines their speculative nature.

A significant additional treatment element for some patients will be work with trauma. Special body-oriented techniques for trauma are often used: these were developed by myself and colleagues for use within a cognitive-behavioral framework (Opitz-Gerz, 2008). Delicate and noninvasive, these help the patient to maintain a level of emotional activation, just sufficient to permit the processing of trauma memories, but not so high as to create excessive anxiety. Room is made for "body memory" manifestations, as well as visual imagery. With children and adolescents, these procedures are frequently combined with the CBT approach to trauma developed by Cohen, Mannarino, and Deblinger (2006; Cavett and Drewes, 2012).

## Long-Term Body-Focused Therapy

The long-term form of Body-Focused Therapy, usually found in private practice settings, lasts typically between six months and two years. It continues with the same techniques as the short-term form, but adds other techniques as well. Not infrequently a patient who has profited from the short-term version in an institutional context, and who desires further treatment, is referred to a therapist practicing the longer-term version.

"Open process" sessions are the most different. The patient lies on a mat or mattress, or stands. Techniques involving work with breathing are employed. The process is "open" in the sense that it is not tied to any initial verbalized theme. The patient and the therapist just see what gradually emerges, on a bodily level, and in what way this manifestation can be linked to any particular verbal theme.

In such sessions, memories from the past can arise fairly easily. These are reflected upon, and worked with, at whatever emotional level appears appropriate. Often, as well, the body "shows" new, more functional body organizing alternatives. If so, these are highlighted and explored. Sometimes, with an important alternative, a plan is made for how the patient might slowly incorporate this more into his life.

Open process sessions require the right readiness on the patient's part, and also plenty of trust in the therapeutic relationship. A limited amount of physical contact may at times be used—e.g., to help draw attention to, or loosen, a tight muscle group that is constricting the breathing. These are sessions that have more of the classic profile of body psychotherapy sessions (Heller, 2012).

Work with dreams is often an additional component of long-term treatment. A procedure akin to, but more body-based than, the approach of Hill (2004) is used. Interpretation is eschewed. The body is used to aid the patient to come into a deeper contact with selected dream images. He is then supported as he investigates his own associations. Interestingly, some dreams, when so explored, quite plainly draw the patient's attention to new possible body organizing alternatives.

Techniques of "imaginative reparenting" are employed at times. What is meant by the term is that the patient, while in contact with a seemingly early vulnerability or fear or such, imagines a more positive parent, and also senses—in detail—how it would feel in his body to receive this kind of caregiving.

This is somewhat similar to what is undertaken in the later stages of Young's Schema Therapy (Young, Klosko, and Weishaar, 2003). A difference is that it is not the therapist who is cast as the "good parent," nor an adult "self-part" of the patient, but simply an imaginative figure, as is done in some CBT imagery rescripting work (Arntz, Tiesema, and Kindt, 2007; Smucker and Dancu, 1999). A second difference is a continued linking of dysfunctional core beliefs with their procedural, body organizing implications.

The concept of body organizing would seem to hold considerable promise for psychotherapy. These short-term and long-term versions of Body-Focused Therapy represent one of what are certainly many possible applications.

## References

Ainsworth, M., Blehar, M., Waters, E., & Wall, S. (1978). *Patterns of attachment: A psychological study of the Strange Situation.* Hillsdale, NJ: Erlbaum.

Arntz, A., Tiesema, M., & Kindt, M. (2007). Treatment of PTSD: A comparison of PTSD with and without imaginal rescripting. *Journal of Behavior Therapy and Experimental Psychiatry, 38,* 345–370.

Beebe, B., & Jaffe, J. (2008). Dyadic microanalysis of mother-infant communication informs clinical practice. In A. Fogel, B. King, & S. Shanker (Eds.), *Human development in the 21st century: Visionary ideas from systems scientists* (pp. 176–187). Cambridge, UK: Cambridge University Press.

Beebe, B., & Lachmann, F. (2013). *The origins of attachment: Infant research and adult treatment.* New York: Routledge.

Bloom, P. (2013). *Just babies: The origins of good and evil.* New York: Crown.

Bronfman, E., Parsons, E., & Lyons-Ruth, K. (2004). *Atypical Maternal Behavior Instrument for Assessment and Classification (AMBIANCE): Manual for coding disrupted affective communication* (2nd ed.) [Unpublished manual]. Harvard University Medical School.

Cavett, A., & Drewes, A. (2012). Play applications and trauma-specific components. In J. Cohen, A. Mannarino, & E. Deblinger (Eds.), *Trauma-focused CBT for children and adolescents: Treatment applications* (pp. 124–148). New York: Guilford Press.

Cohen, J., Mannarino, A., & Deblinger, E. (2006). *Treating trauma and traumatic grief in children and adolescents.* New York: Guilford Press.

Downing, G. (2000). Emotion theory reconsidered. In J. Malpas & M. Wrathall (Eds.), *Heidegger, coping and cognitive science*. Cambridge, MA: MIT Press.

Downing, G. (2005). Emotion, body, and parent-infant interaction. In J. Nadel & D. Muir (Eds.), *Emotional development: Recent research advances* (pp. 429–449). Oxford, UK: Oxford University Press.

Downing, G. (2008). A different way to help. In A. Fogel, B. King, & S. Shanker (Eds.), *Human development in the 21st century: Visionary ideas from systems scientists* (pp. 200–205). Cambridge, UK: Cambridge University Press.

Downing, G. (2011). Uneasy beginnings: Getting psychotherapy underway with the difficult patient. *Self Psychology: European Journal for Psychoanalytic Therapy and Research, 44/45*, 207–233.

Downing, G., Buergin, D., Reck, C., & Ziegenhain, U. (2008). Intersubjectivity and attachment: Perspectives on an in-patient parent-infant case. *Infant Mental Health Journal, 29(3)*, 278–295.

Downing, G., Wortmann-Fleischer, S., von Einsiedel, R., Jordan, W., & Reck, C. (2013). Video intervention therapy with parents with a psychiatric disturbance: January 3, 2014. In K. Brandt, B. Perry, S. Seligman, & E. Tronick (Eds.), *Infant and early childhood mental health: Core concepts and clinical practice* (pp. 261–280). Washington, DC: American Psychiatric Publishing.

Feldman, R. (1998). *Coding interactive behavior manual* [Unpublished]. Israel: Bar-Ilan University.

Frijda, N. (1986). *The emotions*. Cambridge, UK: Cambridge University Press.

Fivaz-Depeursinge, E., & Corboz-Warnery, A. (1999). *The primary triangle: A developmental systems view of mothers, fathers, and infants*. New York: Basic.

Fogal, A. (1993). *Developing through relationships*. Chicago: Chicago University Press.

Fogal, A. (2000). Relationships that support human development. In A. Fogal, B. King, & S. Shanker (Eds.), *Human development in the twenty-first century: Visionary ideas from systems scientists*. Cambridge, UK: Cambridge University Press.

Fonagy, P. (2008). The mentalization-focused approach to social development. In F. Busch (Ed.), *Mentalization: Theoretical considerations, research findings, and clinical implications*. New York: Analytic Press.

Fonagy, P., Gergely, G., Jurist, E., & Target, J. (2002). *Affect regulation, mentalization, and the development of the self*. New York: Other Press.

Geissler, P. (2009). *Analytische Koerperpsychotherapie: Eine Bestandsaufnahme [Analytical Body Psychotherapy: An inventory]*. Giessen: Psychosozial.

Geissler, P., & Heisterkamp, G. (2013). *Einfuehrung in die analytische Koerperpsychotherapie [Introduction to Analytical Body Psychotherapy]*. Giessen: Psychosozial.

Gilbert, P. (2007). Evolved minds and compassion in the therapeutic relationship. In P. Gilbert & R. Leahy (Eds.), *The therapeutic relationship in the Cognitive Behavioral Psychotherapies*. Hove, UK: Routledge.

Gilbert, P. (2009). *The compassionate mind*. London: Constable & Robinson.

Greenberg, L. (2002). *Emotion-focused therapy: Coaching clients to work through their feelings*. Washington, DC: American Psychological Association.

Hackmann, A., Bennett-Levy, J., & Holmes, A. (2011). *Oxford guide to imagery in Cognitive Therapy*. Oxford, UK: Oxford University Press.

Harrison, A. (2013). Psychoanalytic and psychodynamic theory: Play therapy for young children. In K. Brandt, B. Perry, S. Seligman, & E. Tronick (Eds.), *Infant and early childhood mental health: Core concepts and clinical practice* (pp. 111–128). Washington, DC: American Psychiatric Publishing.

Hayes, S., Strosahl, K., & Wilson, K. (1999). *Acceptance and commitment therapy: An experiential approach to behavior change*. New York: Guilford Press.

Heller, M. (2012). *Body Psychotherapy: History, concepts, methods*. New York: W. W. Norton.

Hill, C. (2004). *Dream work in therapy: Facilitating exploration, insight, and action*. Washington, DC: American Psychological Association.

Jaffe, J., Beebe, B., Feldstein, S., Crown, C., & Jasnow, M. (2001). *Rhythms of dialogue in infancy: Coordinated timing in development*. Monographs of the Society for Research in Child Development, Serial No. 265, 66(2).

Kagen, J. (2010). *The temperamental thread*. New York: Dana Press.

Katzow, A., & Safran, J. (2007). Recognizing and resolving ruptures in the therapeutic alliance. In P. Gilbert & R.

Leahy (Eds.), *The therapeutic relationship in the Cognitive Behavioral Psychotherapies.* Hove, UK: Routledge.

Keleman, S. (1975). *The human ground: Sexuality, self, and survival.* Palo Alto, CA: Science & Behavior Books.

Kurtz, R. (1990). *Body-Centered Psychotherapy: The Hakomi Method.* Mendocino, CA: LifeRhythm.

Lester, B. (2013). Behavioral epigenetics and the developmental origins of child mental health disorders. In K. Brandt, B. Perry, S. Seligman, & E. Tronick (Eds.), *Infant and early childhood mental health: Core concepts and clinical practice* (pp. 161–175). Washington, DC: American Psychiatric Publishing.

Lineham, M. (1993). *Cognitive-behavioral treatment of borderline personality disorder.* New York: Guilford Press.

Lowen, A. (1958). *Language of the body.* New York: Collier.

Lyons-Ruth, K., & Jacobvitz, D. (1999). *Attachment disorganization: Unresolved loss, relational violence, and lapses in behavioral and attentional strategies.* In J. Cassidy & P. Shaver (Eds.), *Handbook of attachment: Theory, research, and clinical applications* (pp. 520–554). New York: Guilford Press.

Marvin, R. (1999). *Normative development: Ontogeny.* In J. Cassidy & P. Shaver (Eds.), *Handbook of attachment: Theory, research, and clinical applications* (pp. 44–67). New York: Guilford Press.

Miller, W., & Rollnick, S. (2002). *Motivational interviewing: Preparing people for change.* New York: Guilford Press.

Myin, E., & O'Regan, J. (2009). Situated perception and sensation in vision and other modalities: A sensorimotor approach. In P. Robbins & M. Aydede (Eds.), *The Cambridge handbook of situated cognition* (pp. 185–200). Cambridge, UK: Cambridge University Press.

Ogden, P., Minton, K., & Pain, C. (2006). *Trauma and the body: A sensorimotor approach to psychotherapy.* New York: W. W. Norton.

Opitz-Gerz, A. (2008). Die Bedeutung der Korperdimension fur die Traumaarbeit [The importance of the bodily dimension for trauma work]. *Trauma & Gewalt, 2*(4), 278-287.

Patterson, G. (2002). The early development of coercive family process. In J. Reid, G. Patterson, & J. Snyder (Eds.), *Antisocial behavior in children and adolescents: A developmental analysis and model for intervention,* (pp. 25–44). Washington, DC: American Psychological Association.

Perry, B. (2013a). Child maltreatment: the role of abuse and neglect in developmental psychopathology. In T. Beauchane & S. Hinshow (Eds.), *Textbook of child and adolescent psychopathology,* (pp. 93–128). New York: Wiley.

Perry, B. (2013b). The neurosequential model of therapeutics: Application of a developmentally sensitive and neurobiology-informed approach to clinical problem solving in maltreated children. In K. Brandt, B. Perry, S. Seligman, & E. Tronick (Eds.), *Infant and early childhood mental health: Core concepts and clinical practice* (pp. 21–54). Washington, DC: American Psychiatric Publishing.

Pesso, A. (1973). *Experience in action.* New York: New York University Press.

Riva Crugnola, C., Ierardi, E., Gazzotti, S., & Albizzarti, A. (2014). Motherhood in adolescent mothers: Maternal attachment, mother-infant styles of interaction and emotion regulation at three months. *Infant Behavior and Development, 37,* 44–56.

Riva Crugnola, C., Ieradi, E., Albizzati, A., & Downing, G. (2015, in press). Promoting responsiveness, emotion regulation and attachment in young mothers and infants (PRERAYMI): An implementation of Video Intervention Therapy and psychological support. In Steele, H. & Steele, M. (Eds.), *Handbook of attachment-based interventions.* New York: Guilford.

Röhricht, F. (2000). *Die Koerperorientierte Psychotherapie psychischer Störungen: Ein Leitfaden für Forschung und Praxis [Body-Oriented Psychotherapy in mental disorders: A manual for research and practice].* Göttingen: Hogrefe.

Ryle, A. (1990). *Cognitive analytic therapy: Active participation in change.* Chichester, UK: John Wiley.

Ryle, A. (1997). *Cognitive analytic therapy and borderline personality disorder.* Chichester, UK: John Wiley.

Ryle, A., & Kerr, I. (2002). *Introducing cognitive analytic therapy: Principles and practice.* Chichester, UK: John Wiley.

Safran, J., & Muran, J. (2000). *Negotiating the therapeutic alliance: A relational treatment guide.* New York: Guilford Press.

Segal, Z., Williams, J., & Teasdale, J. (2002). *Mindfulness-based cognitive therapy for depression.* New York: Guilford Press.

Smucker, M., & Dancu, C. (1999). *Cognitive behavioral treatment for adult survivors of childhood trauma: Imagery re-scripting and reprocessing.* Northvale, NJ: Jason Aronson.

Stanley, J. (2011). *Know how.* Oxford, UK: Oxford University Press.

Steele, H., & Steele, M. (2005). Understanding and resolving emotional conflict: The view from 12 years of attachment research across generations and across childhood. In K. E. Grossman, K. Grossman, & E. Waters (Eds.), *Attachment from infancy to adulthood: The major longitudinal studies* (pp. 137–164). New York: Guilford Press.

Stern, D. (1985). *The interpersonal world of the infant.* New York: Basic Books.

Stern, D. (2010). *Forms of vitality: Exploring dynamic experience in psychology, the arts, psychotherapy and development.* Oxford, UK: Oxford University Press.

Tomasello, M. (2009). *Why we cooperate.* Cambridge, MA: MIT Press.

Tronick, E. (2007). *The neurobehavioral and social-emotional development of infants and children.* New York: W. W. Norton.

Tronick, E. (2013). Typical and atypical development: Peek-a-boo and blind selection. In K. Brandt, B. Perry, S. Seligman, & E. Tronick (Eds.), *Infant and early childhood mental health: Core concepts and clinical practice* (pp. 55–70). Washington, DC: American Psychiatric Publishing.

Tversky, B. (2009). Spatial cognition: Embodied and situated. In P. Robbins & M. Aydede (Eds.), *The Cambridge handbook of situated cognition* (pp. 185–200). Cambridge, UK: Cambridge University Press.

Wortmann-Fleischer, S. (2012). Interacktionalses Therapieprogramm fuer psychisch kranke Muetter-Kind-Behandlung in Kliniken fuer Erwachsenenpsychiatrie [Interactional therapy programs for mentally ill mothers-to-child treatment in clinics for adult psychiatry]. In S. Wortmann-Fleischer, R. von Einsiedel, & G. Downing (Eds.), *Stationaere Eltern-Kind-Behandlung: ein interdisziplinaerer Praxisleitfaden [Inpatient parent-child treatments: A practical interdisciplinary guide]* (pp. 94–99). Stuttgart: Kohlhammer.

Wortmann-Fleischer, S., Hornstein, C., & Downing, G. (2005). *Postpartale psychische Storungen: Ein interaktionszentrierter Therapieleitfaden [Postpartum mental disorders: An interaction-centered therapy guide].* Stuttgart: Kohlhammer.

Young, J., Klosko, J., & Weishaar, M. (2003). *Schema Therapy: A practitioner's guide.* New York: Guilford Press.

# 30
## Affective-Motor Schemata

**Andreas Wehowsky, Germany**

**Translation by Katharine Cofer**

**Andreas Wehowsky's** biographical information can be found at the beginning of Chapter 14, "The Concept of Energy in Body Psychotherapy."

George Downing originally introduced the notion of affective-motor schemata (Downing, 1996; see also Chapter 29, "Early Interaction and the Body: Clinical Implications" by George Downing). It is a concept that is full of complexities, and its manifold implications can probably best be understood by first examining its individual components.

## History and Meaning of the Schema Concept

The term "schema" was first introduced to psychology by F. C. Bartlett (1932) and related to the structures of memory contents. Bartlett is regarded as a forerunner of Cognitive Psychology and therefore as an antagonist to the then-predominant Behaviorism. His classic schema theory already conceived of the development of integrated memory structures as a dynamic organization of the psyche. The term became generally known through the work of Jean Piaget, who used it to refer to the action-related aspects of thinking and intelligence (Piaget, 1951). Piaget was interested in describing the cognitive development of the child from a functional perspective—i.e., relating to processes of the systematic development of intelligence and the child's simultaneous adaptation to his environment. Piaget designated the processes of adaptation with the complementary terms "assimilation" and "accommodation." The development of intelligence comprises stages of pre-verbal and verbal skills that were described in particular by the differentiation between sensory-motor and cognitive schemata. Cognitive schemata are complex patterns of perception, assessment, thinking, planning, and action that are the basis for a human being's experience and behavior. In the confrontation with the environment, these schemata change through processes of assimilation and accommodation. Therefore, schemata produce experiences while potentially being changed by them at the same time. Thus, cognitive schemata also represent expectations and attitudes—Grawe (1998) speaks of "potentialities."

Subsequent to Piaget and the "schema" concept based on Bartlett (1932) and developed in U. Neisser's (1967) *Cognitive Psychology,* the term has become widespread in the field of psychology and has attained prominence in various important currents, including cognitive behavioral, psychodynamic, and humanistic schools. With the concept of affective-motor schemata, it has made its indispensable entry into Body Psychotherapy.

The discussion of schema theory today is extraordinarily multilayered and, to some extent, confusing. For this reason, I would like to begin by summarizing its essential points.

## Essential Points

From a neurophysiological perspective, "schemata" correspond to the so-called "cell assemblies" of D. Hebb (1949), a concept that was further elaborated, originally by Hayek and then by von der Malsburg. It is based on the idea that memory contents shape potentialities for specific arousal patterns: synapses in the brain produce inhibiting and arousing functions that form a hierarchical organization and overarching patterns (Grawe, 1998). Among other things, these patterns control complex profiles of muscular contractions.

The neuronal arousal patterns constitute the physiological foundation for ongoing, organized, and organizing knowledge structures in the psyche. Here the important thing is not so much the contents as the self-regulating processes that are based on these structures.

At the same time, these knowledge structures are primarily unconscious, or preconscious, nonverbal patterns that can be attributed to implicit memory. These patterns represent an embodied organization of knowledge, in contrast with verbally conscious representations of knowledge. However, it is possible to become conscious of many implicit structures and to represent them verbally.

Among the fundamental tasks of these structures is the organization of need-oriented action tendencies. For this reason, they are also described as motivational-affective networks. The motivational aspect can be understood as an arc between a need and its action goal, whereas the affective aspect, at a basic level, can be seen as a tension between pleasure and aversion. The schemata are formed through interactions with the environment. In this context, the social environment, of course, is of particular importance. Thus, schemata are knowledge structures that represent automatic action tendencies within relational contexts. For this reason, Grawe prefers to speak of relational schemata rather than motivational schemata (Ibid.). But, in fact, these are two sides of the same coin, which become visible and move into the foreground depending on the perspective from which they are viewed.

As an embodiment of drives and experiences within relational contexts, these schemata are a foundation for the formation of relationships and, as such, contribute to the understanding of transference and countertransference phenomena. Even though, as "coagulated" experience and, therefore, producers of new experience, they always represent a conservative, ongoing structure of "being in the world," they still display potential for plasticity and changeability through accommodation and assimilation.

In accordance with the neurophysiological, hierarchical organization of neuronal arousal patterns, the embodied psychic schemata are also hierarchically organized and capable of forming an integrated and coherent self-organization. Such overarching self-schemata can operate as active organizers of a state that comprises such things as motives, priorities, values, ideas, and feelings. Any such self-schema represents an active, complex configuration of the personality.

Schemata can be activated both volitionally, through top-down, embodying processes of self-regulation, and also through automatic, emergent, bottom-up activation. Both types of activation are triggered by physical, affective, motivational, and reflexive interactions with situational contexts. Schemata represent preconscious and implicit knowledge structures that facilitate ongoing information processing and action regulation on the basis of existing experiential landscapes and their representations.

The hierarchical organization of schemata implies, of course, that they can be described on each individual level. As we know, Piaget made an initial differentiation with the subdivision into sensory-motor and cognitive schemata. Accordingly, there are further differentiations among action, perception, and value schemata.

Of particular relevance for Body Psychotherapy is the concept of "body schema" as distinguished from "body image." In the scientific discussion, there has been repeated confusion due to synonymous use of these terms, which are currently being clarified and reflected upon, particularly in the work of Shaun Gallagher (1998). He points out that the conceptual differentiations are based more on phenomenology than on studies of empirical functions; thus, it is not possible to give a very precise definition of what a body schema is and how it works. Despite all conceptual differentiations, we must assume that body image and body schema are closely related on the level of motor behavior and proprioceptive processes (Gallagher and Cole, 1995).

## Body Schema and Body Image

The term "body schema" was first introduced by Henry Head (1920); he described a system of motor skills and habits that continually enable and regulate body postures and movements. Here, the sensory and motor aspects of experience are hard to separate, as they impact one another reciprocally. After all, as we know, the efferent motor commands are based on afferent inputs from the proprioceptive and vestibular systems (see Chapter 22, "'Body Schema,' 'Body Image,' and Bodily Experience: Concept Formation, Definitions, and Clinical Relevance in Diagnostics and Therapy" by Frank Röhricht).

Although body schemata are innate, their formation nonetheless occurs within the context of a primary intersubjectivity (Gallagher, 2002b). The key to this is imitation, a controlled motor response to interactive perceptions, in particular those that can be described with the categories of body schema, crossmodal perception, and motor representations of other people (Ibid.). Research on the so-called mirror neurons presents an idea of how gestures and movements of other people translate into proprioceptive perceptions in a person's own body, resulting in corresponding motor actions in that person (Gallagher, 2002a; Schultz, 2001). Imitations shape not only expressive movements such as gestures but also the forms of instrumental (e.g., reaching, grasping) and locomotive (e.g., walking) movements. Imitation leads to expressive nuances in movements that initially are intrinsically social. This does not mean that sensory-motor body schemata are nonsocial movements out of which social cognitions later develop, but, rather, that the body-schematic capacities of a child's motor control are social from the very beginning. This system, however, operates beneath the threshold of a self-referential intentionality, although, of course, the system can also support the threshold. A body schema is comprised of preconscious, subpersonal processes that are silently attuned to the environment. Body schemata can have specific effects on cognitive experiences, but they do not have the status of a conscious representation or a belief system per se (Gallagher, 2001, 2002b). By contrast, the term "body image" refers to a complex set of intentional states, the intentional object of which is one's own body. Body image includes perceiving experiences of one's own body, a generalized, culturally shaped, conceptual understanding of the body, belief systems, and emotional attitudes toward one's own body. This list clearly shows that body image includes not only unconscious processes, but also reflective intentionality. Body image as an important component of integrated self-representations, and self-concept is an important foundation of feelings of self-worth and self-confidence. Likewise, it leads to corresponding body-related behaviors that contribute to health-promoting or, conversely, to damaging processes. This fact is vital for understanding the importance of Body Psychotherapeutic work on body image and disturbances thereof.

Whereas the body schema is functionally integrated with a person's surroundings, because it is always directed toward interaction with the environment, body image is more clearly differentiated from the environment, not least because of a person's awareness of bodily boundaries. Body image can also relate to partial areas of the body. By contrast, the body schema functions in a more integrated and holistic manner, because any variation in posture and movement leads to a global adaptation in the entire muscular system. In addition, this global adaptation also corresponds to changes in breathing as well as on the sensory and vegetative levels.

## Schemata and Representations

This contrasting of the terms "body schema" and "body image" also suggests, on a general level, a discussion of the basically complementary terms "schema" and "representation." These terms are often used synonymously, but in some instances are clearly differentiated. The synonymous use of the terms is probably due to the fact that schemata, of course, are representations of experience, whereas, conversely, representations function as schemata of experience and action. The hierarchical organization of both schemata and representations, however, also indicates certain differentiations, for these two hierarchies relate to each other inversely. While the concept of schemata is significant, particularly in the subcognitive and elemental-cognitive areas of the personality, the significance of the term "representation" becomes apparent particularly in the cognitive realms of complex and highly inferent layers of the personality. For a better understanding of this statement, it will be helpful to describe these two or, rather, three areas in greater detail.

At first, approximate differentiation between the subcognitive, the elementary-cognitive, and the highly complex cognitive realms consists in relating these to the "body-near" and "mental" layers of the personality.

The "body-near" subcognitive realm relates to global arousal states and basic components of affectivity such as pleasure and aversion, which are not necessarily mediated by higher cognitive evaluation processes, but do influence them in their activated strength (Kuhl, 2001). The "body-near" elementary-cognitive area comprises systems of intuitive behavior and perceiving/sensing object recognition. These represent learned stimulus reaction associations, habits, and skills.

Within the "body-near" realm, the *Representations of Interactions that have been Generalized*" (RIGs), described by Daniel Stern, are formed. These are presymbolic, psycho-biological (Dornes, 1993), and enactive (Horowitz, 1995) representations of interactive regulation processes that should also, and perhaps more aptly, be termed schemata.

The mental/cognitive realm contains the representational and symbolic forms of knowledge structures and contents, such as goals, plans, expectations, and beliefs. It can be characterized by the personality layers of motives, systems of holistic feeling and analytic thinking, and volitional self-control (Kuhl, 2001).

The initially imaginative symbolic representations in the more complex cognitive realm, which ultimately lead to integrated self-representations, develop only gradually out of the early, schema-forming representations of experiences and actions in the bodily realm. Through such so-called secondary representations, a child becomes able to regulate primal, affective states with a higher degree of autonomy (Fonagy and Target, 2002). The formation of such representations is closely linked with the development of episodic and autobiographical memory, through which holistic experiential landscapes can be assembled out of the individual episodes of experience. This is not, however, a matter of explicit, linguistically reflected and interpreted processing of scenes, but of implicit knowledge structures of experiences that also and above all integrate the internal bodily, affective, and motivational states related to these episodes. Daniel Stern speaks of proto-narrative envelopes and schemata of togetherness (Geissler, 2002). The means of processing such memories is based on extensive, associative neuronal networks in the right brain hemisphere, which enable rapid and preconscious associative access to contextualized and self-relevant life experiences. Thus, the activation of such integrated representations can facilitate effective regulation of affective states, because the processes of the right hemisphere are closely connected with the autonomic nervous system (Kuhl, 2001; Schore, 1997).

Even at this level of cognitive, implicit knowledge structures, the terms "integrated self-representations" and "self-schemata" are often still used interchangeably. The schema concept appears to definitively lose its meaning only where there is a formation of linguistically conscious, explicit representations. In terms of Developmental Psychology, this is the last stage of information processing, which is first linked in the actual sense with thinking and the language centers of the left brain hemisphere. In contrast with the implicit self-representations, here linguistically mediated self-concepts as well as explicit self- and object-representations are produced.

In summary, we can say that, alongside the synonymous use of the terms "schema" and "representation," a tendency toward a meaningful differentiation is becoming visible. This consists of localizing the schema concept chiefly in the subcognitive and elementary-cognitive realm and linking it with generally automatic activations.

By contrast, the development of the notion of representation lies mainly within the cognitive area of meanings and intentions, where we can see superordinate metarepresentations of representations on complex levels of the personality. These metarepresentations can be differentiated into implicit, procedural knowledge landscapes on the one hand, and explicit, analytical linguistic formations on the other. They take over vital tasks in the intentional self-regulation processes.

## Affective-Motor Schemata

The above considerations enable a better understanding of Downing's concept of affective-motor schemata. Downing introduces these as *constellations between motor behavioral patterns (with affective coloration) and cognitive assessments* (Downing, 1996). Thus, these schemata describe an interacting of "sensory, motor, affective, and cognitive levels." They are based on innate potentials, but are shaped, in accordance with primary intersubjectivity, in social interactions and thus form rudimentary self- and object-representations in the form of generalized regulation experiences. These experiences form capabilities for assessing interactions, which manifest as motor convictions, a sort of "implicitly active knowledge" (Downing, 2002). Here, Downing differentiates between connecting and differentiating schemata, through which needs and feelings regarding proximity and distance in interpersonal interactions are regulated. In this context, links with the processes of attachment and autonomy are readily apparent.

This short summary makes it clear that, although affective-motor schemata are indeed related to Piaget's sensory-motor schemata, they are nonetheless markedly different in two respects. On the one hand, the development of these schemata is now embedded in the social interaction, instead of relating to inanimate objects. On the other, they describe configurations that link processes on various levels of the personality.

The interactive and affective nature of physicality means that the development of body postures and movements, of the breath, and of the use of the sensory system is profoundly shaped by communicative experiences and tends to reproduce these as future potentialities of experience and action. Accordingly, body shapes and body postures can be understood as dynamic structures in which the history of repetitive and socially significant experiences and microgestures is reflected. Thus, body postures transport "coagulated" communications into the future as expectations and potentialities; they tend to reproduce what has been experienced. This is why certain schools of Body Psychotherapy, such as Bioenergetics, for example, have made the methodology of body reading a strong component of their work. Of course, conscious perception, mirroring, enlivening, and reflection of body postures generally play a major role in the process of Body Psychotherapeutic work. Over and over again it is a matter of activating implicit movement tendencies in the therapeutic contact by means of a variety of possible methods, and exploring their affective and communicative meaning. Here the client's attention is alternately focused on internal, interoceptive (Craig, 2002) experiences as well as on externally oriented actions.

Within this context the basic forms of movement in contact have always been of primary importance: the approaching movement, or the dependent/clinging movement toward someone; the withdrawing movement away from someone into autonomy or avoidance; the self-affirming, boundary-setting, or attacking movement against someone; and the blocking of movement through contradictory impulses. David Boadella, with his concept of motor fields, has developed these movement possibilities even more thoroughly (Boadella, 1993).

What is true for body postures and movements can also be applied to breathing processes and the use of the sense organs. Every person displays specific patterns of breathing, and the exploration of these patterns enables foundational experiences within schematic interactions, thus making them accessible to innovative change (Wehowsky, 1994). The same is true for the organization of the sense modalities—in particular, of course, with regard to eye contact, tone of voice and forms of listening, the seeking of and reaction to touch, and responses to olfactory perceptions.

These descriptions could be continued in ever-increasing detail. But what is most important to know about affective-motor schemata at this point is, on the one hand, that all these different aspects act conjointly in Body Psychotherapeutic processes, because they affect each other reciprocally. Body postures and movements, breathing, and sense modalities are always engaged in reciprocal action with one other. A therapeutic focus on one of these somatic factors always impacts the other systems. On the other hand, the processes within these somatic systems are intertwined with affective and cognitive layers of the personality. Accordingly, the therapeutic focus can move back and forth between the somatic, affective, and cognitive levels, in both intrapersonal and interpersonal contacts or contexts. In *top-down* processes, we speak of embodiment, in *bottom-up* processes, of emergence, for instance, of hidden feelings, memories, images, and insights (Wehowsky, 2002; Varela, 2000).

The situational activation of the schemata comprises two of the active psychotherapeutic factors identified by Grawe—namely, resource activation and problem activation. Both types of activation are the prerequisite for the conscious, cognitive representation of schemata. It is evident that, with its concept of affective-motor schemata and its numerous possibilities for interventions on all levels, Body Psychotherapy is in an excellent position to do justice both to the requirements for the activation of schemata and to their representational clarification and management.

## Enactments and Moments of Encounter

The concept of activation is closely intertwined with the increasingly important concept of enactment. This term, introduced by Ted Jacobs in 1986, has been finding more and more widespread use in psychotherapy. This is not surprising, seeing as how it expands the possibilities for intervention beyond the very limited realm of verbal interpretation of explicit representations and allows access to the highly relevant work with unconsciously staged actions. Enactments are interactive scenes that take place in the psychotherapeutic process and are jointly designed through the reciprocal interaction between therapist and client. Rather than implicit memories being presented and reflected upon verbally, in an explicit fashion, they are enacted as a reproducing action. Thus, the medium consists chiefly of nonverbal communication, even though speech can be a component of this action dialogue. What is expressed in enactments are often affective-motor schemata that, because of the lack of representation, are not accessible to the language centers of the left brain hemisphere and thus can show up only as manifestations of deeply buried, unconscious transference patterns (Schore, 1997).

The concepts of enactment represent an important contribution toward liberating our understanding of acting out from the status of an undesirable derailment to that of an important and welcome medium of the therapeutic process. This awareness acknowledges the important role of implicit knowledge as a nonverbal and preconscious process for managing experience, regulations, behavior, and action, as well as the fact that one cannot speak about this procedural knowledge before it actively surfaces, manifests, and is lived out in one's own experience. So that all this does not remain unconscious it is, in particular, the role of the therapist to train his or her capacities for precise perception and observation as well as the self-regulating management of positive but also often stressful, negatively affective countertransference responses within his or her own body, and to use them empathically. This empathic use is expressed chiefly through the therapist's own repertoire of rich and flexibly applicable affective-motor schemata. It is essential, however, that this repertoire be expressed contingently—i.e., in temporal proximity and thus in recognizable relationship to expressive utterances of the client. Only in this way can an interactive synchrony occur in which "affective sharing" and "affect attunement/matching" (Kuhl, 2000) can lead to the experience of a dyadically produced, positive affect. This means a careful, rhythmic attunement to one another, which ultimately produces a reciprocal regulation of states.

On the basis of these capabilities, a therapist can make a decisive contribution toward the success of interventions, and the possibility of their leading to intensive "now moments," as Daniel Stern calls them. "Now moments" consist of authentic, specific, and personal responses of interaction partners to one another; and, when therapeutically apprehended and jointly realized, they represent a moment of encounter (Stern et al., 2002). In this moment, through the exchange of affective expressions, an interactive regulation takes place that can affect all levels of the personality, all the way to organismic reorganization. In a sufficiently optimal intersubjective environment, where such moments of encounter occur with regularity, new bodily, affective, and cognitive experiences are created that change the implicit relational knowledge. These experiences favor a willingness to engage in the implicit, procedural representation of new interaction schemata, which can also be verbally integrated in subsequent reflection.

These moments of encounter correspond to the concept of an emotionally corrective experience, which goes back to F. Alexander and is regarded by Heisterkamp as a precursor of enactment theory (Heisterkamp, 2002). Moments of encounter arising from a successful management of enactments lead to a basic shaping of sensory experience, to a "present-moment understanding," in contrast to and as a precursor of a verbally representative understanding (Ibid.). It has always been one of the strengths of Body Psychotherapy that through this intensive work in subcognitive and elementally cognitive areas, where the bulk of an enactment takes place, the preconditions are created for such implicit modes of understanding and for transformational experiences involving affective-motor schemata.

## Stress, Pathology, and Structural Level

Our discussion of implicit relational knowledge, which is closely connected with the schema-forming representations of the right brain hemisphere, has not yet taken into account the fact of complex hierarchies within these neurophysiological systems and their relationships with the hierarchically structured representations and schema formations. These hierarchies can be described as vertical layers within a rough separation of cortical and subcortical structures. One vital system at the interface of these structures, which mediate both elementary and highly complex representations at a psychological level, is the hippocampus. It supports all the cognitive (neocortical) systems, which integrate many isolated pieces of information from external and internal environments into coherent representations (Kuhl, 2001). The formation of integrated self-representations relies on this coherence-producing function of the hippocampus. At the same time, this structure reacts very sensitively to stress. Thus, as an example, anxiety produced by interpersonal stress can impair the hippocampal functions through the secretion of high concentrations of cortisol and thus prevent production of or access to integrated representations. Chronic developmental disorders or trauma can cause structural damage to the hippocampus. Under such conditions, many affective-motor schemata, which then in any case reproduce dysregulating interactions, are prevented from engaging in cognitively symbolic representation formation and remain stuck at an early, presymbolic level.

According to the clarification-oriented psychotherapy of Rainer Sachse, such affective schemata occur only in a sensory-motor code and are expressed as moods, diffuse feelings, bodily reactions and sensations, and visual images. Before they can be explicitly, verbally reflected, they must first be represented in an implicit cognitive code. This is accomplished, among other ways, through the focusing of holistic feeling. By means of the perceptive concentration on the "felt sense," an experience that can be localized in the body, a search for meaning can begin that leads to a "felt shift" as soon as an accurate interpretation is found (Gendlin, 1981; Sachse, 2003). The cognitive elements thus produced in an intuitive/holistic, feeling mode of processing can then later be integrated into more comprehensive concepts through an analytic mode of processing.

Downing also speaks of affective-motor schemata that were prevented from developing appropriately and that display pathological tendencies. They constitute the core of various kinds of bodily defenses, of which the best-known type is represented by chronic tension patterns of holding. Just as important, however, are patterns of chronic hypotension or weakness, reduced breathing, incomplete and underdeveloped schemata, countermobilizations against organic impulses, deactivation of aliveness, kinesthetic avoidance of motor vitality, kinesthetic hyperconcentration on partial areas or aspects of the body, and visual body image constructions that enable an escape from the body.

But Downing also makes it very clear that working with the felt sense is only a limited version of embodiment in psychotherapeutic work. A systematic reorganization of affective-motor schemata requires more than this—i.e., no less than a willingness to engage in interactive encounters, including procedural, nonverbal, bodily micropractices (Downing, 2003). Through such interactive experiences of reciprocal regulation of affective states that reduce overwhelming stress, activated affective-motor schemata can be changed and represented in new, implicit, and self-referential experiential knowledge. Such new, cognitive structures are the foundation for future, self-regulating soothing of intense and generalized affects and dysfunctional action impulses. They represent the key to the treatment of many psychosomatic symptoms, affective disorders, and personality disorders, which according to current research can often be reduced to the common denominator of alexithymia. Alexithymia is a construct that represents a cluster of deficits in the ability to regulate affective processes procedurally and in a self-organized manner, from a cognitive and volitional perspective (Taylor et al., 1999).

## Motivations as Dynamic Coalitions of Personality Systems

The fact that schemata, at whatever level, are goal-oriented distinguishes them, as described above, as motivational schemata. Accordingly, Geissler has correlated the affective-motor schemata with the five or six motivation systems of Lichtenberg, in order to further differentiate Downing's concept with regard to the diversity of human motives (Geissler, 2002). Lichtenberg describes the function of motivational systems as follows: "to develop, preserve, and recreate the coherence of a self or self-organization" (Lichtenberg et al., 2000). This coherence can be understood from two vantage points:

- As an integration of the hierarchically structured layers of the personality. These link body-near sub-cognitive and elemental cognitive stimulus motivations (such as pleasure and aversion, reward and punishment, approach and avoidance) with mental aspects of highly complex cognitive dispositions of the three basic motives: relationship, performance, and power.

- As an integration and linking of experience-oriented systems and goal-building processes with action-oriented, behavior-regulating systems of the personality.

The complexity resulting from these two aspects of a coherent self has been represented by Julius Kuhl in his comprehensive theory of Personality System Interactions (PSI theory). It describes motivation as a dynamic concept that characterizes features of links between four personality-relevant cognitive macrosystems. The latter consist of the two elemental systems of sensate object recognition and intuitive behavior regulation, and the two highly complex systems of analytic thinking and holistic feeling. The motivationally active links between these systems are produced and shaped by the affectively determined flow of energy that moves toward and activates each of these systems (Kuhl, 2001).

Here Downing's core idea—namely, that affective-motor schemata represent specific constellations that are consistent throughout all layers of the personality—is further developed through the description of typical configurations of such constellations, which are produced through varying degrees of intensity in the activation of the macrosystems. Possible perspectives for the future development of the concept of affective-motor schemata include relating the basic forms of affective-motor schemata described by Downing to Kuhl's configurations, and observing more closely the interactions between frequent, automatically activated schemata and volitional self-regulation processes.

## References

Bartlett, F. C. (1932). *Remembering: A study in Experimental and Social Psychology.* Washington, DC: American Psychological Association.

Boadella, D. (2000). Shape flow and postures of the soul. *Energy & Character, 30 (2),* 7–21.

Craig, A. D. (2002). How do you feel? Interoception: The sense of the physiological condition of the body. *Nature Reviews Neuroscience, 3,* 655–666.

Dornes, M. (1993). *Der kompetente Säugling [The competent infant].* Frankfurt: Fischer.

Downing, G. (1996). *Körper und Wort in der Psychotherapie [Body and word in psychotherapy].* Munich: Kösel.

Downing, G. (2002). Die Behandlung von Essstörungen [The treatment of eating disorders]. *Psychoanalyse und Körper [Psychoanalysis and the Body], 1,* 9–35.

Downing, G. (2003). Emotion und Körper: Eine Kritik der Emotionstheorie [Emotion and the body: A critique of the theory of emotion]. *Psychoanalyse und Körper [Psychoanalysis and the Body], 2,* 59–88.

Fonagy, P., & Target, M. (2002). Neubewertung der Entwicklung der Affektregulation vor dem Hintergrund von Winnicotts Konzept des "falschen Selbst" [Reassessment of the development of affect regulation in the context of Winnicott's concept of the "false self"]. *Psyche, 9/10,* 839–862.

Gallagher, S. (1998). Body schema and intentionality. In J. L. Bermúdez, A. J. Marcel, & N. Eilan (Eds.), *The body and the self* (pp. 311–336). Cambridge, MA: Bradford Books, MIT Press.

Gallagher, S. (2001). *Neo-Aristotelian neurobiology.* Presentation, Paris.

Gallagher, S. (2002a). *Understanding understanding: The contributions of hermeneutics and the cognitive sciences.* Lecture at University of Alberta, Edmonton, Canada.

Gallagher, S. (2002b). *Movement and expression in the development of social cognition.* Paper presented at the Piaget Society Meeting, Philadelphia. Retrieved from http://pegasus.cc.ucf.edu/~gallaghr/piaget.html

Gallagher, S., & Cole, J. (1995). Body schema and body image in a deafferented subject. *Journal of Mind and Behavior, 16,* 369–390.

Geissler, P. (2002). Psychoanalyse und Körper: Überlegungen zum gegenwärtigen Stand der analytischen Körperpsychotherapie [Psychoanalysis and the body: Reflections on the current state of Analytical Body Psychotherapy]. *Psychoanalyse und Körper [Psychoanalysis and the Body], 1,* 37–81.

Gendlin, E. T. (1981). *Focusing.* Salzburg, Austria: Otto Müller.

Grawe, K. (1998). *Psychologische Therapie [Psychological therapy].* Göttingen: Hogrefe.

Head, H. (1920). *Studies in neurology (Vol. 2).* London: Oxford University Press.

Hebb, D. O. (1949). *The organization of behavior.* New York: Wiley.

Heisterkamp, G. (2002). *Basales Verstehen [Basal understanding].* Munich: Pfeiffer.

Horowitz, M. J. (1995). *Image formation and psychotherapy.* London: Jason Aronson.

Kuhl, J. (2000). A theory of self-development: Affective fixation and the STAR model of personality disorders and related styles. In J. Heckhausen (Ed.), *Motivational psychology of human development: Developing motivation and motivating development.* Amsterdam: Elsevier.

Kuhl, J. (2001). *Motivation und Persönlichkeit [Motivation and personality].* Göttingen: Hogrefe.

Lichtenberg, J. D., Lachmann, F. M., & Fosshage, J. L. (2000). *Das Selbst und die motivationalen Systeme [Self and motivational systems].* Frankfurt: Brandes & Apsel.

Neisser, U. (1967). *Cognitive Psychology.* New York: Appleton-Century-Crofts.

Piaget, J. (1951). *The psychology of intelligence.* London: Routledge & Kegan Paul.

Sachse, R. (2003). *Klärungsorientierte Psychotherapie [Clarification-oriented psychotherapy].* Göttingen: Hogrefe.

Schore, A. N. (1997). Interdisciplinary developmental research as a source of clinical methods. In M. Moskowitz, C. Monk, C. Kaye, & S. Ellman (Eds.), *The neurobiological and developmental basis for psychotherapeutic intervention* (pp. 1–71). Northvale, NJ: Jason Aronson.

Schultz, S. (2001). Scientists pinpoint neurons as source of "body sense." *Princeton Weekly Bulletin, 90(26).*

Stern, D. N., Sander, L. W., Nahum, J. P., Harrison, A. M., Lyons-Ruth, K., Morgan, A. C., Bruschweiler-Stern, N., & Tronick, E. Z. (2002). Nicht-deutende Mechanismen in der psychoanalytischen Therapie: Das "Etwas-Mehr" als Deutung [Non-interpretive mechanisms in psychoanalytic therapy: The "something more" than interpretation]. *Psyche, 9/10, 974–1006.*

Taylor, G. J., Bagby, R. M., & Parker, J. D. A. (1999). *Disorders of affect regulation.* New York: Cambridge University Press.

Varela, F. J. (2000). Steps to a science of inter-being: Unfolding the dharma implicit in modern cognitive science. In G. Watson, S. Batchelor, & G. Claxton (Eds.), *The psychology of awakening* (pp. 71–89). York Beach, ME: Samuel Weiser.

Wehowsky, A. (1994). Atem-Dialoge: Muster des Atmens als Muster der sozialen Bindung [Breath dialogues: Patterns of breathing as a model of social commitment]. In K. von Steinaecker (Ed.), *Der eigene und der fremde Körper [The own and the foreign body]* (pp. 107–117). Berlin: Edition Lit. Europe.

Wehowsky, A. (2002). Körperpsychotherapie und tiefenpsychologisch fundierte Psychotherapie: Aspekte einer traditionsreichen Beziehung [Body Psychotherapy and psychodynamically oriented psychotherapy: Aspects of a traditional relationship]. *Forum der Bioenergetischen Analyse, 2, 33–44.*

# 31

## Prenatal and Perinatal Psychology

*Vital Foundations of Body Psychotherapy*

### Marti Glenn, United States

**Marti Glenn**, PhD, is co-director of the STAR Foundation, offering intensive retreats to help adults heal early developmental trauma. She is founding president of the Santa Barbara Graduate Institute, the first university to offer postgraduate degrees specializing in Prenatal and Perinatal Psychology as well as Somatic Psychology. A pioneering psychotherapist and educator for more than thirty years, she integrates affective neuroscience with attachment theory, early development, and trauma in her work as trainer and presenter. She often presents at the Esalen Institute in Big Sur, California, and is a frequent speaker at worldwide conferences.

Interestingly, she also co-produced the broadcast documentary: *Trauma, Brain, and Relationship: Helping Children Heal*, and has appeared in such documentary films as: *What Babies Want; What Babies Know; Reducing Infant Mortality;* and *Improving the Health of Babies*.

Since the 1990s, research discoveries from diverse fields have increasingly impacted the clinical principles for effective Body Psychotherapy. Many have provided scientific evidence for the efficacy of our current practices; some are pointing the way to new principles for our art and craft. This research is converging to suggest new paradigms regarding our earliest human development and what it takes to raise relational, creative, and resilient adults and how healing can occur throughout the life span. Research and clinical experience from seemingly disparate fields of epigenetics, Developmental Psychology, affective neuroscience and brain-imaging studies, polyvagal theory, attachment theory, and prevention and healing of trauma are providing us new ways of considering mental and physical health. Particularly highlighted is the *quality* of the infant-caregiver relationship and its lifelong impact on neurological development, self-regulation, the creation of mental models, and the capacity for relationship (Bowlby, 1969, 1988; Ainsworth, 1985; Beebe and Lachmann, 2002; Fonagy and Target, 1997; Fonagy et al., 2002; Lyons-Ruth and Jacobovitz, 1999; Perry, 1999; Porges, 2011; Schore, 1994, 2003, 2012; Siegel, 2012a, 2012b; Stern, 2004; Tronick, 2007). It is important to note that we never want to place blame on parents or the medical system in general. Our goal is to educate and assist in the healing process, given what we know now.

Increasingly, research and clinical practice are looking even earlier than postbirth and infancy for the foundations of health and dis-ease and for practices to prevent and heal maladies throughout life. Much of this research demonstrates that our prenatal experiences lay the foundation for brain development and mental health or illness (Kaplan, Evans, and Monk, 2007; Lupien et al., 2009; O'Connor et al., 2003; O'Connor et al., 2005; Shonkoff, Boyce, and McEwen, 2009; Talge, Neal, and Glover, 2007; Van den Bergh and Marcoen, 2004; Van den Bergh et al., 2008). It is also well established that as humans we are particularly vulnerable to a broad range of effects during the prenatal period (Nathanielsz, 1999; Thomson, 2007; Van den Bergh et al., 2005; Verny and Weintraub, 2002). Prenatal and Perinatal Psychology has been creating and coalescing research and clinical practice in this arena for decades. Given that, in Body Psychotherapy, we know that the body records—consciously or unconsciously—every experience and that this experience forms the foundation for later development, it follows that Prenatal and Perinatal Psychology provides a significant foundation for the practice of Body Psychotherapy (Juhan, 2003; Rand and Caldwell, 2004).

This chapter presents a cursory look at and invites further exploration of the effects of our earliest development, including relationships and environment, with the hope that it might enhance our clinical perspective of the multifaceted and transgenerational influences and provide support for new avenues of healing. In addition, it is imperative that, as clinicians, we continue our own healing process and apply these principles first to ourselves and then to our clients.

## Prenatal and Perinatal Psychology: A Definition

Prenatal and Perinatal Psychology is commonly defined as the study of and clinical practice relating to our earliest development, including preconception, conception, gestation, birth, postnatal experience, and the infant's first postnatal year. Prenatal and Perinatal Psychology considers factors that contribute to optimal beginnings as well as aspects that may relate to stress or trauma patterns that could challenge healthy development. Prenatal and Perinatal Psychology offers best practices to ensure the most favorable outcomes as well as therapeutic interventions to resolve early dysfunctional patterns and trauma in infants, children, and adults (McCarty and Glenn, 2008).

Also included is the intergenerational transmission of early imprints, meaning that parents' foundational experiences and their mental models relating to themselves and the world create the template from which they relate to others, including their infants and children (Siegel, 2012a). We also know that parents who resolve their own early traumas help to give their babies optimal beginnings and a legacy for a lifetime of health.

This interdisciplinary study of Prenatal and Perinatal Psychology provides an understanding of how experiences during this critical period impact lifelong patterns of physical, emotional, cognitive, and social development. It includes the experience of the family system and other caregivers as well as the environment. Our first experiences—energetic, cellular, and relational—form the foundation of our physical, emotional, and spiritual existence and therefore hold the "musculature" of our being: memories, mental models, and our capacity for self-regulation and relationship.

## A Common Tale

Many prenatal and perinatal practitioners discovered the importance of our earliest experiences from our clients. In the late 1970s and early 1980s, I used two modalities that often elicited discoveries of very early trauma: one was Ericksonian hypnotherapy, in which body sensations were key; and the other was body-centered Gestalt Therapy. When we worked with Gestalt principles, on the floor surrounded by lots of pillows, the work was more experience than words. As the client's focus became more internal, we would say, "Let your body do what it knows how to do"; and, while we supported each movement of the body, very often the client would execute what we later discovered was a birth sequence. In hypnotherapy sessions, we would traverse back in time and follow the body sensations, with the suggestion to "Take us back to the source of this difficulty." Very often, clients would have something that seemed like a prebirth experience—for example, a memory of parents fighting, Mom being afraid, and an early decision to take care of her—or clients would spontaneously describe and/or reexperience their birth.

The session with a client whom I'll call Ruth catapulted me into a search for a deeper understanding of these phenomena: it is a graphic story and yet illuminates how our very earliest experiences can affect our physical, mental, and emotional capacities. Ruth came to see me because, although she and her husband had a close relationship, she had become increasingly anxious around sexual encounters, and in fact, her discomfort with being touched had escalated to the point that they had stopped making love altogether. I discovered that her parents had had a solid, caring marriage; she had little trauma growing up and no evidence of sexual abuse.

During a hypnosis session, her only instruction was to "Take us back to the source of this difficulty." In a very deep trance, she began to wince, shake, and make distressing sounds. I asked her if she was OK, and/or wanted to stop. She indicated that this was important and she needed to continue. Then, in a soft and halting voice, she described a horrific scenario: "It's dusk . . . I'm walking down a cobblestone street . . . there's four soldiers . . . Oh, No! . . ." Her body began to writhe and through her tears she made distressing sounds. Again, I asked if she was OK, and she indicated that she needed to continue. Ruth was obviously reliving a dreadful experience. Upon inquiry, she did not remember such an experience and, in fact, had an aversion to even watching scary movies.

I knew Ruth was going to visit her mother over the weekend and so I suggested, if she was comfortable, that she might share her experience with her. The following week she began the session with this account: "On Saturday morning, Mom was making tea for us and I began telling her my experience on the cobblestone street and the four soldiers. She blanched, dropped her teacup, sat down, and with tears in her eyes, told me this story:

> Just after I discovered that I was pregnant with you, I went back to Europe to visit some relatives, and one evening went for a walk down a cobblestone street where I was approached by four soldiers in uniform and they raped me. It was terrifying. I was so humiliated and ashamed that I ran back to my aunt's house, took a hot bath, went to bed, and shook for a long time. *I never told anyone.* Your father doesn't even know."

In therapy, we dealt with the trauma that Ruth had suffered as a result of her mother's assault, and she was able to resume a loving relationship with her husband. After working with Ruth's experience, I began doing some research and looking for my own answers to the questions that this story evoked, and I found that other clinicians were making similar discoveries, and in fact, a whole movement was under way, both in Europe and in the United States, to investigate the effects of our earliest experiences.

## The Evolution of Prenatal and Perinatal Psychology

First, I encountered Thomas Verny's book *The Secret Life of the Unborn Child (1981),* which synthesized findings from many fields of inquiry to suggest that the prenatal child is conscious, feeling, remembering, and very affected by its environment. And, in fact, he espoused, "birth and pre-natal experiences form the foundations of human personality" (p. 118). Delving more deeply into the prenatal experience, I uncovered Otto Rank's book *The Trauma of Birth* (1952, first published in 1923), in which he suggested that adult neuroses and character disorders originate in the anxiety related to the birth process. Since then, Nandor Fodor (1949) and later Francis Mott (1960) headed the modern investigation into prenatal experiences. Soon after reading Verny's book, I also encountered the professional organization he founded, now called The Association for Prenatal and Perinatal Psychology and Health, and discovered numerous like-minded colleagues.

In taking a brief look at the development of this field, we see that several therapeutic modalities emerged during the second half of the last century, including hypnosis, psychedelics, regression therapies, primal therapy, breathwork, and process work. Influenced by the work of Rank, psychiatrist Stanislav Grof (1975, 1985) first used psychedelics in the 1950s and later used breathwork to explore human consciousness, which led to a conceptual framework for Prenatal and Perinatal Psychology. Also in the 1950s, Frank Lake's (1966, 1981) work, like that of Grof, began with psychedelics and later focused on a rapid-breathing technique, and also focused, particularly, on the first three months of gestation and on primal integration. Graham Farrant (1987) resonated further with Lake's findings, being quite specific about cellular consciousness, imprints from conception onward, and their lifelong effects.

Obstetrician David Cheek (Cheek and LeCron, 1968) and psychologist David Chamberlain (1988) began working with adults, using hypnosis to discover and heal experiences relating to birth. Arthur Janov (Janov and Holden, 1975; Janov, 1983) developed his "primal therapy," which involved the reliving of early traumatic events, including birth. Alongside these methods, the 1980s also saw the emergence of other modalities, such as Rebirthing (Ray and Orr, 1983); the psychoanalytic techniques of Leslie Feher (1980), who emphasized the trauma of cutting the umbilical cord; and Martha Welch's (1983) controversial "holding therapy." Although the work was initially focused on adults healing their earliest, often traumatic, experiences, William Emerson (1989), and later Ray Castellino (2000) and Wendy McCarty (2000, 2004), focused on healing early imprints and trauma with infants and children.

## Basic Assumptions of Prenatal and Perinatal Psychology

A basic assumption of Prenatal and Perinatal Psychology is that the developing prenate is a conscious, aware being who is sensing, experiencing, and remembering from the very beginning and can therefore be affected by events even before conception (Lipton, 2005; McCarty, 2000, 2004) as well as *in utero* (Chamberlain, 1988; Janus, 1997; Verny, 1981). Circumstances, such as being unwanted, maternal anxiety, depression, experiences of loss, domestic violence, or states of extreme stress, create imprints on the developing child, with lasting effects. These early imprints carry cognitive, emotional, relational, and somatic consequences, all evidenced into adulthood. Part of implicit memory, these experiences are largely unconscious, as are the mental models that ensue from them, and these ultimately determine our experience of safety, our self-image and self-scripts, and our expectations for how the outside world will perceive and treat us (Schore, 2003). This new synthesis of research and clinical experience invites us to reexamine our current practices to include an understanding of the prenatal and perinatal experience.

As stated, research and clinical experience in Prenatal and Perinatal Psychology have established the fact that our earliest experiences form the foundation of our sense of self, our capacity to relate to others, and our resiliency throughout life. The core foundations of physical and mental health, emotional intelligence, and the ability to develop one's capacities and talents are—we now believe—established between preconception and the end of the first postnatal year (Chamberlain, 1988; Grof, 1975, 1985; Nathanielsz, 1999; Verny, 1981).

Given that brain structures, capacity for self-regulation, social engagement, productivity, and resiliency are all built upon this earliest foundation, it benefits us to examine some of the tenets of the fields of epigenetics, embryology, and affective neuroscience. Here, we discover some of the scientific building blocks of our individual development, and therefore of sound paradigms in Prenatal and Perinatal Psychology, as well as in the practice of Body Psychotherapy.

### Epigenetics

As we reflect on our earliest beginnings, and the creation of optimal health, it is helpful to consider our DNA, the most foundational aspect of our cellular makeup. Epigenetics informs us that our DNA, alone, is not the determinant of our physical structure, capacities, and vulnerabilities, but that gene expression is—to a large extent—determined by the environment: this has the effect of "turning" on or off certain genes. For example, from preconception onward, our biological systems assess the environment for safety or threat, and then choose responses to sustain survival and optimal functioning, given the perceived circumstances and needs (Lipton, 2005; Rossi, 2002). There are implications for not only physical health, but also eventual mental health and/or mental illness. Levels of physical and emotional safety, anxiety, stress, and depression all play a large part in the eventual outcomes of every individual, and these effects begin within our cellular structures, even before conception (Isles and Wilkinson, 2008; Szyf, 2009).

Evolutionary biology research also demonstrates that our earliest development, from conception through to the postnatal, ". . . 'reads' key characteristics of its environment and prepares to adapt to an external world that can vary dramatically in its levels of safety, sufficiency, and peril," including adjusting "set points" in key brain circuits (Shonkoff et al., 2009, p. 2257). Harvard University's National Scientific Council on the Developing Child published a review of the literature in their position papers 3 and 10 (2005, 2010), stating that our earliest experiences can alter gene expression and can affect long-term development; and, as such, excessive stress, maternal or otherwise, disrupts the architecture of the developing brain.

**Consciousness**

International clinical research since the 1980s supports the ancient knowing that we are conscious, aware beings, and also that we are learning and connecting from the beginning of life (Chamberlain, 1988; Hamilton, 2004; McCarty, 2000, 2004). This research is helping us to slowly remove the cloud of Freud's (1899) assumption of infant amnesia and the belief that babies cannot remember and do not feel pain. It was assumed that because the neural structures for explicit memory and perception are not fully developed, infants do not experience pain, and, if they do, they won't remember it. Until the late 1980s, infants were subjected to surgery without the benefit of anesthesia (Anand and Hickey, 1987; Anand et al., 2007). To be fair, it was also not known at the time how to safely administer anesthesia to newborn babies. Chamberlain's (1999) research review illuminates the past century of denial in medicine with evidence that prenates and neonates do remember and certainly feel pain. Merker (2006) and Joseph (2003) highlight the fact that consciousness is possible without a developed neocortex.

Now we know that babies have exquisite *implicit* memory and a heightened sense of awareness (Schore, 2003). Babies are learning *in utero*, during birth and the early moments, and during the months that follow. Our earliest experiences imprint and become our subconscious programming. For example, my client Susan's grandfather died a few months before her birth. As she experienced her mother's grief, she decided that she needed to take care of her mother—which she did; even as a small child, Susan watched her mother carefully and, if there was upset, she would do whatever she could to make it better. She noted how this decision had become a pattern throughout her life of caregiving and denying her own needs.

**Embryology: Earliest Psychological Imprints**

During the first three months of intrauterine life, the embryo is particularly vulnerable to both physical and psychological conditions. At this early time, the neural systems are mainly undifferentiated and are very dependent on a safe and welcoming environment (Anisman et al., 1998; Cicchetti and Tucker, 1994; Cicchetti and Toth, 2009). Brain tissue is growing and differentiating very rapidly during this critical period and is particularly susceptible to its environment (Cicchetti and Tucker, 1994; de Kloet et al., 1996). High levels of maternal stress can change and retard brain development due to elevated levels of maternal stress hormones (Glynn et al., 2000).

**Being Wanted, Being Unwanted, or Abortion Ideation**

Research and clinical experience reveal that whether or not a child is wanted makes a huge difference in the child's early and long-lasting psychological imprints and may also have physiological effects. Clinical case studies as well as research with prisoners have revealed that an experience of the fetus of being unwanted, or the parents considering or attempting abortion, has some long-term psychological influences, as well as potentially causes changes in brain structure and function, thus creating additional vulnerabilities to future stress for neural networks (Sonne, 1997).

An unwanted pregnancy creates stress for both the mother and the fetus. The stress of a couple's ambivalence toward their unborn child can yield negative consequences for the child's later development. An unresolved unwanted pregnancy can seemingly make the child more vulnerable to schizophrenia, and can be a marker for behaviors associated with risk in either the mother or the child (Myhrman et al., 1996). Scandinavian researchers have also found that the stress of an unwanted pregnancy may interfere with fetal development and may result in a higher incidence of malformations (Blomberg, 1980).

*Case Vignette 1*

"Sharon" often seemed both insecure and oppositional: she was, metaphorically and literally, afraid she was going to be annihilated at any time. Through her studies, she began to investigate her earliest experiences, where she connected her anger at the world and the fact that she had been her mother's failed abortion. Her anger was a deep defense against her belief that she was bad, that she hurt people by simply being in their presence, and that she didn't belong anywhere. In order to survive, she believed she had to be confrontational and to seize anything she got. She had difficulty maintaining friends or close relationships. She attended an intensive ten-day healing retreat, where, for the first time, she had an experience of feeling safe in her body, within a caring relationship with the therapist, and so she could differentiate her mother's experience of being unprepared for a child, and see that this was not about her. She also experienced herself as a good and worthwhile person.

**Gestation**

Events during gestation continue to have both physiological and psychological effects on the growing fetus, for good or for ill. Numerous studies consistently support ". . . [the] 'fetal origins hypothesis' that pre-natal environmental exposures—including maternal psychological state-based alterations in *in utero* physiology—can have sustained effects across the lifespan" (Kinsella and Monk, 2009, p. 425). Our concern here is not so much with the physiological outcomes, but the psychological factors that mediate for health and resiliency, or less-than-optimal outcomes. Talge and colleagues (2007) review a number of studies that showed that children of stressed mothers are at higher risk for cognitive or emotional problems, including general anxiety, attention-deficit/hyperactivity disorder (ADHD), and possible language delays. Prenatal conditions, especially maternal dysregulation that accompanies anxiety and/or depression, also play an important role in the formation of the infant's self-regulatory systems (Thomson, 2007). The ensuing hyperreactivity of the fetal defensive reflexes tends to predispose the infant toward a behaviorally defensive stance, resulting in a predisposition toward aggression and survival, instead of creativity and relationship (Davis and Sandman, 2010; Degangi et al., 2000; Fishbane, 2007; Thomson, 2007). Thus, these less-than-optimal beginnings can leave the infant vulnerable to the possibility of mental distress or illness (Kinsella and Monk, 2009).

The mother's psychological and physical state also greatly impacts the quality of the attachment that forms between the mother and the baby. Much has been written about the importance of postnatal attachment. Prenatal and Perinatal Psychology and the science of epigenetics, neuroscience, and Porges's polyvagal theory all emphasize that the attachment structures are laid in place even before birth. In fact, the entire prenatal period lays the groundwork for attachment, giving credence to the importance of supporting not only pregnant mothers' physical health but their psychological health as well (Doan and Zimerman, 2003; Mulder et al., 2002; Porges, 2011; Salm et al., 2004; Sandman et al., 2011; Schore, 2002).

The earliest pioneers in Prenatal and Perinatal Psychology have firmly established that infants are quite perceptive long before birth; are aware of, and sensitive to, the mother's thoughts and feelings, as well as changes in their environment (Chamberlain, 1988; Cheek, 1975; Verny, 1981). For this reason, we encourage expectant parents to speak directly to their prenate, sing, and even read to them, on a regular basis. It is also important that parents protect their developing baby from potentially stressful circumstances, such as loud noises, angry outbursts, any form of domestic violence, or other noxious stimuli (McCarty and Glenn, 2008). Providing such protection and inclusion gives a feeling of safety and belonging, and lays a strong foundation for all attachment relationships.

*Case Vignette 2*

Ryan came to me because, although he liked his job, he was ready to quit, because of the stress he routinely experienced. He reported that his co-workers got into loud, but mostly friendly, arguments and, when he heard their raised voices, he became quite anxious. He wasn't able to concentrate, and found himself "spacing out." As we explored his history, he became aware that from the time he could remember, he overreacted to any conflict, and if criticism was directed toward him, he shut down and completely "disappeared," as he called it. He reported that his home when growing up was "normal," with no unusually harsh treatment, and that his parents rarely argued or fought. We were puzzled about his intense reaction to conflict, so he asked his father about it. His father explained that before he was born, they were under a lot of stress, and he and his wife fought bitterly, almost daily. At one point, they spoke with their minister, who recommended a couples workshop and therapy, where they learned to communicate better, were able to remove some of the stressors, and got the support they needed to become new parents. When Ryan was born, they took a vow that they would never fight in front of him, and had mostly been able to work out their differences amicably.

We worked with the fear he experienced *in utero*, how helpless he felt, and the mental model he had created about himself and the world from that state. He realized that some part of him believed that "Something must be wrong with me; the world is not safe; and I have to guard against causing trouble or something really bad will happen." As he differentiated "then" from "now," and experienced the sensation of safety in his body, he was able to create a new mental model of himself: that he was a deserving and capable person; that he could appropriately discern safety and threat; and that most of the time the behavior of others around him (especially at work) had nothing to do with him. Within the safety of the therapeutic relationship, he gradually found his voice, and experienced himself as a vital part of his work team, even when they were joshing and teasing each other.

## Clinical Assessment and Birth Imprints

Of all the events of our lives, birth is our most important transition, for good or ill. The experience of that journey creates a physiological and emotional imprint and sets a pattern for future transitions, as well as establishes a mental model of ourselves and the world. Childbirth often creates more stress, both emotional and physical, than many later incidents in infancy, with the exception of abuse and severe neglect. There is persuasive evidence, from many fields, that birth is often the most traumatic event of our lives and creates profound psychological and spiritual imprints that are etched in our implicit memory and "profoundly affects our psychological development" (Grof, 2006, p. 131). If we emerge from a safe and nurturing environment, if our passage into the world is unhampered and at our own pace, and if our connection with the mother is unbroken, we are most likely to experience and believe the world is a safe place. Conversely, if our experience has not felt safe and connected, if the process itself is traumatic, and/or if we have had long (enforced) separations from our mother, we are quite likely to create a mental model that "There's something wrong with me, and the world is not a safe place."

Although it may not be obvious, as humans, we seem to always be pushing ourselves toward healing or wholeness. Both as children and as adults, we want to be seen and heard, we want to have someone to help us to acknowledge our pain and difficulties, and to help us make sense of our experience. To that end, consciously or unconsciously, we provide clues to our experience; we act out what has happened to us; we react from our feelings; and we indicate especially anything that is "unfinished" or incomplete. This helps provide significant markers for the possibility of healing.

In addition to a usual assessment, if we hold up the prenatal and perinatal "lens" as we listen to the client's language and their nonverbal cues, this can help us unearth their earliest trauma and subsequent mental models or core beliefs. There are often tips about their early experience that the client is not consciously aware of. We know that every birth is different, and that each reaction depends on a myriad of factors. Although we can never say that a particular birth experience yields a specific outcome, we tend to see a range of patterns that merit consideration.

A number of therapies have evolved to work specifically with birth trauma, each having its own nomenclature and protocols (Castellino, 2000; Chamberlain, 1988; Emerson, 1989; Glenn, 2002; Grof, 1985). Space does not permit the elucidation of any specific model here. However, included below are some examples of clinical observations from decades of work with clients. Simply incorporating a prenatal and perinatal lens into any Body Psychotherapy practice can be quite beneficial.

### Cesarean Section

Adults or children delivered by cesarean section often have difficulty taking initiative: "I usually wait for someone to come and pull me out." "I have trouble knowing when to begin things." Children delivered by C-section, when playing in a tunnel, will most always "pop up" in the middle. It is interesting to note that planned or medically induced C-sections, and emergency C-sections, usually create different dynamics. In planned C-sections, the baby often feels defeated before they begin: their capacity for initiating, and their impetus for movement, is often stymied. They might say things like: "I tend to rely on other people." "I can't do it by myself." There is usually a sudden fear that surrounds an emergency C-section: things move very fast, and either the mother or the baby or both are in danger. Some beliefs might include: "I'm a failure" "I can't get it right" "This must be my fault."

I worked with sixteen-year-old "Tina," who was a patient in our residential treatment facility for repeated episodes of cutting (self-harm) on her forearms. In a family session, I asked her parents, with Tina's permission, to describe her birth. As her mom explained the planned C-section, during which she was to be fully awake, with her husband at her shoulder, Tina curled up on the couch between her parents in a fetal position. When Mom described how they had cut her belly, Tina began to cry, and a tiny girl's angry voice emerged: "Yeah, then they handed me to Daddy, and you disappeared forever!" Mom had had medical complications, and wasn't able to see her daughter for more than twenty-four hours, and only intermittently for the first week. As we worked with this early experience of abandonment, Tina was able to see that her self-cutting was a cry for help: she wanted someone to see how terrifying her ongoing fear of abandonment was.

### Umbilical-Cord Trauma

Having the umbilical cord around the neck may have been a frightening experience. This is sometimes the reason the baby cannot descend into the birth canal. My client, Tom, had an aversion to tight collars, and couldn't stand anything around his neck. He even shouted at his wife, in a particularly difficult couples therapy session where she wanted them to buy a house *now,* "Gee, Jill, you've really put my neck in a noose!" With that clue, we were later able to explore his birth experience, where he felt powerless to take the next step that was required. Another client, Hanna, who was born breech and had umbilical-cord trauma, always wore something around her neck—a scarf or other tie. It was like her security blanket and if she was without it, she began to get anxious. A by-product of her therapy, in addition to increasing her confidence and decreasing her anxiety, was that she began to release her need for the scarves.

### Forceps or Vacuum-Extraction Delivery

The use of a strange-looking pair of clamps that is placed on either side of the baby's head has dwindled as vacuum extraction has become easier to use. Clients who have been delivered with the use of forceps often resist authority or being told what to do. Some phrases might be: "I don't feel I have a choice" "I'm always pushing against [or afraid of] authority." Some phrases expressed by those whose birth included vacuum extraction might be: "I need to be rescued" "People hurt me" "My body is not my own."

### Anesthesia

Common until a few decades ago, general anesthesia is rarely used in birth today. The baby also received the anesthesia, and it could be a frightening experience, a feeling of being out of control and a giving-up or dying. As teens or young adults, they might resort to drugs. Examples of common phrases include: "When it's time for me to take action [or try something new], my energy drains and I'm no longer enthusiastic but just kind of give up on the idea" "I often feel numb."

### Induction

If labor does not progress properly, or if a baby is overdue, drugs are often used to induce or speed up labor. Depending on the amount used, it can be a frightening experience for the baby. Some of the language might include: "I'm a failure. I don't do things right" "I can't do things my own way [or at my own pace]" "I always feel rushed" "What I want [or need] doesn't matter." Seven-year-old Myrna was often angry at her mother, because she felt rushed by her; she also took undue physical risks. Her birth had been induced by prolonged doses of Pitocin. During a play-therapy session, Myrna blurted out, "I don't know where I'm going, but I have to hurry, hurry, hurry."

### Beginning to Work with Patterns

Even more than phrases expressed by the client, we notice life patterns presented in metaphors and stories that echo possible birth experiences. Repeated behaviors that create anxiety, lethargy, helplessness, numbing, or addictions can also have prenatal origins. One important tool, which we call "Linking," which is used to discover and work with early imprints, illuminates the emotional connection between the client's present difficulties and unresolved prenatal and perinatal events. With this tool, we help the client link a current experience with past trauma and unconscious beliefs or an unconscious mental model. For example, when the client speaks about a current issue, such as "I'm really afraid my partner will leave me," we gently guide her to the physical sensation of that experience. After she describes what she notices, we gently ask, "Is this feeling familiar?" Most often, the client will say, "Yes," to which we respond, "Can you imagine an earlier time, maybe as a young adult, when that familiar feeling was present? The situation may be very different, but the familiar feeling is there."

When we've explored that scenario, focusing on the sensation, we ask the client again if she might allow her mind to wander back to an even earlier situation where this familiar feeling was present, and to investigate that childhood experience. Then, we ask her to invite the very earliest scenario she can imagine when her "Little One" might have experienced this sensation. This is often between three and six years of age. Although this is not a birth scenario, it is almost always (somehow) a recapitulation or mirror of that earliest experience. The client then tries to see, sense, or imagine herself as a "Little One," discern what she might have felt at that time (frightened, alone, powerless, etc.), then what she might have been telling herself about herself (e.g., "Something must be wrong with me").

Next, we examine what she might believe about others and/or the world ("They're OK, but I'm not" "I'm not safe"). Finally, we discern how she decided to be in order to get her needs met ("I'll be good" "I'll take care of a parent" "I'll be demanding"). This process helps the client discern her mental model. Having an experience, in relationship with the therapist, in the adult state, readies the client to determine the real truth about her "Little One" ("I am good" "I deserve love" "I can do this" etc.). As you work with this over time, it will be easier to help the client move back into more implicit memories, especially around birth and before.

Frequently, the prenatal or birth experience that created the mental model will appear in a body movement, such as head in hands, slumping over, curling up, pushing away, feeling numb, feeling frozen, etc. The voice sometimes sounds very quiet, and the language is quite young: "They put me in a basket, and Mommy go far, far away" "Get away. I do it" "Does my mommy love me?"

Although facts can be interesting and helpful, it is important to note that it is not the discovery of the story that is the key in working with prenatal and birth imprints. It is going into the experience, as a caring witness, being curious about what will arise, allowing emotions to emerge naturally, while remaining connected in the present moment and staying with the experience until it shifts. Then, peering inside the experience with the client to note what it was like for the "Little One," what she might have (unconsciously) believed about herself and the world, and in some way decided how to be in the world to get her needs met. This is connected to the adult experience and the lifelong patterns of relating.

## An Aside for Further Research

During my two years as clinical director of an inpatient treatment center for disturbed teenagers in the mountains of Southern California, we took extensive family histories of these young people, including such questions as: "Was this a wanted child?" "What were your relationship and your life like during the pregnancy and birth of your child?" "What stresses did you experience during pregnancy?" "Was there domestic violence, drug abuse, or traumatic events prebirth or postbirth?" "What was the birth process like?" "Was the baby allowed to stay with you, or was there separation?"

Much to our surprise, we discovered that every teen—yes, *100 percent*—had experienced some type of trauma between conception and their first birthday. Incidents included events such as: being unwanted throughout the pregnancy; a failed abortion attempt; a very stressful pregnancy; death of a close family member; being placed for adoption; prolonged separation from the mother; traumatic C-section or other birth trauma; time in the neonatal intensive-care unit; surgery at a few weeks or months of age; or abandonment of the family by one parent.

The most gratifying part was that as we worked with the family, with these early traumas that often led to current issues, many of the teens were able to go home and lead productive lives. It seems that during adolescence, being a time of huge transition, many teens amplify or reenact their first transition into the world, and when that pattern and its ensuing mental models are identified and worked with—as they are held in the body and evidenced behaviorally—teens are able to move forward with more self-confidence, connection, and creativity.

It is beyond the scope of this chapter to give full consideration to the principles for integrating Prenatal and Perinatal Psychology into Body Psychotherapy practice. For more specific information, see "*Essential Clinical Principles for Prenatal and Perinatal Psychology Practitioners*" (Glenn and Cappon, 2013).

## Summary

Research from disparate fields over the past several decades offers increasing evidence that experiences from preconception through the first year of life lay the foundation for physical and emotional development, including brain development and mental health or mental illness. We now understand that the foundations for self-regulation, relationship, and resiliency begin even before conception. In Body Psychotherapy, we know that the body records experiences and must be included in the healing process. Prenatal and Perinatal Psychology adds the importance of our earliest development to this understanding and provides a significant foundation for our practice of Body Psychotherapy.

## References

Ainsworth, M. D. S. (1985). Patterns of infant-mother attachments: Antecedents and effects on development, and Attachments across the life span. *Bulletin of New York Academy of Medicine, 61, 771–812.*

Anand, K. J. S., & Hickey, P. R. (1987). Pain and its effects in the human neonate and fetus. *New England Journal of Medicine, 317(21), 1321–1329.*

Anand, K. J. S., Stevens, B. J., & McGrath, P. J. (2007). *Pain in neonates and infants* (3rd ed.). London: Elsevier.

Anisman, H., Zaharia, M., Meaney, M., & Meralis, Z. (1998). Do early-life events permanently alter behavioral and hormonal responses to stressors? *International Journal of Developmental Neuroscience, 16, 149–164.*

Beebe, B., & Lachmann, F. (2002). *Infant research and adult treatment: Co-constructing interactions.* Hillsdale, NJ: Analytic Press.

Blomberg, S. (1980). Influence of maternal distress during pregnancy on fetal malformations. *Acta-Psychiatrica-Scandinavia, 62, 315–330.*

Bowlby, J. (1969/1982). *Attachment and loss: Attachment (Vol. 1).* New York. Basic Books.

Bowlby, J. (1988). *A secure base: Parent-child attachment and healthy human development.* New York: Basic Books.

Castellino, R. (2000). The stress matrix: Implications for pre-natal and birth therapy. *Journal of Prenatal and Perinatal Psychology and Health, 15(1),* 31–62.

Chamberlain, D. (1988). *Babies remember birth.* Los Angeles: Jeremy P. Tarcher.

Chamberlain, D. (1999). Babies don't feel pain: A century of denial in medicine. *Journal of Prenatal and Perinatal Psychology and Health, 14(1),* 145–169.

Cheek, D. (1975). Maladjustment patterns apparently related to imprinting at birth. *American Journal of Clinical Hypnosis, 18,* 75–82.

Cheek, D. B., & LeCron, L. M. (1968). *Clinical hypnotherapy.* New York: Green & Stratton.

Cicchetti, D., & Toth, S. (2009). The past achievements and future promises of developmental psychopathology: The coming of age of a discipline. *Journal of Child Psychology and Psychiatry, 50(1–2),* 16–25.

Cicchetti, D., & Tucker, D. M. (1994). Development and self-regulatory structures of the mind. *Development and Psychopathology, 6,* 533–549.

Davis, E. P., & Sandman, C. A. (2010). The timing of pre-natal exposure to maternal cortisol and psychosocial stress is associated with human infant cognitive development. *Child Development, 81(1),* 131–148.

Degangi, G., Breinbauer, C., Doussard-Roosevelt, J., Porges, S., & Greenspan, S. (2000). Prediction of childhood problems at three years in children experiencing disorders of regulation during infancy. *Infant Mental Health Journal, 21(3),* 156–175.

de Kloet, E. R., Korte, S. M., Rots, W. Y., & Kruk, M. R. (1996). Stress hormones, genotype, brain organization: Implications for aggression. In C. F. Ferris & T. Grisso (Eds.), *Understanding aggressive behavior in children.* Annals of the New York Academy of Sciences.

Doan, H. M., & Zimerman, A. (2003). Conceptualizing pre-natal attachment: Toward a multidimensional view. *Journal of Prenatal and Perinatal Psychology and Health, 18(2),* 109–130.

Emerson, W. (1989). Psychotherapy with infants and children. *Journal of Prenatal and Perinatal Psychology and Health, 3(3),* 190–217.

Farrant, G. (1987). Cellular consciousness. *Aesthema, 7,* 28–39.

Feher, L. (1980). *The psychology of birth.* New York: Putnam.

Fishbane, M. (2007). Wired to connect: Neuroscience, relationships, and therapy. *Family Process, 46(3),* 395–412.

Fodor, N. (1949). *The search for the beloved: A clinical investigation of the trauma of birth and pre-natal conditioning.* New Hyde Park, NY: University Books.

Fonagy, P., Gergely, G., Jurist, E., & Target, M. (2002). *Affect regulation, mentalization and the development of the self.* New York: Other Press.

Fonagy, P., & Target, M. (1997). Attachment and reflective function: Their role in self-organization. *Development and Psychopathology, 9,* 679–700.

Freud, S. (1899). *The standard edition of the complete works of Sigmund Freud.* London: Hogarth Press.

Glenn, M. (2002). *The use of Body-Centered Psychotherapy in working with pre-natal and peri-natal imprints within a group context.* Proceedings of the USABP International Conference.

Glenn, M., & Cappon, R. (2013). Essential clinical principles for Prenatal and Perinatal Psychology practitioners. *Journal of Prenatal and Perinatal Psychology and Health, 28(1),* 20–42.

Glynn, L. M., Wadhwa, P. D., & Sandman, C. A. (2000). The influence of corticotropin releasing hormone on human fetal development and parturition. *Journal of Prenatal and Perinatal Psychology and Health, 14,* 243–256.

Grof, S. (1975). *Realms of the human unconscious.* New York: Viking Press.

Grof, S. (1985). *Beyond the brain: Birth, death and transcendence in psychotherapy.* Albany, NY: State University of New York Press.

Grof, S. (2006). *The ultimate journey: Consciousness and the mystery of death.* Santa Cruz, CA: Multidisciplinary Association for Psychedelic Studies (MAPS).

Hamilton, D. (2004). The nature of consciousness. *British Journal of Psychotherapy, 21(1),* 63–67.

Harvard University National Scientific Council on the Developing Child. (2005). Excessive stress disrupts the architecture of the developing brain: Working paper #3. Harvard University. Retrieved from http://developingchild.harvard.edu/index.php/library/reports_and_working_papers/working_papers/wp3/

Harvard University National Scientific Council on the Developing Child. (2010). *Early experiences can alter gene expression and affect long-term development: Working paper #10.* Harvard University. Retrieved from http://developingchild.harvard.edu/index.php/library/reports_and_working_papers/working_papers/wp10/

Isles, A. R., & Wilkinson, L. S. (2008). Epigenetics: What is it and why is it important to mental disease? *British Medical Bulletin, 85(1),* 35–45.

Janov, A. (1983). *Imprints: The lifelong effects of the birth experience.* New York: Coward-McCann.

Janov, A., & Holden, E. M. (1975). *Primal man: The new consciousness.* New York: Thomas Y. Crowell.

Janus, L. (1997). *The enduring effects of pre-natal experience: Echoes from the womb.* Northvale, NJ: Aronson.

Joseph, R. (2003). Emotional trauma and childhood amnesia. *Consciousness & Emotion, 4(2),* 151–179.

Juhan, A. (2003). *Open floor: Dance therapy and transformation through the 5Rhythms.* (Doctoral dissertation). Union Institute, Los Angeles.

Kaplan, L. A., Evans, L., & Monk, C. (2007). Effects of mothers' pre-natal psychiatric status and post-natal caregiving on infant biobehavioral regulation: Can pre-natal programming be modified? *Early Human Development, 84(4),* 249–256.

Kinsella, M. T., & Monk, C. (2009). Impact of maternal stress, depression and anxiety on fetal neurobehavioral development. *Clinical Obstetrics and Gynecology, 52(3),* 425–440.

Lake, F. (1966). *Clinical theology.* London: Darton, Longman & Todd.

Lake, F. (1981). *Tight corners in pastoral counselling.* London: Darton, Longman & Todd.

Lipton, B. (2005). *The biology of belief.* Santa Rosa, CA: Elite Books, Energy Psychology Press.

Lupien, S. J., McEwen, B. S., Gunnar, M. R., & Heim, C. (2009). Effects of stress throughout the lifespan on the brain, behavior and cognition. *Nature Reviews Neuroscience, 10,* 434–445.

Lyons-Ruth, K., & Jacobovitz, D. (1999). Attachment disorganization: Unresolved loss, relational violence, and lapses in behavioral and attentional strategies. In J. Cassidy & P. Shaver (Eds.), *Handbook of attachment.* New York: Guilford Press.

McCarty, W. (2000). *Being with babies: What babies are teaching us* (rev. ed.), *Vol. 2: Supporting babies' innate wisdom.* Goleta, CA: Wondrous Beginnings.

McCarty, W. (2004). *Welcoming consciousness: Supporting babies' wholeness from the beginning of life—An integrated model of early development.* Santa Barbara, CA: Wondrous Beginnings.

McCarty, W., & Glenn, M. (2008). Investing in human potential from the beginning of life: Key to maximizing human capital. *Journal of Prenatal and Perinatal Psychology and Health, 23(2),* 117–135.

Merker, B. (2006). Consciousness without a cerebral cortex: A challenge for neuroscience and medicine. *Behavioral and Brain Sciences, 30,* 63–134.

Mott, F. (1960). *Mythology of the pre-natal life.* London: Integration.

Mulder, E. J. H., Robles de Medina, P. G., Huizink, A. C., Van den Bergh, B. R. H., Buitelaar, J. K., & Visser, G. H. A. (2002). Pre-natal maternal stress: Effects on pregnancy and the (unborn) child. *Early Human Development, 70,* 3–14.

Myhrman, A., Rantakallio, P., Isohanni, M., Janes, P., & Partanen, U. (1996). Unwantedness of a pregnancy and schizophrenia in the child. *British Journal of Psychiatry, 169(5),* 637–640.

Nathanielsz, P. W. (1999). *Life in the womb: The origin of health and disease.* Ithaca, NY: Promethean Press.

O'Connor, T. G., Ben-Shlomo, Y., Heron, J., Golding, J., Adams, D., & Glover, V. (2005). Pre-natal anxiety predicts individual differences in cortisol in pre-adolescent children. *Biological Psychiatry, 58(3),* 211–217.

O'Connor, T. G., Heron, J., Golding, J., Glover, V., & ALSPAC study team. (2003). Maternal antenatal anxiety and behavioral/emotional problems in children: A test of a programming hypothesis. *Journal of Child Psychology and Psychiatry, 44(7),* 1025–1036.

Perry, B. D. (1999). The memories of states: How the brain stores and retrieves traumatic experience. In J. M. Goodwin & R. Attias (Eds.), *Splintered reflections: Images of the body in trauma.* New York: Basic Books.

Porges, S. (2011). *The polyvagal theory: Neurophysiological foundations of emotions, attachment, communication, and self-regulation.* New York: W. W. Norton.

Rand, M. L., & Caldwell, C. (2004). Integrating pre and perinatal psychology and Body Oriented Psychotherapy. *USA Body Psychotherapy Journal, 3(2),* 50–67.

Rank, O. (1952/2010). *The trauma of birth.* New York: Routledge.

Ray, S., & Orr, L. (1983). *Rebirthing in a new age.* Berkeley, CA: Celestial Arts.

Rossi, E. (2002). *The psychobiology of gene expression: Neuroscience and neurogenesis in therapeutic hypnosis and the healing arts.* New York: W. W. Norton.

Salm, A. K., Pavelko, M., Krouse, E. M., Webster, W., Kraszpulski, M., & Birkle, D. L. (2004). Lateral amygdaloid nucleus expansion in adult rats is associated with exposure to prenatal stress. *Developmental Brain Research, 148,* 159–167.

Sandman, C., Davis, E., Buss, C., & Glynn, L. (2011). Prenatal programming of human neurological function. *International Journal of Peptides, 2011,* Article ID 837596.

Schore, A. N. (1994). *Affect regulation and the origin of the self: The neurobiology of emotional development.* New York: Lawrence Erlbaum.

Schore, A. N. (2002). The neurobiology of attachment and early personality organization. *Journal of Prenatal and Perinatal Psychology and Health, 16(3),* 249–263.

Schore, A. N. (2003). *Affect regulation and the repair of the self.* New York: W. W. Norton.

Schore, A. N. (2012). *The science of the art of psychotherapy.* New York: W. W. Norton.

Shonkoff, J. P., Boyce, W. T., & McEwen, B. S. (2009). Neuroscience, molecular biology and the childhood roots of health disparities. *Journal of the American Medical Association, 301(21),* 2252–2259.

Siegel, D. J. (2012a). *The developing mind: How relationships and the brain interact (2nd ed.).* New York: Guilford Press.

Siegel, D. J. (2012b). *Pocket guide to interpersonal neurobiology.* New York: W. W. Norton.

Sonne, J. C. (1997). Interpreting the dread of being aborted in therapy. *Journal of Prenatal and Perinatal Psychology and Health, 11(4),* 185–214.

Stern, D. (2004). *The present moment: In psychotherapy and everyday life.* New York: W. W. Norton.

Szyf, M. (2009). The early life environment and the epigenome. *Biochimica & Biophysica Acta, 1790(9),* 878–885.

Talge, N. M., Neal, C., & Glover, V. (2007). The early stress, translational research, and prevention science network: Fetal and neonatal experience on child and adolescent mental health. *Journal of Child Psychology and Psychiatry, 48(3/4),* 245–261.

Thomson, P. (2007). Down will come baby: Prenatal stress, primitive defenses and gestational dysregulation. *Journal of Trauma & Dissociation, 8(3),* 85–113.

Tronick, E. (2007). *The neurobehavioral and social-emotional development of infants and children.* New York: W. W. Norton.

Van den Bergh, B. R. H., & Marcoen, A. (2004). High antenatal maternal anxiety is related to ADHD symptoms, externalizing problems, and anxiety in 8- and 9-year olds. *Child Development, 75(4),* 1085–1097.

Van den Bergh, B. R. H., Mulder, E. J. H., Mennes, M., & Glover, V. (2005). Antenatal maternal anxiety and stress and the neurobehavioral development of the fetus and child: Links and possible mechanisms: A review. *Neuroscience & Biobehavioral Reviews, 29,* 237–258.

Van den Bergh, B. R. H., Van Calster, H., Smits, T., Van Huffel, S., & Lagae, L. (2008). Antenatal maternal anxiety is related to HPA-axis dysregulation and self-reported depressive symptoms in adolescence: A prospective study on the fetal origins of depressed mood. *Neuropsychopharmacology, 33(3),* 536–545.

Verny, T. R. (1981). *The secret life of the unborn child.* New York: Summit Books.

Verny, T. R., & Weintraub, P. (2002). *Tomorrow's baby: The art and science of parenting from conception through infancy.* New York: Simon & Schuster.

Welch, M. A. (1983). Retrieval from autism through mother-child holding therapy. In E. A. Tinbergen (Ed.), *Autistic children: New hope for a cure.* London: George Allen & Unwin.

# 32

## Multiple Levels of Meaning-Making

*The First Principles of Changing Meanings in Development and Therapy*

**Ed Tronick and Bruce D. Perry, United States**

**Ed Tronick** is a well-known Distinguished University Professor of Psychology, clinical psychologist, and researcher; director of the Child Development Unit, University of Massachusetts, Boston; lecturer at Harvard Medical School; and author of *The Neurobehavioral and Social-Emotional Development of Infants and Children* and *Infant and Early Childhood Mental Health: Core Concepts and Clinical Practice* (among others). He also developed the "still-face paradigm" as part of a program of investigation into the effects of maternal depression and other affective disorders on infant and child socioemotional development.

**Bruce D. Perry** is the senior fellow of the ChildTrauma Academy in Houston, and an adjunct professor of psychiatry at the Feinberg School of Medicine at Northwestern University, Chicago. He is also a clinician, and a researcher into child mental health. He has written two books (with Maia Szalavitz): *The Boy Who Was Raised as a Dog: What Traumatized Children Can Teach Us about Loss, Love and Healing* (2007) and *Born for Love: Why Empathy Is Essential—and Endangered* (2010).

## Introduction

We see meaning about one's self in relation to the world of people and things, and in relation to one's own self, as a core organizing concept in approaches as varied and contentious as Body Psychotherapies, psychoanalysis, psychodynamics, Cognitive Behavioral Therapy, dialectical cognitive therapies, dyadic therapies, attachment therapies, relational therapies, and others (Tronick, 2007; Harrison, 2003; Ogden, 1997; Modell, 1993). Meanings about one's self are made continuously and simultaneously, in real time, at multiple levels, and by multiple body and brain systems. Loss of any of these meanings—the meaning about one's self to one's self, or one's self to the world—leads to serious psychopathology. Indeed, a failure to "make meaning" is a psychic catastrophe: a trauma (Modell, 1993). More common than failures are the meanings made about more mundane events that distort one's sense of the world and one's self. Such meanings often generate further distortions and increasingly insidious debilitations. Critical to our view is the idea that these endogenous meaning-making processes demand real-time seeking of information through active engagement by the individual with the world of people, things, and the individual's own self in order to apprehend, in both body and mind, the information that is integrated with past meaning into the meaning of the relation of the self to the world. Moreover, and often under-appreciated, meaning-making is a psycho-biological process that involves not only the brain, but other somatic systems that generate implicit meanings and memories that shape our ways of being in the world. Thus, the process of making sense of the world inherently involves the whole individual in an endless and continuous process.

## A Neurodevelopmental Perspective: In Brief

Understanding this meaning-making is no easy task; multiple theoretical perspectives attempt to understand how it is actually carried out; what systems are involved; how meaning-making is distorted, even destroyed; what happens in its aftermath—and, most critically, if the meanings made make for psychic health or illness and how therapy can change the meanings of an ill individual. These different theoretical perspectives all approach these issues from different places. A neurodevelopmental perspective emerges from research on the neurochemical, structural, and organizational view of the functioning brain and the distorting effects of maltreatment and trauma on it (Perry, 1999, 2008). One example emerging from this work is a treatment model of embodied multilevel brain processes, the Neurosequential Model of Therapeutics (NMT) (Perry, 2009). The NMT incorporates a functional assessment of the brain and the individual's developmental experience that sculpted it, which leads to a set of approaches for treatment of areas of brain dysfunction that distort the individual's meaning-making. The neurodevelopmental perspective, because of its focus on developmental experiential processes that sculpt the formation of somatic and neurological systems, holds to a view that *all* current experience, rather than the fifty-minute therapy hour, has to become part of therapy, and to the extent possible the individual should have the choice to determine her engagement with the world and with others on a moment-by-moment basis. In this context, the individual can take hold of information to endogenously create new meanings and ways of being in the world.

## A Developmental-Psychological Perspective: In Brief

The developmental perspective has focused on the infant's and young child's capacity to engage the world, especially the world of people (Tronick, 2007; Tronick and Beeghly, 2011). Researchers have tried to understand the kinds of meanings that even the youngest infants make about themselves in the world. Tronick (2007), for example, emphasizes that the infant does not have explicit processes, but nonetheless makes sense of the world with implicit processes. The approach is to microanalyze infant socioemotional behavior, with the goal of seeing the organization of infant behavior and the relation of that organization to events and their context. This approach reveals that that organization makes it possible to infer the meaning that the child has made about the world, and how that meaning changes with experience and development. Tronick (2007), for example, sees these psycho-biological implicit meanings as assembled into a biopsychological state of consciousness that guides the individual's engagement with the world. His still-face experiment, in which the mother and the infant are face-to-face, but the mother does not respond to her infant, demonstrates that the infant has organized and varied ways to get the mother to change her behavior back to normal and to fulfill his intention to interact with her—"I want you to play with me." And when she does resume her interaction, his behavior changes to smiles and playfulness—"This is fun."

It may seem odd to think of the infant as making meaning, but the infant could not survive in the world if it did not have a way of organizing itself in relation to the world; that means that successfully fitting into the world requires knowing something about the world (see Sander, 1977, for a full explication of fittedness). Rooting to find the nipple of the breast, latching on, and sucking may be labeled as reflexes, but their organization contains powerful meaning about the nipple, the infant, and the world. A ten-week-old covering his face with his hands and ducking away when his mother makes an angry face at him shows us that he has made meaning of the display—threat or danger (we don't know exactly), which has a clearly different meaning from when they engage in mutual smiles. And of course, the meanings made by infants are not the same as the meanings made by adults, and in many ways they are mysteries to us. But when meanings are communicated and shared between an infant and an adult (an amazing accomplishment, given that they are so different developmentally from one another, almost like different species), a *dyadic* state of consciousness is formed such that the infant's as well as the adult's sense of self in the world expands.

## Commonalities of the Two Approaches

Despite the differences of these two approaches, there are commonalities in these neurodevelopmental and developmental-psychological perspectives. The commonalities include the agency of the individual; the multilevel psycho-biological structures and processes involved in organizing the whole individual's (all bodily processes and levels) engagement with the world; the importance of development and past history; the embeddedness of the individual in context; and the critical effects of what goes on in relationships. Both approaches see the infant and the child as able to share meanings with others. Additionally, both approaches see development and therapy as operating similarly: repeated patterned, rhythmic experiences (Perry, 2008, 2009) or chronic, reiterated experiences play a critical role. These commonalities, which organize the individual during development and in therapy, and especially the role of reoccurring experience, are the focus of this chapter.

## Reoccurring Experiences

What do we mean by the reoccurrence of experience? Start with a clinically relevant example of a child getting slapped. The first slap a child receives is not experienced the same way as the tenth; it is unique. It changes the child's state of consciousness about the world—his or her psychic landscape—forever. But so does, and so may, the tenth slap. Moreover, the slaps are not the same, but depend on the motivational state of the child—for example, if she is slapped when she is concentrating on a game and feeling safe; or if she is hiding and in a fearful state; or if she is in an angry state. And any slap is experienced differently at two years of age, than at five years, or at ten years; and differently if, at ten years, it was last experienced at two years, or five years, or never experienced before. Furthermore, whatever actions the child chooses to take—fighting back, running away, freezing, crying—will change the nature of the experience of the slap. So it is not just the event, but the event as it is experienced in context and in the individual's state of consciousness, that makes its meaning.

### Peekaboo

Let's pursue our commonalities in relation to the slap as a way of understanding how it affects the individual and what it suggests for therapy. Because the meaning made of slapping has not been studied, though it is likely that many readers will have had the experience of being slapped, think about how a child comes to learn the game of peekaboo, a recurrent event that has been studied (Bruner and Sherwood, 1976; Commons et al., 1998). Peekaboo may seem quite far away from being slapped, and it is, but—for our purposes—it is not. The game of peekaboo is a dynamic interplay of actions and information between a child and an adult. The game is rule-governed, but flexible in its enactment. Often there are unique individual and familial variations. Despite our saying that a four-month-old plays peekaboo, please recognize that young infants do not actually play peekaboo. It is played "at" the infant, by an adult, who initially plays all the sides of the game. The infant exhibits a large number, and variety, of behaviors and has lots of varying intentions and apprehensions of what is going on, many of which are unrelated to the adult's game-playing actions. The infant looks away when she "should" be looking toward, or she raises her shoe, or looks at her hand. What she is doing is messy—variable, unstable, disorganized. Yet, with reoccurrence, the infant attends, and begins to anticipate the coming "boo," and some of the messiness is pared away. With more reoccurrences and development, the infant begins to become agenic and to control some of the elements and the pace of the game. She comes to signal the timing of the "boo," and her reactions become more complex. As the game is acquired, the infant begins to learn pieces of how to be the "surprisee" and then the "peekabooer." Sequences and rhythms emerge. While all that is going on, the adult continuously makes adjustments (e.g., holding positions longer) in relation to the infant's actions and the adult's intent—what Bruner calls "scaffolding" (Bruner, 1990).

Such scaffolding is intuitive and implicit. The selective assembling of the infant's self-organized actions and intentions *and* her apprehension of the adult's actions and intentions *and* the adult's reciprocal apprehension become incrementally more coherent. And so on, through endless repetitions, until the game is fully "within" the child and at the same time fully within the child-adult dyad. And none of this being within—knowing—is explicit. It is simultaneously embodied in multiple systems at multiple levels.

**Critical Elements in Knowing How to Play a Game**

A few points about the process of acquiring the game: the acquisition of a game depends on the infant being with someone who knows the game and who must be willing to "teach" her the game. Infants cannot teach themselves the game. At any age, the learning of the game is dependent on the repetition of the game, and the development of different capacities, at multiple levels (neurological, regulatory, motor, emotional), that make the acquisition of a game possible; a three-month-old baby does not have the capacities to learn the game no matter how often its reoccurrence. The game is individualized. The adult who is playing it with the infant plays the game in a unique way, and the infant acquires that unique way. Better said, they co-create a unique way of doing the game together. In an important sense, they co-create a unique game of their own. The game, like all children's games, is arbitrary, in the sense that it has a history in a cultural context. It is not built in by evolution. It is a canonical cultural artifact, played in the way it is played in a particular culture (Ibid.). Other cultures play other games in their own cultural form.

More generally and importantly, we see the acquisition of a game by an infant as no different from the infant learning any other cultural form of behavior, or any form of procedural knowing that involves spontaneous—"natural"—interaction; that is their way of being with others. The infant learns the "game" of cuddling, the "game" of feeding, and the "game" of greeting a stranger. They learn the "game" of being demanding; the "game" of the bath; and changing, and nursing, and going to sleep. Each of these "games" reoccurs tens, even hundreds, of times a month. Each has a form that is individualized and culturated. Each changes with development. Each involves learning the "game" with another person. And though hardly a game, these features of learning any game will also apply to learning the "game" of being slapped.

## Systems of Meaning-Making

From a neurodevelopmental perspective, the primary mechanism in meaning-making is the capacity to create associations. When patterns of neural activity co-occur with sufficient frequency, intensity, or pattern, these patterns become "connected" at a synaptic level. The capacity to weave the complex array of sensory, somatic, and cerebro-modulatory patterns of activity into a form of coherence is one of the remarkable qualities of development. Indeed, development requires the sequential creation of associations—essentially, sequential meaning-making—from body to brainstem to cortex (see Figure 32.1). Beginning *in utero,* the meaning-making systems (typically, but artificially, referred to as "body and brain," which is a linguistic dichotomy, not a physiological reality) weave together seamless, multiple, interactive, dynamic systems through multiple molecular mechanisms, including the creation of "activity-organized" synaptic nets that begin to create meaning for the developing organism. In the sensory and somatic rhythms of neural activation, created by the intrauterine environment (warm, fluid, and embracing), the fetus (see Figure 32.1) and the mother (including her ever-beating heart) become associated through the neural activation created when the fetus is "safe and regulated" (i.e., not hungry, thirsty, cold, or threatened). Reoccurring rhythms of somato-sensory activation gain meaning. At the level of the brainstem and diencephalon, then, meaning is made of various patterns of somato-sensory bodily activity; the somatic signals of fetal posture(s) and the somato-sensory signals from rhythmic rocking, for example, have a primordial meaning of "safe," a meaning inherent in coherent somato-sensory organization; and when the frightened or overwhelmed child self-soothes by rocking in the fetal position, it is an attempt to recapture, or may actually create, the primordial meaning of "safe."

Neurodevelopment progresses from the lower (i.e., brainstem and diencephalon) to the higher (i.e., limbic and cortical) area. The timing and pattern of activation of key regulatory neural networks play a crucial role in shaping the functional capacity in all the areas of the brain and body, better thought of as subsystems of the whole individual (see Figure 32.1; Perry, 2001). Perry's neurodevelopmental model provides an understanding of the multiple levels of organization of the embodied processes by which the child comes to learn the "slapping" game. We will start with a two- or three-month-old and then move up the developmental ladder. After we have a picture of how the event's meaning is made at different developmental levels, we will then go on to think about how reoccurrence affects the outcome of being slapped.

**Infant Meaning-Making Systems/Processes**

Even though the young infant's somatic and neurophysiological systems are far from fully developed, she can make meaning. She has states of consciousness, though with no implication of awareness. As such, the infant can fully organize a motivated and embodied state of distress, perhaps even an emotionally fearful state, or a motivated state of pleasure that organize her actions in the world: one state leads to withdrawal and demands for regulatory support; the other to engagement and self-directed action on some object, or communication with another. The process of meaning-making begins with the first experience to create the primary associations (i.e., neural connections) that will organize the infant's world.

During development, this sequential process of meaning-making recruits more complex neural networks in increasingly "higher" areas of the brain, essentially organizing the brain's capacity for increasingly complex and "executive" functions, whereas the lower areas mediate the simpler, more regulatory functions (see Figure 32.1). The bedrock of primary associations that help the infant create meaning is those derived from the somatosensory and regulatory experiences from intrauterine and early postnatal experiences, as well as from ways in which those experiences organize the operation of the regulatory processes that, in their operation, embed meaning. These associations involve a set of crucial regulatory neural networks involved in the stress response (and multiple other functions; see Figure 32.1). These regulatory networks are, themselves, modulated through patterned, repetitive, and rhythmic input from both "bottom-up" (i.e., somato-sensory) as well as "top-down" (i.e., cerebro-modulatory) systems. The brain processes (and acts on) incoming input at multiple levels; although the brain is essentially an open and interactive system, this multilevel process of sensing, processing, and acting on the world basically "begins" at the site of initial input of sensory, somatic, or cerebral input to the lower areas of the brain. It is in these lower systems that prenatal and perinatal experiences shape associations that will influence meaning-making throughout development, as the sequential process of development proceeds. Incoming modulatory input provides a direct route to these crucial regulatory neural networks and can influence the organization, reorganization, and functional status of these key systems. As these regulatory networks (e.g., NE, DA, SER in Figure 32.1) are altered and sensitized by developmental trauma, attachment disruption, and chronic derailing experiences, any therapeutic efforts must be directed at these systems.

As the somato-sensory input from the "experience" enters the brain (see Figure 32.1), there will be an iterative process that involves the sequential processing of this input from the lower neural networks (where all primary somato-sensory input enters the brain) to the higher neural networks and regions. At each level of the different systems, there are opportunities to process, store, and act on the neural "activations" that result from this experience. This complex cascade echoes through the open, interactive, dynamic neural and somatic systems. In other words, the experience of being slapped will result in stored associations—i.e., memory—in all levels of the brain, and there will be an interrelated set of memories of what others often refer to as visceral, sensory-motor, precognitive memory. All networks in the brain involved in processing any experience will be affected. It is, therefore, nearly impossible to experience a meaningful human interaction—especially in infancy—without creating implicit somato-sensory memory components.

In the case of a slap, the first time that the infant is slapped, the image of a hand moving swiftly across the

350 | SOMATIC DIMENSIONS OF DEVELOPMENTAL PSYCHOLOGY

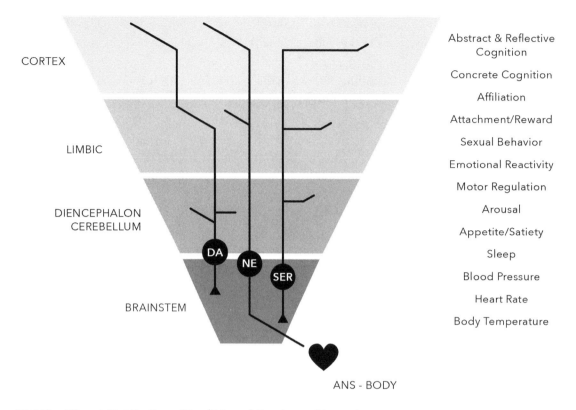

Figure 32.1. The Efferent Distribution of Key (Primary) Regulatory Networks

Human meaning-making systems are organized in a hierarchy that develops in a sequential manner. As the body—including the brain—begins to develop *in utero*, meaning-making begins. At the level of the brain, this process involves the creation of associations (literally, synaptic connections) between neural networks that are simultaneously activated with sufficient pattern, intensity, and duration. Four developmentally distinct regions (brainstem, diencephalon, limbic, and cortical) are woven together by multiple neural networks. These networks, like the monoamine systems (i.e., NE: norepinephrine, DA: dopamine) and other related systems (e.g., SER: serotonin), as well as others like ACH: acetylcholine (not shown in Figure 32.1), originate in lower brain areas and have a widespread impact on widely distributed "upstream" systems in the brain and the "downstream" systems of the body. These regulatory networks play a role in integrating, processing, and acting on incoming patterns of neural activity (Figure 32.1) from the primary sensory networks (such as touch, vision, and sound, which monitor the external environment), somatic networks (such as motor-vestibular, cardio-vascular, and respiratory, which monitor the internal environment), and cerebral networks (such as cortical-modulating networks, which monitor the brain's internal environment). This continuous input from the brain, body, and world must be integrated, processed, sorted, associated, and stored to create coherent states of consciousness for the developing infant. Then they can respond to the outside world—"meaningfully."

visual field has not yet been associated with pain. If the slapper is always the same person, and others never slap the child, the set of somato-sensory associations may generalize to the properties of that person, or the place where the slapping occurs (i.e., the bedroom); the child may begin to feel fearful with the sound of the slapper's voice, the smell of his aftershave, the image of his face, the sound of a door closing, etc. And the child will then generalize, from the slapper's hand, to all hands moving quickly near his face—even if the person is a nurturing caregiver, moving to gently wipe the child's nose. These associations and the resulting threat-related behaviors are mediated by the simpler, lower somato-sensory and action (motor) systems involved in stress and the threat response (see Figure 32.1).

These more generalized and undifferentiated responses can be quite troubling and mystifying, even when the formative experiences are part of the "known but unremembered" aspects of a person's life. Though unavailable in conscious memory, they are nonetheless stored in the brain and in the body's holding patterns, activation preferences, etc., throughout the body and are encoded by implicit neural processes that are remarkably durable. As suggested earlier, traditional talk therapy may not be sufficient to access these subcortical organizers of experience. Directing attentional processes to the body, a core feature of Somatic Psychotherapy, can stimulate neural circuits associated with these memories, providing opportunities to encode new experiences that support a shift in meaning and, subsequently, a shift in experience.

### The Robustness of Early Meanings

This picture of what is going on gives us a critical idea of why early experience has such long-term effects. The meaning-making process in infancy is developmentally robust, because so many meanings are connected to the fundamental regulatory needs and capacities of the child. Thus, many of the associations created early in life are directly linked with these primary regulatory neural networks and primary somatic processes that continue to shape and influence function throughout life (Figure 32.1). Moreover, the infant has less capacity to modulate or shift the meaning, because the higher areas of the brain are not yet fully organized. For example, the infant does not yet have complex time-telling capabilities, or abstract cognition, to allow her to make a more "abstract" or differentiated meaning about the one abusive slapper in relation to other nurturing caregivers.

### Developmental Changes of Meaning-Making

As the child becomes older, and as the limbic and cortical areas of the brain become more organized, the meaning of the slap, the slapper, and the toddler's potential to act in relation to the slapper with behaviors that appear to increase or decrease the probability of slapping change. The infant "learns" (comes to know at implicit, preconscious levels), for example, that crying (a "fight-or-flight," stress-related behavior that should bring a caregiver to ameliorate the infant's distress: i.e., hunger, thirst, cold, pain, etc.) will actually increase the slapping, whereas dissociating (and not crying) will decrease the slapping. As a toddler, she may also learn that overly compliant, almost seductive, behavior will decrease slapping. And she may modify her meaning about slapping. Let's say her mother—a loving but overwhelmed, frustrated caregiver, who never slapped before—slaps her in frustration when she is noncompliant (noncompliance is *not* possible for her with the slapper, but is with the mother). Almost immediately, there will be a physically nurturing and intimate interaction as the guilty mother attempts to repair the empathic rupture (not an unusual dynamic with an overwhelmed mother and an abusive partner—the initial slapper). This change in meaning is now possible because of the development of neural systems previously unavailable to the infant. The "meaning" of the slap evolves.

## Meaning-Making and Therapy

How does the evolution of the complex archaeology of the meaning of the slap, or of peekaboo, or of being with another, or of any way of being, relate to therapy? For us, therapy is about changing meanings. How do we see the change process? Obviously, there are a myriad of driving forces and systems involved that are inherent to making and changing meaning, including somatic and regulatory systems, neural systems, and action systems; the list goes on and on. Our view of therapeutics is very much Vygotskian (1978): optimal development in any domain (e.g., neural, regulatory, motor, sensory, etc.) occurs when the individual is given opportunities and expectations, usually by or with another person, that are neither too familiar and simple, nor too unfamiliar and complex (Perry, 2009; Tronick, 2007). For the individual with a psychic dysfunction, she has to be allowed to select or guide the information that she is presented with, so that it fits to, and can be worked on by, her meaning-making capacities to make new meanings. Tronick (Tronick and Beeghly, 2011) emphasizes that therapeutic work with infants and young children must aim to understand their intentions more deeply and especially the multilevel meanings that children are making about themselves, and how they are making meaning within themselves, and by themselves, with objects and, most importantly, with others. In adults, it is critical to determine where their sense of meaning "resides." It may reside in the prefrontal cortex (as is presumed by cognitive therapies), but we believe that much of it also resides lower down and more unconsciously, in the brainstem and diencephalon, where regulatory and somato-sensory processes tend to operate. These processes will therefore demand forms of therapy that help to reorganize them through reoccurrent (more positive or coherent) experiences that may eventually make the distorting experience available to awareness.

One implication, of multiple levels and different kinds of meaning-making systems, is that therapy cannot simply or solely focus on just one system or another—be it the somatic, or neural, or action, or cognitive, or emotional systems. What development tells us about meaning-making and change is that it involves all these systems, simultaneously operating as a messily organized ensemble. More specifically, change involves an individual who has agency to organize her engagement with the world, especially the world of people, with every level and every meaning-making system she possesses. But development also tells us that therapeutically induced changes in meaning must enact the first principle of reoccurrence. The individual must have the opportunity to engage and reengage in experiences that can change and generate new associations at the core of their meaning.

As the reader can see from this handbook, Body Psychotherapy interventions focus on including the somatic aspects of self-organization. They work with the felt sense of the body, with movement, gesture, posture, etc., to reach those (lower) levels of self-organization(s) and meaning-making that cannot be accessed by explicit mental processes alone. They pay attention to how implicit meanings are held in the body. From this perspective, meaning—for instance, that "the world is a dangerous place"—is held by bodily processes, such as those of the autonomic nervous system (ANS), that were organized or structured by such early experiences, even though the conscious mind does not have access to the early experiences that created that meaning. Work with the body can therefore bring into awareness how the somatic processes—hypothalamic-pituitary-adrenal (HPA) axis, ANS, brainstem—operated during the prior experience, which has biased the individual's view of the world, and makes them desirous of therapeutic work.

This process of changing and creating new associations requires plasticity of neural networks. Fortunately, neurons and neural networks are not only capable of change; they are specifically constructed to change in response to experience. This plasticity underlying both developmental and therapeutic change has conditions that will enhance, and others that inhibit, meaningful change (Kleim and Jones, 2008). Two primary principles of plasticity are specificity and pattern. Simply stated, neural networks that are not being activated with sufficient repetition in a meaningful pattern will not change.

The demand for enough experiences to allow for change is especially critical when we consider early meanings that are interwoven with fundamental somatic and regulatory processes. Admittedly, we don't know what "enough" is, but we do know that there is seldom enough reoccurrent experience in the right systems (i.e., the bedrock associations created by our earliest somato-sensory experiences in the lower areas of the brain). Most targeted therapeutic efforts do not adhere to the core principle of specificity; *non*somatic therapies will not directly and repetitively activate the foundational somato-sensory systems (and related associations) made in early life, and localized in the lowest systems in the brain. This is where somatic and sensory experiences (and somato-therapeutic approaches) can provide direct and nondiffused patterns of neural activity that can play a primary role in reshaping systems that had been negatively impacted by earlier development experience. Yet, somato-sensory repair is, in and of itself, not capable of permeating therapeutic change. The "in and of itself" indeed applies to all therapies, but somato-sensory repair may be most effective in reaching foundational systems. Thus, as we have argued from the beginning, meaning-making and therapeutic change involve systems at all levels of the hierarchical organization of the brain and body simultaneously.

It must now be obvious why we find the idea of bringing the body more fully into therapy to be highly important. We feel treatment will remain needlessly limited, in most clinical contexts, if it cannot reach beyond the domain of the verbal. To the extent that meaning-making capacities, on multiple levels, can be reorganized, therapeutic effectiveness will be increased, we expect. What we find attractive about Body Psychotherapy is how it has embraced this basic insight. By saying this, we are not proposing that Body Psychotherapy is somehow better than other methods. We are not here taking a position about the comparative value of different approaches. Our suggestion is a more modest one, if radical enough: we suspect that there likely exist some types of techniques in the Body Psychotherapy tradition that could be profitably incorporated into, or

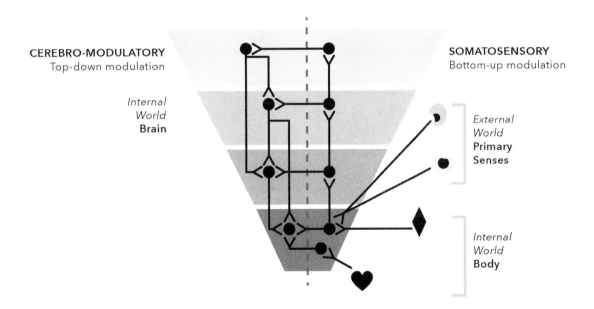

Figure 32.2. Afferent Modulatory "Pathways" of the Primary Regulatory Networks

Figure 32.2 illustrates the afferent (incoming) neural networks that provide input to the set of regulatory neural networks that are in the lower regions of the brain (e.g., NE, DA, SER, etc.). Cognitive behavioral interventions use the cerebro-modulatory routes, whereas somato-sensory interventions (e.g., music, dance, therapeutic massage, physical therapy, occupational therapy, etc.) tend to use primary sensory or somatic routes. In the case of a poorly organized cortex (e.g., due to complex trauma or neglect), or an "unavailable" cortex (e.g., due to high arousal/anxiety), cerebro-modulatory routes will be less effective. Some therapeutic efforts try to use all three routes (e.g., play therapy that integrates somato-sensory activities; EMDR; and the traditional healing rituals of many indigenous cultures).

added to, many treatment modalities (cognitive behavioral, psychodynamic, systemic, etc.).

We also think that the point of view that we have sketched out here might be of use to Body Psychotherapists themselves. It is interesting with respect to this tradition how many theoretical attempts there have been to define what "to reach beyond the verbal" should mean. Notoriously, some of these accounts—e.g., ones positing an esoteric "energy"—ring strange to psychotherapists of other persuasions. However, we sympathize with the motivation for such attempts, even if the results are other than our own way to construe matters. Perhaps a viable alternative might be a theoretical framework that gives more extensive attention to what we have called the various diencephalon and brainstem systems of meaning-making. More generally, our emphasis is on the multilevel psycho-biological nature of meaning-making. This might create a space for plenty of further thinking about what "to reach beyond the verbal" might signify, yet remain within a standard science viewpoint.

The child lives in a world where an hour of any kind of therapy is lost in the welter of all the other hours. If the people in the child's life are not part of the process of change, then change will not occur. Traumatized children face the same dilution, even with weekly hours in therapy. They need an immersion with therapeutic Others. Adults, at some point, may be able to do much work on their own; nonetheless, additional scaffolding of their self-organized work with more contact (sessions) and "work" will enhance their own work. Thus, what makes sense for us as a guide for therapy—for children and adults—is to take our cue from the developmental meaning: approach therapeutic change like learning peekaboo. Do it often, do it in multiple ways that fully engage every level of the individual, and let the individual agencially control the process.

## References

Bruner, J. (1990). *Acts of meaning.* Cambridge, MA: Harvard University Press.

Bruner, J., & Sherwood, V. (1976). Peek-a-boo and the learning of rule structures. In J. Bruner, A. Jolly, & K. Silva (Eds.), *Play: Its role in evolution and development.* London: Penguin.

Commons, M., Trudeau, E., Stein, S., Richards, F., & Krause, S. (1998). Hierarchical complexity of tasks shows the existence of developmental stages. *Developmental Review, 18,* 237–278.

Harrison, A. M. (2003). Change in psychoanalysis: Getting from A to B. *Journal of the American Psychoanalytic Association, 51,* 221–257.

Kleim, J. A., & Jones, T. A. (2008). Principles of experience-dependent neural plasticity: Implications for rehabilitation after brain damage. *Journal of Speech, Language and Hearing Research, 51,* 225–239.

Modell, A. (1993). *The private self.* Cambridge, MA: Harvard University Press.

Ogden, T. (1997). *Reverie and interpretation: Sensing something human.* Lanham, MD: Rowman & Littlefield.

Perry, B. D. (1999). Memories of fear: How the brain stores and retrieves physiologic states, feelings, behaviors and thoughts from traumatic events. In J. M. Goodwin and R. Attias (Eds.), *Images of the body in trauma* (pp. 26–47). New York: Basic Books.

Perry, B. D. (2001). The neurodevelopmental impact of violence in childhood. In: D. Schetky and E.P. Benedek (Eds.), *Textbook of Child and Adolescent Forensic Psychiatry,* (pp. 221-238). American Psychiatric Press, Inc., Washington, D.C. 2001

Perry, B. D. (2008). Child maltreatment: The role of abuse and neglect in developmental psychopathology. In T. P. Beauchaine & S. P. Hinshaw (Eds.), *Textbook of child and adolescent psychopathology* (pp. 93–128). New York: Wiley.

Perry, B. D. (2009). Examining child maltreatment through a neurodevelopmental lens: Clinical application of the Neurosequential Model of Therapeutics. *Journal of Loss and Trauma, 14,* 240–255.

Sander, L. W. (1977). The regulation of exchange in infant-caregiver systems and some aspects of the context-contrast relationship. In L. A. Rosenblum (Ed.), *Interaction conversation and the development of language.* New York: Wiley.

Tronick, E. (2007). *Neurobehavioral and social emotional development.* New York: W. W. Norton.

Tronick, E., & Beeghly, M. (2011). Infants' meaning-making and the development of mental health problems. *American Psychologist, 66(2), 107–119.*

Vygotsky, L. S. (1978). Interaction between learning and development. In: L. S. Vygotsky, *Mind in society.* Cambridge, MA: Harvard University Press.

# 33

## Pattern and Plasticity

*Utilizing Early Motor Development as
a Tool for Therapeutic Change*

### Susan Aposhyan, United States

**Susan Aposhyan** developed Body-Mind Psychotherapy by integrating somatic techniques, particularly Body-Mind Centering, with cognitive and contemplative psychotherapy, as well as with theories from neuroscience, cellular biology, evolutionary theory, and animal behavior. Currently, she maintains a private practice and trains helping professionals internationally in her work. Previously, she developed and directed one of the first graduate degree programs in Somatic Psychology at the Naropa University in Boulder, Colorado. She is the author of *Body-Mind Psychotherapy* and *Natural Intelligence: Body-Mind Integration and Human Development*.

### Vignette

We had hardly begun our work together when Diane began disappearing into a deep, isolated dissociation. In my initial, difficult experiments of interacting with her when she was like this, I discovered that she could remain in this state for extended periods. Ten minutes was the longest that I could stand it. I experienced anxiety—a primitive fear for her safety and a practical fear of responsibility. I wondered about Diane's internal experience.

The universal gesture pantomiming sleep tilts the head to one side, closes the eyes, and rests both hands together against a cheek. When Diane dissociated most fully, her gesture was akin to this. Her head tilted to the side, with her eyes closed. However, rather than having a peaceful expression, she winced painfully. Her hands came up toward her lowered cheek, though not touching her cheek, or each other. Both her head and her hands made tiny, jerky searching gestures—little movements that never found anything to contact.

Once she had dissociated to that degree, it was difficult for her to shift out of it at all. Eventually, I had to pull her to her feet and walk her around my office. Finally, we discovered that if we stood with our backs touching, she would begin to emerge from the dissociation.

### Patterns

All the structures and physiology of our humanness rest upon three and a half billion years of evolved life-forms. These forms are, in themselves, patterns that have developed and elaborated on themselves in nearly endless variations—patterns of molecular structure, patterns of molecular interaction, patterns of cellular structure and interaction, patterns of tissue structure and interaction, and patterns of movement and behavior. Clearly, this process of life's evolution is a dynamic system, and this, therefore, naturally provides patterns that extend into present-day human life.

Practically, we will examine here how these early evolutionary patterns form the basis for the patterns of human organismic structure and human interactions, including psycho-physical, internal psychological, and interpersonal interactions. The fundamental principle is that our adult human movement, behavior, and interactions arise out of this biological foundation of innate patterns. Through an exploration of this foundation, we can discover both resources and pitfalls for human behavioral life. Here, we will particularly explore basic patterns of movement as templates for behavior and interaction.

**Yielding**

From the beginning of life through the first three billion years of evolution, all creatures were unicellular and their movement behavior consisted of pulsation and undulation. These soft, yielding movements were all that were initially needed to exist and procreate. Yielding movements continued to act as potent and foundational organizing schema in the life-forms to follow. In humans, we yield into intimate contact with ourselves, the physical world, and others.

Diane was born to a very young and distressed single mother who was extremely overwhelmed. As a result of these circumstances, the mother was very neglectful, as well as emotionally and physically abusive from day one. One might imagine that, even *in utero*, Diane was not free to yield to her own physiological motility. Instead of softly pulsating and undulating, she embodied the stillness of hiding and the hardening of marinating in her mother's chemical anxiety. When we first met, I noticed how still Diane's chest and belly were, barely moving with her breath. We discussed this, and Diane could mechanically move her breath into her viscera, but no real yielding arose from that. When she touched herself, it was with a poking and prodding quality. I saw my role as recognizing this developmental stage and providing the relational context within which yielding could safely develop. Only years later in our work did Diane begin to yield to her own internal softness and make contact with me and the rest of her world. As with many psycho-developmental processes, we had to move backward from her adult defenses toward her infantile resources and vitality.

**Vertebral Movement Organization**

With the evolutionary advent of vertebral creatures and the development of a central nervous system, life's movement patterns unfolded into new potential structures for interaction. These include spinal, homologous, homolateral, and contralateral movements.

Our early vertebrate ancestors, the fish, mastered their spines, spinal movement, and spinal interactions. **Spinal movements** were used to accomplish all activities of vertebrate life—locomotion, eating, orienting, mating, etc. Yielding motility continued to underlie those spinal movements, and provided a basis of existence, but it was no longer the sole means of existence. One might ask: How does yielding manifest in fish? The answer is: ubiquitously. As far as I can tell, all living fish are continuously pulsating and motile, even when they are hiding from prey.

Figure 33.1. Spinal movement

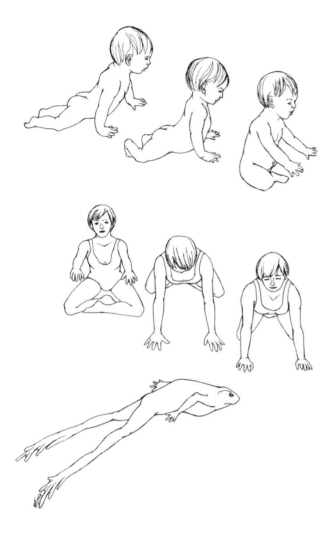

Figure 33.2. Homologous movement

As adult humans, how we live and utilize our spinal patterns reflects our core sense of our self and our ability to communicate with the world from this core. We see the manifestation of spinal behavior in two primary ways: in a sense of its presence, or its absence, manifested by the length and integration of spinal postures and movement; and in a sense of openness, or its absence, in between the vertebrae.

As life emerged out of the sea, vertebrates grew their fins into limbs and began developing movement and interactions based on the abilities of their limbs. Amphibians evolved to use spinal movements to orient, eat, and procreate. Their limbs were used for locomotion, with the lower limbs pushing to jump and the upper limbs reaching to leap. Amphibious limbs are limited neurologically to **homologous movement.** The right and left limbs of amphibians are not differentiated. Therefore, they tend to move in synchrony—i.e., both upper limbs together and both lower limbs together. This is the definition of homologous movement. We see homologous movement in human newborns.

For adult humans, homologous movement provides a strong resource of self-support and differentiation, pushing with both feet to stand our ground and pushing with both hands to protect or separate.

In reptiles, spinal and homologous movements provide a foundation for the next level of neurological function—**homolateral movement,** which differentiates the sides. Left and right limbs are able to push independently; however, the upper and lower limbs of each side are now working in synchrony. For example, when a left lower limb pushes, the movement sequences up to the left upper limb. Homolateral movement provides adult humans with a more permeable boundary than the homologous. We can support ourselves by pushing with just one leg, and thereby leave the other leg free to move in relation to the environment. Similarly, by pushing with only one hand, we can differentiate partially, leaving one hand open to explore and perhaps engage.

Finally, mammals evolved, still utilizing these previous neurological organizations, but with the option to access a fourth pattern of movement sequencing as well—**contralateral movement,** which sequences diagonally, both crossing the midline and connecting the upper and lower body. Relationally, this offers us more complex options that allow us to pulsate between differentiation and contact. These four vertebral movement patterns were first named and delineated by Temple Fay, and are utilized in neurodevelopmental therapy (Wolf, 1968).

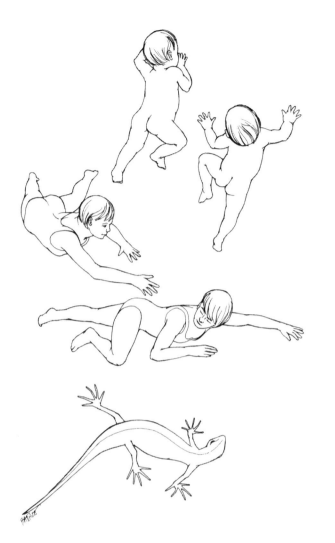

Figure 33.3. Homolateral movement

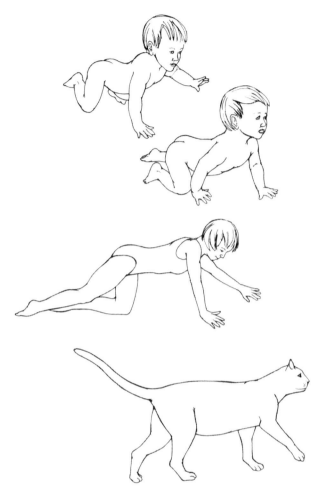

Figure 33.4. Contralateral movement

## Development Recapitulates Evolution

### In Utero

These patterns of movement evolution are echoed in embryonic development. As single cells, both our sperm and our egg are pulsating with life, as are our morula (the initial ball of cells that develops postfertilization) and our blastocyst (the second preembryonic form, approximately five days postfertilization). The pulsating, fluid movements of our earliest development are forms of prevertebral *yielding* movements, pulsating multidirectionally, and recapitulating the patterns of early evolutionary life-forms (Bainbridge Cohen, 1993).

Once we (as a blastocyst) are safely implanted in the uterine wall (at approximately six days), we begin to orient. We develop a front and a back. At approximately fourteen days postconception, we evolve into a tube. Now, we not only have a front and a back, but a top and a bottom: we become spinal creatures. Even as our prototypical spine is developing, we begin to undulate spinally like sea creatures. On a cellular and tissue level,

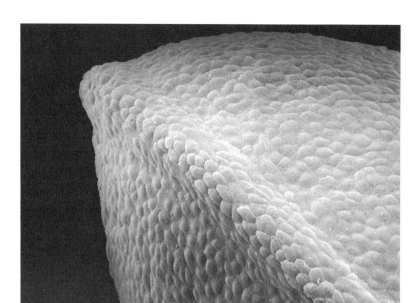

Figure 33.5. Embryological cells sprouting into the ridge of a limb bud

we continue to pulsate fluidly throughout our life span, yielding to the constant growth of this phase of life, but, at a larger organismic level, there is now also a spinal organization to our movement.

Out of this tube, our limb buds sprout (see Figure 33.5), elongate, and eventually practice homologous movements: both hands, or both feet, pushing and reaching together. Later in uterine development, we have moments of one hand or one foot pushing, reaching, grasping, and pulling *in utero,* interacting with our own bodies (hand to hand) or the umbilical cord or sometimes our prenatal twin. Some of these gestures are homolateral: some hint at the contralateral.

### Birth

As we emerge from the womb during birth, we also use this template of evolutionary movement—pushing and reaching with our heads, pushing with our feet, pushing with our pelvic floors, and sometimes pushing or reaching with our arms. These basic neurological actions assist us in navigating through our mother's body and out into the world.

From this early vantage point, it is abundantly clear that we are fundamentally motile creatures—mobile in both structure and function. Movement is primary to life at every level. Movement is communication. Patterns of movement underlie and organize all our organismic communication, accommodation to the environment, and expression of intentionality.

### Ex Utero

Once out of the birth canal, we nuzzle for the breast, pushing with our heads, reaching with our lips, grasping the nipple with our mouths and tongues, pulling nourishment from our mother's body into our mouths, and finally yielding to swallow it into ourselves.

As we mature, these same patterns of yield, push, reach, grasp, and pull are enacted by each of our end points (face/head, hands, feet, and pelvic floor) in the first year of life. Mastery of these movements allows most of us to begin walking at approximately the end of the first year. However, this sequence has been delineated in detail elsewhere (Aposhyan, 1998; Cohen, 1993; Stokes, 2002). During this first year, these basic neurological actions are used not only for locomotion and to perform tasks, but also to communicate with those around us. As we grow, we also learn from the environment whether it is safe to yield to our own impulses and into contact with those around us.

## Vignette Resumed

Initially, in my work with Diane, I experienced directly that yielding was not a safe and pleasurable activity for her. Instead, she had to push quickly, repeatedly, and definitively, both to gain independence and to create a defensive structure around her.

Optimally, as we continue to grow, we learn that it is effective and pleasurable to reach toward what we want in the world, both animate and inanimate. For Diane, as an adult, there was little to reach toward. As we saw, with her truncated self-soothing gesture of hands to face, she would dissociate into unfulfilled reaching and grasping gestures, trying to complete her infantile impulses to make contact nourishment via self or other. Unable to succeed, she dissociated.

During her dissociative states, she grasped with her face, trunk, and viscera, pulling her self into hiding within her core. I speculated that *in utero*, and in early childhood, this might have kept her safer and more contained, less vulnerable to the insensitivity and abuse around her.

## Adult Movement and Interactions

As adults, we come to utilize these same basic neurological actions to interact with the world; and an analysis of how our clients utilize these patterns can tell us how they succeeded at self-usage, and what they learned motorically from their human interactions. We push into a situation, and others take note of us. We reach out to an individual to make eye contact or to connect physically. We grasp and pull to claim ownership, and, hopefully, we have the grace to yield, to soften, to receive and take in from the world.

These movements combine into a dance of neurological possibilities that allow us to perform every movement of which adult humans are capable.

The complexity of hugging a friend might involve pushing homolaterally with a foot, reaching with the face (mostly eyes, but possibly some mouth and ears) and both hands (homologously) and the other foot, grasping your friend with both hands, pulling yourselves closer, pushing a little homologously with both feet to support yourself as you melt (yield) to receive the hug.

The above system of naming these actions was begun by Temple Fay and developed further by Bonnie Bainbridge Cohen, founder of Body-Mind Centering (Bainbridge Cohen, 1993). Many theorists have noted the utility of taking a developmental perspective in psychotherapy (Schore, 1994; Beebe and Lachmann, 2002; Greenspan and Wieder, 1997a, 1997b; Stern, 1985). The particular utility of applying early motor development to psychotherapy has been discussed in detail elsewhere (Aposhyan, 1998, 2004; Frank, 2001; Hartley, 2004).

## THE TWELVE BASIC NEUROLOGICAL ACTIONS

Spinal Push from the Head
Spinal Push from the Pelvic Floor
Homologous Push from the Hands
Homologous Push from the Feet
Homolateral Push from the Hand
Homolateral Push from the Foot
Spinal Reach from the Head
Spinal Reach from the Pelvic Floor
Homologous Reach from the Hands
Homologous Reach from the Feet
Contralateral Reach from the Hand
Contralateral Reach from the Foot

## FUNDAMENTAL ACTIONS

May be performed by the head, pelvic floor, hands, or feet.

Yield
Push
Reach
Grasp
Pull

I developed my work, Body-Mind Psychotherapy, to explore further the psychological aspects of both early motor development, as well as the psychology of our various tissue, fluid, and cellular selves.

Not only do adults utilize these basic neurological actions as building blocks for every movement they perform, but these actions also carry with them the sensual, psychological, and emotional tones of the environment in which they were learned.

Any moment of human interaction may be viewed through the lens of these neurological actions. As these actions are embedded in our neurological structure in a developmental context, they seem to present themselves as a reflection of our adult developmental state. This is a form of character structure that is not fixed, but can potentially develop throughout the life span.

## Vignette Resumed

In her waking, interactive life, Diane was always ready for action—her muscle tone was high, senses alert, limbs were ready to engage with a tremendous amount of push. Her movement was primarily homologous, with both legs and arms pushing simultaneously. This push manifested as muscular armoring, behavioral challenge, and conflict. Fighting and debate figured heavily in her life and our early interactions.

In her more dissociative states, she was simultaneously collapsing into herself and grasping tightly onto her sense of self in order to protect her physical and psychological self from painful and frightening connections to the world. In her dissociative gesture toward connection, she tentatively and incompletely reached out with her hands and made little burrowing pushes with her head, just like a newborn infant, but there was no mother's breast. I lived with her through some agonizing moments during which she relived her experience of an unresponsive human environment and her either futile attempts to connect or defensive attempts to prevent further disappointment and consequential disorganization.

## Plasticity

Happily, there is such a thing as change, growth, and further development. As humans, our unique pattern of about nine months of *ex utero* gestation has also built plasticity into the very foundation of being human. We are born virtually unable to locomote, to feed ourselves, or to function in all the many ways that other mammalian infants are more able to do almost from birth. This means that our nervous system and its innate patterns have to be more plastic than those of other mammals in nature. This plasticity creates more options and thus greater variation in human behavior. Medicine and neuroscience have delighted in this infantile plasticity, but have ignored its persistence into adulthood. Now there is a growing awareness that neuroplasticity is a lifelong trait. We have a greater neurological understanding of adult development and healing, even in the areas of early developmental issues and trauma (Doidge, 2007). From the vantage point of motor development, we can see the potential to grow in our motoric repertoire throughout our life span. I have witnessed octogenarians change deeply, not just a movement or a behavior, but their *way* of moving and behaving, their very character structure. Neuroplasticity is so essentially human that it is embedded to the very foundation of our nervous systems. In our haste to understand human development and behavior, we have tended to overemphasize and freeze the processes of that very development.

Until very recently, we have occupied ourselves with the stability of our nervous systems. We were philosophically and scientifically wedded to the idea of the mature nervous system's strong emphasis on habit. Hebb's Law, paraphrased as "Neurons that fire together, wire together" (Hebb, 1949), formed the basis of that belief. Indeed, the very essence of the nervous system can be seen as a structure for memory (Kandel, 2007). In addition, our observance that new neuronal growth was such a rarity also supported our strong bias toward seeing the adult human nervous system as fixed. Here, one might speculate about the human tendency to choose the psychological safety and political expediency of such a frozen belief when faced with the unpredictability of our own plasticity.

Currently, we have bits of evidence of neuroplasticity as it relates to psychotherapy and mental health (Baxter, 1992). A body of research that relates therapeutic change to adult development is growing. Over time, linking the concepts of Developmental Psychotherapy to neuroplasticity research will allow us to study the intricate dance of plasticity and pattern that forms the very basis of psychotherapy. What are the catalysts that galvanize pattern? Where are the portals that lead us to ways of being so different that they seem to be of a new order? How do we tap into these in a safe manner without therapeutic aggression and retraumatization?

**Vignette: Therapeutic Change**

Diane had an especially tenacious drive toward reaching into contact. Though she spent years pushing me away to see if I would stay, when the moment was right, she was able to integrate and reach out. A particularly significant moment of neuroplastic change occurred during an interaction in which Diane felt secure in her relationship with me, but accessed early feelings of rejection by her mother. At the end of a session, in which she had explored this emotional state, we hugged good-bye. On my back I could feel a tiny, little fluttering of her hands. I recognized this as her characteristic incomplete grasping movements. This was an element in her initial dissociative state described at the beginning of this chapter. Thinking of a primate infant's reflexive grasp into the mother's fur, I said, "Grab my braid." Vaguely, roused a bit out of a minor dissociative stupor, Diane asked, surprised, "What?" "Grab my braid." Diane grabbed on tentatively at first. "It's OK," I said. "Grab as hard as you want to." There was almost an audible neurological click. Diane's grasp was strong and decisive, and immediately it was followed by a yield into our embrace and a deep, parasympathetic breath.

I felt deeply warmed by this moment of safe and spontaneous connection. There was the feeling of having broken fresh ground, and I imagined the possibility that Diane may never have been responded to in this way before. I was able to offer myself, and my body, accurately, effectively, and safely for her next developmental step. This is what many of our clients look for in Body-Mind Psychotherapy—to be recognized in their embodied developmental *now* and to be responded to in new ways that move them back toward or into their own unique developmental flow. Diane confirmed this during our next session by asking incredulously, in the manner of a young child, "How did you know to do that?"

We laughed. I talked to her about primate infants grasping onto their mothers as they swung through the trees. But the real answer to her question was that I had felt, in my own body, her helpless grasp, and an instinctive impulse rose up in me that offered myself to be grasped. In Body-Mind Psychotherapy, therapists' use of their own body is the bridge leading into a depth of contact that allows for new developmental moments.

I would propose that this was a moment in which Diane's neural maps for relationship, safety, and interactional movement were all significantly reorganized. This reorganization formed the basis for further change as the therapy progressed. Out of this moment, Diane began to metabolize her dissociative states. She was able to recognize when she began to dissociate, reach out for physical contact, and continue to talk and listen, thereby reaching out for psychological contact. In this way, we were able to resolve a significant portion of her early traumas and developmental deficits.

**The Therapist's Use of Her Own Body**

In Diane's review of our pivotal moment of her grasping onto me, she asked, "How did you know to do that?" At the time, I gave her a relational answer, meeting her in intimate laughter. The theoretical answer is that I was embodied in the interaction. I was feeling my body respond to her body and to our relationship. I felt—viscerally—the incomplete reaches and grasps that stopped her hands from participating in the good-bye hug. I recognized this as her psychological experience of being unwelcome in relationship.

In Body-Mind Psychotherapy, the therapist's embodiment is foundational to every interaction. By both cultivating an attention to the therapist's internal sensorial world, as well as practicing allowing oneself to act from those physical experiences, one finds a wealth of therapeutic possibilities and potency. It is important to stress that this is not supporting a mindless or unpracticed acting *out* on the part of the therapist, but rather a very cultivated skill of body-mind interface.

## Conclusion

Observing client behavior through the lens of early motor developmental patterns allows us to tap into early development issues in a therapeutic manner. This creates a basis for a developmental view of character structure and therapeutic change. As we move toward understanding the complex dance of pattern and plasticity in human existence, we may further appreciate movement as an excellent medium for promoting change within the therapeutic process. The concept of pattern has developed a negative psychological connotation and yet also provides the basis of stability, predictability, and therefore safety. Our current cultural paradigm polarizes pattern and plasticity. In the modern lexicon, neuroplasticity seems to immediately translate into a drive toward "newness." However, the reality seems to be that pattern and plasticity weave together to form the very structure of human existence. The genetic template for this brain structure that we have now was evolved within a hunting and gathering lifestyle. This lifestyle combines the challenges of hunting and gathering with a deeply embedded sense of season and landscape, and thereby embodies the balance of plasticity with pattern. Penetrating the intricacies of this seeming polarity will support therapeutic theory for years to come.

Furthermore, the therapist's own developmental embodiment is cultivated into an attunement device in the dance of intimacy and the clinical approach to attachment and relational patterns. Embodiment practice as developed in Body-Mind Psychotherapy training weaves the therapist's awareness of self into a stronger attunement with others, providing a developmental platform a lifelong balance of change and stability—plasticity and pattern.

## References

Aposhyan, S. (1998). *Natural intelligence: Body-mind integration and human development.* Baltimore: Williams & Wilkins.

Aposhyan, S. (2004). *Body-Mind Psychotherapy: Principles, techniques, and practical applications.* New York: W. W. Norton.

Baxter, L. R. (1992). Neuro-imaging studies of OCD. *Psychiatric Clinics of North America, 15,* 871–884.

Beebe, B., & Lachmann, F. (2002). *Infant research and adult treatment: Co-constructing interactions.* Hillsdale, NJ: Analytic Press.

Cohen, B. B. (1993). *Sensing, feeling and action.* Northampton, MA: Contact Editions.

Doidge, N. (2007). *The brain that changes itself: Stories of personal triumph from the frontiers of brain science.* New York: Viking Press.

Frank, R. (2001). *Body of awareness: A somatic and developmental approach to psychotherapy.* Cambridge, MA: Gestalt Press.

Greenspan, S. I., & Wieder, S. (1997a). Developmental patterns and outcomes in infants and children with disorders in relating and communicating: A chart review of 200 cases of children with autistic spectrum diagnoses. *Journal of Developmental and Learning Disorders, 1,* 87–141.

Greenspan, S. I., & Wieder, S. (1997b). An integrated developmental approach to interventions for young children with severe difficulties in relating and communicating. *Zero to Three: National Center for Infants, Toddlers, and Families, 17*(5), 5–18.

Hartley, L. (2004). *Somatic Psychology: Body, mind and meaning.* London: Whurr/John Wiley & Sons.

Hebb, D. (1949). *The organization of behavior.* New York: Wiley.

Kandel, E. (2007). *In search of memory: The emergence of a new science of mind.* New York: W. W. Norton.

Schore, A. (1994). *Affect regulation and the origin of the self.* Hillsdale, NJ: Lawrence Erlbaum.

Stern, D. (1985). *The interpersonal world of the infant: A view from psychoanalysis and Developmental Psychology.* New York: Basic Books.

Stokes, B. (2002). *Amazing babies: Essential movement for your baby in the first year of life.* Toronto, Canada: Move Alive Media.

Wolf, J. M. (1968). *Temple Faye, M.D.: Progenitor of the Doman-Delacato treatment procedures.* Springfield, IL: Charles C. Thomas.

# 34

## Attachment Theory and Body Psychotherapy

*Embodiment and Motivation*

**Mark Ludwig, United States**

**Mark Ludwig** is a clinical social worker and Somatic Psychotherapist in private practice in Berkeley, California. Since the 1970s, he has also been one of the most internationally active Body Psychotherapists. He worked as a trainer at the Radix Institute in Ojai, California, and later through the International Institute for Biosynthesis in Switzerland. In these contexts he directed training groups in Europe and the United States. Mark was one of the founding members of the United States Association for Body Psychotherapy (USABP) and was a member of its board and ethics committee for several years. He was also the director of the MA programs in Somatic Psychology at the John F. Kennedy University and was acting chair of the California Institute of Integral Studies, both in the San Francisco Bay Area. As a fellow of the Harvard Children's Hospital, Napa County Infant-Parent Mental Health Fellowship, and as a clinical supervisor, he has focused his work on the clinical implications of infant and infant-parent research for the practice of adult Body Psychotherapy. He has recently been studying in this area with Steven Seligman and Diana Fosha. He is currently a member of the faculty at the California Institute of Integral Studies (CIIS) in San Francisco.

**Editors' Note:** *The original version of this chapter, in the German edition, was written with John May. It has since been extensively revised and updated.*

Body Psychotherapy is an emerging field and is a distinct approach to psychotherapy with a long history and a growing body of literature and research (Reich, 1942/1973; Lowen, 1975; Keleman, 1985; Smith, 1985; Boadella, 1987; Kepner, 1987; Downing, 1996; Hartley, 2008; Heller, 2012). This new field is supported by a growing number of university-level graduate programs in the United States, by national and international professional organizations hosting regular and diverse conferences, and by numerous research projects around the globe. Attachment theory, developing over the past five decades (Bowlby, 1969, 1988; Ainsworth et al., 1978; Main and Solomon, 1986; Hesse, 1999; Cassidy, 1999), and attachment-informed psychotherapy models (Slade, 1999; Fonagy et al., 2005; Wallin, 2007) are now prominent research and clinical paradigms within psychology and psychotherapy.

## Attachment Theory and Body Psychotherapy: Intersecting Approaches

Until recently, Body Psychotherapy and attachment theory have held relatively marginalized positions vis-à-vis the mainstream of psychotherapy. These transdisciplinary fields are supported by underlying theories of systemic complexity and by their shared attempt to integrate objective behaviors with subjective experience, as well as the biological with the psychological. Both paradigms emerged predominantly from within the psychodynamic clinical tradition, which was unable to accept and develop them further for many years. Since 1990, however, attachment theory and attachment research have returned to academic and clinical prominence in mental health and psychotherapeutic circles around the world. Moreover, there is now a greater openness in science for cross-disciplinary and systemic thinking, and within many psychotherapeutic approaches there is also a greater interest in how psychology, genetics, biology, and neurology interplay within the psychotherapy process. The emerging field of Body Psychotherapy, although more than a hundred years old, has only recently begun to self-consciously organize itself into a proper field, and it is now benefiting from many of these same scientific and clinical trends. The two approaches intersect at several points.

Both attachment theory and the Body Psychotherapy paradigm share a deep interest in how *real* experience, as well as symbolized or phantasy representations, becomes organized into inner models of self, the world, and others—models that guide somatic and psychological processes in relationship ("internal working models"; Bowlby, 1969), affective-motor schemas (Downing, 2006), and character styles (Reich, 1933; Johnson, 1994).

Significantly, both paradigms accept that a continuity exists between animal and human behavior and that many human behavior patterns are, at least in part, hardwired and biological or "pre-personal" (Keleman, 1986a). Consequently, attachment thinkers in general understand that positing a bioevolutionary dimension to human behavior does not diminish humanity, but informs us of the complex matrix in which humans develop and live. They therefore share a keen interest with Body Psychotherapists in the biopsychological nature of human motivational systems and the ways that humans organize the fulfillment of genetic, biological, psychological, relational, and emotional needs on an individual and social level.

Finally, both approaches appreciate a larger context for the human condition in which we are embedded. For the attachment theorists, this is the biological process of evolution; and for many of the twentieth-century Body Psychotherapists, it was the infinite permutations of bioenergetic processes.

## Attachment Theory and Body Psychotherapy as Dynamic Systems Paradigms

Body Psychotherapy and attachment theory are complex theories of biopsychological life. Long before the recent ascension of regulation models to the psychological mainstream (Schore, 1994), early body-inclusive psychology pioneers Janet (van der Hart and Horst, 1989) and Reich (1942) and attachment theorists (Bowlby, 1969) recognized the significant extent to which the organism's self-regulating efforts form the substratum of psychological life and mental health. Consequently, both perspectives emphasize theoretically and clinically the centrality of self-regulatory, co-regulatory, and chaotic/nonlinear processes to the life events of the human organism (Boadella, 1987; Heller, 2012).

The dynamic living system concept is a variation of the general systems theory model developed by the Austrian biologist von Bertalanffy (1950, 1969) and others. It challenges the fragmenting reductionistic, mechanical, and linear models of bio-organization, based on static laws. Complex dynamic systems contain a multiplicity of interactive subsystems that operate in a fluid arrangement where dynamically driven state change is constant (homeostatic regulation). Examples of complex dynamic systems are weather fronts, ecosystems, and astronomical phenomena. Dynamic *living* systems are *open,* environmentally embedded systems that require multiple levels of interaction for full functioning. The human organism—with its varied and conflicting needs, multiple developmental domains, and social embeddedness—is an example of a dynamic living system.

The awareness of complex theorizing, and the expansion of the parameters of the scientific frame in the contemporary era, are such that psycho-biological theories have necessarily expanded to continue to provide adequate models for human self-understanding. The "open systems" concept provides a potent working model for comprehending our organism-environment interaction as a nonfragmented whole. Complexity models are already introduced in other spheres of psychological theory and practice (Fogel, 1993; Schore, 1994; Sander, 2002; Seligman, 2005; Tronick, 2007). Body Psychotherapy and attachment theory are two integrative, multidisciplinary models, best comprehended and usable when viewed as dynamic systems models of psychology and psychotherapy.

## Embodied Human Needs and Motivational Systems

The reemergence of attachment theory brings back to our attention the question of embodied "human need" as an organizing force in psychological life. The concept of "basic human needs" (Etzioni, 1968), as motivational systems (Maslow, 1943), has gone out of favor in contemporary human sciences, perhaps because human needs, like its sibling "human rights," is a messy challenge for psychological theorists and other public policymakers. For Body Psychotherapy, however, this is a welcome reunion, as it is the body that persistently expresses a person's needs through its bodily feedback. Fundamental needs, when unmet, are expressed simultaneously and in a global manner, as we can readily see in young children. The stress of adaptation to unmet needs, with their attending failed and often-unconscious "workarounds," is what so often brings our adult clients to therapy in ontological, somatic, and emotional distress.

Recently, the prominent psychoanalyst Joseph Lichtenberg and his colleagues have reintroduced and updated the concept of needs and motivations within psychoanalytic theory (Lichtenberg et al., 2010). Significantly for this chapter, "attachment to individuals" and "caregiving" are listed among those motivational subsystems. Lichtenberg's basic-needs concepts are of considerable interest to Body Psychotherapists, because he describes seven interactive organizing systems that animate and find expression in the whole person: physiological regulation; attachment to individuals; affiliation with groups; caregiving; exploration; the assertion of preference ("Yes") and aversion ("No"); and sensuality and sexuality.

Attachment is one among many motivational subsystems accessed at the somatic level in Body Psychotherapy practice. The securing of needs—biological, psychological, interpersonal, and social—is a full-time, whole-body action. Needs and motives engage the available self-organizing mechanisms and processes that build up through developmental unfolding, experience, and interaction. Theories of human motivation, central to psychoanalytic, psychodynamic, and humanistic psychologies, are the wellsprings of modern Body Psychotherapy. Surprisingly, complex motivational theorizing is not in the current conversations of our field. A treatment of the interplay between attachment theory and Body Psychotherapy offers the possibility of reintroducing and updating a larger discussion about motivational theory—a rich topic for a field promising to contribute to the development of a whole-person model of psychology and psychotherapy.

Body Psychotherapy, or Somatic Psychology, as an embodied theory of experience, behavior, and pathology, inherently involves a complex systems concept. Indeed, one potential principle of any Somatic Psychology metapsychology could be a "whole-person model" of a person and of psychotherapy. Dynamic systems achieve complexity and sustainability when component subsystems are coordinating, communicating, and integrating across time and context. Within this model, as it applies to Somatic Psychology, disease and psychological suffering mean ceasing to function as a whole. (This is also expressed in Winnicott's (1954) model of the intact and healthy "psyche-soma.") Beyond the classic conscious/unconscious and "mind/body" splits, contemporary Somatic Psychotherapists work with *integration* as a primary therapeutic goal: e.g., integration of the three evolutionary brain systems (Carroll, 2003), of "bottom-up" and "top-down" communication (Ogden et al., 2006), of objective biological processes and subjective experience of self (Soth, 2006), of pre-personal, personal, and social selves (Keleman, 1986a and 1986b), and of thinking (ecto)–feeling (endo)–acting (meso) subsystems (Boadella, 1987). In clinical practice, this systemic understanding offers the practitioner a significant number of points of entry into the "life fields" (Ibid.) of the client. This whole-person model, when applied to the attachment subsystem, allows the clinician to organize interventions at the motoric, affective, relational, energetic, cognitive, and imaginal dimensions of the client's attachment system dynamics.

## The Theory of Childhood Attachment

That the relationship between caregiver and child is special has long been known to the arts and in popular culture. However, it became a focus of scientific attention only during the middle part of the twentieth century, after the publication of articles documenting the phenomenon called "hospitalism," especially the famous and widely known studies by René Spitz (1945). These articles made clear that merely providing for the physical needs of children is not sufficient. Children need something more from their relationship with their primary caregiver. If they don't get it, they fail to thrive and may perish. This "something more" that children need has been extensively articulated by numerous theorists and researchers since the 1960s. Winnicott (1956) called it "maternal preoccupation"; Ainsworth (1989), "sensitive parenting"; Schore (1994), "mutual psychobiological regulation"; Stern et al. (1998), "affective attunement"; Sander (2002), "recognition"; Slade (2002), "parental reflective capacity"; and Tronick (2007), "repair." A review of the contemporary relational psychotherapies that have developed a robust literature and practice ethos from this research is unfortunately beyond the scope of this attachment-focused chapter.

John Bowlby (1969) made one of the first comprehensive studies of the relationship that infants form with their caregivers. He called it an "attachment relationship." Since then, attachment theory has been an extremely generative concept, evolving an impressive amount of theory, research, and clinical applications. It has led to many understandings about child development that have become widely accepted in the social sciences. Attempts to understand how the parent-child system functions, including the attachment system, have led to observational studies and theories that are today providing new and important information about child development.

The attachment system is a behavioral system that serves the purpose of ensuring the availability and responsiveness of an animal's caregivers (Kobak, 1999). In other words, the child's behavior is organized around keeping the attachment figure close and responsive to the child's concerns for survival. Indeed, the attachment system has been seen as a part of an even-larger "safety system," organized in polarity with the "fear system" (Slade, 2011), which includes other dimensions such as vigilance, orienting, and proxemics.

Attachment behavior is thought to be instinctive in the full biological sense (Ainsworth, 1989); it occurs in many species, and is highly developed among mammals (see Porges's [2003] related concept of the "social engagement system"). Bowlby's model emerged partially out of earlier research studies of other species: Lorenz's (1981) studies of imprinting in geese, and Harlow's (1958) studies of maternal deprivation in monkeys. In humans, the type and degree of availability desired, and the methods used for obtaining it, develop continuously across the life span, propelled both by innate factors and by environmental learning experiences. That is, attachment is an evolving, emergent source of safety and affect regulation that changes and becomes more complex across the life span. The attachment behavior system is not always active. Distress within the infant (such as autonomic stress and dysregulation) and external danger (such as the threat of bodily damage) are the kinds of states that activate the attachment system (Kobak, 1999).

Modern approaches to the science of infant-caregiver interaction (Tronick, 2007) emphasize the role of co-regulation in the formation and development of these inner organizational systems in humans. Schore (1994, 2001) reviews more than a thousand sources on development and neurophysiology and proposes that attachment is one of several essential regulatory processes in which the secure mother, at an intuitive, nonconscious level, continuously regulates the infant's shifting arousal levels and emotional states. Within this model, the mother is thought to be (under "good-enough" conditions) a "hardwired" participant who is entrained to the child's cues and is biopsychologically responsive by virtue of her own complex behavioral systems, including what Bowlby and Lichtenberg would call her *caregiving system*. This co-regulation facilitates development of the infant's neurological systems that underlie healthy emotional functioning, including the systems that support the capacity for intersubjective knowing and dyadic states of consciousness (Tronick, 2007). Other researchers have explored mutual regulatory patterns between mother and infant from slightly different perspectives (Beebe et al., 2003; Beebe and Lachmann, 2002).

Body Psychotherapy has always been concerned with issues of self-regulation. Reich's early interest in the "economic viewpoint" (Reich, 1942/1973) is, at heart, concerned with emotional and energetic regulation, particularly with regard to the sympathetic and parasympathetic balance of the autonomic nervous system. Organismic regulation systems are therefore a topic that is of considerable interest to Body Psychotherapists, and they bring to this element of attachment theory an appreciation of the extent to which psycho-physical regulatory systems underlie the experience of self and other. The emerging awareness created by attachment research now brings to Body Psychotherapy a new interest in the relational ("body-with-body") realm of mutual regulation (Young, 2012). As this exciting arena is a huge and complex topic, we will be able to do little more than mention some of the findings of the attachment literature and reference some of the interesting speculations in the Body Psychotherapy literature.

## Internalizations, Attachment Styles, and Body Psychotherapy

The attachment behavior system includes not only its outward manifestations but also an inner organization, presumably rooted in neuro-physiological processes. This inner organization develops over time in response to genetic guidance and environmental influences. As the inner organization changes, so do its outward manifestations, the expression of attachment behavior and the circumstances under which it is activated. (Ainsworth, 1989)

Attachment theorists have discussed inner organization using the concept of *internal working models* (Bowlby, 1969). These consist of models of self, the attachment figure, and the environment that capture the actual history of the attachment relationship. This conceptualization contrasted with the dominant psychoanalytic models of the time, which emphasized internal and "phantasmic" dynamic mental representation, rather than actual experience. Bowlby saw these working models as cognitive schema drawn from interpersonal experience (see also Stern's [1985] concept of "representation of interactions generalized"). These attachments emerge during the first year of life, when the child does not yet have verbal symbolic capacities. Thus, they must contain nonverbal (sensory-motor) and subsymbolic elements, which makes them of great interest to Body Psychotherapists.

Within the "whole-person" model of Body Psychotherapy, and via these subsymbolized processes, the concept of "internal models" is elaborated into several somatic realms. The clinician may now locate, and clinically draw out, the client's attachment style as a here-and-now expression in their respiratory rhythms, movement patterns, facial expressions, gestures, gaze, visual tracking patterns, qualities of vigilance, their experience of emotional "closeness" or "distance," etc. In Body Psychotherapy, where the therapeutic dyad's immediate sensory, emotional, motoric, and impulse experience is joined with associations, narratives, joint attention, elaborations, and curiosities, a much wider world for investigation, experience, and discovery can open up.

Downing's (2006) use of the term "affective-motor schema" captures the phenomenology of this emotional-actional-cognitive matrix. He introduces the notion that these schema constitute and express themselves as implicit "body micropractices," emphasizing their procedural and embodied nature. These internal models have sometimes been seen as a type of template through which future relationships are experienced, creating expectations that may be either adaptive or maladaptive. This expanded conceptualization constitutes a significant development of the Reichian Body Psychotherapy "character structure" concept as rigidified adaptations in both the physiological and the cognitive realm.

Individuals develop different "attachment styles." These develop as solutions to their experiential history with their caregiver and their developmental environment (Ainsworth et al., 1978) (see also Boadella's [1987] concept of "the formative process and the organizing field"). Temperamental variations in the infant also affect this process, but the responsiveness of the caregiver to the full range of signals coming from the infant is central and definitive (Belsky, 1999). Four early childhood attachment styles are currently recognized, each having emerged as a stable variant to the "Strange Situation" paradigm developed by Ainsworth, Bowlby's chief collaborator (Ainsworth et al., 1978).

In attachment theory, the internal experience of security is what occurs when one has reliable access to a responsive and sensitive caregiver whenever needed. That experience becomes internally structured as the "secure" attachment type. Significantly, secure infants are then able to use the caregiver as a base for exploration, a necessity for human growth and development. Upon separation, they can also make use of strangers for comfort, in an appropriate manner, but may, on occasion, manifest overt distress and clearly prefer the caregiver. Upon reunion, secure infants seek proximity to the caregiver, and maintain it until their internal feeling of comfort and security is restored.

When an infant does not have reliable access to the caregiver, or when the caregiver is unresponsive or insensitive, the infant experiences insecurity. That experience becomes internally structured as one of three "insecure" attachment types: (1) "Avoidant" infants show reduced affective interaction with the caregiver. Upon separation, there is less distress, and they treat strangers similarly to their caregivers. Upon reunion, avoidant infants show signs of ignoring their caregivers, and they do not seek proximity; (2) Insecure infants of the "ambivalent" type are unable to use the caregiver as a secure base for any exploration; they seek markedly elevated amounts of proximity and contact. Upon separation, they are quite distressed and are unable to use a stranger for comfort. Upon reunion, they seem to want proximity to the caregiver, but are unable to calm down, even with the caregiver. Some sit passively, crying, unable to approach the caregiver. More often, they seek contact, but then refuse it angrily, and it is this pattern that gives the type its name; (3) "Disorganized" infants exhibit disoriented behaviors that suggest an inability to maintain a single coherent attachment strategy in the face of distress. This is no doubt because, for the attachment-disorganized child, the primary caregiver is also the person in the intimate environment who is most frightening. They may exhibit such dramatic responses as behavioral stilling, fear of the caregiver, parentification, and overt aggression (Solomon and George, 1999).

In the interest of depathologizing attachment styles, it is important to hold in mind that attachment styles are styles of "attachment," not of "detachment." Our blend of attachment style expresses the conditions under which we could make some contact and maintain as good as possible attachment security, and, as such, they speak to "connectedness" as much as "defense." All insecure attachment styles are organized ways of coping with insensitive caregiving while maintaining the best-available attachment relationship. These defenses can be seen as organismically organized "resources," akin to other survival skills. Some emerging strength- or resource-based models of developmentally informed clinical practice support client awareness of somato-psychological resources as a platform from which to scaffold further development (Bentzen et al., 1989) and to balance the effects of trauma (Levine, 1997; Ogden et al., 2006).

An impressive body of empirical evidence (Waters et al., 2000; Zhang and Labouvie-Vief, 2004) supports the reliability, validity, and stability of these attachment styles. In studies of later development, general attachment style at year one sometimes predicts a wide variety of developmental, intrapsychic, and interpersonal characteristics. At other times, it does not (Thompson, 1999). The conclusion seems to be that attachment style is a relatively stable characteristic that has the potential to affect the individual broadly. It is subject to modification, however, by innate developmental gains (increased capacities for self-reflection), later interpersonal experiences ("earned security"; see Pearson et al., 1994), and the attachment resources in the current environment.

Attachment security underlies the motoric and psychological dynamics of the child's exploration and return cycles. One of the most powerful findings of attachment theory—indeed, it is part of the definition—is that a secure attachment is used by infants as a "secure base" that facilitates their ability to venture out, to try new experiences, and to explore the world. In a sense, exploration requires, but also challenges, security. The issue of venturing out, moving into the world, and returning to a safe base highlights another possible intersection with Body Psychotherapy, as it has long held that client movement patterns express mental states, internal beliefs, and character attitudes. One possible further contribution to Attachment-Based Psychotherapy might come through the application of the Body Psychotherapy tradition of movement analysis (see also Chapter 86, "Dance Therapy" by Sabine Trautmann-Voigt). Would the application of Boadella's "motor fields" theory (Boadella, 1987), or of Laban's Effort-Shape Analysis (Laban and Lawrence, 1947), reveal movement tendencies native to the various styles of insecure attachments? Judith Kestenberg has already demonstrated such an approach in her work with movement analysis and psycho-sexual development (Kestenberg and Sossen, 1979). Payne (2006) and others are currently looking in this direction as well.

## Adult Forms of Attachment

Attachment research and theorizing initially focused on early childhood experience. Hesse (1999) (also Main and Goldwyn, 1998) and others developed the Adult Attachment Inventory in the mid-1990s. At that time, it was assumed (but not established) that there is a continuation into adulthood of internal working models and behavior styles. Adult attachment is a more difficult and nuanced subject matter, because adult behavior is much more complex and much more highly mediated by a variety of internal factors. Some theorists believe that measures of adult attachment style actually measure the "state of mind" with regard to attachment—this being a reflection of the adult's current state, rather than measuring a continuation of patterns learned in childhood (Hesse, 1999). Adult attachment research is conducted through the use of the Adult Attachment Interview (AAI) protocol. Within that model, avoidant behavior and states of mind are named "dismissive," and ambivalent states are referred to as "preoccupied." In looking at and comparing dismissive and preoccupied insecure patterns in adults, at the body-practice level in clinical interactions, I have made these initial observations of attachment-style manifestations:

**Avoidant/Dismissive**
- Contained eye movement
- Ocular affect relatively flat
- Gaze quality more neutral
- Reduced gesturing
- Stiffness in the spine and neck
- Controlled excitement
- Controlled or hypoventilation
- Emotional expressions short, spasmodic, and pressured
- Reluctance to join
- Active deflection of empathy and other offers of "help"

**Ambivalent/Preoccupied**
- Client actively tracking facial expressions in therapist
- Eagerness for mutual gaze
- Expressive eyes
- Animated in contact
- Excited or hyperventilation
- Longer emotional expressions but without apparent relief
- Actively seeks contact
- Pulls for empathy, but doesn't take it in

Bartholomew and Horowitz (1991) have developed a representative model that defines four types: secure (comfortable with intimacy and autonomy), preoccupied (ambivalent and overly dependent), dismissing (denial of attachment, counterdependent), and fearful (fearful of attachment, socially avoidant).

Describing and challenging these patterns is one natural avenue for intervention. In the various Body Psychotherapies, we have the opportunity to work with these body processes *in situ* and in their somatic manifestations. George Downing, author of the first significant volume (1996) that brought together Body Psychotherapy and developmental research and relational theory, has expressed tentative impressions of these emerging attachment-style models. Downing (2006) offers his own impressions of the attachment-style/character-style connection.

## The Attachment Relationship in Body Psychotherapy

Bowlby was an established psychoanalyst from the object-relations school, and trained and worked at the Tavistock Clinic in London. Though his attachment work was not readily accepted at first, because of its analytic unorthodoxy, attachment theory in its most contemporary form (Fonagy et al., 2005) has returned to take its place among the relationally based multiperson psychologies (Diamond and Marrone, 2003) of the analytic and psychodynamic therapy models (Fosha, 2000; Schore, 2003; Wallin, 2007).

The concerns of relationality in general, and attachment theory in particular, have only recently been represented in the Body Psychotherapy literature (Cornell, 1997; Hilton, 2012; Young, 2012). Reich (1933) briefly addressed the issue of "contact" and "contactlessness" and was an early explorer of somatic transference and countertransference phenomena through his study of "vegetative identification" (Reich, 1933; Boadella, 2005) in the therapeutic relationship. Nonetheless, Body Psychotherapies remained squarely in the one-person psychology camp until the past few decades. Like his contemporaries, Reich did not develop a clear understanding of how interpersonal interaction contributes to the development of healthy regulation. In fact, "other people," individually and collectively, with their character distortions, remained more the problem than the solution. Body Psychotherapy has yet to develop a perspective and a language consistent with its own paradigm that addresses this interpersonal sphere. Skills in mind-body integrative techniques, the subtle tracking of nonverbal expression of the implicit realm, and training in body-to-body communication all offer a fertile ground in which such a contribution might continue to grow and develop. Some steps in that direction have been noted.

Lewis (1974, 1986, 2004) has used Body Psychotherapy concepts to attempt to address concerns similar to those of attachment theory. He described the inability of parents to attune to, and accept, their infant's biological expressions. These descriptions bring to mind the inability to attune to the infant that is discussed in the attachment literature, the self-psychological literature, and the infant-observational literature. Notice how well the conceptualization also seems to anticipate recent work on the infant's reinternalization of affectively tinged images of itself from the parent (Fonagy et al., 2003). Lewis goes on to propose that the infant may experience something that he calls "cephalic shock," a primitive type of somato-psychic holding. According to Lewis (1986), it is also manifest in a specific tension at the base of the skull. Lewis recommends a variety of interventions, but emphasizes the role of relational security in working with this dynamic which he believes is the impact of emotional and physical "mishandling."

Keleman's (1986a) work in *Bonding: A Somatic-Emotional Approach to Transference* uses Somatic Psychology concepts to describe continuing patterns of interaction. His practice, Formative Psychology, achieves some important insights. His vision is one of intimate and immediate mutual interactive effect, used as a method for establishing contact, and occurring mostly unconsciously through a process of self- and co-shaping. He explores somatic relational resonance and the multiple somatic dimensions of transference and countertransference. Although not referring to attachment per se, he tracks how earlier developing forms may persist and how continuing patterns occur. At times, it is an attempt to explain these phenomena on a moment-by-moment basis. This was an important modification to Body Psychotherapy theory, and anticipated much of the intersubjective work being done today.

In attempting to challenge the early arelationality in Body Psychotherapy in a previous piece (Ludwig, 1999), I described a developmental approach to the bioenergetic concept of "grounding" (Lowen, 1975). In suggesting that "we are first grounded in others before we are grounded to the earth, the world, and reality," I directed attention to concerns similar to those in the attachment literature. In the prenatal period, what is the quality of the maternal preoccupation? Does the umbilicus provide us with a secure and regulated attachment to the mother? In the postnatal period, what is the quality of the holding environment? What is the quality of the gaze and mutual awareness, the maternal mirroring, and qualities of touch? (Ludwig and Field, 2013) These are the concerns of the attachment relationship. By altering the concept of grounding, usually understood as a spontaneously emerging individual capacity for self-support, I suggested that true independence may be born from the qualities of the interdependent matrix.

Downing has probably provided the most thorough attempt to relate the recent developmental literature to Body Psychotherapy. His writing and work have integrated Body Psychotherapy with the infant and parent mental health research. A primary structural concept is variously called a "motor belief," an "affective-motor schema," or a "body micropractice" (Downing, 1996). These structures are closely related to memory and information-processing schemas. But Downing emphasizes the sensory-motor nature of these schemas. He compares them to Stern's (1985) "Representations of Interactions that have been Generalized" (RIGs). The principal difference is whether one emphasizes the cognitive aspect (RIG) or the sensory-motor aspect (body micropractice). These are much smaller structures than the Reichian character structure. It is easy to imagine body micropractices as the inner representations that accumulate and become integrated into motor patterns (e.g., approach or avoidance) and implicit inner working models of the attachment relationship. These are the inner structures created by experiences in the attachment relationship, and they become the basis of an individual's attachment behavior and possibly their subsequent character structures.

## Working with the Effects of Insecure Attachment

Reich was a fierce advocate for child welfare and left a significant legacy for the Wilhelm Reich Infant Trust. Prevention and informed early childhood care are strong themes in a number of Neo-Reichian writers (Boadella, 1987; Cooper et al., 2008; Weaver, 2013).

Ventling (2001) attempted to extend bioenergetic approaches in her work with childhood attachment issues. She described a gentle set of experiences intended to encourage maternal prenatal bonding, prepare mothers for the delivery, and help them read their infants more confidently after they are born. The interventions involved such gentle ministrations as providing a holding relationship for the mother, providing education about the delivery experience, and practicing awareness of shape, color, noise, and odor.

Schroeter (2001) also described a body-oriented process intended to encourage bonding. She worked first with the mother regarding her own emotional issues about mothering, and then with the mother and child together. The mother was helped to do such things as explore and observe in which posture the infant preferred to be held. Schroeter also educated her client about the needs and capacities of her baby, and reframed the mother's understandings of infant behaviors.

George Downing (2003) also has much research film on insecure mothers and their relationships with their babies that lead to attachment problems: he uses these films to show the mother the cues that she has missed from the baby, and so that she can see her progress in better attachment processes.

The clinical usefulness of physical touch has often been discussed and debated in the Body Psychotherapy literature, especially with regard to its role in attachment and in interpersonal regulation. Physical touch is, of course, essential to infants, as numerous reports document (Hertenstein and Weiss, 2011; Ludwig and Field, 2013). There is also a growing body of literature indicating that touch can have a regulating and disregulating effect in adults as well (Smith et al., 1998). Although we note that the words "touch," "holding," and "contact" are not even indexed in a major comprehensive review of attachment theory (Cassidy and Shaver, 1999), the strategic use of physical contact as a specific tool of therapy is an important part of many Body Psychotherapy modalities. To what extent is touch a cause of secure attachment or a marker of secure attachment, or both? The extent to which the therapeutic use of touch is an appropriate part of work with attachment wounding at any point in development is an important question to which Body Psychotherapists could make a significant contribution.

I previously noted that secure attachment facilitates exploration of the world (trying new experiences) because it functions as a secure base from which exploration can occur. From an attachment perspective, a productive therapeutic relationship involves the client's capacity to use the relationship as a secure base from which to explore new ways of moving, feeling, thinking, and acting (Slade, 1999). As noted above, it is a parent's sufficiently accurate attunement to the child, emotional availability, responsiveness, as well as the goodness of fit between parent and child that most influence their attachment relationship.

Much the same is true of therapeutic relationships. To the extent that one wishes to make therapeutic use of the benefits of an attachment relationship, and to the extent that one desires to work with a client's attachment issues, then that work will be facilitated by a therapeutic relationship with one therapist that allows a secure attachment bond to form over time. The necessary therapeutic skills involve the ability to read the emotional communications of the client; the ability to "be there" for the client and produce a "good enough" response; and the capacity to give it adequately. This is always a function of the individual training, skill, and humanity of the individual therapist—Body Psychotherapies do not have a demonstrable advantage in the creation of an effective therapeutic relationship, except that their training and personal therapy, being more body-oriented and often more experiential, may have addressed some of their own early attachment issues. However, Body Psychotherapy's emphasis on sensory-motor processes—especially as the field integrates recent developmental, neurological, and traumatological research—may provide Body Psychotherapists with nonverbal-, affect-, and process-tracking skills for the clinicians of the future.

## The Research Road Ahead for a Body Psychotherapy: Understanding of Attachment Styles

One way to proceed in exploring these issues empirically in Body Psychotherapy could involve the instruments that are available for assessing adult attachment such as the Adult Attachment Interview (Main and Goldwyn, 1998). Research samples, be they clients or recruits, could be grouped according to attachment style and then compared on a variety of different Body Psychotherapy evaluative scales. These could range from breathing style, to character type, to quality of eye contact, to response to touch, etc. Another approach would be to measure attachment style in a sample of clients before and after they underwent a course of Body Psychotherapy, and see how it changes. Measures of therapeutic change could be included in such a study, and clients with different attachment styles could be compared to see if they responded to the Body Psychotherapy differently. Alternatively, a group of clients could be assessed for attachment type, then undergo a course of Body Psychotherapy. Measures of therapeutic process, such as the Experiencing Scale (Klein, 1969) or the Client Emotional Arousal Scale (Carryer, 2010) could be applied to their sessions, and comparisons made to see if there were different outcomes among attachment types.

Body Psychotherapy and attachment theory are best understood within a modern dynamic systems paradigm. Attachment theory is a rich tradition that has developed a substantial supportive empirical literature. Body Psychotherapy, on the other hand, is an exciting, emerging clinical field that has yet to develop the conceptual depth and solid theoretical support that characterize attachment theory. Attachment theory is just now penetrating into the areas of sensory-motor interaction that characterize Body Psychotherapy clinical practice. Body Psychotherapy has generated many exciting and interesting clinical speculations that are relevant to attachment theory, and vice versa. There is much work to be done, and these two theoretical traditions have much to offer each other.

## References

Ainsworth, M. D. S. (1989). Attachments beyond infancy. *American Psychologist, 44,* 709–716.

Ainsworth, M. D. S., Blehar, M., Waters, E., & Wall, S. (1978). *Patterns of attachment: A psychological study of the strange situation.* Hillsdale, NJ: Lawrence Erlbaum.

Bartholomew, K., & Horowitz, L. M. (1991). Attachment styles among young adults: A test of a four-category model. *Journal of Personality and Social Psychology, 61*(2), 226.

Beebe, B., & Lachmann, F. (2002). *Infant research and adult treatment.* Hillsdale, NJ: Analytic Press.

Beebe, B., Sorter, D., Rustin, J., & Knoblauch, S. (2003). A comparison of Meltzoff, Trevarthen, and Stern. *Psychoanalytic Dialogues, 13*(6), 805–842.

Belsky, J. (1999). Interactional and contextual determinants of attachment security. In J. Cassidy and P. Shaver (Eds.), *Handbook of attachment: Theory, research and clinical applications* (pp. 249–264). New York: Guilford Press.

Bentzen, M., Jorgensen, S., & Marcher, L. (1989). The Bodynamic character structure model. *Energy & Character, 20*(1), 1–17.

Boadella, D. (1987). *Lifestreams: An introduction to Biosynthesis.* London: Routledge.

Boadella, D. (2005). Affect, attachment and attunement: Thoughts inspired in dialogue with the three-volume work of Allan Schore. *Energy & Character, 34,* 13–23.

Bowlby, J. (1969). *Attachment and loss: Attachment (Vol. 1).* London: Tavistock Institute.

Bowlby, J. (1988). *A secure base: Parent-child attachment and healthy human development.* New York: Basic Books.

Carroll, R. (2003). "At the border between chaos and order": What psychotherapy and neuroscience have in common. In J. Corrigal & H. Wilkinson (Eds.), *Revolutionary connections: Psychotherapy and neuroscience* (pp. 191–211). London: Karnac Books.

Cassidy, J. (1999). The nature of the child's ties. In J. Cassidy & P. Shaver (Eds.), *Handbook of attachment: Theory, research, and clinical applications* (pp. 3–22). New York: Guilford Press.

Cassidy, J., & Shaver, P. (Eds.). (1999). *Handbook of attachment: Theory, research, and clinical applications.* New York: Guilford Press.

Cooper, A., Ludwig, M., & Heineman, T. (2008). Fostering mindful attachment: A relational approach using infant-parent massage. *The Source: Journal of UC Berkeley's National Abandoned Infants Assistance Resource Center, 18*(1), 16–19.

Cornell, W. (1997). If Reich had met Winnicott. *Energy & Character, 28,* 50–60.

Diamond, N., & Marrone, M. (2003). *Attachment and intersubjectivity.* London: Whurr.

Downing, G. (1996). *Korper und wort in der psychotherapie: Leitlinien fur die praxis* [Body and word in psychotherapy: Guidelines for practice]. Munich: Kösel.

Downing, G. (2003). Video Mikroanalyse Therapie: Einige Grundlagen und Prinzipien [Video Microanalysis Therapy: Some basic concepts and principles]. In H. Scheuerer-Englisch, G. J. Suess, & W.-K. Pfeifer (Eds.), *Wege zur Sicherheit: Bindungswissen in Diagnostik und Intervention [Ways to security: Confirmed knowledge in diagnosis and intervention].* Giessen: Psychosozial.

Downing, G. (2006). Frühkindlicher Affektaustausch und dessen Beziehung zum Körper [Early affect exchange and the body]. In G. Marlock & H. Weiss, *Handbuch der Körperpsychotherapie [Handbook of Body Psychotherapy].* Stuttgart: Schattauer.

Etzioni, A. (1968). Basic human needs, alienation and inauthenticity. *American Sociological Review, 33,* 6.

Fogel, A. (1993). *Developing through relationship.* Chicago: University of Chicago Press.

Fonagy, P., Gergely, G., Jurist, E., & Target, M. (2005). *Affect regulation, mentalization, and the development of the self.* New York: Other Press.

Fonagy, P., Target, M., Gergely, G., Allen, J., & Bateman, A. (2003). The developmental roots of borderline personality disorder in early attachment relationships: A theory and some evidence. *Psychoanalytic Inquiry, 23(3)*, 412–459.

Fosha, D. (2000). *The transforming power of affect: A model for accelerated change.* New York: Basic Books.

Harlow, H. (1958). The nature of love. *American Psychologist, 13,* 673–685.

Hartley, L. (2008). *Contemporary Body Psychotherapy.* Hove, UK: Routledge.

Heller, M. (2012). *Body Psychotherapy: History, concepts, methods.* New York: W. W. Norton.

Hertenstein, M., & Weiss, S. (2011). *The handbook of touch: Neuroscience, behavioral, and health perspectives.* New York: Springer.

Hesse, E. (1999). The Adult Attachment Interview: Historical and current perspectives. In J. Cassidy & P. Shaver (Eds.), *Handbook of attachment: Theory, research, and clinical applications* (pp. 395–443). New York: Guilford Press.

Hilton, R. (2012). *Somatic Perspectives on Psychotherapy: May 2012.* somaticperspectives.com/zpdf/2012-05-hilton.pdf

Johnson, S. (1994). *Character styles.* New York: W. W. Norton.

Keleman, S. (1985). Emotional anatomy: The structure of experience. Berkeley, CA: Center Press.

Keleman, S. (1986a). *Bonding: A somatic-emotional approach to transference.* Berkeley, CA: Center Press.

Keleman, S. (1986b). Living your dying. *Psychotherapy Patient, 2(1),* 129–133.

Kepner, J. (1987). *Body process: Working with the body in psychotherapy.* San Francisco: Jossey-Bass.

Kestenberg, J., & Sossen, K. (1979). *The role of movement patterns in development.* New York: Dance Notation Bureau Press.

Kobak, R. (1999). The emotional dynamics of disruptions in attachment relationships: Implications for theory, research, and clinical intervention. In J. Cassidy & P. Shaver (Eds.), *Handbook of attachment: Theory, research, and clinical applications* (pp. 21–43). New York: Guilford Press.

Laban, R., & Lawrence, F. C. (1947). *Effort.* London: McDonald & Evans.

Levine, P. (1997). *Waking the tiger: Healing trauma.* Berkeley, CA: North Atlantic Books.

Lewis, R. (1974). A developmental view of Bioenergetic Therapy. *Energy & Character, 5(3),* 41–47.

Lewis, R. (1986). Getting the head to really sit on one's shoulders: A first step in grounding the false self. *Bioenergetic Analysis, 2(1),* 56–77.

Lewis, R. (2004). *Human trauma.* Retrieved from www.bodymindcentral.com/publications.html#human

Lichtenberg, J., Lachmann, F., & Fosshage, J. (2010). *Psychoanalysis and motivational systems: A new look.* Hove, UK: Routledge.

Lorenz, K. (1981). *The foundations of ethology.* New York: Simon & Schuster.

Lowen, A. (1975). *Bioenergetics.* New York: Coward, McCann & Geoghegan.

Ludwig, M. (1999). Swimming in a human sea: A developmental approach to grounding. *Energy & Character, 21(2),* 46–55.

Ludwig, M., & Field, T. (2013). Touch in parent-infant mental health: Arousal, regulation, and relationships. In K. Brandt, B. Perry, S. Seligman, & E. Tronick. *Infant-family and early childhood mental health: Core concepts and clinical applications* (pp. 237–249). Arlington, VA: American Psychiatric Publishing.

Main, M., & Goldwyn, R. (1998). *Adult attachment scoring and classification system.* Unpublished manuscript, University of California, Berkeley.

Main, M., & Solomon, J. (1986). Discovery of an insecure-disorganized/disoriented attachment pattern. In B. Brazelton & M. Yogman (Eds.), *Affective development in infancy* (pp. 95–124). Norwood, NJ: Ablex.

Marlock, G., & Weiss, H. (Eds.). (2006). *Handbuch de Körperpsychotherapie [Handbook of Body Psychotherapy].* Stuttgart: Schattauer.

Maslow, A. (1943). A theory of human motivation. *Psychological Review, 50(4),* 370–396.

Ogden, P., Minton, K., & Pain, C. (2006). *Trauma and the body: A sensorimotor approach to psychotherapy* (Norton Series on Interpersonal Neurobiology). New York: W. W. Norton.

Payne, H. (2006). Tracking the web of interconnectivity. *Body, Movement and Dance in Psychotherapy, 1(1),* 7–15.

Pearson, J., Cohn, D., Cowan, P., & Cowan, C. (1994). Earned- and continuous-security in adult attachment: Relation to depressive symptomatology and parenting style. *Development and Psychopathology, 6(2), 359–373.*

Porges, S. W. (2003). Social engagement and attachment. *Annals of the New York Academy of Sciences, 1008(1), 31–47.*

Reich, W. (1933). *Character Analysis.* New York: Farrar, Straus & Giroux.

Reich, W. (1942/1973). *The function of the orgasm.* New York: Farrar, Straus & Giroux.

Sander, L. W. (2002). Thinking differently: Principles of process in living systems and the specificity of being known. *Psychoanalytic Dialogues, 12(1), 11–42.*

Schore, A. (1994). *Affect regulation and the origin of the self: The neurobiology of emotional development.* Mahwah, NJ: Lawrence Erlbaum.

Schore, A. (2001). Effects of a secure attachment relationship on right brain development, affect regulation, and infant mental health. *Infant Mental Health Journal, 22(1–2), 7–66.*

Schore, A. N. (2003). *Affect regulation and the repair of the self* (Vol. 2). New York: W. W. Norton.

Schroeter, V. (2001). Improving bonding using Bioenergetics and sensory assessments: A clinical case report. In C. Ventling (Ed.), *Childhood psychotherapy: A Bioenergetic approach* (pp. 19–22). Basel: Karger.

Seligman, S. (2005). Dynamic systems theories as a metaframework for psychoanalysis. *Psychoanalytic Dialogues, 15(2), 285–319.*

Slade, A. (1999). Attachment theory and research: Implications for the theory and practice of individual psychotherapy with adults. In J. Cassidy & P. Shaver (Eds.), *Handbook of attachment: Theory, research, and clinical applications* (pp. 575–594). New York: Guilford Press.

Slade, A. (2002). Keeping the baby in mind. *Zero to Three, 6, 10–15.*

Slade, A. (2011, March 23). *Attachment, fear, and evolution: Better safe than dead.* 6th Annual Robert Wallerstein Lecture, UCSF School of Psychiatry, San Francisco.

Smith, E. W. L. (1985). *The body in psychotherapy.* Jefferson, NC: MacFarland.

Smith, E. W. L., Clance, P., & Imes, S. (1998). *Touch in psychotherapy: Theory, research, and practice.* New York: Guilford Press.

Solomon, J. E., & George, C. E. (1999). *Attachment disorganization.* New York: Guilford Press.

Soth, M. (2006). What therapeutic hope for a subjective mind in an objectified body? *Body, Movement and Dance in Psychotherapy, 1(1), 43–56.*

Spitz, R. (1945). Hospitalism: An inquiry into the genesis of psychiatric conditions in early childhood. *Psychoanalytic Study of the Child, 1, 53–74.*

Stern, D. (1985). *The interpersonal world of the infant: A view from psychoanalysis and Developmental Psychology.* New York: Basic Books.

Stern, D. N., Sander, L. W., Nahum, J. P., Harrison, A. M., Lyons-Ruth, K., Morgan, A. C., & Tronick, E. Z. (1998). Non-interpretive mechanisms in psychoanalytic therapy: The "something more" than interpretation. *International Journal of Psychoanalysis, 79(5), 903–921.*

Thompson, R. (1999). Early attachment and later development. In J. Cassidy & P. Shaver (Eds.), *Handbook of attachment: Theory, research, and clinical applications* (pp. 265–286). New York: Guilford Press.

Tronick, E. (2007). *The neurobehavioral and social-emotional development of infants and children.* New York: W. W. Norton.

van der Hart, O., & Horst, R. (1989). The dissociative theory of Pierre Janet. *Journal of Traumatic Stress, 2(4), 397–412.*

Ventling, C. (2001). Birth and bonding: To be or not to be. In C. Ventling (Ed.), *Childhood psychotherapy: A Bioenergetic approach* (pp. 9–18). Basel: Karger.

von Bertalanffy, L. (1950). An outline of general system theory. *British Journal for the Philosophy of Science, 1, 134–165.*

von Bertalanffy, L. (1969). *General system theory: Foundations, development, applications.* New York: George Braziller.

Wallin, D. (2007). *Attachment in psychotherapy.* New York: Guilford.

Waters, E., Merrick, S., Treboux, D., Crowell, J., & Albersheim, L. (2000). Attachment security in infancy and early adulthood: A twenty-year longitudinal study. *Child Development, 71(3), 684–689.*

Weaver, J. (2013). Sensory Awareness—The heart of Somatic Psychotherapy: From Sensory Awareness to Somatic Psychotherapy. Retrieved from http://judyth-weaver.com/writings/

Winnicott, D. W. (1954). Mind and its relation to the psyche-soma. *British Journal of Medical Psychology, 27(4), 201–209.*

Winnicott, D. W. (1956). Primary maternal preoccupation (pp. 300–305). London: Tavistock.

Young, C. (Ed.). (2012). *About Relational Body Psychotherapy.* Galashiels, Scotland: Body Psychotherapy Publications.

Zhang, F., & Labouvie-Vief, G. (2004). Stability and fluctuation in adult attachment style over a 6-year period. *Attachment & Human Development, 6(4), 419–437.*

# 35

## The Development of Autonomy from a Body Psychotherapy Perspective

Ute-Christiane Bräuer, Germany

Translation by Elizabeth Marshall

**Ute-Christiane Bräuer,** Dipl.-Psych, is a psychological psychotherapist and a child and youth psychotherapist. She is trained in several methods of Body Psychotherapy, Gestalt Therapy, and Group-Analytical Therapy and has practiced since 1976. She belongs to the team in charge of training in Unitive Body Psychotherapy and is active as a supervisor and in various areas of further education. For several years, she has directed a research project entitled "From the Beginning," which studies the relevance of the theory and practice of Body Psychotherapy for educational purposes, both in relation to the earliest learning experiences of babies and toddlers, as well as in the field of education in and out of school. She shares this wealth of experience via vocational trainings and as a consultant for a variety of institutions and educational facilities.

## The Origins of Self-Efficacy and Behavioral Competence in Infants

"Man is an animal of many worlds," states the German philosopher Sloterdijk (1998), and "the appropriation of the world is a continuation of birth process by other means." He emphasizes our ability, as human beings, to be at home in more than one world, as well as the spontaneous and birthlike aspects of the human processes of cognition and development, which—in a whole-body exchange with the environment—can find ever-new, unplanned, and often surprising solutions.

The concept of autonomy derives from the two ancient Greek words *auto* and *nomos* and—in the original sense of the word—means "*he, who gives himself a name.*" How failed attempts at autonomy can be seen to manifest as betrayals of the self is an issue that the psychoanalyst Arno Gruen (1992) has addressed in depth. He defines autonomy as the ability to have a self—a self founded on access to one's own emotions and needs. If we follow Gruen's definition, the question arises: How does such a self develop? The concept of an "autistic phase," in which the infant is regarded as the mere passive recipient of bodily contact and affection, protected by a stimulus barrier, is a thing of the past. As microanalysis has shown, the newborn infant already takes—or at least tries to take—an active role in most interactions.

According to Martin Dornes, we must assume that intentional, will-controlled activity exists from birth onward (Dornes, 1992). Even though newborns are not conscious of their own will, it manifests clearly in expressions of indignation and displeasure when they encounter obstacles in their way or are interrupted in their movements by others.

## Development of Autonomy in Early Life

The development of autonomy is crucially influenced during the extremely sensitive phase before the onset of speech by the infant's experiences with, and within, their own body, as well as in dialogue with the body of the principal caregiver. Fundamental insights regarding the subject have been contributed by the work of Piaget, e.g., his concept of sensory-motor development (Piaget, 1975); the studies of Wallon, on the early tonic dialogue between mother and child; and by Schilder and Head on the origin of body patterns (compare with Gallagher and Cole, 1995).

Recently, George Downing has proposed significantly new ideas: his observations of so-called "body micropractices" constitute a fertile addition to the "Representations of Interactions that have been Generalized" (RIGs), conceptualized by Stern, which—as the infant's representations of interactions that have become generalized—are of a more cognitive nature (Downing, 1996). Whereas Stern addressed the subjective experiences of infants, and was interested in how frequently recurring events and interactive experiences are processed and stored in the developing child's brain (Stern, 1992), Downing's work is generating new impulses in the field of infant research by raising countless questions about the different ways in which subjective experience is being embodied, especially during the first months of life.

According to Downing, structures of knowledge emerge via early somatic experience, as unconscious or preconscious "motoric convictions" that constitute a repertoire of embodied, nonverbal knowledge. Such knowledge—once developed—is then available to us for the rest of our lives, alongside the conscious and cognitively based strategies of action that develop via processes of differentiation only much later. Among other functions, these body micropractices allow the child—in a constant interplay of the sensory, motor, affective, and cognitive levels—to regulate its closeness and distance needs in the interpersonal field. Downing has found a wealth of such strategies, which vary from situation to situation and from child to child, and which depend upon the nature of the specific interactions that the child has with people and with its material environment.

These strategies can be categorized into two groups: schemata of "connection" on the one hand, and those of "differentiation" on the other. These schemata already organize the child's expectation and experience horizon from the very first weeks of life, with regard to fundamental existential issues, such as attachment and autonomy.

Under what conditions these developing body strategies initiate subjective experiences of self-efficacy and autonomy is a question that has been studied by the psycho-motorist Bernard Aucouturier (2001, 2002). He examines the quality of contact engendered by the infant's evolving movements and distinguishes movement from action, which he sees as a dialectic process: an "interaction." He emphasizes that it is not only the child who must learn to adapt to the adult, but also the adult who must be equally prepared to adjust to the child, to be influenced and transformed by the child. It is only within the climate of a gratifying relationship—one in which the effects of mutual impact and change are predominantly experienced as pleasurable and enjoyable—that such transformations can be tolerated and experienced without undue defensiveness. In order to confirm the infant in his experience of self-efficacy, it is indispensable, according to Aucouturier, for the caregiver to attune and familiarize themselves with the logic inherent in the child's nonverbal movement and affects, and to enter into this logic. The infant grasps the world of objects, via his "somatic axis," i.e., through the sensing of his muscles and movement. His behavior originates in each present moment, is absolutely grounded in the present, unlike the behavior of adults, which is informed by values, and is purposeful and intentional.

It is only gradually that the infant becomes aware of its capacity for impact and efficacy, with recurring experiences developing the faculties of recognition and memory and thus evolving from action to thought. If the adult repeatedly makes demands of the infant that require too complex a logic and to which it has as yet no motoric access, then the child is already being deprived, from the outset, of the experience that *it* can be the agent and protagonist of its own development. The child is then robbed of a sense of physical authorship and autonomy (Aucouturier, 2001).

A quite recent realization is perhaps of interest in this context: consistently successful, high-quality attunement to the child is less significant to well-functioning dyadic relationships within the everyday life of the family than the adults' willingness to correct and regulate misattunements in their contact with the child and their capacity to repair ruptures (Tronick, 1998).

## Autonomy as the Discovery of the Lived Body and the Conquest of Space

In recent decades, the findings of attachment research have alerted and stimulated infant observers to concentrate their efforts on the analysis of early mother-child relationships. Since then, detailed insight has been gained as to how the structures of our descendants reflect the transgenerational transmission of our deficits: our own lost abilities and faculties. Modern neurobiology confirms that the human brain is a product of socialization, and that it is programmed by the way it is used. The extent of neuronal connections, especially in the frontal cortex, is crucially dependent on what children devote their attention to, and whether, even as small babies, they are offered varied opportunities to become aware of themselves and of their effect on other people. Uncertainty, time pressure, and anxiety all interfere with the process by which complex patterns of perception and reaction are filtered, integrated, and organized, especially when the neuronal connections are still in the formative stage (Huther, 2002).

As informative as these new approaches are for a more precise understanding of the failure to develop autonomy, they do tend to confine themselves almost without exception to the study of the complex field of interaction between the child and the primary caregivers. Concepts such as microanalytic coding, contingent experience, poor or satisfactory synchronization, fine-tuning to the rhythmic affective exchange, mirroring, matching, tuning in, and mutual coordination play a central role in modern baby research. But current research largely neglects an area of embodied skills that evolve in the early motoric development of children and that generally are *not* established within an interactive framework.

From an anthropological and developmental perspective, there is no other stage in life and human development in which the discovery of the (lived) body is as significant to the proactive process through which both self and reality are formed and generated.

Downing, whose analysis does concentrate on the interpersonal, at least concedes the existence of other micropractices that are less involved with other people and more with the embodied structures of knowledge, and that crystallize out of the challenges of the individual's motoric history and the confrontation with the physical environment. The work of Thelen and Smith is also relevant in this context (Thelen and Smith, 1994). Their research shows that children's activity is much more extensively dependent on context than was previously assumed and that it is continuously determined in its dynamics by the kind of environment that children encounter and what possibilities for movement this provides. The research results strongly suggest that the learning and storage processes in the brain, which are at first strictly related to activity and context, become generalized only gradually and only after the acquisition of differentiated locomotoric skills.

In Europe, the investigation and conceptualization of how we gain knowledge of the world, and develop autonomy in connection with motoric development, have largely been based on the publications of Schilling, Scheid, and Kiphard (Schilling, 1977; Scheid, 1989; Kiphard, 1979, 1998), as well as the long-term studies of several French and Hungarian doctors and psychoanalysts (Pikler and Tardos, 1994; Pikler, 2001; David and Appel, 1995a, 1995b; Szanto-Feder, 2002).

Schilling's theory points to some common characteristics between neglected children, overprotected children, and children from an authoritarian upbringing: they all experience insufficient motoric stimulation, whether they have at their disposal too much or too little space for free development of movement. According to Schilling, it is the varied repetition of different motoric patterns in similar situations, within a wide range of possible movements, that provides the fundamental condition for the acquisition of a rich store of motoric patterns in early childhood. It is this sort of self-determined experience, rather than guided mediation of experience, that forms the basis for the development of an autonomic repertoire of movement (Scheid, 1989).

Jürgen Seewald has also contributed a scientific model for the correlation between physicality, movement, and identity, in which he considers the sensation of movement as central to the experience of groundedness and a sense of core (Seewald, 2000). Following the same track, Ernst Kiphard called for materials appropriate to each relevant developmental stage, for spaces suitable for experiential learning, and for sufficient time for undisturbed exploration in unstructured play (Kiphard, 1979, 1998). As the founder of German Psycho-motorics, he began to oppose, early in his work as a child psychiatrist, the deficit- and function-oriented treatment of behavioral disorders. His work emphasized the dignity of each individual child, and he trusted in their capacity for self-organization. His main goal was to encourage children to cope with their lives proactively and independently and to provide them with stimulating practice materials with which to explore their potential.

In an investigation, Volker Scheid was able to furnish experimental proof that—presupposing a permissive educational attitude—the development of elementary movement patterns in infancy is significantly dependent on the degree of opportunities for sufficient learning experiences with a range of specific situations and materials (Scheid, 1989).

## Self-Efficacy and Free Motoric Development: The Pikler Model

In the course of her clinical observations, Emmi Pikler, a Hungarian pediatrician, recognized, as early as the 1930s, the fundamental significance that free motoric expression of babies has for the development of human autonomy and behavioral competence. Later, as the director of an orphanage in Budapest, she arrived at conclusions that correspond with the findings of Winnicott (1974, 1976), Stern (1992), and many other contemporary researchers and that extend these findings to include one particular aspect essential for the development of autonomy. Pikler was the first to point out both the infant's need, as well as its capacity, to bring about their own development independently, via bodily experience. This requires that the newborn's movements—their spontaneous motoric activity—are allowed to unfold freely from the beginning, precisely because they contain the potential and the strength for the development of autonomy.

Pikler based her theory on the observation that parental behavior not only facilitates the regulation of the infant's physical condition through the provision of feeding, security, and bodily contact, but that it also unconsciously blocks and hinders the infant's curiosity, its cognitive participation in the world around it, its explorative behavior, its wonderment, and its experience of self-efficacy (Pikler and Tardos, 1994; Pikler, 2001). For this reason, Pikler questions commonly accepted practices and forms of adult-child relating whereby, for example, adults make well-intentioned attempts to teach children how to move, to help them sit or stand up, or to play with them, according to the adult's inclinations.

The orphanage and research laboratory Lóczy, in Budapest (founded by Pikler and now run by her daughter, Anna Tardos), is an institution that cares for orphans from birth onward, and is still one of the most provocative and far-reaching institutions in the field of baby research. Informed by the fundamental question of what kinds of behavior toward a child are adults entitled to, the work is based on a code of relational behavior, worked out with near-scientific thoroughness, coupled with an attitude of exceptional respect toward the newborns. In essence, the daily routine is organized to guarantee and maximize the free motoric development of the children. The recognition and respect for the children's rhythms, and these include both daily and developmental rhythms, constitute important points of reference for the structuring of daily life. Right from the beginning, the infants gain the experience that their own wishes and expressions of will are taken seriously. In the case of feeding, for example, the priority is not the successful administering of a balanced diet; the caregivers are interested primarily in the children's appetite for life. Do they open their mouths to signal "I want, I'm hungry"? Or do they reject the food, because the temperature, the consistency, or the moment is not right for them? Allowing sufficient time for eating opens up the possibility for infants to experience the symbolic dimension of assimilating something. Pikler considers this to be an essential condition in which the children's capacity can develop to receive and accept what is given. Acceptance here means that the children are free to take, to push away, to accept or refuse, to grasp, to take possession of, and to make it their own. Also, with regard to the nursing, the children are again given sufficient time to adjust emotionally to the approach of the caregiver, and to prepare for the expected nursing activity. The nurses take care never to move the children into a physical position that they cannot assume of their own accord, in order to prevent the infant from experiencing a loss of their balance and consequent helpless dependency.

Despite the fact that the nursing care facilitates a thorough introduction to the development of relationship skills and autonomy, it was Pikler's deeply held conviction that the development of embodied self-awareness is rooted first and foremost in free and independent play, without well-meaning guidance from adults. Pikler also considered free motoric development, during infancy, to be the main factor in the prevention of damage through (hospital) institutionalization (Pikler, 2001). She describes a setting in which the children are free to spend their time as they wish as a "high school for babies and infants." The newborns are placed on their backs and learn all further movements through their own initiatives.

Pikler had observed that, during their first year of life, infants who are allowed to move freely tend to change their position about sixty times in the space of thirty minutes. Unless they are constricted for long periods of time in the same position by baby bouncers, walking aids, swings, baby seats, straps, or strollers, they will be continuously in motion right from the start of their lives. They will adopt new patterns of motion gradually, in steps and stages.

The practicing of particular kinds of transitional movements that—according to Pikler—are typical for the infant phase plays a decisive part, in parallel to the maturation of the nervous system, because it allows the organism to prepare itself for more highly developed movements, in its own time, and according to its own level of maturity. These transitional, intermediate movements that were first studied in the Pikler Institute include turning from the supine into the side position, and back, turning into the prone position, rolling, rocking, crawling on the belly, crawling on hands and knees, as well as intermediate forms of sitting up and lying down. Each level of motoric ability that follows naturally from the previous one is taken up by the children at their own initiative, in their own time.

This promotes good coordination in which the children attain higher levels of motoric development of their own accord, and furthers both the creativity and the competence of their actions, as well as the gradual ripening of their independence (Pikler, 2001, p. 70). After children are sure of their balance, and their buttocks muscles are sufficiently developed, they can then sit up or stand up without help. However, before they stand up without support and risk taking a few steps, they practice standing, bending over, repeatedly trying out the erect position, as well as innumerable forms of balancing on both feet. In their independent movements, they learn to fall, to deal with unexpected incidents, and to be careful and circumspect.

Their spirit of exploration urges them to touch objects around them and to jumble them up. They want to turn them over, climb onto them, crawl into them, and under them, to discover their form and dimensions, their surface texture, volume, and structure. Children's free play also fulfills the function of dealing with anxiety, helping them to liberate themselves step-by-step from the presence of the "mother." Thus, we can observe how infinite repetitions of the game of "letting themselves fall," associated equally with pleasure and fear, eventually leads to the experience of autonomy. The happiness that children feel, when at last they succeed in letting go of outside support and begin to trust in their inner self, is a significant sign that they are finally able to let go of the "mother" as an external object (Aucouturier, 2002).

The caregivers arrange the playrooms and, apart from their formal nursing functions, practice an attitude of watchful presence and non-intervention. It is precisely because the caregivers resist the temptation to interfere in the children's activities, and refrain from attempts to lead the activities, or to actively stimulate the children with their own suggestions, that the play becomes a real learning situation. This "wait-and-see" attitude gives the children plenty of time, encourages them to look for and find their own solutions, to not give up when things get difficult, and to build up a motoric conviction of their own competence and self-efficacy.

Studies carried out with the support of the World Health Organization (WHO) between 1968 and 1970 on hundreds of former orphanage children (Tardos, 2003), as well as interviews with youths from the Pikler Institute (David and Appell, 1995), and lecture manuscripts from the Pikler-Lóczy Symposium 2003 in Budapest, bear out convincingly that the acknowledgment of the child's need to engage their own development, via their bodily movement experience, contributes substantially to the foundation of emotional robustness, known to specialists as "resilience."

## Conclusions for the Practice of Body Psychotherapy

Many years of experience at the Pikler Institute confirm that the immediate and unspoiled relationship of human beings to their own organism is not necessarily lost after birth. As Body Psychotherapists, we encounter legitimate and reality-adjusted adaptations to a deficient familial and social situation during early formative periods, without access to any precise information as to the basis of the inherent, unconscious motoric convictions that—alongside verbal and visual encodings—seem to have a life of their own. In therapeutic practice, we are frequently confronted with the question of how the reanimation of impaired structures of primal life organization can be achieved, and how early motoric patternings, bound up with deeply buried wishes, unconscious conflicts, and guilt feelings, can be recognized in their symbolic significance, and resolved within the therapeutic context.

Stronger recognition is needed of an organismic perspective about living systems that appreciates their capacity to create autonomous rhythms that function as inner rhythms independently of external stimuli, as a fundamental matrix of autonomous processes (von Uexküll et al., 1997). Wölfl (2001, pp. 136ff.) draws attention to initial therapeutic successes with hyperactive children, whose impaired self-regulation, boundary setting, and communication skills could be improved through developing and rediscovering both their own rhythms and also the rhythms of others.

Body Psychotherapists, too, are increasingly experimenting with the therapeutic structuring of spaces for relating, and for retrospective development, that correspond to the pre-verbal level of experience. Through innumerable studies in German-speaking countries, Ludwig Janus has furthered the scientific conceptualization of a therapeutic practice that turns its attention to the events before, during, and after birth, with the intention of experiencing anew critical phases of psycho-genetic development in a secure environment, thus facilitating the recognition and working through of blocked motor developments in all their symbolic consequences (Janus, 2000).

What kind of faculties and psycho-motor competencies are foundational for human freedom of choice? This is a question we need to ask ourselves if—as psychotherapists—we work toward establishing and reviving the experience of self-efficacy. How can body-oriented therapy introduce and support an awareness of the capacity for autonomous action and physiological agency, or authorship? Successful reorganization of affective-motor patterns requires that we go beyond the level of analytic interpretation, or bioenergetic work on body armor. Taken on their own, these are not sufficient to counter effectively the deep-seated alienation from their bodies that human beings experience when their early biography has been characterized by deficits in the holding environment. It is more important to develop innovative somatic strategies, and to revive fundamental ethical positions:

- In order to restore the connection with the intelligence of the body and to release the healing power of spontaneous liveliness, which in turn promotes the development of autonomy, what is needed, rather than guidance, is an understanding and awakening of awareness in relation to the potentials that are already inherent in us and available to us: an invitation to entrust ourselves anew to the fund of vital knowledge contained in the age-old structures of the bone marrow, the nervous system, the movement of the breath, etc.

- For the alleviation of deep experiences of isolation and relief from primal fears, a trustworthy and bodily attentive therapeutic presence is indispensable. To be therapeutically effective, such a presence must go beyond the usual admonitions to rest in the here and now. It must mean an attitude of openness toward the unknown, a position free of judgment or analysis, free of the need to find a solution or attain a certain goal. This attitude should be based on respect and on trust in the other person's self-organization and, as such, engenders the deeper development of trust in turn.

Facilitating existential development requires the awareness and recognition of the "other" as a fellow human being, with their own original solutions for their development, and able to choose their own timing and directions of movements independently. Moreover, it is important to recognize and accept resistance, too, as a manifestation of individual autonomy. In this context, Gruen has pointed out that impulses toward autonomy reveal themselves not only in explicit rebellion, but also in passivity—for instance, when a well-behaved patient uses their adaptability to try to preserve some secret elbow-room (Gruen, 1992).

In order to free up dormant psycho-motor abilities that have been previously intimidated or undeveloped, and to ensure that impulses toward spontaneous, animated movement are not missed or overridden, it is necessary for the therapist to listen carefully to the client's nuances, and to sense their subtle bodily signals. The therapist must be willing to follow the patient into those subliminal spaces of experience where vague unease indicates a possibly unjustifiable feeling of somehow something being wrong in their world.

In a shared journey of somatic remembering with the patient, they sense their way to a phase of the client's life in which the world was apprehended through movement, through the musculature, and through touch. In the way a person moves, a certain facial expression or gesture, a sudden pause in the breathing, in the reaction to an unexpected touch, the feel or taste of a surprising experience, the therapist recognizes traces of the unspeakable intentions, much earlier and more frequently evidenced than in verbal communication. Body therapists know from their clinical experiences how the stimulation of the muscle or joint receptors can evoke spontaneous body memories, and how, at times, rotation or falling exercises can shake the patient's equilibrium to a degree that archaic feelings and early traumas resurface. Through the unusual kinesthetic experience of being rocked gently, deep truths can suddenly emerge: such as falling off the changing table, the isolation in the incubator, or the experience of being held and carried in infancy.

If the therapist, despite legitimately focusing on the pathological replication of experience and behavior on bodily and biographical levels, succeeds in remaining open to, and aware of, the skills, possibilities, and competencies of the other person, only then does he have his own autonomy at his disposal to a degree that enables him to enter into the give-and-take of authentic motoric dialogue. Through the therapist's mirroring, confirming, and responding to the most subtle motoric impulses, and through the repeated experience of having his freedom not only encouraged in principle, but trusted in practice, the patient ultimately arrives in a place of congruence with his present feelings and needs.

The therapist can now step aside, pull back, and become a witness, one who can help put into words those solutions that the patient has found for himself and that will continue to make him the agent of his own further change and maturation.

## References

Aucouturier, B. & Mendel, G. (2001). *Was bewegt ein Kind?* [What motivates a child?] Bremen: Ed. Doering.

Aucouturier, B. & Lapierre, A. (2002). *Die Symbolik der Bewegung* [The symbolism of the movement]. Basel: Reinhardt Verlag.

David, M. & Appell, G. (1995a). *Loczy—Mütterliche Betreuung ohne Mutter* [Loczy—Maternal care without a mother]. Munich: Cramer-Klett & Zeitler.

David, M. & Appell, G. (1995b). *Vortragsmanuskripte zum Pikler-Loczy-Symposion am 20- 22.3.2003 in Budapest* [Lecture manuscripts for Pikler-Loczy Symposium on 20- 22.3.2003 in Budapest.]

Dornes, M. (1992). *Der kompetente Säugling* [The competent infant]. Frankfurt/M.: Fischer.

Downing, G. (1996). *Körper und Wort in der Psychotherapie* [Body and Word in Psychotherapy]. Munich: Kösel.

Gallagher, S. & Cole, J. (1995). Body Schema and Body Image in a deafferented Subject. *Journal of Mind and Behavior, 16*, 369-390.

Gruen, A. (1992). *Der Wahnsinn der Normalität* [The insanity of normality]. München: DVT.

Hüther, G. (2002): Wohin, wofür, weshalb. In: K. Gebauer & G. Hüther, *Kinder suchen Orientierung* [Children need guidance]. Düsseldorf: Walter.

Janus, L. (2000). *Die Psychoanalyse der vorgeburtlichen Lebenszeit und der Geburt* [Psychoanalysis of prenatal life and birth]. Gießen: Psychosozial Verlag.

Kiphard, E.J. (1979). *Psychomotorik als Prävention und Rehabilitation* [Psychomotorics as prevention and rehabilitation]. Gütersloh: Flöttmann.

Kiphard, E.J. (1998). Psychomotorik als Meisterlehre [Psychomotics is a master teaching]. *Motorik 21 (3)*. Schorndorf: Karl Hofmann Verlag.

Piaget, J. (1975). *Das Erwachen der Intelligenz beim Kinde* [The awakening of intelligence in children]. Stuttgart: Klett.

Pikler, E. (2001). *Lasst mir Zeit* [Give me time]. Munich: Pflaum.

Pikler, E. & Tardos, A. (1994). *Miteinander vertraut werden* [Become familiar with each other]. Freiamt: Arbor Verlag.

Scheid, V. (1989). *Bewegung und Entwicklung im Kleinkindalter* [Movement and development in childhood]. Schorndorf: Karl Hofmann Verlag.

Schilling, F. (1977). Bewegungsentwicklung, Bewegungsbehinderung und das Konzept der Erziehung durch Bewegung [Motor development, mobility disability and the concept of education through movement]. *Sportwissenschaft, 7(4)*, 315ff.

Seewald, J. (2000). Durch Bewegung zur Identität? [Moving to an identity?] *Motorik, 23(9)*. Schorndorf: Karl Hofmann Verlag.

Sloterdijk, P. (1998). *Sphären 1, Blasen* [Spheres 1: Bubbles]. Frankfurt: Suhrkamp.

Stern, D. (1992). *Die Lebenserfahrung des Säuglings* [The life of the infant]. Stuttgart: Klett-Cotta.

Szanto-Feder, A. (2002). *Loczy: Un nouveau paradigme?* [Loczy: A new paradigm?] Paris: Presses Universitaires de France.

Tardos, A. (2003). *Vortrag zum Thema: Die seelische Widerstandskraft des Kindes, das Konzept der Resilienz* [Lecture on the mental toughness of the child, the concept of resilience]. 28.11. 2003 in Frankfurt.

Thelen, E. & Smith, L.B. (2002). *A Dynamic Systems Approach to the Development of Cognition and Action*. Cambridge: MIT Press.

Tronick, E. (1998). Dyadically expanded states of consciousness and the process of therapeutic change. *Infant Mental Health Journal 19(3), 290-299*.

von Uexküll, T., Fuchs, T., Müller-Braunschweig, H. & Johnen, R. (1997). *Subjektive Anatomie: Theorie und Praxis körperbezogener Psychotherapie* [Subjective Anatomy: theory and practice of body-related psychotherapy]. Stuttgart: Schattauer.

Winnicott, D. W. (1974). *Reifungsprozesse und fördernde Umwelt* [Maturation processes and facilitating environment]. Munich: Kindler.

Winnicott, D. W. (1976). *Von der Kinderheilkunde zur Psychoanalyse* [From pediatrics to psychoanalysis]. Munich: Kindler.

Wölfl, A. (2001). Rhythmische Strukturen in Entwicklungsprozessen [Rhythmic structures in development processes]. In: M. Passolt (Ed.), *Hyperaktivität* [Hyperactivity]. Munich: Ernst Reinhardt.

# SECTION V

## Methodological Foundations

# 36

## Introduction to Section V

Gustl Marlock, Germany, and Halko Weiss, United States

Translation by Warren Miller

The chapters in Section V all call attention to a range of different perspectives about an essential characteristic of Body Psychotherapy, a characteristic that has been described using terms such as "experience-oriented," "experience-activating," and "experience-intensifying."

The traditional hallmarks of Psychodynamic Therapy—self-perception, self-reflection, and self-development—are coupled together, over long periods, with movement, bodily experience, dynamic enactments, real gestures and behaviors, as well as with autonomous vegetative processes. Combined, they constitute the dimension of direct experience, which is very deeply grounded in the body. It must be pointed out that the therapeutic processes of Body Psychotherapy cannot be properly understood if these experiential processes are not examined. Furthermore, a large part of the efficacy of Body Psychotherapy is due precisely to the fact that great attention is paid to the multitude of inputs, the different levels of awareness, and the fine interactions of these different components. This gives them an immediacy that differs quite strongly from more cognitively oriented processes.

Of course, the immediate somatic experience has always had its place in the major traditions of psychotherapy, but in a different way. Psychoanalysis, with its focus on the momentary flow of the attention process and on the transferential experience, seeks to ground interpretations and insight in what the client can sense and feel in the moment. Still, most of the work is done as a "top-down" process, as a neuropsychologist would frame these approaches today (van der Kolk, 1994), where memories and narrative recall are processed from the beginning. Body Psychotherapy is almost always approached with a "bottom-up" process, wherein body sensations and movement impulses are explored first, then the emotions, with cognitive meaning-making following after (Fisher and Ogden, 2009).

Cognitive Behavioral Therapy certainly has claimed a firm methodological grounding in the body as well. However, its approach is traditionally concerned with directing learning processes, especially if there is an immediate problem with the body, like managing somatic arousal states, biofeedback, sexual or dysmorphic disorders, and changing the body image. In contrast, Body Psychotherapy understands the body as a general and primary medium for the therapeutic process, and usually supports lingering, deepening, and exploring bodily experience, so that the client can find deeper roots in the somatic realm, start an understanding of its language, and heal through somatic interventions.

**Gustl Marlock,** in Chapter 37, "Sensory Self-Reflexivity: Therapeutic Action in Body Psychotherapy," characterizes the basic working mode of Body Psychotherapy as being a form of sensory self-reflection. He makes reference to the traditions of Sensory Awareness, and **Halko Weiss** builds upon this in Chapter 38, "Consciousness, Awareness, Mindfulness," by elaborating on the central role that consciousness and awareness have for many Body Psychotherapy approaches. This has become more obvious as some of these have also embraced the concept of mindfulness—Hakomi Therapy, in particular, which developed its mindfulness-centered method in the 1970s.

Against this backdrop, **Ron Kurtz,** the founder of Hakomi, describes in Chapter 39 how "Bodily Expression and Experience" are connected in psychotherapy, and how they form some of the basic elements of Body Psychotherapy. The somatic perspective is dealt with further in Chapter 40, "The Experiencing Body," by **Halko Weiss,** describing the body as being the medium of experience.

**Christine Caldwell,** one of the directors of Naropa University in Boulder, Colorado, then illustrates the significance of movement in the process of Body Psychotherapy in Chapter 41, "Movement As and In Psychotherapy," and she exemplifies how movement alone can be a form of psychotherapy by helping the body—and therefore ourselves—to recover, heal, and even transform.

The main methodological concept that underlies **Al Pesso**'s work is that psychodynamic realities structurally have a dramatic form and are tinged by early object-relations. He shows in Chapter 42, "*When* Is Now? When Is *Now*?": Corrective Experiences: With Whom? When? And Where?" how a therapeutic dramaturgy of the unconscious can unfold from bodily experience.

Finally, **Michael Randolph** describes, in Chapter 43, "On Vitality"—written in a literary style that suits this topic—an aspect that many consider *the* key element of Body Psychotherapeutic processes: the restoration of "aliveness."

## References

Fisher, J. & Ogden, P. (2009). Sensorimotor Therapy. In: C. A. Courtois & J. D. Ford (Eds.), *Treating complex traumatic stress disorders.* New York: Guilford Press.

van der Kolk, B. A. (1994). The body keeps the score: Memory and the evolving psychobiology of posttraumatic stress. *Harvard Review of Psychiatry, 1, 253–265.*

# 37

## Sensory Self-Reflexivity

*Therapeutic Action in Body Psychotherapy*

**Gustl Marlock, Germany**

**Translation by Warren Miller and Michael Soth**

**Gustl Marlock**'s biographical information can be found at the beginning of Chapter 1, the Preface to this handbook.

One of the central intentions of psychodynamic and Body Psychotherapeutic practice can be described as an attempt to shed "light" onto the "darkness" of unconscious forces and constellations. Modern ideas of the unconscious can be traced back to romanticism, which equated the realm of the unconscious with night. Romantic thought considered the experience of night as an opportunity to explore a domain that eludes the brightness of Logos-oriented thought (Carus, 1846; Sanchez, 1986).

Without delving into metaphysics, ideas about the "light of consciousness" have existed ever since human beings first strove to understand themselves and the world. We find these ideas throughout mysticism and philosophy in Asia as well as in classical Western philosophy. Through the Enlightenment period and the practical successes of scientism, the light of cognition became more and more strongly reduced to pure rationality. Descartes famously held that pure knowledge could be acquired only after sensory perceptions are excluded.

In developing his practice of interpretation, Freud closely followed this tradition of elevating pure rationality, although his theory of the unconscious was inspired by romanticism and somatic philosophy (Carus, 1846; Schopenhauer, 1918; and others) and their critical attitude toward rationality. Freud's ego-id polarization stands in the tradition of Western rationalism, which Nietzsche had already criticized at the time. Based on an analysis of the myth of Ulysses, Horkheimer and Adorno (1969) later illustrated how the deepest layers of Western cultural history are based on a celebration of control through the mind at the expense of the vitality and the sensuality of the body.

It is interesting to note that, in his attempt to distinguish his own Gestalt therapeutic approach from traditional psychoanalytic practice (not picked up by and reflected much in the secondary literature), Fritz Perls referred back to the metaphor of light (Perls et al., 1981). When speaking of light in terms of the therapeutic process, he emphasizes the difference between a light source—such as a neon lamp, shedding light on things from the outside—and a situation where the light comes from within. He compared the light of the Gestalt therapeutic process to that of a glowing coal. By using this metaphor, Perls was trying to show that he did not emphasize rational understanding, thinking about oneself, and *self-objectifying* insights. Rather, he focused on *awareness* and *becoming aware,* characterized by *contact, sense perception,* and *excitement,* as the conceptual and practical center of Gestalt Therapy.

In 1951, Perls, Hefferline, and Goodman had already given a visionary description of therapy as a progressive process of awareness and growth, based less on rational insights and understanding, but on *sensing and feeling* oneself. This constitutes the core of what in professional jargon is referred to as "experiential activation" or "experiential orientation." The emphasis is on the subject, who is experiencing *through* the senses and sensations.

Perls and Goodman here are formulating the clearest description of Body Psychotherapy's fundamental mode of working and its basic principle. This modus operandi underpins all therapeutic work with the conflictual and relational dimensions of the body. It is an essential underlying principle that—interestingly—is not theoretically obvious and transparent throughout all schools of Body Psychotherapy. The importance of the fact that the body is approached primarily through the experiential mode of "sensing," and the categorical difference this establishes in contrast to the "talking therapies," has remained implicit and somewhat hidden, not so much in terms of practice, but unformulated on a theoretical level, especially by those Body Psychotherapeutic approaches that emphasize the energetic and conflictual or relational aspects of the work. In clearly illuminating these correlations, Gestalt Therapy has explicated—on behalf of the rest of the field—the basic principles and characteristics of a therapeutic mode of working grounded in sense perception and awareness. To highlight the significance of this mode for Body Psychotherapy conceptually, we could refer to it as a process of *sensory self-reflexivity*.[37]

The fact that Perls became known for the theory and practice of awareness is sometimes attributed to the influence of Zen Buddhism. Perls's conceptualization of Gestalt Therapy was, however, well established prior to his visit to Kyoto and his involvement with the early Gestalt movement at the Esalen Institute in the 1960s, where he was inspired by Alan Watts's "translation" of Zen for the West.

The meditation and awareness practices of Zen, with their nonescapist emphasis on presence, share similarities with many aspects of the awareness practice of Gestalt Therapy. Although Zen has a much richer tradition and is more puristic and elaborate than the equivalent Gestalt practices in the "here and now," modern Psychodynamic Psychology has a better grasp of the reasons why success is so scarce in human striving toward *presence;* this is due not only to a lack of discipline, but mainly to the fact that humans are emotionally caught up in unresolved scenes of the "there and then." The *awareness continuum* of Gestalt Therapy certainly echoes the attempt of Zen to counteract the human illusion of a solid, identifiable ego by means of mindful, contemplative concentration on the flow of present experience.

In a discussion of the therapeutic practice of Sensory Awareness or sensory self-reflexivity, there are, however, two other important historical Western sources of influence that must be mentioned: first, Elsa Gindler and her student Charlotte Selver; and second, Wilhelm Reich.

Seven decades before the Zen Buddhist monk Thich Nhat Hanh became known in the West for his slow, walking meditation, Elsa Gindler had developed a method of somatic education in Berlin that focused on creating awareness through slow and conscious movement and sensory experiencing. Reluctant to give her teaching a name, she called it "work on the human being." Elsa Gindler did not want her practice to become understood as a method. She held that the cultivation of awareness works best when it is not practiced as a means to an end. She taught a simple principle of sensory perception: attending to the somatic process throughout the day—sitting, standing, speaking, or remaining silent—how movements and actions occur and whether there are more optimal ways of doing the same things that could be less tiring and more vitalizing. According to Gindler, the full functionality of the body could be developed only by means of complete concentration and attention. The goal of her work was to unfold the vital "responsiveness" (Antwortbereitschaft) of the body. Elsa Gindler's work hinges on a central principle that is a constitutional element in almost all somatic educational systems, ranging from Feldenkrais to Alexander—namely, that the real learning processes unfold through sensing and through sensory perception. This principle can also be found at the heart of Marianne Fuchs's (1994) theory and practice of Funktionelle Entspannung (Functional Relaxation), as well as Helmuth Stolze's (1989)

---

37  I want to thank the Gestalt therapist Hans Peter Dreitzel of Berlin for his far-reaching inspirations that underlie the fusion of these two terms. He has written one of the best books on Gestalt Therapy (1992)

Konzentrative Bewegungstherapie (Focused Movement Therapy).

Forced into exile, Gindler's most famous student, Charlotte Selver, continued Gindler's work in the United States and developed it further under the name "Sensory Awareness," which is now a well-known approach. The programmatic title underscores the relationship between bodily experience and awareness. We could formulate the core message of the tradition of somatic education as a variation of a popular motto: an "alert" mind requires an "alert" body. The key point of Selver's practice was to promote the awakening of the body through the revitalization of its senses: hearing, smelling, tasting, sensing, and touching. Erich Fromm, Fritz Perls, and, interestingly, also Alan Watts were among Selver's early students.

The second source of the theory and practice of sensory reflexivity is Wilhelm Reich. This may come as a surprise, as Reich's practice did not emphasize the kind of mindful, introspective awareness practice, often via slowed-down movement, as propagated by Gindler, Selver, and others. His approach was much more characterized by confrontational impatience and, more importantly, a totally different objective. Reich was aiming at the dissolving of characterological muscular armoring and the establishment of the psychosomatic capacity for sexual surrender. This difference in orientation and goals is not insignificant: although there are some similarities between Gindler and Reich—both, for example, were interested in the reestablishment of natural breathing—there are fundamental divergences between these two approaches. Gindler's and Selver's practice facilitated the unfolding of the self via sensory *learning processes*—i.e., an approach focused on learning. Reich's work, in contrast, was based on a medical frame of reference, viewing the body more from an objectifying perspective in terms of pathology (armoring) and health (orgiastic potency). As a result, his treatment was less oriented toward his patients' subjective experience but was guided instead by intervention-oriented "objective" parameters, such as defense and resistance, and normative notions of health. Reich's objectifying tendency carried over into the Neo-Reichian approaches—something that was vehemently criticized by the Gestalt tradition, which tried to counter these tendencies by emphatically insisting on the self-regulation of the patient. And it was, therefore, Gestalt Therapy that was capable of formulating the recognition that awareness *subjectifies* the body and the therapeutic process—a recognition that is nevertheless essential to all modern Body Psychotherapy.

## Contact and Contactlessness

There is, however, one theoretical aspect of Reich's work that had a significant impact on Perls, and the subsequent development of Gestalt Therapy: Reich's theory of *contactlessness,* as a result of bodily character-armoring, is of central importance in understanding sensory self-reflexivity and its theoretical foundations. In a chapter entitled "Psychic Contact and Vegetative Flow," added to a later (1971) edition of his classic book, *Character Analysis,* Reich describes a number of phenomena associated with characterological armoring: first, the repression of needs and motivations (at the time still referred to as the "demands" of instinctual drives); second, the repressing defense forces; and third, a phenomenon he called "contactlessness."

Contactlessness refers to a patient's—often superficially masked—lack of relational contact with himself and with his environment. The patient experiences contactlessness as a *physiological lack of feeling, inner isolation,* and *inner deadness* (Reich, 1971). Reich describes his observations of *blockages of affect* and *lack of feeling* and sees a connection between them and contactlessness and the concept of dissociation. "Similar conditions of the blocking of the affects or of the development of contactlessness were encountered during the war. They were described by political prisoners who had been subjected to terrorist treatment" (Ibid., p. 313).

Reich hinted at, but did not further develop, the correlations between traumatic experience, contactlessness, and dissociation. Although the significance of these correlations for therapy will be elaborated later, what is relevant here is that the psychic contactlessness described by Reich (and later by Gestalt Therapy) corresponds to a somatic "senselessness" and lack of sensation. This inability to sense the body is caused by the blockage of bodily mobility and sensitivity and expresses itself in subtle or massive "psychic dulling" and "impairment of one's activities and objective interests" (Ibid., p. 316).

Following this premise, the reestablishment of embodiment—the ability to sense one's body and to make contact with one's experience and then contact others from within that experience—can be formulated as a central goal of the therapeutic process and, at the same time, as the therapeutic path *toward* that goal. In the world of contemporary psychotherapy, this approach is still unusual and is even considered strange, as illustrated by the reports of well-trained and practicing therapists who—in the context of workshops on *Funktionelle Entspannung* (Functional Relaxation)—are taking their first steps in sensory exploration and beginning to contemplate their experiences with their own bodily selves:

> For the physicians . . . the experience of their own bodies was a surprise: they discovered that they had entered into foreign territory. This was not the continent of somatic medicine they were familiar with. It also was not the continent of psychological medicine, whose relationship with the continent of somatic medicine has always been puzzling and remains unsolved. In the land of their own body, they experienced feelings and entered spaces which they had never before noticed or entered. They began to sense the vastness of a mysterious landscape with unknown borders. (Uexküll et al., 1994, p. vii)

The majority of traditional psychotherapies—the "talking therapies"—are based on a working mode characterized by somewhat distanced self-observation, rational self-reflection, and *self-objectification*. These processes do not take place via feeling, sensing, or "being" in contact with the bodily self. The emotional suffering that brings people into therapy amplifies this tendency toward distanced self-objectification: in an attempt to avoid pain, we remain distant from our own experience and feeling, taking an *instrumental* stance vis-à-vis our own psychosomatic reality. It is one of the rarely acknowledged secrets of the profession that—therapeutically speaking—there is nothing to be gained from this distancing. The relational stance that we are implicitly taking toward our embodied experience is crucial to the process, and largely unacknowledged. Elsa Gindler has criticized this widespread instrumental stance taken by both clients and therapists:

> In general, people tend to think: "If I do my relaxation exercises, I am relaxed; if I am able to do the breathing exercises, I can breathe; when I make energetic movements, I am moving vibrantly; and when I am making an effort to correct bow-legs or knock-knees, they will be straight." This is not true, and we invariably see failure resulting from these kinds of naive assumptions. (Gindler, 1995, p. 6)

This is the case not only in relation to physical sensations and symptoms; the same is true in relation to emotional states: when strong emotions and affects arise, the clients' relationship to themselves and their bodies tends to remain instrumental. To allow the expression of emotions—perhaps it would be better here to speak of *creating space* for emotional expression—is different from discharging emotions in order to feel better. The significance of this subtle distinction will be further elaborated later with references to Pierre Janet and contemporary trauma research.

## Having a Body—Being a Body

Originally, three approaches of Body Psychotherapy emphasized and further elaborated the fundamental importance of sensed contact, awareness, and sensory self-reflexivity: Konzentrative Bewegungstherapie (Focused Movement Therapy: Stolze), Funktionelle Entspannung (Functional Relaxation: Fuchs), and Gestalt Therapy (Perls and others). Among the more recent approaches, the Hakomi Method (Kurtz), Integrative Leibtherapie (Integrative Somatic Therapy: Petzold), and Unitive Body

Psychotherapy (Stattman) have built upon the Gestalt tradition, accentuating certain aspects. The last two explicitly draw upon existentialism and somatic philosophy, as elaborated by Gabriel Marcel (Marcel, 1985). Marcel's sophisticated philosophy differentiates between *being a body* (in German: "Leib," i.e., soma) and *having a body*.[38]

The latter can become the object of abstract observations, whereas the former can reveal itself only in the immanence of present-moment awareness. According to Marcel, when "being embodied" becomes objectified into "having" a body, the inner unity of being—what some call the soul—fragments. It fragments into an ego that appears to exist by merely postulating and asserting itself, but is nowhere to be found; it also fragments into an assortment of psychic and bodily faculties and capabilities owned by the ego and ascribed to it.

The reason why humans seem to prefer the instrumental "having" mode of relating to themselves over the "being" mode, Marcel suggests, is that the fact of embodiment (incarnation) constitutes a primal situation, which "strictly speaking, cannot be controlled or mastered, and is not even available for analysis" (Ibid., p. 17).

## Body, Defense, and Structure

Having problematized the self-objectifying distancing process from the perspective of existential experience and philosophy, we can return to the clinical context: modern Depth Psychology (Psychodynamic Psychotherapy) approaches this dissociative distancing phenomenon—which constitutes for many people their daily modus of being—as a "defense," and we know since Reich that all defenses are rooted in the body and have a somatic foundation. Whether we use the traditional term "body/mind split," or "disembodiment" in its most general form, a person's defensive relationship to his or her own body pervades their moment-to-moment relationship to all kinds of somatic experience: restricted sensitivity, lack of feeling, and numbness to the point that entire regions of the body disappear from consciousness—all are basic forms of contact avoidance, or contact loss. George Downing, who has described the various forms of body defense in the most comprehensive and systematic fashion, refers to this in general as *kinesthetic avoidance* (Downing, 1996), a defensive operation designed to avoid awareness and perception of painful, frightening, conflictual, or stressful aspects of emotional reality. All that remains are merely vague ego-dystonic background affects, which the rest of the person—mistakenly identified as the self—struggles against. It is one of the fundamental ideas of Depth Psychology (Psychodynamic Psychotherapy) that this kind of internal configuration constitutes preconscious and unconscious conflict: it is what we recognize as the intrapsychic *dynamic* aspect of the pervasive embodied defense against all kinds of moods, vitality affects, emotions, and feelings.

Our understanding of the disorders of the self, and the various forms that conflictual and painful relations to the self take, has been enhanced by recent discussions regarding the structural levels of psychological disorders, particularly in the German-speaking countries (Rudolf et al., 2002). A typological differentiation between conflict-neurotic disorders on the one hand and structural disorders (sometimes also referred to in popular therapy language as "early disorders") on the other, is, of course, based on a rather broad schematization; in reality, the two aspects of conflict and structure are interwoven in multiple ways. In his contribution to an earlier edition of this handbook, Hans-Joachim Maaz shared clinical observations that support the notion that after sufficient emotional depth is reached within the therapeutic process, it becomes apparent that, below the level of neurotic conflict, we invariably find structural deficits due to past failures in the provi-

---

38 Whereas Hilarion Petzold has highlighted the notion of soma (Leib) for good reason, others have kept the term "body" even though it leaves the distinction that Marcel speaks of linguistically undifferentiated. One likely reason for this was the fact that soma (Leib) has not been a term quite without context. Its use reaches back into the miserabilistic history of discourse in Christianity in which soma (der Leib) is associated with the crucified Jesus, whereas normal mortals and the dying were thought of as having "bodies" that were the source of sin and evil in the flesh. These connotations of the term soma (Leib) are therefore in contradiction to the originally clearly hedonistic orientation of Body Psychotherapy.

sion of basic needs. The differentiation between neurotic conflict and structural disturbance is nonetheless useful, and helps us understand more deeply and accurately both bodily defenses and the therapeutic process in general.

The "neurotic-conflictual" level describes a spectrum of psychological suffering that is characterized by blockages in terms of impulses, action, and expression. Due to wounding experiences in early development, behavior is overshadowed by conflict: neurotic compromise consists of an internal organization whereby the person's needs, fantasies, emotions, and behavioral impulses are habitually repressed and denied, due to a fear that these will lead to interpersonal conflict. Ambivalence and a lack of expressiveness, both emotionally as well as behaviorally, are the inevitable consequences and symptoms.

The origins and traditional theories of Body Psychotherapy are oriented toward this neurotic level of psychological pathology, as well as a greater part of Body Psychotherapy's methodological repertoire. On this level, dominated by inhibition and repression, cathartic and expressive methods have both rationale and justification, and Body Psychotherapy has been able to decisively expand psychodynamic theory. A few examples shall clarify this point further:

- Character theory—by addressing holding patterns, postures, and their associated affective-motor schemas—has opened up an embodied perspective on psychological conflicts and how they operate and are maintained: internalized object-relations can be seen to derive their strength and intransigence from the *kinesthetic avoidance* mentioned above—i.e., psychosomatic defenses against emotions, and their associated motor aspects of inhibition, avoidance, and fear.

- Whereas the topological model of psychoanalysis considers the totality of all inhibiting and repressing forces to be located in the superego, Body Psychotherapy has predominantly described this phenomenon as a "turning against the self" (Johnson, 1994)—i.e., aggressive motoric forces that are directed against the self. This perspective facilitates much more dynamic ways of working through than do the necessary, but limited, verbal-mental discovery process and analysis of superego components. Gestalt Therapy has made an important contribution to dynamic theory and practice by explicating the mechanism of retroflection: what psychoanalysis calls the superego derives its force from turning aggressive impulses against the self; in terms of technique, Gestalt has demonstrated how such inhibiting retroflections can be turned back into expressivity through the use of "two-chair" work and other dramatic methods.

- Finally, Body Psychotherapy has accumulated elaborate knowledge regarding the completion of *emotional cycles*. Neurotic conflict and inhibition can be understood as embodied impulses that were interrupted and remain chronically stuck and incomplete. Working through neurotic repression can then be equated with the completion of these interrupted cycles; this can range from the expression of feelings (Lowen), to corrective emotional experiences (Pesso), to the rebalancing of autonomic arousal and its "digestion" (Boyesen).

In addressing this conflictual level of psychological suffering therapeutically, catharsis has its role, but even then we still have to rely significantly on sensory reflexivity. What Gestalt terms "retroflection" is a collection of unconscious, often subtle, bodily operations that George Downing refers to as "countermobilization." These affective-motor schemas and habitualized bodily micropractices cannot be resolved through expressive work alone. Sensory exploration is necessary to make these patterns accessible to consciousness before fundamental revision and change become possible.

Following Reich, Perls emphasized that the expansion of awareness is best facilitated through inquiry into the "*how*" of psychosomatic configurations and their origins, rather than by asking "where from?" and "why?" *How* do people, for example, prevent themselves from crying? *How* does that happen? Do they hold their breath? Do they clench their teeth? Are they "being brave" by tensing the muscles of the trunk, arms, and neck?

Stanley Keleman (1985) has developed one of the most elaborate Body Psychotherapy curricula, based upon a dedicated exploration of the "how" of bodily self-organization. Only through the "felt experience" of "how" a person organizes his or her "self-states," and how these are rooted in physical experience as affective-motor components of the personality, can we shed light on the somatic aspects of unconscious processes. Only this kind of increased awareness can create the possibility for choice and freedom, an understanding that is at the core of how Gestalt defines the concept of "responsibility": only on the basis of new embodied experience can new possibilities of attitude and behavior be discovered, which then opens up new "response-abilities" in a meaningful and nonmoralizing way.

## Dissociation and Association

The significance of Sensory Awareness and reflexivity becomes even more evident when we go beyond the neurotic-conflictual level toward working with so-called "structural disturbances" (or "disturbances of the self"), which refers to difficulties and deficits in emotional regulation, deriving from psychological wounding at formative developmental stages. On this level, psychic suffering results less from the experience of blocked feelings and behavior than from the "behaviors of others that are difficult to bear" (Rudolf, 2004, p. 51).

A therapeutic approach focusing on repression-expression, a sense of agency, and behavioral choices is unlikely to understand and meet this domain of experience, as suffering originates from a sense of being and an unbearable object-world (both internally and externally). Inner states of feeling, agitation, and unbearable tension are triggered through withdrawal of attention, insufficient validation, denial of gratification, or abusive behavior by others, and lead to angry, reactive attacks on the environment, or to flight and withdrawal (Ibid.).

These formulations suggest similarities between this structural level of disturbance and the dynamics of traumatic experiences. Recent theories on narcissistic and borderline disorders describe the defense mechanism of "splitting" as a central feature. When differentiating "splitting" from neurotic defense mechanisms, it becomes apparent that, whereas neurotic conflicts involve the classical repressive superego, splitting does not; instead, denial and splitting fragment the whole structure of the self. Such dissociation can occur when aspects of the self seem unbearable or impossible to integrate, or if they were, and are, unloved.

From the perspective of Body Psychotherapy, splitting always involves a mechanism of kinesthetic avoidance. This form of body defense is particularly important for a sound understanding of narcissistic processes. George Downing (1996) has developed the concept of visual body image construction to address the narcissistic orientation toward the idealized self, manifested as ego ideal and self-image, recognizing that the central reference point in relating to the self is not the actual "lived-in" body, but rather a mental construction. This may explain the fragility and inner peril that characterize the narcissistic position, and also the clinical fact that the unacknowledged suffering of narcissistic personality styles often manifests somatically, experienced as vague fragility, hypochondria, or psychosomatic illness. The pain and cries for help do not manage to reach beyond the somatic level and therefore fail to become associated with the rest of the self.

Psychodynamic theories of personality disorders have shown the severity of dissociation in disturbances of the self. Self Psychology, in particular, has emphasized the lacking cohesion of the self as a key feature of the "structural disorders," exposing vulnerable patients to intense dangers of fragmentation. Etiologically, it can be assumed that early disturbances made it difficult for the child to experience stable self-states of wholeness, reaching back to pre-verbal and primitive developmental stages that are difficult to grasp through a psychodynamic perspective, but will have to be understood on the basis of an embodied developmental psychology of the body, which has yet to be elaborated.

However, in a significant and much-underestimated article on the fundamental principles of bodily development, Petra Grohmann and Andreas Richter describe how basic bodily cohesion and integration grow out of relational resonance phenomena during early infancy (Grohmann and Richter, 1993). They describe how the circulatory and metabolic pulsations in the prenatal child's organism vibrate in nearly complete resonance with the organism of the mother.

After birth, it is during times when the child is being held and fed that these phases of resonance occur. "The rhythms that are stabilized in this manner become the body's own rhythms during times of slumber" (Ibid., p. 125).

During this early developmental phase, the child's brainstem receives converging feedback about the state of the inner organs, as well as still unspecific feedback from the sense organs of the skin, muscular tone, joint positions (proprioception), and the vestibular system. The brainstem regulates and integrates fundamental life processes such as digestion, metabolism and transport of energy, respiration, etc., by utilizing its ability to receive incoming signals and to bundle and integrate them into a unified vibration, which prevents sensory overload. Grohmann and Richter point out that during this phase the child's organism has particular developmental needs in accordance with the functions of the brainstem:

> If these needs are met, a basic rhythm of auto-regulation is established and reinforced frequently. If these needs are not met or there is a delay in meeting them, the basic rhythm remains labile. Needs that foster stabilization are for food, regular and adequate satiation, distinct, close and attentive physical contact, as well as being held, carried and cradled through movements that provide consistent vibrant stimulation of the sense of balance. (Ibid.)

These explanations provide some indication as to how basic experiences of cohesion are developed and stabilized and how they are linked to the pre-verbal regulation of basic developmental needs. Although it would be a misunderstanding to draw reductionist or causal conclusions from these indications, they nonetheless suggest that, from the very beginning, cohesive states of self are constituted via bodily experience and sensations. With structural disturbances, especially in their psychosomatic manifestations, it is this early domain of experience that has been detrimentally affected.

In summary, therapeutic paradigms based exclusively on repression—as classical psychoanalysis and sections of the Body Psychotherapeutic field have been and continue to be—are unlikely to match and meet this early structural level of psychological pathology: disturbances of the self and their corresponding primitive defense mechanisms always involve (or are functionally identical with) disturbed connections to the embodied self, manifesting as an inability to cope with, tolerate, and integrate painful experiences and feelings of injury and hurt, rooted in self-states that involve unbearable bodily sensations that cannot be processed mentally, let alone verbally. Splitting mechanisms indicate that we are not dealing with inhibition and repression of felt impulses, but with *dissociation* of unbearable parts of the self—i.e., affects, emotions, and experiences that threaten both the subjective and organismic sense of cohesion and integrity.

In the earliest version of psychoanalysis, Breuer and Freud, probably influenced by Janet, considered dissociation to be a *resistance against association,* directed against feelings of shame, psychic pain, and a sense of impairment (Breuer and Freud, 1895, p. 268). Reviewing the history of this key phase of modern Psychodynamic Psychology, Bessel van der Kolk was able to show that Janet and some of his important contemporaries, such as James, Piaget, Jung, and Myers, had misgivings about the therapeutic value of catharsis and discharge (van der Kolk et al., 1996, p. 53). As splitting and dissociation indicate that—prior to any work toward expression—a *reassociation* of painful, previously unbearable, and overwhelming affects is needed, thus emphasizing the therapeutic importance of synthesis and integration. Resolution of dissociative contactlessness cannot occur through catharsis, but instead requires *sensing* and *feeling*—i.e., the development of sensory reflexivity. On the part of the therapist, this calls for empathy, compassion, and containment via the ability to create a secure, sustaining environment, rather than for interpretive or energetic skills.

## Loss of Contact and Holes in the Personality

In the preface to the second edition of *Gestalt Therapy,* published in America in 1969, Fritz Perls called attention to the far-reaching repercussions caused by a dissociative loss of contact with the body, or any of its parts and functions. According to Perls, the conflict between our biological and our societal existence, the inability to be who we are, does not primarily manifest in ever more internal conflicts, but leads to pathological states that appear as *holes* in the personality (Perls et al., 1981, p. 8). The loss of contact with the body and the consequent holes in the personality, which also become apparent in projective diagnostic assessments, leave some people "without legs," and limited agency and autonomy. Some people "don't have a spine"; some "don't have ears" and can't listen; some "don't have eyes" and therefore constantly feel observed and judged. As for social relationships, Perls considered the loss of sensory contact with the ears as most debilitating. He writes:

> Those who don't have ears usually find themselves in the company of people who talk and talk and expect that all the world listens. Such people use the expressions of others merely as a prompt for their own reply, if indeed they listen enough to even pick up on that. (Ibid.)

When some people—due to their dissociation and contactlessness—suffer from a "hole" in place of their heart, they tend to believe that there is no such thing as true love in the world. Such convictions are engrained and unshakable and therefore inaccessible to rational discourse. Through sensory experience and the re-association of feelings and qualities that are associated with the heart, therapeutic opportunities can be co-created that allow the person to experience a different reality within his or her own body. These experiences exemplify the contribution that Body Psychotherapy can make to the improvement of the human condition.

## References

Breuer, J., & Freud, S. (1895). Studien über Hysterie [Studies on hysteria]. In S. Freud (1999), *Gesammelte Werke [Collected works]*. Frankfurt, Germany: Fischer.

Carus, C. G. (1846). *Psyche [Spirit]*. Leipzig: Kröner.

Downing, G. (1996). *Körper und Wort in der Psychotherapie [Body and word in psychotherapy]*. Munich: Kösel.

Dreitzel, H. (1992). *Reflexive Sinnlichkeit [Reflexive sensuality]. Cologne*: Edition Humanistische Psychologie.

Fuchs, M. (1994). *Funktionelle Entspannung: Theorie und Praxis eines körperbezogenen Psychotherapieverfahrens [Functional Relaxation: Theory and practice of body-related psychotherapy process]*. Stuttgart: Hippokrates.

Gindler, E. (1995). Gymnastics for people whose lives are full of activity. In D. H. Johnson (Ed.), *Bone, Breath, and Gesture*. Berkeley, CA: North Atlantic Books.

Grohmann, P., & Richter, A. (1993). Was ein Körpertherapeut über Entwicklung weis? [What does a body-oriented therapist know about development?]. In: G. Marlock (Ed.), *Weder Körper noch Geist [Neither body nor mind]*. Oldenburg: Transform.

Horkheimer, M., & Adorno, T. W. (1969). *Dialektik der Aufklärung [Dialectic of enlightenment]*. Frankfurt: Fischer.

Johnson, D. H. (1994). Body, Spirit and Democracy. Berkeley, CA: North Atlantic Books.

Keleman, S. (1985). Emotional Anatomy. Berkeley, CA: Centre Press.

Marcel, G. (1985). Leibliche Begegnung [Bodily encounter]. In H. Petzold (Ed.), *Leiblichkeit [Corporeality]*. Paderborn: Junfermann.

Perls, F., Hefferline, R., & Goodman, P. (1981). *Gestalttherapie. Bd. 1 [Gestalt Therapy (Vol. 1)]*. Stuttgart: Klett-Cotta.

Reich, W. (1971). *Charakteranalyse [Character Analysis]. Cologne*: Kiepenheuer & Witsch.

Rudolf, G. (2004). *Strukturbezogene Psychotherapie [Structure-oriented psychotherapy]*. Stuttgart: Schattauer.

Rudolf, G., Grande, T., & Henningsen, P. (2002). *Die Struktur der Persönlichkeit [The structure of personality]*. Stuttgart: Schattauer.

Sanchez, J. (1986). *Der Geist der deutschen Romantik [The spirit of German romanticism]*. Munich: Pfeil Verlag.

Schopenhauer, A. (1918). *Die Welt als Wille und Vorstellung [The world as will and representation]*. Leipzig: Brockhaus.

Stolze, H. (1989). *Die Konzentrative Bewegungstherapie: Grundlagen und Erfahrungen [Concentrative Movement Therapy: Fundamentals and experiences]*. Berlin: Springer.

Uexküll, T., Fuchs, M., Müller-Braunschweig, H., & Johnen, R. (1994). *Subjektive Anatomie [Subjective anatomy]*. Stuttgart: Schattauer.

van der Kolk, B., McFarlane, A., & Weisaeth, L. (1996). *Traumatic stress*. New York: Guilford Press.

# 38
## Consciousness, Awareness, Mindfulness

**Halko Weiss, United States**

**Halko Weiss's** biographical information can be found at the beginning of Chapter 1, the Preface to this handbook.

## Consciousness and Attention

Since the early days of psychotherapy, a central task of psychotherapists has been, sometimes explicitly, sometimes implicitly, to facilitate their patients in focusing and regulating their attention. Within this context, "focusing" refers to directing the patient's attention to specific objects, whereas "regulating" refers to influencing the quality of the attention process (for example, "free association"). Because attention is an innate capacity of human beings, part and parcel of every interaction, the patient's attention is affected even without any conscious intention or strategy on the therapist's part.

Attention processes themselves are subject to the rules of acquired habitual patterns and the abilities of the central neuronal organization. Consequently, a series of brain regions participate in their functions (Posner and Fan, 2004) and also form according to their use. This adaptive characteristic of the brain is called "neuroplasticity" (Kandel, 1999).

Time and again, psychologists have warned against reliance upon the ingrained, habitually reproduced patterns of consciousness in the attempt to resolve intrapersonal issues. These solutions are problematic (Watzlawick et al., 1974), because the patient's attention tends to return to the same starting points and then follow already-established pathways. Some hypnotic procedures attempt to circumvent consciousness altogether in order to avoid the power of its automatism.

It is being considered that brain networks responsible for attention functions be granted the status of an organ system, because neurobiology has found ways to clearly distinguish and depict them anatomically, and their central role in intelligence and emotional control has become increasingly obvious (Posner and Fan, 2004). This chapter intends to show how focusing and regulating of attention processes is handled in Body Psychotherapy and how these approaches developed.

## Awareness

Consciousness as a contributing agent in effective psychotherapy has been historically proved (see overview in Mahoney, 1991). Body Psychotherapy relies on some kind of guidance of the client's attention by the therapist. Bodily regions or processes that are usually overlooked or discounted by the client are brought to consciousness. As a result, almost every school of Body Psychotherapy places a high significance upon the quality of the client's somatic self-perception.

During the first half of the twentieth century, dance and movement therapists (Duncan, Gindler, Selver, and others) facilitated the growth of consciousness-oriented therapy that also incorporated Eastern paths of liberation. The concept of "sensory awareness" is at the heart of Charlotte Selver's contribution to psychotherapy. Based on her experiences with Elsa Gindler (see Chapter 4, "The Influence of Elsa Gindler" by Judyth Weaver), Selver taught her particular methods for focusing and regulating of attention in service of therapeutic treatment and self-actualization until her death in 2003 when she was 102 years old.

The concept of awareness is broader than the meaning of attention. The term "awareness" involves both heightened sensitivity of sensory experience and increased orientation to the present moment. Gestalt therapist Claudio Naranjo writes, "In the practice . . . , the therapist will not only want to help the patient develop lasting attention for his current experience but will also encourage him to become conscious of his experience . . ." (Naranjo, 1996, p. 45).

Ultimately, Gindler's and Selver's contributions influenced all methods of Body Psychotherapy (such as Gestalt Therapy and other approaches of Humanistic Psychology), either directly or indirectly. Sensory awareness assumes a central position in this historical process, which makes it worthwhile to briefly look at this work: Rather than privileging reflective analysis and psychological interpretation or attempting to directly affect and improve pathological mechanisms, Selver prioritized the fundamental attunement to, and a practice of the mindful, embodied experience of, the self through the senses. Although Selver does not define her work as psychotherapeutic, her goal was to promote the full psychological potential of a human being through conscious living (experiencing). According to her perspective, this is a matter of freeing the forces of our "original nature" from the chains that socialization has placed upon human beings. In a presentation in 1957, Selver describes her observation of a little girl:

> The other day I visited some friends. Among the guests was a couple with their daughter, a little girl of eight—a thoughtful and very graceful child. While we were talking the little girl played in the garden. I had the pleasure of watching her through the window. Then she came upstairs and sat down, one leg hanging down, the other on the couch. The mother: "But Helen—how do you sit? Take your leg off the couch. A girl never should sit like that!" The little girl took her leg down, on which occasion her skirt flew high above her knees. The mother: "Helen—pull your skirt down! One can see everything!" The child blushed, looked down on herself, but asked: "Why, what is wrong?" The mother looked at her quite shocked and said: "One does not do that!"
>
> By this time the atmosphere in the room was completely uncomfortable. The little girl not only had her legs down, but had them pressed against each other. Her shoulders had gone up and she held her arms tight against her body. This went on until she could not stand it any longer; she suddenly stretched herself and yawned heartily. Again, a storm of indignation arose from her mother. By now—this all lasted about ten minutes—the child had changed completely. Her gracefulness had turned into awkwardness; all her movement had become still and stilted; her little body was tense; she hardly seemed to be alive anymore.
>
> What will happen to this child? She will hold her unhappy "pose" for a few minutes before she shakes it off. The next time her mother will admonish her, she will hold it a few minutes longer—until at last she will have repressed her naturalness to the point that she will have forgotten it. The mother will then have reached her goal. She will have educated her to be socially acceptable. As a human being, the child will be greatly inhibited, because just as the mother will shackle her in this direction, she will shackle her in a thousand other directions. (Selver, 1999b)

Charlotte Selver attempts to restore her clients' original and "natural" impulses through refined sensory awareness and through precise attention to the embodied experience of the self; in this process, self-restrictive and repressive mechanisms also come to awareness. Selver emphasizes repeatedly that such "impediments" can be "laid aside" through conscious, mindful experiencing. Her work here thus operates in psychotherapeutic terrain, even though she has never presented herself as a psychotherapist.

Her methodology also leans on spiritual traditions and references sources like Zen Buddhism, D. T. Suzuki, and

Alan Watts. She teaches people to fully feel, sense, and be mindful while "walking, standing, sitting, lying down," as well as through proprioception, touch, and handling objects, moment to moment (Selver, 1999a; Brooks, 1974).

As a concept, the notion of "awareness" involves alertness, concentration, conscious mindfulness, intensive self-perception, wakefulness, and being in the here and now. It is also a skill that can be learned. However, awareness has never been defined in universally accepted terms, although as an epistemological phenomenon it has been explored deeply. In this context, Samuel Bois's research needs to be mentioned. He has emphasized that the concept of the cultural-revolutionary aspects of the awareness is revolutionary in cultural terms because it is based on nonlinear processes where small shifts can produce vast changes. He therefore speaks of the "art of awareness" (Bois, 1996).

For both Selver and Perls, the objective of "awareness" is the dissolution of habitual assumptions about and mental perceptions of oneself, as they are challenged with sensory present experience in the present moment. The attention processes are guided and directed so that what is experienced in the present here-and-now experience can be noticed and observed by both the client and the facilitator. Ultimately, the quality of consciousness is supposed to change so that the patient finds a more authentic and direct access to himself. Perls writes, "It is our goal to reinstate and recover the functions of the self through concentration and to dissolve the rigidity of the 'body,' the petrified self, the 'character armor.'" And he writes a few sentences later, "We all need . . . a return to the natural self" (Perls, 1969, p. 275).

## Awareness and the Body

The body almost always plays a central role in the refinement of the attention processes, because attention needs an object. This is recognized throughout the various meditation traditions, from which many pioneers of mindfulness-oriented therapies have drawn inspiration. In the classical Vipassana meditation, taught by the Buddha, for example, the student first begins by paying attention to the breath, including the flow of air, the movements of the thorax, etc. The practice is initially related entirely to the body (Goldstein and Kornfield, 1989; Nyanaponika, 1976). Only later, when the ability to perceive and focus has increased, the observation of emotions, perceptions, and thoughts is included (Nyanaponika, 1979, pp. 53ff.). The body is therefore the main object of observation in the promotion of mindful states of being.

The coupling of body and awareness in Body Psychotherapy is particularly essential for those approaches that work with unconscious processes, using the body as an avenue to access, reveal, and interpret unconscious experience (Weiss, 2009). An important theoretical basis for body-inclusive procedures is that the body houses both implicit and explicit memories that can be brought to consciousness and then worked through. Therefore, the attention directed toward the body not only sensitizes and supports a more substantial intrapersonal relationship (Hick and Bien, 2008) but also reveals how clients have integrated formative experiences and developed corresponding adaptive and/or defensive patterns. The therapist guides the client's perceptions and awareness in such a way that those states, feelings, thought patterns, images, and memories—which would otherwise have remained concealed—can be reexperienced. Even a simple interpretation of a somatic or psychological phenomenon, or inquiring into the "felt sense" of certain experiences ("How does that feel?"), and similar interventions can direct the client's awareness in ways that circumvent his or her routine processing.

For example, a therapist may notice a client's repetitive gesture and consider it significant; she can decide to direct the client's attention to this movement ("I notice that your hand touches your chest, again and again . . ."). Then she may ask him to stay focused and finely tune in to that movement, which can now come into consciousness in a way that may be quite unfamiliar to him ("Could you perhaps slow that movement down for a moment and explore what sensations are associated with it?").

In many schools of Body Psychotherapy, especially those that de-emphasize interpretations, the focusing of attention continues throughout the entire therapy process. Bodily tensions, sensations, expansions, contractions, and other spontaneous phenomena are observed in increasingly precise and subtle ways. This approach reflects the understanding that the body is the primary ground where emotions are perceived (Damasio, 1999), on the basis of which further nuances of feelings can be elaborated until they then take shape on symbolic levels of images, memories, and language. Experience unfolds from the body and only *then* yields its deeper meaning (Downing, 1996). Thus, a process of uncovering and becoming conscious can be built upon the sustained perception of somatic experience, and the client's attention just requires some guidance and support in order to stay focused on the details of those bodily processes and to keep holding the body as an object of attention.

In bringing conscious and direct influence to bear on the client's shifting awareness processes, Body Psychotherapists pursue the following objectives, among others:

- The promotion of sensory-perceptive states can be understood as salutogenic in itself—basically as a dissolving of the body-mind split (see Chapter 37, "Sensory Self-Reflexivity: Therapeutic Action in Body Psychotherapy" by Gustl Marlock).
- The development of a more precise bodily perception in the service of uncovering unconscious material: making the unconscious conscious.
- Increased consciousness of internal processes of self-organization, including automatic responses and behaviors; being aware of habitual reactions thus creates the option of alternate behaviors for the client.

In addition, some Body Psychotherapies consider certain forms of awareness more beneficial for the therapy process than others. By teaching their clients to be aware of internal, embodied processes, they endeavor to promote—alongside regressive explorations—faculties that support a strengthening of progression and development toward more expanded and mature states of being in general.

## Mindfulness

In the last thirty years of the twentieth century, a great number of therapists, psychologists, and scientists began to research the phenomenon of consciousness and define relevant concepts. Charles Tart, Ken Wilber, Roger Walsh, Frances Vaughan, Daniel Goleman, Ellen Langer, Mark Epstein, Richard Davidson, and many others have intensively explored and written about the interpretation of various states of consciousness, related in particular to psychotherapy and associated fields. In the early 1970s, Body Psychotherapist Ron Kurtz pioneered the use of the more strictly defined term "mindfulness" for Psychodynamic Therapy developed from the Buddhist tradition. He understood mindfulness as being an evolution of the "awareness" concept, and systematically integrated it into his treatment methodology (Kurtz, 1990). In his approach, a central task of a therapist is to help his client build up a skill in mindfulness over the course of time and develop an "internal observer," a role based on the Buddhist concept of the witness. This "observer" is thought to possess the ability to precisely monitor the processes of somatic and psychic self-organization, from a certain inner distance, while the client goes through his or her typical experiences. A "dual" consciousness arises in which the client simultaneously experiences and also observes himself nonjudgmentally, aided by the therapist. Kurtz established precise methodological steps to help his clients to monitor their experience from moment to moment (see Chapter 39, "Bodily Expression and Experience in Body Psychotherapy" by Ron Kurtz).

Since then, the concept of mindfulness has established itself more and more deeply within other pedagogical and psychotherapeutic approaches (Johanson, 2006; Weiss, 2009; Sparks, 2008; Kabat-Zinn, 1999; etc.), alongside its continued use in well-established traditional Buddhist frameworks (see Thich Nhat Hanh [1975] and Nyanaponika [1976, 1979]). Here are some more examples: Psychologist and intelligence researcher Dan Goleman understands "mindfulness" as the main foundation for the training of Emotional Intelligence (Goleman, 1997). Jon Kabat-Zinn, a physician and renowned researcher, has studied and taught patients the use of mindfulness (from within a cognitive behavioral framework) since the 1980s. He reports that:

> . . . they have enjoyed it and that the training means a decisive turning point in their lives. We document the short- and long-term effects of the program by determining the patients' state of health at the beginning and end of the course, as well as periodically examining it afterward. In general, we find a strong decrease in patients' medical symptoms during the eight-week course. Psychological symptoms such as fear, depression, and hostility also decrease significantly. (Kabat-Zinn, 1999, p. 21)

Also within Cognitive Behavioral Therapy, the training of mindfulness has been of growing importance for many years. Renowned researcher Marsha Linehan frequently includes mindfulness training in her treatment plans (Linehan, 1993). Others have also taken up and refined this methodology (Segal et al., 2002; Bennett-Goleman, 2001; Hayes et al., 2004). The same applies within psychodynamic therapy (Siegel and Hartzell, 2004; Siegel, 2007; Germer et al., 2005; Germer, 2006; Safran, 2003), and trauma treatment is greatly improved with the help of mindfulness, as well (Ogden et al., 2006).

Mindfulness is not just a 2,500-year-old Buddhist practice. A good overview of the different modern applications can be found in Mace's (2008) *Mindfulness and Mental Health*. The scientific recognition that has been given to mindfulness in the last decades has unleashed a veritable "attention revolution" (Wallace, 2006).

Recent neuropsychological research reports appear to prove that lasting positive changes in the brain can be gained through the use of mindfulness meditation: the evidence is that neuronal activity that is typically indicative of reduced fear and positive emotional states gets activated (Davidson et al., 2003; Smith et al., 2004). Research at UCLA showed that naming emotions observed in mindfulness produces therapeutic effects (Creswell et al., 2007). The output in research is impressive and ongoing. For updates on recent developments, the websites of the Jane and Terry Semel Institute at UCLA (marc.ucla.edu) and of B. Alan Wallace at the Santa Barbara Institute for Consciousness Studies (sbinstitute.com) are recommended.

For most researchers and authors, the observation of somatic events and processes is a central starting point of any work with mindfulness, enhancing the capacity for self-perception and self-regulation and consequently reducing stress and illness.

## Disidentification

When attention is guided toward observing one's own body and the related psychic phenomena in the therapeutic process, an important question arises: *Who* is observing?

The answer appears almost banal at first: simply "I" or the self-reflective ego, perhaps also consciousness as a whole, or parts of it, and so on. However, on closer inspection, this question reveals itself as much more fundamental and complicated. Several published psychologists (Assagioli, Kurtz, Schwartz, Stone, Wittemann, Freud, Schmidt, von Thun, Marlock and Weiss, and others) posit that our psyche is constructed of parts or states that are clearly distinguishable from each other; each possesses different physical states, feelings, thoughts, intuitive perspectives, etc., and they are related to each other in a "sensitive ecology" (Schwartz, 1997). All of these states (and/or parts) represent certain response potentials to various external situations. These usually develop unconsciously on the basis of past childhood experiences and are reinforced over the course of a lifetime. They are closely related to specific types of experiences and are, in that sense, "partial" in their perspective of reality. This understanding circumscribes a systemic model of a structured psyche that constitutes itself as an integration of dynamically interrelated, differentiated "parts."

Here is a case example: Angie felt torn between two such "parts." On the one hand, she wanted to open up more deeply to a love relationship; yet, on the other hand, she experienced overwhelming fear. One of her identified parts held her longings, hopeful thoughts, memories of closeness, physical openness, etc., that were connected to positive previous experiences. Another part, derived from another set of experiences, contained painful memories, physical manifestations of bodily contractions, and her perceptions of the inherent dangers of relationships. Such parts, or states, as in Angie's case, are often interrelated and conflicted, escalating each other as well as canceling each other out. When her longing increased, a state of fear awakened and became dominant. When her fearful part orchestrated as well as many decisions, her longing intensified. In becoming aware of one state, she was always already identified with the opposing part, which—in becoming alarmed—immediately rejected the other part that she was observing. So what does not occur is true phenomenological—we might say "unreactive"—observation. Angie does not, in fact, have available a metaposition from which she can impartially observe both positions and their interrelationship. This acutely begs the question: *Who* is observing?

Various authors have developed different terms to describe the internal capacity to take a true (or metalevel), transcendent observer position that is separate and differentiated from the various states or parts of the psyche. This position has similarities with the reflexive ego of psychoanalysis, the self (Jung, Kohut, Schwartz, etc.), the conductor (Assagioli), etc. In Body Psychotherapy, correspondences can be found in Al Pesso's concept of "the pilot" and Ron Kurtz's "internal observer." Even if the definitions of the various authors differ somewhat in emphasis, they do agree on one thing: the observing state itself is not distorted, driven, or inundated by somatic states, emotions, or chains of thoughts—whether negative or pleasant (e.g., an anxiety, a sense of contraction, or an image)—but stands apart, and is not affected in its observational stance by the object of observation. The more deeply a person learns to identify with this observer position and the (body-mind) states associated with it, the less he or she will be "overwhelmed" (Schwartz) or "abducted" (Goleman) by difficult and disturbing states. Instead, he or she will develop the ability to "step back" (Linehan) from identifications with such difficult states, and be able to then experience them more consciously and precisely, and consequently to use them more effectively. This witness stance is particularly important in Body Psychotherapy because body-related processes can easily trigger deep regressions that may possibly carry malignant or intensifying effects (see the term "kindling" by Morrell, 1991).

Many types of therapeutic intervention, such as all of the externalization techniques, promote—albeit not always systematically—the development of an observer position, to the point that it can be considered one of the common denominators across the field. American analyst Lewis Aron summarizes this in the following way: "At the end of an analysis, it is not the degree of insight or knowledge or other psychic content that demonstrates the patient's growth or the success of the treatment; rather, it is the capacity for self-reflexivity. Analysts have always known this; we have always said that the goal of analysis is the capacity for self-analysis following termination" (Aron, 1998, p. 27).

Within this context, Aron also emphasizes that he understands self-reflexivity in a way that ". . . includes the dialectical process of experiencing oneself as a subject as well as of reflecting on oneself as an object. It is not, therefore, exclusively an intellectual observational function, but an experiential and affective function as well" (Ibid.).

Despite this, the perennial question remains: What is the part of the psyche that is capable of "doing" this observing and reflecting? Is this part impartial and relaxed, or contaminated by previous experiences that pull the person into some kind of limited "trance" state? Or is it, as Schwartz suggests, a "benevolent," "understanding," and "compassionate" part of a human being, not caught in partial identifications with other parts?

The notion of "awareness," as well as the more precise term "mindfulness," would seem to encompass these qualities, implying a nonpartisan "observer"—a position that can be therapeutically cultivated in such a way that those positive traits of self-relating and "distancing" (Beck et al., 1979) start to develop.

In Angie's case (above), the internal-observer capacity eventually developed to such a degree that she could attend to, understand, and actively support both of the formerly conflicted parts. Schwartz calls this quality "self-leadership," whereby the "impartial" and "observing" state is seen as the authentic "self." This quality of self-reference in the client is systematically promoted with the practicing of awareness and, even more intensively, through the use of mindfulness.

## A Learnable Facility

Continual cultivation of this capacity for self-observation leads to better self-perception and thus makes it possible for habitual processes to be noticed and interrupted, with clear advantages for effective psychotherapy. Over recent years, it has become increasingly clear that a proper conceptualization of the structure of consciousness can be helpful and effective, in both systematic, as well as non-systematic, practice and training.

The early history of psychotherapy both overlooked and downplayed the fact that these capacities for self-observation and awareness depend on skills that can be learned through training and that require deliberate practice. Carl Ginsburg, a well-known Feldenkrais teacher, comments: "mindfulness and awareness . . . require both discipline as well as practice in order to become useful. It is the lack of this discipline in the Western tradition that has led to the early failure of introspection as an exploration method in psychology" (Ginsburg, 1996).

In Body Psychotherapy, Ron Kurtz describes mindfulness as an integral element of the therapy process that must be practiced and honed constantly. A European study on Body Psychotherapy (Koemeda-Lutz et al., 2003, 2006) gave the first indications that this ability can indeed be learned during the course of a Body Psychotherapy process. A study by Grepmair and colleagues (2007) shows that mindfulness training for psychotherapists increased the effectiveness of their therapy and the satisfaction of their clients. By integrating awareness and mindfulness into psychotherapy, therapists enhance:

- the client's faculty for metalevel observation, by directing attention to the body, its emotional states, and its impulses
- the client's capacity to be the "observer" for more precise self(body)-perception in the service of uncovering unconscious material
- the client's ability to support decreasing identification with problematic states
- the client's ability to support a more integrated sense of body/self
- the client's ability to open avenues toward conscious interruption and regulation of habitual processes

Allan Schore (1994) understands the role of the therapist as an "external interactive regulator"; this includes the regulation of states of consciousness, as well as of the body-mind. Awareness and mindfulness become the focus areas for mutual exploration, whereby that regulation can engage directly with those embodied states, vitality affects, and emotions that the client experiences as *needing* regulation. Clients often acutely experience that it is especially automatic, ingrained mechanisms that need special attention, as these states are triggered unconsciously in everyday life and often cause pain and suffering. Through the deliberate induction of, training in, and practice of awareness and mindfulness, the therapist can facilitate experiences that supplant the out-of-control states with new, progressive states that the clients can then begin to regulate themselves, by learning the explicit faculties and skills for doing so. This allows an empowering process for the client that eventually replaces interactive regulation with auto-regulation, as the kind of close interplay of bodily processes and expanding consciousness that characterizes most Body Psychotherapies.

## References

Aron, L. (1998). The clinical body and the reflexive mind. In L. Aron & F. S. Anderson (Eds.), *Relational perspectives on the body.* Hillsdale, NJ: Analytic Press.

Beck, A. T., Rush, A. J., Shaw, B. F., & Emery, G. (1979). *Cognitive therapy of depression.* New York: Guilford Press.

Bennett-Goleman, T. (2001). *Emotional alchemy.* New York: Harmony Books.

Bois, S. J. (1996). *The art of awareness* (4th ed.). Santa Monica, CA: Continuum Press.

Brooks, C. V. W. (1974). *Sensory Awareness: The rediscovery of experiencing.* New York: Viking Press.

Creswell, J. D., Way, B. M., Eisenberger, N. I., & Lieberman, M. D. (2007). Neural correlates of dispositional mindfulness during affect labeling. *Psychosomatic Medicine, 69,* 560–565.

Damasio, A. R. (1999). *The feeling of what happens.* New York: Harcourt Brace.

Davidson, R., Kabat-Zinn, J., Schumacher, J., et al. (2003). Alterations in brain and immune function produced by mindfulness meditation. *Psychosomatic Medicine, 65,* 564-570.

Downing, G. (1996). *Körper und Wort in der Psychotherapie [Body and word in psychotherapy].* Munich: Kösel.

Germer, C. K. (2006, Jan./Feb.). You gotta have heart. *Psychotherapy Networker, 30(1).*

Germer, C. K., Siegel, R. D., & Fulton, P. R. (Eds.). (2005). *Mindfulness in psychotherapy.* New York: Guilford Press.

Ginsburg, C. (1996). The somatic self revisited. *Journal of Humanistic Psychology, 36(3),* 124–140.

Goldstein, J., & Kornfield, J. (1989). *The experience of insight: Simple and direct guide to Buddhist meditation.* Boston: Shambhala.

Goleman, D. (1997). *Emotional intelligence.* New York: Bantam Books.

Grepmair, L., Mitterlehner, F., Loew, T., Bachler, E., Rother, W., & Nickel, M. (2007). Promoting mindfulness in psychotherapists in training influences the treatment results of their patients: A randomized, double-blind, controlled study. *Psychotherapy and Psychosomatics, 76(6), 332–338.*

Hanh, T. N. (1975). *The miracle of mindfulness.* Boston: Beacon Press.

Hayes, S. C., Follette, V. M., & Linehan, M. M. (Eds.). (2004). *Mindfulness and acceptance.* New York: Guilford Press.

Hick, S. F., & Bien, T. (Eds.). (2008). *Mindfulness and the therapeutic relationship.* New York: Guilford Press.

Johanson, G. (2006). A survey of the use of mindfulness in psychotherapy. *Annals of the American Psychotherapy Association, 9(2),* 15–24.

Kabat-Zinn, J. (1999). *Full catastrophe living: Using the wisdom of your body and mind to face stress, pain, and illness.* New York: Delta.

Kandel, E. (1999). Of learning, memory, and genetic switches. In R. Conlan (Ed.), *States of mind* (pp. 151–198). New York: John Wiley & Sons.

Koemeda-Lutz, M., Kaschke, M., Revenstorf, D., et al. (2003). Zwischenergebnisse zur Wirksamkeit von ambulanten Körperpsychotherapien [Intermediate findings on the effectiveness of outpatient Body Psychotherapies]. *Psychotherapie Forum, 11,* 70–79.

Koemeda-Lutz, M., Kaschke, M., Revenstorf, D., Scherrmann, T., Weiss, H., & Soeder, U. (2006). *Evaluation der Wirksamkeit von ambulanten Körperpsychotherapien: EWAK Eine Multicenter-Studie in Deutschland und der Schweiz [Evaluation of the effectiveness of ambulant Body Psychotherapies: A multicenter study in Germany and Switzerland]. Psychotherapie Psychosomatik Medizinische Psychologie, 56,* 480–487.

Kurtz, R. (1990). *Body-Centered Psychotherapy: The Hakomi Method.* Mendocino, CA: LifeRhythm.

Linehan, M. M. (1993). *Cognitive-behavioral treatment of borderline personality disorder.* New York: Guilford Press.

Mace, C. (2008). *Mindfulness and mental health: Therapy, theory and science.* New York: Routledge.

Mahoney, M. J. (1991). *Human change processes.* New York: Basic Books.

Morrell, F. (1991). *Kindling and synaptic plasticity: The legacy of Graham Goddard.* Berlin: Springer.

Naranjo, C. (1996). *Gestalt Therapy.* Nevada City, CA: Gateways.

Nyanaponika. (1976). *The power of mindfulness.* Kandy, Sri Lanka: Buddhist Publication Society.

Nyanaponika. (1979). *The heart of Buddhist meditation: Satipatthna, A handbook of mental training based on the Buddha's Way of Mindfulness.* New York: Weiser Books.

Ogden, P., Minton, K., & Pain, C. (2006). *Trauma and the body: A sensorimotor approach to psychotherapy.* New York: W. W. Norton.

Perls, F. (1969). *Ego, hunger and aggression.* New York: Vintage Books.

Posner, M. I., & Fan, J. (2004). Attention as an organ system. In J. R. Pomerantz & C. M. Crair (Eds.), *Topics in integrative neuroscience: From cells to cognition.* Cambridge, UK: Cambridge University Press.

Safran, J. D. (Ed.). (2003). *Psychoanalysis and Buddhism.* Boston: Wisdom.

Schore, A. N. (1994). *Affect regulation and the origin of the self*. Hillsdale, NJ: Lawrence Erlbaum.

Schwartz, R. C. (1997). *Internal Family Systems Therapy*. New York: Guilford Press.

Segal, V. S., Williams, J. M. G., & Teasdale, J. D. (2002). *Mindfulness-based cognitive therapy for depression*. New York: Guilford Press.

Selver, C. (1999a). *Collected writings (Vol. 1)*. Mill Valley, CA: Sensory Awareness Foundation.

Selver, C. (1999b). Sensory Awareness and our attitude toward life. In C. Selver, *Collected writings (Vol. 1)* (pp. 16–17). Mill Valley, CA: Sensory Awareness Foundation.

Siegel, D. J. (2007). *The mindful brain*. New York: W. W. Norton.

Siegel, D., & Hartzell, M. (2004). *Parenting from the inside out*. New York: Penguin.

Smith, J. C., Davidson, R. J., & Kabat-Zinn, J. (2004). Alterations in brain and immune function produced by mindfulness meditation: Three caveats. *Psychosomatic Medicine, 66(1), 148–152*.

Sparks, T. F. (2008). Observing the organisation of experience. In H. Weiss, G. Johanson, & L. Monda (Eds.), *The Hakomi Method*. Boulder, CO: Hakomi Institute.

Wallace, B. A. (2006). *The attention revolution: Unlocking the power of the focused mind*. Boston: Wisdom.

Watzlawick, P., Weakland, J., & Fish, R. (1974). *Change: Principles of problem formation and problem resolution*. New York: W. W. Norton.

Weiss, H. (2009). The use of mindfulness in Psychodynamic and Body Oriented Psychotherapy. *Journal of Body, Movement and Dance in Psychotherapy, 4(1), 15–16*.

# 39

## Bodily Expression and Experience in Body Psychotherapy

Ron Kurtz, United States

In this chapter, Ron Kurtz describes how present-time, somato-psychic experiences can uncover internal conflicts, and how bodily expressions can be drawn upon to initiate such processes.

**Ron Kurtz,** computer scientist and psychologist, was the founder of "Hakomi," aka "Mindfulness-Centered Somatic Psychotherapy," which is one of the internationally most prevalent approaches to Body Psychotherapy today. He was the founder of the Hakomi Institute in Boulder, Colorado.

He starting studying psychotherapy in the 1970s, and was considered a pioneer in the utilization of the Buddhist technique of "mindfulness" into psychotherapy. Some of his concepts and techniques—for example, the notion of radical non-directivity, or those in regard to the creation of the therapeutic relationship—have facilitated a number of developments, both in the field of Body Psychotherapy and in general. His particular attention was devoted to the development of an experientially oriented therapy process that allows clients to witness their different forms of self-organization and to develop their own corrective experiences in collaboration with their therapists.

During his more than thirty years as a trainer, Ron Kurtz taught his method in many countries around the world. He came to emphasize the significance of a particular kind of presence that the therapist can bring into the therapeutic encounter, a state of being that he called "loving presence." He published a number of books and scientific papers and taught at Indiana University, San Francisco State University, John F. Kennedy University, and the Esalen Institute. Sadly, he died in 2011.

I would like to talk about two aspects of Body Psychotherapy: the role and importance of bodily expression and of experience. Body Psychotherapists give a great deal of attention to their clients' bodily expressions. This focus, as much as anything, gives Body Psychotherapy the great power it has. This is so because these expressions both reveal and provide access to those unconscious structures[39] that have the most profound effects on behavior and experience. These structures contain the models that we hold of who we are, what we can expect from the world, and how we must behave as a result. These models are formed early in life, become habitual, and operate, like all habits, usually outside our awareness. Though unconscious, they strongly influence consciousness and, to a great extent, control what we can and can't experience. Among the things that they control are those bodily expressions we attend to. I'm going to call these inner mental structures "core beliefs." Although they are not stored as statements of fact, as normal beliefs are, they function just as though they were held as such. Habits, which operate without conscious choice, operate "as if" they were expressions of beliefs; and by noticing them, we have the chance to think about the models and beliefs that they are expressing.

---

39 These unconscious structures are called by many names: contextual systems, mental models, cognitive schemata, etc

For profound psychological change, the person we habitually (and unconsciously) believe we are also needs to change. Our unconscious beliefs about what we can expect from the world also need to change. Change has to happen in the unconscious structures (both psychological and somatic) that hold these core beliefs. Therefore, as therapists, we need to understand our clients at these levels. This helps the therapist translate bodily expressions into statements that can be more consciously seen as unquestioned assumptions. Although encoded mainly as emotional and bodily habits, unconscious structures are, in effect, expressions of belief. They operate "as if" the person believes something that makes these habits and emotional reactions appropriate to that belief. This job of observing bodily expressions and inferring core beliefs from them is one of the more important tasks of a Body Psychotherapist.

Due to their unconscious nature and their emotional underpinnings, core beliefs are actively maintained and, when challenged, vigorously defended. Whether beneficial or detrimental, they are deeply ingrained in our psychosomatic structure. They have been with us for a long time. They were learned early, through interactions with caregivers and others close to us. They are the essence of our longest-lasting patterns of being and doing; they are the "core" of our characters, the fabric of our personalities and lifestyles. More than any other thing, they are who we are; they orchestrate the self itself.

The placebo effect is a good example of how powerful an influence beliefs can have. Without powerful emotional events or special practices, core beliefs remain unexamined. They are, paradoxically, most influential and most unknown. ("The fish will be the last to discover water."—Albert Einstein.) It is not that we're just not thinking about them; we are thinking with them. Living them! "The entire world of past experience [is] embodied in the present in the form of character attitudes. A person's character is the fractional sum total of all past experiences . . . The doctor does not need to reconstruct a traumatic moment; the traumatic moment continues to exist in every breath the patient takes, in every gesture he makes" (Reich, 1949).

To work with core beliefs, in the least-violent way, we must first work to establish feelings of trust and safety. Because the most deeply held beliefs are about our identities and our place in the world, bringing them into consciousness is paramount to putting our whole personal identity in doubt. Even to approach this material, a high level of trust is needed. After safety is properly established, we can proceed with the work of bringing elements of the client's core material into consciousness, working with the emotions that are part of it, and translating as much as we can of it into statements of beliefs (Kurtz, 1990).

Experience is important here for two reasons. First, personal experience is always an example of beliefs at work. Experience is organized by habits and emotions that are aspects of the inner structures. So, carefully following the external signs of present experience, the therapist can begin to discern the core material influencing it. Second, the client doesn't need only to understand his or her behavior—as insight theories would have us believe—the client also needs new experiences, in order to feel what a change in belief might be like. Talking about one's past, and what one would like to be different, is no substitute for actually experiencing a change. (See Chapter 12, "Neurobiological Perspectives on Body Psychotherapy" by Christian Gottwald. He clarifies that for change to happen, new neuronal networks have to be activated, which means new experience has to occur.)

And such changes can be helped to happen right in the therapy session, where they can be supported and reinforced. The experiences evoked—like feelings, bodily sensations and tensions, memories, and images—are not always clearly understood at first by the clients. Finding the meanings that those experiences embody for the client is an important part of changing them. By thinking of them as (new) beliefs and verbalizing them, we can go a long way toward understanding them better.

To begin the work of making the unconscious become more conscious, we look for indications of the influence of these core beliefs in habitual, nonverbal expressions. We work to understand what beliefs are being expressed through these unconscious behaviors. As Body Psychotherapists, we use (often) body-oriented awareness and techniques designed to evoke strong, clear experiences that make the organizing beliefs become more obvious to the client. For example, a client with a habit of never asking for help, and with an underlying belief that he cannot expect any such help, we might simply ask the client to be calm and to notice what he experiences when we tell him, "You are not alone." Having done things like this, hundreds of times, I can tell you that it almost always evokes an intense experience of sadness and/or disbelief.

Not all bodily expressions are useful for this: short-lived, momentary gestures, and facial expressions that appear and pass in a moment, are sometimes more useful as indicators of present experience than long-held characterological positions. This channel of communication evidences nonverbal commentaries about the client's present state and (often differing) verbal communications.[40] This channel generally operates quite close to consciousness.

These expressions are a language in their own right, one that speaks about immediate moods, feelings, attitudes, and even ideas. (If you've ever seen the French mime-artist Marcel Marceau, you will know how effective that "body" language can be.) Animal communications are similar.[41] It is possible to discern indicators of core beliefs by paying close attention to short-lived expressions, but it's the more habitual, longer-term expressions that reveal the oldest and deepest belief systems.[42] Contacting or evoking these deeper beliefs will usually evoke powerful experiences or reactions in clients, and it's these experiences, and the work that we do with them, that make Body Psychotherapy so powerful.

Although habitual bodily expressions—like speech patterns, tone of voice, characteristic facial expressions, gestures, postures, tensions, and movement patterns—are all reliable indicators of core beliefs, it should be noted, however, that not all core beliefs need changing. Only some of them are dysfunctional or cause unnecessary suffering; the great majority of them are quite useful and benign.

The ones that do cause suffering can be very influential and are usually easily recognized. Pain, fear, disappointment, grief, frustration, anger, confusion, the feeling of being lost, alienated, etc., can often be read in habitual bodily expressions. When one of these "negative" core beliefs is prominent and persists, it suggests that a core belief needs changing. A very simple, common example is a habit of never looking directly at the therapist: the client's head is always at an angle to the therapist, and the eyes have to look a little bit sideways to compensate. This kind of habit suggests a degree of fear and mistrust and (possibly) reflects a belief that one must protect oneself from potential emotional hurt. Of course, the fact is that the hurt has already happened, and it is this that has shaped the habit we're now observing.[43]

Once recognized, in-depth Body Psychotherapy methods, such as Hakomi, apply techniques to make these core beliefs conscious.[42] Because they are not easily accessible, and because they are contextual systems, these unconscious structures become like prisons. Bringing them into consciousness can be something like a "prison break." Because they are emotionally charged, and because they are limiting, antiquated, and inaccurate, the process of release can be difficult and emotionally painful. The good news is that making them conscious brings with it the discovery that the "chains and bars" of this "prison" are all constructions of the mind and of the body. With that comes relief, a new

---

40  An example of a short-term bodily expression would be this: a person saying, "Yes, I understand," while at the same time holding his arms out to the side, slightly down, with the hands open, palms up. Verbally, he's saying that he understands, while at the same time, his body is making the comment "But there's nothing I can do about it." An example of a long-term expression might be the habit of always speaking quickly and loudly, as if one expects that others won't be generous with their attention.

41  Charles Darwin wrote about this in *The Expression of the Emotions in Man and Animals*.

42  A more detailed discussion of beliefs and unconscious structures is presented later in this chapter.

43  Stephen Porges's work with the "social engagement system" (Porges, 2003) applies to this particular habit.

44  Not all methods take this approach; for example, clinical hypnotists often work directly with the unconscious, but by bypassing consciousness, as a matter of choice.

sense of freedom, and a release of the energy involved in "locking up" these unconscious processes. At this point, all real change begins.

## The Change Process

Here's a short outline on working with bodily expressions and experiences:

1. The therapist maintains an active focus on the client's bodily expressions—such as gestures, posture, tone of voice, coloring, facial expression, mood, and emotion.
2. From these bodily expressions, the therapist gathers information from which inferences about the unconscious structures are made.
3. Using ideas about these unconscious structures, the therapist then creates interventions designed to bring these into consciousness as (often) emotionally meaningful experiences.
4. If this is successful, the therapeutic attention then shifts to working with the emotions and memories evoked by the intervention and that are clearly now being experienced by the client.
5. The experience of the release of emotion, and the realization of the long-term meaning and impact of the material recently made conscious, initiates the beginnings of deep psychological change.

To elaborate: what makes Body Psychotherapy so effective is this: the client's immediate behaviors and experiences provide a kind of information that words alone cannot provide; and this information is a direct expression of the client's unconscious. As Daniel Goleman reports in his book *Emotional Intelligence (1995),* about 90 percent of emotional communication is nonverbal. Bodily expressions are a significant part of this communication, often affecting those receiving the communication as much as, or more than, those expressing it (because of the unconscious component of bodily expressions). This body language conveys the most immediate and available information about the client's "way of being" in the world. Understanding it, responding to it, and exposing it compassionately immensely helps to create a high level of trust within the therapeutic relationship within a short period of time.

The earliest unconscious structures are encoded in "implicit" memory. Psychologist Daniel Siegel, an expert on neuropsychology, has written extensively on this point:

> These [forms of memory] are available early in life and, when retrieved, are not thought to carry with them the internal sensations that something is being recalled . . . Implicit memory involves parts of the brain that do not require conscious processing during encoding or retrieval. When implicit memory is retrieved, the neural net profiles that are activated involve circuits in the brain that are a fundamental part of our everyday experience of life: behaviors, emotions, and images . . . We act, feel and imagine without the recognition of the influence of past experience on our present reality.
>
> With repeated experiences, the infant's brain . . . is able to detect similarities and differences across experiences. From these comparative processes, the infant's mind is able to make "summations" or generalized representations from repeated experiences. These generalizations form the basis of "mental models" or "schemata," which help the infant (in fact each of us) to interpret present experiences as well as to anticipate future ones. Mental models are basic components of implicit memory." (Siegel, 1999, pp. 28–34)

The mental models of implicit memory "do not require conscious processing during encoding or retrieval" (Ibid.). In other words, these mental models are operating (influencing behavior, perception, and perhaps also body sensations) without one being conscious of their doing that. For the individual, these models are just the way the world is, without the luxury of doubt that consciousness affords. Bringing these models into consciousness, where doubt becomes possible, is a first step. The mental models stored in implicit memory, though not normally conscious, are nonetheless controlling, and constantly "speaking" through, behavior and experience. Working with the body makes these models accessible to consciousness.

> . . . emotion is a central organizing process for consciousness . . . any theory of consciousness must have a theory of emotion as one of its linchpins . . . (Watt, 2001)
>
> At some point in brain evolution, behavioral flexibility was achieved by the evolution of consciousness dwelling on events and their meaning, as guided by internally experienced emotional feelings. (Panksepp, 1998)
>
> A vast amount of psychosomatic literature supports the notion that satisfying emotional experiences are a vital part of a happy, healthy life. (Waldstein and Elias, 2001)

In contrast, painful and unsatisfying experiences are what our clients actually bring us. All experiences, whether satisfying or painful, take place within consciousness (one might say they appear in consciousness). For that reason, some discussion of the connections between consciousness and affective experiences is in order.

Consciousness, in both its content and its direction, is effective only when it is guided by affect (emotions and emotional memory) (Damasio, 1994). Without that guidance, without the valuation and purpose it provides, it quickly becomes lost in irrelevancies. Studies of people with a type of brain damage that leaves them rational, but without emotion, show this clearly (Ibid.). Emotion and consciousness are functionally linked. The contents of consciousness are strongly influenced by the "contextual systems" of implicit memory.

Baars's global workspace theory (Baars, 1998; Baars and McGoven, 1997) of consciousness describes these connections: "Global Workspace Theory" is a simple cognitive architecture that has been developed to account qualitatively for a large set of matched pairs of conscious and unconscious processes.

Consciousness resembles a bright spot on the theater stage of working memory, directed there by a spotlight of attention, under executive guidance (Baddeley, 1993). "The rest of the theater is dark and unconscious. 'Behind the scenes' are contextual systems, which shape conscious contents without ever becoming conscious" (Waldstein and Elias, 2001).

Among these "contextual systems, which shape conscious contents" are emotions, moods, memories, and core beliefs. These systems shape all experiences, and most Body Psychotherapy methods have ways to bring them into consciousness. The Hakomi Method brings this unconscious material into consciousness by using a unique state of consciousness called "mindfulness" (see Chapter 38, "Consciousness, Awareness, Mindfulness" by Halko Weiss) and by doing interventions—some physical, some verbal—that evoke memories and emotions while the client is in that state.

All Body Psychotherapies work with present experiences, such as body sensations, emotional reactions, and tensions. Body Psychotherapy is not conversational; it is body-centered, present-centered, emotion-centered, and experiential. In practical terms, this means that although techniques vary widely, from physical interventions such as stress postures and pressure on particular muscles, to "the evocation of experience in mindfulness" used in Hakomi, they are all attempts to use bodily experiential methods to access the unconscious.

The logic of working experientially is this: experience is organized; it is organized by habits that normally remain outside of consciousness; some of these ways of experiencing were formed early, are encoded in implicit memory, and exert great influence over a person's everyday moods, thoughts, experiences, and behaviors (Schore, 1994).

One of the things that we most want to help our clients change is the habitual ways in which they organize unnecessarily painful experiences. One of the criteria of success in psychotherapy is the client's freedom to move away from such dysfunctional experiences. We do that by working *with* the models, and their habits, that organize all such experiences. In this way, Body Psychotherapy is essentially experiential.

In the course of everyday activities, it is not easy (or for that matter, very useful) to focus on how these organizing habits contribute to the creation of our experiences. For that, psychotherapy, or meditation, or mindfulness practice, is appropriate; though these habits are not necessarily within consciousness, they are not always totally repressed—though sometimes that is also the case. It is simply that we need them to function automatically, so we can use our consciousness for other things. And certainly, not all "organizing habits" are worth examining. Only the specific habits that organize unnecessarily painful or dysfunctional experiences are worth working with. In doing so, with appropriate supervision, we can help the client to make fundamental change possible. We make it possible to change the basic experiences of our "selves," of "others," and of the different worlds that we live in.

In psychotherapy, we access unconscious material by helping our clients to study how their experiences are organized. It is the juxtaposition of the ideas and expressions that we use with the experiences that they evoke, and that helps to make it clear (to the client) what these ideas, beliefs, and memories are, and that those are controlling what the client thinks and experiences.

Some methods are designed to help the client to notice how that happens: in Hakomi, for example, we do it by evoking experiences while the client is in a state of mindfulness (Ibid.). For example, in a therapy session, a particular client, while talking about her father, made a gesture that had an "angry" feel to it. She slashed the air with her hand, making what looked like a short karate chop. After pointing that out, and getting permission to work with it, we did a little experiment. I held her wrist, and then asked her to make that same gesture—the chopping motion—while I provided some resistance to it.

This had the effect of evoking, first, an intensification of effort on her part, and then an overwhelming fear of her father (and also memories of his violent abuse of her, which she was already aware of). We first worked with the fear and had a good resolution, one in which she felt compassion for her father and his pain as a child. This simple intervention of providing some resistance to a spontaneous gesture is just one way of physically intervening to evoke meaningful experiences through the body.

Mindfulness is also a way of noticing the moment-by-moment flow of one's experience. With practice, one begins to realize how experiences are put together. Mindfulness is a calm state of mind in which attention is focused on present experience, noticing it, without controlling anything but the noticing. In this state, one simply follows the changing contents of the mind without the intention to control what happens, or what emerges: "Oh, that's interesting" is perhaps the salient perspective. It is a kind of voluntary vulnerability. For us, the important thing is that the practice of mindfulness offers the possibility that core beliefs can become more conscious.

Advanced meditators can stay in mindfulness for extended periods of time, several hours or more, and, in doing so, can reach states of mind in which silence and peace pervade one's whole being; however, that level of mindfulness can take years of practice.

Luckily, for our purposes, only a few brief moments of mindfulness are necessary, and great depth is not necessarily required. We need perhaps ten seconds of mindfulness into which to introduce a statement, a movement, a sensation, or a touch, something simple and short, designed to evoke an experience that will cast light on what the core beliefs are organizing it into. If we have chosen well, our statement (or whatever) will evoke something meaningful, something that reveals core beliefs.

A core belief like "Don't expect help" or "I have to do everything myself" often expresses itself by the client's never asking for support in any way, and doing all of his or her thinking silently, without sharing it with the therapist. Noticing this, an experiential therapist could do this experiment: ask the client to become more mindful and, when he's ready, simply say, "You don't have to do it all yourself." Having done similar experiments many times, I can report that it will often evoke some relaxation, and often a feeling of sadness. Staying with that experience usually brings up memories of being "forced" to "grow up" too soon, taking on adult "experience." This kind of evocation, using the body and mindfulness, is a very effective way to make the unconscious more conscious. Another way to evoke this sort of experience is to provide actual, physical support—again, with the client in mindfulness—such as holding the person in one's arms, or even just arranging that the person can lean on you or on an assistant. That kind of experience can be something the client has always missed, given that the core belief was that such support was just not available.

Some core beliefs cause present-day suffering by limiting those positive emotions that can be experienced. For example, a person with a core belief that says the world is full of danger will be blocked from feeling "safe"—even though they may be. In many situations, recognizably "safe" by any reasonable standards, the person will still not feel safe. His or her blood pressure and heart rate, autonomic nervous system, etc., will still be functioning as if he or she were in danger. If an experience of safety even begins to happen, the habitual state of mind will prevent it from developing any further. Thoughts of peace and relaxation are banished,[45] and a familiar, chronic, low level of mobilization, wariness, and danger is maintained. The very idea of safety is unsafe. The emotionally positive experiences that are prevented by core beliefs are called, in Hakomi, "missing experiences."[46]

A common goal of most Body Psychotherapies is helping clients to recover their capacity to feel—and act on—such missing experiences. We also work to help clients to establish new core beliefs, based on that recovered capacity, and to establish new habits of organization around them. In order to do this, we have to evoke and stabilize the missing experience in the therapy setting. This is done, of course, after the limiting belief has been made conscious, and whatever necessary emotional work (resulting from its evocation) has been done.

For the client who does not feel safe, for instance, there may be a time in the therapeutic process when his therapist will create a perfectly safe situation in mindfulness. Maybe he arranges a physically safe situation with the help of pillows; maybe he contains the client with his own body; there are endless creative possibilities that can be matched to the client's unique experience and done at the client's request.

So, in all these ways, bodily expression and experience are central to the practice of Body Psychotherapy. Bodily expression is the primary language for the communication of unconscious structures. In addition, studies have shown that the single client factor that best predicts success in psychotherapy is whether or not the client can "stay" with his or her experience.[47] If he can't, therapy will not be effective. This one factor is so important because experience is organized by beliefs, which need to be made conscious. It is the therapist's ability to use bodily expressions, and the experiences linked to them, that makes the whole endeavor successful and, by the way, interesting and challenging for those of us who practice in the profession.

## References

Baars, B. J. (1988). *A cognitive theory of consciousness.* New York: Cambridge University Press.

Baars, B. J., & McGovern, K. (1997). Global workspace: A theory of consciousness. In A. F. Colllins & M. A. Conway (Eds.), *Theories of memory.* Hove: Routledge.

Baddeley, A. (1993). *Working memory and conscious awareness.* In A. F. Collins & M. A. Conway (Eds.), *Theories of memory.* Hove: Routledge.

Damasio, A. R. (1994). *Descartes' error: Emotion, reason, and the human brain.* New York: Grosset, Putnam.

Goleman, D. (1995). *Emotional intelligence.* New York: Bantam.

Kurtz, R. (1990). *Body-Centered Psychotherapy.* Mendocino, CA: LifeRhythm.

Lewis, T., Amini, F., & Lannon, R. (2001). *A general theory of love.* New York: Vintage Books.

---

45  Thomas Lewis (Lewis et al., 2001) describes how activation of one neuronal network can suppress others (pp. 128–132).

46  These are often called, in the psychological literature, "corrective experiences."

47  Study done by Eugene Gendlin and his students at the University of Chicago. See E. T. Gendlin (1996). *Focusing-oriented psychotherapy: A manual of the experiential method.* New York: Guilford.

Panksepp, J. (1998). *Affective neuroscience: The foundations of human and animal emotions.* Oxford: Oxford University Press.

Porges, S. (2003). Social engagement and attachment. *Annals of the New York Academy of Sciences, 1008,* 31–47.

Reich, W. (1949). *Character Analysis.* New York: Noonday Press.

Schore, A. (1994). *Affect regulation and the self: The neurobiology of affective development.* Oxford, UK: Oxford University Press.

Siegel, D. (1999). *The developing mind.* New York: Guilford Press.

Waldstein, S. R., & Elias, M. F. (Eds.). (2001). *Neuropsychology of cardiovascular disease.* Mahwah, NJ: Lawrence Erlbaum.

Watt, D. F. (2001). *Emotions and consciousness.* Retrieved from www.phil.vt.edu/ASSC/watt/default.html

# 40
## The Experiencing Body

Halko Weiss, United States

Halko Weiss's biographical information can be found at the beginning of Chapter 1, the Preface to this handbook.

## Experience in Psychotherapy

All forms of Body Psychotherapy base important portions of their technique and methodology on either staying with spontaneously occurring significant experiences and deepening them, or actively engendering them. The underlying principle here is that the here-and-now quality of the client's current felt experience in psychotherapy can be considered to be one of the key elements for its success. The intensity of an experiential piece of work—and the precision with which it constellates and clearly reflects the client's most significant intimate and existential issues, such as their underlying character structure—is rightly understood as pivotal for the extent to which the client's self-organizing process will allow change and development.

Here, I will use the term "experience" in reference to the *qualities of subjectively perceptible events within,* such as emotional nuances and their depth, variations of complex body sensations, or the related networked mental processes. We can think of them as complex body-mind processes, triggered by both external and internal stimuli, and although subjectively many of them may be unconscious and subliminal, in principle they can be perceived and apprehended.

Historically, the experiential perspective was difficult to maintain in academic psychology, because—just as with other concepts of the subjective, first-person dimension—it does not lend itself to being verified through objective measurement. As a result, this factor has largely been ignored in psychotherapy's discourse and theory building, even though it plays a very obvious role in the main streams of psychotherapy—for example, in the transference experience of Psychodynamic Therapy, or in Cognitive Behavioral Therapy, which frequently depends—very specifically—on experience-intensive learning. However, it was Humanistic Psychology that insisted, comprehensively and in grand style, that clients' here-and-now awareness of experience must be at the center of psychotherapy, never mind the fact that it may be hard to define and pin down.

It was only in the last decades of the twentieth century that there were new attempts to comprehend the concept of "experience," when it was afforded a central role by the academic world, with the renowned psychologist Leslie Greenberg assuming a leading role in this process. He explains:

> . . . a dialectical constructivist model of experiential therapy has recently been proposed . . . In this view a person is seen as a *symbolizing,* meaning-creating being who acts as a dynamic system constantly synthesizing information from many levels of processing and from both internal and external sources into self-aware *experience.* Three major levels of processing— innate *sensory motor, emotional schematic memory,* and *conceptual level* processing—are identified . . . In addition people are seen as organizing experience into *emotion-based schemas* that then play a central role in

the creation of meaning and its functions. (Greenberg et al., 1998, pp. 42–43, author's emphasis)

Lately, two other areas of scientific research have been able to contribute important aspects toward comprehending the dimensions of experience.

On the one side, neuropsychology may succeed in developing a reference language that would enable different psychotherapeutic modalities to convey their concepts of "experience" and "experiencing" in a way that supports a "proper" scientific discourse (for example, neuropsychologists like Austin, Damasio, Dennett, Edelman, Gazzaniga, Kandel, LeDoux, Llinás, Panksepp, Schacter, Schore, Siegel, etc.). Neuropsychology considers the "activation" of specific neural networks in the brain, the brain's reciprocal control and inhibition, the role of affect-driven processes, the structure and the role of the "implicit" memory, the function of limbic resonance (interpersonal emotional processes), as well as the close correlation between somatic and central processes, etc. (see Chapter 12, "Neurobiological Perspectives on Body Psychotherapy" by Christian Gottwald). As the term "neuropsychology" already implies, it is apparently possible to create ever more useful links between psychological and neurological processes.

On the other side, the models of system theories, such as the theory of complex adaptive systems (for example, Gell-Mann, Prigogine, Holland, Kauffman, Langton, etc.; see overview in Waldrop, 1992), contribute to a scientifically acceptable language, as well as to a deepening understanding—i.e., when they "assume" that self-organizing systems (such as a human being) learn from "experiences" and, in the process, develop internal models of reality that "anticipate" a specific environment. John Holland, one of the outstanding representatives of this avenue of research, writes:

> Despite the perpetual novelty of the world, we contrive to turn experience into models of the world. We *learn* how to behave, and we anticipate the future, using the models to guide us in activities both common and uncommon. (Holland, 1998, p. 53, author's emphasis)

From a psychological perspective, such models come to light as *response patterns, automatic elements of behavior,* and *affects,* for example. On the basis of these findings by the "hard" sciences of neuropsychology and system theories, we arrive at the recognition that learning—and the reorganization of entrenched patterns—develops through experiences that must contain a certain optimal degree of intensity and significance—a kind of "experiential power" (Spitzer, 2003). Established structures of behavior can change only "*through emotionally moving interactions*" (Roth, 2003, p. 551). The psychotherapy researcher Klaus Grawe (2000) emphasizes the importance of experientially relived memories that should be as concrete as possible, and must be connected to *sensory, motoric,* and *affective* aspects of the experience. Such learning appears to be equivalent to new formations—or re-formations—of the neuronal network architecture (Siegel, 1999, pp. 24ff.). Experiential learning is, therefore, seen as a basic principle of psychotherapeutic change (Mahoney, 1991, pp. 151ff.).

This constitutes support for the assumptions, for example, of classical psychoanalysis that intense transferential feelings, as well as equally intensive *new* experiences, co-created in relationship with the therapist, may be crucial for the success of the therapy.

## The Body as the Medium of Experience

In Somatic or Body Psychotherapy, the body is at the center of attention as the main medium of experience and learning. Of course, words often play an important role, particularly in symbolization processes when meaning is created from experience (Downing, 1996; Kurtz, 1990). However, the very foundations of such a process are embodied perceptions, feelings, and sensations, which—although initially often unclear, vague, and oblique—provide the raw material of new experience. Without exploration and inquiry into somatically based realities, including any impulses and blocks, and without a "felt sense" to start with (Gendlin, 1981), any meaning-making process is hampered by the limitations of being restricted to mental abstractions and shades of "virtual reality."

Transformational change processes, when they occur, substantiate the same principle: a new somatic experience—a more satisfying sense of inhabiting one's being—*precedes* the symbolic articulation. Thus, the somatic experience becomes the reality base for the psychotherapeutic process. Greenberg writes:

> Experience, according to Rogers . . . comprises everything that is happening within the organism, and that is potentially available to awareness. To experience means to receive the impact of sensory or physiological events happening in the moment. Experiencing, according to Gendlin, . . . is the process of concrete bodily feeling. This constitutes the basic matter for all psychological phenomena. Experience is thus what is given; it is what happens as we live. (Greenberg et al., 1998, p. 30)

All Body Psychotherapists take as their perennial starting and reference point the body as the actual place where experiencing takes place, where feelings and moods become perceptible, and where differentiations between different emotional states, nuances between various vitality affects, and distinctions between pleasant and unpleasant states of being are made. There is no access to any sense of being via the brain directly, nor through language, nor memory. Only simultaneous somatic events, occurring in parallel with mental events, lend evident reality to what is being experienced (Damasio, 1999). "Meaning-making" takes place when insights, recognitions, and realizations occurring in therapy acquire a quality of immediacy, congruence, and subjective truth through the client's embodied experience. This is fundamentally different from the (often speculative) explanations derived from merely cognitive reconstructions, commonly relied on in the "talking therapies." This is one of the reasons why Hilarion Petzold has called the quality of such multimodal experiences "vital evidence" (Petzold, 1977, p. 280).

There are recent initiatives in psychoanalysis that are beginning to appreciate the somatic aspects of experience. The contemporary American analyst Lewis Aron refers to Winnicott when he explains, "For him [Winnicott], under healthy conditions, the mind is not located in the head but, rather, is experienced as at one with the whole living body, hence the idea that the mind does not really exist as a separate entity" (Aron, 1998). This is similar to Winnicott's phrase "psyche indwelling in the soma," where he uses the concept of "personalization"—or the infant coming to feel, through loving handling, that his body is himself and that his sense of self is centered in his body (Abram, 2007, p. 197).

Neuropsychology is also beginning to illuminate these connections; among others, the significant participation of the body in everything that happens to the psyche is highlighted by Antonio Damasio, who has introduced the term "somatic markers" for it. He writes, "I advanced the possibility that the part of the mind we call the self was, biologically speaking, grounded on a collection of non-conscious neural patterns standing for the part of the organism we call the body proper" (Damasio, 1999, p. 134). From this perspective, the brain is constantly fed data from the body that constitutes the basis for the current representation of the self (Ibid., pp. 21ff.).

Increasingly, therefore, incorporating the body into psychotherapy is seen as a promising advantage, because the therapeutic process can be directly linked to the client's somatic experiences. It is a peculiarity of human self-organization that this fact is normally largely concealed from consciousness: ". . . we cover the representations of our bodies, of how much mental imagery based on non-body objects and events masks the reality of the body. Otherwise, we would easily know that emotions and feelings are tangibly about the body" (Ibid., p. 29).

Therefore, Body Psychotherapy attempts to bring the body—and its sensations—back into conscious experience, in order to make it possible for us to inhabit the intimate interconnection and mutual reciprocity of the body and mind. For those therapists who work psychodynamically, the goal is to then connect—through various therapeutic strategies—with those levels of the experience that were shaped in the early years of life and that have left their imprint on a person's self-organization. For the purposes of the psychotherapeutic process, it is often relatively easy to evoke intense modes of experiencing by employing such a multimodal combination of the "here and now," the body, and self-awareness, although these elements may oftentimes require strong and decisive support by the therapist. Intense affective, embodied experiencing in the present moment of therapeutic interaction maximizes neuroplasticity, activating neural-network patterns that correspond to previously inaccessible implicit memories that can become reawakened in a session, giving an authentic avenue into the client's formative experiences that shaped their personality structure.

From a Body Psychotherapy perspective, three central criteria can thus be formulated for eliciting such experiential material in a multimodal way:

1. They should touch upon, and be relevant to, the client's core organizing patterns.
2. They should occur within the optimal arousal zone, with a well-calibrated degree of emotional and motoric activation.
3. They should offer opportunities for transformation of the core organizing patterns into new, more satisfying experiences.

## Symbolization and Meaning

In all forms of Body-Oriented and Somatic Psychotherapy, therapists generally observe their clients' bodies very closely. Based on their own experience, as well as specific theories (character theory, functional segments, etc.), a therapist may decide to draw attention to aspects of the client's spontaneous experience in that moment. Client and therapist may then engage in an extended exploration, staying with, and dwelling within, the experience, letting their attention follow the emerging experience as it unfolds and shifts in response to mindful awareness. What usually becomes relevant is the question of *how* the current focus of attention is related to often-lifelong existential patterns. Ron Kurtz, for example, uses the term "indicator" for this kind of key meaningful expression, where a fragment of experience points toward underlying formative character issues (see Chapter 39, "Bodily Expression and Experience in Body Psychotherapy" by Ron Kurtz). A therapist may recognize the significance of a gesture, or other nonverbal expressions, as an "indicator" and pick up on it as a starting point for an experiential exploration that may well lead to formative events in the client's life history.

## Case Example 1

In the eighth session, the therapist draws her client Andy's attention to her observation that he keeps pressing his arms tightly to the sides of his body as he talks—which he does quite a bit. In drawing from her particular therapeutic modality, she suggests an experiential experiment: Andy is invited to observe what is happening internally when he slowly alternates the position of his arms, between slightly lifting them and then returning to pressing them even more firmly into his body. Andy is somewhat confused at first, but then examines the difference in a slow and deliberate way. He begins to report his observations after having experimented for about a minute.

> Andy: It is . . . as if . . . here, in the moment when the arm loses the contact with the body . . . as if . . . there is somehow a fear within me . . . here in the belly . . . a contracting . . . a stinging.

After a couple of minutes of Andy further examining his experience, the therapist invites him to explore the quality of the fear that always seems to arise when his arm is raised.

> Andy: It's more like a secret panic . . . there! . . . a panic! [pause] [He feels what is going on inside himself, his arms now tightly pressed against his body.] . . . It is as if I am afraid to be seen . . . I want to . . . somehow . . . contract . . . slink away.
>
> Therapist: See if you can stay with this for a moment . . . What does that fear actually feel like?
>
> Andy: Like a little boy who wants to hide away . . . There's a panic . . . an expectation of hostile looks . . . eyes that are hard . . . no love . . . [His voice becomes more childlike. It looks as if he wants to start crying.]

In this case, the therapist was addressing an "indicator"— the arms pressed against his body—that directly and quickly led to a relevant "organizing experience." During the rest of this session, the two of them were able to remain with—and explore—a troubling experience from Andy's past, i.e., his relationship with his stepfather. There was a direct experiential link between his original fear, his shrinking away from his stepfather, and his attempts to "hold himself together" with the help of an unconscious somatic habit: the sensation of his arms pressing into his sides was designed to stop himself from feeling his fear and to compensate for a pervasive lack of support. With the help of his therapist, Andy was able to open up to a significant alternative experience of acceptance and safety over the course of the next several therapy sessions.

## Calibration

Today, neuropsychology supports a well-established principle in the tradition of Body Psychotherapy: that there is an optimal range of activation (in the body-mind, as well as in the brain)—often referred to as a degree of "ripeness"—and thus an intensity with which the client's fundamental patterns and essential experiences need to be constellated in therapy—that is a central criterion in the conditions for therapeutic change. Researchers emphasize how essential the activation of neural networks is as a precondition for their restructuring (Nader, 2003). A pivotal question is whether the emerging experiences are *sufficiently intense*, as well as sufficiently *multimodal* (i.e., the combination of body, feelings, memories, etc.) (Gottwald, 2004).

It is relatively easy to trigger intense experiences through body exercises, or through somatic experimentation, when evoked within a framework of awareness or mindfulness. Challenging, stressing, and exhausting the defenses of the muscular armor, the interpersonal charge of touch, with a finely tuned awareness to sensitive body regions, etc., can quite quickly engender forceful body sensations, feelings, and memories. In the history of Body Psychotherapy, the evocation of such strong experiences alone was often (mistakenly) understood to be therapeutic in and of itself. The cathartic approach certainly has its rationale and benefits: the experience and expression of strong emotions, especially if they have been suppressed for a long time, *may* constitute an important step in the therapeutic process. However, in recent decades, it has become increasingly clear that this route can also lead into harmful territory. One of the resulting problems may be "malign" regressions, repetitive and mechanical expressions that—albeit vehement and dramatic—are engaged with little awareness or reflective consciousness and employed mainly as a means of defense (Geissler, 2001; Marlock, 1991).

A related problem occurs in the context of trauma: when a traumatic experience gets triggered (again), it reactivates—and may then reconfirm—the same neuronal pathways that were already established with the original trauma—leading to retraumatization. This is not an uncommon "dead end" of trauma—repetitions through which the traumatic state becomes engrained ever more deeply through progressive sensitization—that has been described as the so-called "kindling" effect (Morrell, 1991; see also Chapter 57, "Risks within Body Psychotherapy" by Courtenay Young).

By contrast, a well-calibrated level of arousal appears to benefit all kinds of learning processes (Siegel, 1999; van der Kolk et al., 1996). Without a minimum degree of activation throughout the corresponding neural networks, no learning can take place at all. Excessive arousal—or insufficient arousal—appears to be detrimental to the therapeutic process, or can obstruct it. In recent years particularly, those trauma therapists who work with the body have shown how the client's level of arousal can be quite well regulated—and with increasing degrees of sophistication (Levine, 1997; Ogden and Minton, 2000; Ogden et al., 2006).

## Transforming Experience

An emerging experience frequently serves to uncover unconscious material; this alone, as shown in Psychodynamic Therapy, can have a beneficial effect. However, many Body Psychotherapists also see the participation of the body in the psychotherapeutic process as an opportunity for offering alternative ("corrective") experiences, as proposed by Franz Alexander (1963). This therapeutic strategy becomes possible only after the activation of already-established experiential patterns—and, if necessary, after working through them and their related meanings. Activated alternative patterns of a corrective experience can then be explored in great detail and depth, to be integrated with the help of the sensate body. Such an approach is based on the assumption that established forms of experiencing (along with their associated internal models of reality) can be differentiated, complemented, and optimized within the therapeutic relationship.

**Case Example 2**

Walter was a thirty-two-year-old "perpetual" student who—during the course of his first twenty-five therapy sessions—had explored his experience of lack of support throughout his life, and the pain of that. Throughout that time, he had repeatedly suffered from depressed and collapsed states that were connected with the memory of how he had lost his mother, through a car accident, when he was six years old. These memories had been conflated with even older ones that were also characterized by feelings of loneliness and abandonment. The therapist spent a great deal of time exploring the related somatic affective states and supporting the development of corresponding narratives. It had become fairly apparent why Walter had never succeeded in becoming involved in a warm, supportive relationship. Around the twenty-fifth session, Walter repeatedly made allusions to how he would love to get to know such a "supportive world" (his expression) at least once in his life.

The therapist offered to sit, back-to-back with him, on the floor, and allow Walter to lean back against him—as a somatic form of "support." This intervention was talked through, and prepared for, in some detail. When they actually tried it out—slowly, and with much awareness—the first thing that surfaced was a series of memories of a long chain of experiences that made it impossible for Walter to feel anything other than tension and fear. These experiences were then explored and shared.

Then, one day—after several more similar sessions of sitting on the floor—Walter suddenly found himself—without anything particularly unusual happening beforehand—"yielding," and he was then able to lean into the therapist easily and without resistance. Then came an avalanche of intense emotions that erupted from within sadness, relief, joy, and pain. During several of the following sessions, the ability to receive "backing" (as Walter called it) finally became increasingly easy and natural. Events outside the therapy room started to confirm this expanded reality.

This example illustrates how the multimodal intensity of embodied experiences can provide opportunities for exploring new and previously unknown reparative modes of "being" and "relating," and how these can be integrated into established structures of character.

## Body Psychotherapy and Experiencing

Body Psychotherapists cultivate, facilitate, and help to shape their clients' processes of experiencing. Many of their techniques are designed to enable, and evoke, a fuller, more comprehensively multimodal possibility of experience, lived with greater awareness. Out of this fuller and richer experience, narratives can be evolved, co-created by the client and therapist, that—in turn—open up avenues toward conceiving new and healing experiences, and integrating them into the established cognitive, emotional, and somatic schemata. The somatic components serve both to uncover unconscious subjective realities, as well as to create powerful and lasting experiences that contradict and counteract the limiting original ones.

## References

Abram, J. (2007). *The language of Winnicott: A dictionary of Winnicott's use of word.* London: Karnac.

Alexander, F. (1963). *Fundamentals of psychoanalysis.* New York: W. W. Norton.

Aron, L. (1998). The clinical body and the reflexive mind. In L. Aron & F. S. Anderson (Eds.), *Relational perspectives on the body.* Hillsdale, NJ: Analytic Press.

Damasio, A. R. (1999). *The feeling of what happens.* New York: Harcourt Brace.

Downing, G. (1996). *Körper und Wort in der Psychotherapie* [Body and word in psychotherapy]. Munich: Kösel.

Geissler, P. (2001). *Mythos Regression* [The myth of regression]. Giessen: Psychosozial.

Gendlin, E. T. (1981). *Focusing.* New York: Bantam.

Gottwald, C. (2004). Bewusstseinszentrierte Körperpsychotherapie [Consciousness-centered Body Psychotherapy]. In S. Sulz, L. Schrenker, & C. Schricker (Eds.), *Die Psychotherapie entdeckt der Körper* [Psychotherapy discovers the body]. Munich: CIP-Medien.

Grawe, K. (2000). *Psychologische Therapie* [Psychological therapy]. Göttingen: Hogrefe.

Greenberg, L. S., Watson, J. C., & Lietaer, G. (1998). *Handbook of Experiential Psychotherapy.* New York: Guilford Press.

Holland, J. (1998). *Emergence.* Oxford: Oxford University Press.

Kurtz, R. (1990). *Body-Centered Psychotherapy.* Mendocino, CA: LifeRhythm.

Levine, P. A. (1997). *Waking the tiger: Healing trauma.* Berkeley, CA: North Atlantic Books.

Mahoney, M. J. (1991). *Human change processes.* New York: Basic Books.

Marlock, G. (1991). Notes on regression. In G. Marlock (Ed.), *Unitive Body-Psychotherapy* (Vol. 2). Frankfurt: Afra Verlag.

Morrell, F. (1991). *Kindling and synaptic plasticity: The legacy of Graham Goddard.* Berlin: Springer.

Nader, K. (2003). Memory traces unbound. *Trends in Neuroscience, 26,* 65.

Ogden, P., & Minton, K. (2000). Sensorimotor Psychotherapy: One method for processing traumatic memory. *Traumatology, 6*(3), 149–173.

Ogden, P., Minton, K., & Pain, C. (2006). *Trauma and the body: The theory and practice of Sensorimotor Psychotherapy.* New York: W. W. Norton.

Petzold, H. (1977). *Die neuen Körpertherapien* [The new body therapies]. Paderborn: Junfermann.

Roth, G. (2003). *Fühlen, Denken, Handeln* [Feeling, thinking, acting]. Frankfurt: Suhrkamp.

Siegel, D. J. (1999). *The developing mind.* New York: Guilford Press.

Spitzer, M. (2003). *Lernen* [Learning]. Heidelberg: Spektrum Akademischer Verlag.

van der Kolk, B. A., McFarlane, A. C., & Weisaeth, L. (Eds.). (1996). *Traumatic stress: The effects of overwhelming experience on mind, body, and society.* New York: Guilford Press.

Waldrop, M. M. (1992). *Complexity: The emerging science at the edge of order and chaos.* New York: Simon & Schuster.

# 41
## Movement As and In Psychotherapy

**Christine Caldwell, United States**

**Christine Caldwell,** PhD, BC-DMT, LPC, NCC, ACS, is the founder and former director of the Somatic Counseling Psychology program at Naropa University, where she teaches somatic counseling, clinical neuroscience, research, and diversity issues. Her work, called the Moving Cycle, spotlights natural play, early physical imprinting, fully sequenced movement processes, the opportunities in addiction, and a trust in the authoritative knowledge of the body. She has taught at the University of Maryland, George Washington University, Concordia, Seoul Women's University, Southwestern College, and Santa Barbara Graduate Institute, and trains, teaches, and lectures internationally. She has published more than thirty articles and book chapters, and her books include *Getting Our Bodies Back* and *Getting in Touch*.

Body-Centered Psychotherapy, often called Somatic Psychotherapy, uses physical and biological processes to build, both literally and metaphorically, its theoretical orientations, its assessment tools, and its therapeutic interventions. Physical processes associated with human development, maintenance, reproduction, creativity, and senescence all play a central role in this psychotherapeutic paradigm. These physical processes possess an inward, intrapsychic element and an outward, communicative, relational element, and represent the human drive for both internal and external cohesion. All these processes require our bodies to be in some kind of motion.

Movement may be our most relevant definition of life. We know we are alive when our heart beats, our lungs expand and contract, and our brains generate electromagnetic waves. If any of these are absent, we are deemed dead or inert. The quality and quantity of movement, from a cellular to an organismic level, may also be our most observable and fundamental diagnosis, assessment, and treatment tool from a psychotherapeutic perspective. This chapter will explore the reasoning for this theory, and postulate practical ways it can be applied therapeutically.

## Coherencies, Cohesions, and Continuums

Our drive for physical cohesion seems to ride oscillatory waves, waves such as the expansion and contraction of the heart, the ebb and flow of the lungs, and the squeeze and release of digestive peristalsis. It may be that oscillatory phenomena help us to range along a continuum of movement that maximizes adaptive responses to a changing environment. Our consciousness tends to follow this wave pattern as well, alternating between attending to internal states and attending to external events, in order to achieve physical, psychological, and social cohesion.

Perhaps one of the best physiological examples of these oscillatory waves is the sensory-motor loop—the continuous cycle of taking in information about the internal and external world, processing it in a way that makes the information coherent, and using this coherent information to determine behavior, or actions. In a real sense, we can translate sensory processing and the resulting responsive behavior into a more primary term—movement. All human activity involves and requires movement, whether that movement is cellular, systemic (digestive, respiratory, etc.), or involving the whole organism (posture, gesture, locomotion, vocalization). Life on all levels, then, begins to look more like an oscillating movement phenomenon (Llinas, 2001).

Biological research has sought to understand and categorize movement across all species, and has arrived at the concept of a mobility gradient. This gradient illustrates that all biological movement can be seen along a continuum, beginning with immobility and ending with complexity and unpredictability, as a result of increased and decreased stereotypy (Golani, 1992). When looking at an intact organism, this continuum begins with a lack of observable movement—immobility—as a result of either a loss of energy, such as unconsciousness, or an increase in bound energy, like muscular tension. "Freezing"—as part of the "fight-or-flight" reaction in a dangerous situation—would be an example of high-energy immobility, and involves simultaneously contracting muscles that perform opposite movements (agonist and antagonist). Thus, an action is both initiated and inhibited at the same time. Movements at this end of the continuum tend to be more primitive, often being processed in the spinal cord and not requiring higher brain functions.

Complex and spontaneous movement, on the other hand, requires motor planning, with the potential of many brain regions being active and cooperating with each other (basal ganglia, cerebellum, corpus callosum, cerebral cortex), and results in more global brain functioning. In this sense, as humans, we tend to oscillate between primitive and complex movement and brain states. Recent research even points to the likelihood that the evolutionary emergence of human intelligence is more a product of an increase in coordinated brain functioning, required by complex motor planning, than it is by, say, possessing an opposable thumb (Calvin, 1998).

Authors have also speculated on a similar movement continuum from highly patterned, inherited, and fixed motor behaviors, such as reflexes and orienting responses (Loeb, 1973), to highly spontaneous, impulsive, and creative movements that are responsive to rapid environmental changes. Play behavior and artistic improvisation occupy this latter category. The highly impulsive nature of free play in mammals and birds has been theorized to be "training for the unexpected" (Bekoff, 2001), whereas reflexive movement is often associated with defense and other autonomic functions. Both facilitate coherency in the organism.

Human development, from a movement perspective, follows a somewhat linear progression from simple to complex behaviors as well, ranging from embryonic pre-neurological pulsations to autonomic/reflexive behaviors to "thought-out," complex, conscious, and volitional ones. The developing fetus is said to move through all the stages of phylogenetic development, from single-cell motion to amphibian to reptilian to mammalian activities. When it is born, it demonstrates many reflexive movements, orienting responses, and a few basic motor plans such as sucking. As it develops postnatally, complexification travels down the spine, beginning with the ability to hold up its own head, then progressing to reaching and pushing with the arms, and on to sitting, to standing, etc. After motor development completes, the child is hopefully able to oscillate its behavior along a continuum from preneurological pulsations to complex and spontaneous play behavior (Stassen Berger, 2000; Ayres, 1972; Hannaford, 1995; Hartley, 1989; Loeb, 1973; Aposhyan, 1999).

As stated before, movement regulates inner, less observable processes such as cell metabolism, fluid circulation, digestion, and respiration, as well as outer, observable behavioral processes such as locomotion, facial expression, and nonverbal communication. Humans are a highly social species, and we also use movement to regulate our relationships with others. We belong to movement communities in the same way that we belong to racial, ethnic, and gender communities. Facial gestures and posture communicate emotion, mood, and intention, for instance. Our use of space and level signal our social status, relatedness, and dominance (Henley, 1977). Coherency, in this sense, runs on a continuum from the biological to the social; humans need movement to take care of their personal needs, as well as their social ones.

There also exists another dimension of movement—the seemingly purposeless behavior of play—done in the moment just for the sake of doing it. Increasing evidence exists that shows that playful movement, wherever it occurs along a continuum from highly organized and ritualized to highly impulsive, is essential for biological, psychological, and social health, extending our continuum of movement toward greater complexity and adaptability (Bekoff and Byers, 1998; Fagen, 1981; Huizinga, 1950).

## Movement Therapy

A central premise of a movement-centered psychotherapy is that consistent disturbance in these organic oscillatory continuums, such that any movement sequence becomes incoherent or absent, eventually results in illness or dysfunction. Western medicine, for instance, is increasingly coming to the conclusion that biological processes can be accomplished only when a system is acting on coherent information (Oschman, 2000). Illness equals incoherency, and may also be called entropy (Nuland, 1993). The same may be true for psychological and social health. Incoherency occurs when any psychologically motivated movement is retarded, accelerated, or distorted (in space, time, or effort) out of the form that allows it to complete desired actions, or to set up conditions for optimal communication or information gathering. Trauma, as evidenced by post-traumatic stress disorder, not only affects thoughts and emotions, but reaches all the way down into the brainstem to alter reflexes and orienting responses, changing the "set point" of activation (hypotonic or hypertonic) in the autonomic nervous system (Ogden, Minton, and Pain, 2006).

Our basic sense of self-efficacy may arise from a sense that "how I move gets me what I want," which ensues from successfully mastered early childhood developmental movements (Caldwell, 2001). By studying movement, we may unlock the essential processes of health and illness. By using movement in psychotherapy, we may get to the heart of how humans heal, grow, and transform.

How do we see a movement-based therapy as increasing coherency in our physical, psychological, and social bodies? In the physical realm, this has largely been done. We value and support such movement-centered practices as physical therapy, exercise, Yoga, Tai Chi, stretching, and other disciplines. We personally understand the relationship between exercise and physical health, for instance (Sapolsky, 1998). In my opinion, psychotherapy has been slower in accepting and developing movement practices that facilitate psychological wholeness (coherency), due largely to the modern Western tendency to separate the body from the mind, and to locate psychological health largely in mental and emotional realms. Movement-based therapies tend to remedy this error by seeing movement as occurring across the spectrum of human existence—that we not only physically move, but also move emotionally, cognitively, and spiritually—and that all these movements live within the context and container of physical movement.

Often, in the throes of an emotion, we say that someone or something "moves us." We try to avoid becoming rigid and fixed in our thinking, and we value people who are able to change their mind, or "move" their thinking. In the realms of the spirit, we strive to move toward that which is greater than ourselves. To see our emotions and thoughts as moving, and not sedentary, implies the same measure of health as the same action in the physical body. In the view of many movement-centered psychotherapists, oscillating along many movement continuums in order to create and maintain coherency may be our most holistic view of human health (Dychtwald, 1977; Needham Costonis, 1978; Pesso and Crandell, 1991; Sheets-Johnstone, 1999; Sweigard, 1974).

Movement-based therapies also go one step further, and postulate that movement in one area of our being promotes movement in the others. We are "of a piece," and what we think influences what we feel, and how we move physically creates a ripple effect into the flow of feelings, thoughts, and basic awareness. This belief, for instance, represents a central tenet of Dance/Movement Therapy (Lewis Bernstein, 1984). Trained dancers literally went into psychiatric hospitals and began to dance with psychotic patients. As the trained dancers adapted their techniques to these fractured people, staff noticed positive behavioral change in the patients, and the patients themselves reported feeling more present, calmer, and more coherent (Chaiklin, 1975). Dance therapists feel not only that the physical act of dance promotes increased movement coherency, but that the creative experience inherent in dance promotes psychological coherency. Here again, we see the idea that creative movement sequences may extend our movement repertoire beyond stereotypy, and this expansion of capacity reflects the nature of healing, as well as the nature of biological development.

Western culture is becoming increasingly more sedentary, and increasingly "cogito-centered," overvaluing mental motion at the expense of physical movement. Aside from the physical-health compromises that this trend engenders, psychological risks may occur as a result of our increased immobility. What also may result from this tendency is a culture that develops the eyes and ears (exteroceptive senses) at the expense of touch, taste, smell, and perhaps most importantly, proprioception and kinesthesia. These last two senses tell us about our balance, muscle tone, position in space, and pressure against objects, all faculties that are essential for movement coherency or for movement intelligence. Interestingly, some researchers postulate that an inability to process proprioceptive information may lie at the heart of the etiology of schizophrenia (Grand, 1982).

It may also be that the ability to move in one realm, and not others, defines what we consider an unbalanced being—someone who is physically coordinated, but stumbles over emotions, or someone who is a mental gymnast, but can't throw a ball. Our definition of a "balanced" person often implies a capacity for movement across physical, emotional, cognitive, and spiritual realms.

## Movement Observation and Analysis

If we see movement as central to human health, we must then find some way to objectively and systematically observe it, in order to assess how to use it in promoting health. Beginning at the turn of the last century, efforts were made to simply describe movement processes objectively (Laban, 2011). These centered on humans' use of time, space, and effort, the hallmarks of mechanical physics. In other words, any movement occurs in time, and exists along a continuum from slow to fast. All movement occupies some kind of space, from large to small. And all movement involves some kind of effort, or expense of energy, from minimal to quite strong.

Rudolf Laban is the grandfather of analysis systems that follow these observations, and the people who have followed him have strongly influenced the field of Dance Therapy (Bernstein, 1972). Observers have refined the basic principles with elements of flow sequencing, such as rising and sinking, scattering and gathering.

Another way to analyze movement is to look at the patterns of action in the muscles. Valerie Hunt, in her work at UCLA, discovered four basic patterns of muscle action that produce movement. They are based on kinesiology, which coined the term "agonist" for the muscle that contracts to produce an action, and "antagonist" for the muscle that must relax or stretch to permit a movement to occur; for instance, in flexing the elbow the biceps is the agonist, and the triceps is the antagonist. Hunt found that four basic patterns of movement result from the actions of agonists and antagonists. They are:

- **Burst:** a strong firing of an agonist, followed by a rebounding contraction of an antagonist. A punch with the fist is an example of a burst movement.
- **Sustain:** a continuous firing of an agonist with minimal or no contraction of an antagonist. The steady motions of Tai Chi are an example of sustained movement.
- **Restrain:** A contraction of an agonist with an almost equally strong contraction of an antagonist at the same time. A slow pushing movement of the arms in the air would illustrate this.

- **Undulate:** an alternating firing of agonist and antagonist, often producing a wavelike motion, such as hula dancing.

These systems hold the advantage of being very observable, and people can be and have been trained to notate and transcribe movement using these principles. These systems have also entered the realm of analyzing these movement elements for their psychological significance. For instance, I conducted a study using Hunt's movement protocol that correlated movement behaviors with personality characteristics (Caldwell, 1976). Several dance therapists have used Laban-inspired systems to postulate psychological states that co-inhabit movement states (Bernstein, 1972; Kestenberg-Amighi et al., 1999). In this way, some clinicians feel that they can infer psychological organization from its observable movement and postural/gestural correlates, thereby creating an assessment tool based in readily observable phenomena (Kurtz and Prestera, 1976; Keleman, 1985). Other clinicians believe that these correlations exist, but are so influenced by personal and cultural history that the therapy involves helping the client to make a map of their own, assisting the individual to know herself better by identifying the ways in which her thoughts, emotions, and physical motions dance together (Caldwell, 1976, 2001, 2010).

Some problems with these assessment strategies are that correlations between physical movements and psychological ones are usually exceedingly complex, culturally influenced, and also contaminated by observer bias, as well as by the fact that there is no hermeneutic theory that would mediate between the observable and the hidden psychic domains (Caldwell, 2010). It may also be difficult to train people to be reliable and valid observers and notators (Koch et al., 2001). However, this is a problem that plagues the psychotherapy field in general, and may be no more unworkable than when clinicians are asked to infer psychological states from verbal statements.

Another criticism of this type of movement analysis is that it is biased toward muscle-mediated movement. Especially when we look at the preneurological and pulsatory cellular level, movements are not muscle-initiated. For several movement-based therapies, this "myo-centrism" represents a critical blind spot, as cellular and fluid movement is seen as the basis for emotion, and perhaps even for consciousness itself. The researcher Candace Pert (1997), for instance, points out that emotions are strongly mediated by the movement of peptides and ligands circulating throughout the body via the blood and lymph systems. She also notes that which fluid-delivered chemicals that a cell accepts or resists through its cell membrane determine the function of that cell, which can ultimately determine the entire organism's perception and behavior. She describes cell receptors as "dancing" with the chemicals that arrive at their gates, and that the resulting *pas de deux* can be seen as determining overall functioning and health.

These processes are largely unconscious and have historically been considered solely autonomic, but Pert and others believe that overall behavior influences these cellular movements, just as much as these cellular movements determine overall behavior. In a parallel to classic understandings of the psyche, we may be coming to an understanding, long held by Eastern disciplines (such as Tai Chi and Yoga), that conscious behavior and movement influence unconscious movement, as well as unconscious movement influencing conscious behavior. By infusing attention and intention into the movement process, we may be increasing coherency and complexity, generating health, which is a well-accepted basis for psychoneuroimmunology (Pert et al., 1998).

Other systems of movement analysis look at developmental sequencing (Aposhyan, 1999; Bainbridge Cohen, 1993; Bernhardt, 1992). It has been well documented that human babies learn complex motor functions in a systematic and largely sequential manner. In fact, many infant and childhood diseases and conditions are routinely diagnosed via observing the developmental milestones of movement behavior such as sitting up, crawling, and walking (Hartley, 1989). In movement-based psychotherapies, theorists believe that each developmental movement process pairs with psychological development. Coordinating a push with the arms, for instance, which is necessary for learning to sit up, forms the behavioral template for the ability to set boundaries, say no, and feel a sense of self-efficacy. If this push movement is interfered with during a child's development, through abuse, neglect, accident, or disease, the psyche has few physical reference points for learning to set its boundaries and feel powerful. Conversely, finding this push in the physical body—in therapy—is often seen as helping a person develop or recover psychological requirements like empowerment and self-esteem.

Assessing developmental movement sequences, and understanding their behavioral sequelae when they are interfered with, was also pioneered and developed by both physical therapy and occupational therapy. Recently, the field of Sensory Integration has also been developed, via physical therapy and occupational therapy. Sensory Integration arose from the understanding that learning, behavior, and memory disorders are often traced to problems in processing sensations and organizing a behavioral response, the infamous sensory-motor loop (Ayres, 1972). Once again, conscious movement practices are often the treatment of choice for people with attention, processing, and behavioral problems (Hannaford, 1995; Hartley, 1989). Several Somatic Psychotherapists have developed their work along these lines, noting that, along with learning and memory, sensory-integration problems may be at the root of some affective and thought disorders.

## Movement-Based Therapies

Psychotherapies that involve physical movement tend to cluster around the premises mentioned above. All of them assume that movement must be made more conscious and deliberate in order to increase coherency and health. Most assume that physical movement often reveals and heals unconscious processes. Many assume that incoherent movements that have arisen from abuse, neglect, accident, disease, or developmental interference need to be dissolved and replaced with more functional forms. Although this chapter cannot discuss all the various movement-based therapies that are available, it can look at the ways this field is generally organized.

It can be a sensitive and tricky task to separate out the therapies that concentrate on physical movement and only tangentially address psychological coherency, via conscious movement, from the "true" Body Psychotherapies. Debate permeates the field as to whether Tai Chi, or Yoga, or Feldenkrais, for instance, can be seen as inherently psychodynamic. Many people in the field feel it would be a mistake to exclude these systems, though most realize that these systems include no psychotherapeutic training or professional codes. It may be best to say that movement therapy lies along a continuum from straightforward physical rehabilitation to highly symbolic and emotionally infused expressions that heal psychic pain. When looking at the movement-therapy continuum, four general types of work emerge:

1. **Creative/Expressive:** Using the healing power of creative movement; e.g., Dance/Movement (Psycho)therapy and psychodramatically based systems (Pesso, Psychodrama, Dance/Movement Therapy, etc.) live here.

2. **Developmental/Physiological:** Forms that work through developmental frameworks or through various body systems; e.g., Body-Mind Psychotherapy (Aposhyan) and Bodynamics (Marcher) are two examples.

3. **Sensory-Motor Processing:** Working with the sensory-motor loop (sensation to sensory processing to behavioral response); e.g., Sensorimotor Psychotherapy (Ogden) and Somatic Experiencing (Levine).

4. **Sequencing/Completing:** Recovering the original movement sequence and moving it until it feels complete; e.g., Moving Cycle (Caldwell).

Most systems blend some of the above categories. All work with attention and intention. Movements that are stereotypic, or chaotic, or cut off are saturated with inattention: these alter consciousness, and oftentimes affect healing negatively. Intentions of courage and curiosity allow one to probe into states that threaten the old movement patterns. As consciousness alters, the unconscious rises up toward visibility. Physical free association ensues, and movement is used as the reference point for navigating and containing the inchoate emergence of unconscious material. By continuing to move one's authentic experience of this previously unconscious state, nonrational and nonlinear elements of the psyche are formed into coherent resources for the conscious self. These new movement resources are then applied to daily life and its persistent problems.

## A Case Study

In a movement-based psychotherapy, the goal is not to find more movement but to help a client recover movement sequences that are natural, effective, and satisfying. I will describe a typical session within the Moving Cycle format, as an example. A session can (and usually does) begin with sensate awareness. The ability to focus attention on and track the progress of sensation forms an essential support for any healing movement process. The client is typically asked to pay attention to her body and to report any sensations present. This may or may not be woven in with the client speaking about themes or issues at the same time. The educational component of asking the client to report her bodily sensations, as descriptively as possible, is crucial here. When a client slips into interpretation or judgment in this early phase, she runs the risk of getting trapped in the same dysfunctional relationship to her body that she likely came in with. So the therapist might coach the client to describe the nuances of the sensations involved in, say, a headache, rather than speculating how she got it, or how the headache reflects on her as a person. The therapist may also add descriptions of what he or she sees in the client that may be relevant to what the client is reporting. For instance, the therapist may observe that as the client was talking about her headache, her brow furrowed and her jaw clenched. The session simply begins with high-quality attention to the client's body, and this in itself engenders an essential healing process.

Next, the therapist and client together begin a "focusing" process. Often, more sensations may arise and more are reported than are feasible to deal with that day, and others may be irrelevant to the emerging theme of the session (the client noticing the pressure of her legs against the chair, for instance); still others may be so subtle that they can easily escape notice.

What distinguishes a skillful therapist is his or her ability to help the client focus on her sensations in a new way. The client is often causing, or worsening, her own suffering by paying too much attention to some sensations and possibly not enough to others. Her perceptual filters screen sensations that are consistent with her previous (habitual) views, fears, traumas, and patterns. By becoming more curious, with the therapist's help, about those subtle, quirky, or avoided sensations, the client can start to break the cycle of her usual attention that has kept her trapped in the problem, rather than finding the way out or a possible solution.

As the focus deepens, the therapist supports the client to tolerate and take care of this or that sensation, witnessing it and listening deeply to it. Again, the ability to care for a sensate experience in this way is often inherently healing, as the client is often more used to a system of judgment and control toward the unfamiliar sensations. What happens when this high-quality attention deepens is that the client's natural healing capabilities start to become accessible, typically in the form of nonlinear and nonrational (but profoundly significant) associations. These associations arise through diminishing thought and increasing attention to the body. Perhaps, as the client pays attention to her headache, an image of water pressing against a dam forms. Or it could be that the client hears a voice that says, "Shut up and sit still!" Or it may be that an emotion such as anger builds. Any of these experiences is considered to be a "coded" message from deeper within the self. It too is greeted with the same high quality of attention and interest.

What tends to unfold naturally at this point is that the association and the attention start to "move" the client in some way. All sensation impels motion as a behavioral response, and this natural process is now identified and supported. The therapist might ask the client what she wants to do, as she works with these sensations and associations. It may be that the image of water pressing on a dam will move her to press her hands and arms out in front of her. Or she could answer that the "inner voice" is telling her to shut up, either verbally or nonverbally. Or she could let her body give shape to the feelings of anger. In this portion of the session, movement and sensation and occasional descriptive reporting form several waves of ever-deepening engagement. The client literally moves herself into a new relationship with her direct experience, letting her inherent healing forces take over. Here again, the process of oscillating between moving and being moved forms the backbone of healing and recovery. And the original, natural movement sequences of a coherent organism start to become recovered and supported.

This model of movement therapy may, or may not, involve some catharsis at some point. Certainly, expression in the form of movement occurs. However, this expressive movement is just as often subtle, or quiet, or gesturally complex. Often, repressed movement can be expressed cathartically, but catharsis also robs a natural movement of its meaningful shape and flow, sometimes falling into the "more is better" trap.

For movement to be healing, client and therapist must work together, over time, to maintain a high state of presence, integrity, and participation at the center of their focus. In this phase of a session, the client's conscious "allowing" of movement to arise spontaneously and authentically, as a result of attention and care, may help to generate a deeper sense of contact and self-efficacy. It may also assist with the development of a deeper sense of wholeness, of coming "home" to the true self, and helping the person to know "Who I really am and what I really want, when I move according to my nature." It may be that the pushing that began in the arms sequences, to full extending of all the limbs, results in the client starting to feel a concrete sense of being able to take up space. She may even reinforce this feeling with statements such as "I am here. I can be here." As conscious movements are tolerated all the way to completion, a sense of self-appreciation often occurs.

The next phase of the session organizes itself—as this is an organic process—around helping the client to tolerate and enjoy any positive affect. Most clients need safe and supportive guidance as to how to stay conscious and involved in their own pleasure or satisfaction, or even just during a small moment of relief from a (negative) symptom. It may be that the client is now coached to breathe more deeply as she says, "I am here." Or she may be asked to let her body celebrate "I am here" any way it wants. Pleasure has a natural shape, and tempo, and effort pattern, and—at this point—the client needs to (re-)explore this natural birthright.

As the session concludes, the "action" phase occurs. No therapy will "stick" unless it is integrated into a client's daily life. In this phase of a session, practical applications to home, work, or relationships are discussed and practiced. It may be that the client practices a feeling of "taking up space" as she imagines talking to her boss. Or the client may choose to do conscious-breathing exercises until the next session so that she can feel more familiar with supporting her experience with her breath.

This application work is crucial for new sensate awareness to occur, awareness that will prepare the client for the next session, or for a more meaningful life.

## Conclusion

All life moves. All life shares movement sequencing as our primary means of creating, maintaining, and extending life. This chapter has looked at health and healing through the lens of biology, and natural movement, as well as psychology. By studying organismic movement, we may be peering into the foundations of the self, an idea supported by Freud when he opined that the first and foremost ego is the body ego. Looking through this biological lens, we can hypothesize that healthy life moves in ways that satisfy, and enrich, and fulfill purpose; and unhealthy life moves in ways that cause frustration and suffering. By consciously attending to and caring for our movement processes on physical, emotional, cognitive, and spiritual levels, we may be better able to heal, recover, and transform ourselves. When we move together with others, we bond; we attune with others (and ourselves), and thus we know ourselves to be more than just individuals. Whether it arises as a knee jerk or an improvisational dance, movement has a significant hand in creating and maintaining our coherency, our identity, and our ineffable grace. Repeated movements are gradually tracked into our systems, creating automatic patterns that may be the physical manifestation of personality. In this sense, momentum may be what creates identity. By both establishing movement patterns and being willing to interrupt their momentum with something new, we may be keeping ourselves more safe, whole, and happy.

## References

Aposhyan, S. (1999). *Natural intelligence: Body-mind integration and human development.* Baltimore: Williams & Wilkins.

Ayres, A. J. (1972). *Sensory integration and learning disorders.* Los Angeles: Western Psychological Services.

Bainbridge Cohen, B. (1993). *Sensing, feeling and action: The experiential anatomy of BodyMind Centering.* Northampton, MA: Contact Editions.

Bekoff, M. (2001). Mammalian play: Training for the unexpected. *Quarterly Review of Biology, 76*(2), 141–168.

Bekoff, M., & Byers, J. (Eds.). (1998). *Animal play: Evolutionary, comparative, and ecological perspectives.* Cambridge, UK: Cambridge University Press.

Bernstein, P. (1972). *Theory and methods in Dance-Movement Therapy: A manual for therapists, students and educators.* Dubuque, IA: Kendall Hunt.

Bernhardt, P. (1992). Individuation, mutual connection, and the body's resources: An interview with Lisbeth Marcher. *Journal of Prenatal and Perinatal Psychology and Health, 6*(4), 281–293.

Caldwell, C. (1976). *Personality characteristics and movement behavior.* Unpublished master's thesis, UCLA Dance Department, Los Angeles.

Caldwell, C. (2001). Addiction as somatic dissociation. In M. Heller (Ed.), *The flesh of the soul: The body we work with* (pp. 213–230). Bern: Peter Lang.

Caldwell, C. (2010). Diversity issues in movement observation and analysis. In S. Bender (Ed.), *Movement analysis of interaction.* Berlin: Logos Verlag.

Calvin, W. H. (1998, Winter). The emergence of intelligence. *Scientific American Quarterly, 9*(4), 86–93.

Chaiklin, H. (Ed.). (1975). *Marion Chace: Her papers.* Columbia, MD: American Dance Therapy Association.

Dychtwald, K. (1977). *Bodymind.* New York: Pantheon.

Fagen, R. (1981). *Animal play behavior.* New York: Oxford University Press.

Golani, I. (1992). A mobility gradient in the organization of vertebrate movement: The perception of movement through symbolic language. *Behavioral and Brain Sciences, 15,* 249–308.

Grand, S. (1982). The body and its boundaries: A psychoanalytic view of cognitive process disturbances in schizophrenia. *International Review of Psychoanalysis, 9,* 327–340.

Hannaford, C. (1995). *Smart moves: Why learning is not all in your head.* Arlington, VA: Great Ocean.

Hartley, L. (1989). *Wisdom of the body moving: An introduction to body-mind centering.* Berkeley, CA: North Atlantic Books.

Henley, N. (1977). *Body politics: Power, sex, and nonverbal communication.* Englewood Cliffs, NJ: Prentice Hall.

Huizinga, J. (1950). *Homo ludens.* Boston: Beacon Press.

Keleman, S. (1985). *Emotional anatomy: The structure of experience.* Berkeley, CA: Center Press.

Kestenberg-Amighi, J., Loman, S., & Sossin, K. M. (1999). *The meaning of movement: Developmental and clinical perspectives of the Kestenberg Movement Profile.* Amsterdam: Gordon & Breach.

Koch, S. C., Flaum Cruz, R., & Goodill, S. (2001, Fall/Winter). The Kestenberg Movement Profile: Performance of novice raters. *American Journal of Dance Therapy, 23*(2), 71–87.

Kurtz, R., & Prestera, H. (1976). *The body reveals: An illustrated guide to the psychology of the body.* New York: Harper & Row.

Laban, R. (2011). *The mastery of movement.* Binsted, Hampshire, UK: Dance Books.

Lewis Bernstein, P. (Ed.). (1984). *Theoretical approaches in Dance-Movement Therapy.* Dubuque, IA: Kendall Hunt.

Llinas, R. (2001). *The "I" of the vortex.* Cambridge, MA: MIT Press.

Loeb, J. (1973). *Forced movements, tropisms, and animal conduct.* New York: Dover.

Needham Costonis, M. (1978). *Therapy in motion.* Chicago: University of Illinois Press.

Nuland, S. (1993). *How we die.* New York: Vintage.

Ogden, P., Minton, K., & Pain, C. (2006). *Trauma and the body: A sensorimotor approach to psychotherapy.* New York: W. W. Norton.

Oschman, J. (2000). *Energy medicine: The scientific basis.* London: Churchill Livingstone.

Pert, C. (1997). *Molecules of emotion: Why you feel the way you feel.* New York: Simon & Schuster.

Pert, C., Dreher, H., & Ruff, M. (1998). The psychosomatic network: Foundations of mind-body medicine. *Alternative Therapies, 4*(4), 30–40.

Pesso, A., & Crandell, J. (Eds.). (1991). *Moving psychotherapy: Theory and application of Pesso System/Psychomotor Therapy.* New York: Brookline Books.

Sapolsky, R. (1998). *Why zebras don't get ulcers: An updated guide to stress, stress-related diseases, and coping.* New York: W. H. Freeman.

Sheets-Johnstone, M. (1999). *The primacy of movement.* Amsterdam: John Benjamins.

Stassen Berger, K. (2000). *The developing person: Through childhood and adolescence.* New York: Worth.

Sweigard, L. (1974). *Human movement potential: Its ideokinetic facilitation.* New York: Harper & Row.

# 42

## "When Is Now? When Is Now?"

*Corrective Experiences: With Whom? When? And Where?*

### Albert Pesso, United States

**Albert Pesso** is considered to be one of the most important living masters of the art of Body Psychotherapy by many of his colleagues. He developed his method, called Pesso Boyden System Psychomotor Therapy (PBSP), in collaboration with his wife Diane Boyden-Pesso beginning in the early 1960s. In contrast to many other methods of Body Psychotherapy, PBSP is not based on the work of Wilhelm Reich, but grew out of modern expressionist dance therapeutic methods, as Al and Diane Pesso had been expressionist dancers and choreographers at the beginning of their careers.

Now in his eighties, Al Pesso continues to teach his method to psychiatrists, psychologists, social workers, and other psychotherapists in three-year-long training programs. PBSP training programs are established in eleven countries, and additionally in many places in the United States. Albert Pesso has published many books and articles on his method. A neuropsychological study has also been conducted at the University of Prague in which functional MRI (fMRI) has been used to examine the effect of PBSP on patients with trauma issues (Pesso and Wassenaar, 1991).

Albert Pesso is the president of the Psychomotor Institute, taught his work in a number of renowned hospitals, and was a faculty member at Emerson College and the Fielding Institute. Over the course of the last fifty years, he has presented his work to thousands of psychotherapists at countless clinics, and at universities and large conferences in the United States, Europe, and South America. He holds a Lifetime Achievement Award from the USABP. His precise and well-founded psychodynamic method has significantly contributed to the establishment of durable bridges between the fields of psychoanalysis and Body Psychotherapy, and has a strong focus on creating a corrective experience, conveyed in this chapter.

When clients enter the therapy room for a session, they bring their entire world and their history with them. They are certainly aware of the therapist as they step in, but what part of the room are they taking in, and what part of the therapist are they seeing? Even further, what part of themselves are they projecting or experiencing? All this awareness, conscious or unconscious, is going on whether this is a one-on-one session, or a group process, as a client steps forward to work.

Memory studies of the brain suggest that the quality and present state of people's lives are the consequence of the complex interaction between their genetic and environmental histories impinging on the present moment. Thus, if clients are intact and have not had brain or memory damage, a huge crowd of people, experiences, and events walk in with them wherever they go—and what an effect that internal crowd has on them. They often behave toward their therapists or the other group members as if they were stand-ins for one or several of the cast of characters who are milling around in the back rooms of their minds. Inevitably, those internally seen and heard characters significantly influence what people are seeing with their present/actual eyes and hearing with their present/actual ears every single, breathing moment of their living present. Of course, psychoanalysts and other schooled psychotherapists understand this situation very well—they clearly know that the client's inner reality will be played out in the transference or through other means over time. The difference with the Pesso Boyden System Psychomotor Therapy (PBSP) is that we attempt to give the client immediate information about their conscious states at the very moment that these are occurring and not wait to attend to those phenomena at a later time.

We believe that it is critically important to attend to the issues of "with whom?" "when?" and "where?" in the corrective experience. In this chapter, I will address the key features of those techniques that support our ability to attend to these issues. These key features are:

- Creating a setting that leads to a believable, corrective experience
- Defining the function and role of the psychotherapist in that healing process
- Establishing the "stage" upon which that healing takes place and the "time frame" within which it is most fruitfully experienced
- Helping clients become conscious of and be able to monitor the "screens" where the corrective experience is lived and represented

A corrective experience is that kind of interactive event that psychotherapists believe can compensate for what had been missing in a client's personal history. In psychoanalysis, that corrective experience is arranged to take place within the transference. The psychoanalytic therapist encourages, or—at least—permits, the client to experience the therapist as the "provider" of what had been missed and what had been longed for during the client's developmental process. In other forms of psychotherapeutic practice, the therapist him- or herself provides those missing and longed-for experiences during real time, within the therapeutic relationship. I would therefore like to present another way that therapists can organize both themselves and the therapeutic relationship that could lead toward a more clearly defined corrective experience. We call that relationship "offering the possibility sphere."

The following explanation of the possibility sphere is from a transcription of one of my teachings:

The possibility sphere is a psychological envelope, rather like a flexible balloon, that we surround the client with, in the relationship that we have. The reason it's called the possibility sphere is that it is a field that is so flexible, and so full of "yeses" to the soul, that it gives the soul the message "Yes, all that is in you is possible, life is possible, life is good, you can feel good, nothing in you has to die. None of your potentiality, your possibility as a person, has to die, or those things that you thought had died in you may still be alive." So it's very much a "yes" to life, and implicit in it is a belief that life is good—so it is an optimistic view that is implicit in the possibility sphere.

When you present this possibility sphere, it's got to be really connected from your heart and from yourself. But, in order to be a tool, it's got also to be separated from the self. Part of the possibility sphere is also to be presented as a countertransference screen, and in order for us to make use of that screen, as a tool, we have to truly be separated from it. On the one hand, we have to have a caring relationship with the clients, and what is surrounding them. On the other hand, we've got to have our own boundaries, our own lives, so clearly distinct from theirs, that we don't get lost and lose our objectivity. Somehow [the possibility sphere] has got to be connected to our hearts, but not become part of the primary part of our lives; otherwise, the client's therapy becomes more important than our own lives. But unless it's connected to our hearts, we are not going to be truly empathic and truly caring; it has to be a professional caring, so that we don't start caring more for them than we do for our own family, or more for them than they even care for themselves.

So the possibility sphere is not something you invent; it's something that has to be truly there, or if it is not, there are ways of recognizing its limited extent, and you can see where it may be worked on. People sense it instantaneously in your presence what they can or cannot do. (Pesso, 1987)

The therapist offering the possibility sphere creates a personal relationship with the client that engenders a state of hope and expectation of goodness. However, we believe it is critical that the therapist does not position him- or herself to be the actual provider of what has been missing in the client's life in the past, in order to avoid clients' dependency on the therapist, and to sidestep the dual pitfalls of regression and of confusion between real events and symbolic events.

We believe the corrective experience should be provided for by "symbolic" figures in a new "symbolic memory" choreographed by the client with the support and assistance of the therapist. This "virtual event" is then installed—with the help of the therapist—in association with the stored memories of past deficits that occurred in "literal past events."

In that collaborative process, client and therapist construct those symbolic (yet body-based, and therefore emotionally impactful) experiences in such a way as to satisfy the basic developmental needs that clients have long awaited. The relationship provided by therapists in offering the possibility sphere certainly supports the *believability* of a corrective experience, although the relationship by itself is not the *actual content* of the healing event.

Our goal then is to create a "symbolic enactment" of satisfaction of remembered needs in the "seeming real time" of the therapy room. We assist clients to learn how to record and internalize the event in such a way as to make it the equivalent of a long-term "actual memory" of the past. We are aided in this endeavor by the powerful, body-based affect that motoric enactment arouses in clients (see Pesso 1991a, 1991b, and 1991c for case studies).

Further, we encourage and support clients to internalize consciously the corrective experience within their "mind's body" database of early emotional states and self-images. What we call the "mind's body" is the storehouse of the interactive, kinesthetic, motor memories of critical periods when the satisfaction of basic developmental needs is actually required and literally longed for (Stern, 1986; Erikson, 1964).

Later, I will elaborate on how the appropriate providers of the corrective experience are created and represented, and in what time frames those healing interactions with those figures are stored as virtual or symbolic memories. But first, let us look at the beginning of a session using these procedures (Pesso 1973, 1995, 1997).

## Micro-Tracking

How do therapists follow all that is going on inside, and how do they help the client attend to the same task? We use a process of what we call MicroTracking to help clients become conscious of their own internal processes, with the goal of helping them to become more in charge of what they are immediately feeling and thinking, as well as what they are emotionally recalling during the course of the session. MicroTracking also helps the client become more aware of the relationship between their emotional and mental states. In addition, MicroTracking helps make the "crowds" of unconsciously felt and seen people (in the client's memories and mind's eye) to become more conscious, externalized, more visible, and therefore more under their conscious control. Thus, the role of the therapist doing the MicroTracking is to assist clients to see and externalize their own set of

- Internal emotional/mental processes
- Internally represented, remembered, emotionally experienced dramas

During Micro-Tracking, therapists also attend to whether their clients are projecting a part of themselves on their therapist, or relating to their therapist as if they were one of the figures in their remembered dramas. If therapists are going to effectively Micro-Track their clients, it is important that they remain clearly *outside and beside* them—not in a typical "therapeutic relationship" with them—in order to assist them to see who and what else they are relating to, as they sit with the therapist, and see the therapist and the rest of the room in the immediate present.

Therapists endeavor to set the stage for their clients so that they can see the inner workings of their own consciousness as well as their bodily reactions that are in response to those states. Therapists can then help their clients to stage and externalize those past times, places, and deficit-laden, interactive events that the clients discover are the foundation for their present distress and distortions, as they live in the "real-time" present. Thus, MicroTracking helps the client distinguish between:

- The emotions they are having now
- Thoughts they are having in relationship to those emotions
- People and events that are associated with that pattern of relationship between those emotions and those thoughts that have arisen in the here and now

This Micro-Tracking of consciousness helps to lead the clients toward affectively associating with those impactful events that are the foundation for their present difficulties—difficulties, and the discomforts accompanying them, that have led them to seek therapeutic help. The next step in the therapy process is to help externalize these and to represent those emotionally laden, internally experienced events and people within the therapy room.

In the Micro-Tracking process, therapists use the notion of a "witness figure" who is positioned to notice the client's moment-to-moment emotional shifts—shifts that are illustrated primarily by the client's facial expressions and vocal tones—to name them, and to place them in the context of what the client is talking about. A standard statement of a witness figure would be "I see how furious you feel when you speak about, or remember how angry you were, at your older brother for attacking you when you were a boy." Such a statement makes it clear that the present anger, felt strongly in the body *now,* is a consequence of remembering that event, "seen" in the mind's eye and also "felt" in the mind's body *then.* This makes it clear that there is a distinction between *then* and *now,* that—though the feeling is *happening now*—it is about *remembering then.* This helps anchor the client's ego in the "actual present"

and helps them have subjective feelings while also seeing themselves objectively through the eyes of the witness figure. Thus, the witness figure becomes the external template for their own objectivity, which we understand as part of the "pilot" function in PBSP—or in neurological terms, that part of the central nervous system that monitors subjective states.

When clients pose a thought that is expressive of a value or a way of being—for instance, saying, "There's no use in getting angry at my brother. He will only take it out on me later"—this thought is presented back to the client via a "voice figure" who simply says back to the client their own exact statement, word for word, but positioned externally as a command. For instance, in the above example, the voice figure would say, in the imperative, "There's no use in getting angry at your brother. He will only take it out on you later."

The point and purpose of this tactic is to externalize that particular life-attitude or formula. This externalization process allows the client to be freer from its effect and in a better position to consider an alternative strategy. In general, thoughts are regarded as if "carved in stone" and are responded to by the self as if they were hypnotic suggestions. When those controlling thoughts are thus externalized, and presented back to clients in the imperative, as external commands, clients are more able to effectively contend with them.

Therapists should not take the route of constructing another, more positive statement (such as an affirmation) in order to offset the effects of that original, negative statement. The above-mentioned negative thought arose in response to a *literally experienced, negative event* that gave birth to that life-attitude and belief. A new, alternative, positive thought should therefore be effective only if it arises out of an alternative event, albeit a *symbolically experienced positive* event. New ways of thinking about possibilities in the future are one of the goals we have in mind in providing the corrective experience.

Thus, one of the goals and results of MicroTracking is to awaken the *people* and the *events* that were the underlying foundation for present emotions, thoughts, and life strategies. When those memories arise, each individual who is spoken about is a signal to the therapist that the client is "seeing" that figure in their "mind's eye" and therefore reacting to that figure in their "mind's body." The engrams associated with that figure and that event are thus likely to be awakened and have been stimulated to "fire" in the brain.

In the past, we would have taken the position of having those scenes represented by role-play in the room, in the belief that reviewing and discharging those old, stored emotions would provide a positive therapeutic effect. Neuroscience has taught us otherwise—that such firing and repetition could have the effect of reinforcing those old memories and patterns of behavior. Of course, back then, we would not stop the process following the discharge, but instead provide an "antidote" experience, opposite to that event and in line with generic expectations in the world. This is the new memory principle that is the basis for all healing in PBSP theory.

Nowadays, the moment that the client mentions the name of anyone, whether it is with loaded emotion or simply stated, we ask the client to choose one of a cluster of stones, shells, or simple objects to be a "placeholder" for all that the client remembers consciously (or unconsciously) about that figure. Thus, it represents not the figure externalized, but the "database" or "filing cabinet" in the brain containing all the memories, associations, etc., connected to that figure.

This difference supports mindfulness—cognitive separation from the emotions associated with those figures. We would say that the client's "pilot" is now awakened to see "its other" parts of the brain's emotional content from a distance. From this standpoint, an alternative, opposite, healing event can be staged, as with an ideal brother, who would never have beaten him, but would have been kind and supportive during his childhood.

Considering the above resolution to past indignities, it is important for the therapist to avoid unwittingly encouraging the client into thinking that the therapist is the "good guy" and would do the right thing for the client that the real figures in the past had not done. This is a very attractive pitfall, for both the client and the therapist; but it doesn't lead anywhere.

In summary, we believe that in order to help keep the clients from becoming confused and overloaded, with transferences and projections on the therapists—as well as on the others present, if it is a group therapy—it is essential that therapists should become aware of, and have effective techniques to handle with clarity, the following critical issues:

- Stages
- Screens
- Time
- Place

Certainly, psychoanalytic psychotherapists are fully aware that history is interwoven with the present, and they pay due attention to that fact in their notions of transference, regression, abreaction, and projection. But they nonetheless have only the one objective stage of reality to view it from and to discuss it from. This third stage (of the "wished-for" there and then) we construct consciously—with the full participation of the client—in the therapy session. On this stage or screen, therapists mount the scenes of the memories of interactive events that are associated with the present-day perceptions and actions taking place in the immediate moment.

More about that in a moment, but now we have to use another theatrical metaphor in order to clarify the next points, which have to do with perception. Here, we would like to use the more modern forms of theater and refer to "screens." Thus, we will be looking at the different arenas where we play out our lives, which are enacted on three different "screens."

In order to fully understand our notion of stages and screens, one first needs an understanding of the notion of time. Time is a relatively recent construct, created by the neurological organization in our brains. This sense of time allows us to experience immediate sensations, which we call the present, and to recall previous sensations, which we call the past, as if they (the present and the past) were part of a timeline stream of seamless, continuous, contiguous, conscious events. Along with this sense of time, people have the innate capacity to develop anticipations and expectations of the future, from an internal review and distillation of the new data of the experienced present, coupled with the stored data of the recalled past. At first glance, this seems simple enough, however, brain studies show that it is not possible to experience the present without unconsciously remembering/reexperiencing parts of the past. These studies also show that when we remember the past now, it awakens the same part of the brain that was active during the past experience of the original event when it happened in the then-present (Edelman and Tononi, 2000). Thus, our experiences in the past inevitably condition and modify our experiences in the events of the present. Further, because the construction and anticipation of the future are dependent on the amalgam of the data of the past and present (Damasio, 1999), one's future will be hugely affected—positively or negatively—by the qualitative contents of past and present input.

We try to attend to these complex facts and time-fusing, potentially confusing, neurological realities by introducing the element of "place" in combination with the notions of "stages" and "screens." We use the term "place" in two contexts: first, in the sense of the stages, arenas, or platforms where life is occurring; and second, in the sense of the screens where that activity is represented. We then describe how to work with all elements to produce a corrective experience, clearly and effectively, in the psychotherapy session.

We posit the notion that there are two, actual-now, stages upon which present reality is enacted or lived; and a third, virtual-then stage—which we construct for therapeutic purposes—upon which not only can the remembered past be reenacted, as it actually was, but a more "environmentally satisfying" past can be symbolically constructed now (in the therapy room) to be experienced and internalized, as if it had taken place then, so it will contribute to an anticipation of a more satisfying future.

But, in order to understand that notion, we must first address the issue of on what stage and in what time does ordinary living take place. Objectively speaking, it takes place on the literal/material stage of the external world: the freshly born, objective present endlessly unfolds anew. Objectively speaking, the present is only what is happening right now: there is only one objective present. This we call "stage 1," the concrete and literal stage of the immediate present where the action of life unfolds in all its complexity, in the outside world as well as in the therapy room. Subjectively speaking, the same as above happens on the literal or material stage of the external world. However, knowing that the subjective present always includes much of the past, we feel obliged to call stage 1 "the platform of the *apparent* here and now."

Internally, there is another stage where living takes place. This theater takes place on the surfaces and interiors of our bodies. The performers in this three-dimensional arena are our sensations, emotions, and "felt states" that are "dancing on" and "swimming in" the surfaces and interiors of our bodies. We call this "stage 2." You might also call this the stage of the "body unconscious." Here, the dancers/swimmers are actually our unconscious body emotions—that swirl of feelings before they become conscious and acted upon—which clients may experience as disturbing, purely physical symptoms. In fact, many of these so-called "symptoms" are caused by sensory awareness and proprioceptive, kinesthetic feedback arising from premotor contractions and muscle tensions, triggered by unconscious emotions and states (LeDoux, 1996). In this light, the freshly born, subjective present also endlessly unfolds anew, but with the inclusion of each individual's personal history and experience combined with it. Thus, there are as many subjective presents as there are living individuals.

The average person is mostly conscious of living on stage 1. He or she has little knowledge that the subjective present is a compound blend of some of the here and now, coupled with some of the there and then, and innocently assumes that the past is over and done with, and their notion of an absolute present is all that needs attending to. They also may pay scant attention to the unconscious theater playing out on and in the stage 2 of their bodies. Further, they may sometimes unwittingly begin living out their apparent here and now on "stage 3" when they unconsciously have a transference reaction to someone, or unknowingly project on someone, and blithely act, feel, and think just as they did in some defining past event. All the while that they are assuming they are simply and entirely in the objective present, they have unconsciously and unwittingly boarded an instant time-machine and are replaying aspects of their past. Some might chalk such situations up to having a "déjà vu" experience. Other, more esoterically minded persons might describe such events as "past-life" effects, rather than the effects of memory of their own personal history.

The "third stage" is the stage that is consciously constructed—in collaboration with the client—where those memories of the past that are interspersed with our perception of the present can be given the time and place to exhibit their history, in the seeming real time of the therapy session. That "third stage" is on wheels—so to speak—it can be made to virtually roll over the stage of the objective reality of the therapy room, per se, and land like a virtual time-machine in any location, at any time, in any moment, of the client's remembered events.

It is upon this "third stage" that the client—with the assistance of the therapist—constructs synthetic, symbolic, "gene-satisfying" memories to offset—point for point— those abuses and deficits of the past that had contributed to the anticipation of a negative future. This "third stage" is a virtual stage, built upon the stage of the actual here and now of the therapy room. That stage is where all the events that are unfolding in the client's mind—that had taken place in the then of the past—can be externalized and staged in the now of the present, as it is seen in the mind's eye and represented in the mind's body.

We define "screen 1" as the actual, literal screen of what our eyes are seeing at the present moment. However, it is clear, as I said above, that every time we see something in the present, it automatically awakens parts of the visual cortex that deal with past images. Therefore, seeing *now* always includes something of seeing *then*. Thus, screen 1 is mostly what is operating when a client is in the apparent here and now of stage 1. The MicroTracking process begins on stage 1, as clients speak about what they are feeling in the present moment. The "witness figure" and the "voice figure" are positioned on stage 1.

"Screen 2" is the screen of the mind's eye. During the MicroTracking process, clients may recall a figure in the past, and their bodies will show the impact of that perception on stage 2: their faces will flush; their breathing patterns will change; and their bodies will become tense or relaxed as their gestures broadcast a changed inner state.

Simultaneous with the awakening of stage 2—that of the surface and inner volume of the actual body—is the awakening of the neurally represented "mind's body," which we refer to as "screen 3." This is where the neurally registered memories of body images and body coordinations are stored and available for recall.

When the corrective experience is organized, choreographed, and experienced on stage 3, therapists assist clients in accessing their body images and body behaviors that are stored in screen 3 of the mind's body. We believe this coupling with the mind's body of screen 3 helps clients anchor the experience of new possibilities with their body memory of when they actually needed to have those events happen. So, though the event is literally taking place in the here and now of the therapy room, it is carefully orchestrated so that as far as part of the psyche and brain is concerned, it is the equivalent of something that should or could have happened back in time. In this way, therapists can carry out the main therapeutic goal of constructing new, symbolic memories of a life-satisfying *past* on that third virtual stage, which we have evidence to believe increases the client's capacity to experience a more pleasurable present, and leads to an increased capacity to anticipate, as well as create, a more life-satisfying future.

It is our hope that clarity in addressing the issues of "with whom?" "when?" and "where?" will provide the foundation for a more effective therapeutic experience for patients in emotional pain and suffering. I hope that the notions and interventions that I have explained in this chapter will help Body Psychotherapists provide a corrective experience in the hypothetical and/or symbolic past on stage 3, without their actual relationship on stage 1 becoming transferentially overloaded. Using these techniques and concepts, therapists can avoid the pitfall of unwittingly enabling clients to fall into a dependent, personally indebted, and vulnerable position where they can become emotionally overattached, and subject to the uncertainties and vicissitudes of the actual, clinical relationship.

## References

Damasio, A. (1999). *The feeling of what happens: Body and emotion in the making of consciousness.* Orlando, FL: Harcourt Brace.

Edelman, G. M., & Tononi, G. (2000). *A universe of consciousness.* New York: Basic Books.

Erikson, E. (1964/1993). *Childhood and society.* New York: Homburger; New York: W. W. Norton.

LeDoux, J. (1996). *The emotional brain: The mysterious underpinnings of emotional life.* New York: Simon & Schuster.

Pesso, A. (1973). *Experience in action.* New York: New York University Press.

Pesso, A. (1987). Teaching workshop transcription.

Pesso, A. (1991a). Abuse. In A. Pesso & J. Crandell (Eds.), *Moving psychotherapy: Theory and application of Pesso System/Psychomotor Therapy* (pp. 169–188). Cambridge, MA: Brookline Books.

Pesso, A. (1991b). Ego development in the possibility sphere. In A. Pesso & J. Crandell (Eds.), *Moving psychotherapy: Theory and application of Pesso System/Psychomotor Therapy* (pp. 51–63). Cambridge, MA: Brookline Books.

Pesso, A. (1991c). Ego function and Pesso System/Psychomotor Therapy. In A. Pesso & J. Crandell (Eds.), *Moving psychotherapy: Theory and application of Pesso System/Psychomotor Therapy* (pp. 41–49). Cambridge, MA: Brookline Books.

Pesso, A. (1995). The realization of hope. *Communication and Cognition, 28*(2–3), 151–164.

Pesso, A. (1997). PBSP-Pesso Boyden System Psychomotor. In C. Caldwell (Ed.), *Getting in touch: A guide to Body-Centered Therapies* (pp. 117–152). Wheaton, IL: Theosophical Press.

Pesso, A., & Wassenaar, H. (1991). The relationship between PS/P and a neurobiological model. In A. Pesso & J. Crandell (Eds.), *Moving Psychotherapy: Theory and application of Pesso System/Psychomotor Therapy* (pp. 33–40). Cambridge, MA: Brookline Books.

Stern, D. (1986). *The interpersonal world of the infant.* New York: Basic Books.

# 43
## On Vitality

**Michael Randolph, France**

**Michael Randolph**, MA, has a private Body Psychotherapy practice in Toulouse, France, and works as a trainer and workshop facilitator in France, England, Poland, and Italy. He received his early therapeutic training in Primal Therapy (Arthur Janov) as well as in the Feldenkrais Method, and then later particularly in Radix Body Psychotherapy, which he learned directly from its founder, Charles Kelley.

Michael Randolph is a co-founder of the European Radix Institute, where he served as the secretary and was the editor of the *Radix Journal*. For many years he has been active in the regulation of and policymaking for psychotherapy in France, and as treasurer for the French national psychotherapy union. Currently, he serves as its general secretary and as editor of its journal, *Actuapsy*. He is a faculty member of the University of Toulouse and has received recognition through numerous publications and significant presentations at conferences.

The search for what divides vital from lethal, and for what separates the spark from the quenched, and the animate from the inanimate, revealed its bottomless complexity almost as soon as it was embarked upon.

To the eyes of Heraclitus in sixth-century BC Greece, there seemed to be no end to the pervasiveness of movement. Flux was; change was; and stability was illusory; the human being was a paltry, storm-tossed waif, clinging weakly to flotsam.

Over the centuries of ruminating about what we are to the world, or what the world is to us, one of the more potent ideas that emerged and took form was that life is everywhere and in everything. For some, this took the form of a theistic certainty: God is Life and Life is God. For others, this intuition enabled a circumventing of the "God problem": there isn't one. Life is God. Or Life just Is—Period.

By the time the infinitesimal machinery of the cell started to yield its secrets in the second half of the nineteenth century, the presence of energetic waves, associated with absolutely everything, throughout all modes of emergence, began to seem self-evident. Nothing is utterly inert. It should be possible to trace anything—from its simplest manifestation, through its ramifications, into the most complex expressions possible—without losing the original keynote. It should also be possible to extrapolate the functioning of the outer reaches of systematized ferment from the very simplest energetic principles. This is a vitalist credo.

Body Psychotherapy evolved out of psychotherapy—that is, out of a movement guided by Sigmund Freud away from the search for pathogens and neurological malfunction (just as DSM-IV and -V are trying to drag it back). The past was the pathogen, and the inability to live outside its narrow walls, the neurosis. This remains—in spite of substantial, illuminating functional additions from asthma and tuberculosis treatment or from the insights gleaned from early stress-reduction initiatives—the thumbprint of the Freud-Reich tradition. The West wasn't a Taoist cradle; Descartes' illuminating awarenesses had been ponderously incorporated into a ubiquitous form of perceptual apartheid, and the inhuman, productionist frenzy into which society had plunged itself widely spawned what Elsworth Baker called *Man in the Trap* (Baker, 1967).

Unlike its Freudian precursor, Body Psychotherapy, at least as Wilhelm Reich began to unfurl its motifs, was not a matter of divining where and why "invisible armies clash by night" (Arnold, 1962), but rather of what had happened to the "green fuse that drives the flower" (Thomas, 1973). Where had all the vitality gone while we, disquietingly, had been busy doing other things?

## Even Partially Life-Deprived

For the psychotherapist (as indeed for those who come to see him or her), the first and most obvious access to an awareness of vitality is through a developed and constantly developing sense of what is devitalized: what aspects of the life here before us—of this energetic instrument, this organism, this social actor, this kaleidoscope of representations, this thread woven into the universal fabric—are disowned, closed, chronically bereft of the nurture of the living? It is a radical bereavement to be even partially life-deprived. Reich, specifically and systematically, taught us about the tremendous dynamic subtlety of this ongoing bereavement. Learning to infer patterns of "armoring," as the sinuous hoops of taut lifelessness were named, became the Body Psychotherapist's cartography. In the clinical setting, in an individual as well as in a group framework, awareness of vitality has something of the importance of the North Star to early explorers of the immensity of the oceans: It's there, even when you can't quite see it—thwarted by cloud, or drowned in brighter bodies' light—and when glimpsed or felt, it validates intensely the personal living experience.

## Life against Death

Evolution in what underpins the precepts that we work with is often not apparent. The famous shifts in the perceptual framework, or paradigms, often creep up on us unbeknownst to ourselves. Over the second half of the nineteenth century and the first two decades of the twentieth, "vitality" as a reference point was gradually covered over by terminology borrowed from linguistics or from the mechanizing and fractioning influence of a Pasteur-informed fascination with germ pathology. For the mainstream, vitality had become a passé word, without an embedded cultural and clinical field of attachment. So what replaced it? Well, nothing did.

Interest in the whole organism waned until quite recently, and even then the intangibility of *Life against Death,* as Norman Brown's 1959 masterpiece (Brown, 1959) called it, remained a major stumbling block. Vitality is a quality of the whole organism in reference to its immediate life-horizon. It is not a characteristic of any one part or function, or any set of parts or functions, of that organism. If Body Psychotherapy, since its beginnings, has remained closely attached to a perception of its pertinence as the central factor of health, it has swum against the stream. From the beginning, what would now widely be called an "intersubjective field" was the core framework of perception in Body Psychotherapy. It served, above all, to hold and express vitality as the quintessential quality of the living.

Perhaps the simplest common denominator of what we call Body Psychotherapy is to call it "expressive psychotherapy," which doesn't systematically disown bodily manifestations. The various currents over time have created an intricate tracery of real and imagined conceptual traditions. Whatever their specificity, aliveness—as a quality—is generally closer to the heart of the endeavor than acceptance. In psychodynamic traditions, on the other hand, analysts seek to attune themselves to underlying psychological dynamics and the intense fields of refusal or denial that often accompany them. The subject, whose fuller psychological emergence is the aim of the therapy, is alive precisely in abandoning his refusal of limitations to the lived experience. His joy is that of becoming unburdened from his illusions. Vitality does not stand alone in this context, but it is qualified and defined by the weight of knowing. In Body Psychotherapy, on the other hand, whether the "green fuse" remains a close or a distant presence, a pronounced or inarticulate goal, it cannot be reneged on, nor denied.

Reich's aim, dating from his days as a training psychoanalyst specializing in resistance, of directly confronting emotional and muscular armoring, or the Lowenian version of posturally "squeezing" it (through stress positions) to bring forth its life-affirming underlay, has subsequently engendered other approaches that are more directly focused on the said life flow, as in Pierrakos's "Core Energetics" techniques.

## The Heart of Growth

Whether and how vitality can be teased out and made in some way tangible is a fraught question. Reich's scientific explorations—a compendious, valiant, sometimes poetic, sometimes ponderous attempt to catch sight of a ToE (as modern physicists call it, a theory of everything)—have remained intensely controversial. A less litigious grounding for a discussion of vitality in human existence can be found in what researchers into infant development have been uncovering over the past few decades. It is a seminal perception that vitality is what can be felt to thrive in the bonding between two people, most specifically between the infant and its mother. More than mirroring, beyond imitation, mutual gaze transactions between a mother and her child of, say, ten months are a veritable pump for growth, aliveness, and a more intensely refined positioning of the infant in the context of his or her world. If it is arguable whether the "green fuse that drives" really stretches the flower's face out toward contact with the face of the sun, there is no doubt possible that the symmetrification of affect between mother and infant is at the heart of growth; it is the groundwork of emergent autonomy. Such autonomy, rooted in intimate exchange, is a good gauge of the pertinent vitality of a subject connected to his environment. The opposite—that is to say, the hallucinated autarchy of the infant, with which much psychoanalytic theorizing (pre-Bowlby, the founder of attachment theory) was impregnated—is a singularly lopsided sketch in which the frenetic, but unvitalized, infant runs through a series of sealed rooms whose mirrored walls reflect nothing but himself in a fragmentary universe (Bowlby, 1971).

Modern infant research helps move us beyond the hopeful toward the palpable: "The mother's empathic attunement to the infant is not only a crucial dimension (of instant and long-term capacity) for affect regulation, but is now understood to play a vital role in the physiological development of brain structure" (Mollon and Parry, 1984).

Both the vitality and the structural/functional dynamism of the organism are in direct relation to the quality of its interactive reality. The question of adaptation to the environment is not then extrinsic to considerations about vitality, because it resides in the "active transactions" between an organism and its environment. A further question is whether vitality, and budding self-regulation, exist merely as counterweights, or do they fundamentally enhance each other?

Vitality used to be conceived of as representing an idea of an outside life force beyond constraint. Part of Reich's deep credo, and a natural outgrowth for him of that, was that the organism has a built-in capacity for self-regulation, and only intense social and emotional pressure could make it abandon this. The bulk of what is unfolding in infant research, coming frequently in a belated echo of Body Psychotherapy practice, points clearly to the emergence of self-regulation out of a "shared" matrix. This awareness takes us a step beyond previous conceptualizations: A new alignment opens up that allows us to distinguish not a retinted cameo, but an observationally rooted vision of the vital molding of life.

## Trajectories

So, perhaps we should really look to the infant in its environment in order to feel brushed by the wings of vitality? If this life force really is everywhere, and of course it must be, why focus on this to the exclusion of other, wider-ranging phenomena? Allan Schore, author of *Affect Regulation and the Origin of the Self,* in the introduction to his book states that developmental and auto-regulatory issues are the key to understanding the organism in the widest sense of the word: "The beginnings of living systems set the stage for every aspect of an organism's internal and external functioning throughout the lifespan" (Schore, 1994, p. 3).

Daniel Stern, infant researcher of renown, muses for his part about the internal world of the infant, which, far from being a meaningless kaleidoscope of sensations—"a blooming, buzzing confusion," William James called it—is probably structured around what Stern calls "vitality contours." This life topography is made up "of the instant-by-instant patterns of shifting intensity and hedonic tone over time, as occasioned by internal or external events. They are more like a musical phrase of feelings in flux, which cannot be captured or even imagined by taking a single note." He talks of "vitality contours" as being "like the trajectory of a desire as it travels to its immediate goal" (Stern, 2000, pp. 85–86). Somewhere between neurohormonal gradients and resonant symbolism, "desire" brings us closer to a vitalistic awareness that we can use.

## The Body's Singular Typeface

Many would argue, of course, that liberating desire from its immediate goal is the only way to gain access to a "reality principle" that we tend, unwisely, to shun and that, in legitimizing the equivocal, merely corroborates what we suspect is the human fate anyway. Body Psychotherapy's principal focus, however, is neither on the desire, nor on its goal, but on the trajectory or process. The trajectory of a butterfly moving toward a bank of bright flowers doesn't typically include a paralysis of its ability to choose one particular one to settle on; the trajectory of a child's Christmas desire, on the other hand, soon includes the deliciously painful procrastination of putting out milk and cookies for Santa as part of the ritual of getting there.

The "caught breath" of the man on the therapy mat, as he seeks to allow his lower back to release, and to release him in turn into a realm of pleasurable pelvic sensations, is a clear manifestation of the reflexive, refractory web in which his personal trajectories have become ensnared. The underlying assumption, from a psycho-sociological viewpoint, is that we have become "trajectory-poor," strangers to all but torpid restlessness and frothing immobility. In reality, when you glide from here to there, or float from here to there, or leap from here to there, contrary to folk wisdom, you don't always look first and there is often a nebulous rationalization. When you hack through, burst out, slither under, clamber over, what you battle toward may be as obscure as a Talmudic maxim, as indistinct as sunken hieroglyphs. "How" is as intrinsically the mind-body's (and body-mind's) deep imprint, its singular typeface, as, or perhaps more so than, "why?"

The tools that the therapist brings to the therapeutic encounter are mainly a capacity to tune in to life patterns. As I stand before the man who has volunteered to be the first of the group to work with me, I may be aware of how little is really voluntary about his presence, how strongly an involuntary army is at work. What connects might be said to consist of one awareness reaching out to another, but more fundamentally, as I perceive it, is the embryonic recognition of the other's vitality and, as we move on, something like the awareness of a vitalistic space that exists between us. By definition, words seek to halt, seize, and define, and we must admit that this vitality that we are referring to tends to refuse all three, but we could say that the "drawing out" of an intense constancy in the space of interaction is part of what both of us are probably experiencing. Attunement modes, as in eye contact, breathing synchronization, and empathic mobility, largely inherent in reflexive human interactions, are undoubtedly a part of the field, but we can consciously override them by choosing empathic ocular avoidance, a stabilizing respiratory anchor, and/or postural solidity, as a counterweight to their frenetic distress, whenever the situation requires. The human organism is deeply sensitive to all aspects of "being in the world" and "being in the world in the presence of the other" (Hobson, 2002, p. 106). These may manifest themselves in elusive changes in skin coloration, imperceptible conjunctions of postural aplomb and suppleness, or a shifting tracery of receptivity across the body's expressive span. This linkage of interoceptive aliveness and interconnective preparedness is the shuttle of the loom of life. In the session, as it progresses, we may be aware, in slightly different ways, either of contact loss, or of vitality loss, or of both. The two intertwine but are not identical. Underlying life-readiness may be present outside contact and, on the other hand, devitalized, depressive, or frenetic contact is common. What is of most concern to the Body Psychotherapist is the above-mentioned "motion" of the loom of life: its process. Human beings are unique in "refusing" this movement, in pulling away from it, thwarting its rhythm, or sliding into the multiple expressions of devitalized intensity that we end up calling "defenses" or, more dramatically, "pathology." This, however, is no inevitability—perhaps Reich's central message—and Body Psychotherapy aims to connect the individual again, over and above his psychological self-involvement, with a more constant access to the vital flow of his existence.

## A Counterpoint to the Other's Music

Clearly, the quality of the interactivity between therapist and client is a potent factor in establishing a credible access to vitality, both within the therapy framework and beyond, in everyday life. When one of Freud's early patients told him to stop interrupting and to listen (thus launching the "talking cure"), she was asking him to override his natural impulses and offer a silent counterpoint to her inner music. Offering a counterpoint to the other's music is a metaphor that Body Psychotherapy could happily and justifiably embrace. Almost by definition, through their present, active involvement, Body Psychotherapists seek to explore both sides of the interactional equation, often with the avowed aim of relaunching the liquid skating of human emotional trajectories.

## Love Heals, Love Fragments

Yes, emotions again! It's hard to dissociate them from vitality, though the decades (since the 1970s) of therapeutic emotional overkill have made many wary of too tight a linkage. "Love heals, love fragments," says Michael Eigen (1999). Emotions do not come complete with guarantees of intent and even less of effect. Nevertheless, real-time somatic and emotional accompaniment is probably both the aim and the barefaced, impossible challenge of Body Psychotherapy. Fortunately, misattunement and reattunement are just as much part and parcel of the original human relational experience as they are of the therapeutic endeavor. Only dire clinical apnea can result from chasing myths of relational and positional exactitude. "Trajectory-spotting" may be a "good-enough" way of describing the core cognitive/intuitive cross-section of Body Psychotherapy training. Like its cinematographic near-namesake, it brings us into contact with the often-impenetrable dialect of the living.

Where has the life drained away to in this sociable, playful woman whose fleshy face and arms appear now fallen in, tinted with a queasy shade of pale? In what fiber of her living might she feel touched, if I slide my hand, palm up, under the middle of her back? Is the tilting forward of her head a shift toward contact, or the mark of an even deeper, more disconsolate misery? As color slowly washes through her, it washes her back up onto the therapy mat in a high, sunny group room in an erstwhile factory in East London, and one can almost hear the crackling of aliveness running from cell to cell as the falling body abruptly feels caught, held, accompanied, and awaited anew.

We cannot, of course, program the presence of vitality into the psychotherapy setting. But avoiding the issue of what sustains aliveness overall is avoiding the particular potential outreach of Body Psychotherapy. Although resistance to aliveness (as both Freud and Reich showed) often contains as much energy as any more directly recognizable expression of it, it **is** part of the therapist's aim—not systematically, not under any particular circumstances, but as a guiding principle—to help disintegrate patterns of retention and reintegrate the connective tissue of vitality. A relatively recent perception, furthermore, common to conceptual evolutions throughout most of the field of psychotherapy, is the unavoidable and even indispensable interweaving of the affect of both patient/client and therapist.

## The Stutter-Step of Attunement

The interaction of a mother and her infant has nothing of that seamless progression that the term "synergy" conjures up. It is a flickering, stammering linkage viewed in slow motion, consisting of innumerable attunements, misattunements, reattunements, crests of elation, and troughs of withdrawal. The therapeutic interaction cannot aim to reproduce, still less retrospectively repair, the original parent-child link. It does, however, aim to connect and to allow breadth and breath to this connection. Here, too, the exchange is choreographed by the stutter-step of attunement, misattunement, and reattunement. Creating, or re-creating, supple, solid somatic and psychological articulations is possible only when we accept the strobelike quality of the therapeutic encounter. Most specifically in Body Psychotherapy, this is being played out in real time. It is impossible for the therapist to master all of his or her proposals or reactions—they inevitably have a life of their own; however, a metaexchange emerges that resonates, of course, far more vibrantly than the sum of its conscious parts.

## A Vibrant Anguish

The eyes of Eliane open wide after a mobilization exercise aimed at stimulating a rapid acceleration of her normal pulse of energetic experience. It consisted of running ever more rapidly on the mat, hitting synchronously with both arms at once, while letting a higher- and higher-pitched vocalization accompany the hitting. Her eyes open wide on an inner world of intense subjective sensation, at an intersection with an outer world that includes the eyes, faces, and bodies of myself and the other group participants. It is a breathtaking moment, literally, in which the collision of excitement and a vibrant anguish of the living is written large.

Without being reductionist, nothing technically definable happens, yet all present are flooded with a sense of the uncoiling potency of this moment. The process of integration of this moment, of this pulse of intensity, winds through its varied and highly personal somatic and verbal way-stations toward an incorporated whole whose resonance is as wide or narrow as the individual process may permit. Body Psychotherapists, by definition, work through body-sourced interactions (which doesn't mean the interaction of two physical bodies). The somatic connection is a theater of the interplay of different vitalities. Its scope, focus, and significance are all predominantly to be found there.

## Somatic Authenticity

By way of comparison, the therapist, in much Psychodynamic Therapy, may be seen, or may see him- or herself, in some important ways as a guardian of the symbolic temple—an archivist, apt to condense and read out the complex time- and sense-loops that individual human history consists of. The interactional quality, in its often-undemonstrative way, may have much of the intensity of the more overtly expressive therapy modes. The rhythmic quality, dictated by a radically different somatic articulation, is, however, very dissimilar. Reinstating the right, reopening the access to a personal trajectory, in both the short and the longer term, is a key element of all psychotherapy processes. It may be that, without the shorter-term flights that Body Psychotherapy is uniquely well fitted to explore, the longer term finds itself starved of somatic authenticity, thus engendering a personal world built against rather than around vitality.

Perhaps, as with the pattern associations that neuropsychologists assure us develop a curious life of their own, trajectory associations build up to give something like a resonant sense, feeling, intuition, etc. This probably contributes in large part to the neurophysiological experience of vitality. In fact, vitality trajectories, to hook up those different elements, can be said to be what provides resonant, recognizable tone to human exchange and, by extension, to personal experience.

Somatic authenticity may thus be seen as the cradle of vitality in the therapeutic setting. An outline of a session focusing on such authenticity might go something like this: At the beginning is the encounter, a contact to be established, including questions of trust, mistrust, projections, verbal reporting of everyday life concerns, etc. Accompanying this is an encouragement to tune in to visual, bodily, energetic, and intuitive awarenesses, as a way of expanding the scope of here-and-now aliveness. Some premobilization might be necessary: some movement and/or loosening in the eyes, chest, shoulders, breathing, and often legs—in general, a preparation for energy flow. The next step could be some "centering"—contact, safety, relaxation, working with images, words, feelings to deepen and broaden the web of proprioception.

A subsequent focus on the distribution and flow of energetic bodily perception—movement, sound, breathing, trembling, vibrations, etc.—may also be necessary—working with the whole body, as far as that is feasible (Reich's orgasm reflex is one model of this), allows a growing openness to the person's core energetic flow. Then there can be a movement into surrender to the flow, either outer or inner, with a corresponding release of emotions: fear, anger, pain, pleasure, excitement, power, rage, despair, etc. This may be connected to working with sounds, words, movements, with a head and face integration with the rest of the body.

There can be moments of deep inner contact, often with timeless, universal feelings. At some stage, the contact with the therapist can be reestablished with its own interpersonal intensity and coherence. It grounds the client's experience and allows an understanding of risk and outreach; a sense of nurturing; of sharing an affirmation, even of love perhaps. Finally, there is a connection back, through words, to a grounding in present-day life, with sometimes a decision and/or a redefined sense of the future. At the end, separation is prepared for, accepted, and carried out. This session template, fairly typical of much Body Psychotherapy practice, is, as stated above, a cradle for vitality, both inwardly experienced and also as an intersubjective shared web of exchange. This sort of exchange enables a revitalization of discrete elements of an organism's functioning and paves the way for a generalized, global, or holistic vitalization that extends through the intrasubjective and on into the intersubjective realm. It is, no doubt, unrealistic to expect to live permanently at this pitch of vital openness, but deep experience of Body Psychotherapy often permits a revitalized underlying awareness, capable of resisting the potently chronic quality of surreptitious emotional and somatic holding, and giving some hope for the future. As Abraham Maslow affirmed, such key experiences have a resonant, transformative effect, out of all proportion to their duration (Maslow, 1964).

## Vitality May Be Enhanced, Not Appropriated

D. H. Lawrence, in one of his essays, talked of writers who "keep their thumb in the pan" (a reference to the cheating of tradesmen with the handheld weighing-scales of his childhood). Lawrence held that an author, deeply attached to his creation, does not treat his characters as so many objects to be manipulated to a predetermined end (Lawrence, 1936). His robust assertion of his characters' underlying, indefinable right to a degree of independence is a reminder that life is not the domain of an omniscient cartographer, with desired outcomes writ large in the margins, but something altogether more ungraspable and that, above all, doesn't belong to the observer. Our clients' (and our own) vitality is something therapy may enhance, but cannot appropriate.

If there is one way in which Body Psychotherapy continues, and will continue, to distinguish itself from other psychotherapies, it will no doubt be through its continued attachment to a concept of vitality—more than acceptance, more than adjustment, more than self-confidence, more than a "contract for living." The endless attempts to track vitality down to its source, to find a title and form for vitality that would put it out of reach of contestation or depreciation, are no doubt in vain. "Unitary vegetative functioning," as Elsworth Baker (1967), a good Reichian standard-bearer, calls his holy grail, is not to be sneered at.

Nor are many other, sometimes tortuous, terminological constructs that have had their day and are subsequently put aside. But the "green fuse" is probably out of reach to all but poets, and is as unlikely to allow itself to be broken in as a rodeo bull. Nonetheless, and for all its impalpability, "vitality" is radically, seminally, and indissociably at the heart of what we call Body Psychotherapy.

## References

Arnold, M. (1962). *Dover Beach. Norton Anthology of English Literature* (Vol. 2). New York: W. W. Norton.

Baker, E. F. (1967). *Man in the trap: The causes of blocked sexual energy.* Houndmills, UK: Macmillan.

Bowlby, J. (1971). *Attachment and loss (3 vols.).* Newark, DE: Hogarth Press.

Brown, N. O. (1959). *Life against death.* Middletown, CT: Wesleyan University Press.

Eigen, M. (1999). *Toxic nourishment.* London: Karnac Books.

Hobson, P. (2002). *The cradle of thought.* Houndmills, UK: Macmillan.

Lawrence, D. H. (1936). *Phoenix: The posthumous papers of D. H. Lawrence (E. D. McDonald, ed.).* New York: Viking.

Maslow, A. (1964). *Religions, values and peak-experiences.* New York: Penguin Books.

Mollon, P., & Parry, G. (1984). The fragile self: Narcissistic disturbance and the protective function of depression. *British Journal of Medical Psychology, 57,* 137–145.

Schore, A. N. (1994). *Affect regulation and the origin of the self.* Hillsdale, NJ: Lawrence Erlbaum.

Stern, D. (2000). Roots of a controversy. In J. Sandler, A-M. Sandler, & R. Davies (Eds.), *Clinical and observational psychoanalytic research (pp. 85–86).* Madison, CT: International Universities Press.

Thomas, D. (1973). *The force that through the green fuse drives the flower. Norton Anthology of Modern Poetry.* New York: W. W. Norton.

# SECTION VI

# The Therapeutic Relationship in Body Psychotherapy

# 44
## Introduction to Section VI

Gustl Marlock, Germany, and Halko Weiss, United States, with Michael Soth, UK

It is now generally accepted across the majority of the psychotherapeutic field that the quality of the relationship between therapist and client plays a central role in the success of the therapeutic process. However, there is much less of a consensus as to what actually constitutes "quality" of relationship and how the therapist contributes to it, manifests it, and embodies it. The main problem in clarifying the complexity of therapeutic relating is that it consists of a multiplicity of diverse and contradictory elements (Clarkson, 1994) that are not yet equally appreciated by everybody across the therapeutic traditions. As a result, "quality" of relating tends to be elevated and absolutized into too much of a one-dimensional fashion through the partial lenses habitually employed by therapists who tend to take their own therapeutic way of relating for granted.

As an example, there has been a growing tendency in some quarters of the Body Psychotherapeutic field to equate "quality" of relating with a nurturing, encouraging, affirming stance, designed to "repair" the wounds of the client's "inner child" and to counter the introjected damage from "not-good-enough" inappropriate or inadequate early parenting. However, if this becomes the dominant or only stance, it is bound to acquire all kinds of countertherapeutic functions and side effects (e.g., infantilizing the client, emphasizing regression rather than maturation and progression, avoiding negative transference, sidestepping dialogic-authentic encounters, exacerbating compliance and power-over dynamics).

What is now increasingly accepted is that the different theories and corresponding techniques of the therapeutic field—despite their traditional schisms and fragmentations—are underpinned by and emerge through a variety of different and conflicting *modalities of therapeutic relatedness*. Both Martha Stark (1998) in the United States and Petruska Clarkson (1994) in the United Kingdom contributed seminal clarifications to this field. They each approached the existing diversity of relational modalities in different and yet complementary ways. Conceptual clarity in this most confused arena of therapeutic discourse requires that we neither separate out and absolutize one particular modality at the expense of any of the others, nor conflate what are distinct and irreducible elements.

For the purposes of this introduction, we can combine these models and distinguish the following "relational spaces"—each of which constitutes an essential and at times critically relevant pillar of the multidimensional therapeutic endeavor:

- A "one-person psychology" and the "treatment modality"
- A "two-person psychology" and the "I-Thou modality"
- A "one-and-a-half-person psychology"
- The transference/countertransference modality
- A reparative (or developmentally needed) modality
- The working alliance

## "One-Person Psychology" and the "Treatment Modality"

Freud took the treatment modality for granted, with the classical psychoanalyst taking a quasi-scientific, quasi-medical position—what Stark calls a "one-person psychology" attitude: based on the dualistic assumption that it is only the patient's psychology (i.e., *their* conflictual intrapsychic dynamic) that is at issue in the treatment, while the analyst provides insight into the patient's pathology via interpretation, from a position approximating the "objective truth." Although the postmodern *zeitgeist* registers dissonance with these hierarchical attitudes, it is possible for this relational arrangement to be experienced as profoundly helpful by the client, especially because "treatment" can nevertheless be administered in a friendly, humane manner (as by a traditional family doctor).

But, of course, the "treatment modality" is not restricted to psychoanalysis: it is taken equally for granted in Cognitive Behavioral Therapy and is a background reality in nearly *all* therapy, if only because of the client's preconceptions about therapy. Although frequently denied and philosophically refuted, it can still be detected as present and influential, even within humanistic and existential approaches.

Within the field of Body Psychotherapy, all approaches that focus on the intrapsychic relationship of impulse and inhibition (such as classical Reichian Vegetotherapy and Lowen's Bioenergetics), as well as most methods that center on the patient's energetic, psychic, and somatic self-exploration, can be categorized as tending toward this one-person psychology modality, with countertransference understood either as merely the therapist's own pathology, or as nonexistent or irrelevant.

## "Two-Person Psychology" and the "I-Thou Modality"

Stark applies the term "two-person psychology" to all approaches that are based upon "intersubjectivity" or a "dialogic" stance. Within psychoanalysis, this perspective developed only recently, through the notion of "mutual recognition," which has become a cornerstone of relational psychoanalysis. However, the crucial inspiration for authentic relating—predating the explicit formulation of intersubjectivity by several decades—came from Martin Buber's dialogical philosophy (1947), which had a fundamental impact on Rogers, Perls, and the humanistic movement.

The essence of proper dialogue between two individuals is the meeting of two "self-possessed" authentic subjectivities—two people who know who and what they are, and who are each aware of what drives them. Arguably, though, in human relationships and especially in therapy, this cannot always be assumed to be a given. Existential therapists find it hard to describe how a dialogic attitude can be maintained therapeutically when one or both of the partners suffer degrees of dissociation, unconscious conflicts, or characterological fixations. Where degrees of transferential blindness toward the other person seem to interfere with mutual recognition, other therapeutic modalities have filled the existential gap.

## "One-and-a-Half-Person Psychology"

Stark's "tongue-in-cheek" label for the transition from the historical phases of a one-person psychology toward a two-person psychology can be seen to comprise the vicissitudes of relating to the client's characterological wounds when the therapist cannot take refuge in a taken-for-granted "objective" position, and when authentic relating alone does not seem helpful either.

The phenomenon of transference becomes an explanatory paradigm both for the absence of mutuality as well as for the lack of recognition by the other, which we can experience in human relating and in the sense that we have become an "object" to them—a fantasy or facsimile in their minds that they are projecting onto us.

When early developmental wounding becomes fixed into a character structure and persists unconsciously as internal object-relations, which are then transferred into the therapeutic space, therapy requires additional modalities to engage the relational complications that we can encounter. To bring the client's wounding from unconsciousness into awareness, and to then transform it (which also involves addressing the developmental deficits caused by the wounding), Clarkson (1994) describes two other modalities: the transference/countertransference modality, and the reparative (or developmentally needed) modality.

## The Transference/Countertransference Modality

The essence of this mode of relating is that the therapist allows himself or herself to be "constructed" as an object by the client's unconscious. Rather than directly engaging as a discrete subjective other in a supposedly mutual dialogue, the therapist allows the client's transferential projections to emerge, which then shape their interactions and the relational space. This process makes the client's biographical fixations more apparent and understandable, and also available to be addressed directly within the therapeutic dyad and thus worked through. Transference hinges on the recognition that the client's wounding will enter the therapeutic space (Soth, 2006), and that the therapist will at times be experienced as the "wounding object."

The question of how transference is "worked through" and transformed, or transcended, has been one of the most productive and polarized issues in the history of psychoanalysis. Whereas the Kleinian position is that the wounding needs to be accepted and mourned (with the therapist refusing to become a "better object" in order to allow the full depth of the client's pain, grief, and rage), Alexander and colleagues (1946) insisted that a "corrective emotional experience" was needed in order to provide more favorable conditions for the wounding to find a new outcome in therapy.

## A Reparative (or Developmentally Needed) Modality

Whatever the original wounding, emotional injury, or traumatic developmental experience was, it invariably created a developmental deficit. As neuroscience is increasingly establishing (Schore, 1994), certain phases and developmental windows in the child's maturation require appropriate relational responses; otherwise, some crucial integration of the child's physical-emotional-cognitive faculties will be lacking.

In this relational modality, the therapist takes a stance that provides the developmentally needed response: if the parental response was too distant, uninvolved, or cold, the therapist provides a warmer, more caring, and engaged presence; if the parental presence was too invested, restrictive, or invasive, then the therapist provides a spacious, allowing, and encouraging presence (Ferenczi, 1999; Rogers, 1951).

## The Working Alliance

Clarkson (1994) puts the working alliance at the forefront of all other modalities, because without it the endeavor of therapy does not have a viable professional frame. The working alliance is the publicly visible business arrangement, which historically has not been well understood. Traditionally, it is referred to as the bond between the health-seeking part of the client (imagined as equivalent to the "rational" part of the ego) and the helpful, knowledgeable part of the therapist, seeking to do what is in the client's best interest. One of the problems with this conceptualization is that it equates "health" with the "rational mind" and thus perpetuates nineteenth-century dualisms. An embodied understanding of the working alliance would need to go far beyond this notion of the ego-ego alliance, and conceive of the bonding that maintains the frame of therapy as a multidimensional body-mind process. There is, of course, also a precondition of a degree of attunement and empathy between therapist and client, which is close to Boadella's (1982) "empathic resonance" in body-mind terminology.

## Relational Modalities in Body Psychotherapeutic Practice

From our perspective, *all* the modalities—as opposite and contradictory as they are—are in principle valid, essential, and complementary in dynamic interplay within the system of the therapeutic relationship. Each has validity in some situations and beneficial therapeutic effects not achievable without them; each also has its dangers and countertherapeutic effects and functions.

The bulk of current Body Psychotherapy—along with the larger field of Humanistic Psychology—remains in a fairly confused and unreflected state regarding the modalities of therapeutic relating. Because some of the relational modalities are not deliberately owned and recognized as such, while others are habitually dominant and taken for granted, the stresses and impasses of the working alliance are not well understood.

Much of the actual practice is focused on developmentally needed interactions; however, one can be caught between "repairing" the client's woundedness, on the one hand, and, on the other hand, apparently exacerbating it by working to bring it to awareness. Transferential pressure is often countered with self-disclosure on the part of the therapist, who is aiming at some kind of authentic relating, but usually ends up avoiding the original wounding and the implicit "bad object."

Considering all aspects then, much of modern Body Psychotherapy tends to operate within a somewhat ill-defined one-and-a-half-person psychology paradigm, neither fully authentic, nor fully addressing the transference. When transference and countertransference are considered by Body Psychotherapists, they often retain the classical one-person psychology definition or position, and do not include modern intersubjective revisions of these concepts. The treatment modality falls into the "shadow," from where it exerts a powerful and decisive influence (Soth, 2006), as the metapsychological frame is oriented toward a humanistically inspired conception of therapy as an expression of the "true self" and "real relating."

Now that the use of mindfulness has entered the arena of therapy, the capacity to reflect on relational dynamics is increasingly informed by the possibility of "witnessing" or "pure observation," which offers—at certain points in the therapeutic process—a potential metaspace of awareness, free from transferential perceptions, allowing more embodied clarity and emotional freedom (Weiss et al., 2015).

## Somatic Theories of Therapeutic Relating

By championing a focus on the body-mind dimensions of the therapeutic endeavor, the discipline of Body Psychotherapy has evolved embodied models and practices quite unique in the field of psychotherapy. But developing these special gifts, now comprehensively confirmed and supported by modern neuroscience, has come at a price: as we see it, Body Psychotherapy has tended to neglect those relational vicissitudes that the nature of therapy would have to entail if we are indeed pursuing characterological transformation in depth. As with everything else in life, the client approaches therapy and the therapist *via* their character, and it would fly in the face of our own theories if we were to presume the possibility of a real or realistic character-free working alliance, both from the client's and from the therapist's side. Both "frightened people in the room" (Bion, 1990, p. 5) bring their own wounds and characterological protections to the therapeutic relationship, inevitably creating an entangled "intersubjective mess" (Soth, 2012) the more we attempt to address the roots and depth of character.

In spite of these acknowledged limitations of the Body Psychotherapeutic field, there has been a passion for continuing learning and an openness toward contemporary trends in other therapeutic approaches that have a more developed sensibility to the potentials and complications of the therapeutic relationship. Partly out of these kinds of dialogues and partly through our own ongoing evolution, Body Psychotherapy is making its own particular and noteworthy contributions regarding an embodied understanding of the therapeutic relationship.

> **Wilhelm Reich** originated the concept of *vegetative identification,* a term that emphasizes the somatic and embodied nature of what other approaches conceive of as understanding and/or empathy. As a nonverbal and prereflexive process, it is a concept that has the potential to explicate and ground somatically any

notions of unconscious communication, including "projective identification." In this way, empathy, resonance, and identification processes may come to be understood as direct bodily interactions. This may help to counteract the currently fashionable neuroscientific overemphasis on the brain, even if it is predominantly the right brain (according to Schore, 1994).

**David Boadella** (1982) has been tireless in reminding us that—beyond the particularities of theory—the therapist's relational style must match their own personality and—much more importantly—that of the client: that it is the therapist's own congruence between their personal and professional selves that then allows them to meet the uniqueness and the needs of the client. He has described the somatic and psychodynamic aspects of the therapeutic relationship in terms of "transference," "resonance," and "interference." Building upon the Reichian character model—with concentric layers of "persona" or "mask," "secondary reactivity," and "primary core" or "self"—Boadella proposed that interactions between these various characterological layers of both client and therapist will tend to generate particular relational and transference dynamics.

**Stanley Keleman** developed a somatic theory of human bonding in the 1990s that was picked up by **Maarten Aalberse** (1993) and applied creatively to the therapeutic relationship. He has described particular bonding and transference constellations for specific character types.

**Jacob Stattman** created the concept of "organic transference and countertransference" and thereby initiated a somatic theory addressing the conscious and unconscious interactions and reciprocities between client and therapist on the nonverbal level (Stattman, 1993).

Some psychoanalysts with an interest in the body (Geissler, 1998) have picked up on **Albert Pesso**'s method of therapeutic enactments, theatrically staging both internalized object-relations and their therapeutic correctives. Such active techniques depart from the classical psychoanalytic setting with its rigid taboo against acting and acting out (Pesso, 1999; Moser, 1999). Where these enactments originate from the body, its moods, and its capacity to symbolize, such techniques can penetrate into the domain of implicit or procedural memory (Stern, 1998; Schacter, 1996).

Different meanings of "enactment" are rooted in a recognition of embodied patterns and their subliminal communication—an area of the therapeutic relationship in which Body Psychotherapy has accumulated extraordinary practical competence. One example of how the whole domain of "nonverbal communication" can be integrated into a two-person psychology approach is **George Downing**'s work (see Chapter 29, "Early Interaction and the Body: Clinical Implications"), based upon developing Stern's infant research further. Another example is the work of the German communication researcher **Siegfried Frey,** which has been made fertile for the Body Psychotherapeutic field by **Michael Heller** (Downing, 1996, 2004; Frey, 2001; Heller, 2001).

In the United Kingdom, a group of Body Psychotherapists, centered mainly around the **Chiron Centre,** have evolved a relational version of Body Psychotherapy that is integrative in several respects: in terms of the multiple levels of body-mind process, in terms of the humanistic-psychodynamic divide, as well as the diverse schools and styles of Body Psychotherapy and other humanistic approaches, especially Gestalt. This developed in the 1990s into a further reintegration with Reich's psychoanalytic origins, which resulted in a multidimensional and multimodal version of Relational Body Psychotherapy (Hartley, 2009; Totton, 2003). The "relational turn" (Soth, 2012) marks a transcend-and-include departure from traditional body-oriented paradigms toward a two-person psychology notion of enactment as understood in relational psychoanalysis.

As has become evident in recent international Body Psychotherapeutic conferences, these developments over the last twenty years or so form one of the growing edges of the field. Contemporary authors, like Robert Hilton (Hilton and Sieck, 2008), Rob Fisher (2002; see Chapter

81, "A Somatic Approach to Couples Therapy") and Courtenay Young (2012), have also contributed to the current discourse.

Coming to the content of Section VI: Chapter 45, "Entering the Relational Field in Body Psychotherapy" by **William F. Cornell,** written from such an intersubjective perspective, demonstrates the implications for both practice and supervision.

Chapter 46, "Enhancing the Immediacy and Intimacy of the Therapeutic Relationship through the Somatic Dimension" by **Richard Heckler** and **Gregory Johanson,** illuminates the kind of intensification of the therapeutic process when attention to the body is actively included in the relationship: situations of marked closeness and intimacy as well as charged transferential processes can arise in quick succession spontaneously and unpredictably. This heightened embodied intensity, which is taken for granted by Body Psychotherapists as the norm, also brings with it the danger of increased enmeshment between therapist and client.

From psychoanalytic perspectives, we know that these enmeshments are often unavoidable, manifesting in enactments of wounding interactions that replicate the dynamics of the client's original character formation. The essence of the "relational turn" lies precisely in the recognition that these kinds of enactments are not only unavoidable, but often necessary for neuroplasticity to become available and for therapy to actually work. Via enactment, characterological core constellations are activated in the here and now and become available for working through. The unpredictable immediacy, intensity, and intimacy of such relational experiences means the stakes are high for both client and therapist—a recognition that places particularly high demands on the therapist's communicative skill, emotional differentiation, and capacities for self-regulation.

**Michael Soth** explores some of these issues in Chapter 47, "Transference, Countertransference, and Supervision in the Body Psychotherapeutic Tradition," and especially the need for and the role of supervision to try to resolve some of these potential complications.

The dangers of entanglement and confusion, which at times also manifest as confused theoretical elaborations, are further increased by another aspect of Body Psychotherapeutic work, which is highly controversial—namely, the issue of touch. Although not all Body Psychotherapists use touch, those who do need to consider the following proposition: What can expand and enrich the possibilities of therapeutic intervention can also increase the demands on the competency and sovereignty of the therapist.

Chapter 48, "Touch in Body Psychotherapy" by **Gill Westland,** and Chapter 49, "The Somatics of Touch" by **Lisbeth Marcher** with **Erik Jarlnaes** and **Kirstine Münster,** respond to the challenge of this dialectic with great commitment and insight, without presenting any generalizing ultimate conclusions.

The last chapter in Section VI, Chapter 50, is a case study by **Tilmann Moser,** "The Empty Voice of the Empty Self: On the Link between Traumatic Experience and Artificiality." He illustrates how the bodily dimension—in particular, enactments—can be analyzed in a differentiated manner in the context of psychoanalytic therapy. He introduces a way of working with the unfolding relational process by using both enactments and concrete embodiments.

# References

Aalberse, M. (1993). Eins-Sein, Dualität und Einheit [Oneness, duality and oneness]. In G. Marlock (Ed.), *Weder Körper noch Geist* [Neither body nor mind]. Oldenburg: Transform.

Alexander, F., French, T. M., et al. (1946). *Psychoanalytic therapy: Principles and application.* New York: Ronald Press.

Bion, W. R. (1990). *Brazilian lectures.* London: Karnac Books.

Boadella, D. (1982). Transference, resonance and interference. *Journal of Biodynamic Psychology, 3,* 73–94.

Buber, M. (1947). *Between man and man.* London: Macmillan.

Clarkson, P. (1994). *The therapeutic relationship.* London: Whurr.

Downing, G. (1996). *Körper und Wort in der Psychotherapie* [Body and word in psychotherapy]. Munich: Kösel.

Downing, G. (2004). Emotion, body and parent-infant interaction. In J. Nadel & D. Muir (Eds.), *Emotional development: Recent research advances.* Oxford, UK: Oxford University Press.

Ferenczi, S. (1999). *Ohne Sympathie keine Heilung* [Without sympathy, no cure]. Frankfurt: Fischer.

Fisher, R. (2002). *Experiential Psychotherapy with couples.* Phoenix, AZ: Zeig, Tucker & Theisen.

Frey, S. (2001). New directions in communications research: The impact of the human body on the cognitive and affective system of the perceiver. In M. Heller (Ed.), *The flesh of the soul.* Bern: Peter Lang.

Geissler, P. (1998). *Analytischer Körperpsychotherapie in der Praxis* [Analytical Body Psychotherapy in practice]. Stuttgart: Klett-Cotta.

Hartley, L. (Ed.). (2009). *Contemporary Body Psychotherapy: The Chiron Approach.* Hove: Routledge.

Heller, M. (Ed.). (2001). *The flesh of the soul.* Bern: Peter Lang.

Hilton, R., & Sieck, M. (Eds.). (2008). *Relational Somatic Psychotherapy: Collected essays of Robert Hilton.* Alachua, FL: Bioenergetics Press.

Moser, T. (1999). Einführung [Introduction]. In A. Pesso, *Dramaturgie des Unbewussten* [Dramaturgy of the unconscious]. Stuttgart: Klett-Cotta.

Pesso, A. (1999). *Dramaturgie des Unbewussten* [Dramaturgy of the unconscious]. Stuttgart: Klett-Cotta.

Rogers, C. (1951). *Client-centered therapy: Its current practice, implications and theory.* Boston: Houghton Mifflin.

Schacter, D. C. (1996). *Searching for memory.* Cambridge, MA: Harvard University Press.

Schore, A. N. (1994). *Affect regulation and the origin of the self.* Hillsdale, NJ: Lawrence Erlbaum.

Soth, M. (2006). What therapeutic hope for a subjective mind in an objectified body? *Journal for Body, Movement and Dance in Psychotherapy, 1*(1), 43–56.

Soth, M. (2012). The relational turn in Body Psychotherapy. *Somatic Psychology Today, 1*(4), 56–60.

Stark, M. (1998). *When the body meets the mind: What Body Psychotherapy can learn from psychoanalysis.* Panel presentation at the 1st National Conference of the USABP.

Stattman, J. (1993). Organische Übertragung [Organic transmission]. In G. Marlock (Ed.), *Weder Körper noch Geist* [Neither body nor mind]. Oldenburg: Transform.

Stern, D. (1998). *Die Mutterschafts-Konstellation* [The maternity constellation]. Stuttgart: Klett-Cotta.

Totton, T. (2003). *Body Psychotherapy: An introduction.* Maidenhead, UK: Open University Press.

Weiss, H., Johanson, G., & Monda, L. (Eds.). (2015). *Hakomi: Mindfulness-centered Somatic Psychotherapy: A comprehensive guide to theory and practice.* New York: W. W. Norton.

Young, C. (Ed.). (2012). *About Relational Body Psychotherapy.* Galashiels, Scotland: Body Psychotherapy Publications.

# 45
## Entering the Relational Field in Body Psychotherapy

### William F. Cornell, United States

**William F. Cornell** is a clinical psychologist and is one of the leading Body Psychotherapists in the United States. He has a private practice in Pittsburgh, Pennsylvania, and works internationally as a lecturer, trainer, and supervisor in a variety of therapeutic cultures. He is a co-editor of the *Transactional Analysis Journal* and has expressed his thoughts on the relationship between psychoanalytic and Body Psychotherapeutic theory and practice in numerous publications.

In a pivotal paper with the title "If Reich Had Met Winnicott: Body and Gesture," Bill Cornell facilitated an early dialogue between psychoanalysis and Body Psychotherapy, at a time when this sort of dialogue was close to unheard-of, as compared to our present time in which such dialogue tends to be welcomed and is becoming more normal. He is particularly interested in highlighting the complementary strength of each tradition, without overlooking their respective biases and blind spots.

> The body is misleading because it leads one into relationship, and so toward the perils and ecstasies of dependence and surrender (Ghent, 1990); it reminds us, that is to say, of the existence of other people. (Phillips, 1995, p. 230)

### Introduction with Case Illustration

Elizabeth and I lay on our backs, side by side on the carpet of my office. I asked Elizabeth to notice any impulses within her body in relation to mine and, if she wished, to explore any of those impulses through movement between her body and mine. This therapeutic invitation, at one level clear and apparently simple, proved to be complex, disturbing, and nearly impossible for Elizabeth.

Elizabeth's therapy did not start on my office floor. We began our work together seated in chairs talking to each other about the ways in which Elizabeth felt immobilized in her life. Successful in her career, with a wide circle of friends, and with warm relationships with her family, Elizabeth lived alone, never having been able to sustain an intimate relationship, never having had a sexual relationship.

She had been in psychotherapy before and had found it very useful. Many things in her life had changed in response to her earlier therapy, but she was still not able to establish an intimate relationship with anyone: her basic relationship pattern had not changed. When first entering psychotherapy, Elizabeth recognized many aspects of herself and her isolation in the pages of trauma-centered self-help books. She spent three years with a trauma-centered therapist searching for some forgotten or dissociated trauma: nothing emerged. Although it was clear that something had gone quite terribly wrong in her emotional and interpersonal development, it did not seem to be the result of some form of intrusive trauma. Her therapist suggested that she work with a Body-Centered Psychotherapist, and she found her way to me.

As we began to work, Elizabeth would say, "I don't know what to do. I don't know what to do with my body. I can't tell if someone is interested in me. I can't tell if I'm attracted to someone. I just don't know how people know these things. It's like everybody knows something that I don't know, like I was looking the wrong way one day when they taught it in school." "I don't know what to do with my body" became the central refrain in our work, so we decided to explore this together: this not knowing what to do. We moved from the chairs to the floor, so as to begin a different kind of therapeutic exploration.

As Elizabeth and I moved to the floor, we moved into the domain of therapeutic activity that is unique to Body-Centered Psychotherapy. The movement of the client's body, and movement between client and therapist, becomes a central feature of the therapeutic endeavor. Body Psychotherapy brings to conventional psychotherapy an informed and skilled attention to the activity, motility, sensory-motoric coherence, and bodily competence of the client. Both the structure and activity of the body are understood within a developmental and/or characterological framework.

A Body Psychotherapist extends the therapeutic repertoire of analytic and cognitive interventions with direct interventions in the client's bodily activity. Body-level interventions are intended to facilitate new sensate, expressive, and motoric experiences within the client's somatic repertoire. In contemporary relational and intersubjectivist models of psychoanalysis, the client is granted increasing access to the psyche—the mental and affective states—of the therapist. While I am aware that the way I work as a Body Psychotherapist is by no means universal, I offer my clients access to, the use of, my actual body. As a Body Psychotherapist, deeply influenced by psychoanalytic and relational models of psychotherapy, I want to offer my clients a somatic dyad—that is, a person with whom literally to move, as well as to think and speak. I seek to provide a safe space within which to experiment with movement, aggression, tenderness, and contact: a space within which one can act as well as think. I want clients to have the opportunity to affect and be affected by the actual body of another, a body different from their own: my body. As a psychotherapist, I want my clients to have the ongoing experience of two different minds engaged in a project of mutual interest. As a Body Psychotherapist, I extend the framework to offer the possibility of two bodies exploring new terrain and possibilities.

When I first started listening to Elizabeth, I often found myself imagining her as an adolescent. I kept these imaginings to myself, trying to learn something about Elizabeth from my internal images and fantasies. I began to realize that I was wishing a new adolescence for her. I wanted her to have that wonderful/awful period of adolescent development in which most of us are so fueled by the frenzy of awakening hormones that we manage to blast through awkwardness and inhibition to figure out some way, somehow, however unskilled and unmannered we may be, to get one's body and body parts in relationship with those of another. Grace and skill are not in the foreground for most adolescents. It was becoming clear to me that, while my mind (not Elizabeth's) was filled with images and urges of adolescence, the dilemmas of Elizabeth's body were rooted in much earlier phases of development. Elizabeth needed a chance to be awkward and de-skilled with her body in relation to another. I became that other.

As we lay side by side that first time, her experience was one that we visited and revisited time and again: "I don't know what to do. I don't know what my body wants. It doesn't have any impulses." As we worked with this apparent lack of impulse, it became clear that Elizabeth experienced her body through what it didn't want. She began to realize that there were clear signals from her body about what "it" didn't want. She could, however, discover no sense of what "it" *did* want. I pointed out that her "not-wanting" was, possibly, an impulse in relation to my body. When she was free to explore this "not-wanting," her body began to feel more alive in the room. Her body was becoming more connected to itself, more able to inform itself. During sessions, we rarely touched. In her day-to-day life, she began to notice how much she defined her experience through *not* wanting rather than wanting ("I knew I didn't want to go to that restaurant/that movie, but I could never say what I *did* want. Somebody else always ended up making that choice").

Gradually, she asked me if I would make suggestions as to what her body could do with mine so that she could find out if she could tell what she liked. The experiments were many: our arms lightly touching, as we lay on our backs; lifting her head onto my shoulder; rolling onto my chest; sitting back-to-back pressing in and pulling away; pressing her head and shoulders into my back; spooning; and wrapping our legs around each other playfully, aggressively, tenderly. She began to differentiate between what she wanted and what she didn't. She began to notice that some of our experiments seemed to stay in her body between sessions, and—most importantly—she began to have fantasies of her own about what she wanted her body to do with mine. She began to initiate the movement experiments between us, though she was often surprised at the results. We didn't do something to achieve a certain outcome; we did something to find out what would happen—how it felt and what it might mean. Often, the sessions had an unmistakable erotic tension to them, experienced in the pleasure of discovery and mutual exploration; there were moments of tenderness and excitement. Her body started to become a source of information for her mind, in relation not only toward me, but, gradually, toward others as well. She began to notice what it was in her body that let her know when she was attracted to someone, and when someone was drawn to her.

## Body and Gesture: Entering the Relational Field

It is a fairly recent development in Body Psychotherapy for the therapeutic relationship itself to be understood as a central mechanism of experimentation and change. My own work as a Body Psychotherapist has been deeply informed by and changed through my reading and supervision in contemporary psychoanalysis, particularly through the work of Donald Winnicott (1965) and Christopher Bollas (1989, 1999). When I was a young clinician, Reich's descriptions of character and muscular armor, as the unconscious mechanisms of defense, helped me begin to understand why and how it was so difficult for people to change. Reich understood character as a "system" of defense and resistance—to be named, analyzed, confronted, and broken through. This was my early training. It was both invaluable and insufficient.

Winnicott's work was also deeply imbued with the centrality of bodily experience and movement. Winnicott offered the metaphor of mother-infant and analyst-patient relationships as psychosomatic partnerships. He described the therapeutic process as a "space within which patients could play, imagine, attack, experiment, fall apart, explore." Winnicott (1965) suggested that the mother provided an adequate "facilitating environment" and an innate psychosomatic partnership when she was able to recognize and respond to the "spontaneous gestures" of her baby:

> Periodically the infant's gesture gives expression to a spontaneous impulse; the source of the gesture is in the True Self, and the gesture indicates the existence of a potential True Self. We need to examine the way the mother meets the infantile omnipotence revealed in a gesture (or a sensori-motor grouping). I have here linked the idea of a True Self with the spontaneous gesture. Fusion of the motility and erotic elements is in the process of becoming a fact at this period of development of the individual. (p. 145)

The responsiveness of these first interpersonal environments with primary caregivers supported the development of an active, embodied sense of a "true self." Environmental failure (i.e., unresponsiveness, in Winnicott's thinking) promoted the evolution of a "false" and a disembodied sense of self. It becomes possible to reconceptualize Reich's (1949) descriptions of resistance and armor as patterns of *interrupted* gestures between self and other. A crucial therapeutic function in Body Psychotherapy, therefore, is not so much the confrontation of armored resistances, as the reestablishment of an interactive, gestural field between (initially) client and therapist, later client and others. Romanyshyn (1998) takes up the phenomenology of gesture in psychotherapy with particularly compelling language:

As such, every gesture is an appeal, an invitation not only to enter into a world, but also to partake of its experience.... What the patient brings into the field of therapy is a body haunted by an absent other, a body whose gestures find no witness, no reciprocal, for their appeal. Addressed to the therapist, these gestures hold in their presence, an absence which yearns for some lost other, an absence which in fact invites the therapist to become that other, an absence which galvanizes a field between patient and therapist. (pp. 51–52)

## Understanding Character within the Relational Field

The repressed unconscious was central to Reich's model and therapeutic work. This is the unconscious of resistance and Character Analysis. Reich emphasized the experience and expression of *invariance* as an organizing force in early development: the psychological and characterological structuring of experience. What was once an "experience in living" is systematically transformed out of a survival or traumatic necessity into a "psychological structure," now deprived of its original fluidity and vitality, and maintained as character structure. In Reich's model, and in most Neo-Reichian systems, "character" was seen as the enemy: deeply engrained patterns of resistance and psycho-pathology that needed to be confronted and broken through. Perhaps the first person to attempt a systematic approach to countertransference within the Reichian Bioenergetic model was Leites (1976), who addressed countertransference as the defensive encounter between the character of the patient with that of the therapist.

The understanding of the nature and function of character is changing within contemporary body-centered and psychoanalytic models (Aalberse, 1997; Boadella, 1997a, 1997b; Bollas, 1992; Johnson, 1985; Josephs, 1992, 1995; Totton, 1998; Young, 2012). The defensive aspects of character are certainly not ignored in contemporary models of Body Psychotherapy, but there is a deeper understanding of character as also providing an organizing and cohering force in the development of personality and relational patterns. There is also an understanding that the quality of attention—the responsiveness—of the therapeutic relationship is one of the crucial contexts that promote the awareness, softening, and transformation of character. Within this context, Marlock and Weiss argue:

> Working therapeutically with these relational conditions can help to support and motivate the natural and necessary gestures and movement towards the world and its objects. If these actions are successful, they strengthen the leadership position of the Self, its sense of affective subjectivity, agency and cohesion ... We want to assert here that the process of dearmouring and deconstruction needs to be supplemented by a more relational and systemic approach that could support the therapeutic accessing of Self-type capacities. (2001, pp. 144–145)

Bollas (1992) writes of *being* a character. Bollas sees character as an accomplishment, not a failure—or, perhaps, as an accomplishment *and* a failure. He writes eloquently and persuasively of the "intelligence of form" captured by an individual's character. I had been trained to see character and form as stupid, overformed, and underinforming. Bollas describes character as "a form of intelligence and a means of unconscious communication." Seeing character from a more directly body-centered perspective, Aalberse describes it as "an embodied narrative [that] can be seen not just as a story full of pregnant words and images, but also as a choreography of resourceful postures, gestures and interactions" (2001, p. 105).

Seen through Bollas's eyes, Reich's conceptualization of character as a static, deadening, and defensive system shifts into an understanding of character as both a simultaneous effort for, and a defense against, communication. Character does not simply constrain a client's expression: a client's character shapes, in many unspoken ways, the interpersonal field between therapist and client. Any given client's "character" pushes the therapist around during the hour, shaping, telling, and demonstrating a lived reality, without often a word being spoken (or, often, in contradiction to the words being spoken). The dance of character is a means of relating, deforming, informing, re-forming. There is the potential for a vitalizing form of unconscious communication in the midst of the deadening intentions of character structure. Character acquires new meaning as a rich field of unconscious communication.

## Therapeutic Relatedness

Bollas (1992, 1999) and McLaughlin (1981, 1987, 1995), each in his own way, articulates a model of therapeutic relatedness that allows for uncertainty, dissonance, and the mutual exploration of unconscious meanings. For these two psychoanalysts, who share a deep respect for non-verbal and unconscious communication, the therapist's countertransferential responses to the client's characterological style are a rich field of data emerging from the therapist's willingness to be moved, infected, affected, and informed by a matrix of unconscious communication and disturbance. Within the body-centered literature, a similar sense of characterological communication is captured in Boadella's (1997a, 1997b) writings on somatic transference, interference, and resonance, and in the descriptions of organic transference and countertransference within the Unitive Psychology tradition (Marlock, 1988, 1990).

Reich's preoccupation was that of the body in relationship to itself rather than of the patient in relationship to him. What Reich failed to grasp was that the "breakthrough into the vegetative realm" (Reich, 1961, pp. 221–264)—i.e., the realm of sensation and affect, of limbic system and autonomic nervous system dominance—was often a simultaneous breakthrough into the realms of infancy and early childhood: i.e., the gestural and interpersonal field. The "breakthrough" into noncognitive and prelinguistic realms is often accompanied by intense anxiety and disorganization. Reich understood his patients as being afraid of their own impulses, aggression, and vitality. He did not seem to grasp the intense fear of "the absence of the other" during periods of extreme disorganization and vulnerability. Emotional availability, empathy, quiet waiting, tenderness, and bodily accompaniment—experiences so needed from the "other" as part of finding reorganization in the midst of disorganization—were rarely a part of Reich's own character or his therapeutic repertoire.

Reich, like Winnicott, had a lifelong fascination with infants and the mother-infant relationship. Unlike Winnicott, he failed to bring his passions and insights about infancy and infant health into his therapeutic process. He did not bring his studies of adult sexuality, on one hand, with his studies of infancy, on the other, into a theoretical or clinical coherence. Reich's clinical thinking remained rooted in the classical Freudian "drive theory." Reich never truly grasped the pre-genital longings and striving for the "other": the fundamental sense of object-seeking and object-relatedness that infuses Winnicott's work. From my point of view, the primary failure of Reich's clinical work is his failure to incorporate his understanding of infancy into a broader vision of human erotic desires, or into his therapeutic theory and technique. Reich worked brilliantly with the client's defenses, with the client's body in its defensive manifestations, but not with the client's relationship to himself.

Many theorists in the Body Psychotherapy domain are now working to articulate a coherent theory and practice of relatedness within direct work with the body (Aalberse, 1997, 2001; Cornell, 1997, 2000, 2002; Downing, 1996; House, 1996; Klopstech, 2000; Marlock and Weiss, 2001). Winnicott recognized that the intrapsychic and interpersonal were deeply and profoundly intertwined. Winnicott described how the baby learned about his or her own body, about the body of another, as well as the nature of relatedness, through the bodily activity between the two. The "internalization" of another comes through the activity between one's self and another. It is this early, largely unconscious, field of interpersonal activity that is often awakened and explored in Body Psychotherapy. Aalberse conveys this aspect of Body Psychotherapy in this way:

> By concentrating on what is not yet clear, we find out that in that first and rather hazy feeling, a surprising intelligence is waiting to reveal itself. After a certain time deeper trust in this intrinsic intelligence and in

the sensing body able to capture this intelligence can develop. (2001, p. 107)

To return to the earlier case illustration, as Elizabeth and I lay on my office floor, she began to use—and, more important, *began to be able to use*—her body in relation to mine. For Elizabeth, this began to open a lived history, a "domain of experience" that she had not been able to access through conscious memory, thought, or language in her earlier treatment. She was able to begin experiencing and experimenting with her very literal experience of "not knowing" what to do with her body, the seeming impossibility of getting her body close to the body of another. Elizabeth and I spent much of our time together in the space of the "yet-to-be-known." Elizabeth was able to get to know her body, in the presence of mine. I did not nurture her, or soothe and comfort her: I paid attention; I waited attentively. I responded actively (and appropriately) to the tentative emergence of her impulses, using my body to help give her impulses force and form, using my language to help give her impulses meaning.

There are significant times in the therapeutic endeavor when, upon entering emergent and novel realms of bodily experience, words may fail, or simply not be available. At these times, the pressure to verbalize may limit (rather than deepen or enlighten) a client's experience. At times like this, patients may need the therapist to enter directly—if temporarily—into the literal syntax of the client's sense and gesture, not in an unconscious enactment, but in a conscious, intentional provision of a wordless, somatic containing, structuring, or formative function.

As relational models have begun to emerge in Body-Centered Psychotherapy, at least in the United States, they have most often developed from such theoretical perspectives as the empathic style of Self Psychology; the safety and empowerment focus of trauma theory; and the maternal idealizations of feminist and mother-infant-centered theories. Here, we have psychotherapy as a form of extended and idealized motherhood that compensates for the sins and environmental failures (of both mother and father) in the past. This new, corrective, "maternal" presence offers safety, holds, soothes, nurtures, mirrors, resonates, attunes, mirrors, and accommodates in respectful and nonintrusive ways. There is a provision of safety and relief. I see this as too often a rather grandiose form of countertransference. Traditional Reichian, bioenergetic, and Gestalt models were certainly not comforting or maternal, but they have also lacked a model and means of therapeutic relatedness.

Martha Stark (1999) has also had a significant influence on the evolution of relational thinking among Body Psychotherapists in the United States. She enters the contemporary discussion about relational processes in psychotherapy by delineating three central and enduring modes of therapeutic action and interaction. Stark defines the therapeutic purposes of different models of therapeutic relatedness, suggesting that a comprehensive psychotherapy requires differing modes of relatedness over the course of treatment. Stark defines the first mode as that of providing knowledge through insight and interpretation, a model based on intrapsychic, structural conflict as in classical psychoanalysis, within which Reich developed the interpretive and confrontational style of his work. The second therapeutic mode is rooted in the models of developmental and/or structural deprivation and deficit, as often represented in feminist, trauma-based, and Self Psychology (Kohutian) theories. In this mode, the primary therapeutic action is that of the therapist's provision of a corrective relational experience, typically articulated through the language of empathy, attunement, and attachment. As summarized by Stark, this second mode stresses: "(1) the therapist's actual participation as a new good object, (2) the therapist's actual gratification of need, and, more generally, (3) the therapist's provision of a corrective (emotional) experience for the patient" (Ibid., p. 28). The third mode of therapeutic interaction, as outlined by Stark, is that of authenticity and intersubjectivity, therapeutic encounters between two real people in the here and now that simultaneously manifest and challenge archaic beliefs and behaviors.

In Stark's delineation of these modes, the deficit model (mode 2) emphasizes the absence of "good" in the client's life, whereas mode 3 examines the presence of "bad" in the client's motivations and functioning. In the third mode:

. . . [the] therapist participates authentically in a real relationship with the patient—the intention being both to enhance the patient's understanding of her relational dynamics and to deepen the level of their engagement. Accordingly, in the third mode, the intersubjectivist therapist might choose to focus the patient's attention on (1) the patient's impact on the therapist, (2) the therapist's impact on the patient, or (3) the here-and-now engagement (or lack thereof) between them. (Ibid., p. 126)

Within this perspective, the therapist pays close attention to how the client—through actual interactions, projections, and fantasized distortions—creates and maintains bad objects and ineffective or destructive relationships.

## Returning to the Case

To illustrate, I return to the ongoing work with Elizabeth. One day, Elizabeth was feeling especially despairing about the progress of her therapy. She told me that she was thinking of leaving treatment; that this was probably as far as she could go; that for reasons she might never understand, her life was going to remain limited. "It's not such a bad life after all," she argued. I responded that, indeed, hers was not a bad life, but it was a sad life. I continued (without giving much thought to what I was about to say), "I think you deserve more, and I'm rather determined to see that you get it. I can be quite stubborn with people I'm fond of." Elizabeth was stunned. "You're fond of me?" "I certainly am," I replied. "Isn't that obvious?" It wasn't obvious to Elizabeth. In fact, the possibility had never occurred to her that I might feel affection for her, or pleasure in working with her. It had simply been a given for her that I was doing my job, that I felt a sense of responsibility to her. She knew, and felt, that I took our work seriously. It did not occur to her that there was pleasure for me in seeing her. Suddenly, a window into her early childhood began to illuminate. She realized that her parents had always been responsible parents, seriously committed to their children, but she never felt herself to be a source of pleasure in their lives. She realized that she never expected to be a source of pleasure or affection to anyone.

Something began to shift for Elizabeth. As we had been working together, she had often expressed the worry of "being too much" for me. She could never really articulate what this phrase meant, but it seemed ever present. I would often suggest that she seemed ashamed of her body and any potential desire. She would insist that she did not feel shame—"That's not part of my repertoire"—but she did worry that I would find her disgusting. After we had stumbled into the reality of my pleasure in being with her, she was faced with her continuing fantasy that I found her disgusting, quite the opposite of what I actually felt. Gradually, she began to realize that the disgust belonged to her mother, that—in many subtle ways—her mother had always seemed ill at ease with Elizabeth, and that Elizabeth had come to feel that she was disgusting. She had had to keep herself away from her mother. Her body knew well how to move subtly away; it did not know how to move close. We had begun to move into the realm of Elizabeth's dynamic unconscious, those feelings and experiences that had to be unconsciously split off and denied because they were too threatening in her early childhood relations. Elizabeth began to see the signs of her mother's discomfort in their present-day relationship. She began to recognize her anger toward her mother, and with the recognition of her anger, Elizabeth began to develop a capacity for more aggression with her friends. She was able to see her mother (rather than herself) as physically and emotionally limited. She did not need her mother to change. She needed to change, both in relation to her body and in relation to others.

## Aggression and Therapeutic Space

Winnicott's writings offer a perspective that breathes life into the rigidities of both the psychoanalytic and the Reichian-based therapeutic models. Winnicott described the complex, and often paradoxical, nature of infancy as a constant tension and interaction between dependency and aggression. Babies do not perpetually seek nurturance and soothing. They do sometimes: but they also seek separation, aloneness, stimulation, excitement, and destructiveness.

The Winnicottian infant, rather like the Winnicottian patient, is a complex creature—not simply the passive recipient of parental (or therapeutic) largesse (Cornell and Bonds-White, 2001). The Winnicottian infant, as are those described in direct infant observation and research, is an active, ambivalent, and aggressive creature, moving away from as well as toward the parent. Winnicott's mother-infant observations and clinical writings were full of exquisite paradoxes. In an article on "Primitive Emotional Development," for example, he observes:

> I will just mention another reason why an infant is not satisfied with satisfaction. He feels fobbed off. He intended, one might say, to make a cannibalistic attack and he has been put off by an opiate, the feed. At best he can postpone the attack. (1958, p. 154)

How often does a therapist offer, wittingly or unwittingly, empathy and comfort—the opiate, the feed—to ward off the ambivalence or aggressiveness of a client?

The Winnicottian infant becomes impatient with holding, with feeding. There is a powerful developmental pressure for exploration, conflict, and differentiation. The primary parental activities shift—often at the infant's initiative—from providing comfort and responses to physiological and affective states, to facilitating and enjoying the motoric activity, independence, and competence of the baby.

Mel Marshak (2002), in her summary of Winnicott's theory of early object-relations, stressed that for Winnicott there are three forms of infant dependence. The first, which seems to get the most attention in the literature, is that of the early survival needs of the infant and his or her dependence on the maternal holding environment and the protective, highly responsive envelope that it offers. The second, which moves into the first experience of space between, is that of transitional space, the nontraumatic weaning of the infant from maternal provision (which is as much at the initiative of the infant as that of the mother). In this second form of dependence, the infant depends on the mother being unintrusive. In this space, the infant is able to be alone in the presence of the other, able to have the space and movement to "generate for himself a matrix for his psychological and bodily experience" (Ibid., p. 11). The third is the infant's dependence (and here is a classic Winnicottian paradox) on the mother's survival of his separateness and aggressiveness. This is a crucial and often misunderstood phase of development in human growth and maturation, as well as within the psychotherapeutic process. The client's aggressiveness and attack against the therapist and/or the therapeutic process are not necessarily a defense, but are often an expression of this third form of "dependency," the need to rely on the other to survive the conflict with interest and care, without retaliation or severing of the relationship. The therapeutic field is one of ever-evolving styles of relatedness, of movement (verbal, emotional, and motoric) toward and away from one another within a space of lively and responsive attentiveness.

## Conclusion

Life is rarely safe; intimacy is not safe; the world is not safe. Life, intimacy, and the world can, however, be and stay alive in the midst of its risks, uncertainties, dangers, and disappointments. This, I would suggest, is the space and function of the therapeutic relationship. True safety for clients in Body Psychotherapy is that of having the room to move and experiment, the opportunity to make mistakes, the reliability of a committed and attentive relatedness, and the therapist's enduring curiosity and interest in the client's unfolding experience. This must include negative experiences with the therapist, and the space to experience and examine aggression and conflict without retaliation.

That grand and resplendent jazz musician, Sun Ra, was famous for his phrase "Space Is the Place," which he transformed into sound, song, chant, and dance in a multitude of variations through his amazing career. It is my understanding that the function of the therapeutic relationship in Body-Centered Psychotherapy is to provide space, a space in which to move, in which to acquire new emotional and sensory-motoric skills. That space is the place, an intrapsychic and interpersonal space for experimentation and exploration. That space is a place to try again, in the presence of a skilled and attentive therapist, to challenge one's psychosomatic rigidities, to revive and complete one's patterns of interrupted gestures.

## References

Aalberse, M. (1997). When eros fails. *Energy & Character, 28*(1), 77–94.

Aalberse, M. (2001). Graceful means: Felt gestures and choreographic therapy. In M. Heller (Ed.), *The flesh of the soul: The body we work with* (pp. 101–132). Bern: Peter Lang.

Boadella, D. (1997a). Embodiment in the therapeutic relationship. *International Journal of Psychotherapy, 2*(1), 33–44.

Boadella, D. (1997b). Psychotherapy, science, and levels of discourse. *Energy & Character, 28*(1), 13–20.

Bollas, C. (1989). *The forces of destiny: Psychoanalysis and the human idiom.* London: Free Association Books.

Bollas, C. (1992). *Being a character: Psychoanalysis and self experience.* New York: Hill & Wang.

Bollas, C. (1999). *The mystery of things.* London: Routledge.

Cornell, W. (1997). If Reich had met Winnicott: Body and gesture. *Energy & Character, 28*(2), 50–60.

Cornell, W. (2000). Transference, desire, and vulnerability in Body-Centered Psychotherapy. *Energy & Character, 30*(1), 29–37.

Cornell, W. (2002). Body-Centered Psychotherapy. In R. Massey & S. Massey (Eds.), *Comprehensive handbook of psychotherapy: Interpersonal-humanistic-existential* (Vol. 3) (pp. 587–613). New York: John Wiley & Sons.

Cornell, W., & Bonds-White, F. (2001). Therapeutic relatedness in Transactional Analysis: The truth of love or the love of truth. *Transactional Analysis Journal, 31*(4), 71–83.

Downing, G. (1996). *Korper und Wort in der Psychotherapie* [Body and word in psychotherapy]. Munich: Kösel Verlag.

Ghent, E. (1990). Masochism, submission, surrender: Masochism as a perversion of surrender. *Contemporary Psychoanalysis, 26,* 108–136.

House, R. (1996). Object relations and the body. *Energy & Character, 27*(2), 31–44.

Johnson, S. (1985). *Characterological transformation: The hard work miracle.* New York: W. W. Norton.

Josephs, L. (1992). *Character structure and the organization of the self.* New York: Columbia University Press.

Josephs, L. (1995). *Balancing empathy and interpretation: Relational character analysis.* Northvale, NJ: Jason Aronson.

Klopstech, A. (2000). Psychoanalysis and Body Psychotherapies in dialogue. *Bioenergetic Analysis, 11*(1), 43–54.

Leites, A. (1976). *Countertransference: A characterological approach.* New York: Institute for the New Age.

Marlock, G. (1988). *Unitive Body Psychotherapy* (Vol. I). Frankfurt: Afra Verlag.

Marlock, G. (1990). *Unitive Body Psychotherapy* (Vol. II). Frankfurt: Afra Verlag.

Marlock, G., & Weiss, H. (2001). In search of the embodied self. In M. Heller (Ed.), *The flesh of the soul: The body we work with* (pp. 133–152). Bern: Peter Lang.

Marshak, M. (2002, June 1). *The use of the object.* Paper presented to Seminars for Mental Health Professionals, C. G. Jung Institute of Pittsburgh, Pennsylvania.

McLaughlin, J. (1981). Transference, psychic reality and countertransference. *Psychoanalytic Quarterly, 50,* 639–664.

McLaughlin, J. (1987). The play of transference: Some reflections on enactment in the psychoanalytic situation. *Journal of the American Psychoanalytic Association, 35,* 557–582.

McLaughlin, J. (1995). Touching limits in the analytic dyad. *Psychoanalytic Quarterly, 64,* 433–465.

Phillips, A. (1995). The story of the mind. In E. Corrigan & P. Gordon (Eds.), *The mind object* (pp. 229–240). Northvale, NJ: Jason Aronson.

Reich, W. (1949). *Character Analysis.* New York: Orgone Institute Press.

Reich, W. (1961). *The function of the orgasm.* New York: Farrar, Straus & Giroux.

Romanyshyn, R. (1998). Psychotherapy as grief work. In D. Johnson & I. Grand (Eds.), *The body in psychotherapy: Inquiries in Somatic Psychology.* Berkeley, CA: North Atlantic Books.

Stark, M. (1999). *Modes of therapeutic action.* Northvale, NJ: Jason Aronson.

Totton, N. (1998). *The water in the glass: Body and mind in psychoanalysis.* London: Rebus Press.

Winnicott, D. (1958). *Through paediatrics to psychoanalysis: Collected papers.* London: Karnac.

Winnicott, D. (1965). *The maturational processes and the facilitating environment.* Madison, CT: International Universities Press.

Young, C. (Ed.). (2012). *About Relational Body Psychotherapy.* Galashiels, Scotland: Body Psychotherapy Publications.

# 46

## Enhancing the Immediacy and Intimacy of the Therapeutic Relationship through the Somatic Dimension

**Richard A. Heckler and Gregory J. Johanson, United States**

**Richard A. Heckler,** PhD, is a Hakomi trainer and was the director of the Hakomi Institute of San Francisco. Previously, he was an associate professor of counseling psychology at John F. Kennedy University, and a faculty member of the Union Institute for Experimental Studies. Aside from Body Psychotherapy, he was trained in family therapy and Gestalt Therapy. His particular interest is in the psychological effects of spiritual practice. His two books—on survivors of suicide attempts (*Waking Up, Alive*), and life-changing, extraordinary experiences (*Crossings*)—made him known throughout the United States, and led to many invitations to talk shows and conferences.

Dr. Heckler works in private practice and as a trainer for Somatic Psychotherapy (Hakomi). In this chapter, he describes one of his first attempts to bring the body into the psychotherapeutic process, and his surprise, at the time, at how fast and deeply this measure facilitated the therapeutic relationship.

**Gregory Johanson's** biographical information can be found at the beginning of Chapter 15, "The Organization of Experience: A Systems Perspective on the Relation of Body Psychotherapies to the Wider Field of Psychotherapy."

## The Body Reveals

Relating to the somatic dimensions of a client's presentation can accelerate the immediacy, intimacy, and power of the therapeutic relationship. This in turn enhances the possibility of more quickly and efficiently deepening the therapeutic process in what may be characterized as in-depth brief therapy (Ecker and Hulley, 1996), or what Peterfreund (1983) characterizes as the "good/effective" hour of heuristic as opposed to stereotypical therapy.

The power and efficiency of attending to somatic expressions are that those expressions are tied more closely to deeper brain structures than the cerebral cortex (Cozolino, 2002; Nadel, 1994; Siegel, 1999; Schore, 1994). Aron (1998b) cites a number of psychoanalytic theorists who underline this truth, leading him to conclude that "one's self or one's self-representation is first and foremost a bodily self" (p. xix).

Winnicott (1949) surmised that the antithesis of mind and body is based on illusion, with self-evolving from bodily sensations connected to the "holding" and "handling" by primary caregivers. This emphasis on self-arising through bodily contact with others has enabled relational-oriented theorists such as Greenberg (1991), Gill (1994), Mitchell (1988), and Aron (1998b), who question Freud's somatic drive theory, to affirm an intersubjective-bodily self. Aron (1998a) further notes the work of Anzieu (1985) on the function of the skin, Eigen (1977) on the function of breathing, and Ogden (1989) on issues of development that are all aspects of what Stern (1985) termed the "core self."

This core self functions to make meaningful sense of our experience, to organize all aspects of our life (Kurtz, 1990; Mahoney, 2003; Stolorow et al., 1987). Not only are our cognition, interpersonal relationships, and dreams organized, but the entire spectrum of our bodily existence: posture, breathing, movement, facial expression, skin quality, gestures, sensations, muscle tone, and more (Kurtz and

Prestera, 1976). Thus, the body provides a readily available revelation of the unconscious, as do one's dreams, thinking patterns, and ways of relating. It is an intriguing revelation that has not been abused and desensitized by overuse, as have many verbal, stereotyped interventions: "How do you feel about that?"

## Deepening into the Revelation

Verbal speech is also further along the distancing line of generalization and abstraction in the transmutation of initial energy stimulation (May, 1982, pp. 179–181). Therapists of many persuasions are familiar with the paradoxical ability of words to both enliven and deaden communication with another (Johanson, 1996). Too often, words—though necessary for meaning—introduce distance into the relationship between oneself and one's own experience, and between oneself and the therapist.

Body-inclusive psychotherapists therefore are, by and large, less interested in hearing the stories of clients, which can recount repetitive, habitual, but unending variations on a theme, than in tracking the body for physical manifestations (Kurtz, 1990) of the core organizers that form the storytellers themselves.

Perhaps, for instance: a slight redness on the neck and tightness of the jaw indicate a deeper anger at perceived disrespect than the person is actually communicating; a spouse, in couples therapy, leaning back and away when her partner is talking indicates a deeper fear than is being admitted verbally; hypotonic muscles in the arm might indicate a fear of being abandoned that won't allow pushing away and setting a boundary; or raised shoulders could reveal a fear of control that will not allow intimacy. Possible somatic indicators are virtually infinite.

After an indicator is identified, and there is an implicit or explicit contract to proceed, Body-Centered Psychotherapists often move to contact, to evoke, or to bring awareness to the somatic manifestation. It is a move meant to establish an immediate, curious (Johanson, 1988), mindful (Austen, 2001; Bennett-Goleman, 2001; Kurtz, 1990; Segal et al., 2002) relationship between the client and his or her present-moment experience, as well as to foster an intimate, live, collaborative relationship between client and therapist.

A typical first step is for the therapist to notice a somatic revelation, and invite the client to bring it into his or her awareness, in an open, reflective, exploratory way. The invitation often functions to bring something outside of awareness into consciousness. For instance, "Some emotion comes into your face as you say that, huh?" "Are you aware that your fists are tightening as you speak of your second son?" "How about experimenting with not locking your knees as you talk with him?" "Notice what it is like talking with me if you hold your chin and head up about a half an inch higher." "Your shoulders appear closed in. Let's check out what it is like as you lay back over this roller on the floor for a while."

Once the therapist and client focus their attention on the present felt experience of the client, there is a palpable immediacy, aliveness, and intimacy that go beyond what is possible when people are offering theories, rationales, justifications, or verbal recitations of their experience. It is the difference in the quality of knowing similar to that of right- and left-brain questions: Right: "What is the quality of sadness in your heart?" Left: "Why do you think your heart is sad?" It is the difference between bringing affective, reflexive self-awareness to one's experience (Aron, 1998a, pp. 3–4) and offering a theory about one's experience.

There is also the clinical, faith-in-process present, confirmed by our clinical experiences, that once there is a felt sense of an experience present, the next step will emerge, as Gendlin (1992, 1996) has noted. That next step will often be a movement closer to the core organizer that was revealed somatically.

## Personhood as a Safe Context

Clients who have consented to enter into a mutual exploration of live, present experience that leads them spontaneously into deep, new places of awareness and possibility, are in many ways undefended, exposed, or naked within the therapeutic bubble or alliance created with the therapist.

The comfort of habitual mental-emotional ways of keeping the other at a distance has collapsed in a courageous and hopeful act of trust. A profound degree of intimacy, openness, and curiosity is achieved between the client and their own experience, as well as between the client and the therapist. This is why the process can accelerate into uncovering the prereflective unconscious at such a fast rate.

There is also the potential for danger here: were the therapist to become defensive, to take transference personally, to get invested in pushing a certain result, to switch from a mutual explorer to a hierarchical expert, or to allow their fear or other forms of countertransference to take over within this therapeutic alliance of trust and vulnerability, the results could be therapeutically disastrous. The worst fears of the person could be confirmed and reinforced. The very possibility of therapeutic change could be buried and despaired of, as betrayed defenses often reengage with a vengeance. Self-destructive and/or self-protective parts could take over, leading to a serious acting out (Schwartz, 1995).

Of course, the signs, especially the somatic ones, of perceived or actual ruptures of empathy can be tracked, contacted, and corrected by the therapist. This can, as intersubjective, relational, and attachment theorists teach (Cassidy and Shaver, 1999; Mitchell and Aron, 1999; Stolorow et al., 1987), be even more powerful in terms of enhancing the client's growth than if the therapist's attunement and limbic resonance (Lewis et al., 2000) never faltered. In general, the power of body-centered interventions to enhance relational processes calls for precise and exquisite training, practice, and supervision. In particular, the deepening of experience and intimacy calls for high levels of safety, provided through learning to honor, respect, support, and explore for their wisdom all hesitancies, anxieties, or fears that are evoked throughout the process (Johanson and Kurtz, 1991, pp. 40–47).

Likewise, comprehensive training would teach therapists the use of body-inclusive methods in the various modes of therapeutic action outlined by Stark (1999). These methods can be used to foster intrapsychic awareness in the client, to integrate new experiential realities from ideal partners, as well as to engage in more mutual forms of relationship (Hedges, 1996; Hycner, 1991; Mitchell and Aron, 1999; Weiss, 1995; Whitaker and Malone, 1953). In the context of this chapter, Stark's last option, called two-person therapy, normally occurs during the integration phase of a therapeutic process when new beliefs or core organizing narratives are experimented with in the real time and space of the client's everyday relationships.

Although there is much more that could be said theoretically of the immediacy, intimacy, and power of body-inclusive methods in therapeutic relationships (Feinstein, 1990; Fisher, 2002; Gilligan, 1997; Lewis et al., 2000; McNeely, 1987; Rosenberg et al., 1985), the following offers a more palpable clinical illustration from the practice of Heckler when he first started exploring the potential of somatic interventions in psychotherapy.

## A Case Example: "Radar": Meeting, Assessing

I was working at a typically underfunded mental health center. That morning, the combination secretary-administrator had assigned to me a new client, 'Catherine,' who was in her late thirties. Catherine arrived on time, something somewhat unusual in our rather laid-back community. She greeted me cordially and formally. Smartly dressed in a beige and brown business suit, she conveyed an air of industry, competence, and confidence. Catherine worked in the corporate sector, and had, in the rather short period of a few years, moved from management to the executive ranks. This was a source of pride—she had worked hard, and had come from humble beginnings—but recently, it was the focus of her increasing anxiety.

A job promotion now required her to travel more, meet many new people, and, sometimes, make presentations to groups of thirty or more. Although no one aspect of this was disconcerting, as we sat down, she explained that together, they seemed to leave her unsettled and enervated by the time she returned home. In time, she began to dread the trips, and a despair about her career encamped within her. She described an attrition that was occurring, below the level of her job performance: she felt she was exhausting her ability to rise to a challenge, and eroding her capacity to remain even-keeled when encountering the inevitable surprises that life "on the road" offered. Something deep and disturbing was being stirred, she felt, and Catherine was at a loss over how to respond.

Early on in our session, I had noticed a quickening within me as I listened to her. She was smart and articulate, and she was serious in her mission to quickly dispel her unease and to return to her career. I imagined that she would need to feel intrigued by our work just to stay with it. I knew that this first session would be crucial, and that joining with her would require a connection beneath typical conversation.

As our first session continued, Catherine described her situation further, and we settled into our traditional roles. As the client, she would provide relevant information, and, as the therapist, I would assemble and reorganize it in some alchemical fashion in order to promote healing. Truthfully, these roles were comforting. She could ease into this new relationship by offering probably well-rehearsed personal material, and I, within the privacy of my own thoughts and risking little, could incubate a cogent response. Yet it was precisely this choreographed predictability that prompted me toward more innovative exploration—first, my training in Family Therapy, and then, training in Somatic Psychology as well.

It was something from my most recent, in-depth training in Somatic Psychotherapy and one of its principal messages on which I began to reflect during our first session. The Hakomi Method of Body-Centered Psychotherapy taught that the body reflects psychological material with uncanny accuracy. Through gesture and movement, posture and voice, even in the way we breathe (or don't), the body more eloquently expresses our deepest beliefs, our most buried memories, hurts, and fears, than our often well-worn descriptions of who we are. I was taught that, if the therapist truly learned the language of the body, and employed the creativity and courage to include the body within the field of exploration, deep and authentic work could result. Fresh from an advanced training, I was anxious to test its capacity with a wide range of clients. Catherine was one of my first opportunities.

In our Body Psychotherapy training, we spent weeks observing the body—statically, in its posture, and then in movement as well. We listened to the voice, its pace and tenor; we watched repetitive gesture, movement, and the range of movement. We were taught to notice how in, or out of, alignment the body was with gravity—indications of extra effort needed to compensate for imbalances, both physical and emotional. Most importantly, we learned how to use this material phenomenologically—to help a client, first, to become aware of "how" they were organized physically, and then to use that awareness to explore the emotional substrate below.

Catherine continued to talk about her situation. Though compelling in its description, something else tugged at my awareness: it was her eyes. When I looked at her, Catherine held my gaze. She seemed direct and forthright. When I looked away, she would visually scan the office. A few times, she just barely returned to me before my gaze met hers. It seemed important to her that I didn't notice. A few times, I saw her entire demeanor change—nervous and almost afraid as she furtively examined the room.

*"What is she searching for?"* I wondered. *"What is she concerned about?"* Further, was this activity significant? However tangential it seemed to the rational mind, could it shed light on her situation? Could it provide a window, an entry point, through which we could explore the more elusive layers of her experience?

**Switching Gears**

A choice point had been reached. We could continue talking 'about' her life, or we could explore, in the present moment, how she constructed it. I was reminded of a favorite couplet in *The Love Song of J. Alfred Prufrock*, by T. S. Eliot: "*Should I, after tea and cakes and ices, have the strength to force the moment to its crisis?*"

With a bit of hesitation, and not sure how it would be received, I mentioned my awareness. I described her behavior in mechanical terms—what she did with her eyes, how she seemed to hold her breath, taking care to avoid judgment—and then added what I imagined . . . that she seemed nervous.

To my surprise, she seemed to melt a bit. Letting out a deep exhale, she said: "I always do this. Ever since I can remember . . . I look around . . . make sure the door is closed, the windows are shut. I try to sit where I can see the whole room, and where my back is against a wall."

I asked if she would be willing to continue scanning, and tell me what else she was aware of: *"I hold my breath as long as I can so I can hear better."* "Hear what?" I asked. *"If anyone is coming unexpectedly. I don't want to be surprised. I also try to keep still."* For the next few minutes, she visually traveled the room, but with this extra awareness. To her list, she added that she senses the skin on her arms, to notice if there is heat—the possibility of an unwanted approach. She listens to the conversation, with as little attention as she can in order to follow it, but most of her awareness is devoted to detecting sudden movement, sound, or vibration. Finally, she tried to do all this (it was before the word "multitasking" had been coined) in a manner that avoided someone noticing. At the end of her description, I asked her if she would give the entire complex of activity a name. Without hesitation, she said, *"Radar."*

I noticed a curious mix of feelings within myself. I felt awe for this complex, enduring, even loyal amalgam of behaviors, created by fear decades ago, and practiced and refined throughout this woman's life. I felt humbled that we as a species are capable of such boundless creativity and intelligence, and yet we can also truncate that range as a desperate though subliminal response to threat. I also felt honored to have been 'let in.' It seemed we could have talked for many sessions and not have arrived at this particular point. It had occurred from simply naming her physical behavior that was happening outside of the content of her story.

## Somatic Experimenting

This sudden intimacy also gave rise to a deep compassion. In that moment, using the tools I had learned, my therapeutic strategy became clear. I asked Catherine if she would teach me how to do the "radar" as well as she did. I asked her to teach me each part, and then check and refine my attempts while I tried to do what she was doing. She laughed (something between a chuckle and a wistful sigh). She seemed intrigued and perplexed, and willing to go along, at least for a time.

As she explained each part, and watched and critiqued my modeling, two significant things happened. She became a bit more playful. Sometimes feigning an imperious judge, she would critique, roll her eyes, bemoan my attempts, and then correct me. We had entered a realm of curious play— light and serious. Joined together in this peculiar project, we both grew animated, focused, and collaborative. At the same time, more color came to her face. More emotion seemed apparent. Sometimes her certain and sure voice would quaver.

After fifteen minutes or so . . . Catherine conceded that I accomplished a fair imitation, although *"Don't let go of your day job"* was implied. Next, I asked her if she would let me do the 'radar' for her, so she wouldn't have to. I told her it was entirely voluntary, but it seemed that only one of us really needed to do the work. She was surprised at such an odd request. I was somewhat surprised that she actually agreed.

These were critical moments. I knew we were working with deeply buried, traumatic material. Within the intimacy of our new and fragile alliance, she was allowing me to take over a secret, lonely, core defense. I knew we had to go slow, and I had to track for overload, dissociation, flooding, the entire host of symptoms that could possibly arise in therapy.

We made a plan. She could decide all the parameters— how long we would experiment, how much she would allow me to 'take over' the radar for her, how deeply she wanted to sense what happened inside her. This was crucial for providing a safe container, operating under the control of her own inner wisdom. In my memory, she said, *"One minute"*: it may have been a bit more or less, but not by much. I told her we could begin when she wanted to, and when the second hand again reached the top of the clock, she said, *"Start."*

Although she could never really know what I was truly doing inside during that time, I felt I must be absolutely true to my word. It was a promise, a kind of sacred vow. Someone in this room needed to be the 'radar' to honor the wisdom of her body. First, I made sure the doors and windows were closed and locked. Next, I looked around the room with quick glances. I tried to hear every sound and vibration—not only in my office, but in the building as well. I slowed my breath and noticed my senses becoming keener. I began to feel less visible, taking up less space, and therefore becoming less of a target. Finally, I felt the skin on my arms—alert for the sudden, unexpected approach of a stranger. It was an odd state—steadying, but filled with fear; resourceful, but utterly lacking true creativity; enduring, but deeply fatiguing. Intellectually, I was enormously intrigued. Emotionally, my heart was breaking for the essential safety that she had somehow lost.

**Relating Deeply**

We never reached our time limit. About thirty seconds into the experiment, I heard a deep exhale, and then tears. I glanced at Catherine to see her place her head in her hands, and fold over in her chair. She began to sob. Her body began to shake. Not wanting to abandon my role just yet, I included Catherine in my scanning, and listened to the sounds coming from a deeper and deeper place within her. I felt a deep empathy and limbic resonance with her.

Truthfully, therapists live for these moments. Our roles dissolve, leaving just two people, humble and very human, deeply connected. The powerful silence is filled with only the most essential sounds, spare and true. These moments are both delicate and robust—inhabited by the pain of ghosts past, and the seeds of authentic liberation and change.

Catherine and I were silent for a while. Her tears had built to a crescendo, and then ebbed. I continued my job for a while, but then let it dissolve, as she seemed quieter and more collected. After what seemed many minutes, she raised her head and softly held my gaze. She began, *"You know, I can't ever remember not having to do that: that radar. I was molested as a child . . . by family and friends of family, and I was beaten too. I don't ever remember a time when I felt carefree and safe. These were the first minutes. This was the first time."*

We continued for three or four more sessions before she came to the closure she had sought. In each of those sessions, she recalled our first encounter. It had become a new reference point: for her, a new, very real experience that represented a new sense of possibility. She could still employ her radar when appropriate, but it no longer needed to be constant and unconscious. She could begin to differentiate situations, and make choices about when it was safe to take the radar off alert status. She ended our work elated, victorious in a gentle way, and for the first time, free.

I still don't believe all of her healing had been accomplished. The breakthrough she experienced would hopefully allow her to finally reenter her past without retraumatization, and truly reevaluate and heal that chapter of her life. Catherine chose to relocate for her job, and that was the last I saw of her. However, this story remains—for this clinician—a pivotal one.

## Enhancing Intimacy

The example of 'radar' illustrates a number of points in the process of deepening immediacy and intimacy in the therapeutic relationship through incorporating the body. Although there are no scripted or linear, preprogrammed steps that guarantee a particular result, the following sequence (described above) demonstrates clinically positive possibilities:

1. Tracking, paying special attention to how bodily manifestations seem to reveal core organizers.
2. Allowing the client's presentation or organization to deeply affect oneself, taking it on with as much somatic resonance as possible.
3. Stepping outside normal conversational habits to bring awareness to what is noticed.
4. Inducing safety, by calling attention to somatic realities in a curious, nonjudgmental way that suggests they should be honored for the wisdom they contain.

5. Proceeding in a collaborative way of mutual exploration that engages the creativity and knowledge of the client's reflective awareness, as well as their more immediate sensations, feelings, and memories.
6. Maintaining an open, experimental attitude that allows present experience to deepen with the cooperation of the unconscious, and prevents premature explanation and theorizing from foreclosing on new discoveries.
7. Consistently honoring and respecting experiences as they arise, as opposed to pathologizing anything, even if they appear defensive or irrational.
8. Allowing connections between bodily experiencing and mental meaning to be made when there is a felt sense of rightness, as opposed to prematurely imposing interpretations.
9. Affirming the narrative meaning that makes sense of the deeper material that was controlling the presenting problem.
10. Assisting the client to experiment with consciously employing the old means of self-protection, as well as discerning when new situations allow for broader possibilities.

The end of the process comes when both client and therapist are touched and energized through intimate contact with the truth of their felt, present experience.

# References

Anzieu, D. (1985). *The skin ego.* New Haven, CT: Yale University Press.

Aron, L. (1998a). The clinical body and the reflexive mind. In L. Aron & F. Sommer Anderson (Eds.), *Relational perspectives on the body* (pp. 3–38). Hillsdale, NJ: Analytic Press.

Aron, L. (1998b). Introduction: The body in drive and relational models. In L. Aron & F. Sommer Anderson (Eds.), *Relational perspectives on the body* (pp. xix–xxviii). Hillsdale, NJ: Analytic Press.

Austen, J. H. (2001). *Zen and the brain.* Cambridge, MA: MIT Press.

Bennett-Goleman, T. (2001). *Emotional alchemy: How the mind can heal the heart.* New York: Harmony Books.

Cassidy, J., & Shaver, P. (Eds.). (1999). *Handbook of attachment: Theory, research, and clinical applications.* New York: Guilford Press.

Cozolino, L. (2002). *The neuroscience of psychotherapy: Building and rebuilding the human brain.* New York: W. W. Norton.

Ecker, B., & Hulley, L. (1996). *Depth-oriented brief therapy.* San Francisco: Jossey-Bass.

Eigen, M. (1977). Breathing and identity. *Journal of Humanistic Psychology, 17(3), 35–39.* Reprinted in *The electrified tightrope.* Northvale, NJ: Aronson, 1993.

Feinstein, D. (1990). Transference and countertransference in the here-and-now therapies. *Hakomi Forum, 8, 7–13.*

Fisher, R. (2002). *Experiential Psychotherapy with couples: A guide for the creative pragmatist.* Phoenix, AZ: Zeig, Tucker & Theisen.

Gendlin, E. T. (1992). On emotion in therapy. *Hakomi Forum, 9, 15–29.*

Gendlin, E. T. (1996). *Focusing-Oriented Psychotherapy: A manual of the experiential method.* New York: Guilford Press.

Gill, M. (1994). *Psychoanalysis in transition.* Hillsdale, NJ: Analytic Press.

Gilligan, S. (1997). *The courage to love: Principles and practices of Self-Relations Psychotherapy.* New York: W. W. Norton.

Greenberg, J. (1991). *Oedipus and beyond.* Cambridge, MA: Harvard University Press.

Hedges, L. E. (1996). *Strategic emotional involvement.* Northvale, NJ: Jason Aronson.

Hycner, R. H. (1991). *Between person and person: Toward a dialogical psychotherapy.* Highland, NY: Gestalt Journal Press.

Johanson, G. J. (1988). A curious form of therapy: Hakomi. *Hakomi Forum, 6, 18–31.*

Johanson, G. J. (1996). The birth and death of meaning: Selective implications of linguistics for psychotherapy. *Hakomi Forum, 12, 45–55.*

Johanson, G., & Kurtz, R. (1991). *Grace unfolding: Psychotherapy in the spirit of the Tao-te Ching.* New York: Bell Tower.

Kurtz, R. (1990). *Body-Centered Psychotherapy: The Hakomi Method.* Mendocino, CA: LifeRhythm.

Kurtz, R., & Prestera, H. (1976). *The body reveals.* New York: Harper & Row.

Lewis, T., Amini, F., & Lannon, R. (2000). *A general theory of love.* New York: Vintage Books.

Mahoney, M. J. (2003). *Constructive psychotherapy: A practical guide.* New York: Guilford Press.

May, G. (1982). *Will and spirit: A contemplative psychology.* San Francisco: Harper & Row.

McNeely, D. A. (1987). *Touching: Body therapy and Depth Psychology.* Toronto: Inner City Books.

Mitchell, S. (1988). *Relational concepts in psychoanalysis.* Cambridge, MA: Harvard University Press.

Mitchell, S. A., & Aron, L. (Eds.). (1999). *Relational Psychoanalysis: The emergence of a tradition.* Hillsdale, NJ: Analytic Press.

Nadel, L. (1994). Multiple memory systems: What and why. An update. In D. Schater & E. Tulving (Eds.), *Memory systems* (pp. 39–63). Cambridge, MA: MIT Press.

Ogden, T. H. (1989). *The primitive edge of experience.* Northvale, NJ: Aronson.

Peterfreund, E. (1983). *The process of psychoanalytic therapy.* Hillsdale, NJ: Analytic Press.

Rosenberg, J., Rand, M., & Asay, D. (1985). *Body, self and soul: Sustaining integration.* Atlanta, GA: Humanics.

Schore, A. N. (1994). *Affect regulation and the origin of the self.* Hillsdale, NJ: Lawrence Erlbaum.

Schwartz, R. (1995). *Internal family systems theory.* New York: Guilford Press.

Segal, Z. V., Williams, J. M. G., & Teasdale, J. D. (2002). *Mindfulness-based cognitive therapy for depression.* New York: Guilford Press.

Siegel, D. J. (1999). *The developing mind: Toward a neurobiology of interpersonal experience.* New York: Guilford Press.

Stark, M. (1999). *Modes of therapeutic action: Enhancement of knowledge, provision of experience, and engagement in relationship.* Northvale, NJ: Jason Aronson.

Stern, D. N. (1985). *The interpersonal world of the infant.* New York: Basic Books.

Stolorow, R., Brandchaft, B., & Atwood, G. (1987). *Psychoanalytic treatment: An intersubjective approach.* Hillsdale, NJ: Analytic Press.

Weiss, H. (1995). The emergence of the other. *Hakomi Forum, 11, 11–26.*

Whitaker, C. A., & Malone, T. P. (1953). *The roots of psychotherapy.* New York: Blakiston.

Winnicott, D. W. (1949). Mind and its relation to the psyche-soma. In D. Winnicott (Ed.), *Through paediatrics to psycho-analysis* (pp. 243–254). New York: Basic Books.

# 47

## Transference, Countertransference, and Supervision in the Body Psychotherapeutic Tradition

**Michael Soth, United Kingdom**

**Michael Soth's** biographical information can be found at the beginning of the "Introduction to the American-English Edition."

## Introduction

How do contemporary Body Psychotherapists work with the transference? What are some of the perceptive, theoretical, practical, and metapsychological tools that distinguish Body Psychotherapy's stance toward transference and countertransference from that of other approaches? How does this manifest in the therapeutic relationship? And how does it manifest in supervision? These are the main questions that I will try to touch upon in this chapter.

The concept of transference comes down to us as a precious and essential gift from the psychoanalytic tradition and its various modern schools. However, in its classical version, it comes packaged with what I have called psychotherapy's "birth trauma" in the *zeitgeist* of the late nineteenth century with its inherent dualisms (Soth, 2006a and 2006b), especially the dualistic conceptions of the mind-over-body and the doctor-patient relationship. There is a growing consensus among psychotherapists regarding the centrality of the therapeutic relationship (Marlock and Weiss, 2006, p. 481), but there is still considerable confusion and polarization regarding the nature of therapeutic relating (Soth, 2007a and 2007b). This is because there are indeed a variety of categorically different and to some extent contradictory relational modalities and kinds of therapeutic relatedness that, in turn, constitute fundamentally different therapeutic spaces (Stark, 1999; Clarkson and Wilson, 1994).

## A Multiplicity of Relational Modalities

Stretching from Freud's original, taken-for-granted "medical model" stance, via various other manifestations of one-person psychology (in which an expert dispenses treatment, often in the form of mental insight, without considering the contribution of their own subjectivity, let alone pathology, to the relationship—and this would largely include Reich and, to some extent, Lowen), to the more modern humanistic and psychoanalytic forms of one-and-a-half-person psychology (in which the therapist monitors and occasionally makes explicit use of their countertransference responses in the service of the client's experiential process), to even more modern and explicit forms of two-person psychology, variously called "I-Thou" relating by the humanistic tradition (Buber, 1937/1970), "intersubjectivity" by Stolorow and Atwood (1992), and "mutual recognition" by relational psychoanalysts (see Aron and Harris, 2011), the psychotherapeutic field comprises a wide range of relational stances. *Each* of these stances can be practiced within a predominantly verbal-cognitive or also from within a holistic, body-mind orientation. Inevitably, the more Body Psychotherapy has cross-fertilized with the ongoing development of psychoanalysis, many mixtures and hybrid forms are conceivable and exist (Sletvold, 2014).

Generally speaking, though, we can say that the bulk of Body Psychotherapeutic history has been characterized by Reich's quite authoritative, quasi-medical stance. The humanistic revolution then countered these one-person psychology influences, and established more egalitarian modes of relating, being more open, authentic, and realistic about the therapist's own wounds and their impact on the therapeutic relationship. However, remnants of Reich's objectifying stance are implicit in both theory and practice and can be found throughout the field to this day, often in hidden and disavowed forms alongside an insistence on dialogic relating, or an explicit philosophical commitment to two-person psychology.

In practice, the relational confusion manifests in therapists shifting their relational stance back and forth, often in the course of one session, without being aware of this (e.g., from an expert stance, providing a diagnostic interpretation or body reading; toward a reparative, nurturing stance of encouragement; toward a self-disclosure of the therapist's own experience, in a spirit of mutuality). Often, this may be precisely what the client's process needs, and the therapist's fluidity between relational stances is then an asset. However, more often than not, on investigation in supervision we find that these shifts by the therapist turn out to be reactions *against* the disturbing heat of the transference, and not at all in the service of the process, but defenses against it (what Strean [1993] calls "counter-resistances," or what psychoanalysis might label "acting in").

In the psychoanalytic tradition, the vocabulary of the counter-transference was used to shed light on such reactions by the therapist, including their handling of the transference, based precisely on the recognition that not all of the therapist's ideas and therapeutic impulses could be trusted to be useful. The notion of counter-transference itself, full of multiple and contradictory meanings, confused and contentious as it has historically been, has been taken up widely by many humanistic therapists, including Body Psychotherapists, but largely in Freud's sense as the therapist's own pathology (which is meant to be kept out of the consulting room so as not to contaminate the client's process).

However, the major paradigm shift that occurred in some branches of psychoanalysis in the 1950s, called the "counter-transference revolution" by Samuels (1993), largely has not yet filtered through into the field of Body Psychotherapy, leaving the supervisory exploration of counter-transference limited and one-dimensional. This is all the more regrettable and ironic, because the Body Psychotherapeutic tradition has developed tools of perceptive embodied sensitivity that are useful and necessary to bring awareness to otherwise-subliminal processes such as projective identification, vicarious traumatization, and "dreaming up" (Mindell, 1982). This will be, therefore, one of the productive growing edges of the field in the coming years: to bring embodied and energetic perception to everything that psychoanalysis subsumes under the label of "unconscious processes," both in therapy and in supervision (where the widely established notion of "parallel process" relies largely on the supervisor's embodied perception of subtle and unconscious processes to become useful and impactful).

The "counter-transference revolution" gave psychoanalysis a more complex and differentiated view of the therapist's internal process. Rather than attributing every disturbance in the client-therapist relationship to the therapist's own pathology entering the room as counter-transference ("What is it about the therapist's own wounding that is interfering with them doing their job properly?"), which was Freud's original position, during the 1950s there was an increasing acceptance that some of the body-mind responses evoked in the therapist contained useful information about the client's inner world (Heimann, 1950; Racker, 1957, 1982). This inevitably lends the supervisory exploration of counter-transference increased complexity—there are a myriad of things going on in the therapist: the relationship between two ordinary humans, the transference, responses evoked by the transference (Racker called them concordant and complementary counter-transferences), the therapist's own wounding and transference to the client, the therapist's reactions both as a person and in the therapeutic role—multiple projections and identifications going back and forth.

A simple key insight of this perspective, however, is that transference and counter-transference *interlock,* in

Racker's terms: the fact that the therapist feels disturbed, a loss of composure or equilibrium, or in danger of losing the therapeutic position is not necessarily indicative of mistakes or incompetence on the part of the therapist. In fact, these feelings can be a sign that the therapist is deeply engaged and affected. Reich understood the first half of that interlocking: that the client cannot help but construct the therapy *via* their character and that the constellation of the negative transference will *need* to lead to disturbances and ruptures in the working alliance. He just did not go as far—and neither has the Body Psychotherapeutic tradition since Reich—as investigating in detail the inner experience of the counter-transference process; it is the object-relations tradition that made a special area of inquiry and expertise out of the precise interlocking of transferential and counter-transferential objects: which aspects of the child's reality and which parental aspects are being projected, evaluated, projectively identified—passed back and forth between client and therapist, and how can precision in this area of therapeutic perception deepen the therapist's understanding of the client's inner world and internal object-relations? So far, Body Psychotherapy has largely not been interested in this exploration.

The recognition that some of the therapist's counter-transference is evoked by being engaged with the client's character conflict does not obviate the need for monitoring the therapist's own contribution to the dynamic, along the lines of Freud's understanding of the counter-transference; it just means that the situation is more complex.

I find it useful to theoretically distinguish between the habitual counter-transference (the therapist's habitual construction of their therapeutic position [Soth, 2007a], irrespective of the particularities of the client in front of them but rooted in their own character) and what I call "situational counter-transference" (everything that is evoked between client and therapist in their particular intersubjective field and thus "grist to the mill"), although in the nitty-gritty of practice these two aspects intermingle and become indistinguishable.

In the history of Body Psychotherapy, the exploration of counter-transference has largely remained tethered to Freud's original conception of it as the therapist's pathology. Any interference in the therapist's smooth capacity to resonate with the client tends to be understood as the therapist's own character resistance becoming activated. In common parlance, supervision then boils down to the question of what is the client's "stuff" and what is the therapist's.

This position is probably the most widespread among Body Psychotherapists, summarized in David Boadella's famous paper (1982) on "Transference, Resonance and Interference," where he explicitly equates resonance with healthy contact, and both transference and counter-transference as interferences to that healthy ideal.

With the benefit of today's hindsight, we might say that such an idealization of harmonious, always-resonant contact (reminiscent of Balint's 1968 notion of the "harmoniously interpenetrating mix") can be understood to be a reaction against what Body Psychotherapists perceived as the disembodied, non-resonant paradigms of psychoanalysis and the behavioral schools that we passionately wanted to counteract. These are some of the—historically situated—reactive, idealizing biases, wounds, and shadow aspects of the Body Psychotherapeutic tradition (Soth, 2005a and 2005b) that directly limit our response to the transference as well as how we address it in supervision.

Today, developmental neuropsychologists studying the early infant-caregiver bond understand rupture and repair as essential to development, both in the child-parent as well as in the client-therapist relationship. So, far from non-resonant ruptures of the bond being in and of themselves traumatic and deleterious interferences, they can be seen as developmental crises that are precisely necessary for growth to occur, and where shifts from interactive regulation toward auto-regulation take place, thus building resilience. This obviously does not deny the crucial recognition that systematic emotional injury and environmental failure in attunement constitute "transmarginal stress" (Boadella) and lead to defensive and self-protective character formation.

The main question then becomes: What will facilitate the transformative repair of ruptures? Typically, the idealization of good therapy as harmonious, resonant contact, attunement, and conflict-free togetherness then becomes an obstacle rather than an aid. This is another area where Body Psychotherapy potentially might have a lot to contribute, as the only way to judge the depth of a transformative experience is through comprehensive perception of the client's multidimensional body-mind. This becomes especially relevant when many of the talking therapies—having taken on board the need for the therapeutic repair of relational ruptures—are rather inclined to take mental shortcuts toward supposedly co-created "meaning-making" out of the "intersubjective mess" that skim the surface of the experience and usually backfire.

In summary, we can therefore say that the field of Body Psychotherapy has its center of gravity somewhere between one-person psychology and one-and-a-half-person psychology. However, there are plenty of exceptions, implicit contradictions, and anomalies, and the picture is confused because—in picking up on recent fashions and developments in the field in general—many Body Psychotherapists are grafting dialogic (authentic, "I-Thou") relating or intersubjective, relational perspectives on top of a largely unchanged foundation of their traditional one-and-a-half-person stance. Put positively, this can be ascribed to the field's openness and willingness to learn and develop further, toward the capacity to inhabit *all* of the relational stances with awareness and fluidity, in a relationally integrative fashion. However, before we can integrate, we need to get clear about the diversity and plurality that we are now landed with—this would require a more differentiated discourse regarding the tensions and contradictions between different relational modalities, especially concerning the tension between intersubjective and objectifying stances (in simple terms: "I-Thou" versus "I-it" relating). Since the humanistic revolution, the field of psychotherapy has been split and polarized between traditional "medical-model" conceptions of "therapy as treatment" versus the historically later humanistic-existential insistence on "therapy as human encounter." Although the humanistic reaction against the "medical model"—its obeisance to a dualistic conception of the patient-doctor relationship, to traditional notions of power-over, and to objectifying assumptions (which reduce the person to a "case"—an object in a supposedly quasi-scientific procedure)—is precious and valid, it has frequently become absolutized as a dogmatic "anti-medical-model" position, which is just as unhelpful as what it protests against. Strongly opposing ideas regarding the handling of the transference arise from these polarized positions.

The phenomenological reality of much of the psychotherapeutic field is that each client-therapist relationship lives in a constant tension between these opposing paradigms of I-Thou and I-it ways of relating—a tension that cannot—and should not—be reduced or short-circuited by ideological positions, one way or the other. As long as the client pays for therapy, they can legitimately expect the therapist to monitor the process, maintain something resembling an "objective" view of it, and take an asymmetrical degree of responsibility for it—thus nudging the therapeutic position closer to that of a doctor. On the other hand, we understand that holding the therapeutic frame and overview is only as useful as the human engagement that actually happens within it (which precisely does not follow scientific or "medical-model" principles). In summary, we can say that psychotherapy cannot afford to jettison the "medical model" altogether, but neither must it subscribe to it as an exclusive paradigm.

Holding the therapeutic space as essentially conflicted between these relational paradigms becomes even more important when we include the body in psychotherapy, as the culturally predominant attitude toward the body is one of objectification. The body as a source of emergent subjectivity is an unknown idea and an alien category of experience; many clients only know attention to their body via an objectifying attitude. Thus, in attending to and championing the client's body, Body Psychotherapy is liable to fall into and exacerbate the client's self-objectification and the therapist's "treatment" of the client's body as an object. According to Winnicott (1949), it is the mother's physical-emotional "handling" of the baby and her capacity for intersubjective "play" at the emergent self-other boundary that help her child toward an embodied existence—an underlying sense of "psyche indwelling in the soma." This requires a relational fluidity in the mother—between sufficiently identifying with her baby one moment in order to accurately attune, and sufficiently disidentifying the next in order to provide solid holding—which ideally is matched by our relational flexibility as therapists between I-Thou and I-it modes of "subjectification" and—when needed—"objectification."

An honest self-evaluation would have to admit that within the Body Psychotherapeutic tradition as a whole, these relational vicissitudes of the therapeutic endeavor are still undertheorized (Soth, 2006a and 2006b). Thus, a holistic and phenomenological two-person psychology as a body-mind process[48] still awaits formulation (Stark, 1999). But I have attempted to provide a starting point elsewhere (Soth, 2007b) by extending the concept of parallel process to include body-mind, intrapsychic, as well as intersubjective dynamics (including, of course, unconscious processes) and generating the integral-relational notion of the "Fractal Self" (Ibid.).

Such a relationally integrative perspective would, of course, assume—as both Stark and Clarkson explicitly do—that rather than presenting a historically linear evolution from an earlier "worse" paradigm toward a later "more enlightened" paradigm, *all* relational modalities have their validity and therapeutic uses in particular contexts. "Later" is only insofar "better" as it *transcends and includes*—in Wilber's terms—*all* stages of development.

For the present moment, this leaves us not only with widely diverging opinions regarding the significance of the transference, but with controversy about what it actually is and how to work with it; with Body Psychotherapy having its roots in both humanistic and psychoanalytic traditions, this controversy is particularly pronounced because the inclusion of the body is commonly acknowledged as having an intensifying effect on the transference.

---

[48] This would extend Reich's functionalism beyond its original one-person psychology frame into dyadic, intersubjective systems, and then beyond that into groups and many-persons psychology.

## Supervision Example 1 (One-and-a-Half-Person Mode)

I will not include here an example illustrating the traditional one-person psychology stance in working with the transference, as any of Reich's brilliant case studies (Reich, 1933) serve to demonstrate just how far such a psychoanalytic approach (which is how he thought about it at the time) can go, when the therapist is rooted in an embodied stance, and proceeds, as Reich advocated, in systematic fashion, always working closest to the ego, layer by layer reversing the original layerings of character formation as they arise in the unfolding process. The following example was chosen because it illustrates a typical one-and-a-half-person mode, by both the therapist and the supervisor, demonstrating the potential as well as the limitations when this is the dominant or exclusive relational mode.

Jenny, a twenty-six-year-old woman struggling to complete a PhD in feminist studies, has been engaged in therapy with Tom, a Body Psychotherapist in his forties, for about eight months. She initially came to seek help in her struggle with and against her tutor for her PhD with whom she was locked in an unhelpful and, at times, destructive relationship, and thus unable to complete her PhD.

Therapy had been going well, with Jenny and Tom establishing a trusting and open relationship. But things had gotten more sticky in later weeks, which is why Tom started bringing his work with Jenny to his weekly supervision sessions with Susie. Tom was well aware that he and Jenny were beginning to replicate—in therapy—her difficult relationship with her tutor: "Although her tutor is a woman, it seems she is transferring her onto me, and that transference is intensifying. Most sessions now, she will end up with this very quiet, mousy voice, almost inaudible, exactly the same way that she describes being with her tutor, becoming invisible, disappearing into the armchair. That means I will have to lean forward to hear what she is saying. So I end up on the edge of my seat, as if I am pursuing her."

Susie suggested that Tom demonstrate Jenny's body posture and her energetic presence in those moments.

Tom found it easy to get himself into Jenny's position: *"She becomes like this,"* he said, slinking down in his chair, *"almost whispering."* He imitated her: *"All my previous tutors have always been supportive and encouraging. For her, I can't get anything right!"*

As Tom spoke these words, Susie saw him swallowing and detected a wave of sadness, his voice almost breaking. *"Is this kind of position familiar to you?"* she asked. *"Whom would you be directing these words to?"*

*"This is rather obvious,"* Tom replied. *"It's my father. He was very ambitious for me, and I could never satisfy his standards."*

*"So it seems you are rather over-identified with Jenny's regressed position and unable to support her in empowering herself?"* Susie suggested.

*"Yes, I guess that's true,"* Tom admitted in a rather defeated fashion.

Susie's intervention, based initially on a physical sense of identification, but then extending into an emotional one, helped to bring to Tom's awareness, without any need for interpretation or criticism, a crucial dynamic in organizing the relational space between Tom and Jenny. We can have no doubt that Tom's own 'stuff' would affect his perception and thus his room for maneuvering as a therapist. Feeling rather defeated at the end of this vignette, Tom is likely to redouble his efforts, in the next session, to lead Jenny toward a more empowering outcome. Although this makes some sense, we will see later that this can also backfire. Susie would have internally been checking resonances with her own life and the therapeutic work that she had done on those, which then enabled her to be decisive and directive in her intervention, as well as informing her conclusion.

This would be a typical example of a one-and-a-half-person intervention in supervision, using very effectively an embodied, experiential mode of working. Susie's task was made considerably easier by the fact that Tom already had a clear and succinct understanding of Jenny's transference—as we will see in other examples, the transference can be a more confusing and multi-headed phenomenon. However, a deeper exploration of layers of transference was foreclosed, as Susie focused only on how Tom's own stuff—in Boadella's words—*interfered* with his capacity to handle the rather simple transference of Jenny's tutor onto him.

But this example also highlights the possible confusions around the term 'resonance,' as, arguably, there is *too much* resonance between Tom and Jenny, not too little. This indicates that, the more we investigate it, resonance turns out to be a much more complex phenomenon, especially when we take into account that there may be different parts—or conflicting internal objects—operating within the client's body-mind, all of which the therapist is liable to resonate with.

A simple formulation of this key insight—arising from thinking through the "counter-transference revolution" in body-mind terms—is that inevitably *the client's conflict becomes the therapist's conflict:* by empathically resonating with *both* sides of the client's internal, characterologically structured conflict, the therapist quite validly and necessarily will have to experience conflict in the counter-transference, ending up feeling torn between both (Soth, 2005b).

Without expanding on it here, a good contrasting example of a psychoanalytic version of a one-and-a-half-person stance, in many ways quite similar as it also builds on character theory, is Kernberg's object-relations version of working with the transference. Because he always already assumes that transference will be arising as a configuration of "relational units" (Kernberg, 1995), replicating the originally wounding relationships, he expects his counter-transference to resonate with the objects in the "primary scenario."

This perspective of "relational units" could usefully and instructively be integrated by Body Psychotherapists, with very little adjustment: by integrating more comprehensively the assumption—foundational across the object-relations tradition—that the wounding objects do indeed become internalized, Body Psychotherapy can then bring a wealth of body-mind perception to "internal objects," explicating in a holistic, embodied way what Object Relations still mainly thinks of as "mental representations" rather than flesh-and-blood realities. Once Body Psychotherapy takes more widely on board the counter-transference revolution, Object Relations, and intersubjectivity, it will have the potential to revolutionize how psychotherapy in general approaches the totality of unconscious processes by attending to them as body-mind processes, both in therapy and in supervision.

## The Conception of Unconscious Processes in Body Psychotherapy and Psychoanalysis

From a Body Psychotherapeutic perspective, we recognize transference as a function of embodied developmental wounding, via character formation (Reich, 1933; Johnson, 1994; and others). Reich's view of character—as the frozen landscape of early experience with its concomitant internal splits, repressions, and dissociations—implies a chronic and systematic distortion of present perception through the (embodied) lens of past painful experiences and their denial.

The purpose of such defense mechanisms is to minimize our awareness of pain and to encapsulate the trauma by dissociating it from consciousness, shielding the ego's functioning against internal disturbances. Reich's notion of character always implied some lack of awareness in the client and—whatever beliefs or definitions we subscribe to regarding unconscious processes—by extending these beyond merely mental representations, the 'unconscious' becomes an embodied concept that can be tangibly perceived and apprehended, thus becoming clinically specific and useful.

Depending in its particular manifestations on the developmental phase, the available resources, both before and after the event, and the intensity of the character-forming wounding or trauma (Johnson, 1994), character theory assumes that some form of projection of the "wounding relationship" into the therapeutic relationship is likely (or almost inevitably) going to occur during therapy, and that, at least, some aspects of that process of projection are unconscious.[49]

This assumption puts the tradition of Body Psychotherapy squarely into the "depth-therapeutic" camp, alongside psychoanalysis, with its emphasis on transference as a crucial factor in any form of psychological process or helping relationship. If we hold out for the possibility of characterological transformation in body-mind depth, an equivalent personal and professional engagement on the therapist's part with unconscious processes, both intrapsychic and interpersonal, is required. It could be argued that—beyond all the profound therapeutic models, techniques, and strategies that we employ as Body Psychotherapists—*how* we actually employ them is structured by the transference—counter-transference dynamic, which is, therefore, at the heart of what makes therapy work—or not.

Beyond Body Psychotherapy's origins in Reich's work as a psychoanalyst—and in spite of their development as separate traditions over the period since Reich's expulsion in 1934 from the International Psychoanalytical Association—we share with psychoanalysis an understanding regarding the etiology of psychological difficulty through developmental theory and the recognition that—inevitably—we will, at some point in the therapeutic process, be confronted with the body-mind reality of the original wounding in the "here and now" of the therapeutic encounter.[50]

As we will see, there is quite a divergence of opinions as to how far-reaching that confrontation is, or needs to be, and how to handle its various vicissitudes and complexities; in simple terms: just how unconscious is unconscious, especially when it comes to the therapist's contribution? That divergence of different approaches (e.g., Transactional Analysis; see Little, 2013; Soth, 2013), even within the Body Psychotherapeutic tradition, is reflected in a wide range of opinions regarding the meaning, significance, and ways of dealing with the transference-counter-transference process between client and therapist. This, in turn, affects our assumptions and priorities regarding the supervisory process, and our actual practice of supervision.

## The Wound Enters . . .

I have elsewhere proposed a simple formulation as to the extent to which psychotherapy has increasingly recognized

---

[49] Reich's "The Development of the Character-Analytic Technique," written with hindsight in the early 1940s, is very clear on this and other similar points.

[50] For a summary of possible steps toward a reintegration of the two traditions, see Soth, 2000.

over the last century that "the wound enters . . ." (Soth, 2006a and 2006b) into the consulting room, the therapy, and the therapist, and then into supervision. This deconstructs the dualistic "medical-model" conception, prevalent in the *zeitgeist* of Freud's late nineteenth century, that the therapist needs to maintain a quasi-scientific "distance" in order to remain objective and uncontaminated by the patient's pathology and irrationality. The history of psychotherapy could be written in terms of the increasing recognition that the patient's "wound" cannot be neatly segregated into the past, the outer life, or the inner experience of the patient, but actually enters into the therapeutic relationship and affects the therapist's being, both as a *practitioner* and as a person, touching the therapist's own character, wounds, and existential issues, as well as his or her various gifts, resources, and talents. The wound even gets replicated, via a parallel process, in supervision.

In Freud's time, we might initially have said, "I can operate on the wound *only* if I can stay separate from it and remain unaffected, uncontaminated, and objective (because otherwise I will get so emotionally entangled that I will become unhelpful)." Today, we might say, from a perspective grounded in the notion of the "wounded healer" and a relational, postmodern, participative universe: "I can work with the wound *only because* I am affected by it and because my own subjectivity is inextricably involved (which helps me to understand the wound from within), therefore entanglements come with the territory."

Via the client's character, aspects, and fragments of the original wounding relationship—because Reich understood it as a process involving *all* levels of the body-mind, rather than merely the conscious mind and the unconscious mind—enter the "here-and-now" experience of the therapeutic relationship *all the time.*

Here is a simple and practical categorization of the ways in which the "wound" can be recognized as manifesting on all levels of the therapeutic relationship, when we conceive of it, through and through, as a relational body-mind system:[51]

---

51 See Nick Totton's recent challenge for body psychotherapy to stop borrowing its conceptual framework from psychoanalysis, and to solidly establish therapy as embodied relational process from the ground up. (Totton, 2015)

The client's "wound" comes into the room and enters into the following dynamics:

1. . . . the client's "here-and-now" experience as a nonverbal process
2. . . . the client's *perception* of the therapist as transference
3a. . . . the client's unconscious *construction* of the therapeutic space as transference not in relation to the person of the therapist, but towards therapy as a relational space and procedure
3b. . . . the client's *experience* of the therapist as embodied transference
4. . . . the therapist's awareness as countertransference
5. . . . the therapist's experience as embodied countertransference
6. . . . the whole client-therapist system as reenactment
7. . . . the supervisor's experience as a "parallel process"

The tradition of Body Psychotherapy is one of the few psychological approaches that benefits from a holistic meta-psychology. Based on Reich's functionalism, we understand that all emotional and psychological dynamics between client and therapist are not just reflected in, but are identical with, a myriad of body-mind processes, reaching all the way from the vegetative, via the emotional, to the mental.

As a tradition, Body Psychotherapy has made enormous contributions to our understanding of points 1, 2, 3a, and 3b (above), and—through developing points 4, 5, 6, and 7 (Soth, 2005a and 2005b)—has the potential to transform psychotherapy into an integral-relational discipline for the twenty-first century (Soth, 2008a and 2008b). This potential depends partly on us, as Body Psychotherapists, and our ability to integrate the sensibilities of other therapeutic approaches into our framework.

## Support for Body Psychotherapy's Holistic Conception of Transference

Many assumptions inherent in Body Psychotherapy's holistic perspective have been comprehensively confirmed by modern neuroscience (Schore, 1994; Damasio, 1994), but have not yet been translated into the psychotherapeutic mainstream. These are discussed throughout this handbook and do not need repeating here, but there are three points that have a specific bearing on the transference.

Statements like "the equal footing of mind and body, as far as they are manifest to the percipient" (Damasio, 2004, p. 217[52]) support the interdependence and mutuality of mind and body, implicit in Reich's functionalism. This essentially puts an end to mind-over-body dualism and might be extended (as a final nail in the coffin) to challenge the widespread notion that the transference is to be "worked through" via insight, interpretation, and mental understanding. Body Psychotherapy's long-held intuitions in this regard are supported by the influential Boston Change Study Group (Lyons-Ruth, K. 1998), which places great significance on "implicit relational knowing" (without, however, spelling out how that might be translated into practice).

The concept of mirror neurons has been used to "explain" subtle processes like "compassion fatigue" (Rothschild, 2006) and the concept of "projective identification." In these endeavors to find the neurological substrate for subtle, subliminal, and pre-reflexive communication, neuroscientists like Schore (1994) are inclined to overemphasize the significance of the brain in organizing the myriad of internal and external body-mind messages that constitute the transference and counter-transference dynamic, and do not sufficiently take into account self-organizing vegetative processes (which are considered to be devoid of consciousness).[53]

The realm of right-brain to right-brain communication, postulated by Schore (1994) as the essential core of the therapeutic relationship, is usually considered subliminal and therefore prior to, and inaccessible to, reflective consciousness. However, from a Body Psychotherapeutic perspective (and substantiated by Neuro-Linguistic Programming's deliberate training of sensory acuity—for example, of eye movements, pupil dilation, and lower lip expansion [Bandler and Grinder, 1979]), the dividing line between what is subliminal and what is accessible to awareness is not a fixed given; rather, it is a function of the therapist's own sense of embodiment, and therefore the degree to which they can use their own body as an instrument of subtle and differentiated perception, thus noticing minimal non-verbal cues, subtly charged body-mind interactions, and Downing's micro-practice. One does not need to be capable of reflectively tracking each and every one of this multitude of pre-reflexive processes in order to get a sense of, and an emotional feel for, the overall relational dynamics established by these processes.

Since the 1930s, Body Psychotherapy has accumulated a wealth of both theoretical and practical expertise in developing practitioners who are both embodied and embedded in—and therefore sensitively attuned to—the subtleties of intersubjective body-mind communications. It is this field of embodied skills, qualities, capacities, and practices that can provide the badly needed ground for the otherwise-disembodied concepts of psychoanalysis. The practice of "body reading" and "body diagnosis" (Berliner, 1994; Geissler, 1994; Kirsch, 1994), well established, for example, in Bioenergetic Analysis, as demonstrated by Alexander Lowen, is only one—in my view, somewhat questionable—formalized expression of a finely honed intuitive capacity taken for granted throughout Body Psychotherapy.

The point in the therapeutic process at which a practitioner perceives the client's wound as entering into the therapeutic space between them is crucially dependent on these subtle, perceptive body-mind skills, as the following example demonstrates.

---

52  "What is Spinoza's insight then? That mind and body are parallel and mutually correlated processes, mimicking each other at every crossroad, as two faces of the same thing."

53  However, this is increasingly being challenged through interdisciplinary efforts in the fields of interpersonal neurobiology (Dan Siegel) and embodied intersubjectivity or enactive intersubjectivity (Fuchs and De Jaegher, 2009).

## Example 2: "Breakthrough" Therapy

A client, whom I shall call "Mona," thirty-four years old, had led a self-sufficient life, and was highly functional and respected in her specialized profession, but was socially isolated, her life being devoid of intimacy. She made many friends and acquaintances, but had no relationships—intimate or otherwise—lasting longer than a few months. In therapy, she presented her life as a failure, dominated by feelings of inadequacy and dejection.

Her therapist, "Clare," found her engaging, intelligent, and self-reflective, keenly taking in the affirmations, reflections, and interpretations that Clare had offered her. This continued for the first few months of therapy, with Clare feeling quite satisfied with the work and good about herself as a therapist.

Toward the end of this period, she began to notice that Mona was coming to sessions looking less presentable than her usual social persona, occasionally disheveled and smelling of drink. Clare concluded that Mona's underlying feelings of loneliness were breaking through, and felt moved by Mona's apparent incapacity to own up to this, let alone share these feelings with her, the therapist. Clare's attention was drawn to Mona's chest area, and especially to the area beneath her collarbones. This is where a hidden and unexpressed regressive wave of emotion seemed to be located. So Clare suggested, *"You look exhausted and drained—why don't you lie down?"*

Mona hesitated and then distracted from the question by talking about her work. Clare insisted, *"You know how we have been talking for months about how you avoid your pain. Well, isn't that what you are doing right now?"* Mona admitted, *"I know. I am no good at anything! I can't bear how useless I am, but it's no use trying to get away from it: even you, my therapist, thinks so!"*

Saying this, Mona looked Clare straight in the eyes, with an atmosphere of challenge. This took Clare momentarily by surprise and made her feel insecure. This was an unusual and crucial moment of directness and immediacy. Clare defaulted to what—in supervision later—would turn out to be her own "credo," or bottom line, for therapy: *"Well, there is an isolated, neglected child in you that is crying out for nurturing and acceptance. Can you feel that?"*

*"Not really. Somebody as useless as me does not deserve any nurturing, anyway. My pain drives everybody away—that's why I always end up alone!"* Clare continued to be surprised by Mona's unusually argumentative and resistant reaction. But she then remembered her perception of Mona's collapsed chest, and said to herself, *"I'm sure that is what she is defending against."*

So Clare gathered up her courage, stood up, and walked behind Mona's chair. Holding her hands gently over Mona's shoulders and collarbones, she said, *"Close your eyes and feel my hands."* For a minute, Mona appeared quite still while Clare intensified and eased the pressure of her hands on Mona's upper chest in the rhythm of Mona's minimal breathing.

Suddenly, without warning and quite shockingly for Clare, Mona erupted into uncontrollable sobbing. But, as this was precisely the feeling that Clare had interpreted as fundamental, she quickly adjusted and encouraged Mona to let it all out, to not hold back, to not go back into her usual defended persona. This cathartic expression continued for about ten minutes, after which the sobbing subsided.

Mona seemed to experience considerable relief, and admitted to being astonished: *"Gosh, I have never experienced anything like it. I feel so light."* However, when she got up to leave, Mona said she felt dizzy and confused, and she nearly forgot her purse.

Clare saw her off and closed the front door behind Mona, and then moments later was shocked to hear a loud crash. On her way out, Mona had reversed her car into the garden wall, with a whole section of bricks tumbling down and leaving a gaping hole in the wall.

### Every Body-Mind Fragment Contains a Whole Story

There are many lessons we can draw from this example. Whatever the subsequent complications, there can be no doubt that Clare's intervention was based on a highly attuned body-mind awareness, not just of the client's somatic experience per se, but also its emotional and regressive—i.e., life-historical—correlates. This is a specific instance of Reich's characterological understanding of how developmental injury is frozen into habitual body-mind patterning: Clare intuitively "read" Mona's child feelings within a holding pattern that Mona herself was entirely unconscious of.

One aspect (which—as mentioned above—is rarely spelled out in the Body Psychotherapeutic tradition) is the recognition that the child's body-mind experience always implies a relational "other" that—according to object-relations theory—has become internalized. We can therefore say that the whole complex, the conscious and unconscious relational configuration between child and adult, is condensed into an apparently innocuous body-mind fragment, such as a "held" upper chest. Like a hologram, which contains the whole image in each part, the whole story of a particular phase in the original parent-child interaction is contained in every charged fragment of the client's body-mind phenomenology. Inevitably, the vulnerability contained in Mona's chest was surrounded by layers of unawareness and numbness, and—when confronted with closer therapeutic attention—included distractions and denials. Clare had to deliberately and determinedly override these "protection mechanisms" in order to get through the guarded perimeter and touch the pain hidden inside the somatic manifestations of Mona's characterological holding patterns.

## The Body Psychotherapist as Enemy of the Client's Ego

What this example also demonstrates is a particular habitual position which the therapist takes, very common throughout the tradition of Body Psychotherapy, in relation to the transference. The validity and uncanny acuteness of the therapist's embodied perception can distract from, override, and occlude the fundamental problems which this therapeutic position tends to create.

Clare had accurately perceived several long-standing manifestations of Mona's character formation: a self-sufficient holding pattern that constantly denies basic needs while also feeding a pervasive internal shaming.

There are two main maneuvers that Body Psychotherapists use to counteract the client's disembodiment: first, there is the "hard," masculine way of cracking the client's character armor by confronting patterns of denial and challenging the client's defenses, provoking catharsis at a primal level by breaking through resistances; and second, there is the "soft," mothering way of melting the client's armor by undercutting the pseudo-autonomy of the social facade by nurturing the neglected (sometimes pre-verbal) self.

As a therapist, Clare had both a well-practiced facility for, as well as a bias toward, reaching out to the regressed, vulnerable child. Her perceptions of that child—in Mona—were well attuned, accurate, and valid. However, she found it difficult to be aware of, and to question, the fairly automatic therapeutic conclusions that she was accustomed to drawing on the basis of these accurate perceptions. It made sense that the tendency toward these habitual conclusions was part and parcel of her own characterological wounding, and a reaction against her own pain. When under pressure, the therapist's habitual relational position and construction of her own role inclined her toward a "default" intervention (from a "reparative" modality, to proactively attend to the "child"). That meant that Clare's therapeutic reactions, at this charged moment, were as automatic as the client's. And, strictly speaking, it was a defensive reaction, which nevertheless seemed to have the desired cathartic outcome—in that particular moment.

However, when—in supervision—Clare reflected on her internal process as a therapist, she became aware of her therapeutic hypotheses regarding Mona's "wound": Mona had a perennial pattern of avoiding her pain, reaching all the way back to her childhood, and the history of that pattern was an established narrative that both client and therapist took for granted. Clare "assumed" that Mona's parents were unresponsive and humiliating whenever Mona was vulnerable and needy, and that—at some point—Mona had learned to turn against herself and her own needs, and acquired a habit of appearing self-sufficient. In reaching out toward the neglected child, Clare was therefore positioning herself as the "opposite" of the real parents, and was—more or less explicitly—encouraging an "anti-parental" philosophy: whereas Mona's basic needs had been originally—and were still to this day being—dismissed and rejected, now, in therapy, it was supposedly safe and "healthy" to feel and express these needs.

This echoes a general bias within the tradition of Body Psychotherapy that could be phrased as *"where inhibition was, there expression shall be."* However, as the example shows, this precious principle—formulated out of Reich's recognition and championing of the life force as an essential aspect of Body-Oriented Psychotherapy—can nevertheless have counter-therapeutic functions and effects within the reality of a particular therapeutic relationship.

In Mona's example, a real cathartic release occurred. However, that release was precipitated by Clare overriding Mona's defenses—prematurely, it could be argued. As Body Psychotherapists perceive the "ego" as the "enemy" and inhibitor of the life force, the therapist tends to position themselves, as in Clare's case, on the side of the spontaneously expressive body, the hurt child, the deep feelings, and so forth—and thus attempts to "champion" the "repressed." This is a "trap" that Body Psychotherapists—urged by the very real "heat" of the transference and its attendant pain and desperate longing for "healing"—are inclined to resort and default to.

As I have suggested elsewhere (Soth, 2006b), for Body Psychotherapists to construct their role as an "enemy" of the client's "ego" typically leads to a series of complications in the therapeutic alliance, and in the counter-transference, that tend to remain under-theorized in traditional Body Psychotherapy.

The symbolic significance of the "breakthrough" and the corresponding "hole in the wall" was not lost on Clare, who was capable of recognizing and owning the defensive nature of her habitual therapeutic position. As can easily be imagined, Mona came back in the next session implicitly blaming her therapist for the confused state that she had been "jumped into" by Clare's intervention, even though it had temporarily transported her into a less contracted and more pleasurable body-mind reality.

This event constituted a major rupture in the therapeutic alliance, which—in time—became a pivotal phase in the therapy. It involved delicate negotiation of the practical level of payment for the damage, but, more importantly, an equally delicate working through of Clare's perceived "takeover" in the session. In time, Clare realized that Mona's mother had not actually responded to Mona's pain by neglect (as she had assumed), but by a kind of frantic activity designed to "make her feel better."

The very real pattern of avoidance of pain was not rooted in Mona's mother shrinking and withdrawing from her, but launching into a display of supposedly caring actions that Mona felt obliged to submit to. Much later, it emerged that Mona's mother was so identified with a persecutory image of having to be a "perfect" mother that she immediately felt guilty about any sign of pain in Mona. For her own reasons, Mona's mother took any manifestation of pain as evidence that she was a "bad mother," and then had to act impulsively to try to get rid of the pain—in Mona.

Clare was eventually able to see, with hindsight, that this was the established pattern through which Mona unconsciously interpreted Clare's intervention and why Clare ultimately submitted, as she had to her mother's form of "care." Far from Clare's therapeutic intentions, her "encouragements" for Mona to feel the pain, and to express and discharge it, resembled the messages from Mona's mother, who could not bear Mona's pain, but had to "do something about it." The therapist's intention was transferentially being misperceived through the lens of Mona's wounding, and actually turned into its opposite.

## Transference: Therapy via Character rather than Operating on It

We can categorize such experiences between client and therapist as aspects of the transference in the widest sense. But here the client's "wound" entered into the therapeutic relationship to a much larger extent than is usually implied by the notion of countertransference, let alone transference.

It makes sense to speak of the "whole dynamic of the wounding relationship" entering—and even taking over—the therapeutic relationship, as implied by the notion of "enactment" (Soth, 2005b, 2006b). The wound does not just enter the counter-transference as a feeling or thought (as some have traditionally presumed), but compels the therapist's whole experience—as a person and as a professional, including their supposedly therapeutic interventions—and manifests as an uncanny and accurate replication of the client's originally wounding relationship.

The recognition of the central and paradoxical nature of enactment at the heart of the therapy—as the very mode of therapeutic action by which therapy does its work in transforming character—has been described elsewhere as the "relational turn" in Body Psychotherapy: "It is impossible to pursue a 'therapeutic' agenda of breaking through the armor or undercutting the ego's resistance *without* enacting in the transference the person whom the armor/resistance first developed against" (Soth, 2006b).

This recognition constitutes a watershed in our appreciation of the transference and counter-transference matrix—as it did for Clare in her process with Mona. Whereas Freud would have located the origins of enactment entirely in the client and their "repetition compulsion," the "counter-transference revolution" begins to formulate a more mutually entangled one-and-a-half-person conception in which the therapist's counter-transference is "role-responsive" to the transference (Sandler, 1973), and thus implicated in the client's "actualization" (Sandler's word for "enactment") of the wounding relationship. Racker's ideas go further than that in terms of the therapist's implication in the enactment, preparing the way for how modern Object Relations (Casement, 1985) views the dangers and potentials of counter-transference enactment, and the therapist's responsibilities in averting and managing its destructive implications.

But, beyond an embracing of the counter-therapeutic effects of the counter-transference, we may now be able to recognize that Clare's unwitting enactment of Mona's mother had an immense therapeutic potential. Initially, Clare was horrified to recognize that—far from encouraging Mona's surrender to her pain—she was being perceived, through the lens of Mona's regressive experience, as trying to get rid of it—*like* Mona's mother. Therefore, Clare could only perceive her intervention as one enormous mistake:

"How can I dare to charge money for this? There I am, trying to help her out of her lifelong prison, based on avoiding pain, and all I do is exacerbate the urge to get rid of it. I'm trying to help her get out from underneath her mother, and all I do is replicate the mother!"

Fortunately, Clare's supervisor was a whole lot more accepting of this apparent disaster than Clare was herself. In the first instance, Clare needed help to not go back the following week and prostrate herself in abject guilt and shame, apologizing—as was her initial impulse—for her miserable and counterproductive professional services (which was how she thought of it). This might have turned into the opposite enactment, replicating the guilt that Mona's mother felt for any hint of being anything less than the "perfect" mother that she felt she had to be. With the help of her supervisor, Clare steered an even course between these extremes and eventually learned to see for herself that the laborious and painful "repair process" that she and Mona had to go through bore unexpected fruit in Mona's life.

The whole issue around the avoidance of pain—which up to this point Mona had simply felt therapeutically criticized for by Clare—acquired a different, more sympathetic complexion between them. At times, Clare even learned to proactively use body-oriented interventions to help Mona avoid emotional pain, occasionally helping her to temporarily dissociate which had a soothing effect, rather than Mona—when left to her own devices—continuously picking at it like a child with a scab. This deepened their alliance, and eventually their roles reversed, to the point that Mona started accusing Clare of being the one who was steering her away from her pain.

This eventually became an "all-out" challenge, not only to Claire but, more importantly, to Mona's mother, with profound consequences. As a result, Clare's notion of the transference deepened and broadened: far from conceiving of her task as merely reparative, in order to counteract a theoretically formulated but, in practice, neglected negative transference, Clare now speaks of different transferential configurations co-existing in the therapeutic space. More importantly, she now recognizes how the client's characterological conflict will inevitably draw the therapist into corresponding dilemmas that require intricate attention to the counter-transference in order for the implicit enactments to be survived and eventually contained.

The recognition of how the "wounding dynamic" not only enters into, but pervades, the whole client-therapist system opens out into a bio-neuro-psycho-social formulation of the therapeutic relationship, where the paradox of "enactment" becomes the hinge of transformation.

# References

Aron, L., & Harris, A. (2011). *Relational Psychoanalysis (Vol. 4)*. Hove: Routledge.

Balint, M. (1968). *The basic fault: Therapeutic aspects of regression*. London: Tavistock.

Bandler, R., & Grinder, J. (1979). *Frogs into princes: Neuro Linguistic Programming*. New York: Real People Press.

Berliner, J. (1994). Psychoanalyse, Bioenergetische Analyse, analytische körpervermittelte Psychotherapie [Psychoanalysis, Bioenergetic Analysis, Analytical Body-Oriented Psychotherapy]. In P. Geissler (Ed.), *Psychoanalyse und Bioenergetische Analyse: Im Spannungsfeld zwischen Abgrenzung und Integration [Psychoanalysis and Bioenergetic Analysis: The tension between separation and integration]*. Frankfurt: Peter Lang.

Boadella, D. (1982). Transference, resonance and interference. *Journal of Biodynamic Psychology, 3*, 73–93.

Buber, M. (1937/1970). *I and Thou*. New York: Touchstone.

Casement, P. (1985) *On learning from the patient*. Hove: Routledge.

Clarkson, P., & Wilson, S. (1994/2003). *The therapeutic relationship*. Oxford, UK: Wiley-Blackwell.

Damasio, A. (1994). *Descartes' error*. London: Putnam.

Damasio, A. (2004). *Looking for Spinoza*. London: Random House.

Fuchs, T., & De Jaegher, H. (2009). Enactive intersubjectivity: Participatory sense-making and mutual incorporation. *Phenomenological Cognitive Science, 8*, 465–486.

Geissler, P. (Ed.). (1994). *Psychoanalyse und Bioenergetische Analyse: Im Spannungsfeld zwischen Abgrenzung und Integration [Psychoanalysis and Bioenergetic Analysis: The tension between separation and integration]*. Frankfurt: Peter Lang.

Heimann, P. (1950). On countertransference. *International Journal of Psychoanalysis, 31*, 60–76.

Johnson, S. (1994). *Character styles*. New York: W. W. Norton.

Kernberg, O. (1995). *Object relations theory and clinical psychoanalysis*. New York: Jason Aronson.

Kirsch, S. (1994). Von der Bioenergtischen Analyse zur analytischen Körperpsychotherapie [From Bioenergetic Analysis to Analytical Body Psychotherapy]. In P. Geissler (Ed.), *Psychoanalyse und Bioenergetische Analyse: Im Spannungsfeld zwischen Abgrenzung und Integration [Psychoanalysis and Bioenergetic Analysis: The tension between separation and integration]*. Frankfurt: Peter Lang.

Little, R. (2013). The new emerges out of the old. *Transactional Analysis Journal, 43(2)*, 138–143.

Lyons-Ruth, K. (1998). Implicit relational knowing: Its role in development and psychoanalytic treatment. *Infant Mental Health Journal, 19(3)*, 282-289.

Marlock, G., & Weiss, H. (2006). *Handbuch der Körperpsychotherapie [Handbook of Body Psychotherapy]*. Stuttgart: Schattauer.

Mindell, A. (1982). *Dreambody: The body's role in revealing the self*. London: Arkana.

Racker, H. (1957). The meanings and uses of countertransference. *Psychoanalytic Quarterly, 26*, 303–357.

Racker, H. (1982). *Transference and countertransference*. London: Karnac.

Reich, W. (1933/1972) *Character Analysis*. New York: Touchstone.

Rothschild, B. (2006). *Help for the helper: The psychophysiology of compassion fatigue and vicarious trauma*. New York: W. W. Norton.

Samuels, A. (1993). *The political psyche*. Hove: Routledge.

Sandler, J. (1973). *The patient and the analyst*. New York: International Universities Press.

Schore, A. (1994). *Affect regulation and the origin of the self*. Hillsdale, NJ: Lawrence Erlbaum.

Sletvold, J. (2014). *The embodied analyst: From Freud and Reich to relationality*. Hove: Routledge.

Soth, M. (2000). The integrated bodymind's view on body/mind integration. *Chiron Centre for Body Psychotherapy Newsletter, No. 17*, 11–15, & *No. 19*, 6–12.

Soth, M. (2005a). Body Psychotherapy today: An integral-relational approach. *Therapy Today, 16*(9), 8–12.

Soth, M. (2005b). Embodied countertransference. In N. Totton (Ed.), *New dimensions in Body Psychotherapy*. Maidenhead, UK: Open University Press.

Soth, M. (2006a). How "the wound" enters the room and the relationship. *Therapy Today, 17*(10), 10–14.

Soth, M. (2006b). What therapeutic hope for a subjective mind in an objectified body? In J. Corrigall, H. Wilkinson, & H. Payne (2006). *About a body*. Hove: Routledge.

Soth, M. (2007a). The implicit relational stance and habitual positions. *CABP Journal, no. 35*, 36–40.

Soth, M. (2007b). *The relational paradigm shift—is it "complete"?* Presentation at CABP conference "The Body and I," Cambridge, UK.

Soth, M. (2008a). Embracing the paradigm clash between the "medical model" and counselling—A response to: "Should counselling be considered a healthcare profession?" by J. T. Hansen (2007), *Therapy Today, 18*(10), 4–6.

Soth, M. (2008b). From humanistic holism via the "integrative project" towards integral-relational Body Psychotherapy. In L. Hartley (Ed.), *Contemporary Body Psychotherapy: The Chiron Approach*. Hove: Routledge.

Soth, M. (2013). We are all relational, but are some more relational than others?—completing the paradigm shift towards relationality. *Transactional Analysis Journal, 43*(2), 122–137.

Stark, M. (1999). *Modes of therapeutic action*. New York: Jason Aronson.

Stolorow, R., & Atwood, G. (1992). *Contexts of being: The intersubjective foundations of psychological life*. Hillsdale, NJ: Analytic Press.

Strean, H. S. (1993). *Resolving counter-resistances in psychotherapy*. New York: Brunner Mazel.

Totton, N. (2005). *New Dimensions in Body Psychotherapy*. Maidenhead: Open University Press.

Winnicott, D. (1949). Mind and its relation to the psyche-soma. In D. W. Winnicott (Ed.), *Through paediatrics to psycho-analysis* (pp. 243–254) New York: Basic Books.

# 48

## Touch in Body Psychotherapy

**Gill Westland, United Kingdom**

**Gill Westland** is the director of Cambridge Body Psychotherapy Centre (CBPC), which is an organizational member of the United Kingdom Council for Psychotherapy and is recognized as an accrediting and training organization. CBPC offers a full training to registration level in Body Psychotherapy, which is underpinned by psycho-spiritual principles and draws on contemporary approaches to (body) psychotherapy.

Westland is a UKCP-registered Body Psychotherapist, trainer, supervisor, consultant, and writer. She has worked as a Body Psychotherapist for many years and has been training Body Psychotherapists for more than twenty-five years. She worked originally as an occupational therapist in the British National Health Service in mental health at the Maudsley Hospital, London, and then at Fulbourn Hospital, Cambridge, as a clinician and later as a manager, clinical supervisor, and teacher. She has extensive experience using touch in psychotherapy in a variety of clinical settings. She is a full member of the European Association for Body Psychotherapy and is an external examiner for the Karuna Institute, United Kingdom, and the London School of Biodynamic Psychology. She is a co-editor of the journal *Body, Movement and Dance in Psychotherapy*, and she has written numerous articles on communication in Body Psychotherapy, contemplative supervision, burnout, and Biodynamic Massage. She was also involved in writing *The Competencies of a Body Psychotherapist* (Boening, Westland, and Southwell, 2012).

Body Psychotherapy has considerable professional expertise about relating through touch. This chapter gives a comprehensive overview of touch in Body Psychotherapy and points toward future directions and research on the subject. Touch is part of most Body Psychotherapies, and some practitioners focus extensively on hands-on work. However, those Body Psychotherapists including touch in their practice will not touch each client in every session, and may not touch some clients at all (Kepner, 1987; Westland, 2009). Although the inclusion of touch in Body Psychotherapy is often seen as a differentiating factor from other forms of psychotherapy, not all Body Psychotherapists touch, nor does Body Psychotherapy require touch (Warnecke, 2009). Body Psychotherapists know how to offer psychotherapy without touch, and some authors give indications, theory, methods, and clinical vignettes of how to do this (Rothschild, 2000, 2002; Aposhyan, 2004; Young, 2005; Ogden, Minton, and Pain, 2006). However, when a Body Psychotherapist does include touch competently, it can be a potent force for change.

### The Historical Perspective: The Context for Present Debates

Prior to the development of psychiatry and psychoanalysis toward the end of the nineteenth century, massage was included in cures for the insane and those suffering from "nerves" and was provided by neurologists and physicians in asylums, spas, and private practices. It was in this context that Freud (1856–1939) developed psychoanalysis. The forefathers of contemporary Body Psychotherapy— Janet (1859–1947), Ferenczi (1873–1933), and Reich

(1897–1957)—all have in common an adherence to an "active" and "tactile" relationship with their patients.

Janet used massage as a way of talking to the client without words and restoring muscle awareness to the hysteric. He writes of the importance of respect for the patient, explaining the massage treatment, and calming any anxieties about it (Boadella, 1997).

Ferenczi experimented with the "active method," which included "relaxation" and "mutual analysis." Mutual analysis attempted to redress the power imbalance in the patient-doctor relationship. Ferenczi also believed that distressed patients sometimes required holding and comfort, and he worked directly with others on the physicality of their defense system. He describes grabbing hold of a man, whose symptom was fainting, as the man was about to pass out: "I shook him quite severely, repeated the sentence he had begun, and forcibly demanded that he should finish his sentence" (Barossa, 1999, p. 197). This proved effective in preventing the patient from escaping his "unhappy reality." Ferenczi was "seriously libeled" by Ernest Jones, who spread rumors about him being psychotic and seducing patients, and it is only relatively recently that Ferenczi's reputation has been restored (Stanton, 1990; Heller, 2012). The basis of these rumors was the "Küsstechnik" (kissing technique), part of the active methods, where patients were purported to have permission to express physical affection for their analyst, provided it did not drift into sexual intercourse. Although Freud wrote admonishingly to Ferenczi about Küsstechnik, this was unnecessary, as active methods did not encourage promiscuity between the patient and the analyst (Stanton, 1990; Schlesinger and Appelbaum, 2000; Heller, 2012).

Reich, of course, also worked directly on the patient's defense system with its tense muscles holding emotions. Boadella (1987) points out that this was not manual manipulation of muscles, but a direct empathic resonance with the emotion of the muscle.

Another major strand of influence on Body Psychotherapy was the Norwegian collaboration between physiotherapy, psychiatry, and psychoanalysis (Braatøy, 1954; Andersen, 1991; Anderson and Jensen, 2007; Heller, 2007), in which psychoanalysts recognized the impact of hands-on work on psychological well-being.

It is also well known that when Freud worked with Breuer, they used touch, hot and cold baths, and hypnosis to stimulate regression, memory recall, and catharsis. In the case of Frau Emmy van N, Freud writes, "I laid my hand on the patient's forehead, or took the patient's hand in my hands and said 'Now it will come to you under the pressure of my hand'" (Freud and Breuer, 1895/2004, p. 113). Later, Freud revised his ideas to emphasize free association, analyst neutrality, the frustration of impulses, and interpretation of the transference. In the 1930s, the rule of abstinence became fixed when psychoanalytic trainings, particularly in the United States, institutionalized the training, and when psychoanalysis became a major approach in psychiatry (Shorter, 1997). The "abstinence rule" protects analysts from "acting out their transferences" and attempting to gratify the instinctual impulses of patients because the analyst cannot bear to be with the patient's pain. This supposedly denies the patient their painful experience, and the expression of feelings about the analyst not giving them what they want comes into the therapy.

Although psychoanalysis is known for not touching, there are notable exceptions (Bosanquet, 1970, 2006; Woodmansey, 1986; Rosenberg, 1995; Pinson, 2002; Toronto, 2006; Orbach and Carroll, 2006). From time to time, psychoanalysis reexamines the place of touch in psychotherapy, and the benefits of not touching tend to be reasserted (Casement, 2002; Schaverien, 2002, 2006), but with some exceptions for more damaged patients, especially "when words are not enough" (Schlesinger and Appelbaum, 2000). This is not very surprising, as few analysts have any training in how to touch empathically or therapeutically.

The development of British object-relations theory (1950s), being "a loosely integrated theory rather than a set approach" (Gomez, 1997, p. 2), shifted the psychoanalytic focus away from the "oedipal" scenario toward the needs of the developing infant. The urge for a tactile relationship was now seen as primary in infants, rather than biological instincts, and this provided different reasons to touch. Object Relations also made links with the American schools of Ego Psychology and Self Psychology, which were more open to the possibility of touching patients/clients.

**Recent Developments**

Until the 1990s, Body Psychotherapy was viewed with suspicion, some admiration, and ambivalence, and also debated somewhat defensively with other forms of psychotherapy. However, new thinking in philosophy, the development of modern technology (enabling more precise research), research into child development, extensive touch studies showing its benefits (such as those conducted at the Touch Research Institute in Miami by Field and colleagues [2003]), and developments in neuroscience (including trauma studies), have all elicited much more appreciation of what skilled touch, including that within Body Psychotherapy, has to offer.

The intersubjective perspective views the client and the psychotherapist as co-creating the interactional field, and relationship as a mutual flow of reciprocal influence. Transferences are seen less as intrapsychically driven, and the unfolding process becomes more important than content (Stolorow et al., 1987). As the intersubjective-relational view gathers momentum, the "touch debate" is shifting significantly, as this perception of a relationship is closer to that of many Body Psychotherapies. It also permits more complexity to come into the discussion (Warnecke, 2011). There have also been calls for open discussion, rather than the polarized positions of touching or not touching (e.g., Pinson, 2002; Carere-Comes, 2007; Fosshage, 2009), and of thinking simplistically of touch as only soothing or sexual.

Since their inceptions, the United Kingdom Council for Psychotherapy (UKCP), the regulator of psychotherapy in the United Kingdom, and the European Association for Psychotherapy (EAP) have included all forms of psychotherapy (including Body Psychotherapy) and have hosted landmark conferences. In this arena, there has also been dialogue and experiential investigation between different psychotherapeutic modalities, including Body Psychotherapy (Corrigall and Wilkinson, 2003; Westland, 2004/2005; Corrigall, Payne, and Wilkinson, 2006). In Britain, there have also been groundbreaking dialogues between relational psychoanalysts (coming from the United States) and Body Psychotherapists (Gauld, 2008).

## Philosophical Underpinnings

Touch is understood differently depending on the philosophical framework and underpinnings of the therapeutic work. Discussions on touch can be confused if these understandings are not made explicit (Westland, 2011). Weber (1990) proposes a model to guide discussion and describes the domains of the physical-sensory, the psychological-humanistic, and the field. The physical-sensory view is reductive and medical, and the psychological-humanistic perspective is closest to phenomenology and existentialism. Buber (1947/2002) describes "I-Thou" relating as "whole-person relating"; thus, "I-Thou" touch involves one's whole being touching another's whole being: touch is thus reciprocal. The field perspective incorporates the other perspectives and fits in more with Eastern philosophy. The intention of the "giver" makes a difference to the touch, and therefore how it is "received." Intention is energetic, impacts on the other, and may be experienced before the actual physical touch occurs. Everything is interconnected, and meaning comes from the context. The client and the therapist, therefore, co-create the field through the contact between them. This constellates and gives the relationship its particular shape in the immediate moment (Parlett, 1991).

## Types of Touch

Touch can be a "bodywork" intervention (physical-sensory model) with specific technical aims (as in physiotherapy). It can also be the chosen vehicle for communication (as between mothers and newborn babies). Touch and verbal communications are not interchangeable (Busch, 2005), and sometimes touch communicates far more than words can possibly capture. Touch can be an aspect of the relationship, and an awareness of the touching can be either the main focus, or in the background. A major consideration is whether the tactile and verbal communications are congruent.

Touch involves using a body part to touch another body part of oneself or another. Touch includes handshakes and hugs, but Body Psychotherapy has developed a vast array of touch communications going beyond these social forms of touching. The client and the psychotherapist may touch back-to-back, foot-to-foot, hand on back, the client's feet on the psychotherapist's belly, the client's back leaning into the front of the psychotherapist, the psychotherapist holding the client's head, and so on. A session may include fairly brief moments of touch, or a whole session of hands-on work.

Touch can include tapping, stroking, rolling, and rocking tissues, squeezing, pressing, gliding across skin, stretching, pulling, pushing (for example, in hand-to-hand resistance work), or moving limbs; or be barely perceptible, as in mirroring work, "following" with the palms of the hands. "Auric" touching of the energy field, without physically touching, is also possible. Consideration may be given to what is being touched (i.e., clothes, skin, connective tissue, or muscle), and whether the touch is moving, or in one place and still. If the touch includes movement, then rhythm, timing, speed, and the "musicality" of the touch can be considered. Pressure is another variable.

Smith (1985) describes "soft techniques," such as lifting and rocking in groups; and "hard techniques," including kneading and "pinching." Brown writes of "catalytic direct touch," an assertive form of touch, and "nurturing touch," a "laying of the hands on the client's skin without the slightest movement or pressure" (Brown, 1990, p. 121). Kepner (1987) follows this dichotomy with "firm" and "light" touch.

Boadella (1986) relates touch to the elements of earth, water, air, and fire. Earth touch communicates solidity, grounding, and support; water touch follows the "liquid movements" of the body; air touch draws the breath into the whole body; and fire touch invites the inner warmth of the client to the surface, or dissipates excess fire into movements. Bräuer (1991) elaborates on this, looking at body therapeutic methods through these four elements, with the aim of not changing the body parts, but making a human relationship. For example, she describes Gerda Boyesen's deep draining massage as touch connecting with the earth element.

Some Body Psychotherapies highlight tactile communications as exploratory experiments and refer to "contactful touch" (Boadella, 1987; Westland, 2004/2005; Warnecke, 2009) and "listening touch" (Rubenfeld, 2000), which has clear intent and purpose and is related to the context. Biodynamic Psychology lists various touch intentions or ranges such as "This is where you begin and end," "Wake up," and "You're all right as you are" (CBPC, 1996). Caldwell (1997) distinguishes the intentions of support, nurture, challenge, reflection, and providing space that can all be combined with the touch types of awareness, working, nurturing, and teaching. Hunter and Struve (1998) list appropriate situations for using touch in psychotherapy, such as: to reorient a client; to emphasize a point; to access memories or emotions; to communicate empathy; to provide safety or calm a client; to assist in enhancing ego strength; to change the level of intimacy; as an adjunct to hypnosis; and to assist in working with past traumatic experience. A contemplative, supervisory perspective of the therapeutic relationship within Biodynamic Massage has been described through the windows of clarity, compassion, and spaciousness (Westland, 1995).

Some Body Psychotherapists have also trained in a particular form of body therapy (e.g., Rolfing, Craniosacral Therapy, Zero Balancing) to enhance their tactile skills. This is not the same as touch in Body Psychotherapy. Body therapies do not work with a psychotherapeutic understanding of relationship, including transferences, and do not maintain a psychotherapeutic framework for their practice. Opinion is divided about whether body therapy is a helpful adjunct to more verbally oriented psychotherapies and nontouching forms of Body Psychotherapy (Durana, 1998), or whether it undermines and muddles both therapies (Staunton, 2009)

At the present time, Body Psychotherapy does not have common language for touch, and sometimes uses the same terms for different phenomena. Brown's "nurturing touch" (Brown, 1990), for example, is not the same as Caldwell's "nurturing touch" (Caldwell, 1997). The professional understanding about touch would be improved enormously by the development of a common vocabulary.

## The Benefits of Touch

The benefits of touch have been very well researched. Some of this research is outlined here.

### Touch in Development

Touch is the "chief" of the languages of the senses: "The communications we transmit through touch constitute the most powerful means of establishing human relationships, the foundation of experience" (Montagu, 1971/1986, p. xv). Research demonstrates that tactile stimulation, cuddling, and skin-to-skin touch are absolutely vital for brain development and affect regulation in infancy. Moreover, the specific quality and emotional content of the tactile input is also important for brain development. Up to nine months old, touch—for a child—is a major source of joy, as expressed in laughter. Without fairly constant and caring touch, infants significantly fail to thrive and can even die. "Harsh touch" in infancy is implicated in aggressive behavior later in life and possibly also in mental health problems (see, for example, Spitz and Wolf, 1946; Harlow, 1958; Bowlby, 1969/1997; Brazelton and Cramer, 1991; Schore, 1994, 2003; Trevarthen and Aitken, 2001; Trevarthen, 2004).

### Therapeutic Uses of Touch

Extensive research into touch, including massage studies, has demonstrated numerous benefits, including lifting mood in depression (including postpartum depression), reducing anxiety, relieving pain, reducing muscular tension, decreasing raised blood pressure, enhancing immune function, improving sleep, decreasing the symptoms of sexual abuse, reducing aggression in adolescents, and improving weight gain in preterm neonates (Field, 2003; Westland, 1993a, 1993b).

### Touch in Psychotherapy

Research on touch from the patient perspective in psychotherapy is essentially positive (Horton et al., 1995; Gelb, 1982). Patients reported feeling accepted, developing better self-esteem, having more contact with external reality, and experiencing greater openness in relationships. These positive views of touch were connected to feeling in control, touch being discussed, and feeling congruence between emotional and physical intimacy.

## Reasons to Touch

The literature across different psychotherapeutic domains describes a wide range of reasons for touch in psychotherapy. These following reasons for touching are all found in the literature (any unattributed reasons are mine):

- *Technical touch:* as a skilled intervention (Totton, 2003); for diagnosis; to gather information (Atkinson, 2004); to facilitate new actions and postural patterns (Ogden, Minton, and Pain, 2006); to break down restrictions in the tissues (Baker, 1980) and to induce movements (Pierrakos, 1987); to cleanse tissues of toxins and emotional remnants, and to improve the flow of fluids (Southwell, 1982).

- *For those who are emotionally defended:* to reflect the defense system; to bring resistance into awareness and to explore it (Kepner, 1987); "taking over" the defense (Kurtz, 1990); to reduce resistance and to provoke emotional expression and release (Reich, 1942/1961, 1949/1970; Lowen, 1975; Pierrakos, 1987; Smith, 1985); to deepen breathing, increase movement in muscular contractions, and increase sensation (Keleman, 1981).

- *For traumatized clients:* containment, facilitation of safety, reorienting, and reality testing (Mintz, 1969; Hunter and Struve, 1998); fear reduction (Liss, 1974); dissipation of the transference and to make the symbolic concrete; to learn to stay present, take charge, and not dissociate (Showell, 2002); to reach frozen clients (Jacoby, 1986); to strengthen boundaries (Warnecke, 2009); to begin to know one's emotions; to build new somatic resources or to support awareness of existing ones; to activate nerve endings on the skin surface to increase or restore awareness of bodily sensation (Ogden, Minton, and Pain, 2006).

- *For those who are emotionally and physiologically dysregulated:* to soothe or enliven, and to balance the autonomic nervous system, including breathing patterns (Eiden, 1998; Warnecke, 2009), and to restore equilibrium (Southwell, 1982); to restore the psycho-physiological repair systems of the organism (Heller, 2007); to create safety and relationship nonverbally, for the client to make a stronger contact with themselves and their inner sensations, and to allow internal movements (Eiden, 1998).

- *For those with childhood developmental deficits and traumas:* symbolic mothering when the client is unable to verbalize (Mintz, 1969; Bosanquet, 1970; Toronto, 2006); mirroring (McNeely, 1987); connection with the suffering "child within" (Jacoby, 1986); to nourish the physical connection and to experience the presence of the therapist (Goodman and Teicher, 1988); to explore, to amplify, and to give feedback (McNeely, 1987), to connect bodily sensations with touch, and to bridge physiological awareness with feelings (Eiden, 1998); to experience a stronger sense of the skin boundary to foster differentiation and separation (Cornell, 1998); to facilitate the capacity for organization, and for sustaining emotional and interpersonal structure (Cornell, 1998); to link eye contact and touch in clients with schizoid protective patterns (Atkinson, 2004); for reparation and replenishment (Atkinson, 2004); to connect with inner objects and to face deficits with a psychotherapist (Busch, 2005).

- *Embodiment of aggression and pleasure:* for controlled exploration of aggression, as in arm wrestling (Mintz, 1969), and wrestling man-to-man; to explore "contactful pushing away," and to discover strength and pleasure in the assertion; to gain a capacity for pleasure, especially with abused clients (Ogden, Minton, and Pain, 2006); to bring energy into the body to experience pleasurable "streamings" (Boyesen, 1976; Liss, 1974; Southwell, 1988); to reconnect with the sensual and sexual self; or to explore revulsion toward pleasurable sensations (Staunton, 2000; Cornell, 1998); to deepen intimacy, and to differentiate emotional and sexual intimacy (Cornell, 1998); to feel the pleasure of being alive (Southwell, 1982).

- *Exploring and deepening experience in relationship:* touch as a collaborative experiment (Kepner, 1987; Ogden, Minton, and Pain, 2006), and to bring experiences to consciousness for exploration mindfully and in awareness (Ogden, 1996), especially by holding attention specifically for a time in one place (Weiss, 2002); touch with mindfulness, to access the unconscious, or implicit information (Johanson, 2006); to focus attention (Older, 1982; Kepner, 1987); to emphasize a verbal statement (Older, 1982), and to increase self-exploration (Pattison, 1973); to encourage and validate emotional expression (Boadella, 1987; Kurtz, 1990); to explore closeness and to discover that closeness does not have to be sacrificed for autonomy; to deepen the client's experience and relational needs (Cornell, 1998); to tolerate pain, and to lessen shame interfering with working through issues (Durana, 1994); to facilitate individual and relational psyche-soma dynamics; to engage with processes evoked by touch either verbally or as cues to engage, mirror, or co-regulate relational tensions (Warnecke, 2009).

- *Increasing energy flow:* to free energy flow and to allow breathing to deepen (Older, 1982; Totton, 2005); to revitalize a client cut off from feelings (Tune, 2005); to put information into the organism, to create energy flow throughout the body, and to increase self-sensation (Davis, 2001); to connect with the spiritual, as described by Carroll (2000), and to come to know oneself deeply as "incarnate spirit" (Southwell, 1982).

- *Touch as the primary way to relate:* choosing touch as *the* vehicle for communication; "being with" without demand, to enhance somatic resonance, to embody the relationship, and to connect with the whole being, not just the thinking/talking part (Rubenfeld, 2002; Atkinson, 2004); to relate to implicit (nonverbal) knowing, especially when words are "too slow" or interfering, and to access deep material from pre- and nonverbal stages of development (Atkinson, 2004); to reach a client and for direct communication; to fully experience emotional pain (Atkinson, 2004), and when the client cannot symbolically experience the presence of the psychotherapist, or the client uses excessive rationalization; to confirm a new state of being (Southwell, 1982); to explore relationship (alter ego, transferential, and dialogic-interactional) (Busch, 2005); to extend beyond the skin boundary, connecting "heavenwards" and "speaking to" the client "at a very deep level of his being" (Southwell, 1982).

- *Real relationship*: to convey a sense of self-worth and to communicate acceptance (Mintz, 1969; Eiden, 1998); to relate to the client as an adult in postoedipal states (Asheri, 2009); spontaneous and natural expression of the therapist's feelings (Mintz, 1969; Smith, 1998); social touching, such as handshakes and hugs (Kepner, 1987).

## Fears and Risks about Touch in Psychotherapy

Concerns about touch within psychotherapy often reflect the position that touch has within society. Poor early childhood experiences of touch, even if "normal," color opinions about touch and can lead to an indistinct or impoverished touch vocabulary. Caldwell (1997) highlights the widespread acceptance in the United States of hitting children. Touch is also often associated with sexual activity (Davis, 1991; Hunter and Struve, 1998) and abuse. Legislation to prevent abuse and attempts to make society safe are fueling caution about touch, but risk aversion has its own problems (Furedi and Bristow, 2008), such as avoiding what would be beneficial (Zur and Nordmarken, 2009).

Within psychotherapy generally, the main concern is that touch might give rise to uncontrollable aggressive and sexual drives in either client or psychotherapist, leading to ethical violations (Hunter and Struve, 1998). Touch might also be misused to satisfy the narcissistic psychotherapist's own needs for power (Kepner, 1987). Touch can also reinforce the power differential between genders in society (Alyn, 1988).

Ethnic and cultural differences about touch have scarcely been discussed so far, and this area requires a much fuller exposition, based on actual practice and research. Touch can encourage dependency and regression. An objectifying touch can be problematic, if unintended. Strong pressure can lead to tissue damage (Pierrakos, 1987), and unskilled touch can rapidly breach the client's defense system, leading to fragmentation and breakdown.

Touch can also gather projections, both positive and negative, often focusing on specific single aspects, and Warnecke (2009) cautions against idealizations of the body and touch, especially in this context.

Psychotherapists skilled in touch develop "Intricate Tactile Sensitivities" (Johnson, 2000, cited in Totton, 2003), tuning in to the subtle communications of clients. The perceptive client also tunes in to the psychotherapist. This can place both parties in potentially intimate, vulnerable, sometimes private, and sometimes awesome situations (Leijssen, 2006). Touch reminds both of their humanness and of the mysteries that can unfold with embodiment.

### Does Touch Lead to Unethical Practice?

Hugging patients "fairly often" was reported by 41 percent of respondents in research by Pope, Tabachnick, and Keith-Speigel (1987). Touch is more prevalent in psychotherapy than is initially recognized by psychotherapists reflecting on their work (Tune, 2001). Worryingly, those with no training and a belief in "abstinence" were sometimes "compelled" to touch, and this touch was unsupervised (Pinson, 2002); and seemingly others, uncomfortable with touch, were doing it anyway (Horton et al., 1995). Caldwell (1997) maps five sorts of touch with their conscious intentions and unconscious counterparts: support or sedation, nurture or codependency, challenge or aggression, reflection or mindlessness, and providing space or abandonment. There are "spectrums of possibility" between these polarities.

Gutheil and Gabbard (1993) regard any touch, beyond a handshake, being the "slippery slope" toward gratifying sexual feelings. However, this is not supported by research

(Milakovich, 1998). Female humanistic psychotherapists using touch do not have erotic contact and intercourse with clients any more than other categories of psychotherapists (Holroyd and Brodsky, 1977). However, psychotherapists using a differential application of nonerotic touching to the opposite sex, and who were sex-biased, were possibly at a higher risk of the touch leading to intercourse with patients (Holroyd and Brodsky, 1980).

Touch, per se, is not unethical, but psychotherapists may be. Denman (2004) asserts that sexual boundary violation is about the "gradual erosion of *customary* boundaries" (p. 298) (my italics). Hunter and Struve (1998) list boundary changes often occurring prior to psychotherapists having any erotic contact with clients. These include changes of time and place, money arrangements, clothing, language, self-disclosure, and physical contact without sound therapeutic reason.

Touching is a process, and an initially soothing touch from the psychotherapist can later become erotic or aggressive. Clients can also intend to hug with affection, but be cut off from themselves and unintentionally aggressive. This has to be explored verbally and unpacked like any other form of communication within psychotherapy. Touch is a subjective experience, and there are therefore no guarantees about how the client will actually receive any form of well-executed and well-intentioned touch (Scott, 2009).

## Best Practices

Best practices—using tactile communications—are exactly the same as those for any other Body Psychotherapeutic or psychotherapeutic interactions—adequate training, personal psychotherapy, thorough assessment, clear contracting, supervision, adherence to professional codes of ethics and practice, self-awareness and monitoring, self-care, and continuing professional development.

- *Training*: Adequate *experiential* training in the technical skills of touch; a theoretical framework and a rationale for including touch; ways of monitoring the impact of touch and discussing it within the therapeutic relationship; and especially discrepancies between spoken and unspoken communications are essential. Additionally, any psychotherapist using touch should have some capacity to anticipate the possible client reactions to touch and to be able to relate to them.

- *Personal psychotherapy:* Ideally, Body Psychotherapists will have experienced touch in their individual psychotherapy (Kepner, 1987). It is a UKCP and EAP requirement for students to experience individual psychotherapy—congruent with the psychotherapy that they are being trained in. It is therefore vital for the Body Psychotherapist to know about their own psychosomatic world (Busch, 2005). This can only come from experiencing it.

- *Assessment and initial consultations:* Those patients/clients requesting Body Psychotherapy bring their own assumptions (and needs) about touch, and these must be explored. A thorough history should be taken, including a touch history, where relevant. Caldwell (1997) recommends gathering information from the client about their experiences of being touched, touching, and witnessing touch.

- *Contracting and reviewing:* At the beginning of any form of psychotherapy, being clear about the mutual contractual obligations creates the therapeutic framework providing safety for both participants. Increasingly, contracts are written and signed by both parties. These often include statements about the boundaries of the work, ways of working, and the right to refuse. The therapeutic contract provides the broad outline for the work, but the specifics arise in the liveliness of the moment in the relationship. Touch should be negotiated generally and then specifically and ongoingly. Regular reviews of the ongoing relationship and of the mutually agreed methods of exploration will keep the process creative and focused, and builds the cooperation of the client. Sometimes a review will lead to revising and recontracting with the client.

- *Supervision:* Regular supervision for a Body Psychotherapist is a requirement for both novices and the experienced alike. The supervisor of a Body Psychotherapist must have experiential training and considerable experience of practice in touch and not be solely reliant on theory.

- *Ethics:* Ethical guidelines and codes of practice in psychotherapy provide a container for clinical work, and indicate acceptable practice to all. Codes are a mixture of clear prohibitions and also of guidelines leaving the practitioner to use sound judgment in the actual practice of psychotherapy. Psychotherapists should be able to give an audit trail of their decision-making processes and should record this in their notes. Sexual relationships with clients are totally unethical, and this is clearly stated in all Body Psychotherapeutic ethical codes. Codes also include statements on the misuse of power, avoiding harm, being respectful, working within professional competencies, self-care, honoring diversity, and the client's right to refuse. The United States Association for Body Psychotherapy's Ethics Guidelines, Section VIII: Ethics of Touch (see Addendum), is one of the most explicit set of professional guidelines about touch in psychotherapy. Ethical codes must also be internalized and be made one's own, rather than feeling externally imposed on the therapist.

- *Self-awareness/monitoring process in the session:* Psychotherapists should be highly attuned to their own bodies and should constantly monitor their somatic, feeling, countertransferential, and energetic cues for any information about the therapeutic relationship and especially about touch (Durana, 1998). An aspect of this is being aware of one's intention and also the context. It is all too easy to objectify another person's body and to implement instrumental touch unintentionally (Busch, 2005).

- *Self-care and continuing professional development:* Leading a full life, including self-care, is part of being a healthy psychotherapist. Regular professional audits by psychotherapists of their work are advisable, and significant continuing professional development is mandatory.

## Further Guidelines

Physical contact should not be happening within psychotherapy unless the psychotherapist is trained, and is comfortable with touch with this particular client, at this particular moment. Touch may be initiated by the client, or by the psychotherapist, but—very importantly—has to be negotiated relationally. The client's request to be hugged, or the psychotherapist's impulse to touch, should be seen as part of the overall relationship. Whereas some choose tactile contact as a way to build the therapeutic relationship from the start (Southwell, 1982), others believe that touch should be graduated (Kepner, 1987), or should be sparing at first (Brown, 1990).

Ball (2002) emphasizes the importance of discussing touch in psychotherapy. The style of the discussion should be consistent with the model being practiced. Rubenfeld (2002) gives an example of such a discussion in a demonstration session. The therapeutic alliance, and the fluctuations in it, should guide the relevance of touch to the psychotherapy at that particular moment (Kertay and Reviere, 1998). Relationships are complex, and the psychotherapist should attend to the multiple levels of meaning that touch may have, and be aware that sometimes feelings arise after the particular event (Westland, 2009). Social forms of touching, at the beginning or end of sessions, and especially outside the consulting room, should usually be avoided (Ibid.) or should be circumspect. They should not become habits that are not able to be discussed within the therapeutic frame.

Brown (1990) recommends caution with "catalytic touch" with sensitive clients, who can become more defensive, maybe distorting reality, and misascribing the psychotherapist's motivations. Correspondingly, "nurturing touch" can sometimes be too passive for people with more rigid structures, and "firm" touch can be too invasive for people with delicate or fragile character structures.

Touch is also contextual. What might be acceptable in a private center may be unacceptable within Britain's National Health Service. Nevertheless, Waterston was able to use Biodynamic Massage within the context of an NHS facility for problem drinkers because he had the backing of his colleagues and superiors for this type of work (Westland, 1994).

Some authors see touch as being contraindicated for the more emotionally disturbed clients, who may be psychotic, perhaps paranoid, and with fragile ego strength (Kepner, 1987), and for hostile or aggressive clients (Durana, 1998). However, each client is unique, and many clients with early attachment issues, or with histories of sexual, physical, and emotional abuse, seek out Body Psychotherapy precisely because Body Psychotherapy has a significant degree of expertise in this area and may include touch that is appropriate and important for their healing process. Some Body Psychotherapists are able to work with some of these clients, depending on their own personality, history, training, experience, the context of the work, the fit between the client and the psychotherapist, the resources of the client, and with the support of robust supervision. Ford (1993) offers a protocol for exploring touch with those who have been sexually abused.

## Case Studies and Research on Touch in Body Psychotherapy

There are numerous case examples and vignettes written by Body Psychotherapists that include touch; but, because touch is often integral to the psychotherapy, it does not show up distinctly as a subject in book indexes (e.g., Keleman, 1981; Boadella, 1987; Pierrakos, 1987; Southwell, 1988; Kurtz, 1990; Brown, 1990). May (2005) and Röhricht (2009) have summarized research in Body Psychotherapy; and Chapter 84, "Research in Body Psychotherapy" by Barnaby Barratt, as well as his book (Barratt, 2010), and several other studies, support the efficacy of touch in Body Psychotherapy. However, a great deal more specific research into touch within Body Psychotherapy and the communications and the subtleties of touch in Body Psychotherapy is needed, and this topic would merit far more investigation.

## Conclusion and Future Directions

Touch is an undeniable and fundamental form of communication. Body Psychotherapy has a long history and well-established practices of relating through touch. Touch is both a technique, and a form of interaction, and the benefits of touch are very well documented. Body Psychotherapy is mostly an experience-driven psychotherapy in which communication through touch is sometimes prominent. This must be balanced with attention to meaning and all the other forms of communication and relating. Relationships are incredibly complex and multifaceted, and, as Body Psychotherapists, our experience is that, if touch can be included, clients are often able to become more whole. The knowledge and methods of Body Psychotherapy—with respect to touch—should be recognized in all forms of psychotherapy, and the debate about whether to touch or not must move into a deeper exploration of the awesome potency of touch, a language in its own right.

## Addendum

### USABP Ethics Guidelines, Section VIII: Ethics of Touch

The use of touch has a legitimate and valuable role as a body-oriented mode of intervention when used skillfully and with clear boundaries, sensitive application and good clinical judgment. Because use of touch may make clients especially vulnerable, body-oriented therapists pay particular attention to the potential for dependent, infantile or erotic transference and seek healthy containment rather than therapeutically inappropriate accentuation of these states. Genital or other sexual touching by a therapist or client is always inappropriate, never appropriate.

1. Body Psychotherapists evaluate the appropriateness of the use of touch for each client. They consider a number of factors such as the capacity of the client for genuine informed consent; the client's developmental capacity and diagnosis; the transferential potential of the client's personal history in relation

to touch; the client's ability to usefully integrate touch experiences; and the interaction of the practitioner's particular style of touch work with the client's. They record their evaluations and consultation in the client's record.

2. Body Psychotherapists obtain informed consent prior to using touch-related techniques in the therapeutic relationship. They make every attempt to ensure that consent for the use of touch is genuine and that the client adequately understands the nature and purposes of its use. As in all informed consent, written documentation of the consent is strongly recommended.

3. Body Psychotherapists recognize that the client's conscious verbal and even written consent for touch, while apparently genuine, may not accurately reflect objections or problems with touch of which the client is currently unaware. Knowing this, Body Psychotherapists strive to be sensitive to the client's spoken and unspoken cues regarding touch, taking into account the particular client's capacity for authentic and full consent.

4. Body Psychotherapists continue to monitor for ongoing informed consent to ensure the continued appropriateness of touch-based interventions. They maintain periodic written records of ongoing consent and consultation regarding any questions they or a client may have.

5. Body Psychotherapists recognize and respect the right of the client to refuse or terminate any touch on the part of the therapist at any point, and they inform the client of this right.

6. Body Psychotherapists recognize that, as with all aspects of the therapy, touch is only used when it can reasonably be predicted and/or determined to benefit the client. Touch may never be utilized to gratify the personal needs of the therapist, nor because it is seen as required by the therapist's theoretical viewpoint in disregard of the client's needs or wishes.

7. The application of touch techniques requires a high degree of internal clarity and integration on the part of the therapist. Body Psychotherapists prepare themselves for the use of therapeutic touch through thorough training and supervision in the use of touch, receiving therapy that includes touch, and appropriate supervision or consultation should any issues arise in the course of treatment.

8. Body Psychotherapists do not engage in genital or other sexual touching nor do they knowingly use touch to sexually stimulate a client. Therapists are responsible to maintain clear sexual boundaries in terms of their own behavior and to set limits on the client's behavior towards them which prohibits any sexual touching. Information about the therapeutic value of clear sexual boundaries in the use of touch is conveyed to the client prior to and during the use of touch in a manner that is not shaming or derogatory.

# References

Alyn, J. H. (1988). The politics of touch in therapy: A response to Willison and Masson. *Journal of Counseling and Development, 66,* 432–433.

Anderson, H., & Jensen, P. (2007). *Innovations in the reflecting process.* London: Karnac.

Andersen, T. (Ed.). (1991). *The reflecting team, dialogues and dialogues about the dialogues.* London: W. W. Norton.

Aposhyan, S. (2004). *Body-Mind Psychotherapy: Principles, techniques and practical applications.* New York: Norton.

Asheri, S. (2009). To touch or not to touch: A relational Body Psychotherapy perspective. In L. Hartley (Ed.), *Contemporary Body Psychotherapy: The Chiron Approach* (pp. 106–120). London: Routledge.

Atkinson, E. (2004). *Psychotherapists' experiences of touch: An exploratory study* (Unpublished research thesis in partial fulfillment of the requirements for the degree of Master of Science, Counselling and Psychotherapy in Health and Social Care). University of Surrey, UK.

Baker, E. (1980). *Man in the trap.* London: Collier.

Ball, A. (2002). *Taboo and not taboo: Reflections on physical touch in psychoanalysis and Somatic Psychotherapy.* Melbourne: Psychoz.

Barossa, J. (1999). *Sándor Ferenczi: Selected writings.* Harmondsworth, UK: Penguin.

Barratt, B.B. (2010). *The Emergence of Somatic Psycholology and Bodymind Therapy.* New York, NY: Palgrave Macmillan.

Boadella, D. (1986, Aug.). What is Biosynthesis? *Energy & Character, 17*(2), 1–23.

Boadella, D. (1987). *Lifestreams.* London: Routledge & Kegan Paul.

Boadella, D. (1997). Awakening sensibility, recovering motility. Psycho-physical synthesis at the foundations of body-psychotherapy: The 100-year legacy of Pierre Janet (1859–1947). *International Journal of Psychotherapy, 2*(1), 45–56.

Boening, M., Westland, G., and Southwell, C. (2012). *Body Psychotherapy Competencies.* Amsterdam: EABP. Accessed 11-Jan-2014: www.eabp.org/pdf/BodyPsychotherapyCompetencies.pdf

Bosanquet, C. (1970). Getting in touch. *Journal of Analytical Psychology, 15*(1), 42–57.

Bosanquet, C. (2006). Symbolic understanding of tactile communication in psychotherapy. In G. Galton (Ed.), *Touch papers: Dialogues on touch in the psychoanalytic space,* (pp. 29–48). London: Karnac.

Bowlby, J. (1969/1997). *Attachment and loss* (Vol. 1). London: Pimlico.

Boyesen, G. (1976). The primary personality and its relationship to the streamings. In D. Boadella (Ed.), *In the wake of Reich,* (pp. 81–98). London: Coventure.

Braatøy, T. (1954). *Fundamentals of psychoanalytic technique.* New York: John Wiley & Sons.

Bräuer, U. C. (1991). The four elements: An attempt to establish a holistic perspective on body therapy methods. In G. Marlock (Ed.), *Unitive Body-Psychotherapy: Collected papers* (Vol. 2), (pp. 119–131). Frankfurt: AFRA.

Brazelton, T. B., & Cramer, B. G. (1991). *The earliest relationship: Parents, infants and the drama of early attachment.* London: Karnac.

Brown, M. (1990). *The healing touch: An introduction to Organismic Psychotherapy.* Mendocino, CA: LifeRhythm.

Buber, M. (1947/2002). *Between man and man.* London: Routledge Classics.

Busch, T. (2005). Therapeutic touch as a maturation-enhancing intervention. In H. Weiss & G. Marlock (Eds.), Handbuch der Körperpsychotherapie [Handbook of Body Psychotherapy], (pp. 517–529). Göttingen: Hogrefe.

Caldwell, C. (1997). *Getting in touch: The guide to new body-centered therapies.* Wheaton, IL: Quest Books.

Carere-Comes, T. (2007). Bodily holding in the dialogic-dialectical approach. *Journal of Psychotherapy Integration, 17*(1), 93–110.

Carroll, R. (2000). Biodynamic Massage in psychotherapy: Re-integrating, re-owning and re-associating through the body. In T. Staunton (Ed.), *Body Psychotherapy,* (pp. 78–100). London: Routledge.

Cambridge Body Psychotherapy Centre. (1996). *Summary of Biodynamic Massage methods and how they can be used with different intentionality.* Cambridge, UK: CBPC Training Paper.

Casement, P. (2002). *Learning from our mistakes: Beyond dogma in psychoanalysis and psychotherapy.* New York: Guilford Press.

Cornell, W. F. (1998). Touch and boundaries in Transactional Analysis: Ethical and transferential considerations. In *"Creating Our Community": Conference Proceedings of the US Association for Body Psychotherapy, Boulder, CO,* July 1998.

Corrigall, J., Payne, H., & Wilkinson, H. (Eds.). (2006). *Working with the embodied mind in psychotherapy.* Hove, UK: Routledge.

Corrigall, J., & Wilkinson, H. (Eds.). (2003). *Revolutionary connections, psychotherapy and neuroscience.* London: Karnac.

Davis, P. K. (1991). *The power of touch.* Carson, CA: Hay House.

Davis, W. (2001). Energetics and therapeutic touch. In M. Heller (Ed.), *The flesh of the soul: The body we work with: Selected papers of the 7th Congress of the European Association of Body Psychotherapy, 2–6 September 1999, Travemünde,* (pp. 59–80). Bern, Switzerland: Peter Lang.

Denman, C. (2004). *Sexuality: A biosocial approach.* Basingstoke, UK: Palgrave Macmillan.

Durana, C. (1994). Bonding and emotional expressiveness in the PAIRS training: A psychoeducational approach for couples. *Journal of Family Psychotherapy, 5*(2), 65–68.

Durana, C. (1998, Summer). The use of touch in psychotherapy: Ethical and clinical guidelines. *Psychotherapy, 35*(2), 269–280.

Eiden, B. (1998). The body in psychotherapy: The use of touch in psychotherapy. *Self and Society, 26*(2), 3–41.

Field, T. (2003). *Touch.* Cambridge, MA: Bradford Books, MIT Press.

Ford, C. (1993). *Compassionate touch: The role of human touch in healing and recovery.* New York: Simon & Schuster.

Fosshage, J. L. (2009). To touch or not to touch in the psychoanalytic arena. In B. Willock, R. C. Curtis, & L. C. Bohm (Eds.), *Taboo or not taboo? Forbidden thoughts, forbidden acts in psychoanalysis and psychotherapy*, (pp. 327–350). London: Karnac.

Freud, S., & Breuer, J. (1895/2004). *Studies on hysteria.* London: Penguin Classics.

Furedi, F., & Bristow, J. (2008). *Licensed to hug.* London: Civitas: Institute for the Study of Civil Society.

Gauld, S. (2008). Chiron Association for Body Psychotherapists Conference, 2007. "Meeting in the flesh": Relational dilemmas and opportunities. *Body, Movement and Dance in Psychotherapy, 3*(2), 119–124.

Gelb, P. (1982). The experience of nonerotic physical contact in traditional psychotherapy: A critical investigation of the taboo against touch. *Dissertation Abstracts, 43*, 1–13.

Gomez, L. (1997). *An introduction to object relations.* London: Free Association Books.

Goodman, M., & Teicher, A. (1988, Winter). To touch or not to touch. *Psychotherapy, 25*(4), 492–500.

Gutheil, T., and Gabbard, C. (1993). The concept of boundaries in clinical practice: Theoretical and risk management dimensions. *American Journal of Psychiatry, 150*(2), 188–196.

Harlow, H. (1958). The nature of love. *American Psychologist, 13*, 673–685.

Heller, M. C. (2007). The Golden Age of Body Psychotherapy in Oslo: From vegetotherapy to nonverbal communication. *Body, Movement and Dance in Psychotherapy, 2*(2), 81–94.

Heller, M. C. (2012). *Body Psychotherapy: History, concepts and methods.* New York: W. W. Norton.

Holroyd, J., & Brodsky, A. (1977). Psychologists' attitudes and practices regarding erotic and non-erotic physical contact with patients. *American Psychologist, 32*, 839–843.

Holroyd, J., & Brodsky, A. (1980). Does touching patients lead to sexual intercourse? *Professional Psychology, 11*, 807–811.

Horton, J. A., Clance, P. R., Sterk-Elifson, C., & Emshoff, J. (1995). Touch in psychotherapy: A survey of patients' experiences. *Psychotherapy, 32*(2), 443–457.

Hunter, M., & Struve, J. (1998). *The ethical use of touch in psychotherapy.* London: Sage.

Jacoby, M. (1986). Getting in touch and touching in analysis. In N. Schwartz-Salant & M. Stein (Eds.), *The body in analysis*, (pp. 109–126). Wilmette, IL: Chiron.

Johanson, G. (2006). *The use of mindfulness in psychotherapy.* Retrieved from www.hakomiinstitute.com

Johnson, D. H. (2000). Intricate tactile sensitivity. *Progress in Brain Research, 122*, 479–490.

Keleman, S. (1981). *Your body speaks its mind.* Berkeley, CA: Center Press.

Kepner, J. (1987). *Body process: A Gestalt approach to working with the body in psychotherapy.* New York: Gardner Press.

Kertay, L., & Reviere, S. L. (1998). Touch in context. In E. Smith, P. R. Clance, & S. Imes (Eds.), *Touch in psychotherapy: Theory, research and practice,* (pp. 16–30). London: Guilford Press.

Kurtz, R. (1990). *Body-Centered Psychotherapy.* Mendocino, CA: LifeRhythm.

Leijssen, M. (2006). Validation of the body in psychotherapy. *Journal of Humanistic Psychology, 46*(2), 126–147.

Liss, J. (1974). Why touch? *Energy & Character, 5*(2), 1–8.

Lowen, A. (1975). *Bioenergetics.* Harmondsworth, UK: Penguin.

May, J. (2005). A review of the objective literature on Body Psychotherapy (2nd ed.): Update/continuation of 1998 review. In *Conference Proceedings, US Association for Body Psychotherapy 4th National Conference, The Body of Life: Body Psychotherapy in the Real World,* June 8–11, Tucson, AZ (pp. 380–398).

McNeely, D. A. (1987). *Touching, body therapy and Depth Psychology.* Toronto: Inner City Books.

Milakovich, J. (1998). Differences between therapists who touch and those who do not. In E. Smith, P. R. Clance, & S. Imes (Eds.), *Touch in psychotherapy: Theory, research and practice*, (pp. 74–92). London: Guilford Press.

Mintz, E. E. (1969). Touch and the psychoanalytic tradition. *Psychoanalytic Review, 56*, 365–376.

Montagu, A. (1971/1986). *Touching: The human significance of the skin.* New York: Perennial, Harper & Row.

Ogden, P. (1996, Summer). Hands-on psychotherapy. *Hakomi Forum Professional Journal,* Issue 12. Retrieved from www.hakomiinstitute.com

Ogden, P., Minton, K., & Pain, C. (2006). *Trauma and the body: A sensorimotor approach to psychotherapy.* New York: Norton.

Older, J. (1982). *Touch is healing.* New York: Stein and Day.

Orbach, S., & Carroll, R. (2006). Contemporary approaches to the body in psychotherapy: Two psychotherapists in dialogue. In J. Corrigall, H. Payne, & H. Wilkinson (Eds.), *Working with the embodied mind in psychotherapy*, (pp. 63–82). Hove, UK: Routledge.

Parlett, M. (1991). Reflections on field theory. *British Journal of Gestalt, 1*, 69–81.

Pattison, J. E. (1973). Effects of touch on self-exploration and the therapeutic relationship. *Journal of Consulting and Clinical Psychology, 40*(2), 170–175.

Pierrakos, J. (1987). *Core Energetics.* Mendocino, CA: LifeRhythm.

Pinson, B. (2002). Touch in therapy: An effort to make the unknown known. *Journal of Contemporary Psychotherapy, 32*(2/3), 179–196.

Pope, K. S., Tabachnick, B. G., & Keith-Speigel, P. (1987). Ethics of practice: The beliefs and behaviors of psychologists as therapists. *American Psychologist, 42*, 993–1005.

Reich, W. (1942/1961). *The function of the orgasm.* New York: Farrar, Straus & Giroux.

Reich, W. (1949/1970). *Character Analysis.* New York: Farrar, Straus & Giroux.

Röhricht, F. (2009). Body Oriented Psychotherapy: The state of the art in empirical research and evidence-based practice: A clinical perspective. *Body, Movement and Dance in Psychotherapy, 4*(2), 135–156.

Rosenberg, V. (1995). On touching a patient. *British Journal of Psychotherapy, 12*(1), 29–36.

Rothschild, B. (2000). *The body remembers: The psychophysiology of trauma and trauma treatment.* New York: Norton.

Rothschild, B. (2002). Body Psychotherapy without touch: Applications for trauma therapy. In T. Staunton (Ed.), *Body Psychotherapy*, (pp. 101–115). Hove, UK: Brunner-Routledge.

Rubenfeld, I. (2000). *The Listening Hand: Self-healing through the Rubenfeld Synergy Method of talk and touch.* New York: Bantam.

Rubenfeld, I. (2002). The Listening Hand: To touch or not to touch. In *Conference Proceedings: The 3rd National Conference of the US Association for Body Psychotherapy, John Hopkins University, Baltimore, MD, June 2002* (pp. 223–235). USABP.

Schaverien, J. (2002). *The dying patient in psychotherapy: Desire, dreams and individuation.* Basingstoke, UK: Palgrave Macmillan.

Schaverien, J. (2006). Transference and the meaning of touch: The body in psychotherapy with the client who is facing death. In J. Corrigall, H. Payne, & H. Wilkinson (Eds.), *About a body: Working with the embodied mind in psychotherapy*, (pp. 181–198). London: Routledge.

Schlesinger, H. J., & Appelbaum, A. H. (2000). When words are not enough. *Psychoanalytic Inquiry, 20,* 124–143.

Schore, A. (1994). *Affect regulation and the origin of the self.* Hillsdale, NJ: Lawrence Erlbaum.

Schore, A. (2003). *Affect regulation and disorders of the self.* New York: W. W. Norton.

Scott, T. (2009). A short history of touch in the time of regulation. *Self and Society, 37*(2), 16–24.

Shorter, E. (1997). *A history of psychiatry.* New York: John Wiley.

Showell, J. (2002). Touch in the right hands. *Psychotherapy in Australia, 8*(2), 46–50.

Smith, E. (1985). *The body in psychotherapy.* Jefferson, NC: McFarland.

Smith, E. (1998). Traditions of touch in psychotherapy. In E. Smith, P. R. Clance, & S. Imes (Eds.), *Touch in psychotherapy: Theory, research and practice*, (pp. 3–15). London: Guilford Press.

Southwell, C. (1982). Biodynamic Massage as a therapeutic tool—with special reference to the biodynamic concept of equilibrium. *Journal of Biodynamic Psychology,* No. 2, 40–54.

Southwell, C. (1988). The Gerda Boyesen Method: Biodynamic Therapy. In J. Rowan & W. Dryden (Eds.), *Innovative therapy in Britain*, (pp. 178–201). Milton Keynes, UK: Open University Press.

Spitz, R., & Wolf, K. (1946). Anaclitic depression: An inquiry into the genesis of psychiatric conditions in early childhood. *Psychoanalytic Study of the Child, 2,* 313–342.

Stanton, M. (1990). *Sándor Ferenczi: Reconsidering active intervention.* London: Free Association.

Staunton, T. (2000). Sexuality and Body Psychotherapy. In T. Staunton (Ed.), *Body Psychotherapy*, (pp. 56–77). Hove, UK: Brunner-Routledge.

Staunton, T. (2009). Touch in a time of regulation. *Self and Society, 37*(2), 5–10.

Stolorow, R. D., Brandchaft, B., & Atwood, G. E. (1987). *Psychoanalytic treatment: An intersubjective approach.* Hillsdale, NJ: Analytic Press.

Toronto, E. L. K. (2006). A clinician's response to physical touch in the psychoanalytic setting. *International Journal of Psychotherapy, 7*(1), 69–81.

Totton, N. (2003). *Body Psychotherapy.* Maidenhead, UK: Open University Press.

Totton, N. (2005). *New dimensions in Body Psychotherapy.* Maidenhead, UK: Open University Press.

Trevarthen, C. (2004). Intimate contact from birth. In K. White (Ed.), *Touch, attachment and the body*, (pp. 1–16). London: Karnac.

Trevarthen, C., & Aitken, K. J. (2001). Infant intersubjectivity: Research, theory and clinical applications. *Journal of Child Psychology, 42*(1), 3–48.

Tune, D. (2001). Is touch a valid therapeutic intervention? Early returns from a qualitative study of therapists' views. *Counselling and Psychotherapy Research, 1*(3), 167–171.

Tune, D. (2005). Dilemmas concerning the ethical use of touch in psychotherapy. In N. Totton (Ed.), *New dimensions in Body Psychotherapy*, (pp. 70–84). Maidenhead, UK: Open University Press.

United States Association for Body Psychotherapy. *Ethics Guidelines.* Approved Oct. 2001, revised Sept. 2007. USABP.

Warnecke, T. (2009). The therapeutic modality of touch and statutory regulation. *Self and Society, 37*(2), 11–15.

Warnecke, T. (2011). Stirring the depths: Transference, countertransference and touch. *Body, Movement and Dance in Psychotherapy, 6*(3), 233–243.

Weber, R. (1990). A philosophical perspective on touch. In T. B. Brazelton & K. E. Barnard (Eds.), *Touch: The foundation of experience*, (pp. 11–43). Madison, CT: International Universities Press.

Weiss, H. (2002). *Mindfulness and renowned research.* Retrieved from www.hakomiinstitute.com

Westland, G. (1993a). Massage as a therapeutic tool: Part 1. *British Journal of Occupational Therapy, 56*(4), 129–134.

Westland, G. (1993b). Massage as a therapeutic tool: Part 2. *British Journal of Occupational Therapy, 56*(5), 177–180.

Westland, G. (1994). Biodynamic Massage. *Complementary Therapies in Nursing and Midwifery, 2,* 47–51.

Westland, G. (1995). An evolving model of supervision for Biodynamic Massage. *Journal of the Association of Holistic Biodynamic Massage Therapists,* No. 4, 4–7.

Westland, G. (2004/2005). An exploration of how touch can be contactful. *Journal of the Association of Holistic Biodynamic Massage Therapists, 8*(1), 10–14.

Westland, G. (2009). Reflections on touch in psychotherapy. *Self and Society, 37*(2), 24–32.

Westland, G. (2011). Physical touch in psychotherapy: Why are we not touching more? *Body, Movement and Dance in Psychotherapy, 6*(1), 17–29.

Woodmansey, A. C. (1986). Are psychotherapists out of touch? *British Journal of Psychotherapy, 5*(1), 57–65.

Young, C. (2005). To touch or not to touch: That is the question: Doing effective Body Psychotherapy without touch. *Energy & Character, 34,* 50–64.

Zur, O., & Nordmarken, N. (2009). To touch or not to touch: Exploring the myth of prohibition on touch in psychotherapy and counseling: Clinical, ethical, and legal considerations. Retrieved from www.zurinstitute.com/touchintherapy.

# 49

## The Somatics of Touch

Lisbeth Marcher with Erik Jarlnaes and Kirstine Münster, Denmark

**Lisbeth Marcher**, a Bodynamic Analyst, was one of the founders and has been a leading force of the Bodynamic Psychotherapy System since 1982; director of training in the United States, Canada, Japan, and Europe; former member of the EABP board and president from 2006 to 2008; former chairperson of the EABP Forum (Body Psychotherapeutic schools in Europe). She has an MA in Psychomotor Education. Her special interests are working with babies and animals, including observations of mother-child interactions. Lisbeth has presented the Bodynamic System at many different conferences in the United States and Europe since 1982, with issues ranging from prenatal and perinatal psychology, to PTSD, Body Psychotherapy, dissociation, and character structure development. She has studied Transactional Analysis in depth, and has had some Neuro-Linguistic Programming training, as well as a lot of training in Gestalt, family systems theory, and Integrative Psychotherapy, and special studies in meditation. She has an ongoing small private practice in Denmark, while teaching all over the world, and also being a therapist and supervisor for students in Holland (the Netherlands) and other countries. She lectures at universities in Denmark and in the United States. David Boadella has praised her as "the Scandinavian legacy of Wilhelm Reich." She is fighting for a truly unified socio-psycho-motor (bio-socio-psycho) therapy rather than seeing "body" as an adjunct to Cognitive Behavioral Therapy. She created the Bodynamic Bodymap, based on five years of study, 1972–1977, and has been involved in an interdisciplinary research project on "bodily learning": *Hey I Can!*, which is a video showing children at different age levels learning new skills. She co-wrote *Body Encyclopedia:* A Guide to the Psychological Functions of the Muscular System (2000) with Sonja Fich.

**Erik Jarlnaes** is a Bodynamic Analyst; manager and co-founder of the Bodynamic System; former general secretary and board member of the EABP; and teacher at the Danish Center for Conflict Resolution and former member of their educational board. He has a BA in Political Science, an MA in Journalism, and an MA in Psychomotor Education. His special interests include: peak experiences, trauma work, communication and conflict resolution, team building, and including the body in all kinds of therapy. He has a small private practice in Denmark and teaches worldwide.

**Kirstine Münster**, MD, is a specialist in gynecology and obstetrics. She also specializes in acupuncture and pain treatment in her private practice in Denmark. She has been head of the Gynecological Pain Clinic (Hillerød Hospital), as well as a massage therapist and a teacher. A former researcher in gynecological endocrinology and epidemiology, she now teaches acupuncture to medical doctors and other health personnel, and teaches functional anatomy and energy work in Russia.

## Touch Influences Psychological Processes

Nearly four hundred years ago, the philosopher Descartes wrote that body and mind (or soul) are effectively separate (Damasio, 1996), creating what we now call a Cartesian dichotomy. The relevance of this viewpoint has since been challenged from many sides, including from the field of Body Psychotherapy.

Body Psychotherapy sees the body and mind as an indivisible unity, operating seamlessly; and thus psychological aspects have a somatic root and somatic interventions have a psychological impact. This is especially true for touch: though it must be remembered that within Body Psychotherapy the different schools and systems (modalities) each have their own way of differentiating touch—i.e., different purposes, impacts, ways, places, and intentions of touch, and a different quality of the muscle tone that is touched; these also differ with respect to different ethical considerations.

The discoveries in the twentieth century of the brain's superior control of the hormone systems, of the neuropeptide hormones, and (from the 1980s) the discovery of the immune system's hormonal signal systems, together with the impact from the interdependence between these three systems, have greatly helped in changing the previously dominant view of body and mind (soul) as separate units. Today, we have a biological basis, from neuroscience, that sheds light on the coherence between mind–soul–psyche and thought on the one side and the functions of the autonomic nervous system and the immune system on the other.

We will begin this chapter by describing a study emphasizing one example of the psychological outcomes of touch in the whole field of Body Psychotherapy.

## A Pilot Study: Some Psychological Impacts from Being Touched

In a pilot study conducted from 1998 to 2002 involving 437 participants in educational groups, we observed the effects arising out of a simple touch exercise. Working together in pairs, A placed one hand on the back of B, and, after one to two minutes, B was asked to state how he or she felt inside. After completing the exercise, the participants were presented with a list of statements about the effect. The top five most frequent answers were:

- Feeling more calm and at ease
- Feeling more present and alive
- Feeling more centered
- Feeling stronger with higher self-esteem
- Feeling more in touch with one's emotions

We will revisit some of these statements later in this chapter, where we will discuss the scientific knowledge and hypotheses concerning the physiology of the body-mind effects of touch. We will also present some cutting-edge research regarding body-mind unifying theory.

## The Psychoneuroendocrinology (PNE) of Touch

The viewpoint that the nervous system, the hormone-producing (endocrine) glands, and the immune system work as a functional, integrated complex has created the field of psychoneuroendocrinology (PNE).

PNE is based on the understanding that the immune system is homeostatically regulated (by that we mean that it constantly tries to achieve a balance within itself, given a broad spectrum of environmental influences), and that it interacts primarily with the nervous system, and with the endocrine glands.[54] This relationship indicates that our psychological state has the capacity to impact the function of the immune system, and also has the capacity to impact different functions that are controlled by the brain, such as appetite, consciousness, sleep, and regulation of temperature (Brinch et al., 2002).

An abundance of PNE research has emerged in recent years, most of which is experimental and carried out in animals, mostly rodents (Pert et al., 1985; Pauk et al., 1986; Uvnäs Moberg, 2000, 2003; Vázquez, 1998). In humans, the

---

54 **Editors' Note:** Several bodily systems can be considered to be "homeostatically regulated": the internal body temperature system; the blood pressure system; the immune system; the digestive system; the nervous system; the endocrine system; the integumentary system; etc.—and all of these systems work together to maintain an overall homeostasis: Each of these body systems contributes to the homeostasis of other systems and of the entire organism. No one system of the body works in isolation, and the well-being of the person depends upon the well-being of all the interacting body systems. A disruption within one system generally has consequences in several of the other body systems.

majority of studies concern massage, acupressure, biofeedback, and other methods within the growing field of energy medicine (Leivadi et al., 1999; Oschman, 2000; Ironson et al., 1996). We are not aware of any studies on specific neuroendocrine effects of the different types of touch. The following section therefore mainly concerns the general biological effects of gentle (noninvasive) touch.

## From the Skin to the Brain

Sensory afferent nerves bring information from receptors in the skin to the central nervous system. These nerves are mainly of two types: receptors for fine touch and for proprioception and receptors for pain and temperature. Both types of receptors generate two nervous impulses, the first of which is carried centrally by thick, coated nerve fibers (A delta fibers). These impulses travel very rapidly in the spinothalamic tract to the thalamus in the midbrain (emotional) limbic system and from there up to the cortex of the brain (Brodal, 1977). These rapidly traveling impulses allow the central nervous system (CNS) to activate inhibitory nerve impulses (efferent muscle reactions) in case the signal is judged to be painful or "too much" (Rosenfeld, 1994). This rapid system might also activate the autonomic nervous system.

Slower-acting C-tactile nerves in uncoated nerve fibers transport the second kind of nervous impulse. This part of the system is ontogenetically the oldest, and new research (Olausson et al., 2002; Wessberg et al., 2003) suggests the possibility that the C-tactiles are able to register the unconscious aspect of the stimulus; you might call it something like the "intention of the touch!" All incoming signals incidentally cross the body midline at different locations in the medulla spinalis—i.e., signals from your right arm are processed in the left part of your brain, and vice versa.

The midbrain processing in the limbic system gives a further emotional flavor to the quality of touch, somewhat dependent on how "triggered" other parts of the limbic system—like the amygdala—are. A gentle touch could therefore be received as pleasant when the person is relaxed, but as "spooky" if the fear index is high.

## From the Brain to the Body

There are various different nervous systems: the outgoing (efferent) parts of the different nervous systems consist of the whole somatic "motoric" system, which regulates a person's movement, muscle actions, and the corresponding feedback loops, and, then there are other sets of totally different (afferent or receptor) sensory nerves, that carry messages to the Central Nervous System (CNS). And then there is the autonomic nervous system (ANS), which regulates all the internal organs without our conscious mind taking any part in this, and this nervous system is divided into two very distinct parts, the sympathetic and the parasympathetic.

The sympathetic system originates from the thoracic and lumbar parts of the spinal cord. The sympathetic nerves are activated by any perceived threat and regulate the "fight-or-flight" set of responses, primarily by means of the neurotransmitter norepinephrine (noradrenaline), as well as cortisol and other cortico-steroids that make up the "stress hormones." When this sympathetic half of the system is activated, the body becomes—instantly—prepared to fight for its life, or to run for its life. The other part, the parasympathetic system, originates in the brainstem and the sacral parts of the spinal cord. The parasympathetic nerves are actively engaged during gentle, everyday activity, rest, and peacefulness, and primarily use the neurotransmitter acetylcholine (Uvnäs Moberg, 2000, 2003).

When the sympathetic system is activated, it is "not open for touch," but if it is "touched" anyway (e.g., by a reassuring hand on a shoulder) it starts to relax a bit. When the parasympathetic system is activated, it is "open for touch," and if it is "touched" (e.g., by a reassuring hand on a shoulder) it starts to relax even more.

## The Brain Responses

The limbic system in the mid-brain might be considered to be an enormous information center, connecting with both the "higher" areas (the cortex) and the "lower" levels (the brainstem) of the brain; it connects with other areas of the brain as well, such as the cerebellum. The limbic system consists primarily of the thalamus, hypothalamus, basal forebrain, hippocampus, and amygdala. Information is processed mostly through neurotransmitters and other peptide substances, and also by direct neural connections (Damasio, 1996, 1999), but all this activity happens mostly somewhat below the level of consciousness. Because all sensory input, especially from the sensory receptors in the skin, comes through the thalamus and the emotional limbic system, all sensory input concerning touch therefore has (or is given) an inevitable emotional content: his or her touch is . . . pleasant / calming / soothing / energizing / harsh / wonderful, etc.

Hypothalamic peptides elicit endocrine responses in the pituitary gland and in glands such as the adrenals. Some of the peptides synthesized in the pituitary are transported to higher levels of the CNS, thus acting partly as neurotransmitters. Neurotransmitters, peptide substances, and hormones all act on receptor molecules in different body tissues, including the brain. Some of the substances have different types of receptor molecules in different tissues. Recent lines of research in neurotransmitters has discovered the astonishing fact that most neurotransmitters are not only produced in the CNS, but also in nearly all parts of peripheral tissue. Candace Pert (1997) writes, "Neuropeptides could be found not only in the rows of nerve ganglia on either side of the spine, but in the end organs themselves" (p. 140); "And the radical discovery we made was that every neuropeptide receptor we could find in the brain is also on the surface of the human monocyte" (p. 182) (i.e., all over the body). Not only does this mean that there is a link between neuropeptides and emotions, but also, because the neuropeptide receptors are found all over the body, that emotions are a bodily "felt" sensation, rather than just "in the mind." Another consequence of this type of connection might also be that manipulation of peripheral tissues—e.g., muscles and joints—might elicit a local production of neurotransmitters—i.e., a proprioceptive "feeling" sensation. The profound effect of acupuncture on internal organs may also be an example of this more total experience of emotions.

## Psychoneuroendocrine (PNE) Substances

If one takes a look at some of the most important substances involved in the mechanisms of touch, these include oxytocin, endorphins, the neurotransmitters, and the steroid hormone cortisol. Nearly all of the body's hormone systems are in some intriguing ways implicated in the different responses to touch, but here we'll concentrate on the most important.

### Oxytocin

One of the most significant hormonal substances is possibly the pituitary hormone oxytocin. Oxytocin is produced in the supraoptic and paraventricular nuclei in the hypothalamus, transported to the posterior lobe of the pituitary, and then into the circulation of the blood. Some of the oxytocin-producing cells in the hypothalamus enhance its effect as a neurotransmitter by transporting the substance to other areas, such as:

- The *hippocampus*, the place where memory is stored and where the stress system is regulated
- The *substantia nigra* ("black substance"), the main center for the production of dopamine, which affects the ability to focus, to sense how it is to be rewarded, and to react emotionally
- The *raphe nuclei*, the main center for the production of serotonin, which has its main effect on one's general mood
- The *locus coeruleus*, the main center for the production of norepinephrine, which among other things is involved in alertness and aggression

For decades, the only known effect of oxytocin was its ability to bind to receptors in the uterus of a pregnant woman, causing contractions and thereby eventually causing the expulsion of the baby, and also in lactation—assisting the production of milk in the female breast. Later it was found that oxytocin, in addition to its role in the pregnant uterus and the mammary glands, also elicits contractions involved in female orgasms.

In recent years, research in both animals and humans has shown that oxytocin has several other behavioral effects (Uvnäs Moberg, 1998, 2000, 2003; Sachser et al., 1998; Pert, 1997; Komisaruk and Whipple, 1998; Henry, 1993b). With higher levels of oxytocin, animals display less anxiety and more curiosity, providing them with courage to establish social contact with other animals without aggression; their mating behavior is increased, and intercourse produces even more oxytocin in both female and male animals (a mechanism most likely also promoting the motility of egg and sperm); bonding behavior is significantly promoted, with feelings of contentment, reductions in anxiety, and feelings of calmness and security around the mate; maternal behavior is promoted, even in animals that have not given birth—and not only toward the animals' own offspring but also toward other youngsters; social memory, i.e., the ability to recognize others, improves; and learning abilities and the ability to retain useful information are promoted. Oxytocin also increases the pain threshold, so the animal has a decreased reaction to any pain stimulus.

Oxytocin has numerous biological effects, including lowering of the pulse rate and blood pressure; redistribution of body heat; stimulation of digestion through stimulation of gastrin, somatostatin, and insulin, and also by affecting the part of the autonomic nervous system that is involved in digestion (the vagus nerve); stimulation of wound healing; and the stimulation of pituitary production of prolactin, growth hormone, and adrenocorticotropic hormone (ACTH). The stimulation of ACTH briefly increases the production of cortisol by the adrenal cortex, but, via feedback-loop mechanisms, the general effect of oxytocin is to stabilize the cortisol at a consistently low level. The production of oxytocin in the body is stimulated by gentle touch, by being in good relationships, by sex, by delicious food and beverages, by pleasurable exercise (most likely connected to the interference between the endogenous opiate system and oxytocin), and by stillness (i.e., in meditative mindfulness).

In Uvnäs Moberg's book, *The Oxytocin Factor (2003)*, she emphasizes the importance of this hormone for health, calm, and love; thus it is essential for "good" human relationships. However, the greatest significance—especially in this context about touch—is that oxytocin is most easily produced by gentle physical contact to the ventral area of the torso: the chest, breasts, and belly. Young animals (like kittens and puppies) know this instinctively as they "knead" the mother's belly to stimulate milk production. Thus, to have a higher quality of life, one needs to touch and be touched.

**Endorphins**

The endorphins are peptide substances, chemically very similar to morphine. (The reason that morphine works is that it is very similar to the endorphins and thus "binds" to the endorphin receptors throughout the body.) Endorphins are produced in the brain and in nearly all kinds of peripheral tissues. Stressful and harmful stimuli immediately generate an increase in endorphin levels in the body. The function of this is obvious: to mitigate pain in order to be able to flee from, or fight against, stressful stimuli. Thus endorphins are also the crucial part of the freeze response, allowing a person to not feel pain in inescapable stressful situations. This can even allow for death without suffering (Henry, 1993a; van der Kolk, 1994; Nabeshima et al., 1992; Rosenfeld, 1994). But the endorphins are also produced in great amounts by nonnoxious stimuli—i.e., by transcutaneous electrical nerve stimulation (TENS), acupressure, acupuncture, massage (including touch), and movement, particularly in continued extreme exercise, such as running long distances (Thoren et al., 1990); they are also produced during orgasm (Pert, 1997, p. 104). These are actually an essential part of the primary pain-reducing and healing mechanism, working in various therapies. The endorphins not only act as painkillers, but they also have psychoactive effects. You may feel more at ease; you get a feeling of floating, and of being able to endure ("I can go on like this forever"). You may be able to defocus your emotional responses in a situation, rendering it easier for you not to be overwhelmed by emotions (Pert et al., 1985). The endorphins are intimately connected with oxytocin. Oxytocin seems to stimulate the production of endorphins, while some of the endorphins suppress a further increase in oxytocin (preventing sleep)

(Daddona and Haldar, 1994). So, to help the production of endorphins, one needs to exercise hard and/or to touch and be touched.

### The Neurotransmitters

As described in the section on oxytocin, various neurotransmitters in the brain are released in response to touch. In addition, neuroscientists are finding that "brain" neurotransmitters exist in nearly all types of peripheral tissues (Pert, 1997). Dopamine and serotonin are the most likely candidates for our clinical experiences, wherein touch renders clients more focused and emotionally stable, and also helps to generate (usually pleasant) moods (Damasio, 1996). It is interesting that the neurotransmitter norepinephrine, generally connected with the sympathetic stress response, also increases in connection with touch. The reason for this is that norepinephrine also has the ability to control the "positive" side of alertness, the ability to stay awake and stay focused. This means that being touched makes you become more present (awake and focused), which is one of the goals of therapy.

### Cortisol

Cortisol is a steroid hormone produced in the adrenal cortex. Cortisol is important in acute stress responses, promoting the mobilization of glucose to working muscles and to the brain, and also speeding up the heart rate. However, if the stress response becomes chronic, a problem can arise: chronically elevated cortisol levels eventually result in high blood pressure, cardiac illness, development of type 2 diabetes, depression, and even dementialike conditions in the brain (Henry, 1993a; Henry and Wang, 1998; van der Kolk, 2000; Vázquez, 1998). It is therefore important to note that several studies in both animals and humans have unambiguously shown that gentle touch and massage can lower the levels of cortisol (Field, Grizzle, et al., 1996; Field, Hernandez-Reif, et al., 1999; Field, Peck, et al., 1998; Field, Schanberg, et al., 1998; Field, Seligman, et al., 1996; Field, Sunshine, et al., 1997; Pauk et al., 1986; Leivadi et al., 1999). So, in order to reduce stress: you can touch and be touched.

### Summary of the Biopsychological Effects of Touch

Touch has been found to be a very efficient method of reducing anxiety and creating a sensation of ease and trust. This is a combined result of producing oxytocin, endorphins, and serotonin as well as regulating other hormones and muscular and nervous systems. The researcher Tiffany Field has long been researching and promoting the benefits of touch in her books *Touch Therapy* (2000) and *Touch* (2003).

Seen from a therapeutic perspective, touch can often strengthen the contact between client and therapist—and help to teach the client better social interaction skills to use in his or her life outside the therapy room. The production of oxytocin, supported by dopamine, helps to achieve this for both client and therapist.

Touching can promote the learning ability of the client through the combined action of oxytocin, the decrease in cortisol level, and the activation of the parasympathetic part of the autonomic nervous system. Touching is one of the ways to support a more internal focusing/presence in the client, assisted biochemically mainly by the release of dopamine and norepinephrine.

Touching also promotes the client's capacity for "staying in" (enduring) high-intensity situations, as the production of oxytocin helps the client experience the intensity as less dangerous. The endorphins can also elicit a feeling of being at your best or "peaking" in intense situations. Norepinephrine helps the client to be alert. Dopamine gives the feeling of satisfaction in this situation. Even cortisol has positive effects on short-term stress in situations of high intensity.

The combined effects of touch suggest that the client's ability to handle feelings, and his or her experience of self-esteem and personal dignity, are further increased. The therapist must therefore consider how to use touch in situations where any of the above themes are active, must be able to know the impact of any touch that he or she might use, and must see touch as an integral part of the goal for therapy, which, in the Bodynamic System,[55] is the

---

[55] Bodynamic Psychotherapy is a body-oriented type of psychotherapy.

building of new resources and the resolving of old issues that prevent one from achieving a satisfactory quality of life (Bentzen et al., 1997). These biopsychological findings match the results of our pilot study described at the beginning of this chapter.

## The Cutting Edge: New Theories Explaining the Impact of Touch

In recent years, two outstanding biomedical scientists, Candace Pert and James Oschman, have each presented integrative concepts detailing how all parts of the human body and mind interconnect, and also how touch influences the mind-body system via a series of bioelectrical and biochemical networks.

Candace Pert, the discoverer of the endorphin receptor in the brain and in the body, describes in her book, *Molecules of Emotion* (Pert, 1997) the concept of a biochemical information network as the agent of the relationship between touch, body, and emotions.

Soon thereafter, the renowned scientist in biophysics James Oschman describes in his book, *Energy Medicine* (Oschman, 2000) the concept of an electromagnetic and structural information network as the agent of the relationship between touch, body, and emotions.

Together, they have been working on a unifying theory to explain how traumatic personal experiences are stored in these information networks and how this results in different degrees of malfunction in the mind and in the body. Furthermore, experimental studies regarding the ability of therapeutic touch to regenerate the malfunctioning networks are being performed.

Both researchers' findings are interesting from a Bodynamic perspective because the peptides act as chemical messengers in both the brain and in the body. The discovery of their significance opens up a set of possible explanations for a major research finding: that there is a relationship between hyperresponsive and hyporesponsive muscles (Fich and Marcher, 1997; Marcher and Fich, 2010) and their psychological content, respectively, explaining how this psychological function is available to the client as a resource, is held back or is rigidly enacted, or was given up or never learned (Bernhardt, 1997a, 1997b; Bernhardt et al., 1997).

Finally, there is a need for knowledge that will document the effect of different ways of touching, including the importance of touch therapies in relation to hyporesponsive and hyperresponsive muscles (Pert, 1997). This could be fundamental for establishing the scientific basis for Body Psychotherapy.

The work of Pert (1997) and Oschman (2000) provides an excellent basis for understanding the often-dramatic effect on psychic and somatic symptoms brought about by energy-based based healing systems—e.g., acupuncture and therapeutic touch. However, in order for healing to result in personal growth, the dissolving of old patterns, and the building of new resources, it is necessary as well for clients to be able to verbalize and to integrate their experiences and insights into personally meaningful frameworks. This is what Body Psychotherapy (which is much more than just a "touch therapy") does and where we believe the future of Body Psychotherapy lies.

## References

Bentzen, M., Jarlnaes, E., & Levine, P. (1997). The body self in psychotherapy. In I. Macnaughton (Ed.), *Embodying the mind and minding the body.* North Vancouver, Canada: Integral Press.

Bernhardt, P. (1997a). The art of following structure. In I. Macnaughton (Ed.), *Embodying the mind and minding the body.* North Vancouver: Integral Press.

Bernhardt, P. (1997b). Individuation, mutual connection and the body's resources (an interview with Lisbeth Marcher). In I. Macnaughton (Ed.), *Embodying the mind and minding the body.* North Vancouver: Integral Press.

Bernhardt, P., Bentzen, M., & Isaacs, J. (1997). Waking the body ego: Parts 1 & 2. In I. Macnaughton (Ed.), *Embodying the mind and minding the body.* North Vancouver: Integral Press.

Brinch, J., Bögeskov, J., & Elleman, K. (*2002*). *Hjernen og stress [The brain and stress].* Copenhagen: Aarhus Hjerneforum [Aarhus University].

Brodal, A. (1977). *Sentralnervesystemet* [The central nervous system] (3rd ed.). Oslo: Tatum Norli.

Daddona, M. M., & Haldar, J. (1994). Opioid modulation of oxytocin release from spinal cord synaptosomes. *Neuroreport, 5(14), 1833–1835.*

Damasio, A. (1996). *Descartes' error*. London: Papermac.

Damasio, A. (1999). *The feeling of what happens.* Orlando, FL: Harcourt.

Fich, S., & Marcher, L. (1997). *Psykologi og Anatomi [Psychology and anatomy]*. Copenhagen: Kreatik.

Field, T. (2000). *Touch Therapy*. Edinburgh: Churchill Livingstone.

Field T. (2003). *Touch*. Cambridge, MA: MIT Press.

Field, T., Grizzle, N., Scafidi, F., & Schanberg, S. (1996). Massage and relaxation therapies' effect on depressed adolescent mothers. *Adolescence, 31, 903–911.*

Field, T., Hernandez-Reif, M., Hart, S., Theakston, H., Schanberg, S., Kuhn, C., & Burman, I. (1999). Pregnant women benefit from massage therapy. *Journal of Psychosomatic Obstetrics and Gynecology, 19, 31–38.*

Field, T., Peck, M., Krugman, S., Tuchel, T., Schanberg, S., Kuhn, C., & Burman, I. (1998). Burn injuries benefit from massage therapy. *Journal of Burn Care and Rehabilitation, 19, 241–244.*

Field, T., Schanberg, S., Kuhn, C., Fierro, K., Henteleff, T., Mueller, C., Yando, R., & Burman, I. (1998). Bulimic adolescents benefit from massage therapy. *Adolescence, 33, 555–563.*

Field, T., Seligman, S., Scafidi, F., & Schanberg, S. (1996). Alleviating post-traumatic stress in children following Hurricane Andrew. *Journal of Applied Developmental Psychology, 17, 37–50.*

Field, T., Sunshine, W., Hernandez-Reif, M., Quintino, O., Schanberg, S., Kuhn, C., & Burman, I. (1997). Chronic fatigue syndrome: Massage therapy effects on depression and somatic symptoms in chronic fatigue syndrome. *Journal of Chronic Fatigue Syndrome, 3, 43–51.*

Henry, J. P. (1993a). Biological basis of the stress response. *News of Physiological Science, 8, 69–73.*

Henry, J. P. (1993b). Psychological and physiological responses to stress: The right hemisphere and the hypothalamo-pituitary-adrenal axis. An inquiry into problems of human bonding. *Integrative Physiology and Behavioral Science, 28, 368–386.*

Henry, J. P., & Wang, S. (1998). Effects of early stress on adult affiliative behavior. *Psychoneuroendocrinology, 23(8), 863–875.*

Ironson, G., Field, T., Scafidi, F., Hashimoto, M., Kumar, M., Kumar, A., Price, A., Goncalves, A., Burman, I., Tetenman, C., Patarca, R., & Fletcher, M. A. (1996). Massage therapy is associated with enhancement of the immune system's cytotoxic capacity. *International Journal of Neuroscience, 84, 205–218.*

Komisaruk, B. R., & Whipple, B. (1998). Love as sensory stimulation: Physiological consequences of its deprivation and expression. *Psychoneuroendocrinology, 23(8), 927–944.*

Leivadi, S., Hernandez-Reif, M., O'Rourke, M., D'Arienzo, S., Lewis, D., Del Pino, N., Schanberg, S., & Kuhn, C. (1999). Massage therapy and relaxation effects on university dance students. *Journal of Dance Medicine and Science, 3, 108–112.*

Marcher, L., & Fich, S. (2010). *Body encyclopedia*. Berkeley, CA: North Atlantic Books.

Nabeshima, T., Katoh, A., Wada, M., & Kameyama, T. (1992). Stress-induced changes in brain met-enkephalin, leu-enkephalin and dynorphin concentrations. *Life Sciences, 51(3), 211–217.*

Olausson, H., Lamarre, Y., Backlund, H., Morin, C., Wallin, B. G., Starck, G., Ekholm, S., Strigo, I., Worsley, K., Vallbo, Å. B., & Bushnell, M. C. (2002). Unmyelinated tactile afferents signal touch and project to insular cortex. *Nature Neuroscience, 5, 900–904.*

Oschman, J. L. (2000). *Energy medicine: The scientific basis*. New York: Churchill Livingstone.

Pauk, J., Kuhn, C., Field, T., & Schanberg, S. (1986). Positive effects of tactile versus kinesthetic or vestibular stimulation on neuroendocrine and ODC activity in maternally deprived rat-pups. *Life Science, 39, 2081–2087.*

Pert, C. B. (1997). *Molecules of emotion: Why you feel the way you feel*. New York: Scribner.

Pert, C. B., Ruff, M. R., Weber, R. J., & Herkenham, M. (1985). Neuropeptides and their receptors: A psychosomatic network. *Journal of Immunology, 135, 8205–8265.*

Rosenfeld, J. P. (1994). Interacting brainstem components of opiate-activated, descending, pain-inhibitory systems. *Neuroscience & Biobehavioral Reviews, 18, 403–409.*

Sachser, N., Durschlag, M., & Hirzel, D. (1998). Social relationships and the management of stress. *Psychoneuroendocrinology, 23(8),* 891–904.

Thoren, P., Floras, J. S., Hoffman, P., & Seals, D. R. (1990). Endorphins and exercise: Physiological mechanisms and clinical implications. *Medicine & Science in Sports & Exercise, 22,* 417–428.

Uvnäs Moberg, K. (1998). Oxytocin may mediate the benefits of positive social interaction and emotions. *Psychoneuroendocrinology, 23(8),* 819–835.

Uvnäs Moberg, K. (2000). *Lugn och beröring: Oxytocinets läkande verkan i kroppen* [Calm and touch: The healing effect of oxytocin on the body]. *Stockholm: Natur & Kultur.*

Uvnäs Moberg, K. (2003). *The oxytocin factor: Tapping the hormone of calm, love and healing.* Cambridge, MA: De Capo Press.

van der Kolk, B. A. (1994). The body keeps the score. *Harvard Review of Psychiatry, 1,* 253–265.

van der Kolk, B. A. (2000). The diagnosis and treatment of complex PTSD. In R. Yehuda (Ed.), *Current treatment of PTSD.* Washington, DC: American Psychiatric Press.

Vázquez, D. M. (1998). Stress and the developing limbic-hypothalamic-pituitary-adrenal axis. *Psychoneuroendocrinology, 23(7),* 663–700.

Wessberg, J., Olausson, H., Fernström, K. W., & Valibo, Å. B. (2003). Receptive field properties of unmyelinated tactile afferents in the human skin. *Journal of Neurophysiology, 89(3),* 1567–1575.

# 50

## The Empty Voice of the Empty Self

*On the Link between Traumatic Experience and Artificiality*

Tilmann Moser, Germany

Translation by Warren Miller

**Tilmann Moser** is perhaps the most prominent psychoanalyst from the German-language area to engage with the field of Body Psychotherapy. He was already a well-known and published psychoanalytic author when, under the influence of Al Pesso, he began to integrate enactments and other elements of Body Psychotherapy (for example, touch) into his work, and into his theoretical publications. At times, he was harshly criticized for these developments, an experience he has become accustomed to over the course of his many years as a passionate author. Since the 1970s, he has challenged the scientific establishment repeatedly with his critical and pioneering books.

Tilmann Moser is a literary scholar, journalist, sociologist, and political scientist. Following his psychoanalytic training at the Sigmund Freud Institute in Frankfurt, Germany, he was a lecturer in criminology and psychoanalysis at the law school of the Frankfurt University. He has been a psychoanalyst in private practice in Freiburg since 1978. Another focus of his work, aside from Body Psychotherapy, is the relationship between psychoanalysis, politics, and society. In this context, he has published on the toxic "sediments" in the deep layers of the psyche that are left over from the experience of the Third Reich, and how the consequences and effects of fascism and World War II continue to reverberate inter-generationally.

## On the Seventh Sense of the Body Psychotherapist

Despite stacks of literature on sensitivity, empathy, identification, and all the other manifestations of our ability to put ourselves into another person's mind (aside from introspection, i.e., our insight into ourselves), I have yet to come across a plausible explanation as to how these mechanisms actually work. Whereas research on sensation and perception has grown into a vast field, spanning multiple disciplines, the question of how and via which channels we receive information about the inner states and stirrings of others remains clouded in darkness. Infant research will likely shed some light on this issue, because the mother and child begin practicing such abilities early on, through a wide range of interactions. And it seems clear that these abilities depend upon a multitude of diverse perceptions; but how these are combined and integrated, although the sum of sensory-perceptual factors is not enough to account for the whole phenomenon?

However, my accumulated working experience allows me to increasingly trust that my sensitivity informs me accurately in most cases, and often it is possible to identify the "noise factor" in the case of misperceptions, such as conflicts, resistances, fatigue, as well as distractions.

Even while I was still working as a classical analyst, I was awed by the bandwidth of "data transference." Concordant and complementary identifications lead us into enactments, into relational scenarios with their scripts and associated affects, which reach us subliminally, as if in small-print stage directions. Brief, high-speed trial identifications, based on trial imitations, are likely to play an important role in orchestrating such scenarios. The ear of the analyst has also been thoroughly trained: through changes in tone and frequency, the client's voice communicates "affects" that we resonate with and that can thus be decoded and maybe even understood.

As we expand our perceptual repertoire through body therapeutic perspectives and body language, the question of how we use our own senses and other less-defined channels of empathic sensitivity gains importance. Nevertheless, the ways in which these channels of communication and their effects work becomes ever more mysterious.

If a well-trained "breath therapist" tries to give a practical explanation regarding the perceptive sources of his diagnostic information to a psychotherapist who has not developed this kind of tactile sensitivity, a beginner will soon find they are lacking an amalgamation of sensory perceptions, whereas such a mechanism is clearly functioning for the expert or the sensitive layperson. In practice, I often simply share the images that I associate with the currently constelled affective images, without particularly investigating where they may be coming from, and often enough they turn out to contain useful comments and even indications for the further development of the process.

Nonetheless, the challenge remains: how we can become more specific and explicit about the ways in which empathy works, the ways it is communicated, and what kind of body-mind processes it is based upon.

In researching the gap between my trust in my body therapeutic sensitivity on the one hand and my inability to precisely describe its factors on the other, I have come across a passage by the novelist Monika Maron (1991) that indicates to me that her knowledge is able to describe the kinds of processes that are central to the case study that I will present. I feel grateful for the sense of validation that comes from recognizing my own felt knowing reflected in her writings. She describes how we find our body involuntarily gripped by another person's emotion, specifically by affects that threaten to damage us, as they reside in the other, in a disordered interpersonal form, not "in me." The body and psyche of the "receiver" seem to be helpless, and therefore liable to fall back on a child's ways of coping, involuntarily imitating what cannot be kept away, kept outside, or excreted quickly enough.

In her novel, *Stille Zeile Sechs* (translated as "Silent Close No. 6"), which I recommend to anyone wanting to learn about the psychic processes in the former German Democratic Republic, she writes:

> On a crowded streetcar an old man was scolding his elderly wife for the bumpy ride: obviously, as if she was responsible. I was standing behind him and could clearly feel the vibrations of his angry body in the air between us. First they penetrated my skin, then my flesh, until they reached my heart, which, suddenly enraged, brought my blood to a boil. It shot through my veins with such force that I could hear it seething behind my eardrums. Just as this anger had invaded me, so now it shot out of me in the man's own grating tones. "What did I tell you, what did I tell you?" I repeated his last phrase like a parrot, startled by my own strange voice, and, when the man and woman looked around at me in disbelief, I tried to cover my words with a rasping cough. (Maron, 1993, p. 12f.)[56]

## A Case Study

There are many events in family life that may result in a child losing the possibility of surviving with a vibrant sense of self. A directly traumatizing event may shock the child, and overwhelm their ability to cope or to defend themselves. But trauma can also be embedded in the coping mechanisms that a family tries to employ in dealing with a traumatic event. This constitutes an additional traumatization, which can take many forms, including vicarious traumatization, abuse in the service of coping, assignment of supportive roles, etc. In any case, the "sacrifice of the vibrant self" can be an act of survival, or of deep loyalty: by empathically making themselves available, or by taking on certain roles apparently required by the system,

---

56  The translation of the Maron quotation was taken from the official English translation, *Silent Close No. 6* (1993).

the child may put themselves at the threatened family's disposal, although such sudden, radical, and confusing shifts in expectations tend to set up fundamental internal contradictions.

It may even be problematic to speak of an "empty self," even though the following case study suggests that kind of notion, because usually fragments of a false self fill the space that remains when the vibrant self is lost. Such fragments may contain vague memories of the pain involved, in terms of both the loss of self, as well as the inherent violence of denial or self-denial; the fear of this pain can emerge as fear of the next step in therapy—in more conventional terms, as resistance.

The term "empty self" is, of course, a mental construct. It conjures up an image of a place in which—by means of psychic violence—contents are changed and replaced. But it can also be associated with Balint's term "new beginning" (Balint, 1970): in particularly safe situations, with deepened trust in the therapist and a strengthened sense of hope that parts of the vibrant self can be recovered, a regression can ensue that goes beyond the fragments of the false self. Such a descent, however, does not automatically lead to the recovery of the vibrant self, or its renewed growth. In Eastern wisdom traditions, and in some of the more recent therapy approaches, stepping into the "void" or into "emptiness" signifies crossing a threshold or stepping into a liminal space that, without support or guidance, feels threatening and eerie, like an unspeakable poverty of the soul, and is accompanied by a deep sense of shame.

The following case study is of a patient who experienced traumatic shock through her father's sudden death when she was six years of age, but whose self had already been weakened by family tensions earlier. As her father had occupied a senior position, with a presence in the public eye, the patient learned early on how important it was to show "composure," to support the mother as a "dignified widow," to act in a "representative" way, to take responsibility for the younger siblings, and to suppress any ambivalence, grief, despair, protest, questions, expressiveness, etc. Symbolically, this manifested itself in the loss of an authentic voice. The patient was left without the ability to resist identification with other significant voices, such as the voice of the mother in a variety of moods, or the family's concert of voices.

A therapeutic challenge in the treatment of such disorders is the fact that the "true self" is often first recovered in feelings of despair, in sounds of lament, whimpering, and a kind of wailing that always brings with it the fear of going insane, or at least the fear of falling to pieces, that originally was defended against by the sacrifice of the vibrant self. The basic question then is: what kind of support is called for when the patient approaches the experience of her trauma and its aftermath?

Through the work of the Body Psychotherapist Albert Pesso (Moser and Pesso, 1998), I found, time and again, how important it is to find both concrete as well as symbolic "holding," a sense of footing and containment to secure against fragmentation, shattering, loss of control, and nameless fear and shame. As the stress level in a family increases, the level of empathy in the family environment decreases, and the subsequent lack of mirroring of the child's experience leads to an experience of terrible and terrifying loneliness. This is one of the reasons why Pesso views the figure of the "witness" as playing such an important role in his therapy groups: the witness represents a figure who recognizes the past inner conditions of the patient, mirrors these back, and offers support, if this role is not played by another figure in the system.

If the therapist is able to maintain the steady conviction that going through the emptiness is not the end of all activity in the psyche, as patients sometimes fear, the way to the recognition of the shock is not that far off. Then a sense of deep hurt emerges, not only through the original events themselves, but through the fact that they since contributed to the patient living a "derivative," inauthentic existence. This can be the case in situations where an important person was lost, even though they may have been primarily hated. A fragmented, secret love was drowned out by so much hatred and disappointment that the death was also experienced as a relief, something that could never be admitted. The repression of the guilt associated with this sense of relief in the midst of the dignified enactment of the family "tragedy," which was acutely threatened by social degradation, called for an additional expenditure of energy, further weakening the vibrant self. The hurt is based on the fact that a person—although long gone and partially unloved—has continued to dominate the course of life and direct its inauthenticity.

On the somatic level, many body therapists recognize shock as a partial freezing of embodiment. Hilarion Petzold (1985) even speaks of a "*de-carnation*" from the body. Sometimes, only certain areas of the body have become numb and expressionless. I have found *interaction within regression* to be the most useful form of support in working with such issues, and this kind of work often needs to happen before symbolic-verbal work can take place.

## The Patient

"Victoria" was a student in her early thirties, studying business administration and having great difficulties in taking her final exam. Although the oldest of three siblings, she did not have a degree. Shortly after starting college, she had lost her father in an accident. He had been a dynamic, loud, and expansive manager who had often been insensitive in relationships with members of the family.

He had also studied business administration. What pained her was that, in her course of study, she felt destined to turn into a man—business administration is a man's world. If she wanted to be successful in her studies, she basically could not be a woman. But that was not the only reason why she still needed to remain "stuck": she continued to be in a symbiotic relationship with her mother.

The mother had made Victoria into a surrogate partner, and now she was feeling the relationship was at risk of being lost. She could hardly differentiate herself from her mother. Every time the mother visited her, Victoria felt out of balance for the next few days, and when the mother called, which happened a lot, to share her worries and successes in the newfound women's work she is doing, Victoria felt unbalanced for the next couple of hours. As Victoria also felt responsible for her younger siblings, with all her attention and empathy directed toward the family, she had remained unaware for a long time that she had no sense of herself.

Only recently in therapy (which had now lasted about fifteen months, one hour per week) could she express how angry she feels toward her brother, who "took advantage" of her care and help while he was doing his studies, and then, after graduating, moved to a different city and now does not even think about returning the favor and helping her. She also feels anger toward her mother, who selected her (the patient) to be the "problem child," and calls Victoria's professors, friends, (and initially myself as well) to tell these people about the fate of her "oversensitive" child, and thereby directs her life from afar. After a number of arguments between mother and daughter, the mother seems to begin to respect Victoria's growing independence, but she still sometimes suddenly overruns these new boundaries, as if to test her receding power once in a while.

In a brief summary of the transference constellation, and its unfolding to date: the sudden death of her father continued to overshadow Victoria's life completely, although for a long time she was unable to acknowledge this. Both her preconscious and conscious mind were occupied by memories of his strictness, roughness, and occasional acts of cruelty. Other memories, close to consciousness, include scenes of her being driven to school in the morning, like a princess in a grand automobile, or her father taking her along to visit customers, or showing her off to his friends.

During the first six months of therapy, a tenacious "princess" fantasy dominated the work, and, according to this, everything should fall into her lap effortlessly. Over time, the loss of her father seems to have even strengthened her sense of entitlement, so that, for a long while, she dreamed of a celebratory reinstitution of her special rights and status (as a "princess") of times past. The father now is less a remembered and internalized relational figure than a guarantor of her elitist status, and is also an archetypal macho-ruffian whose mighty paw on the back of her neck continued to be very "alive" in association with feelings of punishment or threat.

Victoria has remained childlike in parts of her personality. She presents herself as caring and easy to care for, a real sweetheart, and she can experience negative feelings only in the form of sudden, impulsive breakthroughs of "beastliness," or cutting contempt for people with poor taste or lack of intelligence. At times, this contempt hit me out of the blue, so that I found myself taken aback, and cringing with bad feeling. She could be truly and openly mad only when she perceived men making crude transgressions—occasionally, small mistakes on my part would be followed by a mix of sizzling rage and biting contempt.

This led to another person who played a central role in shaping her worldview regarding the psychology of men: not long after the death of her father, a neighbor began a sexual relationship with her mother in their apartment. This relationship was no secret to the children, and had an insistent and compulsive ambience, with the neighbor alternately threatening and courting the children in an atmosphere that the patient experienced as "slimy and disgusting." When she heard the unintelligible and threatening sounds of sexuality coming through the thin walls of her room, the uncontained arousal kept her under its spell, even against her will.

Since then, any form of touch with a man was immediately sexualized as a woman victimized by the ruthless greed of a man out of control. This version of events was also likely to serve to prop up the image of the mother, which otherwise would have become shaky. In the beginning, there were long periods when I seemed to disappear in the image of a salacious predator, only out to get her. Her fear of falling victim to me, should she allow her affection for me to grow, at times made her freeze.

Entirely split off from this hyper-sexualized witness-child, a younger part of herself also began to emerge, connecting with the time before the father's death. This part showed a need for dependency and trust, but also she always had to stay on guard to protect herself against the rough grasp of the father, and the immense emotional pain of being laughed at and ridiculed if she did not meet the father's expectations.

Very early on, at the age of two, her newborn brother displaced her from her former position as the "princess." For the brother, it was easier to identify with the image of the father as a brute, and Victoria continues to describe her brother as "unbearably robust" and still insensitive to this day.

After nine months of weekly individual therapy, I invited her to join one of my Pesso therapy groups (Moser and Pesso, 1998) in addition to her individual sessions. At first, she felt very isolated and awkward, but, after a few months, she was able to integrate herself quite well and now is proud of her "new family." Initially, it was difficult for her to find a place for herself between the two aspects of my dual role, as an empathic individual therapist attending solely to her on the one hand, as well as the stage director of a therapy group on the other.

Equally difficult, but very rewarding each time another small step was accomplished, was the work with the body. The first touch occurred with us sitting back-to-back on the rug when I invited her to allow herself to lean into me for a change, as opposed to taking the role of supporting and carrying others—i.e., the rest of her family. We had spoken and fantasized about this for a while. Finally, she wanted to give it a try. Although I kept myself upright, she had the strong body sense that I was leaning on her in a roughshod way, misusing her to prop me up. She kept having this sense as we continued exploring this experience. Only after repeating the experiment in front of a wall mirror was she able to see that an emotional experience from her childhood and youth had led to a profound distortion in her bodily perception. In this way, a series of somatic interactions with me, which she survived without getting hurt, slowly supported her trust that it was indeed my goal to help her reenter her disowned and estranged body, for her own sake.

The constellation of a narcissistically abused, strongly parentified, and sexually overstimulated female patient with a male therapist is bound to lend Body Psychotherapy a sense of walking on a tightrope, although it can also be particularly useful in facilitating progress in such a difficult case. Any newfound sense of self arising from such interactions, and providing an alternative to the originally wounding experience, is embedded as a physiological imprint, so to speak, which leads to relearning on a fundamental level: the fear that has been felt and survived in relationship turns into a sense of hitherto unknown security, calm, and trust. The therapist always risks being viewed with suspicion, and being massively attacked for making minimal mistakes. He does, indeed, enter the role of seducer, but only partially so, and with the intention of providing experiences of touch that can transcend the old, dominant, internalized patterns and expectations, and, in regression, replace them with new models of fathering or mothering. It is unavoidable that both patient and therapist will, at times, fall into unpredictable holes, as old bodily "engrams" will unexpectedly activate patterns, when innocuous and harmless physical touch—especially in previously untouched areas of the body—can suddenly awaken old fears and memories.

This is one reason why Body Psychotherapy can sometimes turn dramatic, with intensive forms of touch or interaction prompting sudden changes in the transference. A push into regression (or progression) can feel like a fast ride on the elevator of life history, from one developmental age to another. Suddenly, a generally positive transference can flip, in fear and panic, into the perception of the therapist as a mean, depraved, and cruel tyrant. We could say that the therapy of this young woman is indeed a story of ongoing careful and well-considered "transgressions" with the goal to help her learn to experience them no longer as transgressions but as beginnings of new, almost unknown forms of interaction that will eventually lead to a new "map of expectations."

## Victoria's Thirty-fifth Session: Voice Practice

The patient arrives, and I take her waddling, ducklike style of walking as an indication that she is quite far removed from herself. Unconsciously, she presents herself as a droll child in the company of imaginary observers. In the past, such behavior was probably met with mocking or patronizing approval. At the same time, she seems to broadcast something along the lines of *"See, I'm not a woman yet. I'm a waddling duck."* The short walk from the door to the armchair also conveys an obvious, although unconscious, salacious tone. She *does* call attention to her femininity, deformed as it may be, but in a way that is reduced to sexuality: suddenly her pelvis seems to have acquired a life of its own, moving in an ever-so-subtle obscene and provocative way. I perceive something completely different, unconnected, foreign stacked on top of her pelvis: the prepuberty torso of a boy, which—in turn—is surmounted by the head of a young girl, whose locks embrace it with the charm of a young boy.

I find a massive split: what I see is reminiscent of a child playacting a particular, single feature of adult sexual expression that she deems as attracting attention and interest. On the very top, sits the head, from which emanates a flat and alienated voice. The short walk conveys an intensive mixture of seductiveness and complete, childlike innocence. When her boyish features had been noted in a previous session, she reported that, at the age of eight, she had had an intense, adoring friendship with a neighborhood boy who was something of an idol to her. She also recalled later times, when she wished she was a boy, in part because this would have made it easier to protect her mother as the precociously competent substitute husband, and in part because she was convinced that she would have had more chances for affection from the father at an earlier age.

My clearest images are these: I see her dancing on the large, colorful rug in the center of the room, and I am witnessing her with an encouraging attitude. Then I realize that this is a utopian idea that lies far in the future, a kind of wish fantasy of mine, longing for the realization of her dormant feminine charm. At present, it is so fragile that any outward demonstration of it would require me standing next to her and supporting her to lessen her self-consciousness. But it is clear to me that this isn't possible yet: she would interpret such contact as eroticized seduction, or as a "presentation" of the princess by the vain father.

As my thoughts linger on the image of a vibrant girl who is hiding behind these dissociated fragments of identity, she continues to talk hurriedly, with a breathless, flat voice, about her studies, family, a friend of hers, and memories of an ex-boyfriend that she continues to dream of once in a while. Cautiously, I feedback to her the alienated tone of her voice. Immediately, she misunderstands, assuming I want to tell her how ugly her voice is. I tell her that is not what I meant, feeling somewhat startled by the intensity of the disapproval she is expecting—as if I had intended a degree of exposure that seems cruel to me, and suddenly lends to my presence a sadistic complexion. I therefore emphasize that my comment was not at all intended as critical, but as caring, and that she herself might sense that her voice had somehow gotten lost, or become estranged. I remind her of previous sessions when we had identified her voice as being like that of her mother or brother. She agrees, relieved, and turns the whole encounter into a positive experience, as if to quickly get away from the shame. She tells me she is good at imitating voices, but sometimes she gets stuck with one of them and can't shake it off.

Having just returned from an exhausting one-week trip, I am aware that my own voice is not fully present either, which seems to make me particularly sensitive, perhaps via identification, to the way in which her voice seems to have lost all its vitality. As I share with her that I feel somewhat distant from my own voice, and that this might be why I am particularly sensitized, she responds, very awake, clear, but not without heart: *"Yes, usually your voice is fuller and more impudent, but when I listen to you today, you sound like you're reading a newspaper."*

She is satisfied to have noticed it, to have been able to put it so well, and to find that we now share the same issue, and she is not alone with her "disappeared" voice. Historically, she is accustomed to swallowing mean, critical, or gloating comments, in particular from a long-term, critical-pedagogic friend of hers who was constantly nagging at her. I am listening on two levels, the "content" and the "musical" level, and that is why I am not certain whether she brought up the following issues before or after our conversation about voice: she says that she is so low-maintenance and easily malleable that she does things for others that she does not really want to do, only to keep their approval. She finds it very difficult to set limits in relation to her mother when they speak on the phone. Basically, the only way to set limits that works for her is to avoid contact altogether. Then she says that she had a dream the night before, which she has had a number of times. In her dream, she feels surprised and frightened as she finds out that she has unknowingly committed herself to something in the past, such as to sleep with a man, and this man is now standing outside her door, insisting on his right to enter and demanding that she fulfill her commitment.

Waking up in the morning, she feels very insecure, thinking that the man might really be there, waiting for her at the front door. Then she is very unhappy with herself: although she cannot remember making such a commitment, she can imagine herself making such promises, giving her word about the future, in order to buy herself some time and get out of an uncomfortable present. Often, when her sense of self-worth is low, she thinks that the only way of possibly becoming interesting to men is through sexual flirtation.

I silently ponder the interpretation whether a part of her might actually be drawn toward such a compromising union, as it would also relieve her of any sense of responsibility once the commitment is made. But, although this partially rang true, I dismissed it—my feeling was it did not mesh with the overall emotional climate of the session. Victoria seemed to me so much like a toddler that I concluded that this is not an actual erotic longing or fear, but something developmentally earlier that is only cloaked in the image of sexual union. Possibilities might include: intensive cuddling with the mother; parental care of personal hygiene; or gentle or rough-and-tumble contact with her father. Although occurring at a younger age, such longings are fraught with their own fears, because the father, in his inconsistent visits home, used to grab her whenever he felt like it, to briefly shower her with insensitive touch, whereas her mother was almost completely untouchable. To this day, this dichotomy makes it difficult for her physically to express gentleness, or to allow it, especially in relation to other women.

She feels reluctant to explore her voice, while simultaneously giving clear signs that I'm on the right track. She whimpers and experiments with soundings of lament, in effect saying, *"How can you possibly want to engage with this feeble remnant of a voice?"* Other quiet signals contribute to confirm the relevance of the topic. Alongside, her demeanor conveys something like "How can you do something so cruel as to take note of my voice? This can only lead to some kind of torture!"

To stabilize this shaky situation and give her some ground to stand on, I sketch out my attitude toward her: perhaps occasioned by the break in meetings during the previous week, she, Victoria, might have lost something important, something precious that might never have been securely hers in the first place: her own voice. I would endeavor to help her recover it, although searching for it might be difficult and embarrassing at times, as she might have to begin by making whimpering sounds. I might have to hold her, to help her not to get lost and not feel too ashamed. In response, she gets up from her chair and sits down on the rug. This clear sign of regression gives me the sense that she is ready to go along, but that she also needs protective guidance, along with ongoing explanations of where we are and what the next step might be.

Again, she gets into telling stories and speaks of her mother, but her voice meanwhile remains flat; the "patient" is not emotionally present, but speaks of herself, monotonously, as if talking about someone else. Her storytelling includes tales about her voice, which—at times—has gotten lost altogether. I tell her that it might be better to wait until she can clarify these connections at some later date, when she has grown stronger.

I share my images with her: in my mind's eye: I see her lying on the couch on her side, with my back sitting against hers, an arrangement between us that is familiar to her; or I hold her head while she explores the sounds of her voice; or as she initially does not want to look at me, she is sitting at the side of my chair looking in the opposite direction from me, out the window, and she puts her hand on my arm to explore the contact.

Sharing my images with her has multiple purposes: it allows her to feel and fantasize herself in my images and their relational offers, and it gives her time to examine them and let them resonate with her. It gives her the opportunity to appraise my affective state and my degree of equanimity, and creates space to attend to sudden transferential fears before she engages in any concrete interaction of this sort.

Without much deliberation, she chooses to lie down. Repeatedly she asks reproachfully, resigned, helpless: *"How am I supposed to do it?"* As soon as she is lying on the couch, facing the wall, and I am sitting there alongside her, she starts to nag in a clenched sort of way, and whine in an aggressive tone. She jerks her back into mine, hits me, and squeals like a child who can express her rage only in a clenched and restrained way. I call this "squashed rage"—to myself. Then I ask her whether she can sense how much the "emergency brake" is on. At first, she does not understand what I mean, so I demonstrate it to her. Then, she understands. But she is still not able to voice a single strong, natural sound. On the contrary, she gets ever deeper into a rage that seems tight like a compressed tin can where the only way out is via a tiny blast hole, producing a high whirring sound. Her whole jaw seems tight. I ask her where she can sense her imprisoned voice, and whether she might be able to bring that part of her into contact with me, as it surely must be overcharged with all this tension. She responds, *"Only in my head, which feels like it's about to crack open."*

So, I offer to hold her head. She agrees verbally, but her body startles and retracts as if confronted by a big danger. Seeing her response, I say that her body's reaction looked like a message in "pantomime," based on the fact that we had encountered fears in relation to her head being held in the past, and her retraction appears to be a reminder of this, as if to say, *"You know how easily I startle in this area."*

I therefore let her know that I am going to get up, and I will then hold her head while sitting down in my usual chair, behind the couch. So, I put one hand on the pillow, inviting her to rest her head in it. Immediately, she begins to hit my hand with her head and laments that it does not hurt me, but her. She complains, "Your sausage fingers hurt. You are touching my face!" She has pulled her hair over her forehead and cheeks, so that I am only touching a thick curtain of hair. When a movement causes one of my fingers to touch her nose directly, she shows her fingernails like the claws of a cat, and scratches my hand, to teach me a lesson: *"Be warned!"*

Then she vigorously rubs her forehead and eyes. I offer to hold her forehead. To accept, she needs to spread out her hair again in order to prevent any kind of skin contact. Then she fights my hand, pushing like a bull, while intermittently voicing childlike, tight, and high-pitched sounds that remind me of Oskar Matzerath (of *The Tin Drum* by Günter Grass). In response to my question, whether she can also make lower-pitched sounds, she responds with a sad tone of voice, *"But can't you see? I cannot scare anyone. I'm the puny one. Everyone laughs at me!"* Then she asks me to demonstrate to her what a lower-pitched voice might sound like. This is progress. During earlier voice practices, I have always had to remain completely silent, as any sound from me seemed to bother her, or she took it as me mocking her, rather than as encouraging responses or as demonstrations inviting her to go deeper.

Her voice evokes pity in me, as well as disengagement: she is so imprisoned, thin, acidic, and helpless, but also mercilessly aggressive. I ask her whether she could scare me by becoming louder; she responds with a long, tense, high, and fearful sound of wailing. I mention Oskar Matzerath. She laughs in agreement. *"Yeah, I would have liked that: to sing a glass into pieces!"* Then she is silent, and I ask her how she experienced her scream. She tells me that it left her feeling very uncomfortable—as if fog or smoke were clouding her head. She describes her head as being very tense: *"The voice came only from the head, almost completely without any participation from the body."*

This scream occurred while I was still sitting at her head, and the sense of vertigo that followed led her to give me permission to hold her head properly. That calmed her down somewhat. Then her voice grew stronger as I was holding her head and she was pressing it against my hand; and even stronger, especially, after I proposed that she support her voice by movements of her whole body. As she tentatively bends and writhes, her voice gains some coordination with her movements. Previously, I had given her an idea of what this work might be about: the reintegration of voice, emotion, scene, movement, and the body. That had made sense to her, confirming our shared understanding by talking about these aspects as having fallen apart.

After this limited exploration of movement, as if matching it with her voice on a trial basis, she seems to get frightened and suddenly completely withdraws into herself, as if afraid of being beaten. She clasps her arms around herself and looks like a tightly wrapped bundle. I reflect this to her and she whimpers. I ask her if I may try replacing her binding, protecting hands and arms with mine.

The American Body Psychotherapist Albert Pesso, with whom I trained for several years, proposes that patients frequently use body language to signal their needs in terms of holding, touch, resistance, and interaction, making attempts to get these needs met, either concretely or symbolically. Consequently, he offers "scenarios" in which ideal parental figures offer such holding, comforting, or containing gestures. This principle is confirmed in my own practice, giving the patient whose gesture is picked up upon the sense not only that she is being empathically witnessed, but also that she is unconsciously making a useful contribution to the therapeutic alliance.

As she has already taken many risks in this session, and apparently continues to feel held, she agrees to let me hold her. I move back to sit by her side while she is turned toward the wall. I clasp her gently with my arms. As my attention continues to remain with her restrained voice, I ask her if she can free herself from my hold and make sounds along with that. She replies that she finds herself in a comfortable position, and that she does not feel inclined to move out of her "narrow" confinement. This leads me to propose that she take some time to take in that sense of comfort, even though the ring (of my arms) around her chest is quite tight. After a while, I comment that the ring seems like a symbol to me: she is paying for warmth and closeness by putting up with great limitations of movement, pressure, and restrictions of breath and voice. Surprised, she agrees. So, I increase the pressure a little, and now she uses her real strength to free at least one arm from my hold. Her voice becomes stronger and angrier, but also remains high-pitched and angry/helpless. This is "loving oppression" on my part, as when temporarily catching and restraining a child in one's arms to playact "getting away," or to entice resistance. The scene generates great intimacy. In struggling for her freedom, her voice fluctuates between fright and joy. When she rests, many images come back to her, memories of her father, who was very loud and whose roughness was frightening. She despised him for that, and this may be a deep reason for being unable to ever become really "loud." Her face looks entirely different now: less smooth—she is no longer the "user-friendly," pretty, girlish boy, but a rough child who looks strong and vibrant.

Earlier in the session, when she had failed to voice any kind of low-pitched sound, I had suggested that she might also try making ugly or mean sounds. This comes more easily to her—she spits out sounds, her mouth distorted, and really gets into it. But she also wants to hide herself, because she feels embarrassed. She partially buries her head under the blanket that lies next to her.

When she comes to rest again, still with her back turned toward me, she tells me that this is how she wakes up in the mornings, curled up like a fetus. But this posture does not calm her anymore; now she just hurts all over when she wakes up. She feels empty, like a transparent jellyfish. This description touches me, because I, also, see her as an absent presence of a woman, a shell without a center, sad and lacking substance, but still feeling that all the protective covers, including the layers of the false self, have now fallen off.

I think to myself: I have never seen the "empty voice" mirror the whole body-mind this clearly. She appears despairing, as if she has become completely unreal, having lost all her content and holding.

The effect of this powerful holding interaction seems paradoxical: it appears as if she has lost her vibrant self more than ever. But, in my opinion, the experience of feeling securely held, along with the discovery that it is possible to recover aspects of her voice, and thus her self, has enabled her to regress deeper, to a more basic level of self-loss, a place where even movement and struggle are of no avail, and only contact with another body serves to fuel a sense of being.

This consideration leads me to suggest to her that she needs "relational nurture": touch and holding by another, in order to absorb some substance. I propose that she turn around and—while lying down—wind herself around me. Although we have done this before, she laments, "How?" until I explain it to her once more. She curls her body around me, and starts whimpering again, but this time it sounds like "eating," taking in. She calms down, as if she were getting something; the tone gradually sounds more satisfied. I had told her that she could take me in like a jellyfish, or clasp me like an octopus does. As she is "fueling," she speaks of her states of emptiness, and how much she fears that in states like these she would do anything that is asked of her, in particular by men, to become whatever she is expected to be, not having anything to hold on to within herself. Then she asks me, almost enthusiastically, *"Does that mean I can learn to say, 'No, that's not possible right now!'?"* As I nod, she begins practicing, hissing at an imaginary man, *"'Leave me alone. Can't you see that I don't want that now? That's enough.' It took me long enough to feel that, and to find the courage to say that!"*

Near the end of the session, she asks me once more why I was so focused on her voice in this session, and I repeat that it had stood out for me more than usual today, perhaps because (for me) it was likewise. She takes this in with relief; this way she is not as alone with her disorder, which so often causes her to feel ashamed.

I tell her, *"It takes courage, sometimes even some impudence, like it was in your voice just now, to really say 'No' to someone you don't want to lose, or even to disappoint or anger such a person."* And she says, *"Until now, when I've said 'No,' I've made my voice so soft that it almost sounds like a 'Yes,' and no one is offended. But then some men don't hear my 'No' at all and pretend as if I hadn't said it."* So, I suggest that she practice voicing her "No" by imagining children who say "No," and scream, and perhaps even stomp their feet, but she says, *"I can't do that right now. I want to spit my No's into the other's eyes. He's supposed to get it, after all."* It becomes obvious that she holds a lot of pent-up rage: so many unspoken No's, linked with so much humiliation and self-loss, that she fears and hopes her future No's will be like bullets that return some of the humiliation that has built up in her. *"We'll have to continue working on that,"* she says as she leaves, and gives me a friendly slap on the shoulder on her way out.

I am left feeling lighter and enriched. I feel much more present, resting within myself, and no longer worrying that I might become an empty jellyfish myself during the remaining three therapy sessions of that afternoon.

## References

Balint, M. (1970). *Therapeutische Aspekte der Regression: Die Theorie der Grundstörung* [Therapeutic aspects of regression: The theory of the basic disorder]. Stuttgart: Klett-Cotta Verlag.

Maron, M. (1993). *Stille Zeile Sechs* [Silent Close, No. 6]. Frankfurt: S. Fischer Verlag.

Moser, T., & Pesso, A. (1998). *Strukturen des Unbewussten* [Structures of the unconscious]. Frankfurt: Suhrkamp Taschenbuch.

Petzold, H. (1985). *Leiblichkeit* [Corporeality]. Paderborn: Junfermann.

# SECTION VII

# Clinical Aspects of the Therapeutic Process

# 51

## Introduction to Section VII

Gustl Marlock, Germany, and Halko Weiss, United States

Translation by Warren Miller

In Section VII, the clinical practice of Body Psychotherapy will be explored in greater detail. It will therefore be useful to illuminate some of the general facets that are relevant to the clinical practice of Body Psychotherapy a little more comprehensively, as well as those that permeate the variety of treatment approaches.

When proceeding systematically, the question that arises first is one of effective diagnostics. This was touched upon earlier in Section IV, Somatic Dimensions of Developmental Psychology. Many Body Psychotherapists, influenced by Humanistic Psychology, prefer descriptive forms of psycho-diagnostics instead of the more classical medical-psychiatric format. This diagnostic stance assumes that the overall picture of a disorder truly reveals itself only gradually during the therapy, and that the therapist's "diagnosis" therefore emerges progressively in collaboration with the client over the course of the whole therapeutic process.

In Chapter 52, "The Relevance of Body-Related Features and Processes for Diagnostics and Clinical Formulation in Body Psychotherapy," **Frank Röhricht** examines a more rigorous diagnostic form, stemming from his perspective of being the chief physician in a psychiatric clinic, and from the fact that such diagnostics are required in the context of medical health care. The chapter shows how a systematic assessment and evaluation of body-related characteristics can improve the quality of clinical diagnosis.

In Chapter 53, "The Role of the Body in Emotional Defense Processes: Body Psychotherapy and Emotional Theory," **Ulfried Geuter** and **Norbert Schrauth** deal with a central and characteristic concern of Body Psychotherapy—namely, the question of defense against affects. They show the central role that the body plays, both in the regulation and in the repression of these. Dissociation, or a more general regulation of affective experience, and how to work with these affects through the body, in turn, can provide effective access to these emotional experiences that have shaped the client's psychotherapeutic process.

In Chapter 54, "The Spectrum of Body Psychotherapeutic Practices and Interventions," **Ilse Schmidt-Zimmermann** presents a synopsis of the range of methods and the breadth of intervention techniques that Body Psychotherapists can draw upon. As already mentioned, it is quite difficult to organize this methodological material in a sensible manner due to the enormous diversity in theory and practice, along with the divergences among different approaches and schools. To make her task even more complex, this handbook is not conceptualized to present the major therapeutic schools and their approaches, nor is it designed to provide operational instructions to therapists, but instead it is organized around themes that characterize the field as a whole. In this respect, Chapter 54 is of particular significance as it creates a systematic insight into the multiple dimensions of Body Psychotherapy's practical approaches.

This particular diversity also becomes evident in Chapter 55, whereas Chapter 54 focuses on an important differentiation: with the term "psychic structure," a new concept has been introduced into the theory of Psychodynamic Therapy that is used to describe a range of features that the self needs to regulate its relationship with itself and its environment: self-perception, self-regulation, object perception, attachment, communication, etc. The preoccupation with psychic structure has arisen in part through the observation that patients with severe psychosomatic disorders, personality disorders, and psychoses seem to benefit only from classic psychoanalytic interventions—to a certain extent. While the same lack of effectiveness can obviously apply to the classic exposing and deconstructing techniques of Body Psychotherapy, the significance of the question of how Body Psychotherapeutic stabilization techniques work becomes very important. These are techniques that build structure and strengthen the ego.

Due to its intensifying impact on affect, Body Psychotherapeutic work can easily trigger regression, as we have mentioned earlier. Therefore, Chapter 55, "Regression in Body Psychotherapy," by **Peter Geissler** critically examines the potential and dangers of regressive states, and addresses some of the misunderstandings that are widespread within the field of Body Psychotherapy—e.g., regarding the "inner child." His perspective builds more on a concept of "interactional transference," and less on the psychological model of developmental phases, which requires experiencing childhood states. It focuses on a model of "domains" that exist simultaneously and that can be activated through focusing attention in particular ways.

In Chapter 56, "The Unfolding of Libidinous Forces in Body Psychotherapy," **Ebba Boyesen** and **Peter Freudl** address both a historical and contemporary core aspect of clinical theory and practice in Body Psychotherapy, as well as in its metapsychology: the libido. The chapter's main concern is with the question of how the "unfolding" of libido (eros) can be facilitated therapeutically. The authors come from a background in the Biodynamic Psychology tradition, which, perhaps more clearly than other Body Psychotherapeutic approaches, maintains a tradition of thinking along the lines of libido concepts.

In Chapter 57, **Courtenay Young** addresses what is seen as particularly significant, yet what is often not discussed: "Risks within Body Psychotherapy," the main risks of Body Psychotherapeutic methodology that all of its practitioners should become more aware of. All methodologies carry some risks, and patients (or clients) can suffer damage if a therapist handles their therapeutic processes naively. The four main risks typical to Body Psychotherapy are: retraumatization; abusive touch; the breaking down of defenses; and inappropriate or malign regression. Accordingly, along with establishing a proper set of competencies in training, an awareness of the risks and good supervision are critical, if not essential, to ensure safe Body Psychotherapeutic practice.

# 52

## The Relevance of Body-Related Features and Processes for Diagnostics and Clinical Formulation in Body Psychotherapy

**Frank Röhricht, United Kingdom**

**Translation by Warren Miller**

**Frank Röhricht's biographical information** can be found at the beginning of Chapter 22, "'Body Schema,' 'Body Image,' and Bodily Experience: Concept Formation, Definitions, and Clinical Relevance in Diagnostics and Therapy."

Independent of the theoretical and practical orientations of specific schools of Body Psychotherapy, bodily experiences and self-experiences (perceptual, affective, cognitive, and psycho-motor aspects) and their systematic recording and subsequent analysis are an essential component of any form of Body Psychotherapy. Rather than referring to diagnostic criteria for the diagnosis of mental illnesses, according to the standard systems of diagnostic classification (DSM/ICD), the diagnostic perspective on bodily experiences aims to evaluate static, dynamic, and interpersonal body-related features as relevant cues to the patient's body and ego structure, sense of self, and patterns or modes of self-regulation.

Among the foundational theoretical discussions of the pioneers of Body Psychotherapy, considerations about diagnostic relevance of bodily features take a central position (for an overview, see Geuter, 2000). Simultaneously, these considerations indicate a close association between diagnostic and therapeutic processes. In 1933, Reich wrote his pioneering work, *Character Analysis.* In the context of his analysis of character resistances, he proposed that every bodily expression has a corresponding mental attitude and that this would allow one to draw conclusions about personality traits and psychic habitual reactions, and draw conclusions from an analysis of bodily structure (and vice versa). He described for the first time some of the physical (in particular, muscular) processes that participate in the psychic mechanisms of affect regulation and coined the terms "muscular armor" and "character armor." Around the same time and parallel to Reich, inspired by the developments in wellness and body pedagogics—specifically, the work of Gindler—movement-therapeutic approaches that paid close attention to restrictions in vital breathing and movement rhythms were also being developed. Representatives of modern expressionist dance contributed the first movement-analytical approaches to describe expressive contents and the situational significance of movement patterns. One such systematic approach was developed by Laban (1926, 1950), who defined specific categories of movement that can be examined and that form the matrix of therapeutic intervention strategies in Movement Therapy and Dance Therapy.

In Body Psychotherapy, just as in any other healing method, the indication for treatment and a phenomenological or process-oriented therapeutic approach is guided by its methodologically specific (in this case, body-oriented) diagnostic findings. As elsewhere in the clinical practice of psychotherapy, the diagnostic perspective is gradually extended toward a process-oriented analysis of a variety of factors, while paying particular attention to the quality and themes in the continuously changing therapeutic relationship. For instance, Dychtwald's description of his personal experience of discovering the Human Potential Movement can serve as an illustration of this approach toward bodily (or self-) experience:

> It is September 1970. I am standing naked in a room full of men and women of all ages. Dr. John Pierrakos, along with everyone else in the room, eyes my body with tense interest, . . . comes towards me and minutely examines the structure of my skin, and the overall state of my muscular system. He asks me . . . to walk about the room for him to observe my body in movement. In walking I am fully aware of my self-doubt and insecurity . . . After a while that seemed like an eternity, John Pierrakos proceeds . . . to talk about me . . . He describes my general attitudes towards life, love, personal relationships, movement, change, and performance . . . The scary thing about this whole experience was the fact that everything he said, every observation he made, every description he gave, was right on the money. (Dychtwald, 1981, p. 18)

This ideal/typical sketch outlines the basic elements of Body-Oriented Psychotherapeutic diagnostics:

- A rather static element of precise structural analysis, via tactile and visual information (posture, gesture, mimicry, skin coloration, physiognomy, muscular constitution, etc.)
- Assessment of body-oriented thoughts, emotions, and perceptions
- A dynamic element of movement analysis, transitioning into . . .
- A process element of the emerging, specific therapeutic relationship, as unfolding within the therapeutic encounter

As the Body Psychotherapeutic process advances, these diagnostic dimensions of bodily experience flow into one continuous process. In the early stages of therapy, formally descriptive and treatment-planning aspects, along with related working hypotheses, tend to be in the foreground.

As the process unfolds, the cognitive-analytical attitude with which the therapist aims to gain understanding is complemented by the reception of nonverbal, affective communications, which can be utilized as a source that provides "intuitive" understanding and impulses for intervention (in the sense of an interpretation).

In this context, it needs to be emphasized that any diagnostic appreciation of the living body—i.e., the soma—has to acknowledge the epistemological dilemma formed by the ambiguity between having and/or being a soma, making it difficult to describe the subjective experience of the body in precise scientific terms. The situation is further complicated by the complexity of the subjective experience of the living body as a whole. Using operationalized descriptive methods, objective assessment of lived bodily experience can only be artificially approximated. The process of research itself impacts on the subject matter inasmuch as the subjects are human beings responding to the nature of the situation and to the investigation process itself.

The investigation of body-related features usually starts with a body "history" (e.g., traumatic events, adversity, habits and manners, etc.). To allow for further theoretical elaboration, a systematic differentiation of diagnostic elements is used to organize the sections of this chapter:

- Structural analysis (posture, gesture, mimicry, skin coloration, physiognomy, and muscular constitution)
- Assessment of state- and body-related thoughts, beliefs, feelings, and perceptions
- Dynamically designed movement analysis
- Relational (interpersonal) behavioral analysis made up of situational body interpretations and analysis of nonverbal styles of communication (including aspects of "felt sense" and bodily countertransference)

In the context of clinical research, this is furthermore enriched through systematic assessments of partial aspects of bodily experience (body image, body schema, body cathexis), using a range of questionnaires and other instruments.

## Structural Analysis

As previously mentioned, the work of Reich (1933) has been foundational to efforts that aim to describe body-oriented analogies in a system of character structures. In character-analytical practice, we tend to perceive the functioning of the character armor in the form of a chronic, frozen, muscularlike bearing (p. 344).

This model interprets chronic muscular tensions, due to one-sided strain, in the sense of a fixed psychodynamic posture (physically and psychically), with regard to its defensive functions, avoidance strategies, and coping mechanisms (see also Chapter 27, "Shapes of Experience: Neuroscience, Developmental Psychology, and Somatic Character Formation" by Marianne Bentzen). In view of the flexible nature of the movement apparatus, the analysis focuses on the qualitatively different aspect of the specifically, one-sidedly overemphasized, static and isometric movement patterns (static postures, in particular). A variety of structural changes can be described. A lack of use of particular muscle groups or a hypertrophic exaggeration of muscular efforts may be observed. Even though, in specific cases, information can clearly be gained from the observation on the microscopic level of singular body segments, the actual diagnostically relevant picture emerges in the complex interplay of the resulting whole-body gestalt.

I have drafted a comprehensive system of relating muscular body structure and bodily expression and developed detailed suggestions with regard to possible corresponding interventions against the background of the available clinical knowledge and literature (Röhricht, 2000). This system initially presents tables describing the skeletal musculature in its anatomical directions and functions. These descriptions are then linked to bodily expressions that are potentially associated with a muscle or a group of muscles.

Next, the associated psycho-motor functions of chronic tensions—i.e., overemphasis—in the respective muscle groups are discussed. Finally, examples of possibilities for interventions that can be derived from such findings are sketched out, considering the available clinical knowledge base of practitioners' experiences. The large chest muscle, *pectoralis major*, can be mentioned as an example: for the most part, this muscle spreads between the upper aspect of the clavicle and sternum, the costal cartilage, and the upper arm; its anatomical functions include lowering of the raised arm forward, pulling the arm back toward the trunk, and assisting breathing while the arms are pushing.

I have also described the following psycho-motor functions: *"protection of the anterior and upper half of the body by means of contraction of the shoulders (i.e., protection of the area of the heart from direct contact, from attack/injury); also: breath-holding inward posture ('Depression-muscle'); in case of overdevelopment also: psychopathic 'inflation' of the (body-) ego"* (Röhricht, 2000, p. 223). I suggest that corresponding and potentially useful interventions include: *". . . work on the lateral insertion area, opening of the breath and heart-feelings (often mobilization of deep, held back sorrow, feelings of loneliness, neglect, neediness, and heightening of sensitivity as well as compassion, and ability to express love)."* Marcher and Fich (2010) have since published an even more comprehensive *Body Encyclopedia* as a "guide to the psychological functions of the muscular system."

In his comprehensive book review, Boadella comments on a particular problem with this system that is in accordance with the introduction given above: *"The overview is impressive and extremely helpful, given one doesn't use these exercises like a cook book and remembers Wilhelm Reich's warning that it is meaningless to simply press a muscle before one has established a good emotional contact with the function of the character-resistance of the client."* (Boadella, 2000, p. 144)

Interventions that address the body structure are numerous, necessitate a stabile therapeutic relationship, and call for comprehensive practical experience and solid anatomical knowledge on the part of the therapist. *"The notion of a muscular 'armour' that originally served as a defense against and a stabilizing protection from uncomfortable, painful and/or traumatic bodily feelings and experiences demands a careful diagnostic evaluation and weighing of the range of interventions and with respect to the question, if the patient is in a position yet to dispose of these structures, i.e., if the patient has the ability to generate alternative behaviors."* (Röhricht, 2000, p. 193)

I also emphasized the need for further empirical validation of the system that I drafted with reference to findings from experimental psychological affect research. In this regard, the Facial Action Coding System (FACS) studies by Ekman and others are of particular interest. Dornes underlines the significance of the relationship between bodily expression and emotionality for psychotherapy in emphasizing that *"the expression is itself part of the feeling and mentality . . . It is not only an indicator of the feeling, but an integral part of its constitution and as such contributes to the origination as well as to its maintenance"* (Dornes, 1993, p. 114).

In regard to the macroscopic physiognomy—i.e., the whole gestalt of a body posture—a few categorical ordering principles can be identified. Dychtwald (1981) lists so-called cardinal splits in body consciousness: front/back, above/below, right/left, trunk/extremities, chest/pelvis, and body/head. These perspectives can provide valuable indications pertaining to aspects of the personality: the degree of bodily integrity, proportion, balance, congruence, flexibility, consistence, overemphasis of individual aspects (for example, "inflated" chest with psychopathic character structure against the background of a narcissistic conflict; or a "compact," compressed appearance in the bodily structure due to chronically suppressed aggressive-negative impulses against the background of chronically oppressed self-assertion). He also describes observations on the interplay between physiognomy and self-expression. Using the case of two differently formed feet, he develops analogies about the "standing" of an individual—that is, his or her basic bearing in the world. Pelvic positions are discussed as they relate to psycho-sexual experiences and beliefs, and the relationship of the upper chest with the pelvis and the extremities is discussed in the context of personal needs and the degree of self-esteem.

Drawing upon systematic observation of behavioral patterns and findings from analytical Developmental Psychology, Neo-Reichian methods have further refined body-oriented structural diagnostic methods that describe the so-called character structures (schizoid, oral, anal, phallic-narcissistic, rigid, and psychopathic). In this approach, psychic and bodily features are organized into schematic syndromes that are associated with respective character types. Following Reich and Lowen, the diagnostic categorical description can offer cues about likely typical developmental traumas. In this spirit, Lowen (1992) describes behavioral patterns as rigid and predetermined reactions of an individual as an answer to recurrent psychic traumas or crises.

In his book *Character Analysis,* Reich had previously illustrated how much character dispositions and muscular dispositions overlap. He viewed the character tendencies as serving a function—namely, avoidance of (emotional) pain and discomfort. This was regarded as a significant maneuver in the reestablishment—that is, maintenance—of psychic equilibrium. The structures associated with the patterns of chronic discomposure of a psychic and physical-muscular nature ("muscular armor"), on the other hand, led to marked loss of function, or in other words, limitations in psycho-motor agility/fluidity and hence a loss in creativity. In the frame of this chapter, this characterology, which is described in detail elsewhere, can only be outlined briefly. Using the example of "schizoid character structure," we can follow Lowen's (1992) description: The head appears somewhat disconnected from the neck segment, creating an expression of distancing with deep-seated tensions of the muscles at the base of the skull; the face appears masklike, cold, and immobile; the body doesn't take part in interacting and expressive behaviors, and the joints (in particular, the ankles) are often stiffly held: there is an above/below split. In the opinion of these authors, the person's bodily structure corresponds with a psychic attitude of emotional coldness and withdrawal, associated frequently with a biographical background of traumatization of existential needs early in the development of the ego. In accordance with Boadella's warning, Petzold stresses the limits and constraints of this type of approach:

> The stable frame of reference for interpretation that is given through characterology, and the biographical background associated with the character structures

also determine the quality of the therapeutic relationship . . . and this is where the problem with this approach lies: viewing individuals in classes of types narrows the variability of human reality . . . and in that specific structures are paired with a specific set of interventions including techniques and exercises a pathologically oriented "maintenance" of the body is suggested. (Petzold, 1988, pp. 292–293)

Here it becomes apparent how much a diagnostic categorization of psycho-pathological phenomena, along the lines of the medical model of illness (*morbus*), can lead to a dilemma in the psychotherapeutic context. Such a perspective can lead to a mechanistic therapeutic approach at the cost of adequate and situationally derived therapeutic work with dynamic processes and conflictual themes. Therefore, it seems imperative to collaborate with the patient in treatment planning—for example, to set the goals of therapy collaboratively at the onset of treatment so that the diagnostic proceedings can be oriented toward these goals. A phenomenologically or symptom-oriented approach that consciously aims to treat specific disorders, forgoing process-oriented work on a potentially underlying conflict, can in individual cases justify a focused diagnostic perspective. In other words, Petzold's critique of the Reichian and Neo-Reichian method of "body reading" for the purpose of categorization of psychic structures, in consideration of its narrowing of the diagnostic perspective, carries an important factor for consideration. It is, however, in my opinion applicable only if the therapeutic approach isn't disorder-specific, but predominantly follows a process-oriented, psychodynamic paradigm of exploration and change. This dynamic characteristic contravenes the concept of an immutable character structure.

## Assessment of State- and Body-related Thoughts, Beliefs, Feelings, and Perceptions

Considering the particular significance of bodily experience as a determining factor for self-experience, body-related phenomena are assessed descriptively in the contexts of research and clinical settings. Assessment of bodily signs and symptoms against the background of descriptions of typical impairments in bodily experience with specific disorders has proved to be diagnostically relevant with some psychiatric disorders such as anorexia nervosa and schizophrenia (for an overview see, among others: Fisher, 1986; Röhricht and Priebe, 1997, 1998). These findings have led to the development of integral, disorder-specific, and phenomenologically oriented therapeutic approaches (see, for example: Röhricht, 2000).

Due to inconsistent theoretical conceptualizations and a resulting lack of clarity in definitions, the clinical significance of bodily experience remained vague for a long time. Only since the end of the 1970s and beginning 1980s (for example: Shontz, 1974; Meermann, 1985; Bielefeld, 1986), efforts to formulate standardized definitions of terms can be noted (for example: Thompson et al., 1990). Subsequently, a multimodal approach that aims to assess multiple dimensions of subjective bodily experience has gained wider acceptance (Röhricht, 2006). In addition, operationalized definitions of disturbances in bodily experience have come to serve as criteria in the context of Body Psychotherapeutic outcome evaluation (Röhricht, 2000, 2009).

The assessment of therapeutically relevant aspects of bodily experience (indication, contraindication) begins with an individual body-related narrative. It includes the gathering of information about current bodily complaints and illnesses, past medical history including surgical procedures, and the history of accidents and traumas/adverse incidents (e.g., sexual and physical abuse, termination of pregnancy, etc.). Information about the use of medications and other medical treatment will be gathered, with particular reference toward detection of contraindications for specific exercises in bodywork as well as with regard to any significant impairment or disability potentially impacting upon body perception or mobility. Information on general bodily self-care provides further important cues in respect to the patient's relationship to their body. Habitual daily practices, diet, bodily activities (exercising/sports, gymnastics, etc.), sexuality, and the usage of alcohol, nicotine, and illicit drugs should be assessed. Additionally, other relevant bodily experiences are inquired about—for example, changes of the body during puberty or in the context of pregnancy or during the aging process, as well as atypical behavior during childhood—for example, stuttering, bedwetting, and prolonged thumb sucking.

The primary orientation for the planning of further systematic assessment derives from the characteristics of the respective target population. For example, the assessment design for a group of patients diagnosed with psychosis or, more specifically, schizophrenia should take marked dissociative phenomena, (body-)ego impairments, and perceptual impairments into particular consideration, whereas the assessment of patients with depression and anxiety disorders should pay particular attention to commonly found negative cognitions and disorders of affect, as they color the patient's cognitive and affective evaluation of his or her body. In regard to the assessment of bodily experience in general, it needs to be taken into consideration that bodily experience is influenced by basic rhythms and moods, such as the menstrual cycle or seasonal fluctuations in affective self-evaluation. Röhricht (2011) proposed a body-oriented classification of main mental disorders on the basis of phenomenological findings regarding dysfunctional body-mind regulation in response to maladaptive adjustment processes; in this system, patterns of body-mind affect regulation distinguish between embodied disorders (i.e., the body as a burden, overemphasized and lasting as in major neuroses, depressive, anxiety, and somatoform disorders) and disembodied disorders (i.e., the dissociated, split-off, disintegrated "fleeting body in passing" as in psychotic disorders such as schizophrenia); between those polar manifestations, he identified a group of alternating body-mind dysregulation with severe objectifying instrumentalization of the body (i.e., personality disorders). These distinctions can pave the path for a new, syndrome-specific conceptualization of systematic, disorder-specific intervention strategies in Body Psychotherapy.

In order to capture the influence of such factors, the structured assessment of aspects of bodily experience should always include an open interview, which provides patients with the opportunity to describe their bodily self-experience spontaneously. Joraschky and colleagues (1998) describe this as the "narrative element," and emphasize that specific associations can be relevant symbolizations of personal conflicts.

**Overview of Available and Common Methods of Assessment**

Among the methods available for the assessment of bodily experience, we distinguish between projective, verbal (mainly questionnaires), and perceptive methods. Röhricht and Priebe (1998) and Thompson and colleagues (1990) further differentiate between aspects that are of neurophysiological nature belonging to the field of psychology of perception (perception, sensation, autonomic nervous system), and aspects such as cognitions (thoughts, fantasies, concepts, attitudes), emotions, and psycho-motor behaviors (movement patterns, mimicry, gesture, posture, and expressive behaviors).

To my knowledge, structured assessment tools are currently mainly used only in the behavioral branch of Body Psychotherapy (see, for example: Görlitz, 1998). Probably one reason for this is the theoretical concept underpinning the cognitive behavioral approach, lending itself to a more positivistic, empirical approach, in contrast to Body Psychotherapy, which has a predominantly depth-psychological or psychodynamic orientation. Yet, the development of the Operationalized Psychodynamic Diagnostics (OPD) system can be viewed as an example of an increasing recognition that such a diagnostic approach can be utilized in other schools of therapy as well. Among the multitude of assessment instruments that have been developed in the context of research, the following, which will be outlined briefly, present themselves as clinically useful for Body Psychotherapy.

The Draw-a-Person test (Machover, 1949) specifically refers to the body, in that a free drawing of the body structure ("gestalt") of the person is used as an assessment tool for the diagnosis of personality traits. The underlying rationale is that the self-image finds expression in the body image. In a similar fashion, the Body Image Sculpture Test (Joraschky et al., 1998) can provide nonverbal information on bodily experiences. In this projective test, the test subjects are instructed to mold a human body using clay (initially with eyes closed, followed by alterations with visual control). This clay figure is then structurally analyzed in accordance with a formal process that provides quantitative and qualitative data. The test is used for assessment of the body-self, referring to a wide range of body-related experiences, body memories, etc. It is further considered to be an indirect measure of ego identity and ego consistency. The qualitative evaluation is conducted in regard to three dimensions: proportionality, completeness, and connectedness of the figure. Using the Body Image Painting Test [*Körperbild-Mal-Test*] *(*Breitenöder-Wehrung et al., 1998), the therapist can obtain access to an experiential plane that can offer valuable information about the emotional evaluation—that is, the affective and cognitive associations linked with specific parts of the body. In this test, the patient is given a schematic drawing of a body and is asked to fill out this schema using different colors according to a graded catalog of criteria (levels of satisfaction).

From among the vast array of so-called verbal methods (interview techniques and questionnaires), a few can be identified as relevant sources of clinically useful information in the context of Body Psychotherapy. These methods predominantly assess cognitive aspects of bodily experience in a range of given categories (body concepts, attitudes toward the body, body evaluations, body-oriented thoughts, knowledge, fantasies). The categories that thus far have received the most attention are: uncertainties regarding body boundaries, depersonalization, and distancing from parts of the body, changes in size perception, and changes in outward appearance.

In addition, there are questionnaires that specifically assess affectively colored body evaluation, satisfaction with the body, and attention paid to the varying parts of the body—e.g., Body Focus Questionnaire, Body Prominence Score (Fisher, 1970, 1986); Questionnaire for Evaluation of One's Own Body (Strauss, 1983; Strauss and Appelt, 1986); and Body Image Questionnaire (Löwe and Clement, 1996).

Other methods, which haven't been used much to date, even in research, promise further information. For example, in the context of the Body Image Automatic Thoughts Questionnaire (Cash et al., 1987), subjects are presented with negative and positive cognitions associated with bodily experience and are instructed to rate their level of agreement or disagreement with these statements on a five-point scale. The Frankfurt Body-Concept Scales (*Frankfurter Körperkonzeptskalen)* (Deusinger, 1992) comprehensively assesses self-images in regard to concepts including: health, bodily well-being, bodily self-care, bodily efficiency, body contact, sexuality, self-acceptance of the body, and acceptance of the body by others, aspects of outward appearance, and dissimilative body processes.

Due to the complex requirements of the technology needed for the assessment of bodily experience in the area of the psychology of perception, this is currently practicable only in the context of research (e.g., for disorder-specific evaluation studies). An assessment of the body schema would prove to be highly relevant in individual cases of those who undergo Body Psychotherapy. As a proxy, cognitive methods to evaluate body-size perception can be used—for example, the Body Image Screening Scale (Fichter and Meermann, 1981). Following this method, patients are asked to enter the width of the respective areas of different body parts on a scale. Alternatively, pictorial methods—that is, sketched drawings of one's own body—can be used. A relatively new instrument was developed specifically for therapeutic assessments in the context of Concentrative Movement Therapy [*Konzentrative Bewegungstherapie],* an approach of psychodynamic Body Psychotherapy: The Questionnaire on Group Experience in Body Psychotherapy [*Fragebogen zum Gruppenerleben in der KPT*] (Seidler, 1995). This questionnaire assesses the group climate, the therapist's behavior, and the patient's confidence, as well as some group therapeutic curative factors. A number of aspects that are of particular relevance for Concentrative Movement Therapy are also assessed: self-perception, body perception, manner of relating to one's own body and self, emotional evaluation of bodily experience, and body-oriented self-experience. More recent developments are the Dresden Body Image Inventory (Questionnaire DKB-35) (Pöhlmann et al., 2013) and the Evaluation Form for Concentrative Movement Therapy (Schreiber-Willnow and Seidler, 2013). The DKB-35 measures five dimensions of body image—namely, vitality, self-acceptance, self-aggrandizement, physical closeness, and sexual fulfillment; the Evaluation Form for Concentrative Movement Therapy captures therapy processes for individual patients and provides data for quality monitoring. An updated overview of concepts and instruments on body image research is provided within the second edition of *Body Image: A Handbook of Science, Practice, and Prevention* (Cash and Smolak, 2012).

## Dynamically Designed Movement Analysis

Although the efforts to describe different aspects of subjective bodily experience (in the context of the phenomenology of embodiment) have to date focused primarily on static categories (for example, thoughts/attitudes regarding the body, or body perception), the dynamic aspects of bodily self-experience—in particular, movement behaviors—have been rather neglected. In contrast, within the scope of Body Psychotherapy, movement analysis receives significantly more attention. This section will focus on the theme of significant interpersonal movement behaviors, whereas the next section among other issues addresses the interpersonal aspects of nonverbal styles of communication.

As a preface, it is important to keep in mind that, in day-to-day practice of Body Psychotherapy, the diagnostic tools that are described in this section and the next are integral aspects of the clinical practice, rather than more rigidly structured assessments as presented here. In practice, phenomena that newly arise, or attract attention, contribute to an ongoing diagnostic process of clarification, through constant revalidation, reformulation, or invalidation of previous assessments.

Body Psychotherapy is interested in the characteristics of movement in the context of general psychological features, individual biography, and intrapsychic conflicts. Such an analysis includes a range of aspects, such as conduct with one's own body, body openness (versus tight body-boundary setting), and self-expression (for example, in regard to self-confidence, problem areas, and flexibility). Laban (1950) introduced a system of structured movement analysis that has been and is being primarily used in Dance Therapy and Movement Therapy for identification of dysfunctional psychic structures and as a tool for treatment planning and evaluation. Following this method, the movement pattern or image is analytically assessed in respect to qualitatively distinct movement categories (the main components are: drives, form, rhythm, organization, sequencing, space, and use of the body). In his Effort Analysis, Laban described the basic factors of space, weight, time, and flow. These factors are then related to the psychological functions: thinking, feeling, intuition, and sensing. The complexity of this kind of movement analysis and corresponding training requirements has apparently limited the wider dissemination of this method, which by now has become video-based. Lausberg (2006) nonetheless emphasizes the maturity and precision of movement-analysis tools for body schema and body image diagnostics. On the basis of the Laban movement analysis, Martha Davis (quoted in Higgins, 1993) developed a research instrument for the assessment of psycho-pathological features (Davis Movement Diagnostic Scale). This instrument assesses movement in regard to seven given categories of pathological features: fragmentation; diffusion; exaggeration; fixed or invariant movement patterns; bound active control; flaccidity; reduced mobility; and low vitality. The scale bases its evaluations on observations of facial expression and gesture, self-referential movements, instrumentalized and goal-oriented movements, locomotion, and the recognition of abnormal movement patterns.

## Relational (Interpersonal) Behavioral Analysis

This last section addresses the specific aspects of Body-Oriented Psychotherapy in regard to the interpersonal dimension of the therapeutic relationship. Primarily, we are concerned with situational, body-related interpretations, and with interpretations of the transference relationship. Particular consideration is given to the somatic countertransference, and the analysis of nonverbal communication styles. "Interpretation" here refers to the complex interactions that mesh a diagnostic, phenomenologically based understanding of the structures and psychic processes of the patient with the therapeutic effects that the reflection of these findings has on the patient. Within Body Psychotherapy, this reflection/mirroring can occur verbally as well as nonverbally (for example, through facial expression, gesture, qualities of touch, etc.). Body Psychotherapeutic interpretations are directed toward somaticized or repressed psychic contents, toward somatically symbolized desires/needs and the repression of bodily aspects of self, and toward the relationship patterns that emerge within the concrete, embodied patient-therapist relationship.

Again, diagnostic-analytical and therapeutic strategies are closely linked. Petzold elaborates: "Pathogenic scenes therefore must not only be remembered so as to be linked with new meanings via interpretation, they must be repeated within the novel context of the therapeutic relationship and therapeutic group, which support the patient's awareness of the reenactment" (Petzold, 1988, p. 319).

The inclusion of the body as one target of intervention and as a thematic focus of self-experience leads to a very particular kind of therapeutic relationship. Comprehensive discussions of the therapeutic relationship in Body Psychotherapy can be found in Petzold (1988) and Downing (1996), who carefully demonstrate the uniqueness of the "soma-to-soma" relationship in the Body Psychotherapeutic framework of interventions.

Nonverbal styles of intervention or communication behaviors—that is, the abundance of body movements that form a gestalt—are very complex information systems that are strongly shaped by social, cultural, and situational conditions, and that consequently can be understood only within this context. A systematic observation of the therapeutic engagement, utilizing information from movement behavior and nonverbal communication, widens the analysis of conflict constellations to include an important new dimension. Experienced Body Psychotherapists listen to their own somatic countertransference to inform their choice of intervention strategy: a method that has also been referred to as the "seismographic response" of the therapist.

## References

Bielefeld, J. (1986/1991). Zur Begrifflichkeit und Strukturierung der Auseinandersetzung mit dem eigenen Körper [For the terminology and structure of the engagement with one's own body]. In J. Bielefeld (Ed.), *Körpererfahrung: Grundlagen menschlichen Bewegungsverhaltens* [Body experience: Foundations of human movement behavior]. Göttingen: Hogrefe.

Boadella, D. (2000). Book review: F. Röhricht: Body-oriented psychotherapy for mental disorders. *Energy & Character, 31,* 144–148.

Breitenöder-Wehrung, A., Kuhn, G., & Günter, M., et al. (1998). Vergleich des Körperbildes bei gesunden und psychisch bzw. körperlich kranken Kindern mit Hilfe des KBMT-K [Comparison of body image in healthy and mentally or physically ill children using the KBMT-K]. *Psychotherapie, Psychosomatik, Medizinische Psychologie, 48,* 483–490.

Cash, T. F., Lewis, R. J., & Keeton, P. (1987). *Development and validation of the Body-Image Automatic Thoughts Questionnaire: A measure of body-related cognitions.* Paper presented at the annual meeting of the Southeastern Psychological Association, Atlanta, GA (cited by Thompson et al., 1990).

Cash, T. F., & Smolak, L. (Eds.). (2012). *Body image: A handbook of science, practice and prevention* (2nd ed.). New York: Guilford Press.

Deusinger, I. (1992). *Die Frankfurter Körperkonzeptskalen* [The Frankfurt concept of body scales]. Göttingen, Germany: Hogrefe.

Dornes, M. (1993). *Der kompetente Säugling: Die präverbale Entwicklung des Menschen* [The competent infant: The preverbal human development]. Frankfurt, Germany: Fischer.

Downing, G. (1996). *Körper und Wort in der Psychotherapie: Leitlinien für die Praxis* [Body and word in psychotherapy: Guidelines for practice]. Munich: Kösel.

Dychtwald, K. (1981). *Körperbewußtsein* [Body awareness]. Essen: Synthesis.

Fichter, M. M., & Meermann, R. (1981). Zur Psychopathometrie der Anorexia nervosa [About the psychopathometry of anorexia nervosa]. In R. Meermann (Ed.), *Anorexia nervosa: Ursachen und Behandlung* [Anorexia nervosa: Causes and treatment] (pp. 17–31). Stuttgart: Enke.

Fisher, S. (1970). *Body experience in fantasy and behavior.* New York: Appleton Century Crofts.

Fisher, S. (1986). *Development and structure of the body image (Vols. 1 & 2).* Hillsdale, NJ: Lawrence Erlbaum.

Geuter, U. (2000). Wege zum Körper: Zur Geschichte und Theorie des körperbezogenen Ansatzes in der Psychotherapie. Krankengymnastik [Way to the body: The history and theory of body-based approaches in psychotherapy and physiotherapy]. *Zeitschrift für Physiotherapeuten, 52,* 1175–1183, 1346–1351.

Görlitz, G. (1998). *Körper und Gefühl in der Psychotherapie: Basisübungen und Aufbauübungen* [Body and emotion in psychotherapy-based building exercises]. "Leben Lernen" ["Life learning"], 120 & 121. Munich: Pfeiffer.

Higgins, L. (1993). Movement assessment in schizophrenia. In H. Payne (Ed.), *Handbook of inquiry in the arts therapies* (pp. 138–163). London: Jessica Kingsley.

Joraschky, P., Sebastian, S., & Riera, R. (1998). Der Körperbild-Skulptur-Test [The body-image sculpture test]. In: F. Röhricht & S. Priebe (Eds.), *Körpererleben in der Schizophrenie* [Body experience in schizophrenia] (pp. 121–135). Göttingen: Hogrefe.

Laban, R. (1926). *Gymnastik und Tanz* [Gymnastics and dance]. Oldenburg: Gerhard Stalling.

Laban, R. (1950). *The mastery of movement* (L. Ullmann, Ed.). London: MacDonald & Evans.

Lausberg, H. (2006). Körperschema, Körperbild und Bewegungsmuster: Bewegungsanalyse in der Diagnostik von Körperschema—und Körperbildstörungen [Body schema, body image, and pattern of movement: Movement analysis in the diagnosis of body image—and body image disorders]. In P. Joraschky, T. Loew, & F. Röhricht (Eds.), *Körpererleben und Körperbild* [Body experience and body image]. Stuttgart: Schattauer.

Löwe, B., & Clement, U. (1996). Der Fragebogen zum Körperbild (FKB-20): *Literaturüberblick, Beschreibung und Prüfung eines Meßinstruments* [The questionnaire on body image (FKB-20): Literature review, description, and validation of the questionnaire]. *Diagnostica, 42,* 352–376.

Lowen, A. (1992). *Körperausdruck und Persönlichkeit: Grundlagen und Praxis der Bioenergetik* [Body expression and personality: Principles and practice of bioenergetics]. Munich: Goldmann.

Machover, K. (1949). *Personality projection in the drawing of the human figure.* Springfield, IL: Thomas.

Marcher, L., & Fich, S. (2010). *Body encyclopedia: A guide to the psychological functions of the muscular system.* Berkeley, CA: North Atlantic Books.

Meermann, R. (1985). *Körperschemastörungen* [Body schema disturbances] (Unpublished thesis). University of Münster, Germany.

Petzold, H. (1988). *Integrative Bewegungs und Leibtherapie: Ein ganzheitlicher Weg leibbezogener Psychotherapie (Band 1)* [Integrative body therapy: A holistic method of related physical psychotherapy (Vol. 1)]. Paderborn: Junfermann.

Pöhlmann, K., Roth, M., Brähler, E., & Joraschky, P. (2013, Aug. 21). *The Dresden Body Image Inventory (DKB-35): Validity in a clinical sample. Psychotherapie Psychosomatik Medizinische Psychologie, 64*(3–4), 93–100.

Reich, W. (1933/1973). *Charakteranalyse* [Character Analysis]. Frankfurt: Fischer.

Röhricht, F. (2000). *Körperorientierte Psychotherapie psychischer Störungen* [Body-oriented psychotherapy in mental disorders]. Göttingen: Hogrefe.

Röhricht, F. (2006). Ansätze und Methoden zur Untersuchung des Körpererlebens [Approaches and methods for the study of body experience]. In P. Joraschky, T. Loew, & F. Röhricht (Eds.), *Körpererleben und Körperbild* [Body experience and body image]. Stuttgart: Schattauer.

Röhricht, F. (2009). Body oriented psychotherapy—the state of the art in empirical research and evidence based practice: A clinical perspective. *Journal of Body, Movement and Dance in Psychotherapy, 4,* 135–156.

Röhricht, F. (2011). Leibgedächtnis und Körper-Ich: zwei zentrale Bezugspunkte in der störungsspezifischen körperorientierten Psychotherapie [Body memory and body-self: Two central points of reference in disorder-specific Body-Oriented Psychotherapy]. *Psychologie in Österreich, 4,* 239–248.

Röhricht, F., & Priebe, S. (1997). Störungen des Körpererlebens bei schizophrenen Patienten [Disorders of body experience in schizophrenia]. *Fortschritte Neurologie Psychiatrie, 65, 323–336.*

Röhricht, F., & Priebe, S. (1998). Empirische Untersuchungen zum Körpererleben in der Schizophrenie: eine Literaturübersicht [Empirical studies on body image in schizophrenia: A literature review]. In F. Röhricht & S. Priebe (Eds.), *Körpererleben in der Schizophrenie [Body experience in schizophrenia]* (pp. 43–50). Göttingen: Hogrefe.

Schreiber-Willnow, K., & Seidler, K-P. (2013). Therapy goals and treatment results in body psychotherapy: Experience with the Concentrative Movement Therapy evaluation form. *Journal of Body, Movement and Dance in Psychotherapy, 8, 254–269.*

Seidler, K-P. (1995). Das Gruppenerleben in der Konzentrativen Bewegungstherapie [The group experience in the Concentrative Movement Therapy]. *Gruppenpsychotherapie & Gruppendynamik, 31(2), 159–174.*

Shontz, F. C. (1974). Body image and its disorders. *International Journal of Psychiatry in Medicine, 5, 461–472.*

Strauss, B. (1983). Ein Fragebogen zur Beurteilung des eigenen Körpers [A questionnaire for the assessment of one's body]. *Diagnostica, 29, 145–164.*

Strauss, B., & Appelt, H. (1986). Erfahrungen mit einem Fragebogen zum Körpererleben [Experience with a questionnaire on body experience]. In E. Brähler (Ed.), *Körpererleben [Body experience]* (pp. 220–231). Berlin: Springer.

Thompson, J. K., Penner, L. A., & Altabe, M. N. (1990). Procedures, problems and progress in the assessment of body images. In T. F. Cash & T. Pruzinsky (Eds.), *Body images: Development, deviance and change* (pp. 21–48). New York: Guilford Press.

# 53

## The Role of the Body in Emotional Defense Processes

*Body Psychotherapy and Emotional Theory*

**Ulfried Geuter and Norbert Schrauth, Germany**

Translation by Regina Mirvis

**Ulfried Geuter's biographical information** can be found at the beginning of Chapter 3, "The History and Scope of Body Psychotherapy."

**Norbert Schrauth**, MD, is a resident specialist in psychosomatic medicine. His training is in Psychodynamic Psychotherapy, as well as in Biodynamic Psychotherapy, which he completed with Gerda Boyesen and David Boadella. In the 1980s, he studied and worked for three years at the Gerda Boyesen Institute in London. He has been an instructor, and supervisor in Biodynamic Psychotherapy since 1990. In 1999, he became co-founder, board member, instructor, and supervisor at the Tiefenpsychologisches Institut [Depth Psychological Institute], Baden, which offers a psychodynamic-humanistic training for psychologists and doctors. He is also a founding member of the German Association for Body Psychotherapy (DGK) and was on its board of directors. His publications concentrate on the history and methodology of Body Psychotherapy.

Some of the essential starting points of any body-focused intervention in psychotherapy are in the work with the physical side of the defense processes. These are the somatic blockages of perception and the expression of suppressed emotions, as well as the somatic access to the experienced emotion. Thereby, Body Psychotherapy pays heed to the *"shift between the expression of affect and affect analysis,"* which (according to Yalom) defines each and every psychotherapy (Yalom, 2002, p. 177). In contrast to other schools of psychotherapy, the expression of affect, as well as the affect itself, is always seen on the somatic level.

In recent years, experientially oriented psychotherapeutic approaches—such as Neo-Reichian schools of therapy, Dance Therapy, and Gestalt Therapy—have opened up more to psychodynamic and to systemic theories. At the same time, other schools of psychotherapy, such as psychoanalysis and behavioral therapy, have turned toward the emotion dynamics. However, the physical side of the emotional processes is usually neglected. Also, in research literature on emotions, the role of the body in our emotional experience had long been ignored (Downing, 2000). According to Downing, however, there are three reasons why emotional theory cannot do without the inclusion of somatic experience. First, the intensity of emotions cannot be experienced without the body being involved. Second, every person is capable of specifically localizing emotion in a part of his or her body, when asked (see Nummenmaa et al., 2013). Third, some emotions are felt as diffuse bodily sensations that do not clearly point to a specific "about what?" Because each emotion contains a bodily feeling, emotions can be targeted by bodily sensations.

Body Psychotherapy is characterized by the fact that it provides a medium to support the bodily exploration of emotional states ("What do I feel in a situation and what does this say about it?"). It also allows access to emotional reactions via the body and therefore enables one to deepen one's experience. Downing (1996) showed how affective-motor schemes are reorganized by exploring so-called "body micropractices." Gendlin's "focusing" (1996) can be seen as a method of affect exploration using the body, as Gendlin seeks to find answers to emotionally significant questions in the body's "felt sense." Monsen and Monsen (1999, 2000) were able to demonstrate, in a study of pain patients, that Body Psychotherapeutic treatment led to sizable changes in the expression of affect. It also led to an increased awareness of emotions, such as envy, shame, guilt, and joy, as well as to a lesser degree of denial of emotional conflicts.

## Bodily Feeling, Posture, and Emotion

Experimental research findings are increasingly supporting the theory that body percepts (sensations) play a decisive role in emotions (Niedenthal et al., 2005). Martin and colleagues (1992) demonstrated that human beings draw upon their bodily feelings in order to assess social situations. We utilize our bodily self-perception as a source of information for something that is occurring outside of ourselves. The felt intensity of a perceived emotion depends on the extent of bodily arousal. The meaning of the emotions is perceived by motoric feedback—e.g., by the expression of the facial muscles (Ibid., p. 417). During an experiment where the motoric feedback was manipulated experimentally, subjects alter their evaluation of a stimulus even without interpreting the experimental manipulation of their mimicry in terms of emotions. This is in concordance with Damasio's neurobiological theory, according to which so-called "somatic markers" are involved in decision-making processes (Damasio, 1994, pp. 237ff.). An abundance of possible bodily sensations, according to Damasio, warns the person of any negative results of intended actions, or allows the execution of an action. Emotional orientation is phylogenetically older than intellectual reason, and links perception, feeling, and acting without relying on words (Revenstorf, 1985, p. 24).

Stepper and Strack (1993) manipulated the posture of subjects under the pretext of ergonomically testing work furniture: people who received fictitious praise while in an upright position were prouder of a good test result than those who received praise while in a slumped position. Other experiments show that people who experience success in a hunched-over posture have higher test values for depression than do those who experience failure in an upright posture. Body posture accounted more toward a negative emotional experience than did the experience of failure. People also tell different stories about an equivocal image depending on their posture (Döring-Seipel, 1996). Thus, body postures have an immediate activation on emotional schemas in the processing of an experience, without any conscious knowledge of the process.

## Somatic Defense and Body Psychotherapy

Body Psychotherapy started from the notion that the body influences *"emotions and thoughts as well as their dissociation and repression"* (Revenstorf, 2000, p. 209). The psychosomatic physician Georg Groddeck established the concept of "body defense," finding that muscular tensions, breathing restrictions, and chronic holding patterns of muscles can prevent the perception of an impulse (Downing, 1996, pp. 191ff.). The psychoanalyst Sándor Ferenczi, a friend of Groddeck, wrote that neuroses are always accompanied by a strong restriction in motility. Wilhelm Reich (1933) further expanded on these ideas in his concept of muscular armor.

Whereas psychoanalysis saw the processes of defense to be cognitive operations (Geuter and Schrauth, 2001, p. 7), Reich understood them to be mental and body processes at the same time. He assumed that the character armor, initially described on the psychological level, as well as the physical muscular armoring, both serve the same purpose of keeping undesired emotions and affects away from the individual's consciousness. Hence, the impulses to act are held at bay by muscle behaviors developed in childhood: *"Our patients invariably report that they experienced periods in childhood in which they learned by certain exercises in vegetative behavior (breathing, abdominal tension) to sup-*

*press hateful, fearful and loving impulses*" (Reich, 1942).

Thus, the history of emotional repression resides within the tensed-up muscles. Reich characterized the chronic holding of the breath as "the most important tool" in the repression of emotion. This leads to an armoring in the chest area, and to psycho-physically controlling one's feelings. Reich described, in detail, the defense mechanism of "affect block" in which the notion of an affect is dissociated, and the patient remains totally unaffected and appears to be like a "living machine" (Reich, 1933).

Attachment research has shown that very young children with an "insecure-avoidant attachment pattern" showed no emotional expression in an experimental separation situation (the "strange situation") at twelve months of age; however, they showed clear physiological stress reactions (Spangler and Schieche, 1998). Infant research confirms that babies already learn to use physical activities to regulate their emotions in early interactions (Downing, 1996, 2000). Stern (1985) describes the representations of emotional interactions in the body-to-body contact learned in early mother-child engagements. Papousek and Papousek (1979) showed that infants react to a persisting irritation by limiting the depth of their breathing and developing a uniform, almost mechanical, frequency of breathing. We understand this to be a part of the "freeze reaction" or the "startle reflex." Body Psychotherapy sees fundamental emotional defense mechanisms within these patterns, which, upon becoming chronic, can lead to a chronic blockage in breathing. Changes in a client's breathing during a therapy session can indicate some still-unconscious emotional processes. Sometimes these processes can be helped into awareness simply by giving attention to the breathing.

Reich (1933) was the first to give detailed descriptions of the chronically tensed-up muscles as a part of physical defense mechanisms. The blockage in emotions is executed by tensions in those muscles that are normally involved in the corresponding expression of the emotions or gestures. Thus, for example, the learned inability to reach out for help, or to take hold of another person, is held by tensions in the arms, the shoulders, and the chest. Deeply entrenched fear is held by an equally deeply entrenched upward contraction of the shoulders. Suppressed rage is chronically held as a tension in the muscles of the chest and jaw that hold the breath. Gerda Boyesen (1987) emphasized that the defense processes can also settle in other bodily layers, such as in connective tissue, or in the viscera: this can lead to tissue or visceral armoring. The correlation between muscular and visceral tensions and emotional defenses has been confirmed by numerous research findings (Traue, 1998).

Reich's model of character structure, which was further developed by Alexander Lowen (see Chapter 27, "Shapes of Experience: Neuroscience, Developmental Psychology, and Somatic Character Formation" by Marianne Bentzen), connects the body defense theory with Developmental Psychology. This model assumes that frustrations that are typical for an early developmental phase, and their corresponding defense operations, lead to characteristic mental attitudes and—as a result of chronic tensions or expressive movements—physical postures. Keleman (1985) relates chronic postures to stress reactions, and in *Emotional Anatomy* he portrays how repetitive reactions to distress can become a mental and physical habit. Thus, a certain posture can be inferred back to experiences in a client's life.

## Expressive Movement and Emotions

In Darwin's (1872) book, *The Expression of the Emotions in Man and Animals,* he wrote how certain body movements accompany the expression of emotions. However, only recently has experimental research started concerning itself with the question of the extent to which physical expression can be read as an expression of certain emotions. This research is occupied with the identification of discrete emotions and not, as in Body Psychotherapy, with physical postures or movements as a result of emotional-developmental processes.

Although a great amount of research has already been done on how emotions can be read from facial expressions (Wallbott, 1998c), it is rare to find research on the recognition of emotions via postures and movements. Wallbott

(1998a, 1998b) was able to show, in studies with actors, that more than half of the postures and movements employed by them discriminated between certain emotions. Thus, for example: the lifting of the shoulders pointed to euphoria; a forward movement of the shoulders pointed to disgust, despair, or dread; and a backward shoulder movement portrayed revulsion; above all, shame could be very aptly determined by visible movements (Wallbott, 1998a, p. 129). Wallbott also found differences between various emotions in their expansiveness and in the dynamics of movement.

This corresponds to Stern's (1985) notion that affects have dynamic and kinetic qualities that Stern calls "activation contours" or "vitality affects." Stern understands the vitality affects to be general patterns of arousal and activation processes that are characterized by features of intensity, timing, beat, rhythm, duration, and form (spatial characteristics; shape of a motion sequence). They need not be accompanied by attributed affects. In interactive processes, these have great significance, especially in a dialogue with an infant (Stern, 1985, p. 223).

Other experimental studies show that specific emotions can be distinguished by the quality of the voice (Frick, 1985; Klasmeyer and Sendlmeier, 1997). In a study by Banse and Scherer (1996), confusions in emotional recognition were based largely on the proximity of emotions, such as hot and cold anger, sadness and despair, or fear and panic. Bloch, Lemeignan, and Aguilera (1991) discovered specific patterns of breathing depending on certain emotions. Conversely, only certain emotions can be felt during certain breathing and movement patterns: for example, a person who breathes arbitrarily in an excited way, which corresponds to an angry or anxious reaction, cannot feel any sadness at the same time.

## Basic Emotions or Vegetative Affects

Body Psychotherapeutic work with nonperceived or suppressed emotions often deals with those emotions that are classified in research as basic emotions (for more detail, see Geuter and Schrauth, 2001, pp. 9ff.). Lowen (1990) called them "vegetative affects," and Kernberg (1992) simply called them "affects." These affects are: surprise, rage/anger, grief/pain, disgust, fear, joy/happiness, and interest/curiosity. Whether contempt is also one of them is controversial. These emotions can be interculturally identified due to their universal facial-movement patterns, which obviously belong to the biological endowment of human beings. Basic emotions or affects, according to Krause (1996), are of high intensity and short duration and interrupt courses of action (see Mandler, 1984). Neurobiologically, they are operated through the limbic system. The emotions assigned to attachment behavior and exploratory behavior by Bowlby are love, trust, rage, fear, and grief (on the one hand), as well as fright, self-confidence, and disgust: these are largely found in the list of basic emotions (see Revenstorf, 2000, p. 199).

Krause (1996) discerned the basic emotions from the self-reflexive "me emotions." When having these emotions (like pride, shame, guilt, humiliation, arrogance, envy, or jealousy), one internally compares a feeling or behavior with something supposed to be desirable or undesirable.

Many Body Psychotherapeutic interventions focus on freeing the basic emotions. In Neo-Reichian theory, one can have access to free affective or "vegetative" flow if the blockage to the affects is resolved. What is being referred to is the permeability between physical sensations and emotional movement.

Beginning with Reich, Body Psychotherapy initially placed techniques in the foreground, which promoted bodily expression and the cathartic abreaction of blocked emotions. We describe a differentiated model below. In working with the more complex "me emotions," it is more conducive to work with cognitive-emotional clarification, or experimental scenic methods, like role-playing or chairwork. This becomes different if one addresses the primary affects that are often contained in these emotions, such as anger in envy, despair in arrogance, or fear hidden in pride. In daily life, one reacts intuitively to affects such as sadness or anger with physical care, or with physical limitation or calming, whereas when confronted with self-reflexive emotions such as envy, jealousy, or shame, one is more likely to react verbally.

From the Body Psychotherapeutic point of view, these two classes of emotions can be differentiated by their activation contour. Vegetative affects have a temporal-cyclical structure. Clynes and Nettheim (1982), due to results from musicological research, assume a biologically given dynamic form. Vegetative affects arise and subside, either quickly or slowly, severely or mildly. When they persist, one is probably dealing with symptoms of a personality disorder, such as with chronic rage or fear. Most likely, we have an intuitive knowledge about these processes that allows us to judge whether an emotional expression toward something, in regard to its intensity or duration, is pertinent or not. It is also in this manner that psychotherapists are able to estimate the adequacy of a reaction by classifying it along the wide spectrum of healthy and pathological. Therefore, psychotherapists will need to empathize with the individual activation contour of a patient if they want to aid the patient in the reliving and finding closure of an unfinished emotional process.

## Core Affects

Every emotion is basically felt in the two dimensions of activation and pleasure. Perceptions only become emotional if a change in the degree of mobilization or energy and in the hedonic tone of pleasure or displeasure occurs. These two dimensions are called the "core affect" by Feldman Barrett and Russell (1998, 1999). According to their theory, a person is always in a core-affective state of activation and valence. This state is what we call the mood. For instance, on the dimension of activation, a person "senses being somewhere on a continuum ranging from sleep . . . through drowsiness, relaxation, alertness, hyper-activation, and, finally, frenetic excitement" (1999, p. 10). Their two-dimensional model includes four basic states with all nuances in between them:

- High arousal and high pleasure—a state of excitement
- High arousal and high displeasure—a state of distress
- Low arousal and high displeasure—a depressive state
- Low arousal and high pleasure—a state of relaxation

Depending on their state, a person experiences a situation emotionally differently. The same stimulus might not lead to an intense emotional reaction in a person in the latter state of well-being, but might greatly stress a person who is in the state of a background core affect of distress. In the state of well-being, stimuli can reach awareness without resulting in heavily emotional reactions. A person who neither becomes aroused nor feels displeasure will probably not feel fear in a threatening situation.

If a change in the core affect is noticed, without feeling any categorical emotion, a person experiences this as a shift in mood. Only if the feeling on the core-affective dimensions changes intensively, and is attributed to an appraisal of a situation as being sad, alarming, or distasteful, does the perception of a situation become emotional.

Inhibitions of core-affective feelings embrace the entire emotional perception. We describe a person who cannot generally feel changes in arousal as being clinically alexithymic, and a person who cannot change from displeasure to pleasure as depressive. Concomitantly, the main feature of the severely depressed patient is not sadness, but emptiness—the inability to feel attributed emotions by the lack of a core-affective reaction. These core affects also seem to be those that are influenced by antidepressants and other psychotropic drugs that change emotional states.

Russell (2003) distinguishes between affect regulation, as the regulation of the core affect, and emotional regulation, as the regulation of the emotional reaction toward an object or situation. If we speak of charge and discharge in Body Psychotherapy (e.g., Totton, 2003, p. 67), we refer to changing the arousal dimension of the core affect. Working with charge and discharge is independent of the emotional category that we awaken or calm by provoking or soothing arousal. In contrast, categorical emotions can only be changed by emotions (Greenberg, 2011)—for instance, a sadness by feeling the hidden anger or experiencing the missed solace; a rage by feeling the pain about the loss. To change an emotion, one has to face the relation toward the object of the emotion and to change the appraisal of this relationship (Downing, 2000).

A special feature of Body Psychotherapy is to work with the regulation of arousal and hedonic tone and with experiencing emotions in one and the same therapeutic process. Body techniques are often easier means to stimulate or calm arousal than is verbal work. Thus, we may stimulate the general arousal to make a person feel its rage, fear, or joy in order to better perceive and regulate the emotions; or we may help people to settle down from a state of hyperarousal in order to perceive faint emotions hidden by noisy ones.

The following model combines the core-affective regulation of arousal with the vitality affect theory of an emotional cycle and with the regulation of the categorical emotions.

## The Affective Cycle

In a temporal-cyclical model of affective processes (Southwell, 1990; Geuter and Schrauth, 2001), specific defensive operations and blockage points can be pinpointed and can be related to certain process-oriented bodily interventions. The model portrays the course of affective excitation as a curve or circle beginning at a quiescent point from which an arousal is the result of a stimulus. This leads to the buildup of arousal and bodily tensions, which finally leads to the expression or discharge, if the process is completed. After the fall of excitation, there is a phase of rest leading to a new quiescent point. The model assumes that the affective processes are experienced on all of the following levels, which are shown in Figure 53.1:

- Vegetative level (blood pressure, heart rate, digestion, etc.)
- Muscular level (facial expression, gesture, posture, and activity)
- Psychological level (awareness, thoughts, consciously experienced feelings)

This model assumes that the rise of excitation at the beginning of an affective process is predominantly a movement in relation to an object (toward an object as with curiosity or joy, or away from an object as with disgust, or the object away from the subject as with rage). This occurs while the decrease in excitation serves the internal regulation within the relationship of the subject to itself. Ideally, we distinguish seven different points of inhibition or blockage (Figure 53.2) where:

1. A stimulus is not perceived.
2. After perceiving a stimulus, there is no excitation or only a marginal increase.
3. The excitation is subdued, as the emotion cannot be tolerated in its full extent.
4. The expression of an emotional excitation is blocked.
5. An expression of an affect is chronically repeated, without leading to a solution.
6. After the expression of an emotional excitation, a high level of arousal is maintained.
7. Despite the decreasing of arousal, there is no reintegration, nor any recovery of an inner equilibrium.

In Body Psychotherapy, there are a multitude of interventions that are suitable to reduce blockages on all three mentioned levels—vegetative, muscular, and cognitive-emotional. They also serve to complete unfinished affective cycles and thus to achieve self-regulation. Depending on the location of the blockage, there are different possible interventions indicated in the psychotherapeutic process:

1. **Perception Block:** The blockage of perception is addressed using techniques that support the perception of sensations and feelings or that support general awareness. Belonging to these are techniques that explore vegetative changes or physical micropractices: e.g., the sensing of involuntary movements; the awareness of bodily experience in stillness or in movement, with or without being touched by oneself or someone else; the conscious experiencing of breathing; or the technique in

The Role of the Body in Emotional Defense Processes | 549

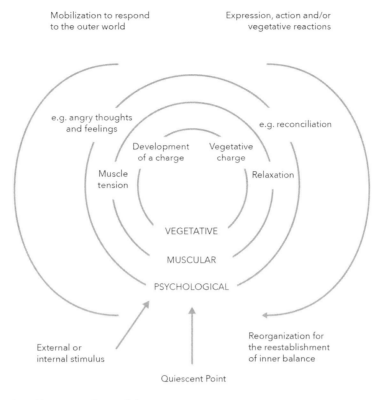

Figure 53.1. The affective cycle model

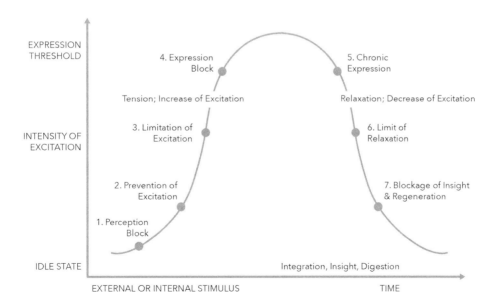

Figure 53.2. The affective cycle (as a curve with points of blockage)

which the therapist physically takes over the visible defense mechanism from the patient in order for the patient to feel the underlying impulse.

2. **Prevention of Excitation:** The fundamental strategy of treating blockages during the buildup of excitation is the so-called strategy of "charging." The patient is encouraged to deepen his or her breathing, to become more active, or to take on a physical stress position that increases emotional tension. This includes working with movements—for example, dancing emotions in Dance Therapy; stress positions in Bioenergetics; orchestration of acting out and role-play.

3. **Limitation of Excitation:** If the resulting emotions are limited or not fully developed, as often with tears of sadness, fearful trembling, or joyful excitement, it is the challenge of the Body Psychotherapist to help the patient maintain his or her emotion and keep it going, to help clarify it and in order to experience a satisfactory release later, without falling into any distracting action patterns. The following factors can assist this endeavor: the help of words; the emotional presence of the therapist; as well as gestures, touch, and physical containment.

4. **Expression Block:** If the expression of an emotion is prevented, due perhaps to shame or fear, the therapist can invite the patient to find a verbal and physical expression of their feeling. The best-known techniques are those from Gestalt Therapy, such as a verbal confrontation with the object of the emotion. Role-plays or interventions for the purpose of activating affect expression—such as hitting, screaming, or longingly stretching out the arms—can also be used here. The therapist must also be able to offer a necessary degree of safety during these interventions, so that the emotional cycle can be completed.

5. **Chronic Expression:** If a patient becomes chronically stuck in a pseudo-cathartic expression, it is the duty of the therapist to explore the compulsion for repetition, or to interrupt the dysfunctional expression, and to characterize it as a defense, in order for the patient to be able to recognize the persistence of the expression as a reaction that is keeping him or her away from finding a solution. There are techniques of de-dramatization, such as bodily interventions that promote contact with reality in the here and now—for example, contact to the floor, or contact with the therapist.

6. **Limit of Relaxation:** If a high level of excitation is perpetuated, although an emotion was adequately expressed, it is vital to calm emotional processes down and help to give them closure. Sitting still, relaxation exercises, soft movements, or certain types of massage can contribute here.

7. **Blockage of Insight and Regeneration:** Verbal work can also be used in order to understand what happened and to achieve integration. This work can, however, relate back to the body by attempting to feel what is cognitively understood within the body, and by relating a word to a physical sensation, and vice versa. This is known as "rooted talking" (Southwell, 1990).

We have indicated different possible bodily interventions for each one of the seven above-mentioned blockage points. At each point in the therapeutic process, verbal interventions, however, often have the biggest share in the work toward helping the person's understanding: a mixture of bodily and verbal interventions is therefore probably better than either one alone.

While working with a body-focused perspective with strong affects, "affect attunement" (Stern, 1985) by the therapist is essential. This means that the therapist must pay attention to the time flow and hit the mark of the "dynamic moment" at which a certain intervention is helpful. If the starting point of a basically correct intervention is badly timed, it may increase the blockages. We know, from daily life, that solace has no effect if a person does not yet feel grief, or if a person has already gone through the experience of grief. It can also be inappropriate to embrace a person who is feeling slightly sad, or only to speak to someone who is experiencing severe grief. This likewise applies to the therapeutic process of properly tuning in to the temporal rhythm and the intensity of a patient's affective processes. In order to loosen the psychological defenses, it is not only necessary to apply certain techniques, but most of all to do so with empathy and resonance.

# References

Banse, R., & Scherer, K. R. (1996). Acoustic profiles in vocal emotion expression. *Journal of Personality and Social Psychology, 70,* 614–636.

Bloch, S., Lemeignan, M., & Aguilera, T. N. (1991). Specific respiratory patterns distinguish among human basic emotions. *International Journal of Psychophysiology, 11,* 141–154.

Boyesen, G. (1987). *Über den Körper die Seele heilen: Biodynamische Psychologie und Psychotherapie: Eine Einführung* [Healing the body through the soul: Biodynamic Psychology and Psychotherapy: An introduction]. Munich: Kösel.

Clynes, M., & Nettheim, N. (1982). The living quality of music: Neurobiological patterns of communicating feeling. In M. Clynes (Ed.), *Music, mind and brain: The neuropsychology of music,* (pp. 47–82). New York: Plenum Press.

Darwin, C. (1872). *The expression of the emotions in man and animals.* London: John Murray.

Damasio, A. (1994). *Descartes' error: Emotion, reason and the human brain.* New York: Putnam.

Döring-Seipel, E. (1996). *Stimmung und Körperhaltung: Eine experimentelle Studie* [Mood and body posture: An experimental study]. Weinheim: Psychologie Verlagsunion.

Downing, G. (1996). *Körper und Wort in der Psychotherapie* [Body and word in psychotherapy]. Munich: Kösel.

Downing, G. (2000). Emotion theory reconsidered. In M. Wrathall & L. Malpas (Eds.), *Heidegger, coping, and cognitive science,* (pp. 245–270). Cambridge, MA: MIT Press.

Feldman Barrett, L., & Russell, J. A. (1998). Independence and bipolarity in the structure of current affects. *Journal of Personality and Social Psychology, 74,* 967–984.

Feldman Barrett, L., & Russell, J. A. (1999). The structure of current affect: Controversies and emerging consensus. *Current Directions in Psychological Science, 8,* 10–14.

Frick, R. W. (1985). Communicating emotion: The role of prosodic features. *Psychological Bulletin, 97,* 412–429.

Gendlin, E. (1996). *Focusing-oriented psychotherapy: A manual of the experiential method.* New York: Guilford Press.

Geuter, U., & Schrauth, N. (2001). Emotionen und Emotionsabwehr als Körperprozess [Emotions and emotional defense as a bodily process]. *Psychotherapie Forum, 9,* 4–19.

Greenberg, L. S. (2011). *Emotion-focused therapy.* Washington, DC: American Psychological Association.

Keleman, S. (1985). *Emotional anatomy: The structure of experience.* Berkeley, CA: Center Press.

Kernberg, O. (1992). *Aggression in personality disorders and perversions.* New Haven, CT: Yale University Press.

Klasmeyer, G., & Sendlmeier, W. F. (1997). The classification of different phonation types in emotional and neutral speech. *Forensic Linguistics, 1(4),* 104–124.

Krause, R. (1996). Emotion als Mittler zwischen Individuum und Umwelt [Emotion as a mediator between the individual and the environment]. In T. v. Uexküll et al. (Eds.), *Psychosomatische Medizin* [Psychosomatic medicine], (pp. 252–261). Munich: Urban & Schwarzenberg.

Lowen, A. (1990). *Spirituality of the body: Bioenergetics for grace and harmony.* New York: Macmillan.

Mandler, G. (1984). *Mind and body: The psychology of emotion and stress.* New York: W. W. Norton.

Martin, L. L., Harlow, T. F., & Strack, F. (1992). The role of bodily sensations in the evaluation of social events. *Personality and Social Psychology Bulletin, 18,* 412–419.

Monsen, J. T., & Monsen, K. (1999). Affects and affect consciousness: A psychotherapy model integrating Silvan Tomkins's affect and script theory within the framework of Self-Psychology. *Progress in Self-Psychology, 15,* 287–306.

Monsen, J. T., & Monsen, K. (2000). Chronic pain and psychodynamic body psychotherapy: A controlled outcome study. *Psychotherapy, 37,* 257–269.

Niedenthal, P. M., Barsalou, L. W., Ric, F., & Krauth-Gruber, S. (2005). Embodiment in the acquisition and use of emotion knowledge. In L. Feldman Barrett, P. M. Niedenthal, & P. Winkielman (Eds.), *Emotion and consciousness,* (pp. 21–50). New York: Guilford Press.

Nummenmaa, L., Glerean, E., Hari, R., & Hietanen, J. K. (2013). Bodily maps of emotions. *PNAS.* Retrieved from www.pnas.org/cgi/doi/10.1073/pnas.1321664111

Papousek, H., & Papousek, M. (1979). The infant's fundamental adaptive response system in social interaction. In E. B. Thoman (Ed.), *Origins of the infant's social responsiveness*, (pp. 175–208). Hillsdale, NJ: Lawrence Erlbaum.

Reich, W. (1933/1970). *Character Analysis.* New York: Farrar, Straus & Giroux.

Reich, W. (1942/1986). *Function of the orgasm: The discovery of orgone, Vol. 1.* New York: Farrar, Straus & Giroux.

Revenstorf, D. (1985). Nonverbale und verbale Informationsverarbeitung als Grundlage psychotherapeutischer Interventionen [Nonverbal and verbal information processing as the basis of psychotherapeutic interventions]. *Hypnose und Kognition [Hypnosis and Cognition], 2(2),* 13–35.

Revenstorf, D. (2000). Nutzung des Affekts in der Psychotherapie [Use of affect in psychotherapy]. In S. Sulz (Ed.), *Von der Kognition zur Emotion: Psychotherapie mit Gefühlen [From cognition to emotion: Psychotherapy with feelings],* (pp. 191–215). Munich: CIP-Medien.

Russell, J. A. (2003). Core affect and the psychological construction of emotion. *Psychological Review, 110,* 145–172.

Southwell, C. (1990). Biodynamische psychologie [Biodynamic Psychology]. In J. Rowan & W. Dryden (Eds.), *Neue Entwicklungen der Psychotherapie [New developments in psychotherapy],* (pp. 198–221). Oldenburg: Transform.

Spangler, G., & Schieche, M. (1998). Emotional and adreno-cortical responses of infants to the strange situation: The differential function of emotional expression. *International Journal of Behavioral Development, 22,* 681–706.

Stepper, S., & Strack, F. (1993). Proprioceptive determinants of emotional and nonemotional feeling. *Journal of Personality and Social Psychology, 64,* 211–220.

Stern, D. (1985). *The interpersonal world of the infant.* New York: Basic Books.

Totton, N. (2003). *Body Psychotherapy: An introduction.* Maidenhead, UK: Open University Press.

Traue, H. C. (1998). *Emotion und Gesundheit: Die psychobiologische Regulation durch Hemmung [Emotion and health: Psycho-biological regulation through inhibition].* Heidelberg: Spektrum Akademischer.

Wallbott, H. (1998a). Ausdruck von Emotionen in Körperbewegungen und Körperhaltungen [The expression of emotion in body movements and postures]. In C. Schmauser & T. Noll (Eds.), *Körperbewegungen und ihre Bedeutungen [Body movements and their meanings],* (pp. 121–135). Berlin: Berlin Verlag Arno Spitz.

Wallbott, H. (1998b). Bodily expression of emotion. *European Journal of Social Psychology, 28,* 879–896.

Wallbott, H. (1998c). Decoding emotions from facial expression: Recent developments and findings. *European Review of Social Psychology, 9,* 191–232.

Yalom, I. (2002). *The gift of therapy.* New York: HarperCollins.

# 54

## The Spectrum of Body Psychotherapeutic Practices and Interventions

Ilse Schmidt-Zimmermann, Germany

Translation by Warren Miller

**Ilse Schmidt-Zimmermann,** Dipl.-Paed, is an accredited psychotherapist and child and youth psychotherapist; and was the president of the European Association for Body Psychotherapy (EABP) from 1998 to 2002. She has a broad training background, including trainings in Unitive Body Psychotherapy, Gestalt Therapy, Group-Analytical Therapy, and Psychodynamic Therapy, as well as continuing education in Bioenergetics and in Stanley Keleman's Formative Psychology.

She is the director of the German training program in Unitive Body Psychotherapy in Frankfurt, and is a lecturer, supervisor, and training therapist in Psychodynamic Therapy. Her professional experience (of nearly forty years), along with her far-reaching knowledge of the various Body Psychotherapeutic approaches, puts her in a very special position to provide an overview of the spectrum of techniques and methods of Body Psychotherapy.

Aside from her work in clinical theory and practice, her presentations and publications—informed by the tradition of Critical Theory (Adorno, Marcuse)—have brought attention to mythic beliefs in psychotherapy and to the relationship between psyche and society.

An infant or toddler does not surrender aspects of its vital organismic and psychic needs without passionate remonstrances. The process in which a child adapts, perhaps neurotically, to an environment that fails, rejects, insults, or neglects it cannot occur without a set of painful mental and physical experiences on the part of the child. Failure, disregard, or more massive restrictions lead to formative imbalances that vary depending on the developmental stage during which they were experienced. Such distortions can be classified as overformations (too much) and underformations (too little). They affect vegetative functions, muscular structure, the grounding of the self in the body and in the world, and contact and relational capacities. "When the natural organizing process of a person is disrupted, this sets off a whole series of reactions—anger, grief, helplessness, and rage" (Keleman, 1987).

If, on the other hand, an infant's or toddler's needs for connection, care, touch, movement, and loving maternal regard are basically met, it will develop a much more stable sense of its body and its self, and will be in a better position to meet the challenges of life and society later in life. If the immediate environment of a child doesn't interfere with its basic organismic rhythms (such as between contact and retreat, waking and sleeping, vibrant activity and relaxed rest, hunger and satiation), but establishes a relational mode, characterized by attunement and resonance, or reestablishes such a relationship after it has been disrupted, the organism of this person will develop the ability to swing back and forth between expansion (e.g., activity, self-expression, contact) and retraction (e.g., recuperation, regeneration, protection).

Developmental research has shown that successful psycho-physical development is a process of recurrent, dynamic attunement. The stimuli and impulses that are processed in this context arise not only from interactions with the primary caregivers and the familiar environment but also from within the person's own body. Because of the complexity of the learning tasks (motor, sensory, verbal, cognitive, and also in regard to sexuality) and the multi-layeredness of childhood experiences, and because these developmental processes always occur in a sociocultural context, there are many possibilities for potential breakdowns and interruptions. Psychotherapy addresses the repercussions that such developmental disturbances have for a client, and Body Psychotherapy focuses not only on the mental consequences but also on their bodily (somatic) manifestations.

Wilhelm Reich (1933), among others, discovered the basic correlation between mental and emotional states and body posture. He concerned himself with character development and the phenomenon of body armoring, and he described in detail how body armoring leads to the freezing, restriction, distortion, or displacement of psychic and vital functions. This line of inquiry was subsequently further elaborated by Lowen (1988), Keleman (1992), and Boadella (1991a, 1991b, 1991c), among others. According to Alexander Lowen, early childhood development can be compromised by three basic kinds of breakdown of the primary relationship, each of which leaves a characteristic trace in the personality of the child:

- Deprivation, which leads to orality
- Repression, which leads to masochism
- Strong frustration, which leads to rigidity

Elsworth Baker (1980), a co-worker of Reich in the United States, brought a fourth kind of disruption to attention:

- Hostility, which leads to withdrawal or splitting

Downing (1996) and others found that inhibition also seems to strongly affect psycho-motor development. Especially in times of transition from one developmental phase to another (e.g., pre-verbal to verbal), a child is less stabile and consequently more vulnerable to inhibitions from his environment. Possible inhibitions also include verbal inhibitions.

Additionally, behavior that is invasive, ambivalent, or rejecting is viewed as compromising development, particularly with regard to the so-called structural disorders. In contrast to the effects of the experience of repression, such childhood experiences cause bodily and psychic patterns that are unstable, confused, and tending toward fragmentation. Desensitization of the senses, numbing, freezing of regions of the body, and restrictions in awareness are also further correlates. Lowen's description of five basic holding patterns can serve well to illustrate the ways the body responds to the developmental disruptions described above:

- *Holding together* is the answer to the fear of falling apart or into pieces. Typologically, this defines the "schizoid" character or the schizoid position. The fear of fragmentation also characterizes a dynamic of the narcissistic personality.
- *Holding on* to someone is a response to the fear of being rejected or abandoned. This defines the "oral" position.
- *Holding up* is the response to the fear of falling into a state of vulnerability that would be experienced as personal failure, and the exposure to the dominance of others. According to Lowen, this defines the "psychopathic" position.
- *Holding in* expresses the fear of being disobedient, of letting go, and of exploding. This defines the "masochistic" position.
- *Holding back* is a response to the fear of renewed wounding and insult through rejection, if one were to let oneself be guided by feelings of love and surrender. This characterizes the "rigid" character position.

Although each individual is much too complex to reflect only one of these character types, one of the patterns can nonetheless predominate. In his chapter on posture and body expression, Wilhelm Reich wrote, *"Each muscular constriction contains the history and meaning of its origination . . . The constriction of musculature is the bodily aspect of the process of extrusion and the basis of its maintenance"* (Reich, 1975b).

## Clinical Example 1

A thirty-five-year-old client presented herself as "held up," not only in a relational sense, but also in her bodily expression. Her reactions to my careful and well-intended interventions were markedly defensive, "like a smart aleck." She attempted, by every means possible, to keep her head "above water," so as not to sink into a sea of emotions, out of her immediate control. We came to a turning point when I realized that the way she was holding her actual head (chin high up) correlated with her character defense pattern. The method of intervention that I chose at this point was Stanley Keleman's five-step practice, which I describe in more detail elsewhere in this chapter. Practically, I invited the client to feel into her head posture and then to exaggerate it somewhat. Through this practice, she could begin to sense which muscles were involved, and how this posture was constituted. She was also able to feel some of the strain involved in constantly needing to keep her head "above water." When I then asked her to gradually lower her chin, in slow, small steps, she was able to identify exactly the point at which her fear set in, and she was able to name the associated psychic contents. Subsequently, after loosening her neck muscles, she began to weep heavily. She could now experience some of the sense of abandonment that she had suffered during her childhood and early adolescence, and was able to share these feelings in contact with me—which was a new experience for her. In further lowering her chin, she was able to identify clearly when her fear turned into panic, associated with flooding and drowning (in her emotions). At this point, the client had an experience of self-regulation—a concept that is considered to be very important in Body Psychotherapy. She learned that she could regulate her panic by returning by just one small step in the direction that she was more familiar with, without having to fall back into the old emotional defense pattern.

This chapter can mention only a few of the many developmental-psychological theories of Body Psychotherapy that are necessary to understand Body Psychotherapeutic interventions. Reich (1975a) established a correlation between his theory of libido and the function of the vegetative nervous system, which operates on the principle of homeostasis (a tendency toward equilibrium) and plays an important role in the regulation of human relationships and emotions such as lust, joy, anger, and fear. The autonomic (or vegetative) nervous system unfolds a spectrum of oscillations, reaching from expansion into the world (contact), along a relaxed retreat into the self, to fearful withdrawal from, or defense against, the world (contraction).

In a modern theory on the vegetative nervous system, the polyvagal theory, Stephen Porges (2011) describes how the different neural branches of that nervous system become activated. Neurologist Antonio Damasio's discovery of somatic markers led him to a new and contemporary theory that supports the notion that basic preferences for psycho-physical development do exist: *"The neurological basis for the internal preference system consists mainly of innate regulatory dispositions that serve the survival of the organism. Ultimately, the task of securing survival overlaps with the reduction of unpleasant body states and the establishment of homeostatic states . . ."* (Damasio, 1997).

Downing (1996) has made a major contribution to the conceptual framework of Body Psychotherapy and the theory of body defenses. He shows how the dynamics of early object-relations, including nonverbal interactions between the primary caregiver and the toddler, lead to the development of "affective-motor schemas" (see Chapter 29, "Early Interaction and the Body: Clinical Implications" by George Downing; see also Chapter 30, "Affective-Motor Schemata" by Andreas Wehowsky), and how already-existing schemas, such as anatomically preformed patterns, can be profoundly shaped or restricted in development. Downing highlights the aspect of affectively charged motor learning (determined by the emotional tone of the affective attachment) and the corresponding cognitive appraisals.

## Divergence of Theories

The field of Body-Oriented Psychotherapy has generated a very broad and partially divergent spectrum of theoretical understanding and methodological practice. Each specific tradition of Body Psychotherapy builds on particular aspects of this spectrum and moves within specific parameters. Whereas some schools approach defenses and character structure in a systematic fashion, others focus more on the process and exploration of the present moment. Some traditions facilitate increased energetic charge and affective expression, whereas others focus on supporting internal vegetative processes. All these methods are working within basic parameters and with categories of Body Psychotherapeutic intervention that—to different degrees—are in common use in the majority of the field of Body Psychotherapy.

## Central Functions and Experiential Practices

For the analysis of presenting psycho-physical structures, and for the understanding of body defenses, the following indicators are of particular relevance:

- Character structure patterns or postural holding patterns
- Emotional expression of body parts (e.g., the eyes)
- Bodily symmetry, asymmetry, and body "splits"
- Muscular hypertonia and hypotonia
- Blocked and restricted movements
- Impairments in the ability to express emotions
- Restrictions and impairments in breathing patterns
- Limited or distorted sense perceptions, numbness
- Splitting off from bodily experience, ego-dystonic perceptions of body regions, depersonalization, and dissociation
- Spontaneously emerging body phenomena such as pain, coldness, warmth or heat, tingling, vibrations, etc.

Further diagnostic indicators and cues for intervention can be found in the symbols that the client uses, such as colors and shapes (common examples include: a lump in the throat, pain in the neck, head in a vice, stomach like a rock, hole in the gut, hole in the heart, things on my chest, etc.). The work of Jay Stattman (1991) and Hilarion Petzold (1988) offer avenues of understanding and therapeutic applications of body-related images, symbols, and imaginations in the process of Body Psychotherapy. In collaboration with Joseph Campbell, Stanley Keleman (1999) illustrates the associations between archetypical images, mythological symbols, and organismic significance in his book *Myth and the Body*. In the treatment of dissociative disorders and post-traumatic stress disorder (PTSD), Body Psychotherapy can also utilize a form of guided imagery (Levine, 1998).

## Levels and Interventions of Body-Oriented Work

In the diagnostic, as well as in clinical, processes, it is useful to distinguish different levels of work. The following represent the basic levels:

    I. Self-awareness
   II. Central functions and experiential practices
  III. Conflict- and process-oriented work

### I. Self-Awareness

Because personal identity is grounded in bodily reality, we could say, *"I know who I am as I experience myself."* Any self-awareness, and therefore also any memory, begins with sensory information. For the process of Body Psychotherapy, self-awareness and self-perception are of central importance. Consequently, many awareness practices play an important role in Body-Oriented Psychotherapy. **Interoceptive** self-awareness (perception of the inner organs), **proprioceptive** self-awareness (perception through the muscular system), and **exteroception** (perception through the five senses) are all practiced, and constitute the foundation of a relationship to the self and the world that is grounded in empirical personal reality, rather than in fantasy or imagination. This reality also contains the necessary resources for change.

Neuropsychology researcher Bessel van der Kolk locates the key to change in interoceptive experiences, because they can influence structures of the brain (limbic system, etc.) that cannot be accessed by means of verbally oriented psychotherapy. Blockages of perception can be addressed by means of a focused sensing of bodily sensations (pleasant as well as unpleasant) and awareness of vegetative processes: through exploration of one's breathing; through concentrated sensing of body parts in response to self-touch or touch by another; and through noticing even minimal movement impulses (which often come to the client's attention only through feedback by the therapist).

The facilitation of sensory perception and self-awareness, as well as the ability to explore bodily experiences and emotional tones at the onset of therapy, creates a good platform for the exploration of regressive experiences later in the course of therapy (see Chapter 37, "Sensory Self-Reflexivity: Therapeutic Action in Body Psychotherapy" by Gustl Marlock).

Gestalt Therapy is aware of the significance of sensory self-awareness as it pertains to the reanimation of repressed aspects of the self. Along these lines, Downing (1996) describes "frozen" or underdeveloped affective-motor schemas that evidence a "will to grow" once the client comes into contact with them.

Aside from sensing, Geissler and Geissler (1993) also focus on how clients put their bodily experiences into words. This process is viewed as contributing to a post-maturation of the ego: "The verbal explication of body experiences skews pathologically distorted perceptions and enhances the ability to differentiate between what is inside and what is outside."[57]

Lastly, kinesthetic sensation (the perception of movement) needs to be noted, because kinesthetic sensation plays an important role in the perception of movement restrictions, the reanimation of psycho-motoric functions, and bodily practices in general.

## II. Experiential Work and Practices of Self-Discovery

The theories of most schools of Body Psychotherapy agree that practices of self-discovery are indispensable when it comes to the psycho-physical process of change. The limitations of neurotic structures consist of restricted *functions,* underdeveloped *abilities,* and immature *qualities.* Practices addressing the different levels of function serve the client as methods of self-exploration, and to gain experiential familiarity with the client's abilities and limits. They also serve the therapist, when in diagnostic mode, as it allows him or her to perceive and experience the client in action. Two kinds of basic bodily practices can be distinguished:

- **General preparatory practices** (such as sensing, perceiving, and slowly immersing); and targeted therapeutic interventions—for example, to deepen emotional experience, or to facilitate the expression of repressed emotions. In regard to the level of conflict-oriented work (discussed in more detail later in this chapter), such practices offer a valuable potential to activate problems and to make the therapy process more dynamic. Such practices can be valuable purely for self-discovery; but, used in the context of psychotherapy sessions, the therapist pays attention to their timing and intensity, so as to integrate them advantageously into the flow of the session. This kind of Body Psychotherapeutic work can further facilitate organismic self-regulation, the development of new affective-motor schemas, and a restructuring of the body. In the following examples, I will describe central functions with corresponding examples of self-discovery practices. Discussion of these functions will simultaneously illustrate some of the conceptual devices that Body-Oriented Psychotherapy operates with.

- **Breathing practices:** Breathing constitutes one of the most essential themes of self-exploration in the context of Body Psychotherapy. The goal of breathwork and associated practices is to deepen the breath, so as to eventually reestablish natural

---

57  Author's translation.

or spontaneous breathing. Because breathing is closely linked with emotional mood and mental state, not only can breathing practices loosen musculature, activate the voice, and intensify breathing, but also the ensuing vitalization can lead to experiences of well-being, evoke other emotional responses, or trigger conflicts and defensive reactions (see Chapter 61, "The Role of the Breath in Mind-Body Psychotherapy" by Ian Macnaughton with Peter A. Levine).

Although some clients execute and perceive these practices in a mechanistic fashion in the early stages of therapy, doing these practices over time tends to lead to a new and expanded sense of one's bodily, or embodied, self. Knowing that one can't make breathing natural, but can only allow this to happen on its own accord, it is advisable to introduce breathwork by selecting practices that match the current emotional state of the client and offer him or her the possibility of experiencing their own personal breathing pattern at that moment in time. This way of proceeding limits the risk of practices becoming drills, or being done by rote. Even practices that merely aim to deepen the breath can initiate self-regulatory processes that can facilitate the unfolding of natural breathing.

**Practice Example 1: Deepening of the Breath via Bodily Vibration**

In a supine position on a level, firm surface, with legs extended toward the ceiling and knees slightly bent, and the hands and arms flat on the surface, bring the soles of the feet parallel to the ceiling by extending (pushing up with) the heels. The legs will soon begin vibrating. These vibrations are maintained by continuing to extend the heels. In this exercise, the breath is enlivened and deepened through the bodily vibrations. After a minute or so, bring the legs back down to the flat surface. This practice can be repeated a couple of times.

*Vitality*

Although a lack of vitality can be an indication of an acute problem, it is also often a sign of unresolved trauma, or an expression of preexisting, character-neurotic armoring and formation, which always leads to devitalization. Just as the blockage of emotions is linked with restrictions in breathing, the lowering of vitality—bioenergetically, we would speak of it as low "energy"—is a consequence of reduction in breathing. The degree of devitalization can differ between layers of the body (endoderm, mesoderm, ectoderm), or the various parts of the body. This lowering ranges from a mild lack of energy to manifest resignation: very tense areas can also be low in energy, because the energy is "locked up" in the tension.

In Body Psychotherapeutic experiential processes involving "charging" and "energizing," it is important to proceed carefully, just as people suffering from hypothermia are not treated by immediately being exposed to great heat. The best approach is to oscillate between vitalization practices and then the reflection on and assimilation thereof. Merely focusing on "energizing" is insufficient. This must be complemented with observation and therapeutic processing of the client's response to heightened vitality, and how the client is able to integrate this. If the capacities for grounding and containment are not yet sufficiently developed, as is commonly the case in people with structural deficits, there is a risk of overstimulation. In people who are overly structured and haven't therapeutically resolved this yet, sole focus on energizing can lead to an "inflation" of existing patterns. This reflective approach is fundamentally different from mechanistically applying techniques.

When referring to aliveness, Reich (1933/1975a) also spoke of vegetative aliveness, to distinguish between vitality based on non-neurotic, authentic, vegetative, mobile, and libidinal embodiment, and "hysterical" forms of vitality—as Boadella calls them (Stumm and Pritz, 2000)—to be observed today in the context of substance abuse (various addictions) or extreme sports (bungee jumping, whitewater rafting, etc.) that stimulate adrenaline-induced vitality. Aside from breathing practices that are equally relevant to all levels of function, the following practice for vitality has stood the test of time.

**Practice Example 2: Rhythmic Leg Beats**

Lying on a mattress in a supine position with legs extended, hit the mattress hard, with alternating legs, not using only the heels. Keep the legs straight without making them stiff or rigid. It is important for the alternating legs to create a rhythm, and to let the movement come from the hips, rather than from the knees, by raising the legs as high as possible. If possible, begin with 60 to 100 beats total, slowly raising that number. Possible questions for the client: "Do your beats feel effective, or do you feel weak as you do them?" "Were you able to sustain the strength of the hits, or did your energy decrease over time?" Regular practice significantly vitalizes the legs, which leads to an enlivening of the whole body.

*Expressiveness*

Although blocked self-expression can be caused by trauma, it also often results from neurotic inhibition, as seen in people who either withhold their movement impulses, affective impulses, emotions, thoughts, and words, or turn their impulses against themselves and their bodies through retroflexion. In such cases, psychic conflicts mainly concern relationships and contact. Often, we also find overarching superego conflicts.

A lack in the capability of being self-expressive commonly indicates insufficiently developed affective-motor schemas. In Gestalt Therapy, we would also consider this as a break in contact with the self or body-self, and a withdrawal behind one's own boundaries with the world. Drawings by children with such problems often show themselves with missing limbs and mouths. Whereas a large number of bodily practices aim to develop body contact and reduce tensions, expressive practices aim to facilitate the expression of emotions. These can be expressions of anger, rage, or frustration, as well as longing.

**Practice Example 3: Gestural Self-Expression: "Longing for Something"**

In a supine position, with bent knees and feet on the floor, reach both arms upward, like a child in a crib longing for its mother. With each exhalation, the arms are extended a little farther. Questions for the client can be: "Can you sense how you are holding yourself back?" "Are you letting your hands hang in a gesture of resignation?" "Can you feel how you are longing?"

*Mobility*

All character-based holding patterns manifest restrictions in mobility and processes of immobilization. These restrictions are not only due to muscular inhibitions, but, additionally, based on limitations in vegetative or pulsatory motility, emotional suppleness, and affect modulation. Contraction and rigidity are organismic answers to mortification. Activation of the stimulus-response cycles in response to stress and alarm reactions is healthy and normal, as it serves survival. However, if the mortification is extraordinarily severe or frequently recurrent, this can induce an automatic immobilization of the involved musculature, among other aspects. The degree of restricted mobility ranges from increased tension and alertness to rigidity and aversion, to total immobility, which expresses itself in flaccidity and resignation. Contraction restricts affective and vegetative excitation that would otherwise inevitably lead to an emotional expression (emotion literally means "to move out"). In certain circumstances, these emotions can become permanently blocked from expression (the Body Psychotherapeutic treatment of traumatic shock is discussed in Chapter 76, "Sensory-Motor Processing for Trauma Recovery" by Pat Ogden and Kekuni Minton).

**Practice Example 4: Breathing Stool**

Immobility in the chest and back can be addressed using a classic bioenergetic practice, with a breathing stool, or alternatively a thick blanket roll placed on top of a waist-high stool. The client lies with his back over the roll, which is placed under the chest or ribs, with the arms stretched back. The pelvis is suspended loosely, and the feet rest on the floor. All the areas of immobility in the area of the neck, chest, and upper back become visible in this posture. The breath goes deep into the abdomen, and painful sensations can be vocalized. A perceived intransigence may be expressed with a "No." With further, deeper breathing, the rigidity of the musculature begins to soften, and body vibrations emerge. After a period of vibrating, the roll is removed. The client then stands, with soft knees, and lets his trunk and head hang down toward the ground.

*Sense-Ability*

The reanimation and refinement of sense-ability is one of the cardinal goals of Body Psychotherapy. Sense-ability brings gracefulness to the body and clarity to the mind. It is a prerequisite for contact with the self, one's own body, and emotions. It also enables contact with the world and other people. Although practices in the area of sensing, and experiencing through the senses, derive primarily from the nonpsychotherapeutic roots of Body Psychotherapy (such as Sensory Awareness: Brooks, 1997), they are nonetheless of elemental significance. Practices use daily activities such as sitting or walking, or facilitate concentration on sense perceptions. The experiential learning derived from such practices allows the practitioner to cut through the level of conceptual, presupposed knowing, which often isn't more than biased opinion, and to access fresh, current information so as to further explore what is immediately and actually present. Gestalt Therapy focuses more comprehensively on this perceptual and experiential work than does Body Psychotherapy in general.

## Practice Example 5: Practices for Self-Perception and Sensing the Self

The client concentrates on what she perceives of herself and speaks of this. For example: "I perceive that my hands touch each other. I sense that my fingers are warm and that my right thumb presses into the heel of the hand. Now I notice that I clench my teeth and press my lips together. Now I take a deep breath and sense that I'm beginning to feel sad." In a practice of pure self-discovery, the client might proceed in this fashion for about ten minutes, but this is also an excellent way to begin a therapeutic process.

*The Ability to Surrender in Sexuality and Love*

Many clients come to therapy because of couples problems, or conflicts relating to their sexuality, and, in many cases, we find the main neurotic blockages in these areas. Conflicts most commonly involve oedipal relational dynamics, gender identity, and problems with the embodiment of gender. Commenting on sexuality, Reich noted the massive degree of societal conditioning in the body. Considering the fact that today a large majority of products are marketed by creating associations with a "sexual body," this topic (the societal command of the body) is more current than ever.

Sexual surrender entails highly affectively charged states of excitation and loss of control by the ego; accordingly, associated fears are often experienced, like the fear of falling. Great muscular countermobilizations are found mainly in the area of the neck, the chest segment, the diaphragm, and the pelvic region. Pierrakos (1974) has come up with some interesting thoughts regarding energetic blockages of the heart region and heart disease (see Chapter 62, "Heart, Heart Feelings, and Heart Symptoms" by Courtenay Young). Pierrakos, as well as Lowen (1993), consider the heart and heart-centered feelings to be the core of what it is to be human. Lowen (1991) developed a series of falling practices that offer therapeutic avenues of addressing the fear of losing control and difficulties with surrender. Reich considers sexuality as the central affective theme of human affairs. The "jellyfish" practice can help to loosen up some of the previously mentioned blockages, particularly in the pelvis and the legs, and to facilitate experiences of body pulsations and pleasurable streaming sensations (Heller, 1994).

## Practice Example 6: The Jellyfish

In a supine position, bend the knees, with the feet flat on the mat. The distance between the pelvis and the feet allows a comfortable, grounded pelvic rotation, upward and backward. The feet and knees are separated by about four inches. With the exhalation (out-breath), allow the knees to spread apart as far as is comfortably possible, creating a stretch of the inner thighs. With the inhalation (in-breath), bring the knees together until they almost touch. With the next exhalation, let the knees open again back downward. Repeat these flowing, pulsing movements, similar to the movements of an anemone or jellyfish (that's why it is called the "jellyfish exercise"), until the legs begin to vibrate. If possible, allow these vibrations to spread toward the upper body to occur for some time while breathing freely and without effort. As a practice of self-discovery, try to do this for eight to ten minutes.

*Aggression, Self-Assertion, and Setting Boundaries*

Along with others, Lowen (1991) emphasizes how important it is for a person to be able to adequately defend themselves, and to be able to say "No," as well as to emphatically say "Yes." He notes that most patients come to therapy with a manifest inhibition against aggression, not only in regard to anger itself, but more generally pertaining to issues such as taking something for themselves, wanting something, or rejecting something. Practices addressing this important issue can make a substantial contribution toward strengthening of the ego and developing the body ego. Because anger and angry self-expression are often laden with feelings of guilt and fear, the positive effect of entering these affective landscapes is not to be underestimated. At times, associated practices have an archaic character. They often evoke images of children in fits of rage, or making efforts to set boundaries.

**Practice Example 7: "Get off my back!"**

Stand with the feet parallel and shoulder-width apart. Bend the elbows and raise them to about shoulder level. Then move both elbows back sharply and vigorously, either together or alternately (as if trying to get something off one's back), and say, "Get off my back!" Repeat this practice a number of times, and express any anger loudly and clearly. Questions for clients: "Could you feel how this practice can help to straighten and strengthen your back?" "Were you aware that you had been a little hunched over, as if you were actually carrying someone (or something) on your back?" "Who or what might that be?"

The levels of function discussed thus far have addressed the expansive and expressive side of the continuum of human experience. The following three functions—grounding, containment, and centering—represent the necessary polar complements (Boadella, 1987).

*Grounding*

The concept of grounding, introduced by Lowen (1988) and Keleman (1980), has become part of the common vocabulary of Body Psychotherapy (see particularly Chapter 66, "Horizontal Grounding" by Angela Belz-Knöferl, and Chapter 67, "Vertical Grounding: The Body in the World and the Self in the Body" by Lily Anagnostopoulou). It refers to the relationship between a person's body and the earth's gravitational field. A successful balance between the force of gravity and muscle tone, along with other upwardly directed forces in the human being, has a twofold effect: It provides stability on the ground, and it makes mobility possible. From the perspective of Developmental Psychology, grounding concerns the transition from the horizontal—dependent—position of early childhood to the achievement of vertical autonomy. The processes of coming "to stand on one's own two feet" and "taking a stand" in the world unfold in the interplay of motoric development, ego development, and the environment. Metaphorically, we speak of whether someone can "stand" himself or something; whether he can "stand up for" or "stand for" himself; or if he "tiptoes through life" or "hovers" around things. According to Lowen (1991), such metaphors have analogies to the ways people actually stand, and—in regard to this—Lowen speaks of good or poor grounding.

The introduction of the concept of grounding (see Chapters 66 and 67) also expanded Body Psychotherapy to include therapeutic work in the vertical dimension. Lowen (Lowen and Lowen, 1977) developed a large number of practices for work in a standing position, having a range of positive effects.

Another aspect of grounding is commonly referred to as horizontal grounding. It speaks to how rooted a person is in their own body, how grounded they are in their own bodily reality, how aware they are of being in the world as an embodied being, and how they can relate—from this position—to others (see Chapter 66).

**Practice Example 8: Basic Practice for Vibration and Contact with the Ground**

While standing, bend forward from the waist with the arms relaxed so that the fingertips can touch the ground. The whole weight of the body remains on the feet, preferably on the balls of the feet, without lifting the toes. Begin with bent knees, and then slowly lift the pelvis (buttocks) until the hamstrings are stretched. Questions for clients: "Does this create a vibration in the legs?" If not, "Can it be helpful to slowly bend the knees a little once more and then straighten them again?" If necessary, repeat multiple times until the muscles begin to release. Breathe easily and allow the vibrations to occur. "Are these vibrations soft or jumpy, smooth or jerky?" Remain in this position for about one minute, and then straighten up, standing with soft (slightly bent) knees. "Has the contact to the ground changed?" "What is the effect of this practice?"

*Containment*

In order to establish personal boundaries, and to develop and maintain a sense of identity and integrity, it is necessary to be able to collect and consolidate oneself. Inner excitement and arousal can be channeled into constructive behavior or contact to the extent that a flexible, non-repressive muscular embrace can contain them. Reich's (1933/1975a) theory was that all bodily contractions are always generated by fear and that this functions antagonistically to sexuality. The concept of containment represents a revision of this idea, as it shows how successful containment is the precondition for all successful expansion. In the context of the therapeutic relationship, containment refers to the establishment of an experiential space that is—simultaneously—secure and open, and thus can hold any of the material that the client introduces into it.

**Practice Example 9: Feeling Your Boundary**

While in a standing position, raise the arms so the hands are in front of the chest, facing outward. Position the hands as if touching the inside of a curved wall or permeable membrane that totally surrounds your body. Imagine that this represents a membrane around the whole of you: it functions as your boundary. You are safe within it and it is permeable, so that you can breathe easily. The muscle tone and the pressure outward of the hands is increased, in small, incremental steps until this membrane is experienced as thickening or stiffening. Then the muscle tone and pressure is decreased again until it is so low that the membrane seems very permeable. The hands can move around a bit to experience other parts of the membrane. Next, begin to oscillate between more pressure (felt as a movement of the hands outward) and less pressure (felt as a movement from the hands back slightly), changing the muscle tone in the hands. This can lead to the experience of a pulsation, possibly in tune with your breathing. The gestural expression of the hands is a microexpression of what is happening on the level of the whole organism. The brief pauses that occur in this kind of bodywork are critical: they allow for the emergence of somatic inner feedback in response to the neuromuscular activity, and they make time for this feedback to be perceived. After some time, a clear sense emerges of how much tension and support the membrane must offer to provide adequate containment and safety. The membrane, as it thickens and strengthens, can also protect you.

*Centering*

Centering means to direct one's attention toward the center of one's own person, in contrast to experiencing what is at the periphery. It means turning toward the biological and ontological core of the self. It also means sensing and perceiving, in contrast to doing and acting; being present in the moment instead of contemplating the future or the past. Because most people are very identified with some aspects of themselves, they might not be aware that they have lost their "center." Only when they enter the above-mentioned fields of experience do they notice the difference. Centering and containment are helpful in the regulation of hyperaroused states, post-traumatic stress, and PTSD.

The process of centering can be facilitated by means of attentional practices—such as a walking meditation or a sitting meditation—in which the attention is focused on the perception of the movement of breath, or at the center of the abdomen. Generally, centering is facilitated by the principle of slowing down.

**Practice Example 10: Centering the Eyes**

Sense your eyes, in exploration of the question as to whether they are straining to look out, or if they are withdrawn and glazed over. Note the differences between the left eye and the right eye. After releasing some tensions in the muscles of the neck, the eyes are centered during the exhalation of the breath. We are working with the image of returning the overly extended eye back to a neutral baseline, whereas the overly withdrawn eye is expanded forward to this point. Questions to the client: "What kinds of perception and what feelings arise through centering the eyes, as compared to the earlier state?" "What effects do centering of the eyes have on the whole body?"

Many of the practices mentioned above are a part of the standard repertoire of many Body Psychotherapy (and other) approaches, and can also be used as methods of self-discovery in the context of groups or dyads. In these contexts, the experienced therapist will need to be alert to note when such practices of self-discovery are no longer merely that, but when they enter a deeper, therapeutic field of experience. Used in the context of psychotherapy, many of these practices have a high potential to be affectively evocative. Therefore, only well-trained Body Psychotherapists should facilitate this kind of practice with their clients. However, some of these practices can be used safely as self-exploratory exercises.

**III. Conflict- and Process-Oriented Work**

Whereas the utilization of Body Psychotherapeutic practices in the two previously discussed levels of body-oriented work (self-awareness, experiential work, and practices of self-discovery) may usually have direct (or indirect) therapeutic effects, the third level (conflict- and process-oriented work) directly addresses Body-Oriented Psychotherapeutic work. In the attempt to categorize the different methodological approaches, demarcations are sometimes a bit crude and oversimplified. If we choose to do so nonetheless, it would be useful to distinguish a primarily process-oriented approach from a primarily conflict- and defense-oriented approach.

The process-oriented, phenomenological approach, similar to the methodological approach of Gestalt Therapy, uses the therapeutic space to facilitate mindful awareness of the client's own inner state, in the present moment, and the unfolding of associated processes. The technical way of proceeding might therefore be described as explorative or permissive.

The Hakomi Method, for example, establishes mindfulness by introducing the image of a neutral inner observer, with whose help a person can explore how their own body-mind is organized (Kurtz, 1985). Similarly, in Al Pesso's Psychomotor Therapy, a fictitious witness is called upon to reflect fine nuances of the client's perceptions and to facilitate processing. Even some time ago, Perls (1974) proposed that it is possible to observe oneself from beyond one's personal, conflictual entanglements—thus, to perceive and understand oneself as different from and wider than those entanglements. This idea can probably be traced back to his knowledge of Zen Buddhism. Gestalt Therapy works with the role of an inner director who is in a position to propose creative solutions for problems that present themselves as insurmountable. These methods draw upon elements of Humanistic Psychology: first, in addressing people's abilities and resources that are often found to be dormant, and second, in facilitating their tendency for self-actualization.

Rollo May (1990) writes, *"This ability is already contained in the word 'exists,' which literally means to come forth. Existence refers to an ongoing becoming, growing, and unfolding...."* This touches upon the existential dimension of work with the body.

The methods more closely associated with the tradition of character-analytical work tend to explicitly focus on conflicts and defenses. Commonly, the goal is to facilitate the emotional expression of repressed affects and feelings that are held in the defenses of the body. In order for an incomplete gestalt, or for interrupted cycles, to be completed, arrested processes of development and maturation are revisited. In this case, the goal of direct interventions with the body is to understand and modulate holding patterns and blockages manifesting at different levels of the musculature, in the autonomic nervous system, and in emotional and cognitive patterns.

The previously mentioned functions present areas of potential conflict. Sometimes such functions and correlating vital abilities and qualities are abandoned, restricted, or insufficiently developed in order to maintain earlier object-relations constellations. Consequently, the bandwidth of emotions that can be experienced is significantly restricted, and the spectrum of unpleasurable affects dominates the emotional landscape. In addition, it is important to note that the blocked organismic mobility, and the reduced sense of self, lead to the development of "pathogenic convictions and dysfunctional behavior potentials" (Rudolf, 2004).

The following illustrates what such a methodological approach might look like in addressing the breath and holding patterns.

*Breath*

The immobilization of the breath plays a central role in the development and maintenance of the psychic structure that is manifested in the body. From an organismic perspective, we find that dysfunctional use of breathing, or restrictions in the process of breathing, are directly correlated with a host of other problems, which include: reductions in sensitivity, emotionality, and the ability to express feelings and vitality in general; repression of sexual and other affective impulses; restriction of the ability to receive something; and limitations in the ability to contain and structure emotions.

> The restriction of breathing is perhaps the most effective body-defense. Its destructive effects can be observed in just about anyone's psychic economy . . . that is why any defensive reduction in breathing is so powerful. It impairs our contact with our selves and with other people. (Downing, 1996)

> With nearly all strong emotions such as crying, rage, fear, and lust, our breathing deepens. So it comes as no surprise that reduction in breathing is a central dynamic whenever someone tries to suppress such emotions. (Boadella, 1991c)

The maintenance of chronically restricted or unbalanced breathing patterns is reflected in tensions of the breathing musculature, particularly in the muscles of the upper back, in the large muscles of the chest, and in the intercostal muscles. Restrictions of breathing through chronic contraction of the diaphragm play a central role in splitting off feelings of sexuality and vitality from the pelvic and abdominal region. Limitations in the functioning of the diaphragm primarily affect spontaneous and autonomous breathing, while the ability to breathe deeply and voluntarily may remain unimpaired.

> The work of Body Psychotherapy calls for a high degree of awareness, sensitivity, and knowledge about the psycho-emotional dimensions of breathing patterns and body defenses on the part of the therapist. Before dysfunctional breathing patterns can fundamentally change, the client needs to understand the emotional and life-historical context of these contractions and feel and process its impacts. (Boadella, 1991a)

The first step in specific work with the breath is to assess the course of the breath wave, and where and how it is blocked—for example, in the chest, in the diaphragm, or in the abdomen. The "how" of the breath shows itself in the way that the breath moves—for example, whether air is sucked in hungrily, or if air is pushed out during exhalation, or if the breath is halting with interruptions, or reduced and in small increments, or full and flowing. Downing (1996) refers to this as the establishment of a client's breath profile. The kinds of contraction present serve to differentiate between the holding patterns of pronounced inhalation versus pronounced exhalation. But hypotonic muscles are just as important as hypertonic muscles.

In many cases, and generally in the case of clients with

structural disorders, it is advisable to first stimulate flaccid, hypotonic muscles before facilitating release in hardened, hypertonic muscles. Some degree of abdominal muscle tone is necessary in order to be able to exhale fully.

## Clinical Example 2

A thirty-four-year-old client presented with a pronounced exhalation posture. Initially, I hadn't noticed this, because the client was tall and shapely, and showed a lively face with alert eyes. I was puzzled, however, that despite her obvious curiosity and intelligence, she worked in an unskilled job at a daycare center. In the analysis of her breath pattern, I noticed that many of the breathing muscles of the trunk were chronically hypotonic. According to Downing, we could refer to this as a massive deactivation—a form of body defense that is not based on holding, but on reduced tension. Viewed in the life-historical context of this client, this pattern made a lot of sense. The client's mother, a pretty and petite model, reigned as the (egocentric) center of the family, and was very much idealized by all members of the family. Because the mother wasn't able to tolerate the client's feelings of competition or rage, the client repressed her negative emotions. This continued even after the parents emigrated abroad, leaving her and her brother, who was two years older than she, alone in Germany, right after she graduated from high school. One of the areas that the therapy focused on was to stimulate her breathing and her hypotonic musculature. This evoked much rage and fury in her. Interestingly, she had practiced a (Yogic) relaxation technique for some time that had emphasized the exhalation. In therapy, she now learned the significance of inhalation. She restored herself, psychologically as well as physically, and began to take her life into her own hands. Equipped with newfound strength, she began to study medicine and graduated successfully. She was also able to end an unsatisfying relationship with a man.

Restrictions in breathing patterns can be directly treated within the context of Body Psychotherapeutic breathwork. Although we know that the expansion of a deeper and fuller breath leads to a deepening of bodily and emotional experiences, we cannot predict what specifically this will stimulate in a client, and we are not to impose any expectations on our clients in this regard. The therapeutic work with breath is one of the best ways to guide clients into a dialogue with themselves, because breath, breath movement, and associated breath sounds have near-seismographic precision in reflecting changes or processes within the body or psyche that may (or may not) be conscious. In the process of therapy, attention can be directed toward these processes at any time. Similar to the method of free association in psychoanalysis, the client can then follow her own breathing process and see what wants to emerge—for example, a feeling, an expressive movement, or a defensive posture.

Aside from proceeding in an explorative and associative fashion, there are many techniques the Body Psychotherapist can select from in order to make direct, body-based interventions with the goal of deepening the breathing. These reach from the conscious modification in breathing tempo (faster or slower), to deliberate, gradual lengthening of the inhalation phase and exhalation phase (for example, by counting), to techniques that expand the breath through the use of voice or movement. They also include the use of the palms to touch the chest or abdomen, where they may lightly press during the exhalation. Lifting the trunk, at the level of the ribs, can further stimulate the inhalation. In the case of a diaphragmatic blockage, the intercostal muscles can be treated with pressure-point massage.

A further, paradoxical, intervention is to intensify the restrictions in the area of the lower ribs by holding this area for about ten seconds. Letting go is often followed by a reflective inhalation, which initiates deepened breathing. If this disorganizes some of the body armor in this area, heavy vibrations or convulsive movements of the body may be observed. These movements either spontaneously link together, or the therapist can guide them in the direction of an emotional expression.

Affects, or feelings, expressed in the movement of emotion can be associated with a specific scene, person, or situation. Commonly, the desire arises to express what was previously repressed in relation to a significant person who is present either symbolically or in memory. The mostly affective memory calls for a completion, the completion of a gestalt, or "unfinished business," as it is referred to in Gestalt Therapy. The affects involved can be positive, such as love, or negative, such as rage or hatred, or grief and longing. Here, the phenomenon of procedural or even participatory memory (Alan Fogel, 2008) becomes apparent.

*Treatment of Holding Patterns*

Tensions and holding patterns, but also hypotonic patterns, are brought to awareness by directing attention toward perception of the client's musculature. Intensifying the tension in the affected muscle groups makes it possible to perceive the associated posture and emotional content more distinctly, and to recognize the movement or behavior that is frozen, or inhibited, in this posture. The question of *how* someone does something—that is, how a client chronically raises his shoulders, how a client makes his chest rigid and hard, or how he collapses his abdomen—all offer the client a new perspective. Postures that were previously viewed as "given," or "fated," can now be seen as generated by actions. When specific movements (e.g., raising the shoulders) are explored and repeated in micromovements, and with deliberate slowness so as to allow time to perceive the inner feedback that responds to these actions, this can initiate a change process in both the body and the mind that can gradually spread to include the whole organism. The following are important questions in this context: What kind of experience arises from a specific body posture? Which functions does this posture serve?

The clarity with which a body posture, or a specific kind of body defense, can be felt and reenacted is mirrored in the clarity of the psychic, emotional, or existential messages it conveys. Such messages arise from the center of the client's own body.

Keleman's (1987) methodological approach might best represent this way of working. Only a few pioneers of Body Psychotherapy have stressed as much as Keleman the clients' own involvement in their growth and change processes as important therapeutic factors and as essential elements in the success of the therapy. Along this line, he proposes that *how* someone participates in a practice, or in the work in general, has a critical impact on the overall experience.

This kind of therapeutic work with the body always begins in the present body posture, or with an apparent behavioral pattern that has been repeatedly observed. A general, psychosomatic pattern, or a local, specific pattern, such as a gesture of the hand or a posture of a particular body part, can serve as starting points. One of Keleman's (1987) basic practices is composed of five steps:

1. Become aware of your body, without changing anything. What posture have you taken? Where have you tensed your muscles, and where have you allowed yourself space? How are you in contact?

2. Intensify this posture by tensing the involved musculature. Do more of what you have been doing anyway. Then you can perceive what you are doing more clearly, which allows you to make new distinctions. How do you perceive yourself in this posture?

3. Starting with this intensified but familiar posture, gradually let it go in small "microsteps." Clearly take note of every step. What are you experiencing and sensing during this process? How does your posture change?

4. Wait! Stay with this experience for a while. Feel what wants to emerge. What resonance arises from within your body when you let go of your habitual way of organizing yourself? What do you experience about yourself that is new to you? With each step of letting go (step 3), you can repeat step 4, listening.

5. Give the new experience and form some more shape by lightly firming up the associated musculature. What did you learn? How do you embody your new experience in the world?

Keleman (in an unpublished 2003 paper) elaborates as follows: "*From a given pattern (extroverted or introverted) we begin to differentiate. The definition and differentiation of the original figure or form leads to its transformation. This is what we might call growth, voluntary muscular efforts opening the door to what was inherited and automated.*"

A different approach—following Reich (1975b), Rosenberg (1989), and others—conceives of "body armor" as a complex system of seven ring-shaped segments of blockages (beginning with the eyes and ending with the pelvic region). Their strategy of confronting these defenses is to "unearth" the affects and feelings that are held in these blockages, so as to bring the conflicts associated with the different segments into consciousness, and then process them in the context of object-relations work. Excessive, chronic muscular tensions also indicate frozen vegetative arousal and reduced emotional motility.

Unspecific body interventions such as bioenergetic stress positions (Koll, 1988), or specific interventions such as the movement of particular body parts (e.g., the eyes or the jaw), or the massage of specific muscles (e.g., the shoulders), in conjunction with deepened breathing, can be used to free muscle groups from their fixations and bring them into greater motility. Although, at first, we may observe only a minimal or unspecific movement, with exploration and therapeutic processing, it can become more distinct and emotional in tone. The therapist is careful to take note of spontaneously arising phenomena, such as movements of the extremities, facial expression, or changes in breathing (for example, taking a deep breath, holding the breath, sudden sounds, etc.). *"Your body speaks its mind,"* says Keleman (1980).

Such things don't occur at random, but signify processes that are often unconscious, whether fear has arisen, triggering increased defensive behavior, and/or previously frozen patterns are now melting, in which case they are manifestations of bodily self-regulation or reorganization. Any such process is to be given undivided attention and regard (respect).

Interventions like these can cause a marked increase in affective charge, which then needs to be handled carefully. Let's say we work with a client for whom the expression of his aggressive impulses is taboo. If we were to work with his arms, shoulders, and upper back, he might want to give cathartic expression to his aggressive impulses by screaming, hitting, kicking, or wanting to choke someone ("I'm going to wring your neck!").

Geissler and Geissler (1993) have commented on this point:

> Additionally, body-work is an appropriate means for working with affects at 'blast furnace temperature.' Such affects, for example murderous rage and strain paralyze the client's ego. Techniques that provide encouragement and permission and the containment offered by boundaries and security . . . make it possible to raise them into consciousness and enact them to that extent. Knowing that no one will be destroyed or annihilated in the process makes a positive experience possible. Subsequently, such omnipotent feelings lose some of their conviction and force, and their repression can be softened. The energetic potential that is contained in these aggressive affects can then incrementally be integrated to support the conscious actions of the ego, thereby strengthening the life functions of the client.[58]

As described above, one way for psychotherapists to address holding patterns in the context of conflict-oriented work is to facilitate the client's self-motion. Another possible route of intervention, based on knowledge of character structures and their specific defensive manifestations, is to create bodily enactments between the therapist and the client. The therapist can "take over" the holding pattern (inhibition) that the client embodies—for example, in her arms, chest, or pelvis—and thereby create some space for the client to develop what was previously blocked. (Please note: Interventions like these are to be employed only by highly experienced therapists, and—in preparation for such an intervention—the therapist needs to inform the client about the procedure, its intention, and the therapist's actions, and to ask for the client's consent to proceed.)

Here is an example of a rather dynamic intervention: The blocked desire for autonomy that is commonly associated with the masochistic theme can be enacted by the therapist preventing the client from walking by briefly

---

58  Author's translation.

holding both of the client's ankles. Lowen (1988) emphasized that the masochistic body structure is characterized by a contraction of the flexor muscles. The tension that would enable erect standing and mobility, if it were toning the extensors, is instead drawn into the viscera in order to generate inner pressure to create a kind of support. The approach outlined above makes the instability caused by such a shift evident, and calls forth some extensor tonus that then enables self-motion. This specific mobilization can generate strong feelings of frustration and rage, which may be transferred onto the therapist. It also cues emphatic expressive movements of the legs. Initially, this intervention will bring to the surface the frustrated and conflict-laden desire for autonomy. As the experience is processed, and the defense is overcome, the client may transition into spontaneous self-motion. If this affective cycle is allowed to "complete" itself, the client may experience a sense of lightness, and possibly great satisfaction over having won her independence. As a matter of course, each affective cycle is followed by a therapeutic phase of verbalization, reflection, and integration.

What is really interesting about Body Psychotherapeutic work is that not only are we challenged to hear and understand the words that are spoken and unspoken, but we also need to learn the individual dialects of the person's body language: their language of posture, gesture, micromovements and macromovements, sounds, breath, the language of their eyes, and facial expressions. Both the therapist and the client can learn these dialects.

Facial and eye expressions can be used therapeutically by guiding the client to overemphasize what is already apparent in the expression of his face (e.g., disgust, mistrust, fear, grief, etc.). In the case of reduced facial expression, the client can be invited to mimic the emotions that are suspected to lie beneath the "facade." Al Pesso (1973) is the founder of Psychomotor Therapy: his method, perhaps most of all, emphasizes the understanding and effective use of facial-expressive messages.

As in any form of psychotherapy, Body Psychotherapy works not only with repressions, where the therapeutic goal is to free up restricted structures, and not only with dissociations, where the facilitation of contact and association can remedy interruptions of contact, but also with deficits and structural weaknesses.

In work with structural disorders, the initial emphasis is not so much on expression as on strengthening the muscular capability to hold the self, what Keleman (1992) referred to as "containment," and also on grounding, so as to increase the ability to bear the self and to tolerate contact with painful aspects of the self. Until the inner ground (access to emotional, mental, and physical resources and the development of new affective-motor schemas) provides a sufficient sense of security, the therapist and the therapeutic relationship can provisionally serve as external ground or support, or as an auxiliary ego, or to offer a corrective emotional experience.

**Practice Example 11: A Grounding Experience with the Therapist**

The client must have developed a reasonable measure of trust in the therapist for this particular practice to work. The client lies on her back, and the therapist kneels at the foot end of the mattress. The client's knees are bent, and her feet touch the front of the therapist's thighs. If the client can tolerate the closeness and the physical contact with the therapist, the client is asked alternately to use her feet to gently press against the therapist's legs with each exhalation. The client is encouraged to find her own rhythm and to follow her own inner process while the therapist attends her carefully.

From a methodological perspective, the therapist can give support by holding the body, or parts of the body, such as the head, shoulders, arms, or feet, where a neurotic postural holding structure is evident. This is true for underdeveloped, as well as for overdeveloped, structures. The therapist's provision of actual emotional and physical support can enable the client to access aspects of inner experience that—having to hold it together on his own—had seemed too threatening to behold.

## Conclusion

This chapter has presented a range of practices and body-oriented interventions that derive from the substantial methodological repository of Body Psychotherapy, in order to illustrate some of the practical work within Body Psychotherapy.

As this has shown, a wide spectrum of methodological approaches can be distinguished. Some of the practices mentioned in this chapter have become part of the standard repertoire of most Body Psychotherapeutic methods by now. The conflict- and process-oriented interventions, described in the last section, include examples of approaches that are creatively designed to fit individual and contextual factors. In the field of Body Psychotherapy, such interventions are just as common as the others, but they can't be described in a similarly systematic fashion, because they vary considerably with the conflicts of the client, the therapeutic relationship, and the present situation.

## References

Baker, E. F. (1980). *Der Mensch in der Falle: Das Dilemma unserer blockierten Energie: Ursachen und Therapie* [Man in the trap: The dilemma of our blocked energy: Causes and therapy]. Munich: Kösel.

Boadella, D. (1987). *Lifestreams: An introduction to Biosynthesis.* London: Routledge, Arkana.

Boadella, D. (1991a). *Befreite Lebensenergie: Einführung in die Biosynthese* [Lifestreams: An introduction to Biosynthesis]. Munich: Kösel.

Boadella, D. (1991b). Schwerkraft, Muskeln, Herzgefühle [Gravity, muscles, and heart feelings]. *Energie & Charakter, 22*(4).

Boadella, D. (1991c). Stile der Atmung [Styles of breathing]. *Energie & Charakter, 22*(3).

Brooks, C. V. W. (1997). *Erleben durch die Sinne: deutsche Bearbeitung von Charlotte Selver* [Sensory Awareness: German edition of Charlotte Selver]. Paderborn: Junfermann.

Damasio, A. R. (1997). *Descartes Irrtum: Fühlen, Denken und das menschliche Gehirn* [Descartes' error: Emotion, reason and the human brain]. Munich: DTV.

Downing, G. (1996). *Körper und Wort in der Psychotherapie: Leitlinien für die Praxis* [Body and word in psychotherapy: Guidelines for practice]. Munich: Kösel.

Fogel, A. (2008). Remembering infancy, in *Theories of infant development*, ed. J. Gavin Bremner and Alan Slater. John Wiley & Sons.

Geissler, C., & Geissler, P. (1993). Praxeologie der Bioenergetischen Analyse [Praxeology of Bioenergetic Analysis]. *Energie & Charakter, 7*.

Heller, M. (1994). Der "Jelly-Fish" und Gerda Boyesen [The "jellyfish" and Gerda Boyesen]. *Energie & Charakter, 9*.

Keleman, S. (1980). *Dein Körper formt Dein Selbst: Der bioenergetische Weg zu emotionaler und sexueller Befriedigung* [Your body shapes itself: The Bioenergetic path to emotional and sexual gratification]. Munich: Kösel.

Keleman, S. (1987). *Embodying experience: Forming a personal life.* Berkeley, CA: Center Press.

Keleman, S. (1992). *Verkörperte Gefühle: Der anatomische Ursprung unserer Erfahrungen und Einstellungen* [Embodied emotions: The anatomical origin of our experiences and attitudes]. Munich: Kösel.

Keleman, S. (1999). *Myth and the body: With Joseph Campbell.* Berkeley, CA: Center Press.

Koll, R. D. (1988). *Grundkurs Bioenergetik: Theorie und Praxis der Selbstbefreiung* [Basic Course Bioenergetics: Theory and practice of self-liberation]. Munich: Goldmann.

Kurtz, R. (1985). *Körperzentrierte Psychotherapie: Die Hakomi-Methode* [Body-Oriented Psychotherapy: The Hakomi Method]. Essen: Synthesis.

Levine, P. A. (1998). *Trauma-Heilung* [Healing trauma]. Essen: Synthesis.

Lowen, A. (1988). *Körperausdruck und Persönlichkeit: Grundlagen und Praxis der Bioenergetik* [Bodily expression and personality: Principles and practice of Bioenergetics]. Munich: Kösel.

Lowen, A. (1991). *Bioenergetik für Jeden: Das vollständige Übungshandbuch* [Bioenergetics for everyone: Full training manual]. Munich: Goldmann.

Lowen, A. (1993). *Bioenergetik als Körpertherapie: Der Verrat am Körper und wie er wieder gut zu machen ist* [Bioenergetics as body therapy: The betrayal of the body and how it is to get well again]. Hamburg: Reinbeck.

Lowen, A., and Lowen, L. (1977). *The way to vibrant health: A manual of Bioenergetic exercises*. New York: Harper & Row.

May, R. (1990). *Sich selbst entdecken: Seinserfahrung in den Grenzen der Welt [To discover themselves: Experience of being within the limits of the world]*. Munich: DTV.

Perls, F. (1974). *Gestalttherapie in Aktion [Gestalt Therapy in action]*. Stuttgart: Klett.

Pesso, A. (1973). *Experience in action: Psychomotor Psychology*. New York: New York University Press.

Petzold, H. G. (1988). *Integrative Bewegungs und Leibtherapie: Ein ganzheitlicher Weg leibbezogener Psychotherapie: Band 1 und 2 [Integrative movement and body therapy: A holistic method of related somatic psychotherapy (Vols. 1 & 2)]*. Paderborn: Junfermann.

Pierrakos, J. (1974). The case of the broken heart. *Energie & Charakter, 5*.

Porges, S. W. (2011). The polyvagal theory: Neurophysiological Foundations of Emotions, Attachment, Communication, and Self-Regulation. New York: W. W. Norton.

Reich, W. (1933/1975a). *Charakteranalyse [Character Analysis]*. Frankfurt: Fischer.

Reich, W. (1975b). *Die Entdeckung des Orgons: Die Funktion des Orgasmus [The discovery of orgone: The function of the orgasm]*. Frankfurt: Fischer.

Rosenberg, J. L. (1989). *Körper, Selbst & Seele [Body, self and soul]*. Oldenburg: Transform.

Rudolf, G. (2004). *Strukturbezogene Psychotherapie [Structure-related psychotherapy]*. Stuttgart: Schattauer.

Stattman, J. (1991). *Kreative Trance [Creative trance]*. Oldenburg: Transform.

Stumm, G., & Pritz, A. (Eds.). (2000). *Wörterbuch der Psychotherapie [Dictionary of psychotherapy]*. Vienna: Springer.

Wehowsky, A. (1997). Konzepte der Erdung: Ein Vergleich zwischen Psychotonik und Biosynthese [Concepts of the earth: A comparison between Psychotonic and Biosynthesis]. In M. Glatzer (Ed.), *Die Psychotonik Glaser im Licht aktueller Entwicklungen [Psychotonic glasses in the light of current developments]*. Stuttgart: Hippokrates.

# 55
## Regression in Body Psychotherapy

Peter Geissler, Austria

Translation by Warren Miller

**Peter Geissler**, PhD, MD, is a psychotherapist in private practice and one of the founding members of the influential Arbeitskreis für Analytische und Körperbezogene Psychotherapie (Research Group for Analytic and Body-Oriented Psychotherapy). He has offered significant theoretical and clinical inspirations and initiatives for the integration of psychoanalysis and Body Psychotherapy and has promoted this discourse through numerous publications and the organization of regular symposiums. As editor of the scientific journal *Psychoanalyse und Körper* (Psychoanalysis and Body), he has created a forum that has a far-reaching influence on psychoanalysis and Body Psychotherapy.

All schools of Psychodynamic Therapy consider regression to be an important phenomenon. From a historical perspective, the idea of regression developed during the early years of psychoanalysis. At the time, it was based on the contemporary psychiatric understanding of brain processes being based on similar dynamic processes within the organism. Regression, then, referred to episodes of organic degradation of the brain. It is unlikely that Freud and Breuer used this metaphor coincidentally, because ideas of biological atavism and the regression of morphological structures were characteristic of the evolutionary thinking of late nineteenth-century biology.

Over the course of decades, the concept of regression has become more theoretically differentiated within the field of psychoanalysis, and its use has not remained limited to psychodynamic methods. Gestalt Therapy and other humanistic approaches have also used the concept, but more in a metaphorical sense than as a theoretically valid construct of therapeutic processes (Geissler, 2001).

Although the concept of regression also came into use in the practice of modern Body Psychotherapy in this manner, its integration into a theoretical framework took longer. This might have been due to the fact that Reich, the grandfather of all Body Psychotherapists, increasingly distanced himself from his original training in psychoanalysis, methodologically as well as conceptually. However, Lowen used regression fairly systematically as a construct in Bioenergetic Analysis in *Fear of Life* (Lowen, 1981), although he did not use it in his earlier theoretical work.

In the field of Body Psychotherapy, careful attention to the body commonly intensifies the affective experience and facilitates regressive processes, which can become very obvious when these processes lead to cathartic discharges of affect. Regression therefore needs to be considered to be a critical phenomenon in any kind of Body Psychotherapy. So it comes as a surprise that regression, within the context of Body Psychotherapy, was not theoretically conceptualized at an earlier point in time.

This state of affairs has led to significant misunderstandings and even to "traps": *"No other therapeutic tradition [has] overestimated the function and importance of regression as much as some parts of the Body Psychotherapy scene"* (Marlock, 1993, p. 147).

Whereas "benign" regressive processes open up important therapeutic opportunities, "malign" regressions can lead to exceptionally destructive dynamics between the client and the therapist and may even include sadomasochistic reenactments that can become intractable. Body Psychotherapeutic approaches have been particularly vulnerable to such malign developments due to a gap between practice and theoretical conceptualization: affect intensification and bodily closeness pose great challenges to the therapist's ability, while the theoretical and conceptual aspects of modern Body Psychotherapy are *"still fairly fragmented and underdeveloped . . . [and] specifically in regard to the phenomenon of regression . . . [are governed by] rather simplistic and primitive conceptual frameworks and treatment protocols"* (Ibid., p. 148).

A differentiated handling of regressive processes, therefore, becomes an essential *sine qua non* condition of skillful and competent Body Psychotherapeutic practice.

## One Regression Is Not Like Another

In 1900, Freud described regression as a ubiquitous aspect of the dreaming process, conceptualizing it in the context of his initial view of the psychic apparatus as a reflex action. At the time, he conceived of the psyche as having a sensory axis and a motor axis, with psychic excitation traveling from the sensory axis to the motor axis, from perception to movement. When dreaming, the normal direction of excitation is reversed and memory traces are being animated in hallucinatory fashion: *"If we call the direction in which the psychic movement proceeds from the unconscious into the waking state 'progredient,' we could describe the dream as having a regrediant character"* (Freud, 1900, pp. 518, 547).

To explain the process of dreaming, Freud initially used a topographic conception of the psychic apparatus: the psyche was described as a space with different areas, similar to a house with different rooms. Regression was seen from a topographic perspective as well: as spatial movement from one area of the psyche to another. Later, the temporal aspect increasingly came into the foreground of Freud's theory, and other schools of therapy picked up on the idea of temporal or genetic regression. In 1914, Freud felt it necessary to differentiate between the topographic, temporal, and formal dimensions of regression. His topographic understanding of regression particularly described the dreaming process. His temporal understanding of regression was linked with the phases of psychosexual development and implied a return to an earlier developmental phase; from then on, temporal regression has played an implicit role in *all* the different approaches built on developmental theory—e.g., the model of Bioenergetic Analysis, as it conceives of specific developmental phases with particular need conflicts that facilitate specific, character-forming structural developments.

Freud's "formal regression" referred to the loss of more structured, mature, or sublimated ways of functioning at the expense of a return to more primitive and less evolved behaviors. From the perspective of classical psychoanalysis, body processes of any kind tend to be seen as regressive in nature, because they jettison the domain of verbal expression and gravitate toward "acting out." Modern psychoanalytic perspectives view the transition from verbal expression to nonverbal and body processes in more differentiated ways, but this will not be elaborated in this chapter.

Regression is an important phenomenon in daily life, as well as in the therapeutic situation. It can have many possible meanings, both productive and destructive: it can be a withdrawal, or stagnation based on fear of the next developmental step, or a retreat for the purpose of recuperation, security, or regeneration, or a reconnecting with a relationship that was disturbed early on. Some regressions envelop the whole person, and some are limited to specific ego functions, the id, or the superego. Some regressions end spontaneously, and some remain for a long time. In a psychodynamic context, regression is nearly always also treated as an expression of transference. Often, precursors of regression are first perceived in the countertransference, including the somatic countertransference, which can provide some of the first cues about the depth of the coming regression (Moser, 2002).

Boadella (1991, pp. 157ff.) and other psychoanalytic authors have noted two ways in which regression can function: as an indispensable engagement in the therapeutic process ("tactical regression"), and as a defensive process as part of the resistance ("strategic regression"). The multiplicity of the phenomenon of regression, and the associated difficulties of defining its meanings, is compounded by another level of complexity: regression has been viewed as a process of pathological development as well as a potentially healing development within the therapeutic process. From this perspective, the development of a neurosis, as well as its treatment, can both move in a regressive direction. Given this situation, and the inflationary use of the term over the course of the last century, regression, as a conceptual term, has lost much of its original meaning. Recent findings from infant research have further contributed to this development. As a curiosity, it can be mentioned that—aside from topographic, temporal, formal, and later also libidinal and phylogenetic—Freud described a bioenergetic regression as well. According to this theory, some phenomena of the psyche are regressions to behaviors of prehuman life-forms. The process of autonomy in salamanders and lizards, for example, is viewed as analogous to castration; the reflex of faking deadness in lower animals, as analogous to trance and stupor.

Infant and early childhood development research has shifted the perspective and theory in recent years—for example, through the development of the concept of preverbal interaction representations, so-called RIGs (Stern, 1992). Under this influence, even authors who continue to use the concept of regression have moved away from a purely temporal understanding. Instead, it is much more common today to speak of structural regression, referring to an activation of older structures of thought and experience and a decrease in the level of structural integration of the psyche. Inner schemas—i.e., representations—contain a variety of levels of abstraction, integration, and processing through symbolization and memory processes, along with age-appropriate modes of processing.

Therefore, in the transference with a structurally sound neurotic patient an aspect of a RIG that has received a relatively high level of processing can be actualized, whereas Borderline patients tend to also activate the earlier aspects of the RIGs, such as lived moments, and traumatic interactional experiences that were directly stored in memory. On this structurally deep level of regression we see simple, unprocessed memories with associated affective reactions that have not been symbolically processed, that can be actualized very rapidly, and can be affectively very intensive. (Bettighofer, 1998, p. 49)

## Regression and Implicit Assumptions

It is important to keep in mind that the idea of regression contains implicit assumptions that are based on respective views on the nature of human beings. Such veiled assumptions occasionally have left Body Psychotherapists (and others) with an "undifferentiated regression paradigm" and an understanding of regression that is fixated on the past (see Petzold and Orth, 1999, pp. 174ff.). Although there is *"no doubt that archaic modes of psychological organization in adults are related to the psychological organizations found in childhood . . . these archaic modes are not identical with their manifestations and occurrences in the young child"* (Stolorow et al., 1996, p. 30).

Contrary to the implications of the "autistic" phase in Mahler's developmental theory, we now know that the autism of adult schizophrenic patients does not have a correlate in normal child development. The psychoanalytic view of the human being during Mahler's time proposed that neurotic disorders during adulthood could be traced back to normal, age-appropriate phases of child development. This view pathologized childhood and infantile behavior as a whole, and under this impression psychoanalytic treatment of the Freudian orientation viewed regression as a burdensome but necessary path, a detour to the patient's mental health. Body and Humanistic Psychotherapies since have developed important alternatives to this stance. In modern psychoanalysis and contemporary analytic Body Psychotherapy, such perspectives also have become outdated: *"the adult psychopathology . . . can not be accurately described as temporal regression to an earlier normal phase"* (Ibid., p. 31).

The most important form of regression was temporal regression, not only for Freud: many forms of Body Psychotherapy have developed techniques and approaches that aim to facilitate a return to the level of the "inner child" of the patient, and to sense into, name, and become able to grieve past deprivations. In this context, the role of positive corrective experiences, mediated by the therapist taking a parental stance, and often including the use of therapeutic touch, have been emphasized. Upon closer examination, however, this perspective can be seen as a double-edged sword: in a positive sense, the experience of bodily presence and the direction of attention to the nonverbal experience of early, pre-verbal scenes, and especially traumatic ones, can be particularly fruitful in deepening the process; particular emotional aspects, such as whole-body grief, can hardly be reexperienced with such immediacy otherwise. Certain kinds of body memory generally emerge only in settings that offer sufficient space for bodily and behavioral associations (see G. Downing's description of "body regression": Downing, 1996). However, Body Psychotherapeutic intervention frequently fails to examine dialectically the other side of the coin, particularly in the vortex of regressive group dynamics—namely, that these settings can also foster dependencies and infantilizations, thus allowing the therapist undue possibilities to exercise power, or at the very least, that such issues are unconsciously brought into play. Particularly worrisome in this regard are early and rather primitive, intensive idealizations of the therapist by the patient that more or less "set up" collusive developments and conditions that are prone to lead to emotional breakdowns of the patient at a later time. This danger *"grows to the extent that the therapeutic model is organized by a regressive orientation"* (Marlock, 1993, p. 149)—the "regressive one-dimensionality of Janov's Primal Therapy" (Ibid.) can serve as a stark example of this point.

Beyond assumptions about the significance of the "inner child," other implicit assumptions come into play:

The idea of temporal regression is most frequently used with respect to psychosexual development. Discussions in which psychopathology is understood as a regression to oral, anal, phallic, or oedipal phases presuppose that the dominant motivational priorities of the patient are identical to those of the child in the earlier phases. There are two questionable assumptions here. The first pertains to the linearity of psychosexual development—the notion that in the adult earlier motivations are normally renounced or relinquished in favor of later ones. It is assumed that maturity requires renunciation and that, indeed, such renunciation is possible. The concept of temporal regression, therefore, implies a failure in renunciation. The second questionable assumption is that an adult whose motivations are dominated by psychosexual wishes and conflicts must be functioning like a child who is traversing the corresponding psychosexual phases. (Stolorow et al., 1996, p. 31f.)

Both of these assumptions can be questioned: a psychoanalytically minted ideology of renunciation can be just as harmful as emotional overindulgence that leads to an addictionlike spiral of malign regression. In the context of corrective experiences, unfavorable regressions occur to the extent that the aspect of gratification is emphasized while the differentiation between the original and substitute needs is neglected.

Alexander Lowen, the founder of Bioenergetics, initially did not consider regression as theoretically noteworthy. In his early discussion of psychoanalysis, *The Language of the Body* (Lowen, 1971), regression isn't even listed in the subject index. Only much later, in *Fear of Life* (Lowen, 1981), does he introduce the term conceptually:

In working with conflicts from the pre-oedipal phase the patient is encouraged to regress to the level of an infant. For example, he might lie on a bed and reach out for his mother with both of his arms. At the same time he is directed to say "mommy" and to surrender to the feeling that these words convey. (Lowen, 1981, p. 223)

Sometimes the language Lowen uses in describing his handling of regressive processes seems somewhat forceful—for example, when he describes one of his techniques as follows:

> In order to break through this unconscious resistance one often needs to press on the tense muscles of the jaw and throat using the hands. Due to the tensions this pressure is experienced as painful, but under the pressure the muscles relax and allow the voice to become stronger and more animated. It is also necessary that the patient inhales deeply, so that the repressed feelings get charged up . . . In almost all cases these measures make it possible for the repressed longing for the mother to reemerge. It is accompanied by a deep sobbing, the cries of an infant for a mother that wasn't there, that didn't respond. When this happens the respective patient experiences himself as an infant in one aspect of his being . . . this is regression in therapy. (Ibid., p. 224)

However, Lowen deserves some credit. The value of his concept of "grounding," which he introduced as a method of Bioenergetic Analysis, goes beyond the concrete bodily metaphor of "standing one's ground." In its existential sense, it forms a link to the reality principle that can be viewed as an opposite pole to infantilizing regressions.

Jay Stattman characterizes positive "functional" regression as follows: *"The key purpose of therapy . . . is . . . to initiate and organize learning processes, which help the client to resolve his fixations and unfold his potentials. The art of therapy lies in the ability to transform the therapeutic relationship and the client's exploration of his bodily and psychological reality into a creative learning environment . . ."* (Stattman, 1993, p. 164).

## Regression and Infant Research: "Body Regression"

In the context of Body Psychotherapy, Downing (1996) has offered the most substantiated theoretical and methodological perspective on regression to date. His theory is based on observations of interactive processes between children and their caregivers. It proposes that processes of exchanging and regulating movements and behaviors form pre-verbal, motor-patterned beliefs. These are referred to as "affective-motor schemas." In order to access and change these beliefs in the context of psychotherapy, a setting is called for that allows for body-oriented interventions. This model views the infant as inherently endowed with active relationship-seeking impulses, oriented toward initiating interaction, referred to as the "competent infant" (Dornes, 1992).

Although there is a genetic predisposition to develop affective-motor schemas, this is a potential that needs to be actualized. During the course of childhood development, affective-motor schemas undergo many transformations until they become part of the child's available repertoire. This learning process facilitates the refinement of movement patterns and the ability "to utilize and regulate the affective component. It is also important to learn to make appraisals, which necessitates the formation of basic beliefs. Of course these beliefs aren't linguistically coded, instead, they are motor-patterned" (Downing, 1996, p. 131).

The young child uses affective-motor schemas to form early representations of self and other. Infant researchers believe that real events play an important role: *"Real events profoundly influence the evolution of the infant's affect-motor schemas, and these in turn jointly form his early self and object representations . . . That doesn't mean that fantasy doesn't play any role. Naturally, the child may have perceived real events in a distorted fashion. Emotions contain an appraisal, and appraisals can be false . . . Nonetheless we would assume that the core of the fantasy, however distorted it may be, in most cases contains an objective truth"* (Ibid., p. 132).

To access therapeutically early affective-motor schemas and motor-patterned beliefs, Downing prefers a way of working in which the client lies on a mat on the floor. In differentiated reflections, he describes body regression as manifesting a "network" of different aspects of consciousness (verbal-cognitive, imagery, emotional, sensory, and motor). He further elaborates on self- and object poles, initial motor impulses, bodily micropractices, the handling of emotions during body-regressive processes, and the necessary therapeutic stance (Downing, 1996, pp. 214ff.).

Rather than working on the mat, other analytic Body Psychotherapeutic colleagues prefer the frame of an "open setting." They use the spontaneous regulation of closeness and distance, as well as bodily association phenomena within the therapeutic relationship, to embody the unfolding relationship, and, depending on ego strength, to systematically work on the transference issues. This approach generally maintains the value of verbal interpretations and the "working through" of scenic interactions.

## Regression and the Therapeutic Frame

In order for the client to be able to "let go" during the therapeutic process, the therapist needs to hold a dialectic tension: the therapist conveys to the client that the client may regress, and that "regression in service of the ego" or "regression in service of progression" is permissible, even desired. At the same time, the therapist maintains the boundaries of the therapeutic frame in such a way that—implicitly or explicitly—it is communicated that regression is only one side of the change process.

Diagnostic assessments, particularly with respect to the level of integration of ego structure, make it possible to deliberately guide the intensity and tempo of a client's regression—for example, by modulating how the therapeutic frame is set. In psychoanalytic contexts, it has been a common practice for a while now to reserve the couch for those clients whose egos are less threatened by regression. In analytically oriented Body Psychotherapy, the ability of the ego to weather the oscillations of regression is also considered to be a key criterion for how to proceed. Depending on a client's ego strength, a therapist may decide to work "in the transference" mode, which puts more stress on the ego, or may offer relational work "on the transference"—for example, by using interventions of scenic enactment—which is much easier on the ego. Other methods—for example, the Pesso method—have developed certain rituals ("disengagement") (see Marlock, 1993, p. 156) that symbolically help to set boundaries for enactments in the "here and now." The method of "grounding," developed from Bioenergetic Analysis, can be viewed in a similar vein. In a theoretical sense, it introduces the reality principle, and, methodologically, it offers a way of "keeping one's feet on the ground" and "feeling rooted" in life.

## Regression in the Interactional Therapeutic Relationship

Proponents of psychoanalytically body-oriented approaches have been noting for some time (to some extent building on early work in this regard by Sándor Ferenczi and Michael Balint) that regression also needs to be considered to be an interactive process: client and therapist are in an ongoing process of behavioral interaction, and on the microlevel, bodily messages are being exchanged on a moment-by-moment basis. In this way, the client's and the therapist's signals mutually influence the other's regulation processes. The bodily reality of the therapist therefore certainly does come into play, although this usually remains unconscious, both to the therapist and to the client. In modern interactive psychoanalysis, this perspective has led to a revision of the concept of transference. A one-sided understanding of transference has been replaced by the notion of an "interactional transference."

From such an interactional perspective, a client's regression then can be used to plumb the depth of the therapeutic encounter, in terms of the client's reality as well as fantasy, by focusing on the client's and the therapist's somatic expressions, taking into account subtle intrapsychic and body defense and resistance processes. Rather than exclusively prioritizing a focus on defenses and underlying anxieties, the therapist can also invite the client to engage through spontaneous bodily impulses, thus attending closely the flow of client-therapist interaction; rather than preceding experience, reflection can then follow the experience of interaction, and fears and resistance can then be analytically explored based upon shared, here-and-now relational experience.

Whether therapists presuppose that clients have an inherent growth potential that will drive maturation after developmental deficits are addressed, or whether they emphasize working with intrapsychic conflicts, a therapist's theoretical orientation and view of human nature will inform the significance and value that is accorded to corrective emotional experience and how this can be facilitated—for example, by actively using touch.

Analytic Body Psychotherapeutic practice makes it increasingly evident that oedipal issues do not have as much significance as was assumed in classical psychoanalysis, affecting the priorities of both theory and practice. The contemporary understanding of therapy, informed by infant research and cognitive science, is that representations of early interactions are spontaneously reenacted between client and therapist, offering possibilities for experiential experimentation in the therapeutic relationship. In the context of regression, it is especially split-off, nonintegrated representations that deserve particular attention. Commonly, they first emerge as incomprehensible expressions of affect or bodily agitation. On the basis of an expanded understanding of regression, such phenomena then can be appreciated as valuable aspects of the therapeutic process.

Handling regressive phenomena in the context of a body-oriented treatment setting often places high demands on the therapist. The intensification of affect that commonly results from attending to the body challenges the therapist's ability to contain the affect. An interactional understanding of transference can be theoretically helpful in this regard. It suggests that a partial relinquishing of the "position of the observing third" is not only permissible, but actually desired. Daniel Stern's (1998) concept of "now moments" can be considered in this light. They are significant in that such moments transform the intersubjective field between therapist and client. Only if the therapist is prepared to tolerate the risk of "not knowing" can the therapeutic process shift from one intersubjective level to the next.

## Outlook: Rather Than Temporal Regression: Foreground and Background

The findings from infant research since the 1990s have offered us a new image of human development, and of infants in particular. Today, we view the infant as socially interactive and competent. In a parallel development, a humanistic perspective has taken hold in the therapeutic landscape across the board, not only with regard to practice, but also with regard to theory development. This paradigm shift has also affected psychoanalysis and the Body Psychotherapies, manifesting, for example, in the fact that the self-psychological movement within psychoanalysis is gaining in popularity. In the Body Psychotherapeutic scene, psychodynamic perspectives on the therapeutic process have become standard practice. Classical one-person psychology approaches have been significantly enriched by object-relations approaches.

Current infant research no longer supports the idea of subsequent phases of development with specific developmental themes. The Freudian theory of psycho-sexual development, as well as Lowen's theory of character development, are based on the idea of development in clear sequential phases. Today, we prefer to think of different domains of experience that remain important, and can become activated throughout life, and that stand in varying background/foreground relationships with one another, although they can be seen to initially emerge sequentially. These domains are the senses of an emergent self, core self, subjective self, verbal self, and narrative self (Stern, 1992). In other words, we have returned to the understanding that Freud began with: psychic spaces among which we move, arranged in variable foreground and background configurations. However, in contrast to a psychodynamic understanding in the sense of impulse and defense, this perspective is focused less on the resolution of repression, or on splitting, than on the training of attention to bodily procedural processes that have often become unfamiliar to adults. Infant research, cognitive science, and Body Psychotherapy synergistically complement each other in this respect.

Such a shift of perspective toward an appreciation of procedural behavioral knowledge—that can be understood to have become neglected and inaccessible through inattention, rather than repression—has far-reaching theoretical, as well as practical, implications, including, for example, a revision of the concept of the unconscious. The idea of a foreground/background relationship can be easily integrated with Gestalt therapeutic concepts: the background is formed by the sum of our experiences that are, in principle, accessible to our consciousness. Against this background, certain—more or less distinct—figures emerge into the foreground, and capture our attention until they are sufficiently explored; then, they recede again, back into the totality of the background. In accordance with a tendency toward self-regulation—that is, inner growth—regression contains the idea of blocked development, or "unfinished business" as Gestalt therapists like to say.

In the context of affective-motor schemas, Downing (1996) also speaks of a tendency toward actualization and completion of insufficiently developed schemas. However, this tendency is not viewed as a movement backward to points of fixation in the past, as implied by the classical idea of developmental phases; rather, it is viewed as an intrinsic oscillation between different domains of our self that are all equally important and necessary to generate a complete experience of wholeness.

> It is no longer necessary to engage in "fantastic" [regressive] time travel in order to gain access to particular psychic configurations only because they were formed in early childhood ... all that is needed is that a person can, on occasion, engender a background–foreground shift between different "domains" of experience. (Staemmler, 2002, p. 93)

This perspective suggests that a revision of character structure theory is needed, based on the idea that character structures are the outcome of a play of dynamic forces. Modern video microanalysis of the early child-parent interaction, as well as therapeutic interaction, as it is being developed, particularly in connection with affective microregulation (see Bänninger-Huber et al., 2002; Benecke and Krause, 2001; Juen and Bänninger-Huber, 2002; Peham et al., 2002), would offer a new scientific support for the significance of body processes in the psychotherapeutic process. The juxtaposition of a dynamic and an implicit unconscious, their relationship with one another, and associated practical considerations might pose an exciting challenge for the coming years.

## References

Bänninger-Huber, E., Peham, D., & Juen, B. (2002). Mikroanalytische Untersuchung der Affektregulierung in der therapeutischen Interaktion mittels Videoaufnahmen [Microanalytical study of affect regulation in the therapeutic interaction by means of video recordings]. *Psychologische Medizin, 13(3)*, 11–16.

Benecke, C., & Krause, R. (2001). Fühlen und Affektausdruck: Das affektive Geschehen in der Behandlung mit Herrn P [Feelings and affect pressure: The affective events in the treatment with Mr. P]. *Psychotherapie und Sozialwissenschaft, 1(3)*, 52–73.

Bettighofer, S. (1998). *Übertragung und Gegenüber-tragung im therapeutischen Prozeß [Transference and countertransference in the therapeutic process]*. Stuttgart: Kohlhammer.

Boadella, D. (1991). *Befreite Lebensenergie: Einführung in die Biosynthese [Lifestreams: Introduction to Biosynthesis]*. Munich: Kösel.

Dornes, M. (1992). *Der kompetente Säugling: Die präverbale Entwicklung des Menschen [The competent infant: Pre-verbal human development]*. Frankfurt: Fischer.

Downing, G. (1996). *Körper und Wort in der Psychotherapie: Leitlinien für die Praxis [Body and word in psychotherapy: Guidelines for practice]*. Munich: Kösel.

Freud, S. (1900). *Die Traumdeutung [The interpretation of dreams]*. GW II/III, 1–642. Frankfurt: Fischer.

Geissler, P. (2001). *Mythos Regression [Mythical regression]*. Giessen: Psychosozial.

Juen, B., & Bänninger-Huber, E. (2002). Therapeut-Klient-Interaktion versus Mutter-Kind-Interaktion: Ein Vergleich [Therapist-client interaction versus mother-child interaction: A comparison]. *Psychologische Medizin, 13(3)*, 17–21.

Lowen, A. (1971). *The language of the body*. New York: Macmillan.

Lowen, A. (1981). *Angst vor dem Leben: Über den Ursprung seelischen Leidens und den Weg zu einem reicheren Dasein [Fear of life: On the origin of psychic suffering and the way to a richer existence]*. Munich: Kösel.

Marlock, G. (1993). Notizen über Regression [Notes on regression]. In G. Marlock (Ed.), *Weder Körper noch Geist [Neither body nor spirit]*, (pp. 147–166). Oldenburg: Transform.

Moser, T. (2002). Seele vorwärts, Seele rückwärts: Zu Peter Geißlers umfassendem Werk über Regression [Soul forward, soul backward: About Peter Geissler's extensive work on regression]. *Psychoanalyse und Körper, 1(1), 131–134*.

Peham, D., Ganzer, V., Bänninger-Huber, E., & Juen, B. (2002). Schuldgefühlsspezifische Regulierungsprozesse in Mutter-Tochter-Interaktionen und Psychotherapeut-Klient-Beziehungen: Ein Vergleich [Guilt-specific regulatory processes in mother-daughter interactions and psychotherapist-client relations: A comparison]. *Psychologische Medizin, 13(3), 22–27*.

Petzold, H., & Orth, I. (1999). *Die Mythen der Psychotherapie: Ideologien, Machtstrukturen und Wege kritischer Praxis [The myths of psychotherapy: Ideologies, power structures and ways of critical practice]*. Paderborn: Junfermann.

Staemmler, F-M. (2002). Diagnose und Therapie regressiver Prozesse aus gestalttherapeutischer Sicht [Diagnosis and treatment of regressive processes of Gestalt Therapy perspective]. *Psychoanalyse und Körper, 1(1), 85–104*.

Stattman, J. (1993). Organische Übertragung [Organic transmission]. In G. Marlock (Ed.), *Weder Körper noch Geist [Neither body nor spirit]*. Oldenburg: Transform.

Stern, D. N. (1992). *Die Lebenserfahrung des Säuglings [The world of the infant]*. Stuttgart: Klett-Cotta.

Stern, D. N. (1998). "Now-moments": implizites Wissen und Vitalitätskonturen als neue Basis für psychotherapeutische Modellbildungen ["Now moments": Tacit knowledge and vitality contours as a new basis for psychotherapeutic model training]. In S. Trautmann-Voigt & B. Voigt (Eds.), *Bewegung ins Unbewußte: Beiträge zur Säuglingsforschung und analytischen KörperPsychotherapie [Movement into the unconscious: Contributions to infant research and analytical Body Psychotherapy]*, (pp. 82–96). Frankfurt: Brandes & Apsel.

Stolorow, R. D., Brandchaft, B., & Atwood, G. E. (1996). *Psychoanalytische Behandlung: Ein intersubjektiver Ansatz [Psychoanalytic treatment: An intersubjective approach]*. Frankfurt: Fischer.

# 56

## The Unfolding of Libidinous Forces in Body Psychotherapy

### Ebba Boyesen and Peter Freudl, Germany

**Ebba Boyesen,** CandPhys, has made significant contributions to the development of Biodynamic Psychology and continues to teach this method today. Her mother, Gerda Boyesen, who died in 2005, founded Biodynamic Psychology, which made her a leading figure of Body Psychotherapy in Europe. The Biodynamic approach grew out of Wilhelm Reich's Vegetotherapy and contributions by his most well-known Norwegian student, Ola Raknes. It includes a wealth of massage techniques, as well as a theory and methodology relating to "visceral armoring" and "psycho-peristalsis"—based on the hypothesis that psycho-vegetative arousal can also be channeled through the digestive tract.

Ebba Boyesen has been a trainer of Biodynamic Body Psychotherapy, and the director of the European School for Biodynamic Body Psychotherapy, since 1975. She is a member of the United Kingdom Council for Psychotherapy and the EABP, and is accredited as a psychotherapist by the European Association for Psychotherapy. She has been working internationally for many years and has published numerous scientific papers. Among her original contributions to Body Psychotherapy are her theory of "segmental emotional anatomy," and "psycho-orgastic" techniques to reawaken the autonomous flow of libido—a topic that will be discussed in this chapter.

**Peter Freudl,** Dipl.Psych, works as an accredited psychotherapist and a training therapist of Biodynamic Psychology in close collaboration with Ebba Boyesen. His area of focus is continuing education and teaching. He is trained in a number of approaches in Body Psychotherapy, as well as hypnotherapy in the tradition of Milton Erickson. He is a co-founder of the Institute for Biodynamic Psychotherapy in Hamburg, and his publications are important contributions to the history and practice of Body Psychotherapy.

*The spirit that gives life to all things is love—Tschu-Li*

Currently, Body-Oriented Psychotherapy seems to be discussed as being helpful mainly in therapeutic work with preoedipal or pre-verbal issues. Yet, especially in its Neo-Reichian forms, Body Psychotherapy has also been exploring the human frontiers of complexity with the intention of experiencing joy and happiness within one's own body and also in mature sexuality and love. In the late 1960s and in the 1970s, when Body Psychotherapy started to blossom again, there was a deep and powerful longing for embodied freedom and alive expression to overcome any authoritarian repression and all the phenomena of alienation from one's bodily existence. And especially in its early days, Body Psychotherapy was concerned with expanding the human possibilities of experiencing sensual and sexual fulfillment and pleasure. It took some time to acknowledge, and—theoretically and practically—to grasp, the difficulties of this path. It also took time to understand the fact that the brave experiments to free the repressed and to tear down the inner blocks against the flow of energy were of limited therapeutic value, or even potentially dangerous for the sanity of a person, if there was not a strong-enough personality structure to contain all the liberated material. And it is especially the gradual implementation of these insights into the theories and therapeutic techniques concerning the libido that constitutes one of the special strengths of Body Psychotherapy.

In the ongoing process of integrating this knowledge, the unique history of Body Psychotherapy (Freudl, 2000) in exploring the human potential of embodied freedom has come up with an attitude toward human happiness that is much more optimistic than the classical view from psychoanalysis.

## Freud and Reich: Different Views: The Concept of Drives

In Freud's early works, the sex drive and its energetic force, which he called the "libido," played a very prominent role. Freud had defined libido as the *"energy of those drives, which have to do with all that can be summarized as love"* (Freud, 1921/1999). Some ten years later, he spoke of libido as a *"name for the energetic expressions of Eros"* (Freud, 1930/1999). For Freud's pupil, Wilhelm Reich, research into the libido became the "red thread" of his early life and work as a doctor, a psychoanalyst, a psychotherapist, a social activist, and a natural scientist.

In December 1929, Reich was giving a speech on the topic of prevention of neurosis in front of the Viennese inner circle of leading psychoanalysts, including Freud. In this speech, Reich stressed that cultural and especially sexual happiness is the essential goal in life, and therefore should also be the purpose of a reasonable social policy for the people. According to Reich, Freud strongly opposed this view. In his book, *Das Unbehagen in der Kultur* [Civilization and Its Discontents] (1930), Freud argued skeptically about the possibility of human happiness. In September 1930, Freud and Reich met for the last time. Freud, who had openly supported Reich up to about 1928, had started to intrigue against him and eventually Reich was expelled from the International Psychoanalytical Association (Fallend and Nitzschke, 1997). Psychoanalysis had turned itself into a meta-psychology in which the energetic life of the body became merely a symbolic and peripheral issue (Kutter, 2003).

Freud's pessimistic view of the human possibilities for happiness is fairly widely known. Yet, in order to clarify some essential differences between the views of Depth Psychology in the Freudian tradition, and current Body Psychotherapy in the tradition of Reich, it may be useful to look at some of the differences concerning the two basic Freudian concepts: drives and the unconscious.

Freud defined "drives" as forces or energies that rested deep within the organic fabric of the body and were consciously perceivable only in their effects—namely, as affects, or ideas. Up to about 1921, Freud thought of these drives as energetic forces that one day might be measured and quantified. It is interesting that Freud saw drives as the *". . . somatic demands onto the life of the soul"* (Freud, 1938). The drive would be *"the psychological representative of the stimuli that come from the body and reach the soul. It is a measure of the demand of work that is put upon the soul because of its connection with the body"* (Freud, 1921).

Meanwhile, in contemporary psychoanalytic discussions, talking about drives has become mostly outdated; however, some Body Psychotherapists have kept the idea of the bodily rooted drive alive. It has become the basis of one of the energy concepts in Body Psychotherapy, which since the 1980s has led to a slow and cautious process of mutual reintegration of Body Psychotherapists' opposing views.

Present schools of Body Psychotherapy have been very active in developing methods in order to facilitate the experience of feeling good within one's own body. In Body Psychotherapy, the Freudian libido concept has been integrated into the concept of the unitary force that governs the "alive" being: it has been variously called "life energy," "life force," the "élan vital" (by Mesmer), "bioenergy" or "orgone energy" (by Reich).

### The Concept of the Unconscious

Freud's concept was: *"Where there is id, there shall be ego."* He stressed that, in order to become a mature grown-up, the basic "pleasure principle" (libido) had to be given up in favor of accepting, and defending, the "reality principle." In its essence, the unconscious (seen through Freud's eyes) is a place of irrational and anti-social forces. The possibility of happiness is therefore considered to be an illusory hope.

Destructiveness is seen as a primary, and not as a reactive or secondary, aspect of human beings. Therefore, the child is looked upon as if it were a wild animal that has to be tamed and adapted to "civilized" culture. Being confronted with these strong inner forces and the demands of society, the psychoanalytic therapeutic task was to strengthen the ego position, with the aim of consciously controlling these unconscious forces (the id).

The view of the unconscious that was developed by Reich and still further elaborated by contemporary Neo-Reichians, like Alexander Lowen, John Pierrakos, Gerda Boyesen, David Boadella, and others, has been very different.

Instead of speaking of an "unconscious life of the soul," Reich spoke of *"unconscious realms of existence"* (Reich, 1956, p. 3). He stressed the point that the unconscious does not exist in a psychological space that is independent of one's bodily reality, but is intimately connected to a somatic or energetic substratum. Reich's understanding seems somewhat self-evident now, but—in his time—it was largely rejected and mocked.

Unconscious "soul" (or spirit) mechanisms are interrelated with physiological processes. The unconscious really is embodied. Reich did not deny Freud's vision of the forces of human destructiveness in the unconscious. Yet, behind and beyond the Freudian unconscious, Reich conceived of his own model of the structure of personality. He claimed to have found a more basic level that he called the "core" level. Here, he identified a natural sociality and sexuality, a spontaneous pleasure in work, and the ability to love.

Reich's core unconscious is governed by a rational and understandable logic and is basically pro-social. Contemporary infant research strongly backs up Reich's view on this point, insofar as no evidence has been found for any primary expression of destructive hostility in small children. Dornes stresses that, in untraumatized children, hostility (defined as an action or impulse to hurt another) cannot be found prior to the age of about fifteen months (Dornes, 1997, pp. 264ff.).

Reich's unconscious is essentially monistic.[59] The unusual phenomena of life are the effects of a more or less impeded flow of energy from the primary core (the essence of the personality structure). This is surrounded by a secondary layer of defenses, created by conflicts between the child, its caregivers, and the society around it. While passing through the secondary and tertiary layers, the primary core energies get distorted and emerge as twisted, inhibited, (positive) sensations, feelings, thoughts, or actions, or as contradictory (or negative) sensations, feelings, thoughts, or actions.

In the wake of Reich, current Body Psychotherapists dropped Freud's idea of a second immanent force in the unconscious besides the libido, which he called the "death instinct" or *thanatos*.

By comparison, Reich's unconscious is constructive and contains progressive tendencies that are the inner, driving forces for developing self-regulation and holistic wellbeing. The "repetition compulsion" is optimistically seen as being presented with a new chance to solve an old issue. Reich's unconscious is able to regulate itself, and—in its liberated form—it is governed by a natural and inherent set of moralities. These morals are naturally pro-social; therefore, the person does not need outer social constraints or inner superego demands. He is ruled by what Reich called a "vegetative consideration" (Reich, 1942/1981, p. 137). Being confronted with the possibility of harming another human being, the "vegetative consideration" would be: "I would not enjoy it; therefore, I will not do it."

One of Reich's basic insights was: *"The diseases of the soul [mental illnesses] are consequences of the disturbance of the natural ability to love"* (Reich, 1942/1981, p. 31). Reich therefore considered the experience of human happiness as a real possibility, though a relatively rare occurrence. In his view, overcoming psychological disturbances was seen as a process of opening, and surrendering to, one's natural human ability to love.

---

59  Reich's basic metaphysical belief system is quite close to the philosophy of Baruch Spinoza. Like Spinoza, Reich assumed that the universe consists of different aspects of only one single substance.

## Self-Regulation, Libido, and the Surrender to the Flow

Neo-Reichian Body Psychotherapists are, to a large degree, united in an optimistic and constructive view of the unconscious. In this view, the possibility of an inner process of self-regulation is a key concept insofar as it strengthens the attitude of seeing therapy as a continuous process of getting in touch with the healthy, creative, autonomous being that potentially we all are.

Since the late 1960s, the psychologist and eminent Biodynamic Psychotherapist Gerda Boyesen, with her theory of psycho-peristalsis, has enriched the concept of organic self-regulation. Her theory states that, in the functioning of the enteric nervous system that governs gastrointestinal functions, the peristaltic (wavelike, rhythmic flowing) activity of the "smooth muscles" of the intestinal walls, with their multitude of nerves connected to the parasympathetic part of the autonomic nervous system, is also capable of helping to "digest" the vegetative aftereffects of important emotional experiences, and—in so doing—helps to rebalance the person both organically as well as psychologically. This form of daily self-regulation facilitates the body-mind connection and has a psychotherapeutic effect in itself, as well as preparing the somatic ground for independent well-being and an effective psychological process of change.

> Technically, the enteric nervous system (the second brain) is the component of the peripheral nervous system, but it is so only by definition. The enteric nervous system can when it chooses, process data its sensory receptors pick up and it can act on the basis of those data to activate a set of receptors that it alone controls. The enteric nervous system is thus not a slave of the brain but a contrarian, independent spirit in the nervous organization of the body. It is a rebel, the only element of the peripheral nervous system that can elect *not* to do the bidding of the brain or spinal cord. (Gershon, 1998, p. 17)

The task of the (Biodynamic) Body Psychotherapist is to be a flexible guide, a midwife, a detective, and a knowing, healing surgeon, all at the same time (IFBP, 1980). The process of the unconscious has to "impinge" from within. *"The energy finds its way by itself. That is simultaneously the most simple and the most difficult thing"* (Boyesen et al., 1995, p. 118). This is done by developing a therapeutic presence that is instrumental and empathic and in accordance with the client and the therapeutic goal: "Only then the process is authentic, original and healthy" (Ibid., p. 129). As Almaas put it: *"This presence is not a static reality"* (Almaas, 1996, p. 33), but is characterized by a marked fluidity and openness toward the person's process.

It is important to note that this process can be initiated, or invited, by a large variety of methods, but once self-regulation of the enteric system is achieved, it continues to function by itself, without any guidance of the process by any psychological or psychotherapeutic technique or intention. Trying to control the organic self-regulation function is counterproductive, insofar as it would very likely stop the beneficial aspects of the process immediately. Allowing the process to happen, and trusting in it, seems to be the key for its functioning in a healthy way. *"When the enteric nervous system fails and the gut acts badly, all seems to fade into nothingness. When the enteric nervous system runs the bowel well, there is bliss in the body"* (Gershon, 1998, p. 17).

The free energetic flow is considered to have a cleansing and "melting" effect, and is often felt as "sweet" and highly agreeable. The movement of libido, or life energy, within one's own body brings with it a feeling of being alive. It may help to overcome an alienated or controlled life, often lived in the head, and to stimulate reexperiencing the life of one's body. Reestablishing this flow tends to bring a feeling of freshness and the radiance of sheer life. *"Pleasure is to feel the life energy circulating. Then life is beautiful"* (Boyesen et al., 1995, p. 167).

In many schools of Body Psychotherapy, there is a strong clinical argument against "pushing the river"—trying to force something with the client. In Biodynamic Psychology, for instance, where this idea is strongly inherent in its orientation, the main method of Vegetotherapy is basically done as a form of "free associations" of the body—i.e., movements and concomitant feelings of the client that impinge and unfold from within (G. Boyesen, 1987). Meanwhile, the therapist is instrumental in supporting, encouraging, and gently directing this process of the unconscious slowly becoming conscious. The basic therapeutic attitude is this: the method can betray the client, but the client can never betray the method.

To illustrate the point of how some specific instruction may trigger the involuntary processes of organismic self-regulation, we include one short piece of a therapy session with Ebba Boyesen.

**Excerpt from a Therapy Session**

The client is a single woman in her mid-forties. She came because of lack of aliveness and of libidinous feelings. Her problem was essentially that the way to get recognition and love from her father, and therefore from other men, was through intellectual achievement. She could not get away from being "the clever girl." Her body seemed rigid and compressed, sporty but not really alive. Ebba's impression was that the woman reminded her of a frozen princess. Midway through a vegetotherapeutic session, with the client lying on the mattress, the following exchange took place:

Therapist: "Let it breathe and see if there is anything your body wants to do or say . . ."

[The client closed her eyes . . .]

Therapist: "Let it breathe . . . from mouth to chest . . . Let it breathe . . . from mouth to belly . . . take your time . . . Let it breathe . . . from the mouth to your pelvic area . . . Let it breathe . . . from your mouth to your knees . . . Let it breathe . . . from your mouth to your feet . . . How does it feel?"

[The client started coughing. The coughing went along with a few, strong, "jerky" movements from the chest to the pelvic area. It was clear that this energetic movement was in connection with the pelvic area and was not coming only from her diaphragm.]

Client: "Oh sorry. I am moving! . . ."

Therapist: "Well—that is fine . . . just let it breathe . . ."

[The client continued to breathe lightly as suggested and then slowly began to laugh. The coughing transformed into laughter, first shy, then more heartfelt and free.]

Client: "Oh my body is moving, oh . . ."

[The client then opened her eyes, lifted her head, looked down at her body with its now-spontaneous movements, and continued to laugh.]

Client: "I can feel I am moving . . . it feels nice . . ."

[It was then that Ebba observed that what she calls the "orgastic reflex" (spontaneous small movements in the body that Reich called "the streamings") was starting to work, and the libido reservoir in the client's body was opening up.]

Therapist: "Close your eyes . . . relax your body . . . let your breath out, lightly as a sigh . . . that's it . . ."

[After a while:]

Therapist: "How does it feel?"

Client: "Like a soft wave . . . and my body is tingling, I feel alive . . . all over, it feels beautiful . . . I feel beautiful . . ."

In the following sessions, Ebba worked with the oedipal material that began to unfold, and slowly the client's connection with her head, heart, and pelvic segments started to reintegrate.

## Surrender and the Orgastic Reflex

Wilhelm Reich was a pioneer in doing research on the bodily and energetic aspect of sexual love. As early as 1927, in the first edition of *The Function of the Orgasm* (Reich, 1927/1944/1985), he talked about the importance of surrendering to involuntary and natural movements of the body, in order to experience deep satisfaction and libidinous sensations. Reich was often misunderstood—and so it's important to add that he stressed that the more love there is between two partners in an intimate sexual encounter (later on, he called it a "full genital embrace")—the more enriching and gratifying the experience would be. The capacity to surrender was deeply embedded in the ability to create, feel, and express a loving relatedness to another human being.

Reich also described what he called the "orgastic reflex" as a spontaneous and very intense, wavelike movement that seized the whole body and was accompanied by a strong feeling of happiness. It was a bodily reaction that was not necessarily connected to sexual intercourse, and could happen spontaneously when in a relaxed and "orgonomic" space.

Though, on the one hand, the orgastic reflex was an important discovery, augmenting our knowledge about the possibilities of independent human sexuality, on the other hand, it had the fate of being turned into a destructive "ideal" of sexual performance that poisoned the sheer pleasure of making love and, even worse, it led away from the basic therapeutic intention to help clients to live a life within a loving relationship, which most of us find necessary in order to experience our life as satisfactory.

Neglecting the work on human relatedness led into the criticism that Body Psychotherapy is based just on one-person psychology, which does not deal with the basic interrelationship in therapeutic encounters. This criticism nowadays seems inappropriate insofar as most Body Psychotherapeutic schools take an interactional stance about transference, countertransference, and the therapeutic relationship (Bettighofer, 2003).

The important message from Reich is that our most intense and holistic moments can happen when we give up voluntary control and surrender to the movements that lie dormant in the depths of our organic existence—that is, letting go of control allows the autonomous inner processes to happen, which is highly effective in helping to restore well-being, fulfillment (and not just sexual fulfillment), and a healthy equilibrium.

Biodynamic Psychology, like Reich, adheres to the notion of the "pleasure principle" (libido) being part of our human birthright and that it has spiritual significance as well. The life energy moves in us, as libido, as the flow of pleasure, and its vibrations lead us through the physical sensations toward emotional freedom, and then to the cosmic or transpersonal level (Southwell, 1981). This view relates to Reich's concept of the essential rightness and aliveness of a person's true nature, with its basically sound, decent, and loving core, and thereby also to Winnicott's concept of the "True Self" (Schrauth, 2001).

While Freudians held to their concept *"Where there is id, there shall be ego,"* Gerda Boyesen took a somewhat liberating and reconstructive position. She put it this way: *"Where there is ego, id shall emerge"* (Boyesen et al., 1995). She coined the term "grip" for the effect of a too-strict superego structure within psychotherapy. This grip needs to be carefully loosened, without putting too much stress on the integrative forces of the client, so that the person may slowly open up to the potential of their libidinous streamings throughout their body. In Biodynamic Psychology there is a concept of "ripeness" that is used to understand which bodily defined process is closest to the ego (in the subconscious) of the person at that moment, and therefore can be therapeutically worked on without endangering the personality structure of the client. Therefore, deeper material, not so close to the person's consciousness, cannot be so easily worked with.

## The Therapeutic "Language of Tenderness"

The potential for the flow of the life energy within the body is always there, as long as the person is alive. In Biodynamic Psychology, Gerda Boyesen speaks of an "independent well-being," and of an inborn, natural, and autonomous circulation of libido within the body that can be disrupted and hampered by unempathic (or abusive) behavior of the parents in childhood, yet it is eminently restorable. The implicit aim of the Body Psychotherapist is therefore to help the person to re-create the merging of tender feelings within their caring adult self, and not to confront or disturb the process unnecessarily. This is not just a verbal "language of tenderness"; it comes across in the therapist's body language, nuances of voice, eye contact, and touch.

## Conclusion

Freud said that the neurosis would melt in the fire of positive and loving transference toward the therapist, and when the therapist allows this trusting, bonding capacity, which is a constructive resonance between the heart of the therapist and the heart of the client, the transference process slowly starts to transcend itself (G. Boyesen, 1987). Thus, it is the therapist's attitude toward the client's feelings that really counts, and this reflects in his or her ability to help transform human sensations into healing qualities (Boyesen, 1990).

## References

Almaas, A. H. (1996). *The point of existence: Transformations of narcissism in self-realization.* New York: Shambhala.

Bettighofer, S. (2003). Intersubjektivität in der Psychotherapie: Therapeutische Beziehung Übertragung und Kontakt im Hier und Jetzt [Intersubjectivity in psychotherapy: Therapeutic relationship and contact transmission in the here and now]. In P. Geissler (Ed.), *Körperbilder* [Body images], (pp. 51–72). Giessen: Psychosozial.

Boyesen, E. (1987). Beyond transference. *Adire,* 2 & 3, 229–234.

Boyesen, G. (1987). *Über den Körper die Seele heilen: Biodynamische Psychologie und Psychotherapie* [Healing the soul via the body: Biodynamic Psychology and Psychotherapy]. Munich: Kösel.

Boyesen, G., Leudesdorff, C., & Santner, C. (1995). *Von der Lust am Heilen* [From the desire to heal]. Munich: Kösel.

Boyesen, M-L. (1990). Übertragung und Gegenübertragung zwischen Mann und Frau in der Biodynamischen Massage [Transference and countertransference between men and women in Biodynamic Massage]. *Dialog des Biodynamische Psychologie,* 2(1), 83–96.

Dornes, M. (1997). *Die frühe Kindheit* [Early childhood]. Frankfurt: Fischer.

Fallend, K., & Nitzschke, B. (Eds.). (1997). *Der "Fall" Wilhelm Reich* [The fall of Wilhelm Reich]. Frankfurt: Suhrkamp.

Freud, S. (1921/1999). *Massenpsychologie und Ich-Analyse* [Mass psychology and the analysis of the ego]. GW XIII, 70–161.

Freud, S. (1930/1999). *Das Unbehagen in der Kultur* [Civilization and its discontents]. GW XIV, 419–506.

Freud, S. (1938). Findings, ideas, problems. New Introductory Lectures on Psycho-Analysis: The Standard Edition, 23. London: Hogarth.

Freudl, P. (2000). What is Biodynamics? Biodynamic Psychology and Psychotherapy. Retrieved from www.gbpev.de/was-ist-die-biodynamik

Gershon, M. (1998). *The second brain: The scientific basis of gut instinct and a groundbreaking new understanding of nervous disorders of the stomach and intestine.* London: Harper.

International Foundation of Biodynamic Psychology (IFBP). (1980). What is Biodynamic Psychology? *Journal of Biodynamic Psychology, 1,* 3–6.

Kutter, P. (2003). Der Körper in der Psychoanalyse [The body in psychoanalysis]. *Psychoanalyse & Körper,* 2(3), 23–44.

Reich, W. (1927/1944/1985). *Die Funktion des Orgasmus* [The function of the orgasm]. Frankfurt: Fischer.

Reich, W. (1942/1981). *Die Entdeckung des Orgons I: Die Funktion des Orgasmus* [The discovery of orgone I: The function of the orgasm]. Frankfurt: Fischer.

Reich, W. (1956). Re-emergence of Freud's death instinct as "DOR" energy. *Orgonomic Medicine,* 2(1), 2–11.

Schrauth, N. (2001). *Körperpsychotherapie und Psychoanalyse: Eine vergleichende Studie am Beispiel von Wilhelm Reich, Gerda Boyesen und Alexander Lowen sowie Sandor Ferenczi, Michael Balint und D. W. Winnicott* [Body Psychotherapy and Psychoanalysis: A comparative study about the work of Wilhelm Reich, Gerda Boyesen, and Alexander Lowen as well as Sándor Ferenczi, Michael Balint, and D. W. Winnicott]. Berlin: Ulrich Leutner.

Southwell, C. (1981). Biodynamic therapy. In J. Rowan & W. Dryden (Eds.), *Innovative therapies in Britain.* Milton Keynes, UK: Open University Press.

# 57

## Risks within Body Psychotherapy

**Courtenay Young, Scotland**

Courtenay Young's biographical information can be found at the beginning of Chapter 7, "The Work of Wilhelm Reich, Part 2: Reich in Norway and America."

A lot of this handbook is about the development and benefits of Body Psychotherapy. However, besides all the numerous advantages, there are also some potential risks within the practice of Body Psychotherapy. The four main areas of risk are: retraumatization; abusive touch; the breaking down of defenses; and inappropriate or "malign" regression.

A differentiation has to be made between the area in which the risk is likely to show up, and problems that then add to, or exacerbate, the risk. Problems in these areas often have, as their root, an abuse of power, which is certainly not confined to Body Psychotherapy. These problems often happen where the cracks, or failings, in professional practice begin to show; and, on many occasions, the inherent risk has been exacerbated by poor or unethical practice. Most professional shortcomings can also be attributed to (previous) inadequate training and supervision, or sometimes to a lack of personal therapy received.

Abuses of the therapeutic relationship, or any power relationship, can occur in any type of therapy (and in many other situations, like schools, religious organizations, offices, etc.), and the main safeguard against any of these potential boundary violations is in the person with power (in this case, the therapist) actively working for the empowerment of the person without power (in this case, the client). There is also an inherent imbalance in this dynamic.

The more that we concern ourselves with the techniques of our work as psychotherapists, the less (perhaps) we are focusing on the power, the wisdom, and the innate good sense of the other person in the room, the client. With the development of much better standards of training, recognizable courses, ethics, and levels of supervision, it is probable that the frequency or incidence of these problems has decreased considerably. However, the inherent risks still remain.

Despite these problem areas, the inherent risks that were listed still exist, all of the time, and the identified risks that are still existing in these areas have often been used (usually incorrectly) as a criticism of Body Psychotherapy—for example, because there are risks in touch, and Body Psychotherapists often touch, Body Psychotherapy is therefore risky. This is faulty logic and should be resisted. Body Psychotherapy—like working with high-voltage electricity—is inherently risky; therefore, risk management, adequate controls, and safeguards need to be clearly put in place.

## Retraumatization

For example, whenever any psychotherapeutic work is being done on resolving an area of particular trauma—in the psyche, or within a specific area of the body, whether this is as a result of repeated, low-level traumatization, or of a single, overwhelming incident—one long-established method of healing was to try to prevent the encapsulation and isolation of the trauma, which is generally agreed to give rise to further problems, by discharging the pent-up feelings in a form of catharsis, and then to integrate these into the person's psyche: a little like (perhaps) lancing a boil.

However, sometimes the therapist allows the therapy process to accelerate too fast, faster than the client can contain and integrate. This acceleration produces more arousal in the client's autonomic nervous system, and this can easily spiral into a form of retraumatization. Body Psychotherapists like Peter Levine (1997), Babette Rothschild (2000, 2003), Pat Ogden and Kekuni Minton (2001), Nick Totton (2003), and various other authors like Bessel van der Kolk (van der Kolk et al., 1996) have done much work in this area and have written well about it; this has helped to change much of our fundamental understanding of how to do trauma work safely.

However, when Body Psychotherapy first started working in these areas, the received wisdom was that by just "going into" the area of the client's trauma and discharging the person's feelings (either by allowing the blocks to dissolve, or by circumnavigating the resistances, or by breaking them down) was sufficient in itself for the traumatized area to be able to access the body's natural processes and therefore for it to heal. This is naive (at best) and dangerous (at worst).

Other therapists, like Janov, wrote (even as late as 1992): "*It is possible to relive these imprinted (painful and traumatic) memories and resolve neurosis and physical disease*" (Janov, 1992, p. xxiii). Several Body Psychotherapies, in those days, followed some of these "discharge" or "cathartic" concepts. It is true that sometimes there were seemingly miraculous "cures" or "insights" using these methods, but—many times—the traumatized person might well have gone away unhealed, or even retraumatized. Sometimes the clients were even accused of failing the method: but really the technique, or the therapist, or a combination of both, had failed them.

One of the inherent risks in working in this way is that the continued effect of such "relivings" of the trauma can progressively extend the damage of the original trauma. This is done by a process called "kindling," the model of which implies a "biological memory" of preceding episodes and where the individual's vulnerability increases with repeated episodes of destabilization. The ". . . symptoms of PTSD are maintained and triggered by day-to-day adverse life experiences" so much so that this can be a "stronger determinant of current levels of symptomatic distress than the original trauma." Damage to and a diminution of the person's ego strength are caused by the reliving or rekindling of the traumatic memories to the extent that "even if the symptoms of the immediate disorder remit, permanent changes may remain in the individual's vulnerability to disordered affect and arousal" (van der Kolk et al., 1996, p. 170).

Many Body Psychotherapists realize that important lessons learned from such PTSD research can also apply, more widely, to other interventions in their clinical work. What we realize—importantly—now is that, in order to help to heal the trauma, we need to stay within, but at the edge of, the client's "safety area" or medium arousal zone.

We must "pace" the client's process: we shouldn't force it. As the traumatic memories come back, the person's arousal levels increase. The stress hormones released then suppress the activity of the hippocampus, which deals with explicit memory and contextual thinking, which are exactly the tools that are needed for integration and healing. So, we need to work very carefully to avoid any retraumatization, or rekindling, in these states of traumatic stress.

Therapeutic themes that need to be observed much more pervasively in such delicate trauma work, either in groups or in individual sessions, to avoid many of the inherent risks of retraumatization can be found, neatly listed, in Babette Rothschild's excellent books, which are heartily recommended. She particularly emphasizes the need for the development of dual awareness, which is when the client "*. . . can address the trauma in the past, even though it may feel as though it is happening now,*" while, at the same time, being "*. . . secure in the knowledge that the actual present environment is trauma free*" (Rothschild, 2000, p. 131).

This way of working is also clearly identified in Pat Ogden and colleagues' excellent book, *Trauma and the*

*Body* (2006), in which they identify that, as responsible therapists, we should not "allow" the client to go outside their "comfort zone." This is very fine, delicate work that can (perhaps) be done properly only by an experienced Body Psychotherapist familiar with the microprocesses of body language, especially in the area of arousal.

## Abusive Touch

As Body Psychotherapy developed, there was an increasing realization of how fundamentally deprived of healthy touch we all are in our Westernized society. Books like *Touching* (Montague, 1971), *The Massage Book* (Downing, 1972), and *Loving Hands* (Leboyer, 1977) emphasized the significance and importance of touch. There is also, more recently, Tiffany Field's (2003) classic work on *Touch*.

For many, this grew into a general myth (among Body Psychotherapists) that almost any touch is better than none. It was not until the late 1990s that cogent books about the ethics of touch and the dangers of inappropriate contact and boundary violation began to appear (Hunter and Struve, 1998; Smith et al., 1998).

There are (obviously) significant risks inherent in touch. In order to touch, or be touched, one has to have allowed someone else to come very close, almost to become intimate. There are also many different forms and different kinds of touch. There are wide-ranging and excellent reasons to touch in psychotherapy, and there are also valid reasons not to touch in psychotherapy (Young, 2005, 2009). There is informed touch, and insensitive touch. Touch can be used therapeutically, or it can be abused, demonstrating power issues (Conger, 1994). Touch can be healing, or it can be erotic. Touch can also be supportive of regressive states. It can be needed, yet when it happens it can also raise anxiety levels (Rothschild, 2000, p. 147).

Whatever way or for whatever reason that touch happens in psychotherapy, it must be done with a very clear, well-defined, and well-informed intention. Body Psychotherapy does not necessarily involve touch. But Body Psychotherapists are also often very well trained in, and quite comfortable with, touch; skilled at touching; knowing many of the "why"s, the "how"s, the "where"s, the "when"s, and also why, how, where, and when not to touch.

Abusive touch is a double insult: it is an abuse of the intimacy of the therapeutic relationship, as well as a physical insult. It is clear that any grandiose attitudes about therapy, any views about one's special (healing) abilities, significant charisma, secret techniques, or whatsoever (however they are self-described) can impinge on the development of the necessary professional and personal humility and conscience that respect the lack of distance between the therapist and the client. It is also clear that feelings of privilege, of being educated, professional, or even above the law, or any particular attitude or social climate that denigrates or works against responsible attitudes will lead to abuse—in any arena—as well as this special area of touch. This has also been thoroughly discussed in another forum (Young, 2003).

The privilege of being able to touch another human being must be totally respected. To be allowed to touch someone is a very intimate situation; and wanting to be touched is to allow oneself to become very vulnerable to another person. Qualities such as love, compassion, empathy, care, respect, and sensitivity must be observed at all times. The use of the word "touch" also has a component that transcends the physical, in being able to be "touched" by someone else or to "touch" someone else deeply. Touch is inherently risky; in therapy, abusive touch is an ever-present risk.

The best method of "risk reduction" is excellent training and supervision, but, beyond that, a finely tuned awareness of the minute signals that come from the other person is essential—for you never know (as a therapist) whether your touch is actually right for the client; but, beyond and below that, underpinning everything, a clear sense of one's self, and one's boundaries, as well as an inherent respect for the other person are fundamental.

## The Breaking Down of Defenses

One of the founding fathers of Body Psychotherapy, Wilhelm Reich, defined our somatic defenses as part of our neurotic character structure and our armoring: the rigid muscles are seen, in effect, to hold all our repressed emotions. This, in his view, is what is wrong with us, and with the world. Vegetotherapy, his particular method of Body Psychotherapy, worked directly on loosening the tense muscles, using (sometimes) quite aggressive techniques to counter the held-in aggression and all the client's other repressed emotions. Through the particular practice of this type of "therapy," the tension is increased to beyond the client's ability to hold the repressed emotions, and so the emotions become discharged eventually, and only then can the muscles relax properly.

The therapist then works systematically down the client's body, on the various armored segments, slowly softening their muscles. Character armor eventually gets broken down, or melts, and the client's true persona, or core personality, is therefore expected to come through undistorted. However, when the client's defenses have been "broken down," that client is incredibly vulnerable again, so—in my view—the therapy only really happens in the second half of Reich's "discharge" cycle: that is, in the integration period after the discharge, when a less armored "body" learns to survive in a very different way. The risk here, of course, lies in focusing much too much on the "breaking down" (or breaking through) part of the cycle, rather than on the more drawn-out, laborious, and delicate reintegration aspects.

Even very gentle and caring Body Psychotherapists, like Jack Painter, speak about how *"Deep bodywork helped me break down my old armour, the contractions dividing my head, heart and desires"* (Painter, 1986, p. 16). Alexander Lowen writes, *"This problem is attacked bioenergetically on several fronts simultaneously"* (Lowen, 1971, pp. 116–117). Language of this type developed a characteristic way of working in which the therapist—to an extent—"attacks" the client's "neurotic" defenses, and gradually and systematically "breaks them down."

Many Body Psychotherapeutic colleagues now prefer to see these "armorings" as somatized and healthy "survival patterns," or previously positive and beneficial coping strategies, some of which may now be redundant or dysfunctional (rather than pathological). This perspective helps such defenses to be identified and gradually discarded, rather like a bad habit.

But when the sort of "breaking-down" imagery and methodology was extended, in the 1960s and 1970s, into various types of "no limits" encounter groups, then that developed into a form of therapeutic violence (Boadella, 1980) where the "breaking down" of the participants' defenses had obviously gone too far. Some of the psychotherapy-oriented cults, as well as some body-oriented therapies and psychotherapies, used methods like distortions of transference; body manipulations of the "no pain, no gain" type; repetitive motions; meditation-based "unstressing" (relaxation-induced anxiety); hyperventilation; various forms of "altered-state" systems of working; and even more traditional brainwashing principles (sleep deprivation, food reduction, etc.), as ways of "breaking down" the old, "neurotic" belief systems and somatized patterns of behavior in order to break down the old, "free the mind," and "liberate the spirit" of their clients and their followers (Singer, 2003, 135–139, 172–181).

Today the "breaking down of defenses" paradigm is still quite pervasive: the risks still remain, even though the abuses have lessened. "Breaking through," not "breaking down," is another frequently found pseudo-spiritual misinterpretation of such types of therapy. Care should even be taken with fairly reputable, or well-tried transpersonal, methods, such as Stan Grof's Holotropic Breathwork, because if there is an insufficient integration period or follow-up support after a workshop, the person's ego structure can still remain quite disintegrated or blown apart by the sought-after "out-of-body" experiences, liberated only when the "spirit is free" from the defended and armored body.

The risks are not just from unethical behavior, power-hungry sects, or inadequate methods. Working directly with the body is extremely powerful, and the techniques can very easily undercut a person's somatic defenses. Therefore, special attention must always be given to the finer points of the client's process, so as to ensure that there is no harm done, and to determine how to take care of what might happen—therapeutically—when a client quite suddenly becomes very vulnerable. As therapists, when we are working with a person's defenses, we really need to focus, at the same time, on aspects such as affirmation of strengths; support systems; self-help; empowerment; working only step-by-step and only one step at a time; and giving plenty of therapeutic space and (more than) sufficient time for integration.

## Inappropriate or Malign Regression

Body Psychotherapy is considered (by some) to contain an inherent tendency toward regression, and there has already been some good writing about this (Marlock, 1991). Also, when touch is involved, some regression almost always emerges from this sort of work, as we (as clients) often revert to more needier times.

John Conger writes, *"Touch is our earliest language, and capable of taking us back instantly to our most primitive universe"* (Conger, 1994). Catharsis and regression have always been present in psychotherapy, ever since Freud and Breuer, and some aspects of regression can be very positive and healing. People like Balint (1968), Keleman (1979), Smith (1989), and Winnicott (1987) have written about this, and their work is still of great value to Body Psychotherapists. So this tendency toward regression, and the inherent dangers (as well as benefits), should be addressed significantly in training and supervision work, and perhaps especially the particular level and direction of the regressive tendency in the chosen modality of Body Psychotherapy.

When it is not used appropriately, regression can occur in a seemingly malign manner from the "ungrounded" therapist. Sometimes the therapist adopts a position of omnipotence, either from the client's expectations, or from the therapist's own self-promotions, or both.

Certain examples of this type of malign usage of regression stem quite directly from the work of Marguerite Sechehaye and John Rosen, who used the innovative methods of regression and reparenting in their work with schizophrenic patients, apparently very successfully, in the immediate post-war era; however, there was a much darker side to their work that did not emerge until much later (Singer and Lalich, 1996).

Janov's influence and the popularity of Primal Therapy were still strong. Around this time, Leonard Orr developed a form of therapeutic and regressive "energy breathing" technique, akin to hyperventilation, which he called Rebirthing, and later Sondra Ray adapted this therapy into a form of spiritual-guidance movement or cult.

There are some very serious criticisms that can be leveled against these types of therapy—least of all, that many times these powerful techniques were taught to unskilled people in weekend seminars. Singer and Lalich judged such work in the following way:

> Rather than helping clients to become stronger and more independent, most regression therapies, and in particular the rebirthing-reparenting sort, induce in the client an abdication of responsibility and a state of sickly dependence on the therapist. This is a blatant abuse and misuse of the power relationship inherent in the therapeutic process; it is in effect the exploitation of the client's emotional vulnerability. The "Mommy" or "Daddy" therapist who is supposed to parent the client correctly is in fact playing with fire, potentially entrapping and crippling their "children," and causing undue suffering and in some cases long-lasting damage." (Singer and Lalich, 1996)

Unfortunately, some of the ideas, methods, and attendant risks of therapy being seen as fulfilling this kind of emotional deficit crept into Body Psychotherapeutic work, especially in the 1970s and 1980s. Unhappily also, a recent, otherwise good, book on Body Psychotherapy (Staunton, 2002) included a chapter on regression and past-life work seemingly incorporating this type of therapy within the field, which many Body Psychotherapeutic professionals would disagree with.

People in any form of therapy sometimes just go into a regression, or into a regressive state, and some Body Psychotherapeutic modalities are much more open to supporting this, as well as open to inducing it. Such a spontaneous regression can be very helpful in uncovering important unconscious material: it can be quite a *gnosis* or an insight moment—a very powerful experience of "being back there," as well as being here, now. The uncovered or emerging material is worked through, and later on integrated into their psychotherapeutic process. Here, and in this way, the regression becomes a healthy aspect of their process.

But regression can also become malignant. If the client starts to identify with their regressive state (for instance, their "child" or their "past-life" persona), or even to take this to be something of their "real" self, then we can start to get into very dangerous areas, or, if the therapist is "hooked" on being powerful, or "effective," through using these powerful techniques. With an inexperienced or unaware therapist, the client may be (possibly inadvertently) invited or encouraged to repeat that experience over and over, to reinforce it, and this will carry their regression more into everyday life. This is not therapy!

Many symbiotically regressive forms of therapy effectively castrate the client's aggression by not "allowing" sufficient space for negative transference whereby the client can gain strength, extract themselves from old habits (negative inner objects), take risks, challenge projections, and test out current reality. Some highly regressive processes often involve aggressive or even sadistic maneuvers by the client with the aim of gaining control or power over the therapy, or even the therapist (Marlock, 1991).

Another of the inherent dangers when working with the body is that clients might use the experiential, affective, somatic-sensing aspect of the bodywork, which is extremely powerful, to seek the regressive states as a defense mechanism from other things: simplistically, it is easier to be a "child" than to face the difficult choices of, say, a bad marriage. It may also be easier for the therapist to remain in a form of benevolent parental role, rather than allowing the client to stand up and walk free. By using methods with a potential regressive component, we may inadvertently allow, or implicitly encourage, the client to retreat into a regressed state in which he or she becomes essentially worse off, sometimes more so than when they entered therapy. Jay Stattman, Balint (1968), Boadella (1980), and others have emphasized that one of the beneficial components of regression is in the challenge of the unknown, or in the goal of being recognized; but when the regression becomes repeated and familiar, or is aimed at gratification, then it loses its therapeutic value and can become malignant.

We really need to look at these fairly extreme situations in order to assess properly the inherent risks of regression in any particular situation, and we also need to maintain more awareness of these risks in our therapeutic consciousness. Some of the burden of, or the responsibility for, this type of malign regressive process can even be "put" onto the client, so that the therapist then does not need to face their involvement or responsibility; this is where the risk transfers into the ethics of our work.

So, finally, there must always be a significant emphasis in the therapy, and self-awareness instilled in the client, of the process of "disengagement" from any regression and eventually from the therapy. Without this separation from the regressive process, the chances of both sides acting out in a regressed, symbiotic relationship are increased significantly (Marlock, 1991).

Thankfully, there are many kinds of spontaneous or semi-induced forms of regression that can be quite beneficial, if handled with skill. These need to be embedded into a context that provides an ethical framework of techniques that allow the therapist to help the client move through their regression, despite some of the attractions of staying there, toward an objective, adult, positive, and more present development. In the end, it is necessary for the client to be able to look back and see those states as a regression, having been able to learn something significant from them, and then step clearly and strongly out of these. This can only really be done with therapists who are fully aware of all the various risks of malign regression.

## Conclusion

These inherent risks within Body Psychotherapy can be added to by any unethical practice, power trips, pervasive theories and doctrines that do not support the empowerment of the individual, lack of awareness, too-hurried forms of working, overly goal-oriented therapy (as distinct from process-oriented therapy), and insufficient time for integration. These risks can be reduced by a much better understanding of theory, much more supervised practice, a greater level of awareness of ethical practice, and significant changes in the culture of the profession.

## References

Balint, M. (1968). *The basic fault.* London: Tavistock.

Boadella, D. (1980). Violence in therapy. *Energy & Character, 11*(1), 1–20.

Conger, J. (1994). *The body in recovery: Somatic Psychotherapy and the self.* Berkeley, CA: North Atlantic Books.

Downing, G. (1972). *The massage book.* Harmondsworth, UK: Penguin.

Field, T. (2003). *Touch.* Cambridge, MA: Bradford Books, MIT.

Hunter, M., & Struve, J. (1998). *The ethical use of touch in psychotherapy.* Thousand Oaks, CA: Sage.

Janov, A. (1992). *The new primal scream: Primal Therapy twenty years on.* London: Cardinal Press.

Keleman, S. (1979). *Somatic reality.* Berkeley, CA: Center Press.

Leboyer, F. (1977). *Loving hands: The traditional Indian art of baby massage.* London: Collins.

Levine, P. (1997). *Waking the tiger: Healing trauma.* Berkeley, CA: North Atlantic Books.

Lowen, A. (1971). *The language of the body.* New York: Collier Macmillan.

Marlock, G. (1991). Notes on regression. In G. Marlock (Ed.), *Unitive Body Psychotherapy: Collected papers* (Vol. 2). Frankfurt: Afra.

Montague, A. (1971). *Touching: The human significance of the skin.* New York: Harper & Row.

Ogden, P., & Minton, K. (2001). *Sensorimotor Psychotherapy: One method for processing traumatic memory. Traumatology: An Online Journal, 6*(3).

Ogden, P., Minton, K., & Pain, C. (2006). *Trauma and the body: A sensorimotor approach to the body.* New York: W. W. Norton.

Painter, J. W. (1986). *Deep bodywork and personal development: Harmonizing our bodies, emotions and thoughts.* Mill Valley, CA: Bodymind Books.

Rothschild, B. (2000). *The body remembers: The psychophysiology of trauma and trauma treatment.* New York: W. W. Norton.

Rothschild, B. (2003). *The body remembers casebook: Unifying methods and models in the treatment of trauma and PTSD.* New York: W. W. Norton.

Singer, M. T. (2003). *Cults in our midst: The continuing fight against their hidden menace (rev. ed.).* San Francisco: Jossey-Bass, Wiley.

Singer, M., & Lalich, J. (1996). *Crazy therapies: What are they? What do they do?* San Francisco: Jossey-Bass, Wiley.

Smith, E. W. L., Clance, P. R., & Imes, S. (Eds.). (1998). *Touch in psychotherapy: Theory, research and practice.* New York: Guilford Press.

Smith, S. (1989). A study of clinicians who use regressive work. *Transactional Analysis Journal, 19*(2).

Staunton, T. (Ed.). (2002). *Body Psychotherapy.* London: Brunner-Routledge.

Totton, N. (2003). *Body Psychotherapy: An introduction.* London: Open University Press.

van der Kolk, B., McFarlane, A. C., & Weisaeth, L. (1996). *Traumatic stress: The effects of overwhelming experience on mind, body and society.* New York: Guilford Press.

Winnicott, D. W. (1987). Metapsychological *and clinical aspects of regression within the psychoanalytical set-up.* In D. W. Winnicott (Ed.), *Through paediatrics to psychoanalysis: Collected papers.* London: Karnac.

Young, C. (2003). *The ethics of touch.* Retrieved from www.eabp.org

Young, C. (2005). Doing Effective Body Psychotherapy Without Touch: Part 1. *Energy & Character, 34,* 50–60.

Young, C. (2009). Embodiment: Doing effective Body Psychotherapy without touch: Part 2. *Energy & Character, 37,* 36–46.

# SECTION VIII

Functional Perspectives of Body Psychotherapy

# 58
## Introduction to Section VIII

Gustl Marlock, Germany, and Halko Weiss, United States

Translation by Warren Miller

Entitled "*Functional Perspectives,*" Section VIII summarizes several areas that are of special interest to the practice of Body Psychotherapy. They relate to central human functions, or functional systems—such as respiration, vision, the regulatory circuitry of the autonomic nervous system, sexuality, etc.

There is a traditional line of thought about the body-mind relationship that does not attempt to interpret mental processes as caused by the bodily constitution, but, rather, strives to understand the body from the point of view of its "functional" role. Body Psychotherapeutic traditions have developed a rich variety of techniques to work with functional systems, and these differ significantly from the techniques of other psychotherapeutic approaches.

The functional perspective on which the methodology of these Body Psychotherapeutic approaches is based has three basic historical sources:

1. The psychological school of "functionalism" was developed in the United States at the beginning of the twentieth century as a countermovement to psychological structuralism (Rey, 1997). Functionalism posits that mental states are identified by what they do, rather than what they are made of. Studying how psychological systems actually work should determine the investigation into how psychology "operates." In Body Psychotherapy, this means that the actual operations of somatic systems are seen as the basic realm of observation and ultimately how these influence the functional quality of the psychic system, as well as the overall system: the human being as a whole.

2. The divergent psychosomatic theories of modern medicine and psychotherapy have also developed in response to Western discourses on body-mind dualism: in their critique of monocausal, linear concepts, a dialogue has developed between alternative, multifactorial models that are able to integrate different functional domains.

3. Wilhelm Reich's idea of *energetic functionalism* postulates both a principle of "psychosomatic identity" and one of "antithesis." According to this model, psychic processes cannot be reduced to somatic processes (as in Behaviorism), nor can somatic processes be reduced to psychic processes (as in some schools of psychoanalysis based on conversion theory). Reich and many of his followers assumed instead that the dimensions of the psyche and soma, despite their differences in manifestation, share the same fundamental energetic processes.

From these theoretical and observational beginnings, perspectives on humans' individual functional systems were then developed in both directions: David Boadella (1987) explored the creative foundations for a dynamic understanding of central human functions; and, in a wider sense, the chapters of a number of the authors included here follow in this tradition.

In Chapter 59, "Energy and the Nervous System in Embodied Experience," **James Kepner** explores what is meant—what he means—by "subtle energy" and how this concept can be applied practically and fairly rigorously within the practice of Body Psychotherapy.

In Chapter 60, "The Role of the Autonomic Nervous System," **Dawn Bhat** and **Jacqueline Carleton** describe processes of this little-known system and the consideration of the functioning of this within the context of Body Psychotherapy. This sort of particular attention to autonomic processes reaches back to the earliest beginnings of the transition from psychoanalysis to Body Psychotherapy, and Reich's significant interest in these processes has already been mentioned. Certain aspects of the functioning of the autonomic nervous system are mentioned in several other chapters as well.

In Chapter 61, "The Role of the Breath in Mind-Body Psychotherapy," **Ian Macnaughton,** with significant inputs from **Peter Levine,** examines the process of breathing as one of the most fundamental functions of any vital (living) human organism. In most Body Psychotherapeutic approaches, the "breath" plays an essential role, either somewhat implicitly (as a function that is held in awareness by the therapist, as well as by the client); or very explicitly, when working with emotional defenses, which—on a somatic level—are substantively organized through the breathing function. In Reich's methodology, the "work" to release—for example—"blocked" breathing, and to re-create a natural and spontaneous pulsation of breathing, takes on a crucial role.

Arising out of Boadella's (1987) writings, and Lowen's (1989) inspirations, Chapter 62, "Heart, Heart Feelings, and Heart Symptoms" by **Courtenay Young,** explores the meanings and functions of the psychological aspects of the human heart that go far beyond those conceptualized within basic physiology and cardiac medicine. This is an essential component of Body Psychotherapy, in that we conceptualize "other" (more emotional or psychological) functions of various organs or senses, besides the purely physiological functions.

In Chapter 63, "Dreams and the Body," **Stanley Keleman** suggests a perspective on dreamwork that not only integrates the body in an otherwise-psychodynamic context, but goes much further: He suggests that the representations of a dream can be experienced as an expression of one's embodied existence.

There are—of course—many different ways of working with dreams in Body Psychotherapy: often as many as the many different modalities of Body Psychotherapy. And, in a particular session, with a particular client, a particular way of working may suggest itself from the client's input, from the background of the therapist, or from the circumstances of the moment. We have chosen to represent just this one way, here, from the Body Psychotherapeutic modality of "Formative Psychology" developed by Stanley Keleman, a pioneer of working with the body.

Vision, or insight, is conceived of as another somatic or "organismic" function that is coupled with far-reaching psychic functions. This notion, and the idea that "the eyes are the mirror of the soul," as pointed out by Lowen (1976), belong to the basic premises of the Body Psychotherapeutic tradition. Chapter 64, "Visual Contact, Facing, Presence, and Expression: The Ocular Segment in Body Psychotherapy," was written by **Narelle McKenzie,** with some inputs from **John May,** *both of whom* originally come from the Radix school of Body Psychotherapy, in which Charles Kelley (1971) developed an elaborate system of Body Psychotherapeutic work particularly with the ocular segment. This work is an excellent example of how interventions that address a limiting immobilization of a somatic function, and the muscular aspects (referred to in Reichian terminology as "blockages") pertaining to these, can initiate and uncover basic psychodynamic emotional processes.

These processes, especially when they evoke memories, are attributed to a specific kind of memory—namely, "body memory." This is a form of "somatization" or embodiment of "issues."

Advances in research (Koch et al., 2012) suggest that this frequently ridiculed "explanation" is not at all absurd, because somatic and emotional components are evidently essential aspects of the integrated neuronal-association processes of memory. The term "ocular segment"—in this instance—simultaneously points to another source of functional thinking within the Reichian tradition: in the conceptualization of Character Analysis, and in reference to body defense mechanisms and their underlying conflicts, Reich described the "armoring" of the body in the order of various body segments: ocular, oral, throat, chest, diaphragm, abdomen, and pelvis. For a long time, the essential characteristic of Reichian therapy was systematic and sequential work with these segments, their functions, and any associated emotional-conflict dynamics (e.g., Reich, 1971; Baker, 1967; Navarro, 1997; Sharaf, 1983; etc.).

A central element of **Jack Rosenberg's** Integrative Body Psychotherapy consists of powerful work with the body's segmental holding patterns and their manifestations in the somatic and psychic dimensions. Together with his wife, **Beverly Kitaen Morse,** he describes the foundations, and the further conceptual advancement, of this approach in Chapter 65, "Segmental Holding Patterns of the Body-Mind."

Historically, as well as presently, the concept of "grounding" has played an extremely important role in the functional thinking of many of the Body Psychotherapies. Alexander Lowen, John Pierrakos, and Stanley Keleman (particularly) developed this concept within the context of an important revision that they undertook in the methodology and the setting of classical Reichian therapy. Reich treated his patients only when they were lying down, which is probably (in part) due to his background in psychoanalysis. Reich's systematic work with patients' blockages, in breathing and in body segments, was to prepare them for what he considered the fundamental goal of therapy: to learn to surrender themselves to the pleasurable sensations of "streaming" and the involuntary movements of the orgastic reflex. This also suggests that this is done "horizontally."

The basic methodological revision came when Lowen (1976) pointed out the fundamental differences between: (1) feelings that are secure within the therapeutic setting; and (2) the much more stressful conditions of the emotionally, less-sheltered reality of everyday life.

This differentiation led the bioenergetic approach to proclaim a need for a therapeutic practice that supported the development of ego strength—defined as a *vertical strength*. In addition, working in the vertical plane came to play a key role in the development of "healthy" aggression. Although it was originally intended to facilitate therapeutically the vertical aspects of human existence (self-reliance, self-support, and autonomy), the concept of (vertical) "grounding" has since essentially become more broad and expanded (e.g., Keleman, 1979). It goes from "having roots," to "being grounded," to being "on the ground"—that is, to be in contact with reality—and has since found its way into common language.

Both David Boadella (1987) and Malcolm Brown (1989), in their respective books, have further expanded the concept of "grounding" by bringing it into relationship with the "dependency phase" of early childhood development. With the additional notion of "horizontal grounding," they explored the question of how stabile, positive "anchoring" in the body correlates with successful "resonance" relationships during the pre-verbal phase of development. They also explored how impairments of this nature can be amended therapeutically.

In Chapter 66, "Horizontal Grounding," **Angela Belz-Knöferl** illustrates how "horizontal grounding" can be understood, and which aspects of post-Reichian therapeutic implications were developed for the basis of this concept, in particular from within the schools of Organismic Psychotherapy (Brown) and Biosynthesis (Boadella). These two schools have made key contributions to the further development of the concept of horizontal grounding.

Chapter 67, "Vertical Grounding: The Body in the World and the Self in the Body" by **Lily Anagnostopoulou,** focuses on the vertical aspects of grounding and its meaning, in particular, for what could be called an "embodied existence."

Functional Body Psychotherapeutic concepts also form the background of the final chapter in Section VIII. **William (Bill) Cornell** reexamines the function of human sexuality—a function that is considered essential, both from the perspective of psychoanalysis, and especially from the perspective of classical Reichian Body-Oriented Psychotherapy. In Chapter 68, "Entering the Erotic Field: Sexuality in Body-Centered Psychotherapy," **Cornell** shows how sexuality, having nearly disappeared from the psychoanalytic and Body Psychotherapeutic field in the 1980s and 1990s, can be appreciated theoretically and methodically, so that both the psychodynamic domain of exploration and the somatic domain can become integrated, largely on equal terms.

## References

Baker, E. F. (1967). *Man in the trap.* Houndmills, UK: Macmillan.

Boadella, D. (1987). *Lifestreams: An introduction to Biosynthesis.* Hove, UK: Routledge.

Brown, M. (1989). *The healing touch: An introduction to Organismic Psychotherapy.* Mendocino, CA: LifeRhythm.

Keleman, S. (1979). *The human ground: Sexuality, self and survival.* Berkeley, CA: Center Press.

Kelley, C. R. (1971). *New techniques in vision improvement: A unique synthesis of vision training techniques from William H. Bates and methods of deep emotional release rooted in the work of Wilhelm Reich.* Stamford, CT: Interscience Research Institute.

Koch, S. C., Fuchs, T., Summa, M., & Mueller, C. (2012). *Body memory, metaphor and movement.* Philadelphia: John Benjamins.

Lowen, A. (1976). *Bioenergetics.* New York: Penguin.

Lowen, A. (1989). *Liebe, Sex und dein Herz [Love, sex and your heart].* Munich: Kösel.

Navarro, F. (1997). *Somatopsicodinâmica das Biopatias [Somato-psychodynamics of biopathies].* Rio de Janeiro: Editora Relume Dumará.

Reich, W. (1971). *Characteranalyse [Character Analysis].* Cologne: Kiepenheuer & Witsch.

Rey, G. (1997). *Contemporary philosophy of mind.* Boston: Blackwell.

Sharaf, M. (1983). *Fury on earth: A biography of Wilhelm Reich.* London: Hutchinson.

# 59
## Energy and the Nervous System in Embodied Experience

**James Kepner, United States**

**James Kepner** is the author of *Body Process: Working with the Body in Psychotherapy* and *Healing Tasks: Psychotherapy with Adult Survivors of Childhood Abuse.* He has moved between Body Psychotherapy and Gestalt Psychotherapy and, more recently, has became involved in subtle energy methods, particularly in energy-healing approaches that work with the chakra system, the energetic body, and the flow of energy through physical tissue. It is this later approach that he writes about here.

Since the late 1980s, explorations in Gestalt Body Process Psychotherapy (GBPP) (Kepner, 1987, 2012) have enhanced our appreciation of the importance of the nervous system to our embodied functioning and experience. These observations have emerged from a refinement of "energetic" techniques that have allowed us to work directly with the human nervous system, rather than through methods more common in Body Psychotherapy, whose effect on the nervous system is somewhat more physical or emotional, and thus more indirect. This chapter is a preliminary report on some of the concepts and principles that have emerged over the last quarter century.

These developments have had a significant impact on our facility, on our effectiveness, and on our use of body-oriented interventions, facilitating our work with the body and character structure, helping us to further connect clients to their embodied experience more rapidly, and allowing us to readily clear trauma responses from the nervous system. The results of this work have transformed the way that we understand what is meant by "embodiment" and also how we practice Body Psychotherapy.

The emphasis in this particular approach is on energy, consciousness, and the experience of embodiment, which may seem peculiar to those whose view of the nervous system is drawn only from biology. But this energetic framework integrates very well with our scientific view of the nervous system, while also helping to anchor us better in the phenomenology (direct experience) of ourselves as embodied beings. Real, felt, embodied *experience* is what lies at the core of our work in Body Psychotherapy. Energetic work with the nervous system gives us a selection of tools to deepen (subtly, but profoundly) our embodied experience while revealing important insights into the energetic aspects of the nature of consciousness itself—the marriage of soul and matter, which is the nature of our humanness.

## Energy, Embodied Awareness, and the Nervous System

Body Psychotherapy has always had a connection with the energy of the body, deriving from our roots in Reichian theory, as the first truly body-oriented psychotherapy (besides Pierre Janet). Reich took on Freud's theory of *libido energy* (very seriously), seeing it being bound up in neurotic processes, and he linked this to the binding of muscular tensions in various character structures. He observed that muscular armoring, as an intrinsic part of neurotic adaptation, reduces vitality, sensation, and feeling, as well as the flow of emotion, and so on. On the other hand, release of muscular armoring reproduced in/stored up in/introduced into a retrieval system or transmitted in any form by any means (electronic, mechanical, photocopying, recording, or otherwise) brought about pulsatory movements and "streaming" sensations.

These are experienced subjectively as a flow of energy, and are experienced objectively as concomitant with such things as increased emotional release, warmth, vitality, and liveliness of tissue. Reich understood this as a functional unity between the bioenergetic process (libido, or what he later termed orgone energy), muscular armoring, and character defense structures. Although many Body Psychotherapies do not use notions of an energetic system in their own theory and understanding of embodiment, the concept of energy has a significant place in the deeper ground of our field.

More recently, in the field of the healing arts, hands-on approaches have evolved from the influence of Eastern systems, such as the chakra system of subtle energy, and the traditional Chinese medicine mapping of the flow of *chi* or subtle energy in the body. These energetic healing arts (see, for example: Krieger, 1979; Brennan, 1993; Bruyere, 1994; Brown, 1998) are based on the well-established practice of the "healer" either manipulating the recipient's "subtle energy" (as in acupuncture) or directing "subtle energy" through their own body and hands into the body of the "recipient." This is a skill that can be demonstrated and taught.

Although the actual nature of what "subtle energy" is is still quite puzzling, scientifically, there is considerable research that suggests that experienced healers appear to be emitting low-frequency electromagnetic fields from their hands, and thus influencing the electromagnetic and bioplasmic fields in and around living tissue within the client's body. There is now a wide array of research indicating that subtle energy work has definite and measurable effects on a variety of medical and psychological conditions, suggesting that it is much more than just a placebo effect, a form of hypnotic suggestion, or a "mystic phenomenon."

Because it is not the purpose of this chapter to review and present the arguments about the reality of subtle energy (which is nonetheless a definitive experiential phenomenon, even if arguably still a controversial one), readers are therefore referred to Hunt (1978, 1982), Becker (1992), Slater (1995), and Benor (2001) for discussion about some of the scientific and research issues in this field; and to Krieger (1979), Brennan (1987), Bruyere (1994), Fahrion (1995), and Brown (1998) for descriptions of various forms of practice. In this chapter, the term "energy" will be used synonymously with "subtle energy."

Subtle energy appears to have certain characteristics of either *flow* (plasmic and waterlike qualities) and/or *field* (coherent and interpenetrating qualities) (see Figure 59.1). Skilled therapists can also affect the frequency, temperature, and tonality of subtle energy by using their practiced intention. The intensity (amplitude) of subtle energy, generated by a particular therapist, also tends to increase over time (with practice) and, generally speaking, the greater the amplitude of energy flow generated, the more effect there seems to be both on the recipient's sensation and on creating actual changes in the recipient's body tissue itself.

Subtle energy, in this sense, may be subtle—in effect—only because of the therapist's lack of skill or experience; and, with practiced operators, it may not be felt as being subtle at all by the receiver. Another factor in the receiver being able to perceive a palpable effect is their degree of kinesthetic numbness to their own body's sensations, which we will understand later in this chapter as being determined (to a large degree) by the blockage of their own nervous system to their flow of energy. The more numb and blocked a person is, the greater the intensity of energy flow that will be required for them in order to "feel something." (Reich also found this with blocked or heavily "armored" patients.) Conversely, the more open they are to the flow of energy, the less intensity of flow will be required to create a palpable experience of energy.

As a student of these methods, I have integrated energetic practices into the hands-on work that we do as a part of GBPP (Kepner, 2000) because of its usefulness in fostering many of the aims of a body-oriented psychotherapy. This includes aims such as: increasing bodily sensation; supporting a sense of interconnection of one's body parts;

## CHARACTERISTICS AND QUALITIES OF SUBTLE ENERGY

**CHARACTERISTICS**

FLOW—Movement along pathways; "like water;" fills muscle, fascia & tissue; spreads down available routes, into available spaces; plasmic qualities

FIELD—Interpenetrates matter; not bounded by the physical; tends to cohere (form a unified whole, stick together) with itself

**QUALITIES**

FREQUENCY—color, vibration, pulsation

TEMPERATURE—warmth to coolness

TONALITY—has tonal qualities e.g. vital, charging, calming, soft, definitive, yin, yang, etc.

EFFECTS—effects both tissue and also subjective experience (embodiment)

Figure 59.1. Characteristics and qualities of subtle energy

the experience of internal flow; and greater access to embodied emotional experience. Energetic techniques also operate with a minimal degree of intrusiveness for the client. This can be an important factor, especially when working with traumatized clients (Kepner, 1995), especially in comparison to more muscle-oriented interventions, such as movement, expressive work, or deep massage, which are typical of many Body-Oriented Psychotherapeutic interventions.

As we have extended this energetic work to being able to direct particular application on, and within, the recipient's nervous system itself, some principles have emerged pertaining to the relationship between energy, awareness, and embodiment. I will discuss these and then present some of our current observations on the phenomenology of different parts of the nervous system as they impact Body Psychotherapeutic work: Figure 59.2 summarizes these principles.

## KEY PRINCIPLES FROM ENERGETIC WORK IN THE NERVOUS SYSTEM

I. The nervous system is also an energetic system.

II. Conscious awareness has energetic properties.

III. Consciousness is embodied via the pathways of the nervous system.

IV. Consciousness is embodied in the nervous system in a cephalo-caudal-peripheral direction.

V. The availability of nervous system tissue to energy determines our capacity for, and experience of, embodiment.

VI. Different parts of our nervous system engender different qualities or aspects of self-experience.

Figure 59.2. Key principles from energetic work in the nervous system

## I. The Nervous System Is Also an Energetic System

In addition to all its physiological functions and the transmission of nerve impulses, the nervous system appears to also serve as a system for distributing energy to body tissues and organs. This is an understanding that has emerged from our exploration of the work of a twentieth-century energy healer named William Gray (Gray, 1947; Kepner, 2001; Montgomery, 1973).

Gray intuitively developed a strange but powerful system of healing, essentially by understanding the nervous system as a distribution network of subtle energy. Our "subtle energy" therapeutic work has evolved from trying to re-create some of Gray's understanding. Nerves and the nervous system tissue appear to be able to readily distribute this form of subtle energy throughout the body and directly into body tissues.

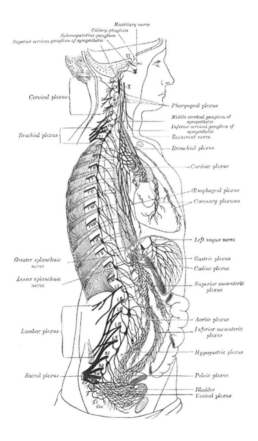

Figure 59.3. The autonomic nervous system (from Gray's Anatomy, 1918)

The concept of the human nervous system as an energy-distribution system is certainly of interest to many energy practitioners and healers, and to those in the somatic therapies, but we are more interested in the impact on Body Psychotherapists.

As we have developed various techniques to "clear" and "open up" these nerves for a better energy flow according to this principle, we have also observed that this often made a major impact on the client's sense of their own embodiment. They experienced themselves as more "in" their body, more physically aware, with increased bodily sensations, and with greater access to emotional feelings. These factors are essential to any Body Psychotherapeutic process and so were of considerable interest to us, especially because the energetic work with the nervous system produced these effects more readily, and with less fuss, than more vigorous physical techniques. In addition, working with the nervous system as an energetic system has allowed us to understand the crucial link between consciousness, energy, and the nervous system, and how this linkage profoundly affects our experience of our embodied self.

## II. Conscious Awareness Has Energetic Properties

Practitioners who have been trained in and are sensitive to touch techniques readily note the difference in the "felt quality" of a person's body tissue, particularly when that person brings their awareness *into* that body area—not just attends "from a distance," but is able to feel "present" in that area. When awareness is present, body tissue feels more vibrant, warm, flowing, and alive. These qualities are almost identical to what other energy healers have observed in the "felt quality" of tissue that has been opened to energy.

Consciousness (conscious awareness) appears to have properties and qualities that are almost identical to those of subtle energy in general; therefore, we have concluded that it, too, is "energetic" in its nature. We term this energetic property of "conscious awareness" the *Energy of Awareness* (EOA). As with other energetic phenomena, a trained practitioner can sense this conscious awareness in terms of its "presence" or "absence" in the client's body. The EOA behaves like other "energetic stuff" in having qualities of flow and presence, as well as frequency and amplitude. Even relatively untrained hands can acquire some sense of this through the following exercise:

**Exercise: Presence/Absence of Awareness in the Shoulder and Impact on the Toucher's Impressions**

Find a partner to work with and have them stand in a relaxed and comfortable position. Stand at their side, facing them, so that you can easily place your hands on either side of one of their shoulders, cupping the shoulder joint with your palms, without reaching and without straining your own shoulders.

First, rub your hands briskly together to warm and sensitize them, then place your hands on their shoulder as described. Continue breathing fully throughout this exercise, rather than diminishing your breathing in order to "focus," because constancy of breathing maintains better sensitivity. Your elbows should be bent and your own shoulders and arms should be relaxed so you don't strain.

Without changing their breathing and without moving in any way, instruct your partner to bring their attention *away* from the shoulder you are touching, not just to ignore that part of them, but to actively draw their attention out of that place and to put all of their focus elsewhere, say, into their other shoulder. Notice how their shoulder feels between your hands as they do this for a minute or two.

Then instruct your partner to bring all of their attention *into* the shoulder you are touching, as if bringing themselves as fully as possible into the space between your hands. Again, pay attention to how their shoulder feels between your hands as they do this, noting any differences for a minute or two.

You might wish to ask them to repeat this sequence so that you can compare and contrast the subtle differences, and because your partner may become more skillful at moving their attention by repeating this a few times, giving you a more distinct difference to notice.

Most people can discern some palpable differences in the sense of vitality, a liveliness or presence, when you (or your partner) withdraw their awareness from their shoulder, compared to when they moved their awareness more fully into their shoulder. It is also this sense of awareness

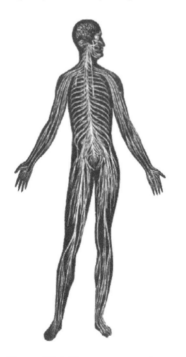

Figure 59.4. The nervous system.

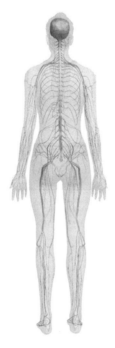

Figure 59.5. Nervous system flow.

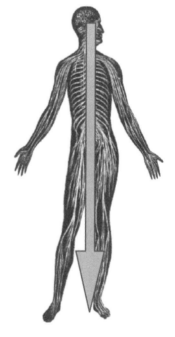

Figure 59.6. Embodiment via the nervous system.

*moving* in and *moving* out of body areas that further gives us the sense that awareness is something that is flowing and energetic in nature.

Consciousness is not like a light shining from a tall tower onto the bodily terrain below. Conscious awareness itself has an energetic quality and literally spreads and moves through mental awareness, as well as through body areas and tissues. Whereas the biological nervous system gives us a "signal" to and from the brain and nerve endings, which results in awareness of our body from that signal, it is the actual energy flow through the nervous system and the ability of our nervous system to carry the EOA that make for the possibility of *awareness in* our body. It is the EOA that gives us a direct felt sense of "being" spread into, and through, our body that we can truly call "embodiment" rather than experiencing ourselves as only perched in our head, observing our bodily experience from afar.

## III. Consciousness Is Embodied via the Pathways of the Nervous System

Although most people would say that they are aware of their body, in the sense of being able to feel their bodily presence and location in a general way, if asked to point to where they live or to locate their "I," they are quite likely to point to their head. For the most part, we experience the center of our conscious awareness as being in the body region of the head, with the rest of our body being experienced at a distance—so to speak, "down there." It is not that we don't have *literal* sensation or control over our body below the head, but that, as a rule, we don't feel rooted "in and of" our body as a whole. Experientially, our "I," our sense of consciousness, is not evenly spread into, embedded in, and living in our bodily being, and we don't fully *inhabit* our bodily "being." Being aware "of" one's body is not the same as living *in* one's body. We don't fully *occupy* our bodily being. The "commonsense" view that a person is their mind and thinking is not a philosophical "mind/body" problem. It is our common experience that our sense of presence, our consciousness, and our EOA is embedded more in our brain and head than elsewhere in our body.

If you look at Figure 59.5, you can observe how the nervous system so beautifully connects all the body areas and parts to the brain and vice versa. You will recall how energy behaves like water in the sense that it flows and fills into tissues—similar to the flow of blood—and spreads, when it has an open channel through which to do so, and provides a carrier vehicle for other "substances," like the EOA.

Imagine that the nervous system is like an open set of conduits or channels. Imagine pouring a stream of water from the brain "downward and outward" (in a cephalo-caudal-peripheral direction), filling all the channels of the nerves. Then picture a drop of blue dye centered in the brain, the particular energy quality of consciousness that we are calling the EOA, spreading downward and out into these watery channels until it filters all the way into the nerve endings and thus into the body tissues.

If the brain is the putative "seat of consciousness," and if conscious awareness is an energetic phenomenon (the EOA), then we can see how the nervous system would be the ready pathway—the highway of light, so to speak—for the EOA to spread into the body.

## IV. Consciousness Is Embodied in the Nervous System in a Cephalo-Caudal-Peripheral Direction

Consciousness is embodied via the pathways of the nervous system in a cephalo-caudal-peripheral (from the head, downward toward the tail, and then outward) direction. It becomes apparent from the description we are developing that the consciousness becomes embodied as the EOA enters into bodily life from the center of consciousness in the brain, via an energetically accessible nervous system in a downward direction (from the point of view of a standing figure). Just as the nervous system of the human embryo grows in a cephalo-caudal (head-to-tail) direction, *conscious awareness spreads into the body from the center of consciousness (in the brain) "downward" through the spinal cord and then "out" into the peripheral nerves, autonomic, sensory, and motoric, and thus into the body's tissues.*

The nervous system is, in this view, the means by which our consciousness connects into matter. As we appreciate the cephalo-caudal-peripheral direction through which awareness spreads throughout the nervous system, this helps us to understand why certain classical Body Psychotherapeutic interventions don't seem to last very long. Grounding is one example of this.

Many body-oriented psychotherapies (like Bioenergetics) do a lot of physical work with the client's legs in order to help them to become more "in their body" and to become connected to the ground, and to the supports of their self, and much more aware of their lower half. These body-oriented psychotherapeutic approaches often work via the muscular system, through stretching and creating tensions, then relaxing, and/or generating vibrations and sensations through vigorous movement.

But, if the nervous system is the main means by which awareness connects downward into the body core and, once there, to the limbs, then the "grounding work" through the muscular system might not be the best approach. Although muscular work certainly creates an energetic charge and sensation in the areas being stimulated, thus creating more temporary signals for the whole biological nervous system, such muscular work may not open the nerves adequately to the resulting energy flow. And, more fundamentally, this may be working in the wrong direction in terms of how consciousness connects into embodiment: from the bottom up instead of from the head down.

Imagine the nervous system being like waxed cloth, such that the cloth can't absorb the "water" of awareness, centered in the brain. If you remove the wax in the leg end of the cloth, it still can't absorb the water from above, because the rest of the cloth is unable to absorb and draw down the Energy of Awareness toward the legs. Muscular work may make muscles more available to energy, but may not sufficiently clear the nerve flow in the legs, making the effects of grounding work dissipate too readily, despite hours of exercise and expressive work. You could wet the cloth, so to speak, by generating energy in the muscles through exercises, breathing, and movement, and the EOA will be carried on the general field of energy that is then present and covering more of the body. But, after you stop, the cloth will dry out again. As the muscularly generated field dissipates again, as it will without the coherency and interconnection provided by the EOA throughout the nervous system, the person would feel himself or herself disconnecting from their legs again. The circuit of awareness is not completed from the inside out, via the natural carrier of the EOA, the energetic nervous system.

In addition, for some clients, all that stimulation and charge generated in their lower body can actually "chase out" their awareness from the nerves in their lower body, because it is fairly overwhelming and so the "ego" retreats from it. This is particularly true for survivors of trauma or abuse: there is an energetic withdrawal inward, more to their core.

Grounding is more rapidly facilitated and is actually longer lasting by energetically clearing out the nervous system, especially the big nerves in the legs, and making it more accessible to the EOA coming from the "head-down" direction.

## V. The Availability of Nervous System Tissue to Energy Determines Our Capacity for, and Experience of, Embodiment

The relative availability of our nervous system tissue to energy largely determines our capacity for, and experience of, embodiment. It is obvious to anyone who works with bodily experience that, whereas everyone is aware *of* their body to a greater or lesser degree, many people do not prove to be *embodied* in the sense of feeling truly *in* their body. Some parts of us feel more "distant" from our sense of "self"; some parts of us we barely feel at all, let alone feel "present" in. Put in the terms of this chapter, our EOA is often not spread evenly throughout our nervous system and into our body tissues.

When our nervous system tissue is readily available to energy flow, we experience ourselves as more connected to, and truly able to occupy, our physical being. Conversely, when our nervous system tissue is limited in energy flow, we experience our bodily life more at a distance and indirectly, or hardly at all. One observation from the Body-Oriented Psychotherapies—that we are commonly less aware of, and less "in," some parts of our "bodily being" than others—is a function of just this availability of our tissue to energy and awareness. Just as muscular tension can block the flow of energy and emotions in the body (as Reich observed), so too can nervous tissue become blocked and less permeable to the flow of energy and thus also to (the flow of the energy of) awareness.

The "waxed cloth" metaphor (used in the previous section) appears at times to be all too accurate a description for our nervous system: impervious to the watery flow of lived-in awareness. As we have worked in the nervous system energetically, it has become apparent for many of our clients, and for ourselves as well, that (1) their nervous system is not particularly open or available to energy flow, and (2) their EOA literally *can't* get into their body in any deep way.

It is not necessarily that they are resistant or defensive to bodily awareness, so much as they are stuck in their brain and, as the punch line of an old joke goes, "They can't get there from here." A process that may have originated for defensive purposes may result in the nervous system being unavailable to the EOA, even when the client is willing and ready to release the defensive function.

As we connect to body areas that were vacated for defensive purposes, we must learn to distinguish defensive avoidance from the incapacity to experience. Therapists are often too ready to attribute ongoing incapacity to defensiveness, blaming the client for their inability or for their lack of "readiness." It is as if, would they only be less defensive, they would be able to feel, or sense, or express emotion. The two may exist concurrently, and the client will tend to experience defensive avoidance only when their incapacity to experience their bodily nature via the nervous system exists.

## VI. Different Parts of Our Nervous System Engender Different Qualities or Aspects of Self-Experience

Different parts of our nervous system engender different qualities or different aspects of self-experience, and our degree of consciousness in these parts of our nervous system (mediated by the energetic availability of these parts of our nervous system) affects our psychological functioning and sense of self. So far, we have spoken only of the *general* availability of the nervous system to the EOA and to our general sense of being embodied.

Body-Oriented Psychotherapists have long noted that the specific location of a person's awareness, and the degree to which it occupies their body, has a significant impact on their psychological functioning. For example, as a way to cope with physical or sexual trauma, a person may withdraw their awareness from specific traumatized body areas, which may result in being unable to make that area function as fully available in their lives. Feeling numb and disconnected from the pelvis and sexual organs, as a result of sexual trauma, or feeling less present in body areas associated with surgery or disease, are just two examples of this mode of coping.

The obverse can also occur where some particular dimensions of embodiment are emphasized, to the exclusion of others, making this dimension of self-experience and contact predominant. We see this in character adaptations—for example, where a person's neuromuscular dimension of embodiment is the most energetically available part of them, predisposing them to relating to the world through *activity,* but leaving them relatively unaware of their visceral inner sensations and therefore relatively cut off from their emotional life. Someone who is "all action and no sense" may seek high-intensity and dangerous situations in order "just to feel" or "just to have an experience!" as one man put it to me in the course of therapy.

Our experience through each of our different body systems creates important nuances that somatically anchor us to different aspects of the self: our experience of having a solid place to stand in the world is mediated through our experience of our legs; our feelings and emotions are felt as resonant in our visceral organs; our feeling of our "depths" and "insides" is intrinsically connected to our capacity to sense our organs, bones, and muscles. We will have a clear sense of being "in" that part of us, and we will have access to the self-experience of that part of us, if that part of our nervous system is available to, and occupied by, our EOA. This is true even with the autonomic nervous system, even though we have regularly been told (by our scientific educationists) that we cannot be consciously aware of this system.

608 | FUNCTIONAL PERSPECTIVES OF BODY PSYCHOTHERAPY

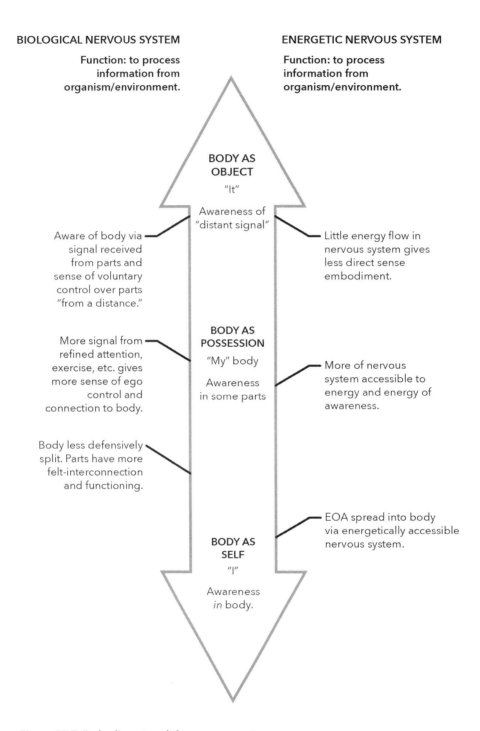

Figure 59.7. Embodiment and the nervous system.

Although the *functions* of our autonomic nervous system are not governed by aware cognition, in our work we have found we can have a surprisingly detailed awareness of our autonomic organs when the EOA has access to them by way of the autonomic nerves.

By opening the nervous system to the flow of energy, we gain access to awareness of our bodily life and we find new resources for experience, claim self-capacities, and bring our aware self into contact with issues in need of resolution. By bringing the EOA into our bodily life through an available nervous system, we come to live in the world and in ourselves more fully, making the pathway for our soul to manifest into a fully "lived" life.

The table in Figure 59.8 summarizes the two natures of our nervous system, and shows their contribution to the issue of embodied awareness and ownership of embodied life.

## The Phenomenology of the Embodied Self and the Nervous System

As we have noted, different parts of our nervous system engender different qualities or aspects of self-experience, and our degree of consciousness in these parts of our nervous system (mediated by the energetic availability of each part of our nervous system) affects our psychological functioning and sense of self. We could broadly term this the "phenomenology of the embodied self through the nervous system." In this, both the biological and energetic aspects of the different parts of our nervous system integrate into embodied qualities of experience.

### The Experience of "Basic Being": The Brain and Existence: The Brain and Feeling Located

From a Body Psychotherapist's point of view, the primary experience of being an embodied self is like those three things said to be needed to sell any real estate: it is very much about location, location, location. To exist is to have a sense of location inside a body. To "incarnate" derives from the Latin *in carne* ("to be flesh"). Our first sense of being located in a body derives from our sense of being inside our skull looking out. From the view of this chapter, our

**BRAIN**
Basic being

**SPINAL CORD AND MAJOR MUSCULO-SENSORY NERVES**
Being in the world

**MUSCULAR NERVES**
Self as activity
External focus

**AUTONOMIC NERVOUS SYSTEM**
Having insides
Internal feeling focus

**VAGUS NERVE**
Inner presence and substance

**PELVIC PARASYMPATHETIC NERVES**
Earthy, primal self

**SYMPATHETIC NERVES**
Sense of inner charge and excitement
Self as centered in body core

Figure 59.8. Experience of embodiment through the nervous system

sense of being located in the head comes from the way in which nerve tissue carries the EOA. Because the brain is the biggest mass of nervous tissue, it acts as a kind of big reservoir for consciousness and the EOA. It is this sense of presence, derived from the concentration of consciousness in the brain, that gives us the very fundamental grounding experience of "I am." Descartes' famous phrase could be phenomenologically restated as *"I feel my sense of location in my head, where I think that I think, and therefore I am."* Had Descartes been more embodied, I daresay that the course of Western philosophy might have been different!

This brain-location sense of our fundamental being is usually so key to the very nature of human existence that it is infrequent for clients to lack even this much sense of their fundamental existence. One exception is some dissociative clients who may at times withdraw their EOA so completely (in order to flee embodied life) that they experience being located outside of their body. To be so dislocated clinically suggests early, pre-verbal childhood trauma and shock, or perhaps prenatal problems that significantly disturbed the very process of fusing consciousness to matter in the developing nervous system.

## The Experience of "Being in the World": Filling Down into the Spinal Cord and Major Sensory-Motor Nerves

Our experience of *basic beingness* is followed by our movement into embodied life as the EOA extends "down" into the spinal cord from the brain (in the cephalo-caudal direction referred to earlier). The best nerve pathways for energy are through the bigger nerves of the body[60] and those that flow most directly to the seat of conscious awareness in the brain. These nerves include the spinal cord, the brachial nerves stemming from the cervical spinal cord, the large somatic nerves of the back, and the sciatic nerves of the legs. As we "*fill into ourselves*," we establish a sense of our outline and a sense of being "present" in a bodily form. That is to say, as we have a sense of our back, arms, legs, and basic skin container via these major nerve pathways for energy and awareness, we also have the experience of being in the world as a bodily being. As the "fullness" of energy and EOA increases, we carry a greater sense of presence in our sense of being here on earth, as an embodied being.

This process of acquiring "fullness" can be done momentarily, as in an exercise or a workshop, but takes regular practice over time to become more constant and sustainable.

## The Experience of Our "Insides": The Autonomic Nervous System and a Core Self

The sense of our being in the world—which comes from the basic spinal cord, sensory, and muscular nerves—could be described as our experience of our bodily self as agent and container; but as embodied beings we are both container

and contents, a phrase used by Bonnie Bainbridge Cohen (1993). Our experience of having contents or insides comes from our autonomic nervous system, the combination of parasympathetic and sympathetic nerves that enervate our internal organs. Most of us have been taught (in biology and physiology) that this part of our nervous system, in both sensory and motor forms, is completely unaware and is not accessible to conscious awareness or control. Medical doctors have even told me that we have awareness of internal-organ sensation only under conditions of disease, such as gastric pain or indigestion! But even on the biological level, nerve signals from our internal organs are registered by our brain, and certainly visceral sensations such as fullness, hunger, arousal, fear (via increased heart rate, respiration, and so on), and others are commonly perceived autonomic sensations.

As the autonomic nervous system is made more accessible to energy, our sense of "having insides" becomes even more clear and pronounced. We also have greater access to our inner life, our inner emotions, our gut feelings, and a textured response to our living, which comes from registering this dimension of our embodied being. Psychotherapy patients who present symptoms such as "I am empty inside" frequently turn out to be energetically blocked to significant parts of their autonomic nervous system and so register a blank spot in their bodily field of awareness, which they interpret as "empty."

On more careful exploration of their body senses, this actually turns out to be a lack of sensation, like an area of the mouth numbed by dental anesthetics, so that these people are simply unable to *feel* their insides. In our current view, this is because they don't have access to their autonomic nervous system via an available energetic connection.

An open energy flow from our central nervous system into the autonomic nerves creates a clearer sense of *having insides*: registering our inner sensations and processes. As our EOA spreads into the nerves of our autonomic nervous system, we shift from the experience of *having* insides to *being* inside, and begin to feel that we are *living from the inside out*. We have a sense of our core, our depths, in a way

---

60   It appears that literal nervous tissue volume has something to do with how much energy can be carried through the nervous tissue. Larger nerves tend to carry more energy and awareness, and also tend to open first to flow as we clear the nervous system.

that is not just metaphorical as these terms are often used in psychotherapy, but real in a physical sense. Our "depths" are literally our nerves and organs deep in our body core. "Deep inside me" is the feeling of sensation and consciousness embedded in one's autonomic nervous system. "My core" is the feeling of being anchored in the literal location of the central axis of the torso through the sympathetic nervous system.

The most direct neural routes for the EOA, from the brain into the body core (torso) and the visceral organs, are through the nerves of the autonomic nervous system, especially the sympathetic ganglion chain and the vagus nerve. The sympathetic chain, which descends on either side of the spine inside the body cavity, and the vagus nerve, which descends from the brainstem and branches into the heart, lungs, and midabdominal digestive organs, both have direct cranial connections to the brain. It is from the quality of energy and awareness through these nerves, as well as the less conscious sensory nerve signals, that we have a sense of our insides, our inner gut feelings, and our visceral sense of experience.

Sensory nerve signals alone may give us some vague form of inner visceral sensation, but it is not sufficient to give us a sense of being inside ourselves, rooted in our inner presence and substance. Only when the EOA is connected to, and spread down into, our visceral organs via the autonomic nervous system does this sense of inner presence and substance become tangible and specific. When the EOA is *not* connected to and spread into our autonomic visceral nerves, we may feel autonomic stimulation and emotions, but they are experienced as coming from "down there" rather than "inside *me*." We experience our feelings and emotions as "rising from below" without a clear connection to our own ongoing processes. For example, in panic and anxiety disorders, the person feels himself or herself as being taken over by a wave of anxiety—rising up from the solar plexus or chest—that occurs "from nowhere." As we open the nerve pathways to energy flow, and thus create access for the EOA, clients experience a greater sense of their insides, and find more connection to their emotions and their inner life.

## The "Vagal Experience": Parasympathetic Nervous System Experience

The vagus nerve, really a nerve system in some ways, is one of the longest nerves in the body with direct cranial connections. It originates in the midbrain and descends down the interior of the torso all the way to the umbilical area, with branches to the eyelids, middle ear, salivary glands, heart, bronchial tubes, stomach, liver, pancreas, and parts of the large and small intestines. It covers a tremendous amount of our body interior.

The experience of being energetically present and connected to the vagus nerve is that of having inner presence and substance. We feel a sense of being filled into ourselves, of having inner substance. It tends to be a softer-edged quality than our sense of connection to our sympathetic nerves. Much of our vagal experience of self is related to the sensations and processes of feeding and ingesting food: an open and receptive quality of experience in the eyes and mouth; a sense of moving down and into one's soft body core; a suffusing warmth in the chest that comes with slowing cardiac activity and bronchial dilation; and the sensations of interior satisfaction and fullness that come from the esophageal and intestinal presence. A lot of what (in psychotherapy) is referred to as "oral" is more properly "vagal" in nature.

Contact with yearning, longing, heartfelt wounds, difficulty with self-comforting and self-soothing, difficulty with love and relatedness, lack of an internal sense of sufficiency, and so on, are often related to energetic blockage and lack of presence in parts of the vagal system.

## Lower Parasympathetic Experience

The lower parasympathetic nerves, which emerge from the sacrum, enervate the lower digestive and pelvic organs. Our internal experience through these nerves is not as specific as that arising from the vagus nerve, whose major organs—the heart, lungs, upper digestive tract, and transverse colon—seem to give us more definite and distinctive qualities of experience. We might best describe the registry of our lower parasympathetic nervous system experienc-

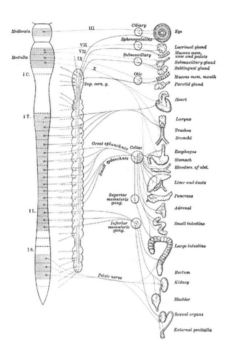

Figure 59.9. Diagram of autonomic nervous system (from Gray's Anatomy).

ing presence of, and in, our "earthy" self, because of the connection to sexuality and digestion. Another quality is a sense of our "depths." The sense of having a deep, inner well of feeling comes from being connected to and living from (the EOA spread into) our lower parasympathetic nervous system.

### The Experience of the Sympathetic Nervous System

Physiologically, the sympathetic branch of the autonomic nervous system is responsible for arousal states, and for preparing us for high-output activity, the so-called "fight-or-flight" reaction. This involves increased heart rate, increased blood pressure, increased respiration, a decrease in peristalsis and digestive activity (to free metabolic energy for the brain and muscles), a massive increase in adrenaline, an increase in cortisol and other secretions, and many other changes in the metabolism.[61] Phenomenologically, this creates a general internal sense of charge and excitement, a feeling of being energized and actively engaged or a feeling of readiness for engagement. It can also be experienced as great fear: but not so great a fear that paralyzes one (that is a third sympathetic variant, "fright").

Our energetic experience of being in our sympathetic nervous system is, in part, related to this physiological sense of arousal, but is also related to the anatomical structure and location of one of its primary components: the sympathetic ganglion chain. The sympathetic ganglion chain descends all the way from the upper cervical vertebrae bilaterally on either side of the spine, but anterior to it, just inside the body cavity, from the spine all the way to the sacrum. Thus, it defines a kind of internal axis just in front of the spine, on the interior of the body. Nerve roots at each vertebral level connect from the spinal cord to the various ganglions.

Please recall that our main route of incarnation or inhabitation into embodiment is first from our brain downward into our spinal cord. When we energetically inhabit our spinal cord, and our sympathetic ganglion chain, we begin to have a very clear sense of being centered in ourselves and aligned with our axis. This sense of our axis is tremendously stabilizing to our personality, and we can feel much more able to hold our personal ground, unswayed, when we have this sense. A lot of issues that psychotherapists in our era have framed as being about "boundaries" are not really about how we manage interaction at our edges at all, but rather are about how we feel displaced from this central axis in our body. If we are not adequately anchored in our sympathetic/spinal axis through these parts of our nervous system, we can easily "lose ourselves" and center upon the experience or agenda of others.

As energy can spread into the sympathetic nerves that connect from the ganglions to the various organs, we have a sense of organ tone and internal support. The quality of "charge" that is characteristic of sympathetic nervous system energy carries a felt quality of being "pumped up." We feel filled out inside, not just with a sense of internal

---

61 Overall, an increase in sympathetic nervous system activity tends to decrease parasympathetic activity, although in some areas both of these are required, as in sexual arousal, during which increased heart rate and peripheral vasodilation (for erection and genital swelling) co-occur.

presence (as occurs from the connection of our parasympathetic nerves to the organs) but with a sense of being somewhat expanded, internally defined, and toned.

## The Experience of "Self as Activity": The Neuromuscular Connection

When the Energy of Awareness (EOA) is engaged in the musculoskeletal nerves, the sense of one's self as a definitive and bounded being, as well as of one's self as being about activity, becomes paramount. The sensory signal generated by our muscle tone, when our muscle tone is adequate, leaves us with a sense of having a definite boundary—an elastic "shell," so to speak—that has vibrancy and strength. If you have lifted weights at all, this sense of "I am" that comes from charged and toned musculature is quite familiar. Our sense of personal capacity and strength, which importantly relates to the feeling of our coping capacity, comes, in part, from our muscular and movement capacity and especially from the neurosensory feedback that we derive from an active, charged musculature.

In addition to feedback and self-definition, the quality of energetic emphasis on our "muscular" being also affects our focus. To have a more open energetic pathway out into our muscles—our periphery—is to focus more of our consciousness outward into our activities and into the world, so to speak. How much we live in our shell, our action in the world versus our action in other dimensions of our being, is an important contribution to character style and can be worked with from the energetic–nervous system direction.

For example, in the autonomy structure,[62] the emphasis on guarding against manipulation by engaging the social world defensively through high-output actions or charm radiating outward from the body directs all the energy of the personality toward the outer world.

The inner world, here understood as the autonomic nervous system and the body core, does not get accessed

---

62  This term "autonomy structure" is derived from Bodynamics. The equivalent term used in Reichian theory is the psychopathic character structure.

by awareness and is not "lived in" or inhabited by the EOA. Body therapeutic work that attempts to work through the musculature in this character structure usually reinforces this defense by mobilizing more energy output to this body "shell." It does little to connect safely with and make accessible their inner being, which in essence is their autonomic nervous system, particularly the parasympathetic realm of experience that they are so defended against. Energetic work on the autonomic nervous system goes more directly to the heart of the matter for this kind of character structure.

In contrast, the need (oral) structure has the opposite problem. This structure must develop stronger energy and conscious connection to their muscular capacity and shell. Without this, they feel weak, impotent, unbounded, and unable to mobilize energy and self-support. Muscular development alone does not make for a continuity of energy consciousness through the nervous system. Working energetically at the boundary between nerve endings and muscles helps people with this character structure acquire a more stable and lively connection to their muscular, and thus more proactive, nature.

## Reformulation of the Process of Body-Oriented Psychotherapy

Body Psychotherapists have worked to develop clients' bodily awareness through physical means (touch-based work, movement, exercises, breathing, etc.) and often understand these as a way of working with a defense or adaptation. These techniques are predominantly muscular in nature, seeking to release defensively held tensions and emotional patterns, or seeking to flood the body systems with an energetic charge via breathing, the use of movement and touch, and so on. The effect on the nervous system is usually indirect and secondary. Under the terms of the current discussion, it appears that until the nervous system is accessible to energy, and to the EOA, the person *can't* readily be "in" their bodily self. It is not resistance, so much as an inability. The muscular system *per se* seems to be an indirect means to accomplish this.

From the view presented here, much of the emphasis in Body-Oriented Psychotherapy on dissolving armor and working muscularly appears to be working from the wrong end of the system of human awareness. Our historical theory base, which has oriented more from our muscular nature, has predisposed us to certain kinds of interventions. These may have misled us as to the critical system through which our work operates.

Therapeutic aims that have appeared to require large movements, dramatic discharge, and high-amplitude breathing might be accessed with more subtle interventions if the awareness function can be accessed through its native energetic body system. The therapeutic work referred to here is, in my experience, equally deep as such high-amplitude discharge work, even though it may not have the dramatic quality that some have confused with authenticity. Also, it avoids the "collateral damage" that can come from excessive reenactment, regression, flooding of traumatized systems, retraumatization and imprinting, and so on—the iatrogenic problems inherent in certain forms of body therapeutic work.

## References

Becker, R. O. (1992). Modern bioelectromagnetics and functions of the central nervous system. *Subtle Energies, 3(1),* 53–72.

Benor, D. J. (2001). *Healing research: Vol. 1, Spiritual healing: Scientific validation of a healing revolution.* Southfield, MI: Vision.

Brennan, B. A. (1987). *Hands of light.* New York: Bantam Books.

Brennan, B. A. (1993). *Light emerging.* New York: Bantam Books.

Brown, C. (1998). *Afterwards, you're a genius: Faith, medicine, and the metaphysics of healing.* New York: Riverhead Books.

Bruyere, R. (1994). *Wheels of light* (Vol. 1). New York: Simon & Schuster.

Cohen, B. B. (1993). *Sensing, feeling and action.* Northampton, MA: Contact Editions.

Fahrion, S. E. (1995). The clinical face of energy medicine. *Subtle Energies, 6(1), i–iii.*

Gray, H. (1918). *Anatomy of the human body* (20th ed.). Philadelphia: Lea & Febiger.

Gray, W. E. (1947). *Know your magnetic field.* Pomeroy, WA: Health Research.

Hunt, V. (1978). Electronic evidence of auras, chakras in UCLA study. *Brain/Mind Bulletin, 3(9),* 1–2.

Hunt, V. (1982). Scientific research on psychic energies at the Department of Kinesiology, UCLA. *Journal of Holistic Health, 6,* 47–54.

Kepner, J. I. (1987). *Body process: Working with the body in psychotherapy.* Cleveland, OH: Gestalt Institute of Cleveland Press.

Kepner, J. I. (1995). *Healing tasks: Psychotherapy with adult survivors of childhood abuse.* San Francisco: Jossey-Bass.

Kepner, J. I. (2000). Touch in Gestalt Body Process Psychotherapy: Purpose, practice and ethics. *Gestalt Review, 5(2),* 97–114.

Kepner, J. I. (2001). *The highway of light: Energetic healing through the nervous system: A guide to the principles and practices of the work of Bill Gray.* Self-published paper.

Kepner, J. I. (2012). *Nervous system energy work in Gestalt Body Process Psychotherapy.* Retrieved from www.jimkepner.com/wp-content/uploads/2012/08/NSEWB-PKepner.pdf

Krieger, D. (1979). *The healing touch.* New York: Prentice Hall.

Montgomery, R. (1973). *Born to heal.* New York: Fawcett Crest.

Slater, V. E. (1995). Toward an understanding of energetic healing: Parts 1 & 2. *Journal of Holistic Nursing, 13(3),* 209–238.

# 60

## The Role of the Autonomic Nervous System

**Dawn Bhat and Jacqueline Carleton,**
United States

**Dawn Bhat**, MA, MS, NCC, holds graduate degrees in General Psychology from Queens College in New York City and in Clinical Mental Health Counseling from Long Island University in Brookville, New York. She received her bachelor of science degree from the University of Florida in Gainesville. She is a National Certified Counselor (NCC) and is a Yoga Alliance (RYT-500) registered Yoga teacher. Dawn is a research writer for *Somatic Psychotherapy Today* and has training in neuropsychology and Somatic Psychology. She has been a psychotherapy researcher under the guidance of Jacqueline A. Carleton, PhD, of the USABP since 2010, and currently receives clinical supervision from Dr. Carleton.

**Jacqueline A. Carleton,** PhD, is editor of the *International Body Psychotherapy Journal: The Art and Science of Somatic Praxis,* and has been in private psychotherapy practice in Manhattan since the 1970s. She attended Smith College and MIT, and holds a PhD from Columbia University. Since the 1980s she has taught both Body Psychotherapy (Core Energetics) and the principles of Psychodynamic Psychotherapy internationally. Since the turn of the century, she has utilized Somatic Experiencing, a neurologically based treatment for trauma. She practices and lectures on Somatic Experiencing in the United States and in Europe and the Middle East. She is also on the Executive Committee of the Integrative Trauma Treatment Program of the National Institute for the Psychotherapies (NIP) in New York City, where she works on curriculum development. She is co-authoring a book applying Somatic Experiencing techniques to early developmental (attachment) trauma.

This chapter outlines the theoretical development of the autonomic nervous system (ANS) in Body Psychotherapy. Historically, attention to the ANS in psychotherapy stems from the work of Pierre Janet and Wilhelm Reich. Modalities of Body Psychotherapy that have emerged since Reich's time have utilized the ANS as a vehicle for organismic regulation. The ANS operates largely out of consciousness at the level of the reptilian brain or brainstem, which controls involuntary body processes (i.e., heart rate, respiration, digestion, etc.). Some modalities of Body Psychotherapy focus on the body-mind experientially—that is, the inner awareness of the viscera, soma, or bodily states.

The self-regulatory functions of the ANS include homeostatic regulation of bodily functions, emotional balance, and an enhanced capacity for social engagement. ANS regulation restores the nervous system to a healthy cycle of activation and deactivation through the reciprocal workings of the sympathetic (SNS) and parasympathetic (PNS) branches. Contemporary neuroscience acknowledges that there are, in addition, two branches of the PNS, which are mediated by the dorsal and ventral branches of the vagus nerve, and that the latter gives rise to social engagement (Porges, 2011). The quality of the attachment relationship between an infant and its caregiver contributes to the early neural development of the self-regulatory functions of the ANS.

In this chapter, we will explore select modalities of Body Psychotherapy that work with the ANS explicitly and implicitly. Finally, we will discuss contemporary efforts toward integration within the field of Body Psychotherapy and among forms of verbal psychotherapy to work holistically with the underlying neurology and the whole person, physically, mentally, and relationally.

## The Autonomic Nervous System (ANS) in Body Psychotherapy

For many Body Psychotherapists, the ANS is intimately involved in, if not central to, a client's process when working from a somatic point of view. To understand the importance of the ANS in Body Psychotherapy is to become familiar with the influential—albeit, historically, undervalued in mainstream psychotherapy and psychoanalysis—theoretical perspectives originally put forth by Wilhelm Reich and subsequently by others. Reich developed concepts describing the "vegetative nervous system," which is commonly known today as the ANS. The concept of self-regulation is particularly significant for many modalities of Body Psychotherapy as are other regulatory functions of the ANS, including stress modulation.

Body Psychotherapists today not only work with the expression of cognitions and emotions in the neuromuscular system, but also focus directly on ANS processes. Integrating what MacLean (1990) described as the "triune brain" in psychotherapy allows the clinician to work with the hierarchical functions of the whole underlying neurology (Ogden, Minton, and Pain, 2006). The reptilian, limbic, and neocortical regions of the human brain are related to sensory-motor, affective, and cognitive processes, respectively. As such, there is neuropsychological evidence for applying a "bottom-up" approach, which essentially targets the ANS.

One aim in Body Psychotherapy is to increase the capacity of the ANS to remain within a "window of tolerance" (Ogden, Pain, and Fisher, 2006), restoring a state of homeostasis and ultimately increased resilience in the physical body, which enhances one's connection to oneself and one's relationship with others. The notion of the "window of affect tolerance" was elaborated some years ago by Allan Schore (2001, 2003), based on the influence of relational perspectives to working at the "edge of the window of tolerance" where the therapeutic dyad is "safe, but not too safe" (Bromberg, 2006, pp. 153–202).

## Historical Roots of Attention to the ANS in Body Psychotherapy

The historical roots of working with the ANS in Body Psychotherapy can be traced back to the French psychologist Pierre Janet, who greatly influenced Freud, Jung, Adler, Piaget, and Reich. In a seminal article by David Boadella (2011), this legacy of Pierre Janet is treated at length. Janet, who lived from 1859 to 1947, was a contemporary of Freud, and ran Charcot's experimental laboratory on physiological psychology. Janet claimed that psychoanalysis stemmed from his development of a system that he originally called "psychological analysis." Janet published his case studies in 1886, the first examples of a cure by catharsis. He was influenced by F. A. Mesmer and his eighteenth-century ideas on the psychotherapeutic use of hypnosis.

Janet may in fact be called the grandfather of Somatic Psychology and Body Psychotherapy (Boadella, 2011), as he held the position that the body and mind are inseparable such that psychology could not be divided from physiology (the body). Boadella (2011) suggests that *"Janet was not just a primary inspiration for psychoanalysis, analytical psychology and individual psychology, he was the first of the new generation of psychological analysts to focus on the centrality of understanding the involvement of the body in psychotherapy"* (p. 57). A number of topics Janet investigated involved the ANS in general, and respiration and dissociation in particular. Janet identified the diaphragmatic block in neurotic patients, which influenced the work of Bleuler, who coined the term "schizophrenia" stemming from *schizo* (split) and *phren* (diaphragm). Contemporary researchers, such as Bessel van der Kolk and Pat Ogden, writing on post-traumatic stress and dissociation, are validating Janet's early ideas.

Janet's interest in the body-mind connection was evident in his insightful ideas on massage, embryological development, muscular consciousness, kinesthetic sense of self, and the relation between movement and intentionality—some of which are foundational in many schools of Body Psychotherapy (Boadella, 2011). In describing the principles of psychotherapy, Janet (1924) investigated the functioning of the ANS as an important direction for scientific endeavor. Janet talked about visceral consciousness (Boadella, 2011) and explored the relationship between visceral sensations and emotionality. Janet had a gastrointestinal theory of neurosis (later developed by Gerda Boyesen) wherein he saw intimate connections between the peristaltic functions of the gut and emotional expressivity (Ibid.).

Since the early twentieth century, there have been many other theorists speculating about the interrelated functions of the ANS in physical and mental health. Walter Cannon (1871–1945), an American physician, was a contemporary of Wilhelm Reich (1897–1957). What Cannon called the ANS, Reich called the vegetative nervous system. While Cannon, who coined the term "fight-flight," continued his investigations and built his theories (i.e., the Cannon-Bard theory of emotion), Reich developed approaches to psychoanalysis that took into consideration the physiology of the body.

## The Evolution of the Work of Wilhelm Reich

It is the work of Reich that bridges the historical developments of Janet to contemporary modalities of Body Psychotherapy. For Reich, the rhythm of the body is the expansion and contraction leading to genital pleasure or cardiac anxiety, respectively. Reich formulated the orgasm as mechanical expansion, bioelectric charge, bioelectric discharge, and mechanical relaxation—a basic form of vegetative (autonomic) functioning. This movement of life was echoed in Reich's observations of the plasmatic movements of the amoeba. The nervous system in animals operates in parallel to the expansion or elongation and contraction or rounding up of the pulsation in protozoa. From this,

the theoretical basis for Reich's psychosomatic research emerged.

In the 1930s, Reich looked toward the physiology of the ANS, chemistry of anxiety, electrophysiology of the body fluids, and hydromechanics of plasma movements in protozoa to generate a theory of the antithesis of vegetative life (Boadella, 1973/1985). Reich was concerned with the contrast between the anxiety syndrome caused by the adrenal reaction and the cholinergic effect of pleasurable relaxation. During the 1920s, Ludwig Robert Müller had described the two divisions of the ANS: the sympathetic and parasympathetic nervous systems (Neundörfer and Hilz, 1998). The sympathetic effects were identical to the adrenal effects, also associated with anxiety reactions, whereas the parasympathetic effects were identical to the cholinergic effects or the relaxation response, which we discuss in more detail later in this chapter.

Reich was primarily concerned with which ANS division is involuntarily predominant in the organism and the associated voluntary reactions that may or may not occur. Reich's clinical observations revealed bodily expressions corresponding to a person's mental attitude. Repression or inhibition of aggression, pleasure, and anxiety among other strong emotions were also associated with body musculature and tension. For Reich, "character armor" and "muscular armor" became functionally equivalent. Reich was the first analyst *"to introduce an exhaustive study of just what bodily mechanisms were involved in the dynamics of repression, dissociation, and other defenses against feeling"* (Boadella, 1973/1985, p. 116). Reich emphasized the strong impact of the ANS on respiratory function and emotional balance and the role the ANS played in the functioning of the whole person, physically, mentally, and relationally. In this, he took Müller's work to a psychological and clinical level.

In Reich's therapeutic work with character defenses, energy in the ANS was released, liberating the patient from the effects of repression, enhancing their capacity for self-regulation, and giving greater resilience in the nervous system. Vegetotherapy, developed by Reich from about 1934, was a set of techniques designed to dissolve the person's muscular armoring (Boadella, 1973/1985). For Reich, at the end of therapy, the patient should be able to surrender to their deepest feelings. A free flow of orgone energy throughout the body defined this state (Blasband, 2005). For Reich, vegetative self-regulation (a healthy ANS) was also a principle of healthy adult functioning throughout their life span, optimally commencing in infancy and childhood (Carleton, 2008).

## Self-Regulatory Functions of the ANS

Because of the complexity and interconnectivity of the body's systems, there are many regulatory functions of the ANS, including organismic homeostasis, emotional balance, and social engagement. ANS processes operate mostly unconsciously, involuntarily, and automatically. Homeostasis is achieved via regulation of blood pressure, heart rate, gastrointestinal responses (i.e., peristalsis), contraction of the bladder, focusing of the eyes, the immune function, and thermoregulation, to name just a few. The ANS innervates cardiac muscle, smooth intestinal muscles, and various endocrine and exocrine glands, influencing most tissues and organ systems throughout the body (McCorry, 2007). By and large, the ANS is clearly implicated in many, if not most or all, visceral functions.

## A Basic Overview of the Neural Aspects of the ANS

A comprehensive understanding of the nervous system—from a neuroscientific point of view—has become a key component in many training programs for Body Psychotherapists. Before we discuss the techniques developed to target ANS (in)activity, we will provide some general background that is essential in effectively identifying and treating any dysfunctions associated with the ANS.

The ANS is very basic or primitive, coordinated mainly by the "reptilian brain" (i.e., brainstem, medulla, pons) involuntarily, and has most interconnections with the right hemisphere of the brain (Schore, 1999, 2000, 2009) and the limbic system, which is part of the midbrain, sometimes called the "emotional brain." The hypothalamus (a part of the midbrain) is very much involved in regulating ANS processes, such as stress, arousal, basic survival needs, including hunger, thirst, and sexual behavior, as well as aggression, pain perception, and the experience of pleasure. The hypothalamic-pituitary-adrenal (HPA) axis will be discussed in more detail later in this chapter, as it relates to the regulation of the stress response and traumatic stress.

The unconscious activity of the ANS is mainly interconnected within the right hemisphere of the brain and the limbic system (Damasio, 2000). In the limbic brain, the amygdala and hippocampus are necessary for the storage and processing of emotional and traumatic memory to be recorded in the brain's cortex. The amygdala plays a distinct part in fear conditioning (LeDoux, 1998), and becomes active when there is a threat, which signals the survival system leading to ANS preparation for the fight, flight, or freeze reaction. The body remembers traumatic events through emotional sensations and ANS arousal (Rothschild, 2000). When ANS arousal is high, releasing stress hormones, the activity of the hippocampus, storing cognitive aspects of memory, is suppressed.

A function of the orbitofrontal cortex (OFC) in humans is the control of the ANS (Schore, 1999). The OFC is structurally and functionally linked to the interconnectivity within the right cerebral hemisphere with connections with the hypothalamus, autonomic areas, and the brainstem. Functions of this fronto-limbic cortex include arousal reaction, homeostatic regulation, drive modulation, and suppression of heart rate and anger. In terms of ANS activity, the OFC is implicated in parasympathetic decreases in cardiovascular activity and inhibitory influences on the sympathetic system. Furthermore, this structure is involved in socioemotional behaviors, regulation of the body and motivational states, adjustment of emotional responses, and neurodevelopment of the attachment process. It is important to note, however, that a self-regulatory system consists of many different regions in the brain, including those beyond the realm of the structures that regulate the ANS (Young, 2007).

ANS functions are also modulated by neurochemicals and neurohormones. The sympathetic nervous system is associated with increased blood levels of the catecholamines (norepinephrine and epinephrine), adrenaline, and calcium. The parasympathetic nervous system is associated with increased blood levels of acetylcholine and potassium (Heller, 2012). The synthesis of epinephrine is adrenaline, which is greatly enhanced during stress. Neurohormones and neuropeptides such as cortisol and other corticosteroids are also involved in ANS regulation. A goal of many Body Psychotherapeutic interventions is a return to an easy alternation between the sympathetic and parasympathetic nervous systems. Cycles of intense (aerobic) activity followed by profound rest may help offset any imbalances in the regulation of the ANS by regulating levels of neurohormones (i.e., cortisol) and neurochemicals (i.e., catecholamines) and thus alleviating psychosomatic pathology.

## Sympathetic and Parasympathetic Nervous Systems

For Body Psychotherapists, familiarity with the distinct and reciprocal roles of the two branches of the ANS is extremely helpful in assessing and treating psychological manifestations of ANS dysfunction, frequently seen in mood disorders, including anxiety and depression, and traumatic stress disorders (among others). In a healthy organism, the function of the sympathetic nervous system (SNS) is connected with fear or arousal and initiates instinctive emergency-response activity as well as any conscious effort. In contrast, the function of the parasympathetic nervous system (PNS) supports processes such as everyday gentle activity, normal digestion, deep relaxation, and sleep. While the "fight-or-flight" response is associated almost totally with the SNS, the "freeze" response (also "playing dead" and including dissociation) is associated more with the PNS, as a reaction either immediately before or after SNS stimulation.

### The Stress Response and Traumatic Stress

The stress response activates the SNS or adrenergic half of the ANS and the hypothalamic-pituitary-adrenal (HPA) axis. The regulation system manages states of arousal, and consists of the hypothalamus and regions of neurochemical mechanisms within the brainstem and basal forebrain. Three of the major chemical messenger systems that influence cortical arousal in the brain include: (1) norepinephrine or noradrenergic, which supports sensory alertness; (2) dopamine, which supports prediction of reward and motor activity; and (3) serotonin, which supports autonomic control and emotion. The primary connections occur within the amygdala, regulating emotional reactivity and memory as well as meaning, along with the prefrontal cortex in the executive system, which controls motor and behavioral activity (Lillas and Turnbull, 2009). The main chemical messengers for the remainder of the body are cortisol for the heart and adrenaline for the rest of the body.

However, this is not just a "brain" function. Adrenaline, cortisol, and corticosteroids flood throughout the whole body: stimulating the heart rate and contractility of cardiac cells; closing down some of the blood vessels in the periphery (skin) and making much more blood available for any intense muscular activity; as mentioned, the digestive system shuts down, the blood supply is shut off, and all intestinal sphincters are contracted (including the urinary sphincter); the bronchioles of the lungs are inflated to achieve greater oxygen exchange; the pupils of the eye are dilated, so as to allow more light to enter the eye and to enhance distance vision. All the external (skeletal) muscular systems also receive a "tweak" to prime them for almost instant physical activity: they become tense, ready to "fire."

When the brain perceives a threat, it activates these physiological and behavioral responses, which could result in promoting adaptation or allostasis. However, if stress is sustained or increases over time, the allostatic load causes damaging changes to the body that can lead to disease and long-term psychological or physiological imbalances (McEwen, 2006, 2007). Acute stress facilitates adaptation and survival by activating the necessary neural, cardiovascular, autonomic, immune, and metabolic system responses. In contrast, chronic stress often (or nearly always) has damaging effects resulting in dysregulation of the same systems. As a result of sometimes massively acute and often chronic stress, there is altered structure and chemistry in the hippocampus, prefrontal cortex, and amygdala, which may be relatively easily reversible if the chronic stress lasts only for weeks. However, prolonged stress over months or years may have almost irreversible effects on the brain (McEwen, 2008).

During traumatic stress, the limbic system activates the SNS. When "fight-or-flight" responses are not instantly possible or appropriate, the limbic system activates the "freeze" response. This frozen or death-like state often occurs in victims of child sexual abuse, rape, and torture when they are unable to fight back or escape from physical violence. The nervous system stores undischarged energy experienced as a state of being overwhelmed and frozen in fear. If this is frequent or becomes chronic, the inability to return to equilibrium and balance afterward may become the primary difficulty involved in the process of recovery from emotional trauma (Levine, 2008; Rothschild, 2000).

### The Freeze Response and the Relaxation Response

Levine (2010) provides evidence that the "freeze response" immobilizes an individual in the face of trauma, which gives rise to the most debilitating somatic symptoms, such as numbing, being shut down, dissociation, feelings of entrapment, and helplessness. During extreme arousal of the SNS, the PNS is also activated, slowing down or even shutting down body systems: in animals, this can be seen as "playing dead." When people are numb, they are dissociated and not "in" their bodies. Trauma manifests in the body as tightened, contracted energy, often locked into the muscles or viscera, which is similar to what ethologists call "tonic immobility" (Levine and Frederick, 1997). Keleman (1985) also explored this in his classic book, *Emotional Anatomy*. Animals in their natural environment, when faced with a threat, can rebound far more easily than humans can. Unfortunately, humans are much more vulnerable to being overwhelmed and traumatized by the inactivity of the neocortex, often giving rise to somatization. As such, the body does not release the pent-up energy, which then becomes a focus of Body Psychotherapeutic techniques.

Under normal conditions, the PNS regulates various everyday, healthy, relatively relaxed responses. Associated with activation of the PNS is the healthy relaxation response (relative to the activation response), or essentially the "back-to-normal" response. In most circumstances, the PNS is the "default" mode; the SNS is the "emergency" defensive response.

The relaxation response is a state of deep rest (Benson and Klipper, 1975) that decreases metabolism, heart rate, and blood pressure. In addition, levels of nitric oxide increase. When the relaxation response (under the influence of the PNS) is elicited, the muscular tensions of the body can relax and soften; blood flow is returned to "normal"; the digestive system starts up again; and the hormonal "switch" from adrenaline to acetylcholine takes place. The whole nervous system is restored to a healthy, normal level of functioning, and any of those stress hormones that are still present (being unused) can then be metabolized (digested).

The SNS and PNS seem to manifest in three patterns of interaction: reciprocal inhibition, mutual antagonism, and unilateral activity (Schore, 1999). Discharging high ANS arousal and returning to rest and balance have been goals in much Body Psychotherapy. In addition, the ANS branches are coupled with the social engagement and attachment systems, and so therapy also involves coupling and uncoupling the branches of the ANS in social and relational engagement situations.

### The Social Nervous System

Polyvagal theory (Porges, 2011) proposes that the vagus nerve has different neurophysiological roles that are related to three phylogenetic subsystems in the mammalian autonomic nervous system: communication, mobilization, and immobilization. The vagus nerve is located in the brainstem, but, in the mammalian brain, there are two vagal systems, dorsal and ventral. Porges explains that the more primitive phylogenetic unmyelinated dorsal vagus is present in all vertebrates and is associated with mobility (i.e., fight-or-flight) and immobility (i.e., vegetative states, the freeze response, or playing dead) as a survival function. In the mammalian brain, however, there is a myelinated ventral vagal pathway that serves an evolutionary function linked to adaptive social, affective, and communicative behaviors.

The myelinated ventral vagal complex innervates the supradiaphragmatic structures (larynx, pharynx, soft palate, esophagus, bronchi, and heart) via the nucleus ambiguus, a neuroanatomical substrate unique to the mammalian brain. It also regulates the striated muscles of the head and face, including emotional expressiveness, eye gaze, listening, and prosody, which are part of the social engagement system. The unmyelinated dorsal vagus innervates the subdiaphragmatic structures (stomach, intestines, among others) via the dorsal motor nucleus. Based on the evolutionary function of the myelinated ventral vagal complex, Porges asserts that the complexity of social interactions is regulated via the visceral state (Ibid.)—and vice versa.

Neural regulation of the heart rate is linked to the detection of fear and safety (Ibid.). When the environment is perceived as safe, cardiac output is inhibited, the PNS is activated, and the organism perceives internal states as calm, enhancing social engagement. When there is a perceived (real or unreal) environmental threat, cardiac output is disinhibited, stimulating the heart via activation of the SNS in order to support adaptive survival functions, mobilizing to fight or flee, or immobilizing (i.e., playing dead). Communication and positive social behavior can occur ("please and appease") when the defensive limbic structures are inhibited. Additionally, respiration, an involuntary process controlled by the medulla in the brainstem, is closely connected with cardiac activity, which when taken under conscious control decreases heart rate variability.

Neuroception, a physiological state operating outside of conscious awareness, may determine a range of experience and behavior (Ibid.). It is accessed in some modalities of Body Psychotherapy to enhance awareness and discharge ANS energy. Polyvagal theory thus helps to shed light into some of the neurophysiological mechanisms involved in Somatic Psychotherapies, such as Somatic Experiencing, developed by Peter Levine, which accesses the "felt sense" and tracks visceral sensations to achieve ANS regulation.

## Early Development of the Social Nervous System: The Neuroscience of Attachment

Bowlby (1969) hypothesized that secure attachment relationships are the foundation for the growth of self-reliance, the capacity for emotional regulation, and also social competence (Sroufe, 2005). As a regulatory theory and a motivational system, attachment promotes an interactive regulation of biological synchronicity between organisms (Siegel, 2001; Schore, 2000). Resilience is a strong coping adaptation that is highly correlated with secure attachment (Bowlby, 1990), where there is a physiological sense of security and safety (Siegel, 2001).

The function of the attachment system is to compel the infant to seek proximity to a caregiver for protection from, for instance, harm, starvation, unfavorable temperature changes, distress, and separation (Ibid.). Given that this is a highly responsive system to danger, the internal experience tends to be that of anxiety or fear, which can be elicited by any perceived (real or not real) or actual frightening experience. Attachment relationships are essential in the organization of inner experience, as well as in neuronal and brain development, including the stress response of the HPA axis. Uncoupling the attachment system and the defense/arousal system is often the target of modalities of Body Psychotherapy that incorporate healing attachment wounds (Heller and Carleton, in process of publication).

The development of a resilient nervous system is central to the attachment relationship, and the attachment relationship is based on a resilient nervous system, so impairments in this connection can be, of themselves, a source of traumatization (Scaer, 2005). Secure attachments are a protective barrier to stress, whereas insecure attachments perpetuate the stress response (Goldberg, 2000). Stress regulation in infancy is dependent on the quality of attachment relationships (Beebe and Lachmann, 2002; Tronick, 2007; Gold, 2011). Recent research by Tharner and colleagues (2013) revealed that higher levels of maternal depression were associated with lower resting respiratory sinus arrhythmia (RSA). If a caregiver is not present, not attuned, or depressed, the infant may not be given an opportunity to interactively regulate stress, thus impeding the development of a resilient nervous system and the capacity for self-regulation.

Autonomic control is the outgrowth of the experience-dependent maturation of the OFC (Schore, 2001). The OFC represents internal working models, a cognitive set that allows for affect regulation and stress adaptation (Schore, 1999). The PNS in the frontal lobes develops more slowly than the SNS. Schore (1999) posits that, "under optimal conditions the two branches, initially uncoupled, become progressively coupled during development, especially in the postnatally maturing OFC" (p. 324). In suboptimal conditions, there is inhibition and repression of unconscious affect. The ability to shift in and out of ANS states, or alternating between SNS dominance and PNS dominance, is known as the stress-state recovery mechanism and may result in either underregulation or overregulation disturbances. Optimally, affect regulation, mentalization, and a sense of self (Fonagy et al., 2004) develop.

A self-regulated child engages in the process of self-determination of the body and its functions. Reich noticed that children who were not allowed to "self-regulate" stored the memories of repression within their nervous and muscular systems and, as a result, were more prone to mental and emotional symptoms such as anxiety, neurosis, and depression as well as improper immune function and diseases of the body (Neill, 1960). Orgonomists believe a parent must be relatively self-regulated themselves to raise a self-regulated child (Carleton, 1991). We might translate that in current conceptualizations as "securely attached." *"Early life events, especially the mother-infant bond, are crucial for maturation of the experience-dependent cortical, sub-cortical, and autonomic nervous systems"* (Carleton and Padolsky, 2012). In attachment trauma, the SNS is constantly in a state of over-arousal. The body needs to complete interrupted physiological sequences related to threat in order to allow the SNS and PNS to alternate appropriately.

The coupling between a healthy stress response and healthy attachment relationships is supported by oxytocin (Pierrehumbert et al., 2010). Oxytocin is also associated with stability in new romantic relationships up until approximately six months. Higher levels of oxytocin were present in couples who stay together longer than six months and can be enhanced through interactive reciprocity, which includes affectional touch (Schneiderman et al., 2012). In a similar vein, maternal touch has been shown to improve antonomic functioning in premature infants (Jean and Stack, 2012), supporting the early work of Eva Reich, who explored gentle, nurturing infant touch in preventing armoring and expanding energy while also promoting attachment and regulation. Touch in psychotherapy is a powerful technique (Young, 2007) used in many modalities of Body Psychotherapy (e.g., Rubenfeld Synergy Method, Biodynamic Psychotherapy, and Bioenergetics) and has been utilized to repair attachment disruptions (Carleton, 2010).

Irrespective of disrupted attachment style, there is a capacity in every human being to repair the self via corrective emotional experiences and to promote secure attachment, creating healthy adult relationships. A Body Psychotherapist can try to lower the person's arousal, meet some of the unmet needs on an attachment level, and then move, through time, to integrate all this into the present. As attachment wounds are healed, the authentic self engages more in the present (Heller, 2010) and the body also realigns its autonomic regulatory systems.

## The Role of the ANS in Awareness of Body and of Self

Body Psychotherapists pay careful attention to how a client perceives visceral information and feelings from their body, which is an implicit, subjective process. The sense of the physiological condition of the body has been called interoception (Craig, 2003). The British physiologist Charles Sherrington (1906) described proprioception (awareness of one's own body) as an integration of exteroception (sensory awareness from outside the body) and interoception (awareness of organs and processes from inside the body). The conscious awareness of emotions and feelings (Damasio, 2000) is located in the dorsal posterior insula, which perceives the body, including pain, temperature, touch, muscular and visceral sensations, vasomotor activity, hunger, and thirst (Craig, 2003). The right anterior insula may also provide the basis for the subjective image of the material self as a feeling entity (Ibid.).

This interoceptive awareness is intrinsically involved in meditation and mindfulness practices, which are explicitly integrated in some Body Psychotherapies (e.g., Hakomi) (Heller, 2012). Mindfulness, a concept often associated with Buddhism, is practiced to enhance happiness and to gain insight into the true nature of one's existence. Mindfulness has been defined as the nonjudgmental awareness of experience in the present moment (Kabat-Zinn, 2003). The practice of mindfulness encompasses focusing one's entire attention on the experience of thoughts and emotions, as well as bodily sensations, with curiosity, openness, and acceptance. Improving inner awareness facilitates self-regulation, an inner sense of security, a reduction in anxiety, and resiliency in the autonomic nervous system (Bhat and Carleton, 2013).

Mindfulness practices activate the prefrontal cortex, and a mature prefrontal cortex (PFC) allows one to focus, concentrate, attend, and imagine (Graham, 2013). The PFC regulates the autonomic nervous system, the flow of emotions, and the surge of feelings; calms the activated amygdala; allows attunement to other people, empathy for self and others; and allows for insight and awareness. Implicit, automatic, and reflexive patterns are brought into awareness and when one notices this, one can choose to change them intelligently and sensitively.

Finally, it has been postulated that mindfulness creates a secure attachment with the self (Siegel, 2007). This felt sense of security for the self has been compromised in many clients seeking Body Psychotherapy. In addition to mindfulness training, many Body Psychotherapists apply some aspect of the Focusing techniques developed by Eugene Gendlin (1998). Focusing takes mindfulness a little further to involve the body and a new kind of experience, the felt sense. The felt sense is a freshly forming whole-body sense of one's life situation, which has great transformative power (Cornell, 2013).

## Self-Regulation in Body Psychotherapy

Since the 1970s, pioneering thinkers in Body Psychotherapy (Levine, 1979a and 1979b; Liss, 1979) have written about the regulation of ANS functions in *Energy & Character,* the only publication for many years dedicated to disseminating the breadth of knowledge within the field of Body Psychotherapy. They (Levine, 1979a, 1979b; Liss, 1979) have pointed out that there is an energetic relation between the SNS and PNS that influences organismic regulation.

Cognitive, affective, and sensory-motor processes can also impact the ANS indirectly via neural projections from the neocortex. For example, movement may be intentional, one can decide to "calm down," and respiration can be taken under conscious control. According to Heller (2012), this explains why individuals can influence these systems by indirect modalities, such as breathing exercises, relaxation, Yoga exercises, and mindfulness. Basically, *"the vegetative system [ANS] is a part of the mechanisms of organismic regulation. It is consequently used in all of the interactions between the dimensions of the psyche and the body"* (Ibid., p. 198).

When tension and stress are chronic and prolonged, the "relaxation" stage does not fully engage and the organism stays somewhat stressed: if this persists, then this "somewhat-stressed" position becomes the person's "usual" resting state, but this is a state of relative hypertension. If there is further stress that does not get fully resolved, then another "resting" state is created, but at a higher level of stress and bodily tension. We can thus build up layers and layers of emotional distress and physiological stress and tension.

Prolonged relaxation, or combinations of relaxation and physical therapy (like massage), are then needed to restore the organism to a "healthy" level of balance and functioning. Awareness of this is key to any Body Psychotherapeutic approach, and many approaches combine both emotional work, psychological and cognitive aspects, with actual physical techniques to assist a proper rebalancing of the ANS by helping to regulate visceral functions. Notable here is the work of Gerda Boyesen and her development of Biodynamic Psychotherapy (Boyesen and Boyesen, 1980).

Emotional balance arises from the self-regulatory functions of the ANS. According to Totton (2003), "affect" (in psychology, affect is the experience of feeling and emotion and the resulting presentation of the person) *"is more and more deeply understood as a complex neurological phenomenon—one which, just as it philosophically marries mind and body, neurologically marries the CNS and ANS, the voluntary and involuntary aspects of our embodiment"* (p. 34).

## Organismic Regulation and Emotional Balance

Physical and mental health are both associated with emotional balance and the efficiency of energy expenditure. The reciprocal interaction of the SNS and PNS branches of the ANS is an energetic one. The SNS spends energy through action, and the PNS regains energy through rest. These two systems work basically alternately. Spending energy is also known as "sympathetic discharge," and regaining energy is "parasympathetic discharge" (Liss, 1979).

Positive and negative emotions are associated with both SNS and PNS dominance (Ibid.). When the body is reactive, sympathetic dominance generates the positive emotions of pleasure or active joy. When the body is receptive, parasympathetic dominance generates the positive sense of melting pleasure (joy), as in making love. On the other hand, negative emotion or distress caused by sympathetic dominance may present as rage, anger, frustration, irritability, etc. Distress caused by parasympathetic dominance may present as hurt, fear, sadness, shame, or guilt. After the "completion" of the active emotions (sympathetic state), rebound occurs and the person feels relaxed, warm, and receptive (parasympathetic state).

Emotional discharge or expression is often not sufficient (is incomplete) without the presence of another person to help one rebound from the more vulnerable feelings of hurt, fear, and sadness and restore regulation and resilience. Unhealthy emotions and their tensions stay in the body, manifesting as "knots" rather than transforming into warmth and wellness through the process of emotional release. That is, when there is no rebound between the SNS and PNS, repression, contraction, and tensions may become chronic. When an individual is chronically unhappy, a whole array of somatic symptoms has the opportunity to emerge. When these systems do not alternate effectively or discharge energy simultaneously, the organism is dysregulated and in an abnormal state. Breathing is irregular. In addition, depression can be understood as energy depletion due to the lack of rebound between these two systems.

Incomplete and/or simultaneous discharge within both branches of the ANS may generate disturbances in emotional well-being. Symptoms associated with incomplete sympathetic discharge are aggression, palpitations, and nervousness. Symptoms associated with incomplete parasympathetic discharge are depression, fatigue, gastrointestinal troubles, nausea, vomiting, diarrhea, and constipation. During simultaneous activation resulting in the freeze response or a vegetative state, blood pressure decreases, muscles become flaccid, numbness and dissociation occur, affect may be flat, and memory storage, processing, and retrieval are impaired, manifesting in some level of amnesia (Levine, 2009).

The body speaks through contraction, immobility, or hyperarousal triggered by trauma. The therapist assesses the functioning of the client's ANS and, based on these evaluations, makes inferences about the client's brain functions. Through reading the body, the therapist systematically identifies the regions of chronic muscular holding and constricted breathing patterns. Therapeutic objectives involve softening or opening each armored segment and breaking the feedback loop, which activates the fight/flight/freeze response from the *locus coeruleus* (containing norepinephrine neurons) in the brainstem. As a result, the relaxation response occurs, sensations start to flow through the body, and numbness or hyperarousal is corrected. In addition, body-oriented techniques are utilized to assist the patient to develop a conscious awareness of emotional trauma so that it can be therapeutically resolved (Young, 2008).

## Modalities of Body Psychotherapy Working with the ANS

The focus on the ANS in Body Psychotherapy can be attributed mostly to the pioneering work of Wilhelm Reich and his followers in pre–World War II Norway, and then later in other parts of Europe, and in America, post–World War II. In this next section, we will highlight some of the therapies that were developed from this impetus of Reichian therapy. There are many more modalities of Body Psychotherapy that warrant attention in this section; however, to review any more would be too exhaustive for the scope of this chapter.

## Bioenergetic Analysis

Alexander Lowen and John Pierrakos studied directly with Reich in America, and together they developed the method of Bioenergetic Analysis, describing bioenergy as a "force," the energy dynamics in life processes. Bioenergetic techniques include breathing, grounding, expressive movement, exercises, physical contact, sound, and touch, through which emotional and psychological blocks become expressed and feelings become more felt within the psychodynamic processes (Lowen, 1976). These techniques focused on "breaking down" some of the chronic (sympathetic) tensions, but they did not explicitly incorporate much stimulation of the (parasympathetic) aspects in relation to the ANS, except for the grounding exercises.

Modern Bioenergetic theorists (Baum, 2011) note that people strive to experience pleasure and aliveness, not just to release unpleasant tension. Although there is a paucity of literature within the field of Bioenergetic theory on working with the ANS explicitly, Bioenergetic therapists' work with the ANS is implied, such that "aliveness, the embrace of energy and charge, and the possibility for the connection to goodness and benevolence, to love and joy, are at the center of our work" (Ibid., p. 8).

## Biodynamic Psychotherapy

Developed by Gerda Boyesen, Biodynamic Psychology and Psychotherapy works "with" the client's life force, or their vital energy, rather than "against" the tensions. The Boyesen approach also offers a unique contribution to Body Psychotherapy: the theory of "psycho-peristalsis" (Boyesen and Boyesen, 1980). The concept of gastrointestinal (GI) functioning is especially relevant to mental health practitioners, as many psychiatric disorders in the *Diagnostic and Statistical Manual of Mental Disorders* are associated with GI complaints (American Psychiatric Association, 2013). Biodynamic Psychotherapy operates under assumptions similar to those of Reichian therapy as to the function of the orgasm, but also theory particularly emphasizing the role of the ANS in self-regulation. In healthy regulation, both branches of the ANS alternate in a complementary fashion to mediate vasomotor and emotional cycles forming the patterns of emotional regulation.

In Biodynamic Psychotherapy, any physical release of the ANS—such as yawning, crying, sweating, shivering, relaxing, etc.—also opens up the possibility for associated peristaltic movements and borborygmi (tummy rumblings). Boyesen focused on stimulating the parasympathetic side of the ANS, particularly through her Biodynamic Massage. Psycho-peristalsis is the body's way to digest both emotions and stress hormones. When a vasomotoric cycle is not completed (i.e., emotions go unexpressed), the emotional "charge" is stored in the body as some form of physical tension and stress. In Biodynamic Psychotherapy, massage is used along with listening to these borborygmi through a stethoscope. The therapist's "goal" here is to help to increase the peristaltic sounds, a process that is indicative of the release of uncompleted emotional or vasomotoric cycles and a "switchover" from sympathetic (holding) to parasympathetic (release). As such, the primary regulator of bioenergy is thus found in the intestinal organs, and the "emotional" digestive system is the body's own method of daily emotional self-regulation.

Recent research (King, 2011) described borborygmi as a body phenomenon and an embodied reaction. When the therapist explicitly addresses borborygmi, by engaging in verbal commentary, the therapeutic process can deepen and fresh new material may emerge. Early prenatal experiences may be a somatic entrance to deepen the psychotherapeutic process, as the fetus constantly listens to the mother's borborygmi. Somatic Psychotherapists are aware of the connection between the mind and the gut, so this study complements Boyesen's development of Biodynamic Psychotherapy and the discovery that peristaltic sounds are part of the self-healing or self-regulating ability of the body.

## Biosynthesis

In the 1970s and 1980s, David Boadella developed a form of Body Psychotherapy that he called Biosynthesis, which he defines as an integration of life that is founded on the understandings derived principally from Reich and also from embryology (Boadella, 1987). It is understood that the basic patterns of expansion and contraction occur in all life-forms. One somatic technique in Biosynthesis that addresses hyperactivity of the sympathetic nervous system, whereby chronic states of tension persist, is "centering," to establish a functional rhythmic flow of metabolic energy and homeostasis in the ANS: the internal organs are all endodermic in origin. Another is "grounding," which establishes a relationship with the (mesodermic) voluntary and involuntary movement systems within the body to address hypertonicity and hypotonicity. The former is associated with chronic activation of the sympathetic nervous system, and the latter is associated with negative symptomatology connected to the parasympathetic nervous system, such as lethargy and depression. "Facing," the third somatic technique, addresses imbalances in the ectodermic structures (brain and skin), manifesting as oversensitivity and undersensitivity to sensory information by directly working with eye contact and integration of language in perception. Finally, the integration of centering, grounding, and facing—associated with the affects of the endoderm, mesoderm, and ectoderm, respectively—has a profound effect on the person's somatic energy, on their emotional balance, and in moving their life forward.

## Rubenfeld Synergy Method

The Rubenfeld Synergy Method (RSM) combines gentle touch and talk therapy. After several sessions of the Alexander Technique, Ilana Rubenfeld developed her method after she found herself bursting into tears and was flooded with memories that the Alexander Technique, a primarily somatic method, did not address (Medina and Montgomery, 2012). So, Rubenfeld sought help from a psychoanalyst to deal with the psychological manifestations of the touch therapy. She then synthesized Gestalt Psychotherapy with Feldenkrais's work (Rubenfeld, 2000). Rubenfeld believed that, *"emotions and feelings arise hand in hand within the brain and the body. To grasp them, the patient needs touch and talk"* (Medina and Montgomery, 2012, p. 74).

During the application of passive therapeutic touch (the "Listening Hand"), the patient will feel something happening in his or her body and is invited to express the experience verbally. This combination of talk and touch during the session aids the practitioner in attending to the patient more wholly (Medina and Montgomery, 2012). Integration of touch and talk therapy into the present moment during a session can release tension from the body, bring the person to a state of relaxation, and achieve body-mind connection—goals aligned with those of Somatic Psychotherapists working with the ANS.

## Sensorimotor Psychotherapy

Ogden and colleagues (Ogden, Minton, and Pain, 2006; Fisher and Ogden, 2009) describe Sensorimotor Psychotherapy, another form of Body Psychotherapy that encourages the client to understand how movement, physical response, and posture are related to accompanying thoughts, beliefs, and emotions, especially in connection to trauma. The client becomes aware of how beliefs can affect posture and how posture affects thoughts and emotions. Therapists utilize a "bottom-up" process to address more primitive, automatic, and involuntary functions underlying the client's traumatic and post-traumatic responses.

In Sensorimotor Psychotherapy, as the therapist assists the client to track his or her sensory-motor experience, physiological signs of arousal are reduced or increased, but only at levels that are manageable for the client. Clients observe and report interactions between their emotions and physical sensations. Top-down cortically mediated functions are utilized as clients observe and report the interplay of bodily sensations, emotions, and thoughts; while bottom-up processing of trauma-related sensations, arousal, movement, and sensory-motor responses within the client's window of tolerance facilitates adaptive responses (Ogden, Pain, and Fisher, 2006).

## Somatic Experiencing

Peter Levine (2010) described the treatment goal of Body Psychotherapy as the activation of the innate capacity for self-regulation. According to him, survivors of emotional trauma need to develop tolerance for all sensations, whether pleasant or unpleasant (Levine, 2008). Survivors are encouraged to complete their fight-or-flight responses, in the form of minute movements of the arms or legs, to engage their self-protective reflexes. The brain registers this new experience, and equilibrium is restored in the nervous system; natural resilience is activated, which heals trauma. Empirical studies have shown the efficacy of Somatic Experiencing in working with trauma (Leitch, 2007; Parker, Doctor, and Selvam, 2008; Leitch, Vanslyke, and Allen, 2009; Whitehouse and Heller, 2008).

In the Somatic Experiencing paradigm, there are principles designed to aid in attending to the experience of visceral sensations and to discharge residual ANS energy (Bhat, Carleton, and Hippel, 2013). Somatic Experiencing techniques (Levine, 2009) may be utilized to promote healthy stress responses affecting the biological defense system and the attachment system and subsequently affective and cognitive functioning. When the body is highly dysregulated, stuck in chronic patterns of activation, traditional verbal therapy alone may often be unsuccessful or sometimes even contraindicated. In Somatic Experiencing, narrative is used to track autonomic activation, not to search for memories. The therapist must work within a range of resilience by never pushing through the client's resistance or promoting catharsis.

Somatic Experiencing techniques and principles explicitly focus on regulation of the ANS. Pendulation facilitates an individual to pendulate effectively between states of resource and states of highly charged traumatic energy. Pendulation is utilized to shift bodily awareness from regions of relative ease to those of discomfort and distress, based on innate rhythms of contraction and expansion of the ANS, alternating between the SNS and PNS. *"Resourcing"* is used to develop the ability to tolerate what has been impossible to tolerate. Because the present moment is a resource in Somatic Experiencing, just tracking what goes on in the session may in itself lead to more organization and greater coherence. Additional resources are identified and alluded to throughout the treatment. The patient's resources are reparative and aid in the process of titration. *"Titration"* involves introducing traumatic material in small amounts to prevent retraumatization. It keeps the nervous system activation within the "window of tolerance." The energy locked into the system by trauma is most effectively released gradually. In this way, unpleasant, distressing sensations are followed by comfortable, relaxing sensations that work on the levels of both the SNS and PNS.

It is important for the therapist to be able to recognize signs of discharge without inhibiting them in either oneself or the client. Some signs of discharge of traumatic activation may be sweating, crying, shaking and trembling, coughing, etc. Somatic Experiencing practitioners strive to bring awareness to as many elements of experience as possible. As such, the discharge of trauma activation can occur through awareness of any of the following five elements: sensation, image, behavior, affects, and meaning. The therapist allows significant amounts of time for the nervous system to reorganize itself after each intervention.

The goal of the therapist is to find where in the sequence completion of the traumatic response was thwarted, and to guide the client through to relaxation and a sense of triumph and relief. If the therapist is more embodied, the client's wish to heal draws from the therapist's state (Napier, 2011). Similar to many therapies, in Somatic Experiencing the client responds more to how the therapist is, not what the therapist says: assuming that wisdom rests in the client, the therapist is letting the experience of the client guide the therapy session.

The role of the breath in ANS regulation has long been a cornerstone of Body Psychotherapy. Levine asserts that neocortical interventions may restore the regulatory functions of the nervous system; however, rigidly controlled breathing may prevent deeper homeostasis. Levine stresses that, when you feel like you need to take that deep breath, feel the sensation that wants you to take the deep breath instead. As such, the culminating experience of working with the breath is coherence or a full-bodied breath resulting in shifts in consciousness (Somatic Experiencing Trauma Institute, 2012).

## Integration in Body Psychotherapy

Based on the experience of many Body Psychotherapists, utilizing somatic techniques that target ANS processes penetrates to the physiological roots of suffering and helps the client to reattain a healthy balance that extends to the emotional and psychological as well. Trauma resolution, using recent somatic techniques, leads to greater resilience and increased life satisfaction—freeing the person from the "emotionally heavy obstructions within our nervous system that hinder our potential for a healthy, thriving, and generative development" (Carleton, 2010).

### Cultural Considerations in Discharging ANS Energy

Crying is a primitive reflex and is a discharge of sympathetic activation. As such, allowing the impulse to cry may serve to restore fight responses. If clients have a fixed pattern of crying, the therapist might ask them to simply stay with the impulse to cry in order to help them learn to contain and integrate the emotion (Levine and Frederick, 1997). Other clients might be emotionally shut down, and it is very useful for the tears to flow. Crying may be an unspoken voice, indicative of dispelling trapped energy from the body (Levine, 2010).

By thinking culturally, Somatic Psychotherapists can connect deeply with a client, especially when working to move a client through a painful, distressing event. After a client cries, the body can relax. However, depending on what culture a client may identify with, there may be differences in working with releasing the ANS. Though tears are an innate human phenomenon, not everyone cries the same (van Hemert et al., 2011), as cultural differences in freedom of expression explain differences in crying rather than actual distress or suffering.

### Integration and Research

Utilizing an integration of techniques designed to balance the ANS from different modalities of Body Psychotherapy promotes deep healing and transformation on somatic, affective, cognitive, intrapersonal, and interpersonal levels. Within the field of psychotherapy, researchers and practitioners are moving beyond a single-school approach and toward assimilation of techniques and theories into more of an integrative approach (Stricker and Gold, 2002). This kind of integration is frequently happening in the field of Body Psychotherapy.

The convergence of phenomenological experience with empirical verification is a developing interest within the field of Body Psychotherapy (Bhat, Carleton, and Hippel, 2013). There are ongoing collaborative efforts of the European Association for Body Psychotherapy and the United States Association for Body Psychotherapy that include the development of research initiatives to provide greater evidence for some of these theories and clinical techniques of the various institutes, most of which originated outside of academia.

## References

American Psychiatric Association. (2013). *Diagnostic and statistical manual of mental disorders* (5th ed.) (DSM-V). Washington, DC: Author.

Baum, S. (2011). *Modern Bioenergetics: An integrative approach h to psychotherapy* [Monograph]. New York: Society for Bioenergetic Analysis.

Beebe, B., & Lachmann, F. M. (2002). *Infant research and adult treatment: Co-constructing interactions.* Hillsdale, NJ: Analytic Press.

Benson, H., & Klipper, M. Z. (1975). *The relaxation response.* New York: Avon.

Bhat, D., & Carleton, J. A. (2013). *Promoting resiliency: Clinical applications of neuroscience, attachment theory, and mindfulness.* Paper presented at the annual meeting of the American Mental Health Counselors Association, Washington, DC.

Bhat, D., Carleton, J. A., & Hippel, B. (2013). *Somatic Experiencing: Theory and technique for integration in psychotherapy.* Paper presented at the annual meeting of the Society for the Exploration of Psychotherapy Integration, Barcelona, Spain.

Blasband, R. A. (2005). Working with the body in psychotherapy from a Reichian viewpoint. *AHP Perspective.* Retrieved from http://orgonomictherapy.com/working-body-psychotherapy-reichian-viewpoint

Boadella, D. (1973/1985). *Wilhelm Reich: The evolution of his work.* Chicago: Regnery.

Boadella, D. (1987). *Lifestreams: An introduction to Biosynthesis.* Hove, UK: Routledge.

Boadella, D. (2011). Psycho-physical synthesis at the foundations of Body Psychotherapy: The 100-year legacy of Pierre Janet (1859–1947). In C. Young (Ed.), *The historical basis of Body Psychotherapy* (pp. 53–70). Galashiels, Scotland: Body Psychotherapy Publications.

Bowlby, J. (1969). *Attachment and loss: Vol. 1: Attachment.* PEP Web.

Bowlby, J. (1990). *A secure base: Parent-child attachment and healthy human development.* New York: Basic Books.

Boyesen, G., & Boyesen, M-L. (1980). The Biodynamic theory of neurosis. *Journal of Biodynamic Psychology, 1*(1), 56–71.

Bromberg, P. M. (2006). *Awakening the dreamer: Clinical journeys.* Hove, UK: Routledge.

Carleton, J. A. (1991). Self-regulation. *Energy and Consciousness, 1*(1), 15–46.

Carleton, J. A. (2008). *Is Reich still relevant? Self regulation from Wilhelm Reich to Peter Levine.* Paper presented at the Society for the Exploration of Psychotherapy Integration conference, Boston, MA.

Carleton, J. A. (2010). *Somatic Experiencing and attachment trauma program.* Paper presented at United States Association for Body Psychotherapy 6th Annual Conference: Unraveling Trauma: Body, Mind and Science, Concord, CA.

Carleton, J. A., & Padolsky, I. (2012). Wilhelm Reich's theoretical concept of mother–infant attachment as the origin of self-regulation: A neurophysiological perspective. *Body, Movement and Dance in Psychotherapy, 7*(2), 1–12.

Cornell, A. W. (2013). *Focusing in clinical practice: The essence of change.* New York: W. W. Norton.

Craig, A. D. (2003). Interoception: The sense of the physiological condition of the body. *Current Opinion in Neurobiology, 13*(4), 500–505.

Damasio, A. R. (2000). *The feeling of what happens: Body and emotion in the making of consciousness.* New York: Mariner Books.

Fisher, J., & Ogden, P. (2009). Sensorimotor Psychotherapy. In C. A. Courtois & J. D. Ford (Eds.), *Treating complex traumatic stress disorders: An evidence-based guide,* (pp. 312–328). New York: Guilford Press.

Fonagy, P., Gergely, G., Jurist, E., & Target, M. (2004). *Affect regulation, mentalization, and the development of the self.* London: Karnac Books.

Gendlin, E. T. (1998). *Focusing-oriented psychotherapy: A manual of the experiential method.* New York: Guilford Press.

Gold, J. (2011). Attachment theory as a foundation for psychotherapy integration: An introduction and review of the literature [Special issue]. *Journal of Psychotherapy Integration, 21*(3), 221.

Goldberg, S. (2000). *Attachment and development.* London: Hodder Arnold.

Graham, L. (2013). *Bouncing back: Rewiring your brain for maximum resilience and well-being.* Novato, CA: New World Library.

Heller, D. P. (2010). How attachment affects trauma with Diane Poole Heller. Interview by Ruth M. Buczynski. National Institute for the Clinical Application of Behavioral Medicine.

Heller, D. P., & Carleton, J. A. *Nervous system, attachment system: Crossing the bridge to now.* (currently in process of publication).

Heller, M. C. (2012). *Body Psychotherapy: History, concepts and methods.* New York: W. W. Norton.

Janet, P. (1924). *Principles of psychotherapy.* New York: Freeport.

Jean, A. D. L., & Stack, D. M. (2012). Full-term and very-low-birth-weight preterm infants' self-regulating behaviors during a still-face interaction: Influences of maternal touch. *Infant Behavior and Development, 35*(4), 779–791.

Kabat-Zinn, J. (2003). Mindfulness-based interventions in context: Past, present and future. *Clinical Psychology: Science and Practice, 10,* 144–156.

Keleman, S. (1985). *Emotional anatomy: The structure of experience.* Berkeley, CA: Center Press.

King, A. (2011). When the body speaks: Tummy rumblings in the therapeutic encounter. *British Journal of Psychotherapy, 27*(2), 156–174.

LeDoux, J. E. (1998). *The emotional brain.* New York: Simon & Schuster.

Leitch, M. L. (2007). Somatic Experiencing treatment with tsunami survivors in Thailand: Broadening the scope of early intervention. *Traumatology, 13*(3), 11–20.

Leitch, M. L., Vanslyke, J., & Allen, M. (2009). Somatic Experiencing treatment with social service workers following Hurricanes Katrina and Rita. *Social Work, 54*(1), 9–18.

Levine, P. A. (1979a). Autonomic stress and vegetotherapy, I. *Energy & Character, 10*(2), 10–19.

Levine, P. A. (1979b). Autonomic stress and vegetotherapy, II. *Energy & Character, 10*(3), 24–30.

Levine, P. A. (2008). *Healing trauma: A pioneering program for restoring the wisdom of your body.* Boulder, CO: Sounds True.

Levine, P. A. (2009). *Somatic Experiencing Training Manual.* Boulder, CO: Somatic Experiencing Trauma Institute.

Levine, P. A. (2010). *In an unspoken voice: How the body releases trauma and restores goodness.* Berkeley, CA: North Atlantic Books.

Levine, P. A., & Frederick, A. (1997). *Waking the tiger.* Berkeley, CA: North Atlantic Books.

Lillas, C., & Turnbull, J. (2009). *Infant/child mental health, early intervention, and relationship-based therapies: A neuro-relational framework for interdisciplinary practice.* New York: W. W. Norton.

Liss, J. (1979). Emotions and the human energy system. *Energy & Character, 10*(1), 41–48.

Lowen, A. (1976). *Bioenergetics: The revolutionary therapy that uses the language of the body to heal the problems of the mind.* New York: Penguin Books.

MacLean, P. D. (1990). *The triune brain in evolution.* New York: Plenum Press.

McCorry, L. K. (2007). Physiology of the autonomic nervous system. *American Journal of Pharmaceutical Education, 71*(4), 1–11.

McEwen, B. S. (2006). Protective and damaging effects of stress mediators: Central role of the brain. *Dialogues in Clinical Neurosciences, 8*(4), 367–381.

McEwen, B. S. (2007). Physiology and neurobiology of stress and adaptation: Central role of the brain. *Physiological Reviews, 87,* 873–904.

McEwen, B. S. (2008). Central effects of stress hormones in health and disease: Understanding the protective and damaging effects of stress and stress mediators. *European Journal of Pharmacology, 583,* 174–185.

Medina, L. L., & Montgomery, M. J. (2012). Touch therapy combined with talk therapy: The Rubenfeld Synergy Method®. *Body, Movement and Dance in Psychotherapy, 7*(1), 71–79.

Napier, N. (2011/2012). *Introduction to Somatic Experiencing* [Presentation]. New York. Retrieved from: www.nancyjnapier.com/Downloads/SE%20Intro%20Flyer_NY,%20NY_%20Sept%2024,%202012%20(Napier).pdf

Neill, A. S. (1960). *Summerhill School: A new view of childhood.* London: Penguin Books.

Neundörfer, B., & Hilz, M. J. (1998). Ludwig Robert Müller (1870–1962)—a pioneer of autonomic nervous system research. *Clinical Autonomic Research, 8*(1), 1–5.

Ogden, P., Minton, K., & Pain, C. (2006). Hierarchical information processing: Cognitive, emotional and sensorimotor dimensions. In P. Ogden, K. Minton, & C. Pain (Eds.), *Trauma and the body: A sensorimotor approach to psychotherapy,* (pp. 1–50). New York: W. W. Norton.

Ogden, P., Pain, C., & Fisher, J. (2006). A sensorimotor approach to the treatment of trauma and dissociation. *Psychiatric Clinics of North America, 29,* 263–279.

Parker, C., Doctor, R. M., & Selvam, R. (2008). Somatic therapy treatment effects with tsunami survivors. *Traumatology, 14*(3), 103–109.

Pierrehumbert, B., Torrisi, R., Laufer, D., Halfon, O., Ansermet, F., & Beck Popovic, M. (2010). Oxytocin response to an experimental psychosocial challenge in adults exposed to traumatic experiences during childhood or adolescence. *Neuroscience, 166,* 168–177.

Porges, S. W. (2011). *The polyvagal theory: Neurophysiological foundations of emotions, attachment, communication, and self-regulation.* New York: W. W. Norton.

Reich, W. (1942/1973). *The function of the orgasm: Sex economic problems of biological energy.* New York: Farrar, Straus & Giroux.

Reich, W. (1945/1972). *Character Analysis.* New York: Farrar, Straus & Giroux.

Rothschild, B. (2000). *The body remembers: The psychophysiology of trauma and trauma treatment.* New York: W. W. Norton.

Rubenfeld, I. (2000). *The Listening Hand: How to combine bodywork and psychotherapy to heal emotional pain.* New York: Bantam Books.

Scaer, R. C. (2005). *Trauma spectrum: Hidden wounds and human resiliency.* New York: W. W. Norton.

Schneiderman, I., Zagoory-Sharon, O., Leckman, J. F., & Feldman, R. (2012). Oxytocin during the initial stages of romantic attachment: Relations to couples' interactive reciprocity. *Psychoneuroendocrinology, 37*(8), 1277–1285.

Schore, A. N. (1999). *Affect regulation and the origin of the self.* Hove, UK: Routledge.

Schore, A. N. (2000). Attachment and the regulation of the right brain. *Attachment and Human Development, 2*(1), 23–47.

Schore, A. N. (2001). The effects of early relational trauma on right brain development, affect regulation, and infant mental health. *Infant Mental Health Journal, 22*(1–2), 201–269.

Schore, A. N. (2002). Dysregulation of the right brain: A fundamental mechanism of traumatic attachment and the psychopathogenesis of posttraumatic stress disorder. *Australian and New Zealand Journal of Psychiatry, 36,* 9–30.

Schore, A. N. (2003). *Affect regulation and the repair of the self.* New York: W. W. Norton.

Schore, A. N. (2009). Right brain processes in development: The interpersonal neurobiology of secure attachment. In D. Fosha, D. J. Siegel, & M. F. Solomon (Eds.), *Healing power of emotion: Affective neuroscience, development, and clinical practice*, (pp. 112–144). New York: W. W. Norton.

Sherrington, S. C. S. (1906). *The integrative action of the nervous system.* New Haven, CT: Yale University Press.

Siegel, D. J. (2001). *The developing mind: How relationships and the brain interact to shape who we are.* New York: Guilford Press.

Siegel, D. J. (2007). *The mindful brain: Reflection and attunement in the cultivation of well-being.* New York: W. W. Norton.

Somatic Experiencing Trauma Institute. (2012). *SE Master Class Series: The role of breath with Peter A. Levine, Ph.D.* Boulder, CO: Somatic Experiencing Trauma Institute.

Sroufe, L. A. (2005). Attachment and development: A prospective, longitudinal study from birth to adulthood. *Attachment and Human Development, 7*(4), 349–367.

Stricker, G., & Gold, J. R. (2002). An assimilative approach to integrative psychodynamic psychotherapy. In F. W. Kaslow & J. Lebow (Eds.), *Comprehensive handbook of psychotherapy: Vol. 4. Integrative/eclectic*, (pp. 295–316). New York: Wiley.

Tharner, A., Dierckx, B., Luijk, M. P. C. M., van Ijzendoorn, M. H., Bakermans-Kranenburg, M. J., van Ginkel, J. R., et al. (2013). Attachment disorganization moderates the effect of maternal postnatal depressive symptoms on infant autonomic functioning. *Psychophysiology, 50*(2), 195–203.

Totton, N. (2003). *Body Psychotherapy: An introduction.* Maidenhead, UK: Open University Press.

Tronick, E. (2007). *The neurobehavioral and social-emotional development of infants and children.* New York: W. W. Norton.

van Hemert, D. A., van de Vijver, F. J. R., & Vingerhoets, A. J. J. M. (2011). Culture and crying. *Cross-Cultural Research, 45*(4), 399–431.

Whitehouse, B., & Heller, D. P. (2008). Heart rate in trauma: Patterns found in Somatic Experiencing and trauma resolution. *Biofeedback, 36*(1), 24–29.

Young, C. (2007). The power of touch in psychotherapy. *International Journal of Psychotherapy, 11*(3), 15–24.

Young, C. (2008). The history and development of Body Psychotherapy: The American legacy of Wilhelm Reich. *Journal of Body, Dance, and Movement in Psychotherapy, 3*(1), 5–18.

# 61

## The Role of the Breath in Mind-Body Psychotherapy

**Ian Macnaughton, Canada**

with Peter A. Levine, United States

**Ian Macnaughton,** PhD, has been a teacher and practitioner of Somatic Psychotherapy since the 1970s. He is a Somatic Experiencing Practitioner and a Bodynamic Analyst and trainer. He is also an adviser to families in business, families of wealth, and to various organizations, and is a Fellow of the Family Firm Institute. His clients include many government ministries and corporations.

Ian is an associate faculty member of the City University (Vancouver site) and has taught at a number of universities and colleges at both the undergraduate and graduate levels in psychology and in business. His publications include two edited books: *Embodying the Mind and Minding the Body* and *Body, Breath and Consciousness: A Somatics Anthology*. His writings on family business have been published in a number of venues, as well as his work in systems science, which has been published as part of a NATO Advanced Research workshop on education.

**Peter A. Levine,** PhD, is a forerunner in body-oriented approaches to trauma. He is the developer of Somatic Experiencing®, a naturalistic approach to healing trauma that he has developed since the 1970s. He has received the Lifetime Achievement Award from the United States Association for Body Psychotherapy, in recognition of his original and pioneering work. He also received an honorary award as the Reiss-Davis Chair for his lifetime contributions to infant and child psychiatry.

Dr. Levine served as a stress consultant for NASA during early space shuttle development and has served on the APA Task Force for responding to large-scale disasters and ethnopolitical warfare. He is the author of several best-selling books on trauma, including *Waking the Tiger: Healing Trauma*, published in at least twenty-four languages; *Healing Trauma*; and his most recent book, *In an Unspoken Voice: How the Body Releases Trauma and Restores Goodness*. He has also published two books on children, including *Trauma through a Child's Eyes* and *Trauma-Proofing Your Kids: A Parents' Guide for Instilling Confidence, Joy, and Resilience*.

Breath has long been an essential part of the quest to understand the human condition, to promote health, and to alleviate suffering. Over thousands of years, Taoist and Yogic philosophers and adepts have evolved their techniques to enhance people's awareness of their breathing as an aid to reaching different levels of consciousness. Today, Yoga, Buddhist mediation, Tai Chi, other martial arts, as well as various relaxation approaches, have contributed to the prevalence of breathing practices in Western cultures. We will be differentiating the term "breathwork" (as consciously modifying the amplitude and rate of breath) and breathing *awareness,* dealing with breath "as it is."

Whereas Eastern cultures and other traditions spent centuries using breathing awareness, among other techniques, to improve human functioning, Wilhelm Reich's twentieth-century venture into the therapeutic applications of breathing practices in psychiatry and therapy is comparatively recent. Reich used active breathing patterns, as well as the provocation of muscles through deep pressure, to dissolve what he termed "character armor" (Macnaughton, 2004). He discovered that, while paying attention to the patterns or types of breathing, his patients unconsciously displayed useful information. Reich also found that intervening in their breathing patterns helped move them toward self-regulation and a "felt sense" of safety, wholeness, and wellness (in other words, coherence).

According to Levine (1976, 2010, and ongoing clinical observations) and Porges (2011), coherence is a measurable state (e.g., noted as respiratory modulation of heart rate and blood flow to parts of the body inhabiting conscious breath) that serves as an indication of health. They noted that a relationship exists between behavior and coherent flow states under the control of the myelinated vagus nerve, known as the ventral vagus (Porges, 2011). The development of these understandings has allowed us to move beyond the historically interesting paradigm of Reich's structures toward a more sophisticated way of viewing coherent organismic function.

An understanding of some basic physiology helps to clarify the role of consciously modified breathwork and to elucidate the effect of different breathing patterns on individuals' resources and their ability to self-regulate. In this chapter, our focus is on the neurophysiological underpinnings of respiration and the therapeutic implications and effects of various breathwork interventions. We will discuss breath interventions by addressing: (1) developmental issues within Alexander Lowen's bioenergetic character structure framework, which was adapted from Reich's armoring theory; (2) the use of breathing awareness; and (3) contraindications for breathwork.

## Reich's Vital Contribution

Studying originally with Sigmund Freud, Wilhelm Reich was perplexed as to why various patients did not respond favorably to Freud's "talking cure." Reich began to notice his patients' nonverbal body language—how they presented themselves, how they held their musculature, and how they modified their breathing patterns. He began experimenting with movements that would allow the muscles and breath to loosen for fuller natural expression.

Reich developed his groundbreaking ("Reichian") therapy initially while living in Austria in the 1920s (see Chapter 5, "The Work of Wilhelm Reich, Part 1: Reich, Freud, and Character" by Wolf Büntig). He later worked directly with the body to unveil "repressed" emotions underlying character neurosis. Ultimately, he sought to harmonize and balance the client's "bioenergy" system. His primary objective was to enhance a patient's physical, emotional, and spiritual sense of well-being.

Encouraged by these results, he developed a therapeutic model of optimal health, restoring the "wisdom of the body" and the capacity for self-regulation. Reich realized that the body operates as an energy system, in harmony with the energy of the natural environment. He called this "orgone" energy. To the degree that this energy system operated efficiently and effectively, throughout the organism, patients reported that they felt better and functioned more spontaneously. According to Reich, ready access to "orgone" was essential for all living organisms because it was the vital energy of life—the *élan vital* or "life force," as it will be called in this chapter.

To Reich, the human dilemma lies in learning how to surrender to this life force by allowing it to flow freely. Put another way, achieving well-being implies learning how to not block the free flow of this "current" of life force, instead opening to it with receptivity. Ultimately, Reich theorized, blocking this energy flow causes dysfunctions in health, both physical and emotional.

As the emerging psyche tries to handle its developmental frustrations, throughout childhood, muscular contractions suppress and deaden the emotions associated with that thwarting. Reich noted that the blockage of energy flow occurs when we "armor" ourselves (physically and psychically) against experiencing our deep feelings of connection to the life force. He then developed his theory of "segmental armoring," which correlated somewhat to the chakra systems of Eastern philosophies. (See Chapter 65, "Segmental Holding Patterns of the Body-Mind" by Jack Rosenberg and Beverly Kitaen Morse.) Reich employed this schema to address what he called "character-armoring." This block against emotional and energetic experiences results in either rigidity or a collapse in the body and a constriction of emotional contact. For an excellent review of all of this, see Heller (2012).

Reich felt that the comfortable, pleasant sensations of feeling the soft pulsations of energy within oneself had become so foreign to his patients that they were frightened and braced against these deeply pleasurable pulsations. In other words, pleasure and ease had become "alien"; and tension, anger, sadness, depression, and pain had become the "familiar" or "normal" experience. This state of "disease" became the "normal" tone of feeling! All other sensations were thus experienced as unusual or abnormal and, therefore, threatening. Next, we look, briefly, at the role of the breath in various types of "armoring."

## Character-Armoring: Character Structures

According to Reich, character-armoring manifests in body postures, gestures, voice, and also breathing patterns. These "character structures" reveal how individuals handle their need to love, their reaching out for intimacy and closeness, and their striving for competence and pleasure.

Seen in this light, the different character structures form a spectrum. At one end of the continuum is the *schizoid* position, embodying an almost total withdrawal from intimacy and closeness because these are seen as too threatening. At the other end of the spectrum is emotional health. Here, there is little holding against the impulse to reach out openly for closeness and contact. The various character types fit into this spectrum, or hierarchy, essentially according to the degree that they allow for intimacy and contact.

Alexander Lowen, one of Reich's many students, reinterpreted his teacher's work to create the therapeutic system he called "Bioenergetic Analysis" (see Chapter 14, "The Concept of Energy in Body Psychotherapy" by Andreas Wehowsky). It also examines character and personality in terms of the body's energetic processes. Lowen (1994) defined character as a fixed pattern of behavior—the typical way individuals handle their striving for pleasure and connection. These prototypical striving manifestations are structured in the body in the form of chronic and (generally) unconscious muscular tensions that block or limit our impulses to reach out.

Character, according to Reich and Lowen, is also a psychic attitude, buttressed by a system of denials, rationalizations, and projections. The functional identity of psychic character and bodily structure (or muscular attitude) is the key to understanding personality; it enables therapists to read the character from the body and to explain a body attitude by its psychic representations, and vice versa.

In the Bioenergetics nomenclature, the different character structures are classified into five basic types. Each has a special pattern of defense, both on the psychological and muscular levels. Finally, Reich understood that hidden beneath the individual's unique character structure blend is their pure "life force," an animating birthright of vitality and joy fueling their capacity to live and to flourish.

It is important to note that this is a classification of defensive positions, not of people. It is recognized that no individual is a pure type, and that all people combine some or all of these defensive patterns within their personality and physical structure. No two individuals are alike, in either their inherent vitality or their patterns of defense (which have arisen from aversive or conflictual life experiences). Nevertheless, we speak in terms of types for the sake of clarity. The five types are termed *schizoid, oral, psychopathic, masochistic,* and *rigid*. These terms are used because of their historical significance, though they clearly lack much that is known from the contemporary fields of child development and neuroscience.

### The "Schizoid" Character Structure

"Schizoid" describes a person whose sense of self is severely diminished, whose ego is weak, and whose contact with the body and its feelings is greatly reduced (also known as the Unwanted Child). It is probable that the schizoid structure is formed by overwhelming stress during the perinatal period and includes attachment frailty. It is maintained primarily through a large reduction of breath and a conservation of energy, breathing only enough to barely sustain life and breathing very shallowly.

### The "Oral" Character Structure

A personality is described as being "oral" when it contains many traits typical of infancy—the oral period of life. These regressive traits are weakness in the sense of independence, a tendency to cling to others, a decreased assertiveness, and an inner feeling of needing to be held, supported, and cared for (also known as the Needy Child). The fear of annihilation is less severe than with the schizoid structure. The breath here is also quite diminished, though less so than for the schizoid structure.

### The "Psychopathic" Character Structure

The essence of the "psychopathic" attitude is the denial of feeling. There is, in all psychopathic characters, a great investment of energy in one's own image. The other aspect of this personality is the drive for power, and the need to dominate and control others (also known as the Controller/Leader). Their breath pattern is equally controlled.

### The "Masochistic" Character Structure

The "masochistic" individual is one who suffers, whines, blames, or complains but remains submissive. Submissiveness is the dominant masochistic tendency. Although the outward behavior of the masochistic character shows a submissive attitude, the opposite is harbored within (as in the passive-aggressive personality). This deeper emotional level holds strong feelings of spite, negativity, hostility, and superiority (also known as the Endurer) and correspondingly represses, or suppresses, their breathing.

### The "Rigid" Character Structure

The concept of rigidity derives from the tendency of these individuals to hold themselves stiff, possibly with pride. Thus, the head is held fairly high and the backbone straight. These would be positive traits were it not for the fact that the hardened pride is defensive, the rigidity unyielding. The rigid character is afraid to give in, equating this with submission and weakness. Rigidity can also become a defense against an underlying masochistic tendency (also known as the Perfectionist/Obsessional), and the rigid person's breathing is designed to maintain this state, with little proper release and relaxation.

## Breathwork with Character Structures: The Importance of Understanding the Physiology of Breathwork

Breath has the unusual capacity to bridge voluntary and involuntary realms—it is the autonomic function that we have the most control over. Humans can, at will, breathe rapidly, slowly, deeply, superficially, abdominally, or thoracically. As we ready ourselves to run, our breath prepares us for this exertion. In different emotional states, our breathing patterns vary. Shakespeare, the Great Bard, in *As You Like It,* describes "... *lovers sighing like a furnace.*" In fear, we gasp and hyperventilate to the point that we may even pass out. In anger, we breathe strong, full breaths and prepare our body for an energetic response. All of these breath experiences are on the gray border between voluntary and involuntary.

The deep, involuntary control of breath, on the other hand, is orchestrated primarily by two factors: the respiratory "pacemaker" in the medulla of the brainstem (which stimulates the basic respiratory rhythm), and the level of carbon dioxide in the blood. It is *not* the level of oxygen, as is so often presumed, but the CO2 levels that are crucial in the chemical and physiological regulation of the breath.

### The Bohr Effect

An important phenomenon associated with carbon dioxide (CO2) levels in the blood (and hence associated with respiration) is known as the "Bohr effect." This effect describes the dynamic in which hemoglobin molecules pick up oxygen from the lungs (in the alveoli of the lungs) and transport it to all the cells of the body, where it charges the ATP.[63] This molecule, in turn, fuels the energy pro-

---

[63] Adenosine Tri-Phosphate (ATP) is a nucleoside triphosphate that transports chemical energy within cells and plays a signaling role in the central and peripheral nervous systems

duction in the mitochondria of the cells. Efficient oxygen transfer, release, and utilization depends on the level of $CO_2$ (within a specific optimal range). Any departure from these $CO_2$ concentration levels reduces the oxygen available to the brain and the body. In other words, when you have *either* too high or too low $CO_2$ levels, the amount of oxygen being transported and delivered to the cells is reduced. The notion that people need to breathe deeply, or to speed up their respiration, to get more oxygen is physiologically incorrect. Reduced $CO_2$ also diminishes the inner (i.e., involuntary) urge for a spontaneous breath. If we mechanically override the spontaneous interplay of the breath pacemaker and $CO_2$, we interfere with the normal physiological role of $CO_2$ to regulate the breath. What we really want is regulated breath—a self-regulated breath under a sort of "pacemaker" regulation (within normal levels of $CO_2$). This dynamism, expertly and spontaneously, helps us to manage our responses to a multitude of encounters and experiences.

## Hyperventilation and Emotional Flooding

Reich knew that breathwork evoked deeply rooted psychological and emotional material. He frequently had patients overbreathe in order to build a charge, leading to catharsis and "de-armoring." He seemed less aware that "the reduction or dissolution of the patient's armor can disorganize his whole system of adaptation and coping" (Macnaughton, 2004, p. 371). Today, there are many therapeutic uses of voluntary hyperventilation, some constructive, and some destructive.

From a physiological perspective, hyperventilation causes vasoconstriction of the blood vessels in the brain (Lowry, 1967). The brain responds first by shutting down activity in the neocortex, second in the limbic system, and then, finally, in the brainstem, where oxygen starvation would be lethal. When less oxygen is delivered to the brain, the neocortex goes "offline" first. One of the important functions of the neocortex is to inhibit the lower centers. This control is, therefore, diminished due to hyperventilation. With this inhibition reduced, the limbic system and brainstem became destabilized, and a flood of primitive sensations, emotions, and images is released. Some of these may be trauma-related and many, including attachment styles, are pre-verbal. This disinhibition can be of therapeutic value, as it allows one to get in touch with various emotions and procedural (body) memories that are normally unconscious. However, it can also lead to flooding, panic attacks, and potential (re)traumatization.

This experience of disinhibition can be dramatic, a bit like taking a hallucinogenic drug such as LSD. In addition, patients can become almost addicted to hyperventilation, because it evokes such intense experiences. This overbreathing can set up a pattern of seeking this kind of dramatic catharsis with its primitive sensations, emotions, and strikingly vivid imagery. Hyperventilation, then, becomes a habitual way of accessing these emotions; however, simply "getting them out" does not necessarily give rise to deeper integration and regulation. The habitual cathartic venting of emotions can produce dead-end results where patients do not sense a deeper connection to their felt inner world. They do not learn from experiencing the subtleties of their sensations and emotions and then expressing them effectively in relationship. They may feel better immediately after these catharses; however, problems of destabilization may arise in the next hours or even days or weeks following such sessions.

What the effective use of hyperventilation requires is that the patient has the capacity to hold a "charge" and also the (limbic) feeling and the observational (neocortex) functions, all together, in full play. None of these brain regions can be sacrificed to the other. Whereas talk therapy overemphasizes cognition, and some body-based therapies overemphasize emotion, it is the balance of all these levels ("bottom-up" and "top-down" processing) that leads to truly integrative and holistic therapy. An optimal therapeutic approach maintains all three regions in concert. Bodily sensations (upper brainstem and thalamus), the emotions (limbic system), and the observing/thinking/reasoning capacity (neocortex) can work together to manifest deep integration and to develop a coherent narrative that furthers the individual's emerging capacities (Levine, 1997, 2010).

## Character Structure and Breathwork: Hyperventilation and Hypoventilation

Strategies for working with patients depend on their psychological makeup and on their character structure. For instance, in the *schizoid* and *oral* character structures, voluntary overbreathing is not generally a good approach for uncovering unresolved developmental issues. In the other structures—*psychopathic, masochistic,* and *rigid*—voluntary overbreathing is more useful; the patient has the resources to integrate its impact, having developed more ego strength and autonomic stability at the earlier developmental stages. These later character structures tend to have issues around surrender, which breathwork can help to address.

There will be, necessarily, somewhat different intervention strategies for each of the character structures. When a charge is built up, a *schizoid* structure type may believe he is going to "fall apart," die, or disintegrate. He may become terrified of explosion (fragmentation) or implosion (collapse inward). He may contact an even greater fear of getting stuck in one of these terror states. Supporting the patient verbally, and with gentle touch as he breathes, can result in shifts in activation without falling apart. This experience can move him toward a more organized and functional way of being in the world.

On the other hand, a patient with a *rigid* structure will try, without success, to push through a charge, yet often fails to achieve discharge and relaxation. This patient requires some degree of "provocation," possibly via (mutually agreed) manipulation of musculature (particularly of the jaw, neck, shoulders, and back) as well as a continuation of breathwork.

Patients with a *masochistic* structure are likely to be most aware of the tension, whereas those with a *rigid* structure will be more aware of excitement, the ability to handle the energetic sensations, and the subsequent movement into surrender. When working with these patients, (especially the *masochistic* structure), therapists need to be both firm and gentle. They may need to assist the patient, perhaps freeing the breath using various touch techniques such as massage, to diminish the patient's overthinking activity, to promote a sense of ease and stillness, and to allow her to let go into surrender to her softer sensations and feelings.

Therapeutic interventions are used to help the patients' transition from a sympathetic state of arousal and holding to a parasympathetic (ventral vagal) state of release. In the parasympathetic state, patients begin to notice and experience sensations besides pain, bracing, and tension. They start to realize that there is another world available to them. They are now able to experience a broader range of sensations. Later, they can learn to access these sensations and feelings without their habitual overbreathing. They become aware of more subtle, softer sensations, and those of flow, aliveness, connection, yearning, and healthy aggression.

Some further guidelines with regard to these structures include having patients lying down with their eyes closed, attending to their inner experiences, as they increase their breathing. This typically allows them to pay more refined attention to discovering awareness of emergent life energy, sensations, feelings, images, and thoughts. It's also important, at the same time, that patients become aware of the therapist's presence and the overall container of safety that the therapist provides (Porges, 2011). Asking patients to report on what they are discovering, as the process proceeds, while also attuning their felt sense and maintaining some visual contact with the therapist, can assist in reinforcing the therapeutic alliance, social engagement, and safety for patients.

As a general rule, interventions should be made in gradual steps with patients trying out different breathing patterns, taking a few breaths, then resting and reporting on their experience, their sensations, images, and feelings. They then repeat that cycle, pacing the level of integration. These steps help patients develop a foundation of awareness (both cognitively and somatically) so that they can build on that foundation in a timely, relational sense of discovery and safety. With each phase of exploration and pausing, integration is enhanced vertically (brainstem, limbic system, and prefrontal cortex) and horizontally (left and right brain).

It is helpful to include interventions such as asking patients for their awareness of how and where they experience their breath—i.e., shallow or deep, slow or fast, whether in the chest or in the belly, or both—as well as encouraging them to report if their breath is experienced in their back, their front, or to their sides. What sensations, feelings, or images arise? What meanings are associated? These questions assist patients in developing a more coherent narrative of their embodied experience and increasing their appreciation and discovery of their capacity for expansion and for various states of consciousness.

It is often tempting to view the character structure in a layered, linear manner through life's developmental stages. In fact, although there is a discrete domain to these stages of development, each with its own challenges and opportunities, the whole system of development is actually nonlinear, moving (back and forth) between later and earlier structures. For example, an earlier structure may well depend on the stability of later structures for its capacity to self-regulate, even if in a limited way. In addition, it is important not to "undo" a (later) character structure without considering the effect on destabilizing earlier structures. Further, understanding the functions of more hyporesponsive muscular patterns and the hyperresponsive patterns of compensation for hyporesponsive (weaker) tension patterns in muscle fascia and in organ systems requires precise assessment and more delicate interventions (Marcher and Fich, 2010).

## Hyperventilators

People who tend to overbreathe (hyperventilate) are generally from the later-developed structures (*psychopathic, masochistic,* and *rigid*). They often do not believe in meaningful experience without a tangible, concrete anchor (*"It's not rational"* or *"I'm trying but can't seem to find it"*) and may express disillusionments, because they have tried to change their reality and nothing has happened. They can use breathing as a tool to discover the more subtle levels of their felt experience. In these cases, a therapist can work directly with breathing to build up a charge. Eventually, patients will start going into deeper discharge experiences, altered states of awareness, and suspended respiratory states ("still points"). They may begin to see "eidetic" images and may experience subtle bodily sensations associated with "near-death states."

Relaxation happens when patients navigate the excitation or charge successfully and are able to drop into deeper states of consciousness. This kind of deep relaxation can support hypermnesia and the ability to make more flexible associations and can loosen up the superego, our critical censor and critical judge. When patients yield to deep relaxation, they are able to access more core material: memories associated with how they see their self, how they feel, and how they experience the difference between the public and private self, the heart, feelings, and desires. They also often begin to develop an interest in spirituality and seek to explore these dimensions through various spiritual practices.

Because *rigid* structure patients need to learn to move through the tension and experience the charge, the therapist must work with their tension and help to ease the hold of the musculature, so as to achieve a free flow of sensation. Once patients begin to accept and feel comfortable with new sensations and to gain confidence derived from successful experiences, they will be able to gradually release their patterns of holding their breath and muscular armoring.

## Hypoventilators

*The earlier-developed structures, the schizoid* and *oral* character structures, generally hypoventilate (though they may have periods of unstable hyperventilation and panic attacks). They need to be strongly encouraged, supported, and helped to breathe more deeply. The first benefits that the hypoventilator will experience from increasing respiration is having more oxygen. This enables him to get more energy, to hold more charge, and to sense some greater vitality, core feeling, and satisfaction. It is crucial for the hypoventilator to learn to develop self-support. This can be done with a little gentle awareness work with ankles, with feet, and on the chest. If the therapist places his hands gently on the sides of the patient's chest, it encourages the patient to engage in "side breathing" (expansion of the rib cage), which is usually more spontaneous and expansive. The patient may need only two or three breaths before experiencing a noticeable sense of charge in his nervous system.

By staying with that experience until the charge becomes fully associated as a sensation or feeling, the patient can move toward integration. The patient may become a little dizzy, or slightly uneasy at first, and may need external contact or support. The therapist can also encourage some movement work at this time to help the patient titrate the experience gradually. As the patient opens up feelings contained within his body, these then become more grounded in meaning and in mutual connection. At this point, the goal of therapy is to develop some further sense of containment, grounding, and energy flow, and to reinforce the ability of the patient to handle the increasing charge without fragmentation. This is an important corrective experience, because it reorganizes the patient's basic belief in himself, and his capacity to be in the world.

It is important to give these individuals a strong sense of security, so they will not feel that they are flying apart when they experience increased intensity. They need to learn to feel directly within their body and then work at containing the sensations. Their natural tendency will be to escape from the increased sensations, so it is necessary to build up feeling a little at a time, helping patients to stay with their experiences. This initially invites a positive transference and supports them to develop a good therapeutic alliance. Occasional breathwork (as contrasted with breathing awareness), at this point, can help patients develop the strength to reduce flooding by sensations and any spontaneous emotional material that may emerge. As they learn to control the charge and tolerate it, the experience becomes one of developing increased resilience and healthy boundaries.

It is also important that therapists take care not to push the *schizoid* structure into dissociation or catharsis (actually a different form of dissociation). Therapists need to work at a level where patients are able to contain and tolerate the charge, via "titration" in the Somatic Experiencing model (Levine, 1997, 2014), and cited as the "window of tolerance" (Ogden, Minton, and Pain, 2006). It is critical to work within the patient's observable ability to self-regulate and co-regulate without dissociation.

## Titration: Differentiating Procedural Memory and Self-Management of Activation

Understanding the role of the breath, within the therapeutic environment, is an important framework for differentiating between declarative (explicit) and procedural (implicit) memories. Procedural (implicit) memory is unconscious; it is the language of the body, and oversees self-management of activation. Procedural memories include defending one's self, setting boundaries, retracting, fighting, fleeing, and freezing. The respiratory and autonomic procedural memories are also deeply rooted procedural memories that need to be carefully titrated, and worked with at the level of bodily sensations (Levine, 2010, 2014).

Regardless of the precipitating event, patients are going to have procedural (implicit) memory cues related to past overwhelming experiences. One of these might be cued as, *"I can't breathe"* (the primal fear of suffocation). After they move through the procedural memory of not being able to breathe and realize, *"Ah yes, my breath does come in on its own,"* their anxiety lessens and the breath can flow more freely, allowing a state of coherence to develop. Working with breathing awareness (rather than breathwork) is, generally, the best approach here.

Optimally, therapists want the arousal state to go up and then to come down on its own. The goal is to reestablish dynamic homeostasis and a flexible physiological respiratory pattern, and a physiological balance between the sympathetic and parasympathetic (ventral vagal) nervous systems. Attention to respiration is critical because it is intrinsically tied to anxiety, to different kinds of specific traumas related to the fear of suffocation.

Primal (core) anxiety is the experience of suffocation. Therefore, pausing between the exhalation and inhalation is a useful exercise. One might suggest, *"OK, let's just see what* happens . . . I know it feels like you need to take a breath, but let's just see if you can feel what happens just before you take a breath." or *"OK, when you feel like you need to take that deep breath . . . see if you can delay it for a bit. Just feel the sensation that wants you to take that deep breath . . . just see if you can trust in that difficult moment."* Generally, as patients do this, their respiration resets to be more physiologically regulated, rather than taking conscious effort. It may also be useful to use "self-talk"—phrases like *"I can allow a deep breath." "I can relax." "I can calm myself."*

## Breathing Awareness

Generally, with early structures, and in cases where there is unresolved (shock) trauma or physical pain, awareness of breath is the most valuable approach. What follows are some descriptions of simple breathing awareness exercises:

### Just One Breath

The goal is to watch the breath without consciously trying to change it. Have the patient simply follow the sense of the breath as it moves in and through the body, and again as the breath moves out, just as waves lapping on the beach flow in and out. Have her notice what changes in her body during that one inhale/exhale cycle. Repeat the cycle, following the pathway of a second breath as it moves through the body as it comes in, and then goes out, again sensing it to be like the tides of the ocean that ebb and flow. Again, focus on what changes are noticed in the body this time. (Levine and Phillips, 2012, pp. 33–34)

### Circle Breathing

This exercise is used to open up pathways of movement and flow in the body to begin counteracting the constriction of fight, flight, and freeze. First, have the patient take a few moments to connect with the overall sense of his body. Then practice breathing up the middle (midline) of the body, imagining that the inhalation starts at the base of the pelvis and rises up to the nose and face. Then imagine breathing out, down through both sides of the body, through the shoulders, arms, and hands, and down through both legs and out through the feet. Repeat this process for three to four breaths and then do a check-in.

If problems exist in the cervical, thoracic, or lumbar spine, another technique involves imagining breathing up the middle of the front of the body to the top of the head. As the patient breathes out, have him sense the breath moving down the back of his head, neck, midback, through the lower back, and out through the tailbone; finally, imagine it cascading down both legs. Repeat this several times. Then do a check-in: what are the effects? (Levine and Phillips, 2012, pp. 25–26)

### An Exercise for Patients to Practice at Home

After working with the therapist on exploring the sensation to breathe and resist, this exercise can help patients find relief from anxiety through a simple, three-step model: Pause, Take One Breath, and Choose.

When the patient becomes aware of an increase in anxiety, the first and most important step is to pause. Really get a sense of pausing and slowing everything down. The next step is to take one breath with full awareness and to notice what happens in the body as she takes only one full breath, pauses at the end of the inhalation, and then exhales, pacing the release of air with the inhalation rate, and pausing at the end of the exhalation. After that breath, or perhaps after several more, she will be in a position to make choices—to use other techniques to stay with the sensations through the discharge or to regulate it as necessary for the current situation. (Levine and Phillips, 2012)

Rather than focusing on resistance, understanding, or emotional release, clients can learn to sense their body in a way that helps to awaken undeveloped resources, resources that have been given up or that were never learned. The acquisition of these new resources (which are exactly the ones needed, but missing) greatly facilitates the resolution of developmental/relational issues. At the same time, it empowers patients to take new actions in daily life, including developing the ability to reposition themselves within their family of origin and their social context.

## Contraindications

A Body-Oriented Therapist must know something about the somatic organization making up character structure, health status, and psycho-pathology—enough to recognize when not to use controlled breathwork. For example, breathwork is rarely appropriate in working directly with shock trauma. As previously mentioned, however, it can be useful in some situations to help develop resources and to uncover previously unconscious material. This holds true particularly for individuals with the later character structures. Nonetheless, it is important for the therapist not to push these clients through to these discoveries prematurely. Put simply, breathing *awareness* can be used in traumatic and schizoid/oral structures to help clients tune in to their respiration and autonomic nervous system rhythms, and to develop a sense of beneficial resources. A therapist may choose to do this before working with the shock itself. It is not appropriate to introduce overbreathing techniques for clients under the effect of extreme, unresolved birth and intrauterine stress. It is important for the breathing to start from the generation of spontaneous biological rhythms, rather than rhythms imposed by the therapist.

The patient may have been respirated at birth. If the therapist introduces an external (voluntary) respiration pattern, the patient may become even more locked into that shock pattern. It is important to realize that these interventions must be put into the appropriate context. A therapist should not, for example, do a "rebirthing" session if a patient is still exhibiting birth stress or shock. However, if the patient has worked through some of his birth and intrauterine stress, gentle belly breathing, followed by a light, panting pattern, can be used as a resource, to recapture some degree of "womb bliss."

It is essential to monitor the patient's breathing patterns closely—what appears to be hyperventilation may be a transitional phase that will actually take the patient back to equilibrium. Or a patient who is barely breathing may start to hyperventilate to avoid going through the experience of "nonbreath." Working with this is similar to the situation of patients with dissociative states. Instead of the patient going fully into the state, the therapist needs to support the patient as she touches into it and comes back out.

Careful monitoring and titration are essential and will prevent runaway cycles of hyperventilation followed by shutdown. The principle of establishing safe resources with patients, both in terms of the relationship with the therapist and through "enough" stabilization of the nervous system, provides a foundation for forward progress. It is important to slow the process down, to take it in little bits, and to calibrate interventions in response.

Breathwork may be contraindicated, or be a cause for concern, in the presence of certain medical conditions or in cases of entrenched personality disorders. For instance, it is difficult to know what meaning a patient will place on the altered-state experience, especially if he has a borderline personality or a dissociative identity disorder. This patient may take a few breaths and become flooded with traumatic images, projecting them onto the therapist. Such a patient needs to connect more slowly, in terms of transference, rather than have a rapid projection provoked by hyperventilation.

Hyperventilation can cause the blood sugar to drop precipitously, which can be significant for patients with diabetes and hypoglycemia. The increased stress of prolonged hyperventilation could, possibly, precipitate a heart attack in those with certain heart problems, including particular arrhythmias. Hyperventilation could conceivably also increase the rate of spread of cancer within the body. Autoimmune and endocrine problems are most likely a result of hypothalamic-pituitary-adrenal (HPA) axis central nervous system dysregulation. If too much energy is introduced, through overbreathing, the therapist may not be able to control HPA destabilization. Hence, it is possible to reactivate symptoms of lupus, multiple sclerosis, Graves' disease, and other autoimmune disorders. A patient with certain kidney problems who is exposed to hyperventilation could, potentially, experience kidney failure, because the hyperventilation can force the kidneys to secrete additional carbonate ions, putting more stress on the kidneys. These are not necessarily absolute contraindications, but they are serious concerns and caveats for therapists to consider carefully.

Indeed, breathwork, along with breathing awareness, can have a considerable positive impact, informing various Body-Oriented Therapies. A therapist can provide trustworthy support to patients; help them to secure healthy attachment, psychodynamic development, and movement out of trauma patterns; promote self-regulation; contact core energy pulsation; and help in restoration of the deep self (Levine, 2010).

# References

Heller, M. C. (2012). *Body Psychotherapy: History, concepts, and methods.* New York: W. W. Norton.

Levine, P. A. (1976). *Accumulated stress, reserve capacity and disease.* PhD thesis, Department of Medical and Biological Physics, University of California, Berkeley.

Levine, P. A., (1997). *Waking the tiger: The innate capacity to transform overwhelming experiences.* Berkeley, CA: North Atlantic Books.

Levine, P. A. (2010). *In an unspoken voice: How the body releases trauma and restores goodness.* Berkeley, CA: North Atlantic Books.

Levine, P. A. (2014). *Trauma and memory.* (in progress).

Levine, P. A., & Phillips, M. (2012). *Freedom from pain: Discover your body's power to overcome physical pain.* Boulder, CO: Sounds True.

Lowen, A. (1994). *Bioenergetics: The revolutionary therapy that uses the language of the body to heal the problems of the mind.* New York: Penguin Arkana.

Lowry, T. (1967). *Hyperventilation and hysteria: The physiology and psychology of overbreathing and its relationship to the mind-body problem.* Springfield, IL: Charles C. Thomas.

Macnaughton, I. (Ed.). (2004). *Body, breath and consciousness: A somatic anthology.* Berkeley, CA: North Atlantic Books.

Marcher, L., & Fich, S. (2010). *Body encyclopedia.* Berkeley, CA: North Atlantic Books.

Ogden, P., Minton, K., & Pain, C. (2006). *Trauma and the body: A sensorimotor approach to psychotherapy.* New York: W. W. Norton.

Porges, S. (2011). *The polyvagal theory: Neurophysiological foundations of emotions, attachment, communication, and self-regulation.* New York: W. W. Norton.

# 62

## Heart, Heart Feelings, and Heart Symptoms

**Courtenay Young, Scotland, UK**

**Courtenay Young**'s biographical information can be found at the beginning of Chapter 7, "The Work of Wilhelm Reich, Part 2: Reich in Norway and America."

The feeling of love is traditionally located, by nearly every culture, within the human heart. Love is seen as one of the most powerful and fundamental of all human feelings; therapy is deeply connected with love, and the need for therapy is often connected with lack of love (Pierrakos, 1974). So what is the role that "heart feelings" play within Body Psychotherapy, and how can we help people with their heart feelings and symptoms?

There are different perspectives of the heart within Body Psychotherapy, and they fall into three major categories: these are therefore the three essential ways that we can generally use the word "heart" and can work with "heart feelings."

## The Heart as a Psycho-Physical Center

The first is the psycho-physiological way, where the heart relates to the pump, circulating blood, fluid, energy, nutrition, and oxygen—the essentials—to every part of the body. In character-analytical work, founded by Wilhelm Reich and still followed by many Body Psychotherapists today, the heart is seen as being located in the fourth "armored" segment of the body. This segment contains the upper torso or trunk of the body, the heart, the lungs (breathing), and the arms. Such Neo-Reichians, like Lowen, see the heart as being ". . . boxed in between the tensions in the roof of the chest, at the neck, and the tensions in the floor of the chest, at the diaphragm" (Boadella, 1987, p. 67), and these two rings of "tension" are therefore primarily involved in blocking off one's feelings (heart) from one's perceptions.

Another psycho-physical perspective dates back to the psychoanalysts who saw disturbances of the autonomic nervous system, including the heart, as "strangulated affects," "hysterical organ neuroses," or "psycho-physiological disorders." Thus, related illnesses were signals from the heart; therefore, treatment meant analysis "of the body signs so as to effect their translation into verbal symbols" (Lake, 1966, pp. 540–547). Ripples of this type of approach still exist today in Body Psychotherapy.

The Western world especially has a high (and escalating) incidence of coronary heart disease—apparently a "unique phenomenon of contemporary man [which] is the most common cause of death in the industrialized world" (Sinatra and Lowen, 1988, p. 32). However, they go on to say, "Cigarette smoking, hypercholesterolemia and hypertension, well-known cardiac risk factors, deserve considerable merit in the etiology of atherogenesis. Additional research studies, however, have disclosed that certain individuals are more prone to coronary disease than others. Such disease-prone individuals have a special pattern of behavior (see Friedman and Rosenman, 1974; Friedman and Ulmer, 1984). It is a pattern of behavior that helps people cope with competitive structures, rapidly changing social mores, and environmental imbalances" (Ibid.). We have here the beginnings of a bio-psycho-social model.

Sinatra—who is CEO of the New England Heart and Longevity Center and chief of cardiology at Manchester Memorial Hospital, Manchester, Connecticut—writing in collaboration with Alexander Lowen—develops this theme a little: the major repressed emotions (as the psychosomatic component of sustained hypertension, he claims) are anger, frustration, and hostility (Rosenman, 1985). "Sudden emotional repressed rage associated with the feeling of loss of control was recently seen in a case of acute hypertensive aortic dissection" (Sinatra and Chawla, 1988). Coronary-prone individuals are unique because in addition to repressing anger, hostility, and rage, they have struggled with the heartbreaking experience of the loss of love and subsequent loss of vital connection. Such feelings of heartbreak imply great sorrow, grief, and anguish that are subsequently expressed in one's evolving behavior, body, and character. Thus, negative reactions can hurt the body. Channeled correctly, however, emotions can also heal. For instance, in animal studies (Lynch, 1979), simple contact, companionship, love, and affection altered hemodynamics, assuaging cardiac indicators of fear and pain.

This is an interesting early attempt to get some sort of scientific backing and mainstream support for the Bioenergetic (Bio-psychodynamic) perspective. The author goes on to emphasize that these "conditions" were probably caused by lack of love or affection in childhood, etc. This lack of love or affection apparently causes, in such people, a drive to achieve in order to overcome their low self-esteem due to these early "rejections." This is the basis of the type A personality, which is relationally prone to, but not a totally causal factor in, coronary heart disease. First described in the 1950s, this perspective is still quite prevalent.

In Body Psychotherapy, there were also several early attempts to work with heart symptoms by Reich and several of his colleagues. These centered around clients with heart problems and the effects on them of the "orgone energy accumulator"; the listed results, again while not being conclusive, show some interesting improvements (Boadella, 1973, pp. 205–207).

Some later attempts toward treatment have also been made using focused relaxation techniques with patients who have undergone heart surgery (Achinard, 1997, p. 198): again, nothing absolutely conclusive. Much of the early research work (by Friedman and others) was done on middle-class, white males. Although there were some significant results, these cannot necessarily be extrapolated to other populations.

Later developments in Body Psychotherapeutic work with the heart are characterized more by one of David Boadella's psychotherapeutic principles in Biosynthesis, which is to try to integrate the three centers of the body: the head (the seat of the intellect), the heart (the seat of emotion), and the *hara* (an Eastern word for the center or core of the person, often located in the belly; the seat of identity) (see also Alimohamed et al., 2001). Energetic connections can be made with these three centers from the thymus gland and the cardiac plexus. Shiatsu and the acupuncture meridians are also very connected with the heart and with the body's fourfold circulation flow that moves in and out of the heart center.

So the heart here is mostly seen not just as an anguished organ caught between intolerable tensions, nor as a static thing to work with and fix if broken (like a transmission of a car), but the center, source, and receptacle of very powerful emotions and a sense of life and well-being. If these powerful flows get blocked, physiologically, emotionally, or psychologically, then problems may well occur.

When we look more specifically at a person's breathing, the heart center is related to thoracic breathing. "In thoracic breathing the chest is pumped up and held in an inflated position. Feelings are held back, creating a sense of over-containment. There is a fear to breathe out fully; letting go would feel like dying (expire), like dissolving the boundary and falling into more self-expression. Paradoxically, this sense of thoracic pressure actually creates a risk of dying, since the over-inflated inspiratory breathing pattern is frequently associated with Type A (rigid) personalities who are prone to high blood pressure and heart-attacks" (Boadella, 1987, p. 78). Stanley Keleman writes:

> Blood is an electrified fluid that is given tidal thrust by the heart and its vessels. Blood circulation is a

generalized function with a specialized local organ, the heart. Blood and gas exchange takes place all over the body, yet the heart is the central pump. The heart and its main branch, the aorta, send energized fluids through the body. The aorta, accompanied by the esophagus and the vagus nerve, pierces the diaphragm. Here the intimate relationship between the heart and the dome of the diaphragm is established; breathing and the heartbeat communicate directly. The location of the vagus nerve also makes clear that breathing and heartbeat give rise to sensations that flood the whole organism. (Keleman, 1985, p. 42)

We should also not forget that the blood (and everything else in the body) is carried in tubes, and the formation of these tubes—their elasticity or rigidity, their pressure, and the strength or weakness of their walls—is crucial to the healthy physiological functioning of that person, so the heart is a central part of a very complex capillary tubular system that extends (amazingly) about 62,500 miles with about 75,000 square yards of membrane surface area (Salmanoff, 1963).

> The internal tubes and organs are affected by overbound or underbound muscle states. Inside of cardiac and smooth muscle tubes are holes, channels, or lumina through which food, air, and blood pass . . . With rigidity, these holes narrow in spasm . . . In swollen structures the muscle tube cannot create resistance . . . The lumina inside the various tubes lose shape and differentiation. In collapse or atrophy, the body wall implodes, crumbles, loses form. (Keleman, 1985, p. 84)

Keleman's central theory, in *Emotional Anatomy*, is that it is our unique life experiences and our emotions that give our bodies their shape and form. "The shapes seen throughout this book are consequences of human attempts to love and be loved" (Keleman, 1985, p. 85). And our heart reactions are a core [sic] part of this process.

In Body Psychotherapy, we take the person's etiology and these associations and juxtapositions very seriously. We see the body as an interconnected whole and, while a different function may be happening in one organ alongside another, there may also be a distinct relationship between the two. Here, we see clearly that the heart and the breathing are closely related: the bloodstream carries the energy of the breath to every part of the body; the capillaries and membranes play an essential part in our general health. Emotions are also intimately connected with the heart and with the breathing.

Going one step further, we know that aerobic exercise is the best form of antidepressant there is, and it also burns off stress hormones. Regular aerobic exercise—of almost any sort—is therefore one of the best "therapies" that a person can give themselves. Combine this with some healthy relaxation, also on a regular basis, and you are essentially rebalancing your own autonomic nervous system and taking a major step toward physical and mental health (Young, 2010). This is also a form of cardiovascular work.

### The Heart as an Emotional Center

This leads us to the second understanding of the heart. Boadella writes: "Secondly there is the heart center in the body, the center of feeling . . . The heart in the second sense begins to be contacted in any therapy that works with 'opening the feelings.' You can work down towards the feelings by loosening the cramps in a person's mind, or you can work up towards the feelings by improving his contact with the ground and the body" (Boadella, 1987, pp. 162–163).

Because the word "heart" is so central in our language, and to our emotions, we must consider also the language of the body that Alexander Lowen writes about:

> The richness of expression involving the word heart shows how important its extra-mechanical aspects are to people. Here are some of them. In the expression "go to the heart of the matter" we equate the heart with the concept of essence. It also connotes the center or core as in the expression "You have reached my heart," which we assume means a person's deepest, most central aspect. "With all one's heart" indicates

total commitment, since it involves the deepest part of a person. Everyone knows we associate the feeling of love with the heart. "To lose your heart" is to fall in love; "to open your heart" is to take in the love of another person. "To wear your heart on your sleeve" is to look for love. So far it is used largely symbolically. But the heart is not just associated with feeling; it is, according to our language, a feeling organ. When we say, "My heart shrank within me," it conveys a proprioceptive sensation, which another person can sense within himself as donating an extreme of anxiety and disappointment. The heart also expands with joy, and this is a literal statement, not just a figurative one. If that is the case, does the expression "You have broken my heart" donate a real and physical trauma? I tend to believe it does but also that broken hearts often mend themselves. The word "break" does not necessarily mean "break into two or more pieces." It could mean a break in the sense of the connection between the heart and the body's periphery. The feeling of love no longer flows freely from the heart to the world. (Lowen, 1975, p. 85)

Sinatra and Lowen write:

It is the sacrifice of true deep feeling, denial of feeling, or suppression of feeling that contributes to coronary-prone behavior and subsequent cardiovascular risk. This lack of awareness by adults established in childhood is very typical of coronary-prone patients. The memory of the heartbreak may be repressed but the body will reveal the truth in its somatic expression . . . Heartbreak is directly and indirectly responsible for coronary disease. Direct responsibility is evident in the sudden unexpected death of an individual upon learning of the loss of a loved one. (1988, p. 34)

To a divided, distorted, or dysfunctional person, any expression of spirituality or finer feelings can be exaggerated in order to take one's attention away from the lack of heart feelings, healthy sexuality, and their contact with their body, just as sexual expression can sometimes be overemphasized, which keeps one's attention away from expressions of the heart or the spirit, but firmly locked into the flesh. However, both these polarities lack "heart"; therefore, the main goal of any form of Body Psychotherapy should be to help restore a dynamic "flow of energy" and feelings from the head to the heart and from the heart to the rest of the body, and back again. This energy can be forms of bioenergy, or it can be the energy found and gained in relating to someone "from the heart," and having them "touch" one's heart.

As therapists, we may—almost certainly—have to learn to model this in ourselves and in the therapeutic relationship (Hubble et al., 1999; Wampold, 2001). Working with people's bodies and bodily manifestations in Body Psychotherapy is a richly rewarding experience, and more so when we touch their hearts, and especially when our hearts are touched by their work on themselves. Some of the more graphic case studies illustrating this type of work, and the complexities of Body Psychotherapeutic work, can be found in Barbara Holifield's account of working with Delores in "*Against the Wall/Her Beating Heart: Working with the Somatic Aspects of Transference, Countertransference, and Dissociation*" (Johnson and Grand, 1998, pp. 59–84).

Holifield writes, "*Similar to dreams, the body expresses a raw, elegant poetics. At times this wordless language is harsh and primitive, like the disturbing occurrence of heart problems, or the deeply upsetting quality of a recurring, gruesome and murderous dream.*"

When we consider working with these feelings in therapy, we must consider the means of expression of the feelings of the heart. In Lowen's form of Body Psychotherapy, Bioenergetics, it is felt that the primary channel of expression for heart feelings is through the throat and mouth. If these are "blocked," no really effective work is possible, and thus work on these areas is a prerequisite to working with the heart feelings. The baby's first channel of communication is also through the heart, he claims, "*. . . as it reaches with its lips and mouth for the mother's breast. However, a baby . . . also reaches with its heart*" (Lowen, 1975, p. 86).

As therapists, we can help the client to become more conscious of how they block themselves in this heart area and what the obstacles to that sort of expression may be. The second main channel of expression for our heart feelings (in Bioenergetics) is through the arms and hands, as they reach out to touch, and as they receive other people's touch. For love to flow, the channels of that flow must be "open," and often we find difficulties in "reaching out" from our heart to express compassion to others. Tensions in the shoulders, extensor muscles, and wrists and hands can all block these expressive heart feelings in many subtle ways, turning a reaching into a grabbing, or a caress into a possessive stroke, or creating a rigidity that is off-putting to the other's embrace. "Here too, if the action is to be an expression of love, the feeling must come from the heart and flow into the hands. Truly loving hands are highly charged with energy" (Ibid.). We also find a section in an early article by David Boadella (1987) on "Gravity, Muscles and Heart Feelings" relating to this sort of analysis, where he writes:

> Lowen has described the sense of bristling in the back when a surge of aggressive energy is free to flow along it. In a back which is free to yield to the rhythm of flexor and extensor movements, which is neither spastic nor flaccid, but in healthy tonus, pleasurable streaming movements can be felt: the back becomes orgastic. John Pierrakos has described how an overdeveloped will center in the back leads to an overdriving, but withheld, person who cannot commit his heart fully. The extensor tensions in the upper region of the back hold back both the aggressive impulses to strike, and the loving impulses to reach out and caress, from flowing down the arms …
>
> Lowen relates to the tender feelings of the heart: "I linked these movements in a common pulsation which had its center in the heart. These are feelings which seem to stem from the heart. Heart feelings are tender feelings which draw the individual into relationships for charge or discharge." …

John Pierrakos has pointed out in his article on heart troubles,[64] that these are commonest in people in whom either aggressive or assertive impulses are bound up, or who have to repress their longing. That is, if the chest is cramped by tension to contain either explosive feelings of rage or the longing to reach out and make contact, this can set up the basis for a heart condition. John Olesen has shown how vital the tonus of the musculature is in determining the strength of the vein-pump, and with that the vitality of the circulatory system as a whole. The connection between the muscular system and the circulatory system is an intimate one: there are two ways in which the circulatory system is usually modified and induced to pump more or less blood through the body: one way is through muscular work, the other way is through vegetative stress. If a man who is angry can discharge that anger through vigorous movements (it need not be an actual fight, it could be—as in the case of many animals—a threat display); or if a man who is sexually aroused can express the sexual charge in love-making and orgastic movements, then the circulation benefits, the heart temporarily increases its output and relaxes again afterwards. Both muscular work and regular love-making are recommended as antidotes to heart disease. Where anger and love are blocked by the rigid refusal to surrender, however, we have muscular tension leading to cardiac stress. (Boadella, 1977, pp. 75–77)

However stilted or defined by their times these presumptive descriptions are, they still carry some elements of basic truth. These were people reporting from a huge caseload of experience. Arnold Mindell's Process-Oriented Psychotherapy work also illustrates some further client work on people with heart attacks, though this is not based

---

64  J. Pierrakos (1974). The case of the broken heart. *Energy & Character, 5(3)*. Also in D. Boadella (1976). *In the wake of Reich*. London: Coventure.

on any particular theory of the heart. The underlying theory here is (still) that the person has developed an "edge" against feeling. However, when current events drive the person into a feeling state,

> ... Now, Paul is disturbed by a lot of things, now he is hurt by all sorts of problems, but will not admit it. He is unconsciously acting like a tough guy, saying nasty things about himself, being hard and critical, and he does not admit he is hurting himself. So, right now, the pattern for his heart attack process is still going on. His "mother," his primary and sober realism, is hurting the ordinary guy, the patient, his "secondary" process who has troubles. This is a common program for people with heart attacks." (Mindell, 1988, p. 142)

Another way of expression of the heart feelings, in Bioenergetics, is downward into the pelvis and genital area. Sex is an act of love, and one's heart should therefore be involved. When the heart connection fully happens, *"the sexual experience has an intensity and reaches a level of excitement that makes climax or orgasm an ecstatic event ... a full and satisfactory orgasm is possible only when one is totally committed. In such a case one can actually feel the heart leap (leap for joy) at the moment of the climax"* (Lowen, 1975, p. 87).

In women, Lowen states, the heart area also has a direct connection with their breasts, which respond erotically or glandularly to the impulses flowing from their heart as the functions of the breast also become involved in either sexual expression or nursing one's child—a clear expression of maternal love.

More recently, with the advent of neuroscience, the emphasis has moved from the muscular flows and blocks, to the hormonal flows. There is increasing evidence that the role of oxytocin is very significant in love and in bonding relationships (Carter, 1998; Uvnäs Moberg, 1997). Because oxytocin is also the hormone that stimulates the production of breast milk, we probably have another "heart" connection here.

There are therefore many complexities and differences of perspective involved with the heart when seen as a psycho-physiological organ or as an emotional center.

## Polarities of the Heart

This is not as simple as "I love you and I hate you." David Boadella goes into further complexities here. He relates the four basic qualities of the heart that are found in Tibetan Buddhism—love, joy, compassion, and balance or equanimity—to a bipolar deviation (one often an opposite and one a slight distortion) of each of these qualities and then uses the resulting eightfold schemata to help direct a person's therapy. Thus, love (nonpossessive, goodwill) deviates into either possessive love (the opposite) or oral-compensated love or codependency (the distortion). Joy and happiness deviate into either helpless misery or frivolous excitement. Balance deviates either to overemotionality or to indifference and apathy. And compassion deviates to the misuse of power or to sentimentality.

Boadella teaches that centering in the heart quality will help to neutralize its opposite, and thus we have a direction for the therapy of heart feelings. But where the person is caught up in the distortion, it is better to center on a different heart quality to create a better balance: love is used to counteract apathy; joy to counteract sentimentality; balance to counteract frivolity; and compassion to counteract symbiotic dependency. Boadella further relates these eight emotional states coming from the four heart qualities to the developmental time in life when the distortion of the heart quality first manifested, and he connects these to the four main character patterns: the schizoid-hysteric (in the first six months) upsetting inner balance; the manic-depressive (in the second six months) upsetting the sense of joy; the narcissistic-borderline polarity (manifesting in the second year) upsetting the sense of love for others; and the compulsive dominant/submissive polarity coming from distortions (in the third year) destroying the sense of compassion for and empathy with others (Boadella, 1995, pp. 5–20).

I tend to try to help people move beyond the simple polarities of "I love you—I hate you"; "We are together—we are apart"; "I want your babies—you can't have visitation with the kids"; etc. This is what I call the "either . . . or . . ." type of thinking. There is another way, more open, less proscribed: the "both . . . and . . ." way of thinking—so the polarities above become something like: "I do love you, and sometimes—like right now—I dislike you intensely"; "We are really good together, and sometimes I also need to be alone"; "I know you love the children, and—because we are separating—their need for a stable environment, and lots of looking after, means that I can do this better than you, as you are away working so much: let's see what sort of visitations we can work out."

This sort of thinking does not deny the good feelings because of the necessity for survival (which the "either . . . or . . ." pattern tends to do), and it leaves a lot more space for a negotiated settlement in which everyone's "heart needs" get recognized.

A lot of the early Body Psychotherapists adapted the basic Reich–Lowen–Pierrakos model of a tri-layered psyche: with a surface or social "mask"; then a layer of powerful secondary feelings, often repressed and "negative" (thus necessitating the "mask"); and a primary "core" level—where the heart feelings truly reside. Depending on the strength of the secondary layer, due essentially to the level of repression, these inner-core, heart feelings can sometimes get blocked and turned back (made secondary), or just give up. However, later, we Body Psychotherapists have also learned from the Gentle Bioenergetics of Eva Reich, from the "mindfulness" practice of Ron Kurtz, and from people like Gerda Boyesen that we do not have to "break down" the psychic armoring; we can allow it to melt, by going to (and making contact with) the "core" and stimulating and encouraging the "heartfelt" feelings that are always latent there. It is just a different way of working, often involving seeing the person less as a character-armored pathological specimen and more as a locked-in person in the here-and-now who is struggling to get out.

In a book called *The Warmth of the Heart Prevents Your Body from Rusting: Ageing without Growing Old* (de Hennezel, 2011), a French psychologist who works with the elderly recommends that we savor the moment, keep our curiosity, and slow down a little, and thus start to enjoy life a little more. If we can maintain the energy of our hearts, and believe a little more in the power of joy and human warmth, we can transform both ourselves and the way that we look at the world. She is not a Body Psychotherapist, though maybe she now deserves to be thought of as one. But, however all this theory is used, finally one comes to the inner sense of the heart, in the ability to feel one's inner essence and the connection with things much greater than the self.

John Conger writes, "Loving is not feeling or gushing or romance, but an awareness that gives meaning, which may be as cool as a glass of water on a summer day. Like water, love fills the shape of what is needed. When the mind is not braced against the heart, we have vision in our words" (Conger, 1994, p. 224). He also advocates a growing sense of loving and feeling coming through the integration of the head, the heart, and the rest of the body, for it is not just a mind-body duality that has to be worked against, but the unfeeling and hardness that come with the cut-off heart. I shall leave the last word here to Lowen, who writes:

> I have discussed the heart at some length because it is central to all therapy. People come to therapy with various complaints: depression, anxiety, a feeling of inadequacy, a sense of failure, etc. But behind each complaint is a lack of joy and satisfaction in living. It is popular today to talk of self-realization and the human potential, but such terms are meaningless unless one asks—potential for what? If one wants to live more fully and more richly, it is possible only if one opens his heart to life and to love. Without love—for one's self, for one's fellowman, for nature and for the universe, a person is cold, detached and inhuman. From our hearts flows the warmth uniting us to the world we live in. That warmth is the feeling of love. The goal of all therapy is to help a person increase his capacity to give and receive love—to expand his heart, not just his mind. (Lowen, 1975, pp. 88–89)

# References

Achinard, M. (1997). Assessment of current training in psychosomatics: Primary-care medical practice. In J. Guimón (Ed.), *The body in psychotherapy: International Congress, Geneva, February 1–3, 1996.* Basel, Switzerland: Karger.

Alimohamed, S., Talebi, H., Beutler, L. E., Malik, M., Harwood, T. M., Noble, S., & Wong, E. (2001). *Therapist variables: A meta-analysis.* Paper in panel, University of California, Santa Barbara.

Boadella, D. (1973). *Wilhelm Reich: The evolution of his work.* London: Vision.

Boadella, D. (1987). *Lifestreams: An introduction to Biosynthesis.* London: Routledge.

Boadella, D. (1995). Inspiration and embodiment: Quality levels of expression in Body Psychotherapy. EABP Congress Paper, Carry-le-Rouet, 1995. Printed in *Energy & Character, 26*(1).

Boadella, D. (1997). Gravity, muscles and heart feelings. *Energy & Character, 8*(3), 74–78.

Carter, C. S. (1998). Neuroendocrine perspectives on social attachment and love. *Psychoneuroendocrinology, 23*, 779–818.

Conger, J. P. (1994). *The body in recovery: Somatic Psychotherapy and the self.* Berkeley, CA: Frog.

de Hennezel, M. (2011). *The warmth of your heart prevents your body from rusting: Ageing without growing old.* London: Pan.

Friedman, M., & Rosenman, R. (1974). *Type A behavior and your heart.* New York: Alfred A. Knopf.

Friedman, M., & Ulmer, D. (1984). *Treating Type A behavior and your heart.* New York: Alfred A. Knopf.

Hubble, M. A., Duncan, B. L., & Miller, S. C. (Eds.). (1999). *The heart and soul of change: What works in therapy.* Washington, DC: APA.

Johnson, D. H., & Grand, I. J. (1998). *The body in psychotherapy: Inquiries in Somatic Psychology.* Berkeley, CA: North Atlantic Books.

Keleman, S. (1985). *Emotional anatomy.* Berkeley, CA: Center Press.

Lake, F. (1966). *Clinical theology: A theological and psychiatric basis to clinical pastoral care.* London: Darton, Longman & Todd.

Lowen, A. (1975). *Bioenergetics.* Harmondsworth, UK: Penguin.

Lynch, J. (1979). *The broken heart.* New York: Basic Books.

Mindell, A. (1988). *City shadows: Psychological interventions in psychiatry.* London: Routledge.

Pierrakos, J. C. (1974). *The case of a broken heart.* New York: Institute for the New Age of Man.

Rosenman, R. (1985). Health consequences of anger and implications for treatment. In M. Cheaney & R. Rosenman (Eds.), *Anger and hostility in cardiovascular and behavioral disorders* (pp. 103–135). Washington, DC: Hemisphere.

Salmanoff, A. (1963). Secret wisdom of the body: Bompiani: translated from Russian to Italian by Dr. Mario Mancini; mentioned in L. de Marchi, Sexual repression and individual pathology. In D. Boadella (Ed.). (1991), *In the wake of Reich* (2nd Ed.). London: Coventure.

Sinatra, S., & Lowen, A. (1988). Heartbreak and heart disease. *Energy & Character, 19*(2), 32–35.

Uvnäs Moberg, K. (1997). Oxytocin linked antistress effects: The relaxation and growth response. *Acta Physiologica Scandinavica, 640*, 38–42.

Wampold, B. E. (2001). *The great psychotherapy debate: Models, methods and findings.* Mahwah, NJ: Lawrence Erlbaum.

Young, C. (2010). *Help yourself towards mental health.* London: Karnac.

# 63
## Dreams and the Body

**Stanley Keleman, United States**

**Stanley Keleman's biographical information can be found at the beginning of** Chapter 21, "The Maturation of the Somatic Self."

The body dreams of its future: the body, as a process, is always imagining and dreaming of its next shape, and how further to incarnate itself. Dreams are important because they are direct statements of our deep somatic reality, and they present suggestions of how to continue our somatic, emotional, and cognitive growth. Dreams are also connected to the various stages of our embodied life; they display what is becoming, but what is not yet fully embodied. Working somatically with people reveals this interconnection between dreams and embodiment.

Our destined shapes are always a potential within us, and we are always in the process of forming the next stage of our embodied self. Dreams, as a language of the body speaking to itself, offer clues about behaviors seeking to be embodied, or constitutional issues seeking to be resolved. The insight that the language of the body, interacting with itself, is revealed in the neural, muscular, imagistic, and feeling states that we call dreaming allowed us to find another application of the dynamics of Formative Psychology, and to develop a new avenue for helping people use their bodily experience to participate in the forming of their lives.

Within the Formative Psychology paradigm, the main function of dreams is to influence the soma's behavior in the service of developing our human dimension in its infinite evolutionary aspect and in its finite personal aspect. In this, I have grounded a psychology of dreams in the body's own processes of individuation and evolution. The body and its experience are my starting point and reference, rather than borrowing from other theories of psychology that want to include the body. In other words, the body gives rise to its own psychology, rather than psychology offering the body a way to understand itself.

Forming a personal life, both subjective and social, with its own values and meaning is the goal of Formative work. Years ago, I was struck by the notion "man is not yet; he is but a promise." I took this to mean that humans, by nature, are unfinished, and over a lifetime each of us must continue to form ourself. In my 1987 book, *Embodying Experience,* I laid out the practical principles of the Formative dynamic, and, for more than thirty years, I have been applying these Formative principles to work with dreams.

Dreaming presents us with "how" the somatic self is signaling itself to organize and change its way of being in the world. Dreams are the soma's interiority seeking embodiment—our inside reality using the language and images of society, embedded in non-societal time and space. An underformed expression of the soma has a hunger for more body, and it announces this in the dream. To work somatically with a dream is to voluntarily mimic the dream characters in order to decipher the intended actions.

The soma develops itself through feedback of both its inherited biological program and its learned somatic interactions. The innate ability of the soma to influence itself, to learn from its involuntary metabolic activity, and to adapt its structures and responses is also the basis of voluntary self-influence. The learned ability for self-influence is what I call "voluntary cortical muscular effort." Using voluntary effort to influence involuntary and habitual behaviors is a way for individuals to change their anatomical patterns, behavioral responses, and feeling states. This voluntary Formative process is the ground floor of the psychology of the body that I have developed. This is the basis of how I use dreams to help people empower themselves.

Dreams are a form of motile anatomy expressed in social images and feeling states. They are fast moving and often ephemeral. When motile dream expressions are slowed down (as in the retelling of them), they become more stable, and we are able to remember and make connections to past and present behavior, and to conceive possibilities for new behavior. Using the principles of the Formative process means learning to differentiate and slow the action of a dream figure through this sort of voluntary effort. Deliberately using muscle and cortex to organize discrete changes in anatomical shapes makes new neural pathways that eventually become new memory structures. Voluntarily slowing and stabilizing gradations of change, within a pattern of action, becomes the experienced continuity of how we know ourselves. This makes it possible not only to know our past structural history, but also to alter our structure and to form new experiences and meaning.

Our embodied life is its own subject, as well as its own personal creation. The cortex gathers the body's metabolic excitation and sequences it into a narrative of image, expression, and feeling. The dream process connects the body we are with the one we are becoming. Dreams, then, are a part of the reality of the life of the body.

Jorge Luis Borges (1962), the Argentinean writer, tells a story about a man who wished to have a son. The man began his creation by dreaming him, part by part, over a period of many nights. When he was finished, he prayed to the god of fire to animate the son that he had dreamed. The story ends when the dreamer discovers that he, like his created son, is also a creation of some dreamer.

Borges's tale offers insights into the role of dreams in the body's development of itself. His story also tells us something about inner experiences: the body uses its own experience, of which dreams are an expression, to develop its own subjectivity. The body's ability to remember its own dream, and to reenact a dream figure, demonstrates the relationship that the body has to itself. Thus, we learn that dream figures are related to how the body forms its own expressions and deepens its experience.

There is a continuity between body process and dream figures. The body speaks to its cortex, and the cortex offers images and suggestions for the body to voluntarily change itself. Borges's dreamer, who wants a companion, writes not only about a literal offspring, but also about an inner brother or son. His theme parallels both the Christian story of resurrection (where God sends his only son) and the Hebrew story of the Golem (about the making of a human-like creature). This theme of self-generation is part of the most recent thinking about epigenetic evolution.

These stories also share a common matrix: the relationship between the limbic emotional and brainstem reflex centers, and the ability of the cortex to differentiate the body's expressions in the service of creating new possibilities. The brain makes an image of the body and then asks the body to give it more structure and experience. Borges's story deepens the theme of voluntary participation in the formation of the shapes of our existence from youth to full adulthood to maturity and old age.

We can learn from our dreams when we can reorganize our somatic emotional structure and thereby create new meanings and associations. Although many people try to decode dream images symbolically, they do not learn to experience dreams as an inner environment, or to use them as expressions of bodily states. As the body develops its own dream images, it grows its subjectivity, and uses its cortex to embody new shapes, new meanings, and new behaviors to form a personal future.

Two aspects of our body's process, the body itself and its cortex, interact to organize and form a somatic subjectivity. This relationship of the body with itself forms an embodied life of personal and unique expression. Our body is the subject of its own living, the source and reference point for forming a personal existence. The body, as a process, has an intimate relationship with itself. Dreaming is becoming more intimate with oneself.

Working physically with a dream figure, by organizing a muscular model to mimic the figure, or feeling its shape proprioceptively, uses voluntary muscular-cortical effort (VMCE). How we prepare for and execute an intentional action always calls for a dialogue between brain and muscle, a dialogue that usually happens below our level of awareness. However, introducing voluntary effort into the dialogue changes the game by opening the door to personalizing an instinctual, inherited act.

By using cortex and muscle to voluntarily re-create a dream figure, and then slowly, step-by-step, differentiating its muscular shape, a person is able to influence their inherited or learned behavioral patterns, and, in this way, form a personal present, as well as develop possibilities for original behavior in forming the next stage of their embodiment. VMCE is a powerful tool for influencing one's Formative journey. It is a solid foundation for generating experience and embodying new acts by giving them a concrete anatomical shape.

By organizing a dream figure, a person learns how they can use both cortex and muscle to prepare for and enact their expressions. This is the experiential foundation for understanding how the organizing of an action creates the experience of learning, by laying down the anatomical structures (neural pathways) of memory, as well as the rehearsing of future acts.

When a dream figure is voluntarily "bodied up" by making a muscular model and "stabilized," which is to give it duration by holding the muscular pattern in place, then the process of differentiation and creation begins. Using small, slow, step-by-step gradations in muscular pressure (intensity), layers of slightly different shapes are created within the original shape. Using the dream figure as the body's suggestion of how it desires to form itself, and using voluntary effort to differentiate the figure's muscular shape, brings to the fore a cornucopia of new insights and possibilities. The ability to voluntarily differentiate a somatic shape and to use the ensuing changes of behavior and feeling becomes the basis of personalizing a life and forming a future.

## How to Work with a Dream

The Formative method of working with a dream is to connect it more fully to its own source—the body. In this approach, the focus is on bodily experience, rather than on meaning and interpretation. Dreams are about organizing how we use our bodies to be in the world, and how we inhabit the body we live in. We use dreams to grow a personal self and a complex subjectivity that embraces multiple realities.

In working with the dream somatically, we begin by making a muscular model of a dream figure. Through this voluntary act, we engage both the cortex and the muscular patterns controlled by the brainstem. We begin to become intimate with how we experience our given body, and also with the body images within our brain. This approach generates feelings and memories associated with those postural patterns.

Working with the dream by choosing a dream figure, organizing it muscularly, and then slowing the act vivifies both feeling and imagination. The slowing of a behavioral pattern of a somatic shape not only brings a subjective aspect to our bodily life, but also increases the choices for behaving. The practical application of this practice has five steps:

1. Recollect the dream, in language and in bodily expression.
2. Make a muscular model of a dream figure.
3. In slow, measured, discrete steps, increase and then decrease the muscular intensity of the figure. Slow, small changes are important.
4. Wait and contain the experience to incubate somatic subjectivity.
5. Notice any new form that you may want to give expression to.

Here is an example of working "formatively" with a dream: "Betty," a forty-year-old single woman who has a "porous" shape dreamed of an endomorphic, pear-shaped woman with a large, rounded pelvis. In the dream, there was a nonverbal voice of an older woman saying, "Now is the time to get pregnant." Betty told me that she was deeply touched by the dream's announcement, but does not recognize herself as the endomorphic "dream figure," and feels that something is beyond her control.

I asked her to tell me the dream. She paused at the shape of the woman, so I suggested that she make a muscular model of this dream figure. I encouraged her to begin by gently making a soft fist that could resemble her dream figure's endomorphic pelvis. Next, I asked her to make the fist tighter, which is "rigid," then looser, which is "porous," then tighter again. Repeating this pattern of action mimicked the organization of rigidity that functioned to contain and manage her porosity.

Porous individuals often have a somatic organization of malleable boundaries. They do not contain excitement well, and they have difficulty sustaining their own form: being an adult is identified with compromise and adaptation.

As we worked with the dream figure's porous, womanly shape, a shy, yielding posture became present in Betty. I asked her to make a muscular model of this new shape and to slowly intensify it. Because she had been able to make the hand gesture with more and less tension, she could duplicate this same muscular act in the abdominal and pelvic muscles and allow her inner organs more room to pulse.

This influenced her whole body. She felt more receptive, softer. After a few repetitions of working muscularly with her dream figure, she experienced a wave of excitement rising from her pelvis that threatened her ability to contain porosity. She said, *"I fear I cannot sustain this firm shape. I want to yield to the wave."* I took this to mean that she wanted to give more body, more firmness, to her shape, in order to contain her porosity.

Next, I suggested that she again increase the muscle tone with small, discrete steps, with more intensity and less intensity in a measured way, and to pause between the steps to emphasize the discrete stages of muscular form. In this step-by-step procedure, voluntary muscular effort enabled her to give firmness to her porosity. As she repeated her voluntary efforts, her cortical brain went back and forth between porosity and rigidity, and she was actually using her dream figure to organize another adult identity for herself.

When I suggested again that she firm up her posture with microcontractions to make it slightly more rigid, she again experienced a swell of arousal that this time gave her a sense of power. When I told her that she had formed a shape of power, a sadness appeared, and she said, *"I fear I can't sustain it. It's a demand that I don't know how to fulfill."*

I reminded her that, in learning how to increase muscular contractions and lessen them in small doses, she can minimize the threat of being overwhelmed.

Over time, and with continued practice, Betty learned to tolerate more and more intensity. Doing so evoked excitement, optimism, and anxiety. She learned to play with the varying degrees of her muscle tone and its intensity. Practicing in this way, she learned to influence her underformed, porous adult shape by organizing different degrees of intensity and duration of containment and assertion. Working with her dream figure muscularly created a wider choice of behavior for her adult identity: the porous yielding, the porous receptive, and the firm, fuller-formed, embodied woman who could contain her excitement.

Learning to use voluntary self-influence became the experience of Betty's own personal Formative dynamic. In working with the dream figure in a Formative way, her body became more able to embody its own desire.

I would like to share another example of the Formative principle applied to working with a dream. "Wilma" is an older woman who had worked with me over many years and who was now in a transition phase from her mature form to an older, aging stage of her life. Wilma had been working with her aging, and with feelings of despair and helplessness in terms of shrinking. As often happens, the dream occurred as part of how she was engaging herself physically. The dream offered her a way to deepen her experience and reconnect with an inner vitality. Working Formatively gave her an experiential basis for shaping her current experience and using it to form the next stage of her living. She kept a journal and shared the following:

> The relationship I have with my shrinking pattern, how I organize it and then disorganize it, shows me the relationship I have with myself. Now I understand

shrinking is actually my habitual pattern of density. A habit of self-protection I use to prevent too much excitement or to ward something off. When I slowly shift the muscle intensity of my shrinking, using small steps, I am able to feel the continuity between my more intense, dense, and less intense shape. In this way I vivify the experience of myself in my different somatic shapes and notice changes in my feelings and thoughts. Now, after some practice, I can differentiate the dense pattern inside my mouth and down my throat, and the collapse in my chest and viscera. More intensity brings a kind of collapsing that then brings feelings of resignation in my brain and thinking. When I use voluntary effort to alter the dense patterns, slowly bit by bit, there comes a swelling, a warm pulse that fills me. Working with my self in this bodily and formative way brings me a serenity that wells up from my chest and abdomen and then I feel more free in my mind.

During this period of working with herself, Wilma had a dream that we used to deepen her experience.

The dream: I am standing in my house on the ground floor looking outside through the window. Dusk is coming and the sun is disappearing. I become sad. I am standing there in a sort of depressed stance, with sunken chest and pressed lips, I have an unworthy feeling and a kind of fear is in me to lose the light of the sun. Immediately, I feel an urge to ascend the stairs to observe the sun longer. Arriving at the upstairs window, I see a small slice of the sun shining above the darkness that seems to be covering it. I experience stiffening in the head and face and hands. I'm clinging to prevent my body from fading like the sun. In this moment, a deep longing rises in me, it is a longing not to lose the view to the sun. I climb up to the next floor, the top floor, with more urgency and alarm. Here, a larger window than downstairs permits a wider view of the sunset. Now the sun presents itself as a wonderful big orange ball, slowly moving down into the dark clouds of the coming night. My heart is beating fast; my eyes and mouth are wide. I am fascinated by the way the sun blends into the dark and how the bright colors of the sun disappear.

The following is excerpted from her journal and letters:

The formative work we have done using my "sun dream" is ripening in me and I want to share what is happening as I work with it. I have been working with my postures: Standing in front of the window looking at the sun, the shrinking and fear of the loss, and the pattern of dense clinging to prevent collapse. First doing it more, then slowly undoing the shrinking pattern and lessening the intensity of the clinging. Over the past week, I have been practicing many times the differentiating of these patterns and lately in the steps of less intensity I begin feeling a pulse of warmth rising from inside. You asked me where is the sun in my body and to make its shape. So I spread my arms and hands slightly bigger than my chest. I then increased the muscular intensity of my arms and chest and belly, little by little, so I could experience different shapes. As I went back and forth in small steps between more and less intensity warm swells arise from my belly to my chest, even filling my arms and face. It feels like the inside of my body is a sun filling me with warmth. This gave me the feeling that my body is part of this beautiful orange sun.

Over the next weeks, she continued to use her experiences and wrote again:

The compelling fascination with the sun disappearing makes me fearful, but when I use the practice to change my shape the warmth fills me and penetrates the darkness of my brain. When the orange heat penetrates my darkness and my shrinking body becomes receptive to my own swells, I sometimes even feel optimistic. *A later entry:* I am understanding to be like a sun, with different settings; these experiences are akin to having had different bodies each with their time to be here. Now I experience how the sun in the dream is me, it is my body shining with different intensities at different stages of my life. Working with this dream the sadness of the ground floor disappears and the longing to follow the sun fills me. Having the power to influence my shrinking shape helps me be part of a process—not lost or abandoned by my body. Now I know in a deep experiential way my body has a rising and setting pattern. The knowledge that I am able to reorganize my shrinking and fear brings me a feeling of inner security and serenity.

This dream reveals the soma's anatomical subjectivity. It is a personal experience of the body organizing from its own process, and indicating an alternate way to relate to an emerging and fading shape. The body is dreaming of itself, and its cortex offers suggestions in the images of a woman who is fearful and sad to lose the sun. The dream figure alludes to how the body responds to a challenge or a threat. An instinctive urgency is organized into an intense, dense pattern, almost to the point of implosion and collapse.

Using the protocol of the Formative dynamic, imitating and differentiating a muscular model of the dream figure, Wilma was able to identify her somatic emotional postures of despair and fear. Over time, she learned to influence her state and to have a Formative relationship to her aging. Empowering herself to influence her body shape and thereby altering her responses, she was able to personalize nature's developmental process. From these somatic experiences grew a new source of security and serenity, a new perspective, and optimism about the future.

Perhaps the single most important ability that a person can have is the experience of self-influence. Voluntary self-influence, even in small amounts, is an antidote to fear of the unknown, and is the basis of hope and optimism during any phase of transition or stage of living. Many people who want to change their situation often do not know that they have limited themselves to behaving only in ways that are instinctual or socially habituated. Experiencing themselves as anatomical, emotional, cognitive, and feeling beings is a revelation, but it is learning to use the Formative protocol of voluntary effort and muscular modeling that is the basic and essential tool for personal empowerment. It is the basis of sustainable behavioral change—and gives rise to the possibility of forming a personal life of meaning and satisfaction.

## References

Borges, J. L. (1962). *Ficciones [The circular ruins].* New York: Grove Press.

Keleman, S. (1987). *Embodying experience: Forming a personal life.* Berkeley, CA: Center Press.

# 64

## Visual Contact, Facing, Presence, and Expression

*The Ocular Segment in Body Psychotherapy*

Narelle McKenzie, Australia

**Editors' Note:** *This chapter was originally written in conjunction with John May, who has subsequently asked to be removed as an author, as his interests now lie in a different direction.*

**Narelle McKenzie,** MA, is a registered psychologist and accredited psychotherapist from Melbourne, Australia. She is the director and a senior trainer of the Australian Radix Training Centre and the Radix Institute, North America. In that capacity, she represents a classic Body Psychotherapeutic method that goes back to Charles Kelley and through him to Wilhelm Reich. Although the functional appreciation of the segments is an important element of this tradition in general, Dr. Kelley considered the ocular segment to be of particular importance. As a psychologist, he had specialized in the area of vision, and this specialization then became reflected in the critical role that he assigned to the ocular segment in the theory and practice of Radix work.

Throughout her professional career, Narelle has also devoted particular attention to the ocular segment. Like Kelley, she considered "presence" in the eyes to be a central diagnostic tool when deciding on how to progress and how to deepen work with clients, and the client's capacity for an easy pulsation of the life force in the eyes to be necessary for mind/body integration. Her theoretical perspective makes a link to Winnicott's notion of "the sparkle in the eye of the mother," which he regarded as very important. Narelle trained in and taught Developmental Psychology at universities in Australia and is heartened that her perspective on the significance of the eyes is validated by current findings in infant research that point to the central role of eye contact in the relationship of mother and child. Narelle has published a number of articles.

Wilhelm Reich (1945/1972) described several perspectives from which one could view the body-mind relationship. One was the "structural model," in which he described the muscular armor as organized into seven segments: ocular, oral, cervical, thoracic, diaphragmatic, abdominal, and pelvic. His pupils Baker (1967), Kelley (1975), and Lowen (1975) were all heavily influenced by this perspective. All shared the basic Reichian perspective that defined a segment as *". . . those organs and muscle groups which have a functional contact with one another and which are capable of accompanying each other in the emotional expressive movement"* (Reich, 1945/1972, p. 370). The life energy in the body was seen as flowing longitudinally through the body; tensions within these segments were seen as the action of the muscular armor to block the energy flow.

Thus, when one speaks of the ocular segment, one is speaking from Reich's structural model. One is also implying the existence of some sort of "economic model," concerned with the regulation and flow of some energy, or emotion, aliveness, activation, vitality, etc. It quickly becomes clear, however, that a number of other, different perspectives can be used to approach the role that the structures of the ocular segment have in daily functioning and in psychotherapy. Among these, two will be emphasized here: the functional model and the relational model. These models are not mutually exclusive, and they interact to provide a rich, textured description of the role the ocular segment plays in life and in Body Psychotherapy.

## A Structural Approach to the Ocular Segment

Reich was the first to define the ocular segment (Reich, 1945/1972, Chapter 14), and Lowen wrote on the importance of the eyes (Lowen, 1975, pp. 279ff.). But perhaps Chuck Kelley—a Certified Bates Method Teacher, an academic experimental psychologist who specialized in vision, and founder of the Radix Institute—emphasized the importance of the ocular segment more than any other Body Psychotherapist.

He defined the ocular segment by drawing a line from the base of the skull in back, where it joins the neck, along the sides of the skull, above the ears, above the temples, under the eyes, to the bridge of the nose. The region of the body above this line, including the internal spaces and organs, constituted the ocular segment (Kelley, 1998a). Kelley, Reich, and Baker regarded the ocular segment as the most externally directed of the body segments. Hence, they regarded work with the visual system as especially important in relational contact (especially at a distance) and for the reality function. *"Vision, broadly conceived, is the purpose function, the conceptual function, the function that looks ahead in space and time, looks to our future"* (Kelley, 1998c, p. 2). For Kelley, this was not only because of the role the eyes have, but also because major portions of the brain are located in this segment. Thus, he thought of the ocular segment in connection with internal events such as distortion, fantasy, imagination, and dreaming. He felt there was a powerful link between visual functioning and psychological functioning. He empirically demonstrated that psychological factors can have a role in visual problems, as well as the effectiveness of Body Psychotherapeutic techniques in ameliorating them, specifically myopia (Kelley, 1962).

More recently, Shapiro has made notable use of the connection between the eyes and mental processing in her EMDR approach. Although many clinicians today would agree that other types of movement can be substituted in that approach, there is no doubt that the importance of the ocular segment is recognized there (Shapiro and Forrest, 1997). The technique reminds one of the eye movements seen in the Bates Swings Technique incorporated into Radix by Kelley (1998a), and in the flashlight exercise originated by Barbara Goldenberg (cited in Baker, 1967, p. 68). In all of these approaches, work with the eyes is part of a program that affects a person's psychology.

Reich, Baker, Kelley, and Lowen all agreed that, from a structural perspective, one should "peel the onion," working from the external surface layers to the deeper internal layers. For Reich, Baker, and Kelley, this meant a top-down approach, emphasizing the ocular segment first. Kelley, in particular, felt that successfully working through blocks in the ocular segment is crucial to establishing a working relationship with the client, and that working on deeper material before one worked through blocks in the ocular segment actually intensified blocks there (Kelley, 1978).

## The Ocular Segment in Character Structure

The ocular segment can be used either as part of a system of character structure, or as a way of diagnosing it. Baker (1967) considered the ocular segment to be the first of four erogenous zones to be cathected by the developing infant. He also described an ocular character type containing several subtypes: schizophrenia, essential epilepsy, and voyeurism. Lowen felt that he could identify five character types by the typical look of the eyes:

* Schizoid character: The typical look can be described as vacant or unexpressive. It is the absence of feeling in the eyes that characterizes this personality . . .
* Oral character: The typical look is appealing—an appeal for love and support . . .
* Psychopathic character: Two looks are typical . . . One is the compelling or penetrating look seen in those individuals who have a need to control or dominate others . . . The other is the soft, seductive, or intriguing look that beguiles . . .
* Masochistic character: The typical look is one of suffering or pain. However, this is often masked by an expression of confusion . . .
* Rigid character: This personality generally has fairly strong, bright eyes. When the rigidity is marked, however, the eyes become hard without losing their brightness. (Lowen, 1975, pp. 285–286)

As a Bates Teacher, Kelley began a process of articulating sets of characteristics that were typically seen in hyperopes and myopes. He went on to develop a characterology that proposes three types, which were defined by which of the primary emotions that the structure seemed organized around blocking. He described the typical eyes of an "anger-blocking structure" as shiny but hard, immobilized, looking straight ahead, hyperopic, and possibly having a projective, bulging, piercing, or penetrating quality. They have a quality that seems alive to the therapist, as if the person is really there. The brows tend to be held downward and inward, as in a tiny bit of a frown (Kelley, 1998b). In a "fear-blocking structure," the eyes are myopic, wide open with dilated pupils, relatively lacking in tension, but also lacking in sparkle, having a quality that feels deadened to the therapist, as if the person may not really be there. The brows may be raised in a tension that runs up the forehead and over the scalp to the rear of the neck, adding to the wide-eyed effect (Kelley, 1975). And finally, the eyes of a typical "pain-blocking structure" were described as crinkling and pulling wide, if not closed and clinched (Ibid.).

It should be noted that the above ideas have not been adequately tested empirically. Thus, they should be used cautiously. Some Body Psychotherapists do not approach their work in the systematic, structural way described by Reich, Baker, Lowen, and Kelley, and thus do not emphasize the ocular segment in the way they did. For instance, one finds no reference to it in Kurtz's (1990) text on Hakomi, nor does one find it in Totton's (2003) introductory text on Body Psychotherapy. Nonetheless, this systematic structural approach is one of the founding contributions made by Body Psychotherapy. It continues to be useful in understanding how the body reacts, even when one does not apply a structural approach in one's work.

## A Functional and Relational Approach to the Ocular Segment

There is no comprehensive list of the functions in which the eyes play a central role. Obviously, the eyes are for seeing. But this is not as simple as it sounds. Seeing is thought to include much more than the automatic process outlined in medical texts by which light enters the eye, is processed into electrical impulses by the retina, and is transmitted via the optic nerve to the visual cortex. In contrast, one is truly "seeing" when one's thoughts, emotions, sensations, and general awareness are focused on what is happening in the present moment, in front of one's eyes, not on the past, nor the future. There seems to be an energy in the body, particularly in the eyes, that is pulsing and flowing. Consequently, consciousness easily shifts between our inner and outer worlds. One is present to oneself, connected inside, yet also in contact with what is happening in the surroundings. If one has learned to sense it, there can be a subjective sense of reaching out to the other with the eyes and also a letting in with the eyes. It is an active process, not static.

### Contact

One important function of the eyes is contact. We probably all know of times when we had eyes physically focused on another person or object, clearly saw the object (if the object was another person, perhaps we even made fleeting eye contact), processed information based on what was seen, and even took action, all the while not being "really there." This is basically a lack of contact. It is at least partially an ocular phenomenon involving issues of focus, convergence between the eyes, tensions in the muscles around and inside the eye, and other even more subtle energylike effects. Contact and its absence are often described subjectively. Contactful eyes can light up, seem bright, seem alive, dance, pierce, penetrate, search, devour, soak up, invite, be receptive, be warm, or be inviting. They can be deep, limpid pools. Contactless eyes seem dead, lifeless, dull, vacant, staring, or distracted.

There are at least two potential objects one may contact: the inner world (self) and the external world (others). Most people need a balance of contact between these two. One can interfere with the other, however. Too much contact out through the eyes can cause one to lose contact with oneself, and vice versa (McKenzie, 1999). In addition, the issue of contact with others raises the issue of boundaries. To be able to make contact with others through the eyes, one must also be able to create boundaries with the eyes. Unbounded eye contact can be intense; too much can be overwhelming. Consider the following vignette:

> As I (McKenzie) anticipated my first meeting with Ian, a 40-year old medical student, I expected that he would find eye contact easy. But this was not the case. Within minutes of sitting down, Ian started to "go away." His eyes had a vacant stare, and he started to squirm. He was caught between trying to look calm, in control, and feeling that the direct eye contact with me was too overwhelming. We talked about this process and worked with it. He moved around the room exploring different distances and postures in relation to me, and he had me move around in a similar way. Finally it ended with us sitting opposite each other at a fair distance but with Ian holding a large soft toy rabbit in his lap, around which he would both peek and hide as he shared his history with me. Ian was able to use the stuffed rabbit to create the boundary he needed, but in his everyday life where no rabbit was available, he would go blank in the eyes to create the same boundary.

In addition, external contact proceeds in two directions: one comes out through the eyes to contact the other, but also allows the other in through the eyes to contact oneself. The eyes have such an important role in this function that we have the saying *"The eyes are the mirrors of the soul."* Davis reminds us that being seen is not a passive process, but active *". . . in the sense that one is present and receptive . . . One must stay present with oneself and be available to contact with the other. If you are not in contact with yourself, how is it possible to show yourself—to be seen . . . It is like having something locked away in the attic, inviting someone over, standing at the front door with them (not letting them past the eyes) and expecting them to know what is in the attic"* (Davis, 1988, p. 2).

Another client of mine (McKenzie) had learned at a young age not to let people know that they mattered to her. When she started therapy, it became obvious that when she felt emotionally touched or started to feel more intimate, her eyes would glaze over and she would put on a poker face. With time she learned how to soften her eyes and let others in when she felt strongly connected, knowing that she could restore the barriers when she needed to.

Assessing and establishing the level of contact that matches what the client can tolerate are important therapeutic tasks that must occur early in the work. Too much contact, and the client may be frightened and overwhelmed (as in the vignette with Ian above). Too little, and the client will feel abandoned, unable to connect, or that the therapist isn't really contacting what needs to be contacted (as in the vignette with Patti below). Cultural variations in eye contact also need to be considered: for instance, depending on status and position in the tribe, eye contact can be taboo among Australian aborigines. Additionally, underbounded clients and clients with a history of trauma often find eye contact early in the therapy to be too intense.

It can be useful to work actively and consciously on manipulating the amount of contact in session. Clients can move around, choose how they want to sit or orient themselves, decide if they want something to hold in their lap or across their chest, cover their eyes and peek through their fingers, decide if they want a blanket or other wrap to cover themselves, position us (the therapist) in the room, and tell us how they want us to look at them (or sometimes, away from them).

Sandra, a client of mine (May) felt the need to hide, but to have me present. She sat behind a large chair in my office, surrounded by a bookcase, table, and curtain. She made contact with me by sticking her hand out through a gap and having me hold it. It re-created for her a scene from her childhood when she often hid in this way at home. But in those instances, she desperately missed someone who would make contact with her in the way she needed.

On the other hand, Patti needed just the reverse. She came to me (May) from two previous therapies where she had felt unable to connect with the therapists at the level she needed. Our exploration of how she wanted to sit, look at me, and have me look at her took parts of several sessions, resulting in the two of us sitting closely side by side, facing opposite directions. This was a much closer, more intimate arrangement than I would have chosen, but it fit her needs and her work has proceeded productively from there.

If given no attention, these various negotiations will occur unconsciously. But if done mindfully, they reinforce clients' contact with self; they begin the process of learning adaptive ways of seeing and of regulating contact. In addition, they send a powerful and important message regarding the therapeutic relationship: *"You (the client) don't have to ignore what is actually going on here in order to have a relationship with me (the therapist). Your needs deserve a response. You don't have to protect the two of us from seeing how interacting with me makes you feel. In fact, I am interested in it, and willing to help you with it as I can."* Of course, the paradox is that such negotiations about seeing mean that the therapist sees something that has previously been hidden. In that sense, even these negotiations contain the potential to be too intense, or possibly shaming. Thus, they need to be managed with sensitivity.

## Expression and Containment

A second important function played by the eyes is the expression of a wide range of emotions. The emotional importance of the face—and of the eyes, in particular—has been widely discussed ever since Darwin's (1872) The Expression of the Emotions in Man and Animals. This may be partially because the face is a part of the body easily open to observation by others. Baker, Lowen, and Kelley all emphasized the role of the eyes in emotional expression. Kelley, in particular, thought that, although all segments of the body could express the basic emotions, the higher one went in the body, the more refined the expression. The eyes, in particular, could express *". . . typical or unique feelings that have a cerebral component. The eyes express not only anger, fear, pain, and their opposites, they show suspicion, amusement, detachment, contempt, pride, and dozens of others"* (Kelley, 1998a).

The reverse of expression is containment. Whereas early Body Psychotherapeutic traditions tended to emphasize emotional discharge, recent work has also emphasized the importance of containment, modulation, centering, and grounding (e.g., McKenzie, 2001). Often, people withdraw from the eyes when experiencing powerful feelings; and when they do, these feelings can easily become escalated and unfocused. Consciously learning to keep the ocular segment focused and in contact with others can be very helpful to such clients.

For instance, before seeing me (McKenzie), Geoff was capable of expressing anger very fully, yet he never felt a sense of completion, release, or re-regulation. When he expressed anger, he seldom inhaled and his eyes glazed over. I encouraged him to imagine that his anger was located in one small part of his body (he chose his left hand). Then I helped him establish a particular rhythm of breathing, pushing into the mat with his left hand, and expressing his anger out through his eyes to me. Although the expression of his anger became much more contained, I experienced it as far more focused and effective. It took many attempts before he could actually experience what it meant to express anger with his eyes. When he succeeded, he experienced a much greater sense of completion, release, and re-regulation than from his previous escalated and unfocused tantrums.

## Imagery and Fantasy

As previously noted, some people have difficulty connecting to the real world through their eyes, and dissociation from the eyes is one way in which this difficulty occurs. Another occurs when the inner process becomes overconnected to fantasy. Leslie, one of my (McKenzie's) clients, had powerful expectations and fantasies about how her close friends should act, and her behavior often related to these fantasies rather than to the actual reality. She was constantly frustrated. We explored this by having her role-play three of these people. The key work came as she imagined actually looking with her eyes and describing the specifics of what she saw, rather than connecting to the usual expectations. She began to see her friends as they actually were.

Others, however, have difficulty generating and connecting to images, fantasies, and dreams. This is a powerful deficit that greatly impoverishes inner life. In Chapter 80, "Subsymbolic Processing with an Alexithymic Client," May describes and analyzes a piece of work with such a client. In addition, doing fantasy work in session can help clients practice developing and connecting to their inner world. An important element in such work is working to help the client gain the inner sense of actually connecting with the visual images rather than just watching them from a distance.

## Development

It has primarily been outside of Body Psychotherapy that the importance of the eyes for the psychological development of children has been most studied. According to Kohut, the founder of Psychoanalytic Self Psychology, "mirroring," including the lighting up of parental eyes with delight in the child, establishes one of the poles of a healthy self. The child, through repeated exposure, comes to internalize the approving eyes as the origin of self-esteem (Kohut, 1984). Similar negative internalizations occur when the child is repeatedly exposed to hostile, critical, or shaming eyes.

Additionally, a substantial literature has suggested that emotional regulation is an interpersonal process as well as intrapersonal. Direct infant observation by Stern, Beebe, Tronick, and others has demonstrated that this emotional regulation occurs between mother and child through nonverbal affective displays occurring over fractions of seconds, forming a complex, mutually regulating process (Stern, 1984; Beebe and Lachmann, 2002; Tronick, 1989). Schore (1994) has discussed the role that these mutually regulating interactions have in the creation of the self and the neurological networks supporting it. All of the above-mentioned authors recognize the central role of the eyes. Schore (1994) has even speculated about a specific ocular developmental need to see a glint in the mother's eyes. Love activates the parasympathetic nervous system, which dilates the iris, allowing light to enter and be reflected off the retina—the same mechanism that causes a cat's eyes to shine in the dark. As discussed above, it seems that such a glint is a much more complex phenomenon.

Recently, in his book *The Science of the Art of Psychotherapy,* Schore (2012) confirms the significance of the eyes and the ocular segment for early social and emotional development. He states, *"Through visual-facial, auditory-prosodic, and tactile-gestural communications, caregiver and infant learn the rhythmic structure of the other and modify their behavior to fit that structure, thereby co-creating a specifically fitted interaction"* (p. 56); and later, *"During mutual gaze episodes of bodily based affective communications, the spatiotemporal patterning of the primary caregiver's exogenous sensory stimulation is synchronized with the spontaneous expressions of the infant's endogenous organismic rhythms"* (p. 264).

Later, when addressing the neurobiology of relational trauma, Schore (2012) discusses the process of dissociation: *". . . a second later-forming reaction to infant trauma is seen in dissociation, in which the child disengages from stimuli in the external world and attends to an 'internal' world. Traumatized infants are observed to be 'staring off into space with a glazed look'"* (p. 266).

These developmental theories have been entering Body Psychotherapy through the work of several authors, including Cornell (1997, 2004), Downing (1997), Marlock and Weiss (2001), and Pitzal (1999). How are these developmental and mutual regulatory processes affected by dead or lifeless eyes that are unable to sustain eye contact, or that are chronically piercing and frozen in hostility? Weinberg and Tronick (1998) suggested that the deadened faces of depressed mothers may be harmful to the development of their children, but until recently there have been no direct studies involving the eyes.

This gap appears to be being addressed with Schore's (and others') research work on the functioning of the right and left brain. With respect to visual-facial attachment communications, it is now established that mutual gaze is critical to early social development (Trevarthen and Aitken, 2001). The development of the capacity to efficiently process information from faces requires visual input to the right (and not left) hemisphere during infancy (Le Grand et al., 2003). At two months of age, the onset of a critical period during which synaptic connections in the developing occipital cortex are modified by visual experience (Yamada et al., 2000), infants show right-hemispheric activation when exposed to a woman's face (Schore, 2012, p. 344).

All of the above suggests that healthy development in the child may be enhanced through contact with healthy, alive eyes in the parent—eyes capable of intense contact but that also have boundaries; eyes capable of reading, joining in, and reflecting the emotional state of the child; eyes capable of freely expressing the love and delight the parent feels toward the child. One can only speculate that such mutually related ocular engagement between therapist and client is equally significant for the healing process.

## References

Baker, E. (1967). *Man in the trap: The causes of blocked sexual energy.* New York: Avon Books.

Beebe, B., & Lachmann, F. (2002). *Infant research and adult treatment: Co-constructing interactions.* Hillsdale, NJ: Analytic Press.

Cornell, W. F. (1997). If Reich had met Winnicott: Body and gesture. *Energy & Character, 28*(2), 50–60.

Cornell, W. F. (2004). Entering the relational field in Body Psychotherapy. In G. Marlock & H. Weiss (Eds.), *Handbuch der Körperpsychotherapie* [Handbook of Body Psychotherapy]. Stuttgart: Schattauer.

Darwin, C. R. (1872). *The expression of the emotions in man and animals.* London: John Murray.

Davis, W. (1988). *Seeing and being seen: Collection of papers.* California: Author.

Downing, G. (1997). *Korper und Wort in Psychotherapie* [Body and word in psychotherapy]. Munich: Kösel.

Kelley, C. R. (1962). Psychological factors in myopia. *Journal of the American Optometric Association, 33*(11).

Kelley, C. R. (1975). *Opening the feelings: The functional approach.* Radix Institute Training Program. Albuquerque, NM: Radix Institute.

Kelley, C. R. (1978). *Orgonomy, Bioenergetics and Radix: The Reichian movement today.* Self-published book available from: Kelley Radix, 13715 SE 36th St., Vancouver, WA 98684.

Kelley, C. R. (1998a). *Seminar 9: The ocular segment.* Radix Institute Training Program. Albuquerque, NM: Radix Institute.

Kelley, C. R. (1998b). *Seminar 20: Functional approach: Anger and love.* Radix Institute Training Program. Albuquerque, NM: Radix Institute.

Kelley, C. R. (1998c). *Seminar 27: Vision and sexuality: Functional integration.* Radix Institute Training Program. Albuquerque, NM: Radix Institute.

Kohut, H. (1984). *How analysis cures.* Chicago: University of Chicago Press.

Kurtz, R. (1990). *Body-Centered Psychotherapy: The Hakomi Method.* Mendocino, CA: LifeRhythm.

Le Grand, R., Mondloch, C. J., Maurer, D., & Brent, H. P. (2003). Impairment in holistic face processing following early visual deprivation. *Psychological Science, 15(11),* 762–768.

Lowen, A. (1975). *Bioenergetics.* New York: Coward, McCaan & Geoghegan.

Marlock, G., & Weiss, H. (2001). In search of the embodied self. In M. Heller (Ed.), *The flesh of the soul: The body we work with.* Bern, Switzerland: Peter Lang.

McKenzie, N. (1999). Our eyes: Windows of the soul, shields from the world, integrators of life. In L. Glenn & R. Muller-Schwefe (Eds.), *The Radix reader.* Albuquerque, NM: Radix Institute.

McKenzie, N. (2001). *The therapeutic goals and basic concepts of Radix work.* Radix Institute Training Program. Albuquerque, NM: Radix Institute.

Pitzal, W. (1999). Contact and relationship. In L. Glenn & R. Muller-Schwefe (Eds.), *The Radix reader.* Albuquerque, NM: Radix Institute.

Reich, W. (1945/1972). *Character analysis* (3rd ed.). New York: Touchstone Books.

Schore, A. (1994). *Affect regulation and the origin of the self.* Mahwah, NJ: Lawrence Erlbaum.

Schore, A. (2012). *The science of the art of psychotherapy.* New York: W. W. Norton.

Shapiro, F., & Forrest, M. (1997). *EMDR: The breakthrough therapy for overcoming anxiety, stress, and trauma.* New York: Basic Books.

Stern, D. (1984). *The interpersonal world of the infant: A view from psychoanalysis and Developmental Psychology.* New York: Basic Books.

Totton, N. (2003). *Body Psychotherapy: An introduction.* Maidenhead, UK: Open University Press.

Trevarthen, C., & Aitken, K. J. (2001). Infant intersubjectivity: Research, theory and clinical applications. *Journal of Child Psychology and Psychiatry and Allied Disciplines, 42(1), 3–48.*

Tronick, E. (1989). Emotions and emotional communication in infants. *American Psychologist, 44*(2), 112–119.

Weinberg, M. K., & Tronick, E. (1998). The impact of maternal psychiatric illness on infant development. *Journal of Clinical Psychiatry, 59(Suppl. 2), 53–61.*

Yamada, H., Sadato, N., Konishi, Y., Muramoto, S., Kimura, K., Tanaka, M., et al. (2000). A milestone for normal development of the infantile brain detected by functional MRI. *Neurology, 55, 218–223.*

# 65
# Segmental Holding Patterns of the Body-Mind

### Jack Lee Rosenberg and Beverly Kitaen Morse, United States

**Jack Lee Rosenberg,** PhD, is a psychotherapist who was initially trained in dentistry. He has had a close relationship to the Esalen Institute (Big Sur, California), where he has been teaching since the 1970s. At Esalen, he witnessed the work of and studied with colleagues who were foundational in the Human Potential Movement: Fritz Perls, Abraham Maslow, Alexander Lowen, John Pierrakos, Rollo May, Carl Rogers, Moshe Feldenkrais, and Ida Rolf.

From 1968 to 1973, he was a training therapist at the Gestalt Institute in San Francisco, and the first name he gave to his work was "Gestalt Body Psychotherapy." Through a series of books, trainings, and workshops over many years, he has made his approach become one of the most renowned methods of the field. His method of Integrative Body Psychotherapy (IBP) embraces psychoanalysis, object-relations theory, Gestalt and Reichian therapy, Bioenergetics, Self Psychology, the Feldenkrais Method, Transpersonal Psychotherapy, and Eastern philosophies and practices.

Today, there are IBP institutes in North America, Canada, and Europe. The focus of Jack's work is on individuals, relationships, sexuality, and release techniques for holding patterns in the body-mind, which are somatically based on energetic and psychological models. Dr. Rosenberg was on the faculty of the first department of dental psychology at the University of California Dental School, where he was teaching and doing research. He is the founder and clinical director of the Rosenberg-Kitaen Integrative Body Psychotherapy Central Institute in Los Angeles and teaches the IBP method that he developed worldwide. He is the author of *Body, Self, and Soul* and *Total Orgasm*. He wrote this chapter in collaboration with his partner, Dr. Beverly Kitaen Morse. Together they elucidate how psychological holding patterns can be active in the different segments of the body, and by what means they can be released.

**Beverly Kitaen Morse,** PhD, works as a Somatic Psychotherapist and trainer, and is vice president and executive director of the Rosenberg-Kitaen Integrative Body Psychotherapy Central Institute in Los Angeles. Aside from training in Body Psychotherapy, she is informed by trainings in Gestalt Therapy and Self Psychology. Over the years, she has specialized in couples therapy and human sexuality—subjects that she has taught at Ryokan College, Los Angeles. She has co-authored a book on these topics, *The Intimate Couple,* with Dr. Jack Lee Rosenberg.

Morse has played a significant role in the development of IBP. She also has a private practice in Santa Monica, California, and teaches as a trainer in Los Angeles, at the Esalen Institute, and in other locations in North America, Canada, and Europe.

## Holding Patterns

Important grounding assumptions of Body Psychotherapy are: the emotional memories that are stored in the brain and throughout the body influence how we view our self, one another, and the world; they influence how we feel, move, breathe, walk, make love, and dance. These memories, shaped by what we have learned from our generational themes, what happened to us, and what we have observed, traumatic or nurturing, form our belief system, our way of being. Our habitual beliefs, fears, longings, and behaviors are not held just in our brain alone. They form repetitive patterns throughout the body. When repetitive patterns support our natural full functioning, we tend to feel a sense of integration in our body. In this state, we experience a sense of well-being and resilience, heightened and fulfilling aliveness. It forms clarity of knowing, and a stabilized sense of self. Some repetitive patterns, however, do not support our full function and well-being. When these faulty patterns cause us to tighten, shut down, or dissociate, they can become interruptive to our well-being and full functioning. When repetitive patterns become rigid, they form holding patterns that disrupt our natural somatic functions.

Holding patterns can retain and rigidify faulty beliefs, fears, and responses to archaic emotional or physical injuries. Holding patterns can create areas of the body that are emotionally or physically numbed, therefore inhibiting awareness and full and fluid functioning. Most rigid holding patterns are due to emotional and/or physical trauma. By dividing the body into segments, we can more easily identify these embodied emotional traumas and the emotional and physical repetitive patterns that they perpetuate.

To clarify our inner guiding voice, holding patterns and the information that they retain must be brought into awareness and resolved. Otherwise, when we look inside for guidance to make sense of our everyday life experiences, we are more likely to be informed by lingering embodied (often traumatic) memories than by a clear, well-founded perspective. Early traumas to the body and mind classically influence our perceptions of events and of other people, particularly in our interpersonal relationships.

Attachment theory, as illustrated by Daniel Siegel (1999), who is a leading attachment theory representative, emphasizes that the foundation for our emotional development takes place through relationship to our primary caregivers in the first years of our life, perhaps even *in utero* (Siegel, 1999). Most Body Psychotherapists have long believed that our body-mind holding patterns are also laid down at this time. Yet, the ramifications show up in our everyday life even today.

If a holding pattern in any segment of the body is constricted, we are not able to identify our subtle inner feelings. For example, if we are stressed at work and our chest is constricted, when we come home to our intimate partner, we are not likely to be able to feel our subtle emotions of love and tenderness. If our pelvis becomes constricted, we are not likely to feel sexual, particularly loving sexuality. We may believe that the problem is a loss of love, rather than notice that our body has become temporarily constricted and numbed because of a nonassociated stress.

As we prepare to discuss these body-mind segments and their holding patterns, we must first point out that—as Body Psychotherapists—our center of attention is not exclusively focused on the individual body segments; it relates primarily to the whole person. Working with the body, mind, and soul, in an integrated fashion, is what makes Body Psychotherapy so effective and profound.

> People make distinctions between thought and emotion in the same way they make distinctions between the mind and body. However, despite our deeply ingrained assumptions, these distinctions don't actually exist. Body, thought, and emotions are intimately bound together through intricate networks, and function as a whole unit to enrich our knowing. (Hannaford, 1995)

Inflexible emotional patterns are "held" in the body, and these rigid body patterns affect the mind. Psychological themes represent and perpetuate holding patterns in the body. This interlinking perpetuates the person's emotional patterns and limits any interior exploration or spiritual quest. Body-mind-spiritual patterns are reciprocal. For every holding pattern, there are psychological, emotional, somatic, and spiritual-existential components. All these components are important aspects with which to work.

## The Release of Holding Patterns

Chronic holding patterns, both physical and psychological, can cause dysfunction and disorder, and can even lead to disease in the body. A muscular holding pattern may inhibit a segment of the body from operating normally, not allowing it to fulfill its purpose or function. A therapist can help a client to release these (mainly muscular) holding patterns. There are many approaches, which include: awareness through verbal-cognitive means; self-release systems; a therapist's direct manipulation of muscular and energetic holding patterns; and applied stress exercise movement techniques.

Some holding patterns are transient and situational. These are rather more easily released when the psychological-emotional component is addressed. Others are more chronic, and these are not so easily amenable to release. For instance, the release of early pelvic holding patterns often involves a complex understanding of development and early psychological and emotional attachment injuries that formed the patterns and that have been compounded by later traumatic events.

Such chronic holding patterns often require release techniques that physically soften the fixed muscular pattern. After many years of experimentation, we concluded that the less a therapist physically touches the body in order to bring about the physical and emotional release, the more productive the therapeutic process. Therefore, awareness and self-release techniques that include breath and movement are now generally applied before any physical, hands-on release techniques are used. These less invasive techniques tend to empower the client and do not create a dependent transference.

Although chronic holding patterns can sometimes be physically released, often quickly and dramatically, the emotions released can become overwhelming and therefore act to fortify the pattern further. This can render a holding pattern inaccessible to change. Therefore, it is best to release these patterns physically, with caution, in phases that allow for the exploration and emotional integration of the repressed material that is made accessible through the release.

In the early 1960s, when Body Psychotherapy was reintroduced to the Western world, most therapists focused primarily on the release of "energy," as Reich called it. This was done with the belief that energetic release alone could create or initiate a healing process. And indeed, these openings of the body often did create a marvelous release and a sense of well-being . . . for a limited period of time. With experience, we have found that physical release alone is not sufficiently productive. When the emotional and psychological components are not simultaneously attended to, and linked to generational and developmental themes to form a coherent narrative, the physical openings often become severely fixed. Thus, the holding patterns of the (original) trauma, and the subsequent (distorted) emotional, relational patterns, can often become retraumatized and reinforced by the lack of emotional release: we build layer upon layer of repression.

Fixed holding patterns in the body are an attempt to provide a form of protection from the original trauma. They can mute the offending emotions and sensations, and they can sustain the protective strategies. Therefore, a major problem experienced is that the release of a fixed holding pattern can leave a person feeling very vulnerable, often in despair, emotionally naked, and alone. Any such body openings made without professional psychological support, attunement, and an understanding of the person's interior structure can "drop" a client into a deep well of fragmenting regression. They may find themselves floundering, almost drowning, in the wake of re-experiencing the powerful emotions, thoughts, fears, beliefs, and behaviors surrounding the old trauma or injury. The disturbance of these "protective" holding patterns can also leave an already internally fragile person without their necessary or habitual defenses. This can be terrifying to the client and sometimes also to the therapist.

Body Psychotherapy is an approach with powerful techniques: and these therefore inevitably carry some risks (see Chapter 57, "Risks within Body Psychotherapy" by Courtenay Young). We must be aware of who can benefit from and tolerate this work, and who can't. We must know how to respect and support, rather than overwhelm, a fragile sense of self. We now know that for each opening, we must help our client sustain an interior sense of stability or constancy. When a holding pattern is released, so is the energy that has been "locked up" in it, or that has been used to "hold on" for so long. These restrictions have limited our energy, and thus this released energy, albeit beneficial, can initially feel quite overwhelming. When our entire body is reasonably limber, toned, and alive, the potential amount of energy that it can contain is greatly expanded. This energy is then available for feelings of a sense of self, well-being, health, and aliveness. As we age, we can no longer afford to waste our energy on outgrown, unnecessary holding patterns.

It may be worth noting here that energetic patterns can also be "held" within the soft inner tissues of the body, as well as in the muscles (see Keleman, 1983).

## The Segments of the Body

Using a segmental approach helps us to visualize and organize the types of injuries and their resultant holding patterns held in the body-mind. Wilhelm Reich was the first in the Western world to lay out a segmental system of the body when working with psychological themes. Although developed independently, his system of seven segments correspond somewhat to the Eastern "chakra" system of Kundalini Yoga practices. However, the Reichian segments are based more on the physical holding patterns, even though they also include concepts of energy. Chakras can be seen more as ways of "being" in the world, and their energy as somewhat more transcendent. Reich believed that these holding patterns contained muscular constrictions, which he called "armoring." Armoring limits or reduces breathing, movement, feeling, and expression, and perpetuates psychological attitudes and dysfunctions. It can change the flow of energy, causing those areas of the body to lack, or exaggerate, feelings and sensations.

We unconsciously protectively armor ourselves in many different ways. Armoring can take the physical form of becoming too fat, too muscular, too tight, or too thin. All are attempts to hide our feelings away. These protective coverings can feel cold, hot, flaccid, rigid, tense, dry, moist, tender, or numb. Reich also believed that muscular constrictions are the historical and cultural indications of our psychological and physical experiences. He theorized that the body is "organized" into seven lateral segments:

- Ocular: eyes, eyebrows, and forehead
- Oral: mouth and chin
- Cervical: neck, throat, shoulders, and upper chest
- Thoracic: upper chest, arms, hands, heart, lungs, and upper back
- Diaphragmatic: lower chest, midback, diaphragm, and solar plexus
- Abdominal: lumbar area, stomach, and colon
- Pelvic: buttocks, anus, genitals, ovaries, uterus, legs, and feet

It is not difficult for a therapist to heighten the level of aliveness or energy felt in the client's body, or to move energy from one segment of the body to another. A lack of energy or movement in any part of the body can originate

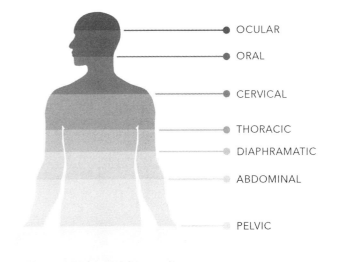

from two opposite types of body defenses: one is "hyper-," an increased holding of tension in the area; the other is "hypo-," a lack of muscular tension or tone in the segment. When a particular segment is released, it is best to keep in mind a whole-body concept—and work as well with the associated or adjoining segments in order to maintain the openness and the flow of energy and to prevent the holding pattern from re-forming.

All the body segments are connected, with varying degrees of interdependence. Many common holding patterns are not adjacent, but act in a reciprocal fashion. With the following conditions, for example, interdependent segments must be worked with for positive results:

- **Eyes–feet:** The more present we are (with our eyes), the more grounded we will be (with our feet and legs) and vice versa.
- **Neck–pelvis:** Holding in one segment may cause a block in the other, and releasing one can release or tighten the other.
- **Head–heart:** Sometimes people can think very well but can't feel their emotions, or the other way around.
- **Head–heart–pelvis:** When these are not balanced, they will affect our sexuality and intimate relationships.
- **Anterior–posterior (front/back split):** Holding in the pelvic segment—the anus, for instance—will affect genital holding patterns and vice versa.
- **Right–left or top–bottom:** These splits can make one feel off-balance, stronger, weaker, or more sensitive on one side than the other.
- **Ticklish areas:** These are usually an indication of a holding pattern; these can be in just one area of the body.

Working on one part of a reciprocal pattern affects the other part(s). In fact, a block that is holding emotional trauma may be more resistant to letting go because of a fear of the release of uncomfortable feelings. Therefore, it can be more effectively released by working with a reciprocal holding pattern. For example, a neck or throat block can indicate a pelvic block. If the trauma is held in the pelvis, the block may be more effectively released by working with the less vulnerable neck and throat. Then again, if a tenacious block is held in place to maintain an emotional or psychological "speed limit," or emotional "set point," releasing one end of the block, such as the neck, can actually cause the other end, the pelvis, to close down. One function of almost any block is to maintain homeostasis, or to preserve the status quo. Therefore, for any change to transpire, especially the release of both blocks, the underlying or originating psychological component must be resolved.

**First Segment, Band 1: Top of Head and Forehead**

The first (uppermost) segment (sometimes called the "ocular segment") can be considered as being divided into two bands: Band 1, the top of the head, the forehead, the scalp, and the back of the head; and Band 2, the eyes. A fascial sheath runs from the forehead *frontalis* muscle, attaching to the scalp, running over the top of the head, attaching to the *occipitalis* muscle located at the back of the head. Thus, both *frontalis* and *occipitalis* muscles influence the nature of the expression and function of the eyes.

Another muscle in this band is the *temporalis,* which fans up the side of the head. It is one of five muscles used to close the jaw (oral segment). It is possible to keep this muscle tight even when the jaw is relaxed. Holding in the *temporalis* can make the eyes (Band 2) look hard, even if one doesn't feel angry. Anger or resentment may be felt with the release of the *temporalis* muscle.

Emotions associated with the contraction of the forehead include: wondering, worrying, perplexity, despair, intense forms of thinking, and feelings of suffocation, overwhelm, or fear of "blowing one's top." A releasing in Band 1 allows the client to move some of the energy in the holding pattern down into Band 2 (the eyes).

**First Segment, Band 2: Eyes**

The eyes are probably the most exciting place to work, because this is where the sense of aliveness, soul, and being can shine through (Rosenberg et al., 1985). Opening this segment first allows the client to make some emotional contact with the therapist. It also allows a client to see the world in an emotional "technicolor," rather than in polarized black and white.

Ocular communication functions in two ways: the eyes take in what they see, or they send out feelings from within. Certain blockages are deeper and more chronic; others are more superficial. The eyes are very private, sometimes called "the windows of the soul." A glazed look is usually more temporary and superficial; and a deadened, flat look is often deeper and more "guarded." The deadness is often a sign of an early developmental trauma. When these bands are relieved, pent-up emotions can be released, and the eyes become more open for expression, compassion, or love, including erotic expression and aliveness. Reich often talked about "softening" the eyes.

### Oral Segment: Mouth, Jaw, and Chin

For an infant, from immediately after birth, the mouth is the part of the body that makes the first significant contacts with the world. The mouth has many functions, including nourishment, respiration, expression, and aggression. It can also be considered to be a sexual organ. Our mouth is also associated with biting, spitting, gagging, swallowing, and sucking. With our mouth, we cry, laugh, smile, eventually talk, and express attitudes of dependency or holding on. The major muscle circling the mouth is the *orbicularis oris*. This muscle and several smaller ones attached are responsible for moving the mouth and for many expressions of emotion.

The action of sucking (and all the associated lip movements) may produce a number of longings, and may also stimulate feelings of aggression or sexuality; it may also soothe, or comfort, depending on one's early state-bound experiences. Biting and chewing can heighten expressions of aggression. The muscles at the floor of the mouth and in the throat influence "swallowing." Metaphorically, this can connect to a swallowing of toxic or pleasant substances (and the emotions attached to these), or a swallowing of expressions of one's self. It may cause an inability to receive nurturing, or even information. The mouth can hold expressions of sadness or hurt, by pulling the muscles at the corner of the mouth down. The *masseter* muscles of the jaw often hold anger, defiance, stubbornness, and attitudes of maintaining control. The *mentalis* muscle of the chin participates in crying. It quivers; expresses worry, doubt, dismay, gloom, and can even engender pity in others.

With awareness, facial muscles can break down the false self or "mask" of emotional holding. The facade of a fixed smile, disgust, omnipotence, or powerlessness, when released, may reveal more of the longings underneath than some clients can handle easily.

Touching the face directly affects the efferent fibers that go to the brain. It profoundly stimulates the brain, directly arousing emotional responses. This is why it is such an affront to be hit in the face, or so emotional when one's face is touched in a caring fashion. Unlike other parts of the body, the muscles of the face are attached directly to the skin without a fascial layer for protection. For this reason, kissing and stroking are more intensely felt on the face.

### Cervical Segment: Neck, Throat, and Upper Shoulders

The muscles of the throat are important because of the reciprocal relationship between the throat and pelvic blocks. Throat blocks are often a result of early emotional injuries, due to attitudes of repression, invasion of boundaries, or sexual (or other) instances of pelvic distress. A block in the cervical segment, or throat, can often be heard in the sound of the voice, or the quality of the breath. Because the throat and neck hold many vital and sensitive structures—including the jugular veins, the carotid arteries, the thyroid and parathyroids, and the *carotid sinus* that regulates blood pressure—it is best not to do any muscular releases in the front part of the neck: there are also often emotions associated with strangulation, or attack, located here. A much firmer pressure can, however, be used on the back of the neck.

### Thoracic Segment: Chest, Upper Back, and Arms

The thoracic segment, or the chest area, is known as the home of the heart—the doorway to the sense of self, the witness, the "I am" experience, the site of well-being, compassion, love, joy, and empathy. In opening the body, the eyes are first released for contact and presence. Next, in order to build any sort of real interpersonal relationship, the release of the heart area, the thoracic segment, is essential (Rosenberg and Morse, 1996). Releasing the thoracic segment, in conjunction with breath, opens the way for emotions to flow more freely: these can include trust. It is always a good idea for trust to be firmly established before any attempt is made to open up any other segments, particularly in the pelvic area. This softening of the heart allows the other segments to open more easily.

The thoracic segment extends from the diaphragm (in the front) to the scapulae (shoulder blades) in the back. It includes the lungs, heart, and rib cage. The arms and the hands are extensions and are used primarily for reaching out, holding, defending, and doing. Major muscles in this segment are the *intercostal* muscles (between the ribs), the *pectoralis major* and *minor,* the *latissimus dorsi, rhomboids, trapezius,* and *teres major* and *minor.* These are relatively easily identified[65] and form a complex set of interconnected muscles around the upper half of the torso.

An injured or "broken" heart might engender sadness, longings, pity, pain, and sorrow. People who breathe shallowly, and "hold in" their chest, tend to lack energy and depth of emotion. Remember, as in the other segments, the holding goes all the way around, so the back part of the same segment must also be taken into consideration. Muscle spasms or knots in the back can represent holding back or a carrying of burdens. The back and chest often express attitudes of self-esteem, or a protective mode. A concave chest can express a "giving-up," and a puffed-up chest can indicate an attempt to bolster one's self-image. Rounded shoulders can indicate an overburdening of emotions.

## Diaphragmatic Segment: Lower Chest and Diaphragm

The diaphragm is directly related to the regulation of our breathing patterns, and to the level and flow of our energetic aliveness and emotions. It is important to the whole organism that the diaphragm moves freely. The diaphragm, and its movement through breath, is where the autonomic and the central nervous systems coincide. Because the breathing function is both automatic and controllable, the diaphragmatic segment is the best place of access for influencing the autonomic nervous system through one's breath and movement. The diaphragm is a broad, flat, sheetlike muscle that originates at the rib cage and attaches to the spinal column. It functionally divides the top and bottom halves of the body. Certain types of Yoga and breathing techniques, such as those taught to professional wind-instrument musicians and opera singers, can strengthen or even "armor" the diaphragm. Deep diaphragmatic blocks are very common and are relatively resistant to change. Holding in the diaphragm can cause pain and nausea. At times, it can also produce a pain in the chest, similar to that felt with coronary artery disease.

When experiencing anxiety, people often hold their breath and tighten their diaphragm, reducing or eliminating uncomfortable "gut" feelings in the belly and possible sexual feelings in the pelvis, creating a split between the heart and the pelvis (loving and sexual feelings) so they are not felt at the same time. When this somatic body/mind split is not resolved, one cannot love the person they feel sexual toward, and they can't feel sexual toward the one they love. When anxieties are not dealt with, they can become internalized and create stress.

Many people hold their breath during sexual arousal, thereby decreasing their ability to build excitement and feel pleasure. This diaphragmatic holding pattern cuts off feelings in the pelvis. Some push down with the diaphragm to force an orgasm, or pull the diaphragm up to refrain from releasing into orgasm (Rosenberg, 1973).

## Abdominal Segment: Major Intestinal Organs

The abdominal segment runs from the diaphragm to the pelvis. The primary muscle, the *rectus abdominis,* shields and stimulates many vital organs beneath it. This is a most vulnerable and unprotected segment. Many emotions are stored here, and to avoid uncomfortable feelings, both positive and negative, people often tighten these muscles.

---

65   See also: www.innerbody.com/anatomy/muscular/upper-torso.

Tightening in one side will affect the other. The abdomen holds deep, strong, "gut" emotions: hunger, longings, assertion, aggression, anger, and the deep, sobbing tears of sadness. Stress felt in this area can cause digestive disorders and back pain. Reich often spoke about attaining a "soft belly": an interesting contrast to the desired "six-pack" of many modern bodybuilders.

## Pelvic Segment: Buttocks, Anus, Genitals, Ovaries, Uterus, and the Legs and Feet

The pelvis should not be worked with early on in therapy, not until a foundation of trust is established within the therapeutic alliance and there is support from the other segments. All body segments are directly associated with psychological and emotional patterns, but none compare in intensity to those stored in the pelvis: sexuality, eroticism, desire, trust, vitality, empowerment, identity, safety, anger, and freedom. The pelvic region is intricately entwined with all other segments and subject to our moment-by-moment emotional body-mind state.

If any segment of the body is shut down, the risk of the pelvis closing as well is almost inevitable. "Opening" the pelvis is not difficult. Yet, no amount of physical or emotional prodding, begging, or force can sustain, and maintain, the release of the pelvis . . . especially when the emotional component is not resolved. As with other segments, pelvic holding has a reason. There are many muscles that can be involved in a pelvic block, including the *psoas, rectus abdominis, inguinal, pubococcygeus, levator ani, gluteus maximus, urethral sphincter,* and *ani externus.* Pelvic blocks are brought about by emotional and/or physical trauma. Certainly sexual abuse at any age can cause the pelvis to close, whereas lesser-known body-mind traumas are due to childhood enemas, early toilet training, and almost any continual boundary infringement.

Toilet training before the anal sphincter control is properly attained at about eighteen months of age can cause a block by requiring the contraction of contiguous muscles of the thighs and buttocks, a pulling up of the pelvic floor, and respiratory inhibition. Punishment for sexual curiosity or masturbation as a child often fosters feelings of guilt or shame. It can create a holding pattern as the child turns to secrecy to hide any feelings of sexual desire.

For women, one of the primary sites for holding emotional tension is in the uterus. This can cause a block and the resulting lack of desire. For both men and women, a fear of or loss of a pregnancy (no matter how long ago), an inability to sustain comfortable limits, sexual or otherwise, with a partner, a lie in an intimate relationship, either partner having an affair, gender prejudice, etc., are all examples of themes that can cause pelvic blocks and an array of sexual dysfunctions. A block in the pelvic segment can diminish natural emotional affect and erotic sensations and expression in the pelvis. A healing of this block can provide a foundation for sustaining pelvic opening and sexual awakening. Some people enjoy Latin dancing and belly dancing for these reasons.

The legs and feet form an extension of the pelvic segment, and provide a sense of "grounding," a foundation from which our energy will return and recycle through our body, rather than dissipate. It is important to bring awareness and energy to our legs and feet. This helps one to feel stable and to contain higher levels of aliveness. On a psychological level, grounding yields a feeling of confidence, trust, and clarity within. Our feet and eyes have a strong energetic connection. When one segment is closed, the other is affected, and both influence grounding. When we are grounded, we can stay present more easily and can tolerate higher states of well-being, sexuality, and aliveness.

For instance, standing with locked knees tilts the pelvis forward, causes the spine to curve forward more in the sacral area, and sets up numerous postural tensions. Relaxing the knees, as in a Tai Chi "first position" stance, can help grounding and also help allow feelings to descend more into a deep-belly, self-centered position.

There are an infinite number of causes for why our bodies become inhibited as we grow up. Almost everyone has some holding in his or her body, especially in the pelvis. Yet, we most surely did not come into the world holding back our aliveness, or our sexuality. Somehow and for some reason, we learned to do this. But we do not have to stay that way.

When holding patterns are resolved, we can become more integrated. Our body can contain more flowing energy so that we will feel more alive and have more presence. With openness, our energy can spread throughout the segments for function and healing. This helps our body systems perform better with greater fluidity and inner balance. With inner balance, our immune system becomes more resilient, and we have greater access to health. This incorporation creates an inner state of constancy or consistency of being that allows us to reintegrate disowned parts of the self and often leads to a shift of consciousness to deal with the existential issues of life.

## References

Hannaford, C. (1995). *Smart moves: Why learning is not all in your head.* Arlington, VA: Great Ocean.

Keleman, S. (1983). *Emotional anatomy.* Berkeley, CA: Center Press.

Rosenberg, J. (1973). *Total orgasm.* New York: Random House.

Rosenberg, J., & Morse, B. (1996). *The intimate couple.* Atlanta, GA: Turner.

Rosenberg, J., Rand, M., & Asay, D. (1985). *Body, self and soul.* Atlanta, GA: Humanics.

Siegel, D. (1999). *The developing mind: Toward a neurobiology of interpersonal experience.* New York: Guilford Press.

# 66
## Horizontal Grounding

Angela Belz-Knöferl, Germany

Translation by Regina Mirvis

**Angela Belz-Knöferl**, MA, was trained in Organismic Psychotherapy (developed by Malcolm and Katherine Brown), as well as in other Humanistic Psychotherapy methods. She has been working in private practice as a Body Psychotherapist since 1980 in Nuremberg, Germany. Her practice comprises individual and group therapy, supervision, and further education in Organismic Psychotherapy. In 1985, she co-founded the German Association for Organismic Psychotherapy.

In addition, she has been very active in professional policy-making: she was a board member of the German Association for Body Psychotherapy (DGK) for seven years beginning in 1996, and from 1999 to 2012 she was chairperson of the Ethics Committee and a board member of the European Association for Body Psychotherapy (EABP).

The term "*horizontal grounding*"—being in a connection with the earth—is a substantive theoretical and practical concept in Body Psychotherapy, one that is not seen as anything separate from "vertical grounding" (see Chapter 67, "Vertical Grounding: The Body in the World and the Self in the Body" by Lily Anagnostopoulou). Both versions describe dimensions of human existence that complement, influence, and mutually determine one another, on a polar level, as parts of a higher form. If one transfers both of these dimensions of existence into the image of daylight as an active and productive element, and nighttime as a passive-receptive element, one can describe "day" as "vertical grounding" and "night" as "horizontal grounding." As an experiential quality, the latter represents tranquility and contemplation, joy of being, and a feeling of internal security. It represents a deep connection with oneself and the world, and the ability to surrender oneself trustfully to the flow of life. In contrast, vertical grounding builds up a form or charge and expends energy. It can be characterized as an inner feeling of security in an exchange with the outside world, the joy of independence, as a focused perception of and ability for goal-oriented action.

Using the image of a polarity, it becomes clear that one of these cannot exist without the other. There is a cycle, a flow, a pulsation that can be compared with expansion and contraction, with breathing in and breathing out, or as Stanley Keleman (1992) describes it, "In a never far from incessant flow, we turn to the world and return to ourselves."

According to the viewpoint of Depth Psychology, horizontal and vertical grounding represent, simply stated, two consecutive developmental phases of life: Horizontal grounding forms itself in the prenatal, perinatal, and postnatal phase. Vertical grounding comes into the foreground, in the literal sense, during the autonomy phase of the toddler. The extent to which horizontal and vertical grounding have been established in an individual is an important criterion for diagnosis and treatment in psychotherapeutic practice.

## Development of the Concept

Horizontal grounding, as we know and use the concept today, entered into Body Psychotherapeutic theory in about 1985. It is interesting to take a brief look at the history of this methodological concept. Even in early Freudian psychoanalysis, there existed an idea of "grounding": each child must grapple with the gravitation toward "Mother Earth" and the feeling of "being securely carried by her." Balint and others believed that an occurrence of insecurity in this early developmental stage could become the prototype for later anxieties (Smith, 1989b, p. 137).

Alexander Lowen and John Pierrakos, as well as Stanley Keleman, all assimilated the concept of "grounding" into Body Psychotherapy in the United States at the end of the 1950s. Lowen and Pierrakos created an innovative idea within the scope of their experiments on themselves during their development of Bioenergetics. At that time, their joint further development of their Reichian legacy was to get the patient to leave the (horizontal) therapy couch and, instead, to work while standing vertically. The actual physical experience of "standing on your own two feet" supports the feeling of being connected to the earth, both in its literal and in its metaphorical and symbolic sense.

Body Psychotherapeutic practices that support the strengthening of the ego, independence, and aggression (in its original literal sense: *aggredi* = moving forward) were the basis for the new concept of grounding, known from today's point of view as "vertical grounding." In addition, the emphasis on ego functions mirrors the *zeitgeist* of the 1960s—in contrast to the "laid-back" California counterculture—the pressure to succeed and the necessity for self-assertion characterized by the New York scene.

Over the course of the next twenty years, both David Boadella and David Smith rendered outstanding work on their complementary expansion of understanding the concepts of both types of grounding (Smith, 1989a, pp. 137ff.). They developed a new therapeutic method, stemming from Frank Lake's synthesis of the Reichian character structure model and from object-relationship theories, as well as incorporating the latest embryological research (and Laban's analysis of movement [Smith, 1989a, pp. 89ff.].). According to this understanding, new states of being and new relationship patterns begin to form in the intrauterine developmental phase. Due to their forming at such an early point in time, they have a massive impact on the basic mental-physical and psychological development of a human being.

At the same time, in the growth of the Human Potential Movement, the relevance of the human potential and its resources—instead of focusing solely on pathological structures—moved more into the focus of developmental therapeutic work. David Boadella describes grounding as "inner ground" in his definitive book (1987b), *Lifestreams:*

> We must . . . find the inner ground. That is the source, through which he (the human) splutters his own healing energy. This grants him strength to integrate himself anew, despite all that he has learned about it. (p. 108)

Virtually all the important Body Psychotherapeutic schools have adopted the overall concepts of both horizontal and vertical grounding, albeit these are received differently and with varying theoretical and practical main focuses. The most important of these schools in Europe (apart from that of David Boadella's "Biosynthesis") were Gerda Boyesen's "Biodynamic Psychology" (Boyesen, 1987), Malcolm and Katherine Brown's "Organismic Psychotherapy," (Brown, 1985), Jay Stattman's "Unitive Psychology," (Stattman, 1988) and Jerome Liss's "Biosystemic Psychotherapy" (Liss, 1989); these were followed by Lisbeth Marcher's "Bodynamics." There were similar developments in the USA, which also used the concepts of grounding in various ways (e.g. Pat Ogden's "Sensorimotor Psychotherapy," Al Pesso's work, Chuck Kelley's "Radix" work, Thomas Pope's "Lomi Psychotherapy," Ron Kurtz's "Hakomi," and Ilana Rubenfeld's "Rubenfeld Synergy").

## Horizontal Grounding Theory

If we, now, turn toward the theoretical fundamentals of horizontal grounding, it makes the most sense to describe this Body Psychotherapeutic concept with images that are taken from embryology. This is because they represent the most early developmental and innovative aspects of grounding: "When observing therapy from an embryological point of view, it can be considered one of the most extensive ways to understand our somatic organization" (Boadella, 1987b, p. 30). We are (horizontally) "grounded" in our basic biology and embryology. Our essential organizational systems are developed from, and follow, the three basic embryological layers, as described below. Our development in the womb, and our mobility outside of the womb, also follows the basic embryological development from: first the amoeba, then the jellyfish, the fish, the lizard, the mammal, and then (only eventually) the upright humanoid. These developmental components all tie us into our essential "horizontal grounding."

[**Editor's Note:** *See also chapter 33 in this volume, by Susan Aposhyan: "Pattern and Plasticity: Utilizing Early Motor Development as a Tool for Therapeutic Change."*]

## Grounding and Embryology

An embryo is composed, at a certain point in its early development, of three blastodermic layers: these are called the ectoderm, mesoderm, and endoderm. Further physical systems develop from each blastodermic layer:

- From the *ectoderm (outer) layer* evolves the skin, all the sense organs, nerve cells, and the brain. The brain is later in charge of *thinking* and *feeling*. That is to say, this "system" is responsible for perception of the outside world, and all aspects of mental processes, yet also for desires, dreams, symbols, analyses, self-awareness, etc.
- From the *mesoderm (middle) layer* evolve muscles, bones, vasculature, and the heart. This "system" is responsible for *action* and *movement*. It bonds structure and organs. It defines the form of the body, strength and mobility, and task-oriented posture. Essentially, this is later responsible for vertical grounding.
- From the *endoderm (inner) layer* evolve tissues that influence the metabolism of energy: digestive organs and lung tissue (visceral organs). This organic system is responsible for *energy creation* and *energy depletion,* as well as for the basic level of energy.

The metabolization of energy correlates with one's emotions. One can therefore label the endodermic system, on a psychological level, as the "center of emotion" of the body. "Emotions have a somatic architecture" (Keleman, 1992, p. 8).

An emotionally balanced state is somatically regulated by the vegetative or autonomic nervous system. Its two branches—the sympathetic and parasympathetic—have very different effects: the sympathetic branch is energy consuming and is responsible for action, strength, and the joy of doing; when a person is under stress, the situation is managed by either the "fight" or the "flight" mechanism, which is then connected to feelings of rage, fear, and irritation. The parasympathetic branch ensures balance and rebuilds energy: flight or fight are forsaken in favor of "letting go," "resting," and "digesting." It is positively connected to the feelings of "being soft," "being relaxed," and to the "joy of being." Negatively, it is connected to pain, grief, desperation, etc.

In a healthy state, the transition between the two branches is rhythmic and constitutes the somatic basis of self-regulation. This natural rhythm is disturbed in all neurotic and psychotic structures (compare with Nathan, 1985/1986). More recent research by Stephen Porges (2001) expands the polarity of both branches of the vegetative nervous system (sympathetic–parasympathetic) into a hierarchy. According to his model, the parasympathetic branch can be split into two parts: an "intelligent" vagus and a—phylogenetically older—"primitive" vagus. In summary, there are three fundamental energy currents in the body:

- The ectoderm current as the flow of perception, thoughts, and images
- The mesoderm current as the flow of movement through the muscles
- The endoderm current as the flow of emotional life

Wilhelm Reich had already discovered the therapeutic significance of unhindered flow, current, and pulsation as one of *the* basic functions of life. Every simple organism (e.g., monad) regulates its reaction to an external stimulus through pulsation by means of either expansion (flow toward the stimulus) or contraction (withdrawal from the stimulus). Stanley Keleman states, *"The pulsation and its form are the cornerstones of the organismic process as well as for intra- and interpersonal forms"* (Keleman, 1992, p. 181).

The intrapersonal form allows the pulsation, in connection with the blastodermic layers, to give a very differentiated statement about what occurs when the energy currents between the endodermal, mesodermal, and ectodermal systems cannot properly, or can only partially, flow. To describe these effects in detail would be beyond the scope of this chapter. In short, one can describe adult morphology as a reduced or suspended connection between feeling, acting, and thinking:

- If the connection between the endoderm and ectoderm is affected, this means either acting without emotional association, or having feelings that are not implemented in the action.
- If the connection between the endoderm and ectoderm is limited, either feelings are held in the belly that do not want to be consciously perceived, or there is a fixation on mental processes that are not in keeping with the emotions.
- If the mental and motor systems separate, the result is: either an identification with thought structures that do not implement into action; or actions that remain not reflected.

## The Developmental Process of Horizontal Grounding

### Prenatal Phase

The interpersonal form of pulsation is in turn dependent on the quality of encountering the world—for an embryo, this is the connection to the mother. Upon implantation in the womb, the unborn is directly connected to the mother and her blood flow. *"At the beginning of life there exists a powerful pulsation pattern between mother and child"* (Keleman, 1992, p. 39). This connection not only transports nourishment and oxygen but also transmits emotional states.

Ideally, a child experiences "intrauterine bonding" as physically unhindered growth and trust in its self-regulatory abilities. Psychologically, the child experiences the world as a pleasant place; relationships are something positive, and its existence is welcomed. Frederick Leboyer labeled this phase of life as the "golden age"; Stanislav Grof, as "paradise"; and Wilhelm Reich spoke of "oceanic emotions" and "cosmic currents" (Boadella, 1987b, p. 44).

As useful and important as it may be in the daily practice of psychotherapy to have a concept of ideal growth and life conditions, it is in the essence of psychotherapy to deal with more or less serious deviations thereof.

The intrauterine phase is characterized by maximal dependence. If the mother is exposed to stress over a long period of time—labeled as "adrenalized womb"—this does not remain without consequences to the embryo. Factors that could cause stress include:

- External circumstances, ranging from a difficult family life situation to war or conflict
- Inner states of being, ranging from rejection of the pregnancy to the point of acute or chronic physical-psychological problems
- Toxification from medications, alcohol abuse, or toxins such as nicotine and other drugs

The unborn child cannot evade any of these unpleasant or even threatening influences. The child cannot change its situation by "fight or flight," as it is biologically programmed to do by the vegetative nervous system. It also does not yet possess muscles (Davis, 1997/1998), which it could tense to protect its core. Fear, pain, and discomfort can be made tolerable only by reducing (or freezing up) its impetus to live, its pulsation, and its expansion. Such an experience in the first matrix of "being in the world" can leave profound traces in the organism and can have immense consequences on later attitudes toward life. Upon pondering how an organism can "perceive" what is occurring at all in this stage of development, Boadella writes in *Lifestreams*:

> With high probability are the fetus' arousal patterns, pleasant and unpleasant and the reflexes associated with them, stored in some form . . . we do not need to limit the ability to remember to the brain. Organisms without brain tissue or nervous systems have experiences. They are able to sense, react to their environment and act accordingly. It seems that . . . cells of a certain system possess a primitive ability to remember past organic states. (Boadella, 1987b, p. 40)

**Perinatal Phase**

As we leave the intrauterine phase of growth and turn toward the "meanings" (and consequences) of birth and the extrauterine attachment procedure, the second important phase of development for horizontal grounding starts.

Leboyer's groundbreaking book, *Birth without Violence*, reminds us of fundamental knowledge about the meaning of birth and how important it is to grant a baby a harmonious transition from the amniotic world into an existence on earth dominated by external forces, including gravitational forces (Leboyer, 1981).

The newborn experiences not only changes in sensations (dark/light, quiet/loud, warm/cold), blood circulation (it must breathe on its own), and, as already mentioned, gravitational forces (fear of falling perhaps has its origin here), but also changes in nutrition (the child must now actively seek its own food source). Birth can sometimes be a traumatic event, possibly due to complications, or possibly due to an abrupt separation from the mother. Another quotation applicable here is: "*. . . when the first fundamental rooting of a human being is a shocking or frightening experience, one in which the contact organs only reluctantly expand or do not expand at all, the foundation of feeling secure in being in the world, in one's own body, or in the midst of others' bodies is weakened, undermined or even destroyed*" (Boadella, 1987b, p. 74).

**Postnatal Phase**

The phase after birth is much better researched and much more present in general knowledge than the prenatal phase. This is thanks to various therapeutic models, such as (for example) from current infant research, attachment theory, object-relationship theories, and psychoanalytic theories. Therefore, we will concentrate here only on the essentials.

The smallest common denominator of all these theories is the assumption that loving contact to and with the mother—and increasingly also to other members of the family—is the foundation for a baby to feel accepted into this world with all its differentiating needs. It is essential for the further development of horizontal grounding, whether a degree of self-regulation can be continued, and the way in which it is continued. Ideally, the baby learns that it can trust its impulses on a physical level:

- The umbilical-cord pulsation can differentiate itself in the rhythm of breathing, sucking, and digesting (endoderm system).
- Contact to the skin aids the sensing of body contour forms and stimulates the ectoderm system.
- Eye contact supports the connection between the sense organs and the feeling of being recognized (ectoderm-endoderm connection).
- The reflex movements of the fetus are replaced by tension and relaxation in the forming musculature (mesoderm).

Resonance (from those around) with an infant's different needs is a prerequisite for the development of self-regulation: in the emotional relationship with the mother; the availability of the attachment figure; the right timing (the baby determines when it needs how much of what); and the physical-energetic exchange with the mother—these are the basic requirements for successful self-regulation.

In the same way, as an embryo can positively experience having the "right to exist," a baby can also experience the "right to its needs." In order for the baby to be able to trustfully rest within itself, and from within itself seek contact with the world, the infant needs to feel seen, be held, and be loved—unconditionally.

Disorders in this phase center around themes of loss of the mother, lack of attention and support, encroachments, and non-solvable conflictual situations. In contrast to the embryonic phase, a baby is more able to protest. If there is a repetitive lack of, or inadequate, reaction in response to the protest, the baby will little by little abandon its attempts to call attention to itself. Despair and withdrawal can result. In order to survive (physically and emotionally), the baby will superficially adapt to the situation; however, the price for this survival strategy is high (compare with Aalberse, 1991). This requires self-denial, true to the motto *"If my needs only cause me pain, then I will not have them"* (Johnson, 1990, p. 150).

On the other hand, this also signifies a limitation of pulsation on the physical level. This pulsation connects different organ systems: *"Such a person breathes less, does less, does not expend much energy; 'depression instead of expression' becomes the solution"* (Ibid., p. 150).

The foundation of a harmonious evolution toward vertical grounding is effected well, leading to the detachment from the mother into greater autonomy. Depending on the degree of deprivation, vertical grounding either does not develop at all, or *"the child . . . strides . . . prematurely towards individuation"* (Ibid., p. 151). The escape of moving forward and becoming independent—as quickly as possible—turns vertical grounding into a defense mechanism against a lack of internal security.

## The Practice of Horizontal Grounding

### General Comments

Body Psychotherapy has a definite strength in treating disorders based on the personality structure, especially those that arose long before speech development. General statements can, however, be made only to a limited extent, such as how Body Psychotherapy works practically with horizontal grounding. As mentioned earlier, grounding concepts from the original schools—and, in the meantime, from newly arisen schools—were incorporated in different ways according to each one's different approach and focus. Accordingly, they differ in their actual work methods. This has happily led to a plethora of methods since about the 1980s, but makes it rather challenging to speak of *the* (or any *one*) Body Psychotherapeutic practice of horizontal grounding.

Despite the many different "characteristics," the theory allows for the creation of a type of "matrix" or a specification of the practical work in regard to its objectives and methods. The main objective of Body Psychotherapeutic work is to resolve dissociations from primary impulses and affects that originated in the earliest life experiences. A further objective is to return the patient to the possibility of the varying forms of expression of being—feeling, acting, thinking—into a merged, meaningful whole.

The focus of work on the physical level is to restore a basic pulsation that expresses itself in a self-regulating flow and rhythm. The person's metabolic energy needs to be able to express itself between "being active in the world" and a "passively contemplative display." In the emotional arena, it is imperative to support the feeling of security in one's existential being, and trust in one's own experience and wants and actions, from which important relationships can be shaped.

With regard to the therapeutic relationship, as a transference and as a learning model, it is particularly important to have a secure framework and a sufficient establishment of trust. Lost trust cannot be restored with words; restoration of trust requires at least one significant concrete experience, along with much time and patience. As in real life, trust must be experienced in the therapeutic relationship "in each and every cell." Beyond knowledge and techniques, this presupposes a therapist's high measure in their ability to be mindful and compassionate.

On a physical level, this requires what Wilhelm Reich called "vegetative identification" and what Stanley Keleman (1975) called "somatic resonance." What is meant here is the ability to feel something of what the client is experiencing in one's own body, yet at the same time not losing the necessary distance that one needs while working professionally. Therapists who do not know both grounding dimensions within themselves, and who do not know how to balance them in a specific situation, will have difficulties working successfully with this concept.

In addition to the verbal working through of the structures of needs and their defenses, Body Psychotherapy differentiates two basic approaches of how emotional tension can be relieved:

- Cathartic methods that are meant to release suppressed feelings and to relieve tension and blocks in the body
- Harmonizing techniques that serve to develop greater inner balance

The main emphasis of the work with horizontal grounding is on the harmonizing and developing side. Components of the work are: contact through touch; massage; support-giving exercises—either alone or with the therapist; breathing work, which is the simplest method to access better pulsation; and eye contact, as a representation of "being seen in one's nature." These components are found in all Body Psychotherapeutic schools of work in one form or another.

## Case Study

Horizontal and vertical grounding are, for example, seen as central working concepts in Organismic Psychotherapy. Vertical grounding is somatically classified as belonging more to the back of the person's body, whereas horizontal grounding is classified as belonging more to the front: face, chest and belly, etc. Both are additionally differentiated in "being centers" that communicate different "ways of being in the world."

How the work with horizontal grounding may look in the practice of Organismic Psychotherapy is illustrated here with an example of a client with particular deficits in this area. Using a selection of therapy sessions that extend from the second to the fourth years of the therapeutic process, it becomes understandable how the mental, emotional, and physical aspects of the client began to reconnect with each other.

The client, a thirty-seven-year-old computer specialist, came to therapy due to emotional and physical problems. He was single, barely had any friends, and strongly longed for an intimate relationship; professionally, he suffered from panic attacks when he had to *"say something in front of everyone."* He characterized himself as "sociophobic" and "felt foreign (like an alien) on this planet." He suffered physically from chronic back pain and migraines.

After one year of seated dialogic work and the building of a sufficiently good therapeutic relationship, the client expressed the desire to begin doing some bodywork. He chose to lay himself down and asked that I should sit next to him, so that he could look at me whenever he needed to do so. His otherwise-dominant flow of words stopped; the breath was shallow. At my request, he focused on his breathing, and his perception went more within himself. The breath deepened only minimally; he "sensed and felt nothing." After a certain amount of time resting, an image surfaced in him: he saw himself in an underground room, standing and wrapped like a mummy; his family members were also in the same room, yet were not in contact with each other.

**Commentary**

*It became clear in this session the extent that his ectoderm (mental, symbolism-giving) system was separate from the endoderm (emotional) and mesoderm (motor) system in his personality: The image (of a mummy) was torpid; neither was it connected to an emotion, nor were any movement impulses found in the image, nor in the body of the client.*

In the following year, the client's healing process involved repeating the same patterns over and over again—a procedure that is typical for this kind of disturbance. Through this repetition, the client could reestablish a sense of internal security and a rudimentary trust in his own experience: the client experienced living through and enduring feelings of horror, fear, loneliness, and helplessness, all arising from his internal images, all within the safety of the therapeutic relationship. Thus, the therapeutic manner of working with infantile disorders can be compared with the way that one deals with an infant: only through constant repetition of the same or similar actions does a baby become confident in its way of being in its self, in its body, in its environment, and with its care attachment figures. The following session demonstrates a further important stage of development.

The client is lying—almost as always—on his back. While focusing on his breath, which has considerably increased in its expansion to the abdomen, the client begins to feel his feet as being perceivably cold as ice and *"as if they are not associated with the body."* At first, I held his feet with my hands. After a while, the warmth that spread through his feet felt "very comfortable" to him. Almost unnoticeably, movement came into his feet; I responded to this movement with gentle counterpressure. Hence, a kind of movement game developed whereupon the impetus that was coming from the client flowed into a bending and stretching movement in his legs. The permanent, warm counterpressure from my hands "felt very good" and "made moving myself around fun," as stated by the patient.

After a period of rest initiated by him, the client brought up how little stability and support there was in his family and how sad he was about that.

**Commentary**

*The increasing connection between perception, movement impetus, and emotions demonstrated that not only did the separation (block) between the ectoderm and endoderm system continue to dissolve, but also the mesoderm system was slowly being incorporated as well. Furthermore, the spontaneous alternation between movement and rest clearly demonstrated that a self-regulation in the vegetative nervous system, between the sympathetic and parasympathetic branches, was beginning to become attuned. In the following time period, a change took place in the personal life of the client.*

His relationship to his work colleagues was improving; he became less fearful to speak "before an audience." His migraine attacks occurred less often and were less intense, similar to his back pain. Moreover, he began an intimate relationship in which he experienced himself as being "warm and open," although he consistently also experienced deep doubt and guilt about whether he was capable of loving.

In this phase, an increasing number of issues of an existential nature entered into the therapy, such as, *"Who am I?"* and *"What is the point of me being in the world?"* These became an urgent concern, and were repeated over and over. The dialogues that evolved from these questions left the client with a *"deep feeling of satisfaction."*

It must be noted that existential and spiritual themes often emerge in people with infantile disorders. If these themes are not included in the therapeutic process, a potential for "grounding" to "the source of all being" is passed by and not integrated.

The client initiated further progress in his integration process: he said that he *"holds on in his head,"* and this hinders him in responding to his needs: *"I so want to let go."* So, he again began with the bodywork while lying down. By placing attention on his breath and small head movements, he noticed that the center of his tension was not where he assumed it to be, in the shoulders and neck, but rather was localized at the base of the skull. In accordance with my suggestion, the client attempted to see if any change occurred when alternating between holding his head and massaging the tension. After fifteen to twenty minutes, spontaneous sighs and gurgling intestinal sounds emerged, indicating a relaxing vegetative reaction. Shortly afterward, the client described the expansion of a gentle, flowing feeling in his chest and abdominal cavity: he wept silent tears.

**Commentary**

The experience of flowing physical feelings, and the ability to allow them without a defensive reaction, is a milestone along the path toward horizontal grounding. These feelings are ultimately those of love, warmth, acceptance, and relatedness to an embodied form of existence. In the therapeutic process, they are the quality of experience that in time helps to dissolve dissociations and blocks in the body from "within."

## Conclusion

The varying insights into the developmental process of the client give only a limited depiction of the complexity of these worked-through themes. The time frame of three years, by itself, clearly shows that the "working through" of deficits in people with horizontal-grounding issues can be a difficult, long-term, and drawn-out process.

The social environment is often not conducive toward this kind of profound work. The general trends in psychotherapy are moving toward short-term therapy; the scales of values in our society are increasingly those of efficiency, speed, and performance. Even "free time," which should serve for relaxation, reflection, recreational idleness, and the assimilation of countless stimuli, is becoming filled with the demands of the "fit-for-fun" ideology. Pharmaceutical products, alcohol, and other "quick fixes" offer (apparently) easier alternatives.

The factors needed for these existential processes that actually deliver profound change are relatively time-consuming, and the consistently difficult passages, and/or bottlenecks or "edges," are neither properly appreciated nor accepted. Basic trust in oneself cannot be created "just now," if it can be successfully created at all. If a human being needs both grounding and centering, both "roots and wings" for a purposeful life, this requires that consciousness overrules some of the necessities of modern life, and different ways of "being," in order for our mental and physical health to improve significantly. Body Psychotherapy can make an important contribution here.

## References

Aalberse, M. (1991). Die dunkle Nacht der Seele [The dark night of the soul]. In G. Marlock (Ed.), *Weder Körper noch Geist [Neither body nor mind]*. Oldenburg: Transform.

Boadella, D. (1987a). Life energy and blood. *Energy & Character, 18(2)*, 1–21.

Boadella, D. (1987b). *Lifestreams: An introduction to Biosynthesis*. London: Routledge.

Boyesen, G. (1987). *Über den Körper die Seele heilen [Healing the soul through the body]*. Munich: Kösel.

Brown, M. (1985). *Die heilende Berührung [The healing touch]*. Essen: Synthesis.

Davis, W. (1997/1998). Biological foundation of the schizoid process: Parts 1 & 2. *Energy & Character, 28(1)*, 57–76, & 29(1), 55–75.

Goodrich-Dunn, B., & Gould, E. (2002). A history of Body Psychotherapy. *USABP Journal, 1(1)*, 34–73.

Johnson, S. (1990). *Character transformation*. Oldenburg: Transform.

Keleman, S. (1975). *The human ground*. Palo Alto, CA: Science and Behavior Books.

Keleman, S. (1992). *Verkörperte Gefühle [Embodied feelings]*. Munich: Kösel.

Leboyer, F. (1981). *Geburt ohne Gewalt [Birth without violence]*. Munich: Kösel.

Liss, J. (1979). Emotions and the human energy system. *Energy & Character, 10(1)*, 41–48.

Liss, J. (1989). Vertical and horizontal grounding. *Energy & Character, 20(1)*, 21–44.

Ludwig, M. (1990). Swimming in a human sea. *Energy & Character, 21(2)*, 46–55.

Porges, S. (2001). The polyvagal theory: Phylogenetic substrates of a social nervous system. *International Journal of Psychophysiology, 42*, 123–146.

Smith, D. (1989a). Biodynamics and object relations. In D. Boadella (Ed.), *Maps of character*. London: Abbotsbury Publications.

Smith, D. (1989b). Movement and character. In D. Boadella (Ed.), *Maps of character*. London: Abbotsbury Publications.

Stattman, J. (1988). Organic transference. *Energy & Character, 19(1)*, 27–41.

# 67

## Vertical Grounding

*The Body in the World and the Self in the Body*

**Lily Anagnostopoulou, Greece**

**Lily Anagnostopoulou**, PhD, is a psychologist and psychotherapist and an international trainer in Biosynthesis. She is the founder and director of the Greek Biosynthesis Centre and has been working for thirty-five years as a psychotherapist in private practice and for twenty years as a trainer in Biosynthesis in various countries. She has trained with David and Silvia Boadella in Biosynthesis, and with Alexander Lowen in Bioenergetics. She has had extensive trainings in hypnosis with Ernest Rossi and in Jungian dream analysis with Winifred Rushforth. She has also trained in Family Systems Therapy, Group Analysis, and Rogerian counseling. She has worked as a school psychologist for twenty years and taught at the University of Indianapolis, in their master's program in psychology, at the Athens Campus. She is founder and director of a residential retreat and healing center in Corinth and lives in Athens, Greece.

The grounding concept developed within the field of Bioenergetics by Alexander Lowen (1958), who emphasized the importance of working with patients while they are standing erect. Having people "stand on their own two feet," he could examine posture and movement and help them become aware of the connection between somatic function and psychological problems. It became a principle of Bioenergetic Analysis to start from the ground up, because legs and feet are the foundations of support and movement of the human body. The feelings of security and independence that well-balanced legs offer are equal to a sense of autonomy and control over one's life. Legs and feet are the foundation of the ego structure that is responsible for handling reality. Having one's "feet on the ground" means to be in contact with reality.

The term "grounding" was introduced later (Lowen, 1972), and it was borrowed from physics. Lowen saw grounding as serving *"the same function for the organism's energy system that it does for a high-tension electrical circuit. It provides a safety valve for the discharge of excess excitation"* (Lowen, 1976, p. 196). Stanley Keleman started using the term at around the same time, emphasizing this aspect of contacting our biology, becoming aware of our organismic function (expansion-contraction), and realizing how we shape ourselves from the inside to counteract gravity (Keleman, 1979, 1985). David Boadella expanded the notion of grounding—as a downward flow of discharge—to a feeling contact with the holding environment, a flow of movement upward and downward, to all organs, of charge and discharge (Boadella, 1987). Lisbeth Marcher and her colleagues studied grounding and reality testing as an ego function related to muscles, character, and inner sensing. Muscles end up being hyperresponsive or hyporesponsive depending on the conditions of mastering a specific developmental task: stand on the floor, separate reality from fantasy, embody extrasensory perception, etc. (Marcher and Fich, 2010).

Today, almost all schools of Body Psychotherapy consider the function of grounding to be of primary importance.[66] They use it both diagnostically and therapeutically.

---

66 See, for example, Biodynamics, Bioenergetics, Biosynthesis, Bodynamics, Core Energetics, Hakomi, Integrative Body Psychotherapy, Organismic Psychotherapy, Radix, Unitive Psychology, etc. For further information, refer to the References.

The emphasis is placed on all inner and outer, physical and conceptual, "ground." Inner ground is the ground of our being—meaning, values, inner intention, and essential qualities. Grounding, in the inner ground, requires an unimpeded flow of charge toward our center. The outer ground is the reality of our daily life, home, work, relations, and nature. It requires an outward flow to meet the world. The physical ground is the earth, so physical grounding requires a relation to gravity in standing and moving—a downward flow of expressing and releasing. The conceptual ground is our language and belief systems, so conceptual grounding requires a relation to reality in handling and understanding emotions, needs, and behavior—an upward flow of charge and discharge.

## Basic Concept

Grounding is an energy concept and a psychological metaphor. Thus, "grounding" a person is both a physical and a psychological process. In its basic function, grounding refers to a feeling contact between the feet and the ground: a flow of excitation that allows the body's weight to pass down through the legs and feet into the ground, pulled by gravity.

The awareness of one's feet pressing the ground offers a sense of solidity and knowledge of where one stands, and offers acceptance of who one is. One is in contact with the basic reality of existence: rooted in the earth, supported by its solidity, identified with one's body.

The downward flow of excitation is the discharge process of the body. However, muscular spasticities do not allow for a full discharge to occur. These can be found in the legs, the ankles, the feet, but also the back, the chest, the shoulders, the base of the skull, the neck, the throat, and the jaw. *"Every therapeutic approach that aims to ground a person must effect a significant release of these muscular tensions"* (Lowen, 1972, p. 60).

The therapeutic task of grounding is not a simple one. It requires one to open up the pelvic connection to the legs, by restoring the respiration wave throughout the whole body, allowing feelings to develop deeper in the belly and to touch the pelvic floor. In order for the legs to become active organs of relating, instead of a simple mechanical support, the full motility of the pelvis has to be regained. This process stirs deep anxieties that have to be processed. These can be: fear of loneliness and lack of support for daring to stand as an individual, resisting parental and societal demands; fear of falling and failing; fear of surrender and collapse and never being able to get up again; fear of sadness and despair; deep pain due to lack of love, comfort, and security, held in the belly as a need to cry; fear of dissolution, melting, and streaming sensations; sexual anxieties and orgasm anxiety held in the pelvic floor.

These fears do not allow for centering in the lower abdomen, which is the natural body center for balance. By pulling in the belly, people support themselves from the gut, instead of from the back and the legs; or they pull their energy up, causing an upward displacement, functioning more with the head, without contact to the lower part of the body. This is lack of grounding, lack of any feeling contact with their body, their sexuality, their human nature, and Mother Earth. Thus, grounding a person is a major task of the whole psychotherapeutic process.

People can also be helped by exercises, which they can do regularly by themselves, to promote their process of grounding. Lowen suggests two exercises (see below) as an imperative for grounding, and he has created other exercises that can be used in addition to the psychotherapeutic process (Lowen, 1972; Lowen and Lowen, 1977). Other therapists over the years have developed more exercises and tools to help people with their grounding.

### Two Basic Bioenergetic Exercises for Vertical Grounding

Many people report a lot of benefit from these two exercises, especially when they experience anxiety or panic attacks.

1. Stand with knees slightly bent for two minutes. Feet have to be parallel, shoulder-width apart. The weight of the body is balanced between the heels and the balls of the feet; the body is straight, erect.

If the knees stay locked, they immobilize the lower body. Open the mouth to help the breathing. Let the belly out and the buttocks hang loose. You will slowly experience involuntary movements, vibrations, shaking, tremors, in the legs and/or the body due to the flow of feeling as the body gets more charged and alive by fuller and deeper breathing. When tired, change to the second exercise.

2. With bent knees, feet eight inches apart, toes slightly turned inward, bend forward for one to two minutes. Fingertips touch the ground, to keep balance with no weight for support, head hanging. Straighten the knees slightly, but not fully extended, until vibrations start.

## Grounding as Contact

Building on the psychoanalytic concept of the "holding environment" (Winnicott, 1964, 1971), which is later internalized and defines our relationship to the world, David Boadella offers a broader definition of grounding: *"Grounding is related to the holding environment which the person has available around him, and how he can internalize this holding environment so that the body becomes a true home"* (Boadella, 1997, p. 11). *"Grounding is concerned with what happens when energy flows out towards the surface of the body and the quality of contact it finds there"* (Boadella, 1987, p. 93). He speaks of the many grounds that a child contacts as it develops. Mother's body and abdomen when held, Mother's breast while sucking, Mother's eyes and face when looking at her, language in speaking. At the same time, during these interactions the child is grounding different parts of its body or aspects of its being: legs, arms, mouth, eyes, and ideas.

The prototype of grounding is physical, but as we grow, the ground diversifies from the physical to the psychological (energetic, emotional, mental, spiritual) (Wehowsky, 1998, pp. 14–22). Grounding, in this sense, relates to our contact with the body, the earth, nature, other human beings, family, work, country, culture, God. The supportive function of the many forms of grounding is of primary concern in Body Psychotherapy, similar to the "holding environment" in psychoanalysis. Physical ground refers to the stability of our legs on the earth; sexual ground, to our contact with another's body; relational ground, to the network of our social and emotional relationships (family, community, work). Conceptual ground refers to our language and belief systems; and spiritual ground, to the meaning of our life. In all these aspects of life, *"grounding refers to our intentional and behavioral connection"* to these realities (Ibid., p. 11). Programmed to meet them on the basis of our prototype of grounding—as a "holding environment"—in our therapeutic work, we try to create experiences of recontacting the ground in a new way. We try to liberate the inner thrust for contact that was deformed by negative experiences of contact in an unsupportive holding environment. We try to help our clients to experience the basis of their groundedness as a flow of energy to their feet, but also as a directedness, focus, and strength of action in each one of the many grounds that life offers. *"The work of grounding distributes energy out towards all the contact points of the organism"* (Boadella, 1987, p. 100). The aim of therapy here is to release habitual contracting patterns that block contact and expression. Thus, grounding work involves breathing, and working with legs, feet, pelvis, back, arms, sound, and eyes, and offers the possibility for a more secure connection with our inside and outside reality.

## Muscle Tone and Character

How we handle gravity in every expression of our life—sitting, standing, moving, lying down—is a task that we accomplish by our postural alignment and muscle tone. In every moment, we have to deal with the force of the earth pulling us toward its center. Proper body alignment uses gravity for balance and makes movement easy, gracious, and effortless.

Deviations from alignment cause body parts to compensate for balance, resulting in a struggle with gravity, expending a lot of energy. Ideal alignment in the erect posture is on an axis connecting the top of the head with the middle points of the ear, the shoulder, the hip joint, the knee, and the ankle. In this way, each body part supports the one above it. If misaligned, each part has to handle the gravitational pull by holding up against it or being pulled down by it.[67] *"To be grounded well is to be in postural balance with just the amount of muscle tone needed to maintain the body against gravity. More leads to overstressing, less leads to weakness and insecurity"* (Boadella, 1987, p. 51).

Muscle tone refers to the condition of the muscle, informed by the muscle spindle, relating to the need for action. So, the muscle tone might be appropriate for the action at hand, or unbalanced in the direction of too much tension or too little tension. This results in hypertonic or hypotonic muscles, which affect the quality of grounding in the direction of too much or too little. David Boadella speaks about two extremes for people: being "overgrounded" or "undergrounded." Overgrounded people have spastic hypertonic muscles, which feel tense, knotted, rigid, and ready to fire in any moment at all times. They can build charge, but they cannot relax. They are trapped in security, protection, stability, or roots, but they cannot dream, fly, or open their boundaries and make contact. Undergrounded people have overly flexible, hypotonic muscles, which feel slack, spongy, and oversluggish. They pull energy from the muscles into the head, resulting in a rich fantasy life, but they are open to invasion, cannot easily build a charge, nor hold their ground. Both types express disturbances of the grounding function as an energy current in two directions: downward flow (physical grounding) and upward flow (conceptual grounding) (Boadella, 1987; Kurtz and Prestera, 1976).

Both types defend against each other. Overgrounded people relate to rigid structures with their strong egos, not allowing themselves to experience weakness and vulnerability. Undergrounded people have a tendency to regress, collapse, or hold on, preventing themselves from contacting their power and establishing autonomy. In their therapeutic work, they need to be helped differently. Overgrounded people need opportunities to express more, whereas undergrounded people need opportunities to resist more. *"The therapist works to release energy from over tense muscles by transferring the tension into expressive movements and to draw energy into overslack muscles by increasing the tonus through dynamic resistance against the ground of the earth or the ground of the therapist's body"* (Boadella, 1986, p. 15).

Rebalancing the muscles in this way may lead to eutony, which releases patients from their character defenses. Our usual state of muscle tone is an expression of our history: hypotonic muscles indicate deprivation and understimulation; hypertonic muscles reflect invasion and overstimulation. A balanced muscular state allows the true self to express itself in movement.

Marcher and her colleagues have also studied the polarity of hyporesponsive / hyperresponsive muscles in relation to character structure (Marcher and Fich, 2010). They have mapped the whole body, listing the muscles that relate to different developmental stages of a child, connecting hyporesponsiveness to early disturbances and hyperresponsiveness to late disturbances of the relevant stage. Hyporesponsive muscles resign from expression, whereas hyperresponsive muscles block expression (Marcher and Fich, 2010; Bernhardt et al., 1996a, 1996b, 1996c).

## Grounding, Ego Development, and Sense of Self

Lowen explicitly related grounding to ego strength: *"Having one's feet on the ground is body language revealing that the person is in touch with reality"* (Lowen, 1958, p. 185). He considered the legs and feet, physically and psychologically, to be the support and foundations of the ego structure. The function of grounding, releasing excess energy to the ground, is—for him—the safety valve of our energetic system. Grounding an electrical circuit into the earth does not allow any excess charge to blow the system. In the same way, a strong ego is helped by grounding to contain strong emotional charges, without breaking or splitting.

Another way of relating ego development to grounding is offered by the combination of Developmental Psychol-

---

67   Moshe Feldenkrais, Ida Rolf, and Thérèse Bertherat all studied extensively how to help the body realign, from a purely physical aspect, not ignoring the psychological implications of their work (Feldenkrais, 1977, 1985; Rolf, 1977; Bertherat, 1976, 1989).

ogy and object-relations theory. Developmental Psychology studies the sensory-motor development of the child, which object-relations theorists consider to be the basis for the maturation process of a developing ego. Freud was the first to speak of ego as a "body ego." Body Psychotherapists work with the body ego, and they know that the social and the biological systems mature hand in hand. Each developmental task is associated with specific bodily states and motor patterns.

The process from lying to sitting, to crawling, to squatting, to standing, signals the psychological transition from emergence and dependency toward autonomy. A step taken is usually a step away from the mother. Body Psychotherapists working with their clients can offer them the opportunity to complete developmental tasks bodily and to use some of the motor and sensory skills that were not allowed to mature in their early development. Seen from this perspective, ego functions—the ability to say "No," boundary formation, bonding, reality testing, self-support, self-assertion, direction, orientation, focusing, containment of energy and emotions, managing sexuality, understanding, dignity, and identity—all depend upon the mastering of the developmental movements, from lying to standing, from horizontal to vertical grounding. Every developmental stage depends on the one before, and whatever was not adequately mastered is transferred as a deficit to the next. In Body Psychotherapy, one can correct these developmental deficits and work with grounding and strengthening the ego.

Keleman's theories and practice are close to Winnicott's idea of grounding the self in the body: *"Motility has to be appreciated from the inside . . . True identity does not arise sensorily, from muscle movement patterns or the approval of others, but rather it arises from the quality of sensation from the internal pulsatory waves of the smooth muscles of organs. Feeling and sensation that arise from the inside tell us 'this is who I am'"* (Keleman, 1985, p. 28). This concept of interiority is more relevant to the process of self-formation. The ego integrates the self as the infant accepts the body as part of the self. *"Embodied self-awareness—through exploration of inner sensations, vegetative reactions, impulses and subtle movements—provides a clearer sense of boundaries and leads to a stronger sense of self. Tuning in to these inner sensations and feelings, which we call 'anchoring in the body,' enables a deepening of contact to oneself and to others"* (Hartley, 2009, p. 19).

Bodily awareness is the foundation of consciousness. One's self originates in a "felt sense of being." A child, through mastering new motor skills, changes its consciousness; and adults in therapy learn to sense themselves more deeply and to participate in their formative process. Keleman eloquently describes anatomy as self-identity: *"The various tubes and layers, pouches and diaphragms act together to give a feeling of one's self . . . hollow, soft and dense tissue produce different sensations and feelings. There is a dialogue of sensations from hollows to solids, from liquid chambers of the brain to densely packed muscle cells. This overall relationship generates a basic tissue state that forms a continuous pattern of consciousness"* (Keleman, 1985, p. 58).

Marcher and her colleagues incorporated all these lines of thought in their Bodynamic System. They see psycho-motor development in the context of relations and the world. *"The healthy individuated self moves naturally towards greater grounding in reality and greater connectedness with the world"* (Bernhardt and Bentzen, 1995, p. 54). They trace grounding from the initial contact of the fetus to the womb, through the pushing of the legs during birth, to the contact of an infant's belly in lying, and its pelvis in sitting. As the child grows and starts to move, grounding is mastered through its arms and legs, and then this involves adjustments of the pelvis when standing. The body is being used for grounding the emerging self (internal awareness), and the developing ego (voluntary processes). From the physical ground, the child develops *"to ground himself in his opinions and still later in peer relations, group formation and cultural norm building"* (Ibid., p. 56).

### Case Illustration

Dimitra is a twenty-seven-year-old woman. She attended a two-day workshop in Body Psychotherapy that used the method of Biosynthesis. In these workshops, the participants work in small groups of three people under the guidance of a trained therapist. In her session, Dimitra introduced herself and said that she lives in Athens but her dream is to move to an island to start her own business there. She is immobilized by her relationship with her mother, whom she takes care of emotionally. In her session, she is sitting stuck, sad, desperate, and very angry about this situation. She is asked to imagine her mother sitting opposite her, and the main hook is in what she sees in her mother's eyes. With the encouragement of her therapist, Dimitra changes to a standing position, still facing the mother. The therapist is supporting her back, and she is developing an awareness of her feet on the ground, the supporting function of her legs, and the strength of her back. She is encouraged to use her hands and arms to explore the space around her and to make a little more distance from her mother. Gradually she is instructed to use her eyes to contact the surroundings and to orient herself in the room, finding something interesting to look at other than the mother. With the support of the therapist holding her hand, Dimitra tries to turn her back to the mother and she takes a few steps, keeping her awareness in the power and strength of her legs and back. She feels the urge to leave the room, and she is instructed to do this slowly while staying in contact with her bodily sensations. She is very happy to orient herself in another place, symbolic of her wish to move to the island. She feels empowered and free. Later in her life, she could also take this step and make the changes that she wants, which she tried for the first time in that session.

## Grounding as a Resource in Trauma Work

Grounding is of major importance in trauma work.[68] Traumatized people are typically ungrounded. They have had to disconnect from a traumatic reality in order to survive, and now they disconnect from their body sense. Internal sensations or memories flood them, causing them to vacate their bodies and to live in their heads. They feel disconnected, insubstantial, and vulnerable, and are also experienced as such by other people. They are trapped in the trauma cycle, not allowing themselves to experience their rhythm and their constantly changing flow of internal sensations. Grounding in trauma work usually takes two directions: (1) grounding in the here and now, increasing their contact with reality; and (2) grounding in their body, increasing their feeling of safety in their physical presence.

In (1), one can emphasize feeling the chair on which they sit, the ground on which they stand, and their feet on it, looking around the room that they are in, becoming aware of the therapist's presence; these are some examples of what therapists can use, especially in the early phases of the therapeutic work, to help their clients ground themselves in the present time and space. This is later used as a main resource to help them when (if) they start dissociating. Thus, grounding in the here and now helps them to navigate their traumatic experience whenever it becomes overwhelming and sucks them in, causing them to flee from their present reality.

In (2), reconnecting with resources in one's body is a way of working with bodily awareness, sensations, and feelings in the body, moving from the periphery (skin) to the center (internal organs). Contacting the pulsation of contraction and expansion in their body rhythm, they can move from a sense of powerlessness, vulnerability, and helplessness to one of strength, empowerment, and competence. To achieve this, therapists often use images of a safe environment in which clients can start exploring their bodily sensations and movements with some initial security. For example, images of running to a safe place and experiencing their legs doing this, or visualizing actual supportive people, produce a shift in their feelings. Experiencing various body parts positively now becomes a new resource. Their body can be a safe home. Following their body's natural potential to swing between states, from positive to negative, their sensations moving slowly from one pole to its opposite, they regain their trust in their body's ability to change the way that it feels. Later, this is a main resource to be used for releasing their trauma, because they tend not to feel stuck anymore. A traumatic experience can

---

68  See, for example, Levine, 1997, 2005, 2010; Levine and Kline, 2007; Kepner, 1987, 1996; Ogden et al., 2006; Aposhyan, 2004.

be unlocked, because the body now has a broader context, and as a result even painful events can be left behind when the flow of sensations can be trusted and allowed to move.

## Conclusion

Grounding is a basic concept and practice in Body Psychotherapy, but its applications go far beyond our field. In recent years, the sciences of psychology and of neuroscience have been dealing with grounding the mind in the body. Damasio states that the mind is being built through its caring for the body, and psychology theorists speak about "grounded cognition" (Damasio, 2000; Barsalou, 2007). We are coming to a time of grounding our theories more in our experiences, and grounding our experiences more in our theories:

"*Give me a place to stand on, and I will move the earth.*" Such is the significance of grounding, as beautifully stated by Archimedes, the ancient Greek mathematician. If we can find our ground, we can safely practice our dreams. We can be all that we are, and this is the most.

## References

Aposhyan, S. (2004). *Body-Mind Psychotherapy.* New York: W. W. Norton.

Barsalou, L. (2007). Grounded cognition. *Annual Review of Psychology, 59,* 617–645.

Bernhardt, P., & Bentzen, M. (1995). Waking the body ego: Lisbeth Marcher's Somatic Developmental Psychology. *Energy & Character, 26*(1), 47–59.

Bernhardt, P., Bentzen, M., & Isaacs, J. (1996a). Waking the body ego: Part II. *Energy & Character, 27*(1), 38–50.

Bernhardt, P., Bentzen, M., & Isaacs, J. (1996b). Waking the body ego: Part III. *Energy & Character, 27*(2), 61–76.

Bernhardt, P., Bentzen, M., & Isaacs, J. (1996c). Waking the body ego: Part IV. *Energy & Character, 28*(1), 108–121.

Bertherat, T. (1976). *Le Corps à ses Raisons [The body with its reasons].* Paris: Éditions du Seuil.

Bertherat, T. (1989). *Le Repaire du Tigre [The tiger's lair].* Paris: Éditions du Seuil.

Boadella, D. (1986). What is Biosynthesis? *Energy & Character, 17*(2), 1–23.

Boadella, D. (1987). *Lifestreams: An introduction to Biosynthesis.* London: Routledge & Kegan Paul.

Boadella, D. (1997). *Common ground and different approaches in psychotherapy.* Paper presented at 7th European Congress of Psychotherapy, Rome.

Damasio, A. (2000). *The feeling of what happens.* London: Vintage.

Feldenkrais, M. (1977). *Awareness through movement.* New York: Harper & Row.

Feldenkrais, M. (1985). *The potent self.* New York: Harper & Row.

Hartley, L. (2009). *Contemporary Body Psychotherapy.* Hove, UK: Routledge.

Keleman, S. (1979). *Somatic reality.* Berkeley, CA: Center Press.

Keleman, S. (1985). *Emotional anatomy.* Berkeley, CA: Center Press.

Kepner, J. (1987). *Body process.* New York: Jossey-Bass.

Kepner, J. (1996). *Healing tasks.* Cleveland, OH: Gestalt Press.

Kurtz, R., & Prestera, H. (1976). *The body reveals.* New York: Harper & Row.

Levine, P. (1997). *Waking the tiger.* Berkeley, CA: North Atlantic Books.

Levine, P. (2005). *Healing trauma.* Boulder, CO: Sounds True.

Levine, P. (2010). *In an unspoken voice.* Berkeley, CA: North Atlantic Books.

Levine, P., & Kline, M. (2007). *Trauma through a child's eyes.* Berkeley, CA: North Atlantic Books.

Lowen, A. (1958). *The language of the body.* London: Penguin Books.

Lowen, A. (1972). *Depression and the body.* London: Penguin Books.

Lowen, A., & Lowen, L. (1977). *The way to vibrant health.* New York: Harper Colophon.

Marcher, L., & Fich, S. (2010). *Body encyclopedia.* Berkeley, CA: North Atlantic Books.

Ogden, P., Minton, K., & Pain, C. (2006). *Trauma and the body: A sensorimotor approach to psychotherapy.* New York: W. W. Norton.

Rolf, I. (1977). *Rolfing.* New York: Harper & Row.

Wehowsky, A. (1998). Cultivating grounding, centering and facing. *Energy & Character, 29(1), 14–22.*

Winnicott, D. W. (1964). *The child, the family, and the outside world.* London: Penguin Books.

Winnicott, D. W. (1971). *Playing and reality.* London: Tavistock.

# 68

## Entering the Erotic Field

### *Sexuality in Body-Centered Psychotherapy*

**William F. Cornell, United States**

**William F. Cornell**'s biographical information can be found at the beginning of Chapter 45, "Entering the Relational Field in Body Psychotherapy."

## Introduction with Case Illustration

It was like a small miracle that Chloe and Phillipe ever got together in the first place. Phillipe had lived in a deeply symbiotic marriage for more than forty years. His was a marriage in which he and his wife had created a buffer against the "dangers" and uncertainties of the world outside their suburban home; theirs was a relationship that served to manage their anxieties about themselves and life. It was a comfortable and highly predictable life. Theirs had not been a particularly passionate or sexual relationship, but more an arrangement of mutual caregiving. Phillipe satisfied his sexual interests through pornography, as his wife seemed to prefer being left alone with regard to sex. The marriage endured quite successfully. Then Phillipe's wife died.

Chloe had lived alone with her dogs for more than thirty years, after a failed and sometimes violent marriage. Phillipe, born in Europe, described himself as being afflicted with "weak nerves" and subject to nervous collapse whenever life got too difficult for him. Chloe described herself as suffering from PTSD, the contemporary American equivalent of "weak nerves." She limited the scope of her life so as not to trigger her PTSD and subsequent anxiety attacks.

Unable to grieve his wife's death, Phillipe became severely depressed. Mutual friends introduced him to Chloe. After dinner with their friends, Phillipe asked Chloe if she would like to go to dinner and a movie with him. *"Yes,"* she replied, *"as long as you don't expect to have sex."* Phillipe assured her that sex was not on his agenda; it was hard enough to ask her to the movies. They began to date and, in spite of their best efforts to the contrary, fell in love. They rather rapidly became sexual and, somewhat to their mutual amazement, found themselves having quite a good time. The good times, however, tended to alternate rapidly with bad times. The bad times were marked by profound anxiety reactions for each of them. Chloe and Phillipe sought couples therapy.

It was very clear from the initial session that they each were having a very hard time tolerating the intensity of stimulation that this relationship brought to them. A key goal of therapy, I suggested, would be to deepen their capacity to feel and enjoy more stimulation and pleasure in life. They each made a serious commitment to their therapy together. Having made this commitment, things rapidly became worse. Both complained of suicidal thoughts. Chloe became increasingly suspicious that Phillipe was sleeping with other women and using pornography. Phillipe insisted he was faithful and now had no need for pornography. At the same time, Phillipe began to miss and grieve his wife, which he felt was somehow disloyal to Chloe, and he felt quite guilty. Chloe was also growing more distressed and anxious. Both were feeling that they had been better off before getting involved with each *other*. *"Why is this happening? Why are we feeling suicidal?,"* they asked me.

What Phillipe and Chloe were probably experiencing is what Wilhelm Reich would have called "pleasure anxiety." Although I never used that term directly with them, I began to talk with them about how frightening it might be to begin to open up one's body, heart, and emotions to another person, especially after decades of careful constriction. I worked with them gradually to try to both respect, and reflect upon, their individual defenses. Each could begin to see how their reactions to, and fears of, the other were projections of their fears of themselves, of their own emotions and needs. Reich wrote eloquently of these forms of anxiety—pleasure anxiety, falling (surrender) anxiety, and orgasm anxiety. It was an enduring clinical question for Reich: *"How is it that those aspects of life and relationship that can be so intensely pleasurable seem to be at the roots of our most determined and vigorous defenses?"*

Joyce McDougall (1995, 2000), the French psychoanalyst whose work is deeply engrained in the exploration of bodily experience, echoes Reich's observations about the anxieties arising during intense bodily pleasure and orgasm when she writes, *"I learned that the terrors of dissolving, of losing one's bodily limits or sense of self, of exploding into another or being invaded and imploded by another, were both frequent and revealing of the buried links to archaic sexual and love feelings originating in earliest infancy"* (1995, p. xvi).

Like Reich, McDougall explores the unquiet waters of adult sexuality, infused with ageless desires and conflicts. These were the waters that Chloe and Phillipe were entering into their psychotherapy. The therapy work with Phillipe and with Chloe was delicate, focused—in the present, within each session—on how their deepening relationship both frightened them and precipitated their defenses.

Seen from a body-centered perspective, Phillipe's psychological and somatic organization was quite fragile and fragmented. Typical of the schizoid style of defense, Phillipe was profoundly identified with his mind, while describing his emotions and his body as sources of weakness. He had learned to keep a careful, subtly disdainful distance from those around him, so as to not be too disturbed or disorganized by emotional relatedness. I would watch carefully for the moments when, and the means by which, Phillipe created a distance from Chloe (or me) within the session. I would catch those moments "live," as they occurred, inquiring as to what it was that he had begun to feel and then warded off. What was he afraid of Chloe seeing about him? I worked to bring the process of Phillipe's distancing more and more to his conscious awareness, and then to bring him into deeper contact with his emotions. Part of the work was to develop his experience of his body as a resource, rather than a threat or an embarrassment.

Phillipe began to realize that his growing love for Chloe evoked his split-off love for his deceased wife, that—as he began to feel love again with Chloe—his experience of grief for his dead wife was inevitable. He began to realize that his grief was not a betrayal of Chloe, but it was really her gift to him. He needed to grieve his wife in order to be able to fully give himself to Chloe. In session, I would observe how he would hide his eyes from view, and also constrict his jaw and throat to cut off sobbing. With my gentle encouragement, he was able to cry in front of Chloe, and then to move physically toward her, rather than away, while he was in pain. He began to see that he had always kept a careful distance from people; his caregiving of his wife for more than forty years had meant that he never fully opened up to her. He was starting to experience something with Chloe that both touched and terrified him. He began to understand that Chloe did not want, or need, the constant protection that his wife had demanded, but that what she wanted was to be *met* emotionally.

Chloe, quite correctly, described herself as obsessive-compulsive. Seen from a bodily perspective, she carried a high emotional and energetic charge with intense, rigid body defenses, both to contain herself and to avoid exploding in anger, or disintegrating in fear. She feared loss of control, above all else, and her many years of living alone could be seen as seeming to ensure a degree of control over her life. Chloe began to see how terrified she was of her loneliness, even as she was terrified of giving it up. She was frightened of her sexual desires. Chloe feared the loss of control during sex, even as she craved evidence of Phillipe's love and wanted to demonstrate hers to him. Her sexual urges in her teens and twenties had always propelled her into the arms of selfish, controlling men, whose superficial appearance of strength had enticed her. It felt safer to look constantly for evidence of Phillipe being untrustworthy, as a hedge against her losing control, or (again) making a bad judgment in the choice of a partner.

She was afraid of the force of her desire; Phillipe likewise was afraid of his. Each, in their own way, would begin to feel excited—and then feel as if they were being overwhelmed, falling apart, disintegrating. When Chloe felt threatened, she tended to close her eyes and go off in a flood of memory and fantasy that escalated her distress. All she could think of to do, to alleviate her distress, was to flee. Direct work with her body in distress began to foster alternatives. As we worked together, I stressed the importance of her maintaining eye contact whenever she got upset, to come *to* me with her eyes, rather than go into her mind. I, in turn, held her in my gaze, never looking away from her (as Phillipe usually did) when she became upset. As I was a more neutral figure than Phillipe, I was less a source of anxiety. It was easier for her to work directly with me, with Phillipe observing the two of us. Gradually, bit by bit, Chloe was able to experience fear, anger, or desire, and then to express them (to me) in words and with body movements. In contrast to her habitual use of retreat and obsession to reestablish a sense of boundedness, she began to experiment with reaching toward me, pressing against me, pushing me away. She began to learn to use her body—in relation to mine—to establish a sense of boundedness *while in contact* with another person.

They each learned to slow down; to look at each other when they spoke of difficult things; to respect their own and the other's physical and emotional limits; and to feel some tenderness toward the other's limits. This was the heart of the therapeutic work with their pleasure and orgasm anxieties. Much of the work with Chloe and Phillipe was actually individual Body-Centered Psychotherapy, in the presence of one another. Each learned to understand each other better and to open up their emotional and body processes—in the work with me. Each learned to understand the other better, through witnessing the work with me.

Chloe and Phillipe are hardly alone in their struggle to embrace their sexual and loving desires. Desire, pleasure, and love are incredibly complex, and often conflicted. Desire, pleasure, and love are frequently messy. Desire, pleasure, and love are often what carry us through the disappointments and vicissitudes of life among other people. In the undoing and overstepping within erotic relations, in being naked to one another, we are continually invited to undo ourselves, and to revisit, undo, and (hopefully) re-do the history of our loves, desires, dependencies, and moments of madness and fury. These undoings and fragile re-doings are the source of profound hope and anxiety.

## Reich and Sexuality

We need only to look at some of the titles of the various books that Wilhelm Reich published over the course of his lifetime—namely: *The Sexual Revolution* (1945), *The Function of the Orgasm* (1961), *The Invasion of Compulsory Sex-Morality* (1971), *Sex-Pol: Essays* (1972), *Genitality* (1980), *The Bioelectrical Investigation of Sexuality and Anxiety* (1982), *Children of the Future: On the Prevention of Sexual Pathology* (1983), etc.—to see the centrality of sexuality in Reich's perspective on emotional and relational health. From his earliest writings, as a psychoanalyst, Reich began to explore the relationship between pleasure and sexuality, on the one hand, and the antitheses, anxiety and hostility, on the other.

He postulated that the deepening of one's capacities for tenderness, intimacy, and sexual pleasure is essential for the resolution of, and freedom from, characterological and muscular defenses. The freeing up of one's capacities for intimate and orgasmic surrender was among the explicit goals in psychotherapy for Reich, especially during the 1920s and 1930s.

In the 1960s and 1970s, Alexander Lowen (1965, 1970), Kelley (1972), Keleman (1975, 1994), Baker (1967), and Mann and Hoffman (1980), among others, took up Reich's attention to sexuality. During these decades, active work with clients' sexual attitudes, behaviors, and relations was central to Neo-Reichian therapy. The work with sexuality in these later years—despite the sexual revolution of the 1960s—was often deeply confrontative, and frequently quite mechanistic. Clients could feel "faulted" for not having sex "in the right way" —for falling short of the Reichian ideal of orgiastic potency. Often, the styles of (therapeutic) intervention were pathologizing, intrusive, or transgressive of clients' sexual limits and vulnerabilities. In the guise of sexual freedom, sexual misconduct between therapists and clients, or between trainers and trainees, was also often excused, or even justified.

During the 1980s, the attitudes about sexuality within psychotherapy and society began to change again, spurred by the growing recognition of the frequency of domestic violence and especially sexual abuse and trauma. It was an important recognition, and yet it forced the pendulum of clinical attention to move to an extreme. Sex had become a field of potential intrusion and trauma. Sex had become threatening to a new generation, in contrast to being considered sinful and immoral by earlier generations. The trauma of aggression, violence, and abusive sexuality was typically located in the behavior and attitudes of *the other,* the self typically cast in the place of the victim. Little attention was paid, in the clinical literature during the 1980s and much of the 1990s, to the trauma, the disturbance, the intrusiveness of one's *own* sexual urges and desires on another. Sexuality can be exquisitely enlivening and intimate; however, it can also be profoundly disturbing and disorganizing. In the face of the trauma-centered concerns of society, psychotherapy, and the reemergence of spiritualism under the rubric of the "New Age" in psychotherapy (Marlock, 1996), direct work with and support of sexuality nearly faded away from the therapeutic landscape.

Reich worked actively within the social and political arenas of his time, as well as the therapeutic, to develop services in support of sex education, counseling, and birth control. Reich founded the Socialist Society for Sex Consultation and Sexological Research, operating free clinics for the working class in Vienna. These clinics were then expanded by his work in Germany with the Communist Party, before Reich was forced to emigrate by the Nazis' takeover.

He later moved to Norway, where he continued his social and psychotherapeutic work with sexuality, and also initiated research into the bioelectrical nature of sexuality (Reich, 1982), which involved the direct observation and physiological recordings of couples during lovemaking, foreshadowing (by several decades) the pioneering research of Masters and Johnson.

Reich had challenged the prevailing norms of sexuality during the 1920s and 1930s. He was convinced that most political, social, and religious institutions were invested in the repression of healthy sexuality—primarily to foster the chronic attitudes of depression and resignation that promoted a compliant citizenry with authoritarian social structures and families. For Reich (1961), pleasure anxiety was a social, religious, and political creation that thwarted the healthy expression of love and the natural development of children, and thus created emotionally maimed and dependent adults. The suppression of pleasure anxiety necessitated the development of somatic and both intra- and inter-personal armoring. This type of psychic armoring thus assured the individual of a place within the family, and in society, but also created the emotional foundation for loneliness, sexual misery, resignation, impotent hostility, sadism, fear of responsibility, and a craving of outside authority (Reich, 1945).

## The Crucial Function of Erotic Pleasure and Surrender

Contemporary infant and neurological research offers powerful validations of Reich's clinical observations and theoretical speculations about the developmental and interpersonal centrality of pleasure, both in infancy and throughout the course of one's life. Stern (1990), for example, stresses the crucial, formative role of joy and pleasure in an infant's experience:

> Observations of infants rekindle this question [of the explanatory power of the pleasure principle] because it is so widely recognized that infants seek stimulation that arouses, excites, and activates them. They will,

in fact, expend much time, energy, and ingenuity to create and maintain heightened states of delight and joy. (p. 14)

Stern (1985, 1990), Emde (1988a, 1988b, 1999), and Panksepp (1993, 1998, 2001) have each emphasized the importance of bodily and interpersonal pleasures in healthy human development. Pleasure, joy, and positive emotions become encoded neurologically and motorically, are internalized as crucial relational schema, and evolve into psychological representational structures that guide thought and action. It seems clear that the successes and failures of these primary, organizing experiences of infant and childhood joy and pleasure are deeply evoked, for good or ill, during adult sexual relations as primary, orienting passions.

While it was mainly during the 1920s and 1930s that Reich wrote most consistently about sexuality, sometimes he wrote as a psychotherapist and psychoanalyst, but in those years, he often wrote as a socio-political polemicist, or even as a scientist. As a result, his language was often politically strident or stiffly scientific, in the fashion of those times. He wrote far more often from his fury than from his tenderness. He rarely wrote of these matters from his heart. But, what he was attempting to describe and valorize, long before his psychoanalytic colleagues could tolerate it, was the centrality of love and loving surrender to the other person as an essential component to emotional health and physical well-being. He wrote of orgiastic potency, but what he was truly writing about was *the capacity to love with heart and "flesh"* (Heller, 2001, p. 14).

In his classic book *The Function of the Orgasm,* Reich (1929/1961) challenged the definition of the sexual intimacy of his day. From his perspective, most of what passed in the psychoanalytic circles of his day as healthy sexual functioning was, in fact, deeply neurotic and impaired. For Reich, the mere capacity to "perform" was not the indicator of healthy sexuality. He studied and described the qualitative experience of sexuality in both the emotional and the physiological experience.

Boadella (1973, pp. 17–18) summarized Reich's observations about the *quality* of sexual experience as shown in Table 68.1. Reich's concept of orgiastic potency has often been caricatured and criticized, but as Boadella observed, "Orgasm in this sense is nothing less than one of the most sensitive areas of human relationship that one could find" (1973, p. 22).

## The Infantile Roots of Sexuality and Its Adult Echoes

In Reich's writings about the genesis of sexual inhibition and dysfunction, we find a twofold explanation. The first, as discussed above, was the social and political "functions" of sexual inhibition. The second theme in Reich's account was that of the infantile roots of sexuality. This is not to suggest that sexuality was seen as regressive or infantile in its intent. Quite to the contrary, Reich was convinced that a healthy, enlivening, erotic relationship between mother and baby was perhaps the greatest assurance of that a young child was developing an intact, vital sense of his or her body and sexual pleasure.

Nearly four decades ago, Dorothy Dinnerstein (1976) was challenging the impact of traditional gender arrangements in infant care in the United States and in most Judeo-Christian societies. She argued that these socially sanctioned child-rearing practices were actually maiming the emotional health of our children, and straining, and often crippling, our erotic capacities as adult lovers. Her writing powerfully describes the infantile root of adult sexuality and also deeply evokes the spirit of Reich:

Our most fleeting and local sensations are shot through with thoughts and feelings in which a long past and a long future, and a deep wide now, are represented. . . . But our sexuality [as humans] is also characterized by another peculiarity, one that is central for the project of changing our gender arrangements: *It resonates, more literally than any other part of our experience, with the massive orienting passions that first take shape in pre-verbal, pre-rational human infancy.* (pp. 14–15; emphasis as in the original)

| PHASES OF DEVELOPMENT OF EXCITATION | ORGIASTIC POTENCY | ORGIASTIC IMPOTENCE |
|---|---|---|
| 1. Foreplay | Biological readiness. "Calm excitement." Mutual pleasurable anticipation. | Over- or underexcitement. "Cold" erection. "Dry" vagina. Foreplay either insufficient or overprolonged. |
| 2. Penetration | Preceded by a spontaneous urge to enter, or to be entered, by the partner. Bodily tenderness. Increase of pleasure. | Either: sadistic piercing by the man or rape fantasy by the woman. Or: fear of penetrating, or of being penetrated, and decrease in pleasure at point of penetration. |
| 3. Voluntary phase of sexual movements | Movements are voluntary but effortless and rhythmic, unhurried and gentle. Extraneous thoughts are absent; there is absorption in the experience. Pleasurable sensations continue to increase. Periods of rest do not lead to a decrease of pleasure. | Violent friction, nervous haste. Extraneous thoughts or fantasies are compulsively present. Preoccupation with a sense of duty to one's partner and fear of "failure" or determination to succeed. Period of rest likely to lead to a sharp drop in excitation. |
| 4. Involuntary phase of muscle contraction | Excitation leads to involuntary contractions of the genital musculature and similar contractions of the vagina (which precede ejaculation in the man and lead to the climax for both). The total body musculature participates with lively contractions as the excitation flows from the genitals back into the body. "Melting" sensations in the body. Clouding of consciousness at the climax. | Involuntary movements greatly reduced or in some cases absent altogether. Sensations remain localized in the genitals and do not spread to the body as a whole. Involuntary responses may be simulated for the benefit of the partner. Squeezing and pushing, with spastic contraction, to achieve a climax (for the man). Head remains in control, and the clouding of consciousness is absent. |
| 5. Phase of relaxation | Pleasant bodily and mental relaxation. Feeling of harmony with the partner. Strong desire for rest or sleep. "Afterglow." | Feelings of leaden exhaustion, disgust, repulsion, indifference, or hatred toward the partner. Excitation not fully discharged, sometimes leading to insomnia. The body after orgasm is depressed. |

Table 68.1. Types of Sexual Experience

Her phrase "massive orienting passions" vividly conveys the sense of somatic and emotional forces that underlie our love and gender arrangements, our sensual and sexual experiences.

Bollas (2000), a psychoanalyst and an important writer within the British psychoanalytic community, vividly describes the impact of a mother who cannot enter the erotic realm with her infant:

> Specifically, the mother experiences intense ambivalence towards the infant as a sexual being, especially towards the genitalia, which cannot be sensorially celebrated. Maternal care is in this respect a "laying on of hands" and the mother in this case cannot eroticize her infant's body through her own hands. . . . If the mother then refuses the infant's genital sexuality—not sonically celebrating it, averting her gaze, stiffening her touch—thereby displacing it to other parts of the body . . . she has removed the core of erotic life and sought surface sexuality as a defense against deep sexuality. . . . As maternal love is the first field of sexual foreplay, the hysterical mother conveys to her infant's body an anguished desire, as her energetic touches bear the trace of disgust and frustration, carrying to the infant's body communication about sexual ambivalence, "rolfed," as it were, into the infant's body knowledge, part of the self's unthought known. (pp. 46–48)

I would suggest that, like the mother described above, we do our clients a disservice when we, too, avert our gaze, our minds, our language, and the attention of our clients from the realms of the sexual and erotic. It is, indeed, tempting to avert our gaze from the sexual—and many models of psychotherapy do exactly that, on a regular basis. Muriel Dimen, a prominent feminist and psychoanalyst in the United States, challenges her psychoanalytic colleagues' detached and clinical writings on sexuality with the question, *"What happened to the heat?"* (1999, p. 419). There is "heat" in adult erotic passions. Dinnerstein uses the phrase "massive orienting passions" to capture the evocative power of sexuality as it is drenched with infantile echoes and wrenched with hope, desire, vulnerability. Essential to both the disturbance *and* the excitement of our erotic desires is the simultaneous evocation of the infantile underpinnings of our somatic emotional experiences, as well as the force and complexity of adult love and passion. Dinnerstein captures the heat and the anxiety, as well as the warmth and the caring, in the passions of our infantile attachments and longings, in her use of our "massive orienting passions."

## The Body Psychotherapist in the Erotic Field

The impassioned desires and fears of the erotic field, infused with the force of the adult body, emerge and reemerge with relentless vitality within our sexual relationships, and also in the transference and countertransference dynamics of in-depth Body Psychotherapy. To enter the realms of the erotic within the therapeutic relationship and to enter fully into adult sexual relations, one has to invite the full force of life's vicissitudes, replete with fantasy, idealization, disappointment, frustration, aggression, excitement, and unpredictability. Passionate sexual engagement with one's own body, and that of another, is an undoing of the insulated self, an undoing of the ordinary.

The relentless pressures of developmental forces during infancy, childhood, and adolescence repeatedly disorganize and reorganize the body and mind. Children learn, in the most fundamental ways, through their bodily activity. The grammars of mind and language follow the grammars of sensory-motor activity and bodily experience. In adulthood, our somatic, emotional, and interpersonal processes become more stable. More than any other aspect of adult life, sexuality is the most profoundly somatic force: simultaneously intimate, exciting, disorganizing, and sometimes frightening. It is within our sexual relations that we, as adults, can experience ourselves in the most directly, fully embodied way. Reich emphasized the capacity for sexual and orgasmic surrender as the most significant evidence of emotional health. Ghent (1990) suggests that "there is something like a universal need, wish or longing for what I am calling surrender, and that it assumes many forms"

(p. 114). Sexual surrender, in particular, brings one to one's own body and unites it with that of another, rife with excitement, desire, wounds, and also anxiety.

Sexual surrender is both deeply gratifying and disruptive. Disruption is often managed defensively, through avoidance and deadening, as we saw with Chloe and Phillipe. Disruption can also be received and incorporated in change and growth through bodily responsiveness and experimentation. It is perhaps most effectively, in this regard, that Body Psychotherapy provides unique avenues of approach and work with sexuality and its consequent patterns of excitement, anxiety, disorganization, and reorganization.

A Body Psychotherapist utilizes multiple modes of attention and intervention, and the particular attention to the actual, lived processes of the body can be an enormous advantage to working with such sexual issues. Body Psychotherapy has a keen sense of both the disorganization and the opportunity created in sexual relations. In addressing sexual concerns and problems, a Body Psychotherapist not only asks, *"What makes you anxious?"* but also, *"How do you become anxious?"* A Body Psychotherapist creates new developmental opportunities, at a direct body level, experimenting with changes in body movement and expression that do not overwhelm the client. The therapist monitors the level of anxiety and disorganization, seeking to find the edge of disorganization that creates the occasion for new experience, rather than a level of anxiety that evokes defensive avoidance and deadening. Like most psychotherapists, a Body Psychotherapist will also examine any beliefs, feelings, and interpersonal patterns that inhibit any sexual expression and intimate contact. Unlike most psychotherapists, a Body Psychotherapist will have a repertoire of skills to intervene and work directly at a body level, as we saw in the work with Chloe and Phillipe.

A Body Psychotherapist seeks to foster an alive and increasingly skilled body in their client: a body that is skilled in "being" a body, with all its capacities for vitality, contact, and surrender. Psychotherapists usually form a new and (hopefully) creative alliance with the client's mind; a Body Psychotherapist provides a further form alliance (or resonance) with the client's body. Body Psychotherapy develops the means—through exercises and increased awareness—with the client in session, as well as support for their newfound emotional communication, bodily movement, and (possible) engagement with a partner's body—to reduce their anxiety and tension and thus help to promote greater pleasure and sexuality within their sexual and erotic fields of experience.

## References

Baker, E. (1967). *Man in the trap: The causes of blocked sexual energy.* New York: Macmillan.

Boadella, D. (1973). *Wilhelm Reich: The evolution of his work.* London: Vision.

Bollas, C. (2000). *Hysteria.* London: Routledge.

Dimen, M. (1999). Between lust and libido: Sex, psychoanalysis, and the moment before. *Psychoanalytic Dialogues, 9,* 415–440.

Dinnerstein, D. (1976). *The mermaid and the minotaur: Sexual arrangements and human malaise.* New York: Harper & Row.

Emde, R. (1988a). Development terminable and interminable: I: Innate and motivational factors. *International Journal of Psychoanalysis, 69,* 23–42.

Emde, R. (1988b). Development terminable and interminable: II: Recent psychoanalytic theory and therapeutic considerations. *International Journal of Psychoanalysis, 69,* 283–296.

Emde, R. (1999). Moving ahead: Integrating influences of affective processes for development and psychoanalysis. *International Journal of Psychoanalysis, 80,* 317–339.

Ghent, E. (1990). Masochism, submission, and surrender. *Contemporary Psychoanalysis, 26*(1), 108–136.

Heller, M. (2001). Presentation: The organism as physiology, body, flesh and soul. In M. Heller (Ed.), *The flesh of the soul: The body we work with* (pp. 9–32). Bern, Switzerland: Peter Lang.

Keleman, S. (1975). *The human ground: Sexuality, self and survival.* Palo Alto, CA: Science and Behavior Books.

Keleman, S. (1994). *Love: A somatic view.* Berkeley, CA: Center Press.

Kelley, C. (1972). Primal scream and genital character: A critique of Janov and Reich. *Journal of Humanistic Psychology, 12*(2), 61–73.

Lowen, A. (1965). *Love and orgasm.* New York: Macmillan.

Lowen, A. (1970). *Pleasure.* New York: Coward-McCann.

Mann, W., & Hoffman, E. (1980). *The man who dreamed of tomorrow: A conceptual biography of Wilhelm Reich.* Los Angeles: J. P. Tarcher.

Marlock, G. (1996). Reich, Humanistic Psychology and the New Age: Part I. *Energy & Character, 27*(2), 1–14.

McDougall, J. (1995). *The many faces of Eros: Psychoanalytic explorations of human sexuality.* New York: W. W. Norton.

McDougall, J. (2000). Sexuality and the neosexual. *Modern Psychoanalysis, 25*(2), 155–166.

Panksepp, J. (1993). Rough and tumble play: A fundamental brain process. In K. MacDonald (Ed.), *Parent-child play: Descriptions and implications* (pp. 147–184). Albany, NY: State University of New York Press.

Panksepp, J. (1998). *Affective neuroscience.* New York: Oxford University Press.

Panksepp, J. (2001). The long-term psychobiological consequences of infant emotions: Prescriptions for the twenty-first century. *Infant Mental Health Journal, 22,* 132–173.

Reich, W. (1945). *The sexual revolution.* New York: Orgone Institute Press.

Reich, W. (1929/1961). *The function of the orgasm.* New York: Farrar, Straus & Giroux.

Reich, W. (1971). *The invasion of compulsory sex-morality.* New York: Farrar, Straus & Giroux.

Reich, W. (1972). *Sex-Pol: Essays 1929–1934.* New York: Random House.

Reich, W. (1980). *Genitality in the theory and therapy of neurosis.* New York: Farrar, Straus & Giroux.

Reich, W. (1982). *The bioelectrical investigation of sexuality and anxiety.* New York: Farrar, Straus & Giroux.

Reich, W. (1983). *Children of the future: On the prevention of sexual pathology.* New York: Farrar, Straus & Giroux.

Stern, D. (1985). *The interpersonal world of the infant: A view from psychoanalysis and Developmental Psychology.* New York: Basic Books.

Stern, D. (1990). Joy and satisfaction in infancy. In R. Glick & S. Bone (Eds.), *Pleasure beyond the pleasure principle.* New Haven, CT: Yale University Press.

# SECTION IX

Body Psychotherapeutic Treatment of Specific Disorders

# 69

## Introduction to Section IX

Gustl Marlock, Germany, and Halko Weiss, United States

Translation by Warren Miller

One of the ways to determine the value of a therapeutic modality is to look at the extent to which it expands and improves the options of treatment of specific disorders. Consequently, there is a need to differentiate both the theory and the practice from the point of view of specific disorders, as well as specific symptoms. That is certainly true for Body Psychotherapy: the particular somatically oriented treatments for anxiety, depression, or post-traumatic stress disorder vary accordingly. Therefore, it seems necessary to take steps to develop a much more specific clinical theory and to intensify empirical research. Body Psychotherapy—very much like other approaches, from Psychodynamic Psychotherapy to Systemic Therapy—finds itself facing this challenge. In Section IX, various authors write about the treatment of diverse disorders, their special authority stemming from their vast experience in dealing with each specific disorder, as well as their publications on the topic.

We have not attempted to systematically cover all types of psychological symptoms and disorders, as is the case with many other handbooks. Instead, the aim is to present a list of therapeutic approaches that can provide a representative insight into the diversity and breadth of potential Body Psychotherapeutic strategies.

Section IX commences with Chapter 70, "Body Psychotherapy for Severe Mental Disorders" by **Frank Röhricht**, about the potential of Body Psychotherapeutic treatment of people with such diagnoses in a hospital setting: Frank—being a psychiatrist and working with such populations—presents an excellent perspective. In Chapter 71, **Guy Tonella** adds to this theme by describing the use of "Body Psychotherapy and Psychosis," as developed within the context of a research project.

**In Chapter 72, "Body Psychotherapeutic Treatments for Eating Disorders," Sasha Dmochowski, Asaf Rolef Ben-Shahar, and Jacqueline A. Carleton** elaborate on a specifically Body Psychotherapeutic perspective on the treatment of eating disorders. These are increasingly common disorders that still challenge the psychotherapeutic community today, as much as "hysteria" did in Freud's time.

The following two chapters explore somatic approaches to equally demanding challenges. In Chapter 73, "Body Psychotherapy with Narcissistic Personality Disorders," **Manfred Thielen** investigates Body Psychotherapy in relation to the very difficult topic of working with people with narcissistic personality disorder. In Chapter 74, **Xavier Serrano Hortelano** provides a number of interesting insights into working with "Vegetotherapy with Psychosomatic Disorders: Functionalism in Practice," followed by **Guy Tonella** presenting a specific method of treatment for "Oral Depression" in Chapter 75.

Particularly noteworthy in Section IX is Chapter 76 by **Pat Ogden** and **Kekuni Minton,** "Sensory-Motor Processing for Trauma Recovery," about a particular Body Psychotherapeutic approach to the treatment of post-traumatic stress disorders (PTSD) that has received a great deal of acclaim.

As noted several times earlier in this handbook, the most promising contributions to the treatment of trauma (aside perhaps from the reported success of EMDR) come from the field of Body Psychotherapy. Therefore, besides Pat Ogden and colleagues (2006), Bessel van der Kolk (1997), Peter Levine (1997, 2008), Hilarion Petzold (2000), Petzold and colleagues (2002), and Babette Rothschild (2000) must all be mentioned here, as they are all linked to the field of Body Psychotherapy and are also major contributors to the currently very rich discourse about this topic of trauma.

## References

Levine, P. (1997). *Waking the tiger: Healing trauma.* Berkeley, CA: North Atlantic Books.

Levine, P. (2008). *Healing trauma: A pioneering program for restoring the wisdom of your body.* Boulder, CO: Sounds True.

Ogden, P., Minton, K., & Pain, C. (2006). *Trauma and the body: A sensorimotor approach to psychotherapy.* New York: W. W. Norton.

Petzold, H. (2000). Integrative traumatherapie [Integrative trauma therapy]. In B. A. van der Kolk, A. C. McFarlane, & L. Wisaeth (Eds.), *Traumatic Stress: Grundlagen und Behandlungsansätze. Theorie, Praxis, Forschung zu posttraumatischem Stress und Traumatherapie [Traumatic stress:* Fundamentals and treatment approaches. Theory, practice, research on post-traumatic stress and trauma therapy]. Paderborn: Junfermann.

Petzold, H., Wolf, H. U., & Landgrebe, B. (2002). *Das Trauma überwinden [Overcoming trauma].* Paderborn: Junfermann.

Rothschild, B. (2000). *The body remembers: The psychophysiology of trauma and trauma treatment.* New York: W. W. Norton.

van der Kolk, B. A., McFarlane, A. C., & Wisneath, L. (Eds.). (1997). *Traumatic stress:* Fundamentals and treatment approaches: Theory, practice, research on post-traumatic stress and trauma therapy. New York: Guilford.

# 70

## Body Psychotherapy for Severe Mental Disorders

**Frank Röhricht, United Kingdom**

**Translation by Elizabeth Marshall**

**Frank Röhricht's biographical information** can be found at the beginning of Chapter 22, "'Body Schema,' 'Body Image,' and Bodily Experience: Concept Formation, Definitions, and Clinical Relevance in Diagnostics and Therapy."

The Body-Oriented Psychotherapeutic treatment of severe mental illness (SMI) has a long and controversial tradition of scientific theory and practice orientation. At the beginning of the twentieth century, fifty years before the introduction of the first psychotropic drugs, and particularly inspired by the increasing popularity of psychoanalytic theory, there was a lively and creative struggle for psychologically oriented treatment strategies for severe mental disorders. The advent of the "neuroleptic era" with subsequent discoveries of other psychotropic treatments and, in consequence, the relatively speedy remission of, for example, florid psychotic symptoms heralded the age of biological psychiatry, later referred to as "the decade of the brain." Following the introduction of Cognitive Behavioral Therapy and Family Therapy into the portfolio of mental health care for SMI patients and because of ongoing problems with lack of response to somatic treatments, there are renewed and growing efforts to evaluate alternative psychotherapeutic approaches for the treatment of severe mental disturbances (particularly therapy for psychosis, chronic conditions, and personality disorders).

In the diffusely defined category of "severe mental disorders," which forms the basis for this chapter, the following illnesses are grouped together: (1) schizophreniform and manic-depressive psychoses (acute mania and severe depressive episodes with or without accompanying psychotic symptoms); (2) personality disorders with psychosocial malfunctioning or destructive and/or self-harming behavior; (3) acute or severe anxiety disorders; and (4) severe psycho-reactive crises.

Attempting to organize the state of our knowledge about severe mental disorders, systematically and for the field of Body Psychotherapy, we must differentiate between the treatment of acute phases of illness and the outpatient therapy of often chronic and incurable (untreatable) diseases. In Europe, despite growing evidence supporting the effectiveness of psychiatric outpatient community care (crisis services, Soteria models, home treatment, recovery-oriented services, etc.), acute disorders are still usually treated in psychiatric hospitals, with psychotherapy often being delivered as group therapy; therefore, this setting will be a main part of the focus of this chapter.

Another level of differentiation is related to the question of available evidence regarding the efficacy and effectiveness of Body Psychotherapeutic approaches. But, most importantly, the theoretical underpinning for body-oriented intervention strategies is based upon a novel paradigm in respect to the nosological categories used to distinguish between types/groups of severe mental illness: Fuchs and Schlimme (2009) and Röhricht (2011) describe mental illness as disorders of embodied self-regulation.

Applying a basic phenomenological approach of functional psycho-pathology, three main groups of disorders can hereby be distinguished:

- Embodied disorders (the body as the source of suffering—e.g., severe neurosis)
- Alternating and instrumentalized body-mind regulation (personality disorders, eating disorders, etc.)
- Disembodied disorders (the body in passing, the dissociated body: psychosis)

Body Psychotherapy employs several different, syndrome-specific approaches for the treatment of those three main groups, aiming to facilitate greater body-mind, self-affect regulation. According to most recent reviews of the literature (Loew et al., 2006; Röhricht, 2009), the current evidence base for Body Psychotherapy in the treatment of severe mental illness can be summarized as follows: Body Psychotherapy seems to have generally good effects on subjectively experienced depressive and anxiety symptoms, somatization, and social insecurities. Patients who are treated with Body Psychotherapy appear to benefit in terms of improved general well-being, reduced muscular tension, and enhanced activity levels. There is substantial evidence for the efficacy of functional relaxation on psychosomatic disorders (asthma, tension headache, irritable bowel syndrome), and evidence from one randomized controlled trial (RCT) that Bioenergetic Analysis may be specifically effective for somatoform-disorder patients (Nickel et al., 2006). At least three RCTs have also demonstrated that chronic schizophrenia patients with predominantly negative symptoms respond to manualized Body Psychotherapy (or Body-Oriented Psychological intervention strategies, such as Movement Therapy), improving their psycho-motoric behavior, social interactions, and emotional openness; one multicenter trial across the United Kingdom will also be completed sometime in 2015: others include Nitsun et al., 1974; Röhricht and Priebe, 2006; and Priebe et al., 2013. The most recent pilot RCT of Body Psychotherapy for conditions of chronic depression demonstrated good effects in comparison with a waiting list control group only receiving treatment as usual, despite the fact that the participating patients had more than ten years of ongoing severe symptoms and even though both pharmaceutical and other psychotherapeutic treatments failed to improve their conditions (Röhricht, Papadopoulos, and Priebe, 2013; Papadopoulos and Röhricht, 2013).

## Treatment Concepts for Specific Disorders

Principles for Body Psychotherapeutic interventions for specific disorders have been identified in recent publications, both on the basis of distinct Body Psychotherapeutic schools and corresponding practice variations (see 2012 book edited by Röhricht: "Disorder-Specific Concepts in Body Psychotherapy," in German) and also from integrated, overarching perspectives across schools (EABP Science and Research Committee; e.g., Röhricht, Gerken, Stupiggia, and Valstar, 2013; and Röhricht, Butler, Gerken, Grassmann, Valstar, and Young, 2014).

This chapter discusses individual illnesses in relation to their distinctive, disease-related characteristics. A short sketch of the cardinal symptoms and body image phenomenology is followed by a summary of various models of psychological etiology; on this basis, I will develop disorder-specific Body Psychotherapeutic intervention strategies.

Furthermore, I would like to point out that reference to the confusing diversity of Body Psychotherapeutic schools seems quite irrelevant for the purpose of this chapter, especially because much of the available literature on Body Psychotherapy in SMI is integrative in concept. Body Psychotherapeutic interventions for severe mental illness are specific to the disorder, based on the clinical phenomena and the experiences of the patients, and aim primarily for symptom reduction, improvements in patients' subjective quality of life, and reconsolidation of functional capacities. At the same time, Body Psychotherapy works in the context of individual narratives and, in the case of individual therapy, is centered on biographical and functional self-exploration whereby Body Psychotherapy is oriented toward affect/self-regulation. With respect to the phenomenological focus, I will refer to those specific psycho-pathological symptoms for which a Body Psychotherapeutic strategy can be developed. The intervention strategies are related to specific body-oriented phenomena—i.e., disturbances of bodily experience and body-mind regulation disorders (see Röhricht and Priebe, 1996, 1997; Priebe and Röhricht, 2001; Röhricht et al., 2002; Röhricht, 2011). Body Psychotherapeutic interventions are also increasingly integrated with and used as part of mainstream modalities, especially in analytical and in depth-psychological methods but more recently also in the context of Cognitive Behavioral Therapy (CBT) approaches like mindfulness (e.g., Moser, 1989; Geissler, 1998; Klinkenberg, 2000); but that cannot and should not be the issue here.

## Mania (and Bipolar Disorder)

These affective illnesses have been practically disregarded in the development of psychotherapeutic techniques per se; nonpharmaceutical interventions are therefore limited mostly to supportive therapy and psycho-education. In the second edition of the *New Oxford Textbook of Psychiatry,* currently the most comprehensive psychiatric textbook, Paykel and Scott (2009) summarize the evidence as follows: "Psychotherapy has not been evaluated in manic patients and the benefit in bipolar disorder is for relapse reduction when delivered during euthymia" (p. 677). Also, there are no identifiable publications in the Body Psychotherapeutic field that explicitly address this type of condition.

From a clinical perspective, and on the basis of theoretical considerations—e.g., the psychodynamic connection between depression and mania (keyword: manic defenses)—we can identify potentially useful body-oriented intervention strategies, considering the evaluation of a strategy directly aimed at core symptoms, such as psycho-motor hyperactivity. This is not—as is psycho-pharmacologically customary—directed primarily at suppressing the agitation and tension, but at trying to help patients in facilitating the expression of motor impulses and exploring meaningful alternatives. In this context, it is interesting to acknowledge the clinical observation that manic impulses or behavioral tendencies are often reinforced by the ever-increasing level of psycho-pharmacological suppression in a kind of vicious circle. This can result in rather bizarre conditions in which the patient is psycho-motorically "numbed" or "frozen" (noticeable mainly through evident side effects), but at the same time is mentally "resisting" and "fighting against" being quieted down or suppressed. One could also deploy psychodramatic role-playing, which enables manically ill patients to confront themselves with the various aspects of their dysregulated body-self, aiming to gradually develop a range of alternative and corrective bodily experiences. As for symptoms such as excessive speech and thought disorders, Focusing techniques and/or exercise sequences from Concentrative Movement Therapy could be utilized with a view to supporting the rebalancing of impulsive and restrictive tendencies.

## Depressive Disorders

These illnesses are symptomatically determined by pervasive feelings of grief, loss, hopelessness, loss of interest/drive, thought blocks, and a multitude of bodily vegetative symptoms (loss of vitality; functional organic disorders such as somatoform pain, low muscle tone, inhibited gait, and motor retardation; and occasionally also agitated psycho-motor activity). There are specific forms of depression featuring mainly bodily symptoms (masked depression). In addition, empirical studies show a pronounced negative assessment of, and preoccupation with, the body as failing, with negative (affective) cathexis or satisfaction (Marsella et al., 1981; Angsmann and Schroer, 1983; Röhricht et al., 2002).

There is no one unified theory to explain depressive symptoms and their etiology; in fact, there are a number of different contributory or precipitating factors identified, ranging from the organic (biological and genetic) to psychological, evolutionary, and social influences. The theoretical models describing psychological processes leading to depression do not explicitly or systematically refer to the body-mind nature of depressive syndromes; and with the exception of mindfulness-based CBT, the treatments focus entirely on either verbal interventions or physical interventions such as exercising. This is contrary to the theoretical notion and empirical findings of embodied cognitive science, which emphasize the embodied, enacted, and environmentally embedded nature of mental and somatic phenomena (e.g., Niedenthal, 2007; Röhricht, Gallagher, et al., 2014).

Psychological, psychodynamic etiology models show that, if basic needs such as nurturing, attachment, and acceptance are not sufficiently satisfied in early childhood, this can lead to oral or narcissistic deficits with subsequent neediness or low self-esteem (accompanied by an increased focus on and preoccupation with the body). The latter should be distinguished from those traumas that stem from overprotectiveness, in which the child is effectively instrumentalized as an object for regulation by, and satisfaction of, caregivers, often leading to a distinct inhibition of the child's expansive motor impulses (muscular hypotonia in the neglected child versus hypertonia and successive shortening of those muscle groups of the extremities nearer the torso in the overprotected scenarios).

The projection of negative cognitions or unconscious conflict into the somatic sphere is also under discussion as a component of the manifold bodily symptoms of depressive patients; important in learning theory is the so-called "cognitive triad" (Beck) with negative attributions toward or expectations of the (body-)self, the world, and the future; and the model of "learned helplessness," which was derived from animal experiments and shows the successive exhaustion of mental and biological coping mechanisms. In the extreme case of a dynamic psychotic derailment, such as nihilistic delusion, the body can be experienced as dying or dead. Co-morbid symptoms of anxiety are often related to the body in the form of hypochondriacal complaints, when in extreme cases patients voice the conviction that they are severely (or even terminally) physically ill.

General principles of Body Psychotherapy for depressive disorders have been identified, encompassing the following main components (Röhricht, Butler, et al., 2014):

* Explorative movements, exercises, and increased sensory awareness (to address lack of affect and reduced psycho-motoric activity—lack of drive/initiative).

* Techniques derived from Neo-Reichian Body Psychotherapy, Movement Psychotherapy, and Psychodrama: exploring, enacting, revitalizing, and transforming—particularly, suppressed negative/aggressive impulses, especially those presenting as self-destructive/suicidal tendencies; enhancing patients' affective modulation and psycho-motoric expressiveness, and fostering healthy self-regulation.

* Interventions focusing on bodily strength, capabilities, and other healthy resources aimed at rebalancing patients' negative self-evaluation, and strengthening self-demarcation.

* Working against gravity (physically and metaphorically) to counteract feelings of heaviness and the unbearable weight of emotional/mental pain;

* Body Psychotherapeutic work directed toward biographical backgrounds, with a specific focus on unmet physical/emotional needs, lack of nourishment, and traumas (i.e., separation/loss), enabling patients to identify how self-destructive tendencies can be "diverted" in order to identify a range of more constructive responses and solutions.

On that basis, more specific phenomenon-oriented Body Psychotherapeutic treatments for severe depression can be distinguished for three different clinical manifestations, which often overlap:

### Adynamic, Inhibited Conditions:

*Profound Sadness or Feelings of Insensitivity, Psycho-Motor Retardation, and Lethargy, with Oral Deficits and Depressive (Dependent) Personality Structure*

The guiding principle for therapy here is the resource-oriented strengthening of the person's self-potential, the developing of a forward-oriented and uplifting ("aggressive") position and a shift of emphasis away from "taking" toward "giving." There is some—albeit controversial—evidence from evaluation studies regarding the efficacy of physical exercise on the depressive mood (Ernst et al., 1998; Mead et al., 2009).

Body Psychotherapy for this depressive subtype focuses on working with facial expression and behavioral, interactive gestures, aiming to achieve an initial improvement in muscle tone (e.g., working in front of a mirror or with video feedback on mirrored—i.e., guided—alternative behavior). Psycho-dramatic enactments help patients to connect with lived experiences; a variety of different scenarios are triggered within group therapy frameworks in particular, enacting primary feelings (such as joy, grief, anger, surprise, disgust) with corresponding facial expressions and body gestures, using voice intonation and other expressive body language exercises for further exploration. The direct and careful use of tactile stimulation, such as massage techniques (only with the consent of the patient), as well as directly aimed interventions on the skeletal muscles in the context of exercises conducive to emotional expression, are further important components in developing a stronger energetic position, which can help patients to access their range of emotions, particularly more negative feelings. At the same time, exercise sequences from play therapy and sports therapy (especially the use of balls in various ways) furthers the awareness of patients' physical potential, which creates an important counterbalance to the cognitive knots of negative (bodily) self-images. Here, dance-therapeutic elements are also important, in which patients at first just sense their body rhythms (pulse, breathing), and are then guided into contact with musical rhythm or movement impulses. With regard to the (often indirectly expressed) demands for attention and the tendency toward symbiosis and dependent life structures, it does seem important to help patients experience these hidden impulses through expressive gestures (demands) in their body schema (e.g., reaching-out or begging gestures, or expressing desire through the eyes).

Over the course of therapy, the encouragement of self-expression, empowerment, and an awareness of the possibilities for activating their own physical resources become increasingly important. Patients with dominant hypertonic-hypertrophic physical defense structures whose adynamic position is a result of chronically suppressed mobility (see above: a depressive pattern through overprotective mother/parent behavior) could be treated by strengthening their own mobility and autonomic movement impulses. Furthermore, it is essential to encourage expansive motoric movements so that patients can develop greater confidence in their own physicality—for example, slowly accentuating movements into the room, movements directed upward against gravity and clinging to the ground, or movements symbolically against lingering in the "morass" of the (maternal) body space, as for example through hopping and jumping—all of those integratively relate to personal/biographical narratives as they emerge during the therapeutic process.

When working with individual psychodynamic patterns or biographies in individual sessions, Body Psychotherapy often uses exercises that have an emotional, expressive character as a starting point for further exploration. Through confrontation with the physical experience of the facial or bodily expression of the feeling of hopelessness and the accompanying tendency to sink into resignation, patients can build up, somewhat paradoxically, a motor tension with the potential to be used for other patterns of movement. In this way, patients can make contact both with the emotional-affective content of the underlying conflict (e.g., oral deficits) as well as with the suppressed psycho-motor reactions to it, described and labeled by Downing (1996) as "affect-motor schemata" (e.g., adequate movements, crying for help).

### Agitated-Aggrieved Conditions: Severe Crises of Self-Esteem and Self-Degradation

The basic Body Psychotherapeutic principle here is characterized by an effort to achieve a position of "satisfaction," and Body Psychotherapy works particularly on the patient's tendencies to act out their narcissistic anger against the self, and thus to ward off the feelings of grief.

In the therapeutic process (particularly in group therapy), the focus is on the positive intensifiers of the bodily realities, such as gestures of (self-)respect, or relaxation exercises to reduce the arousal level or to make room for other—i.e., sad and needy—feelings. In psycho-dramatic activities, patients can enact their self-(body) posture, which again, when paralleled in their individual therapy, is helping patients to recognize and reflect on their underlying conflicts more explicitly, embodied, and experientially.

*Conditions of Dynamic, Psychotic Derailment*

This clinical syndrome is characterized by feelings of insensitivity, nihilistic and inhibited thought schemata, delusional hypochondria, and guilt feelings.

Here, the Body Psychotherapist must be much more active and directive in the therapeutic process and should endeavor to "relieve" patients of their unbearable state of mind as much as possible (e.g., with exercises in which patients are encouraged to let go of their weight by lying down or leaning on/toward someone or an object, seeking containment and support physically and metaphorically). Also, the therapist can temporarily assume the function of an auxiliary ego function and can offer emotional containment through guidance. Body Psychotherapy in psychiatric settings works either in individual or in group therapy with more basic tasks for this condition, aiming to reestablish secure anchor points within (bodily) reality first. Similar to the phenomenon of an initial stimulation effect through the administration of antidepressants, but leaving the depressive mood still unchanged, active and stimulating Body Psychotherapy can potentially amplify suicidal tendencies to a level at which the patient may act on them. Therefore, it is essential that the patient is continuously observed and also questioned about any self-harming or suicidal thoughts and tendencies.

Breathing exercises are used to treat severe disorders of ego vitality, and external, tactile stimulation—always administered with an attitude of respectful attention—plays a major role here as well. After a containing therapeutic relationship and basic grounding have been established and reality testing is improved, the experienced Body Psychotherapist can use guided interventions leading to a regressive re-experiencing of the essential, unsatisfied primary needs; the group can function here as a "good family" environment, thus allowing for a kind of symbolic (wish) fulfillment.

## Anxiety Disorders

This group of mental illnesses includes conditions with dominant, free-floating anxiety, phobic anxieties, and feelings of panic, often accompanied by considerable adverse effects on patients' social life. Similarly to the depressive disorders, anxiety disorders present as hyper-embodied disorders with numerous physical sensations that can be described as "somatic anxiety equivalents"; moreover, circumscribed disturbances in bodily experience are also reported by these patients (Röhricht et al., 2002), mainly negative body cathexis and body image disorders (weakening of body boundaries and somatic depersonalization).

Psychological, psychodynamic models refer to biographical/traumatic memories, especially existential threats experienced in early childhood, as, for example, the lack of fulfillment of basic needs or overstimulation due to the intensity of exposure to threatening or even dangerous situations, whereas in later stages the dynamics that underlie the primary fear will be suppressed (e.g., conflict, embodied response schemes, basic motor impulses), leading to the transformation of concrete fear into nameless anxiety. Thus, within the theory of psychodynamic psychotherapy (depth psychology), anxiety is understood as the consequence of an unsuccessful, neurotic conflict resolution (possibly with weak and unstable primary ego functions). From the perspective of learning theory, other processes are more important, above all the conditioning of negative learning experiences through intensifying mechanisms (e.g., physical symptoms of anxiety) with an assumed sensitivity to stimuli.

Whereas body therapies aim to reduce stress levels associated with heightened anxiety through, e.g., aerobic exercises or relaxation techniques (Lahmann et al., 2010), Body Psychotherapy engages patients in relational embodied psychotherapy in order to address the complexity of underlying psychological processes. General Body Psychotherapeutic principles in the Body Psychotherapy of anxiety disorders have been identified, encompassing the following main components (Röhricht, Gerken et al., 2013):

* Initially in Body Psychotherapy, therapeutic engagement is facilitated through exploration of bodily experiences and movement/breathing patterns; particular attention is paid to bodily equivalents of anxiety such as muscular tension, increased heart rate, and hyperventilation. Body Psychotherapy for anxiety relates to the common denominator of hyperarousal while exploring a range of alternative expressive behaviors relevant to the neuropsychological axis "fear-flight-fight-withdrawal/learned helplessness."

* Based upon psychodynamic roots in Body Psychotherapy, this includes careful clarification of traumatic memory backgrounds and personal deficits as trigger factors for what patients experience as unrealistic, unfounded fear. It is based on the observation that root causes have been dissociated, separating subjective feelings from physiological reactions.

* Clients are guided toward improved reality testing through grounding movements, establishing a firm "stance" in the world. This enables individuals to relate to anxiety-provoking thoughts/experiences from a position of self-awareness, tolerating and enduring anxiety without being "overtaken" by it.

* Body Psychotherapy facilitates shifting of a (holding, inward-bound) breathing/movement pattern, suggesting a range of expressive body movements (supportive, releasing, directive, etc.) and rhythmic integration. Interventions include direct body contact (self-soothing/protection/shielding) as well as exercises aiming to confront the perceived threat/aggression/danger in self-defense. This process enables reevaluating reality on a complex conceptual and organismic level, whereas the anxiety syndrome was bound in negative self-evaluations and disempowerment. Hereby, emphasis is given to "normalize" anxiety symptoms as a necessary, natural, and functional part of organismic functioning, basic to encountering the threat of (inter)personal damage.

From a Body Psychotherapeutic perspective for this group of mental health problems, various possible intervention strategies can be employed corresponding to specific problem constellations. In the sense of a guideline for the embodied psychotherapeutic processes for anxiety disorders, the principle of a modified exposure treatment is important (in the form of a psychodramatic reenacting of the situation that causes the anxiety and exploration of corresponding bodily expression). Initially, in the per-acute stage of the illness, the focus will be on grounding, so that the patients can experience reliability of their own musculoskeletal system and the weight-bearing capacity of the floor. In addition, the emphasis or focus is on the emotional and bodily expression (as far as is possible) of the underlying, inadequately repressed affect-motor impulses/schemata, especially those with an aggressive content (from Latin *aggredi* = to approach, *gradus* = a step; therefore, going forward in the most positive sense of the meaning). By relating to the primary (emotional = affect-motor) reaction patterns as motor responses to the experience of threat—i.e., by searching for fight-or-flight patterns latent in the musculoskeletal system—we can reestablish naturally created, healthy reactions and thus establish a more constructive, mature range of responses to adversity and break the cycle of negative reinforcement. Body Psychotherapy offers many interventions that explore, foster, and encourage these primary reactions to assert themselves and thus make space for emotionally correcting experiences, reevaluation, and reorientation.

Another focal point of Body Psychotherapy is concerned with the maturation process of weakly developed ego functions, which are often found in people of an anxious disposition. Here, we can employ, for example, Bioenergetic treatment techniques (such as grounding and falling exercises), tactile-sensory self-explorations, and physical endurance training, to mention only a few. Less indicated—although sometimes recommended—are, in my opinion, methods that promote contemplative relaxation, as this can reinforce the experience of passivity in the face of a threatening situation. Instead, we endeavor to mobilize and successively reestablish active reaction patterns in order to rebalance the overdeveloped psycho-physiological arousal levels.

Patients can practice self-defense and protective and confidence gestures that can be used in individual therapy in confrontation or exposure to the anxiety-triggering stimuli (e.g., support exercises, imagination: "Journey to My Strengths," ritual dances to "banish" fear). Over the course of psychodynamic background work, it can be useful to personify the anxiety in psychodramatic role-playing (e.g., placing the fear-carrying role with a different person or with the therapist). In view of the fact that anxiety usually manifests itself in complex social situations, the therapy group can be used as an important framework for social experiments (see the "support-confront," "catwalk," and "jostling" exercises—Görlitz, 1998; Röhricht, 2000—for working with social phobias). In therapies that work almost exclusively on the verbal level, it is difficult to deal with unconscious "frozen" anxiety, which usually manifests as phobic avoidant behavior. If, however, the patient is "well grounded," then it is possible to mobilize the affective material through Body Psychotherapeutic methods (e.g., hyperventilation techniques or the dyad exercise "shock-shield-face," whereby the partners sit opposite each other, hands in front of their faces with the fingers spread out, portraying a combined shock/protection reaction). The instinctive fight-or-flight reaction patterns, or the otherwise-mobilized aggressive affects, which appear to lie as root-cause phenomena behind chronic anxiety, can be reintegrated through the Body Psychotherapeutic process and pave the path for alternative behavioral solutions that are more adequate for the present-day adult. Other ways of achieving more conscious perceptions of avoidance behavior are those interventions whereby the muscular-postural schemata (observed by the therapist) are reinforced or overaccentuated and so become very clear (e.g., progressive muscle relaxation, which we have modified for our own purposes).

## Schizophrenic Disorders

This very heterogenic group of mental illnesses is characterized by a "disorder of the identity," a dissociation of psychological processes that leads to the development of heterogenic clinical conditions, including symptoms such as hallucinations, delusions, depersonalization, affective disorders, formal thought disorders, and psycho-motor disturbances. Although descriptive psycho-pathology pays little attention to it, the phenomenon of disturbed bodily experiences in schizophrenia is clinically significant to the point of describing schizophrenia essentially as a "disembodiment disorder" (e.g., Fuchs and Schlimme, 2009; Röhricht et al., 2011). This is especially important in the light of theories that regard schizophrenia as a disease of the ego/self.

Specific disorders of the experience of the body have been identified empirically: centralized body schema with underestimation of the lower extremities and a corresponding disturbance of the body image, cenesthopathy (qualitatively abnormal bodily feelings), and—less specifically—loss of the boundaries of the body and desomatization (Fisher, 1986; Röhricht and Priebe, 1997; Priebe and Röhricht, 2001). The existence of a subtype of schizophrenic illness with a dominant body-related psycho-pathology is under discussion (e.g., Röhricht and Priebe, 2002).

A multifactorial etiology/pathogenesis, with a central (genetically determined?) vulnerability on the basis of diverse neuroanatomical and biochemical abnormalities of the central nervous system, is now considered proved; other factors regarded as significant in the development of the illness are perinatal injury and peristatic (psychosocial) influences.

Psychoanalytic theory refers to a model of impaired ego psychology that assumes a premorbid (primary or acquired) weakness of the prereflexive self and ego functions, resulting in primitive defense mechanisms (projection, splitting, isolation); this model is furthermore assuming very early incompatible traumas and insufficient structuring of the self, resulting in an ambivalence conflict between the symbiotic desire for fusion versus an intensive need for distance (and homicidal fantasies). Cognitive behavioral approaches concentrate on disturbances in information processing that develop over the course of the illness, on the influences of the family on the illness (e.g., high levels of expressed emotion), and on the dysfunctional meaning-attribution processes and inadequate coping styles of the schizophrenic patients.

The essential principle of Body Psychotherapies for schizophrenia is related to the concept of "ego consciousness" with an emphasis on disintegrative tendencies as described by Scharfetter (1981) and the essential phenomenological features of disembodiment, as described above. The intervention strategy primarily focuses on ego-reconstructive measures using the development of an integrated, embodied self as a prerequisite for self-development and adequate (functional) self-management. In a further step, the patient's body can be utilized as a medium for reality checking and as an anchor point for connection to the world. It is important to bear in mind that the direct reference to the body always constitutes a balancing act for schizophrenic patients between (1) developing new structures on the one side and (2) a process of destabilization on the other, because the body as the location of perceptive and affective experience not only serves as the basis of the relationship with the world, but is also the experiential site of the conflictual or traumatic and threatening aspects of embodied connectedness for the schizophrenic patient.

Additionally, many patients with schizophrenia suffer from severe ambivalence conflicts when it comes to making social contact, which is all the more significant when the contact is physical. So, we must modify our treatment techniques considerably to suit the special requirements for this particular patient group. Essentially, the strategy of Body Psychotherapy is based—in the initial phases—on the principles of sensory self-awareness, grounding, and mirroring, or of moving supportively with the patient, which means to follow the postures and movements of the patient directly and creatively in the sense of providing an auxiliary or supportive ego function, supported by the use of various objects. This is mainly work on the surface of the body to improve the awareness of boundaries and also work on the joints or the transitions between the segments to encourage the experience of inner coherence.

As for the disorders of bodily experience mentioned above, Body Psychotherapy employs strategies of guided perception, sometimes including external stimulation with balls or natural materials, introducing a range of tactile sensations with which patients can compare the experience of their own bodies, serving as a real counterbalance to the predominance of abnormal bodily experiences. This can be differentiated further individually in therapy—for example, with regard to the delusionary significance connected to the bodily experiences. For instance, hallucinations can be transformed into dance segments, thus substantiating and materializing them, whereby they become more of an integrated aspect of the self, losing influence and power, and/or the patient becomes less afraid of them. Many movement exercises help patients to strengthen their autonomy in action. Body Psychotherapy works on issues related to the centralized body schema, both through exercises stimulating the surface of the body, and through cycles of expansive movements (stretching and extending laterally and vertically), while working with external objects as a comparison. Also, modeling body image sculptures from clay creates a visible and tangible corrective; it allows psychotically ill patients to materialize their most personal self-experiences virtually, to confront in reality their way of relating to the body, and then to question and correct it gradually over time.

Scharfetter (1981) developed a classification system of five fundamental functional aspects of self-consciousness (ego-vitality, -activity, -coherence/consistence, -demarcation, -identity), and their corresponding pathologies, later validated empirically (Scharfetter, 1995), which (not only) Body Psychotherapists refer to extensively. The central principle of Body Psychotherapeutic treatment of disorders of ego-vitality is to focus on body rhythms (breathing, circulation, etc.). Nonspecific physical activity (fitness training) also promotes the perception of liveliness and an improved ego-vitality. Sports therapists accentuate the positive effects of sports on social behavior, time structuring and recreational activities, self-esteem, bodily sensation, and physical performance (summary in Längle et al., 2000). Tactile self-exploration, guided and commented on by the therapist, addresses aspects of not only ego-vitality, but also ego-demarcation. The "body-ego technique" described and evaluated empirically by May and colleagues (1963) is eminently suitable for disorders of ego-vitality and -activity. In this technique, the actions of the patients can be developed through directed movements, imitation, and verbalization of their own actions, so that they can more easily differentiate between subject and object. Disturbances in ego-coherence or -consistence can be treated in Body Psychotherapy with guided whole-body movements (e.g., various balancing exercises, like balancing a sand sack on the head while moving around the room, or balancing the body weight in a circle with ropes, or working with large parachutes), whereby the experience of an integrated and functioning body gestalt can be used as a center of experience around which the ego/self can organize itself. Dance-therapeutic interventions are likewise especially suitable, as the focus is on coordination and the flow of movement. Ego identity disorders respond well to visual exposure with whole-body mirroring. Here, too, recognizing parts of the body as belonging to oneself can be used therapeutically.

A clinically significant syndrome that has a decisive influence on the prognosis of schizophrenic illness comprises the phenomena summarized under negative symptoms: *anergia* (emotional withdrawal, psycho-motor retardation, blunted affect) and *anhedonia* (inability to experience pleasure), as well as ambivalence. Nonverbal therapies, such as Body Psychotherapy, seem particularly well suited to meet the ambivalence of schizophrenic patients with regard to constructive social contacts. Examples for this are: the use of musical instruments as a medium for making contact; or the "mirroring" intervention that was originally developed and described by Chace (see Scharf-Widder, 1983). This intervention refers discretely as a theme to early forms of mother-child communication. In the framework of this body dialogue, it is often much easier to establish a positive, nonthreatening social contact and ultimately a trusting therapeutic relationship.

Other forms of Body Psychotherapeutic mobilization techniques that simultaneously promote the feeling of having a "firm stance" in the world are elements from Dance/Movement Psychotherapy, such as: using the body as a sound box for music; using rhythm in the group for passive movement stimulation; working with a sheet that is set in motion by the whole group; playing with balls; etc.

## Personality Disorders

This collective term comprises a group of exceedingly heterogenic mental disorders that are often difficult to distinguish from one another, and, before the introduction of the diagnostic classification used today, were described in the literature as "psychopathy," "character neurosis," or even "core neurosis." The schizoid and narcissistic personality disorders are dealt with elsewhere in this handbook (see Chapter 71, "Body Psychotherapy and Psychosis" by Guy Tonella, and Chapter 73, "Body Psychotherapy with Narcissistic Personality Disorders" by Manfred Thielen), and in another chapter (Chapter 72, "Body Psychotherapeutic Treatments for Eating Disorders" by Sasha Dmochowski, Asaf Rolef Ben-Shahar, and Jacqueline Carleton) the possibilities of Body Psychotherapy to treat self-harming behavior are examined; this is a symptom that is often found in patients with an emotionally unstable personality disorder. Therefore, I will make only a few general remarks on the use of Body Psychotherapy for these patients with such personality disorders.

The vast majority of hitherto-published information on Body Psychotherapy for personality disorders refers to borderline and narcissistic disorders, which are summarized together as "early wounded." For these illnesses, a fragile ego structure is described that expresses itself in (for example) an unclear sense of ego boundaries. Body Psychotherapeutic strategies that seek to help the ego mature retrospectively, with non-verbal communication or interaction, can intervene successfully here.

A basic therapeutic attitude of empathy and support, sometimes functioning as an auxiliary ego, is specifically important while working with these patients; and (at least, at first) all interventions that explore or mobilize feelings, or are aimed at a cathartic discharge, should be avoided, as there is not enough ego control available to integrate the experiences. Because this group of patients (especially those with schizoid personality disorder) has not been able to occupy the periphery of their bodies and often present a contracted basic posture, a manifested splitting-off in their experience of the body (right/left, horizontal/vertical, above/below), and an unstructured (fragmented) occupation of the body, the use of integrative Body Psychotherapeutic techniques seems well indicated here: regulation of closeness and distance behavior; encouragement of "vessel-forming, containment oriented" (Schroeter, 1994); and movement patterns that help establish a secure contact with the ground. The splitting experiences of the patients are directly addressed (e.g., through specific verbalization of the perceived distance between feeling and body, thinking and head). It is very important to work directly—i.e., including the bodily reality—with the existential need for supportive contact. Only on the basis of a previous improvement in the basic foundations of embodiment should the therapist start to address—in individual therapy—the, often severe, negative affects (self-harming, self-destructive, or disintegrative tendencies, including "murderous" rage) in a regulated, channeled, and systematic manner, so that patients can articulate those negative affects and then integrate them into a more coherent self-experience. Such a process presupposes that the therapist possesses a great deal of experience and structuring ability, so that he or she can contain the formidable tendencies of the patients toward disintegrative acting out.

## Contraindications

Just as for any other therapy, there are also definite contraindications for Body Psychotherapy, on a continuum between relative and absolute contraindications.

Ascertaining contraindications must always be done from the perspective of our current knowledge, which is in a constant state of flux and which depends—furthermore—on the specific characteristics of the illness, the provisions of the treatment setting and environment, and the individual (self) experience of the therapist.

The following groups of patients are, in my opinion, not suitable for Body Psychotherapeutic treatment, as they are in an acute state of mental disorder:

* Those patients with acute manic disorders in which their self-control is severely impaired
* Those patients with personality disorders, when the impulse control is underdeveloped and who have an observable tendency to "act out"
* The acute, suicidal patients
* Patients with schizophreniform diseases, when a severe disorder of the ego structure or disorganized behavior determines their condition
* Those patients who are suffering from a structural ego deficit and are in danger of either being flooded with primary or process material, or of complete ego disintegration

## Conclusion

A significant shift within the humanities and social sciences from cognitive science to embodied cognitive sciences; findings from neuroscience regarding neuroplasticity; change processes in psychotherapy that require simultaneous addressing of cognitive, perceptual affective, and motor processes; and the growing evidence base for the efficacy of Body Psychotherapy in the treatment of severe mental disorders—all have firmly established Body Psychotherapy as an important modality in the mainstream landscape of psychotherapeutic treatments.

The intervention strategies are now being more specifically developed to address disorder-specific pathologies, while retaining their resource-oriented focus and personal-growth strategy as a humanistic psychotherapy. In respect to specific mental disorders, manualized intervention strategies in Body Psychotherapy have now been developed and are becoming available for research and practice.

## References

Angsmann, K., & Schroer, B. (1983). *Körpererfahrung und Depression: Eine kontrollierte klinische Studie* (Unveröffentlichte Diplomarbeit, Fachbereich Psychologie, Universität Münster) [Body experience and depression: A controlled clinical trial (Unpublished thesis, Department of Psychology, University of Münster, Germany)].

Downing, G. (1996). *Körper und Wort in der Psychotherapie: Leitlinien für die Praxis* [Body and word in psychotherapy: Guidelines for practice]. Munich: Kösel.

Ernst, E., Rand, J. I., & Stevinson, C. (1998). Complementary therapies for depression: An overview. *Archives of General Psychiatry, 55,* 1026–1032.

Fisher, S. (1986). *Development and structure of the body image (Vols. 1 & 2).* Hillsdale, NJ: Lawrence Erlbaum.

Fuchs, T., & Schlimme, J. E. (2009). Embodiment and psychopathology: A phenomenological perspective. *Current Opinion in Psychiatry, 22,* 570–575.

Geissler, P. (Ed.). (1998). *Analytische Körperpsychotherapie in der Praxis* [Analytical Body Psychotherapy in practice]. Munich: Pfeiffer.

Görlitz, G. (1998). *Körper und Gefühl in der Psychotherapie—Basisübungen (Reihe Leben Lernen, Nr. 120) und—Aufbauübungen (Reihe Leben Lernen, Nr. 121)* [Body and emotion in psychotherapy—basic exercises (Life Learning, No. 120) and—building exercises (Life Learning, No. 121)]. Munich: Pfeiffer.

Klinkenberg, N. (2000). *Feldenkrais-Pädagogik und Verhaltenstherapie (Reihe Leben Lernen, Nr. 133)* [Feldenkrais pedagogy and behavior therapy (Life Learning, No. 133)]. Munich: Pfeiffer.

Lahmann, C., Röhricht, F., Sauer, N., Ronel, J., Noll-Hussong, M., Henrich, G., Nickel, M., Tritt, K., & Loew, T. (2010). Functional relaxation as complementary therapy in irritable bowel syndrome: A randomized, controlled clinical trial. *Journal of Alternative and Complementary Medicine, 16,* 47–52.

Längle, G., Siemssen, G., & Hornberger, S. (2000). Die Rolle des Sports in der Behandlung und Rehabilitation schizophrener Patienten [The role of sports in the treatment and rehabilitation of schizophrenic patients]. *Rehabilitation, 39,* 276–282.

Loew, T., Tritt, K., Lahmann, C., & Röhricht, F. (2006). Körperpsychotherapien—wissenschaftlich begründet? Eine Übersicht über empirisch evaluierte Körperpsychotherapieverfahren [Body Psychotherapy—scientifically proved? An overview of empirically evaluated Body-Oriented Psychotherapies]. *Psychodynamische Psychotherapie, 5,* 6–19.

Marsella, A. J., Shizuru, L., Brennan, J., & Kameoka, V. (1981). Depression and body-image satisfaction. *Journal of Cross-Cultural Psychology, 12,* 360–371.

May, P. R. A., Wexler, M., Salkin, J., & Schoop, T. (1963). Non-verbal techniques in the re-establishment of body image and self-identity: A preliminary report. *Psychiatric Research Report, 16,* 68–82.

Mead, G. E., Morley, W., Campbell, P., Greig, C. A., McMurdo, M., & Lawlor, D. A. (2009). Exercise for depression. *Cochrane Database of Systematic Reviews,* No. 3, art. no. CD004366.

Moser, T. (1989). *Körpertherapeutische Phantasien: Psychoanalytische Fallgeschichten neu betrachtet* [Therapeutic body fantasies: Psychoanalytic case histories revisited]. Frankfurt: Suhrkamp.

Nickel, M., Cangoez, B., Bachler, E., Muehlbacher, M., Lojewski, N., Mueller-Rabe, N., et al. (2006). Bioenergetic exercises in inpatient treatment of Turkish immigrants with chronic somatoform disorders: A randomized, controlled study. *Journal of Psychosomatic Research, 61,* 507–513.

Niedenthal, P. M. (2007). Embodying emotion. *Science, 316,* 1002–1005.

Nitsun, M., Stapleton, J. H., & Bender, M. P. (1974). Movement and drama therapy with long-stay schizophrenics. *British Journal of Medical Psychology, 47,* 101–119.

Papadopoulos, N., & Röhricht, F. (2013). An investigation into the application and processes of manualised group body psychotherapy for depressive disorder in a clinical trial. *Body, Movement and Dance in Psychotherapy.*

Paykel, E. S., & Scott, J. (2009). Treatment of mood disorders. In M. G. Gelder, N. C. Andreasen, J. J. Lopez-Ibor Jr., & J. R. Geddes (Eds.), *New Oxford Textbook of Psychiatry* (2nd ed., Vol. 1) (pp. 669–680). New York: Oxford University Press.

Priebe, S., & Röhricht, F. (2001). Specific body image pathology in acute schizophrenia. *Psychiatry Research, 101,* 289–301.

Priebe, S., Savill, M., Reininghaus, U., Wykes, T., Bentall, R., Lauber, C., McCrone, P., Röhricht, F., & Eldridge, S. (2013). Effectiveness and cost-effectiveness of Body Psychotherapy in the treatment of negative symptoms of schizophrenia: A multi-centre randomised controlled trial. *BMC Psychiatry, 13,* 26.

Röhricht, F. (2000). *Körperorientierte Psychotherapie psychischer Störungen: Ein Leitfaden für Forschung und Praxis* [Body-Oriented Psychotherapy mental disorders: A guide to research and practice]. Göttingen: Hogrefe.

Röhricht, F. (2009). Body Oriented Psychotherapy—the state of the art in empirical research and evidence based practice: A clinical perspective. *Body, Movement and Dance in Psychotherapy, 4, 135–156*.

Röhricht, F. (2011). Leibgedächtnis und Körper-Ich: zwei zentrale Bezugspunkte in der störungsspezifischen körperorientierten Psychotherapie [Body memory and body ego: Two central reference points for disorder-specific Body-Oriented Psychotherapy]. *Psychologie in Österreich, 4, 239–248*.

Röhricht, F. (Ed.). (2012). *Störungsspezifische Konzepte in der Körperpsychotherapie* [Disorder-specific concepts in Body Psychotherapy]. Giessen: Psychosozial.

Röhricht, F., Beyer, W., & Priebe, S. (2002). Störungen des Körpererlebens bei akuten Angsterkrankungen und Depressionen: Neurotizismus oder Somatisierung? [Disturbances of body experiences in acute anxiety disorders and depression: Neuroticism or somatization?]. *Psychotherapie Psychosomatik und Medizinische Psychologie, 52, 205–213*.

Röhricht, F., Butler, S., Gerken, S., Grassmann, H., Valstar, J., & Young, C. (2014). Body Psychotherapy: Clinical roundup: Selected treatment options for depression. *Alternative and Complementary Therapies, 20(1), 52–59*.

Röhricht, F., Gallagher, S., Geuter, U., & Hutto, D. D. (2014). Embodied cognition and Body Psychotherapy: The construction of new therapeutic environments. *Sensoria: A Journal of Mind, Brain, and Culture, 10*. doi: http://dx.doi.org/10.7790/sa.v10i1.389

Röhricht, F., Gerken, S., Stupiggia, M., & Valstar, J. (2013). Body Psychotherapy: Clinical roundup selected treatment options for anxiety. *Alternative and Complementary Therapies, 19, 340*.

Röhricht, F., Papadopoulos, N., Holden, S., Clarke, T., & Priebe, S. (2011). Clinical effectiveness and therapeutic processes of Body Psychotherapy in chronic schizophrenia: An open clinical trial. *Arts in Psychotherapy, 38, 196–203*.

Röhricht, F., Papadopoulos, N., & Priebe, S. (2013). An exploratory randomized controlled trial of Body Psychotherapy for patients with chronic depression. *Journal of Affective Disorders, 151, 85–91*.

Röhricht, F., & Priebe, S. (1996). Das Körpererleben von Patienten mit einer akuten paranoiden Schizophrenie: eine Verlaufsstudie [The bodily experience of patients with acute paranoid schizophrenia: A follow-up study]. *Nervenarzt, 67, 602–607*.

Röhricht, F., & Priebe, S. (1997). Störungen des Körpererlebens bei schizophrenen Patienten [Disorders of bodily experience in schizophrenic patients]. *Fortschritte Neurologie Psychiatrie, 65, 323–336*.

Röhricht, F., & Priebe, S. (2002). Do cenesthesias and body image aberration characterize a subgroup in schizophrenia? *Acta Psychiatrica Scandinavica, 105, 276–282*.

Röhricht, F., & Priebe, S. (2006). Effect of Body Oriented Psychological therapy on negative symptoms in schizophrenia: A randomised controlled trial. *Psychological Medicine, 36, 669–678*.

Scharfetter, C. (1981). Ego-psychopathology: The concept and its empirical evaluation. *Psychological Medicine, 11, 273–280*.

Scharfetter, C. (1995). *The self-experience of schizophrenics: Empirical studies of the ego/self in schizophrenia, borderline disorders and depression*. Zürich, Switzerland: Privately published book.

Scharf-Widder, S. (1983). *Interventionen in der Tanztherapie: Untersuchung tanztherapeutischer Interventionen am Beispiel der Arbeit mit schizophrenen Klienten* [Interventions in Dance Therapy: Study of Dance Therapy interventions with the example of working with schizophrenic clients]. Rauenberg: Selbstverlag.

Schroeter, B. (1994). Körperpsychotherapie mit Frühstörungen [Body Psychotherapy with early interventions]. In Verein für Integrative Biodynamik (Eds.), *Körperpsychotherapie zwischen Lust und Realitätsprinzip* [Body Psychotherapy between pleasure and the reality principle] (pp. 102–113). Oldenburg: Transform.

# 71

## Body Psychotherapy and Psychosis

Guy Tonella, France

Translation by Warren Miller

**Guy Tonella,** PhD, is considered to be one of the most articulate French Body Psychotherapists. He was a professor of psychology and a researcher at the Universities of Paris, Toulouse, and Montpellier for many years. Today, he works as a psychotherapist in private practice, and as a supervisor and trainer.

Dr. Tonella's psychotherapeutic training includes Rêve Eveillé Dirigé ("directed waking dream"), Psychodrama (Moreno), group dynamics, psychoanalysis, and, most importantly, Bioenergetic Analysis. He is a trainer for Bioenergetic Analysis and, in this role, works in France, Portugal, Italy, Switzerland, Belgium, and Brazil. He is on the faculty and the board of the International Institute for Bioenergetic Analysis in New York, and is also on the board of the Wilhelm Reich Institute in Paris, as well as being certified to teach psychotherapy by the national syndicate of French psychotherapists in Paris. His diverse publications on Body Psychotherapy are highly regarded.

Since the early 1970s, Dr. Tonella has utilized Body Psychotherapeutic methods at the Hôpital Marchant in Toulouse. Subsequently, he also brought these methods into his private practice with people diagnosed with severe mental disabilities, like schizophrenia, pre-psychotic conditions, borderline conditions, and severe depression.

From 1987 to 1990, he was a collaborator in a research project at the hospital of the University of Purpan-Toulouse that studied the effect of body-oriented/affective methods on young adults with psychosis. The therapeutic work in small groups was recorded on video and later appraised by a psychiatric team using a rating method. The outcomes were published in 1990, and are reflected in this chapter.

This is essentially a written account of work with a group of people diagnosed with psychosis. More specifically, this work took place with a group of young adult psychotic patients at an inpatient psychiatric unit (under Professor M. Escande, University Hospital Purpan, Department for Adult Psychiatry, Toulouse, France). There, Virginie Jacomini and I co-facilitated a psychotherapy group that met once a week for ninety minutes and offered body and movement meditations. These group meetings were observed and completely recorded on film over the course of two years. The documentation on film was used for staff training and research purposes.

The diversity of our training backgrounds (psychoanalysis, psycho-motoricity, body language, Bioenergetic Analysis, and Gestalt Therapy), previous experience of psychotherapy with psychotic populations—in which I had focused on body language at Hôpital Marchant in Toulouse in 1971—and a few cases from private practice formed the basis on which I formulated my working hypotheses (Tonella et al., 1989). The following discussion is based on our clinical work and research.

## Etiology of the Psychotic Process

The pathology revealed in psychosis is caused essentially by a structural weakness of the self, with a structural weakness of attachment and interactive bonding.

The *structural weakness of the self* manifests as a significant deficit of co-integration between the various body-mind functions that together form the foundation of a core identity: the energetic function (gradation of activation/deactivation of the organism); the sensory function (gradation between cold/hot, hard/soft, joy/despair, etc.); the tonic function (gradation between hypotension and hypertension); the emotional function (gradation between love and hatred); and the representational function (gradation between good environment/bad environment). Ongoing linkages of these functions during the first two years of life constitute the fundamental process that facilitates the development of the self: energetic variations usually trigger sensory changes that also lead to changes in muscle tone. The changes in tone in turn affect the emotional state and evoke further representations in imagery or language. Psychotic patients lose this *continuity of body and psyche, and consequently lose their somatically based "felt sense" of a core identity. These functions are missing these mutual linkages* (Robert-Ouvray, 1993; Tonella, 1995). What remains instead is a more or less severe discontinuity between some or all of these functions. Without a coherent sense of self, patients experience an extraordinarily frightening state of non-integration, instability, and confusion.

But there is a second reason for the underlying sense of disintegration: as well as remaining fragmented and unlinked with each other, each function oscillates radically between polar extremes, without a coherent and gradual sense of an organic process along the gradation curve. In terms of *all* of these functions, the psychotic person remains trapped in the bipolar, elemental schema of the newborn, which flips from one extreme to the other without the possibility of intermediate steps or variations: it is either hard or soft; either hostile or loving; either good or bad; etc. In the psychotic person, the psycho-physiological bipolarity that is normal and adaptive during infancy has turned into a chronic pathological split. This "either-or" experience of internal polarization and discontinuity makes any form of interpersonal attunement precarious, leading to frequent breaks in relational attachments. The resulting inability to form relationships leaves the psychotic person in a state of extreme fear and loneliness.

The *structural weakness of attachment and interactive bonding* (Bowlby, 1969) reveals itself in the great difficulty (or complete inability) in forming strong, lively, and stable relationships with other people (Tonella, 2000). The psychotic experience is based on a lack or deficiency in terms of the internal behavioral schema underpinning relations to an object. These schemata usually emerge in infancy over the course of the lived relationship with the caregiver and consolidate as the primary attachment and interaction "working models" (Bowlby, 1969). However, when the infant is deprived of the opportunity to construct such schemata, the psychotic "developmental wound" results, manifesting across the spectrum of relational possibilities. The infant lacks experiences of shared joy (Watson, 1973; Bower, 1977), or maternal regulating and holding functions (Brazelton, 1982; Stern, 1974). What the infant experiences in the present moment is not internalized as a resource via memory, available for recall at a later time, so as to contribute to the establishment of a vital experiential and relational web. Instead, the infant remains frozen, on the outside, cut off from any prospect of contact and interaction. The infant desires relational contact, but is tormented, even terrorized, by fear, based on its earliest experiences of relationship at the beginning of its life: the unmet desire for love, body contact, and emotional contact (Winnicott, 1957), and the failure of its longing to lead to the experience of an enduring love—i.e., "constancy of the love object" (Mahler, 1975).

## Transformation of Innate Adaptation Mechanisms into Defense Mechanisms

Psychotic individuals defend themselves against this threat from within and the terror of the "Other" outside by using a range of defense mechanisms. These are developed as early as the first months after birth, by converting innate, adaptive, and basic psycho-tonic and psycho-motor mechanisms for defensive and self-protective purposes.

The adaptive capacity for protective encapsulation, which manifests in the body's prominent flexion pattern (curling up), is transformed into a *psychotic withdrawal* by de-energizing and immobilizing the connective tissue system: the "paralysis" of the main connective tissue systems is a somatic defense against the "lysis" of these systems—i.e., the necessary loose mobility of this system becomes frozen, as fluidity is experienced as threatening the dissolution of the foundations of being.

The innate tonic bipolarity (hypertonicity of the flexors, and hypotonicity of the paravertebral muscles) is transformed into a tonic split: either all-out hypertonicity, or complete hypotonicity without the possibility for eutonia—i.e., a well-balanced and responsive muscle tone. This tonic split is the somatic underpinning of the split (schizophrenic) self.

The psycho-physical discontinuity, which is a normal characteristic of immature neurophysiology, morphs into a pathological *dissociation* of the self. Keeping the muscles of the neck region very tight, producing a sort of neck grab, maintains the dissociation between the head and the body by preventing the perception of one's own body (sensations and emotions). The normal non-integration of sensation and perception after birth then functions like a *perceptual denial*, both of the person's own body, as well as the personified Other. This denial is also maintained in the body, specifically by strong suboccipital tensions, and thereby is patterned into the structure of the psychosomatic self.

A physical and psychological hardening of the self (catatonia) forms the backdrop to an effort to free the self from strong projections. We find both processes of pathogenic *introjections* on the one hand, and on the other of fighting against such introjections, in place of the innate adaptive processes of assimilation. In this sense I see "adaptive assimilation" (Piaget, 1936) in juxtaposition with "introjection" (Klein, 1948). I consider the latter as part of a pathological process in which a foreign object is inserted into the self without being assimilated. Assimilation enriches the self, whereas introjection is alienating. The self of the psychotic person is an estranged self, filled with unmetabolized and indigestible introjections. The disappointed expectation for the needs of the self to be met by unconditional responsiveness can lead to two possible outcomes:

1. An *autistic,* completely *mute resignation,* which expresses unbearable loss, or
2. A self-sufficient and *extremely hallucinatory* behavior, which blots out the deprivation and its terror and replaces them with sensory and emotional hallucinations that produce self-generated satisfaction.

The disappointed desire for mutual affection—which enables the self to construct its sense of internal security, self-confidence, and self-esteem—has led to a *self-destructive encapsulation,* which manifests in a tendency toward violence and impulsively hostile or self-mutilating behaviors, unless this encapsulation flips into *grandiose idealizations:* the psychotic person is then possessed by either "God" or the "Devil."

The unknown desire for affection and recognition has transformed into a desire for renunciation, and an idealization of the powers of the Other, which are often fantasized, or experienced, as omnipotent.

## Trauma as a Cause of the Psychotic Process

Initially, the psychotic process is a defensive, psychophysical, structural process. It is a protective reaction against traumatic experiences, by an emerging self, which is physiologically, emotionally, and psychologically dependent.

The kinds of trauma that can be considered pathogenic from the perspective of structural formation and interaction are characterized by frequently misattuned intrusions of the caregiving environment into the homeostatic system of the infant. This "cumulative trauma" (Khan, 1974) manifests in the infant's sensory and emotional experience as terrifying and corrosive. The infant reacts by disowning its sensory-emotional states and withdrawing from human contact. In this way, the infant constructs a split structure that is strongly founded on primary psycho-motor and psycho-tonic mechanisms of adaptation and defense; these in turn promote an avoidance pattern in regard to attachment and interactive bonding.

## The Therapeutic Process and Psycho-Physical Structure Formation

For the reasons outlined above, psychotic individuals need a therapeutic process that helps them to establish the previously missing psycho-physical continuity, which in turn allows a core identity to emerge gradually. This process includes the formation of interactive attachment bonding schemata.

These kinds of therapeutic experiences can be facilitated in the context of therapeutic art groups that offer drawing, collage-making, painting, or working with clay (Broustra, 1987). However, I am thoroughly convinced that it is also essential to bring the body into these activities. With behavior, the sense of our action and who we are is woven into the texture of our body dynamic in the form of sensory-emotional and interactional experiences. Therefore, the body apprehends and undergirds this process of "making sense." Because the defense mechanisms of the psychotic person are rooted and organized in the body, the integration of the body and its movements into the therapeutic process facilitates experiences that can change these mechanisms and replace them with more flexible and regulatory mechanisms. The originally metabolic (regulation of heart and respiration) and tonic mechanisms (experience and regulation of tonic variations) are transformed into organizers of emotional expression, precognitive exploration, and interactional communication. These mechanisms are designed to adapt, assimilate, and accommodate their environment for the creation of the self, the object-world, and intersubjective exchange.

Reich (1949), reporting a clinical case of a schizophrenic patient, came to the following conclusion at the end of this work:

The schizophrenic cannot recognize the internal source of primary, bio-physiological sensations and plasmatic streamings, and therefore interprets them poorly and distortedly. In other words, he takes it, that these stirrings—sensations, tingling, inner disturbances—are to be attributed to external causes. He might believe, for example, that enemies try to kill him by electrocution. He perceives his bioenergetic emotions, but interprets them poorly.

The growing awareness of her bodily experience allowed one patient to identify these experiences as "her own powers," which then lessened her hallucinations and instead began forming the sense of bodily continuity that she was missing.

In my individual and group work with psychotic people, I have frequently come across these kinds of misattributions. For example, at the end of one session, a woman who had previously appeared wax-like beamed at me and said, *"For the first time I can feel my heartbeat!"* I was happy to hear that, and shared that with her. She added, *"Would you like to feel how it's beating?"* I agreed. Then she took my hand and guided my hand toward her genitals. Obviously, I was rather surprised. I told her, *"Your heart seems to be sitting rather low!"* She laughed, but reaffirmed her proclamation. She had mistaken the perception of her pulsating vagina as the perception of her beating heart. Nonetheless, this was of great significance for her, as it indicated the waning of her bodily numbness and emotional emptiness, which had been with her for as long as she could remember. She was happy to discover sensations, and she shared her sensational finding with me in an expression of emotion.

In the group setting, we often work with discoveries of individuals so as to establish a setting of exploration for everybody else in the group, too. At the beginning of one group session, Stephan appeared wide-eyed: with a restrained voice, he said, *"What I most fear about relationship is the first step."* So, I proposed that he should stand up and position himself facing me at a certain distance, and then to take a step toward me. This was very hard work for him: he was frightened and frozen. He then risked taking that first step: the experiment was successful. It was repeated in numerous variations, and was offered to others in the group, with more or less success depending on the individual. This way of proceeding is focused on the affect-motor interaction and will usually pay off over time.

We have also worked with movement, sound, and vocal games. For most, access to their "scream" is critical: to scream and also to hear screaming. We played a lot, so as to bring each other to laughter, to scare each other, to be mean, or to be nice. Experiences erupted, waiting to be identified. Feelings were expressed among the participants and in relation to the familiar observation team. Fine threads of psychosomatic continuity were tied, undone, and renewed, creating a formless "archegonium" (Tonella, 2002) form and assimilating all of this into the self.

## The Therapeutic Process and the Formation of the Intersubjective Relationship

An essential principle of this therapeutic work is that of deeply psychosomatic *work in relation to a relationship.* It leads to awareness and creative formation of the original streamings that emerge from the interstitial spaces between the connective tissues and reverberate throughout the human organism. These forces, which had previously been locked up, suddenly start to break free: at first, they find expression in behavior (rather than in reflective thought); in breathing and heart rhythms; in postural erection; in sensations shuttling up and down the spine, or around the tightly held neck; in the flow of emotions arising from within; and in the eyes that harden, or that can get "glassy." Because these phenomena emerge in the context of the therapeutic relationship, they can eventually become intersubjective phenomena, and eventually acquire personal meanings. The experienced exposure, which can also be thought of as a protosymbolic process, paves the way for another form of expression, which belongs more to the domain of the psyche. This other form allows for nondelusional verbal expressions that build on and reorganize the experiences of muscle tone, sensation, and emotion.

The emergent "archegonium" is form-generating. At first, it is rooted in the body's structure and is carried by emotion; later, meanings and images begin to be associated. If it is perceived in this way, the sensory-emotional process is primary to the thought process, and thus begins to seek relationship. What is new and different in this case is that the "archegonium" now is no longer archaic: it has form, gestalt, and intersubjectivity: it is no longer psychotic, fragmented, or fragmentizing.

At this point, the "archaic transference" challenges the therapist to be not only affectively, but at times also physically, engaged in the relationship. The therapist needs to hold the ropes to guide the pulsating "archegonium" in its search for the relationship to the transference object—i.e., initially the therapist. The therapist's responses must be attuned to, and in accordance with, the situation (Stern, 1985), in order to weaken and defuse the patient's archaic defense reactions. Such reactions defend against the eruption of this pulsating *prima materia,* and are associated with fears of annihilation, falling into emptiness, rejection through hostile and paralyzing eye contact, as well as a fear of destructive and reactive aversions, and of violence that threatens everything alive (including the relational contact) with the longed-for object.

The archaic transfer calls upon the therapist to pay very careful attention and to ready his or her hands, arms, even the whole body if need be, to provide what Winnicott referred to as *"holding, handling, and object presenting":* indeed, anything that offers the patient presence, support, vitality, and relationship when the unformed force breaks free.

The therapist's "countertransferential space" offers the patient the possibility to embody and surrender to his or her experiences, and to form the relational self into something creative and constructive. The way in which the therapist emotionally and psychically receives and responds to the patient (i.e., the countertransference in relationship with the client) is determined by the extent to which the therapist has familiarized him- or herself with their own pre-verbal space in the context of their own therapy, so that he or she is able to navigate this terrain without fear or danger of getting lost. To the extent that this is given, the therapist can enter the archaic space of the client and communicate with them, even though this is—essentially—a pre-verbal space: a space without words.

## Psychosis and the State of Our Research

Our findings with these "psychotic" patients can be summarized as follows:

* Over the course of two years, the frequency of incidental interactions rose by 42 percent. This includes interactions with therapists, as well as among patients.
* Individual behaviors within the group expanded in range and became more subjective, as evidenced by mutual support and cooperation behaviors, and divergence and conflict behaviors. Seventy percent of the patients developed spontaneous co-therapist behaviors, in comparison with the therapists' interventions. Patients supported other patients who were struggling, and shared their experiences among each other, indicating an expansion of intersubjective processes.
* All patients demonstrated greater physical mobility to varying extents: some demonstrated a changed body posture; some evidenced more gestures during speech; some exhibited more expressive facial expressions; etc.
* All patients developed subjective expressiveness to varying degrees: in interactions with the therapists or among patients; and sensory-emotional states, such as fear, terror, grief, despair, hatred, rage, longing for love, loneliness, etc., emerged and could gradually be identified.
* All patients also attended a weekly, verbally oriented therapy group under the supervision of Mr. Girard, the unit's lead psychoanalyst. In the first year of the body-oriented group, patients began making linkages in their verbally oriented group to their experiences in the body-oriented group. This was a novelty. Because these psychotic patients had previously not been able to remember experiences from their other weekly groups, Mr. Girard notified us of this change. The ability to remember—that is, the ability to recall experiences and process them with some distance—increased. These patients with psychosis began to own their experiences, to have a representational awareness of them, and to be willing to discuss their possible meanings—i.e., they began to symbolize.

From this, I can conclude that: the self gradually emerged and "weaved a texture"; that psycho-physical continuity grew; and that the various—energetic, sensory, tonic, emotional, and representational—functions began to be linked together, thereby creating an inner structure, which is almost synonymous with the integration of the self.

This supports my hypothesis that going beyond the psychotic structure necessitates (re)construction of psycho-physical continuity, which includes sensory, tonic, affective, and interactional therapeutic work.

## References

Bower, T. G. R. (1977). *Le développement psychologique de la première enfance* [The psychological development of early childhood]. Brussels, Belgium: P. Mardage.

Bowlby, J. (1969). *Attachment and loss: Vol. 1. Attachment.* New York: Basic Books.

Brazelton, T. B. (1982). Le bébé: Partenaire dans l'interaction [Baby: Interactive partner]. In T. B. Brazelton, B. Cramer, I. Kreisler, et al. (Eds.), *La dynamique du nourrisson* [The dynamics of infancy] (pp. 11–27). Paris: ESF.

Broustra, J. (1987). *Expression et psychose* [Expression and psychosis]. Paris: ESF.

Khan, M. (1974). *The privacy of the self.* London: Hogarth Press.

Klein, M. (1948). *Contributions to psycho-analysis.* London: Hogarth Press.

Mahler, M. (1975). *The psychological birth of the human infant.* New York: Basic Books.

Piaget, J. (1936). *La naissance de l'intelligence chez l'enfant* [The birth of intelligence within the child]. Neuchatel, Switzerland: Delachaux et Niestlé.

Reich, W. (1949). The schizoïd disintegration. In W. Reich, *Character Analysis*. New York: Orgone Institute Press.

Robert-Ouvray, S. (1993). *Intégration motrice et développement psychique* [Integration matrix and psychic development]. Paris: EPI.

Stern, D. (1974). The goal and structure of mother-infant play. *Journal of the American Academy of Child Psychiatry, 13,* 402–421.

Stern, D. (1985). *The interpersonal world of the infant.* New York: Basic Books.

Tonella, G. (1995). Symptôme psychosomatique et intégration psychocorporelle [Psychosomatic symptoms and psycho-physical integration]. *Les Lieux du Corps, 2,* 59–84.

Tonella, G. (2000). The interactive self. *Clinical Journal of the International Institute for Bioenergetic Analysis, 11*(2), 25–59.

Tonella, G. (2002). Théorie clinique de la régression en Analyse Bioénergétique [Clinical theory of regression in Bioenergetics Analysis]. *Revue de la Société Française de Gestalt, 23.*

Tonella, G., Jacomini, V., Girard, M., et al. (1989). L'emergence de la douleur/souffrance en psychothérapie à médiation corporelle et motrice chez le psychotique [The emergence of pain/suffering in psychotherapeutic body mediation and palsy in the psychotic]. *Psychologie Médicale, 21*(6), 698–700.

Watson, J. S. (1973). Smiling, cooing and the game. *Merrill Palmer Quarterly Journal of Behavior and Development, 18,* 323–339.

Winnicott, D. W. (1957). *The child and the family: First relationships.* London: Tavistock.

# 72

## Body Psychotherapeutic Treatments for Eating Disorders

Sasha Dmochowski, United States, Asaf Rolef Ben-Shahar, Israel, and Jacqueline A. Carleton, United States

**Sasha Dmochowski**, MA, is currently pursuing a PhD in Drew Anderson's Weight and Eating Disorders Laboratory at the State University of New York at Albany. At the New York State Psychiatric Institute (NYSPI), she was a research coordinator for a comparative therapy study of individuals whose primary diagnosis was post-traumatic stress disorder (PTSD), with outcome data from interpersonal, exposure, and relaxation therapy. She also helped to conduct research at NYU School of Medicine's Brain, Obesity, and Diabetes Lab (BodyLab) in a study that investigated the impact of obesity, insulin resistance, and type-2 diabetes, on the brain and on cognition. A former professional ballerina with Boston Ballet and American Ballet Theatre, she received her BA in Psychology from Columbia University and an MA in General Psychology from New York University.

**Asaf Rolef Ben-Shahar**, PhD, is an Israeli-born psychotherapist living both in Israel and in the United Kingdom. He is the training director of the Relational Body Psychotherapy Programme at the Israeli Centre for Body-Mind Medicine, and runs a parallel program in London called "Touching the Relational Edge" with the Entelia Institute. Additionally, Asaf teaches and lectures in clinical and academic settings in Israel and Europe. He is on the editorial board of *Body Psychotherapy Publications, Self and Society, Body, Movement and Dance in Psychotherapy,* and the *International Body Psychotherapy Journal.* Asaf has published extensively in the fields of Body Psychotherapy and relationality. His first book, *An Anatomy of Therapy,* was published in 2013 in Hebrew, and an expanded and updated version of this book, *Touching the Relational Edge,* was published in 2014 in English.

**Jacqueline A. Carleton**'s biographical information can be found at the beginning of Chapter 60, "The Role of the Autonomic Nervous System."

With the population of people with eating disorders (ED), more than those with other disabilities, it is the language of the body that is both incisive and integral to recovery—it is the language through which treatment can most effectively be conducted. The complexities of the condition obscure a clear path to recovery; and even for the most experienced clinician, untying the interwoven layers of body image, self-esteem, anxiety, depression, and self-destructive behaviors that are associated with eating disorders presents an intricate challenge. Other than anecdotal and case study data, very little is currently known about how we can fully heal an eating-disordered individual specifically through the somatic experience itself. The cluster of symptoms that are usually classified as "eating disorders" include the three best-known, but very different, disorders: *bulimia nervosa* (BN) (characterized by binge eating and purging); *anorexia nervosa* (AN) (characterized by an irrational fear of gaining weight, a distortion of body image, and extreme food restriction); and *binge eating disorder* (BED) (characterized by recurrent/persistent episodes of uncontrolled binge eating with distress but without the inappropriate compensatory behaviors of BN). However, the variety of anorexic thought patterns, purging disorders, ruminations, *orthorexia nervosa,* etc., can also be included in the eating-disorders category.

Disordered eating, and the related behaviors of these disorders, serve as a collection of symptoms by which an individual may express their affective states nonverbally. To be able to communicate effectively with these conflicted self-states, as treatment providers, it is essential that we learn how to communicate subsymbolically and at a level that the somatic body can recognize and respond to (Bucci, 2005, 2008, 2011). The variety of Body Psychotherapeutic techniques that have been used in the treatment of eating disorders have included: Yoga, the Alexander Technique, breathwork, Sensory Awareness, Hakomi, Gestalt, massage therapy, eye movement desensitization and reprocessing (EMDR), Sensorimotor Psychotherapy, mindfulness, and Dance/Movement Therapy, among many others. All of these various methods have (anecdotally) managed to alleviate symptoms of these conditions, but none have been shown to be comprehensive treatments of eating disorders, in their entirety. Although various psychoanalytic traditions (Freudian, Self Psychology, attachment-based) all offer a methodological understanding of the processes, little attention has been given to the body—not merely as a symbolic participant, but as the part that actually "speaks" about the disorder. As Body Psychotherapists, reinvention of any preexistent theory is not necessary; instead, our aim is to dialogue with those theoretical and clinical understandings and to integrate our embodied knowledge of the etiology and clinical practice with what is already understood.

Some eating disorders (ED) develop as a result of childhood traumas, sometimes stemming from some sort of physical or sexual abuse; other etiologies include a variety of combinations of biological factors (including genetic and epigenetic), biochemical factors, psychological factors (including attentional bias and personality traits), or sociological/environmental factors (including maltreatment, social isolation, parental influences, peer pressure, and cultural pressure [e.g., media portrayals of "ideal" (but very thin) fashion models]). Regardless of etiology, the somatic experience of the individual who is eating-disordered usually includes deficits in self-regulation. Most theories of ED also agree that sufferers have complex attachment patterns, particularly with their mothers, and difficulty differentiating themselves (e.g., Bachar, 2001). Geneen Roth, developer of the nondiet approach, who made issues of emotional eating accessible to the public, claimed that preoccupation with food and weight often stemmed from difficulties in creating intimate interpersonal relationships (Roth, 1984, 1992).

Lowered self-esteem, poor or distorted body image (i.e., body dysmorphic disorder), preoccupation with body weight and size, self-criticism, depression, and anxiety are some of the more typical and co-morbid symptoms presenting within these disorders. Given the efficacy of different Body Psychotherapeutic treatments used with individuals who have experienced trauma, there may be a parallel benefit in the use of the same types of treatments for those with eating disorders. In using somatic techniques, the hope is to reconstruct a more positive relationship with the body, to develop an increased ability to regulate mood, and to facilitate the integration of emotion with somatic experience.

Because various Body Psychotherapeutic modalities differ in their theoretical orientations, this chapter's purpose is not so much to present a cohesive understanding of ED, but instead focuses on the potential clinical contributions that Body Psychotherapy has to offer in working with ED patients. We shall discuss some of these more promising Body Psychotherapeutic techniques that appear to effectively alleviate eating-disorder symptoms, highlighting ways in which to incorporate somatic methodology into enhanced and more comprehensive paths to recovery. These will include techniques focused on self-regulation, as well as some dyadic-regulation techniques that may be incorporated by psychotherapists from different modalities.

## The Body in Eating Disorders Has Often Been Neglected

Currently, approximately 1–5 percent of female adolescents in the United States suffer from an eating disorder (Carei et al., 2010), with higher estimates when including feeding and eating disorders that are not elsewhere classified within the DSM-V (Stice et al., 2013). Within a culture that praises avid exercise, going to the gym, and working out, the predominance of EDs among men is likely to be higher than that which is currently reported and remains masked by societal acceptance. Preoccupation with muscular development and the desire to maintain an optimal weight for training are more acceptable for men; and, with this gender-specific bias, it may be harder to engage with and diagnose men therapeutically, and their clinical presentation may be with co-morbid conditions. When beginning the treatment of individuals, with any form of eating disorder, the priority must always be, first, a degree of medical stabilization and the restoration of weight to within healthy norms.

The client/patient must obviously and clearly be "safe"—both in eating and weight terms (i.e., not at risk in any way, with a body mass index (BMI) of at least about 18.5), and with no risk of cell or tissue damage through inadequate nutrition, or due to secondary effects like a risk of infections through physiological depletion; and they must also be "safe" psychologically, in that any form of lying about food intake, or induced vomiting, or especially any self-harming tendencies, are all discussed openly and are kept under reasonable control. There are no treatments undertaken in any variation or combination of cognitive, pharmaceutical, or somatic methods that will be effective, if the body and mind are essentially being malnourished. In some medically oriented protocols for working with ED, the priority on medicalization highlights the body, and places the psychological phase of healing as secondary. But, after weight is restored and the psychological component of therapy can begin, it is imperative that the body is not kept secondary, nor treated simply as the garbage can *"for that which the psyche cannot handle"* (Orbach, 2004, p. 14). Clinical work with the patient's somatic experience must continue on levels that are both personally and uniquely embodied.

For those readers who find the Reichian-based character structure system (Lowen, 1958; Reich, 1933; Totton and Jacobs, 2001) useful, we can find both schizoid (particularly because of the highly dissociative nature of ED) and, of course, oral characteristics when considering eating disorders. Both represent forms of psychic wounding at stages at which the primary wound concerns dyadic regulation and premature establishment of self-regulatory techniques, leading to compensatory defense mechanisms (Rolef Ben-Shahar, 2013). Hence, the therapeutic work would involve an emphasis on stabilization, safety, and clear boundaries (necessary for the schizoid character), as well as attending to needs and learning to tolerate emotions and gradual individuation (for the oral character).

Although there are differences in their symptomatology and process, the three main forms, AN, BN, BED, and all other forms of eating disorders, share, as a core feature, the presence of a disturbance in the body image, inaccurately perceiving their own body image (usually claiming it is larger) and also retaining an overevaluation and preoccupation with body weight and shape. Particularly in anorexia, any motivation to restore body weight to a level at which effective therapy may begin is low, but even when medical stabilization and weight restoration are achieved and therapy for the psyche can be instituted, clinicians who have experienced the relative recovery of their eating-disordered patients will still concede that, as of yet, there is no ideal treatment course—no silver bullet, magic wand, or best way, to treat eating disorders.

That is not to say that Western medicine is without a viable treatment protocol. Currently, the most common treatment for eating disorders is composed of a program of Cognitive Behavioral Therapies (usually coordinated by a team with a psychologist and/or psychiatrist, a primary care physician, and a nutritionist), varying—by way of their structural components—to provide inpatient or daycare programs, and include individual, as well as group and family, therapy. Some clinicians have reported success with medication therapy, particularly selective serotonin reuptake inhibitors (SSRIs): antidepressants that seem to work on all EDs and that seem to work reasonably well in conjunction with psychotherapy (de Zwaan and Roerig, 2003), and even with psychoanalysis. But most treatments today still fall within a combination of the cognitive behavioral realm with twelve-step components. Despite these programs being the most highly relied upon, based on their comparative efficacy, only about 50 percent of ED patients fully recover (Carei et al., 2010).

Body Psychotherapists tend to prioritize that healing the body should be done through the body, which may be why the programs that do not prioritize the somatic experience itself within the recovery process may fall short. Moshe Feldenkrais (1977), originator of the Feldenkrais Method, commenting on the nature of our self-image, proposed: *"In reality our self-image is never static. It changes from action to action, but these changes gradually become habits; that is, the actions take on a fixed, unchanging character"* (p. 11). According to Feldenkrais, it is through movement that we learn to better bridge the inner and outer aspects of self-image, thus advocating awareness education through movement. Most Body Psychotherapeutic approaches to ED will indeed include some experiential learning (or relearning), and because the basic ED symptomatology is embodied, the course of treatment will address embodied realms and images as well.

Keeping a food-log, or speaking about body image and the negative cognitions associated with ingestion, are known to be necessary and effective tools within cognitive behavioral programs, but such conversations can be a trap in the intellectualization of the disorder. While specific symptoms differ, individuals with anorexia, bulimia, binge eating disorder, and not-otherwise-specified eating disorders demonstrate little awareness of their interoceptive state. Eating too much, or too little, lacks a sensitive, embodied self-awareness, and filling the gastric system too much, or too little, creates experiential states that serve adaptive functions—often suppressing painful feelings of loss, or experiencing a "high" from binging and dissociation, or experiencing starvation that can also feel palliative.

Stephen Gilligan (1997) speaks of the "relational self" as a bridge between the cognitive and somatic selves, claiming that many human difficulties arise from loss of rapport between the two. People with eating disorders clearly express a loss of rapport between their cognitive and embodied self-states, and thus, merely addressing the former will not necessarily contribute to any long-term improvement of the latter. What is missing in the treatment of EDs is a bridge between the two. Expansion of bodily awareness, movement, breathwork, and touch—each within an alive and embodied therapeutic relationship—all serve to re-create and rehabilitate those connections and bridges. Individuals with ED struggle with affect regulation and the way that their nervous system manages stress and energy; food (or lack of it) can become a means to manage that excess arousal. Chronic hyperanxious arousal (alarm and trauma) can be soothed by the use of eating behaviors, either by binging or by obsessive restriction. The counterregulative state, hypoenervation, allows for a dissociative use of eating behaviors that can create a welcome loss of corporeal reality (Bromberg, 2006). Linking the bodily state to emotion is a matter of being able to tolerate the feelings that have been suppressed, while maintaining a healthy relationship with food and with one's own bodily needs. Reversing bodily numbness, and the lack of interoception that is coupled with the individual's profile of emotional and sensation suppression, is an important way that Body Psychotherapeutic treatments can become salient within a treatment course.

## Possible Treatment Methodologies: An Introduction

Any therapeutic alliance with an eating-disordered individual must include the realm of the physical body. Whereas the patient determines whether the therapist can be trusted, the therapist must help the patient to integrate on all levels, including the visual, which can be particularly difficult if the patient is either malnourished or obese. Integration on a relational level must include a respect for the patient's initial lack of motivation (particularly in anorexia), as well as an understanding of the individual's underlying resistances. Barring the need for hospitalization that might be necessitated for medical stabilization, to begin addressing such cognitive issues as food preoccupation and food phobias, the therapist must offer the patient a safe space, free from other demands. Once this positive therapeutic alliance has been established, body-to-body relational treatment can be challenging, considering that usually by the time treatment is sought, the physical form of eating-disordered individuals has become their metaphoric battlefield. Some individuals experience disordered eating with no apparent history of trauma, but in all cases, the body is undoubtedly a particularly sensitive zone. As such, linking somatic experience with affective states, and then putting those into words, is a therapeutic goal; but this cannot be the starting point. Nevertheless, it is feasible to invite the possibility of bringing about long-lasting change without such links. Neither addressing the body on its own (as an object), nor addressing the underlying emotional problems on their own, seems sufficient. Moreover, before conceptualizing the language of the body into an analytic language (i.e., turning subsymbolic processes into symbolic or secondary processes), we might be required to speak to the body in a form of body language—to intervene somatically, and not just analytically.

## Transference Dynamics

Along with the therapist and the patient, the patient's body itself becomes a third component in the treatment room. How a patient feels about her body, and also her therapist's body, may include objectification, idealization, devaluation, competition, fear, curiosity, or envy. With this scope of emotions, unique to the language of eating disorders, is the comparing and contrasting of the body and its appearance. Objectification and identification, attachment and distancing, and the ties that form between the two bodies—patient and therapist—are key to the therapeutic alliance and can be enhanced by any Body Psychotherapeutic technique that aligns the two bodies energetically.

Forms of regulation within the therapeutic relationship will include the patient's self-esteem, self-knowledge, self-image, self-regulation, and affect regulation—all will be played out using the patient's and the therapist's physical forms. Alignment of the patient and the therapist on a somatic level, within the therapeutic alliance, can serve as a catalyst for change. Somatic resonance (being in your own body) and somatic countertransference (identifying what is your own body and what is that of others) are related and essential to this foundational empathy between the therapist and the patient.

The therapist's body thus becomes a potential source and/or resolution of the patient's negative emotions—envy or scolding, idealization or demonization—and one therapeutic task may concern extensive self-regulation of the therapist, who serves as a self-object (Orbach, 2004; Pizer, 1997; Rolef Ben-Shahar, 2012). Bringing the body into therapy is thus an invitation for the therapist to, not only deeply engage in her own somatic countertransference, but also work through her own body image issues in order to support the client's endeavors. If, for example, the therapist, who might have previously appeared polished, sometimes seems vulnerable and not entirely in control of her body, then the patient with anorexia might feel encouraged, through the therapeutic skill of mirroring, to abandon the rigid control that she usually retains in her physicality, and to enter into a more fluid relationship with her own physical form. The therapist thus attempts to normalize humanity, in all of its embodied forms.

Relational Body Psychotherapist Ronen Levy (2012) relates to the transferential relationship with food in his work with Shlomit, a client whose binging episodes (always on her own) left no "space" in her body for relationships; food was easier to trust than people. Levy suggested to Shlomit that they "eat together," both concretely and symbolically, thus conceptualizing the dialogue in therapy as dining together. This approach demonstrates a different quality of attachment-based and psychodynamic interventions in Body Psychotherapy when working with eating disorders. Perhaps, what Levy points us to is worth looking at in a broader sense. Eating disorders are not just an intrapsychic condition; they are also a pattern of relationship. The bodies of anorexic clients "shout" their suffering to everybody surrounding them, and all but the client herself can notice the volume of the shout. Bulimic clients engage in secrecy, and the obsession and pain of the rituals oftentimes remain hidden from all. These dynamics repeat themselves outside their eating habits, including in the clinical practice. We would like to suggest that, at times, the therapeutic relationship assumes "anorexic" or "bulimic" qualities (Rolef Ben-Shahar, 2013): overengagement with the symptom (eating, diet, body weight) could easily take over the therapy, leaving the relationship, and the client, behind. Collusion with the symbiotic wish, denial, overemphasis on doing and fixing, or being pulled into protocol-like psychotherapy in which we deal with an eating disorder and not a client, are all possible transferential traps for Body Psychotherapists working with eating-disordered clients.

## Traumatic Symbolization of Embodiment: EMDR

Processing distressing memories by way of EMDR techniques and reducing their presence has found some research support mainly for disorders caused by distressful life experiences, such as post-traumatic stress disorder (PTSD), but it has also shown some efficacy when used with negative body image in eating-disordered inpatients (Bloomgarden and Calogero, 2008). The fuel for body image disturbance can come from a heightened level of self-criticism and self-consciousness due, in part, to the sociocultural emphasis on thinness and beauty in modern Western culture. Ultimately, negative body image is clearly associated with the core pathology of eating disorders, regardless of how it is produced or exacerbated. Body image distortion is also the most tenacious and often the last symptom to yield to treatment. Although more research is necessary to discern the mechanisms of action that bring about change, it is reasonable to conclude that incorporating EMDR techniques, with or without bilateral stimulation (i.e., eye movement), into a standard course of inpatient treatment may reduce distress about specifically targeted negative body images (Bloomgarden and Calogero, 2008; Kiessling, 2013).

## Reorganizing Psychosomatic Habitual Forms

Eating disorders can be seen as essentially a means of voicing oneself without speaking. Particularly in cases of *anorexia nervosa,* individuals will have a profile that suppresses emotion and retains gestural language, posture, gaze, hand movements, and muscular organization that are fairly contained and rigid. Integrating dance with therapy has proved to facilitate both the fluidity of the conversational therapy, as well as overall integration of the body, into the recovery process (e.g., Krantz, 1999). Psychoanalyst Wilma Bucci (2008, 2011) termed this language "subsymbolic," pointing to an organized language that is nonetheless nonverbal. Such language is immanently different from primary process—and whereas psychoanalytic theory was able to discuss such communication, psychoanalytic technique is relatively limited when speaking directly with those bodily communications: this is where Body Psychotherapy can contribute significantly. When our client speaks with the body (as so clearly occurs in eating disorders), the Body Psychotherapist can answer in the same language, through movement, breathwork, touch, or bodily awareness, rather than insisting on translating the communication (which is somatic) into the therapist's own symbolic or verbal conceptualization.

Eating disorders are coping devices whereby the body and its nourishment become the vehicle for whatever cannot otherwise be expressed. Blanche Evan, one of the pioneers in the field of Dance Therapy, considered the body to be a repository, a point of reference, and a vehicle for expression where the interaction between the psyche and the body is two-directional—movement both expresses the inner space of the psyche, and also influences the external, physical, and emotional states (Krantz, 1999). The clinical experience of many dance/movement therapists also suggests that sexual conflicts are intrinsic to EDs, whether or not abuse has occurred (Krantz, 1999; Pallaro, 1999).

For all humans, food plays a very significant role in our early nurturing, as well as later in our romantic life: meals are historically a part of courtship, and appetites for food and expressions of love are inherently linked. This is the case for everyone, but magnified and distorted for those with eating issues. Many ED individuals are inhibited about touching their bodies and feel as if they are fat, ugly, and despicable to others. Individuals with AN tend to display a more prim and proper approach to sexuality and are often inhibited when expressing themselves sexually, as well as tending to have sexual relations less often with their partners, compared to normal controls, or to BN counterparts. Overall, ED patients report less sexual satisfaction, greater performance anxiety during sex, and lower sexual self-esteem than normal controls (Zerbe, 2008).

However, it should be noted that some sexual dissatisfaction relates to endocrine function deficits in those who are starving, and even at normal weight, bulimics may be malnourished from their eating habits and purging behavior. Interestingly, even in weight-restored AN cases, there is a higher dopamine binding (indicating less dopamine in the system) and less experience of sexual and overall pleasure. We cannot of course be sure if this chemical imbalance was present before the restriction of food began. Expressing oneself through movement that can either be narrative (to represent the conflict with food), or interpersonal (with another), or simply abstract, can start to free up any rigidities and lead to increased comfort with the concept of the body as being sexual.

## Further Interventions: Balancing Self-Regulation with Dyadic Regulation

The body can be considered to be a closed system in the way that the diverse internal dimensions interact with each other in many different ways. But it may also be considered—at the same time—to be an open system, regulated by both internal and external influences. For a Body Psychotherapist, evaluating the postural behavior of a patient can be a useful way of using the biomechanics of the body to understand better the impact that posture may have on the other dimensions of the system, and the communication strategies that the posture represents and participates within (Heller, 2012).

Given the manner in which the container of the physical body is held, within this frame, the disorder itself has become an important self-object. If patients obviously do not feel ready to relinquish the powerful role that food (or the disorder) plays in their internal world, they may first need the therapist to act as a bridge to replace that self-object until they themselves feel as if they can do it on their own. The therapist may need to "demonstrate" that the bridge is "safe." This brings into play the question of boundaries and to what extent personal disclosure (by the therapist) may be helpful, assuming the therapist has any personal experience either with eating disorders or with a distorted relationship to food; it may be necessary to express the emotions that their food behavior has suppressed or replaced. Patients might need the therapist to feel viscerally and to express emotionally first, what they have—as yet—been unable to.

## Self-Regulation: Bioenergetic Analysis

Bioenergetic Analysis (often referred to as Bioenergetics) was developed by Alexander Lowen, a student of Reich, and included the importance of "grounding"—of having a strong connection to the earth through the feet and legs. Most body-oriented methods of therapy (following the Reichian tradition) divide the body into segments that are differentiated by the function of the large joints of the skeleton such as the pelvis, thorax, and shoulders, and the mobility of the large vertebrae that connect the neck to the trunk. The diaphragm that separates the ventral and thoracic sections of the trunk is pivotal in respiration, and, along with other segments (like ocular organization and gaze orientation), can play into postural dynamics (Heller, 2012). Eating-disordered individuals typically show muscular tension and rigidity in the way their body is "held," often in a manner that will affect postural dynamics, and disrupt general circulation as the body relates to the gravitational pull. In Lowen's (1958) character structure system, these dynamics would be understood as schizoid or oral/schizoid. It would be simplistic to say that emotions are made manifest through the expression of the body, and—yet to some extent—we know this instinctively and anthropomorphically, as humans, from the (imprinted) history of our evolution. We learned to protect ourselves when we see aggression, to approach when we feel welcomed by a smile. The posture of an individual with anorexia reflects control—their need, not necessarily to control others, but their desire to control themselves, and to control the factors that dictate their environment. When tension is released from the jaw, neck, and shoulders, from the hips and other major joints of the body, the emotional release is that of often extreme vulnerability and openness. It is an opening, to a beginning, to be able to express some of the emotions that have been controlled, and often the anger, frustration, hate, envy, desire, etc., that was contained and not able to be expressed. The following account illustrates how physical training of the body can take advantage of the natural rigidity of an anorexic, and channel food into fuel that "makes sense" to an eating-disordered individual:

> My mom and I made a deal that if I got to a certain weight I can start having personal training sessions so I can gain the remainder of the weight in muscle. I started training with a great trainer, Jody, and instantly fell in love with strength training. During my workouts, I would be so focused on my form and the movement that I would not hear the eating-disordered thoughts that continuously bombarded me throughout the day. It allowed me to get away from my ED while also releasing the tension and energy stored in my body. After every session, I felt the endorphins surge through my body, resulting in a better mood, greater energy, and an easier time at the next meal. I loved learning new exercises, practicing, and perfecting them. Although it is partly due to my eating-disorder drives, I intensely enjoyed weight training and working on strengthening my body. Not only does it relieve stress and release endorphins, but also it has been a really big motivation factor for me. It was really interesting to see my strength increase and my body change shape as I gained weight and weight trained. Every time I eat now, I think of it as, "I must eat if I want to fuel my body for my next workout and increase my strength." What is the point of lifting weights if you are going to starve your body so it eats your muscle? It also gave me another aspect to contribute to my identity. It was one of my passions that I could talk about and share with others. (personal communication, June 2012)

Another promising treatment approach involving Body Psychotherapy includes a significant component of psycho-education, especially about the neurobiological components (Ventling, 2004). Helping the patient to self-regulate can also mean reeducating them a little (or a lot). By feeding the mind, we can help to feed the body. Ventling recommends a seven-point treatment plan focusing on several body-oriented points: (1) *not* discussing food, diets, eating patterns, or weight, etc. (as that reinforces the "illness"); (2a) building up a trusting relationship—as already mentioned—and (2b) educating the patient about her disorder (assisting cognitive self-regulation); (3) naming the depression and explaining it—though Ventling says this ought to be dealt with first; and, if the patient agrees, trying antidepressants; (4) working on the pleasurable aspects of the body, especially the negative body image, and making the body come alive; (5) focusing on the real (emotional) hunger and its (probably early) origin; (6) working on building up other resources (creativity, interests, talents, social engagement, etc.)—i.e., "normalizing" the person and getting rid of the "patient"; (7) occasionally checking on hunger and satiety feelings—i.e., returning to a "normal" hormonal balance.

## Yoga and Mindfulness

Individuals with *bulimia nervosa* are generally more responsive to a number of different modalities of treatment, possibly because anorexia has complex secondary benefits related physiologically to starvation and cultural approval. Endorphins, which are naturally released when the body enters into a state of deprivation, often provide a sort of positive reinforcement by decreasing anxiety and thus help to cause an individual who is experiencing this "high" to be more difficult to engage in treatment. These endorphins can be offset chemically by antidepressants that target dopamine and serotonin, but these antidepressants cannot ultimately prevent reoccurrence of the sought-after high. Individuals with EDs often attempt to control these fluctuations in endorphins, and attempt to control their anxiety, depression, and food preoccupation, by way of rigorous exercise (which also releases endorphins). More specific to bulimia, exercise is sometimes coupled with purging, and this adds a further dimension to possible treatment that may complicate therapies and can lead clinicians not to advise treatments that involve potential calorie expenditure.

One small study (Carei et al., 2010) showed that Yoga had a possibly beneficial effect on people with ED; another (Clarke, 2008) combined Yoga and discussion reasonably successfully for BN patients. As BED is a new classification in the DSM-V, few research studies have focused on the potential effects of Yoga and mindfulness specifically on this population. The mindfulness practice of Yoga can help to address the anxiety and depression found co-morbidly in ED, and, although most research that has attempted to determine the efficacy of meditation interventions has focused on the treatment of anxiety and depression alone, it is possible that the efficacy could be generalizable to the eating-disordered population.

In a study of anorexia symptoms, Bruha (2010) found that individuals with anorexia experience less attention to and awareness of their present state, and a tendency toward engaging in restricted or blunted consciousness that limits emotional and physical availability. With decreased attentional capacity, there is limited cognitive space for individuals with eating disorders to process either external or internal stimuli. It is possible that what they may attend to most are the physical sensations of "fatness" and thus they may be more mindful of their body dysmorphia than any other emotion or sensory experience. There is no conclusive evidence that these individuals have limited attentional capacity, prior to the onset of their disorder, but regardless of whether individuals enter into acute *anorexia* or *bulimia nervosa* with a deficit in present-state awareness, the disorder itself increases this dysregulation.

Mindfulness focuses our attention, and allows us to create intentional states of brain activation: it also encourages a focus onto what bodily sensations there actually are in the present in a nonjudgmental way. Altering ingrained neural pathways is an arc from effortful concentration to greater self-observation, a path that ultimately cultivates the ability to uncouple and disengage maladaptive cognitive pathways. In a practice such as Yoga, the body and mind are activated in resonance with one another, in a way that allows an individual to mobilize dimensions of posture, breathing, relaxation, mental concentration, physiology, and intellectual knowledge (Heller, 2012), all of which may help to reset attentional dysregulation.

## Working with Somatic Transference Dynamics (Dyadic Regulation)

The following is a summary of a vignette demonstrating the use of somatic transference and countertransference, first published in the *International Body Psychotherapy Journal* (Rolef Ben-Shahar, 2012):

> During our second session, when I asked Elle whether she was bulimic, she shook her head vigorously: "No, I just hate my body and hate being fat, but I don't throw up." Elle was a stunning thirty-year-old woman and everything seemed to go smoothly and easily for her. During the first two months of therapy, and although Elle was quite distressed, my main feelings towards Elle were envy and jealousy. Her unhappiness made me angry. During the first year of therapy we discovered that her mother, whom she at first considered "my best friend, my soul mate, my twin sister" always used Elle to regulate her own emotional life. Elle was expected to comfort her mother from a very early age, to perform perfectly "to make mummy happy," or else her mother would slip into her depressive slopes.
>
> Elle therefore never attained appropriate differentiation, she continued to exist as a partial-system, unable to regulate herself on her own, entering symbiotic relationships where she disconnected and felt betrayed and lonely. Israeli Self-Psychologist Eitan Bachar (2001) explored bulimia in terms of the dif-

ficulty to occupy space. He claimed that the role-reversal, commonly observed between the bulimic client and her early attachment-figures, represented a parental tendency to excessively use the child as self-object. Interestingly, my empathetic failure was similar to her mother's and this powerful transferential dynamic was, as my supervisor helped me to realise, an expected reenactment of her attachment dynamics.

In order to help Elle I had to survive myself, to self-regulate. Going back to basics, when she entered the room and I was bombarded with self-loathing internal dialogues, I would practice conscious breathing techniques (Hendricks, 1995), and a lot of inner-child work. The need to push Elle into saying things decreased. Her suffering was more apparent to me, and it was relieving to feel my therapeutic empathy returning and therapeutic positioning regained. About that time, Elle admitted to having been bulimic for five years: "it's just that your questions seemed invasive at first, I didn't even know you," she said.

If we are willing to look at the therapeutic relationship through relational eyes, we can appreciate, as relational Body Psychotherapist Michael Soth explained, that enactment is inevitable (Asheri et al., 2012). With eating-disordered clients, it means that the therapeutic dyad will inevitably manifest bulimic or anorexic patterns. It also means that we can change the pattern from inside (Rolef Ben-Shahar, 2012)—that therapy can become the healing agent. If we are able to introduce change into the relationship; if we are able—as therapists—to relate better to our own bodies and body image in the presence of the client; if we can transform the disordered eating of the therapeutic relationship, then something deeper can transform in the client as well. Could such deep patterns of relationship—with the self, the other, and the world—change just behaviorally? Do we not perpetuate the body/mind split that we have come to attend to when we focus merely on behavioral patterns?

Perhaps, from a relational and attachment point of view, the role of the Body Psychotherapist who works with eating disorders is far less technical than accumulating sophisticated knowledge, or applying therapeutic techniques. Perhaps, what we are mostly called to do is simpler and much harder: to love our bodies in the presence of our clients; to accept and love the beauty of our bodies and the body of the relationship, without needing to change it, to make it better, or to shape it until it is acceptable and lovable. Perhaps a kindly embodiment of the therapist, and of the therapeutic relationship, is the one meaningful act of therapeutic grace that we can genuinely aspire to.

## Self- and Mutual Regulation: Grounding, Centering, Belonging

Asking a patient to keep a food journal is *not* just a matter of recording what they eat (that is crossing over to medical treatment), but rather to help them to reflect on how their body feels before, within, and after the experience of eating. Many patients will not be able to experience hunger or satiety normally, or will not know when to initiate eating healthfully, without an affective or environmental trigger, and may even fear the feeling of hunger. Carolyn Ross (2009), author of a body-oriented binge eating disorder workbook, offers these five "relationship skills" for those readers who are practicing the exercises that she suggests: active attention, listening, communicating, give-and-take, and active loving. Ross describes ways in which these skills can be attuned to, not with others, but rather in relationship to one's own body.

In one study (Morgan Lazarro-Smith, 2008), nine psychotherapists and seven ED clients were asked to compare their experiences with healing eating disorders using Body Psychotherapeutic treatments. In-depth, open-ended, semi-structured interviews were used to collect data on central themes and subthemes that emerged within the treatment process. Several correlations emerged in relation to the thesis question of how Body Psychotherapy can be a useful element in the treatment of EDs.

Among all of the patients surveyed in this study, the relationship to the body encompassed estrangement and fear, a mind/body disconnect, a tendency toward intellectualization, body hatred, shame, and dissociation. Among these patients, the relationship to emotion was one of disconnection, and the eating disorder was often used, either to avoid or further disconnect from emotion, or to manage excessive anxiety. Participants cited self-judgment for feeling emotion, and a fear of being oneself, a fear of relationships with others, and a self-imposed pressure to perform/succeed. Body Psychotherapeutic techniques that were found to be helpful centered around self-regulation techniques that enhanced relaxation, mindfulness, breath, grounding, and containment, the ability to identify satiety cues, as well as to identify dissociation cues and emotional needs.

To be connected with the body in a manner that matches one's perceptual experience is considered crucial to an ED patient. This is demonstrated in the following description of a client's experience with phototherapy:

> Phototherapy was honestly the most beneficial part of my recovery. I scheduled to see the photographer and get professional photos taken. For me, I wanted to wear a bikini so I can see every part of my body. I took my first set of photos at around ninety-two pounds. I brought my photos to my therapy session, where we discussed them in depth. What do I see/like/hate? What does he see? I would look at the photos and look in the mirror at the same time. Was I seeing in the mirror a body that was somewhat similar to the one in the picture? The answer was absolutely not. I didn't think I would be any less distorted by looking at my body in a picture; however, I saw the bones sticking out and the muscle missing in certain places. From there, I took a new set of photos every five pounds I gained. We would do the whole process again and compare the photos of the first set to the second set, etc. It was shocking to see how little a difference the five pounds made. I couldn't tell the difference in the first set and the second set. Now on my fourth set and twenty pounds heavier, I can see the difference—but it is a positive difference. I love my most recent set of photos and am the happiest I have ever been with my body. I look at my first set when I am having a bad day and they scare me to death! I see a gross, unhealthy, and emaciated body. It has truly done wonders for me. I still have more weight to gain, more photos to take, and more progress to make. The photos helped me see the physical manifestation of the internal and mental afflictions I was suffering due to my eating disorder, which gave me the motivation to work toward a healthier physical appearance and mentality. Although I can't say I am happy with how I look all the time, I don't think any person can say that! (personal communication, June 2012)

Using embodied (and concretely bodied) techniques to challenge a distorted body image equips the therapist with powerful tools for intervention (Rolef Ben-Shahar, 2010). At the heart of Body Psychotherapy is a belief that experiential learning (and affect-laden processing) results in deeper and more thorough implementation of insights than cognitive processes alone. The originator of Formative Psychology, Stanley Keleman (Keleman and Adler, 2000), wrote: "Life is a process of forming. There is a continual reshaping of our bodily self, from the unformed infant to the formed adult. Either we live this forming unreflectively, or we volitionally participate in influencing our inherited responses" (pp. 50–51). Keleman (1985) went even further in claiming that, "without anatomy, emotions do not exist. Feelings have somatic architecture" (p. xii). In the context of the last case study mentioned above, the therapeutic dyad helped to create a kinder set of internalized eyes, by changing the anatomy cognition through a therapeutic intervention that combined concrete (primary and subsymbolic) as well as cognitive (secondary process) elements within it.

These Body Psychotherapeutic techniques, along with Dance Therapy, Movement Therapy, Yoga, and mindfulness—practices that all enhance embodiment and interoceptive awareness—have shown great promise in the potential treatment course for individuals with eating disorders. "Dis-ease" and "well-being" are individual courses in the unique somatic experience along each human continuum. In prescribing any form of treatment—but most vitally in the realm of eating disorders, the ultimate course of therapy taken must be reflective of, and conducted by way of, each unique body in order to attempt a comprehensive, holistic, and successful chance of recovery.

## References

Asheri, S., Carroll, R., Rolef Ben-Shahar, A., Soth, M., & Totton, N. (2012). *Relational Body Psychotherapy panel presentation.* The Body in the World, the World in the Body—13th International EABP Congress of Body Psychotherapy. Cambridge, UK: Owl Productions.

Bachar, E. (2001). *The fear of occupying space: Self-psychology and the treatment of anorexia and bulimia* [Hebrew ed.]. Jerusalem: Hebrew University: Magness Press.

Bloomgarden, A., & Calogero, R. (2008). A randomized experimental test of the efficacy of EMDR treatment on negative body image in eating disorder patients. *Eating Disorders: The Journal of Treatment and Prevention, 16*(5), 418–427.

Bromberg, P. (2006). Treating patients with symptoms, and symptoms with patience. In P. Bromberg, *Awakening the dreamer* (pp. 108–127). Mahwah, NJ: Analytic Press.

Bruha, J. (2010). The effects of body experience and mindfulness on body-image disturbance and eating disorders. *USABP Journal, 9*(2), 54–68.

Bucci, W. (2005). The interplay of subsymbolic and symbolic processes in psychoanalytic treatment: Commentary on paper by Steven H. Knoblauch. *Psychoanalytic Dialogues, 15,* 855–873.

Bucci, W. (2008). The role of bodily experience in emotional organization. In F. S. Anderson (Ed.), *Bodies in treatment: The unspoken dimension* (pp. 51–76). Hove, UK: Analytic Press.

Bucci, W. (2011). The interplay of subsymbolic and symbolic processes in psychoanalytic treatment: It takes two to tango—but who knows the steps, who's the leader? The choreography of the psychoanalytic interchange. *Psychoanalytic Dialogues, 21*(1), 45–54.

Carei, T., Fye-Johnson, A., Breuner, C., & Marshall, M. (2010). Randomized controlled clinical trial of Yoga in the treatment of eating disorders. *Journal of Adolescent Health, 46*(4), 346–351.

Clarke, D. P. (2008). *Assessing finding Om: A Yoga and discussion-based treatment for binge eating disorder.* ProQuest.

de Zwaan, M., & Roerig, J. (2003). Pharmacological treatment of eating disorders. *Eating Disorders, 6,* 223–314.

Feldenkrais, M. (1977). *Awareness through movement: Health exercises for personal growth.* Harmondsworth, UK: Penguin.

Gilligan, S. G. (1997). *The courage to love: Practice and principles of self-relations psychotherapy.* New York: W. W. Norton.

Heller, M. C. (2012). *Body Psychotherapy: History, concepts, methods.* New York: Norton.

Hendricks, G. (1995). *Conscious breathing: Breathwork for health, stress release, and personal mastery.* New York: Bantam Books.

Keleman, S. (1985). *Emotional anatomy.* Berkeley, CA: Center Press.

Keleman, S., & Adler, S. (2000). Couples therapy as a formative process. *Journal of Couples Therapy, 10*(2), 49–59.

Kiessling, R. C. (2013, March). *Using the EMDR approach (with and without all that BLS) for the treatment of eating disorders.* Presented at iaedp Symposium 2013: What's New Under the Sun? Innovative Approaches to Treatment. Henderson, Nevada.

Krantz, A. (1999). Growing into her body: Dance/Movement Therapy for women with eating disorders. *American Journal of Dance Therapy, 21,* 81–103.

Levy, R. (2012). If you eat alone, you die alone: The body's voice [Regular column; in Hebrew]. *Haim Acherim [A Different Life], 193,* 66.

Lowen, A. (1958). *The language of the body.* New York: Macmillan.

Morgan Lazarro-Smith, B. (2008). Healing eating disorders with body-centered therapies. *USABP Journal, 7*(2), 33–42.

Orbach, S. (2004). What can we learn from the therapist's body? *Attachment and Human Development, 6*(2), 141–150.

Pallaro, P. (Ed.). (1999). *Authentic Movement: Essays by Mary Starks Whitehouse, Janet Adler and Joan Chodorow* (Vol. 1). New York: Jessica Kingsley.

Pizer, B. (1997). When the analyst is ill: Dimensions of self-disclosure. *Psychoanalytic Quarterly, 66,* 450–469.

Reich, W. (1933/1972). *Character Analysis.* New York: Noonday Press.

Rolef Ben-Shahar, A. (2010). *In the body we know: Using Body Psychotherapy for working with eating disorders and distorted body-image* [Hebrew]. Retrieved from www.betipulnet.co.il

Rolef Ben-Shahar, A. (2012). The relational turn and Body Psychotherapy: IV. Gliding on the strings that connect us: Resonance in Relational Body Psychotherapy. *International Body Psychotherapy Journal, 11(1),* 12–24.

Rolef Ben-Shahar, A. (2013). *A therapeutic anatomy: Body Psychotherapy* [Hebrew Ed.]. Haifa, Israel: Pardes.

Ross, C. C. (2009). *The binge eating and compulsive overeating workbook: An integrated approach to overcoming disordered eating.* Oakland, CA: New Harbinger.

Roth, G. (1984). *Breaking free from compulsive eating.* London: Grafton.

Roth, G. (1992). *When food is love: Exploring the relationship between eating and intimacy.* New York: Plume.

Stice, E., Marti, C. N., & Rohde, P. (2013). Prevalence, incidence, impairment, and course of the proposed DSM-5 eating disorder diagnoses in an 8-year prospective community study of young women. *Journal of Abnormal Psychology, 122*(2), 445.

Totton, N., & Jacobs, M. (2001). *Character and personality types.* Buckingham, UK: Open University.

Ventling, C. (2004). Health-threatening *bulimia nervosa* and a promising new treatment approach. *USABP Journal, 3*(2), 82–100.

Zerbe, K. J. (2008). *Integrated treatment of eating disorders: Beyond the body betrayed.* New York: W. W. Norton.

# 73

# Body Psychotherapy with Narcissistic Personality Disorders

Manfred Thielen, Germany

Translation by Warren Miller and Michael Soth

**Manfred Thielen**, PhD, is an accredited psychotherapist equally committed to clinical work, research, professional policy, supervision, and teaching therapy. As chairman of the German Association for Body Psychotherapy (DGK), the German national association of the EABP; chairman of the Institute for Integrative Biodynamics; a member of the board for accredited psychotherapists in Berlin; and a delegate to the German Federal Board of Psychotherapy, he has tirelessly engaged himself in the promotion and recognition of Body Psychotherapy in Germany. He is on the editorial board of the German journals *körper–tanz–bewegung* and *Psychotherapeutenjournal,* and the *International Journal of Body Psychotherapy.*

Dr. Thielen is trained in Body Psychotherapy (Integrative Biodynamics), client-centered psychotherapy, Cognitive Behavioral Therapy, and Psychodynamic Psychotherapy. He is a co-founder of and a trainer at the Institute for Body Psychotherapy in Berlin, which offers training and continuing education in Body Psychotherapy. He has taken part in the scientific discourse by contributing numerous publications, by organizing relevant conferences, and through his teaching role at the psychology department of the Free University of Berlin. He has been in practice since 1982, and, in recent years, has devoted his particular attention to the clinical and social aspects of narcissistic personality disorder. In a series of publications, including three books (Thielen, 2002, 2009, 2013), he has highlighted the importance of the therapeutic relationship and the value of integration of Body Psychotherapeutic approaches in the treatment of this condition.

## General Features of Narcissism

The main features of narcissistic personality disorder (NPD) are a pervasive pattern of grandiosity in fantasy or behavior, hypersensitivity to the appraisal of others, and a lack of empathic capacity (Sass et al., 2003, p. 781). Many research findings lend support to this phenomenological description and describe further traits, such as fluctuations in self-worth, labile affect, search for recognition and validation, and domineering behavior, among others (Sachse, 2002, pp. 156ff.; Maaz, 2012, pp. 23ff.).

The narcissistic person's feelings about themselves commonly fluctuate between grandiosity and inferiority. They commonly feel empty, numb, and depressed, and are highly susceptible to feeling insulted. In relationship to themselves, as in relationship to others, they are subject to the mechanisms of idealization and devaluation, and their unstable sense of self-worth wavers between these two polarities. Depending on the degree and intensity of these internal oscillations, they suffer from their isolation of affect, and it tends to be difficult for them to maintain satisfying relationships, if they manage to form proper relationships at all. They generally try to cope with their oversensitivity and susceptibility as to how they are being evaluated in the eyes of others by "isolating" their feelings and numbing their affective experience.

## The Concept of Narcissism and Its Historical Development

The concept of narcissism in psychotherapy, as a category of psychological pathology, goes back to Freud. Having initially proposed it as an early phase of the psycho-sexual stage of development, Freud's definition of narcissism, and his ideas about it, changed over the years as his theories evolved. In 1914, Freud distinguished between primary and secondary narcissism: he saw "primary narcissism" as a stage in development during the first months of life, when the infant's libido is—quite age-appropriately, in Freud's view—entirely directed toward itself and not yet capable of being oriented toward other people or "objects." In Freudian terms: in primary narcissism, the libido cathects the ego. In contrast, "secondary narcissism" is pathological: libido is withdrawn from the world after a phase of having been turned toward the object-world (Freud, 1914, pp. 41ff.).

In 1923, Freud considered the id as the original reservoir of libido and the source of primary narcissism. He proposed that in secondary narcissism the ego takes hold of the libido that ought to cathect the objects (Freud, 1923, p. 312f.). Psychoanalytic theorists of narcissism, such as Kohut (1971, 1976, 1977) and Kernberg (1983, 1995, 2004), among others, picked up Freud's theory of primary narcissism and further differentiated the concept. So did Mahler (1979), who described the first weeks of the infant as the "normal autistic phase," and compared this with Freud's metaphor of a bird in its shell.

Regardless of the finer points of definition, Freud's conceptualization of primary narcissism has been empirically refuted by modern developmental research. As soon as the infant is born, it is in relation with others, its close caregivers. Its self is a "self with other" (Stern, 1992). Likewise, Freud's idea that a stimulus barrier protects the infant from environmental stimulation during the first months of life lacks any empirical evidence. From the time of its birth, the infant has significant traits of subjectivity, using all its senses and is in constant, active, and reciprocal interaction with its primary caregivers (Ibid., pp. 324ff.). Rather than being motivated solely by the pleasure principle and the drives of the id, as Freud had presumed, the infant's "ego functions"—such as patterns of exploration, curiosity, perceptual preferences, novelty-seeking, and the desire for mastery—are all equally important in regulating behavior (Stern, 1992; Dornes, 1998, 2000, 2006, 2012). Infants are social beings, subjects who actively establish relationships with their caregivers and their environment.

Narcissistic development must then be viewed as a secondary phenomenon that arises ontogenetically from disordered interactions between the primary caregivers and the child. As we will see in some detail later, within the field of Body Psychotherapy, Lowen (1985, 1986), the founder of Bioenergetics, proposed precisely this understanding of narcissism, both before and independently of any research findings that now support it.

Although Kohut (1976) distinguished a healthy form of narcissism, viewing healthy narcissism as self-love, and considered this as a mature stage of development. as a mature stage of development and an expression of self-love, common parlance—deriving from the Greek myth of Narcissus—emphasizes the pathological aspects of narcissism, associating it with vanity and self-absorbed self-admiration (Wahrig, 1970, pp. 25–38). This is the meaning used in this chapter: a healthy person—in contrast to the narcissist—is able to direct love both toward him- or herself as much as toward other "loved objects."

Narcissistic development in an individual must also be viewed in the sociocultural context that the individual lives in. Demeanor, values, norms, and the ideologies of postmodern society shape the specific interactions between the primary caregiver and the child. The narcissism of the individual thus always reflects (or develops in the context of) the narcissism of society at large (Wirth, 2011; Maaz, 2012).

Modern cultural norms tend to prioritize outer appearance, success at any cost, and "image," over any inner qualities, like authenticity, peacefulness, and harmony with nature. Power, status, and symbols of wealth count more than solidarity in human relationships. Instrumentalization of the "other" is not only a manifestation of narcissistic behavior, but also of economic commodification (Lasch,

1982; Wirth, 2011; Maaz, 2012). We may be in an "epidemic of narcissism" (Twenge and Campbell, 2009).

## Body Psychotherapeutic Theories of Narcissism

### Wilhelm Reich: Oedipal (Phallic) Narcissism

In 1933, when writing *Character Analysis* and still thinking mostly in psychoanalytic terms, Reich began to conceptualize the "phallic-narcissistic character." At that time, no research on the structural disorders had been done yet. Reich (1933/1989, pp. 271ff.) analyzed narcissism as the manifestation of an oedipal disorder. He described the phallic-narcissistic character as confident, at times arrogant, flexible, strong, athletic, often imposing, and with a marked degree of aggressiveness. According to Reich, such a person tends to attack, to preempt being attacked. The ego of the phallic narcissist is completely identified with his phallus, and he expresses his aggression sexually in relation with women to get revenge. The desire for revenge originates from experiences of thwarted love in relation to his mother. The female narcissist takes revenge on her father, for having rejected her as a worthy heterosexual object.

Reich emphasized the inability to love as the most characteristic trait of the narcissistic personality. Through "acting out" in sexually promiscuous ways, narcissists get revenge for having been emotionally and sexually rejected by their parents. Reich identified that this tended to manifest in the transference as a strong devaluation of the therapist, which is generally recognized as a common feature of the countertransference in working with narcissists. Based on what we know now, Reich overemphasized the aggressive aspect of the narcissist, while neglecting to note the depressive aspect. Only to a certain extent was Reich able to recognize the core problem of lability between grandiosity and inferiority. Depression and the associated sense of inferiority are the flip side of the sense of grandiosity. As the narcissist continues to fail to live up to his own ideals, he devalues himself and may fall into depressive states.

In his vegetotherapeutic phase (beginning in 1934), Reich developed Body Psychotherapeutic interventions to address such characterological issues. In the case of the narcissist, whom he considered to be "contactless," these interventions were aimed at restoring the ability to love, and reestablishing the energetic contact between the heart and the genitals.

Because the narcissist's impaired ability to form attachments commonly manifests in a lack of ability to surrender sexually, Reich's objective of restoring the capacities for both love and attachment continues to play a central role in the Body Psychotherapeutic treatment of this disorder today.

### Alexander Lowen: A Developmental Spectrum of Narcissism

Lowen (1986) distinguished different kinds of narcissism according to their respective degree of ego strength (strength of the self) and the depth of emotional denial. According to his classification, the phallic-narcissistic character suffers from only a relatively mild form of narcissism because of what Lowen sees as a relatively high degree of functioning. His classification of narcissism comprises the narcissistic character, the borderline personality, the psychopathic personality, and the paranoid personality. The severity of narcissism—in the form of grandiosity, lack or denial of emotion, lack of a sense of self, and impairment in reality testing—is most pronounced in the paranoid personality and least pronounced in the phallic-narcissistic character. In contrast to the mental-psychological conceptions of Psychoanalytic Self Psychology, Lowen defined the self as the "living body, which includes the mind" (Lowen, 1985, p. 7). The narcissist thinks of his body as an instrument of the mind and subjects it to his will. With the body being treated more like a machine, it loses vitality—the main reason why the narcissistic person feels "lifeless" and "empty."

Lowen rejected Freud's concept of primary narcissism without being able to refer to the findings of infant research that are now available. He considered the genesis of narcissism to be a *secondary* phenomenon, a result of a disturbance in the pattern of interaction between the mother (or primary caregiver) and the child. The parents have not only been neglectful (deficit model), but also actively wounding (by denigrating aspects of the child), while also demanding their "performance" in various ways. According to Lowen, the core problem that the narcissist struggles with is that he was socialized to live in his false self, his "image," and thus to deny his real feelings and true self. He diagnosed this as *narcissistic alexithymia,* a severe inability to feel; but it needs to be stated that people with a narcissistic personality do not necessarily suffer from general alexithymia, but can be alexithymic in relation to specific feelings that they are particularly defended against, such as grief, fear, dependency, etc.

Lowen saw the task of the bioenergetic "treatment" of narcissism to be the reanimation of the body and its feelings, and the development of the patient's "true self." According to Lowen, the denial of feeling is reflected in body-based defense mechanisms, especially in the form of strong rigidities. The musculature is chronically tense (hypertonic), in particular at the base of the skull, at the intersection of head and neck. These tensions cause an extreme split between the head and the body: the breath becomes restricted and the intake of oxygen is reduced, and so the metabolic rate is lowered. Due to the inhibition of the early impulses to suck or bite, the muscles of the jaw are usually quite tense. All these contractions are designed for, and result in a repression of the need for, closeness and contact. Years of diagnostic and therapeutic experience led Lowen to theorize that the upper body of narcissists is usually quite well developed. The chest appears inflated, while the lower body is disproportionally weaker, and also appears that way. This split between upper and lower body is also commonly reflected in a blockage in the pelvis and unsatisfying sexuality. The narcissist's rigidity serves to repress his unpleasant feelings, especially those that do not fit into his image of himself. In particular, sadness, dread, humiliation, helplessness, neediness, lovelessness, horror, and feelings of insanity are also repressed.

## Gerda Boyesen: Narcissistic Rigidity throughout All the Body Systems

Clinical experience over recent decades has thrown doubt on the idea of a uniform narcissistic body type. Lowen's finding of a marked rigidity throughout the body, on the other hand, has become a commonly accepted notion in Body Psychotherapy. This rigidity expresses itself not only in the muscular, but correspondingly also in the vegetative, system (early on, Reich had described vegetative dystonia in correlation with strong rigidity).

Having studied with Ola Raknes, a student of Reich's in Norway, Gerda Boyesen (1987) devoted particular attention to the vegetative aspects of psychological disturbances. In her system of Biodynamic Psychotherapy, rigidity can also be seen to manifest in congestions of the lymphatic system and the digestive system. She developed the concept of the "emotional vasomotoric cycle," in which any emotional expression involves activations, not only in the muscular system, but also in the vegetative systems of the body, including the autonomic nervous system. Rage, for example, is expressed motorically in the form of a fist, or an angry face, but also depends upon a corresponding vegetative arousal (including metabolic and physiological activations), manifesting in angry feelings. Inhibition of emotional expression has consequences on all three levels: muscular contractions (through suppression of the motor impulse); vegetative stasis (as the charge that has built up is not being discharged); and psychologically, as the unexpressed rage may be compensated for by it being converted into an indirect expression, such as contemptuous dismissal. Stress reactions trigger the release of adrenaline and noradrenaline in the lymphatic system, and affect many organs throughout the body. If these hormones are not worked off through physical expression, or drained off by normal digestive processes, toxic residues will remain in the system and will build up over time. These residues are considered to be the vegetative factor in the multifactorial causation of psychosomatic disorders. Geuter and Schrauth have further developed Boyesen's concept of the emotional vasomotoric cycle, into the notion of the "affect cycle" (see Chapter 53, "The Role of the Body in Emotional Defense Processes: Body Psychotherapy and Emotional Theory").

In order to dissolve or reduce blockages in vegetative flow, Boyesen developed several different types of Biodynamic massage, aiming to facilitate organismic and psychological self-regulation. In the treatment of narcissistic personality disorder, this Biodynamic approach can be useful, as it bypasses the kinds of resistance commonly found in Bioenergetic treatment. With the Bioenergetic focus on the muscular system and the pulsatory principle of charge and discharge, the activated charge usually is accompanied by a degree of stress. Because narcissists are often achievement-oriented, Bioenergetic stress-practices can thus intensify their defensive structures by adding to the already-existing internal pressures to perform "properly."

In contrast, the Biodynamic combination of massage and psychotherapy is a psychosomatic dialogue with the patient, and usually helps patients to enter a state of deep relaxation. The patient's mental autonomy and muscular self-regulation are both stimulated, opening up a potential space in which feelings can emerge. The different kinds of Biodynamic Massage address blockages and congestion at different levels and in different systems, and thus facilitate more of a general motility and flow.

Although Lowen viewed alexithymia as the key feature of narcissistic disorders, manifesting especially in a lack of feeling for others, clinical experience suggests that beneath the facade there are also feelings of pronounced self-pity (see Thielen, 2002, 2004). Because of early experiences of humiliation, narcissists are easily offended, take criticism as an insult, and tend to experience it as a fundamental attack on the self, leaving them feeling potentially victimized and treated unfairly. So, they often "attack" back relentlessly, as these feelings are unacceptable.

**Narcissism in the Theories of Other Body Psychotherapists**

Along with Reich, Lowen, and Boyesen, other pioneers of Body Psychotherapy, such as Pierrakos, Boadella, Kurtz, Keleman, and Moser, have all shed further light on the narcissistic dynamic. Downing (1996, 2003, 2006) identified body-based defensive strategies that narcissists tend to utilize to protect themselves against the awareness of unpleasant feelings. Geissler (1995), Trautmann-Voigt (1997), Krüger (2001), Maaz (2012), and Marlock (2012), among others, have submitted further contributions (see also: Geuter, 2002, pp. 114ff.) to the elaboration of the narcissistic dynamic.

In addition to the Neo-Reichian schools, the more perceptual schools of Body Psychotherapy, such as Concentrative Movement Therapy and Functional Relaxation and those that integrate body and movement therapy as well as Body Psychotherapy, have, among other things, delivered further understandings of the narcissistic paradigm. Both directions of Body Psychotherapy have come together in a common training curriculum as part of the DGK.

## Early Childhood Genesis

Narcissism theorists and researchers generally are in ongoing controversy about the question of which particular developmental phase in early childhood corresponds to the origin of narcissism. From a client-centered orientation, Sachse (2002, p. 149) proposes that narcissistic developments begin only in early adulthood. In contrast, the various schools of psychoanalytic theory—such as Self Psychology (Kohut, Tolpin, and Wolf, among others), object-relations theory (Kernberg, Jacobson, Mahler, Masterson, and Winnicott, among others), and Ego Psychology (A. Freud, Hartmann, and Blanck and Blanck, among others)—all agree that narcissistic developments originate in early childhood. Johnson (1987, 1988) integrated humanistic, psychodynamic, and Body Psychotherapeutic perspectives in his description of the development of narcissism. Drawing upon Mahler's theory of development, which posits the phases of normal autism, symbiosis, and individuation (Mahler et al., 1980), Johnson identified the phase of rapprochement (fifteen to twenty-four months) as the time during which narcissism originates.

The infant researcher Daniel Stern (1992) has critiqued and relativized these conceptualizations. Neither an autistic phase, nor a symbiotic phase, can seemingly be supported by findings from infant research. The infant is a competent "actor" who signals its own state to its parents through facial expressions, vocalizations, and gestural behaviors. The infant perceives its ability to influence its primary caregivers, not only as reflective of its agency, but, in the extreme, as a sense of omnipotence. Stern developed a complex interactional model that describes the interactions between infant and caregiver (Ibid., p. 143). According to Stern, grandiosity can develop when the mother responds only to the enthusiastic expressions of the child, amplifying those, while suppressing and denying any depressive expressions.

From the perspective of Developmental Psychology, feelings of shame are considered to play an important role in the genesis of narcissism. Adult narcissists are ashamed of their feelings, in particular their feelings of grief and dependency. Beginning at about the fifteenth month, children confronted with their mirror image show precursory reactions of self-reflexive shame. Shame reactions, such as expressions of a developed self, can first be detected at about two years of age (Hilgers, 1997, pp. 194ff.). In healthy child development, the emergence of shame facilitates maturation and identity formation; but in narcissistic socialization, it inhibits emotional expression (Thielen, 2004).

Whichever developmental phase is theorized to be the precise origin of narcissism, there is a general consensus regarding the following patterns of disturbance in the empathic attunement between the primary caregiver and the child:

* The child wants to be loved by its parents or primary caregivers for its whole being, and not just for its doing. The child wants all its needs and feelings to be acknowledged and accepted. But, in a narcissistically skewed development, only some aspects of the child are loved.

* Therefore, the child's innate need for attachment is met only selectively. Usually, the emotional attunement between the parents and the child strengthens their attachment. To a large extent, this process occurs on a bodily level. From the way in which the primary caregivers touch the child, support it, take it into their arms, stimulate it, or set boundaries, the child forms cognitive representations and generalizations (referred to by Stern as "RIGs") (Thielen, 2003, 2009, 2013).

* Adequate interaction necessitates that the parents are able to empathize with the child. In narcissistic development, this empathic attunement is severely impaired. The child is "required" to fulfill the ideal expectations of its parents. If the child does not respond emotionally as expected (for example, if it responds with rage to the experienced pressure to perform), the parents punish it by depriving it of their love, and/or by devaluing, ridiculing, or (emotionally) abandoning the child.

* If this negative experience is recurrent, the child withdraws into itself. It develops the sense that it is faulty, and it becomes ashamed of itself and its feelings, as these are not acknowledged by its parents. In order to avoid this acute disappointment, and the rage that comes with it, the child develops a number of compensatory strategies. It withdraws from actual contact and, age permitting, flees into a fantasy world in which it dreams of itself as a "hero." Its core belief becomes: "I don't really need anyone," which is the result of this rejection and withdrawal and humiliation.

Narcissists are caught up within themselves and the outward appearance of their—empty—bodies. Their emotional withdrawal and their flight into grandiosity are reflected in their body image. The lack of emotional nourishment during early childhood also manifests itself on a body level. Their childhood was characterized by a lack of affectionate physicality, authentic touch, caresses, and loving attention. Consequently, they experience their bodies, not as a container in which feelings can move around, but as vague, empty, void, or even as a broken vessel (Busch, 2002).

The core conflict of narcissistic people is that they cannot genuinely reach out from their isolation in order to make contact with people, but remain withdrawn in an imagined, virtual world, revolving only around the centrality of their own self-image. So, even when they are among people in social situations and appear to be involved and communicative (which they become very good at faking), they actually feel removed and isolated internally. Therefore, one of the essential aims of therapy is to support the patient in approaching others more authentically (Busch, 2000). This approach has psychological and bodily aspects, as it calls for an integrated sense of self, as well as emotional opening and movement. Aggression—in the sense of *aggredi* (Latin: to go out, or explore)—is usually what supports their movement toward others, but the previously described disappointments and emotional wounds tend to inhibit and foreclose any more vulnerable initiatives and divert the impulses of healthy expressions into often what are experienced as devaluations of the other and a focus on their own self-importance.

## Body Psychotherapeutic Practice

The practice of Body Psychotherapy operates at the interface between relational work and body-oriented work (Thielen, 1994, 2002, 2009, 2013). A stable therapeutic alliance and a trusting therapeutic relationship are therefore preconditions for any effective Body Psychotherapeutic work. Body Psychotherapeutic techniques are integrated into the relational work, and the transference and counter-transference processes are given as much attention as the genuineness and authenticity of the therapeutic contact.

One of the basic challenges in any psychotherapy with narcissistic patients is to reach and "touch" them emotionally, behind their firm defenses, which may include alexithymia. To stand any chance of addressing these defenses successfully, it is imperative that the therapist be empathically attuned, taking into account the patient's emotional resources and vulnerabilities (including their tendency to easily feel criticized and diminished by all kinds of "therapeutic" interventions), and have respect and appreciation regarding the function of their defenses as a sensible protection for the vulnerable and underdeveloped core. To facilitate the patient's process of gradually reclaiming their bodily self, a variety of embodied practices can become useful, designed to strengthen realistic awareness of the patient's own body (including different forms of self-touch) and awareness of self and others generally.[69]

These practices can help the patient: to perceive sensations that arise from within his body; to learn to differentiate among them; and to link them with corresponding emotions. Current research findings regarding the neurobiology of alexithymia (Damasio, 2000) suggest that the alexithymic's brain isn't actually able to link bodily signals with emotions. This ability therefore might need to be relearned. A useful exercise, for example, is the Bioenergetic "bow," which can be utilized to promote self-awareness, as well as to facilitate emotional expression. The bodily signals that are being generated, such as tension, warmth, or vibration, can then be successively associated with emotions. This process of realignment leads to the formation of new synaptic connections in the emotion-processing areas of the brain, such as the amygdala (Hüther et al., 2006; Siegel, 2006; Schore, 1994, 2009).

After a degree of self-awareness has been restored, the narcissistic patient needs to learn to become increasingly nuanced in differentiating between himself and others. A qualitative empirical study (Stehle and Körber, 2002, pp. 144ff.) classified the range of techniques and interventions into four main groups, and then validated their efficacy:

The first group involved Biodynamic massages, in the Boyesen tradition, which can help to "melt" the somatic defenses or "slip through" the narcissistic patients' strong defenses and resistances. Early childhood and childhood experiences that are stored in the body, but remain verbally inaccessible, can also be activated in this way. In the context of this empirical study, this kind of intervention is usually well received by patients. They tended to experience it as being very comforting and relaxing, as well as quite revealing emotionally. This form of systematic bodily touch can significantly help narcissistic patients to restore contact with their split-off, inaccessible feelings, and their self. As predicted by the theory of the emotional vasomotoric cycle, self-regulation becomes activated and supported. Often, this kind of massage (and the associated psychotherapy) brings new, unconscious material to light, which can then be examined biographically and verbally, and thus cognitively integrated.

The second group was described with the title "emotional expressive work." This group comprised Body Psychotherapeutic practices and techniques that facilitated the

---

[69] Group Body Psychotherapy can be very useful for people with narcissistic problems (see Thielen, 2013).

expression of previously inhibited emotions. Such inhibitions, manifesting both in muscular and in vegetative systems, can be loosened or dissolved with the help of this type of intervention. In vegetotherapeutic, emotionally expressive work, the patient usually lies down on a mattress and slows, deepens, and lengthens her breathing. Shallow breathing is one of the most common ways to dilute charge and suppress feelings. Usually inhalation, as well as exhalation, are flattened and restrained. Depending on the patient's established (characterological) breathing pattern, different breathing practices, focusing more on inhalation or more on exhalation, can allow charge to accumulate beyond the patient's established routine, which usually leads to increased emotionality. Bioenergetic grounding work aims to bring the lower body, in particular the feet and legs, into better contact with the ground. This can enhance awareness of physical sensations and boundaries, and of the body-self in general, by reanimating split-off feelings.

Narcissistic patients reported feeling actively supported in this type of therapy work with their aggression, which is usually quite deeply repressed. There are a number of effective Body Psychotherapeutic practices and techniques to this end (see Röhricht, 2000). The work of emotional expression helped those patients who were interviewed in the context of a study to get in better touch with their repressed and split-off feelings. In addition to getting in touch with their aggression, they gained access to other feelings, such as grief, sorrow, dependency, etc. Narcissistic patients seem to need bodily interventions, because their feelings are very difficult to access solely by verbal means. They have no (or only a little) relationship with their feelings and their body. The reanimation of their "lifeless" body—that is, their body-self—leads to the enlivening of their emotional responsiveness.

The third group encompassed therapeutic forms of physical, as well as psychological, holding or containment. On a bodily level, there are various ways to provide containment, such as the psychotherapist putting his hand on the patient's back or abdomen, sitting or standing back-to-back, or the patient leaning their back against the therapist's chest (if the specific regressive situation indicates this). Containment gives support and facilitates belated maturation, which occurs on a psychological, as well as a body, level. In the postexperimental inquiry, patients reported that they had experienced these kinds of interventions as very soothing, and that participating in such supportive work—without having to reciprocate—helped them to feel more accepted. They described it as a very important, potentially corrective, experience, because—during their childhood—regard, attention, and care had been contingent on their behavior.

The fourth group comprised body-oriented or biodramatic role-plays. These practices can help consenting patients to reenact biographically rooted core conflicts with their parents. Feelings that were split off or repressed in the past can—in this way—be made accessible to the patient and thus can be redirected toward the object-world. In contrast to Moreno's type of Psychodrama, these forms of Biodrama focus on the body, and reenactments can be expressed through the body. For example, rage against the parent may be expressed through hitting a large cushion, or the chest of the therapist (which is protected by a pillow), often while maintaining eye contact to encourage the relational feelings to emerge. Such practices allow the patient to experience that, although his father or mother punished him for his rage, he is now being more accepted—aversive feelings and all. Or the patient can lean on the therapist, in the transference role of the good father or mother, enabling him to mourn his past lack of parental backup and support.

When the Body Psychotherapist is able to affect the narcissist's dissociation from feelings through the reanimation of the body-self—and the ensuing emotional revitalization—this signifies a significant degree of progress. Grounding through the body, as well as grounding in social contact, can neutralize the narcissistic fantasies of grandiosity and can facilitate a more realistic and viable sense of self. Narcissistic isolation becomes transcended by means of positive aggression and expression, in the form of an active movement toward the other. If the anger due to childhood disappointments, and the destructive rage due to the humiliations experienced at the hands of the parents, can actually begin to be expressed safely, the mechanism of devaluation can gradually be transformed to permit the expression of primary emotions. Devaluation is a secondary process, and the expression of rage has gone cold. The task of Body Psychotherapeutic work with narcissistic clients is therefore to reanimate the primary emotions by reestablishing contact with the "hot" rage, directed mainly against the parents (or one of the parents) in response to the child's disappointment and lack of acceptance. If the narcissist can risk expressing that kind of rage, directly and appropriately, then the compensation mechanism of devaluing both self and others will become progressively superfluous.

To nourish their attachment and relational capabilities, the narcissist should be supported in developing deeper levels of self-love. Only from this basis can his or her ability to love others be developed further. As recognized by Reich and Lowen, the reconstruction of the energetic connection between the heart and the genitals is another important step in the development of the capacity to love fully and sexually. Thus, a range of Body Psychotherapeutic techniques can be used to dissolve the chronic tensions and blockages in the chest and pelvic regions. These may be complemented with cognitive suggestions and techniques using imagery (or visualizations). If the narcissistically hurt person can learn to "open" their heart again, allowing and directing their love toward objects (people) other than the self, a major goal of successful psychotherapy will have been accomplished. If he or she can further learn to view their narcissistic dilemma with humor and a degree of self-reflective distance, another transformation of the narcissistic process will also have been completed.

## References

Boyesen, G. (1987). *Über den Körper die Seele heilen: Biodynamische Psychologie und Psychotherapie* [Through the body, heal the soul: Biodynamic Psychology and Psychotherapy]. Munich: Kösel.

Busch, T. (2000). *Charakter und Persönlichkeit: Aspekte des narzisstischen Persönlichkeitsstils* [Character and personality: Aspects of the narcissistic personality style]. Writings on education and training of the Institute for Body Psychotherapy, Berlin: Unpublished manuscript.

Busch, T. (2002). Narzissmus: Selbstentfremdung und leibseelische Wiederbelebung des Selbst [Narcissism: Self-alienation and body-soul revival of the self]. In M. Thielen (Ed.), *Narzissmus: Körper-Psychotherapie zwischen Energie und Beziehung* [Narcissism: The relationship between energy and Body Psychotherapy]. Berlin: Ulrich Leutner.

Damasio, A. R. (2000). *Ich fühle, also bin ich* [I feel, therefore I am]. Munich: List.

Dornes, M. (1998). *Die frühe Kindheit* [Early childhood]. Frankfurt: Fischer.

Dornes, M. (2000). *Die emotionale Welt des Kindes* [The emotional world of the child]. Frankfurt: Fischer.

Dornes, M. (2006). *Die Seele des Kindes: Entstehung und Entwicklung* [The soul of the child: Formation and development]. Frankfurt: Fischer.

Dornes, M. (2012). *Die Modernisierung der Seele: Kind-Familie-Gesellschaft* [The modernization of the soul: Child-Family-Society]. Frankfurt: Fischer.

Downing, G. (1996). *Körper und Wort in der Psychotherapie* [Body and word in psychotherapy]. Munich: Kösel.

Downing, G. (2003). *Early affect exchange and the body.* Unpublished manuscript.

Downing, G. (2006). Frühkindlicher Affektaustausch und dessen Beziehung zum Körper [Early childhood affect exchange and its relation to the body]. In G. Marlock & H. Weiss (Eds.), *Handbuch der Körperpsychotherapie* [Handbook of Body Psychotherapy] (pp. 333–350). Stuttgart: Schattauer.

Freud, S. (1914). *Zur Einführung des Narzissmus: Studienausgabe Bd. III* [On narcissism: An introduction. Study edition Vol. III]. Frankfurt: Fischer.

Freud, S. (1923). *Das Ich und das Es.* Studienausgabe Bd. XIII [The ego and the id. Study edition Vol. XIII]. (1982). Frankfurt: Fischer.

Geissler, P. (1995). Ein narzisstischer männlicher Klient [A narcissistic male client]. *Zeitschrift für Körperpsychotherapie, 2*(5), 13–25.

Geuter, U. (2002). *Deutschsprachige Literatur zur Körperpsychotherapie: Eine Bibliografie* [German-language literature for Body Psychotherapy: A bibliography]. Berlin: Leutner.

Hilgers, M. (1997). *Scham: Gesichter eines Affekts* [Shame: Faces of emotion]. Göttingen: Vandenhoeck & Ruprecht.

Hüther, G., Storch, M., Cantieni, B., & Tschacher, W. (Eds.). (2006). *Embodiment: Die Wechselwirkung von Körper und Psyche verstehen und nutzen* [Embodiment: Understanding and utilizing the interaction of body and mind]. Bern, Switzerland: Huber.

Johnson, S. M. (1987). *Humanizing the narcissistic style.* New York: W. W. Norton.

Johnson, S. M. (1988). *Der narzisstische Persönlichkeitsstil* [The narcissistic personality style]. Cologne: Edition Humanistische Psychologie.

Keleman, S. (2002). *Formen der Liebe* [Forms of love]. Berlin: Leutner.

Kernberg, O. (1983/1993). *Borderline-Störungen und pathologischer Narzissmus* (7. Aufl.) [Borderline disorders and pathological narcissism (7th ed.)]. Frankfurt: Suhrkamp.

Kernberg, O. F. (1995). *Borderline conditions and pathological narcissism.* Lanham, MD: Jason Aronson.

Kernberg, O. F. (2004). *Aggressivity, narcissism and self-destructiveness in the psychotherapeutic relationship: New developments in the psychopathology and psychotherapy of severe disorders.* New Haven, CT: Yale University Press.

Kohut, H. (1971). *The analysis of the self: A systematic approach to the psychoanalytic treatment of narcissistic personality disorders.* New York: International Universities Press.

Kohut, H. (1976/1992). *Narzissmus: Eine Theorie der psychoanalytischen Behandlung narzisstischer Persönlichkeitsstörungen (8. Aufl.)* [Narcissism: A theory of psychoanalytic treatment of narcissistic personality disorders (8th Ed.)]. Frankfurt: Suhrkamp.

Kohut, H. (1977). *The restoration of the self.* New York: International Universities Press.

Krüger, A. (2001). Narzissmus und analytische Körperpsychotherapie [Narcissism and Analytical Body Psychotherapy]. In H. J. Maaz & A. H. Krüger (Eds.), *Integration des Körpers in die analytische Psychotherapie* [Integration of the body in analytical psychotherapy] (pp. 28–47). Lengerich: Günter Molz.

Lasch, C. (1982). *Das Zeitalter des Narzissmus* [The age of narcissism]. Gütersloh: Bertelsmann.

Lowen, A. (1985). *Narcissism: Denial of the true self.* New York: Macmillan (Collier Books).

Lowen, A. (1986). *Narzissmus: Die Verleugnung des wahren Selbst* [Narcissism: The denial of the true self]. Munich: Kösel.

Maaz, H. J. (2012). *Die narzisstische Gesellschaft: Ein Psychogramm* [The narcissistic society: A psychological profile]. Munich: C. H. Beck.

Mahler, M. S. (1979). *Symbiose und Individuation: Band 1. Psychosen im frühen Kindesalter* [Symbiosis and individuation: Vol. 1. Psychosis in early childhood]. Stuttgart: Klett-Cotta.

Mahler, M. S., Pine, F., & Bergmann, A. (1980). *Die psychische Geburt des Menschen: Symbiose und Individuation (Aufl. 1992)* [The psychological birth of the human being: Symbiosis and individuation (1992 ed.)]. Frankfurt: Fischer.

Marlock, G. (2012). *Körperpsychotherapie im Humanistischen Paradigma* [Body Psychotherapy in the humanistic paradigm]. Keynote speech at the AGHPT Congress: "Humanistische Psychotherapie: Einheit und Vielfalt" [Humanistic Psychotherapy: Unity and diversity]. Retrieved from www.aghpt.de/index.php/vortraege

Reich, W. (1933/1989). *Charakteranalyse* [Character Analysis]. Cologne: Kiepenheuer & Witsch.

Röhricht, F. (2000). *Körperorientierte Psychotherapie psychischer Störungen* [Body-Oriented Psychotherapy and mental disorders]. Göttingen: Hogrefe.

Sachse, R. (2002). *Histrionische und Narzisstische Persönlichkeitsstörungen* [Histrionic and narcissistic personality disorders]. Göttingen: Hogrefe.

Sass, H., Wittchen, H-U., Zaudig, M., et al. (2003). *Diagnostisches und Statistisches Manual Psychischer Störungen: DSM-IV TR* [Diagnostic and statistical manual of mental disorders: DSM-IV TR]. Göttingen: Hogrefe.

Schore, A. (1994). *Affect regulation and the origin of the self: The neurobiology of emotional development.* Hillsdale, NJ: Erlbaum Press.

Schore, A. N. (2009). *Affektregulation und die Reorganisation des Selbst (2. Aufl.)* [Affect regulation and the reorganization of the self (2nd ed.)]. Stuttgart: Klett-Cotta.

Siegel, D. (2006). *Wie wir werden, die wir sind: Neurobiologische Grundlagen subjektiven Erlebens und die Entwicklung des Menschen in Beziehung* [How we become who we are: Neurobiological bases of subjective experience and the development of man in relationship]. Paderborn: Junfermann.

Stehle, S., & Körber, S. (2002). Körperpsychotherapie aus der Sicht ehemaliger KlientInnen: Zentrale Ergebnisse einer empirischen Untersuchung über Integrative Biodynamik [Body Psychotherapy from the perspective of former clients: Key results of an empirical study available via Integrative Biodynamics]. In M. Thielen (Ed.), *Narzissmus: Körperpsychotherapie zwischen Energie und Beziehung* [Narcissism: Between energy and relationship in Body Psychotherapy]. Berlin: Leutner.

Stern, D. (1992). *Die Lebenserfahrung des Säuglings* [The world of the infant]. Stuttgart: Klett-Cotta.

Thielen, M. (1994). Zwischen Röhrentierchen und Bewusstseinswesen: das Menschenbild in der Körperpsychotherapie [Channels between animals and beings of consciousness: The human image in Body Psychotherapy]. In Verein für Integrative Biodynamik (Eds.), *Körperpsychotherapie zwischen Lust und Realitätsprinzip* [Body Psychotherapy between pleasure and the reality principle]. Oldenburg: Transform.

Thielen, M. (Ed.) (2002). Narzissmus: Körperpsychotherapie zwischen Beziehungs- und Energiearbeit [Narcissism: The Body Psychotherapy relationship between work and energy]. In M. Thielen (Ed.), *Narzissmus: Körperpsychotherapie zwischen Energie und Beziehung* [Narcissism: Between energy and relationship in Body Psychotherapy]. Berlin: Leutner.

Thielen, M. (2003). *Bausteine einer körperbezogenen Entwicklungspsychologie: Hauptvortrag auf dem 2. Kongress der Deutschen Gesellschaft für Körperpsychotherapie 18–21.09.2003* [Building blocks of body-related Developmental Psychology: Keynote address at the second Congress of the German Society for Body Psychotherapy, Sept. 18–21, 2003]. Unpublished manuscript.

Thielen, M. (2004). Trauma, Krise, Chance, Neubeginn: Körperpsychotherapie bei narzisstischen Selbstwertkrisen [Trauma, crisis, opportunity, new beginnings: Body Psychotherapy for narcissistic self-worth crisis]. *Journal der Gesellschaft für Biodynamische Psychologie / Körperpsychotherapie* (GBP e.V.), 10 Jahre GBP e.V:, Trauma und Kränkung. Beiträge der 9.Fachtagung der GBP e.V. in Schermau 1.-3.10.2004.

Thielen, M. (Ed.). (2009/2010). *Körper-Gefühl-Denken: Körperpsychotherapie und Selbstregulierung, 2. rev. Hrsg.* [Body-feeling-thinking: Body Psychotherapy and self-regulation, 2nd rev. ed.]. Giessen: Psychosozial.

Thielen, M. (Ed.). (2013). *Körper-Gruppe-Gesellschaft: Neue Entwicklungen in der Körperpsychotherapie* [Body-group-society: New developments in Body Psychotherapy]. Giessen: Psychosozial.

Trautmann-Voigt, S. (1997). Elefanten auf dem persischen Markt oder: Der kleine Dott auf Reisen. Tanztherapie bei einer narzisstischen Persönlichkeit [Elephants on the Persian market, or: The Little Dott on trips: Dance Therapy with a narcissistic personality]. In E. V. Siegel, S. Trautmann-Voigt, & B. Voigt (Eds.), *Tanz- und Bewegungstherapie in Theorie und Praxis* [Dance and Movement Therapy in theory and practice] (pp. 137–172). Frankfurt: Fischer.

Twenge, J. M., & Campbell, W. K. (2009). *The narcissism epidemic: Living in the age of entitlement.* New York: Simon & Schuster.

Wahrig, G. (1970). *Deutsches Wörterbuch* [German dictionary]. Gütersloh: Bertelsmann.

Wirth, H.-J. (2011). *Narzissmus und Macht: Zur psychoanalyse seelischer Störungen in der Politik (4. Aufl.)* [Narcissism and power: For psychoanalysis of mental disorders in politics (4th ed.)]. Giessen: Psychosozial.

# 74

## Vegetotherapy with Psychosomatic Disorders

*Functionalism in Practice*

Xavier Serrano Hortelano, Spain

Translation by Warren Miller

**Xavier Serrano Hortelano** is a well-known Body Psychotherapist based in Valencia, Spain. As is often common in Latin countries, he was strongly influenced by classical Reichian therapy and carries on in the tradition of his teacher, Federico Navarro. His work is informed by a functional and energetic perspective, and a classical, medical-model understanding of the therapeutic process. This chapter makes it evident how a structured diagnostic process and a goal-oriented intervention shape the therapeutic process.

Serrano Hortelano is a clinical psychologist, a character-analytical psychotherapist, an orgone therapist, and a trainer in Vegetotherapy and character-analytical brief therapy. He is the director of the Escuela Española de Terapia Reichiana in Valencia, is the editor of the journal *Energía, Carácter y Sociedad* [Energy, Character, and Society], and has contributed to the international discourse on Body Psychotherapy by means of many publications and conference presentations. His area of specialization is the Body Psychotherapeutic treatment of psycho-pathological, sexual, and psychosomatic disorders.

## Theoretical Frame

In clinical practice, we consistently observe a close linkage between emotional problems and the development of an array of medical disorders. Wilhelm Reich, and later Federico Navarro, defined this phenomenon as "somato-dynamic functionality." Character-Analytic Vegetotherapy is based on the theoretical foundations that Wilhelm Reich laid out in his "orgonomic functionalism." Taking an ecological perspective, Fritjof Capra finds that Vegetotherapy "is a system that shows remarkable similarity with the new scientific paradigm" (Capra, 1996).

In brief, the theory proposes that, as an infant comes into the world, it is influenced by demands coming from the social ecosystem that surrounds it. These demands do not necessarily match the infant's instinctual impulses and biological needs, leading to the development of a strong conflict, which, in turn, causes marked "distress" (pathological stress). This understanding led Navarro to the following proposition:

> Vegetotherapy strives to rebalance patients. Specific muscle-based interventions ("Actions") facilitate autonomic-emotional processes, which can restructure the unfolding of vitality impulses and the flow of life-energy that were bound up in conflict since birth. Treatment takes place in a specific setting and with guidance of a qualified therapist. (Navarro, 1990)

Emotional problems are one of the sources of such intersystemic interferences. When emotional conflicts are resolved by means of neuromuscular Actions, the functioning of the therapeutic relationship, the application of character-analytical methods, group therapy, ongoing observation of the breath, and structural communication can all be reestablished. In the following illustrations, the application of this theoretical framework is illustrated by presenting clinical case studies of patients with the following "functional problems": cephalalgia, gastrointestinal ulcer, and vaginismus.

## Cephalalgia: Involving the First Three Segments[70]

Cephalalgia is a medical term for a headache. Headaches commonly arise from muscular tension in the shoulders and neck and can manifest as severe pain in the forehead and temples, or throughout the whole head. When someone has a headache, strong muscular tensions can often be palpated where they feel pain. Such headaches occur in the absence of systemic diseases such as diabetes, cancer, high blood pressure, etc. Specialists such as Friedman, Wolf, Martin, and the Orgonomist A. Nelson are of the opinion that

> . . . the onset of headaches can often be linked to a specific stressful situation (given that the above-mentioned conditions are ruled out [note by the author, Nelson]), and it is likely that emotional stress causes such tensions in the neck and head. Chronic muscular contractions can cause headaches, and emotional factors play a significant role. In all cases of cranial muscular contraction, a feeling of fear is somatized as evidenced by increased muscular tension. (Nelson, 1974)

Navarro hypothesizes:

> The clinical manifestation of headaches is caused by a hyper-orgonotic blockage. Its dynamic is as follows: The primary fear of the first moments of life causes a loss of tone leading to a dilation of the cranial arteries (vasodilation). This dilation potentiates a subsequent constriction (vasoconstriction) so as to reestablish homeostasis. If the vasodilation were to persist this could lead to death. Cephalalgia can be the symptom of a hysterical conversion or suggest a psychotic core. Headaches and migraines can be traced back to muscular resistance in the eye segment (*locus minoris resistentiae*), which is the first segment, and impairments in vision, hearing, and smell are common co-occurrences. Headaches are an expression of hostility and a consequence of a general state of fear, whereas migraines are the result of a specific fear. The main task of therapeutic intervention is to work with the first segment to unblock the fear. (Navarro, 1988)

The first case is that of Anna, a thirty-five-year-old woman, divorced for three years, who lives with her six-year-old son. She came to see me because she felt completely overwhelmed with her office job, and she felt that her colleagues were criticizing and excluding her. She was very preoccupied by these ideas, she could not sleep well, she felt fatigued, and she was unable to care for her son properly. In her life, there was no record of any sort of trauma, and her sexuality was normal. After separating from her husband, she had had only brief, very unsatisfying, sexual affairs, without being able to establish a stabile relationship. Following the Diagnóstico Inicial Diferencial Estructural (DIDE) diagnosis (Serrano Hortelano, 1990), she presented with a neurotic, masochistic, and hysterical character structure. Recently, Anna felt increasingly emotional, and had paranoid tendencies, strong feelings of fear, and sexual inhibition and dissatisfaction. The separation from her husband came as a surprise to her, and she had to resign herself to accept it. But, since he left her for another woman, she had felt depressed. She started suffering from insomnia, headaches, pain in her shoulders and back, and heavy menstrual bleeding. In sessions, she presented as tense and restless. Her breathing was irregular, and her smile appeared contrived. Her behavior was characterized by contact avoidance, self-pity, and apprehensiveness. She further reported symptoms suggesting a vegetative disorder, including constipation, tingling in her hands and feet,

---

[70] **Editors' Note:** Reich's segmental armoring theory (and thus Reichian Character-Analytic Vegetotherapy) sees the body as being functionally (energetically) divided into seven horizontal segments; from the top down, the first three segments are the "ocular," the "oral," and the "cervical"; then come the "thoracic," the "diaphragmatic," the "abdominal," and finally the "pelvic" segments. Incidentally, this system has a reasonably similar correlation to the Eastern system of the seven chakras.

transient discomfort in the area of her heart, and strong tensions in the areas of the eyes, neck, and diaphragm. The patient appeared to strongly hold back her sadness and rage, but there were no indications suggesting a risk of depersonalization.

Under consideration of her motivations, financial situation, and time availability, I proposed a Brief Character-Analytic Psychotherapy (a so-called "focal BC-AP"; Serrano Hortelano, 1992, 2007, 2011), which consists of one session per week for six months.

In the first session, as she recalled the separation, her emotional turmoil increased; so did her headaches and insomnia subsequently. In the fourth session, I was gathering specific information about her biography, sexual aspects, and object-relations. She told me that her father was mostly absent, and her mother was hysterically irritable. For expressive neuromuscular movement practice (Actions), the patient had to lie down on her back, allow her mouth to fall open, raise her arms above her head, and fixate her eyes on one point on the ceiling. After four minutes, she spontaneously began to cry. She furrowed her brow and frowned, so I encouraged her to surrender to her emotions and I assured her that she was protected. Her crying grew stronger and turned into an uncontrolled sobbing. After completion of the bodily practice, she told me that she clearly saw her father, playing sports with her brother, while she had to stay at home because she was a girl. She associated the behavior of her father with that of her ex-husband, who preferred going out with his friends instead of going out with her, and who rationalized this by telling her that someone would, after all, need to care for the child. Anna felt very sad.

Over the course of the following sessions, her headaches continued to increase in severity and duration. Her sense of grief deepened, and she came to realize how painful the separation from her husband had been for her, how much she immobilized herself, and how much she despised herself. She also came to see that it was she who was bringing her own feelings of vulnerability and incompetence to her workplace. We understood that she also brought these feelings into the relationship with me, in the context of the therapy. This so-called "triangular circulation" (Serrano Hortelano, 1992) helped us to work through the material.

She was then sick and stayed home for a few days, during which time she recuperated physically and mentally. Gradually, she learned how her avoidance of aggression was based on a fear of rejection, and she gained some awareness of the superficial layer of the masochistic aspect of her personality. In the tenth session, I instructed her in the following bodily practice: She lay down on her back and pulled up her legs while her head and neck hung down over the edge of the couch. Involuntarily, her breath became increasingly rapid and she felt afraid. Anna began screaming (like a child) and felt very alone and weak. In the verbal reflection that followed, she realized how much others, including her ex-husband and people at work, have gained from making her feel vulnerable, which had also kept her docile and compliant. She came into touch with her anger, which became increasingly explicit. I encouraged her to lift her arms high, and to hit the mat with outstretched arms, simultaneously saying "I" over and over again.

At first, this felt ridiculous to her, but then she started screaming more loudly and hitting the mat with strength and rage while her eyes were wide open and her breath was flowing and at times was actually quite "free." After seven minutes, when this bodily practice (Action) came to a close, she told me that she could clearly feel a strong resolve to no longer allow the opinions and judgments of others to influence her—not those of her father, nor of her ex-husband, nor those of colleagues—and that she had had enough of restricting her life because of fear.

In the two sessions that followed, we repeated the same bodily practice, in the same order. Then I introduced a new practice in which she had to look all around her body, in a circular fashion, with her eyes wide open. At first, she experienced this movement as very painful, but, in the end, she felt it had had a comforting and calming effect. She reported that she could sleep better again; her headaches were receding; and she was more of an upbeat person, able to do her work and care for her son. She found that she liked her own body, began masturbating again, and resumed going out with her girlfriends. She ended the treatment within the agreed-upon time frame, and the agreed-upon goals had been met.

Over the following eight months, she came to see me once every other month for some follow-up sessions. None of the symptoms that caused her to seek therapy reappeared, but her sense of dread and apprehension persisted. However, she was now more aware of her personal boundaries. A year later, she was promoted at her work, and she considered deepening her therapeutic process. She decided to begin a character-analytical vegetotherapeutic training.

In this case, we can see how a focused therapy, working on the level of the bodily structure, can lead to some progress. The symptoms that the patient presented with could be traced back to a somatic reactivation of an inner state of stress and emotional restriction, which caused the headaches. They were the result of relational conflicts and an activation of the masochistic-compulsive aspect of the patient's character at the moment of separation, which blocked her natural expression of grief and rage. These, in turn, originated from experiences of disappointment and lack of caring attention, which led to the formation of the mechanisms of "behavioral inhibition" and "armoring."

Another case study further illustrates aspects of cephalalgia. Isabel was a thirty-year-old biologist. She came to my practice because of a strong conflict with her boss, which blocked her career development and had triggered a severe depression. Since her youth, she had suffered from strong headaches in the area of her forehead and neck. The DIDE diagnosis indicated a borderline structure with a depressive-psychotic core, underlying a masochistic-phallic surface presentation. Her relationship with her parents was very strained, characterized by postnatal stress, an absent mother, and an authoritarian and distant father. The fear that was at her core was the root cause of her symptoms. Further facets of her disorder included strong ocular and oral tensions, a hypotonic diaphragm, shallow breathing, and an accordingly low vital and orgonotic pulsation. The diagnosis suggested that her symptoms were only the tip of an iceberg of a core relational conflict that could not be resolved by means of a brief-focused psychotherapeutic intervention (BFP). Accordingly, I recommended a course of Character-Analytic Vegetotherapy (CAV). This takes two years in order to facilitate sufficient relaxation in the first two segments for the headaches to recede. Over the course of this process, her energetic charge increased, which lessened her core fear. Her sense of fear was reactivated whenever her structure could not carry an emerging conflict.

Based on these two case studies, we can see that a symptom can often reflect different kinds of logic, meaning, and hidden codes. Therefore, it is important not to overgeneralize the etiology of specific symptoms, but to see them as reflections of the autopoietic (self-sustaining) structural conflict (Maturana and Varela, 1990). Symptoms can thus be a point of reference to guide the therapist in customizing the therapeutic approach to the individual patient.

## Gastrointestinal Ulcer: Involving the Fifth and Sixth Segments

Gastrointestinal ulcers are highly prevalent in our contemporary society, even more so than headaches. Medical research suggests that this disorder is caused by a bacterial infection. This finding, however, does not rule out the possibility of a functional disorder. In order for such a bacterial infection to develop, the autonomic and emotional systems must be out of balance, as Wilhelm Reich was able to show (Reich, 1950). Cases of healing through Body Psychotherapy confirm this hypothesis. We must not forget that the vagus nerve co-regulates all mechanisms that facilitate gastric motility and secretion, including local parasympathetic reflexes, as well as the secretion of digestive fluids.

This case study concerns Enrique, a thirty-five-year-old architect. He was married and had two sons. He was very active in sports and tried his best to keep his family life and sports activities in balance. He wanted to begin a course of Vegetotherapy because he hoped to "diminish his blockages, so as to improve his technique in tennis"—he competed in tournaments. Healthwise, he felt very well. The only thing bothering him in this regard was a stomach ulcer, which had been causing him trouble since his graduate training in architecture. He assumed that this ulcer was due to a blockage of the diaphragm, and because the diaphragm also plays a large role in breathing, Enrique assumed that this was what restricted his breathing when he was playing tennis.

Enrique had an athletic body and a self-assured demeanor. His breathing was thoracic, and he presented with strong tensions in the area of the neck and the pelvis. A very loving but stern father, and an easily irritated and tense mother, characterized his parental object-relations. He had warm, loving feelings for both of them. His father (who was very interested in politics) wanted Enrique to study law, but Enrique decided to study architecture instead. This led to a rupture in their relationship, and Enrique had moved out from his parents' home to study in a different city at that time.

The DIDE diagnosis suggested a neurotic-compulsive-phallic character structure. Based on the patient's capacity for insight and his character structure, the prognosis was quite good. The symptom could be treated via a BFP or a CAV; the goals of the latter are much further reaching and effect greater structural change, so a course of CAV was chosen.

Years earlier, the patient had participated in a psychodynamic focused therapy that had helped him in some respects, but was not able to cure his stomach ulcer. The case of Enrique is relevant for this discussion, as it illustrates the relationship between oral issues and the diaphragm, and, more specifically, between oral stress and fear held in the area of the diaphragm, leading to the above-outlined dynamic and autonomic repercussions.

There was an interesting and significant key session: The patient lay on the couch in the standard CAV-therapy posture and followed my Action instructions to act like a fish. (The patient fixates his eyes on a point on the ceiling and moves his lips outwardly, as fish do, or the way it can be observed in infants that are being breast-fed. In this exercise, the patient is instructed to do this at his own pace and in his own way.)

After a few minutes, the patient experienced a gag reflex, along with a strong sense of fear (apprehension), cold sweat, and disgust. I encouraged the patient to continue, and I showed him a basin in which he could vomit if that were to happen. The mouth practice (Action) let the patient experience his lips moving involuntarily, almost as if by magic. Based on this experience, he felt completely defenseless and helpless, in stark contrast to his usual self, being a very rational man who likes to have everything under his control. After sixteen minutes, the patient had overcome his intellectual resistance, and the mouth practice was nearing its completion, but he still could not vomit and was feeling increasingly apprehensive and miserable. Then some memories began to surface. His younger twin brothers were born when he was twelve. He remembered seeing his mother bottle-feeding them in a tense and curt way. Then he recalled another scene, seeing the same image—but instead of his mother, it was his sister-in-law with her one-year-old son. He began to feel rage toward these figures.

In the following sessions—always facilitated by this same Action—he was able to vomit involuntarily. (This is one of our clinical goals. From our perspective, in Vegetotherapy, such body processes occur in harmony with the patient's autonomic rhythms, and therefore one might have to wait a while for them to take place.) He experienced strong rage that got even stronger when a new bodily practice (Action) was introduced. In this Action, he was encouraged to strongly bite into a towel. Every time the rage emerged, so did the fear—and the impulse to gag.

Then the diaphragm tensed up, so as to inhibit the impulse, but thereby this triggered a state of alarm. The patient realized that his mother had very likely treated him in the same way. But, because he had always been very dependent on affect figures within the family (such as in the past his parents, and today his wife), he balked against the rage that he felt in relation to his mother. He tended to idealize the family situation in order to avoid stirring up conflicts. Now he also understood the meaning of the symptom of getting an ulcer: by not openly working through the conflict with his father, but choosing his graduate training on his own, he had gotten into a chronic state of stress.

Within the therapeutic relationship, the patient first developed an oral transference, which later changed into an oedipal transference. And again, the relationship between the mouth, diaphragm, and pelvis became more apparent, specifically as the fear of authority was worked through in the transference relationship. To this end, the patient was instructed in an Action in which he was to say "No" while moving his head from side to side. As Enrique did this practice, his experience of fear and the impulse to gag reemerged, and he pulled in his pelvis and the anal sphincter. He became aware of an existential dissatisfaction, which he maintained by way of his compulsions and sexual inhibitions. During coitus, he could not fully surrender to the orgasm reflex. He thought of himself as a good lover, but gradually discovered the difference between his familiar and known "streams of energy" and the complete, fearless surrender to another person. It took three years of two sessions per week (lasting one and a half hours each) for him to gain this awareness. His stomach aches disappeared after the completion of the practices for the neck and chest area had led to an indirect relaxation in the fifth and sixth segments. During breathing practices and movement practices for the pelvic region, these pains occasionally reemerged. After completion of the therapy, and regular follow-up sessions over the course of two years (one session every two to three months), the problems did not return. Medical diagnostic assessments cleared him of any organic dysfunction.

## Vaginismus: Involving the Seventh Segment

Vaginismus is a very rare and painful sexual dysfunction that some women suffer from. It is characterized by muscle cramps in the vagina that are triggered by the experience of sexual arousal. The cramps occur with masturbation, and also in sexual contact with a partner, in the absence of any physiological disorder. This restricts these women's capacity to live out their sexuality, and also constitutes a considerable risk factor during childbirth.

On occasion, one comes across patients with neurotic structures who present with a reactive form of vaginismus. Commonly, they have masochistic sexual revenge fantasies and present with strong tensions in the areas of the neck, diaphragm, and pelvis (third, fifth, and seventh segments). These can be caused by problems in familial object-relations, or through a history of sexual molestation or abuse in their childhood or youth. In such cases, BFP can effect positive changes. In the more common cases of vaginismus, however, the contraction of the smooth musculature of the vagina is based on a core structural disorder beginning during the oral phase of development in which strong sexual fear is displaced into the vagina. This form of vaginismus could be said to be due to a "genitalization of orality." In such cases, a CAV therapy is indicated.

Such was the situation in the case of Elisa, a twenty-five-year-old teacher, who was not married but had been in a stabile partner relationship for a few years. The partners had a sexual relationship that excluded vaginal penetration. Elisa suffered from this situation, as both of them wished to have an unrestricted sexual relationship. Both would have liked to get married quite soon and would have liked to have a child together. The patient had always suffered from vaginismus. She had no experience with masturbation practices, and, as she was not able to use tampons, she had to use feminine napkins. A gynecological examination had not been possible, which is why her gynecologist had referred her to psychotherapy.

The DIDE diagnosis revealed a borderline structure with a depressive core and a masochistic-phallic-hysterical superficial layer. Over the course of the therapy, the links between the mouth and the vagina became more apparent: fear of the mother, severe problems with her sexual identity, and, of course, her vaginismus.

Her mother suffered from hysterical episodes (*charcotianos*, named after J.-M. Charcot), with occasional episodes of amnesia, and public sexual provocations, and was constantly critical of her two daughters. She had been hospitalized in psychiatric clinics twice, for long periods of time, when her daughters were at a difficult age (the age difference between the two sisters was one year).

Elisa had come consciously to reject her mother out of social shame, but simultaneously held a strong, affect-charged, but repressed longing for closeness. Due to the small difference in age between the sisters, Elisa had been weaned prematurely. We practiced the following Action: Lying on her back with her mouth opened, arms raised, and hands open, the patient fixated on a point on the ceiling and got in touch with ambivalent feelings of neediness and rage, which indicated a strong oral split. While acting like a fish, she experienced fear and had muscle cramps that totally immobilized her mouth, so that she was no longer able to move it. She realized that she could not approach her mother, nor receive love from anyone else. She also experienced vaginal cramps, and associated fear, while simultaneously projecting sexual longings onto the therapist. It became clear how much she had had to deny her mother in order for her to be herself. She even felt closer to her father, when her mother wasn't there, sometimes (possibly) too close. Throughout the whole session, there was strong "splitting" going on, and this was also reflected in the relationship with the therapist. During the bodily practice involving biting into a towel, and again later, when we were working in the chest area and she had to say "No," she fell into a deep depression, with suicidal ideation. Her body image was completely distorted and empty, and she considered herself unsalvageable.

Later on, as she was hitting the couch in the context of a different Action, she began expressing the rage that she felt in relation to her father. He had not sufficiently validated her and, because of his affective absence, her anger had previously expressed itself only in the form of a strong apprehension. Gradually, the vaginal musculature began to relax, and, in the second year of therapy, she had her first masturbation experience by inserting her fingers into her vagina and experiencing this as pleasurable. At that time, she separated from her boyfriend and had some lesbian episodes.

We were working in the area of the pelvis and diaphragm as follows: She did a breathing practice (Action) by making rowing movements, and, as she said "No," she hit the couch with her legs. In this way, she gradually integrated her oral and genital sexuality. She began defining herself as a woman and developed a feminine identity. She began feeling closer to her mother, accepting her body, and developing her ability to make love. She experienced herself more as herself, and no longer as her mother, and had learned to enjoy life. Finally, Elisa began a relationship with a man whom she later married. Five years after completing her therapy, she got pregnant and delivered a daughter through a natural birth without any complications.

## Conclusion

The case studies described in this chapter show that psychosomatic disorders can be treated successfully by using Body-Oriented Psychotherapy. Freeing the unconscious of blockages, and integrating the experiences that emerge in this process into consciousness by working through it analytically, help to reestablish the person's neuromuscular functionality, autonomy, and emotional balance.

## References

Capra, F. (1996). *The web of life.* New York: Anchor Books.

Maturana, H., & Varela, F. (1990). *El árbol del conocimiento: Las bases biológicas del entendimiento humano [The tree of knowledge: The biological basis of human understanding].* Madrid: Editorial Debate.

Navarro, F. (1988). *La Somatosicodinámica [Psychosomatic dynamics].* Valencia, Spain: Publicaciones Orgón.

Navarro, F. (1990). *Metodología de la Vegetoterapia Caracteroanalítica apartir de Wilhelm Reich [Methodology of the Character-Analytic Vegetotherapy of Wilhelm Reich].* Valencia, Spain: Publicaciones Orgón.

Nelson, A. (1974). Functional headaches. *Journal of Orgonomy, 8(1), 35–42.*

Reich, W. (1950). The orgonomic functionalism. *Orgone Energy Bulletin, II(1–3), 1–15, 49–62, 104–123.*

Serrano Hortelano, X. (1990). El diagnóstico inicial diferencial en la orgonterapia [The initial diagnosis differential in Character-Analytic Psychotherapy]. *Revista Energía Caracter y Sociedad, 8, 22–39.*

Serrano Hortelano, X. (1992). La psicoterapia breve caracteroanalítica (P.B.C.) [Brief Character-Analytic Psychotherapy]. *Revista Energía Caracter y Sociedad, 10, 4–19.*

Serrano Hortelano, X. (2007). *La Psicoterapia Breve caracteroanalítica [Brief Character-Analytic Psychotherapy].* Madrid: Editorial Biblioteca Nueva.

Serrano Hortelano, X. (2011). *Deepening the Reichian couch: Vegetotherapy in Character-Analytic Psychotherapy [Profundizando en el divan Reichiano: La Vegetoterapia en la Psicoterapia Caracteroanalítica]. Madrid: Editorial* Biblioteca Nueva.

# 75
## Oral Depression

**Guy Tonella, France**

**Translation by Warren Miller**

**Guy Tonella's biographical information** can be found at the beginning of Chapter 71, "Body Psychotherapy and Psychosis."

What characterizes the personality structure of people with oral depression is that they've experienced a lack of motherly love, and their oral needs were not satisfied in childhood. Such oral needs include suckling, nursing, being looked after, being held, feeling the warmth of the mother's body, experiencing her unconditional, constant, and anxiety-free love, and experiencing a shared sense of pleasure arising from tactile, visual, acoustic, and motoric interactions and play.

The infant experiences the lack of motherly love as deprivation, separation, or premature loss of bonding with the mother, which deeply impacts the dynamics of the self at the level of metabolic energy production, the transmission of excitation, functional activation, and behavior itself. Depression affects all functions of the psycho-physiological continuum, including energy, muscle tone, sensation, emotion, and cognitive representation. This is the case no matter how a depression manifests specifically in an individual person—in the form of melancholia, manic-depressive psychosis, depressive neurosis, or reactive depression.

### Etiology of the Depressive Process

Psychoanalytic theorists were the first to propose an energetic, affective, and psychological understanding of depression. During his study of manic-depressive disorders, K. Abraham (1912) hypothesized that when the mother frustrates the infant's needs, the infant experiences this as a loss of motherly love, which evokes strong feelings of hostility in it toward the mother. As it represses this hostility, it deprives itself of its aggressive energy, and subsequently develops passive modes of behavior as an adult.

Later on, direct observations of depressed children confirmed this hypothesis. R. Spitz (1945) observed six-month-old infants after the separation from their incarcerated mothers: first they began to cry, then they screamed (expressing aggression). After being separated for three months, and lacking emotional resonance, they became increasingly withdrawn, their faces looked frozen, they were lamenting monotonously, and finally they entered into states of lethargy. Unable to cope with the loss of body contact with the mother, they developed what is referred to as "anaclitic depression."

J. Bowlby (1961) also observed children who were separated from their mothers between the ages of six and thirty months. He found that if the separation persisted, the child developed a depressive reaction, characterized by aversion, nonparticipation, and apathy.

T. B. Brazelton (1981) and D. Stern (1989) were able to show that the mother-child interaction is an essential source of activation for the child. It stimulates bodily excitation, motor activity, and breathing, provokes sensory-emotional transfers, and thus forms the basis of identity.

If this kind of body contact is insufficient or irregular, and the relationship does not provide sufficient patterns of care and interaction, the child is deprived of stimulation and lacks experiences of sensation, arousal, and emotion. The child then progressively loses contact with its own body and its environment. It loses vitality and enters a process of childhood depression that manifests at all levels of the self: in energy, sensation, muscle tone, emotion, and cognitive representation. This is equally true for the child as it is for the adult (Tonella, 2000).

## The Search for Illusions

The depressed adult unconsciously continues to expect that his unmet childhood needs for love and validation will become satisfied; therefore, he lives in a state of deep inner insecurity. The idea that he can move others to meet his unmet needs is very exciting to him, and he is disappointed and depressed when he realizes that others don't unconditionally do so, that they are not the "good mother" that he continues to long for. This disillusionment leads to an eventual collapse. The patient falls into a depression and loses all hope. He starts to feel that he is "nothing" and has no worth at all.

The search for illusions is carried forward by this unmet desire for recognition. Whereas some depressed adults may recognize this, others project their own dependency onto other people, such as their partners. In this case, the other is seen as needing security: "She needs me." Perceiving himself as needed, the depressed adult then feels entitled to avowals of love and recognition, while unconsciously expecting the satisfaction of his desire for complete security. If these needs aren't met, secret feelings of hostility, bitterness, and disrespect can then arise.

## The Conflict between the Ego and the Body

Having had the early childhood experience of not getting his sensory-motor-emotional needs met, and having surrendered the concept of getting them met, the depressed person does not trust his body. *He learned early on to control his bodily and motor impulses when asserting his needs.* In his effort to endow his life with a necessary, while illusory, meaning, *he braced himself with his mental functions as soon as he could.* That's how he fortified himself, and that's where he continues to be entrenched.

Therefore, the depressive person organizes his relationships with the environment by relying much more on his intellect than on his emotions, even while his underlying expectation is directed toward ongoing affective reward, and his whole demeanor is asking for attention, validation, and acknowledgment. His problem lies in the difficulty he has in directing his impulses externally toward the world, specifically his aggression. Being able to express his impulses would allow him to take an affirmative and spontaneous stance, instead of being reactive and controlling.

Lowen (1979a) says, *"In the depressed individual this force has been sapped by the subjugation of the body to the authority of the will and by the suppression of feeling in the interest of an ego image,"* (p. 113).

Attributing his depression to a failure of will, rather than an energetic exhaustion of his body, the depressed person's primary concern is to regain courage and resolve—at any price—even if this means that he has to sacrifice the recuperation of his body, which would allow him to restore his energy. He can keep this up for only so long before the next depressive crisis hits.

## The Loss of Feeling and Self-Expression

The state that the depressed person gets into is, in part, caused by *an inability to vibrate.* This lack of responsiveness is something that distinguishes depression from all other emotional states. The depressed person describes himself as having fallen into a hole and having a sense of inner emptiness.

And indeed, in a state of depression, breathing is shallow and the person's metabolism is compromised. As the energetic charge is markedly reduced, connective tissues and muscles are only minimally activated, and consequently only minimal sensations can be felt. This leads to a *loss of feeling* and great *difficulties engaging in behavior.* In a body sense, depression is a state of inner collapse. The organism can only muster weak and rare impulses in response to environmental stimuli. Emotionally, as well as bodily, the patient is defeated and exhausted. He is capable of only a little expression or action.

## Lack of Energy

In speaking of energy, I first used the concept in the same sense as Reich (1969), but when I use it in its functional sense, I am referring to Keleman's (1985) usage. In this context, I define the concept of "energy" as the "fuel" that is produced in the process of metabolism. This fuel circulates through the organs and tissues in the form of liquid and gaseous streams that serve the functions of the various organs. A predominantly muscular pumping system makes it possible for these streams to flow in all the directions that serve the needs of the organism—that is, from the center to the periphery, and from up to down.

From an energetic perspective, depression is characterized by markedly reduced metabolism that compromises all organic functions:

* The *breath* is shallow. This reduces oxygenation and the metabolic rate, which in turn leads to loss of appetite.
* *Motility* (movements of streaming and exchange within the organism) is reduced, as low muscle tone and strong abdominal contractions inhibit the pump effect that drives the circulation of energy streams.
* *Motor behavior* is restrained; spontaneous gestures are inhibited, the face lacks expressiveness, the eyes are dull, the voice is without timbre, the facial features are lax and show sadness, and the skin lacks tone. In the case of severe depression, the patient may remain motionless, inert, weakened, and collapsed.

The loss of energy that is characteristic of depression can occur rapidly. Such rapid loss occurs when the defense system (the manic defense) that was previously able to prop up the ego despite depressive tendencies breaks down. This pattern is characteristic of the manic-depressive personality structure.

## The Manic-Depressive Dynamic

A phase of exaltation followed by a crash into depression: this is what characterizes the depressive reaction. As the excitement becomes overstretched, it breaks down and the patient tumbles into depression. Basically, the manic-depressive process is composed of such oscillations between manic phases of excitation and depressive phases of exhaustion. The phases are more or less pronounced, depending on the specifics of the case. Lowen (1979a, 1979b) was the first to describe the underlying energetic mechanisms of this process:

1. In the manic phase, the excitation continues to rise. It over-stimulates thoughts and psycho-motor activity, which manifests in hyperactivity and pressured speech. Driven to reestablish the feeling of omnipotence that was lost during childhood, the excitation gets into the patient's head and generates false perceptions ("You are there for me") and possessiveness ("I take you into my arms, and you are mine"). The overstimulated child, youth, or adult is in a state of heightened expectation, as if an unusual or magical event were about to occur. He is like a child who has been separated from his mother and now eagerly awaits her return. This unconscious hope for the restoration of motherly love is what triggers this sudden, gushing rise of energy. In this phase, there is an unconscious expectation that goes out toward someone, anyone, in place of the mother. As such, a hyperactive high is exhausting for the individual himself, as well as for his environment; others begin to distance themselves, which the manic person perceives as a rejection. His sense of self-confidence and self-esteem collapses, and a depressive reaction ensues.

2. The depressive collapse is an energetic phenomenon as well. Literally, "depression" is a "lack of interorganismic pressure." The streams of energy that overstimulated the head and motor activity have now exhausted themselves. The energy needed for survival withdraws into the center of the organism, but without reaching the lower body, as strong abdominal tensions are held in place to repress the childhood feelings of insecurity,

loneliness, sadness, and hopelessness. The experience that this state of affairs leaves available to consciousness is that of an empty stomach from which no impulses arise at all. The sense of having "no guts" generates a fear of general incompetence: self-esteem, self-confidence, and self-security all collapse.

The omnipotence of the ego transforms into a sense of impotence; hyperactivity transforms into rigid passivity. The trough of the "depressive wave" ("to be in the valley of the wave," "to be at the bottom of the well," "to hit rock bottom," etc.) has important correlations with the lower half of the body. The high tension in the abdomen, with low tension in the legs and feet, create the sense of losing traction, which—in turn—generates the fear of not having a viable basis or support to stand on. This is the case even though the depressed person never had a particularly firm ground beneath him in the first place.

The depressive collapse imposes a rest, which facilitates the recuperation of strengths, and solicits care and support from the environment. These changes can lead the patient to believe that he was able to restore his ego and regain the love and respect of his environment. Encouraged in this way, he finds himself right back in his illusion, which may initiate the next shift from the depressive phase back into a phase of manic excitement.

## The Refusal to Feel Helpless

In his infancy or childhood, the patient had experiences in which he felt helpless and threatened in his existence. With enormous effort of will, he was able to prevail, despite his distress. If his willpower collapses today, he will again feel tragically helpless. He cannot draw upon his vitality-based aggression, because it is repressed or is orally fixated. As his attempts to lift himself out of his state of defeatedness fail, his chances of feeling embarrassed rise. The auto-destructive functions further exacerbate this situation. But he can't accept his helplessness; if he did, he would have to acknowledge that he is dependent on others. He would have to face the suffering that his condition has caused him,

the hopelessness, fear, and hostility—all feelings against which he has battled all his life and that he has learned to repress in order to survive. *The refusal to feel helpless fuels the condition of depression and ensures its maintenance.*

## Symptomatology

### Drug Addiction

Drug abuse is based on an illusory search for experiences of body and emotional contact with the lost love object. The "trip" lifts the patient out of her state of burdened exhaustion.

### Alcoholism

States of intoxication by alcohol are no different from those caused by other drugs. They are caused by an effort to lift the patient out of her state of dejection, and artificially create a state of manic enthusiasm.

### Suicide Attempts

In the context of depression, suicide attempts can occur when a patient not only loses her vitality, but also temporarily her will to live. From a dynamic perspective, a suicide attempt can be understood as follows:

> *It expresses the conflict between the ego and the body:* The ego turns against the body, which doesn't live up to the patient's self-image. The discrepancy between reality and the ideal image causes a strong sense of failure, which can then lead to a suicide attempt.

> *It signifies a hostile act in relation to the environment.* Freud noted that any effort to understand the relationship between depression and suicidal tendencies needs to take the issue of repressed hostility into consideration.

Lowen (1979a) comments that the depressed person *"is like a swimmer with an anchor attached to his leg. No matter how hard he struggles to rise to the surface, the anchor drags him down. The suppressed negative feelings with their accompanying weight of guilt are like the anchor in the analogy. Release the swimmer from his anchor and he will rise naturally to the surface. Release the suppressed negative feelings in a depressed person and his depressive reaction will be over"* (p. 90).

## Therapeutic Process

The first step in treatment is to support the patient in regaining her energy. It is difficult to help the depressed person find sufficient interest in getting out of her apathy. Her *resistance* consists mainly of feelings of weakness and exhaustion based on a lack of energy. These in turn are based on negative attitudes that were repressed in earliest childhood to ensure survival and that remain repressed. The organism is like an "empty battery" in need of a recharge. Vitality and depression are mutually exclusive of one another.

To this end, it is important *to increase the (metabolic) energetic charge of the whole organism,* which is done mainly by breathwork. In particular, the lower half of the body (including the abdomen, pelvis, and legs and feet) needs to be recharged so that the patient can find a footing in reality and begin to sense that she can support herself.

Furthermore, it is important to reestablish an optimal flow of energy. Movement, voice, and interactive play can all be part of this process of "reanimation." The goal of psychotherapeutic bodywork is to help the patient perceive herself as she is—that is, to know her depressive tendencies, and to understand their meaning and cause. Work in the following areas facilitates progress toward this goal.

### Activation of the Sense of Loss and Deficit in Care

In the first year of life, the energetic-motor-sensory-emotional continuum of the infant depends on active support from the mother to organize itself and grow. If this support is not provided, or is lost, the preconditions of depression are set up. In the transference role of the mother or father, the therapist accepts the patient's need for care, love, security, and recognition.

No one, no matter how great and truthful they may be, can replace the sense of security that was lacking during early childhood. But we can contribute significantly to the establishment of a foundation upon which adult self-confidence, self-trust, and self-respect can be based.

Stabilized in this way, the patient becomes able to face the deprivations and losses of her childhood, and to experience, express, accept, and finally integrate the sensory-emotional states and inner images that derive from these past events. We facilitate this process to help the patient overcome her childhood fixations and live in current reality, rather than in the illusions of the past.

It's not that we try to compensate for the losses experienced during childhood. Instead, we support the patient in no longer repressing these experiences, and in expressing her associated fears, feelings, images, and movement impulses. Therapeutic work aims to help the patient to love herself, to accept herself, and to develop a trust in herself, all of which can start to take the place that was left vacant by her parents.

### Grief Work

The point of the grief work is *to express childhood emotions* that were previously repressed. Repression restricts the flow of life energy, leads to the loss of bodily sensation, and reduces expressiveness. A repressed, depressed person risks becoming a living dead. The two major feelings evoked by the loss of the loved one are *deep pain and rage.*

> If no anger is felt at a loss, no real grief can be experienced and a proper mourning will not take place. It is the nature of human beings to protest their pain. (Lowen, 1979a, p. 154)

### Recognition and Expression of Repressed Feelings

Because the depressed person was previously unable to express his emotions, he was not able to properly grieve. When he cried as a child, he did so alone. He did not feel understood in his *sorrow and hurt* and therefore needed to repress them. The same is true for the *indignation and rage* that he felt over losing his mother. In addition to sorrow and rage, the depressed person commonly experiences *fear* or *horror* when considering what other adults might think of him (disapproval, contempt). He may further experience *isolation and a feeling of loneliness,* the *hardship* of not having a refuge, and *despair* over seeing no alternatives.

All these emotions can be given recognition, can be experienced, and can be expressed in the context of the therapeutic relationship. Speaking, moving and voicing these repressed feelings can reestablish the patient's contact with the body and his emotional and expressive vitality. If this work is not done, the self remains caught up in childhood attitudes, laden with deep grief, immense despair, and, perhaps, moments of refusal to go on living.

The specific practices and situational role-plays that can facilitate the therapeutic work with repressed feelings emerge from the process of therapy. They may include practices such as alternately sucking and biting on the corner of a towel; lying on the back, reaching up with the arms, and calling "Mama"; hitting alternately with the legs or arms while screaming "Why?"; wringing out a towel with full force; standing and hitting a pillow with a bat; lying on the back and hitting the mattress with the pelvis; etc.

### Centering in the Body and Sexuality

As a child, the depressed person repressed his sobs and rage by strongly contracting his abdomen. These contractions maintain a permanent reduction in sexual sensations. Relaxation of the abdominal muscles restores sensitivity in the depths of the lower abdomen and the pelvic floor, and so enables an awakening of sexuality. To meet the oral needs of the adult means to allow bodily experiences of excitement to spread throughout the body. Whereas genital sexuality is only one dimension of the functional unit "sexuality," sexuality in its entirety is a function of the whole body. Sexual sensations in the whole body facilitate an excitation or charge, whereas sexual sensations in only the genital apparatus facilitate a discharge.

Therapeutic work aims to ground sexuality (and later on, genital sexuality) in the body, in particular in the abdomen and pelvis. We strive to help the depressed person recover his excitable, vibrating, and lively body. The work with the lower half of the body is done with specialized practices that serve to reestablish the natural mobility of the pelvis.

### Centering in Reality and in One's Own Legs

The reestablishment of the body's ability to become aroused (sexuality), the relaxation of the abdomen, and the possibility of energetically charging the pelvis (genital sexuality) make it possible for sensations to stream through the pelvis and genitals into the legs.

Work with the lower half of the body—supporting relaxation, energizing, and enlivening of the legs and feet—is very valuable in this regard. In this way, passive limbs—simple, lifeless posts propping up the pelvis and trunk—can be transformed into active, lively legs. As such, they return to their original functions of giving secure support on the ground and serving mobility. The patient feels grounded and psycho-motorically, emotionally, and psychologically in balance. *He realizes that in reality his body, his sexuality, and the earth are in contact and form one whole.*

## Therapeutic Relationship

Depression is a response to loss of contact. The child's initial loss of contact with the mother's love leads to a loss of contact with one's own body. The therapeutic answer to this is a reversal of this process, in which the reestablishment of caring contact that a therapist makes with his patient reawakens the patient's emotional life.

Love, warmth, human kindness, and understanding can be communicated through body contact. This superbly fits the needs of the depressed patient. She finally gets what she has wanted for so long. Her self can become reengaged and can proceed on the path of maturation. The therapist uses his own body directly and skillfully, such as by taking the patient into his arms and holding her tight while maintaining professional boundaries. The depressed patient, in turn, wants to have their love object (in the transference, this is the therapist), wants to hold him in her arms, hold him tight, and keep him.

I believe this relational pattern between mother and child is fundamental: owning, and being owned. This pattern seems to be the theme of spontaneous play between mother and child. The experience of owning motherly love (practically owning the loved body of the mother) pervades the child's body and suffuses the structure of its self. It constitutes a precondition for the development of self-confidence, self-trust, and self-respect within the child. In the context of therapy, it constitutes the same platform upon which these abilities can be founded in the adult self.

We are not pretending to be the "good, repairing mother" (which would be more a countertransference reaction), but strive to be an authentically "loving source of support" in our function as therapists. This means that we offer the depressed patient an adult relationship in the here and now, which allows the exchange of feelings and the expression of longings. The patient can eventually transfer this pattern of "loving and being loved" from the therapeutic relationship to her daily life outside of the therapeutic setting. Accessed in her daily life, it constitutes a remedy for the depressive process.

## References

Abraham, K. (1912/1965). Préliminaires à l'investigation et au traitement psychanalytique de la folie maniaco-dépressive et des états voisins [The preliminary investigation and the psychoanalytic treatment of manic-depressive and similar states]. *Oeuvres Complètes: Vol. 1907–1914*, Paris Payot (pp. 212–227).

Bowlby, J. (1961). Processes of mourning. *International Journal of Psychoanalysis, 42*, 317–340.

Brazelton, T. B. (1981). *Infants and mothers: Differences in development.* New York: Dell.

Keleman, S. (1985). *Emotional anatomy.* Berkeley, CA: Center Press.

Lowen, A. (1979a). *Depression.* Munich: Kösel.

Lowen, A. (1979b). *Bio-Energetik* [Bioenergetics]. Reinbek: Rowohlt.

Reich, W. (1969). *Die Funktion des Orgasmus* [The function of the orgasm]. Cologne: Kiepenheuer & Witsch.

Spitz, R. (1945). Hospitalism: An inquiry into the genesis of psychiatric conditions in early childhood. *Psychoanalytic Study of the Child, 1*, 53–74.

Stern, D. (1989). *Le Monde Interpersonnel du Nourrisson* [The interpersonal world of the infant]. Paris: PUF.

Tonella, G. (2000). The interactive self. *Clinical Journal of the International Institute of Bioenergetic Analysis, 11(2),* 25–59.

# 76
## Sensory-Motor Processing for Trauma Recovery

**Pat Ogden and Kekuni Minton, United States**

**Pat Ogden** is the founder and director of the Sensorimotor Psychotherapy Institute in Broomfield, Colorado, where the body-oriented method of trauma resolution that she developed is taught. Sensorimotor Psychotherapy, along with a number of other approaches to the treatment of trauma such as those of Peter Levine and Hilarion Petzold, is internationally well recognized. Dr. Ogden has presented her work in many international trauma conferences, often in main presentations with Bessel van der Kolk, Peter Levine, and others.

Dr. Ogden began her professional career as a bodyworker (Rolfing, Reichian massage, and other methods). She holds a PhD in psychology, an MA in education, and a BA in sociology, and she has clinical experience from her own practice and from her work as a prison psychiatrist. She is a faculty member at Naropa University, the first Buddhist university in the West, and was a trainer at the Ergos Institute, and at the Hakomi Institute, which she co-founded in 1980. She worked at the Hakomi Institute internationally for many years as a senior trainer before developing her own treatment approach to trauma. She is the author of a book on trauma therapy (in collaboration with Kekuni Minton), as well as a number of other publications. The first scientific study of her form of PTSD treatment was published in 2006 (Ogden et al., 2006).

Dr. Ogden is a member of the advisory counsel of the United States Association for Body Psychotherapy (USABP).
**Kekuni Minton** is a clinical psychologist, a faculty member of Naropa University, a former Hakomi trainer, and a trainer at the Sensorimotor Psychotherapy Institute, where he works in close collaboration with Pat Ogden. He is a licensed Body Psychotherapist, and is internationally active as a trainer and as a presenter at many conferences.

In addition to his academic background (a PhD in psychology, and an MBA) and training in Hakomi Experiential Psychotherapy and Integrative Body Psychotherapy (Jack Rosenberg and Marjorie Rand), Dr. Minton is also trained as a meditation teacher.

Two of the pioneers of the modern tradition of psychotherapy, Janet and Freud, postulated theories of top-down and bottom-up influences in psychology. In Freud's language, the ego and the superego were on the "top" and modulated the influence of the survival and sex drives—the id—on the bottom. Janet's "psychology of action" describes hierarchically organized actions ranging from primitive and reflexive to highly cognitive and sophisticated. Post-traumatic stress disorder (PTSD) fits such hierarchical models in many ways. In PTSD, reflexive, bottom-up "sensory-motor" elements such as hyperarousal commonly disrupt adaptive functioning. Traumatized individuals are plagued by the return of truncated, dissociated, or ineffective sensory-motor, or somatic, reactions in such forms as intrusive images, sounds, smells, bodily sensations, physical pain, constriction, numbing, and the inability to modulate arousal. These symptoms often render the survivor helpless to take control of his or her life, because they disrupt the executive capacities of top-down cognitive processing.

Janet wrote extensively about the effectiveness of somatic, bottom-up interventions to "prevent or remove mental troubles." But Freud indicated analyzing and sublimating the survival instincts (the id)—an approach for resolving this conflict between top-down and bottom-up components of the psyche that is insufficient, in our opinion, to resolve dysregulated bottom-up processes. Rather than helping to resolve these symptoms, attempts to process traumatic events by describing them in words or by venting the associated feelings can precipitate "somatic remembering" in the form of physical sensations, numbing, dysregulated arousal, and involuntary movements. Typical psychotherapeutic approaches to trauma recovery favor emotional and cognitive processing over body processing, despite the fact that trauma profoundly affects the body and despite the fact that many PTSD symptoms are somatically based. In addition, trauma-related sensory-motor reactions often persist and disrupt the client's functioning even after long-term "talk therapy" approaches and articulation. Is it possible that cortical-cognitive approaches to therapy are not completely effective because they may fail to directly address the physiological and somatic elements—dysregulated arousal and animal defensive reactions—that often drive the symptoms of PTSD?

In recent times, approaches to working psychotherapeutically with trauma that address nonverbal, implicit elements, including somatic phenomena, have begun to surface—e.g., Sensorimotor Psychotherapy (SP), founded by the authors of this chapter; Somatic Experiencing (SE), founded by Peter Levine (1997); somatic-oriented interventions, proposed by Babette Rothschild (2000); as well as approaches that process trauma through nonanalytic protocols: e.g., eye movement desensitization and reprocessing (EMDR), founded by Francine Shapiro (1995); Thought Field Therapy (TFT), originated by Roger Callahan (1981); neurofeedback; and many others. These approaches access noncognitively controlled levels of processing that are thought to support the client's ability to resolve implicit memories and alleviate symptoms of trauma such as dysregulated arousal. All of these methods are "exposure" methods—that is, they work with the state-specific processing associated with trauma-related dysregulated arousal rather than just the cognitive thoughts about the trauma. Therefore, the results are thought to accrue on many levels rather than just cognitive understanding and emotional resolution.

In this chapter, we discuss the use of Sensorimotor Psychotherapy for resolving the debilitating effects of trauma, as well as early attachment injuries. Sensorimotor Psychotherapy, as well as the methods mentioned above, aim to integrate unassimilated (bottom-up) sensory-motor reactions. EMDR, SE, and Rothschild's approach all work with processing somatic abreactions and intrusions, and modulating dysregulated arousal. Thought Field Therapy and neurofeedback have shown promise in the regulation of trauma-related dysregulation as well; and EMDR, SE, and Rothschild's work all highlight resource installation. Sensorimotor Psychotherapy emphasizes processing traumatic somato-sensory intrusions, self-regulation of arousal, and installing resources, as well as addressing attachment disturbances.

In sensory-motor treatment for PTSD, bodily experience becomes the primary entry point for intervention, while emotional expression and meaning-making arise out of the subsequent somatic reorganization of habitual trauma-related responses. That is, sensory-motor approaches like the methods mentioned above work from the "bottom up" rather than from the "top down." By attending to the patient's or client's body directly, it becomes possible to address the more primitive, automatic, and involuntary functions of the brain that underlie traumatic and post-traumatic responses. Sensorimotor Psychotherapy is founded on the premise that "the brain functions as an integrated whole but is comprised of systems that are hierarchically organized. The 'higher level' [cognitive] integrative functions evolved from and are dependent on the integrity of 'lower-level' [limbic and reptilian] structures and on sensorimotor experience" (Fisher, Murray, and Bundy, 1991).

The capacity of human beings for self-awareness, interpretation, and abstract thought and feeling exists within this developmental and hierarchical relationship to the instinctual and nonconscious responses of the body. These hierarchically organized, interconnected responses range from instinctual arousal and mammalian defenses, feelings, and affective expression to thoughts, reflective self-awareness, and meaning-making. Wilber's (1996) notion of hierarchical information processing describes the evolutionary and functional hierarchy among these three levels of organizing experience: cognitive, emotional, and sensory-motor. In neuropsychology, MacLean (1985) has conceptualized this hierarchy as the "triune brain," or a "brain with a brain within a brain." In MacLean's theory, the human brain is the product of evolutionary, hierarchical development: first to develop in the human infant is the reptilian brain (composed of the brainstem and the cerebellum), which governs arousal, homeostasis of the organism, reproductive drives, sensation, and instinctual movement impulses, the heart of sensory-motor experience. The "second" brain is the "paleo-mammalian brain" or "limbic brain," found in all mammals, which anatomically surrounds the reptilian brain and serves to regulate somato-sensory experience, emotion, memory, some social behavior, and learning (Cozolino, 2002). Last to develop phylogenetically is the neocortex, which enables cognitive information processing, self-awareness, executive functioning, and conceptual thinking (MacLean, 1985).

This hierarchical organization results in two distinctly different directions of information processing—from the "top down," and from the "bottom up"—and the interplay between them holds significant implications for the treatment of trauma (LeDoux, 1996). Schore (2002a) notes that for adults, in nontraumatic circumstances, "higher cortical areas" act as "control centers," such that the orbitofrontal cortex hierarchically dominates subcortical activity with "veto power" over limbic responses. Thus, top-down processing enables us to outline plans, determine what to accomplish for the day, and then structure time to meet particular goals. Emotions and sensations, such as feelings of frustration, fatigue, or physical discomfort, may be overridden in order to accomplish these priorities. It is as though, most of the time, we hover just above our somatic and sensory experience, not allowing it to be the primary determinant of our actions without conscious decision-making. For the traumatized individual, however, the intensity of trauma-related emotions and sensory-motor reactions often disorganizes the individual's cognitive capacities, interfering with the ability for cognitive processing and top-down regulation. This phenomenon has been described as "bottom-up hijacking" and is a frequent source of problems for trauma survivors (LeDoux, 1996).

The interplay between top-down and bottom-up processing holds significant implications for the occurrence and treatment of trauma. Because traumatized people have difficulty articulating and regulating their experience, the therapist must serve as an "auxiliary cortex" (Diamond, Balvin, and Diamond, quoted in Schore, 1994, pp. 29–30) for the client through observing and articulating the client's sensory-motor experience and in this way teaching the client to notice, track, and describe these experiences herself. The therapist intervenes in the client's inability to modulate arousal and metabolize trauma-related stimuli by interrupting the flow of the narrative to implement noncognitive protocols that facilitate bottom-up processing. Until clients are able to perform these functions adequately and independently—which helps to restore a more or less healthy balance between top-down and bottom-up processing and thus helps them to begin to self-regulate sensory-motor and emotional experience—the sensory-motor reactions of arousal and defensive responses are subject to becoming either hyperactive or hypoactive, as we shall see in the following section.

## Physical Defensive Responses

Trauma calls forth two general types of physical defenses, which may be active (mobilizing) such as fight-or-flight, or passive (immobilizing) such as freezing and feigned death, or both (Levine, 1997; Nijenhuis, 1999; Ogden, Minton, and Pain, 2006).[71] When mobilizing defenses are impossible or ill-advised, they are typically replaced by

---

71 Whereas Levine (1997) states that hyperarousal and active defenses precede passive defense and immobility, both Nijenhuis (1999) and Porges (1995, 2000) note that frozen states are not always preceded by active defenses or arousal: Ogden et al., (2006) theorize that it is necessary to stay within the "comfort zone." In some cases, the individual might automatically engage passive defenses without first attempting the active defense.

immobilizing defenses such as feigned death, submission, automatic obedience, numbing, and freezing (Nijenhuis and van der Hart, 1999; Nijenhuis, 1999). These immobilizing defenses often prove to be the best option for survival in instances when a victim is unable to fight or outrun an assailant, or in cases of early attachment trauma, when the child is developmentally ill-equipped to fight or flee or when such actions exacerbate the trauma. No one defensive response is "better" than another: all are potentially adaptive and effective at diminishing threat, depending on the situation and the capabilities of the individual. We propose that inflexibility among these defensive subsystems and their overactivity in the absence of threat involve chronic dysregulated arousal and contribute to the traumatized person's continued distress after the traumatic event is over.

The mobilizing defenses that might have enabled escape or the warding off of danger have been rendered ineffective or interrupted and left incomplete, and these incomplete actions of defense may subsequently manifest as chronic symptoms. As Herman (1992) states, "Each component of the ordinary response to danger, having lost its utility, tends to persist in an altered and exaggerated state long after the actual danger is over" (p. 34). If a person, when endangered, experiences the instinct to fight back or to flee but is unable to execute these actions, this uncompleted sequence of possible defensive actions may persist in distorted forms. The individual may experience his "fight-or-flight" muscles held in a chronically tightened pattern, heightened and unstable aggressive impulses, or a chronic lack of tone or sensation in a particular muscle group. In addition, many, if not most, patients come to therapy exhibiting chronic immobilizing defensive tendencies in their body, which in turn profoundly influence their emotions and cognitions.

Unresolved trauma insidiously predicts the individual's future before the future has happened. Bromberg (2008) asserts, "When self-continuity seems threatened, the mind adaptationally extends its reach beyond the moment by turning the future into a version of past danger" (p. 342). The body also predicts the future through patterns of tension and dysregulated arousal. The future has been pre-scribed as hopeless by the past, as indicated by chronic immobilizing defenses. Until an abused patient can experience the satisfaction of performing her active defensive actions fully, her future seems to hold only further abuse and disappointment as she continuously fails to defend herself. Rather than insight alone, it is the actual *experience* of mobilizing action with conscious intention and awareness, while simultaneously addressing the cognitive distortions and emotional reactions, that helps effect such change.

In Sensorimotor Psychotherapy, patients are helped to rediscover their truncated mobilizing defensive impulses through tracking their body movements and sensations that emerge during the therapy session. For example, a patient who had to submit to her caregiver's sexual abuse as a child, in therapy discovered her forgotten, dormant impulse to push away and flee to protect herself. As she mindfully re-experienced how her body ultimately did not resist the abuse and automatically submitted, she noticed a tightening in her jaw accompanied by muscular tension that went from the jaw down the neck into her shoulder and arm. In response to the therapist's encouragement to continue studying her tension, the tightening continued to increase, and her hands curled up into a fist. Being able to observe and attend to how her body wanted to respond then, she became aware of the previously aborted physical urge to not only punch at her father but also run away, reflected in a tightening of and a feeling of energy in her legs. These physical impulses that she did not—could not—act upon at the time of the abuse appeared spontaneously as she became meticulously aware of her physical sensations and impulses as she recalled the abuse in therapy. As she subsequently discovered, the truncated, lost impulses to resist had become encoded not only in the praxis of submission, but also as beliefs or automatic assumptions of "I don't deserve to defend myself."

## Bottom-up Dysregulation and the Window of Tolerance

The characteristic components of the trauma response—a poor tolerance for stress and arousal with consequent affect dysregulation—render traumatized individuals either hyperaroused, experiencing "too much" activation, or hypoaroused, experiencing "too little" (van der Kolk et al., 1996). The top and bottom lines of Figure 76.1 depict the limits of a person's optimal degree of arousal, or "window of tolerance," within which "various intensities of emotional arousal can be processed without disrupting the functioning of the system" (Siegel, 1999, p. 253).[72]

When a person's arousal is outside the window of tolerance at either end of the spectrum, upper levels of processing will be disabled, and will be replaced by bottom-up reflexive action. As Siegel notes, "In states of mind beyond the window of tolerance, the prefrontally mediated capacity [cognitive processing] for response flexibility is temporarily shut down. The 'higher mode' of integrative [cognitive] processing has been replaced by a 'lower mode' of reflexive [sensory-motor] responding" (Ibid., pp. 254–255).

Hyperarousal tends to disrupt cognitive and affective processing as the individual becomes overwhelmed and disorganized by the accelerated pace and amplitude of thoughts and emotions, which may be accompanied by intrusive memories. As van der Kolk and colleagues (1996) state, *"This hyper-arousal creates a vicious cycle: state-dependent memory retrieval causes increased access to traumatic memories and involuntary intrusions of the trauma, which lead in turn to even more arousal . . ."* and there will be a tendency to *"interpret current stimuli as reminders of the trauma"* (p. 305), perpetuating the pattern of hyperarousal.

Although hyperarousal symptoms and intrusive re-experiencing are commonly considered to be the hallmark symptoms of trauma, not all trauma patients respond to trauma reminders with hyperarousal; in one study, 30 percent of subjects responded with hypoarousal and with emotional symptoms when hearing their trauma scripts read to them (Lanius et al., 2002). The perceptual distortions and losses for the hypoaroused patient can involve not only a sense of separation from the self, as in derealization and depersonalization, but also motor weakness, paralysis, ataxia, numbing of inner bodily sensation, as well as cognitive abnormalities, such as amnesia, fugue states, and confusional states (van der Hart et al., 2004) and decreased mobility in facial muscles (Porges, 1995). Cognitive and emotional processing are disrupted by an overall numbing: clients complain of a reduced capacity to sense or feel even significant events, an inability to accurately evaluate

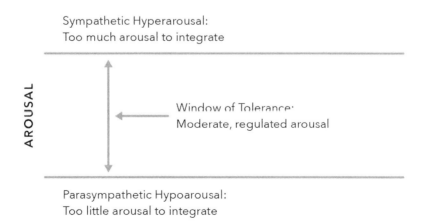

THE WINDOW OF TOLERANCE

---

72  It is important to note that the emotional level of information processing, in its middle position between the cognitive and the sensory-motor levels, may be considered either "higher" or "lower" depending on the context

dangerous situations or think clearly, and a lack of motivation. Additional long-term and debilitating symptoms might include *"emotional constriction, social isolation, retreat from family obligations, anhedonia and a sense of estrangement"* (van der Kolk, 1987, pp. 2–3).

The extremes of autonomic arousal that might have been adaptive at the moment of danger ultimately become the source of therapeutic impasse when the patient cannot maintain arousal within the window of tolerance (Chefetz, 2000). Especially in cases of extreme or prolonged trauma, or in the context of subsequent inadequacies in soothing and relational support, the individual may have difficulty recalibrating autonomic arousal (Cloitre et al., 2004; Herman, 1992; Nemeroff, 2004; van der Kolk et al., 1996). The traumatized individual's arousal level may remain primarily either above or below the parameters of the window of tolerance, or may swing uncontrollably between these two states (van der Kolk, 1987, p. 2). This biphasic alternation of hyperarousal and hypoarousal may become the new norm in the aftermath of trauma, thus further diminishing the quality of life.

It is our view that failed active defensive responses, along with the inability to modulate arousal, contribute to the distressing symptoms of trauma; and because these symptoms are bottom-up phenomena, they appear to be alleviated through sensory-motor processing.

## Sensory-Motor Processing Example

Sensory-motor processing necessitates (1) regulating affective and sensory-motor states through the therapeutic relationship, and (2) teaching the client to auto-regulate by mindful awareness and articulation of sensory-motor processes. The former is a prerequisite for the latter. The therapist's ability to become an "interactive psycho-biological regulator" for the client's dysregulated state gradually facilitates the client's ability to verbally label their affective and sensory-motor experience (Schore, 2002b).

To accomplish this, the therapist must help clients to become aware of and to describe inner bodily sensations that are signs of potential defensive responses or dysregulated arousal. However, when clients are asked to describe sensations, they frequently do so with words such as "panic" or "anger," which refer to emotional qualities rather than to sensation itself. When this occurs, clients are asked to verbally label how they experience the emotion physically. For example, panic may be felt in the body as rapid heartbeat, trembling, and shallow breathing. Anger might be experienced as tension in the jaw, or as an impulse to strike out accompanied by a sense of heaviness and immobility in the arms.

Mindfulness is the key to sensory-motor processing. In Sensorimotor Psychotherapy, the client's cognitions are engaged to evoke mindful observation of the interplay of their perceptions, emotions, movements, sensations, impulses, and thoughts (Kurtz, 1990). Mindfulness is a state of consciousness in which one's awareness is directed toward here-and-now internal experience (see Chapter 38, "Consciousness, Awareness, Mindfulness" by Halko Weiss). To teach mindfulness, the therapist asks questions that require mindfulness to answer, such as, *"Where exactly do you experience tension?" "What sensation do you feel in your legs right now?" "What happens in your body when you feel frightened?"* Questions such as these encourage the client to come out of dissociated states and past- or future-centered ideation and experience the moment-by-moment changes in the body. Intentionally focusing attention in this way engages the cognitive faculties of the client in support of sensory-motor processing, rather than allowing bottom-up trauma-related processes to escalate and take control.

Definitions of mindfulness usually describe being open and receptive to *"whatever arises within the mind's eye"* (Siegel, 2006) without preference. "Directed mindfulness" (Ogden, 2009) is an application of mindfulness that directs the patient's awareness toward particular elements of present-moment experience that are considered to be important to therapeutic goals. When patients' mindfulness is not directed, they often find themselves at the mercy of the elements of internal experience that appear most vividly in the forefront of consciousness—typically, the dysregulated aspects, such as panic or intrusive images, which cause further dysregulation, or their familiar attachment-related patterns. To illustrate: when working with a dysregulated patient, an example of nondirected mindfulness would be a general question: *"What is your experience right now?"* An example of directed mindfulness that guides a patient's attention toward meeting the goal of becoming more grounded would be, *"What do you notice in your body right now, particularly in your legs?"* The patient quite probably will report that she cannot feel her legs, which paves the way for generating sensation and movement in her legs, thus stabilizing arousal by promoting the therapeutic goal of "groundedness."

Sensory-motor processing is illustrated in the first therapy session with Mary, a client who had been repeatedly raped as a child by a family member. At first, it was difficult for Mary to be mindful of her bodily sensations, because when she tried to do so, the hyperarousal, shaking, panic, and terror became overwhelming. The therapist knew that if Mary could fully experience a physical defensive sequence, these symptoms might subside considerably, especially because Mary's defenses had been overwhelmed during her abuse. To accomplish this, the therapist asked Mary if she would be willing to push with her hands against a pillow held by the therapist, who directed her to temporarily disregard all memories and simply focus on her body to find a way of pushing that felt comfortable. By having Mary focus only on her body, the therapist facilitated the regulation of arousal. Mary's sense of control was increased as she was encouraged to guide this physical exploration by telling the therapist how much pressure to use in resisting with the pillow, what position to be in, and so on. Eventually, Mary experienced a full sequence of active defensive responses: lifting her arms, pushing tentatively at first with just her arms, then increasing the pressure and involving the muscles of her back, pelvis, and legs. After experiencing the defensive sequence—which Mary described as a strong *"No!"*—she was able to be mindful without becoming overwhelmed. Her arousal level was now within the optimum zone of the Modulation Model (see Figure 76.1) and she thus could process information more effectively.

Later in the session, Mary reported that her hand wanted to become a fist. Sensing this impulse from the hand itself is very different from the thought or imagery of the hand becoming a fist, or a potentially resourcing directive from the therapist to have the client make a fist. The client feels the impulse arising organically from the body (bottom-up processing) itself. These impulses arise from the sensory-motor areas of the brain and are not cognitively directed or managed. The therapist said, *"Feel your hand becoming a fist and just notice what happens next in your body,"* instructing her to track her sensations and impulses as they changed or "sequenced." As Mary simply tracked and allowed involuntary micromovements and gestures to occur, rather than "doing" them voluntarily as when pushing against the pillow, she reported an impulse to "hit out" accompanied by increased heart rate and tension in her arm, which began to shake quite strongly. Sensory-motor sequencing was occurring spontaneously through mindful attention to bodily sensations and impulses and by harnessing cognitive direction in suspending memory content and emotion in order to support the body's processing. Gradually, Mary's sensations and movements began to quiet and soften, and her heart rate returned to baseline. Only when this sensory-motor experience had settled was she asked to describe additional content, as emotional and cognitive processing was included. Following this session, Mary stated that she felt more peaceful and that she was able to sleep through the night for the first time in weeks. Through the course of these sessions, Mary learned to mindfully monitor her own levels of arousal, interrupt escalating arousal, and use her body as a resource to process past trauma.

## Conclusion

Sensory-motor processing is an essential part of Sensorimotor Psychotherapy, a method that integrates sensory-motor processing with cognitive and emotional processing in the treatment of trauma. By using the body (rather than cognition or emotion) as a primary entry point in processing trauma, Sensorimotor Psychotherapy directly treats the effects of trauma on the body, which in turn has a positive influence on emotional and cognitive processing. This method was developed entirely from clinical practice, and although there has been no formal empirical research at this time, there are many anecdotal reports from both clients and therapists that attest to the efficacy of the technique. Professionals using Sensorimotor Psychotherapy report that it often reduces PTSD symptoms such as nightmares, panic attacks, aggressive outbursts, and hyperarousal, and that the ability to track bodily sensation helps clients to experience present reality rather than reacting as if the trauma were still occurring.

Through sensory-motor processing, the therapist interactively helps the client regulate arousal and eventually gain the skill of auto-regulation, improving the integration of, and healthy interplay among, sensory-motor, emotional, and cognitive processing, which is the overriding goal of this approach. We believe that if the use of insight, understanding, and somatically informed top-down management of symptoms is thoughtfully balanced with bottom-up processing of trauma-related sensations, arousal, movement, and emotions, the complex effects of trauma are more likely to respond to treatment.

## References

Bromberg, P. M. (2008). Shrinking the tsunami: Affect-regulation, dissociation, and the shadow of the flood. *Contemporary Psychoanalysis, 44,* 329–350.

Callahan, R. (1981/2004). A rapid treatment for phobias. In R. Callahan, *Thought Field Therapy: The early papers.* La Quinta, CA: Callahan Techniques.

Chefetz, R. A. (2000). Affect dysregulation as a way of life. *Journal of the American Acadamy of Psychoanalysis, 28*(2), 289–303.

Cloitre, M. K., Stovall-McClough, M. R., & Chemtob, C. (2004). Therapeutic alliance, negative mood regulation and treatment outcome in child abuse-related posttraumatic stress disorder. *Journal of Consulting and Clinical Psychology, 72*(3), 411–416.

Cozolino, L. (2002). *The neuroscience of psychotherapy: Building and rebuilding the human brain.* New York: W. W. Norton.

Fisher, A., Murray, E., & Bundy, A. (1991). *Sensory integration: Theory and practice.* Philadelphia: Davis.

Herman, J. (1992). *Trauma and recovery.* New York: Basic Books.

Kurtz, R. (1990). *Body-Centered Psychotherapy: The Hakomi Method.* Mendocino, CA: LifeRhythm.

Lanius, R. A., Williamson, P. C., Boksman, K., Densmore, M., Gupta, M., Neufeld, R. W., et al. (2002). Brain activation during script-driven imagery induced dissociative responses in PTSD: A functional magnetic resonance imaging investigation. *Biological Psychiatry, 52,* 305–311.

LeDoux, J. (1996). *The emotional brain.* New York: Simon & Schuster.

Levine, P. (1997). *Waking the tiger: Healing trauma.* Berkeley, CA: North Atlantic Books.

MacLean, P. D. (1985). Brain evolution relating to family, play, and the separation call. *Archives of General Psychiatry, 42,* 405–417.

Nemeroff, C. B. (2004). Neurobiological consequences of childhood trauma. *Journal of Clinical Psychiatry, 65*(Suppl. 1), 18–28.

Nijenhuis, E. R. S. (1999). *Somatoform dissociation: Phenomena, measurement, and theoretical issues.* Assen, Netherlands: Van Gorcum.

Nijenhuis, E. R. S., & van der Hart, O. (1999). Forgetting and re-experiencing trauma: From anesthesia to pain. In J. Goodwin & R. Attias, *Splintered reflections: Images of the body in trauma.* New York: Basic Books.

Ogden, P. (2009). Emotion, mindfulness, and movement: Expanding the regulatory boundaries of the window of affect tolerance. In D. Fosha, D. Siegel, & M. Solomon (Eds.), *The healing power of emotion: Affective neuroscience, development and clinical practice.* New York: W. W. Norton.

Ogden, P., Minton, K., & Pain, C. (2006). *Trauma and the body: A sensorimotor approach to psychotherapy.* New York: W. W. Norton.

Porges, S. (1995). Orienting in a defensive world: Mammalian modifications of our evolutionary heritage. A polyvagal theory. *Psychophysiology, 32,* 301–318.

Porges, S. (2000). Emotion: An evolutionary by-product of the neural regulation of the autonomic nervous system. *Annals of the New York Academy of Sciences, 807,* 62–77.

Rothschild, B. (2000). *The body remembers: The psychophysiology of trauma and trauma treatment.* New York: W. W. Norton.

Schore, A. (1994). *Affect regulation and the origin of the self: The neurobiology of emotional development.* Hillsdale, NJ: Lawrence Erlbaum.

Schore, A. N. (2002a). Dysregulation of the right brain: A fundamental mechanism of traumatic attachment and the psychopathogenesis of posttraumatic stress disorder. *Australian and New Zealand Journal of Psychiatry, 36*(1), 9–30.

Schore, A. N. (2002b). The right brain as the neurobiological substratum of Freud's dynamic unconscious. In D. Scharff (Ed.), *The psychoanalytic century: Freud's legacy for the future* (pp. 61–88). New York: Other Press.

Shapiro, F. (1995). *Eye movement desensitization and reprocessing: Basic principles, protocols and procedures.* New York: Guilford Press.

Siegel, D. J. (1999). *The developing mind: Toward a neurobiology of interpersonal experience.* New York: Guilford Press.

Siegel, D. J. (2006). *The mindful brain: Reflection and attunement in the cultivation of well-being.* New York: W. W. Norton.

van der Hart, O., Nijenhuis, E., Steele, K., & Brown, D. (2004). Trauma-related dissociation: Conceptual clarity lost and found. *Australian and New Zealand Journal of Psychiatry, 38,* 906–914.

van der Kolk, B. (1987). *Psychological trauma.* Washington, DC: American Psychiatric Press.

van der Kolk, B., McFarlane, A. C., & Weisaeth, L. (Eds.). (1996). *Traumatic stress: The effects of overwhelming experience on mind, body and society.* New York: Guilford Press.

van der Kolk, B., van der Hart, O., & Marmar, C. (1996). Dissociation and information processing in posttraumatic stress disorder. In B. van der Kolk, A. C. McFarlane, & L. Weisaeth (Eds.), *Traumatic stress: The effects of overwhelming experience on mind, body and society.* New York: Guilford Press.

Wilber, K. (1996). *A brief history of everything.* Boston:

# SECTION X

## Some Areas of Application of Body Psychotherapy

# 77

## Introduction to Section X

Gustl Marlock, Germany, and Halko Weiss, United States

Translation by Warren Miller

In this section, Section X, we present specific areas of clinical application of Body Psychotherapy that tend to go beyond the conventional setting of classical psychotherapy (the therapeutic treatment of individual adults).

We start by closely examining Body Psychotherapeutic work with children in regard to three different age groups. Eva Reich's "butterfly massage" for infants (Overly, 2004) was an example of valuable pioneering work that prepared the ground for contemporary approaches in working with new borns and infants. Her work inspired, among others, **Thomas Harms** (2000), who developed it further and who played a key role in the founding and establishment of the first outpatient clinics for families with chronically crying babies. Since then, other similar clinics have established themselves, and these can be found in many places, mostly in Germany and Switzerland. Harms describes a very successful Body Psychotherapeutic approach to working with infants in Chapter 78, "Body Psychotherapy with Parents, Babies, and Infants." This form of treatment is—aside from early pioneering work, for example, by Wilhelm Reich—a more recent enhancement of this type of therapy. The approach is distinguished by a particularly sensitive understanding of the emotional and somatic effects of traumatic birth experiences.

**Nicole Gäbler** then addresses the area of therapeutic work with children from the toddler age to puberty. In Chapter 79, "A Return to the 'Close Body': Child Somatic Psychotherapy," she makes references to Bernard Aucouturier, the grand seigneur of French psycho-motoric work, who established one of the most interesting links between sensory-motor bodywork and therapeutic work that focused on central fears, complexes, and developmental requirements of early childhood (Esser, 1995).

Chapter 80, "Subsymbolic Processing with an Alexithymic Client" by **John May,** from St. Louis, is a case study demonstrating one way of working with Body Psychotherapy. He illustrates some aspects of modern therapeutic methodology that are also significant and representative for a number of other traditions and their practice. These aspects are of a dialogic, intersubjective method with a phenomenological orientation, and the main focus of this approach is, not on interpretation or practice, but rather on helping patients decode and become incrementally more conscious of their somato-psychic realities.

In his reflection on this process, May refers to the work of Wilma Bucci (1997), who has attempted to develop a theory of subsymbolic perception: in therapeutic processes, meaningful configurations often emerge gradually from fragments of subsymbolic bodily experience. Therefore, May's case study is trendsetting in its important implications for a more precise theory of phenomenological practice in the future.

In Chapter 81, "A Somatic Approach to Couples Therapy," marriage and family therapist **Rob Fisher** shows how work with couples can be enlivened and deepened when the somatic dimension is used to provide substantial new information in some very concrete ways.

In Chapter 82, Wilhelm Reich's daughter **Eva Reich,** in collaboration with **Judyth Weaver,** presents her classical concept of "Emotional First Aid." It illustrates what effective medical and Body Psychotherapeutic ad hoc support can look like in acute crises that have a psychic-emotional background.

In Chapter 83, **Michael Soth,** one of the co-editors of this handbook, examines how the body can be worked with in the context of group therapy processes. When discussing "The Use of Body Psychotherapy in the Context of Group Therapy," there is a widespread tendency to view Body Psychotherapy as merely individual work within a group setting. Soth shows how a theoretical perspective on Body Psychotherapeutic group therapy can be developed to go well beyond this perceived limitation.

To conclude Section X, we have included a chapter by **Barnaby Barratt,** a well-respected South African academic and researcher. In Chapter 84, "Research in Body Psychotherapy," he not only examines the inappropriateness of modern scientific research parameters, mostly designed more for pharmacological trials than to assess the efficacy of psychotherapy, but also looks at the actual research studies that have been done on the efficacy and effectiveness of Body Psychotherapy. His conclusions and criticisms—that many of the previously conducted research studies in Body Psychotherapy were rather poorly done—are very valid; but there are a few studies that he mentions, especially the Koemeda-Lutz and the three Röhricht studies, that do have much greater validity and relevance, both within Body Psychotherapy and also within the pseudo-scientific parameters that constrain all psychotherapeutic research. It is therefore clear that there is still a lot of work to be done in this area.

## References

Bucci, W. (1997). *Psychoanalysis and cognitive science.* New York: Guilford Press.

Esser, M. (1995). *Beweg-Gründe: Psychomotorik nach Bernard Aucouturier [Grounded movement: Psychomotorics by Bernard Aucouturier].* Munich: E. Reinhardt.

Harms, T. (Ed.). (2000). *Auf die Welt gekommen: Die neuen Babytherapien [Coming into the world: The new baby therapies].* Berlin: Simon & Leutner.

Overly, R. C. (2004). *Dr. Eva Reich's butterfly touch massage.* Ashville, NC: Lifestyle Press.

# 78

# Body Psychotherapy with Parents, Babies, and Infants

**Thomas Harms, Germany**

**Thomas Harms** is a psychologist and Body Psychotherapist living near Bremen. He has been working in the field of preventive Body Psychotherapy with babies and parents for many years. Various schools of Body Psychotherapy and the findings of modern baby and attachment research have been important influences in the development of what he calls Emotional First Aid. In 1993, Harms founded the first walk-in clinic for crying babies and their parents in Berlin.

Since 1997, he has been directing a therapeutic and educational center in Bremen, the Zentrum für Primäre Prävention (ZePP) [Center for Primary Prevention]. He is also the editor of the book *Auf die Welt gekommen: Die neuen Babytherapien* [Coming into the World: The New Baby Therapies]. His second book on this topic was published in 2008: *Emotionelle Erste Hilfe: Bindungsförderung, Krisenintervention, Eltern-Baby-Therapie* [*Emotional First Aid: Attachment Aid, Crisis Intervention, Parent-Baby Therapy*].

Research on newborn babies and their early relationships has gradually moved into the focus of attention since the middle of the twentieth century. The results of contemporary infant, attachment, and brain research clearly substantiate the view that the psychic and bodily health of the growing child is fundamentally determined by the quality of its first attachment experiences. The increasing helplessness and bafflement of many parents in coping with their babies has meanwhile found its way into general awareness. Issues such as crises with screaming babies, the ever-rising rate of cesarean sections worldwide, and news of cruel child murders have come to center stage for public discussion. The twenty-first-century boom in modern baby research and the radically changed attitude toward accepting the concept of a "competent infant" (Dornes, 2011) have led to an intensified discussion as to how the essential tools of modern psychotherapy (and especially Body-Oriented Psychotherapy) could be deployed in the field of prevention, crisis intervention, and trauma therapy with parents and children (Cierpka and Windaus, 2007; Harms, 2000). It is the intention here to outline some of the practical possibilities offered by the Body Psychotherapeutic approach in building up and supporting stable attachment relationships between parents and child.

## History of Parent-Child Body Psychotherapy

The beginnings of parent-child Body Psychotherapy are closely interwoven with the history of modern Body Psychotherapy. Despite having barely been acknowledged by contemporary infant research, there was significant pioneering work done on parent-child dynamics in the research on psychosomatic problems and their prevention by the physician and natural scientist Wilhelm Reich (1897–1957).

At a time when René Spitz, John Bowlby, and other psychoanalytic researchers were beginning to study the momentous impact on children's personality development when deprived of maternal care, Reich was already concerned with the basic preconditions of what constitutes that maternal love: good emotional and body contact and the ability of the mother to empathize with the needs of the child (Boadella, 2008; Bowlby, 2010). Having already made a major contribution to the development of a Body-Oriented Psychotherapy in the 1930s and 1940s (Reich, 2010), from the mid-1940s on—triggered by the birth of his son Peter—Reich became increasingly interested in the study of the natural expressions of babies, the preconditions for the development of emotional armoring, even in the nursing phase, as well as the possibility of employing vegetotherapeutic techniques on babies, infants, and their parents. In December 1949, together with forty colleagues from the specialist fields of medicine, obstetrics, and social work, Reich founded the interdisciplinary research project "Children of the Future," with the goal of conducting a long-term study of the self-regulatory processes of and the conditions for the preservation of basic emotional health in babies and in older children. This comprehensive research project focused on the following four main themes (Reich, 1987):

1. Prenatal counseling and preventive Body Psychotherapy for pregnant women and parents-to-be
2. Attentive monitoring and supervision at the birth and during the first days of life of the newborn baby
3. Prophylaxis of early armoring in the first five to six years of life
4. Long-term study and further observation of the children until the end of puberty

In the context of this research, Wilhelm Reich describes the case of a five-week-old baby, in which he describes the gentle use of vegetotherapeutic techniques to undo the first signs of an incipient emotional withdrawal on the part of the baby:

> Our infant was pale, its upper chest was "quiet." The breathing was noisy, and the chest did not seem to move properly with respiration. The expiration was shallow. Bronchial noises could be heard on auscultation. Generally the infant appeared uncomfortable. Instead of crying loudly, it whimpered. It moved little and looked ill. . . . On examination of the chest, the intercostal muscles felt hard. The child seemed oversensitive to touch in this region. The chest as a whole had not hardened, but it was held in inspiration with the upper part bulging forward. . . . Upon slight stimulation of the intercostal muscles, the chest softened, but did not yield fully when pressed down. The infant immediately started to move vigorously. The breathing cleared up appreciably, and the child began to sneeze (bursts of sudden expiration), smiled, then coughed several times vigorously, and finally urinated. The relaxation increased visibly; the back, formerly arched, curved forward and the cheeks reddened. The noisy breathing stopped. (Ibid., pp. 106–107)

In this first practical example of bioenergetically-based baby therapy, alongside the reflection about the child's "affect," expression, and body language, Reich utilized mainly gentle bodily touch in a playful way to release the tense muscles and tissue blocks and to open up the original expressivity of the child. In this first case study, it is the reestablishing of the child's natural pulsation and its ability to relate that is the benchmark of the therapeutic intervention (Reich, 1985).

His daughter, the pediatrician and obstetrician Eva Reich (1924–2008), continued the tradition of her father's bioenergetic baby and infant research (Reich and Zornansky, 1993; Overly, 2005). In the "butterfly touch" baby massage that she developed, important elements of the vegetotherapeutic work were systematized into a specific treatment sequence; she also introduced the concept of neurosis prevention into the work with expectant women, parents, and newborns (Reich and Zornansky, 1993; Deyringer et al., 2008).

In Scandinavia, a Norwegian student of Reich, Nic Waal, had developed and popularized Reich's concept of a form of Somatic Psychotherapy in the field of child and adolescent psychotherapy, particularly for the treatment of autistic children (Waal, 1970).

From the beginning of the 1980s on, influenced by recent infant and attachment research, the first integrative models of parent-child psychotherapy were being developed that combined the approaches of attachment theory, Prenatal Psychology, Depth Psychology, and mindfulness-based psychotherapy with concepts of Body-Oriented Psychotherapy (Brisch, 2013; Brisch and Hellbrügge, 2008; Diederichs and Jungclaussen, 2009; Downing, 2003; Harms, 2008; Terry, 2006; Thielen, 2009, 2013; Trautmann-Voigt and Moll, 2010; Ventling, 2001).

## Body and Attachment

Most modern approaches to parent-child psychotherapy are in agreement about the need to improve the regulatory and attachment capacity of parents and babies; the various ways of achieving this are, however, very different. A distinctive feature of the Body Psychotherapeutic approach to this work is the consideration of the neurovegetative basis of early relational and attachment processes between babies and parents. Wilhelm Reich had already seen that the ability of the infant and parents to communicate was firmly rooted in the regulation of the autonomic nervous system (ANS) (Reich, 2010). The two fundamental branches of the ANS, the parasympathetic and the sympathetic, can be divided into basic behavioral strategies. The stress and alarm mode of a young, insecure mother expresses itself in hyperexcitation, motor agitation, pronounced hypervigilance (constant scanning of the environment for danger), and a permanent concentration of her attention on the child. Feelings of distress and harassment while in contact with the child are other phenomena of the stress and alarm division of the ANS. In contrast, a secure attachment between parents and child presents itself predominately in a relaxed body, an enhanced awareness and sensitivity, as well as an increased receptiveness and willingness to be in contact with the child. One essential focus of parent-child Body Psychotherapy consists of utilizing the body to access and to directly influence the vegetative response of both parents and child and the natural disposition to open up that is connected with it (Harms, 2013).

The American psycho-physiologist Stephen Porges shows in his recent research that the classical perspective of a two-branched ANS needs to be comprehensively reexamined (Porges, 2010). In his polyvagal theory, he differentiates *three* neural circuits involved in regulating stress and safeguarding the survival of the human organism; these neural circuits come into operation in a hierarchical sequence.

He describes two different strands of the vagus nerve next to the sympathetic nervous system. The phylogenetically younger branch—the ventral vagus—is seen alongside the older, dorsal branch. The ventral branch of the vagus controls those bodily functions that are necessary for communicating with others: among others, the function of gaze direction, spontaneous facial expression, turning the head in the direction of the partner we are relating to, and modulation of hearing to the frequency range of the human voice.

In contrast to these functions of the "social nervous system" (Porges, 2010), there exists an older—in terms of evolutionary biology—variation of survival safeguarding that comes into effect when younger adaptation strategies (social contact, or the "fight-or-flight" strategy) have failed to avert danger. In this situation, when the stress is overwhelming, the older branch, the dorsal vagus, regulates the shutting down and "switching off" of the organism. This freezing mode, such as what people experience in a state of shock paralysis, is the organism's oldest and most inflexible adaptive system. Thus, in his new concept of the autonomic nervous system, Porges describes a continuum of different regulatory organismic states, which are connected to conditions of safety, threat, and mortal danger (Porges, 2010).

In Body Psychotherapeutic work with parents and children, we utilize an exact diagnosis of the body and behavior of both parents and child; this enables us to track and to evaluate continually the vegetative regulatory states in the course of the therapeutic process (Ogden, Minton, and Pain, 2010). By determining the regulatory mode of the body within the parent-child relationship in a situation where a parent is holding the screaming child, we can, for example, determine more specifically when the small window of tolerance that the parents have for contact with the child in this state is going to collapse and also what must be done to maintain the parents as adequate co-regulators of the baby.

## Three Levels of Parent-Child Body Psychotherapy

The form of Body Psychotherapeutic work done in Germany with parents and children is based on three fundamental principles:

1. Observing behavior
2. Focusing on mindfulness
3. Touching the body

The **first level** of therapeutic work with babies and parents consists of the nonjudgmental observation of the body language and expressive language of the relevant partner(s) in the interaction. In the context of "reading the baby," the work focuses mainly on ascertaining the behavioral and regulatory condition of the child. When does the baby refuse eye contact? How does it react to being touched in specific zones, areas, and segments of the body? Which activities trigger stress (e.g., when the baby is picked up abruptly and without warning; when the caregiver comes too close, too fast; etc.)? Is the baby capable of returning to a state of bodily relaxation after a few moments of stress? There is an art to reading the bodily signals of the baby, and it becomes an important source of information in determining whether the child is in a more receptive, open state, or in a more withdrawn, closed state.

When working with the parents during the initial phase of the therapeutic process, we explore the spectrum of their behavior in contact with their child. The focus of this behavior-oriented perspective is on the degree of sensitivity that the parents show in their responses to the child's body and behavioral reactions. Do the parents show a direct, or a delayed, response to signs of distress in the child? Are their responses appropriate to the respective developmental stage of the baby, or are they in length and intensity, overwhelming or indifferent and inappropriate for the welfare of the child?

When exploring the behavior of the parents, we concentrate on those critical moments in contact with the baby, especially when they reach the limits of their coping strategies. For example, how does a young mother react when continuously offering the breast is no longer enough to calm the agitation and crying of her three-week-old baby? What does she do exactly when the baby's screaming gets worse and her own experience of stress and disorientation increases? By observing the behavior of these parents—their breathing patterns, the way they use eye contact, and other forms of emotional expression—we can make initial assumptions about their characteristic stress and attachment patterns and therefore begin to develop suitable therapeutic procedures.

The **second level** of Body Psychotherapeutic work with parents and babies consists of supporting the parents in developing their connection to themselves and promoting their perceptive abilities. In this mindfulness-based approach, the parents focus their attention on observing and identifying their different bodily sensations in the various relational contexts with the child (e.g., the baby's screaming fit). While the insecure mother is cradling the child, she can now begin to feel the constriction in her abdomen, the increased agitation in her chest, and how her breathing flattens. In this approach, it is important to link specific parental behavior with corresponding reactive bodily states. As in the observation of behavior, establishing an accepting, nonjudgmental attitude in the mindful observation of the body is crucial for both parents and child (Harms, 2013; Levine and Kline, 2005; Weiss et al., 2010).

The **third level** of parent-infant Body Psychotherapy includes the application of various forms of bodily touch that we use to improve the capacity for contact and attachment of both parents and child. We can differentiate between two areas of bodywork here: on the one hand, the classical methods of skin and body stimulation (e.g., the "butterfly touch" massage of Eva Reich; see Wendelstadt, 2000), and the Biodynamic Massage of Gerda Boyesen (see Claussen, 2000), etc., that essentially focus on developing the ability of both parents and child to relax. These approaches use touching techniques on the child's body primarily as techniques to strengthen the parasympathetic, releasing function of the ANS in both parents and child, which also generate oxytocin in the parent (Unvas-Moberg, 2003). By supporting the relaxation and regulatory quality of the body, we can improve the capacity of the parents and the child for opening up and relating.

On the other hand, in the contemporary approach of parent-infant Body Psychotherapy, touch is also used as a medium to establish a state of secure and safe attachment (Harms, 2013; Renggli, 2013). Especially in working with the parents, touch is used to open up an inner state that makes intuitive contact with their baby easier. In this method, the use of touch to foster attachment is always combined with mindfulness techniques. The goal is not to achieve an externally induced relaxation, but rather to encourage a subjective awareness of the altered state of openness and capacity for relating that have been activated in the course of the attachment-facilitating bodywork.

## Parent Focus versus Infant Focus in Body Psychotherapy with Parents and Infants

We can differentiate modern concepts of integrative parent-infant Body Psychotherapy according to their focus in the work with parents and children. In the prenatal and perinatal baby therapies (Emerson, 1996, 2000; Schindler, 2011; Terry, 2006), direct bodywork and relational work with the baby play a major role. In a safe relational situation, babies are invited to recapitulate any of their unfinished pregnancy and birth experiences and express them through body language. In this baby-centered approach, the child sets the pace, and chooses and processes the various themes in therapy. The accompanying work with the parents cognitively integrates the developmental origin of the body and the expressive processes of the baby. The goal of this method is to enable the adult caregivers to reevaluate the child's expressive language with empathy (e.g., *"Now I can see how distressed my daughter was, as she was stuck in the last stage of birth. I see her desperate screaming fits in another light now"*).

In contrast, other parent-infant Body Psychotherapeutic methods approach the work from the outset from both sides, paying equal attention to both the parents and the baby (Diederichs and Jungclaussen, 2009; Harms, 2008, 2013). Body Psychotherapeutic breathing, touch, and awareness techniques are used with the parents to heighten their perceptiveness and sensitivity toward the child. In turn, the focus moves to the infant, especially if the baby changes from a relaxed condition to a fit of screaming, while the therapist explores the stress situation with the parents.

However, we find the strongest focus on the parents in those Body Psychotherapeutic approaches that combine body-based techniques of psychotherapy with specific video-analytical methods (Downing, 2003, 2006; Trautmann-Voigt and Moll, 2010). Here, microanalyses of video sequences are used to study how well the parents interactively match (or miss) the child's signals and the internal, psychosomatic, and experiential content that these interactions produce (Ruegg, 2007).

## Instruments of Parent-Infant Body Psychotherapy

### 1. Bodily Awareness and Stress Exploration

As mentioned, mindful bodily awareness is utilized in parent-infant Body Psychotherapy to explore the bodily and emotional experiences of the parents during specific attachment and regulation difficulties. By targeting particular body perceptions, the objective behavioral processes of the caregivers (e.g., hectically rocking the baby in their arms) can be connected to inner emotional and bodily states (Harms, 2008; Levine, 2010). We can show an insecure mother how, in contact with her baby, to concentrate on her inner bodily and organic sensations instead of on the mesmerized, questioning gaze of the child. We thereby connect the parents' specific coping strategies ("holding and rocking the baby") with inner bodily states ("tightness in the chest") and with affective aspects of their attachment experience with the child ("feelings of helplessness and estrangement").

In contrast to classical Neo-Reichian therapy, with its emphasis on the expression of repressed affective states, the attachment-based approaches of modern Body Psychotherapy focus on the perception and integration of unconscious and preconscious experiential content. As the parents learn to "somatically mark" and localize (Damasio, 2006) both positive and negative states of being with their child, they are then able to recognize much earlier when they are on the verge of losing the attachment, or the contact, and can work systematically to prevent this from happening.

Body perception, in itself, is also used as a tool to help develop a state of inner calmness and dual awareness on the parents. In the course of the therapeutic work, parents are trained to use guided attention to perceive their bodies as a source of inner information, and thus to care for and modulate the current contact between them and with their child. Together with behavior observation and the reading of the body, this internal "body scan" is one of the most important tools for the parents in reestablishing sensitivity and their capacity to relate with the child.

## 2. Respiration and Strengthening Attachment Bonds

Respiration has always played a central role in the spectrum of methods used by Body Psychotherapy. Originally, breathwork was used to soften the psychic defense system and to facilitate the expression of repressed feelings. In the framework of parent-infant Body Psychotherapy, breathwork is now utilized in various ways. We can differentiate among three basic areas:

### 2a. Encouraging the Ability of the Body to Relax

Parents are trained to shift their attention during the inspiratory phase to their abdomen while in contact with the baby. Modulating the breath in this way strengthens the parasympathetic division of the autonomic nervous system. Bodily relaxation—a general slowing down of external activity and an improved capacity for resonance and contact in the parents—is a direct result of this method. Respiration functions here as a means of influencing the deeper vegetative regulation of the body, so that the intuitive competence of the parents is more able to assert itself.

In his attachment-oriented concept, Harms (2000, 2008) emphasizes abdominal breathing, whereas other clinicians and authors (Diederichs and Jungclaussen, 2009; Wendelstadt, 2000) focus more on supporting the expiratory phase. Ultimately, both methods seem to function fairly well. Unlike expression-oriented methods of Body Psychotherapy, this work is less concerned with releasing repressed emotions and more about developing an inner frame of mind that facilitates parental contact with the child.

### 2b. Respiration as a Means of Guiding Attention

Breathing can also be used to guide the attention, mainly toward the inner life. The parents are trained to align the breathing with direct body perception. With the baby lying on the mother's belly, she tries to sense **from the inside** how, when she breathes in, her belly snuggles up to the child's body. The breathing helps the mother to focus her attention on the interior of her body. Even after only a few breaths, the mother who earlier was feeling very insecure has a softer face, her shoulders relax, and her respiratory movements are more flowing and connected. She is amazed and says, *"I suddenly notice how my belly is full of warmth, just as if a warm liquid was flowing through me. Now I feel intimate and close to my baby. It's as if the outer borders weren't there anymore."* The vagotonic effect of the respiration facilitates the inner perception of the body. It becomes easier for the client to identify and describe inner bodily and affective states.

### 2c. Respiration as an Early Warning System

When the parents have learned to observe their breathing continuously from the inside, it becomes somewhat of an early warning system for the imminent breakdown of their relational capacity. For Harms (2008, 2013), the inner connection to abdominal breathing is a parameter for the existence of an adequate receptivity and capacity for contact on the part of the child's caregivers. Losing the connective thread to breathing is a signal that the stress and alarm system of the organism is beginning to take over. So, when the parents are coping with their agitated and frantically screaming child, they can also ensure that they stay available as co-regulators for the baby, through repeatedly making contact with their own abdominal breathing.

One mother described it during a session in the crybaby clinic: *"When my baby's crying gets so strident and shrill, after a certain point I only function automatically. I rush around the room, sit on the gymnastic ball, moving around all the time. In this phase, I cease to exist, I'm not myself anymore. When I then concentrate on the breathing, I can get myself back down. I have a focus where I can concentrate in all this craziness with my baby. Through the breathing, I find a certain kind of safety and I start to sense myself again. Even if my child goes on crying, I don't feel so alone with it all."* For many parents, two things are important: on the one hand, they can integrate the abdominal breathing technique into their everyday life; on the other, they can do something in those difficult phases, they can experience self-efficacy, and they are in a position to influence their own relational capacity constructively.

## 3. Bodily Touch and Security

In contemporary parent-infant Body Psychotherapy, **bodily** touch is used to improve the parents' experience of security and bonding. In the model of "safety stations" (Harms, 2008), therapists collaborate with the parents to find a specific part of the child's body that, when touched, conveys an optimal feeling of safety. The search process is in itself an important exercise that encourages parental sensitivity. By actively trying out various areas to be touched, the clients not only identify safe and coherent places on their body, but also an inner state of secure attachment, which is then communicated both directly and through "emotional contagion" to the baby.

Another area where bodily touch can be effectively employed is in Body Psychotherapeutic work with trauma-burdened parents. Their own traumatized areas are often reactivated by the crying and agitated state of their baby, leading to temporary dissociative states. This intermittent state of panic or freezing interrupts the relational thread between parent and child. In these cases, the body and breathing techniques already discussed are of little practical use.

In this context, Harms (2013) discusses a further method whereby the therapist can utilize the established "safety station" to "log in" to the parental system. In practice, this means that, through contact with the "safety station," the therapist continuously monitors the inner situation of the client. If the contact thread grows "thinner" or "breaks off," this represents the weakening of the bond in two ways: first, it is a sign of the loss of the alignment between therapist and client; and second, it represents the weakening of the "umbilical-cord bond" and an instable connection between the parent and child. By continuously observing, naming, and evaluating the "umbilical-cord bond" in this process of dual awareness, the therapist can help to reveal and resolve any imminent breakdowns in contact with the child. Thus, through bodily touch, the therapist temporarily assumes the regulatory function of the overwrought parent. To put it another way: the professional helper becomes the bodyguard and auxiliary ego of the temporarily overwhelmed caregiver.

## 4. Strengthening the Bond through Imagination

One difficulty in parent-infant psychotherapy is that the problem with the child, as described by the parents, does not directly present itself in the treatment setting. This is especially true of regulatory disturbances in the child's sleeping patterns. It applies similarly to crying fits that occur in the evenings and then overwhelm the parents. It often happens that, while they are describing the stressful crying and sleep situations, the "real" baby is behaving perfectly quietly. In these cases, various approaches of parent-infant psychotherapy utilize imaginative techniques to gain access to those moments when parent and child are well bonded. Here, the visualizing of "successful" relational moments plays an important role. Parents are asked to imagine a lovely situation with their child and, at the same time, to observe the inner reactions in their bodies. Imagining the early-morning cuddling situation with the newborn baby leads to an "expansive" sensation in the chest, connected to a spreading feeling of happiness and contentment. Those parents who have almost permanently lost their relationship thread to their baby have particular difficulties in carrying out this exercise, even though there may still be "successful" and encouraging moments with their infant. Positive imagination weakens the hold of negative self-judgment and can introduce a more realistic reevaluation of the relationship to the child.

Imaginative techniques are also used to observe problematic situations from a "safe" distance in a "neutral" way. In the imagined situation, this method alternates continually between external observation of the parent's behavior and their body, and an exploration of their inner bodily and emotional experiences. While her four-month-old son is asleep at the breast, a mother imagines his screaming fits. In her imagination, she can recognize how the imagined body is expressing tension and distress. During the imagining of the situation, she can, through a change of the focus of attention, also perceive her present bodily and emotional state. As she watches the inner images, the mother can feel the constriction in her chest and her faltering breath. With the help of the therapist, she can connect the "now experience" of her body with the "evening stress" situation with the child.

Another possibility is to connect interventions on the body level with the imaginative work. The mother is asked to transfer her awareness to the quiet, expansive breathing movements of her abdomen. After she has felt how a state of warmth and relaxation has spread out in her body, she is asked to "take this up" into the imagination of the "stressful evening" situation when the baby is crying. The mother can now see how she is currently holding her baby in her arms in an attitude of inner communion and, at the same time, how relaxed and calm she looks. By combining imagination and bodily experience, the client develops a new perspective for dealing with problem situations in daily life (Harms, 2008).

## 5. The Baby as the Focal Point of Parent-Infant Body Psychotherapy

Next to the body-oriented consolidation of the sensitivity and relationship capacity of the parents, Body Psychotherapeutic work—directly with babies—shows the essential differences of this modality from, say, cognitive behavioral approaches to parent-infant psychotherapy. In order for the body and relational work with the child to become the focal point, it is necessary that the parents have sufficient capacity for their own self-connection and emotional regulation. Only this can ensure that, if regressive states are activated through the baby, the parents will not flounder in a maelstrom of dissociative and projective defenses against negative parts of their personalities.

## Various Methods of Baby-Oriented Body Psychotherapy

### Strengthening the Bond and Catharsis

Babies react quite differently when their parents develop stronger self-connection and capacity for contact. In one aspect, the easing of tension in the parents and their increased availability is "contagious" and positively affects the baby, who reacts to the heightened parental sense of safety by "letting go" when in contact with them and surrendering to the relaxation process.

In another variation, the baby responds to the improved receptiveness of the parents with strong affective-bodily abreactions and expressive processes. In other words, the return of the parents to a state of enhanced openness is the starting signal for the child—bodily—to express hitherto-repressed experiential material. In clinical work with parent-infant therapy, this often leads to a paradoxical situation: while the parents are feeling better and experiencing an increase in security, the baby is going through an intensive (re-experiencing) process in which the pain, helplessness, and existential distress of the bonding and developmental traumas can now be more easily expressed through its body language.

In parent-infant Body Psychotherapy, the above-mentioned methods of breathing, perception, and grounding work are used during the baby's massive crying processes to keep this window of optimal attentiveness and emotional availability open. At the same time, it is important to support continuously the parental capacity for self-connection for two reasons: on the one hand, the bodily attachment and the "staying put" of the parents creates a framework that allows the baby to recapitulate its feelings of internalized separation, birth, and pregnancy injuries in a securely bonded and contained environment.

On the other hand, maintaining that self-connection creates a security system for the parents so that, during the baby's screaming cycles, they are not overwhelmed by the "ghosts" and traumas of their own attachment biography. Preserving the inner thread of contact creates the basis for the baby to be recognized and mirrored with empathy in its reliving of feelings of helplessness, abandonment, and pain.

### The Recapitulation of Terror

As soon as the parents' co-regulation capacity is sufficiently developed, babies begin to come in contact with them and the therapist in order to "tell the story" of their pregnancy and birth. Prenatal baby therapists focus on specific bodily signals and expressive processes of the baby that provide an indication of the time, form, and content of the stress in the particular phases of pregnancy and birth.

Babies spontaneously relive, in the therapeutic birth experiences, those body positions that were connected to particularly high-stress experiences during the stages of their birth. They communicate, with body language, where and when it was "too much" for them and they were in real distress, but also what support they would have needed in order to complete the birth process themselves.

In baby-oriented process work, the therapist remains in constant dialogue with the child. The therapist "mirrors" the body language of the baby and translates it into a language that enables the parents to see the origin of the respective "problematic" behavior (e.g., the baby's uncontrollable and never-ending crying) from a different perspective and to experience it emotionally in a new way.

Due to space restrictions here, this can be only a brief description of baby-centered work in parent-infant Body Psychotherapy.

## Conclusion

Nowhere can the self-regulation of life be so vividly and directly experienced, and "health" understood so directly, as in psychotherapeutic work with babies and infants. Babies are masters of the present moment, of slowness, and of the essential encounter. Eva Reich, the daughter of Wilhelm Reich and a qualified pediatrician, wanted to make it a condition of training in Body Psychotherapy that all students should work for a while with babies, so as to gain a deep impression of their expressive language. Experiences gained in this sort of therapeutic work with babies create a new perspective on the people that we encounter as adults in psychotherapy. They give us an idea of the wounds that often originate in the earliest phase of human development, but they also provide a vision of the healthy, authentic self that exists in each of us.

## References

Boadella, D. (2008). *Wilhelm Reich: Pionier des neuen Denkens* [Wilhelm Reich: Pioneer of new thinking]. Darmstadt: Schirner.

Bowlby, J. (2010). *Frühe Bindung und kindliche Entwicklung* [Early attachment and child development]. Munich: Reinhardt.

Brisch, K. H. (2013). *Schwangerschaft und Geburt: Bindungspsychotherapie: Bindungsbasierte Beratung und Therapie* [Pregnancy and birth: Psychotherapy bond: Bond-based counseling and therapy]. Stuttgart: Klett-Cotta.

Brisch, K. H., & Hellbrügge, T. (2008). *Die Anfänge der Eltern-Kind-Bindung: Schwangerschaft, Geburt und Psychotherapie* [The beginnings of the parent-child bonding: Pregnancy, birth and psychotherapy]. Stuttgart: Klett-Cotta.

Cierpka, M., & Windaus, E. (Eds.). (2007). *Psychoanalytische Säugling-Kleinkind-Eltern-Psychotherapie:*

Konzepte–Leitlinien–Manuale [Psychoanalytic infant-toddler-parent psychotherapy: Concepts–Guidelines–Manuals]. Frankfurt: Brandes & Apsel.

Claussen, H. (2000). Biodynamische Arbeit mit Eltern und Babys– Theorie und Praxis von Babymassage in Gruppen [Biodynamic work with babies and parents – the theory and practice of baby massage in groups] In T. Harms (Ed.), *Auf die Welt gekommen: Die neuen Babytherapien* [Coming out into the world: The new baby therapies] Berlin: Leutner-Verlag.

Damasio, A. (2006). *Der Spinoza Effekt: Wie Gefühle unser Leben bestimmen* [The Spinoza effect: How emotions affect our life]. Berlin: List Taschenbuch.

Deyringer, M., Eckert, A., & Koch, K. (2008). *Bindung durch Berührung* [Bonding through touch]. Berlin: Leutner.

Diederichs, P., & Jungclaussen, I. (2009). Zwölf Jahre Berliner SchreiBabyAmbulanzen: eine Positionierung körperpsychotherapeutischer Krisenintervention und früher Hilfen [Twelve years of Berlin cry-baby clinics: A positioning Body Psychotherapeutic crisis intervention and early support]. In M. Thielen, *Körper–Gefühl–Denken* [Body–Feeling–Thinking]. Giessen: Psychosozial.

Dornes, M. (2011). *Der kompetente Säugling: Die präverbale Entwicklung des Menschen* [The competent infant: The pre-verbal human development]. Frankfurt: Fischer Taschenbuch.

Downing, G. (2003). Video Microanalyse Therapie: Einige Grundlagen und Prinzipien [Video Micro Analysis Therapy: Some basic concepts and principles]. In H. Scheuerer-Englisch, G. J. Suess, & W-K. Pfeifer (Eds.), *Wege zur Sicherheit: Bindungswissen in Diagnostik und Intervention* [Ways to security: Bonding knowledge in diagnosis and intervention]. Giessen: Psychosozial.

Downing, G. (2006). Frühkindlicher Affektaustausch und dessen Beziehung zum Körper [Early childhood emotional exchange and its relationship to the body]. In G. Marlock & H. Weiss (Eds.), *Handbuch der Körperpsychotherapie* [Handbook of Body Psychotherapy]. Stuttgart: Schattauer.

Emerson, W. (1996). *Collected works I: The treatment of birth trauma in infants and children*. Petaluma, CA: Emerson Training Seminars.

Emerson, W. (2000). *Collected works II: Pre- and Perinatal Regression Therapy*. Petaluma, CA: Emerson Training Seminars.

Harms, T. (Ed.). (2000). *Auf die Welt gekommen: Die neuen Babytherapien* [Coming into the world: The new baby therapies]. Berlin: Leutner.

Harms, T. (2008). *Emotionelle Erste Hilfe: Bindungsförderung, Krisenintervention, Eltern-Baby-Therapie* [Emotional First Aid: Attachment aid, crisis intervention, parent-baby therapy]. Berlin: Leutner.

Harms, T. (2013). Eltern-Baby-Körperpsychotherapie im Spannungsfeld von Trauma und Bindung [Parents-baby Body Psychotherapy at the interface between trauma and attachment]. In M. Thielen (Ed.), *Körper–Gruppe–Gesellschaft: Neue Entwicklung in der Körperpsychotherapie* [Body–group–society: New developments in Body Psychotherapy]. Giessen: Psychosozial.

Levine, P. (2010). *Sprache ohne Worte: Wie unser Körper Trauma verarbeitet und uns in die Balance zurückführt* [Language without words: How our body handles trauma and leads us back into balance]. Munich: Kösel.

Levine, P., & Kline, M. (2005). *Verwundete Kinderseelen heilen: Wie Kinder und Jugendliche traumatische Erlebnisse überwinden können* [Children heal wounded souls: How children and young people can overcome traumatic experiences]. Munich: Kösel.

Ogden, P., Minton, K., & Pain, C. (2010). *Trauma und Körper: Ein sensumotorischer orientierter psychotherapeutischer Ansatz* [Trauma and body: A sensorimotor approach to psychotherapy]. Paderborn: Junfermann.

Overly, R. C. (2005). *Bioenergetics: Theory and tools for everyone*. Asheville, NC: Gentle Bioenergetics Press.

Porges, S. (2010). *Die Polyvagal-Theorie: Emotion. Bindung. Kommunikation und ihre Entstehung* [The polyvagal theory: Emotions, attachment, communication and its development]. Paderborn: Junfermann.

Reich, E., & Zornansky, E. (1993). *Lebensenergie durch Sanfte Bioenergetik* [Life energy through Gentle Bioenergetics]. Munich: Kösel.

Reich, W. (1985). *Die Entdeckung des Orgons II: Der Krebs* [The discovery of orgone II: The cancer biopathy]. Frankfurt: Kiepenheuer & Witsch.

Reich, W. (1987). *Children of the future: On the prevention of sexual pathology*. New York: Farrar, Straus & Giroux.

Reich, W. (2010). *Die Entdeckung des Orgons I: Die Funktion des Orgasmus* [The discovery of orgone I: The function of the orgasm]. Cologne: KiWi Paperback.

Renggli, F. (2013). *Das goldene Tor zum Leben: Wie unser Trauma aus Geburt und Schwangerschaft ausheilen kann* [The golden gate to life: How to heal our trauma of childbirth and pregnancy]. Munich: Arkana.

Ruegg, J. C. (2007). *Gehirn, Psyche und Körper: Neurobiologie von Psychosomatik und Psychotherapie* [Brain, mind and body: Neurobiology of psychotherapy and psychosomatics]. Cologne: Schattauer.

Schindler, P. (Ed.). (2011). *Am Anfang des Lebens: Neue körperpsychotherapeutische Erkenntnisse über unsere frühesten Prägungen durch Schwangerschaft und Geburt* [At the beginning of life: New Body Psychotherapeutic insights about our earliest imprints through pregnancy and childbirth]. Basel, Switzerland: Schwabe.

Terry, K. (2006). Therapeutische Arbeit mit "Schreibabys" [Therapeutic work with "cry babies"]. In G. Marlock & H. Weiss (Eds.), *Handbuch der Körperpsychotherapie* [Handbook of Body Psychotherapy]. Stuttgart: Schattauer.

Thielen, M. (Ed.). (2009). *Körper–Gefühl–Denken: Körperpsychotherapie und Selbstregulation* [Body–feeling–thinking: Body Psychotherapy and self-regulation]. Giessen: Psychosozial.

Thielen, M. (Ed.). (2013). *Körper–Gruppe–Gesellschaft: Neue Entwicklungen in der Körperpsychotherapie* [Body–group–society: New developments in Body Psychotherapy]. Giessen: Psychosozial.

Trautmann-Voigt, S., & Moll, M. (2010). *Bindung in Bewegung: Konzept und Leitlinien für eine psychodynamisch fundierte Eltern-Säuglings-Kleinkind-Psychotherapie* [Attachment in movement: Concept and guidelines for a sound psychodynamic parent-infant-toddler psychotherapy]. Giessen: Psychosozial.

Unväs Moberg, K. (2003). *The Oxytocin Factor: Tapping the hormone of calm, love and healing.* Cambridge, MA: De Capo Press.

Ventling, C. D. (Ed.). (2001). *Childhood psychotherapy: A Bioenergetic approach.* Basel, Switzerland: Karger.

Waal, N. (1970). A special technique of psychotherapy with an autistic child. *Energy & Character, 1*(3), 34–43.

Weiss, H., Harrer, M. E., & Dietz, T. (2010). *Das Achtsamkeitsbuch: Grundlagen, Anwendungen, Übungen* [The mindfulness book: Fundamentals, applications, and exercises]. Stuttgart: Klett-Cotta.

Wendlestadt, S. (2000). Wege ins Leben – Bioenergetischer Kontakt, Quelle der emotionalen Entwicklung des Neugeborenen [Paths in life—bioenergeticcontact, source of emotional development of the newborn]. In T. Harms (Ed.), *Auf die Welt gekommen: Die neuen Babytherapien* [Coming out into the world: The new baby therapies] Berlin: Leutner-Verlag.

# 79
## A Return to the "Close Body"

*Child Somatic Psychotherapy*

**Nicole Gäbler, Germany**

**Translation by Siljoy Maurer and Carla Spannbauer**

**Nicole Gäbler** is a certified psychologist and psychological psychotherapist, and is in the rare and perhaps singularly unique position to have worked for many years in a psychosomatic clinic that enables both parents and children to simultaneously receive Body Psychotherapy. This method has allowed her to treat intensively the child in direct conjunction (for the most part) with the mother. Gäbler, a lecturer for clinical motor-therapy and a child/adolescent therapist, is also a certified Hakomi Therapist and is a member of the Hakomi Institute faculty.

In addition, Gäbler possesses educational knowledge of the French Psychomotor Therapy (Aucouturier), Gestalt Therapy, the Pesso Boyden System Psychomotor, and systemic couples and family therapy. She has a long-standing clinical experience with children, adolescents, and adults through her work in psychiatric and psychosomatic hospitals, as well as in her own private practice that was established in 1995.

This chapter clearly demonstrates how Body Psychotherapeutic methods are also applicable for children. At the same time, it sheds light on the more basic question of just how very present the bodily dimension is in child development, and how that is a decisive factor in the development of the self.

## The Growing Self

If we were to observe the world from a child's perspective, we would notice that the child accesses the world through the body and its movements. Until the age of about seven to eight years, the child senses and grasps the world mainly through its body, with the "close-body" senses (tactile, deep sensibility, balance) and the "far-body" senses (smell, taste, sight, hearing). The child perceives the world physically and mentally through its senses; things and objects are experienced related to what the body feels. The child takes an active part in the world through its body and movements. This entire developmental process is also a complex learning process—a multilayered "playing together" of neurological maturing, self-regulation, and processes of interaction, as well as psychological development. The dynamics and contacts are established through the inner and outer movements of the child, and this factor is decisive for the establishment of the child's sense of identity.

The dialogue between the inner and outer world, between the inner and outer movements, is determined by the quality of the child's individual activities, which are oriented around its basic needs, and are based on the quality of the primary relationship. The child's neurological and psychic structures are formed through a multitude of experiential possibilities, and through activities that include play and that are physical and movement-oriented; the ability to plan, organize, and direct are also developed. "The capacity to properly order the sensory impressions, to process them and to use them in a sensible fashion" is defined by the American psychologist and occupational therapist A. J. Ayres (Ayres, 1984; Fisher et al., 1998, p. 4) as "the process of sensory integration." This is a very important criterion for sensory-motor and cognitive learning. Ayres found that a relatively small imbalance in the child's sensory integration can lead to a considerable impairment and disturbance in childhood development. In this respect, she is convinced that the basic order—that is to say, the basic structure of the central nervous system—depends on the deeper-lying, sensory impressions that are unconsciously processed in the brainstem. The optical and acoustical sensory impressions are essentially built on these basic senses. Generally, disturbances in the processing that occur in the brainstem can then spread to the other parts of the brain. This can lead to a learning problem, which can occur in spite of a normal intelligence level and the brain's compensatory abilities. That means if there are sufficient possibilities for the child to experience the "close-body" senses, and if these senses are addressed individually—through internalized relationships with others, brought into interaction over and over again—only then will the developmental process of the self unfold in its healthiest dynamic.

Developmental Psychology and recent findings in newborn child research indicate that what is learned will be held fast in the body-affective patterns and will be repeatedly formed and imprinted through actual interactions. These affecto-motor patterns form the early "representations of self and of the other" and are based on the experience of early childhood relationships (Downing, 1996, p. 131; Stern, 1992).

Thus, the development of the ego (body image and self-perception) is dependent on a continuous reassuring input from all the senses, on sensory integration, and on the resulting dialogue with the child's environment. Damasio, an important neuro-psychologist, designates this feeling of identity as the "sense of one's self," and he describes the development of consciousness. According to him, the sense of the self and the "nuclear self" have a biological predecessor, the so-called "proto-self," which continuously represents all bodily functions necessary for survival. In addition, it forms the basis—i.e., the origin—of the ego. The "sense of self"—that is to say, the "nuclear self"—combined with the autobiographical self—is not only necessary for the process of recognition but, in reverse, continually influences the biological processes, the representations of the organism, and the "proto-self" (Damasio, 2002).

The picture that one has of oneself, or our self-representation, is thus established from our physical perception and is a reflection of our body image (Aron and Anderson, 1998, p. 19). It was clear for Winnicott (1949) that, in early childhood, these body perceptions are strongly influenced by the quality of the "holding" and "handling" of the caregivers (the "holding environment"), that our self is therefore to be viewed—first and foremost—as a "body self," being reflected through the holding and handling of others: "our self in an inter-subjective body self" (for comparison, see Aron and Anderson, 1998).

## Disturbances in Somatic Self-Development

This knowledge demonstrates the importance and basic meaning of the Body Psychotherapeutic work, which can be observed in psychotherapists` work with children in psychosomatic clinics and in private practices.

Children who come into the psychological practice have behavioral and school problems, often also have problems relating to and perceiving reality, and are often movement impaired. There are also children with ADD; children with psychosomatic complaints, such as headaches and/or stomach pain, sleeping and/or eating problems; and children who are already experiencing grave personality disorders. Some are restricted in their motor activities and in their emotional expression: they retreat into a fantasy world, where they keep their suffering to themselves. Such children are hyperactive, impulsive, and overly fixated on the repetition of certain movement games and symbolic play. Through their past story of suffering, they hold their environment in check, often without showing any expression or emotion of their own. These children are psychologically and physically unbalanced, and their deficits and needs almost always have a strong bodily component (Bovensiepen et al., 2002).

## A Case Example: Christoph

A single working mother comes with her eight-year-old son, asking for help: she feels overwhelmed in dealing with Christoph, who demands too much attention, does not follow rules, shows a lack of respect, and is aggressive toward her. Christoph would scream at her, without any reason, insult, and hit her. At school, he would have concentration problems and would be easily distracted; e.g., his daydreams would often prohibit him from finishing his schoolwork. In his contact with other schoolchildren, he would seek fights, react with aggression, and demonstrate a low tolerance of frustration. He would take personally even the smallest jostle, and he would show strong physical reactions. His parents had been divorced for three years, and Christoph had good and regular contact with his father. During their period of separation, the mother had already sought advice from a child/adolescent psychological practice, where in-depth diagnostics established that Christoph had a typical childhood emotional disturbance and ADD, against the background of a disturbed inner-family communication.

Almost all children in our Western culture—like Christoph, in this example—are somewhat insecure in their fundamental sense of self, their ability to act, their sense of autonomy, and their relational experiences. Their perception of their own internal conditions (the processes regarding their self and "proto-self"), as well as the actual assessment of these, are often diffuse and foggy. In the innermost core of their affective experiences, they do not discriminate between "what belongs to me," "who I am," and "what belongs to others." There is often a disturbance in their self-evaluation and self-perception. Their body senses are either hypersensitive or show a lack of sensitivity. They have difficulty perceiving and structuring themselves, as well as having some difficulties entering into relationships with others. They often encounter an environment in their lives that does not properly understand their signals and psycho-motor expressions, and that is frequently unwilling to accommodate or change to meet the child's needs. The children therefore become increasingly frustrated, unmotivated, disturbed, and lonely. If this persists, they feel pushed to the edge, left alone with all their destructive drives and overwhelming anxieties. They can become violent, depressive, and too unmotivated to assimilate the world of knowledge (Aucouturier and Lapierre, 1995; Aucouturier, 2002).

**The First Hours with Christoph**

In the first free play and movement situations, Christoph arranges blocks and balls of different sizes around the room. With great strength and persistence, Christoph circles these on his skateboard, or repeatedly kicks the balls haphazardly around the room. He shows great enthusiasm when the balls crash into each other, or when they hit me, and also when our simultaneously hit balls collide. Through my active participation, a dialogue begins about the activity, which I comment on verbally and with empathic interaction. This brings about a sense of togetherness (a "one-with-anotherness"). In addition to the games of catch that follow, Christoph repeatedly wants to be pulled through the room and flung against the balls and the built-up foam-rubber mats. At this point, it can be observed that Christoph often loses his balance and falls from the skateboard. It takes great effort for him to adjust to the fast and furious directional changes, and his body seems very tense, as well as being active. Due to his deficient self-regulation, as related to his lack of muscle tone (caused by a hyposensitivity of the deep sensitivity and the vestibular system of perception), Christoph's sense of self and thus his feeling about himself is quite limited and undifferentiated.

During the play session, Christoph develops the idea of building a spaceship to take off and land at will, enabling him to have a view of the whole world. So, we turn a trampoline upside down and put it on four skateboards, then clothe it with many blankets, pillows, and foam-rubber parts. We use sticks, ropes, and a large blanket to build a roof. Christoph climbs in the narrow space inside and wants me to pull him through the room and hurl the spaceship against the foam-rubber mats, which are leaned up against the walls. During this interaction, I give a empathetic running observational commentary on his activity while remaining oriented to the sensory-motor needs of Christoph (which means being oriented as to how strong certain stimuli need to be for his optimum sensory integration/self-regulation). I remain open to what can develop, and accompany the results with empathy. For example, I ask Christoph how he is feeling after crashing into the wall, whether he is hurt. I make sure to show concern by inquiring about and checking on his physical intactness. After multiple repetitions, Christoph becomes more peaceful and speaks less; he becomes more introverted, relaxed, and momentarily satisfied in his being. This is a palpable moment of wellness and satisfaction, an arrival and growing awareness of the actual self on a deep somatic level.

His tense, and often overwhelming, family situation seemingly puts Christoph under pressure. His restlessness and lack of concentration are, on the one hand, an expression of a lack of self-regulation on the sensory level; on the other hand, it is certainly an expression of inner tension. The wish to be autonomous and independent from his parents (especially from his mother) contrasts with his need for security and parental care. In this respect, Christoph experiences no clear-cut developmental orientation for his process of individualization.

## Play, Movement, and Experience

Children come to the therapy sessions seeking strong sensory-motor stimuli and strong affective ties. They want to be repeatedly flung around on their skateboards, or to be swung as much as possible, or shaken in wild, stormlike movements in the hammock. They jump from high self-constructed towers and love to fall into soft pillows. They hide, and then want to be found again. They roll themselves up in blankets, or build themselves narrow, dark houses, which can be understood as the need to feel their boundaries and to experience a moment of relaxation and safe rest. Through their "close-body" psycho-motor dialogue, they begin to relate their individual story of suffering.

Bernard Aucouturier, one of the most important representatives of the psychodynamic understanding of childhood motor activity, assumes from his own psycho-motor practice that, for many children, symbolic play in therapy is not far-reaching enough to alleviate tensions and undo fixations (Bortel and Esser, 1995). Achieving authentic representations is possible only when deep-set emotions and tensions can be mobilized and then set free through body-oriented experiences.

Aucouturier believes that the loss of one's union with the mother creates an archetypical anxiety that is present in all humans. He designates this archaic fear as the "angst of the loss of one's body" (Aucouturier, 2002). Examples of such archaic fears are the fear of dissolving, the fear of being divided up or spread around, the fear of losing the body's skin covering, the fear of being chopped into pieces, and also the fear of falling (Esser, 2000). These are representations of the first experiences that the child has with relating to others—e.g., to food intake, or to the experiences of being carried, held, cared for, or cuddled—or not. These experiences are limited to the body shell, because in this early stage of life, mental representations are not yet possible. Such archaic fears are stored as subconscious images pertaining to the body—even before the development of speech—and form the "subconscious memory of the body" (Aucouturier, 1989).

Aucouturier shows in his research, time and again, that the basic themes of the human relationship are the longing to merge, autonomy, aggression, and identity. These are all originally bound in body processes, and are later transported to the mental and the cognitive level. Children repeat their archetypical fears in play; thus, they release tensions and thereby reduce (i.e., compensate for) their fears. Through these "emotional-tonic games" and also "games of fundamental reassurance," as Aucouturier names them (hiding/reappearing, devouring/being devoured, filling/emptying, destroying/rebuilding, catching/being caught, among others), a deeper dimension of the self can be worked through and bonded affects can be set free (Esser, 2002).

Aucouturier understands the movement behavior of the child to be the expression of its early affective-emotional history. The pleasurable and the unpleasant experiences that the child has had in life, especially in the first relationship with its mother, are imprinted in the body, in its motor activity, and in the muscle tone, among other areas. These ever-present experiences are imprinted in the body of the child, and seek their expression through the body in psycho-motor skills. They influence and shape—possibly also destabilize—the being, the actions, feelings, and thinking in all later phases of life (Bortel, 2001).

Drawing from his clinical observations and practical experience with children, from age three months to nine years, Aucouturier explored the structural process of the holistic conception of the "self" body as being the first step in the identity development of the child.

> The ability to act and communicate is based on a successful exchange between mother and child: only in interaction does a movement become a meaningful gesture; only in interaction does behavior take on meaning. (Esser, 2000, p. 24)

Aucouturier sees the child's behavior as being a representation of the "other," as a representation of dealing with the "other," which is deeply imprinted in the subconscious of the child.

## A Sustainable Relationship

The mutual process of change, in terms of communication between mother and child—this joyfully experienced interaction of "I can cause something to happen" and "My actions have an effect on the inner and outer world" (see Esser, 2000)—is existentially necessary for the physical relationship with the mother to be lived out satisfactorily and to be internalized. This is vital for the child, in order to be able to move out and beyond direct physical contact with the mother, to integrate symbolic forms of communication, and to increasingly develop the self. In play and in activity, the child represents the internalized oneness with the mother; the child keeps seeking the successfully or inadequately experienced "oneness." Children with psycho-motor disturbances lack the internal dynamic to find the lost "oneness." They remain captured in their movement, as do hyperactive children. Their emotions are repressed, they do not form their own representations, they have little capacity for relationships, and they have great problems overcoming their fears (Esser, 2000). These children remain subconsciously fixated on the primary relationship: the integration of the sensory-motor and mental processes fails. To ensure the success of a therapeutic process, a "sustainable relationship" is imperative.

Being with the child, and acting in a mutual "emotional tonic resonance," as described by Aucouturier (Bortel, 2001)—in which the child can develop a feeling of security, become aware of its own self (proto-self), and confirm and develop this own self (nuclear self) in all its options—for many children means the first step into a new dynamic of living and acting. That explains why therapeutic attempts on the behavioral level have a short-term regulatory effect on the child's behavior, but in the long run cannot successfully treat the surmised causes that occurred in the early bonding development. The child needs the physical and emotional presence of another person—i.e., that of the therapist. Thus, when our own self is a physical self, then it follows that our relational experiences are mainly physical experiences (Aron and Anderson, 1998, p. 46).

This was also true for Christoph. As can be concluded from his biography, early developmental communication problems arose due to sensory imbalances regarding his self-regulation and a lack of mother-child interactions. Communication problems, aggravated by the parents' separation, developed into various behavioral symptoms. As a result of his limited self-perception, many of Christoph's experiences were with a reduced differentiation of his own self. Despite his high intelligence, Christoph's restricted ability to act constantly exposed him to overly demanding situations, which he compensated for by clownery, through refusal, or through his cognitive abilities. Going back to the first sessions with Christoph, sensory self-regulation is motivated through strong stimuli to the "close-body" senses. His feelings about himself, and about others, are perceived and interpreted more clearly this way, which establishes greater relaxation, well-being, and security on the somatic level, which is the basis of the proto-self. As a result, the ego (i.e., the nuclear self) can develop more specifically, or even be restructured. Christoph becomes quieter and more attentive to his psycho-motor skills, willing and curious to further shape his actions and thoughts, as well as being able to confront his insecurities and fears.

## The Activity Room

Body-Oriented Psychotherapy offers a wide variety of opportunities for children and adolescents to give expression to their abilities and/or deficits. In addition to the use of role-playing and storytelling, playing with hand puppets, and the use of kneading and drawing materials, the activity (therapy) room is equipped with such materials as foam-rubber cubes, trampolines, skateboards, hammocks, climbing and swinging equipment, cloth scarves, blankets, ropes, balls, etc. All this presents the child with a whole gamut of possibilities for movement and perception. The child thus has the time to experiment with its body, experiencing needs and limitations. The child is also given the opportunity to feel competence in the area of its emotional "close-body" dialogue, making clear how important influences are in the development of the self and the self-consciousness of the child. By swinging, spinning around, falling, climbing, and jumping, the child experiences tension/relaxation and balance/imbalance; through this, its "close-body" senses become activated (balance, deep sensitivity, and surface sensitivity), which are closely connected to the deep emotional past experiences of the child. The "close-body" dialogue, especially with a female therapist, is reminiscent of the early mother-child relationship and thereby allows thematic material and problems to arise, such as separation/individuation, presence/absence, appearance/disappearance, holding on/letting go, being emptied/being filled. These are all symbolically expressed through the child's play.

The awakened and remembered emotions and experiences are deepened and worked through in symbolic play, so that new and healing experiences can be made and integrated. New experiences can cause organic changes in the brain and in the cellular structure if the exact needs of the child are met. Indispensable for this process are the development of the physical prerequisites and of the organism's self-regulation, as well as therapeutic intervention (Roth, 1997, 2001). The subconscious basic concepts (Kurtz, 2002) can be changed; and new, individual freedoms for social interactions become possible.

Through the inclusion of "close-body" senses in psychotherapy with children, new knowledge is won that is relevant for the psychological development of the child, pertaining to the naturally occurring needs of children. The elements of the "proto-self" and the "nuclear self" are learned, assessed, and integrated through this experience. Based on recent neurobiological findings, the incorporation of the body in child therapy is indispensable.

## Society and Its Relationship to the Child's Body

In today's society, the role of the body is culturally neglected, especially in communications with children. The importance of the "close-body" senses is simply not adequately taken into consideration and addressed. The "far-body" senses are often overstimulated (through TV, computers, iPads, tablets, cell phones, etc.), and thus the gap between body and mind continues to grow.

Children today exist in an impoverished life situation. As a result, they are lacking motor, emotional, bonding-establishing, calm, and sustaining contacts and interactions (Hurrelmann, 1982). If their surrounding world is not willing or able to change, then the children's self-development and their ability to act and cause an effect will further decrease.

The individual, instinctive, intuitive sensation—that is, the perception of one's own self—is strengthened through the "close-body" senses. This enables the child to take steps into new dynamics of living and acting. "A return to the 'close-body' senses" means to do justice to the process of self-regulation, which is relevant for the child's development, and to the activation of the self-healing and self-forming powers, as well as to the development of the child's identity.

# References

Aron, L., & Anderson, F. S. (1998). *Relational perspectives on the body.* Hillsdale, NJ: Analytic Press.

Aucouturier, B. (1989). Vortrag in Bonn am 23.8.1989 [Lecture in Bonn, Germany, on Aug. 23, 1989] (Personal notes).

Aucouturier, B. (2002). Über Kinder, die leiden [About children who suffer]. *Praxis der Psychomotorik, 27(1), 32–34.*

Aucouturier, B., & Lapierre, A. (1995). *Symbolik der Bewegung [Symbolism of movement].* Munich: Ernst Reinhardt.

Ayres, A. J. (1984). *Bausteine der kindlichen Entwicklung [Building blocks of child development].* Berlin: Springer.

Bortel, D. (2001). Die psychomotorische Beobachtung in der psychomotorischen Praxis Aucouturier [Psychomotoric observation in Aucouturier's practice]. *Praxis der Psychomotorik, 26(3), 140–151.*

Bortel, D., & Esser, M. (1995). Grundlegende Intervention im psychomotorischen Ansatz von Aucouturier [Basic approaches to intervention in Aucouturier's psychomotoric method]. *Praxis der Psychomotorik, 20(1), 6–13.*

Bovensiepen, G., Hopf, H., & Molitor, G. (Eds.). (2002). *Unruhige und unaufmerksame Kinder [Restless and inattentive children].* Frankfurt: Brandes & Apsel.

Damasio, A. (2002). *Ich fühle, also bin ich [I feel, therefore I am].* Munich: List.

Downing, G. (1996). *Körper und Wort in der Psychotherapie [Body and word in psychotherapy].* Munich: Kösel.

Esser, M. (2000). *Beweg-Gründe: Psychomotorik nach B. Aucouturier [Grounded movement: Psycho-motorics according to B. Aucouturier].* Munich: E. Reinhardt.

Esser, M. (2002). Von Bruno bis heute [von Bruno today]. *Praxis der Psychomotorik, 25(2), 84–86.*

Fisher, A. G., Murray, E. A., & Bundy, A. C. (1998). *Sensorische Integrationstherapie: Theorie und Praxis [Sensory Integration: Theory and practice].* Berlin: Springer.

Hurrelmann, K. (1982/1994). Das Schwinden der Sinne: Fernsehfilm [The disappearance of the senses: TV movie]. In *Mototherapie: Im Verein zur Förderung von Bewegung und Spiel* [Movement Therapy: The Association for the Advancement of Movement and Play]. Münsteraner Schriften zur Körperkultur, Band 22, LIT [Munich Writings on Physical Culture, Volume 22, LIT].

Kurtz, R. (2002). *Hakomi: Eine Körperorientierte Psychotherapie [Hakomi: A Body-Oriented Psychotherapy].* Munich: Kösel.

Roth, G. (1997). *Das Gehirn und seine Wirklichkeit [The brain and its reality].* Frankfurt: Suhrkamp.

Roth, G. (2001). *Fühlen, Denken, Handeln [Feeling, thinking, acting].* Frankfurt: Suhrkamp.

Stern, D. N. (1992). *Die Lebenserfahrung des Säuglings [The world of the infant].* Stuttgart: Klett-Cotta.

Winnicott, D. W. (1949/1995). Mind and its relation to the psyche-soma. In D. W. Winnicott, *Through pediatrics to psychoanalysis: Collected papers* (pp. 243–255). New York: Basic Books.

# 80

## Subsymbolic Processing with an Alexithymic Client

**John May, United States**

**John May** is an accredited clinical psychologist with training in Psychodynamic Psychotherapy and the Radix school of Body Psychotherapy—one of the earlier approaches of Body Psychotherapy that came from Charles Kelley's work with Wilhelm Reich.

Since 1981, Dr. May worked as a Radix teacher in private practice. His particular interest lies in the question of ethics in psychotherapy. He has taught professional ethics at Webster University, St. Louis, and has published a book on this topic. He has also been an active participant in the ethics committees of the Radix Institute, the United States Association for Body Psychotherapy (USABP), and the Missouri Psychological Association.

Another focus of his work has been on the development of a scientific base for Body Psychotherapy. In this regard, Dr. May has made contributions through his own research, by publishing an overview of empirical research on Body Psychotherapy, and in being a member of the research committee of the USABP. He was the publisher of the Radix Institute journal and has authored a number of publications. He retired as a Body Psychotherapist in 2008.

Though many attempts have been made to describe the therapeutic process, recent theoretical models offered by the Process of Change Study Group (Stern et al., 1998) and by Wilma Bucci (1997, 2001, 2002) hold promise for describing both body-oriented processes and more traditional verbal ones. The following vignette and discussion focus on showing how a Body-Oriented Therapeutic process and these theories illuminate each other.

### Clinical Material

JL, a white male in his mid-forties, consulted me because he was experiencing bouts of crying that would come upon him unanticipated and at unpredictable times. He was unaware of any reason for the crying, and was unable to connect it to any meaning or words. It quickly became clear that he had no awareness of an inner life of any sort, was subclinically depressed, and suffered from a variety of somatic problems/experiences that were reactive to his unknown inner state. Reich understood problems experiencing and expressing feeling to be related to the muscular and character armor (Reich, 1945/1972). In contrast, the psychoanalytic approach has focused on the inability to represent emotion symbolically. The specific condition that JL experienced was given the name "alexithymia" by Sifneos and De M'Uzan: the word literally means "without words for feelings" (for a discussion of alexithymia, see Finell, 1997).

JL and I have worked together for several years, and he has made progress. He now recognizes somatic sensations and events that he was not aware of previously. He has learned that they sometimes indicate that he is sensing some sort of emotion, and, in many cases, he can directly experience the emotion. Connecting these experiences with symbolic content, either imagistic or verbal, remains a challenge, possible in some instances, not in others.

The vignette starts about twenty-five minutes into a session in which JL discussed an uncomfortable interaction with his wife. He had felt bossed around in front of his mother-in-law. An attack of colitis had followed. He discussed whether the colitis was a response to the interaction with his wife, then started to switch topics. As he did so, his voice seemed to quaver for a moment. Usually his vocalization had a dry, deadened quality. I drew his attention to this unusual vocalization and asked what had happened. He recognized that he felt angry with his wife. In switching topics, he was trying to put it aside and ignore it. As we recognized this dynamic, he felt something that he had difficulty articulating. He could not easily put words to it, but became aware of a movement that seemed to go with it. He leaned forward with his elbows on his knees, his head in his hands, and with his fingers covering his ears. In an attempt to feel what this posture was communicating, I imitated it. As JL saw me do that, he became aware of the posture as a despairing gesture that sought to block out the experience by covering his ears. The words "I don't want to hear that!" came to his mind.

For much of the session up to that point, his posture and affect had seemed to lack energy, to be collapsed and shut down. As he entered this experience, I became even more aware of it. He was hunched forward, his breathing was slow and shallow, and his shoulders were slumped. He seemed resigned to enduring the experience, keeping it out as best he could. Based on previous experience, I became concerned that, if I only continued to sit with him and empathize (quietly feel my way into his experience), he would not experience it as empathic attunement, and we might create an experience of emotional abandonment—like what he had experienced as a child. I wondered how I could help him. I considered several options, eventually deciding to intervene at the body level to counter the physical constriction I was observing. I invited him to lay backward over an exer-ball (a large, inflated plastic ball that people lie over for stretching and exercising).

He lay on his back, with the ball centered just below his shoulder blades, and I held his hands to support his arms. He spontaneously made an "Ahhhhh . . ." sound as he exhaled. I told him that the ball produced a stress position, and this stress would do all the work that needed to

be done. He needed to do nothing except to be aware of his body, especially where he was holding tension, and do what he could to let go. As he became aware of tensions in his body and found the mental "switches" that controlled the muscles, he relaxed bit by bit. As he did, a constriction during his exhale became more and more evident. It produced a constricted, wheezing sound in the "Ahhhhh . . ." noise that he was making. It was also in his diaphragm (and probably in the intercostal muscles of the rib cage), where it produced a jerky, spasmodic exhalation. I brought the constriction to JL's attention. I suggested that he let himself become more aware of the holding there, and when he was ready, to do what he could to let it go. As he did, his exhale slowly became smoother and more relaxed, and the "Ahhhhh . . ." sound became immediately clearer, louder, and less harsh in quality.

Within about fifteen seconds of this change, he began to experience jerks in his diaphragm, and these quickly developed into sobbing. He cried for a moment while still over the ball, and then the crying began to change. He became restless, and a holding-back quality reentered what he was doing. I asked where the holding was now. He indicated the side of his face and head. I put my hands on this area and rubbed very gently, and he began crying again. Then he began to bare his teeth, and his face contracted into a grimace. He began to make a hissing sound, which developed into something between a growl and a roar. The grimace transformed into a snarl. The mouth opened wide, the eyebrows were highly arched, the muscles of the cheekbones lifted high, and the tongue began protruding. As I watched this develop, I privately associated it to an image of Linda Blair growling and sticking out her tongue on the bed in *The Exorcist*. I have had this association before with this client; he was expressing a rage that felt almost demonic to me. There was also something about it that had a psychotic-type quality. I'm not saying he was either demonic or psychotic, but that whatever he was experiencing and expressing brought up those associations in me. At no time did he lose contact with his current surroundings, experience hallucinations or delusions, etc.

The episode ran its course, the emotional expression died away, JL's body softened and quieted, and he rolled down off the ball. The process described, from the odd vocalization to rolling off the exer-ball, took less than fifteen minutes. After giving him a few moments to quietly experience himself, we talked for another ten minutes. He had experienced the emotions and sensations of all that occurred, but had connected no images, thoughts, or words with them. We discussed the specific sensations that he had experienced, where in his body he felt them, and exactly how he felt them. As we talked, he still did not contact images or words to go with his experience. He noted, however, that he felt much better than before going over the ball. He was more relaxed, felt less despair, and was less burdened. His reports of his inner state matched my observation that his face looked softer, and his shoulders were not held as high as previously. We also discussed his feelings about me and about my suggestion that he lie over the exer-ball. He has at times experienced me as demanding and critical, and has associated me with intrusive figures from his past (insensitive athletic coaches, his critical parents, etc.). This time he had felt skeptical of lying over the exer-ball, but found the intervention useful, and noted with pleasure that he did not resent it.

The following week he reported a change. He seemed to experience his affects less as general tensions affecting areas of his body (e.g., the left side of his head and neck), and more as tensions in specific muscles in those areas (e.g., specific muscles in his neck). Although it was more difficult to describe to me, he reported a similar change in his direct awareness of his affects. Instead of a global feeling of anger, he experienced a more specific sense of anger at a specific thing.

## Discussion

### An Intersubjective Perspective

Early Reichian approaches understood the therapeutic relationship through concepts like transference and orgonotic contact. They saw "meaning" within a session as emerging from the client's physical and character structure, which was released by the therapeutic process (e.g., Reich, 1945/1972, 1942/1973; Baker, 1967; Lowen, 1958). Keleman (1986) outlined, but did not fully articulate, an evocative theory of "embodied transference," which attempted to use structural and characterological concepts to describe the relational emergence of meaning in a session along unconscious sensory-motor pathways of communication. More modern Body Psychotherapists provide beautiful and dramatic descriptions of relational processes in Body Psychotherapy (e.g., Cornell [see Chapter 45, "Entering the Relational Field in Body Psychotherapy"]; Downing, 1997; Pitzal, 1999; Totton, 1999). Their work tends to describe the therapeutic relationship as a particular type of space or field in which the client's blocked development is able to unfold.

Many body-oriented theories have also emphasized phases that are expected to occur in many, if not most, sessions. Reich set a tone for this with his "*orgasm formula*," describing the four phases of tension, charge, discharge, and relaxation (Reich, 1942/1973). Kelley (1998a) followed this lead, teaching that Radix Intensives should have a structure consisting of five phases: warm-up, pulsation and charging, transition, discharge, and follow-through. Even Downing (1997), who does so much to integrate the infant-observational literature into Body Psychotherapy, suggested that physical techniques alter respiratory patterns, leading to the phases of incubation, trembling, emotion, and larger movements.

In contrast, the Process of Change Study Group describes meaning in psychotherapy as developing out of the implicit interaction between therapist and client along (mostly) sensory-motor pathways. In this theory, meaning and structure self-organize (Thelen and Smith, 1996) out of factors relating as much to the therapist as to the client, and to the unique interaction between them. No two sessions would be expected to develop the same structure, nor, to an even greater extent, would the sessions of one therapist with different clients, or of one client with different therapists.

## The Emergence of Meaning

My session with JL unfolded through a succession of individual moments, most of which were not marked in a fully conscious manner by either JL or myself. The Process of Change Study Group calls such incompletely comprehended individual instants "*present moments.*" In any psychotherapy session, there is a continual succession of such present moments over time. Heller and Haynal (1997) found that more than a million bits of information are exchanged between therapist and client during a one-hour session, just considering facial expression. Various authors have emphasized the impossibility of being aware of each bit of information in a discrete fashion. Rather, it appears to be processed as a sensory-motor flow (Bullinger, 1997; Bucci, 1997; Beebe and Lachmann, 2002). This flow has been called "*moving along*" (Stern et al., 1998). In the vignette with JL, the original moving along consisted of our discussion of his interaction with his wife and the attack of colitis that followed. While I attended to the content of his narrative, I did not fully attend to all of the various sensory-motor communications that accompanied it. It is not really possible to do so. Rather, I processed the flow, the general tone of the moving along, which struck me as deadened and dry. Alexithymic clients often have an emotionally deadened quality, and often evoke similar feelings within the therapist.

Thus, when JL's voice quavered, it stood out from the preceding flow and entered the foreground of my awareness with sufficient force to cause me to inquire about it. This moment emerged from the flow as somehow more meaningful, more important. This is called a "*now moment*" (Ibid.). Note how this now moment emerged from the particular flow of moving along in this session. It was a function of the quality of JL's speech, the quality of my listening, the general therapeutic environment between us over time, and the specific flow of this session. Thus, a now moment self-organizes (Thelen and Smith, 1996) out of various parameters of a specific process, including both client and therapist.

## Moments of Possibility

A now moment is a moment of potential, of possibility. It is "lit up" affectively and subjectively. If both parties seize it, it can lead to a *moment of meeting,* a moment of heightened emotional interaction out of which the creation of meaning and therapeutic change are possible. These are moments of potential because, in Wilma Bucci's language (see below), they involve the activation of the subsymbolic elements of an emotion schema, leading to the possibility of either further understanding or change. JL did not seem to seize the now moment that emerged between us, but I did: I stopped him from changing the subject and asked him about the quaver in his voice. We began creating a moment of meeting, and meaning began to emerge: JL became aware of being angry with his wife, of trying to avoid it, and then of a feeling to which he could not give words, but that he could express through a posture. He put his elbows on his knees, his head in his hands, and covered his ears with his fingers.

JL's inability to describe his experience through words when he could embody it should be familiar to most Body-Oriented Psychotherapists. Theoretically, it draws attention to the various levels at which information can be processed. Here, "information" is being used as it is used in cognitive science, to indicate the "stuff" on which mental processing occurs, be it thought, sensation, image, etc. For JL to be able to express his experience verbally, he would have to have access to it along *verbal, symbolic* pathways, the most conscious, abstract, and symbolic of all types of information processing (Bucci, 1997). Alternatively he could have described his experience through metaphors, images, or memories that were somehow similar in feeling tone. This level of processing is the *nonverbal symbolic* level (Bucci, 1997). It makes use of material that has been sufficiently processed by the mind to be used for symbolic purposes, but that remains embedded in a specific sensory-motor pathway. JL did not have access to his inner experience at either of these levels, however. He had access to it only in subsymbolic pathways. In contrast to the previous two levels, the subsymbolic level of processing does not involve symbolic content. It involves flows of information embedded within sensory-motor systems that are processed not as discrete events, but as variations in the flow. Information is processed at this level (and at the other two levels as well) in many parts of the organism simultaneously, each in its own different way. Information processed at the sub-symbolic level, however, constitutes the vast majority of information processed by the organism (Ibid.).

**Mirroring**

JL had access to his emotional experience only at the sub-symbolic level at first. Feeling sufficiently comfortable to explore in this way, he enacted or embodied the experience by actually assuming the posture. I responded by mimicking his posture, assuming it myself. This is a ubiquitous Body Psychotherapeutic technique. Reich described its use in his chapter on the masochistic character structure (Reich, 1945/1972), using it in one instance as a confrontation of resistance, and in another as equivalent to an interpretation. I had two goals in using it with JL. I hoped that mimicking JL's posture would enhance my emotional connection to what he was experiencing. This purpose is consistent with the use of this technique as described by Keleman (1986), who called it "*somatic mirroring*"; by Chodorow (1991), who called it "*mirroring*"; and by Totton (2003), who called it "*emotional attunement.*"

By assuming JL's posture, I would connect to sub-symbolic sensory-motor schemas within myself that go with the posture. Bucci's theory says that these sub-symbolic elements should be associated with or connected to each other and to material at the nonverbal symbolic and verbal symbolic levels. This is called the "*referential process*" (Bucci, 1997, 2001). In this way, material in various widely distributed sub-symbolic pathways, plus material in the two other levels, is thought to be connected through associative links into a single, meaningful structure called a "*schema.*" An "*emotion schema,*" the particular kind of schema that JL was experiencing, is particularly powerfully connected to subsymbolic material from the internal viscera (interoception), from the joints and muscles (proprioception), and from motor pathways. This is what gives emotion its particular and distinctive quality. These pathways are called the "*emotional core*" (Bucci, 1997, 2001, 2002). JL's posture thus formed part of an emotion schema. However, in JL, the necessary connections to symbolic levels did not exist or were blocked. On the other hand, they might be open within me, allowing me to make fuller meaning of the posture.

The second reason that I imitated JL's posture was that I was aware that he would see me do so. In this way, it would constitute empathic *mirroring*. Totton describes this as amplifying the client's material, but I did not desire to amplify JL's experience. Rather, I sought to communicate my empathic attunement. This appears closer to Chodorow (1991) or Keleman (1986). On the other hand, Carl Rogers (1951) and Heinz Kohut (1984) are the two theorists most closely associated with the concept of mirroring. They defined it by the effect of communicating emotional attunement, and each described therapeutic models that emphasized it as a central therapeutic technique. Their approaches are primarily verbal, and I could have verbally mirrored the feelings that JL seemed to be experiencing. I elected to stay in subsymbolic sensory-motor pathways for two reasons. One is that as a Body-Oriented Psychotherapist, I am interested in this level of processing. It is the unique contribution of the body-oriented approach. Second, because JL was experiencing at the subsymbolic level, my response had the potential to be a better empathic match than would switching to a more symbolic level.

JL responded by becoming aware of his experience in a new way: he recognized it as "not wanting to hear that." Some might say his wife's bossing is what he didn't want to hear. Others might say his anger is what he wanted to avoid. And still others might point to the transference: my interventions are what he didn't want to hear. Perhaps all three are correct. They are different aspects of one emotion schema. The various elements of this emotion schema were initially not connected to each other with associative links. This *dissociation,* whether it involves the failure to make such connections in the first place, or the disconnection under stress of links that had been previously formed, is one of the major underlying problems that brings people into therapy (Bucci, 1997, 2001).

## Staying in Subsymbolic Pathways

To summarize the process of the vignette to this point: an emotionally pregnant moment of meeting was emerging out of our process of moving along: I had helped JL to become aware of the emotion he was experiencing. But what now? How could I help this emotionally deadened man give life to his experience?

In what followed, JL and I elected to continue working in the sub-symbolic domain: I invited him to lie with his back over the exercise ball, and he did so. The rationale for this specific intervention is complex, involving many factors, such as the type of person JL is, what he wants from his therapy experience, our previous experience together in similar situations, my clinical reading of the current situation, and how we were each feeling that day. Theoretically, one can understand this decision in two ways. First, Body Psychotherapists have traditionally emphasized the predominant role that sensory and motor activation play in psychological phenomena. This goes back at least as far as Reich (1945/1972), but finds elaborate expression in the work of modern Body Psychotherapists as well (e.g., Downing, 1997; Totton, 1999). This view is finding a place in more traditional neurophysiological and psychological approaches, too (e.g., LeDoux, 1996; Damasio, 1994; Schore, 1994; Tronick, 1989; Beebe and Lachmann, 2002). In Bucci's language, it forms the affective core (Bucci, 2001). If JL's experience was a psycho-physical one that depended on that particular physical posture, perhaps this intervention would open it to exploration or change. Second is the concept of the muscular armor, which was first described by Reich and which has been elaborated by many others (Reich, 1945/1972; Baker, 1967; Lowen, 1958; Kelley, 1975; Kurtz, 1990). If JL's posture involved a muscular constriction against underlying feelings, perhaps I could help him become aware of the constriction and release the defenses, making it possible for us to work with the underlying feelings.

Constriction in the breathing has been an interest of many authors in the field of Body Psychotherapy (e.g., Reich, 1945/1972; Lowen, 1958; Kelley, 1998b). They have described the various muscles involved and the role all of this has in blocking the expression and experience of emotion. The specific technique of laying a client backward with a support under the upper back was developed and described by Lowen (Lowen and Lowen, 1977). It enabled JL to "shine the spotlight" of his awareness on the muscles involved and to find the mental "switches" to release them. When he did so, the repressive barrier was lessened, and he made an enhanced connection to the subsymbolic level of the emotion schema. JL began crying, then snarling in rage. Earlier, I had asked what JL hadn't wanted to hear when he placed his hands over his ears, concluding that there were probably several things. This snarling rage, however, is clinically the first, the most immediate, and the most direct answer to that question. We had found a way to give this emotion schema life, though we did not yet understand its meaning.

JL's work over the exercise ball was primitive and unmodulated. Some readers may be frightened, concerned, or put off by such raw material. I have taken the vignette far enough along to indicate that JL did not experience this process as destructive or disturbing, but rather as helpful. The work activated subsymbolic elements of emotion schemas in me that produced symbolic associations: I saw it as demonic and psychotic-like, and an image from the movie *The Exorcist* popped into my mind. This association is another example of emotional communication occurring, as discussed above. To me, the unique focus of the body-oriented approach is not the use of subsymbolic sensory-motor pathways for knowing and experiencing by the therapist, but rather the emphasis on those pathways for processing, intervening, and interacting.

## The Effects of the Work

What effect did JL's experience over the exer-ball have within him? He felt better afterward, and looked softer, less tense. The "resetting" effect of catharsis has been noted by many theorists, but is probably most closely associated with the work of Wilhelm Reich, Alexander Lowen, and Charles Kelley. In addition, over time this type of process is felt to loosen or dissolve the muscular armor. Although the above vignette is too brief to testify to this issue, JL's work with me over time would support that theory.

His experience over the exercise ball did not immediately activate his referential process and connect to symbolic meaning within him. Perhaps the material was not yet sufficiently processed to form connections to symbolic parts of the emotion schema. Perhaps unresolved repression blocked potential connections. Or perhaps the material was too traumatic, and it inhibited brain mechanisms by which the referential process occurs (Rothschild, 2000). I thought the first possibility to be the most likely. Thus, as JL and I talked afterward, we discussed the specifics of his sensory-motor experience in detail. I view this as facilitating the "chunking" process that is required to develop raw sensory-motor information into prototypical images, which must occur before material can be worked into symbols (Bucci, 1997).

JL's report the following week supported this understanding. Both his sensory-motor experience and his direct emotional experience seemed to have been "chunked" into more discrete elements. As a result, both had become more refined and conscious. Bucci believes that the central work of psychotherapy involves the use of story and of images to encourage the referential process (Bucci, 1997, 2001). Although certainly useful, the telling of stories and images requires an already-existing connection to the verbal level. But that connection may not exist, especially in an alexithymic. I believe that the sensory-motor process of developing the flow of subsymbolic material into prototypical images is equally important. It is a process that is not systematically addressed in many types of psychotherapy. I believe it to be the unique contribution of a body-oriented approach.

A detailed discussion of our process over time, and how JL has and has not changed, is beyond the limits of this chapter. Let me simply say that this sort of process—emotional experience followed by discussion of the specific sensory-motor elements—has constituted a large and important part of our work. Most often it emerges directly out of JL's experience, although sometimes, as in this instance, I suggest we try something. As we process, sometimes I label or name emotions that he does not seem to recognize, but typically I listen as he explores the experience for himself. In Bucci's system (1997), the referential process is an intrinsic motivation; the organism will process information into more complex forms when given the opportunity. In this way, at first JL could report sensations and movements at only a very basic level. Over time, however, he recognized recurring patterns of experience and sensation involving particular regions of his body. Thus, he created what Bucci calls "*protosymbols*," information that has been chunked into recognizable units, but that remains embedded in the sensory-motor channels of the subsymbolic level. JL originally had no names for the patterns; but as he gained familiarity with them, he created names according to how he subjectively experienced them. Thus, he connected them to the symbolic, and even the verbal, levels. Simultaneously, he began to recognize relationships between these patterns of experience, and began to associate them with other events, behaviors, and experiences. He began recognizing the patterns as emotions with consensually defined names last of all, but when he did, it seemed to accelerate his growth process. None of these processes are completed. Sometimes we seem to cycle through them in session. Other times, our work seems to embody them all at once, though we cannot possibly pay full attention to them all at the same time.

Although more remains to be done, JL has grown emotionally—immensely. He has an increased ability to experience emotion in himself and to read it in others, and to use that experience as information to guide his daily interactions. This change has been much like the change he reported the following week—a gradual, incremental development over time. As a consequence, his relationship with his spouse is less conflictual and more cooperative than before. He has been able to feel himself capable of being a father, whereas before he refused to have children due to fears that he would not be an adequate parent. Indeed, he and his wife had their first child last year. His performance at work has improved, and he has gone to work for a more prestigious employer at an increased wage. Subjectively, he reports that his experience of life is richer. He tells me it is as if he had been seeing the world in tones of gray all his life, but now has discovered a whole new world of color.

# References

Baker, E. (1967). *Man in the trap: The causes of blocked sexual energy.* New York: Avon Books.

Beebe, B., & Lachmann, F. (2002). *Infant research and adult treatment: Co-constructing interactions.* Hillsdale, NJ: Analytic Press.

Bucci, W. (1997). *Psychoanalysis and cognitive science.* New York: Guilford Press.

Bucci, W. (2001). Pathways of emotional communication. *Psychoanalytic Inquiry, 21*(1), 40–70.

Bucci, W. (2002). The referential process, consciousness and the sense of self. *Psychoanalytic Inquiry, 22*(5), 766–802.

Bullinger, A. (1997). Sensorimotor function and its evolution. In J. Guimon (Ed.), *The body in psychotherapy.* Basel, Switzerland: Karger.

Chodorow, J. (1991). *Dance Therapy and Depth Psychology.* London: Routledge.

Damasio, A. (1994). *Descartes' error: Emotion, reason, and the human brain.* New York: Quill.

Downing, G. (1997). *Korper und Wort in Psychotherapie* [Body and word in psychotherapy]. Munich: Kösel.

Finell, J. S. (1997). Alexithymia and mind-body problems. In J. S. Finnell (Ed.), *Mind-body problems: Psychotherapy with psychosomatic disorders.* Northvale, NJ: Jason Aronson.

Heller, M., & Haynal, V. (1997). The doctor's face: A mirror of his patient's suicidal projects. In J. Guimon (Ed.), *The body in psychotherapy.* Basel, Switzerland: Karger.

Keleman, S. (1986). *Bonding: A somatic emotional approach to transference.* Berkeley, CA: Center Press.

Kelley, C. R. (1975). *Education in feeling and purpose.* Private publication.

Kelley, C. R. (1998a). *Seminar three: Structure of the Radix Intensive.* Radix Institute training program. Albuquerque, NM: Radix Institute.

Kelley, C. R. (1998b). *Seminar four: Pulsation and charge.* Radix Institute training program. Albuquerque, NM: Radix Institute.

Kohut, H. (1984). *How analysis cures.* Chicago: University of Chicago Press.

Kurtz, R. (1990). *Body-Centered Psychotherapy: The Hakomi Method.* Mendocino, CA: LifeRhythm.

LeDoux, J. (1996). *The emotional brain.* New York: Touchstone Press.

Lowen, A. (1958). *The language of the body.* New York: Grune & Stratton.

Lowen, A., & Lowen, L. (1977). *The vibrant way to health: A manual of bioenergetic exercises.* New York: Harper Colophon.

Pitzal, W. (1999). Contact and relationship in infant development and Body Psychotherapy. In L. Glenn & R. Muller-Echwefe (Eds.), *The Radix Reader.* Albuquerque, NM: Radix Institute.

Reich, W. (1942/1973). *The function of the orgasm.* New York: Farrar, Straus & Giroux.

Reich, W. (1945/1972). *Character Analysis,* 3rd Ed. New York: Simon & Schuster.

Rogers, C. (1951). *Client centered psychotherapy.* Boston: Houghton Mifflin.

Rothschild, B. (2000). *The body remembers: The psychophysiology of trauma and trauma treatment.* New York: W. W. Norton.

Schore, A. (1994). *Affect regulation and the origin of the self.* Mahwah, NJ: Lawrence Erlbaum.

Stern, D., Sander, L., Nahum, J., Harrison, A., Lyons-Ruth, K., Morgan, A., Bruschweiler-Stern, N., & Tronick, E. (1998). Non-interpretive mechanisms in psychoanalytic therapy: The "something more" than interpretation. *International Journal of Psychoanalysis, 79,* 903–921.

Thelen, E., & Smith, L. (1996). *A dynamic systems approach to the development of cognition and action.* Cambridge, MA: MIT Press.

Totton, N. (1999). *The water in the glass.* New York: Other Press.

Totton, N. (2003). *Body Psychotherapy: An introduction.* Maidenhead, UK: Open University Press.

Tronick, E. (1989). Emotions and emotional communication in infants. *American Psychologist, 44*(2), 112–119.

# 81

## A Somatic Approach to Couples Therapy

**Rob Fisher, United States**

**Rob Fisher**, MA, MFT, is a distinguished body-oriented couples therapist, a trainer of the Hakomi Institute, and an adjunct faculty member at John F. Kennedy University, Berkeley, California, and the California Institute of Integral Studies in San Francisco. He has been publishing a journal for couples therapy for many years, and in 2002 he published a book on body-oriented couples therapy (*Experiential Psychotherapy with Couples*), which applies Hakomi Experiential Psychology to psychotherapy with couples.

Fisher holds an MA in counseling psychology and is a licensed marriage and family therapist. He is a CAMFT certified supervisor. His training background includes Process-Oriented Psychotherapy (Mindell) and Integrative Body Psychotherapy (Rosenberg). He is the publisher of the *Couples Psychotherapy Newsletter,* and has given presentations on work with couples at many conferences.

A somatic approach to couples therapy can vastly expedite, deepen, and enliven the psychotherapeutic process. Much of the communication between intimate partners takes place on a nonverbal level (Brothers, 2001). This can be in a pleading look, an angry gesture, the rigidity or collapse of posture, or the slow turning toward, or away from, the other person—to name just a few examples. These somatic signals, which often take place just below the awareness of both partners, radically influence couples' interactions. If a therapist focuses only on the verbal content of a couple's dynamics and ignores the wealth of nonverbal interactions, the therapy will be limited, and much of the underlying communication will remain unaddressed. Additionally, each somatic element is an entry point, not only into the systemic dysfunction of the couple, but also into the characterological organization of each person in relation to the other. If, for instance, a man turns away from his wife after a harsh comment directed toward him, this movement is an outwardly observable indication of a whole, unseen, internal process that can be explored therapeutically. The effect on his wife of his turning away may be unspoken but still quite impactful. By mindfully bringing to consciousness, and then exploring, a simple somatic element such as this, the therapy can be expedited and underlying issues brought easily into a couple's awareness. This chapter is designed to present a number of practical approaches that make use of the body in couples therapy to explore the interactional and intrapsychic elements inherent in couples' relationships.

### Vignette

To provide a sense of this, the following is a condensed version of an actual session that illustrates some of these procedures:

> Jack: (speaking to the therapist): "We are here because Marie is very depressed and I believe that this is because I have failed in my role as her husband."
>
> Marie: "It is just that Jack spends so much of his time playing games on the computer. I feel so alone in our relationship."

In addition to the important content of their disclosure, the therapist notices that they are sitting very close to each other. Jack's arm is around Marie's shoulders, and she is sitting in such a way that one of her legs dangles over the top of his thigh. Their bodies form a perfect somatic representation of fusion.

> Therapist: "You (Jack) seem to feel responsible for her, is that true? And you (Marie) look a little bit frustrated and alone, huh?" (Connecting with their present experience.) "The two of you are sitting quite close together. Why don't we find out what it would be like if you sat even closer together."

The therapist here is treating their somatic signal as an important communication from their unconscious and uses it to connect with them below the surface of the words. He uses this as an opportunity to explore how they are organized around each other. The therapist then suggests that they pay close attention to what happens inside (emotionally) as they perform this simple action. Marie moves in closer toward him. Jack looks uncomfortable and burdened. The therapist contacts each of their internal states as follows:

> Therapist: "Marie, you like being close to Jack, huh? And Jack, you now seem to feel a bit uncomfortable?"

Marie nods while Jack says in a flat, resigned voice, *"It's OK."* The tone of his voice speaks much more loudly than his words. The therapist then suggests they try moving farther apart to see what this is like for them. This time, Jack disengages and moves to the corner of the couch. He breathes a big sigh of relief, which the therapist notices and says, *"Something just relaxed inside, huh?"* Marie looks at Jack forlornly with pleading eyes. Her facial expression has tremendous impact on her partner.

> Jack: (his energy changing from relief to deadness): "I feel like I should be close to her." (He drags himself back to her side and sighs deeply.)
>
> Therapist: "Jack, it looked like you really enjoyed the space for a moment, but then, when you looked at Marie, it seemed you started feeling guilty and obligated and moved back toward her. Did I observe correctly that you went from feeling a moment of freedom to feeling burdened?" (The therapist here is simply mirroring Jack's experience.)

As the session progressed, and as the result of this somatic intervention, Jack found out that his sense of obligation eroded his desire for connection with his wife. This drove him to seek autonomy by playing hours of computer games, unwittingly opening up, for Marie, an old wound of abandonment. By experimenting with the physical distance between them, Marie became aware of the depth of her feelings around abandonment, not only cognitively, but in an emotionally connected way as well. She realized that this drove her to reach out to him in increasingly intrusive ways—to which he responded with obligatory contact, followed by his continuing affair with the computer. This could all be seen by the initial fused relationship of their bodies, as well as the results of the little experiments that entailed moving closer or farther away from each other. This uncomplicated experiment allowed some of the subtle, transferential (Goldbart and Wallin, 1994, pp. 198–199), underlying feelings that drove their interaction to come into direct consciousness in a fashion that was more real to the clients than by simply talking about their interpersonal dynamic. Having feelings and beliefs in live experience also provided more immediate visceral information for each person.

## Rationale for the Use of Live Experience in Psychotherapy

There is a vast difference between a conversation and an experience. Conversation tends to be one step removed from the individual and their internal world. For instance, the actual taste of chocolate is exponentially more impactful than a conversation about it. Talking about sex is a very different experience from engaging in it. By working with the body and live, present-time experience, a therapist has the ability to explore at a level underneath conversational consciousness and to generate opportunities for substantive change to occur. When this is applied to couples therapy, as illustrated above, the therapist can intervene in a way that accesses more psychological material and is more alive and impactful than by simply working with the partners' communications or discussions about the issues (Fisher, 2002, pp. xv–xviii). Several chapters in this handbook extensively cover this history (see the contributions of G. Marlock, U. Geuter, D. H. Johnson, and R. Kurtz, in particular).

## The Importance of Nonverbal Communication

Much, if not most, of communication is nonverbal in nature. This is particularly clear in couples' interactions:

> For example, all Helen needs to do is squint her eyes a fraction of a centimeter and John will understand that she is angry—a familiar emotion from which he quietly recoils internally. Of course, his withdrawal, although silent, is not lost on Helen, who notices the slight tensing of his jaw muscles and the flatness of his tone when he speaks. This reminds her of her withdrawn father. The rest of their evening together is history (so to speak). (Satir, 1972, p. 60)

Although words have tremendous power between individuals, the continual nonverbal commentaries on the relationship have deep effects on each partner. In Body Psychotherapy, it is important, therefore, to notice, bring awareness to, and explore the effects of nonverbal types of communication, most of which takes place below conscious awareness and is symptomatic of unconscious characterological organization. These include, but are not limited to, elements such as pace, voice quality, muscular tension and relaxation, movement, increase or decrease in energy or presence, emotions, posture, gestures, longings, changes in breathing patterns, psychological expansion and contraction, etc. Here is an example of part of a session that utilizes some of these factors:

**Case 1:** Hal and Ruby were overly involved with his mother in a way that eroded their relationship. The mother called frequently to find out how the couple was doing and always made sure to say something of a poisonous nature to her only son about his new bride. His wife was incensed that he engaged in these conversations in which she was vilified. It did not take long for this sensitive subject to surface in therapy. No matter how much they discussed it, however, it never seemed to resolve. I thought that maybe we could go underneath the repetitive verbal sequences by approaching the problem somatically.

To shed more light on the subject, I asked them to sit on the floor and for him to draw a chalk circle around both of them that symbolized a boundary around their relationship. The purpose of this was to bring their psychological dynamic into the physical world, a process that often reveals hidden elements. I asked them both to study what occurred in their bodies as they felt the effect of the boundary drawn around the relationship. This is different from simply discussing their boundaries, in that they receive live information directly from their immediate somatic experiences rather than only cognitive information. I could see her face soften and relax as soon as the boundary appeared. She smiled briefly at him. I contacted the internal state that went with her smile by saying, *"Feels better, huh?"* She agreed. I asked her just to feel the sense of relief in her body and to make contact with Hal from this new place. I asked if her hands could have a conversation with his that spoke of her appreciation of the new boundary. They joined hands and by using touch, pressure, and stroking she was able to show him her gratefulness about this. He very much appreciated her new softness around this.

They were beginning to build a new dynamic around this issue; however, I could hear tentativeness in his voice that told me that he still felt worried. He couldn't quite identify the source of his anxiety. In order to further duplicate the relational dynamic and to obtain more visceral information and insight, I asked them both to become mindful of their somatic experience as we placed a teddy bear that symbolized his mother on the outside of the circle. By participating in this, he was able to viscerally feel the effect of having his mother outside of his immediate family. We had brought the dynamic into present-time reality instead of just discussing it. Psychotherapy became *in vivo* rather than *in vitro*. He could actively feel his sense of loyalty to his family, as well as to his mother. I put the mother/teddy bear into the circle along with him and his wife. He then started noticing a strong sense of intrusion. His hands came up in a pushing-away gesture. I asked him to notice what his hands wanted to do, what was the impulse. He felt that it was difficult to breathe with the teddy bear in the circle, and he had a feeling of wanting to push her out. We let him do it in a way that felt right to him, and again notice the effect on him, Ruby, and their relationship. He began to like the effect that having the boundary circle had on his wife (she softened toward him) and on himself (he could breathe), so we practiced having him keep his mother out in appropriate and compassionate ways. Without my suggesting it to him, he then went home, called his mother, and announced that he was no longer going to discuss his marital relationship with her. She was initially very upset about this change in the rules, but gradually adjusted.

## Cautionary Note

Before applying somatic interventions, or any type of intervention for that matter, a therapist must first have an accurate assessment; be able to establish a sense of safety, care, and understanding with his clients; and, because of the dramatic nature of experiential, body-inclusive approaches, be vigilant in a dedication to nonviolence in the therapeutic relationship. Being able to include both the systemic elements and the individual psychodynamic elements in assessment is quite helpful in generating appropriate interventions in couples therapy. Being able to join with clients on the level of their immediate experience (as opposed to the content of their words) is essential to the formation of the therapeutic container.

## Somatic Interventions with Couples

Therapy comes alive when the therapist works with live experience. One important way of accessing experience is through the body. Other ways involve carefully attending to the internal, moment-by-moment experiences of each individual as well as noticing the systemic, interactional patterns as they occur between the partners in present time. Below are some examples of how a therapist might use posture, pace, tensions, movement, and a variety of other experiential techniques to access core relational issues (Fisher, 2002, pp. 23–75). Also included are some examples of how working with present-time experience is an effective method to quickly access deep individual characterological issues. This list is far from exhaustive, but is designed to give the reader a flavor of some of the possibilities of using Body-Oriented Psychotherapy with couples.

### The Use of Mindfulness in Couples Psychotherapy: Acting In versus Acting Out

All of the interventions detailed below rely on each individual in a couple having some degree of observing ego. As most couples therapists have observed, this is not always the existing condition when a couple enters therapy. This is, in fact, one of the major hurdles in couples therapy. However, the couple's observing ego can be readily accessed by using mindfulness. The use of mindfulness in couples therapy helps clients to move from conflict and volatility toward self-exploration. Mindfulness is an ancient Buddhist practice that involves carefully turning one's attention toward one's inner world and observing, without trying to change or judge what one notices (Kurtz, 1992, pp. 67–69).

In psychology, the correlate of mindfulness is the "observing ego." One of the difficulties in couples psychotherapy is that couples lose a sense of self-observation as they become consumed with transferential feelings and beliefs. They then act toward each other in regressed, attacking, defensive, and extreme ways that result in alienation. By asking a person to take a moment to turn his or her attention inside, toward his or her experience, the "acting out" can be transformed into an opportunity to explore how each person is organized in relation to the other. Mindfulness can be directed toward the immediate experience in the body. This allows the information, history, and wisdom inherent in a person's posture, tensions, movements, and other somatic experiences to be brought into consciousness and then used to unlock repetitive, destructive couples patterns. Exponentially more information becomes available when the client is in a mindful state compared to being in ordinary conversational reality. In mindfulness, the client can pay close attention to the ever-changing flow of thoughts, feelings, sensations, images, and memories that are often unconscious in normal consciousness. Accomplishing this switch from outer-oriented blame to inner exploration is one of the keys to successful couples therapy. (For more information on mindfulness, see Chapter 38, "Consciousness, Awareness, Mindfulness" by Halko Weiss.)

Here is another example:

**Case 2:** Edward was complaining to Samantha about how she never listened to him. She was busy defending herself from his attack by pointing out all the times she had indeed listened to him—all the while becoming increasingly agitated. A behaviorally oriented therapist might teach her how to listen reflectively; a stucturalist might explore the cycle of blame and accusation; or a narrative therapist might empathize with her and then ask Edward for alternative stories of feeling listened to; etc. If one were to use the tool of mindfulness, however, the therapist could say to her, "Samantha, take a moment to go inside. You might want to close your eyes and just notice what is happening inside you as Edward complains to you. You can allow yourself to go underneath the impulse to correct his impressions and let yourself experience whatever feelings, thoughts, sensations, tensions, images, or memories might be arising." And to him: *"Edward, you might take a moment inside as well, letting yourself feel how upset and angry you are when it seems like Samantha is not listening to you. Stay with that feeling, and let's see what is familiar about it."* Notice that I am asking each person to enter into conversation with me, rather than with each other at this point, because, when in contact with each other, their reptilian brains are probably more activated than their neocortexes. This does not lead to much more than two lizards snapping and hissing at each other! I am asking them to enter into a state of self-observation to notice in the present moment, and to become curious about, the internal material that is activated by their partner's actions.

## Types of Somatic Interventions

### Pace and Movement

One key to recognizing characterological influences on a couple is the pace with which each person conducts him- or herself. Here is an example of this:

**Case 3:** Allison would burst into the therapy office followed slowly by Stanley. It was clear from the pace with which each of them walked, and the relationship between these two paces, that there was a problem between them created by their different relationships to time. Not surprisingly, the content of their conversation centered around her desire to get married right away and his reluctance. I suggested an experiment in which each of them could become more aware of how their pace affected their partner. After evoking mindfulness, I asked them both to stand up and for her to lead him around the room to see what happened in each of their experience. She jumped up, grabbed his hand, and started pulling him. He stood up slowly, taking his time, and reluctantly followed along while providing continual slight resistance. This was a physical representation of a psychological dynamic between them. This experiment helped them to viscerally become aware of how they created a relationship together in which she felt chronically frustrated by his reluctance, and he felt chronically resentful of her pushing. They could also see how the other partner's reaction made sense in light of their own actions. We went on to explore how he needed to slow down to preserve his sense of himself, and she needed to speed up because she held a deep belief that there was no time for her. These beliefs affected much of their lives. The clients were able to become aware of their models of the world that impacted their relationship. Then, through additional experiments around slowing down and speeding up, they developed more flexibility around the beliefs and began experimenting with different kinds of paces between them to see what could work better.

Simply by noticing and exploring the interface of their individual paces, we were able to focus on the intrapsychic issues and the system in which they had become entrenched.

## Tension

Attending to bodily tensions and relaxations can be very important in revealing underlying themes and missing experiences that each member of a couple hopes to have, but does not say verbally.

**Case 4:** Jim was still unsettled about a fight he had had with Marilyn the previous night. I asked him where that upset still lived in his body. He placed his hand on his chest above his heart. *"It's still tense in there,"* he said. When clients touch themselves, it is often representative of wanting to be touched by their partner. Based on this thought, I asked him if he would like Marilyn to place her hand there. He said emphatically, *"No!"* So much for my hypothesis! I asked him then if she could just send some good wishes to the place in his chest instead. This felt nourishing to him. I asked her if she might like to do this (already being fairly sure that she would like the sense of connection). She responded affirmatively. As she sent her compassion and generosity to this place in his chest, I suggested that he become mindful and notice what came up spontaneously. He started to shake and then to tear up. This place in his chest held a sense of injury about not feeling safe with his girlfriend and with the world in general. At the same time that he was experiencing the danger to his spirit with which he regularly lived, he also felt the comfort of finally having someone attend to it. As the minutes went by, the fear subsided and was replaced by a sense of warmth that he felt from her. He finally let her hand touch his chest. I asked him what her hand might say to his chest if it could speak. He said, *"I don't want to hurt you."* She repeated this out loud to him, and they sat quietly together feeling close to each other. These words began to deconstruct a limiting model of the world that he had developed, a basic conviction he held about life and other people.

## Posture

Noticing each person's posture and how it relates to the other person's can be an important assessment procedure that reveals characterological issues as well as indicates opportunities for intervention.

**Case 5:** After several sessions, I finally noticed that Allen held his chin slightly elevated whenever he spoke to his wife, Sylvia. I began to wonder how this affected their relationship. In order to explore this further, I asked them both to become mindful. While they were in this state, I asked Allen to allow his head to tilt down approximately two inches. At first it was difficult for him to do this. When he finally succeeded, Sylvia breathed a large sigh of relief. I contacted her about this by saying simply, *"Relieved, huh?"* She said, *"Yes, I feel like I finally have a partner."* Turning toward him, I asked what it was like for him with his chin level. He said on the one hand it was nice to be down on the earth, and on the other hand it felt really scary. This opened up an opportunity for us to explore Allen's disinclination to be in contact with other people whom he experienced as threatening and critical, and how he took refuge in superiority. It also began to address Sylvia's frustration with his "unavailability." Simply by having him tilt his chin downward, we were able to experientially access his fear of connection. Having it available in the moment made it possible to work with it without theories, interpretations, or guesses about its true nature.

## Couples Sculptures: A Picture Is Worth a Thousand Words

Virginia Satir would instruct families to create sculptural representations of the family's psychological structure by using their bodies. In the case of a blaming/placating/distracting system (Satir, 1972, p. 63), she might ask one person to stand up and point accusingly downward, as another kneeled at their feet looking upward with pleading eyes, and as their child ran around flapping her arms in an effort to distract the parents from their grim roles. Clearly, this is a somatic and experiential intervention. With couples, one can ask them to "generate their own sculptures" of the psychological places in which they become entranced, or, conversely, of their psychological resources that can be brought to bear on the issues at hand. This is different from "telling" them how to stand or to look, in that a sculpture can be created from their own psyches rather than from the therapist's. Here is an example:

**Case 6:** Peter and Jane were stuck. Peter wanted to leave the marriage, while Jane wanted to find a way to continue it. They both looked to me to adjudicate their dilemma. Instead of announcing a judgment, I asked them to each go inside themselves and imagine a fine sculpture that captured their feelings about the issue. The sculpture Jane came up with entailed Peter standing on the threshold of the office door, with one foot in the waiting room and one foot inside the office. In Jane's sculpture, she sat on the floor, desperately grabbing onto his remaining available ankle. I asked them to mindfully stay with this sculpture for a moment and to notice whatever came up for each of them. In the process of this, Peter could deeply feel and explore his ambivalence that prevented him from moving in either direction. Jane remembered that as a teenager, whenever she wanted to go out with her friends, her mother would try to keep her at home. She felt just like her mother in this situation, so she turned to her husband and said, *"I don't want to keep you here anymore."* New information became available as a result of this somatic intervention that might not have come to consciousness through normal conversation. The sculpture led to her childhood memory and the decision to not be like her mother.

### Supporting Client Activity

The therapist can ask a partner to take over an activity that their spouse is performing internally or externally for him- or herself:

**Case 7:** For instance, Mandy was quite angry at Sam. She began to express her feelings while patting herself slowly and gently on her upper chest. Instead of encouraging her to further communicate her feelings to her husband, who was becoming increasingly defensive, I asked her if she would like him to pat her in the way she was doing for herself. She agreed to try this, and he was relieved to no longer be the target of her emotional barrage. He sat on the couch behind her and gently patted her with exactly the pace, rhythm, and pressure as she had done for herself. She dissolved into tears. After twenty minutes, she turned to him and said to him, *"That's all I wanted from you."* By paying attention to how she was touching herself, and assuming that it was a communication to Sam, the therapist was able to intervene at a level that quickly resolved the issue and taught them a new approach to dealing with upset in their relationship.

### Facial Expressions

Facial expressions communicate loudly without words. Rolling one's eyes in contempt, relaxing the chin or tensing it to inhibit grief, narrowing the eyes in anger, furrowing the brow with worry, even holding the facial muscles still so that one's partner can't tell what is going on—all are consciously, or more commonly subliminally, noticed by one's partner. Failing to address these in psychotherapy exposes the therapist as inattentive or afraid to comment. Here is an example:

**Case 8:** I noticed that whenever Cindy dropped into a rage with Charles, she looked at the ground while she talked to him in a loud, biting, and aggressive tone. Curious about this, I asked her to carefully and slowly alternate between gazing at him directly and then looking at the ground, and to notice how each affected her emotional and relational state. As she explored the difference, she noticed that she was unable to hold the image of him as cruel and heartless when she looked at him directly, yet it was easy when she looked at the ground. This aroused her curiosity and observing ego. It gave us the opportunity to have her explore the history related to the negative projection while she looked at the ground, and then look up at him and separate who he actually was from the negative image. This allowed her ultimately to reown her projection and to speak to him in more collaborate and connecting ways that helped to enlist his compassion and to resolve the problem rather than exacerbating it.

**Gestures**

Gestures can also be very indicative:

**Case 9:** Toward the end of therapy, Laura sat on the couch about three feet away from Gavin. She had been very closed to him for a long time. As they talked, her hand slowly crept across the open space toward him. I hypothesized that this gesture was neither casual nor coincidental, but representative of an emerging closeness between them. It was not really my job to interpret it, but rather to use it as an opportunity for the couple to explore how they related. First, I simply commented on it: *"Your hand is moving toward him."* She replied, *"Yes, I feel closer to him, but not sure that I want to invest too heavily."* I said, *"How about I'll help hold your hand back, and you can see what that's like inside."* I was volunteering to help her hold herself back, so that she could become more aware of the part of her that wanted to connect. I was supporting, rather than opposing, her defense. After asking her specific permission, I held her arm back by gently holding onto her sleeve while she reached out to Gavin. As we worked, the intensity of her reach slowly increased. I asked her if there were words that went along with my holding her back. She said, *"Yeah, 'Never depend on a man again.'"* I asked her permission to take over that function as well, and had her teach me exactly how it sounded inside so that I could accurately duplicate her internal voice. I held her sleeve back and whispered this phrase to her. I explained to him what I was doing, so that he did not feel like I was taking an adversarial position to him. As we proceeded, she asked me to stop talking, as this no longer really represented what she wanted in her relationship with Gavin. This was the result of my helping her to hold a defensive position. By my doing this, her energy was able to cathart to a more libidinous part of herself. She also asked that I decrease the amount of strength holding her back, so that she could touch him. She was becoming more in touch with her desire to connect with him and more willing to take the associated risks. We ended the session with my having a light touch ("Just to remind her") on her sleeve while she snuggled with her friend.

## The Flow of the Process

The interventions cited above illustrate how one can assess somatically and experientially, and begin the process of exploring each person's psychodynamics as they interface with their partner's. There is an underlying assumption here that by staying with one's present experience, the natural intelligence and healing capabilities of the psyche will allow the process to unfold in a fashion that provides for increased flexibility in characterological and interactional patterns. The process generally starts with establishing safety, then joining the clients by mirroring their present-time experience. It then proceeds to finding a specific area of difficulty, asking the clients to become mindful, and performing a simple experiment—the results of which evoke underlying material. Staying with their experiences allows the next level of feelings, beliefs, and other organizing material to start to become clearer and more flexible. Awareness and understanding are increased between the partners, and they can begin to try new options for relating to each other and to their internal maps of relationship. Although few sessions follow this routine exactly and sequentially, this provides a basic model of how to proceed.

**Case 10:** For instance, when Jen had a certain tone of urgency in her voice, Barry would react angrily in an instant (the theme). To explore this, we simply had him become mindful, and, when he was ready, had her say something with this same kind of urgency (the experiment in mindfulness). He began to explore what happened inside when she spoke like this. It brought back feelings of his father's moral superiority and lack of consideration for Barry's sense of direction. This, of course, enraged Barry, who could not express it to his father without dire consequences. The feeling was transferred into the present with Jen. We continued to make room for the feelings, the words, and the impulses from the historical relationship (staying with the experience). As Barry was able to feel and express this, it became clear that he needed to slow things down with Jen so that there was room for his own sense of direction, and he needed to know from her if she valued his opinion (new options). He addressed this with her directly and tried out what it was like for her to let him know she was aligned with him in these issues.

## Conclusion

In summary, psychotherapy with couples can benefit greatly from active use of the tremendous storehouse of information available from the body. Physical posture, the tightening of facial muscles, or even a small gesture can be encoded with not only each individual's history and characterological organization, but also unconscious communication to their partner that heavily directs and influences the couple's interactional patterns. By accessing this kind of material, drawn from the body, a therapist can help bring into consciousness and modify deep patterns and unconscious organization that affect a couple's functioning.

## References

Brothers, B. J. (2001). *Couples and body therapy.* New York: Haworth Press.

Fisher, R. (2002). *Experiential Psychotherapy with couples: A guide for the creative pragmatist.* Phoenix, AZ: Zeig, Tucker & Theisen.

Goldbart, S., & Wallin, D. (1994). *Mapping the terrain of the heart.* Reading, MA: Addison Wesley.

Kurtz, R. (1992). *Body-Centered Psychotherapy: The Hakomi Method.* Mendocino, CA: LifeRhythm.

Satir, V. (1972). *Peoplemaking.* Palo Alto, CA: Science & Behavior Books.

# 82
## Emotional First Aid

### Eva Reich and Judyth O. Weaver, United States

Similar to Freud, Wilhelm Reich also had a gifted daughter, following in his work, **Eva Reich,** who has made her own, unique contributions to Body Psychotherapy. When she was fourteen years old, in 1938, she emigrated to the United States. Later, she joined her father at Orgonon, where, after finishing medical school, she became his research assistant. Marriage did not lessen her commitment to the "new science" of Orgonomy (which is what Reich called his work), or to the field of pediatrics in which she had qualified. Working as a physician in a rural area, she devoted her particular attention to prenatal education, natural birthing, and, especially, infant massage. This focus grew out of her aspiration to prevent the formation of neurosis from the very beginning of life, and thereby to contribute to the "humanization" of humanity. Her commitment to the establishment of birthing clinics led her to travel the world many times.

Dr. Reich was known for her selfless dedication to children and to people living in poverty. After a very busy life, she lived in relative seclusion, being looked after by her daughter and other caregivers in Hancock, Maine. She passed away peacefully at the age of eighty-four, in August 2008. She has enriched the field of Body Psychotherapy by means of three important contributions: (1) through her original contribution to infant therapy: the "butterfly massage," which inspired many of the forms of infant massage that we know today; (2) through her gentle method of working with adults, which she called "Gentle Bioenergetics"; and (3) through what she termed "Emotional First Aid."

It is this third contribution that is the subject of this chapter, which describes cases from her work as a rurally based physician, and it is meant to illustrate how a physician with a Body Psychotherapeutic perspective can provide immediate and effective support to a patient with acute symptoms of illness or distress.

**Judyth O. Weaver's biographical information** can be found at the beginning of Chapter 4, "The Influence of Elsa Gindler."

Emotional First Aid is a term that can be used for a type of body-mind integrative therapeutic process used in situations calling for immediate, direct response, such as what a person might need in an acute or subacute situation of distress or overwhelm. An effective response to such a situation must, by necessity, call into consideration as many aspects of the whole person and his or her life as possible. In long-term therapy, one may take one's time and move slowly from the psyche to the soma; but in an urgent situation, knowledge of a wide variety of ways to work—and surely the inclusion of the physical and the energetic body—is as important as, if not more important than, history and emotions.

 The need for such work arises in a transient society where people with whom we will not have the chance to work with at length or develop a long-term relationship may approach us for therapeutic intervention. This situation brings possibilities of helping that person, and also the difficulties of not having much time or the opportunity to go as deep as we might like. In such situations, it is essential that we have the support and assistance of all the bodily, sensory, and energetic aspects as they are experienced, and the realization of the resources they can afford. In fact, in severe situations, the client may not be able to give us much other information.

In addition to listening to what the client does have to say, we also have assistance through the assessment of the subtle languages of the body, such as posture, prosody, and gestures, which are among the myriad of indicators that are available to us. Understanding prenatal and perinatal patternings, as well as having knowledge of other early developmental and movement stages, is very helpful in accessing the client's situation and in which way it would be best to work. Emotional First Aid is important because it is not meant only for a specific therapeutic setting. Instead, it suggests the possibility of helpful procedures in various situations where people who are under a high emotional strain can be helped spontaneously and quickly. The special potential of working somatically, and using the wealth of information from the body (as well as the mind) to create relief, without extending the work to long-term psychotherapy, is of great assistance as a form of crisis intervention in the psychological or medical professional settings, useful in the fast-moving, highly pressured societies in which we live today.

## Emotional First Aid

The concept of Emotional First Aid was first outlined in an article entitled "Emotional First Aid: Implications of Orgone Therapy to a General Medical Practice" (Reich, 1977). Here are some illustrations of the process:

**Example 1:** A middle-aged man stops at my office "off the road" because of acute pain in his stomach. Blood pressure normal, heart sounds strong, normal, and regular, he looks basically well. No diarrhea, vomiting, or fever and not a tender abdomen.

As we talk and question, he says that he is just returning from the funeral of a beloved friend who had died suddenly. No, he didn't permit himself to cry there. ("Boys don't cry.") I do a rectal examination to check on normality of prostate. His sphincter is tense. I tell him that I believe his "swallowed feelings" may be causing the pain in the epigastrium, that maybe we can improve things by letting go of the retained emotion. He is willing to try. (I am sure he does not even know what "psychology" means. He is a laborer, gnarled hands, wearing his saved, single, outdated "best suit.") While pressing on the rib margin of his fixed, high, emphysematous chest, I encourage him to "make faces"—"*Just let your face do what it wants to do by itself*"—"*Can you wrinkle and move your scalp?*" While he tries, I massage his facial muscles, gently, with what I call a "butterfly touch." "*Now open your eyes wide, like scared, and then close them tight . . . open wide and close tight . . . keep doing this.*"

Then we work on his tight jaw and neck muscles—"*Can you let your voice roll out?—like singing one note—like a big out-loud sigh?*" He is embarrassed and reddens in the "blush area." "*It's OK to have feelings, it is better for you to own them, to allow them.*" I am the strange lady doctor, but he has placed me in authority by coming to the office. There isn't time to work through the defenses, all the layers, all the whys and wherefores. This is an acute emergency, possibly an early heart attack? (coronary occlusion), gallbladder attack? or acute peptic ulcer? If nothing happens soon, I'll have to sedate him (Demerol 100 mg. SQ2) or admit him as an emergency to the nearby hospital (then forty miles distant). I don't tell him my thoughts. I try to keep a calm and reassuring manner. Very doctorate. I only tell him, "*We are trying something new—let us see for a little while whether we are on the right track—let us see whether this helps before we use a drug.*" Now he gets pale, begins to heave, nausea. I ask him to gag himself "*. . . with one finger tickle the back of your throat at the end of the breath, with a sound*" . . . "*Like this*": I demonstrate a gag reflex, which results in my upper and lower body jerking toward one another (the orgastic reflex). He tries, once, twice, three times, it is a struggle. He perspires, saliva flows into the emesis basin. He is on his side (pillow to keep head straight). He heaves, the reflex goes through, the crying comes, he cries bitterly in that racking way of one who has not cried for a *long* time, a lifetime.

After he subsides, I offer an antacid, a sedative. He doesn't need it. He rises, visibly shaken: *"Thanks, Doc. Yes, I feel so much better, all better, but all shook up."* There is a "recovery" bedroom upstairs, but he doesn't need it. He is ready to drive home, several hundred miles farther. I write a note to his family doctor. Time—forty-five minutes. No follow-up (Ibid., pp. 10–11).

**Example 2:** As an intern, on the private medical service (1949), I am ordered to do a routine admission examination on a middle-aged Philadelphia housewife. She is lying on her hospital bed in a dazed state, having been given a quarter grain (15 mg.) of morphine recently for acute back pain. Her admitting physician has diagnosed possible dislocation of a thoracic intervertebral disk. I begin to examine: the routine, head-to-toe, all-over quickie, since she's already well known to her own doctor, no challenge, I'm bored and tired and exhausted, irritated at my useless routine work.

As I check her, we talk. She tells me what a hard time she has been having with her son, who has metastatic carcinoma. *"What a pity, such a young wonderful son, just graduated from college, I can't bear to see him suffer so, and the doctor says he will die soon."* She states this with a flat, detached, monotonous voice. Her emotion has been "somaticized" in the extreme tensions of her body. Her head, neck, and thorax move as one. Her arm stays up in the air and doesn't drop when released. Her muscles are "hard as a board." I get interested. Could it be that the acute muscle pain is directly due to the catastrophe in her life? That "to keep going" she has increased the armor to the point of causing an unbearable pain crisis? She likes me. I tell her that I am just learning about a way of releasing feelings that are repressed and causing "knots" in muscles, that I'd like to help her to bear and feel her feelings. She agrees that she feels "uptight" all the time. We work. She goes into breathing, moaning, then begins to *scream*. She screams like a pig being pierced to roast, like a woman being murdered, like a "crazy in a loony bin" . . . The cry, at first shrill through tense vocal cords, begins to broaden and turns into a huge guttural moan from below the diaphragm.

There is no soundproofing in a hospital. The nurses come running. I'm reported to the administration, the private doctor is notified . . . The patient is now having a tantrum on all fours; all the pent-up anger at being a victim is turning into rebellion against an inhumane medical system . . . I defend her "right to emote" against all comers—by simply saying, "We are letting some repressed feelings out."

Eventually spent, she relaxes. Having been listened to, having been given "permission to be herself," she is lying now exhausted, but relieved, real, all soft, awake, and aware. Her back is soft. Her neck is soft. Her face has become beautiful though still sad. She *knows* now how she created the back pain: by hiding the immensity of her own grief from herself. She is glowing, she reports tingling sensations all over, especially in her lower body! We worked a few more times. She underwent various X-ray examinations, all with negative results, and she left the hospital in a few days, feeling expanded and ready for the future. The pain did not return. Why did her own physician have no knowledge of the connection between repressed emotion and muscular tension? This is not taught in medical school (Reich, 1977, pp. 11–12).

## Conclusion

By integrating the entire organism, and the accompanying energetics, and recognizing their place in a situation that combines emotional and bodily dynamics, we are able to work more efficiently and practically and realize changes more quickly than through a therapeutic process that does not include the entire person's experience.

This work was initially called "Emotional First Aid" to describe the urgent need for care that could relatively quickly reach deep into the client's soma and psyche and allow some acute and immediate relief. It might also include other quick assessment and therapeutic tools such as: clarifying a trauma lifeline (from conception when possible); various energetic balancing and/or grounding techniques, such as Qigong exercises or breathing exercises (Chuen,

1991); Craniosacral therapy (Sills, 2002); and, especially when working with babies, "butterfly massage" or "Gentle Bioenergetics newborn massage" (Wendelstadt, 1998).

Most importantly and essentially, it does require a good rapport to exist between the client and the therapist. Trust is paramount, even for the shortest period of time. The therapist must be sure to create a situation where the client feels safe. Understanding the client's desire is important, and mutual agreement on the intention of the work to be addressed is essential. Clear boundaries and frequent eye contact will greatly help to provide these requirements (Reich, 1977, 1978).

It is also vital for the therapist to be very skilled at understanding emotional and energetic dynamics and their relation to acute and sometimes life-threatening states and symptoms. It is also essential that the therapist be able to monitor his or her own reactions to the situation, and to have a clear understanding of transference and countertransference issues.

The ability to help a person in hyperarousal, or some other crisis, to become more aware of their physical reactions, to become more in touch with their breathing (or lack of it), to feel their feet on the ground (or realize that they aren't), can all be very helpful in assisting the client toward coming back into the present moment, so that they may move away from their overwhelm and come closer to the reality of the current situation. Opening the possibilities to a client of finding some degree of relief and resources in their actual somatic realizations can go far in helping them out of their crisis reactions and bringing them more in touch with their present resources. This then allows the person to deal with the actual situation more realistically and practically.

In those instances where a rapid survey of soma and psyche are required, incorporating knowledge of the structure and function of the body, understanding of emotions, and heartfelt empathy and consideration can be quickly integrated into a way of working with people in distress that could be called a genuine Emotional First Aid.

Emotional First Aid is different in each situation. There are only three rules: (1) to be open-minded to the possibility that very severe or acute bodily symptoms may be caused by acute emotional repression or arousal; (2) to be on the lookout for clues in the actual life situation of the person who comes for help; (3) to know that words alone cannot always relieve the energy stasis.

## Appendix: Extracts from Eva Reich's Obituary

Eva applied many of the principles she had learned from her father with good results. Together, she and her husband also operated a small organic farm, where they were forerunners in the organic food movement. In many ways, Eva was always ahead of her time, preaching the benefits of natural food, gentle birth, and mother-child bonding long before these ideas found the main stream.

> Eva, who had studied infant emotional health under her father's tutelage and as a primary care physician, developed a gentle orgonomic treatment for upset infants and colicky babies. She coined the term "butterfly baby massage," since the touch used was as gentle as the touch used to pick up a butterfly. This method has been taken up especially in Austria and Germany. In Berlin there are special "ambulances" that rush to houses where babies are crying inconsolably, using Eva Reich's methods to calm babies. She found that this level of touch worked with both adults and children, melting the body armor, rather than breaking it down.
>
> She believed in starting with the wanted child, natural nonviolent birth, prepared parents, bioenergetic therapy for the traumatized newborn, and self-regulation as a guiding principle in educational and all institutions. Throughout her life Eva championed peace, stating that peace on earth begins in the uterus.

*Renata Moise (Eva Reich's daughter), EABP Newsletter, Summer 2009, p. 20. (The full text is available at www.eabp.org).*

## References

Chuen, L. K. (1991). *The way of energy.* New York: Simon & Schuster.

Reich, E. (1977). Emotional First Aid: Implications of Orgone Therapy to a general medical practice. *Energy & Character, 8(3), 10–12.*

Reich, E. (1978). Suicide prevention. *Energy & Character, 9(2), 69–71.*

Sills, F. (2002). *Craniosacral Biodynamics.* Berkeley, CA: North Atlantic Books.

Wendelstadt, S. (1998). Emotional First Aid: Healing a birth trauma. *Clinical Journal of the International Institute for Bioenergetic Analysis, 9(1), 85–96.*

# 83

## The Use of Body Psychotherapy in the Context of Group Therapy

**Michael Soth, United Kingdom**

**Michael Soth's** biographical information can be found at the beginning of Chapter 47: "Transference, Countertransference, and Supervision in the Body Psychotherapeutic Tradition."

A review of the literature and an internet search suggest that very little dialogue, let alone cross-fertilization, has occurred between Body Psychotherapy and the various traditions of group psychotherapy. Therapeutic groupwork with a thematic focus on body image (e.g., eating disorders, addictions) is common; and body-oriented work in groups exists in a variety of forms—for example, Feldenkrais, Body-Mind Centering, Pilates, dance and movement styles like 5Rhythms and Laban, and Eastern practices like Yoga, Tai Chi, and Qigong; many of these only tangentially or implicitly attend to psychological and relational dynamics.

There are also Body Psychotherapeutic approaches practiced in groups, both within the Reichian tradition and outside it (e.g., Pesso Boyden System Psychomotor, Psychodrama, Process-Oriented Psychology, and Gestalt). However, in Body Psychotherapy, as defined by the EABP and the USABP, groups are seen mostly as a "mode of delivery," rather than an integral aspect of what is being delivered. Little attention has been paid to the specific therapeutic terrain of the group itself.

Groups become a microcosm of each member's life patterns and therefore manifest, mirror, and bring to awareness *in vivo*, in immediate relational experience, a large proportion of the very issues that participants seek therapy for. At the same time, a creative and well-facilitated group dynamic in and of itself can have transformative and sometimes healing effects on its members, in that it contradicts and counteracts earlier traumatic or damaging group experiences, in adult life or earlier in school or in our very first group experience: our families of origin. In this case, simply being present in such an emotionally healthy group can engender therapeutic changes that do not even rely on direct interaction with the therapist.

These are principles well established in group psychotherapy, which, of course, exists as a recognized discipline in its own right, comprising an ensemble of therapeutic modalities that include both humanistic approaches, such as encounter groups (Rogers, 1973; Schutz, 1966), T-groups (Lewin, 1948), and Worldwork (Mindell, 1992), and psychoanalytic approaches, including the tradition originated by Bion at the Tavistock Clinic (Bion, 1961) and the somewhat different methodology of Group Analysis pioneered by Foulkes (Foulkes and Anthony, 1965; for comparison, see Ancona, 1996).

Historically, Body Psychotherapy has identified itself largely with the humanistic wing of psychotherapy (Totton, 2002), though some reintegration between psychoanalysis and Body Psychotherapy has been taking place since the early 2000s (Totton, 1998; Soth, 2004, 2005). However, Body Psychotherapy as a whole has been only very slightly influenced by *any* tradition of groupwork, analytic or humanistic.

There is a wide gulf between the largely verbal focus of established groupwork practice on the one hand, and the body-mind paradigm, concepts, and techniques of Body

Psychotherapy on the other. Any formulation of Group Body Psychotherapeutic principles needs to straddle this gulf and consider how the two disciplines can inform and cross-fertilize each other.

This chapter is an attempt at a broad-spectrum integration of diverse approaches to group psychotherapy that is specifically grounded in modern Body Psychotherapy and practically relevant for the Body Psychotherapist as group leader. It is viewing the group as a complex body-mind organism constituted by individual body-mind organisms, and subject to field phenomena and collective and systemic processes not readily grasped by the individualistic focus of the psychotherapy field in general, nor traditional Body Psychotherapy in particular.

## The Humanistic Influence on Body Psychotherapy and Its Limitations Concerning Group Therapy

Body Psychotherapy owes much to the humanistic revolution, which also placed big hopes on working in groups, as these played a central role in the youth culture and counterculture of that time. However, alongside the many precious gifts we derive from the humanistic influence, we also inherit some fundamental limitations to our understanding of groups and group therapy. These limitations will be addressed by differentiating three related and overlapping polarities that group therapists need to be capable of embracing and responding to flexibly and fluidly.

One of the inherent contradictions of the humanistic revolution is its emphasis on groups and the collective, while also championing individual freedom from social constraints. As necessary and liberating as both of those elements were, arguably the underlying tensions were not fully resolved, and therefore humanistic aspects of groupwork practice remain influenced by that unresolved dichotomy, as well as a reactive bias against authority and any kind of hierarchy (see Bly, 1996). This, I suggest, is reflected in unconscious attitudes toward three key issues in group work: (1) the conflict between individual and collective perspectives; (2) the tension between paradigms that assume or allow power differentials and those that invite or insist on equality; and (3) the dialectic between structured and unstructured space. Any formulation of Group Body Psychotherapy would therefore need to resolve, or at least address, these inherent dichotomies to the point where both the productive and the defensive aspects of each of the polarities can be appreciated.

Whether such conflicts are held and resolved or polarised and acted out can significantly influence the development of the field. My early training was impacted by an organizational crisis at the Boyesen Centre in the 1980s, which led to a split and the departure of a group of trainers, who then formed the Chiron Centre, when the inherent paradigm clashes between biodynamic and psychodynamic approaches to group and organizational dynamics could not be contained.

## Individual versus Collective

As made explicit throughout this handbook, therapeutic theories and values are informed by their social and historical context. The more that the prevailing *zeitgeist* sees human pathology as an individual issue, rooted in individual psychology, the more we tend to use therapy to work out our own "private salvation," probably resulting in therapeutic adjustment of the individual to the social climate.

However, the more we see psychological dysfunction as a healthy response to a dysfunctional social environment (Foucault, 2001; Laing, 1990; Szasz, 1984), the more that our conception of a comprehensive therapeutic approach needs to include groupwork. It is in the group, as a "mini-society," that humans as social beings can become aware of, and possibly resolve, distressing and dysfunctional interpersonal patterns. To the extent that both the origins and the manifestations of psychological pain are socially constructed and transcend dyadic relating, groups can be considered to be the ideal setting that both constellates and confronts, as well as helps us to work through, some of these issues at their root.

The first perspective—espousing the capacity for individual freedom (as, for example, suggested by Gestalt)—

holds that group members need to take responsibility for the ways in which their individual psychology contributes to the group dynamic. The other polarity—emphasizing the power of the collective over the individual (as, for example, suggested by a systemic perspective)—sees the group as creating certain roles that—in the extreme—need to be filled by *somebody,* and that individual psychology merely influences which role a group member is more prone to being drawn or pushed into. Yalom, in one of the seminal texts within the field, says:

> Does group therapy help clients? Indeed it does. A persuasive body of outcome research has demonstrated unequivocally that group therapy is a highly effective form of psychotherapy and that it is at least equal to individual psychotherapy in its power to provide meaningful benefit. (Yalom, 2005, p. 1)

In spite of its awareness of socio-cultural influences, humanistic practice has often focused on the individual and their "inner" capacity for change. Thus, the traditional methodology of Reichian, Neo-Reichian, and Gestalt Therapy was focused primarily on the individual *within* the group, resulting in what might be called "public individual work." Typically (and with some significant exceptions like Estela Welldon, and Jacob Stattman [1989, 1991] from Unitive Psychology), the group leader would conduct individual sessions in the middle of the group, with the other group members functioning as props, stand-ins for significant others, and/or sources of feedback after the work. Undoubtedly, this can be a powerful way of working. As sessions are conducted by the therapist, and therefore usually uninterrupted, this allows the work to find both depth and resolution, thus often triggering other group members' own material and leading to further sessions in the middle. And even group members who do not work in the middle can derive significant relief and learning from witnessing other people's resolution.

However, with the focus of the group leader mostly on individuals, or at best on the relationships between individuals within the group, large areas of the group's therapeutic potential remain unexplored. With most of the communication flowing through the therapist, as the hub of the group, the two principal areas that get neglected within this format are: (1) the spontaneous unstructured and unmediated interactions between group members; and (2) the dynamics of the group as a whole.

In established group therapy practice, it is precisely these two areas that are seen as essential: *"One of the most important underlying assumptions . . . is that interpersonal interaction [between group members!] within the here-and-now is crucial to effective group therapy"* (Yalom, 2005, p. xv), and *"There is little question of the importance of group-as-a-whole phenomena"* (Ibid., p. 193).

A first principle for Group Body Psychotherapists would, therefore, have to be the capacity to work across a whole spectrum of formats, including *both* conducting individual sessions in the middle *and* attending to the spontaneously unfolding group dynamic between participants as well as the group as a whole.

## Power Differential versus Equality

The term Group Body Psychotherapist does not yet—properly—exist. Humanistic groupwork uses the term "facilitator" to convey the implicit notion that no imposed guidance of the group by a "leader" is required, and that the group is quite capable of organizing and regulating itself, with the catalytic help of a facilitator. The term "facilitator" (Heron, 1999) thus reflects an important, anti-authoritarian, and anti-patriarchal perspective on groupwork and collective reality, and circumscribes a long-established body of knowledge, attitudes, and practice. However, it could be argued that—deriving as it does from humanistic influence—the term "facilitator" does not sufficiently include the legitimate function and purpose of authority, as would be implied in the roles of "group therapist" or "group analyst." There may be aspects of the group's reality that cannot be accessed or disclosed by the facilitator's egalitarian stance, which such group practice may therefore remain oblivious to. One of the dividing lines between the humanistic "facilitator" and the analytically oriented "group therapist" is the question of what group and leadership functions are required to perceive, reveal, and work with the "unconscious," both of the individuals and of the group as a whole?

The more emphasis is placed philosophically and theoretically on the opaqueness and the vicissitudes of the unconscious, the less likely it is that a purely catalytic facilitator function is sufficient to create the necessary safety for unconscious dynamics to manifest fully in the first place, let alone to make it possible to address them. Considering that much human pain originates in relationships characterized by power differentials, the humanistic emphasis on equality, and its bias against oppressive authority, often leads to the superficial avoidance of power issues, rather than their radical transformation.

A second underlying principle for Group Body Psychotherapists is the capacity to remain unbiased in terms of power differentials versus equality, and to hold the tension between these polarities in such a way that the group unconscious can be allowed to "co-construct" the therapist according to the prevailing, emergent dynamics within the group. This means that the group therapist does not unilaterally determine the group's stance based on the therapist's *own* beliefs and principles, but remains susceptible to the transferential realities called forth and required by the group. Any premature declarations of the group leader's own convictions and preferences regarding power issues tend to have the effect that uncomfortable power dynamics are sidestepped and minimized, rather than recognized, owned, and worked through.

## Structured Groupwork versus Unstructured Space

Although nearly all Body Psychotherapeutic training happens in groups—a tradition that has accumulated considerable group experience over the decades—both the content and the educational purpose of the training modules often tend to discourage the open, unstructured space required for therapeutic attention to the group itself, as well as to the transferential position of the combined tutor–leader–group therapist.

One specific advantage of psychoanalytically influenced group theories is the significance that they give to unconscious dynamics and their impact on the group leader (Anzieu, 1984). Unconscious dynamics, generated by particular individuals or the whole group, tend to create uncomfortable conflicts for group leaders, who can find themselves implicated in what feels like impossible dilemmas. One way of avoiding these dangers is for leaders to overstructure the therapeutic space by providing a constant stream of activities that require the giving of instructions and directions, somewhat like a preschool teacher.

This does not deny the value of the wealth and breadth of creative group exercises being used by humanistic facilitators and therapists, within both the Body Psychotherapeutic tradition and its surrounding field. In their emphasis on experiential exploration, participants can discover themselves and gain awareness in many powerful ways, reaching from body-oriented work to psychodramatic techniques. The therapist assumes the beneficial role of providing activities that—within an overall reparative framework of positive transference to the group and to the leader—enable safe and productive exploration and individual development. One ingredient in such a framework often is the unwritten assumption that the group is conceived of as the positive "anti-family" to the originally damaging "bad family."

However, through participants consistently cooperating *within* the structures set up by the leader, powerful unconscious forces may be stopped from manifesting, in relation both to the group and to the therapist. By providing a consistent flow of nurturing and enlivening structure and taking a proactive, guiding, and facilitative-educative stance as an unquestioned, benign, and parental figure, the therapist is protected from anything other than compliant responses on the part of the participants.

But we notice that *any* given structure, when employed habitually, will tend to be used and usurped by participants' defense and control mechanisms, as participants quickly learn to adapt and "play the game." Some flexibility and fluidity between structure and structurelessness, and a commitment to both as part of the group experience, is best suited to bring out such rigid and defensive adaptations and to maximize the potential for addressing these effectively.

Body Psychotherapists are conversant with the tension between an educative, guiding, interventionist therapeutic stance, on the one hand, and an allowing, receptive, patient presence, on the other. The latter, called—for example—the "midwife approach" by Gerda Boyesen (1994), relies on the creation of an unstructured space that trusts "being" and invites the "impinging of impulses from within."

The same tension between contradictory stances on the part of the therapist applies to groups: providing structure from within an energetically attuned, involved position can be experienced as facilitative and reparative in itself. But open, unstructured space is equally required and has many benefits: it allows and invites spontaneity and communicates both acceptance and faith in "what is." By allowing unmediated, spontaneous impulses to manifest in the group, deeply conditioned shadow aspects or regression to primitive realms of experience may emerge, as well as unthought-of new ways of relating. Thus, unstructured space allows and invites what Winnicott considered to be a crucial therapeutic ingredient—play: "A freely interactive group, with few structural restrictions, will, in time, develop into a social microcosm of the participant members" (Yalom, 2005, p. 31).

This spontaneous emergence both of the participants' self-sabotaging interpersonal patterns in relation to each other, and of the often-unexpected self-regulating and self-healing capacities of the group, can be "structured out of existence" by a facilitator who is too active and central. Once unstructured space has allowed participants' patterns to manifest, there ". . . is no need for them to describe or give a detailed history of their [interpersonal universe]: they will sooner or later enact it before the other group members' eyes" (Ibid.).

Group therapy is therefore an effective avenue into characterological issues and how they organize a person's relationships. It is in the fluidity between these poles of structured and unstructured space that group therapists can maximize both containment and spontaneity, security and novelty.

A third working principle for Group Body Psychotherapists is the capacity to be familiar with the advantages and disadvantages of both structure and structurelessness, and to hold the tension between these polarities.

## Toward an Integration of Group Therapy and Body Psychotherapy

A dialogue between the estranged traditions of Body Psychotherapy and group psychotherapy involves:

1. Bringing a group perspective (Bach, 1954; Houston, 1994) to psychological and therapeutic areas neglected by Body Psychotherapy
2. Making the theories and techniques of Body Psychotherapy accessible and available to a field that is still largely steeped in body/mind dualism, by applying a holistic perspective to group phenomena and approaches

Beyond the simple mutual cross-fertilization of the two estranged traditions, a possible integration of body-mind and group perspectives may generate a new sensibility and new ways of framing the therapeutic endeavor altogether, by addressing more explicitly its sociopolitical context and by opening up new ways of perceiving, understanding, and intervening therapeutically within the "body politic." For this purpose, we need a socio-bio-neuro-psychological metamodel of therapy that is relevant not only to groupwork, but to the underlying assumptions governing the modern practice of therapy in all its forms.

## Body Psychotherapy's Contribution to Groupwork

By including the body as one significant ingredient in the therapeutic encounter, Body Psychotherapy has developed certain central attitudes that not only are relevant to specifically body-centered work, but have a contribution to make for *all* therapy and therapists (Totton, 2005).

## "Bringing in the Body"

The most obvious and basic contribution of Body Psychotherapy is, quite simply, to *include* the body, welcoming and attending to the bodily experience of participants and leaders in just the same way that one might do with any other aspect of experience. Thus, group members are encouraged to share and explore bodily sensations, impulses, and symptoms, just as they might share emotions, fantasies, and thoughts; and these bodily experiences are considered to be valid and important contributions to the group's knowledge of itself, as well as to the individual's self-understanding. In parallel, the leaders will consult their own embodied experience, asking themselves how shifts and alterations in the flow of their embodiment express countertransference responses to the group and its members.

Beyond and arising out of this attention to and sharing of bodily awareness, Body Psychotherapy follows and surrenders to "embodiment" as it manifests in all kinds of spontaneous processes. Many group cultures require members to participate mainly through contributing impulses that have been reflected upon and suitably channeled or censored. But because group members allow for and arrange themselves around everybody else's defense mechanisms, an exploratory space of "play" is unlikely to emerge without judicious encouragement of spontaneous impulses and their expression.

Psychotherapy has a traditional bias toward symbolization and reflection, equating action with "acting out," and discouraging spontaneity in the supposed pursuit of "meaning," which is understood to be mental. Although Body Psychotherapy is pervaded by an equivalently strong but opposite bias, leading to an oversimplified notion of spontaneity (Soth, 2000), it can nevertheless help to counterbalance this bias and encourage the emergence and the creation of meaning through following spontaneous impulses (see Chapter 13, "Body Psychotherapy as a Revitalization of the Self: A Depth-Psychological and Phenomenological-Existential Perspective" by Gustl Marlock).

**Example 1:** J. had consistently been the quietest group member throughout the first six of twelve weekly sessions. Nobody—not even herself—had noticed what was obvious in hindsight: having a tendency to arrive late, she never sat anywhere other than opposite T., easily the most verbal and intellectually articulate participant. Tonight, she finally took issue with what she perceived as his self-involved, alienating, and abstract ruminations. Compared to him, she felt inferior and less entitled to the group's attention.

Their interaction started with T. talking at great length, rather like a king holding court, being consciously preoccupied with reflections on his place in and contribution to the group. In the middle of his soliloquy, J. broke into a wild coughing fit, which—to begin with—she politely smothered in her handkerchief. She begged the group to continue and to ignore her coughing, but there was something about her self-effacing manner that some members of the group, including the facilitator, found funny. For all his usual composure, T. was offended—he looked hurt, as if the laughter were exclusively meant for him, referring to what he had said. He became distinctly quiet.

The facilitator noticed that his own laugh had acquired several meanings. He felt caught between what both J. and T. were making sure was most certainly not a confrontation. He also noticed that—apparently—his laugh carried more weight with both J. and T. On the surface, this was an issue between two individuals, and the facilitator initially pursued it as such, asking J. to experiment with coughing "at" T. The cough soon became a direct challenge and an open expression of her hostility toward him. The dynamic between the two of them was quickly established and took its time to unfold, with both J. and T. owning their mutually negative feelings toward each other. This was a moving exchange, but with a deeper layer of significance: later in the work, the facilitator began to think of J. and T. as the protagonists of two quite polarized ways of being, both in the group and in the world.

On the simplest level, their relationship reflected the polarization between "articulate mind" and "inarticulate body," and the question whether—in Gaie Houston's words—the "verbal self" is used "as a tool to enlightenment rather than neurosis-maker" (Houston, 1994, p. 82). It was through the leader not only trusting, but actively encouraging, J.'s coughing that an apparently meaningless and otherwise-unconscious element of the group dynamic, carried in the body, could unfold and reveal its relational meaning. Where verbal exchange is taken for granted as the dominant or exclusive mode of interaction, such a bodily symptom could easily have been overlooked as "irrelevant data"; it requires a particular holistic sensibility, as developed in Body Psychotherapy, to notice and value J.'s spontaneous bodily expression as a form of communication, especially in contrast to T.'s defensive, disconnected mind.

For sure, there are many other facets to the polarization between J. and T., rooted in their contrasting individual identities, reflecting their particular life stories, and especially how they each found different ways of coping with pain while getting some form of attention. But, if we do not reduce such conflicts to individual issues only, we recognize that one dimension that groups often polarize around is the body/mind split, dividing the group into one faction essentially afraid of the body and identified with the rational mind, over and against spontaneity, and an opposing subgroup identified with vitality, expressiveness, and impulsivity. The first group needs to control the body, whereas the second feels imprisoned, unless it is given free rein. The group thus manifests and plays out unresolved cultural conflicts that none of us can entirely escape. Each participant's identity is bound to have been organized in partial and biased ways around these painful conflicts, and each participant will therefore tend to maintain and defend that identity, inexorably drawn toward a particular characteristic position in the unfolding group dynamic.

A crucial step for the facilitator is to think of these polarizations as manifesting not only between people, but also within each group participant. Using the group sculpture technique (which is infinitely adaptable to a whole range of situations), the leader suggested that everybody line up with either J. or T., depending on whom they felt more identified with. A lively interaction between the two sides of the room ensued, with a predominantly goading and raucous, rather than hostile, undertone. The group ended feeling energized, as one unexpected aspect of the exercise was that people found themselves repeatedly switching sides.

An essential skill for the group leader is therefore the capacity to recognize the parallels between intrapsychic, interpersonal, group, and cultural dynamics, and to see how each level reflects the others. The group leader is then able to use each level flexibly, as an avenue into the others, shifting backward and forward between internal and external, individual and collective, using appropriate techniques in each domain. When group participants present partial identities, specializing in one or the other domain to the exclusion or neglect of others, the leader can thus facilitate a group awareness that is oriented toward a wholesome embrace of both individual and cultural splits.

### The Group as a Whole: The Group as an Organism

The perception of the group as a whole entity, rather than just a collection of individuals, is of course central to systemic (Agazarian and Peters, 1981), field theory (Lewin, 1951), and psychodynamic approaches to groups:

> As Bion (1961) noted, we may observe individual gears, springs and levers and only guess at the proper function, but when the pieces of machinery are combined, they become a clock, performing a function as a whole, a function impossible for individual parts to achieve. Appreciating the group as a whole requires a perceptual shift on the part of the observer or consultant, a blurring of individual separateness and a readiness to see the collective interactions generated by group members. (Banet and Hayden, 1977, p. 157)

However, Body Psychotherapy sees the whole group, not as a "clock," but as a living organism, or energetic entity. In contrast to mechanistic models of groups, this picks up on the important fact that the group members are organisms, and suggests that the group is an emergent entity no less complex—and embodied—than the individuals who make it up.

Like an organism, a group is a complex living system that needs to change and develop in order to sustain its evolving dynamic integrity. Like an organism, it needs both to interact with its environment by opening its boundaries, and also to maintain its separate identity by closing them.

**Phases of Group Development: The Orgasmic Cycle**

Like an organism, one of the most basic features of a group's experience is that its development can be seen to go through cycles and that the group itself has a life cycle. Since its inception, groupwork theory has generated—mainly linear—models of the phases and stages of group development (Bennis and Shepard, 1978; Feder and Ronall, 1980; Houston, 1994, the most famous one being captured by Tuckman's (1965) phrase *"forming–storming–norming–performing."*

Body Psychotherapy has made its own contribution to our understanding of the cyclic aspect of any living process and relationship. Reich's original "orgasm formula," the process by which "energy metabolism takes place in a four-beat rhythm of tension, charge, discharge, and relaxation" (Reich, 1983), was developed further in a variety of ways and appears in Gestalt, Hakomi, Biosynthesis, and Biodynamic Psychology models, among others.

Southgate and Randall's pamphlet (1980) entitled *Co-operative and Community Group Dynamics—Or: Your Meetings Needn't Be So Appalling* explicitly applies the Reichian concept of the orgasmic cycle to group life (focusing mostly on various kinds of workgroups rather than therapy groups), but distinguishes further between the "creative orgasmic cycle" and the "destructive orgasmic cycle": groups begin with the process of nurturing, move on to "energizing," then reach a "peak," after which the group moves into "relaxing." A destructive group, however, follows the same cycle, but with a different emotional tone: "destructive nurturing" involves smothering, withholding, paternalism, and dependency; "destructive energizing" is dominating and conspiratorial; the "destructive peak" is explosive and fight-or-flight; and "destructive relaxing" is false and illusion-based. This model combines Reich's four-phase cycle with Bion's understanding of the destructive potential of the "basic assumption group" (Bion, 1961).

An embodied perspective can thus bring an added dimension to models of group development, first theoretically by complementing linear models with the cyclic phenomenology of living systems, and second by translating these principles into embodied group practice—whether over a weekend, or over a year of weekly meetings—through "energetic perception" and an understanding of each member's characterological barriers to certain phases of the group cycle (see Chapter 93, "Existential Dimensions of the Fundamental Character Themes" by Halko Weiss).

**Group Energy**

Southgate and Randall's model of group life is basically an "energetic" model, consistent with Reich's functionalism, and tying together the life of the body and that of the mind: therefore, physical, physiological, neurological, and sexual processes are seen as being interwoven with, and functionally identical with, emotional, imaginal, and various mental processes in a dynamic whole that can be tangibly experienced.

> Our energy is our aliveness. It is the stuff that creates the continuity of our life. We wake up with it, we go to bed with it, it is present in our waking and sleeping dreams. . . . It is the ground from which our living emerges. . . . In a way energy is nothing special, but it is the glue that binds everything together and connects us to our essential self. (Heckler, 1984, pp. 58–59)

The equivalent in a group context—and one that is employed by many who are not Body Psychotherapists—is to talk about "the energy in the room" and what it "feels like"—even what it "wants" or is "trying to do."

In many ways, the term "energy" is co-extensive with what we might call emotional tone—what Daniel Stern calls "vitality affect" (Stern, 1985, pp. 53–60). The ability to read vitality affect is central to group facilitation, and there are many passages in Reich's work that anticipate the significance of vitality affects (Totton, 1998, pp. 166–169) and how they interweave with sensations and movements. Reich often likened the energetic functioning of the human body-mind to a pulsating amoeba, a notion that is echoed throughout our tradition:

> Energetically speaking, the whole body can be viewed as a single cell with the skin as its membrane. Within this cell excitation can spread in all directions... One can experience the flow of excitation as a feeling or sensation which often defies anatomical boundaries. (Lowen, 1971, pp. 51–52)

Attention to this basic level of aliveness underpins and informs the group therapist's perception: there is the energetic state of the particular participants, and also that of the group as a whole, the "emotional weather" of the group. In the 1960s and 1970s, political meetings often appointed someone to act as "vibes watcher" and to give periodic reports on the emotional atmosphere—in particular, to bring awareness to "stuck," "heavy," "anxious," or "jumpy" vitality affects.

## "Charge" as an Embodied Relational Notion of Energy

As has been explored elsewhere in this handbook (see Chapter 14, "The Concept of Energy in Body Psychotherapy" by Andreas Wehowsky), rather than being clearly defined, the range of meanings that the term "energy" holds within the Body Psychotherapeutic field is diverse, contradictory, and probably best understood as "multidimensional."

In trying to overcome the body/mind split, the Body Psychotherapeutic tradition has often swung from one extreme to the other: from mind-over-body dominance into body-over-mind, leading to oversimplified notions of "spontaneity" (Soth, 2000) and "energy." Imagining the therapeutic task as "liberating the animal" and its life energy (Reich, 1983) implies taking a polarized position in the conflict between mind and body. As I have suggested elsewhere, following in the footsteps of Reich's "mission," generations of Body Psychotherapists have tended to construct their therapeutic position as an *"enemy of the client's ego"* (Soth, 2005). While consciously working to overcome the client's body/mind split, it is perfectly possible for a Body-Oriented Therapist to actually end up exacerbating it, or enacting it relationally, precisely by polarizing *against* the dualism inherent in the split (Soth, 1999, 2006). In siding with the body against the mind, we have tended to favor cathartic expression, aliveness, and the flow of energy over inhibition, numbness, and stuckness. Although this has provided a useful counterbalancing to the disembodiment structured into our culture, it is—as Perls criticized (Perls, Hefferline, and Goodman, 1973, pp. x–xi)—not always a therapeutically productive position, nor one that actually facilitates true spontaneity. Rather than favoring expression over inhibition, Perls therefore insisted on therapeutic attention *to the conflict between* body and mind, *between* flowing and blocked energy, *between* aliveness and "resistance" (and pointed out the degree of energy contained *in* resistance).

Contrary to Reich's own metapsychological conception of mind and body as being antagonistic expressions of an underlying functional and energetic unity (Reich, 1983), in actual Body Psychotherapeutic practice, the notion of energy has often been reduced to the vitality of the body alone. Consequently, the associated concept of "charge" is usually understood to refer to the degree of energetic aliveness in the client's physical body, which can be influenced through conscious breathing, physical exercises, and stress positions, and is observable, and even measurable, from the outside. However, this fails to take into account both the "charge" in the mind (Lowen's notion [1971] of the brain as a "condensator" of energy) and the relational charge arising from the subjective and inherent meaningfulness of contact—with the environment, with an "other," or with the self (in Perls's phrase [Perls, Hefferline, and Goodman, 1973], "inherently vibrant contact").

If we expand the notion of charge beyond Reich's very literal, body sense of libido (Totton, 2003; Soth, 2005), it can become a helpful, embodied-relational term to describe the body-mind phenomenology of *both* intrapsychic and interpersonal dynamics, including transference and countertransference: a crucial ingredient in the therapist's awareness and attention. Reflection on countertransference often boils down to a contemplation of charged moments in the therapeutic relationship.

These considerations become relevant for the group therapist because—by a reverse parallel process recognized in group dynamics—the group often expresses the leader's own unconscious processes. As long as Body Psychotherapists operate from within a habitually biased, one-sided notion of energy, the group will tend to reflect this bias by splitting into compliant and resistant factions: one part of the group favoring expressiveness and impulsivity, the other tending to be more withdrawn, inhibited, quiet, and feeling shamed and unsupported.

Perls' focus on awareness of the conflict, rather than on siding with the supposedly "alive" body against the supposedly "deadening" mind, as well as Gestalt's paradoxical principle of change ("change happens when we accept what is": Beisser, 1970), gives the group therapist a more balanced, less habitually proactive position, suited to allowing the group's unfolding in "unstructured space," as well as still retaining the group therapist's capacity for decisive and determined intervention. Our embodied countertransference can then guide our attention to how the conflicts between body and mind, aliveness and numbness, expression and inhibition, engagement and withdrawal, are being played out within the group. Individual and collective issues around "charge" and "contact" are being expressed in the here and now, and manifest patterns of ambivalence around aliveness and relatedness.

**Example 2:** In a supportive group atmosphere, P. had, over some weeks, increasingly gotten in touch with how much he had missed just such an atmosphere in his life, and in his family of origin. *"I always thought my longing for a more loving family was a pipe dream, an impossible ideal. I did not think it might actually happen."* He then fell into a phase of depression, with the "wasted years" weighing heavily upon him, and feelings of despondency and hopelessness actually beginning to separate him from the group. One evening, the group encouraged him to contact his passion and aliveness, which they vividly remembered from just a few weeks before, but the more they tried to rescue him and nudge him toward an apparent group consensus of "health," the more he felt dead, isolated, and misunderstood. The group leader noticed P.'s impulse to draw his knees to his chest and curl up. Encouraged to follow this, P. started rocking and finally rolled onto his side into an isolated fetal position. The therapist drew P.'s attention to his breathing, which had nearly stopped. This prompted P. to remember how, as a child, he used to lie on his bed like this, and experiment with holding his breath: how long could he survive without air?

What eventually allowed some transformation was the further insight that the impulse behind these breath experiments went right back to his parents' divorce: an almost superhuman desire to control the one thing in his life that might not be out of his control: his breath. Although his body felt dead and immobile, there was a lot of charge in the recognition that these attempts at control were still continuing to this very day, right here in the group. The charge then moved into his contact with the group: the love he had received in the group threatened his lifelong established identity, and provoked this regression into an accurate replication of what had actually been his childhood reality.

But was he now going to allow another outcome? This question precipitated an opening of the floodgates, and he broke down into profound and uncontrollable sobbing. Some group members spontaneously came toward him, and he allowed himself to be held and rocked. The group surrounded him and touched him until naturally he felt soothed and his crying subsided. As the group continued during the following months, nobody was in any doubt that this session constituted a profound turning point in P.'s life. This example illustrates various points:

- The importance of the facilitator *not* siding with the group in its definition of "health," but giving attention to the charge as both an embodied *and* a relational phenomenon: by not reducing charge to "energy in the body," the therapist allowed the possibility that there can be a lot of charge in the reflective and contactful awareness of a frozen, paralyzed state of embodiment, or even disembodiment.

* The importance of touch: the group had created enough safety for disinhibition and spontaneous gestures, to allow members to respond warmly and authentically to P.'s distress. Had he been left alone in the isolated state, his "felt sense" of the group would simply have been a reenactment of his childhood scenario. At such times, the group transcends the individual therapist and, to some extent, functions as a substitute parent, without some of the major transference implications that would be inevitable in individual work. It opens up touch as a culturally neglected and underrepresented avenue of social interaction, and reinstates its essential function in human bonding.

* The transference implications: although, in this case, no major transference fallout seemed to occur in the further development of the group process, such a possibility cannot be ruled out. Whether the group, or the therapist, becomes an idealized "good object" as a result of such a session, and then becomes locked into a demand for further, potentially collusive gratification, depends on many factors, not the least of which are whether the regressive experience was forced prematurely, whether it involved a degree of compliance or self-conscious cathartic "performance," and whether it was completed and integrated. An organic, containable, and transformative unfolding of regression within the group context is supported by the therapist modeling attention to both resistance and cooperation, inhibition and expression, spontaneity and reflection, as valid modes of contact.

## Emergence ("Going with the Flow")

Whereas, in the past, leadership and the process of change were seen as "top-down" affairs, the science of complexity has discovered and postulated the emergence of new patterns from the "bottom up." Ideas such as dependence on slight variations in initial conditions (the "butterfly effect"), self-organization in complex systems ("autopoiesis"), bifurcation and strange attractors—all point to a new understanding of how change comes about, and what the leader's role may be in it (Coveney and Highfield, 1995; Maturana and Varela, 1987). Rather than painstakingly pushing incremental, linear change, leaders can attend to emergent processes in the system as indicators of impending discontinuities and quantum leaps of nonlinear change by following the intuitive impulses of the body (Durkin, 1981).

Body Psychotherapists are at home with the notion that transformation need not be an imposed effort, a disciplined application of will; for decades, we have been working with "emergence," the idea of "going with the flow." As illustrated above, we have learned to trust and follow spontaneous bodily impulses, even if—to begin with—they do not yet make sense. Complexity theory thus confirms many of Body Psychotherapy's basic assumptions regarding self-regulation and the body-mind relationship (Carroll, 2002). Emergent process tends to announce itself in subtle, almost imperceptible ways, arriving outside established structures, group norms, and dominant awareness (Mindell, 1995). The participants' bodies and their subliminal cues are a principal route for emergence—an area in which Body Psychotherapists have the perceptive and emotional skills to profoundly affect groupwork practice.

## Projection

A group can also work as a projection screen for each member's "inner world," a complex social organism onto which inner figures and relationships can readily be projected. This, in turn, can become a fertile ground for the therapeutic work of reowning projections, leading to increased self-awareness. Body Psychotherapy can contribute important perceptual, theoretical, and technical skills to this work—for example, the subliminal nonverbal anchoring of projection mechanisms, the body-mind characterological basis for repetitive patterns of relating in groups, and the energetic-cathartic working through of such patterns. These skills put facilitators in a better position to notice, access, and pursue the shifting tapestry of projections as they follow each other in rapid-fire succession; and this helps the group to become more like "real life" and thus to go deeper.

**Example 3:** In the last hour of a first group session, participants were invited to move through the room, experimenting with gazing at and not gazing at each other. They were asked to notice the three people in the group they experienced the most "charge" with—whether pleasant or unpleasant—and to trust their physical and gut reaction to each person. In the next session, this was explored further, through each participant imitating, mimicking, or quietly miming the three people whom they had picked the previous week. This provided material for the group, both through the accuracy of the imitation (for the imitated person), and through bringing attention to the nonverbal anchors for projection (for the imitating person).

G., for example, mimed S.—one of the women who would later be recognized as being given high status by the group—as gesturing and moving in a slow, deliberate, and composed fashion. In G.'s mind, this connected S. to G.'s older sister, M., who had been frequently abused and traumatized, leaving her in a semi-catatonic state. G. had only recently found out about the abuse, but, throughout their lives, had always felt guilty about being impatient with M.

The non-verbal exploration drew attention to a nascent projection on G.'s part that was distinctly different from how other members perceived S.: they felt impatient and irritated with what they perceived as S.'s slow speech and hypercontrolled, deliberately calming manner. In this case, G.'s projection of her sister M. onto S. had several functions: on the one hand, it was a competitive attempt to weaken S.'s position in the group, but, on the other hand, it gave a profound insight into a hidden side of S. During the exercise, when others imitated her, S. discovered the degree to which her posture and mannerisms resembled those of her controlling mother, whom she had introjected. G.'s perspective on this high-status, domineering behavior later opened up important avenues for understanding that behind the controlling attitude of S.'s mother lay buried hidden trauma.

This example is, of course, not meant to suggest that nonverbal work preempts and avoids projections, but rather that it *deepens* them, connecting them to their preconscious roots in sensory and body-mind processes. All of the projections involved would have occurred subliminally anyway, but working through the body allowed both their explicit, felt recognition, and the transformative potential of the kernel of perceptive accuracy.

## Character Styles as Embodied Interpersonal Patterns within the Group Dynamic

Character patterns are both communicated and perceived—as well as experienced in the first place—in predominantly somatic ways. Their restrictive inertia is felt, and perceived by others, as "embodied." Because these patterns are frequently experienced as "normal" (or "egosyntonic"), the group provides a profound feedback system against which the pattern can stand out as something that can be questioned rather than taken for granted.

**Example 4:** T. and R. developed an intense love-hate relationship throughout the course of a group. T. was a tall, skinny, languid, shy man in his late twenties with a history of medium-term relationships with older women who basically mothered him. This would develop into a downward spiral, with both partners increasingly resenting his dependency. R., a woman in her late thirties, who had joined the group after her divorce from a man she felt bullied by, was the perfect match for T.'s pattern. She found his reluctant helplessness quite cute, and certainly unthreatening, and he appreciated her steady attention and nurturing attitude. Bion (1961) observed that such pairing is a common reaction in groups, often serving a defensive function and helping both people avoid engagement with the group. This "coupling" can shut out the rest of the group, setting up rivalries and envy of the "special" intimacy. In this case, T. and R. could be seen to fit what character theory describes as oral and masochistic holding styles, respectively.

Rather than directly interpreting the defensive aspects of T.'s and R.'s pairing, the facilitator used their body language, when sitting next to each other, to draw attention to how they were shutting the group out. They were turned toward each other, their backs rounded and shielding the space between them. This developed into a scenario where the two of them were given special attention by the therapist while the group crowded around at a distance. In both allowing and embodying the dynamic, interpretation became unnecessary: through attending to a shared sense of diffuse bodily tension, T. and R. discovered how much they were already protecting themselves in anticipation of envious attacks. The therapist encouraged them to deliberately and actively protect themselves; after explicitly confronting and jointly shouting at the rest of the group, it became obvious to both of them how, in their different ways, they were projecting a hostile family environment onto the rest of the group: T. felt ignored and neglected, whereas R. expected shaming and humiliating responses denying her right to intimacy. The short-term effect was that T. and R. began to see each other more realistically, including each other's defensiveness, rather than being united against a common "enemy"—the group.

### Regression and Transference Processes

The number of conscious and unconscious, verbal and nonverbal messages communicated in a group increases exponentially as compared with one-on-one contact, making any attempt at control a hopeless undertaking. Beyond a group size of ten, we are confronted with such a multitude of dynamics that it approximates a "mini-society"—a sense that some people find containing and that others find utterly threatening.

The uncontrollable diversity and complexity of collective process overwhelms the individual ego and explains the regressive potential of groups. Another source of regression is the intense, pervasive, and culturally neglected longing for a sense of community—what Paul Goodman, one of the co-creators of Gestalt, called the *communitas* aspect of therapy (Goodman, 1947).

Regression has long been recognized as a powerful and valuable therapeutic tool, though a double-edged one. If anything, Body Psychotherapy intensifies and enhances regressive tendencies: *"Touch is our earliest language, and capable of taking us back instantaneously to our most primitive universe"* (Conger, 1994, p. 13). We commonly find that if an individual resists awareness, then any movement toward embodiment will be regressive (or at least experienced as such). Although regression does entail dangers of re-traumatization, one can assume—like Winnicott—that it can allow *"an unfreezing of an environmental failure situation"* (Winnicott, 1954, p. 287), and that transformation of deep, structural, psychic wounds cannot occur entirely without it.

In a group context, regression and associated transferences can take on a particularly trauma-laden, primal quality. In particular, there can be a form of "transference onto the group as body," including "the group as the body of the mother": because the group is so much "bigger" than the individual, the transference is frequently infantile, with qualities of needy dependence, destructive envy, or helpless terror. Leaders can, of course, have similar countertransference experiences of the group.

We can usefully distinguish between several levels of transferences: a primitive, potentially more overwhelming transference *to the group as a whole* and more differentiated transferences *toward particular people within the group,* including the facilitator. An intermediate level, which in practice constitutes the bulk of the work in ongoing group situations, is *to the group as family,* with each member experiencing the group as a re-creation of their "primary scenario" (Rosenberg, 1989).

All levels, of course, co-exist and intermingle in the group and in each individual, but a detailed exploration of transference-countertransference as body-mind processes is beyond the scope of this chapter (but see Soth, 2005, 2006).

**Example 5:** In a group facilitated by two therapists, one was working with a conflict between L. and D., which had been brewing for most of the morning. She supported them in fully expressing the anger they felt toward each other, culminating in some lively (still predominantly controlled) pushing and shoving, together with a lot of shouting and swearing. This dramatic scene riveted the group's attention. Fortunately, though, as it turned out, the other therapist noticed that G., on the far side of the group, was pale and tearful. The therapist sat with him and silently supported him while the scene played out, then asked whether he could share what had been happening for him throughout the process. His bystander reaction of helpless shock was picked up by several other participants, and turned out to be a crucial turning point in the group process, bringing out the fearfulness that had been hidden within L. and D.'s interaction, and in the group generally.

This example hints at the complexities involved in doing justice both to individual experience as well as to group processes. At one extreme, the individual outsider, or even scapegoat, may be the last bulwark against a mob-like group psychosis, and may function as the "disturber" who is the harbinger of new group consciousness (Mindell, 1995). At the other extreme, the degree and depth to which individual pathology with its blind projections interferes with a "longing to belong" may never be thrown into starker relief than against the backdrop of the collective wisdom of a healthy and containing group.

The group therapist needs to be open and sensitive across the whole range of pathologizing dynamics, from the individual caught in a pattern of "poisoning" the group, to the group driving the individual mad with peer pressure and demands for conformity.

## A Socio-bio-neuro-psychological Paradigm: Beyond Individual Therapy?

Bridging the intrapsychic and interpersonal and social domains, as well as the biological-neurological and psychological, has been intuited as a possibility since the inception of our discipline. But the beginning of the twenty-first century may herald our capacity to actually achieve such an integration within ourselves, in our therapeutic theory, and in our practice. Metamodels, such as Wilber's integral theory, drawing on holographic systems theory (see Chapter 15, "The Organization of Experience: A Systems Perspective on the Relation of Body Psychotherapies to the Wider Field of Psychotherapy" by Gregory Johanson), as well as neuropsychoanalysis (Schore, 1994), based on detailed scientific investigation of the biochemical and anatomical systems of the brain, indicate the degree to which such integrations are being pursued and are now considered feasible and necessary.

In therapeutic practice, however, such grand integrating models have remained fairly abstract and inconsequential in their influence. Undoubtedly, there are many reasons for this, but the traditional absence of the body within the field of psychotherapy is crucial: without a holistic body-mind paradigm, the integration of the various domains remains theoretical. Postmodern and feminist discourses (Merleau-Ponty, 1969; Orbach, 2006; O'Loughlin, 2006) have long recognized the social construction of the body: the body-mind processes organizing our social identity are largely taken for granted, as they are preconscious and pre-reflective. But it is precisely because they are embodied, and communicated as such, that the inclusion of the body in a collective therapeutic context is required if we want to bring into awareness these otherwise-implicit sociocultural forces.

## Extending Theories of Dyadic Resonance and Embodied Attunement into a Social and Group Context

In recent years, neuroscientific research into infant development has extended our understanding of the social construction of subjectivity, and how deeply ingrained and embodied in our experience these early influences are, reaching all the way down into the anatomy and physiology of our brains.

This has both confirmed and further stimulated Body Psychotherapeutic thinking about the interdependence of biology and psychology, indicated by the phrase "nature *via* nurture" (Ridley, 2004). The nonverbal and somatic roots of emotional and relational experience have been studied mainly in the dyadic "embodied attunement" between baby and caregiver. Stern (1985), Trevarthen (1993, 2001), Schore (2001), Porges (2005), Downing (Chapter 29, "Early Interaction and the Body: Clinical Implications"), and others have explored how, in Stern's words, "*All learning and all creative acts begin in the domain of emergent relatedness*" (1985, p. 67). As an example of what he calls "affect attunement"—frequently repeated interactions in which the baby acts in one expressive channel and the adult responds in a different channel, but with the same rhythm or activation profile—a ten-month-old girl finally gets a piece in a jigsaw puzzle:

> She looks towards her mother, throws her head up in the air, and with a forceful arm flap raises herself partly off the ground in a flurry of exuberance. The mother says, "YES, thatta girl." The "YES" is intoned with much stress. It has an explosive rise that echoes the girl's fling of gesture and posture. (Stern, 1985, p. 141)

This sort of interaction occurs spontaneously in all human relationships, and evolves throughout the life cycle, with later developmental stages building on and elaborating this basic, nonverbal, relational dance into the complexity of our verbal, social, and mental-reflective selves. But primitive experience and its embodied communication continue, of course, throughout our lives, although—in a largely disembodied culture—they are relegated to the subliminal shadow, from where they exert an unrelenting, decisive, and often destructive influence.

The—now scientifically validated—recognition of these aspects of human experience and interaction has not yet been extended from the dyadic context (infant-caregiver or client-therapist) into the social domain, and into the realm of group and organizational dynamics.

But Body Psychotherapy has a long-standing tradition of subtle and energetic perception, and helps us to translate and apply neuroscientific insights regarding embodied attunement and resonance to the group context. Although such attunement occurs prereflexively, right brain to right brain, and relies on a myriad of subtle messages that are both communicated and received subliminally, it is possible for therapists to develop and sharpen awareness of such nonverbal communication, and—as Neuro-Linguistic Programming (NLP) has shown—to *"clean up our perceptive channels"* (Bandler and Grinder, 1979).

Thus, we can perceive a complex, embodied weaving of intersubjectivity as operating in the background of all group processes, creating a "shared manifold" (Gallese, 2003)—a collective "soup" of unconscious and subliminal communication—defining the group atmosphere and its affective tone. Group life is the emergent product of multiple experiences of resonance and dissonance, attunement and nonattunement, at each level, from the dyad to the whole group. This is how the "group organism"—referred to above—actually comes into being: wavering in and out of existence as the group resonance patterns shift between order and disorder, separate experience and collective entrainment. Such phenomena will ensure that shifts in the embodied process of one member affect the embodied process of the whole group.

## Conclusion

Groups raise energy: concentrated collective attention intensifies *everything,* all experiences, interactions, and group contributions. This heightened awareness can bring stark recognition of basic life scripts, character styles, and interpersonal patterns, thus allowing for deep work. The group context also tends to lend more weight and significance to any resolutions and transformative moments that occur, allowing for easier and more comprehensive translation of therapeutic experiences into "real life."

The primitive, nonverbal, and subliminal roots of human suffering—and its transmission to other people and generations via significant relationships—have remained inaccessible to predominantly verbal modalities of therapy. Body Psychotherapy, with its accumulated expertise in the subtleties of embodiment versus disembodiment, has the potential to reach into and generate transformational impact on both the individual and the collective depth dimensions of human experience. It provides an ideal foundation from which to bridge and integrate diverse disciplines into a new and larger whole: a comprehensive socio-bio-neuro-psychological paradigm that brings together—among many others—group dynamics, relational psychoanalysis, neuroscience, and attachment theory with Body Psychotherapy's established holistic theory and practice and its inherent countercultural social commitment.

Our challenge is to forge a creative and undogmatic interdisciplinary therapy, unrestricted by traditional segregations into individual work versus groupwork, that is capable of addressing the pain of social and cultural splits as experienced in the depth of the individual *psyche*, precisely because as practitioners we are embracing, holding, and transcending those splits on both personal and professional levels.

Such an approach does not just apply the principles of individual work to group practice, but can redefine, more comprehensively, our vision of what therapy is about: a socially transformative and evolutionary practice that can fluidly interweave between individual and social identity and does justice *both* to the depth of the individual "inner world" and to the significance of interdependent, intersubjective social relating.

## References

Agazarian, Y., & Peters, R. (1981). *The visible and invisible group.* London: Routledge Tavistock.

Ancona, L. (1996). Psicoanalisi e Gruppo-analisi a confronto [Comparing psychoanalysis and Group Analysis]. *Gli Argonauti, XVIII(68),* 29–47.

Anzieu, D. (1984). *The group and the unconscious.* London: RKP.

Bach, G. (1954). *Intensive group psychotherapy.* New York: Ronald Press.

Bandler, R., & Grinder, J. (1979). *Frogs into princes: Neuro Linguistic Programming.* New York: Real People Press.

Banet, A. G., & Hayden, C. (1977). A Tavistock primer. In: J. E. Jones & J. W. Pfeiffer (Eds.), *The 1977 annual handbook for group facilitators*, (pp. 155–167).

Beisser, A. (1970). The paradoxical theory of change. In J. Fagan & I. Shepherd (Eds.), *Gestalt Therapy now: Theory, techniques, applications.* New York: HarperCollins College Div.

Bennis, W., & Shepard, H. (1978). *A theory of group development.* In: L. Bradford (Ed.), *Group development.* La Jolla, CA: University Associates.

Bion, W. R. (1961). *Experiences in groups and other papers.* London: Tavistock.

Bly, R. (1996). *The sibling society: The culture of half-adults.* New York: De Capo Press.

Boyesen, G. (1994). *Über den Körper die Seele heilen: Biodynamische Psychologie und Psychotherapie [Through the body, heal the soul: Biodynamic Psychology and Psychotherapy].* Munich: Kösel.

Carroll, R. (2002). At the border between chaos and order: What psychotherapy and neuroscience have in common. In: J. Corrigall & H. Wilkinson (Eds.), *Revolutionary connections: Psychotherapy and neuroscience.* London: Karnac.

Conger, J. P. (1994). *The body in recovery: Somatic Psychotherapy and the self.* Berkeley, CA: Frog.

Coveney, P., & Highfield, R. (1995). *Frontiers of complexity: The search for order in a chaotic world.* London: Faber & Faber.

Durkin, J. (Ed.). (1981). *Living systems: Group psychotherapy and general systems theory.* New York: Brunner-Mazel.

Feder, B., & Ronall, R. (1980). *Beyond the hot seat: Gestalt approaches to group.* New York: Brunner-Mazel.

Foucault, M. (2001). *Madness and civilization* (2nd ed.). New York: Routledge.

Foulkes, S. H., & Anthony, E. J. (1965). *Group psychotherapy: The psychoanalytic approach* (2nd ed.). Harmondsworth, UK: Penguin.

Gallese, V. (2003). The roots of empathy: The shared manifold hypothesis and the neural basis of intersubjectivity. *Psychopathology, 36,* 171–180.

Goodman, P. (1947). *Communitas.* New York: Random House.

Heckler, R. S. (1984). *The anatomy of change: East/West Approaches to Body/Mind Therapy.* Boston: Shambhala.

Heron, J. (1999). *The complete facilitator's handbook.* London: Kogan Page.

Houston, G. (1984). *The red book of groups.* London: Rochester Foundation.

Houston, G. (1994). *Being and belonging: Group, intergroup and Gestalt.* London: Wiley.

Laing, D. (1990). *The divided self: An existential study in sanity and madness.* New York: Penguin.

Lewin, K. (1948). *Resolving social conflicts: Selected papers on group dynamics.* New York: Harper & Row.

Lewin, K. (1951). *Field theory in social science.* New York: Harper Brothers.

Lowen, A. (1971). *The language of the body.* New York: Prentice Hall.

Maturana, H. R., & Varela, F. J. (1987). *The tree of knowledge: The biological roots of human understanding.* Boston: Shambhala.

Merleau-Ponty, M. (1969). *The visible and the invisible.* New York: Northwestern University Press.

Mindell, A. (1992). *The leader as martial artist.* San Francisco: HarperCollins.

Mindell, A. (1995). *Sitting in the fire: Large group transformation using conflict and diversity.* Portland, OR: Lao Tse Press.

O'Loughlin, M. (2006). *Embodiment and education: Exploring creatural existence.* New York: Kluwer Academic.

Orbach, S. (2006). *Fat is a feminist issue.* London: Arrow Books.

Perls, F., Hefferline, R., & Goodman, P. (1973). *Gestalt Therapy: Excitement and growth in the human personality.* London: Pelican.

Porges, S. W. (2005). The role of social engagement in attachment and bonding: A phylogenetic perspective. In: C. S. Carter, L. Ahnert, K. E. Grossman, S. B. Hrdy, M. E. Lamb, S. W. Porges, & N. Sachser (Eds.), *Attachment and bonding: A new synthesis* (pp. 33–54). Cambridge, MA: MIT Press.

Randall, R., Southgate, J., & Tomlinson, F. (1980). *Co-operative and community group dynamics: Or, your meetings needn't be so appalling.* London: Barefoot Books.

Reich, W. (1983). *The function of the orgasm.* London: Souvenir Press.

Ridley, M. (2004). *Nature via nurture: Genes, experience and what makes us human.* London: Harper Perennial.

Rogers, C. R. (1973). *Encounter groups.* Harmondsworth, UK: Penguin.

Rosenberg, J. (1989). *Body, self and soul.* New York: Humanics.

Schore, A. N. (1994). *Affect regulation and the origin of the self.* Hillsdale, NJ: Lawrence Erlbaum.

Schore, A. N. (2001). Effects of a secure attachment relationship on right brain development, affect regulation and infant mental health. *Infant Mental Health Journal, 22(1–2),* 7–66.

Schutz, W. C. (1966). *The interpersonal underworld.* Palo Alto, CA: Science & Behavior Books.

Soth, M. (1999). The Body in Counselling. *Counselling News,* Jan. 1999, p. 15-17.

Soth, M. (2000). The Integrated BodyMind's view on 'Body/Mind Integration'. *AChP Newsletter.*

Soth, M. (2004). Integrating humanistic techniques into a transference-countertransference perspective: A response to "Humanistic or psychodynamic—what is the difference and do we have to make a choice?" by Lavinia Gomez. *Self and Society, 32(1),* 44–52.

Soth, M. (2005). Embodied countertransference. In: N. Totton (Ed.), *New dimensions in Body Psychotherapy,* (pp. 40–55). London: Open University Press.

Soth, M. (2006). What therapeutic hope for a subjective mind in an objectified body? In: J. Corrigall, H. Payne, & H. Wilkinson (Eds.), *About a body,* (pp. 111–131). London: Routledge.

Stattmann, J. (1989). *Unitive Psychology, Vol. 1.* Frankfurt: AFRA Verlag.

Stattmann, J. (1991). *Unitive Psychology, Vol. 2.* Frankfurt: AFRA Verlag.

Stern, D. (1985). *The interpersonal world of the infant.* New York: Basic Books.

Szasz, T. (1984). *The myth of mental illness: Foundations of a theory of personal contact.* London: Harper Perennial.

Totton, N. (1998). *The water in the glass: Body and mind in psychoanalysis.* London: Rebus/Karnac.

Totton, N. (2002). Foreign bodies: Recovering the history of Body Psychotherapy. In T. Staunton (Ed.), *Body Psychotherapy* (pp. 7–26). London: Brunner-Routledge.

Totton, N. (2003). *Body Psychotherapy: An introduction.* Maidenhead, UK: Open University Press.

Totton, N. (2005). Embodied-relational therapy. In N. Totton (Ed.), *New dimensions in Body Psychotherapy* (pp. 168–181). Maidenhead, UK: Open University Press.

Trevarthen, C. (1993). The self born in intersubjectivity: The psychology of an infant communicating. In U. Neisser (Ed.), *The perceived self: Ecological and interpersonal sources of self-knowledge* (pp. 121–173). New York: Cambridge University Press.

Trevarthen, C. (2001). Intrinsic motives for companionship in understanding: Their origin, development, and significance for infant mental health. *Infant Mental Health Journal, 22, 1–2.*

Tuckman, B. W. (1965). Developmental sequence in small groups. *Psychological Bulletin, 63, 384–399.*

Winnicott, D. W. (1954/1987). Meta-psychological and clinical aspects of regression within the psycho-analytical set-up. In D. Winnicott, *Through paediatrics to psychoanalysis: Collected papers* (pp. 278–294). London: Karnac.

Yalom, I. (2005). *The theory and practice of group psychotherapy* (5th ed.). New York: Basic Books.

# 84
## Research in Body Psychotherapy

Barnaby B. Barratt, South Africa

**Barnaby B. Barratt**, PhD, DHS, is the senior research fellow at the University of Cape Town and is the visiting professor of psychology at the University of the Witwatersrand. He is a psychoanalyst practicing in Johannesburg, South Africa, and an active clinical member of both the International Psychoanalytical Association and the United States Association for Body Psychotherapy. Among his publications is *The Emergence of Somatic Psychology and Bodymind Therapy* (2010).

In our contemporary world, research into the effects of any clinical intervention or treatment modality has dual purposes. It serves to stimulate, direct, and support advances in the specific discipline. In this respect, clinical practitioners may learn to improve their methods in response to scientific findings. It also serves to document the effectiveness of particular techniques, strategies, or clinical methodologies. This latter challenge has a double aspect. It is ethically important to us, as practitioners, as well as to the population of clients or patients, to know that our healing practices do in fact bring relief from suffering, as well as fresh openings for personal growth. It has also become pragmatically important for us, as professionals, to be able to prove to external entities, such as governmental and corporate institutions, that the clinical work we do warrants legal protection and financial support—and this can all too easily become a political matter in which the tail wags the dog.

This chapter will describe the stringencies associated with the classic or conservative "evidence-based medicine" standard of research into the effectiveness of clinical interventions, followed by a brief review of what has thus far been accomplished in terms of this sort of support for the methods of Body Psychotherapy. I will then point to three vital areas of current scientific investigation that are powerfully significant for the advances of Body Psychotherapy. These areas of research provide a theoretical basis on which to believe that Body Psychotherapy will eventually be demonstrated to be efficacious in ways that behaviorist or cognitivist methods cannot be; in this respect, the practices of body movement and awareness, as well as a psychodynamic or psychoanalytic understanding of the human condition, are critical. The question of whether the clinical practices of Somatic Psychology and other body-mind therapies should, or should not, be held to the classic or conservative standards of evidence-based medicine remains open and needs to be more actively debated.

### Research on Treatment Effectiveness

The paradox of this topic is that there is a wealth of clinical reports and anecdotal evidence testifying to the effectiveness of Body Psychotherapeutic practices. In short, as practitioners, we know it works! However, in our contemporary culture, such evidence fails to convince the skeptical and financially motivated forces of governmental and corporate institutions, which demand that all clinical interventions should meet the same rigorous standards of evidence-based medicine as are supposedly required of the pharmacological industry (American Psychological Association, 2006; Kopec, Sinclair, and Matthes, 2011; Sackett, Straus, Richardson, Rosenberg, and Haynes, 2000).

In the past decade, however, the application of these standards to the processes of psychological therapies has been challenged (e.g., Gupta, 2003; Holmes, Murray, Perron, and Rail, 2006; Bickman, 2008; Rosner, 2012; Seidman et al., 2009; Slade and Priebe, 2001; Becker et al., 2011), and the debate over this issue is becoming more heated (e.g., Kazdin, 2008; Loewenthal and Winter, 2006; Norcross, Beutler, and Levant, 2006). Outside the domain of Somatic Psychology, it has often been excessively challenging for general psychotherapeutic research to meet these methodological stringencies (e.g., Goodheart, Kazdin, and Sternberg, 2006; Meltzoff and Kornreich, 2007; Roth and Fonagy, 2005), except perhaps in relation to brief, symptom-focused treatments in the behaviorist and cognitivist tradition (including Cognitive Behavioral Therapy).

However, recent studies not only demonstrate the effectiveness of psychodynamic and psychoanalytic treatments, but furthermore suggest ways in which they are successful where behaviorally oriented approaches are not (e.g., Bateman and Fonagy, 2008; Clarkin, Levy, Lenzenweger, and Kernberg, 2007; Leichsenring and Rabung, 2008; Muller and Tillman, 2007; Milrod et al., 2007; Shedler, 2010); these studies also counter the long-standing belief that psychotherapies may be effective, but that the modality of treatment (i.e., what kind of therapy) makes no difference (Luborsky, Singer, and Luborsky, 1975).

In the context of the conservative or classic model of evidence-based medicine, a compelling quantitative-experimental investigation of the effectiveness of a Body Psychotherapeutic modality should, if at all possible, meet the following five criteria:

1. The use of valid and reliable evaluative instruments that can measure behavioral or psychological change objectively. Studies that ask subjects to report on the benefits of a treatment they have received (or that ask practitioners to assess the effects of a treatment they have administered) lack scientific credibility—as do survey instruments that merely have content or face validity.

2. The establishment of pretreatment levels of the variables to be evaluated and then the assessment of immediate post-treatment as well as delayed post-treatment levels. Too many studies in our field merely assess change at the end of the treatment (at the termination of a three-month therapy, at the end of a weekend workshop, and so forth). The provision of a delayed assessment (for example, evaluating change six months or a year after the termination of treatment) indicates whether the positive benefits of the procedure are actually durable.

3. The use of a placebo treatment with a control group.

4. Random assignment of subjects to one group or the other. This is notoriously difficult in psychotherapeutic research, especially because there are ethical issues involved *both* in giving subjects a therapy of unproven efficacy *and* in withholding from subjects a therapy that is believed to be efficacious.

These difficulties are compounded by:

5. The need to make every effort to eliminate expectation effects. It is for this reason that, in pharmacological studies, neither the subjects nor the persons giving the treatment know whether the agent being administered is the experimental drug or the placebo. Obviously, this double-blind procedure is impossible to replicate in psychotherapeutic research. Nevertheless, convincing studies of therapeutic effectiveness need to control response biases (such as the subject's wish to please the researcher, the practitioners' motivation to demonstrate the successes of their labors, etc.).

Unfortunately, a review of the database maintained by the *European Association for Body Psychotherapy* and of the references generated by other search engines (for example, ProQuest, PsychiatryOnline, ISI Citation Index, PubMed) reveals that there is virtually no research on the effectiveness of Body Psychotherapeutic modalities that meets the stringent rigor of these sorts of evidential criteria.

Too many studies have used only retrospectively collected data (e.g., Gudat, 1997; Ventling and Gerhard, 2000), and an embarrassing number of studies have relied too greatly on the therapists' ratings of their own successes (e.g., Ventling, 2002; Ventling, Bertschi, and Gerhard, 2008). These studies have typically examined one modality of Body Psychotherapy applied to a range of clinical conditions, whereas some of the more promising lines of research on therapeutic effectiveness have focused on the treatment as applied to a particular condition, such as: chronic pain (e.g., Monsen and Monsen, 2000); anxiety (e.g., Berg, Sandell, and Sandahi, 2009); post-traumatic stress (Price, McBride, Hyerle, and Kivlahan, 2007); as well as the somatoform disorders, including eating disorders and body image aberrations (see Röhricht, 2009). Other systematic investigations have used rigorous methodologies, but with only a small number of subjects or with a brief treatment duration; for example, Kaplan and Schwartz (2005) used the Pragmatic Case Study Method to report the gains made by two subjects as a result of a twelve-session treatment.

## The Current Evidence Base

A longitudinal series of studies by Koemeda-Lutz and her colleagues offer some of the best evidence currently available. In their preliminary report of what they call a "naturalistic prospective field study," the investigators described the administration of a battery of standard measures (at the beginning of treatment, after six months of treatment, and at the end of treatment) to 157 German and Swiss subjects participating in various modalities of outpatient Body Psychotherapy (Koemeda-Lutz et al., 2003). The 78 subjects who completed the battery of measures after six months reported significant improvements on various measures (e.g., anxiety, depression), and the 21 subjects who were assessed after two years of treatment showed more substantial positive gains on all scales. The investigators' subsequent report indicated similar results with 342 participants at the beginning of the investigation, 253 after six months, and 160 after two years of treatment (Koemeda-Lutz et al., 2006).

Although these results are indeed promising, not only suggesting that the effects of Body Psychotherapy can be evaluated with some of the standard instruments generally used in psychotherapeutic research (e.g., the Beck Depression Inventory), but also indicating that the beneficial effects of therapy can be maintained over a significant period of time; however, the problematic attrition rate unavoidably limits the value of the study. Put simply, we do not know what happened to the large number of subjects who began treatment, participated in the research program, but dropped out before the end of the six-month timeline, or between that and the two-year evaluation. This, of course, is precisely one of the major challenges of demonstrating the effectiveness of any psychotherapeutic modality that is not brief (and not necessarily symptom-focused).

There are also two or three studies that have been published in mainstream (scientific) journals on the outcome of Body-Oriented Psychotherapeutic research with particular populations. These have met the "evidence-based" criteria required of other psychotherapies and—as a result—Body-Oriented Psychotherapy has been accepted as a valid treatment for these conditions (Röhricht and Priebe, 2006; Röhricht et al., 2011, 2013).

## Other (Future) Studies

Although interventions that are somewhat related to Body Psychotherapy, such as Yoga and EMDR, have generated a small amount of research literature convincingly demonstrating their effects, Body Psychotherapy continues to lag, as was indicated previously in reviews by May (2005) and by Röhricht (2009).

It is clear that if Body Psychotherapies are going to court the engagement and endorsement of third-party payers (e.g., employee benefit programs managed by corporate entities, or health care and governmental organizations, etc.), substantial programs of quantitative-experimental research (outcome studies that demonstrate conclusively the effectiveness of these modalities to achieve behavioral change) will be needed. Indeed, studies that demonstrate the cost-effectiveness of this modality, compared with behaviorist, cognitivist, and pharmacological treatments, will also be necessary. We also have to face the possibility that future quantitative-empirical investigations might show some approaches within this heterogeneous field to be more effective than others (even if this does not correspond with our experience as practitioners).

Nevertheless, it does not serve Body Psychotherapists, as practitioners, to remain under the illusion that anything less than such rigorous research programs will be required—programs in which the criteria of success are those of symptom relief, and in which economic profitability is taken as the additional hallmark of successful treatment. However, research programs of this sort, in the field that we know to be so precious, do not appear to be on the horizon in any volume, and this is undoubtedly because intervention studies are very costly and also because research on Body Psychotherapy is not well funded (in contrast with studies of the latest psychotropic drugs).

Despite our culture's predilection for numbers, steps toward better support for the sort of research that might satisfy corporate entities and governmental agencies might be undertaken by using qualitative methodology (Harper and Thompson, 2011).

Although anecdotal material is not highly regarded in the world of evidence-based interventions, it might even be helpful, as a preliminary tactic, to collect such material in a more systematic manner than has typically been achieved hitherto. Johanson reminds us that, as long ago as 1986, Gendlin advocated the establishment of a data bank of cases, but it is not clear where, if anywhere, this has been done systematically; and perhaps we all need to discuss more actively how such data might be mined and publicized in order to meet the hegemonic standards of evidence-based medicine (Weiss, Johanson, and Monda, in preparation).

## Areas of Scientific Research Relevant to Body Psychotherapy

Body Psychotherapy has developed rapidly in the past hundred years, deriving its practices from several sources. Historically, these have included psychoanalytic and somatic psychodynamics, philosophical and cultural studies (including phenomenological and humanistic psychologies), European and North American traditions of bodywork, increasing knowledge of Eastern healing disciplines, shamanic and transpersonal practices, and advances in the neurosciences (Barratt, 2010; Marlock and Weiss, 2006; Röhricht, 2008).

Today, three areas of research seem of particular significance to the further evolution of our discipline and, in the case of the neurosciences, perhaps lend credence to the proposition that Somatic Psychology and body-mind therapies have a type of effectiveness lacking in behaviorist and cognitivist treatments.

### 1. Research on the Psychodynamic Sensuality of Embodiment

The area that I will mention first concerns sexuality and the sensuality of embodiment, as well as new ways of considering the processes of engenderment. Although there are exceptions, this is unfortunately an area of research with which many Body Psychotherapists avoid association, perhaps due to a failure of courage in the face of public prejudice and stigmatization—and despite the fact that some of the field's most notable leaders, such as Reich (e.g., 1927, 1933, 1936), very clearly understood libidinality as the embodied life force energies that animate and sustain human life.

In the 1980s and 1990s, there was a return of interest in the psychodynamics of erotic experience (e.g., Breen, 1993; Bullough, Bullough, and Elias, 1997; Butler, 1990, 1993, 2004; Chodorow, 1994; Domenici and Lesser, 1995; Dumas, 1997; Francoeur, 1991; Frosch, 1994; Goldenberg, 1990; Green, 1997; Kestenberg, 1995; Lingis, 1994, 1995, 1996; McDougall, 1995; Morin, 1995; Nancy, 1990–1992; Segal, 1997; Spicker, 1995; Stoller, 1992; Warner, 1999). These studies included some remarkable presentations of cross-cultural evidence concerning impressive variations in the human capacity for sensual experience, which were much needed (see also: Gregersen, 1983).

Sadly, this wave of renewed interest occurred mostly far outside the field of Body Psychotherapy. However, it has been followed by diverse, but theoretically psychodynamic or psychoanalytic, reconsiderations of the sexuality and sensuality of human experience (e.g., Barratt, 2005, 2012; Blechner, 2009; Bloom, 2006; Butler, 2004; Ferrari, 2004; Lingis, 2000, 2005, 2011; Mollon, 2005, 2008; Nancy, 2003; Ragland, 2004; Saleci, 1994; Sandfort and Rademakers, 2001; Stauntson and Kyratzis, 2007; Stoller, 2005).

Despite their diversity, these scholarly developments are profoundly relevant to the practices of Body Psychotherapy, because they focus on the significance of the subject's embodied experience and demonstrate the extent to which Freud (1923) was correct in asserting the foundational primacy, for all aspects of human functioning, of what he called the "body ego." These investigative developments also point to the way in which the "voicing" of our sensual experience comes to be suppressed or repressed in the course of our socialization and acculturation (Barratt, 2005, 2012). Such research contributes strongly to the axioms that have guided the development of Body Psychotherapy in the past century.

## 2. Research on the Psychodynamics of Relating

The sensuality of embodied experience, which is our sexuality (using this term in a broad sense), constitutes the dynamic basis of human relationships, both with one's self and with others (Efron, 1985); as one student expressed it, "human contact, especially when it involves intimacies, proceeds more from the gut and the groin than the head." Historically derived from object-relations perspectives in psychoanalysis (e.g., Bowlby, 1969–1980), a range of contemporary investigations into attachment processes and interpersonal relations thus provides a wealth of information directly or indirectly relevant to the practices of Body Psychotherapy (e.g., Beebe and Lachmann, 2005; Cassidy and Shaver, 2010; Karen, 1998; Stern, 2000, 2004, 2010; Tschacher and Bergomi, 2011). The literature in this area is voluminous.

Such research demonstrates the significance of relationships as linked to embodied experience. Obviously, the implications for clinical practice are open to much further discussion, and perhaps may be controversial, even within the heterogeneous field of Body Psychotherapy. For example, although scientific investigations demonstrate the necessity of touch for healthy development (e.g., Field, 2001; Jablonski, 2008), whether and how this might imply that the clinician should touch the patient or client still remains debatable (Hunter and Struve, 1998).

## 3. Research from the Neurosciences

As with research into the sexuality of human embodiment, the investigations of attachment and relational processes connect, quite clearly, with recent neuroscientific developments. The impact of neuroscientific findings on our understanding of the significance of embodied approaches to psychotherapy is considerable (e.g., Aposhyan, 2004; Cozolino, 2006, 2010; Damasio, 2012; Schore, 2012; Siegel, 2007, 2012; etc.). Additionally, the contemporary shift from Cartesian dualism to a more holistic "body-mind" view of human functioning strongly supports the need for psychotherapeutic approaches that do not, so to speak, remain "in the head" without attending to the subtleties of embodied experience (Damasio, 2008).

Specific studies that have been the focus of neuroscientific research also lend credence to body-mind therapies. Examples would include recent investigations in psycho-neuroimmunology (Ader, 2006), neurophysiology (Blum and Rutkove, 2010), psycho-physiology (Andreassi, 2006), and psycho-endocrinology (Nelson, 2010). In particular, we might note the significance of recent work on polyvagal theory by Porges (2011), which provides just one of the many clear links between these advances in neuroscience and the issues of emotional attachment, touch, and bodily awareness that are the distinctive healing practices of Body Psychotherapy.

In sum, many of these sorts of neuroscientific advances are highly suggestive with respect to the effectiveness of embodied approaches to healing. However, in most cases, the precise implications of neuroscience for the actual methodologies of clinical practice have yet to be sufficiently specified or clearly indicated. What one can say, probably, is that the findings of neuroscience definitely dispute the aforementioned Cartesian dualism and, more radically, they might even contest the validity of any psychotherapeutic practice that is committed to purely behaviorist or cognitivist assumptions. To express this differently, the direction in which the neurosciences are advancing leads one to believe that the future lies with Body Psychotherapy, with Body Psychoanalysis, and also with the interesting work being done in neuropsychoanalysis (Bernstein, 2011; Kaplan-Solms and Solms, 2001; Northoff, 2011; Solms and Turnbull, 2002).

## Special Considerations and Concluding Note

Assessing the state of research in Body Psychotherapy, it would be facile to conclude that "half of the glass" is abundantly full, but the other "half of the glass" remains challengingly empty. Despite the fact that recent developments in sexuality research, attachment research, and neuroscientific research would lead one to conclude that the future of Body Psychotherapy (especially if conducted psychodynamically) and of neuropsychoanalysis is bright, it is nonetheless clear that if Body Psychotherapy—as a set of psychotherapeutic healing modalities—is to compete in the contemporary marketplace with the changes offered by psycho-pharmacology, with or without the use of other therapeutic approaches (e.g., Cognitive Behavioral Therapy, short-term verbal psychotherapy, etc.), then much further research in the form of rigorously conducted outcome studies is needed. However, some practitioners might legitimately want to argue that this is not a competitive marketplace into which their particular mode of healing should seek to enter.

Although its assumptions are frequently covert, the arena of evidence-based clinical interventions not only commits us to an attenuated understanding of personal change in terms of observable behaviors, but also measures success in terms of criteria of social adaptation (symptom relief, etc.). On philosophical grounds, some theorists of the body-mind therapies might dispute the worthiness of such criteria (Barratt, 2010, 2012).

For example, it could be argued that the personal-growth processes and the health and well-being perspectives, that are facilitated by Body Psychotherapy involve phenomena that are not readily observable (for example, greater awareness of, and ability to listen to, the "voices" of our embodiment). It could also be claimed that success in these treatment modalities might not be measurable in terms of the individual's adaptive functioning in the contemporary marketplace, nor in terms of adjustment in a culture that promotes our alienation from the processes of our embodiment. Indeed, some modalities of Body Psychotherapy, especially those that refer to subtle energy systems, might be understood better as spiritual practices than as devices promoting or compelling behavioral change (e.g., Ray, 2008).

In conclusion, if Body Psychotherapeutic practitioners wish to follow the demands of the marketplace, substantial investment (in time, energy, and money) needs to be made in rigorous and systematic research demonstrating the effectiveness of these different methods. However, philosophical issues also need to be debated further, because it can be argued that, in attempting to meet such demands, aspects of what is most precious about the methods and processes of Body Psychotherapy can be overlooked, dismissed, and thus lost. Although this conclusion may be scientifically premature and thus somewhat speculative, the available research suggests that three processes in particular that characterize some, but not all, modalities of what is called "Body Psychotherapy"—namely, movement, sensorial awareness, and psychodynamic understanding of the human condition—are indeed precious in their power to facilitate deep and lasting personal transformation. We just need to produce the evidence to substantiate this.

## References

Ader, R. (Ed.). (2006). *Psychoneuroimmunology* (2 vols.) (4th ed.). Waltham, MA: Academic Press.

American Psychological Association: Task Force on Evidence-Based Practice. (2006). Evidence-based practice in psychology. *American Psychologist, 61, 271–285.*

Andreassi, J. L. (2006). *Psychophysiology: Human behavior and physiological response* (5th ed.). Mahwah, NJ: Lawrence Erlbaum.

Aposhyan, S. (2004). *BodyMind Psychotherapy: Principles, techniques, and practical applications.* New York: W. W. Norton.

Barratt, B. B. (2005). *Sexual health and erotic freedom.* Philadelphia: Xlibris/Random House.

Barratt, B. B. (2010). *The emergence of Somatic Psychology and Body-Mind Therapy.* Basingstoke, UK: Palgrave Macmillan.

Barratt, B. B. (2012). *What is psychoanalysis? 100 years after Freud's "Secret Committee."* London: Routledge.

Bateman, A., & Fonagy, P. (2008). Eight year follow-up of patients treated for borderline personality disorder: Mentalization-based treatment versus treatment as usual. *American Journal of Psychiatry, 165,* 631–638.

Becker, K. D., Chorpita, B. F., & Daleiden, E. L. (2011). Improvement in symptoms versus functioning: How do our best treatments measure up? *Administrative Policy in Mental Health, 38,* 440–458.

Beebe, B., & Lachmann, F. M. (2005). *Infant research and adult treatment: Coconstructing interactions.* London: Routledge.

Berg, A. L., Sandell, R., & Sandahl, C. (2009). Affect-focused Body Psychotherapy in patients with generalized anxiety disorder: Evaluation of an integrative method. *Journal of Psychotherapy Integration, 19(1),* 67–85.

Bernstein, W. M. (2011). *A basic theory of neuropsychoanalysis.* London: Karnac.

Bickman, L. (2008). A measurement feedback system (MFS) is necessary to improve mental health outcomes. *Journal of the American Academy of Child and Adolescent Psychiatry, 47(10),* 1114–1119.

Blechner, M. J. (2009). *Sex changes: Transformations in society and psychoanalysis.* New York: Routledge.

Bloom, K. (2006). *The embodied self: Movement and psychoanalysis.* London: Karnac.

Blum, A. S., & Rutkove, S. B. (Eds.). (2010). *The clinical neurophysiology primer.* New York: Humana.

Bowlby, J. (1969–1980). *Attachment and loss* (3 vols.). New York: Basic Books.

Breen, D. (Ed.). (1993). *The gender conundrum: Contemporary psychoanalytic perspectives on femininity and masculinity.* London: Routledge.

Bullough, B., Bullough, V. L., & Elias, J. (Eds.). (1997). *Gender blending.* Amherst, NY: Prometheus Books.

Butler, J. P. (1990/2007). *Gender trouble: Feminism and the subversion of identity* (10th ed.). London: Routledge.

Butler, J. P. (1993). *Bodies that matter.* London: Routledge.

Butler, J. P. (2004). *Undoing gender.* London: Routledge.

Cassidy, J., & Shaver, P. R. (Eds.). (2010). *Handbook of attachment: Theory, research, and clinical applications.* New York: Guilford Press.

Chodorow, N. J. (1994). *Femininities, masculinities, sexualities: Freud and beyond.* Lexington: University of Kentucky Press.

Clarkin, J. F., Levy, K. N., Lenzenweger, M. F., & Kernberg, O. F. (2007). Evaluating three treatments for borderline personality disorder: A multi-wave study. *American Journal of Psychiatry, 164,* 922–928.

Cozolino, L. (2006). *The neuroscience of human relationships: Attachment and the developing social brain.* New York: W. W. Norton.

Cozolino, L. (2010). *The neuroscience of psychotherapy: Building and rebuilding the human brain.* New York: W. W. Norton.

Damasio, A. (2008). *Descartes' error: Emotion, reason, and the human brain.* New York: Penguin.

Damasio, A. (2012). *Self comes to mind: Constructing the conscious brain.* New York: Vintage.

Domenici, T., & Lesser, R. C. (Eds.). (1995). *Disorienting sexuality.* New York: Routledge.

Dumas, D. (1997). *Sons, lovers, and fathers: Understanding male sexuality* (A. Trager & C. Fleischner, Trans.). Northvale, NJ: Jason Aronson.

Efron, A. (1985). The sexual body: An interdisciplinary perspective. Special issue of *Journal of Mind and Behavior, 6(1 & 2).*

Ferrari, A. B. (2004). *From the eclipse of the body to the dawn of thought* (I. Ghigi, Trans.). London: Free Association Books.

Field, T. (2001). *Touch.* Cambridge, MA: MIT/Bradford Press.

Francoeur, R. T. (1991). *Becoming a sexual person* (2nd ed.). New York: Prentice Hall.

Freud, S. (1923). The ego and the id. *Standard Edition of the Complete Psychological Works of Sigmund Freud, 19,* 1–66.

Frosch, S. (1994). *Sexual difference: Masculinity and psychoanalysis.* London: Routledge.

Gendlin, E. (1986). What comes after traditional psychotherapy research? *American Psychologist, 41,* 131–136.

Goldenberg, N. R. (1990). *Returning words to flesh: Feminism, psychoanalysis, and the resurrection of the body.* Boston: Beacon Press.

Goodheart, C. D., Kazdin, A. E., & Sternberg, R. J. (Eds.). (2006). *Evidencebased psychotherapy: Where practice and research meet.-* Washington, DC: American Psychological Association.

Green, A. (1997/2000). *The chains of eros: The sexual in psychoanalysis* (L. Thurston, Trans.). London: Rebus Press.

Gregersen, E. (1983). *Sexual practices: The story of human sexuality.* New York: Franklin Watts.

Gudat, U. (1997). Bioenergetische Analyse als ambulante Psychotherapie: Anwendungsbereiche und Wirkungen [Bioenergetic Analysis as outpatient psychotherapy: Applications and effects]. *Psychotherapie Forum, 5,* 28–37.

Gupta, M. (2003). A critical appraisal of evidence-based medicine: Some ethical considerations. *Journal of Evaluation in Clinical Practice, 9,* 111–121.

Harper, D., & Thompson, A. R. (Eds.). (2011). *Qualitative research methods in mental health and psychotherapy: A guide for students and practitioners.* Hoboken, NJ: Wiley-Blackwell.

Holmes, D., Murray, S. J., Perron, A., & Rail, G. (2006). Deconstructing the evidence-based discourse in health sciences: Truth, power and fascism. *International Journal of EvidenceBased Healthcare, 4,* 180–186.-

Hunter, M., & Struve, J. (1998). *The ethical use of touch in psychotherapy.* Thousand Oaks, CA: Sage.

Jablonski, N. G. (2008). *Skin: A natural history.* Berkeley: University of California Press.

Kaplan, A. H., & Schwartz, L. F. (2005). Listening to the body: Pragmatic case studies of Body-Centered Psychotherapy. *USA Body Psychotherapy Journal, 4(2),* 33–67.

Kaplan-Solms, K., & Solms, M. (2001). *Clinical studies in neuropsychoanalysis: Introduction to a depth neuropsychology.* New York: Other Press.

Karen, R. (1998). *Becoming attached: First relationships and how they shape our capacity to love.* Oxford, UK: Oxford University Press.

Kazdin, A. E. (2008). Evidence-based treatment and practice: New opportunities to bridge clinical research and practice, enhance the knowledge base, and improve patient care. *American Psychologist, 63,* 146–159.

Kestenberg, J. S. (1995). *Sexuality, body movement, and the rhythms of development.* Northvale, NJ: Jason Aronson.

Koemeda-Lutz, M., Kaschke, M., Revenstorf, D., Scherrmann, T., Weiss, H., & Soeder, U. (2003). Preliminary results concerning the effectiveness of Body Psychotherapies in outpatient settings: A multi-center study in Germany and Switzerland. *Psychotherapie Forum, 11,* 70–79. [Reprinted in *USA Body Psychotherapy Journal, 4(2) (2005), 13–32*]

Koemeda-Lutz, M., Kaschke, M., Revenstorf, D., Scherrmann, T., Weiss, H., & Soeder, U. (2006). Evaluation der Wirksamkeit von ambulanten Körperpsychotherapien EWAK: Eine Multizenterstudie in Deutschland und der Schweiz [Evaluation of the effectiveness of outpatient Body Psychotherapies: A multicenter study in Germany and Switzerland]. *Psychotherapien Psychische Medizen Psychosomatic, 56,* 480–487. [Reprinted in *Hakomi Forum, 19 (2008), 20–21*]

Kopec, D., Sinclair, E., & Matthes, B. (2011). *Evidence based design: A process for research and writing.* New York: Prentice Hall.

Leichsenring, F., & Rabung, S. (2008). Effectiveness of long-term Psychodynamic Psychotherapy: A meta-analysis. *Journal of the American Medical Association, 300,* 1551–1565.

Lingis, A. (1994). *Foreign bodies.* London: Routledge.

Lingis, A. (1995). *Abuses.* Berkeley: University of California Press.

Lingis, A. (1996). *Sensation: Intelligibility in sensibility.* Atlantic Highlands, NJ: Humanities Press.

Lingis, A. (2000). *Dangerous emotions.* Berkeley: University of California Press.

Lingis, A. (2005). *Body transformations: Evolutions and atavisms in culture.* London: Routledge.

Lingis, A. (2011). *Violence and splendor.* Evanston, IL: Northwestern University Press.

Loewenthal, D., & Winter, D. (Eds.). (2006). *What is psychotherapeutic research?* London: Karnac.

Luborsky, L., Singer, B., & Luborsky, L. (1975). Comparative studies of psychotherapies: Is it true that "everybody has won and all must have prizes"? *Archives of General Psychiatry, 32*, 995–1008.

Marlock, G., & Weiss, H. (Eds.). (2006). *Handbuch der Körperpsychotherapie [Handbook of Body Psychotherapy]*. Stuttgart: Schattauer.

May, J. (2005). The outcome of Body Psychotherapy research. *USA Body Psychotherapy Journal, 4(2)*, 93–115.

McDougall, J. (1995). *The many faces of Eros: A psychoanalytic exploration of human sexuality.* London: Free Association Books.

Meltzoff, J., & Kornreich, M. (2007). *Research in psychotherapy.* Chicago: Aldine Transaction.

Milrod, B., Leon, A. C., Busch, F., Rudden, M., Schwalberg, M., Clarkin, J., Aronson, A., Singer, M., Turchin, W., Klass, E. T., Graf, E., Teres, J. J., & Shear, M. K. (2007). A randomized controlled clinical trial of psychoanalytic psychotherapy for panic disorder. *American Journal of Psychiatry, 164*, 265–272.

Mollon, P. (2005). *EMDR and the energy therapies: Psychoanalytic perspectives.* London: Karnac.

Mollon, P. (2008). *Psychoanalytic energy psychotherapy.* London: Karnac Books.

Monsen, K., & Monsen, J. T. (2000). Chronic pain and psychodynamic body therapy: A controlled outcome study. *Psychotherapy: Theory, Research, Practice, Training, 37(3)*, 257–269.

Morin, J. (1995). *The erotic mind: Unlocking the inner sources of sexual passion and fulfillment.* New York: HarperCollins.

Muller, J. P., & Tillman, J. G. (Eds.). (2007). *The embodied subject: Minding the body in psychoanalysis.* Lanham, MD: Jason Aronson.

Nancy, J-L. (1990–1992/2008). *Corpus* (R. A. Rand, Trans.). New York: Fordham University Press.

Nancy, J-L. (2003/2008). *Noli me tangere: On the raising of the body* (S. Clift, P-A. Brault, & M. Naas, Trans.). New York: Fordham University Press.

Nelson, R. J. (2010). *An introduction to behavioral endocrinology* (4th ed.). Sunderland, MA: Sinauer.

Norcross, J. C., Beutler, L. E., & Levant, R. (Eds.). (2006). *Evidencebased practices in mental health: Debate and dialogue on the fundamental questions.-* Washington, DC: American Psychological Association.

Northoff, G. (2011). *Neuropsychoanalysis in practice: Brain, self and objects.* Oxford, UK: Oxford University Press.

Porges, S. W. (2011). *The polyvagal theory: Neurophysiological foundations of emotions, attachment, communication, and selfregulation.-* New York: W. W. Norton.

Price, C. J., McBride, B., Hyerle, L., & Kivlahan, D. R. (2007). Mindful awareness in Body-Oriented Therapy for female veterans with post-traumatic stress disorder taking prescription analgesics for chronic pain: A feasibility study. *Alternative Therapies in Health and Medicine, 13*, 32–40.

Ragland, E. (2004). *The logic of sexuation: From Aristotle to Lacan.* Albany: State University of New York Press.

Ray, R. A. (2008). *Touching enlightenment: Finding realization in the body.* Boulder, CO: Sounds True.

Reich, W. (1927). *Genitality in the theory and therapy of the neuroses* (P. Schmitz, Trans. from *The function of the orgasm*; M. Higgins & C. M. Raphael, Eds.). New York: Farrar, Straus & Giroux.

Reich, W. (1933/1950). *Character Analysis* (T. P. Wolfe, Trans.). London: Vision Press.

Reich, W. (1936/1951). *The sexual revolution: Toward a selfgoverning character structure-* (T. P. Wolfe, Trans.). London: Vision Press.

Röhricht, F. (2008). *Die körperorientierte Psychotherapie psychischer Störungen: Ein Leitfaden für Forschung und Praxis* [Body-Oriented Psychotherapy in mental disorders: A manual for research and practice]. Göttingen: Hogrefe.

Röhricht, F. (2009). Body Oriented Psychotherapy: The state of the art in empirical research and evidence-based practice. *Body, Movement and Dance in Psychotherapy, 4(2)*, 135–156.

Röhricht, F., Papadopoulos, N., Holden, S., Clarke, T., & Priebe, S. (2011). Clinical effectiveness and therapeutic processes of Body Psychotherapy in chronic schizophrenia: An open clinical trial. *Arts in Psychotherapy, 38*, 196–203.

Röhricht, F., Papadopoulos, N., & Priebe, S. (2013). An exploratory randomized controlled trial of Body Psychotherapy for patients with chronic depression. *Journal of Affective Disorders, 151(1)*, 85–91.

Röhricht, F., & Priebe, S. (2006). Effect of Body Oriented Psychological Therapy on negative symptoms in schizophrenia: A randomised controlled trial. *Psychological Medicine, 36,* 669–678.

Rosner, A. L. (2012). Evidence-based medicine: Revisiting the pyramid of priorities. *Journal of Bodywork and Movement Therapies, 16,* 42–49.

Roth, A., & Fonagy, P. (2005). *What works for whom? A critical review of psychotherapy research* (2nd ed.). New York: Guilford Press.

Sackett, D. L., Straus, S., Richardson, W. S., Rosenberg, W. M. C., & Haynes, B. (2000). *Evidencebased medicine: How to practice and teach EBM.-* Edinburgh, UK: Churchill Livingstone.

Saleci, R. (Ed.). (1994). *Sexuation.* Chapel Hill, NC: Duke University Press.

Sandfort, T. G., & Rademakers, J. (Eds.). (2001). *Childhood sexuality: Normal sexual behavior and development.* London: Routledge.

Schore, A. N. (2012). *The science of the art of psychotherapy.* New York: W. W. Norton.

Segal, L. (Ed.). (1997). *New sexual agendas.* New York: New York University Press.

Seidman, E., Chorpita, B. F., Reay, W. E., Stelk, W., Garland, A. F., Kutash, K., Mullican, C., & Ringeisen, H. (2009). A framework for measurement feedback to improve decision-making in mental health. *Administrative Policy in Mental Health.*

Shedler, J. (2010). The efficacy of Psychodynamic Psychotherapy. *American Psychologist, 65,* 98–109.

Siegel, D. J. (2007). *The mindful brain: Reflection and attunement in the cultivation of wellbeing.-* New York: W. W. Norton.

Siegel, D. J. (2012). *The developing mind: How relationships and the brain interact to shape who we are* (2nd ed.). New York: Guilford Press.

Slade, M., & Priebe, S. (2001). Are randomized controlled trials the only gold that glitters? *British Journal of Psychiatry, 179,* 286–287.

Solms, M., & Turnbull, O. (2002). *The brain and the inner world: An introduction to the neuroscience of subjective experience.* New York: Other Press.

Spicker, S. F. (1995). *The philosophy of the body: Rejections of Cartesian dualism.* Malabar, FL: Krieger.

Stauntson, H., & Kyratzis, S. (Eds.). (2007). *Language, sexualities and desires: Crosscultural perspectives.-* London: Palgrave Macmillan.

Stern, D. N. (2000). *The interpersonal world of the infant: A view from psychoanalysis and Developmental Psychology.* New York: Basic Books.

Stern, D. N. (2004). *The present moment in psychotherapy and everyday life.* New York: W. W. Norton.

Stern, D. N. (2010). *Forms of vitality: Exploring dynamic experience in psychology, the arts, psychotherapy and development.* Oxford, UK: Oxford University Press.

Stoller, R. (1992). *Observing the erotic imagination.* New Haven, CT: Yale University Press.

Stoller, R. (2005). *Sweet dreams, erotic plots.* London: Karnac.

Tschacher, W., & Bergomi, C. (Eds.). (2011). *The implications of embodiment: Cognition and communication.* Exeter, UK: Academic Imprint Press.

Ventling, C. D. (2002). Efficacy of bioenergetic therapies and stability of the therapeutic result: A retrospective investigation. *USA Body Psychotherapy Journal, 1(2),* 5–28.

Ventling, C. D., Bertschi, H., & Gerhard, U. (2008). Efficacy of Bioenergetic Psychotherapy with patients of known ICD-10 diagnosis: A retrospective evaluation. *USA Body Psychotherapy Journal, 7(2),* 13–32.

Ventling, C. D., & Gerhard, U. (2000). Zur Wirksamkeit Bioenergetischer Psychotherapien und Stabilität des Therapieresultats: Eine Retrospective Untersuchung [Efficacy of Bioenergetic Therapies and stability of the therapeutic result: A retrospective investigation]. *Psychotherapeut, 45,* 230–236.

Warner, M. (1999). *The trouble with normal: Sex, politics, and the ethics of queer life.* Cambridge, MA: Harvard University Press.

Weiss, H., Johanson, G., & Monda, L. (in preparation). *These many realms: Mindfulnesscentered Somatic Psychotherapy: The Hakomi Method.-* Mill City, OR: Hakomi Educational Resources.

# SECTION XI

# Interfaces with Other Modalities of Psychotherapy

# 85
## Introduction to Section XI

**Gustl Marlock, Germany, and Halko Weiss, United States**

Translation by Warren Miller

As previously mentioned, one cannot draw a completely clear dividing line between the field of Body Psychotherapy and other modalities or methods of psychotherapy. For one thing, this is partially due to the history of Body Psychotherapy, which is closely interwoven with the history of Depth Psychology, Humanistic Psychology, and various other approaches. Additionally, many forms of psychotherapy, ranging from psychoanalysis to family therapy, from systems approaches to Cognitive Behavioral Therapy, are now striving to integrate the body into their psychotherapeutic work in new, different, or more explicit ways.

There exist quite a few basic modalities in psychotherapy that do not define themselves as Body Psychotherapeutic, but nonetheless strongly take the body, its movements, and its emotional expressivity into account. One such example is Psychodrama; its basic dramaturgical direction can be found as having had an influence on, for example, Al Pesso's (1994) Psychomotor Therapy, as well as on the so-called "enactments" in analytic Body Psychotherapy. However, Dance Therapy and Gestalt Therapy are perhaps more pertinent to the immediate context of Body Psychotherapy.

"Dance/Movement Therapy" (DMT)—depicted in Chapter 86, "Dance Therapy" by **Sabine Trautmann-Voigt**—directly originates from the German Life Reform Movement, perhaps more so than many of the Body Psychotherapeutic approaches themselves. However, it has other strong influences, as well as significant and successful applications in clinical work with people in psychiatric hospitals.

DMT stresses, first and foremost, the body's expressivity and its capability for symbolization. DMT is not so much concerned with Depth Psychology's concepts of defenses, of resistance, and of character, but rather more with the question of the significance of the person's body movements and their expression of self. Although DMT can be seen as a Body-Oriented Psychotherapeutic method, it has always made it a point to maintain and defend its independent identity, so much so that it is establishing itself totally separately, especially in the United Kingdom, as a uniquely registered psychotherapy, Dance/Movement *Psycho*therapy. Be that as it may, Chapter 86 tells a lot about how this modality works, and how we can also consider the moving body in psychotherapy.

Similar material about the moving body can be found in Susan Aposhyan's (2004) Body Psychotherapy that emerged from Bonnie Bainbridge Cohen's Body-Mind Centering work (see also Chapter 33, "Pattern and Plasticity: Utilizing Early Motor Development as a Tool for Therapeutic Change" by Susan Aposhyan); Christine Caldwell's "the Moving Cycle" (see also Chapter 41, "Movement As and In Psychotherapy" by Christine Caldwell); and the German Concentrative Movement Therapy (Gräff, 1983; Budjuhn, 1992).

The overlapping between Gestalt Therapy and Body Psychotherapy is even more evident and long-standing: both methods evolved out of psychoanalysis. Both Perls and Goodman (the founders of Gestalt Therapy) were strongly influenced by Wilhelm Reich. Core concepts such as the integration of the motor system, emotional expression, and self-regulation all go back to Reich's concepts. Even the shift of the therapeutic focus to the present, which characterizes Gestalt Therapy, is found in Reich's Character Analysis. Nevertheless, Gestalt Therapy developed its own independent theoretical, practical, and organizational identity. It distinguishes itself in its conceptualization of the regulation of need and contact on the basis of the Gestalt perceptual model, while taking a more existential stance. At the same time, there are a number of elaborations of Gestalt Therapy that exhibit considerable common ground with Body Psychotherapy. For example, James Kepner (1997) and Edward Smith (2001) have both made comprehensive contributions toward a Gestalt therapeutic understanding of Body Psychotherapeutic processes. On the other hand, integrative schools of Body Psychotherapy such as Integrative Body Psychotherapy (Rosenberg et al., 1985) and Unitive Psychology (Marlock, 1989, 1991) have embedded the core elements of Gestalt Therapy into their theories and practices. In Chapter 87, *"The Significance of the Body in Gestalt Therapy,"* **Wiltrud Krauss-Kogan** discusses significant commonalities, as well as conceptual tensions and differences, between the "sister" modalities of Gestalt Therapy and Body Psychotherapy.

Wide overlaps also exist between purely body therapeutic modalities and Body Psychotherapy. In addition to their shared focus on the somatic dimension in clinical practice, they arose from common historical roots that led to mutual influences. Direct, manual bodywork has often been found in immediate proximity to—and as a supplement to—more psychotherapeutically oriented practice: well-known examples include the Norwegian Bülow-Hansen method and the work of Ida Rolf (1992), to whom Fritz Perls often referred his clients and students. Direct work with the body, as practiced in Rolfing, Craniosacral Therapy (Kern, 2005), Hellerwork (Heller and Henkin, 2004), Postural Integration (Painter, 1985), and Rebalancing or Kinesiology (Levy and Lehr, 1996), frequently invited therapists to also address the psychological (or psychic) dimension, as these treatments often trigger strong, spontaneous emotional processes. Whereas some pioneers such as Ida Rolf or Moshe Feldenkrais (1991) had good reasons to keep psychotherapeutic work and bodywork separate, other body therapeutic approaches have attempted to integrate the psychological dimension in various degrees.

**Ilana Rubenfeld,** a student of both Moshe Feldenkrais and Fritz Perls, explores the roots of direct somatic work on the body with **Camilla Griggers** in Chapter 88, *"Somatic Emotional Release Work among Hands-on Practitioners."* In a second step, they consider how emotional processes can be integrated into such somatic work, and investigate this on a very fundamental level that penetrates the neurobiological, as well as the psychoanalytic, aspects of their synthetic approach.

The next two chapters inquire into the links between Body Psychotherapy and other mainstream forms of psychotherapy. **Serge Sulz,** in Chapter 89, *"Cognitive Behavioral Therapists Discover the Body,"* describes an increasing interest in working with the body from within the amalgam that is called Cognitive Behavioral Therapy (CBT).

To conclude Section XI, **Nossrat Peseschkian,** in Chapter 90, *"The Positive Management of the Body: A Salutogenic and Transcultural Perspective,"* illuminates the salutogenic and transcultural significance of the body from the psychodynamic perspective of Positive Psychotherapy.

## References

Aposhyan, S. (2004). *Body-Mind Psychotherapy: Principles, techniques and practical applications.* New York: W. W. Norton.

Budjuhn, A. (1992). *Die psycho-sozialen Verfahren: Konzentrative Bewegungstherapie und Gestaltungstherapie in Theorie und Praxis* [The psycho-social processes: Concentrative Movement Therapy and art therapy in theory and practice]. Dortmund: Verlag Modernes Lernen.

Feldenkrais, M. (1991). *Awareness through Movement: Easy-to-Do Health Exercises to Improve Your Posture, Vision, Imagination, and Personal Awareness.* New York: HarperCollins.

Gräff, C. (1983). *Konzentrative Bewegungstherapie in der Praxis* [Concentrative Movement Therapy in practice]. Stuttgart: Hippokrates.

Heller, J., & Henkin, W. (2004). *Bodywise: An introduction to Hellerwork for regaining flexibility and well-being.* Berkeley, CA: North Atlantic Books.

Kepner, J. (1997). *Body process: A Gestalt approach to working with the body in psychotherapy.* Cleveland, OH: Gestalt Press.

Kern, M. (2005). *Wisdom in the body: The craniosacral approach to essential health.* Berkeley, CA: North Atlantic Books.

Levy, S., & Lehr, C. (1996). *Your body can talk: How to listen to what your body knows and needs: The art and clinical application of Clinical Kinesiology.* Prescott, AZ: Holm Press.

Marlock, G. (Ed.). (1989). *Unitive Body-Psychotherapy: Collected papers* (Vol. 1). Frankfurt: Afra Verlag.

Marlock, G. (Ed.). (1991). *Unitive Body-Psychotherapy: Collected papers* (Vol. 2). Frankfurt: Afra Verlag.

Painter, J. (1985). *Postural Integration: Transformation of the whole self.* Mill Valley, CA: Bodymind Books.

Pesso, A. (1994). *Introduction to Pesso Boyden System Psychomotor.* Franklin, NH: PS Press.

Rolf, I. (1992). *Rolfing: Re-establishing the natural alignment and structural integration of the human body for vitality and well-being.* Rochester, VA: Healing Arts Press.

Rosenberg, J. L., Rand, M. L., & Asay, D. (1985). *Body, self and soul: Sustaining integration.* Atlanta, GA: Humanics.

Smith, E. W. L. (2001). *The body in psychotherapy.* Jefferson, NC: McFarland.

# 86
## Dance Therapy

**Sabine Trautmann-Voigt, Germany**

Translation by Martina Wolf and Isabel Aitken

**Sabine Trautmann-Voigt** has achieved widespread acclaim in Germany through her academically ambitious papers on the integration of psychodynamic theory and practice in Dance Therapy. She also works as a resident psychologist and psychotherapist for children and adolescents, as well as a lecturer and supervisor, at the Cologne-Bonn Academy for Psychotherapy (KBAP), a state-recognized educational institution for psychologists and medical professionals. Her duties there include the coordination and supervision of courses.

Dr. Trautmann-Voigt received her dance-therapeutic education in the United States, where she studied under Susan Wallock, Joan Chodorow, and, above all, Elaine V. Siegel. She also wrote her PhD dissertation on the subject of Dance Therapy. She is founder and director of the German Institute for Depth Psychology, Dance Therapy, and Expressive Therapy (DITAT), and is a regular guest lecturer at a number of academies and colleges.

In 1994, she founded, and began publishing, the magazine *Zeitschrift für Tanztherapie* [Journal for Dance Therapy], which became a new professional publication, *körper–tanz–bewegung: Zeitschrift für Körperpsychotherapie und Kreativtherapie* [Body–Dance–Movement: Journal for Body Psychotherapy and Creative Therapy] in 2013.

Dr. Trautmann-Voigt has published a sizable number of articles and books, focusing mainly on infant research, attachment theory, and movement/interaction analysis. She currently supervises some research projects on these topics in collaboration with the Universities of Cologne and Bonn.

### Dance Therapy: An Overview

The roots of Dance Therapy (sometimes also referred to as "Dance/Movement Therapy") can be assigned to the expressive therapeutic methods that originated as part of the humanistic movement in the United States in the 1960s and 1970s. New concepts in psychotherapy regarding "authentic perception," "empathy," and "awareness" began to be developed at that time. In an atmosphere receptive to such concepts as "sensing one's body" and "holistic experiences in the here and now," possibilities were being explored regarding the potential of using body language, movement, rhythmic-dynamic expression, and the ability to express oneself using artistic symbolism to treat psychological and psychosomatic disorders. Thus, Dance Therapy, with its focus on artistic expression, was developed as one of the newest Body-Oriented Psychotherapeutic methods. It was first established as an independent university degree in the United States. Dance Therapy has been defined by the American Dance Therapy Association (ADTA)—the first international professional association of dance therapists, founded in 1966—as "the psychotherapeutic use of movement to further the emotional, cognitive, physical and social integration of the individual" (ADTA, 1972). Practitioners of this method focus on behavioral processes and experiences where emotions become visible through movement and nonverbal interactions.

Visible movement, as well as the spoken word, structure interpersonal communications: body language contains signals, wishes, demands, stories, and more. To be able to better understand and to classify these signals and their communicative intent or effect in a biographical context, as well as in the context of actual relationships, and possibly help to alter them, is the goal of modern Dance Therapy.

The basis of dance and motion in Dance Therapy is the body: in its interplay of movement, perception, and meaning. The therapeutic focus lies on physical experience and perceptive qualities in movement expression, within the context of their verbalization. Dance Therapy focuses on associative self-expression through movement, as well as "formulated" ideas, "shaped" feelings, and "articulated" perceptions, all assuming visible shape in danced representations. Dance Therapy has nothing to do with rehearsing or reproducing various dance styles.

## Aims and Uses of Dance Therapy

The aim of Dance Therapy is to promote the ability to convert emotions and internal experiences into perceptible movements, visual symbols, and/or language and, by doing so, to intensify the process of being in touch with both oneself and others, as well as to be able to diversify the means of communication. The objectives of Dance Therapy interventions include: expanding movement vocabulary; improving physical self-perception and perception of others; and raising awareness of atmospherically compacted experiences. In addition to being used in hospital settings, Dance Therapy can be used in preventive settings, in curative (remedial) education, and in related fields to further development and to act as a supportive measure. In those fields that are not strictly defined as psychotherapeutic in terms of the psychotherapy directives, Dance Therapy is now being seen as a full-fledged, independent method that is to be taken seriously.

The praxeology of Dance Therapy is well conceived, but, due to its relatively short history and a widespread lack of research interest, it is still seriously lacking a sufficient amount of supplementary research. Dance Therapy can be used in a variety of ways, regardless of the setting (Trautmann-Voigt, 2003, 2007; Trautmann-Voigt and Voigt, 2007, 2012):

- The *exercise-centered approach* is used to structure physical perception—for example, in the treatment of psychotic patients, to help optimize the functioning of their body, or to enable them to experience their boundaries.
- The *experience-centered approach* is used to experience the physical self—e.g., in all advisory and educational or therapeutic fields, to stimulate and encourage self-expression.
- The *conflict-centered approach*, in the strict psychotherapeutic sense, is used to treat neurotic disorders, including gaining insight into biographical connections and releasing blocked emotions through mobilization of muscular tension.
- The *trauma-centered approach* can be used as a part of trauma therapy in both inpatient and outpatient settings with the aim of stabilization, fostering the use of resources, and promoting communication about traumatic physical or emotional experiences.

## German Expressionist Dance: Emigration and Reimportation

At the beginning of the twentieth century, the German expressionist dance movement comprised a changed understanding of the body, as well as some innovative ideas for the feminist emancipation movement. Authenticity, expressive representation of personal experiences, and communicative elements—all marked this new form of dance in which especially women publicly celebrated their individuality and self-liberation (possibly for the first time) and started to turn away not only from the tight corsets of ballet costumes, but also from restrictive social conventions. Isadora Duncan imagined the dancer of the future to be "*. . . a woman whose body and soul . . . are developed harmoniously.*"

> Dance is a living language that is spoken by humans and tells of the people, it is an artistic statement, to speak at a higher level in images and parables of what moves us and urges us to express ourselves. (Wigman, in Trautmann-Voigt, 1998)

Expressionist dance, with its main representatives, Isadora Duncan and Mary Wigman, is consistently cited in literature as the artistic root of Dance Therapy. They believed that the free movement of the body allows the internal aspects of the person, their soul, to become free as well: rhythmic improvisation should bring the body to a plane of movement where it is possible to fantasize and symbolize; the body should become the instrument—dance was "the keyboard of emotions," as Daniel Stern would call it much later, and from a very different perspective (Stern, 1992, 1998, 2005, 2011).

A sequence of motions, which resembles chains of associations that spread through the room, is supported by rhythms, sounds, and notes. These processes are developed further into creative compositions; the design process itself is seen as a revival of subconscious characters, albeit from a different angle; and so dance choreography made visible what had previously been locked away in stillness and emotionally closed off.

Many expressionist dancers associated with Mary Wigman had emigrated to the United States before the Second World War to escape the Nazi terror. There, they tried to earn a living as dancers, with varying degrees of success. They found opportunities for work in psychiatric hospitals, which were—at that time—open to new creative and socially inclusive proposals. In the United States, the expressive and communicative ideas of German expressionist dance met a respectful and open-minded *zeitgeist* that was willing to experiment in a way that would have been inconceivable in Europe (Siegel et al., 1999, pp. 9–16).

However, a second-generation expressionist dancer, Chinese-born Fe Reichelt, was a master student and teacher with Mary Wigman (Reichelt, 1990) and has lived in Germany since the age of eleven. Based in Berlin, she has developed her own approach—in which she combines breath, dance, and special education. But the American impulses that molded the previously exported expressionist dance movement into the modern Dance Therapy that we know and predominantly refer to today returned to Europe only in the wake of the youth movement—as a third-generation reimport—in the late 1970s, bringing with it group dynamics, Gestalt Therapy, and other humanistic impulses (Kamper and Wulf, 1982).

## The "West Coast Approach"

### Trudi Schoop: "Come Dance with Me": Dance Expression Heals!

Trudi Schoop (1903–1999) was a Swiss-born dancer and mime artist with her own troupe, touring Germany and Switzerland until the outbreak of the Second World War. Following her emigration to the United States, and extensive artistic work there, she finally settled in California in 1952, and later began working with psychotic patients in Los Angeles. Her work used the basic elements of dance itself: posture, gait, gesture, movement, body image, rhythm, breathing, tension, and relaxation:

> Only by expressing yourself will you gain insight into your own feelings. If you do not communicate your feelings, if you merely stand there like a mummy, secretly dying on the inside, nothing happens. And we are simply meant to be with others. We need to communicate with other people . . . Improvising brings up the feelings inside, fear or sadness or joy. But as long as you improvise, you will always be in this state. Only when you start to say: "Right, so here's the stage. I'm out there, and I want it to be like this"—so only if you design, if you concentrate it, something happens to you. . . . I think if you can extricate your feelings, if you can communicate, if you can show another how you feel, this will be an important process in healing. (Schoop, 1989, pp. 170–171)

And, significantly, Schoop always rejected the formulation of dance-therapeutic theories (Schoop, 1989, p. 175).

## Mary Whitehouse and Her Successors: "Movement in Depth": Authentic Movement Frees Life Energy

Also working on the West Coast, Mary Whitehouse (1911–1979) based her work on C. G. Jung's "active imagination." She was influenced both by Martha Graham and by Mary Wigman, focusing on developing new forms of self-awareness by a gradual process of individuation through movement, aiming at the integration of polar opposites. *"If you follow your innermost feelings and let these impulses room to develop into physical action, then this would be Active Imagination in motion, just as the visualization of internal images represents Active Imagination in fantasy"* (Whitehouse, 1963).

Whitehouse let her mostly adult and "averagely neurotic" clients experiment with polarities such as up/down, closed/open, left/right, and release/hold, and gradually led them toward "authentic movement." This term describes the perceptive internal urge to move, which leads to the perception of being moved through one's own emotional experience: *"I am particularly interested in that moment when people who are in motion at that point, including dancers, realize that they are being moved"* (Whitehouse, 1991, p. 147).

With her ideas, Whitehouse deliberately countered the notions of perfection in movement and conscious body control. It should instead be the subconscious, with its images, figures, and dreams, that should be allowed to evolve through spontaneous movement. *"Since this process is made up of the growth of the individual and conscious wholeness, it is useless to give excessive verbal commands or explanations"* (Whitehouse, 1991, p. 154).

Her own experiences with Jungian analysis and dance improvisation led Whitehouse to a form of Dance Therapy that was also, in part, inspired by Eastern philosophical traditions. She aimed to free people from their rational and/or functional one-sidedness and to encourage the unhindered flow of positive life energies. This approach—to find the authentic, or "real," movement—still has many adherents; however, it is missing a more in-depth theoretical foundation, just like the original approach by Schoop. The "West Coast approach" went through a more theoretical development only through the work of Joan Chodorow and her "Jungian approach" to Dance Therapy, as well as through Janet Adler's form of "Authentic Movement."

Chodorow worked as a psychoanalyst and taught at the C. G. Jung Institute in San Francisco. She was the first to systematically present primary emotions and expressive movement (Chodorow, 1991) and integrated Jung's theories regarding the collective unconscious, the personal unconscious, and the shadow, as well as fairy tales, myths, and symbols, into her dance-therapeutic sessions with children and adults.

> A move in which the shadow [the personal unconscious] manifests itself can usually be recognized by their seemingly random occurrence... Even when a pattern emerges, the mover [i.e., the moving client] and the witness [the therapist is seen as a witness] may be confused about where it comes from and what it means. Because of their idiosyncratic nature, a move that comes from this layer of the unconscious can only be understood with the help of associations and memories of the movers themselves. On this psychological level, we see the expression of unconscious conflicts, and the most painful of them seemed to be related to complex feelings within the family. (Chodorow, 1994, p. 26)

Chodorow connects five "stages of development of the Ego-Self Axis" to symbolic movement interactions between the mover and the witness. With this concept, she provides a link to the theory of Erich Neumann (1988), who uses the concept of "Ego-Self Axis" to describe the dynamic relationship of the two "centers of personality" (that is, intelligence and shadow, or conscious and unconscious).

Janet Adler continued to place the idea of Authentic Movement quite firmly in the tradition of Whitehouse, and referred much more vaguely to Jungian psychology:

> This way we may begin to see the evolution of the development of collective consciousness through the experience of each body to the extent to which the

unconscious material mover (the one who is actively moving) or the witness . . . are aware of the presence of others . . . The foundation of this branch of authentic movement is the relationship between mover and witness. (Adler, 1994a, p. 6f.)

The exploration of the self is the central concern. Ego and superego structures make up only a part of the self; the personal unconscious and the collective unconscious are additional parts that together make up the self that can be accessed through self-exploration and self-actualization in an authentic, real movement coming from inside. The mover usually works with his or her eyes closed, and focuses entirely on his or her internal impulses. The witness-companion "practices the art of seeing." The witness does not look at the mover, but, because she had previously internalized the mover, is able to focus on her own experience of judging, interpreting, and projecting, in relation to the mover acting as a catalyst.

> The witness practices the art of seeing. Seeing clearly is not about knowing what the mover needs or must do. The witness does not "look at" the mover but, instead, as she internalizes the mover, she attends to her own experiences of judgment, interpretation and projection in response to the mover as catalyst. As she acknowledges ownership of her experiences, the density of her personal history empties, enabling the witness at times to feel that she can see the mover clearly and, more importantly, that she can see herself clearly. Sometimes . . . it is grace . . . the witness embodies a clear presence. (Adler, 1994b, pp. 194–195)

Ultimately, this is about dealing with bodily countertransference, which, in this approach, has not been reflected upon in great detail. The approach is still well known today. A just criticism of this methodology would be that only therapists who had gone through extensive additional training in Psychodynamic Psychotherapy would be in a position to use the implications of Authentic Movement that invite you to a kind of "free association" *psychotherapeutically,* through the medium of movement (Siegel, 1994).

Penny Lewis Bernstein had formulated one of the first rigorous textbooks for Dance Therapy in the 1960s and 1970s (Lewis Bernstein, 1972). Judith Kestenberg, a child analyst who had designed a well-known motion-analysis system, initially inspired Lewis Bernstein, who became the first to connect object-relations theory, developmental theory, and movement analysis. Later, she pursued a Jungian art therapy approach that integrated, among other things, dancing, sand play, and painting (Lewis Bernstein, 1999).

## The "East Coast Approach"

### Marian Chace: The "Chace Circle" Rhythmic Relatedness Fosters the Ability to Communicate

Marian Chace (1896–1970) started working in psychiatric hospital settings as early as 1942, which puts her work even before that of Trudi Schoop. Trained in Modern Dance with Martha Graham, Chace worked as part of an experimental dance troupe in Washington, DC. In her own dance school, she met people who were keen to express their psychological and emotional needs through the medium of dance and movement, without aiming for professional careers in dance themselves. This led Chace to develop a set of teaching principles that were intended to help her students to increase their self-confidence. A number of local psychiatrists then started sending their own patients to her studio.

At St. Elizabeth's Hospital in Washington, DC, the very same place where Moreno had introduced Psychodrama, Chace started working with psychiatric patients. Here, she developed the foundation of modern group Dance Therapy for more than twenty years.

The "Chace Circle" was a fixed feature of all her sessions, using the process of nonverbal movement communication: as part of a "warm-up" in the circle, every participant introduced him- or herself and his or her movement, thus inviting the other participants to imitate. As the movement was passed from one person to the next, eye contact was mandatory, maintaining a feeling of community. In a Chace Circle, the therapist makes use of the technique of mirroring, imitating certain movements, structuring, intensifying, or modifying them, stimulating variations on the movements offered, etc. Long before mirror neurons were discovered, and prior to gaining insight from modern-day infant and attachment research in regard to affect attunement, resonance, and nonverbally communicated self-efficacy, Chace had been structuring and focusing interpersonal contact.

During the course of a session, certain movement themes would begin to dominate; these themes could also be addressed verbally by the therapist, or focused by associations from within the group. The circle could be disbanded momentarily; small groups or pairs could form, connected via rhythmic movement, with or without music, when required. One of the most important structural elements in Chace's sessions is the so-called "group rhythm," which would rise to a peak and then continue wavelike until eventually reaching a natural conclusion.

Communication through dance (i.e., a common development of movement at the level of nonverbal behavior, motoric actions and reactions, and eye contact), and an actively induced fostering of experience and expansion of the range of motion, led to a significant improvement of the symptoms of severely disturbed and difficult-to-treat psychiatric patients: all this at a time when there was a gradual move away from electroconvulsive therapy, despite a continuing lack of available antipsychotics.

Later, Chace worked with the Neo-Freudians Frieda Fromm-Reichmann and Harry S. Sullivan, who had developed the concept of "participant observer." Chace's methodology was inspired by Fromm-Reichmann. As early as 1950, Chace wrote that *"Patients should be encouraged to observe their sensory perceptions and physical symptoms and communicate when and how these manifest themselves, or when they occur"* (Chaiklin, 1974, p. 76). Against this background of psychoanalytic assumptions, Chace interpreted *"posture, muscle tension, breathing patterns and coordination difficulties as external manifestations of inner conflicts"* (Siegel et al., 1999, p. 13). Chace did not write down her methodology herself, but Chaiklin documented her work, laying the groundwork for the so-called "East Coast approach." Chace's methods subsequently became more and more open to theories founded on a sound psychoanalytic approach.

It was Chace, together with Mary Whitehouse and other dance therapists, who pushed for the foundation of the American Dance Therapy Association (ADTA). One of her most important goals was the professional recognition of Dance Therapy and dance therapists in the United States. This meant that admission to ADTA would be granted only to those who had graduated from a U.S. university with a degree in Dance Therapy, or the equivalent.

### Liljan Espenak: "Personal Development through Creative Expression—Integration through Movement"

Liljan Espenak (1905–1988), who also trained with Wigman, found yet another approach in her work toward the foundation of modern Dance Therapy. She discovered, just as Chace had, that there were some elements in psychoanalytic theory that were lending some structure to the sometimes seemingly chaotic expressive dance moves of conflicted individuals, who would have otherwise had to cope with their so-called "inner material" on their own. Espenak had also trained as an Adlerian. She developed a theory of psychosomatic movement, based on Depth Psychology, which she called "psycho-motor Espenak" (Espenak, 1985). Her aim was to increase the degree of freedom of movement for her clients through deliberate coordination of their body parts and rhythmic improvisations, which in turn should facilitate changes at a transference level, which should then affect their way of living.

It was up to Espenak's student Elaine V. Siegel to conceptualize the first fully developed and sophisticated approach to Dance Therapy, "Psychoanalytic Dance/Movement Therapy," based on psychoanalysis and extended to include both object-relations theory and developmental theory.

## Elaine V. Siegel: Psychoanalytic Dance/Movement Therapy Becomes Dance Therapy–Based Psychoanalysis

Until the 1970s, Dance Therapy had, first and foremost, been a supporting therapy in the United States. It was mainly thanks to Elaine V. Siegel, a second-generation dance therapist, that Dance Therapy outgrew this status and, at the same time, burst free of the restrictive framework of psychoanalytic methods as a body-related extension, just like other Body Psychotherapeutic approaches. A student of both Espenak and Chace, and a classically trained dancer and dramaturge, Siegel later trained as a psychoanalyst. After obtaining her PhD in psychology, she worked as a senior analyst and a training analyst at the New York Center for Psychoanalytic Training. She ran the Suffolk Child Development Center at the State University of New York for almost fifteen years and had her own private practice in New York until the end of the 1990s. Siegel had lived in Germany until she was eighteen, but, just like many Jews of her generation, she had had to flee the country due to the war and the political situation in Germany at the time. She was involved in the theoretical foundation of Dance Therapy within ADTA from the very beginning. From the 1990s onward, she began to push for a consolidation of psychodynamically based Dance Therapy in Germany, too. She influenced one of the first depth-psychological-oriented academies in Germany.[73] There she initiated numerous discussions between Dance Therapy and modern infant research (Stern, 1992, 1998) and Self Psychology (Lichtenberg, 1998, 2002; Siegel, 1996, 1998, 2002), respectively, to further this goal (Trautmann-Voigt and Voigt, 1998).

As in classical psychoanalysis, her initial focus was on the processing of transference and resistance. Working through those issues, however, takes place primarily through nonverbal, dancelike behavior in the context of a moving dialogue. She goes beyond the beliefs of traditional Dance Therapy that a change in personality would directly follow any changes in the patterns of movement and lead to an improvement in expressive movement in patients. According to Siegel, this belief is lacking an "echo of the past in the therapeutic present."

> I have found that these dance therapy analyses work just like actual human development. Patients talk much at first, often struggle with their resistance to movement and dance with enthusiasm and full of affectivity when they regress. Others use dance as resistance and only manage to verbally associate when their physical boundaries have been established. (Siegel, 1994, p. 89)

In her treatment room, Siegel offers both the couch and a "free space to move." As a psychoanalyst, she believes in meeting often, as much as two to four hours per week, giving her patients the freedom to choose how they would like to communicate—i.e., they can get up and move whenever they like. Her motility concept contains three theoretical assumptions based on the experiences of the patients:

- Movement acts as an indicator of the current developmental stage of the patient.
- Movement gives expression to inner conflicts.
- Movement contains traces of the patient's every reaction to their life experiences and transports those from the past to the present.

Although it would be impossible to include, in detail, the information gathered in numerous publications of an approach that has been thoroughly tested with decades of work with psychotic and neurotic patients of all ages, I would like to highlight two phenomena that Siegel designed primarily for the psychotherapeutic discussion as a dance therapist and psychoanalyst, alongside physical transference and countertransference: body image and creative play in dance dialogue. Below is a summary of the most important facts, including the sources used by Siegel and references to current developments, and explain why this dance-therapeutic approach is to be understood as a specific approach to Body Psychotherapy.

---

[73] DITAT: Deutsches Institut für Tiefenpsychologische Tanztherapie und Ausdruckstherapie [German Institute for Depth Psychology, Dance Therapy, and Expressive Therapy].

## Body Image as a Part of the Self-Image

To what conceptual framework does the body image belong? How is body image defined? The totality of all bodily experiences acquired over the course of individual development—including the cognitive, affective, conscious, and unconscious ones—are summarized by the term "bodily experience." In an attempt to differentiate between varying bodily experiences, one can use the distinction between "body schema" and "body image." The body schema includes the neurophysiological aspects of bodily experience as well as the perceptive-cognitive achievements of the individual. These include information about "body orientation," "body extension," and "body knowledge." Paul Schilder (1923) wrote about body image and the mutual relationship between body and psyche. His concepts acted as a base for Siegel's ideas regarding the development of dialogue-based interventions related to the perception of one's body. As early as 1923, Schilder had pointed out the extremely libidinous relationship between the development of body attitude and body image, and he regarded the relationship between the mother and her child as a central influencing factor in the development of an internal body image. Margaret Mahler later described how especially touch and motoric exploration, the first means of exploration of the body by infants and children, play a major role in developing one's separate identity (Mahler et al., 1980). From the 1970s onward, Elaine V. Siegel drew on both of these authors in her early works, highlighting the importance of body image work for Dance Therapy. In her practice with her own patients, she established connections with and combined painting and movement with verbal analysis.

In the narrower sense of the word, as used in Dance Therapy, that is based on psychodynamic principles, "*body image*" includes the psychological and phenomenological parts of bodily experience—i.e., all emotional-affective acts of the individual, *bodily awareness, spatial awareness* (or perception of oneself as being a separate individual), and *body image*:

- *Bodily awareness* is the mental representation of the body, or its parts, in one's awareness or in the attention concentrated on the body.
- *Spatial awareness* relates to the perception of body boundaries—i.e., to the experience of one's physical self as clearly separate from the environment. In psychotic patients, this perception is often distorted.
- *Body image* describes the conscious perception of one's physical appearance, especially satisfaction/dissatisfaction with one's own body. Biographical influences—e.g., parents' approach to the body, parental values, and social norms, among others—would be included in the term "body image."

Body image should therefore be regarded as an internal model that evolves and changes and acts as a basis for the body perception one experiences at any given moment. It shapes the conscious, as well as the unconscious, self-image. Because of this, one's current body image will often become the dominating factor in Dance Therapy. The therapist might frequently ask: *"How does that feel just now?"* or *"Which bodily experience would you link with this statement?"* or *"When you increase, or reduce, or vary this movement . . . do you notice a change in your breathing, your posture, or your level of feeling?"* These questions can also be found in many other Body-Oriented Psychotherapeutic methods. Dance-therapeutic work on body image can influence the perception of bodily awareness as follows:

- By making the patient more aware of his or her own body and self-perception
- By the stabilization of body boundaries
- By changing the attitudes toward one's own body
- By increasing one's acceptance of one's body
- By changing the way we judge our physical appearance
- By encouraging a more realistic perception of the body
- By accessing physical sensations
- By increasing the ability to experience emotionally
- By raising awareness of the concept of "body"

In practice, this could also be achieved by drawing a picture of your own body, or by creating a full-size body representation, together with the patient. Awareness exercises that focus especially on the body parts selected by the patient might follow, such as getting various body parts to carry out movement; working with the feelings of heaviness, power, and slowness in individual limbs; encouraging feeling one's body in space, on the ground, and in motion, focusing on the perception of body boundaries.

Dance Therapy, with its interventions, directly draws on body image. These are based on an interplay of the unconscious and the conscious body image with the public image of the body. The unconscious body image represents the unconscious ideas and feelings one has of one's body. It shapes the posture, the movement-related appearance, and how we deal with our bodies. Movement improvisation and thematic movement exercises offer a Dance Therapy–specific way to gain access to the unconscious body image. Body image and body memory form an inseparable connection, as countless case studies have shown (Trautmann-Voigt and Voigt, 2001, 2012).

## Play, Creativity, and Body Fantasy as Resources

The observation of children at play presents us with a lot of learning material that therapists working with artistic methods could use. Right from infancy, children can already link *funktionslust* (functional pleasure, or doing something for the sake of feeling satisfaction) and playful curiosity to achieve positive physical and emotional sensations. One goal of Dance Therapy is to reidentify such positive physical and emotional sensations—especially in depressed, traumatized, anxious, or emotionally isolated persons—once again to reawaken and foster curiosity and a sense of pleasure in one's actions and their results. The seven- to eight-month-old infant, for example, shows playful pleasure in a game of "peekaboo," which also deals with important issues of identity formation. Similarly, teasing, chasing, pursuing, and games of hide-and-seek can be tried and rearranged into dance games. Through these dance games, playful, joyful regression, bodily pleasure, and a primal sense of resources may be experienced. After all, creativity is referred to as the creative ability that expresses itself as a person's ability to solve problems and to be original. The problem-solving processes of artistic creativity lie in being able to process emotional conflict, or in an intent to communicate, which addresses other levels of human perception, analogue levels, and thus the right hemisphere of the brain (Rapp, 1997).

The theory of innate motivational systems (Lichtenberg et al., 2002) can be used to capture and use movement themes that are mirrored in motor development in a psychotherapeutic setting (Trautmann-Voigt and Moll, 2011).

Elaine V. Siegel has been dealing with body memory and body fantasy on the basis of psychodynamic concepts since the 1960s and concludes: *"By movement association, i.e. improvisation, dance therapy analysts themselves reach a sore spot within the transference. Motility is used as an ego function that leads to remembering, fantasizing and working through one's issues and can additionally be influenced by interpretations"* (Siegel, 1999, p. 39).

Siegel's achievement is to have laid down a thorough conceptual framework for Dance Therapy as a psychodynamic method—including a full discussion of fundamental essentials of the dance: playfulness and creativity. Thus, Dance Therapy is a form of Body Psychotherapy, with special emphasis on symbolization and expression of nonverbal communication.

## Rhythmic-Dynamic Active Dialogue

### Integration of Infant Research, Neurological Research, and Self Psychology into Modern Dance Therapy

Since the start of the twenty-first century, a number of discussions have taken place regarding scenic representations, enactments, and active dialogue in Dance Therapy (see also Drews, 2000). Dance Therapy has brought to these discussions the concept of rhythmic-dynamic active dialogue—particularly with reference to infant research, as well as to recent findings in neurobiology and systems theory (Trautmann-Voigt and Voigt, 1996, 1997, 1998, 2001, 2002, 2007, 2010, 2012). The rhythmic-dynamic active dialogue takes into account basic psychoanalytic phenomena (transference, countertransference, defense mechanisms, etc.), as well as all three levels of communication during the therapeutic process: on the verbal, semantic, and procedural level, referring among other things to neurobiological networking theories (Damasio, 1994, 2003; LeDoux et al., 2005). The emotional level is called the rhythmic-dynamic address at the procedural level, which is difficult to access by the conscious or the visual unconscious, where the rhythmic-dynamic models of interactive episodes or scenes tend to lie dormant. For example, dance movement, supported by music, is a way to not only revive stored atmospherically condensed memories (Stern's "Representations of Interactions that have been Generalized": RIGs) in a transference and countertransference scene, but also to contribute to their reorientation. How the combination of pictorial, verbal, and procedural work—including music and dreams, and taking into account specific movement analysis—would work in practice has been described in detailed dance-therapeutic vignettes (as summarized by Trautmann-Voigt and Voigt, 2012).

## Movement and Interaction Analysis

It is beyond the scope of this overview to go into the different approaches of clinical movement analysis in more detail. Movement analysis dates back to the German expressionist dancer Rudolf Laban, who developed Laban Movement Analysis (LMA) in the 1920s. Movement is recorded in the way that it relates to drive and shape, and in terms of its fundamental determinants: in space, at a certain intensity, and in its particular rhythm. For clinical work, the Kestenberg Movement Profile (KMP), by the psychoanalyst Judith Kestenberg, and the Emotive BodyMind Motility Paradigm (E-BMMP), by Yona Shahar-Levy, have also been developed. Both models are well operationalized and can provide advice for a sound diagnosis of movement and interactive behavior (reviewed in Trautmann-Voigt and Voigt, 2012; see also Voigt and Trautmann-Voigt, 2001). Opinions are more divided when it comes to motion analysis: it requires precise vision, the ability to accurately verbalize motoric phenomena, and a high degree of physical self-awareness. It is also a core piece of Dance Therapy: no other Body Psychotherapeutic approaches have such an elaborate "language of movement"!

## Case Study: "That's it! I need to leave now!"

A thirty-five-year-old female patient was complaining about her listlessness and inability to unpack about fifty cardboard boxes that had been piled up in her new home following a recent move. In the second session, I asked her to demonstrate how she saw herself in her new home, using ropes and scarves. She created a circle made of three jump ropes around the armchair in which she had been sitting, took a woolen blanket, put it over her head, and sat back down. When asked about how she felt, she stated that she had noticed a feeling of unpleasant heat, darkness, and tightness in her chest, exactly like she felt in her house. But rather than getting rid of a part of the blanket over her head, she seemed to have settled beneath it. I sensed movement and so I asked her if she would consider changing anything of this position. She replied, *"On the one hand, it's terribly tight in here; on the other hand, I do not have to see anything or do anything. This is very comfortable."* She managed to stay in this position for four, almost unbearably long, minutes before throwing off the blanket and practically screaming, *"I never wanted to move into this house. Once again, I only ever do what everyone else wants me to do. I never studied what I wanted to study, I did not have children because my husband did not want that, and now I have to live where I never wanted to go! I want out, I want to get away!"*

*"How would it look in motion if you were to escape from this place now?"* I asked. The patient jumped up and ran around the room at a fast pace until she was out of breath. I asked her about her physical perception of herself once more. She could breathe now. *"It felt good,"* she said. I asked her if any suitable music would support this pace: *"What kind of music do you like?"* She laughed and said, *"How do*

*you know that I always dance around the living room when I can't take it anymore?"* Then I turned on the radio and searched for a station playing something suitable. I put on a current pop song, in the vague hope of finding something that might "fit." She laughed, nodded, and remarked, *"Yeah, that's the one with the glasses. Don't you think she's terrible, too? But the music is good!"*

She ran, jumped, and suddenly seemed like a completely different person. After the music finished, she let herself fall back into the chair and said, *"I can only get this feeling when I move, when I walk . . . That's it! I need to leave now!"*

Feeling frozen in immobility, the suggestion to move again was something that could be embraced by the young woman. She realized immediately what this was about. The implementation of her "theme" in action quickly brought forth the theme her entire therapy would eventually revolve around. The patient was able to work out later, during transference sessions, that the narrowness of her marital relationship had already been a repetition of stifling family dynamics.

The multimodal approach in Dance Therapy and the focus on the body–rhythm–room–experience often act as a "safe haven" in which to develop or consolidate experiences quickly. The focus is on process orientation in this work in an open room, according to Winnicott (1987), and a body-friendly and responsible attitude of the therapist characterized by her own movement-related experience.

## References

Adler, J. (1994a). The collective body. In S. Chaiklin (Ed.). (1994). *Marian Chace: Her papers.* Columbia, MD: American Dance Therapy Association.

Adler, J. (1994b). The collective body. In P. Pallaro (Ed.). (1999). *Authentic Movement: Essays by Mary Starks Whitehouse, Janet Adler and Joan Chodorow.* London: Jessica Kingsley.

ADTA. (1972). *Dance Therapy* [Brochure]. Columbia, MD: American Dance Therapy Association.

Chaiklin, S. (1974). *Marian Chace: Her papers.* Columbia, MD: American Dance Therapy Association.

Chodorow, J. (1991). *Dance Therapy and Depth Psychology: The moving imagination.* London: Routledge, Chapman & Hall.

Chodorow, J. (1994). Der Körper, die Psyche und die Emotionen [The body, the mind and the emotions]. In N. Spandau (Ed.), *Erster Internationaler klinischer Kongress für Tanztherapie in Berlin* [First International Congress on Clinical Dance Therapy in Berlin]. "Sprache der Bewegung": Anwendung der Tanztherapie in der psychiatrischen Klinik ["Language of movement": Use of Dance Therapy in the psychiatric clinic], Sept. 1–4, 1994, pp. 17–34.

Damasio, A. (1994). *Descartes' Irrtum* [Descartes' error]. Munich: List.

Damasio, A. (2003). *Der Spinoza-Effekt* [The Spinoza effect]. Munich: List.

Drews, S. (Ed.). (2000). *Zum "szenischen Verstehen" in der Psychoanalyse: Hermann Argelander zum 80 Geburtstag* [To the "scenic understanding" in psychoanalysis: Hermann Argelander on his 80th birthday]. Frankfurt: Brandes & Apsel.

Espenak, L. (1985). *Tanztherapie: Durch kreativen Selbstausdruck zur Persönlichkeitsentwicklung* [Dance Therapy: Through creative self-expression for personality development]. Dortmund: Sanduhr.

Kamper, D., & Wulf, C. (1982). *Die Wiederkehr des Körpers* [The return of the body]. Frankfurt: Suhrkamp.

LeDoux, J. E., Markowitsch, H. J., & Welzer, H. (2005). *Das autobiographische Gedächtnis: Hirnorganische Grundlagen und biosoziale Entwicklung* [Autobiographical memory: Organic brain basics and biosocial development]. Stuttgart: Klett-Cotta.

Lewis Bernstein, P. (1972). *Theory and methods in Dance-Movement Therapy: A manual for therapists, students, and educators.* Dubuque, IA: Kendall Hunt.

Lewis Bernstein, P. (1999). *Schöpferische Prozesse: Kunst in der therapeutischen Praxis* [Creative processes: Art in therapeutic practice]. Zürich, Switzerland: Walter.

Lichtenberg, J. (1998). Modellszenen und Motivationssysteme—mit besonderer Berücksichtigung körperlicher Erfahrungen [Model scenes and motivation systems—with particular reference to physical experiences]. In S. Trautmann-Voigt & B. Voigt (Eds.), *Bewegung ins Unbewusste: Beiträge zur Säuglingsforschung und analytischen Körper-Psychotherapie* [Movement into the unconscious: Contributions to infant research and analytical Body Psychotherapy], (pp. 110–128). Frankfurt: Brandes & Apsel.

Lichtenberg, J. (2002). Worte und Musik: Bewegung gelebter Erfahrung. Ein Kommentar zur Fallgeschichte von Herrn K. [Words and music: Movement of lived experience. A commentary on the case history of Mr. K.]. In S. Trautmann-Voigt & B. Voigt (Eds.), *Verspieltheit als Entwicklungschance. Zur Bedeutung von Bewegung und Raum in der Psychotherapie* [Playfulness as a development opportunity: On the importance of movement and space in psychotherapy] (pp. 47–52). Giessen: Psychosozial.

Mahler, M., Pine, F., & Bergmann, A. (1980). *Die psychische Geburt des Menschen: Symbiose und Individuation* [The psychological birth of the human being: Symbiosis and individuation]. Frankfurt: Fischer.

Neumann, E. (1988). *The child: Structure and dynamics of the nascent personality.* London: Karnac Books.

Rapp, W. (1997). Ein ganzheitlicher Zugang zur Person über Psychoanalyse und analytische Bewegungsund Tanztherapie [A holistic approach to the person in psychoanalysis and analytical Dance/Movement Therapy]. In S. Trautmann-Voigt & B. Voigt (Eds.), *Freud lernt laufen: Herausforderungen analytischer Tanzund Bewegungstherapie für Psychoanalyse und Psychotherapie* [Freud learns to walk: Analytical challenges in dance and exercise therapy for psychoanalysis and psychotherapy] (pp. 173–212). Frankfurt: Brandes & Apsel.

Reichelt, F. (1990). *Atem, Tanz und Therapie: Schlüssel des Erkennens und Veränderns* [Breath, dance and therapy: Key of cognition and change]. Frankfurt: Brandes & Apsel.

Schilder, P. (1923). *Das Körperschema: Ein Beitrag zur Lehre vom Bewusstsein des eigenen Körpers* [The body schema: A contribution to the theory of awareness of one's body]. Berlin: Springer.

Schoop, T. (1989). Tanztherapie [Dance Therapy]. In H. K. Moscovici (Ed.), *Vor Freude tanzen, vor Jammer halb in Stücke gehen: Pionierinnen der Körpertherapie* [Dance with joy, with sorrow, half go to pieces: Pioneers of body therapy] (pp. 157–186). Frankfurt: Luchterhand.

Siegel, E. V. (1994). Die Brücke zwischen Leib und Seele: Psychoanalytische Tanztherapie [The bridge between body and soul: Psychoanalytic Dance Therapy]. In N. Spandau (Ed.), *Sammelband der Beiträge des 1. Internationalen Klinischen Kongress für Tanztherapie in Berlin* [Keynotes from 1st International Congress on Dance Therapy in Berlin: "Language of Movement"] (pp. 87–96).

Siegel, E. V. (1996). Klinische Vignetten aus der psychoanalytischen Tanztherapie und aus der Psychoanalyse [Clinical vignettes from psychoanalytic therapy and dance from psychoanalysis]. In S. Trautmann-Voigt & B. Voigt (Eds.) *Bewegte Augenblicke im Leben des Säuglings—und welche therapeutischen Konsequenzen?* [Moving moments in the life of the infant—and what therapeutic consequences?] (pp. 75–82). Cologne: Claus Richter.

Siegel, E. V. (1998). Gedanken über scheinbar Unvereinbares: Psychoanalyse, Bewegung und Tanz [Thoughts on the seemingly impossible: Psychoanalysis, movement and dance]. In S. Trautmann-Voigt & B. Voigt (Eds.), *Bewegung ins Unbewusste: Beiträge zur Säuglingsforschung und analytischen Körper-Psychotherapie* [Movement into the unconscious: Contributions to infant research and analytical Body Psychotherapy] (pp. 97–109). Frankfurt: Brandes & Apsel.

Siegel, E. V. (1999). Körperliche Gegenübertragung: Einfühlungsvermögen und Bewegungsempathie [Physical countertransference: Empathy and empathy movement]. In E. V. Siegel, S. Trautmann-Voigt, & B. Voigt (Eds.), *Analytische Bewegungsund Tanztherapie* [Analytical Dance/Movement Therapy]. Munich: Ernst Reinhardt.

Siegel, E. V. (2002). Gedanken über Spielen im Alltag und in der Therapie [Thoughts on games in everyday life and in therapy]. In S. Trautmann-Voigt & B. Voigt (Eds.), *Verspieltheit als Entwicklungschance: Zur Bedeutung von Bewegung und Raum in der Psychotherapie* [Playfulness as a development opportunity: On the importance of movement and space in psychotherapy] (pp. 17–22). Giessen: Psychosozial.

Siegel, E. V., Trautmann-Voigt, S., & Voigt, B. (1999). *Analytische Bewegungsund Tanztherapie* [Analytical Dance/Movement Therapy]. Munich: Ernst Reinhardt.

Stern, D. N. (1992). *Die Lebenserfahrung des Säuglings* [The world of the infant]. Stuttgart: Klett-Cotta.

Stern, D. N. (1998). "Now-moments": implizites Wissen und Vitalitätskonturen als neue Basis für psychotherapeutische Modellbildungen ["Now moments": Tacit knowledge and vitality contours as a new basis for psychotherapeutic model training]. In: S. Trautmann-Voigt & B. Voigt (Eds.), *Bewegung ins Unbewusste* [Movement into the unconscious], (pp. 82–96). Frankfurt: Brandes & Apsel.

Stern, D. N. (2005). *Der Gegenwartsmoment, Veränderungsprozesse in Psychoanalyse, Psychotherapie und Alltag* [The present moment: Processes of change in psychoanalysis, psychotherapy, and everyday life] (E. Vorspohl, Trans.). Frankfurt: Brandes & Apsel.

Stern, D. N. (2011). *Ausdrucksformen der Vitalität* [Expressions of vitality]. Frankfurt: Brandes & Apsel.

Trautmann-Voigt, S. (1998). Tanztherapie—Frauensache? Oder: Anmerkungen zum Zeitgeist der "goldenen 20er Jahre" und zur Zweischneidigkeit von Sonderwelten [Dance Therapy—woman thing? or: Notes to the spirit of the "roaring 20s" and the double-edged nature of special worlds]. *Zeitschrift für Tanztherapie—Körperpsychotherapie, 9*, 20–25.

Trautmann-Voigt, S. (2003). Tanztherapie: Zum aktuellen Diskussionsstand in Deutschland [Dance Therapy: The current discussion in Germany]. *Psychotherapeut, 48*(4), 215–229.

Trautmann-Voigt, S. (Ed.). (2007). *Zeitschrift für Tanztherapie—Körperpsychotherapie (1994–2006)* [Journal of Dance Therapy and Body Psychotherapy (1994–2006)]. Cologne: Claus Richter.

Trautmann-Voigt, S., & Moll, M. (2011). *Bindung in Bewegung: Konzept und Leitfaden für eine psychodynamische Eltern-Säuglings-Kleinkind-Psychotherapie* [Attachment in movement: Concept and guidelines for a sound psychodynamic parent-infant-toddler psychotherapy]. Giessen: Psychosozial.

Trautmann-Voigt, S., & Voigt, B. (Eds.). (1996). *Bewegte Augenblicke im Leben des Säuglings—und welche therapeutischen Konsequenzen?* [Moving moments in the life of the infant—and what therapeutic consequences?]. Cologne: Claus Richter.

Trautmann-Voigt, S., & Voigt, B. (Eds.). (1997). *Freud lernt laufen: Herausforderungen analytischer Tanz und Bewegungstherapie für Psychoanalyse und Psychotherapie* [Freud learns to walk: Analytical challenges: Dance and exercise therapy for psychoanalysis and psychotherapy]. Frankfurt: Brandes & Apsel.

Trautmann-Voigt, S., & Voigt, B. (Eds.). (1998). *Bewegung ins Unbewusste: Beiträge zur Säuglingsforschung und analytischen Körper-Psychotherapie* [Movement into the unconscious: Contributions to infant research and analytical Body Psychotherapy]. Frankfurt: Brandes & Apsel.

Trautmann-Voigt, S., & Voigt, B. (Eds.). (2001). *Bewegung und Bedeutung: Anregungen zu definierter Körperlichkeit in der Psychotherapie* [Movement and meaning: Suggestions for a defined physicality in psychotherapy]. Cologne: Claus Richter.

Trautmann-Voigt, S., & Voigt, B. (Eds.). (2002). *Verspieltheit als Entwicklungschance: Zur Bedeutung von Bewegung und Raum in der Psychotherapie* [Playfulness as a development opportunity: On the importance of movement and space in psychotherapy]. Giessen: Psychosozial.

Trautmann-Voigt, S., & Voigt, B. (Eds.). (2007). *Körper und Kunst in der Psychotraumatologie. Methodenintegrative Therapie* [Body and art in psychotraumatology: Method-integrative therapy]. Stuttgart: Schattauer.

Trautmann-Voigt, S., & Voigt, B. (2010). Entwicklung, Abstimmung, Regulation: Tiefenpsychologisch fundierte Psychotherapie im Rhythmisch-dynamischen Handlungsdialog [Development, reconciliation, regulation: Depth Psychology-based psychotherapy in a rhythmic-dynamic action dialogue]. In W. Wöller & J. Kruse (Eds.), *Tiefenpsychologische Psychotherapie: Basisbuch und Praxisleitfaden* [Depth Psychology-based psychotherapy: Basics and practice guide]. Stuttgart: Schattauer.

Trautmann-Voigt, S., & Voigt, B. (2012). *Grammatik der Körpersprache: Ein integratives Lehr- und Arbeitsbuch zunm Embodiment* [The grammar of body language: An integrative textbook and workbook about embodiment]. Stuttgart: Schattauer.

Voigt, B., & Trautmann-Voigt, S. (2001). Tiefenpsychologische Aspekte der Körpertherapie und der Tanztherapie [Psychodynamic aspects of physical therapy and Dance Therapy]. *Psychotherapeut, 46*(1), 60–74.

Whitehouse, M. S. (1963). *Physical movement and personality.* Lecture for the Analytical Psychology Club, Los Angeles, CA.

Whitehouse, M. (1991). C. G. Jung und Tanztherapie: Zwei Hauptprinzipien [C. G. Jung and Dance Therapy: Two major principles]. In E. Willke, G. Hölter, & H. Petzold (Eds.), *Tanztherapie: Theorie und Praxis: Ein Handbuch* [Dance Therapy: Theory and practice: A manual] (pp. 139–164). Paderborn: Junfermann.

Winnicott, D. (1987). *Vom Spiel zur Kreativität* [Play and creativity]. Stuttgart: Klett-Cotta.

# 87
## The Significance of the Body in Gestalt Therapy

Wiltrud Krauss-Kogan, Germany

Translation by Warren Miller

**Wiltrud Krauss-Kogan**, Dipl. Paed., is a State-certified and -licensed child and adolescent psychotherapist (Psychodynamic), European-certified psychotherapist (ECP/EAP), and Gestalt therapist in private practice in Germany. With her husband, Dr. Gerald Kogan, she was a co-founder and co-director of the Gestalt Education Network International (GENI), and a co-founder of the German Association of Gestalt Therapy (DVG). She also has been a trainer of Gestalt Therapy in Europe, Israel, Asia, and Australia for three decades.

She trained in Gestalt therapy at the Fritz Perls Institut in Germany, the "original" Gestalt Institute of San Francisco (GISF), the former Gestalt Institute of Los Angeles (GTILA), and—in particular—with Laura Perls. She also trained in Gestalt Body Process Therapy with Jim Kepner, in Family Therapy (with Martin Kirschenbaum and others), in Family Constellation Work with Albrecht Mahr in Germany, in Psychotraumatology (EMDRIA), and in Psychodynamic Psychotherapy in the U.S.A. and Europe. She is the author of various articles on Gestalt Therapy.

As her experiences with Gestalt Therapy reach back to the mid seventies, she can be counted among a select group of Gestalt Therapists who are characterized by in-depth knowledge of the history, theory, and practice of the traditions of both Gestalt Therapy and Body Therapy, which makes her particularly qualified to illustrate the commonalities as well as the differences between Body Psychotherapy and Gestalt Therapy.

## Body-Oriented Psychotherapy and Its Roots in Gestalt Therapy

From its very beginning, Gestalt Therapy has considered itself to be a body-oriented approach, or more precisely, a holistic approach that views the body, mind, and spirit as an indivisible whole. It had been psychoanalysis' neglect of the somatic dimension, its exclusion of biological events from the psychotherapeutic process, that finally led the founders of Gestalt Therapy, Fritz and Laura Perls, both originally trained in psychoanalysis, to turn away from that orthodoxy. In 1936, Fritz Perls wrote an article on "oral aggression," attempting to expand psychoanalysis to include the somatic dimension, at least in theory, and this led to their separation from the psychoanalytic association—i.e., both Fritz and Laura Perls resigned their memberships. In his article, Fritz Perls emphasized the significance of bodily aggression, specifically oral aggression, for human development and outlined parallels between psychological and physiological functioning in metabolism and resistance processes.

This "Revision of Freud's Theory and Method" was further elaborated in *Ego, Hunger, and Aggression*, published in 1942, which became one of the foundations of Gestalt Therapy. In this book, Perls elaborated on Reich's position that any drive contains an element of aggression, and devoted particular attention to the fundamental and universal psycho-physical hunger drive that all organisms share. The element of aggression ". . . *not only serves self-preservation, like a defense, but also fosters expansion of the self by destructuring those materials and resources available in the environment, that need to be absorbed for growth to be sustained. Rather than swallowing and introjecting the environment unchanged, this is about biting, chewing through, preparing for absorption, and assimilating*" (Bocian, 1994, p. 24). Perls also views the hunger drive as a *"synonym for the structural similarity between the stages of food intake and our mental assimilation of the world"* (Perls, 1978).

Fritz and Laura Perls got their first impulses for a theoretical framework that takes the biological dimension of human beings into consideration, and that supports a body-oriented, holistic theory of human beings from the work of Kurt Goldstein. Goldstein was a physician and ("gestalt") psychologist who, in the 1920s, treated soldiers with brain injuries from World War I. Fritz Perls had been his assistant in 1926. It was Goldstein who expanded the primarily perceptual model of Gestalt Psychology and applied it to the whole body. In his work on organismic theory, Goldstein was able to show that every organism functions in accord with a number of specific Gestalt-psychological principles (Krauss-Kogan, 1983, p. 14).

Working with soldiers, Goldstein found that their brain injuries, not only caused the loss of specific functions, but resulted in an overall disturbance of the organismic equilibrium. He found that such "unfinished business" forces the organism to find new ways to reestablish organismic homeostasis. With the organism, as a whole, pressed to adapt to a new situation, a kind of organismic transformation ensues that leads to new ways of functioning within the environment.

Goldstein recognized that the principle of organismic self-regulation, including the ability to adapt creatively, is an inherent characteristic of all forms of life, and that, within limitations relative to the severity of the impairment, every organism is able to adapt to changed internal or external conditions. Organismic theory further proposes that the "figure-ground" distinction is the primary organizing function of the organism. This theory later became a cardinal principle in the practice of Gestalt Therapy: the organism operates on the basis of priority: the need that is most pressing for the achievement of homeostasis becomes the "figure"; the rest becomes the "ground" or background (Kogan, 1976, p. 240).

Goldstein's organismic theory, which also included the notion of organismic striving toward growth and self-actualization, forms the foundation of Gestalt Therapy and the whole range of its body-oriented interventions. The task of any therapy based on such a holistic theory is to engage with, and address, disorders and blockages of organismic self-regulation. This is what Gestalt Therapy attempts to do.

## Perls and Reich: Sketch of a Controversial Relationship

When, some years later, Fritz Perls continued his training as a teaching analyst, he went to Berlin and entered into analysis with Wilhelm Reich. He became acquainted with Reich's *Character Analysis* in the early 1930s, at a point when it was at the "zenith of its development as a bridge between psychoanalysis and the first steps towards Wilhelm Reich's own method of body therapy" (Knapp-Diederichs, 1997, p. 3), and he was deeply impressed. Reich also began using the concept of "self-regulation" around that time.

Perls was particularly struck by Reich's "discovery" that the recovery of memories is always accompanied by respective somatic changes, and Reich's assumption that painful emotions manifest in the form of a muscular armoring of the body. Following his work with Reich, Perls adopted new goals for therapeutic work: the ego functions were to be reestablished by means of "biological concentration" (that is, by consciously focusing attention—such an awareness being considered to be a faculty of both the ego and the unconscious) to dissolve the rigidity of the body, the petrified ego, the character armor.

Perls, however, did not agree with Reich that muscular armor can only be discharged cathartically in order to liberate the organism. He particularly disagreed with the implicit notion that uncomfortable emotions—and muscular resistance against such emotions—were cumbersome obstacles on the way toward liberation. On the contrary,

Perls viewed emotions and resistances as natural elements of the organism's self-regulation and manifestations of creative adaptation (in the sense of Goldstein's concept of self-regulation). So, Perls came to the conviction that nature just wasn't wasteful enough to create emotions without purpose that are an unnecessary nuisance (Krauss-Kogan, 1983, p. 6). *"Without emotions, we are dead, bored, and disinterested machines"* (Perls, 1981, p. 52).

Perls was also concerned that the cathartic "material" that is expressed and comes to light by breaking through the muscular armor would remain unintegrated and would continue to be experienced as alien, as something "foreign," particularly if such breakthroughs were accomplished forcefully, as a result of therapeutic pressure (Krauss-Kogan, 1983, p. 6).

Although Fritz and Laura Perls did see therapeutic value in emotional expression, they were much more interested in facilitating the present awareness of "being embodied in the world," and leaving it up to the organism to regulate when, to what extent, and at what pace it would allow such expression and loosening of the armor to occur (Ibid.).

Interestingly, toward the end of his life, Reich came round to a position that is closer to that of Fritz Perls and admitted:

> Looking back, I understand it. It is very dangerous. You see, the armor, as thick as it is and as bad as it is, is a protective device, and it is good for the individual under present social and psychological circumstances to have it. He couldn't live otherwise. That is what I try to teach my doctors today. I tell them I am glad they don't succeed in breaking down that armor because people, who have grown up with such structures, are used to living with them. If you take that away, they break down. They can't, they just can't live any longer. They can't function, you see. It will take a long time—maybe decades, maybe centuries, I don't know—until we have generations whose structures will be different. (Higgins and Raphael, 1968, p. 110)

According to Laura Perls, the work is not about discharging tension, but about the reorganization of charge, as *"charge is energy, and energy is a much too valuable resource to just get rid of, energy must become available for the necessary and desirable changes in behavior. It is the work of therapy to provide sufficient support for the reorganization and rechanneling of this energy"* (L. Perls, 1978, p. 2).

To some degree, she was talking about direct support of the patient by the therapist (in the sense of encouragement), especially at times when the patient comes into contact with new and unfamiliar material, but fundamentally what she had in mind was "support for self-support." Laura Perls implied a holistic understanding of self-support, across all levels of human experience, but always rooted in the body: this is expressed even in language: the German word "Stütze," meaning "support," also refers to physical support, as in buttress, pillar, or prop: *"Stütze begins with the primary physiology such as breathing, circulation, and digestion, proceeds with the development of the cortex, the embedding of the teeth, sensitivity and mobility, upright posture, speech and use of language, habits, customs, and even and especially the inhibitions and blocks, which were originally formed to serve supportive functions"* (L. Perls, 1978, p. 111).

This reconceptualization of patients' "inhibitions and blockages," traditionally also referred to as "defense reactions, defense mechanisms, and resistance," into "support functions" has far-reaching therapeutic implications for the handling of these phenomena in the context of both Gestalt Therapy and Body Psychotherapy. Considering that they were originally formed as "support" functions, which subsequently became "automatic" or "unconscious," the process of Gestalt Therapy strives to "deautomatize" these secondary automatisms by means of conscious exploration. In particular, the exploration of bodily manifestations leads to a greater body-mind awareness and an embodied understanding where, and to what end, these patterns are anchored in the body and continue to operate (Perls, L., 1989, p. 94f.). The goal of therapy is to allow these supports to become more flexible, not to abolish them.

This is the process by which Gestalt Therapy derived its body orientation from Reichian Character Analysis, along with its *active* therapeutic stance, and in contrast to the very passive treatment approaches of orthodox psychoanalysts. In addition, Gestalt Therapy promoted an emphasis on the patient's current life situation, and how it manifests in the body—a shift away from an exclusive focus on the "why" (past content) toward "how" (present process, and bodily expression) (Smith, 1976, p. 9). Gestalt Therapy also integrated Reich's idea of working from the outer layers toward the core. Fritz and Laura Perls further maintained Reich's dictum that techniques cannot be standardized, but that they need to be derived from the context and situation of each patient individually, thus validating the dignity of each individual growth process (Ibid.). The body therapeutic techniques of Gestalt Therapy were significantly modified and developed to reflect these other influences and became the roots of Gestalt Therapy.

## The Influence of Laura Perls

Laura Perls's orientation to the body came from her background and lifelong experience of Rudolf Steiner's "Eurythmy," as well as from Modern Dance; her *"knowledge of the Alexander and Feldenkrais methods long before the development of Bioenergetics and other body-therapies"* (L. Perls, 1989, p. 108); her early studies of Ludwig Klages's expressive movement and creative force work (*Ausdrucksbewegung und Gestaltungskraft*) (Ibid.); and also her studies with Elsa Gindler, while living in Berlin from 1931 to 1933.

Elsa Gindler (1885–1961) is still widely considered to be a pioneer in the field of body therapy (Franzen, 1995, p. 3). She came from a background in the pedagogic reform and gymnastics movement that significantly influenced artists, educators, physicians, and some psychoanalysts—among others, Erich Fromm and Laura Perls—in the first third of the twentieth century, particularly in Berlin. Beginning in 1917, Elsa Gindler researched the interplay between external movement, breath, inner participation, mode of consciousness, and human development. She discovered the significance of mindful awareness, deep sensory contact, and organismic self-regulation, and the conditions for their emergence. She explored these concepts with her students in an "experimental situation," as she liked to call it. Instead of providing structure and giving the students exercises, she encouraged experimentation and the gathering of findings. She called this work "*Nachentfaltung*"—"later unfolding" (in the sense of delayed unfolding, making up for earlier lack of it) (Franzen, 1995, p. 3).

The principles that Gindler discovered, as well as her process-oriented perspective on experiential learning as an explorative body process of *"allowing unfolding with trust in one's own organizational capacities and vitality,"* are also guidelines for the orientation of Gestalt therapeutic work with the body. Her description of the process of making contact, the "coming into contact with the laws of nature," with intention, readying, behavior generation, behavior completion, returning to calmness, reverberating/recuperating, and late effects (Ibid., pp. 3ff.) are reflected in Laura Perls's description of the contact cycle with its phases of fore-contact, contacting, final contact, and post-contact (Perls et al., 1951/1979, pp. 190ff.), which has become a core concept in the Gestalt therapeutic theory of personality.

The Gestalt therapeutic contact cycle model, also referred to as the "homeostatic need cycle" or the "cycle of experience," describes the process of organismic self-regulation (which was originally adapted from Goldstein's theory). Although it has often been misunderstood and criticized as being too simplistic or biologistic, it is precisely this biologically rooted (and therefore body-) and process-oriented perspective that provided the embodied frame and model for working with the body in Gestalt Therapy: "embodiment" and sensory experience were emphasized as a focus for both the therapist's and the patient's awareness. Fritz and Laura Perls viewed the "contact cycle" as a working model that was open for further development.

Many people who were able to get to know Laura Perls in person will remember how her work with sensing, experiencing, and becoming aware was very much in the spirit of Gindler's "experimenting through the senses and sensation," applying these notions to Gestalt practice.

Fritz Perls came into contact with Gindler's work only years later in New York, and even more so when at Esalen, through Charlotte Selver's work. She called this "Sensory Awareness" (Brooks, 1984) and it is, to some extent, based on the work of Gindler. Fritz Perls took some classes with Selver and was so impressed by her work that he assimilated many of her core principles into his work and integrated Sensory Awareness practices into a standard element of Gestalt therapeutic workshops, even if this was not as clearly reflected in his own therapeutic approach.

His rather provocative and confrontational style has been attributed to Reich's ongoing influence on his work. Reich felt that when resistance emerges in the process of therapy, it is one of the tasks of the therapist to be directive and to confront the patient with the "how" and "what" of the patient's resistance behaviors (Smith, 1976, p. 8).

In contrast, one of the working principles of Elsa Gindler's work, as well as Charlotte Selver's work, was to always remain open to unexpected procedural developments and not to superimpose static body-diagnostic schemas and classifications of psychic character structures on the client's process.

This aversion against rigid character classifications is echoed in Gestalt Therapy. Following Fritz and Laura Perls, many later generations of Gestalt therapists have struggled with the task of developing a Gestalt therapeutic diagnostic that maintains the process orientation and avoids rigid and stigmatizing categorizations.

## Further Developments of Body-Oriented Work in Gestalt Therapy

Despite the holistic and body-oriented foundations of Gestalt Therapy, there are many Gestalt therapists, and whole subschools of Gestalt, that give very little attention to the body. In these cases, therapeutic attention to the body might be limited to noticing changes in facial expression, or tone of voice, or body language, and addressing these therapeutically.

To some extent, this development is due to some Gestalt therapeutic schools emphasizing particular foundations of Gestalt Therapy over others. Whereas these aspects are expanded upon or developed into specializations, other aspects are relatively neglected. Such developments are reflected in modifications such as "relational Gestalt Therapy" or "analytical Gestalt Therapy," etc.

Aside from individual preferences, one factor in this development is that, after initially being enthusiastically received in the 1960s and early 1970s, the public profile of body-oriented work deteriorated. Many Gestalt therapists, in particular in the United States, wanted to promote the clinical legitimacy of Gestalt Therapy within the wider field of psychotherapy, and turned toward other modes and possibilities of Gestalt therapeutic work. Another determining factor of the extent to which body-oriented work does, or does not, feature in modern Gestalt is a question of lineage—when, and from whom, each new generation of Gestalt therapists received their training.

Isadore From, for example, one of the founding members of the New York Institute for Gestalt Therapy, viewed bodywork, particularly Reichian bodywork in combination with Gestalt Therapy, as an "inexcusable step backwards" that could not be a part of psychotherapy, as it "reintroduced the split between body and mind under the pretense of being part of a progressive development" (Müller, 1993, p. 40). From, who trained and influenced generations of Gestalt therapists, apparently considered bodywork as nothing else but an effort to manipulate and improve an already-functional body posture. He felt that such an attempt carried the risk of "once again imposing something upon a person, which is the kind of thing that formed the character in the first place" (Ibid.).

However, the main reason why many Gestalt therapists distanced themselves from body-oriented work is that such techniques had not sufficiently been developed from within Gestalt's own principles and theories, and therefore remained relatively rudimentary. Attempts at combining Gestalt Therapy with other body therapies were made, sometimes by therapists who deemed the process of change through growing awareness of the body-self to be too slow.

However, this usually led them into a bind, because these methods were not always compatible or consistent with Gestalt Therapy, theoretically as well as in practice.

In 1980, Gerald Kogan published *Your Body Works* in an effort to list body therapies that could be harmonized with Gestalt Therapy's process orientation and theory of organismic self-regulation, and that might contribute to Gestalt Psychotherapeutic work (Kogan, 1980).

From the mid- to late 1980s, a number of Gestalt therapists attempted to develop a specifically Gestalt therapeutic form of bodywork that was to reflect the theoretical foundations and principles of Gestalt Therapy. They were trying to expand the repertoire of body therapeutic techniques and to further the knowledge of handling body phenomena.

Edward Smith was the first to make such an effort in his book *The Body in Psychotherapy*. He uses Gestalt Therapy's concepts of the organism-environment field and the contact cycle as frames of reference and integrates Neo-Reichian procedures—in particular, body diagnosis and a number of specific Reichian interventions (Smith, 1985). Smith successfully shows how Gestalt Therapy can offer a good frame of reference for body-oriented work; at which points in the contact cycle interruptions might be observed; and what kind of body-oriented interventions can be applied in these situations. However, he does not quite achieve a satisfying and consequent integration of the Reichian material into Gestalt Therapy. Although descriptions of organized structural patterns manifesting in the body do not necessarily contradict the Gestalt approach, such descriptions should not lead to rigid concepts of pathology, as in Reich's description of character structures. Smith was not able to develop an independent Gestalt therapeutic terminology and a working model that is based on, and compatible with, the foundations of Gestalt Therapy.

In 1987, Jim Kepner was the first Gestalt therapist to describe a clear and predominantly Gestalt therapeutic form of body-oriented work in his book *Body Process: A Gestalt Approach to Working with the Body in Psychotherapy*. He was also able to show that it is a characteristic of Gestalt Therapy to be able to lift bodywork into the conscious process of the client, thereby enabling the client to make choices, which stands Gestalt Therapy in contrast to many other body-oriented methods. Joseph Zinker describes Kepner's work as follows:

> The client starts with his/her awareness of self, including sensory experience of the physical self. When attended to, the physical side changes and, at the same time, awareness changes.... Muscular-skeletal change and postural stance change with increased awareness and sense of one's own choices, complexity, and richness. These changes are whole, involving the total organism, and appear to last for many years. (Zinker, 1987, p. xxiv)

He continues: "Change in character structure does not come about from the charismatic directives of the therapist as to how to breathe, stand, or walk, but from the client's own awareness-directed experimentation" (Ibid.). Kepner thinks of his work as involving *"guiding, touching, and experimenting in an atmosphere of intimate contact"* and shows *"enormous respect for the client's moment-to-moment process and for the client's integrity and dignity as a human being"* (Ibid.). He is able to apply the Gestalt therapeutic principle of dialogue, based on the work of Buber, into a dialogue with the client's body-self.

> Kepner supports resistance as an integral part of the self in that he gives it the "somatic voice" needed for the client to learn something very important, specifically as an expression of self that is allowed to emerge consciously, choicefully, and deliberately. Resistance is seen as a disowned part of the body-self that needs to be brought into awareness and reintegrated into the person's total functioning. (Ibid., p. xxv)

In Gestalt therapy, the self is thought of as a mental and embodied sense of agency. Although I might be more than my body, I am also my body. The body is the place where I perceive, experience, and receive the world; it is the instrument with which I apprehend and comprehend the world, with which I move in the world and make contact. The body as self, or more precisely as an aspect of the self, can be viewed as identical to the contact functions. Without my body my access to the world is limited, I am limited. As so many people have split off, interrupted, or desensitized this access route to the world, Gestalt therapeutic body-process work primarily focuses on resensitizing the body by means of directing concentrated attention towards the body. Observation of its structure and process in breathing, movement, exercise, experimentation, the use of embodied language, mirroring, and touch fosters sensation and therefore awareness, which then leads to a reowning of the split-off aspects of the body-self. (Kepner, 1987, p. 11)

Sometimes sensitivity is limited by structural restrictions; and deliberate sensing alone, or other previously mentioned methods, do not lead to the degree of awareness necessary to effect change. In the context of Gestalt therapeutic body therapy, it can be particularly valuable to touch these restricted areas, assuming that the client gives permission, which should always be ascertained before using touch interventions. Often it is only through touch, which is a bodily form of communication, that a response is evoked and leads to a sensory experience in the client's body (Ibid., p. 76).

From a developmental-psychological perspective, touch is the most primary form of human contact. Western culture, deprived and phobic of touch as it is, almost completely excludes touch. In Gestalt bodywork, "contactful" touch by the therapist, or self-touch by the client, can lead to increased awareness of particular aspects of embodiment, such as breathing or tension patterns, and thereby facilitate a deepening of experience. Western culture tends to be a low-touch culture anyway, where touch is often sexualized. Nonetheless, Kepner decided to reintroduce touch into his approach, because it is sometimes the only way, aside from mindful breathing, to reanimate those regions of the body that are desensitized and split off, and to make them accessible to awareness.

What is emphasized in the context of Gestalt therapeutic bodywork is the fact that this kind of work is possible only if the therapist is conscious of his or her own embodiment. The therapist uses their own body as an instrument for modeling and reflection of the client's body therapeutic processes, and this can be effective only if the therapist's own bodily experiences can be distinguished from those of the client. Early on, Laura Perls noted how important it is for therapists to know their own self-supports.

To optimally support the patient, a Gestalt body therapist tunes into and senses the client's breathing patterns, body postures, movements, etc., and then searches for an embodied language to express these experiences. The therapist gives the patient time to experiment and to adjust this as necessary until the patient, who often lacks language for her experience, feels recognized in her experience and develops her own sufficient awareness. In an ongoing dialogue, Kepner collaborates with the patient to expand the possibilities of self-expression, to complete arrested movements, to dissolve fixed postures, and to expand the psycho-physical boundary of the ego (Kepner, 1987).

This sort of body-oriented work needs to be adjusted depending on the setting (field), the client, and the client's problems. It also needs to be adapted to the individual client and is not applicable to all clients. Sometimes it takes many hours without body-oriented work before the possibility of using the methods of Gestalt body-process work emerges.

Inspired by their teacher, Leland Johnson, the Gestalt therapists Staemmler and Bock developed a different Body-Oriented Therapeutic approach in the late 1980s. It is based specifically on Perls's conceptualization of the layers of neurosis, and its main focus is to lead the patient through the "impasse" (also referred to as the dead end or blockage) using body-oriented methods. They described their approach in 1987 in the book *Neuentwurf der Gestalttherapie [The Redesign of Gestalt Therapy],* and revised it in 1991 in *Ganzheitliche Veränderung in der Gestalttherapie [Holistic Change in Gestalt Therapy]* (Staemmler and Bock, 1987, 1991).

Perls's own body disorder, which had manifested as angina pectoris, led him to a physical treatment by Ida

Rolf and also to experience a breakthrough of his own "impasse." Under the influence of this very "delightful experience," he formulated the "layer model" of neurosis during the last months of his life. This model was initially only a rough draft, which is why most Gestalt therapists did not take much note of it. Considering that Perls developed this model based on his personal "liberation experience," it is concluded that this was not given the credit it deserves, and Perls's layer model was developed into a structural model that describes change processes in five phases (Fagan and Shepherd, 1971). Each of these five phases was linked with associated energetic qualities. Particular interest was directed toward the transitions between the phases, and body-oriented methods were developed to facilitate these transitions.

Ruella Frank's "Somatic Therapy" is another Gestalt body therapeutic approach that deserves particular attention. Frank builds her work on Gestalt Therapy's roots in movement education, which have mostly been neglected elsewhere, and this makes it very applicable for Gestalt therapeutic work with children. Frank describes her approach in her book *Body of Awareness* (2001). It is founded on an expansion of Laura Perls's concept of "primary supports" for contact in relation to coordinated movement patterns, and Paul Goodman's concepts of unified sensory-motor-affective reactions within the client-therapist field. She explores the development of children's movement experience from the earliest developmental stages and their influence on experience later in life. She finds that the organizing principles of early childhood development functionally mirror those of adults. Illustrating her point with careful case studies, she shows how movement plays a critical role in the development of self-awareness, in children as well as in adults. She further points out the general links between movement and psychological development, and specifically how they come into play in regard to therapeutic change.

## Conclusion

From the very beginning, body-oriented work has been an intrinsic aspect of the theory and practice of Gestalt Therapy. Since its original formulation, a number of different and promising approaches have further developed, refined, and intensified the bodywork aspects of Gestalt Therapy, which have contributed to bringing Gestalt Therapy ever closer to what—since its beginnings—it has claimed to be: a holistic psychotherapeutic method for integration of the whole being (including the body).

## References

Bocian, B. (1994). Gestalttherapie und Psychoanalyse: Zum besseren Verständnis eines Figur-Hintergrund-Verhältnisses: Teil I [Gestalt Therapy and psychoanalysis: For a better understanding of a figure-ground relationship: Part I.]. *Gestalttherapie, 8(2).*

Brooks, C. (1984). *Erleben durch die Sinne [Experience through the senses].* Paderborn: Junfermann.

Fagan, J., & Shepherd, I. L. (1971). *Gestalt Therapy now: Theory, techniques and applications.* New York: Harper & Row.

Frank, R. (2001). *The body of awareness: A somatic and developmental approach to psychotherapy.* Cleveland, OH: Gestalt Press.

Franzen, G. M. (1995). "Werden Sie wieder reagierbereit!" Elsa Gindler (1885–1961) und ihre Arbeit ["Get ready to react again!" Elsa Gindler (1885–1961) and her work]. *Gestalttherapie, 2,* 13–18.

Higgins, M., & Raphael, C. M. (1968). *Reich speaks of Freud.* New York: Farrar, Straus & Giroux.

Kepner, J. I. (1987). *Körperprozesse: Ein gestalttherapeutischer Ansatz [Body process: A Gestalt Therapy approach].* Cologne: EHP.

Knapp-Diederichs, V. (1997). Wilhelm Reich: Richtige Fragen zur falschen Zeit? [Wilhelm Reich: Correct questions at the wrong time?]. *Gestalttherapie, 11(1).*

Kogan, G. (1976). The genesis of Gestalt Therapy. In C. Hatcher & P. Himelstein (Eds.), *The handbook of Gestalt Therapy.* New York: Jason Aronson.

Kogan, G. (Ed.). (1980). *Your body works*. Berkeley, CA: Transformations Press.

Krauss-Kogan, W. (1983). *Entstehungsgeschichte der Gestalttherapie [The genesis of Gestalt Therapy]*. Frankfurt: Arbeitspapier des GENI Institut für Gestalt-Bildung e.V.

Müller, B. (1993). Isadore Froms Beitrag zur Theorie und Praxis der Gestalttherapie [Isadore Froms contribution to the theory and practice of Gestalt Therapy]. *Gestalttherapie, 4(2)*.

Perls, F. S. (1978). *Das Ich, der Hunger und die Aggression [Ego, hunger, and aggression]*. Stuttgart: Klett-Cotta.

Perls, F. S. (1981). *Gestalt Wahrnehmung [Gestalt perception]*. Frankfurt: Verlag für Humanistische Psychologie.

Perls, F. S., Hefferline, R., & Goodman, P. (1951/1979). *Gestalt Therapy: Excitement and growth in the human personality*. London: Souvenir Press (repub. *Gestalttherapie*. Stuttgart: Klett-Cotta).

Perls, L. (1978). Begriffe und Fehlbegriffe der Gestalttherapie [Terms and false concepts in Gestalt Therapy]. *Integrative Therapie, 3–4*.

Perls, L. (1989). *Leben an der Grenze [Life on the edge]*. Cologne: EHP.

Smith, E. W. L. (1976). The roots of Gestalt Therapy. In E. W. L. Smith (Ed.), *The growing edge of Gestalt Therapy*. New York: Brunner.

Smith, E. W. L. (1985). *The body in psychotherapy*. Jefferson, NC: McFarland.

Staemmler, F., & Bock, W. (1987). *Neuentwurf der Gestalttherapie [The redesign of Gestalt Therapy]*. Munich: Pfeiffer.

Staemmler, F., & Bock, W. (1991). *Ganzheitliche Veränderung in der Gestalttherapie [Holistic change in Gestalt Therapy]*. Munich: Pfeiffer.

Zinker, J. (1987). *Bauen am Prozessselbst. Vorwort zu: Kepner, J. I.: Körperprozesse: Ein gestalttherapeutischer Ansatz [Building on the process self. Foreword to: Kepner, J. I. Body process: A Gestalt Therapy approach]*. Cologne: EHP.

# 88

## Somatic Emotional Release Work among Hands-on Practitioners

Ilana Rubenfeld with Camilla Griggers, United States

**Ilana Rubenfeld**, PhD, studied at the Juilliard School of Music, where she received the Frank Damrosch Award for Outstanding Conducting. After ten years struggling with both the bias against female conductors and a troublesome back, she changed her profession and developed the Rubenfeld Synergy Method (RSM), a system for integrating soma, mind, emotions, and spirit. During her career, she trained with Fritz and Laura Perls in Gestalt Therapy; with Judith Leibowitz in the Alexander Technique; with Moshe Feldenkrais in the Feldenkrais Method; and with Charlotte Selver in Sensory Awareness. Ilana trained hundreds of people in RSM between 1965 and 2005 and has received the Pathfinder Award from the Association for Humanistic Psychology (1998), the Lifetime Achievement Award from the United States Association for Body Psychotherapy (2002), as well as an honorary doctorate in Transpersonal Psychology from The International University, Missouri (2003). She is the author of *The Listening Hand* (2000), as well as numerous chapters and articles. For decades, Ilana presented workshops at the Omega Institute in Rhinebeck, New York, and the Esalen Institute in Big Sur, California, as well as in many places around the world. She moved from New York City to Oregon in 2000, and retired in 2009. Now, late in life, she has returned to her first love: music. She is on the board of directors of the Rogue Valley Symphony and the Youth Symphony of Southern Oregon.

**Camilla Griggers**, PhD, trained with Ilana Rubenfeld from 1998 to 2002, and practiced the Rubenfeld Synergy Method for a decade in Santa Monica, California. During this time, she taught courses in Bodymind Communication and Body Stories at the Institute for Psycho Structural Balancing in Los Angeles and at the Santa Barbara Graduate Institute Somatic Psychology Program. She received her doctoral degree from the University of Florida, and has taught writing, media studies, gender studies and cultural studies at Carnegie Mellon University, Carlow University, and California State University at Channel Islands. Her university experience led her to believe we need more physical and emotional thinking in education. She is the founder of TheHealist.com, an online resource for chronic disease prevention education, and the author of *Becoming-Woman* (1997), *The Superfeed Superfeel Detox Challenge* (2015) and *Sustainable Humans* (forthcoming)

Hands-on, somatic-based approaches to therapy and education help clients and students to learn to become more functional and adaptive by cultivating greater balance, relaxation, and integration in their whole self. Practitioners help clients to release their holding patterns and blockages that cause discomfort, pain, and loss of function. Because human beings contend with constantly changing environments, gravity, and the necessity to adapt, there are forces to be reckoned with in every single moment of waking consciousness. For somatic practitioners, the psychological aspects of human experience arise from deep within the features of our physiology. We cry, laugh, and grimace with emotion; we stand up vertically on the earth; we touch and manipulate the world with fine motor movements of our fingers and opposable thumbs; we communicate through a complex verbal and body language; we reason; we form somatic patterns and transpersonal bonds; and we also experience multiple dimensions of consciousness.

The somatic practices reviewed in this chapter include: Rolfing, the Alexander Technique, Sensory Awareness, the Feldenkrais Method, and the Rubenfeld Synergy Method. Each has contributed to a greater understanding of how human beings learn and adapt. Each has helped to shape the field of psycho-physical education. Developments in this field show an evolution from separating the body, mind, emotion, and spirit to a unity of all aspects of the self. Our understanding of somatic practices has evolved from a Newtonian view of the physical body as an object in space to a quantum physics view of the acoustic body-mind (see Rubenfeld and Griggers, 2009).

## Part One: Somatic Traditions That Excluded the Emotions

### Ida Rolf's Structural Integration

Ida Rolf's Structural Integration (also referred to as Rolfing) took an outside-in approach, characteristic of the medical model. The Rolfing technique applies a firm touch—often working deep within the tissue, and into the muscle fascia, and sometimes stimulating intense moments of pain. After the first decades, trainings were refined, and practitioners were taught to work less intensely. Clients lay on a massage table, unclothed and draped. Rolf formulated a ten-part sequence that began with surface layers of connective tissues, then moved to deep core tissue, and then to full-body integration sessions. This ten-part sequence was designed to enhance organic coordination and movement (Rolf, 1989).

Rolfing sessions produced dramatic effects that surpassed those associated with traditional massage. Whereas massage and deep-tissue work might provide immediate relief of physical discomfort and pain, these effects would typically diminish within a few days. Some of the original symptoms would eventually begin to reappear. Rolfing didn't replace the need for massage, by any means, as the benefits of ordinary massage are very well documented and include: stimulating the blood flow; the metabolic flushing of waste material through the lymphatic system; and the calming of the autonomic nervous system.

However, Rolfing opened a whole new door in bodywork—one in which *fascia* (the connective tissue that surrounds all the muscle fibers and holds us together) became the primary focus of Rolf's therapy. Rolfers were taught to "manipulate the fascial web of connective tissue" in order to release blocked holding patterns and create better alignment and balance.

Rolf's approach was physically and structurally integrative. It focused on the way the soft muscles and the hard skeleton are held in relationship with an internal structure of connective tissue. She believed that when an event blocked the natural flow of movement in the physiological body, it would be felt (and sometimes become held) in the fascia. If clients could be helped to release these blockages and holding patterns in their connective tissues, they would create an opportunity to build a new fabric of both internal relationships within their own structure, and possibly also external relationships, as well.

The implication of this integrative approach on emotional processes was quite profound. Emotional releases were commonly reported during Rolfing sessions, during which intense waves of feelings would rise up and pass through the bodies of clients as fascial holding patterns were released. From her many years of firsthand clinical experiences, Rolf came to understand that the body holds memories of past experiences in its connective tissues. However, perhaps because she applied the medical model of manipulation (in which the practitioner is seen as *doing* something *to* the patient) and because this manipulation could trigger effects throughout the person's entire being, Rolf did not work with emotional release directly as part of her structural integration sequence. Rather, Rolfers were trained to observe emotional events without becoming directly involved in the client's affective process. Rolf was known to say, "Get in and get out!" Her paradigm remained clearly focused just on manipulation on the physical level of connective structures.

We theorize that Rolf may have taken this approach because she was applying, consciously or unconsciously, causal mechanical laws of Newtonian physics to the body. She understood the body's relationship to gravity in terms of "objects" (bones, muscles, fascia, etc.).

The idea of the emotions as waves passing through the space-time of the bodymind may not have occurred to Rolf (Wolfram, 2002). Yet Einstein's general theory of relativity, which predicted the existence of gravitational waves, was published in 1915. His special theory of relativity established the equivalence of mass and energy ($E = mc2$), but by the 1920s, physicists also knew that subatomic high-energy particles do not obey Newton's laws of motion, but rather laws of quantum mechanics, in which particles behave as waves (Witten, 2002).

At the time of this writing, the Rolf Institute's official website still reflects the incongruity between the Newtonian mechanistic paradigm applied to the bodymind and the actual somatic affective experience of Rolfing. The reader is told:

> It is impossible to touch the physical body without touching the emotional body. All individuals develop compensatory patterns, ways of the body holding and defending itself against a variety of physical and emotional traumas.
>
> For most Rolfers, emotional catharsis is not something consciously desired nor intended for their clients. Rather, the person is approached with reverence and compassion. When emotionally charged areas of the body have been identified by the client, or intuited by the practitioner, they are normally accessed slowly and with constant communication between the Rolfer and the client.
>
> Sometimes, however, repressed memories or experiences will arise for which the client and the Rolfer may not have any advanced warning. In this situation, the goal of the Rolfer is to provide a safe container for their release, taking the requisite time to integrate the experience into the physical and emotional body in a way that promotes maximum resolution and minimal trauma to the system. (Rolf Institute, 2014: www.rolf.org)

This contradiction between Rolfing's "intentions" and the actual functional effect of the work can be seen again a few sentences later in a statement about the emotional and psychological effect of Rolfing:

> Rolfer's are trained to ease a client through such an experience but are not trained as therapists. The nature and quality of accessing and resolution of emotionally charged material may be the most profound portion of a client's Rolfing experience. However, the client should not enter the Rolfing process with anticipation of such a major release but should remember that the Rolfer's area of expertise is integrating and balancing connective tissue. The emotional component, as attractive or dreaded as it may be, remains an ancillary aspect of the Rolfing process and not its primary intention. (Ibid.)

## F. M. Alexander's Use of the Self

Rolf was not the only somatic innovator to encounter the phenomenon of emotional energy without fully integrating the emotions into a somatic practice. F. M. Alexander reached the same impasse with his technique for the "use of the self." In the 1890s, he was one of the first teachers in somatic education to articulate the relationship between perception and bodily function. His technique raised awareness about what clients were actually doing, in relation to what clients thought they were doing.

Alexander was a stage actor who had healed himself of chronic laryngitis, and—in the process—articulated a method of somatic education. The approach that he taught continues to be popular among performance artists. Alexander Technique (AT) lessons are done fully clothed, in front of a mirror, usually in private sessions or in groups. AT teachers are trained to touch lightly, only in order to increase their clients' awareness of what is actually happening in their bodies in the moment. AT teachers also focus on everyday movements, such as sitting, standing, and walking.

Alexander's innovation was how he comprehended the role of *habit* in the somatic patterning of the nervous system. His method included subconscious patterns as a significant aspect of the body's mechanics (Barlow, 1965). The clients' own perceptions, therefore, were the key to releasing their holding patterns. This was a significant breakthrough in psycho-physical educational methods.

Perception, followed by *conscious direction,* could create a *pause* between stimulus and habitual response. That *pause,* in turn, created the possibility of a different choice. This method is intended to help clients break their habitual misuse of their bodies and thus the self.

Although Alexander saw that mental and physical aspects of the self are connected, he did not include the person's emotions into his method, even though some students experienced emotional releases during their lessons. From his point of view, somatic patterning included subconscious patterns, but did not include emotional patterning. The emotions were therefore conceived of as a separate element. *Body mechanics* did not include the *wave mechanics* of emotional information moving through the space-time of the bodymind. In this regard, we can conclude that his technique reflected a predominately Newtonian model of physics that was indeed quite mechanical. In spite of the split between soma and emotion, however, he understood—and demonstrated—that physical aspects of the self are relative to, and connected with, perception.

However, remnants of Cartesian thinking may have led him to assume that the mind controlled the body. To correct a misuse of the self, Alexander instructed his clients to forget about trying to learn something new. Instead, he directed them to focus on just stopping what they were presently doing, and then heightening their awareness in the moment (Alexander, 1932). In instructing students to think *No* to dysfunctional habitual patterns, the Alexander Technique reflects a hierarchy in which intellectual cognition dominates consciousness. Likewise, the head dominates the trunk. Intellectual understandings were seen as the means for *managing* ourselves and bringing unconscious patterns under *conscious control.* The key to the Alexander Technique was *cortical inhibition of habitual use.*

This was a leap forward from Rolfing. In the Alexander Technique, a cortical release of a holding pattern could be stimulated without ever actually touching the fascial network. Students were doing their own work to shift structures from the inside out.

**Charlotte Selver's Sensory Awareness**

Charlotte Selver shared the fundamental principle of physical awareness education as a tool for changing the self. However, she decentralized the authority of the head and intellectual cognition in this process of integration. For Selver, awareness is distributed throughout the bodymind, and the head and intellect do not carry the main control function. She believed that integration follows naturally from heightened sensory awareness, without the verbal command to "stop" (as Alexander had taught). This approach can be traced back to her teacher, Elsa Gindler, the German gymnastics and psycho-physical educator, who taught focusing and awareness in her psycho-physical training from the 1920s until her death in 1961 (Loukes, 2006). Whereas Gindler was known for working with gymnasts, Selver took her form of work to the United States. She called it "Sensory Awareness," and popularized it by offering experiential group workshops to the public, in such places as the Esalen Institute in Big Sur, California, the Omega Institute in Rhinebeck, New York, and her New York studio.

Heinrich Jacoby, musician, educator, and Zen teacher, was a longtime collaborator with Gindler, and also influenced Selver's work. He had worked closely with Gindler before he had to flee Nazi Germany to Switzerland in 1933. Gindler and Jacoby brought together both sides of the awareness equation. They believed that when you change awareness, you also change physical performance and function. And equally so, if you change a sensory-motor sequence, you can change bodymind awareness.

When Selver brought Gindler and Jacoby's "focus and awareness" techniques to the United States, she advanced somatic education to a new level, and developed ways to free one's perception. She popularized Sensory Awareness techniques among everyday people, not just athletes and performers. Charles Brooks, Selver's longtime colleague, noted Selver's influence on the Human Potential and Zen movements in the United States in his book *Sensory Awareness* (Brooks, 1986). These lineages intersected at the Esalen Institute in Big Sur, California, in the 1960s. The Sensory Awareness Method involved fully clothed peer-to-peer contact and many hours of lying on the floor. When asked, *"Why are we spending so much time lying on the floor?,"* Selver was known to retort in her wonderful Viennese accent, *"Because something's going to change, and it won't be the floor!"* (Rubenfeld, 1990).

Selver's method was aimed at peeling away layers of somatic conditioning. Her exercises were designed to help the client develop a more organic, authentic, and direct experiencing of the world. Without the pressure of performance (as in the Alexander Technique), importance could be placed on the freedom to explore, rather than attaining specific abilities. She sought to heal the division between body and spirit, by locating authority within the individual's feeling self (Selver, 1999).

Selver's philosophy mirrored the anti-authoritarian structure of Gindler and Jacoby's teachings. Both of them took strong positions against the prevailing National Socialist (Nazi) factions in central Europe in the 1930s. Their tradition emerged partly as a response to the mechanistic mass production of obedient social subjects, epitomized in the Nazi Youth Program.

In the United States, as a sociopolitical contrast, Selver and Brooks taught students Sensory Awareness as a method for mitigating the way that culture inscribes itself on our nervous systems. While students were guided to become conscious of the way they were breathing, lying, sitting, and standing, they were also learning to become more aware of being full-hearted and open to contact with others (Ibid.).

Like Rolf and Alexander, Selver distinguished emotional impulses from sensory input, and did not address any form of emotional processing. In fact, Selver warned teachers and students against "chasing the release." Emotions were seen as "distractions" from the primary aspects of bodily awareness (Brooks, 1986).

## Moshe Feldenkrais's "Functional Integration" and "Awareness Through Movement"

Moshe Feldenkrais, albeit a scientist, carried on the somatic tradition of awareness training, having studied both Judo and meditation techniques with Heinrich Jacoby, as well as the Alexander Technique. Feldenkrais's main focus was on the connection between movement and awareness. His student and colleague Yochanan Rywerant (1983) stated that "sensory discrimination remains the decisive event" (p. 20). Although he shared F. M. Alexander's emphasis on perception, Feldenkrais was critical of Alexander's assumption that Western somatic patterns (e.g., the notion that sitting was done in chairs, rather than on the floor) were universal. Feldenkrais's operating principle was that the quality of muscle movements can reveal the quality of function in the person's nervous system (Feldenkrais, 1949, 1977). In his book *Awareness Through Movement* (1972), he stated his belief that movement is the basis of a person's awareness.

Feldenkrais created awareness experiments for groups, in the form of floor sequences that he directed with verbal cues. He also called this process "Awareness Through Movement," and developed tactile manipulation techniques for private clients, lying prone and fully clothed, that he called "Functional Integration." Sometimes he communicated verbally during these sessions, though he also advised practitioners to keep verbal communication to a minimum (Rywerant, 1983).

Influenced both by his advanced study of Judo and by his formal training in physics, Feldenkrais used movement to help clients distinguish differences among reflexive, habitual, and conscious responses. In both Awareness Through Movement classes and Functional Integration sessions, he focused on slight movements that heighten sensory discrimination, which, in turn, stimulate structural changes in the bodymind. Often the movements were so subtle that they were barely perceptible.

This two-tiered method helped his clients to distinguish undifferentiated movements from differentiated ones. For example, a client might move the entire leg in one plane, while isolating the hip joint. Later, the client would be guided to move his foot, knee, and hip at the same time, in different planes. This process of specifically differentiated movements helps clients to become aware of possibilities for more differentiated movements. Clients often release unconscious holding patterns by performing such simple movements, learning to discern between a gross, habitual overresponse and a finer, conscious response. In *Body and Mature Behavior* (1949), Feldenkrais described the successful act of *learning* as an "adjustment." The achievement of a *proper* response was not seen as the attainment of the average response, but rather as the most *adaptive* response for a present situation (Feldenkrais, 1949, p. 47). He described his contribution to psychology as shifting attention from phases of adjustment in the development of a mature person to the biophysical processes of adjustment itself.

While Feldenkrais valued bodymind integration, he also deliberately sidestepped direct emotional processing. He assumed that physiological responses and sensory-motor functions are primary, whereas other functions are secondary. He wrote, *"A fundamental change in the motor-basis within any single integration pattern will break up the cohesion of the Whole and thereby leave thought and feeling without anchorage in the patterns of their established routines"* (Ibid., p. 39).

Feldenkrais also believed that emotional releases followed changes in neuromuscular functioning. However, emotions were not recognized by him to be *primary* aspects of bodily awareness. Ironically, the emotions were not seen as expressions of *movement*—even though emotions have a direct impact on the muscles.

## Part Two: Including the Emotional Process
### Incorporating Feelings in Somatic Work

Crying, laughing, snickering, glaring, grimacing, and smiling directly affect movements of the facial muscles, diaphragm, and vocal cords, and often trigger expanding or contracting motions of the entire spinal column. These emotions result from impulse signals traveling from the premotor cortex straight to the muscles of the body. Emotions are the first *mother tongue* of all human beings. They are very potent communications. Emotions are movements of *information,* as well as *energy,* traveling through sensory pathways that are located throughout the body. These are not just *muscular,* but include hormonal changes as well (e.g., Pert's [1997] *Molecules of Emotion*).

Muscle-movement patterning that accompanies emotional expression evolved to communicate a person's needs quickly, obviously, and unambiguously. When people *feel* strong emotions, they are *feeling* both movements of energy (expressed as muscular contractions or releases), as well as biochemical reactions (between peptide chains and receptors that might stimulate these muscular reactions).

These emotional and biochemical reactions move throughout the sensory body, throughout the gut, throughout the heart, throughout the brain, and throughout the craniosacral system (Pert, 1997). Emotions naturally *move* through every aspect of the self.

According to social anthropologist Chip Walter (2006), crying is an emotional *grammar* denoting weakness, vulnerability, distress, and need. Across cultures, the common human response to someone crying is usually empathy and sympathy, unless social conditioning has taught otherwise. Walter notes that only humans cry emotional tears. These tears are biochemically distinct from the reflex tears and basal tears that protect our eyeballs from injury and infection.

*Emotional* tears are loaded with prolactin (a limbic bonding hormone). Prolactin also affects mirror neurons in the brain. These mirror neurons allow us to imagine what another person might be feeling. Neuroscientists speculate that the evolution of mirror neurons developed our ability to form complex social bonds and to learn complex social behaviors from each other. This aspect of our emotional nervous system helps us to have a sensory experience of what it might feel like to *be* someone else (empathy) (Ibid.).

From a holistic, systemic perspective, we can conclude that *emotional* responses reflect the quality of the nervous system as much as *muscular* responses do. Habitual emotional responses can be released by developing finer sensory discrimination, in the same way that habitual muscular responses can be released by finer sensory discrimination. These elements cannot be separated: we have a degree of plasticity, even in the later years of life.

Separations of the self into body, mind, emotion, and spirit are mental constructs that don't actually exist in our experience. They exist only within the confines of a Cartesian logic of separation. This separation is then imposed upon our perception of reality. Semiotician Alfred Korzybski warned against mistaking these mental constructs for reality in *Science and Sanity* (1933) (noting that insanity could result from confusing the two).

In the medical and psychoanalytic field in Germany, Wilhelm Reich challenged this logic of separation of the unified bodymind. He courageously crossed the Cartesian boundaries between body and mind and *treated the emotions directly*. He did so as a medical doctor, at a time when dualistic philosophy was very strong. His understanding of people's bodies *included* their emotional structures (Reich, 1933/1990). However, in the field of bodywork, purely somatic practitioners repeatedly bypassed or downplayed the emotions.

The *hierarchy of control theory* dominated early somatic practices. According to this theory, the evolved neocortex brain (known for rational thought and logic) *controlled* the older reptilian and limbic brain structures. The assumption was that the *logical mind* was able to make better decisions than purely *emotional* or *instinctual* responses.

Neurologist Paul MacLean (2002) helped to displace the *hierarchy of control theory* with a *nonhierarchical paradigm* through a lifetime of publications on the "triune brain." His work reevaluated the role of the limbic and reptilian brains. For example, when people flinch and swerve a car away from oncoming traffic, the reptilian brain's split-second instinctual response is the most appropriate and adaptive. Rational thinking in such a situation would be less adaptive, not more.

By the same token, in the face of overwhelming grief, emotional crying (not rational thought) may be the most adaptive response. Emotional crying releases prolactin, manganese, and proteins from the brain. A crying release may help a person to detoxify, adapt, and return to balance more quickly after an intense shock (Walter, 2006).

Emotions may have been segregated from bodywork for so long because trade guilds separated the professions. Bodyworkers were taught anatomy and how to touch, but were not supposed to process *emotional situations* verbally, or to therapize their clients: this was supposed to be the role of the psychotherapists. On the other hand, psychotherapists were expected to aid their clients in processing emotions verbally (the *talking cure*), but were not supposed to use any specific forms of *touch*.

Somatic practitioners are also typically not trained to work with transferential and countertransferential dynamics that may occur during sessions. Without such training, purely hands-on somatic practitioners may feel ill-equipped to respond to the emotional releases that occur quite naturally when working with the body. Hence, they tend to witness emotional releases, without engaging.

The Cartesian model of *splitting* the mind and body also educates somatic practitioners to be guardians of the *body*, but not the *mind*. *Emotions* complicate this binary, polarized system.

In sum, the avoidance of emotional processing by somatic practitioners is the return of the repressed split between mind and body known as "Descartes' error." In his book, *Descartes' Error: Emotion, Reason, and the Human Brain* (1994), neurologist Antonio Damasio wrote, "The mind is embodied, in the full sense of the term, not just embrained" (p. 226). The *emotions* provide a third dimension that breaks apart the old duality—opening the door to integration methods that recognize the unity of the whole self.

### Part Three: The Rubenfeld Synergy Method

This is Ilana Rubenfeld's personal account of the development of the Rubenfeld Synergy Method (RSM):

> I took a different path into somatic work, one that would lead me to the healing model and direct emotional processing through touch. While others came from the medical model, from bodywork, psychology or from psychotherapy, I came to somatic-emotional

processing as a musician—graduating as a conductor from the Juilliard School of Music in New York. Because I began as a musician, my method was based on harmonics. I was comfortable working directly with emotional processing while introducing verbal interventions and touching the body simultaneously. At that time in my life, practicing as a conductor, I suffered from back problems that eventually led me to study the Alexander Technique. When I experienced a somatic-emotional release and started crying one day during an Alexander Technique lesson with my teacher Judith Leibowitz, she promptly referred me to a psychotherapist. "I can touch you," Leibowitz said somewhat apologetically, "but I can't talk to you." I went to her psychotherapist and he said, "I can talk to you, but I can't touch you." I had the "Ah-Ha" realization that one person could process physical and emotional changes simultaneously, without compartmentalizing them. I therefore made somato-emotional integration the core of my work (adding the spiritual dimension later).

Another formative moment in the development of the Rubenfeld Synergy Method happened when I studied Gestalt Therapy with founders Drs. Fritz and Laura Perls in the 1960s. Fritz Perls encouraged me to touch his fully clothed clients while he talked to them. What became apparent was that their bodies reacted (muscles became tensed or relaxed) to what Perls was saying. I discovered various ways to touch the whole person—including when a person was in the middle of an emotional release. This type of light touch became known as the "Listening Hand."

I found validation for my intuitive touch-based approach to somatic-emotional release in the publications of Manfred Clynes, a scientist, mathematician and musician. He developed one of the first machines to measure brain wave frequencies. Clynes coined the word "transducts" to express movements of emotional energy through the hands. In his book *Sentics: The Touch of Emotions* (1989), Clynes asserted that the emotions comprise a universal language, "hardwired" into the human bio-physiology. He even designed a machine to measure emotions in the fingertips. These machines demonstrated a consistency in the emotional responses of hundreds of different musicians to the vibrations of various types of music. Clynes' research on "Sentics" validated my sense that I was working with an underlying structure that could be touched—the language of the emotions. The "Listening Hand" technique worked in the same way instrumentalists and singers move and express their feelings and the instrument's vibrations through their hands. I realized I could express the feeling of empathetic listening and emotional support through my hands. And similarly, I could feel the vibrations of people's emotions through my hands.

As important as touch is to RSM, in actuality, I was using much more than my hands. I was integrating touch, vocal communication, facial gestures and body language to try to help people move emotional energy through the whole Self. It was Buckminster Fuller who gave the word "synergy" to my work. "You are no longer doing integration," he said to me in a conversation in 1978, "you are doing synergy." I foolishly asked him what synergy was, and he reached for a copy of his book *Synergetics: Explorations in the Geometry of Thinking* (1975) to give me, taking the time to write the following inscription: "To Ilana Rubenfeld . . . in Mystery and Faith in the Integrity of Universe." I came to understand that "synergy" refers to the behaviors and effects of whole systems that cannot be predicted from the behaviors and effects of their parts. For example, when you bake bread, you may take milk (which has one characteristic), flour (which has one characteristic), and water (which has one characteristic). When you mix them all together, that is integration. When you add heat, the process of the integration of ingredients turns into bread, which is a form of synergy.

To emphasize the synergy of tactile-verbal-emotional resonances, I often return to my early years at the Juilliard School of Music, and my studies with the cellist and conductor Pablo Casals. Whether he demonstrated on the cello, or analyzed the music, or touched my arm and cajoled me to play, his intention was always crystal clear. We were creating a musical dialogue of universal themes that elevated our spirits. Over many years, I've witnessed that whenever a therapist and client join forces (energies) in a clear intention to move through barriers together, they experience a special kind of harmony that is often beyond words. (Rubenfeld, 1997)

### Example of an RSM Session: Vignette

In one RSM demonstration for a training class, a participant (whom I will call Mary) accessed a core somatic memory. In just a few minutes of contact with words, facial gestures, intonation and the listening hand (gently touching her shoulder and upper back in the area of her heart), a wave of sadness emerged. With a trembling voice and a flushing face, Mary remembered hiding under her mother's grand piano as a young child, sitting quietly listening to her mother practicing for hours. Expressing the feeling of that memory, Mary promptly got up off the cushioned table where she was sitting and crawled underneath it. I followed her and engaged her in that emotional posture. Using touch, verbal and nonverbal expression, I contacted the vibrating energy stored in Mary's bodymind with my intention to listen, witness and support. Mary suddenly burst into tears—releasing a deep well of suppressed feelings of abandonment. After this cathartic release, Mary felt less comfortable hiding under the table. Hiding had become her life's metaphor. After decades of isolation, she opened up to the possibility of change. The entire session was about forty-five minutes from beginning to end. (Rubenfeld, 2000)

### Conclusion: The Acoustics of Emotional Processing

The "musical" approach to emotional processing (which characterizes the Rubenfeld Synergy Method) harmonizes with certain developments in the "new physics," because, at the quantum level, emotions are energy. *String theory* (first expounded by quantum physicists in the 1970s) proposes that each "elementary" component of matter is actually "a loop of vibrating string," much like a violin or piano string (Witten, 2002). Each string is capable of operating in several dimensions and expressing different harmonics. These harmonics determine the form of expression of particles. Whether a particle of matter is an electron, photon, neutrino, quark, or graviton depends upon the *vibration* of that string (Ibid.). In other words, everything in the universe is quantum phenomena of *acoustic vibrations*. Physicist Daniele Amati, in a paper on string theory's acoustic model entitled "*The Information Paradox,*" asserts that even space and time are quantum phenomena determined by acoustic harmonics (2007, p. 4).

Shing-Tung Yau and Steve Nadis, authors of *The Shape of Inner Space* (2012), published the article "String Theory and the Geometry of the Universe's Hidden Dimensions" (2011). In this article, they describe working with topologist and geometer Edward Witten to try to figure out the shape (or geometry) of the six *extra* dimensions of the ten dimensions that string theory proposes: three large spatial dimensions (height, width, depth) plus time (the fourth dimension), and then the six additional dimensions hidden in every point in real space (even though one can't see them). According to Yau and Nadis, the shape of *inner space* defines the properties of the universe and our experiences in it. String theory's acoustic, multidimensional model of inner space helps to explain the physics of the bodymind far better than the earlier Newtonian model does.

Joachim-Ernst Berendt, musician and author of *The World Is Sound—Nada Brahma: Music and the Landscape of Consciousness* (1991), agrees that sound oscillation (or vibration) is a better paradigm for understanding the consciousness of the world inside us. He describes matter (at the subatomic level) as a continuous dance of energy changing into different states. We live in (and actually *are*) a resonating cosmos of dynamic interrelationships of varying degrees of harmony and disharmony (what physicists call quantum coherence and decoherence).

From a quantum perspective, it is quite easy to realize the harmonics of emotions, and that emotions express waves of energy directly throughout the body-mind (Rubenfeld, 2000). Authentic emotions are vibrations that correspond to harmonies and disharmonies in the world around and within us. Suppressed emotions mark distinct moments of incomplete movement and blocked energy in the person's bodymind. In the somatic language between infants and adults, the nervous system learns to anticipate responses from outside the self to emotional expression. There is a basic need for completion (in the sense of emotional impulse). This may be the definition of *limbic bonding*. Anything that blocks the natural harmony between emotional impulses from within (crying, grimacing, laughing, glaring, etc.) and timely responses from without (empathy, nurturance, connection, or distance, etc.) may disturb the harmony of a person's being—from their emotional states to their physical movements to the vibration of receptors in cell walls.

In the musical approach of the Rubenfeld Synergy Method (RSM), sound oscillation provides a useful paradigm to understand emotional release and integration. Emotional resonance is natural and intuitive. Like a musical instrument, the human body receives vibrations from the quantum field, and it also generates emotional vibrations that travel back into the field. Emotions are as palpably felt as musical chords. The songs of our experiences vibrate in all bodies. And emotions can be touched and moved as tangibly as cradling a baby, or crying on the shoulder of a loved one in a moment of grief.

The Rubenfeld Synergy Method provides a way for people to bring themselves into *harmony* in all dimensions of their being. RSM integrates emotional harmonics with listening hands and Gestalt therapeutic language. Fully clothed clients can lie down on a cushioned table, sit, stand, sing, cry, or crawl. By paying attention to their bodymind awareness, movements, and emotional releases, they can practice shifting their *emotional vibrations* from within to expressing themselves outwardly. Clients can learn to laugh at themselves, for example. They can learn that various situations in which they once were crying can be *funny*—if they change their emotional vibration. Likewise, those who learned to bury their cries can explore what it feels like to share vulnerability. All of these changes occur in an atmosphere of safety. By playing the full range of the emotions, clients learn to explore and express nonhabitual responses that can help them be more adaptive and authentic—more in harmony (in *synergy*) with the universe.

In conclusion, hands-on somatic therapies and psychophysical educational methods have contributed a vast body of knowledge about the bodymind's healing process. Ida Rolf's *Structural Integration* revealed the importance of fascia or connective tissue in body memory. F. M. Alexander's *Alexander Technique* explored the use of cortical inhibition to change somatic patterning. Charlotte Selver's *Sensory Awareness* offered experiential techniques for mitigating the effects of society on the nervous system. Moshe Feldenkrais's *Functional Integration* and *Awareness Through Movement* showed the biophysics of how we learn, pattern, and adjust. And the Rubenfeld Synergy Method integrates much of the above with emotional resonance, and adds synergy. The overall development of Somatic Therapy has moved beyond a Cartesian logic of separation to a unity of the whole self, and from a Newtonian paradigm to a quantum acoustical paradigm. As a result, all somatic practitioners/therapists are challenged to do their work in a nondualistic spirit, one that includes the emotions. Likewise, psychotherapists are challenged to do bodywork synergistically with the biophysical aspects of the emotional process.

## References

Alexander, F. M. (1932). *The use of the self.* New York: E. P. Dutton.

Amati, D. (2007). The information paradox. In M. Gasperini & J. Maharana (Eds.), *String theory and fundamental interaction.* Heidelberg Springer.

Barlow, M. (1965). *The teachings of F. Matthias Alexander.* The Annual F. M. Alexander Memorial Lecture: The Medical Society of London. Nov. 9, 1965.

Berendt, J-E. (1991). *The world is sound—Nada Brahma: Music and the landscape of consciousness* (Helmut Bredigkeit, Trans.). Rochester, VT: Destiny Books.

Brooks, C. (1986). *Sensory Awareness.* New York: Felix Morrow.

Clynes, M. (1989). *Sentics: The touch of emotions.* New York: Doubleday.

Damasio, A. (1994). *Descartes' error: Emotion, reason, and the human brain.* London: Putnam.

Feldenkrais, M. (1949). *Body and mature behavior: A study of anxiety, sex, gravitation, and learning.* Berkeley, CA: Somatic Resources, Frog.

Feldenkrais, M. (1972). *Awareness Through Movement.* New York: Harper & Row.

Feldenkrais, M. (1977). *Body awareness as healing therapy: The case of Nora.* Berkeley, CA: Somatic Resources, Frog.

Fuller, B., & Applewhite, E. J. (1975). *Synergetics: Explorations in the geometry of thinking.* New York: Macmillan.

Korzybski, A. (1933). *Science and sanity: An introduction to Non-Aristotelian Systems and General Semantics.* New York: Institute of General Semantics.

Loukes, R. (2006). *Concentration and awareness in psychophysical training: The practice of Elsa Gindler.* Cambridge, UK: Cambridge University Press.

MacLean, P. (2002). *The triune brain in evolution.* New York: Springer.

Pert, C. (1997). *Molecules of emotion: The science behind mind-body medicine.* New York: Touchstone.

Reich, W. (1933/1990). *Character Analysis* (3rd ed.). New York: Farrar, Straus & Giroux.

Rolf, I. (1989). *Rolfing: Reestablishing natural alignment and structural integration of the human body for vitality and well-being.* Rochester, VT: Healing Arts Press.

Rolf Institute of Structural Integration. (2014). *About Rolfing SI: Frequently asked questions: What about the emotional and psychological effects of Rolfing SI?* Retrieved from www.rolf.org/about/faq

Rubenfeld, I. (1990). Public speech at Charlotte Selver's birthday gathering.

Rubenfeld, I. (1997). Listening hands: The healing power of touch: An interview with Richard Simon. *Family Therapy Networker: Psychotherapy and Modern Life.*

Rubenfeld, I. (2000). *The listening hand: Self-healing through the Rubenfeld Synergy Method of talk and touch.* New York: Bantam Books.

Rubenfeld, I., & Griggers, C. (2009). Bodymind is one word. *Somatics, 16*(4), 4.

Rywerant, Y. (1983). *The Feldenkrais Method: Teaching by handling.* Laguna Beach, CA: Basic Health Publications.

Selver, S. (1999). *Learning through sensing.* Retrieved from www.sensoryawareness.org

Walter, C. (2006). *Thumbs, toes, and tears and other traits that make us human.* New York: Walker.

Witten, E. (2002). Universe on a string. [Updated from *Astronomy (June 2002), 42–47*]. Retrieved from www.sns.ias.edu/~witten/papers/string.pdf

Wolfram, S. (2002). *A new kind of science.* Champaign, IL: Stephen Wolfram.

Yau, S-T., & Nadis, S. (2011). String theory and the geometry of the universe's hidden dimensions. *Notices of the American Mathematical Society, 58*(8), 1067–1076.

Yau, S-T., & Nadis, S. (2012). *The shape of inner space: String theory and the geometry of the universe's hidden dimensions.* New York: Basic Books.

# 89

## Cognitive Behavioral Therapists Discover the Body

**Serge K. D. Sulz, Germany**

Translation by Warren Miller

**Serge K. D. Sulz**, PhD, MD, is one of the well-known and distinguished representatives of Cognitive Behavioral Therapy in Germany, both scientifically speaking, as well as in regard to the politics of the profession. As a specialist in psychiatry, psychotherapy, psychoanalysis, and psychotherapeutic medicine; as an accredited psychotherapist, a Balint group facilitator, an examiner for qualification as a specialist in psychotherapeutic medicine, and a supervisor; and as a teaching therapist for Cognitive Behavioral Therapy as well as Psychodynamic Therapy, his approach embraces a wide spectrum. As director of the Center for Integrative Psychotherapy (CIP) in Munich, which offers postgraduate training for psychotherapists, he draws upon this background.

Dr. Sulz established the Bavarian Academy for Psychotherapy (BAP) and is its executive director. He has been the president of the German medical society for Cognitive Behavioral Therapy since 1999, and is a highly productive author of many books and other publications.

Based on recent bio-psychological research findings, Dr. Sulz holds the view that in the future Body Psychotherapeutic perspectives and interventions will be indispensable to any form of psychotherapy, and that Body Psychotherapy should be a mandatory aspect of psychotherapeutic training in general. In this chapter, he describes why the body is viewed as playing such an important role from the perspective of a cognitive behavioral therapist.

### Anxiety in the Body

During the early development of behavioral therapy, when cognitions weren't yet considered to be behaviors, the center of observation and investigations was the emotions and motor behavior. A phobia was defined by an emotional component (fear) and a behavioral component (flight or avoidance).

Both of these components include some somatic aspects, which behavioral therapy assessed in its analysis and then targeted for change. Along with the patient's reported self-assessment of the intensity of his anxiety in a specific fear-evoking situation (by giving it, for example, a percentage figure), muscular tension (assessed by EMG readings), increased heart rate, the increased systolic blood pressure (indirectly caused by the higher heart rate), skin conductivity (assessed by PGR readings), as well as decreased temperature in the hands and fingers were all considered to be the particular components of anxiety.

Flight and avoidance behavior was assessed through direct behavioral observation. The goal of behavioral therapy was to get all components of anxiety out of the range of the phobic response: no more emotion of fear, no more muscular tension, no more heart racing, no more high blood pressure, no more cold hands and fingers, no more increased skin conductivity, and no more flight and avoidance behaviors of the previously phobic situation.

This illustrates that, from its beginnings, behavioral therapy has been working with the bodily aspects of experience and behavior. A bodily reaction is a form of behavior triggered by a situational stimulus and maintained by negative or positive reinforcement. Tension headaches, for example, are triggered by a frustrating, stressful situation, and the symptom is then maintained by internal or external permissions that are used to justify withdrawing, instead of having to face a confrontation. For many years "Progressive Muscle Relaxation" was a standard element of *anxiety therapy* (Paul, 1966). Relaxation was used as an antagonist to anxiety (Wolpe, 1959) because where there is relaxation, there can be no anxiety. This, clearly, is a body-oriented treatment approach, which by now has become one of the best-researched methods, and which has proved particularly successful in the treatment of pain syndromes (Rehfisch and Basler, 1990).

Just as anxiety comes with muscular tensions, there are different forms of muscular tension patterns that over time can become the cause of pain conditions such as tension headaches, or syndromes of the cervical or lumbar spine. Muscular tensions are neuromuscular changes that prepare the body for movement. The body gets ready for action: in the case of fear, it prepares for flight; in the case of anger, for fighting.

A behavioral analysis of hypertensive patterns shows that this symptom arises particularly when muscular agonists and antagonists are contracting simultaneously (Sulz, 1998). In a situation full of anger, the body readies itself for attack through the buildup of muscular tensions. Simultaneously, the fear of the other's aggression leads to a neuromuscular inhibition through contraction of the antagonists. Movement is stopped, and the musculature remains in a state of tension.

The continuing presence of this tension overnight, sometimes for days and weeks, is an indication that a tendency to resist a perceived attack continues to exist and that this tendency continuously needs to be reinforced by a fear of counteraggression. If the impulse to fight would subside, the musculature could simply relax. This would be the simplest way to complete a movement that is not being allowed to happen. Muscular tensions are therefore a sign of conflict between fight and flight, anger and fear, tension and relaxation. Stress, too, consists of both an anger and a fear component, and its bodily manifestations can be categorized into these fear and anger reactions. Jacobson (1990), the developer of *Progressive Muscle Relaxation,* discovered that the effect of muscle relaxation reaches way beyond the muscles themselves. Today we know that the whole cluster of stress reactions responds very well to muscle relaxation, which additionally leads to very good psychological relaxation (Meichenbaum, 1985). The reciprocity between muscular tensions and emotional stress (fear and anger) causes tensions; and muscle relaxation causes psychological relaxation and then more pleasant feelings: all of which has long been known to behavioral therapy.

## Affective and Somatic Schemas

The cognitive era of Cognitive Behavioral Therapy began when researchers began to turn their attention toward the influence of thoughts on emotions and behavior (for example, Goldfried, 1971). In this context, Lazarus (1976) came to postulate that all modes of behavior—emotional, cognitive, somatic—and any drugs or medications, should be taken into account in every treatment plan, based upon the recognition that although these modes strongly affect each other via reciprocal relationships, they show little correlation between themselves. Piaget's (1945) theory of cognitive schemas gathered increasing interest. It showed how separation from a protective caregiver could be appraised as dangerous, and how a situation (for example, a train ride in the context of a weekend getaway) could activate this latent cognitive schema and trigger a panic attack. Among others, Margraf and Schneider (1990) have emphasized the influence of cognition on panic disorders: "*The vicious cycle of cognitive interpretation of an external phobic situation, fear, body reactions, the proprioceptive perception of these reactions, their interpretation as further signals of danger, fear etc., shows the reciprocal causality between cognition, emotion, and the body.*"

Aside from cognitive schemas, Piaget (1945) also described "emotional schemas." These are psychic structures that optimize the mastery of recurring situations.

If a person repeatedly gets into similar situations, there is no need and it is not economical to process the novelty of each specific new situation as if he had never experienced it before. He's already formed a schema, which helps him to respond to the situation more swiftly and effectively. He repeats applicable perceptions, logical cognitive conclusions and interpretations. He automatically re-experiences the same emotions as the last time, and feels the same impulse to act that led to mastery of the previous situation. His expectations of the consequences of his actions are also part of this matrix or schema. Every time the usefulness of his matrix bears out, its correlating reactions are neurally patterned together, that is, the schemas are consolidated. Assimilation ensues. If the schemas no longer fit or do justice to frequently arising situations, they are then changed. This change is the process of accommodation. (Ibid.)

Piaget (1945) was the first to describe and research these processes. He differentiates between cognitive and affective schemas. The latter develop during childhood, primarily during the toddler years, before complex psycho-social events can be grasped cognitively, and before emotionally mature processing becomes possible. Because the schema is characterized by abstraction and generalization, it is readily available—if the reactivating situation varies only slightly from the original one. In this way, recurring events with similar meaning can lead to recurring emotions. Such psychic structures are used to master current situations better, and this psychological organization is a process serving adaptation to the environment (Sulz, 2000, p. 14).

Aside from cognitive, emotional, somatic, and behavioral schemas, we also need to consider complex motivational schemas (for example, need satisfaction, achievement, competition, etc.). A schema can be activated through a single aspect of a remembered or current situation. This schema then activates subschemas, which tend to be specific to certain modes (e.g., often leading first to bodily reactions, which, in turn, trigger emotional, behavioral, and cognitive schemas). As a whole, these subschemas activate a complex motivational schema, which is associated with a multimodal memory of an event, as described by Damasio (1990), with his notion of an inner scenario. Schemas can be triggered not only by external situations, but also by internal ones, proprioceptively. A specific body posture, such as standing with legs apart and fists on the hips, can be a component of a schema that is emotionally associated with anger or challenge, and cognitively with thoughts of hurting or standing up to someone; if the other fights back, the body's posture may be associated with behavioral and motoric schemas for physical attack or defense.

## How Cognitive Behavioral Therapists Work with the Body

Cognitive behavioral therapists use the affect-evoking effects of body postures and reactions in the technique of *emotion exposition*. This is an intervention that amplifies the emotion in order to facilitate the patient's ability to regulate the respective emotion. Using anger as an example: a patient who does not have conscious access to his anger is asked to tighten his loose fists somewhat more vigorously, and then to turn his attention to his emotions; then to tighten his fists even more, and again to turn to the experience of his emotions; to consider the behavior of his opponent; to name any detrimental effects in relation to that person; to return to paying attention to his emotions; and to sense what movement impulses and behaviors then want to arise. This is (cognitively) focusing on the somatic and emotional aspects of a behavior.

Based on the findings of current cognitive and neurobiological research, this approach aims to activate "schemas" that are stored in implicit, emotional-procedural memory, and to confront them with current experiences that cannot be assimilated into these schemas, so that the (dysfunctional) schemas have to be modified through accommodation. Thus, new schemas may be formed that fulfill the demands of adulthood.

A man can experience great fear as he strongly objects to his wife for the first time. He may have the same physically painful bodily sensations as in the past, in a similar situation with his mother, and he is convinced that the relationship will now be "lost" and that he will be rejected forever. As his wife responds with surprise and (perhaps even) a willingness to compromise, his fear falls away, his body grows larger and stronger, and a sense of valor emerges.

One form of Cognitive Behavioral Therapy, Dialectical Behavior Therapy, applied to a particular type of patient, that of borderline personality disorder. Linehan (1996a, 1996b) views the body as playing a very significant role in therapy. From the bodily self-harm quite common in borderline patients, to the "half-smile" derived from Zen meditation as a strategy for affect regulation, working *with* the body is a natural part of this approach.

In principle, we presently use *imaginative methods* to evoke scenic fantasies and memories that are particularly apt to capture experience and behavior on a body level. In the exploration of such scenes, a number of questions are of particular interest: What is the distance between people? What are their postures and movements? How do these movements feel? Which behaviors do they correlate with? Which meanings do these behaviors have? What thoughts and emotions arise?

We then return our attention to their bodily experience and any changes that have occurred (for example, Sulz, 2002b). A patient imagines that her father approaches her. In her fantasy, she lets him stop at a distance of two yards; she does not want him any closer. All the while her body posture is open, with her lower arms and hands subtly reaching out toward him. Aware that he remains far away and does not move, she pays attention to her bodily experience and begins to sense her wish for him to come closer so that she can feel safe in his proximity.

*Role-play* can be used to enact difficult interpersonal situations, and in role-play body postures and body perception are important variables to consider. First, we explore the past experience of these encounters and what nonverbal messages were sent. For example, a man with a soft, hesitant voice, lowered head, looking down, with collapsed shoulders and weak muscle tone wants to approach a colleague to confront him about his unfair behavior. To begin with, we explore what sense of self such a bodily state creates, and what kind of complementary reactions and positions are evoked in the other. Next, a different bodily stance is experimented with that brings about a new sense of self. Then the confrontational situation is reapproached with this newfound sense of self, along with supportive cognitive self-instructions. Lastly, the successful interaction is repeated and re-created numerous times to embed it neurally and thereby stabilize the new behavior.

## How Brain Research Has Changed Cognitive Behavioral Therapy

At present, Cognitive Behavioral Therapy builds on the scientific findings of psychology, including findings from perceptual, personality, social, and emotional psychology, as well as neuropsychology and neurobiology (see Sulz, 2002a). This inclusion expands behavioral theory in the direction of *systems theory* (Grawe, 1998). Its subject is no longer restricted just to behavior, but now includes both experience and behavior, as an expansion of Grawe's functional model of the psyche shows. Damasio's (1990) construct of somatic markers elucidates the interface between classical Cognitive Behavioral Therapy and body therapeutic work. On the one hand, *somatic markers* support behavioral analysis in revealing affective meanings of a person or a situation, and in facilitating the conscious perception of associated emotions and needs. On the other hand, they help to evaluate the outcome of change. It is not the cognitive "OK" that counts, but the affective affirmation that is perceived through a positive somatic marker (Storch, 2002, 2003).

Here it is important to note that Cognitive Behavioral Therapy, rather than being based on a psychology of consciousness, holds that the most important psychic processes, among them behavior-regulating cognitions, occur unconsciously. Although cognitive behavioral therapists use the analytic-sequential functions and the top-down information processing of conscious cognitions, behavioral plans, and intended actions, which are mediated by the left brain hemisphere, more than other therapeutic orientations, we now use behavioral analysis to activate implicit memories, mediated by the right hemisphere, with its networklike, holistic information processing, its scenic, bodily, and emotional contents, and associated (not consciously intended) behaviors, interactions, and communications, before utilizing left-hemispheric functions. We are concerned primarily with fast, automatic, primary emotional processing, not mediated by the neocortex, as it is this kind of processing that sheds light on "unconditioned responses" (UCR) and "conditioned responses" (CR). In this context, the sequences of danger–fear–flight and frustration–rage–attack, as well as hope–love–closeness, are especially relevant.

The slower, secondary emotional processing, mediated by the neocortex, is shaped by social, cultural, motivational, and behavioral schemas. It is primarily these schemas that have become dysfunctional during adulthood in many people who seek treatment with us.

The case of the husband who begins to speak up to his wife can illustrate this sequence in the form of a *micro model*:

* Situation: Making plans for the weekend during dinner. The wife again rejects his request to cancel the visit of her parents, and to go on a big weekend outing instead.
* Primary emotion: rage.
* Primary behavioral impulse: attack.
* Anticipation of consequences: She will leave me.

* This leads to a fantasized scene that evokes highly aversive somatic markers, which in turn evoke a secondary emotion (Greenberg, 2000; Sulz, 2002b) of fear and guilt along with a body sense of weakness and paralysis.
* A secondary behavior follows: giving in, silencing.
* At some point, this is no longer sustainable: symptom formation occurs—for example, as depressive dysthymia acting as a last resort to avoid an aggressive confrontation.

Cognitive behavioral therapists can use such somatic markers to facilitate change. Patients learn to sense these somatic markers, then—beyond that—they become aware of associated emotions, and recognize the emotional meaning of a situation in this way. Aversive markers can be used to help patients become active, in order to prevent bodily discomfort. Positive markers show patients that they have achieved their goal. The therapist's guidelines therefore are:

* Create the somatic markers that trigger the wanted behavior.
* Stop striving for a change in behaviors that trigger negative somatic markers.

These kinds of changes in the theory and technique of Cognitive Behavioral Therapy signal its return to the body, indicating that the turn toward cognition has run its course. Heckhausen's (1987) Rubicon model of behavioral motivation (Figure 89.1) can be expanded accordingly.

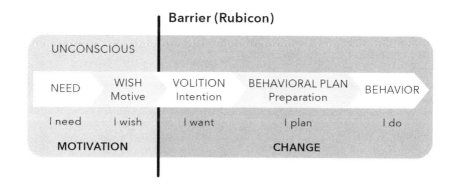

Figure 89.1. Barrier (Rubicon) 1: Somatic Markers (adapted from Heckhausen, 1987)

We begin by shedding light on unconscious motives so that a clear, nonambivalent, volitional intention can emerge, which initiates the longed-for change and leads to an effective behavioral plan and successful follow-through. Initially, motivation is clarified and conflicts between various motives are resolved, such as a conflict between the wish for a harmonious relationship and the wish for more personal space that makes room for endeavors independent from the partner. To discover the conflicting motives, somatic markers are attended to—that is, the chain of reactions is traced back to its origins (see Figure 89.2).

This backtracking implies that we inquire about the emotion that is expressed by the observed behavior. From there, patients are guided to sense their somatic markers and to unfold their respective inner scene. This scene then reveals the unconscious wish and its underlying need. In this process, the body forms the bridge across the Rubicon, between conscious emotion on the one side and the underlying motivational processes, which are not consciously known, on the other.

A young woman may have a need to feel valued. In relationship to her boss, this generates a wish in her to have her achievements validated. An inner scenario has her proudly presenting her work while he impatiently brushes it off. A tension arises in her body, along with a sense of weakness. Her conscious emotion is timid fearfulness. Her behavior—namely, the presentation of her work—becomes apprehensive and is not convincing. In therapy, as the situation is scenically re-created using role-play, she can grasp the nature of her struggle, and gets in touch with her anger as she lets go of her dependency. She can then use her anger to face the situation with a newfound sense of assertiveness and conviction that is supported by associated appropriate body postures and experience.

With the integration of Piaget's (1945) schema theory, the issue of development, and bodily aspects of develop-

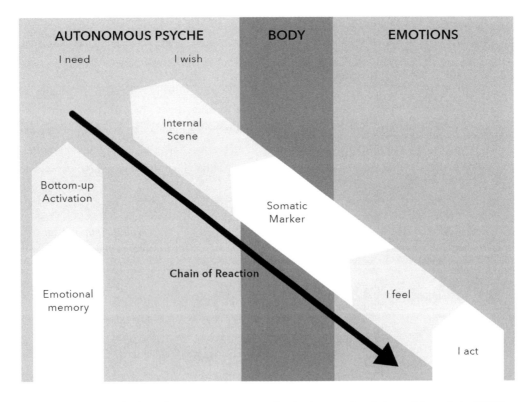

Figure 89.2. Barrier (Rubicon) 2: Autonomous psyche, body, emotion (adapted from Sulz, 2000)

ment in particular, has gradually gained greater recognition in the field of Cognitive Behavioral Therapy. Following the Neo-Piagetian developmental theory of Robert Kegan (1986), we experience and respond primarily with our skin, mucous membranes, and viscera during the ingesting stage; during the impulsive stage, it is often the movement apparatus that shows a reflex-like response; during the imperial stage, we show complex behavior that is voluntary and mediated by neocortical parts of the brain; and lastly, during the interpersonal stage, we can respond holistically and integrate analytic-sequential intentions. Thus, intimacy becomes possible (Sulz, 1994, 1999).

## Conclusions

After the cognitive era and its turn toward the psychology of emotion, Cognitive Behavioral Therapy—like psychoanalysis—is now drawing closer to Body Psychotherapy. Important impulses for this movement come from Piaget's schema theory and Developmental Psychology, as well as from contemporary brain research. With Cognitive Behavioral Therapy being framed as systems theory, its task becomes the consequent examination of the "organism variable," and to define behavior in a way that views bodily responses as an important aspect that plays a central role in behavior. There have been several efforts to use bodywork in Cognitive Behavioral Therapy in order to bring emotions into awareness and to facilitate behavioral change (see, for example, Görlitz, 1998, 2001; Miethge, 2002; Sulz, 2005).

## References

Damasio, A. R. (1990). Synchronous activation in multiple cortical regions: A mechanism for recall. *Seminars in the Neurosciences, 2,* 287–296.

Goldfried, M. R. (1971). Systematic desensitization as training in self-control. *Journal of Consulting and Clinical Psychology, 37,* 228–234.

Görlitz, G. (1998). *Körper und Gefühl in der Psychotherapie: Aufbauübungen, Leben Lernen [Body and emotion in psychotherapy: Building exercises, life learning].* Stuttgart: Pfeiffer bei Klett-Cotta.

Görlitz, G. (2001). *Körper und Gefühl in der Psychotherapie: Basisübungen, Leben Lernen [Body and emotion in psychotherapy: Basic exercises, life learning].* Stuttgart: Pfeiffer bei Klett-Cotta.

Grawe, K. (1998). *Psychologische Therapie [Psychological therapy].* Göttingen: Hogrefe.

Greenberg, L. S. (2000). Von der Kognition zur Emotion in der Psychotherapie [From cognition to emotion in psychotherapy]. In S. K. D. Sulz & G. Lenz (Eds.), *Von der Kognition zur Emotion [From cognition to emotion]* (pp. 77–110). Munich: CIP-Medien.

Heckhausen, H. (1987). Wünschen–Wählen–Wollen [Wishing–Weighing–Wanting]. In H. Heckhausen, P. M. Gollwitzer, & F. E. Weinert, *Jenseits des Rubikon: Der Wille in den Humanwissenschaften [Beyond the Rubicon: The will in the human sciences]* (pp. 3–9). Berlin: Springer.

Jacobson, E. (1990). *Entspannung als Therapie: Progressive Muskelrelaxation in Theorie und Praxis [Relaxation as therapy: Progressive Muscle Relaxation in theory and practice].* Stuttgart: Pfeiffer bei Klett-Cotta.

Kegan, R. (1986). *Die Entwicklungsstufen des Selbst: Fortschritte und Krisen im menschlichen Leben [Stages of the self: Progress and crises in human life].* Munich: Kindt.

Lazarus, A. (1976). *Multimodal behavior therapy.* New York: Springer.

Linehan, M. (1996a). *Dialektisch-Behaviorale Therapie der Borderline-Persönlichkeitsstörung [Dialectical Behavior Therapy of borderline personality disorder].* Munich: CIP-Medien.

Linehan, M. (1996b). *Trainingsmanual zur Dialektisch-Behavioralen Therapie der Borderline-Persönlichkeitsstörung [Training manual for Dialectical Behavior Therapy of borderline personality disorder].* Munich: CIP-Medien.

Margraf, J., & Schneider, S. (1990). *Panik [Panic].* Berlin: Springer.

Meichenbaum, D. (1985). *Intervention bei Stress: Anwendung und Wirkung des Stressimpfungsprogramms [Intervention for stress: Use and effects of stress inoculation program].* Bern, Switzerland: Huber.

Miethge, W. (2002). *Heilsame Gefühle: Trainingsbuch für die Arbeit mit Emotionen [Healing emotions: Training book for working with emotions]*. Munich: CIP-Medien.

Paul, G. L. (1966). *Insight versus desensitization in psychotherapy*. Stanford, CA: Stanford University Press.

Piaget, J. (1945). *La formation du symbole chez l'enfant [Symbol formation in children]*. Neuchatel, Switzerland: Delachaux et Niestlé.

Rehfisch, H. P., & Basler, H. D. (1990). Entspannung und Imagination [Relaxation and imagination]. In H. D. Basler, C. Franz, B. Kröner-Herwig, et al. (Eds.), *Psychologische Schmerztherapie [Psychological pain therapy]* (pp. 448–468). Berlin: Springer.

Storch, M. (2002). Die Bedeutung neurowissenschaftlicher Forschung für die psychotherapeutische praxis: I. Theorie [The meaning of neuroscientific research for psychotherapeutic practice: I. Theory]. *Psychotherapie, 7*, 281–294.

Storch, M. (2003). Die Bedeutung neurowissenschaftlicher Forschung für die psychotherapeutische Praxis: II. Das Zürcher Ressourcenmodell (ZRM) [The meaning of neuroscientific research for psychotherapeutic practice: II. The Zurich research model]. *Psychotherapie, 8*, 45–59.

Sulz, S. K. D. (1994). *Strategische Kurzzeittherapie: Wege zur effizienten Psychotherapie [Strategic Brief Therapy: Way for efficient psychotherapy]*. Munich: CIP-Medien.

Sulz, S. K. D. (1998). Entspannung durch Progressive Muskelrelaxation [Relaxation by progressive muscle relaxation]. In S. K. D. Sulz (Ed.), *Das Therapiebuch: Kognitiv-Behaviorale Psychotherapie in Psychiatrie, Psychotherapeutischer Medizin und Klinischer Psychologie [The therapy book: Cognitive-Behavioral Psychotherapy in psychiatry, psychotherapeutic medicine and Clinical Psychology]* (pp. 236–247). Munich: CIP-Medien.

Sulz, S. K. D. (1999). *Als Sisyphus seinen Stein losließ—oder: Verlieben ist verrückt [As Sisyphus letting his stone go—or: Falling in love is crazy]*. Munich: CIP-Medien.

Sulz, S. K. D. (2000). Emotion, Kognition und Verhalten: zur homöostatischen Funktion der Emotion und zu ihrer Bedeutung bei der Symptombildung [Emotion, cognition and behavior: The homeostatic function of emotion and its role in symptom formation]. In S. K. D. Sulz & G. Lenz (Eds.), *Von der Kognition zur Emotion: Psychotherapie mit Gefühlen [From cognition to emotion: Psychotherapy with feelings]* (pp. 5–76). Munich: CIP-Medien.

Sulz, S. K. D. (2002a). Neuropsychologie und Hirnforschung als Herausforderung für die Psychotherapie [Neuropsychology and brain research as a challenge for psychotherapy]. *Psychotherapie, 7*, 18–33.

Sulz, S. K. D. (2002b). *Praxismanual zur Veränderung des Erlebens und Verhaltens [Practice manual for changing experience and behavior]*. Munich: CIP-Medien.

Sulz, S. K. D. (Ed.). (2005). *Die Psychotherapie entdeckt den Körper [Psychotherapy discovered the body]*. Munich: CIP-Medien.

Wolpe, J. (1959). *Psychotherapy by reciprocal inhibition*. Stanford, CA: Stanford University Press.

# 90

## The Positive Management of the Body

*A Salutogenic and Transpersonal Perspective of Positive Psychotherapy*

**Nossrat Peseschkian, Germany**

**Translation by Warren Miller**

**Nossrat Peseschkian,** Prof. h.c., MD, Dr. med, German board-certified specialist in psychiatry, neurology, psychosomatic medicine, and psychotherapy, was born in 1933 in Iran, and received his psychotherapeutic training in Germany, Switzerland, and the United States. He was the founder of the Wiesbaden Academy for Psychotherapy, one of the largest postgraduate state-licensed training institutes for psychotherapy in Germany.

He became internationally known as the founder of Positive Psychotherapy, which is fundamentally based on a transculturally and salutogenically oriented psychotherapeutic perspective.

He authored a large number of books and scientific papers, and had a reputation for enriching psychotherapeutic theory and practice in surprising ways by relating it to the wisdom contained in the simple and paradoxical stories of the East. He taught physicians and psychotherapists in postgraduate training programs in more than sixty countries. Sadly, he passed away in 2010.

## The Salutogenic Model

Although most psychotherapeutic approaches are based on the understanding of disorders and diseases, and are thereby founded on deficiency-oriented perspectives, it makes sense to view human abilities as primary and essential to their development. Abilities that are suppressed, or one-sidedly developed, can turn into sources of conflict, stress, and intrapsychic disorder. They can also manifest as depression, fears, aggression, stress, behavioral problems, and psychosomatic disorders.

The salutogenic approach (which is generating growing interest in the fields of medicine, psychiatry, and psychotherapy) inspired many specialists and methods, such as the scientist and medical sociologist A. Antonovsky (1997) and the development of Positive Psychotherapy (Peseschkian, 1977, 1987), and was a fundamental paradigm for psychotherapy and psychosomatic medicine. Positive Psychotherapy focuses on the factors that support human health and well-being, rather than on pathologies, and is thus a humanistic, psychodynamic psychotherapeutic method (Peseschkian and Remmers, 2013).

The basic question that this model is concerned with is why some people are on the positive end of the health-illness continuum, and why, irrespective of where they are located on the continuum, some people are moving steadily toward the positive pole of the continuum.

The salutogenic perspective considers specific attitudinal patterns—for example, what Antonovsky (1997) referred to as *the sense of "coherence"*—an essential for a discussion of such questions. Such basic attitudes are the conditions that contribute to the ability to lead a successful life and to cope with crises in a positive manner. Others include:

- The *sense of comprehensibility:* In this regard, cognitive-processing patterns are of significance.
- The *sense of manageability:* This area includes the different resources of coping with stress and conflict. Lifelong experience determines the extent to which such resources are available or underdeveloped, and often it is psychotherapy's task to "actualize" underdeveloped resources.
- The *sense of meaningfulness:* This aspect concerns the emotional-motivational component of human life and behavior.

The salutogenic model constitutes a change in perspective. Aside from asking for the pathogenic factors of illness, the emphasis is on inquiry into the salutogenic resources of the person's health. The leading question is *"What contribution can an individual make to overcome their illness, based on their individual resources?"* Furthermore, we ask, *"How can situations of conflict and exposure to pathogenic stressors be transformed into health-oriented challenges?"* Whereas the traditional medical model views the human being from the perspective of a deficit model, thus seeing a passive object of physical processes, the salutogenic perspective views the ill or suffering person as a subject, and as an agent, of health.

The body plays a very central role in the psychodynamically grounded approach of Positive Psychotherapy: as a realm of experience, as an arena of pathological attempts to resolve conflicts, and in regard to the realization of untapped resources.

## A Holistic Perspective

Whereas in psychotherapy and medicine, particular perspectives often stand alongside each other, frequently overestimating the value of their own procedures, Positive Psychotherapy's role has been to assimilate the various aspects of human existence into an integrated treatment approach. One of its fundamental propositions is that the human body and mind are related in a dynamic interplay. Consequently, the approach assumes a fundamentally psychosomatic orientation, deriving inspiration from Western medicine and Body-Oriented Psychotherapy, as well as from the traditional healing arts of the East. The East traditionally paid more attention to the obvious correlations between social, mental, and physical conditions than is common in Western medicine.

The following story of Avicenna, the famous Persian philosopher and physician, illustrates the case. The story goes that he was called to attend to the severely ill nephew of the ruler, Ghaboos ibn-Wushmgir:

> All the doctors had given up hope, none of their treatments had shown any curative effects. Then Avicenna said that to treat the young man someone who knew all the city's streets and alleys, and all the people that lived in them, would need to be present. While the doctor interviewed the locals about the different districts of the city, he took the patient's pulse. When they arrived in a certain district, the patient's heart rate increased. The same happened when they got to a particular street, and the pulse also identified a specific house, and a young girl that lived there. "Very good," said the physician, "I now know the young man's ailment and it is easy to heal him. Go and get the girl and ask her to be his wife." (Peseschkian, 1986, p. 81)

That the cause of the young man's disease was identified as a broken heart is not as much a characteristic of psychosomatics as of this past Eastern society's penchant for this theme, similar to our contemporary inclination to identify stress as the mental cause of physical disorders.

What has remained the same, then and now, is the skepticism toward conventional methods. The logic of conventional therapy is simple: if there is pain, for example, it must be eliminated; once the symptom is cured, that completes the intervention. The questions behind this—what meanings such pain might have, which disorders in the bodymind organism it can indicate, what potentials for the future it might hold, and what opportunities it opens up—remain largely unexplored by this "medical" approach.

The story that was quoted has the character of a teaching story, and as such serves an important function in "popular medicine." It shows what an important role the language of the body (in this case, the accelerated heart rate) plays and how much therapeutic success depends on the ability to link nonverbal bodily signals and symptoms of the physical "dis-ease" with the mental, psychological, and social domains of life. All these domains remain interwoven at all times. In a short-term, psychodynamic, and conflict-oriented approach, these different domains can be systematically investigated and treated.

## The Different Forms of Coping with Conflict

On the surface, people show a wide array of responses to conflict. However, the range of possible responses they have been able to learn during the course of their life's history essentially determines how they will respond. Such socialization processes are shaped by cultural factors. The influence of culture-specific educational practices on the common behavior of a society, and the range of behaviors that is available to its individual members, has been demonstrated in the work of M. Mead (1970) and E. H. Erikson (1966, 1971). They were able to show that every human society reproduces itself not only biologically, but also in regard to its social rules of engagement. These norms make it possible for individuals to orient themselves within a group. These social norms are passed on, less in abstract codes or through cognitive explanations, but more by a form of osmosis, or *hautnah* (through immediate skin contact): especially in the way that (for example) a mother handles her child, and how she gratifies its tactile and oral needs (Harlow and Harlow, 1967; Spitz, 1967); how the child is received by its father; how its siblings accept it; and how homogeneously these intrafamilial relations are extended into the interfamilial and societal forms of relationship.

However, despite all cultural and social differences, we can also observe that all humans draw upon typical forms of coping with conflict (Kirmayer, 2007). Personal problems, stressors, and frustrations can be expressed in the following four ways of coping with conflict that are correlated with four respective *methods of knowing*. They show how people perceive themselves, and their environments, and in which ways they can reality-test their knowledge:

- Body (method of the senses)
- Achievement (method of reason)
- Contact (method of tradition)
- Fantasy (method of intuition)

This model is aimed to provide a perspective that can help to structure and orient the diagnostic process and to lead to the formulation of a holistic diagnosis that takes into account the symptom and its causes, as well as other mediating factors, such as life situation, environment, family, subculture, and culture. Beyond that, a salutogenic model needs to account for the healthier aspects (of the person and their environment) that hold resources for healing, and the person's abilities and energies for the management of disease and changes in their life situation. In other words, the whole spectrum of human responses and behaviors should be taken into account. On the one hand, the four ways of coping indicate in which direction a flight has taken place: Unconscious and unmanageable-appearing conflicts lead to escapes into illness (somatization), escapes into activity or work, escapes into isolation or sociability, or escapes into fantasy. On the other hand, these four poles also map out the essential domains of the abilities, potential, and resources of an individual, in a general way. As human resources, they are of fundamental importance to the salutogenic approach.

## The Body as an Integrated Element

As we bring closer attention to the domain of the body and the senses, we find the body-ego experience in its foreground. How is the person's own body perceived? How are the various sense impressions from the environment experienced? The information that is collected through the senses is also censored by the values that the individual has acquired. Distinct sense qualities can be charged with conflict, through association with the individual's values and/or their biographical experiences. Very early imprints can significantly shape later developments. The sleep-feeding rhythm of the infant, for example, can shape the adult's sense of being on time, and his or her relationship to timeliness.

Bodily reactions in response to conflicts include bodily activities, such as sports, physical efforts, or (alternatively) the couch-potato phenomenon. Bodily reactions can also manifest in sleep patterns. Conflicts might be "overslept," or sleep disorders might emerge that can be viewed as based on an "overalertness." If the function of eating has been affected, conflicts can manifest as binge eating, weight gain due to sorrow, or a refusal to eat. If sexuality is involved in the conflict dynamics, this can manifest in "Don Juanism" (satyriasis), nymphomania, or sexual defensiveness, which can manifest in various ways, ranging from constipation and migraine headaches to frigidity and erectile dysfunction. In surveying the spectrum of such bodily reactions, the expansive area of functional disorders of the body, along with psychosomatic diseases, need to be considered. The following elaboration on this subject can serve as an example.

Bodily psycho-pathological symptoms include: a lack of drive, a lack of energy, and the dejectedness of depression, or agonizing vital feelings of constraint, inner restlessness, and tension, which are based on elevated muscle tonicity. Psycho-motor symptoms include: psycho-motor tics and psycho-motor restlessness. Vegetative symptoms include: breaking out in a sweat, tachycardia, diarrhea, high blood pressure, decrease in libido and sexual potency, etc. In this context, it needs to be mentioned that the body itself can become the object of fear and worry, as in cases of hypochondria, in heart neurosis, or in the case of a twenty-four-year-old woman who worked as a model and said, "The idea that my body, the flesh of my hand, that my breasts, my stomach could decay makes me disgusted of myself. Although I know that I won't experience this, I cannot let go of the thought."

Were holistic thinking more common in the fields of medicine and psychotherapy, it would not be necessary to point out that one-dimensional forms of conflict management affect the other dimensions of human existence. Hypertrophy of one form of conflict management pushes other forms into the background. In addition, these other forms are negatively impacted by pathological overemphasis of only one mode of coping with conflict. It doesn't take a lot of imagination to plot out the effects that the above-mentioned body-symptomatic forms of coping with conflict have on the areas of work and achievement, contact and relationships, and fantasy (which, positively viewed, includes one's hopes for the future).

Likewise, the effect of flight reactions on the other three forms of coping negatively affects the experience of the body and the accessibility of the resources it holds. Let's look at the form of coping with conflict through achievement and reason, which is particularly common in the industrialized societies of Europe and North America. These cultures have developed distinct norms of achievement that individuals integrate into their concepts of self. Thinking and reason, viewed as positive human resources, enable people to solve problems in a systematic and focused fashion, and to optimize outcomes in this way. Two diametric conflict reactions are possible:

- Escape into more work and achievement
- Escape from the demand(s) to be productive

Symptoms that typically arise—including stress reactions, burnout syndrome, lack of challenge, or feeling overwhelmed—often affect bodily well-being and can manifest in a wide array of bodily complaints, from difficulties in concentration to severe illnesses. The culturally widespread strategy of using alcohol and drugs to cope with stress can also manifest secondary disorders in time.

In the area of contact and relationships, the withdrawal from relationships and the distancing from other human beings create a particularly negative influence on the experience of one's own body. Lack of human closeness and warmth is often compensated for through excessive eating and alcohol intake. In the frame of Positive Psychotherapy, this lack of warmth is often drawn upon for the positive symptom interpretation of diabetes: the comment that this bodily symptom can also be viewed as the ability to give oneself the warmth that is lacking often is surprising to patients and evokes their curiosity to take a closer look at their emotional situation and the ways they are coping with it.

Fantasy and intuition are associated with the psychic processes involved in dreaming, and present another form of coping with problems and conflicts. These reach beyond the immediate present, and can include everything that we attribute meaning to, such as any number of activities, life itself, and the future, including death. From a salutogenic perspective, intuition and fantasy are important human resources. However, an overdevelopment of these abilities can lead to a neglect of the body and bodily needs (asceticism), and thus the contact with reality that is established through the body. Extreme forms of escape into fantasy, as manifested in the delusions of schizophrenia, are always accompanied by a loss of a positive relationship with the body.

Aside from the combinations of different areas of human life that are characteristic of an individual, cultural factors play a very important role. Transcultural observations have led me to believe that, whereas in North America and Europe there is a tendency to resort to coping through the *body* and *achievement,* people in the East tend to assign higher value to *contact* and *fantasy.* For example, if one considers the very common symptom of depression, with all its bodily parameters, central Europeans and North Americans tend to become depressed because they lack contact, are in isolation, and are experiencing a lack of emotional warmth. Dominant themes in this kind of depression include social isolation, order, cleanliness, and, in particular, frugality. In the East, depressions tend to develop because people come to feel overwhelmed by the restrictions of their social obligations. Contents in the foreground of these depressions include fears regarding infertility, social reputation, and the future.

## How Do Psychosomatic Disorders Develop?

If one examines the concepts that a psychosomatically ill patient holds toward her body as a whole, toward particular organs, or regarding specific organ functions, and how she views health and illness in general, how her psychosomatic illness manifests (i.e., her organ choice) begins to make sense. A wide-angle perspective on their conflict dynamics shows that these views determine why one person responds with the heart, another with the stomach, the respiratory system, the skin, etc., and why some people escape into illness, while others use all their might to deny signs of bodily weakness or illness.

Positive Psychotherapy has developed a five-stage integral treatment strategy for a conflict-centered brief therapy approach that, within a short time, efficiently expands patients' resources and coping strategies (Peseschkian and Deidenbach, 1991). In the *first stage,* the symptom manifestation is interpreted positively. Rheumatic symptoms, for example, might be interpreted as the ability to use the body to cope with tensions and conflicts. In the *second stage,* stressors, challenges, and, particularly, microtraumas (life events) that took place over the course of the past five to ten years are explored. The ways of coping that are commonly unconscious are brought into consciousness and put into context with biographically acquired attitudes and behavioral patterns. In *stages 3, 4, and 5,* these coping strategies are systematically expanded, ultimately leading to an expansion of the patient's life goals.

To continue with the example, while staying body-oriented, patients with rheumatic symptoms learn to expand their conflict-loaded psycho-social norms of order, achievement, and obedience toward greater calm and relaxation. In this context, Body Psychotherapeutic methods can help patients to sense and "comprehend" better how ideals of obedience and submissiveness can translate into body postures that in turn contribute to the development and maintenance of their symptoms. Methods and approaches that facilitate relaxation can therefore be therapeutically useful at this time. In addition, different avenues are explored that can lead patients to experience their bodies as more positive and libidinous.

Knowledge of the relationship between emotions and the motor system—that is, the manifestations of emotions in the body—is also valuable for the goal of expanding aggression-inhibited politeness behaviors, as in the old Eastern story of the "Healing of the Caliph":

> A severe illness had come over the king. All efforts to cure him failed and, finally, the revered physician Razi was consulted. He asked the king to let him do his treatment as he saw necessary and to provide him with two of his fastest horses. He ordered that the king be transported to a renowned bath the following morning. Then he lowered the king, who couldn't move, into a bathtub and in short succession poured hot water over him. Simultaneously, he poured into the king's mouth a syrup that raised the patient's temperature. Suddenly, Razi began badmouthing and insulting the king in the most vile of ways. In his unbelievable perturbation, the king moved. When the doctor noticed this, he drew his knife and threatened to kill the king. In his fear, the king tried to save himself, which gave him the strength to get up and flee. Then the king passed out. Razi and his student fled the scene on the king's two horses. When the king woke up he felt freer and was able to move. He was so angry that he yelled for his servant, got dressed, and rode back to the palace. Eight days later, the king received a letter from the physician in which the latter described his treatment: "I did everything that I've learned as a physician. When all these methods failed, I artificially raised your body temperature and made the strength of your rage available to you, which made it possible for you to move your limbs. I ask you, not to call on me to come and see you, as I am very aware of the unfair and mean insults I hurled at you, and I am deeply ashamed for having done so." (Peseschkian, 1986, pp. 75–76)

The activation of emotional engagement (which this story describes) is a core element of Body Psychotherapy and, likewise, is also a very old medical intervention: Razi, the renowned Persian physician, supposedly was the first person to use the term "psychotherapy." His treatment wasn't actually "cathartic" in the narrow sense of the word, as it did not rely on discharging pent-up emotions. Instead, Razi, with his insults and threats, was the one to arouse the king's affect, which was then used as a driving force in the healing process.

A salutogenic perspective is thus oriented toward developing the resources and potentials that enable patients to withstand adversity and cope with conflicts. Salutogenic perspectives are always based on the idea of a dynamic inner balance that people need to maintain in the face of the challenges life confronts them with. Bodily and mental well-being is no static arrangement. Instead, the process of human mental and bodily development calls for an ongoing reestablishment of dynamic inner balance. In regard to the bodily dimension, this ultimately refers to the ability to experience the body as a libidinal body, which as such contributes to the maintenance of physical health.

## References

Antonovsky, A. (1997). *Salutogenese: Zur Entmystifizierung der Gesundheit* [Salutogenesis: Demystifying health]. Tübingen: Deutsche Gesellschaft für Verhaltenstherapie.

Erikson, E. H. (1966). *Einsicht und Verantwortung: die Rolle des Ethischen in der Psychoanalyse* [Insight and responsibility: The role of ethics in psychoanalysis]. Stuttgart: Klett.

Erikson, E. H. (1971). *Identität und Lebenszyklus: Drei Aufsätze* [Identity and the life cycle: Three essays]. Frankfurt: Suhrkamp.

Harlow, H. W., & Harlow, M. K. (1967). Reifungsfak-toren im sozialen Verhalten [Maturational factors in social behavior]. *Psyche, 21,* 193–210.

Kirmayer, L. J. (2007). Cultural psychiatry in historical perspective. In D. Bhugra & K. Bhui (Eds.), *Textbook of Cultural Psychiatry* (pp. 3–19). Cambridge, UK: Cambridge University Press.

Mead, M. (1970). *Kindheit und Jugend in Neuguinea* [Childhood and adolescence in New Guinea]. Munich: Deutscher Taschenbuchverlag.

Peseschkian, H., & Remmers, A. (2013). *Positive Psychotherapie*. Munich: Reinhardt.

Peseschkian, N. (1977). *Positive Psychotherapie: Theorie und Praxis einer neuen Methode* [Positive Psychotherapy: Theory and practice of a new method]. Frankfurt: Fischer.

Peseschkian, N. (1986). *Oriental stories as tools in psychotherapy.* Heidelberg: Springer.

Peseschkian, N. (1987). *Positive Psychotherapy: Theory and practice of a new method.* Berlin: Springer.

Peseschkian, N., & Deidenbach, H. (1991). *Psychosomatik und Positive Psychotherapie* [Psychosomatics and Positive Psychotherapy]. Heidelberg: Springer.

Peseschkian, N., & Deidenbach, H. (2013). *Psychosomatics and Positive Psychotherapy.* Wiesbaden: Peseschkian Foundation.

Spitz, R. A. (1967). *Vom Säugling zum Kleinkind* [From infant to toddler]. Stuttgart: Klett.

# SECTION XII

# Existential and Spiritual Dimensions of Body-Oriented Psychotherapy

# 91

## Introduction to Section XII

Gustl Marlock, Germany, and Halko Weiss, United States

Translation by Michael Soth

The final three chapters of this handbook go beyond the usual frame of clinical theory and practice, addressing more fundamental questions concerning the deeper meaning and context of our lives—in terms of our evolution, our relationship with nature, and the essence of our spirituality. These are questions that are usually considered to belong either to the realm of philosophy, especially existential philosophy, or to the more religious and spiritual traditions, though Transpersonal Psychotherapy has also impacted on this area. As a tradition, Body-Oriented Psychotherapy has always been open to and inspired by these questions, on both theoretical and practical levels.

In some of his early work, Wilhelm Reich already discussed the far-reaching connections between the metapsychology of psychotherapy and psycho-social, political, and anthropological questions (Reich, 1986). In focusing on the embodied experience of orgasm, he began to touch on dimensions of experience that went far beyond Freudian perspectives and were later captured in Abraham Maslow's (1962) terminology as "peak experiences." Reich emphasized that, in surrendering to the depths (or heights) of unrestricted sexual union, it becomes possible to experience deeper dimensions of life and love that transcend the experience of the normal waking consciousness of the ego. Here Reich was inspired by an intuition or inspiration that can be found in much more elaborated and mature forms in the Eastern mysticism of love and sexuality.

In a renowned interview with Kurt Eissler, Reich used the term "oceanic feelings" to describe these dimensions of transcendence and union (Reich, 1967). In an exchange of letters between Romain Rolland (the French philosopher who won the 1915 Nobel Prize for Literature) and Freud, Rolland had first used this phrase when he challenged Freud's critique of religion, *The Future of an Illusion,* pointing out that Freud had altogether ignored oceanic feelings as a source of religious sentiment. Freud then admitted, in the opening chapters of *Civilization and Its Discontents,* that he himself had no access to these dimensions of experience, but insisted on locating them in infantile development, thus reducing them to the regressive loss of the capacity to clearly distinguish between inner and outer, or self and the world. Reich would have been aware of this correspondence.

Viktor Frankl, one of the founders of Existential Psychotherapy, also challenged Freud's position, seeing it as based upon a one-dimensional worshipping of reason and the rational, instrumental mind, corresponding to a "repression of religious feeling" (1987, pp. 63ff.).

Wilhelm Reich, in his later work, elaborated on the limitations of such disembodied rationality, which he saw as a mechanism to exclude emotion and the felt sense of being as well as any intuition of cosmic dimensions; this led him to consider spiritual questions and the nature of the divine (1966, 1972), which he approached predominantly through his studies of life energy. Although Reich's reflections remained largely constrained within a scientific-materialist and reductionist paradigm, lacking the differentiation of later and current discourse in relation to spiritual experience (Maslow, 1962; Wilber, Engler, and Brown, 1986), his work nevertheless contained seeds of developments that became manifest in the last decades of the twentieth century in an increasingly postmaterialist cultural climate.

It was the Human Potential Movement of the 1960s and 1970s that brought the tradition of Body Psychotherapy decisively into contact with these transpersonal and spiritual questions. From the mid-1960s, Western psychology began—to a degree previously unheard-of—to look for inspiration beyond the realms of the prevailing, traditional, Judeo-Christian European and American cultures.

Abraham Maslow's "psychology of being" (2011), as well as the tradition of Transpersonal Psychology, which he helped to initiate, transcended the traditional frame of psycho-pathology and its treatment strategies, opening psychotherapy to questions of meaning, altered states of consciousness, and concerns about the ultimate—realms of thought and experience that had previously been the exclusive domain of the religious and philosophical traditions.

Alan Watts (1975) is known as one of the authors who pioneered the meeting between Western psychotherapy and Eastern spirituality, alongside Erich Fromm's dialogue with Zen Buddhism (Fromm et al., 1970). Another major influence in this context was the first Buddhist teachers who came to the West in the late 1950s and early 1960s, like Chögyam Trungpa (2004) and Shunryu Suzuki (2006). The extent to which their lasting impact has rippled through Western culture in a silent, unspectacular way can be recognized in the current popularity of mindfulness practice, which has been "adopted" by Cognitive Behavioral Therapy and which is also being enjoyed in much wider fields.

Chapter 92, "The Awakened Body: The Role of the Body in Spiritual Development," was written by **Linda Krier and Jessica Moore Britt,** two senior teachers of the "Diamond Heart" tradition, the spiritual teaching initiated by A. H. Almaas (1998), which incorporates Body Psychotherapeutic influences alongside psychoanalytical concepts in its curriculum. This chapter elaborates how the awakening of the body is a crucial part of the awakening aspects of the psyche on its spiritual developmental journey.

Chapter 93, "Existential Dimensions of the Fundamental Character Themes" by **Halko Weiss,** co-founder of the Hakomi school of Body Psychotherapy (which has placed mindfulness at the core of its theory and practice since the 1970s), takes a—so far noticeably lacking—existential perspective to investigate the character-analytical models that have been fundamental for many Body Psychotherapy modalities. Rather than considering character structures primarily as neurotic defenses, as clinical theory is accustomed to doing, Weiss reveals the existential challenges at the heart of such characterological "organizations," which every human being is confronted with during different phases of his or her life and which require an existential-embodied response, whatever their particular manifestation.

**Daniel Brown** is a renowned psychotherapist, as well as a meditation researcher and one of the leading Western teachers of Buddhist meditation. In Chapter 94, "Body Meditation in the Tibetan Buddhist and Bön Traditions," he describes the changing role of the body throughout the unfolding process of meditation: whereas initially the body becomes the focus and object of concentration practice, later—when the "body" is being recognized as a label or as an identification—it loses its sense of solidity and fixed reality and is then experienced much more as a dynamic aspect of aliveness within the person's "field of awareness." Brown discusses how the process of ongoing meditational practice reveals the nature of mind as an "awakened awareness" and how (bodily) feelings and sensations, alongside emotions and thoughts, can be realized as living expressions of that awareness.

# References

Almaas, A. H. (1998). *Essence with the elixir of enlightenment: The Diamond Approach to inner realization.* New York: Weiser Books.

Frankl, V. (1987). *Der Unbewußte Gott* [The unconscious God]. Munich: DTV.

Fromm, E., Suzuki, D. T., & De Martino, R. (1970). *Zen Buddhism and psychoanalysis.* London: HarperCollins.

Maslow, A. (1962/2011). *Towards a psychology of being.* Floyd, VA: Sublime Books.

Reich, W. (1966). *The murder of Christ.* New York: Farrar, Straus & Giroux.

Reich, W. (1967). *Reich speaks of Freud.* London: Souvenir Press.

Reich, W. (1972). *Ether, God and Devil and cosmic superimposition.* New York: Farrar, Straus & Giroux.

Reich, W. (1986). *The function of the orgasm.* New York: Farrar, Straus & Giroux.

Suzuki, S. (2006). *Zen mind: Beginner's mind.* Boston: Shambhala.

Trungpa, C. (2004). *The collected works of Chogyam Trungpa* (Vols. 1–8). Boston: Shambhala.

Watts, A. W. (1975). *Psychotherapy East and West.* New York: Random House (Vintage).

Wilber, K., Engler, J., & Brown, D. P. (1986). *Transformations of consciousness: Conventional and contemplative perspectives on development.* Boston: Shambhala New Science Library.

# 92

## The Awakened Body

*The Role of the Body in Spiritual Development*

**Linda H. Krier and Jessica Moore Britt,
United States**

**Linda H. Krier** has been a teacher of the Diamond Approach (a contemporary spiritual school, founded by A. H. Almaas) since 1983, and an Aston-Patterning teacher since 1976. Linda currently has a private practice in Boulder, Colorado, teaches Diamond Approach groups and classes in the United States and internationally, and is on the training staff of the Ridhwan Foundation. She is a former faculty member of the Aston Training Center and has served as an adjunct faculty member at Naropa University.

**Jessica Moore Britt** has been a student of A. H. Almaas, founder of the Diamond Approach, since 1978. A Diamond Approach teacher since 1985, she is presently a training director and leads ongoing groups in Europe and the United States. From 1981 to 1989, she was on the Gestalt staff of the Esalen Institute as a certified Reichian practitioner, creating an integration of Reichian and Gestalt work. As a nurse in the 1970s, she specialized in the field of childhood sexual and physical abuse. She studied Reichian Breathwork with Phil Curcuruto and David Boadella.

What is the role of the body in spiritual development? This rich and fascinating question takes us to frontiers of our understanding of the nature of the body itself. The body has become a focus of attention in the modern world in various ways. There is a great deal of interest in how we look, how to be healthy and fit, and how to age well. This interest is supported by new scientific information about the nature of the body as a physiological, anatomical, biological, biochemical, and neurological system. This burgeoning knowledge is helping us understand the stunning, intelligent harmony of the physicality of our body. Furthermore, in the last decades, the fields of psychotherapy, and of Body Psychotherapy in particular, have expanded our view of the body to include the intricate and profound ways that our physiology and psychology intertwine in what we could call the "psycho-physical nature" of the body.

In this atmosphere, where the interrelatedness and inseparability of different aspects of the body are being discovered, we can ask new, deeper questions about the relationship of our body to our spirituality: In what ways are our body and spirituality related? Is there a spiritual aspect to the body? If so, what is it and what does it mean? Does the body have a role in spiritual development? Can spiritual development impact the body? Is spirit alive, and, if so, how does it live?

## Spirit and Matter

In asking these questions, we run headlong into the commonly held view that spirit and matter are a fundamental duality: with spirit, God, and heaven in one realm; and matter, our bodies, and the world in another. This way of looking at the body, which essentially started with Plato, has influenced the development of the Western view of body and its relation to spirit.

There are many cultural, philosophical, religious, and phenomenological ramifications of this perspective that are deeply embedded in the consciousness of our culture. Those of us who grew up in this context have been influenced in both subtle and unconscious ways. One common assumption is that turning toward the spiritual realm requires turning away from the material world, and that turning toward the world is turning outward, away from one's inner spiritual life. Seekers of spiritual realization often assume that they will find it someplace other than within the nature of their body. Even those who have found a rich spiritual life as part of an embodied practice are influenced by these beliefs in invisible ways.

## Turning from Body to Spirit

The belief that turning toward the spiritual means turning away from the pull of the flesh is valid on an important level, as it is based, in part, on the well-known fact that the instinctual drives for survival, pleasure, and relationship are compelling motivations that cause us to be consumed by our physical needs and appetites. We turn to the physical world for the satisfaction of these desires. Therefore, many spiritual teachings and practices focus on ways to contend with, overcome, and refocus from the flesh, in order to orient toward our more fundamental spiritual nature.

In addition to the strong pull and the external focus of our instinctual drives, there are other important phenomena that lead us to believe that spiritual experience and physical life exist in separate realms. One very simple one is how different our body usually feels to us compared to our felt sense of spiritual experience.

The spiritual dimension has many realms and qualities that we experience in different ways. In general, there is a deep sense of connection to something beyond our usual day-to-day sense of self, something much more in the moment, a fresh reality. There can be an experience of profound sacredness, heartfulness, spaciousness, openness, and luminosity—a vastness that we sense is not bound by the physical world, is not "of the world" and, therefore, we presume is not of our body.

Experiencing these inner realms can bring a sense of liberation from our usual life, our familiar sense of self, our limitations, our sufferings, the burdens that we associate with physical life. We feel connected, lighter, freer, and unencumbered by the pain and hurts of the body.

In contrast to this more spiritual sense of the "lightness of being," our body can at times feel thick, heavy, opaque, and burdened. Our body appears to be an earthbound material object, a source of pain, suffering, and trouble. Our body is often evaluated, compared, judged, and monitored. If not the antithesis of the lightness and liberation of spiritual reality, this sense of "body as object" feels closer to suffering and limitation than to a sense of freedom. The freedom of spiritual reality can begin to be seen as freedom from the body itself.

Our belief in this dichotomy impacts our experience of ourselves in deep and far-reaching ways. It creates a painful quandary in the fabric of our consciousness in which two precious and fundamental aspects of who and what we are seem to be in irresolvable conflict with each other. We can feel pulled back and forth between our spiritual life and our physical life.

This begs the question: Is this dichotomy fundamentally true? Is it true that our body is simply a "material object," a kind of shell or vessel that seems empty of intrinsic value, that lacks the lightness, freedom, and depth of spiritual reality? Conversely, is spirituality inherently devoid of living, juicy substantiality, and of the concreteness of the physical dimension? Are our spiritual life and physical life necessarily two different lives? Or is it possible that our spiritual life and our physical life could become—could *be*—the same life?

## Body as a Form of Spiritual Consciousness

Certain types of experience that can arise in our spiritual journey challenge the view that body and spirit are two separate realms. In these kinds of realization, we begin to perceive that this assumed separation is not the most fundamental truth about our body, nor about physical reality as a whole.

At these times we can see that, although reality appears in many varied forms, shapes, and flavors—as rocks and trees, as people and animals, as experiences such as suffering and bliss—all these forms are fundamentally made out of the same pure consciousness. This consciousness is not simply a function, but rather a medium, a field of sensitivity.

In this condition, we can perceive that physical reality in general, and our own physical bodies in particular, are not separate from this field of consciousness. We can directly experience that our body, down to the smallest detail, is made of awake, translucent, luminous consciousness. Our body *is* alive, luminous consciousness, in physical form, walking, talking, eating, sleeping, etc. Our body is not an object. It is a particular, unique, but inseparable expression of this fundamental reality, this vast living "beingness," which is the true nature of reality itself. Furthermore, we can see that our physicality cannot be separated from the medium of consciousness. That just can't happen. It can't happen any more than our body can be separated from its protoplasm, its nervous system, or its circulatory system.

In these experiences it becomes clearer that our body is always a form of living consciousness, regardless of our state of health, age, weight, fitness, and outer appearance. This is true whether we've worked on our body or not, or even whether we are aware of our body or not. Becoming conscious of this reality makes an immense difference. It is deeply liberating, settling, relaxing, integrating, and healing. It alters our very experience of life and our self.

We know that many spiritual practitioners are able to have this deeply satisfying spiritual experience without working directly on their body. We have also seen that this experience of the spiritual nature of the body is not dependent on the body's condition. What then is the purpose of working with the body in spiritual work?

## The Value of Directly Including the Body in Spiritual Work

Often we are blessed with such awakened experiences when we are quiet and still, such as sitting on a meditation pillow, in deep prayer, or when absorbed in a pristine natural environment. All spiritual practitioners know that these realizations, however clear and certain, tend to come and go.

Frequently, it is when we get up and start moving, talking, or going about our daily lives that we forget the totality of our spiritual experience. We can blame our daily life, our body, for pulling us away from our spiritual realization, back into normal or conventional life.

This experience is so common that we have to ask whether there is something about the usual experience of the body that takes us away from our awakened experience. How is it that we can lose our experience of the physical world, and most intimately our own body, as a form of consciousness itself? When we are not experiencing our body as a form of spiritual consciousness, what are we experiencing that we are calling "our body"? This fundamental question invites us to explore openly what we believe we know about our experience of the body.

We are tempted to think that when we sense our body we are experiencing our physical condition. But what does this really mean? When we consider it, on the purely physical level, we are not usually aware of much detail. Most of the functions that are considered to be essential physical aspects of the aliveness of our body—such as the flow of blood through our veins, the electrical impulses traveling through our nerves, the passage of oxygen and nutrients through cell walls, etc.—occur below our level of consciousness. Close examination also reveals that we experience only a part of the total geography of our physical body. For example, someone might experience most of the front of their body, but not very much of their back, or have little awareness of their feet, or sense their muscles but not their organs, etc. Importantly, whatever we do experience, we consider to constitute "our body." We don't realize that there is much more to the body that we could experience.

## The "Experienced Body"

Looking closely at our direct experience, we find that we are often experiencing a gestalt of sensation that has a certain pattern that is familiar to us. Consequently, we consider that *pattern of sensation* to be our body.

This patterned gestalt is composed of many individual elements that we are normally not even aware of. There are a myriad of simple sensations, such as where our arms brush our sides when we walk, how our tongue sits in our mouth, our inner landscape of tensions and pains, the experience of our posture. These together compose a whole inner world of sensation that is our experience of our body.

We are so familiar with this patterned gestalt that we become unaware of the degree to which we believe it to *be* our body. We do become aware of the familiar gestalt if it begins to change. For example, we might have an experience of feeling more alive than we ever have, or more grounded in our feet; these change our experience of our body. Or we might have a minor car accident that leaves our body feeling rearranged in some way. Our new bodily sensations can be so surprising and unfamiliar that we don't even recognize our bodies. We can have the sense that "this doesn't *feel like* my body" or even "this *isn't* my body."

Our response to this unfamiliarity reveals both how deeply we believe our familiar sensory pattern to be what our body is, and how compelling our habitual body patterns are. We tend to seek to return to a familiar pattern of body, no matter how positive and powerful our body shifts are, or how sublime our spiritual experiences and insights.

Recognizing this raises new questions. Why do we often find it disturbing when our body pattern changes? Why are we compelled, consciously or unconsciously, to return to the familiar form of our "experienced body"? What is it that determines this form, this pattern, this habit that we seem so attached to?

## Body and Self

Our sense of our body as a totality of familiar physical patterns of sensation is an expression that has evolved through our lifetime. It has formed as the innate tendencies of our body and psyche have interacted with our physical and relational environments. Our basic genetic code, which carries our racial and cultural ancestry, is just one part of the picture. Our body's physical history (whether we played soccer or studied ballet; whether we had small falls or big breaks) is another ingredient. Our responses to past and present relational fields (whether we felt loved, accepted, rejected, or neglected) are also key influences that shape our body and psyche.

Perhaps the most profoundly significant determinant of our familiar pattern, and the one that makes it most compelling, is the way the body is literally connected to, and expresses, our sense of self. Our sense of self is deeply embedded within the body and, in particular, within the body pattern, or the "experienced body."

Wilhelm Reich articulated this phenomenon with his insight that body patterns are a reflection of the person's character. He saw further that these patterns are held in place by a network of tensions that can restrict the freedom of breath, and control and limit the flow of energy, emotion, sensation, and aliveness.

The freedom and pattern of the flow of energy through the body is one factor that both determines, and is determined by, areas of hypertonic and hypotonic muscles. This configuration of tensional and energetic elements gives the body a certain shape and contributes to the unique character and texture of our "experienced body."

The specifics of these shapes have precise meanings to us, as adaptive patterns, and as expressions of early identifications, decisions, and beliefs rooted in our history. These particulars compose our historical sense of self. It is *this* body that we then live our lives in, from, and as.

We can even go so far as to say that the ego structure does not exist independently of the physical patterns that express it. Keeping these patterns in place in the body has the function of keeping the ego structure—our sense of self—the same. This fact helps us understand our attachment to returning to a familiar body pattern. On a deep and unconscious level, we take this pattern to be not only our body, but also *our self*.

It is important to recognize that this structuring process of the body is normal and necessary to ego development. The forming ego needs a relatively stable pattern of inner experience to secure the developing sense of self. At the same time that this process is normal and universal, it is also at the very core of what separates us from the direct experience of spiritual reality.

In the process of becoming this relatively fixed, historically based self, we gradually lose touch with the immediacy of the present moment, where the purity of spiritual experience lies. We become a self that feels separate from spiritual reality.

## Spiritual Realization and the Ego Self

The experience and belief that we are a self that is other than spiritual consciousness, a "separate self," is well known to be a primary barrier to spiritual realization. We are seeing how this sense of self is formed within, expressed in, and reinforced by the experience of the body as a fixed form in time and space: also that the usual way that this separate self experiences its reality differs in a basic way from the experience of spiritual realization. We can begin to appreciate how conventional, or normal, experience and spiritual experience feel like two different realities or two separate worlds.

When we have experienced spiritual realization beyond this divided self, we begin to know ourselves in a more profound way, as beingness itself. We know that we are not just a bounded historical self, nor is our body only a heavy encumbrance. When we find ourselves once again caught in the conventional view, spiritual teachings often instruct us to continue different levels of awareness or mindfulness practice and, if possible, to disidentify with the familiar sense of self that continually returns. This step of being able to disidentify from our past, our ego self, even our physical body, is a significant step toward realizing our spiritual nature. The recognition that our ego is not fundamentally who and what we are starts to make room for a deeper reality, and a more expanded awareness, whenever the strong, habitual ego patterns arise.

The wisdom and necessity of disidentifying from the ego self and the habitual bodily structure take on a particular significance when we recognize that, while the body continues to preserve its patterns of ego identity, it is continually reinforcing the unconscious belief that this familiar shape and form is "who I am." The belief that I am this person, with my own specific history, pattern, and flavor—the ego identity itself—is unconsciously encapsulated and reinforced in each breath and every step. It returns again and again—and is confirmed in the way the weight passes across our feet when we walk, the familiar pattern of our breath, the angle of our eyes when we greet a friend, and how much energy and aliveness we experience. We could see it as an unconsciously repeated mantra: "*This is who I am; this is who I am; . . .*" In these simple, invisible, but ubiquitous expressions, we are pulled back into the experience of our historical self. When disidentifying from this pattern, we counter with a different conscious mantra: "*This is not who I am; this is not who I am . . .*"

When we recognize that the pattern of the ego in the body is not the body itself, and that this limiting pattern can change, another possibility begins to emerge: the familiar unconscious body mantra can become silent. In this silence, what would the mantra of our steps, our gestures, our glances become?

In this condition we find that a different kind of freedom becomes possible. Our body becomes an active transformative ally, rather than a hindrance or something to be transcended on our spiritual path.

As the body reveals layers of our undigested history and limiting beliefs, it brings them into consciousness in a way that they can be met freshly, and worked with concretely and directly. When the ego patterns are released, and the roots of the patterns at the emotional and structural levels are no longer held in the body, the impression of the past is, in the present moment, *gone*.

In this moment, there is no anchor for our history. The old identity, the old belief, is nowhere to be found. We then start to experience a body that is not the body of history, but a new body, living in a new moment, in a new experience of reality. The body's perceptual capacities and senses are thus liberated, bringing new possibilities of unexpected experiences of our nature and the nature of reality. A spiritual freedom that is a bodily reality emerges, not as spiritual experience contained in a bounded body, but as a new experience of what our body really is—embodied life. We begin to discriminate the *form* that the body has taken from something more fundamental about the body's *nature* as a living, revelatory aspect of our consciousness. This realization is a quantum shift, and is a great blessing on the spiritual journey.

## The Body of Being

Releasing some of the invisible effort, tensions, and restrictions that are required to maintain the habitual pattern liberates more of the basic energy, the life force, within the body. In this more vital condition, we can see that this sense of being a "fixed object" is not an inherent part of physicality; rather, it is part of the patterned structure that we took to be our body. The body no longer feels as bounded, separate, thick, heavy, painful, and dense.

We can experience our body not only as the repository of ego, defenses, and suffering, but as a revelatory organism of the totality of our consciousness, as a form of living consciousness, inseparable from infinite consciousness. Our body is now revealed to be the intimate, dynamic, living, precious, immediate manifestation of the depth, breadth, and fullness of who we are. Our body becomes more awakened, more scintillatingly aware, and more sensitive to some of the more subtle forms of energy. Our body feels more transparent, more conductive, and more alive. This body knows, and has the potential to reveal, all aspects of our consciousness in the moment, including the various qualities of spiritual Presence.

This deeper experiential understanding of the relationship between the physical and spiritual dimensions can initiate a profound maturational process with regard to our instinctual energies. These powerful forces, which previously turned our attention away from spiritual realization, now begin to reveal their potential, not only to support our survival and well-being, but also to fuel the spiritual journey.

We can begin to discover different ways, known to various spiritual traditions, that the body is also designed as a conduit for subtle energies. The energy of shakti, *chi*, orgone, kundalini, etc., resonates in the physical realm, and can open us to spiritual dimensions.

We can start to become more aware of a spiritual anatomy (which doesn't appear in anatomy books) that includes various subtle centers such as the chakras, and centers called *lataif* in the Sufi tradition, which are portals to specific spiritual states. We are able to feel energetic channels through which subtle energies flow through the nervous system and tissues of the body. These centers and channels tend to be more or less active and more or less developed depending on where we are in our own particular spiritual journey.

## Working with the Body: How the Body Can Open to Its Inner Nature

There is a wide range of ways and paths to involve the body in spiritual practice that have been developed over centuries in different spiritual traditions. Without attempting to describe any specific practices, we can see that certain principles are important to any practice that works with the body in the process of spiritual realization.

First, our orientation toward our body is significant. Approaching our body as a valuable and integral dimension of our sacred wholeness has a powerful impact on the consciousness of the body itself. If we maintain an attitude that the body is a barrier to spiritual realization, the body will conform to that belief, and will remain a barrier.

Practicing with the attitude that our body is a precious living expression of our individual consciousness, a sacred form, brings deeper respect and appreciation for what our body really is and for what it can reveal. Loving attention, honor, and compassion for its difficulties are appropriate to the profound and magnificent consciousness that our body is. A genuine interest in understanding the body's needs, difficulties, fears, wounds, and energies invites the body to reveal aspects of its history and our consciousness. When touched by our welcoming curiosity and love of truth, the body willingly and naturally reveals unexpected inner dimensions of reality.

Second, these attitudes are also expressed by bringing our conscious awareness more deeply into our body. This is the simple practice of being more aware of whatever sensations are there as we focus our attention on our kinesthetic, intrasubjective experience. We are not looking for something profound or important; we are simply more aware of whatever sensations we find. This practice of awareness can be part of a meditation, and can also become an integral part of how we live our life.

To involve the body in the fullness of spiritual practice is an engaging, "up close and personal" process. The kind of awareness that is needed is not a "witnessing from a distance," but is one that brings a sensing, witnessing consciousness deep into the immediacy of the body's experience. It includes a willingness to participate deeply in what is actually arising in our somatic presence, from the perspective of wanting to understand and see the truth of our embodied experience.

Third, when we become intimately present and curious about what the body is expressing, we begin to understand more fully what is actually being revealed. Inquiring sincerely, wanting to know, not in a detached, intellectual way, but with a heartfelt interest in the body, and its truth, begins a process of deepening and unfolding of our embodied consciousness. As the meaning and origin of the habits and restrictions that are held in the body are understood, and as these habits and restrictions are contacted by our awareness and loving presence, the underlying aspects of our true nature and the nature of the body can begin to come forward. Gradually allowing ourselves to be with, and in, the full range of physical experience, inhabiting different parts of the terrain of our body, is the process of becoming more fully incarnate—the flesh being penetrated by consciousness in a palpable way.

We find that entering deeply into the body in this way takes us into a sense of a greater Presence, and its various manifestations, in a remarkable and profound way. The body itself becomes a portal to new possibilities of consciousness.

Fourth, the process of the body opening to its inner nature is a gradual one. The body opens, insight by insight, releasing one belief, or one self-image, or one idea at a time, expanding into new types of freedom one step at a time. This process has its own organic timing and intelligence that we can listen to, and follow, rather than trying to direct or control with our mind.

Fifth, because the body is a multidimensional form of consciousness, it needs to be addressed in its totality. Physical needs and limitations, energies, feelings, psychological structures with their meanings and experiences, as well as the organic, evolutionary impulse—all need to be respected and included. When the totality of the body is recognized, an organic process of unfolding arises that includes all the dimensions of our embodied experience in an intelligent and harmonious integration. This process of integration also needs time, and proceeds at its own pace.

## The Awakened Body: The Body of Spiritual Experience

We come to see that working with the body as an integral dimension of who and what we are not only releases us from the patterns and structures of the past that define us, but it also opens doors to who and what we are at the spiritual ground of our being. Through our bodies, we enter the vast terrain of our consciousness, including not only the painful and pleasurable parts of our history, but also our whole belief system, identity, the core of our life force, and spiritual realms that we could not previously imagine. We enter into the great mystery of the marriage of body and soul, spirit and matter.

This marriage is not a matter of bringing two separate things together. It is more that we come to see through our mistaken belief that that separation exists in the first place. We can experience that consciousness and the body are actually like two sides of the same coin. The body is a conduit for consciousness because it *is* consciousness manifesting through and *as* the body. This is a radical realization that allows many hidden possibilities of embodied life to become palpable, lived realities.

In this awakened condition, the body itself is experienced differently. Our physicality feels lighter, both in its sense of weight, and in its sense of luminosity. Also, our experience of our body is different in different states of realization. For example, we can experience our body as being made of a light, fluid, loving presence: the presence of Divine Love. In this condition, we can perceive the world as made of the same loving light. Or we can experience our body as a spacious, full consciousness that is Presence itself, a "palpable hereness," a substantial realness without a sense of burden, of limitation, of thickness. Or we can experience the body as an exquisite, luminous emptiness that brings a deep sense of gratitude, connection, and well-being. In certain deep spiritual realizations, we experience our particular body as a multidimensional hologram, containing the totality of Reality from the most physical to the most subtle, here, now, and totally transparent to all levels of Being.

At the same time that we experience our body differently, our experience of spiritual conditions takes on a fresh dimension. Without working with the body, spiritual states tend to appear as light, transparent, empty, clear, or even sweet, flowing, and blissful, while somewhat ephemeral. Integrated into the body, this clarity and bliss become more substantial, palpably full, dynamically sensual, more richly textured, with a sense of sturdy groundedness and powerful rootedness.

Spiritual presence can attain a sense of density, as if it is more condensed, concentrated, and fully there or present. There is a tangible sense that our spiritual realization is more complete, stable, established, and certain. We sense a "through-and-throughness": a sense of nothing being left out, nothing being excluded.

At the same time, we can find that we are physically present in our current reality in a more palpable, concrete way. Our awakened body helps us to emerge from our imagination of what is here, into what is really *here now* in our present environment.

## Physical Life as Spiritual Life

Our body can therefore become a conduit for spiritual qualities to manifest in life in ways that are both more ordinary and more profound than we might normally expect. Then our body is not only housing our consciousness, our life, but is made of our life. Spiritual consciousness comes into form, and expression, and lives in the world through our own unique physical body.

For example, we often think of compassion as a tenderness of heart that can be expressed in overt acts of kindness to others. We can find that it is also possible for the exquisite, sensitive tenderness of loving-kindness, as a substantial quality, to literally flow through the body itself, giving our whole embodied consciousness the sense of being the source of an exquisitely sensitive and gentle radiation. This compassionate lovingness then permeates the simplest gesture of fingers and eyes, radiates through the countenance, fills the voice, and is breathed out with the breath. As we integrate various spiritual qualities, they often spontaneously begin to function in our lives and become an expression of our spiritual maturation.

The embodied qualities then not only inform our actions toward others, but their manifestation is expressed in the totality of what our body is, and how it moves: for example, peace comes into the world as we breathe in and out, as we open a door, as we lift our spoon; strength is expressed through the clarity of our steps, the resonance of our voice, and the presence in our handshake. The inner felt sense is that *being* that Presence is no different from these simple actions of everyday life.

The heart—with its qualities of joy, love, compassion, value, and contactfulness—is not confined to the center of the chest, but can permeate the whole body. The intelligence, openness, clarity, and spaciousness of the mind are not confined to the brain or the head, but can permeate the entire body with its brilliant knowingness and its open receptivity. The alive sensuality and firmness of our belly supports, strengthens, and enlivens our whole, integrated beingness.

Everyday simple movements become the outflow of Being. We can sense that this living beingness animates our first, small, awakening movements, the flexing of fingers and toes, the stretching of the spine, as we reinhabit the body upon awakening. All that we are, know, and feel is expressed as we turn between our sheets, as our feet touch the floor, as we wash, sit, eat, greet, dress, drive, work, rest, and play. Every act is an expression of the dance of Being and its manifestations; our body and consciousness are inseparable, each fulfilling the other in a deep inner union. In this condition of the unity of spirit and matter, of our consciousness and our body, living is the same as Being. The body takes its true place as the lived and living, known and knowing, revealed and revealing presence of spiritual reality.

Within this experience, we can see that embodied life is a living mystery whose potentials are being extended in the moment through our own embodiment. How completely our physicality can express and reveal the Presence that we are, how deep this unity goes, how singular we truly are, is a matter of constant discovery. At this time in human evolution, as we set our feet on the path of embodied realization, we can participate in the evolution of this great mystery: the potential of embodied life as a living fulfillment of the precious and fundamental truth of the spiritual nature of human consciousness.

# 93
# Existential Dimensions of the Fundamental Character Themes

**Halko Weiss, United States**

Translation by Warren Miller

**Halko Weiss's** biographical information can be found at the beginning of Chapter 1, "Preface: The Field of Body Psychotherapy."

## Normal and Pathological Development

In many forms of Body Psychotherapy, the theory of character development plays an important role. Traditionally, just as in the rest of psychotherapy, the focus is directed toward pathological development—an obvious tendency when one is concerned with healing.

Clinical conceptualizations direct our attention toward presentations of dysfunctionality. Pathologizing descriptions are the norm throughout the field—a statement by Wilhelm Reich from 1933 is typical: "Almost all forms of active male and female homosexuality, most cases of so-called moral insanity, paranoia, related forms of schizophrenia, and, moreover, many cases of erythrophobia and manifestly sadistic male perverts, belong to the phallic-narcissistic character type" (Reich, 1933, p. 209).

Such descriptions create absolute rifts between supposedly "healthy" and supposedly "sick" categories of people, which not only allow, but positively indulge, the healing and helping professions—as well as many others drawing on psychological terminology—to elevate and distance themselves. As a result of such "labeling," a deeper understanding of people's problematic psychological developments and the extent of human suffering gets distorted.

Although not dismissing the need for and the productive use of pathologies and diagnoses altogether, it is—on the whole—more realistic to view both "pathological" and "normal" development as differentiated only by degrees. We can assume that the fundamental themes and dilemmas of the human condition affect everybody, leaving their complications, scars, and traces in every development, whether "healthy" or "disturbed," and resulting in similar psychological mechanisms—to greater or lesser degrees, perhaps. Contrary to the usual diagnostic approach, we could emphasize what humans have "in common," and how this "commonality" sometimes takes extreme forms or triggers extraordinary states. Freud used to say that the privileged perspective of the doctor allows a view of the human condition from which the patient's suffering *in extremis* reveals more clearly and starkly the less apparent principles of psychological functioning in the normal person.

In many forms of psychotherapy, the diagnostic stance has changed markedly in the last few decades. Through the influence of Carl Rogers's teachings in Humanistic Psychology (Rogers, 1973), and Heinz Kohut's teachings in the psychoanalytic tradition (Kohut, 1977), Body Psychotherapists—just like therapists of other orientations—have learned to approach their clients with much less analysis and interpretation and with a much more empathic resonance. This is now considered valuable—if not essential—for the collaborative relationship, especially if therapists can personally grasp something of the existential dimension of the other person, and experience it within themselves. Such empathic relating creates a climate of security and bonding, decreases resistances, and makes sensitive dynamics more easily accessible.

The intersubjective approach of psychoanalysis (Stolorow et al., 1987) and the dialogic approach of Gestalt Therapy (Friedman, 1985; Hycner, 1991; Fuhr et al., 1999) are good examples of this development. From these perspectives, therapists' awareness of the common existential ground between them and the client deepens the relationship they can offer. In fact, a therapeutic relationship that is based on an attitude of equality and empathy on the part of the therapist is often considered to be a key element in the healing process (Stolorow et al., 1987; Doubrawa and Staemmler, 1999; Weiss, 1992).

The modern discourse of Developmental Psychology has shifted toward an emphasis on the universal human nature of such lifelong issues as trust, attachment, and autonomy. Daniel Stern, for example, notes that the formative phases of childhood development are not just "windows" wherein imprinting occurs, but that these basic themes remain active throughout life, and in all areas of human relationship (Stern, 1985, p. 34). His description of the mother-child dyad does not view character development in terms of defenses, but as a set of creative coping mechanisms, or strategies, that continue to evolve throughout life. These can develop into a positive life strategy, even if they are based on experiences of deprivation (Stern, 1995).

Informed by these more recent perspectives on developmental disturbances, this chapter presents a description of each individual's quest for a role in the world, both in general and in existential terms, in such a way that anyone will be able to recognize some of their own life themes and struggles. Psychoanalytic theorists have grappled with the existential dimension for a long time—among them, Rollo May (1969), Ludwig Binswanger (1956), Fritz Riemann (1984), Erich Fromm (1956), and Viktor Frankl (1978). Irvin Yalom describes existential conflicts as ". . . neither a conflict with repressed instinctual drives, nor with internalized significant adults, but instead, a conflict arising from the confrontation of the individual with the given facts of existence" (Yalom, 1989, p. 18). He is referring here to the "four existential concerns": death, freedom, isolation, and meaninglessness. It is no surprise that many authors pursuing such ultimate concerns arrived at similar or related themes and issues.

To begin with, I want to emphasize that this chapter does not demarcate the existential perspective as categorically coming from drives and internalizations, as Yalom proposes; instead, encounters with one's own drives and their limitations, for example, are viewed as further "given facts of existence" that cannot be avoided in life. My interpretation of the existential, therefore, pertains to all issues that every human being is confronted with, and therefore needs to deal with, either consciously or unconsciously. The intention is to invite the reader into an exploration: "How have you learned to deal with the fundamental issues of your life?" "Where was it easier and where was it more difficult?" "How did you find your own solutions, and how could these solutions be further improved?" This invitation particularly includes therapists, as it is a way for them to learn to identify with and empathize with their clients' fundamental formative experiences with greater ease and accuracy.

## Character, Types, and Themes

In Body Psychotherapy, the uniquely organized shape or structure—we might say, "body-mind matrix"—of an individual's emotional, symbolic, and behavioral repertoire is generally referred to as "character." Character—in this sense—is the distinct architecture of personality, with its inner dynamics and modes of processing. Body Psychotherapy offers an additional perspective—largely neglected by other therapeutic approaches in their description of schemas, personality types, and habitual patterns as an integral aspect of character: the appreciation of the body in its development, self-organization, and structure.

Different schools of Body Psychotherapy have evolved slightly different developmental typologies (see Chapter 28, "The Main Variants of Character Theory in the Field of Body Psychotherapy" by Andreas Sartory, Gustl Marlock, and Halko Weiss), but all share the principles of a holistic, embodied understanding of character, initiated mostly by

Reich. These typologies describe how children, faced with similar environmental challenges, develop similar coping strategies. As these strategies are chronically fixed, habitual, and fairly automatic, we can recognize these typologies in practice, helping us to anticipate, understand, and engage the client's reactions and behaviors. For the most part, the commonly identified character structures correspond to the so-called "personality disorders" on Axis II of the DSM-IV (Revenstorf and Peter, 2001).

However, even in these Body Psychotherapeutic formulations of typologies, deriving partly from psychodynamic, but predominantly from humanistic, traditions, which are otherwise more critical of "pathologizing" attitudes, the emphasis is still on pathological aspects of character, leading to notions of failed development and deviant behaviors: "schizoid," "oral," "masochistic," "psychopathic," "hysterical," and "phallic" are derogative designations and labels that are supposedly used to characterize actual people (Reich, 1933; Lowen, 1958; Kurtz, 1990; Kurtz and Prestera, 1970; Weiss and Benz, 1987). Accordingly, clients (or patients) are then often identified as a "psychopathic type," or as having a "hysterical character." The modern trend is to see "character" from a much more complex and ambivalent perspective, recognizing both the creative and protective components of the "character armor" (Totton and Jacobs, 2001).

In contrast to these widespread tendencies, the assumption in this chapter is that every client is involved in a variety of attempts to resolve certain thematic issues and that all possible associated strategies are used, probably both simultaneously and sequentially. Some of the themes may be more charged than others, and may thus appear to dominate the person and his or her life, due to the intensity of the underlying traumatic experiences. But even then, we can recognize that the degree to which any respective character style manifests (or prevails) varies from situation to situation, from time to time, and almost certainly from relationship to relationship.

Each of the person's life themes that we explore has the capacity to create conflicts that can overwhelm a person's resources and coping capacities to such a degree that they cause pathological developments. So, the intention here is to illustrate the relationships between:

- The underlying existential themes
- The psychological dilemmas and inevitable conflicts they engender, and
- The variety of strategies toward their resolution, including neurotic forms of self-organization

## Character Theory and Practice

From the perspective of Hakomi Experiential Psychology and its character theory (on which this chapter is based), the consolidation of a century of therapeutic experience along these developmental lines (from Freud—Reich—Lowen and Pierrakos—Kurtz) has led to a formulation of basic human themes, familiar to all of us, and fairly self-evident, as long as we approach each other with an open mind toward this existential dimension.

This theory holds that even young children actively process their experiences and intuitively consolidate them into unconscious perspectives of the world. Corresponding theories on self-organizing systems propose that such systems develop inner "models" of reality designed to anticipate the future (Holland, 1998). Character theory also accords with a variety of other well-known psychological theories, such as Cognitive Behavioral Therapy (Piaget calls them "cognitive schemas") and modern development theory (Stern's concept of "RIGs").

However clear the differentiation of character styles is in theory, in practice we find that over the course of therapy, depending on the stage in the person's process, new and different themes will emerge in the client's life, and in the relationship in the consultation room—all of which can unexpectedly refine and revise the initial impression and "diagnosis" of the client's character. Usually, several of the major themes are touched upon in the course of a therapy. This indicates, from the start, that a person is not just an "oral" type, or just has a "masochistic" personality.

Instead of working with "a psychopathic type," for example, we adopt an attitude of working with a person, say, during the beginning phases of treatment, when we may perceive, in the client's presentation, ways of relating to a range of "psychopathic" elements, along with their associated themes. However, later in therapy, we may discover that other themes, not suggested by the initial presentation, become much more relevant, often unexpectedly so, and we then want to be open, sensitive, and receptive to engaging with them. As we increasingly relinquish simplistic correlations between the patient and their "disorder," we learn to approach each person in a more unique and idiosyncratic engagement with *all* of their great existential themes of life. Many psychodynamically oriented Body Psychotherapists have come to this more differentiated and existential view regarding the complexity of character, and how to adapt and refine their basic theory and techniques to make them serve both their practice and the individuality of each client.

## A Five-Dimensional Space

"Characterology" in the Body Psychotherapeutic tradition can now be distilled into five existential themes that every human being has to engage throughout their developmental process. In the framework of the Hakomi approach, these were termed "safety," "support," "freedom," "authenticity," and "worth." Because we are dealing with complex themes, these terms are to be understood merely as pointers.

As the following systematic presentation is derived from academic psychology, it may require some explanation for those from other occupational backgrounds: each of the above themes is viewed as a factor that, along with the other factors, can describe a person's "state of being" along a spectrum, plotted on an axis with two poles. For example, the factor "security" can vary between an "extremely threatened" state on the right end of the axis (charge: 1) and "completely secure" on the left (charge: 0). A person's state could then be described by locating their position on each of the five axes. The positions are understood in body-mind terms, through the so-called "charge" that they hold for the person (for example, 0.5)—and, of course, this can change from moment to moment.

By giving each of these five axes a dimension and then combining them, with a variable degree of charge in each

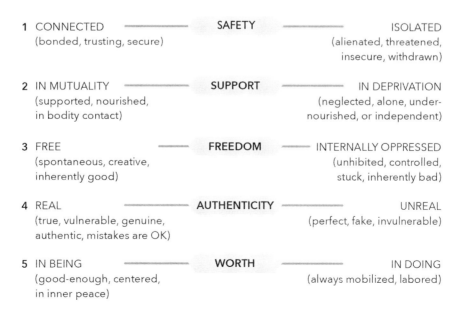

Figure 93.1. Basic developmental themes and their polarities

of the dimensions at any one point in time, a person's state can be visualized as a point in a five-dimensional space. The proposed five dimensions of this "character space" are illustrated in Figure 93.1. It is, of course, possible to use this diagrammatic representation to gauge oneself in these five dimensions and between the respective polarities. For each dimension, I can ask myself: "Where on the continuum between the two poles do I find myself?" "How is it in this particular moment?" "How is it in general?" "How is it in different situations?"

If there are areas and positions where I find myself most often or almost always, the respective dimension will indicate a habitual characterological issue, holding a considerable emotional charge for me around the corresponding theme, and most likely a large amount of pain and struggle, with the troubling character disturbances showing themselves as more extreme and lasting charges over on the right-hand side. But, even in this case, it is interesting to observe how inner and outer events may affect this and shift my position in "character space," revealing that the underlying existential themes are inherently relational and contextual.

## The Five Themes: Phenomenology, Body, and Genesis

As the Body Psychotherapeutic character typologies have already been described earlier in this handbook (see Chapter 27, "Shapes of Experience: Neuroscience, Developmental Psychology, and Somatic Character Formation" by Marianne Bentzen; and Chapter 28, "The Main Variants of Character Theory in the Field of Body Psychotherapy" by Andreas Sartory, Gustl Marlock, and Halko Weiss), the focus here is on the existential life themes that are woven into character types and that manifest through them.

### Existential Life Theme: "Safety"

This dimension represents a person's ability to feel in contact with the world. In other characterologies, the theme is commonly referred to as "schizoid." The theme reflects the existential question of to what extent we can afford to entrust ourselves to the world, and whether we have had to deal with significant and impactful experiences, suggesting that we might also have a tendency to withdraw and keep our distance from the world.

According to character theory, difficult circumstances at birth, rejection by the mother, early experiences of war, hospitalization, etc., trigger unconscious and involuntary movements away from the world. Contact with the world—for example, through the senses, but also contact with one's own feelings—becomes interrupted, inhibited, or split off. The theory implies that breaking contact is one of the early mechanisms available to human beings in order to effectively protect themselves from uncomfortable or overwhelming experiences. These mechanisms remain functional throughout life and can interrupt or distort internal information processing when they are triggered, for example, by traumatic experiences.

The dimension of "safety" reflects how all experiences relating to one's personal sense of security and belongingness, as a whole, are processed, digested, and integrated. If these are predominantly positive experiences, a person can afford to make deep contact with what is out there in the world, and to react with fear and withdrawal only when real, acute threats trigger the relevant defense mechanisms. People are marked by this theme when they have experienced predominantly traumatic, repeated experiences, especially of a hostile and invasive nature, that (unconsciously) suggest that the maintenance of the corresponding protective defenses of withdrawal from the world should be used as a permanent or default solution.

Phenomenologically, people touched by the theme of safety are described as follows: lacking expressiveness; socially insecure; having a hard, contracted body; shallow breathing; with blockages in the ocular segment; etc. The prominence of such characteristics depends on the intensity of the past formative experiences and how these were processed.

### Existential Life Theme: "Support"

This dimension comprises the charge and processing of all those issues related to the fundamental fact that we are existentially dependent on other people. It presupposes that every person is dependent on interactions with others in order to satisfy their needs, and that nobody can survive otherwise. As the poet John Donne wrote, "No man is an island."

The first and foundational experiences regarding this existential condition occur early on in life. In the first few months, infants live in a state of total dependency on their caregivers. Following character theory, how our emotional and relational environment handles and responds to an infant's need for others (Klein, 1987) becomes a template from which unconscious "lessons" are drawn, informing our lifelong encounter with this existential theme.

If these experiences are predominantly characterized by deprivation—for example, when a baby isn't held enough, or is neglected in terms of feeding or comfort, or when the caregivers don't have enough time for intimate developmental play—then the baby's needs aren't sufficiently taken care of, forcing it to adapt. In this process, it will develop appropriate defense mechanisms. In many psychodynamic traditions, character conditioned by significant restrictions around this theme is referred to as "oral."

Learning not to expose itself to the deepest layers of its needs, the child develops the characteristic "oral" self-organization, blocking these layers of experience, but thus also any possibility for its needs to be met and fulfilled later on. Because the core defense simultaneously protects and blocks, the person is cut off from nourishment even when it is available, and therefore becomes "unnourishable," with an ensuing state of chronic depletion. This can result in different coping strategies and relational patterns: an ongoing search for support from other people, but an inability to accept what is offered, although it is longed for (based on the unconscious maxim: "Never again at someone's mercy!"); or, if the organism is strong enough, a determined striving toward independence, avoiding all sense of need and developing as a supposedly "strong" persona instead.

Although the same theme lies at the core of the person's character, two very different organizational tendencies can develop:

* One that tends to lack energy, constantly searching, pleading, with a rather collapsed body, overextended knees, tilted pelvis, and a strong sense that something is lacking.
* One that is independent, geared toward appearing strong, with an erect, energized body organization. In this pattern, the person hardly notices that they might need to receive something.

**Existential Life Theme: "Freedom"**

It is an essential element of a holistic, embodied perspective on character that the various life themes emerge and are first encountered during particular phases of neuro-anatomical development and the corresponding social and relational stimulations. Allan Schore has developed a useful scientific basis for this perspective (Schore, 1994, pp. 27–33, 62–67), confirming in great detail an assumption, long held across the field of Body Psychotherapeutic traditions, that neural and psycho-motor mechanisms "come online"—as it is called—sequentially, by building on the maturational achievements of previous phases. We can recognize various developmental windows, rooted in biological and anatomical changes, that circumscribe periods during which the child will be especially sensitive to particular life themes. Although the theme will continue to be processed and will remain relevant throughout life, the conditions of the child's first encounter can set a blueprint for further development.

This is also true for the encounter with the issue of "freedom." Only when the child has developed the motoric capacity and a degree of mobility that allow it to follow its own impulses and discover the exterior world through trial and error (i.e., when the child becomes able to make autonomous choices) can fundamental experiences associated with this theme begin to accumulate. The child—typically, we can imagine a toddler—is learning at this stage whether it is accepted for going its own way, for experimenting and following its own spontaneity, even if mishaps occur, and thus beginning to develop its own will and experience as to what is desirable and what is undesirable. Here, as in all other developmental phases, the first encounters with the underlying life theme are not always positive: a mother is bound to curtail the child's freedom and impose her will should she, for example, find the child about to poke an electrical outlet with a fork.

This phase in the child's development is therefore crucial in forming unconscious beliefs as to how much freedom is allowed, or not. If the parents are very dominating and authoritarian, there will not be much room to move, and any rebellion is likely to result in complete defeat, with associated (imposed) guilt feelings, and the parents withdrawing their affection. If, on the other hand, they allow a lot of space, the child will integrate this experience into its intuitive view of the world, creating an ability to explore and inhabit its freedom.

A person whose early experience was dominated by restrictions tends to harbor feelings of resistance, rage, and inherent badness, pervaded by shame and a sense of humiliation. The body becomes organized as more compact and downwardly contracted, the buttocks are pulled in, and the upper back is often muscular while the shoulders droop. The body is held in with inhibitions, diminishing any spontaneous expressions of liveliness.

Traditionally, this form of self-organization is referred to as "masochistic." However, the underlying existential issue of freedom affects everybody across the life span, and how we respond to unavoidable experiences of limitation will be shaped by the intuitive image of reality that was formed early on in our first encounters with this theme.

### Existential Life Theme: "Authenticity"

During the further course of development, beginning approximately with the third year of life, when children begin to sense and develop their individuality, the question arises whether the peculiarities of this identity, including "weaknesses" of various kinds, are welcome and manageable. To a greater or lesser extent, social pressure is always present, inclining the child toward "acceptable" ways of being. In an open, tolerant, interested environment, the child can afford to reveal itself, thus fostering self-acceptance. However, the stronger the message that it is not acceptable as it is, but that it should be different, the more the child will intensify its internal efforts to hide and deny itself and will attempt to present outwardly a more "ideal" person—stronger, "cooler," more intelligent, etc.—than it really feels it is. In the extreme, this can lead to an utter shaming of the authentic self and its almost total abnegation. A social "mask" is created and maintained, with which the person later appears to become identified: the person becomes the "mask." Every human being is exposed, to a greater or lesser extent, to this "narcissistic" force field, between what is expected and what is real. And every person gets into states when, at times, "camouflage" seems more important than openness, honesty, or authenticity.

Traditionally, a style of self-organization that is shaped and colored by this theme is referred to as "psychopathic." The embodied manifestations of this theme range from very domineering, controlled forms (body: "pumped-up" chest, intensive eyes, chin up, etc.) to very soft, adaptive, "chameleonlike" forms (body: hyperflexible).

As with the other styles, it is assumed that everyone encounters certain elements or aspects of this theme, at times, and that nobody can always be authentic, real, congruent, and transparent.

### Existential Life Theme: "Social Worth"

Finally, every person—consciously or unconsciously—is faced with the issue of their "value" or "worth" in relation to the community to which they belong. Biologically, as well as psychologically, we are embedded in our social environment and interconnected with it. Whether a person, in their complex, multifaceted being, is able to take their place within their social context is therefore a question of existential significance for everybody. Will he or she drop out, remain unrecognized, not be worth anything? Where in the social "pecking order" are they placed? Many unconscious processes are activated around this theme, essentially revolving around a comparison between oneself and others, and one's acceptance of oneself.

The Body Psychotherapeutic tradition has found two fundamental versions of this theme, manifesting as concerns around achieving or maintaining personal value: some people live in a state of constant tension in the pursuit of "performance"; others are preoccupied with being "interesting" to others. These two themes correspond to what used to be called the "phallic-rigid" and the "hysteric" aspects, respectively.

For people with strong formative experiences in regard to one or both of the above themes, it is difficult to let things be and to surrender to states of "being." They feel driven, are often very energetic, and feel perpetually under pressure. They feel they need to achieve and *earn* their worth, having lost their intuitive sense that the mere fact of their existence might be considered valuable in itself. They can become very stressed and overworked, and thus their bodies tend to carry tension, with high tonus throughout their musculature, manifesting in an overextended back and shoulders; they tend to be energetic, with lots of movement, often athletic. During very difficult phases, a form of "breakdown" can appear imminent and be a real risk.

## Existential Encounter

In conclusion, it can be asserted that theories of character patterns are underpinned by existential life themes that will be encountered by all human beings throughout life, and that each such encounter—beginning with formative experiences in very early development—can leave more or less apparent traces. Recent developments throughout the various Body Psychotherapeutic approaches have encouraged therapists to become more conscious of how these themes play out in their own lives, which in turn helps them to resonate and empathize with their patients when these themes arise in extreme—and sometimes extremely painful—forms in the life of the client and in therapy.

Such an existential characterological perspective, while avoiding unhelpful labeling and pathologizing, still uses well-established diagnostic correlations between somatic and emotional, as well as psychological, manifestations connecting visible indicators with internal experience. For example, a person's "inflated" chest may well be taken as a valid indication that they have had difficult experiences around being authentic that may have shaped their body-mind organization. It refrains, however, from taking an analytic-interpretive stance. Instead, the emphasis is on the endeavor to empathically comprehend the various, often sequentially arising, life themes in their unique and individual manifestations. The diagnostic process then becomes dialogic and procedural (Staemmler, 1999): hypotheses are developed as the therapist meets his patient with compassion, and new discoveries are made. Drawing upon his own personal experience, the therapist can meet the client with ever-deepening insights into shared existential themes, and these become increasingly accepted and integrated.

It seems, therefore, that the distinction between "healthy" and "ill," "functional" and "dysfunctional," is now less categorical than it was fifty or ninety years ago, when Reich first formulated character theory. The gap between patient and therapist shrinks, while the quality of the relationship deepens.

## References

Binswanger, L. (1956). Existential Analysis and psychotherapy. In F. Fromm-Reichmann & J. Moreno (Eds.), *Progress in Psychotherapy.* New York: Grune & Stratton.

Doubrawa, E., & Staemmler, F-M. (Eds.). (1999). *Heilende Beziehung [Healing relationship].* Cologne: Peter Hammer.

Frankl, V. E. (1978). *Der Wille zum Sinn [The will to meaning].* Bern, Switzerland: Huber.

Friedman, M. (1985). *The healing dialogue in psychotherapy.* New York: Jason Aronson.

Fromm, E. (1956). *Die Kunst des Liebens [The art of loving].* Frankfurt: Ullstein.

Fuhr, R., Sreckovic, M., & Gremmler-Fuhr, M. (Eds.). (1999). *Handbuch der Gestalttherapie [Handbook of Gestalt Therapy].* Göttingen: Hogrefe.

Holland, J. (1998). *Emergence.* New York: Oxford University Press.

Hycner, R. (1991). *Between person and person.* Highland, NY: Gestalt Journal Press.

Klein, J. (1987). *Our need for others and its roots in infancy.* London: Tavistock.

Kohut, H. (1977). *The restoration of the self.* New York: International Universities Press.

Kurtz, R. (1990). *Body-Centered Psychotherapy.* Mendocino, CA: LifeRhythm.

Kurtz, R., & Prestera, H. (1970). *The body reveals.* New York: Harper & Row.

Lowen, A. (1958). *The language of the body.* New York: Collier Books.

May, R. (Ed.). (1969). *Existential Psychology.* New York: Random House.

Reich, W. (1933/1973). *Charakteranalyse [Character Analysis].* Frankfurt: Fischer.

Revenstorf, D., & Peter, B. (Eds.). (2001). *Hypnose in Psychotherapie: Psychosomatik und Medizin [Hypnosis in psychotherapy: Psychosomatics and medicine].* Berlin: Springer.

Riemann, F. (1984). *Grundformen der Angst [Basic forms of fear].* Munich: Ernst Reinhardt.

Rogers, C. (1973). *Die klient-bezogene Gesprächstherapie [The client-centered talk therapy].* Munich: Kindler.

Schore, A. N. (1994). *Affect regulation and the origin of the self.* Hillsdale, NJ: Lawrence Erlbaum.

Staemmler, F-M. (1999). Verstehen und Verändern: Dialogisch-prozessuale Diagnostik [Understanding and transformation: Dialogic-procedural diagnosis]. In R. Fuhr et al. (Eds.), *Handbuch der Gestalttherapie [Handbook of Gestalt Therapy]* (pp. 673–687). Göttingen: Hogrefe.

Stern, D. N. (1985). *The interpersonal world of the infant.* New York: Basic Books.

Stern, D. N. (1995). *The motherhood constellation.* New York: Basic Books.

Stolorow, R. D., Brandchaft, B., & Atwood, G. E. (1987). *Psychoanalytic treatment.* Hillsdale, NJ: Analytic Press.

Totton, N., and Jacobs, M. (2001). *Character and personality types.* Buckingham, UK: Open University Press.

Weiss, H. (1992). Die heilende Beziehung [The healing relationship]. In B. Maul (Ed.), *Körperpsychotherapie [Body Psychotherapy]* (pp. 378–382). Berlin: Verlag Bernhard Maul.

Weiss, H., & Benz, D. (1987). *Auf den Körper hören [Listen to your body].* Munich: Kösel.

Yalom, I. (1989). *Existentielle Psychotherapie [Existential Psychotherapy].* Cologne: Edition Humanistische Psychologie.

# 94

# Body Meditation in the Tibetan Buddhist and Bön Traditions

### Daniel P. Brown, United States

**Daniel P. Brown**, PhD, is associate clinical professor in psychology, Harvard Medical School. He maintains a private practice in psychology in Newton, Massachusetts. His specialties are trauma and abuse, forensic psychology, and behavioral medicine. He has also studied the Indo-Tibetan Buddhist tradition for forty-three years, including translating numerous meditational texts from Tibetan. He teaches meditation retreats all over the world in the Pointing Out style of Indo-Tibetan Buddhism. He is the author of fourteen books, including the award-winning *Memory, Trauma Treatment, and the Law* (1998), as well as *Pointing Out the Great Way: The Stages of Meditation in the Mahamudra Tradition* (2006), and has co-authored *Transformations of Consciousness* (1986) with Ken Wilber and Jack Engler. Dr. Brown is currently translating both the *A Khrid* and *Six Lamps Bon po Dzogs Chen* teachings into English.

The body can be used as an object of meditation at every stage along the path of meditation from the very beginning to its end point in Buddhahood.

## The Body as a Concentration Object

The goal of concentration meditation is to stabilize the mind (Gendun Lodro, 1998). Anything can be used as an object to concentrate on, including taking the entire felt sense of the body as a whole as the sole concentration object. Staying-calming meditation (*zhi gnas*)[74] entails directing and repeatedly redirecting the mind toward the concentration object—in this case, the body as a whole—and away from any distracting mental content, until the mind stays (*gnas pa*) continuously and completely on the concentration object, and all extraneous activity of thought and other distracting mental content become calm (*zhi ba*). The skilled practitioner learns to intensify (*sgrim pa*) their mind on the concentration object—i.e., to stay progressively more and more closely engaged with the concentration on the body as a whole in such a way that the mind is so busily engaged with all the subtle detail of the concentration object that there is little occasion to get distracted elsewhere. As a result, staying on the concentration object becomes continuous, and extraneous thought elaboration becomes calm.

As concentration deepens, the concentration object will seem less solid and more energylike. The body as the concentration object becomes more like energy in space, and its energy is dynamic and ever-changing. In this sense, the body as a whole becomes harder to fixate on as an object of concentration. This stage of concentration is called "concentration without support," because the ever-changing body energy serves as less of a support for concentration. Nevertheless, the skilled practitioner is able to find the imprint of the concentration object throughout all the energy and change and to deepen concentration. Eventually, concentration becomes automatic on a very orderly flow of unfolding "one-pointed" energy, and the focus of awareness, with the precision and quickness of a laser beam, will stay on whatever is intended, for as long as

---

74  Tibetan technical terms are given in parentheses in italics.

is intended, with no extraneous activity or reactivity of the mind. The epitome of concentration is making the mind serviceable. Fully stabilized concentration now becomes a tool with which to gain insight into how the mind constructs experience.

## Insight Meditation: Seeing Beyond the Constructions into the Nature of Awareness

Insight meditations (literally "seeing beyond": *lhag mthong*) in Tibetan Mahayana Buddhism pertain to emptiness (*stong ba*). Emptiness is best understood as a synonym for "just a construction of mind." The ordinary mind is constructive in nature. The ordinary mind constructs representations for a sense of self (emptiness of self); constructs representations for mental content (emptiness of phenomena), such that thought, emotion, and perceptions like sights, sounds, tastes, smells, and bodily sensations all constitute types of mental constructions; and also constructs representations for time (conventional time). These ordinary structures of mind are a form of relative reality. The sense of self becomes a central organizing principle. For example, I organize most of my daily experience around "Dan." Likewise, conventional time becomes a central organizer for our social world—for example, to get to places on time or to meet deadlines. Although operating out of these conventional structures of mind is useful in negotiating everyday relative reality, the problem, from a Mahayana Buddhist perspective, is reification (*dngos 'dzin*).

We make the epistemological mistake of forgetting that these are constructions, and thereby we behave as if they have independent self-existence. For example, we take the convention of time as all too real. We think that there is an external cosmic "time clock," and we even locate it in Greenwich. We also think that the sense of self is all too real. According to Mahayana Buddhism, there are two experiential consequences to reification. The first is the experience of "grab" (*'dzin pa*). The sense of self has a lot of grab, and grab is the source of attachment and suffering. Time—for example, "running late"—likewise has grab and is thus a source of suffering. The body, likewise, has a lot of grab as a source of attachment and suffering. Second, reification has the capacity to obscure (*mun pa*) the real nature of the mind. From an ultimate perspective, everything that seems to exist is a manifestation of primordial wisdom's awakened awareness (*rig pa'i ye shes*) and its liveliness (*rtsal*).

In Mahayana Buddhism and in Bön, awakened awareness has two dimensions—the knowing aspect of awareness (*shes rig*) and the dynamic energetic aspect of awareness, its liveliness (*rtsal*). Whenever we take any ordinary structures of mind as too solid or too real, this obscures the possibility of "seeing beyond" (*lhag mthong*) these empty constructions into the real nature of the mind's lively awakened awareness, manifesting itself to itself and knowing its awakened nature moment-by-moment through its own lively manifestation. In Great Completion Meditation (*rdzogs chen*), everything ultimately is the play (*rol ba*) of lively awareness manifesting itself to itself and knowing each manifestation with brilliant awareness. Innate awakened awareness is like the sun that shines all the time, but cannot be seen if covered by clouds. Emptiness meditation allows the practitioner to see beyond all seemingly solid and reified constructions of mind, until awakened awareness shines forth.

As an actual meditation practice, emptiness meditation is a high-speed, negative search task. The search begins by positing a target for the search—for example, the sense of sense, or personal identity: "Dan," in my case. As humans, we have the capacity for self-reflective awareness. I can evoke "Dan" as an object of reflection and get a direct general sense of "Dan-ness." Having become familiar with the target of the search, the practitioner uses awareness as the medium of the search. Awareness operates at a much higher speed than ordinary thought, and thought itself cannot serve as an effective medium for genuine insight. With the precision and lightning speed of awareness, cultivated from concentration training, the practitioner rapidly and thoroughly searches through the field of bodily sensations and mental content for the target of the search. Can an independently existing, solid self—or thing-in-itself—be found anywhere? His Holiness the Dalai Lama says that "the essence of emptiness as a meditation practice is 'unfindableness' ('chor med)." In other words, this rapid, high-speed search, with awareness, typically results in the experience of the target of the search slipping away and receding from awareness. If you think you can find the target, break the area into smaller units of analysis until the target recedes. For example, if you think you find the self somewhere in the brain, search into each region, then the cells, then the molecules in the cells, until getting to the experience of unfindableness.

In Mahayana Buddhism, emptiness meditation is described as an affirming negation—i.e., you negate some seemingly reified construction of mind in order to affirm something about the real nature of awareness that has been obscured by reification. Therefore, at the point of directly experiencing unfindableness, the practitioner looks directly into the field of awareness itself, and will discover something new. With respect to emptiness of self, the practitioner discovers a level of awareness no longer obscured by the sense of self. This "awareness itself" (*rang rig*) now becomes the basis of operation for subsequent meditations—awareness itself, instead of "Dan," guides the subsequent meditations.

With respect to emptiness of thought, emotion, and perception, these various emptinesses of phenomena meditations clean up the tendency to reify thought and emotions so that we don't get lost in them. But, more importantly, they affirm that all seeming thought, emotion, and perception is ultimately none other than the liveliness of primordial wisdom's awakened awareness. The practitioner is able to see beyond these seemingly solid structures of mind into the real nature of lively awareness manifesting itself to itself and knowing itself through its own lively manifestations.

With respect to the convention of time, the practitioner is able to see beyond time (as a reified structure) into the changeless, boundless nature of this oceanlike field of awareness that is always right here. It is important to remember that emptiness meditation doesn't get rid of anything. The emptiness meditator still has a sense of self, still thinks and emotes, and still operates within conventional time. Emptiness meditation doesn't get rid of these constructions; it only gets rid of their capacity to obscure seeing beyond them to the real nature of awareness.

## Emptiness of the Body

Emptiness of the body is a type of emptiness of phenomena meditation. It is generally considered more difficult to realize emptiness of the body, as compared to emptiness of thought, emotion, or perception, because the body is ordinarily taken to be solid and real. The most popular emptiness-of-body meditation in Mahayana Buddhism is attributed to Shantideva. In essence, the practitioner takes the body as the target of the search process. With high-speed awareness, the practitioner thoroughly searches through various regions of the body (as above), until having the direct experience of a "body" as unfindable. At that point, the practitioner looks into the field of awareness and affirms the body as an aspect of the liveliness of the field of awareness, still existing in a relative sense, but ultimately insubstantial. The body becomes "lively awareness" manifesting as "body," insubstantial yet occurring as the pure energy of manifestation. In Prāsaṅgika Mādhyamaka practice, emphasis is given to the fact that "body" is merely a label or designation. In other words, the practitioner learns how language and labeling serve to reify constructions of mind. If we call it a "body," the body becomes reified (Hopkins, 1996).

## Inner Fire Practice as a Support to Pointing Out the Mind's Awakened Nature

The essential point of all emptiness practice is to clean up the seeming solidness and reification of all constructions of mind and to see beyond into the real nature of awakened awareness. A boundless ocean of awakened awareness, or love, is always right here. This real nature is innate, like the sun that always shines. Emptiness practice, when applied to all constructions of mind, clears away the clouds everywhere, enough to see beyond and to experience awakened awareness directly, like seeing the sun shining when the clouds clear away. There are two ways to recognize awakened awareness. At some point, the practitioner may realize a shift in their basis of operation, so that he or she is no longer operating out of the constructs of individual consciousness, but operating out of "being" that boundless ocean of awakened awareness, or love—a place that is no place, has no location, and has no reference points; or at some point, the practitioner may recognize that there is something very distinct about awakened awareness, as compared to ordinary awareness, in its brightness (*dwangs ba*), awakeness (*hrig ge*), or sacredness (*dam pa*). These qualities are variations on the theme of the "lucidity" (*gsal ba*) of awakened awareness. The practitioner must come to recognize awakened awareness in a genuine way, and then stabilize and develop that awakening to the point of having awakened awareness, not ordinary awareness, as the basis of operation at all times and in all situations.

"Energy channels and energy current meditations" (*rtsa lung*) are often used at this point in the overall practice in support of the recognition of the lucidity of awakened awareness. Effective energy meditations brighten the field of awareness, so that, after such practice, the lucidity of awakened awareness becomes more obvious. There are many types of energy meditation practice (Tsong-kha-pa and Mullin, 1996; Thupten Yeshe and Courtin, 1998). One popular type of Great Completion Meditation utilizes the five main branches of energy channels (*ru-shan*): the practice consists of five movement meditations, done in a sitting position. Each specific movement is designed to activate and regulate the flow of subtle energy in these five pathways: the upward-moving channel, associated with the throat chakra; the life-force channel, associated with the heart chakra; the fire channel, associated with the navel chakra; the all-pervasive channels, associated with the skin; and the downward-moving channel, associated with the secret chakra (sex organs). These meditations, using the five main-branch energy channels, indirectly activate the energy currents in the central channel: the consequence of which is a greatly increased lucidity of the field of awareness. The aim is to practice the movement meditations repeatedly, and then look into the field of awareness in order to recognize the lucidity of this awareness, and ultimately to directly know

awakened awareness for what it is. A detailed description of *ru-shan* practice, along with a CD, can be found in Tenzin Wangyal's *Awakening the Sacred Body* (2011).

Central-channel practices are far more direct, but they can be dangerous and should best be done under the guidance of a teacher. The central-channel system consists of two main side channels, each about the diameter of a drinking straw. The right channel is red in color and contains the impure elements of the body-mind. The left channel is white in color and contains the pure elements. The central channel is about the diameter of the index finger and slightly larger on top, like a Tibetan brass horn. The central channel extends from just above the secret chakra, past the heart, past the throat, through the center of the brain, ending at the crown protuberance. It runs about an inch in front of the spinal column. It is blue in color. The two side channels join the central channel in the "vase" region (*bum pa*) just below the navel and above the secret chakra. This vase region looks like the bulb of a fennel plant. The side channels extend upward along the sides of the central channel and open on each side of the crown protuberance. The central energy channel is said to be largely inactive throughout the person's lifetime. Most of the energy from the side channels flows into the central channel during the dying process. The only exception is that the energy becomes active in the central channel at any point in the person's lifetime when they engage in deep concentration and/or energy meditation.

Central-channel meditation begins with visualizing the three main energy channels until this can be done easily. Next, the practitioner imagines "energy drops" (*thig le*) about the size of a pea, stacked just above the mouth of each side channel. After expelling stale air, the practitioner draws the breath into the vase, while simultaneously visualizing the energy drops descending down each side channel, mixing together in the vase, and then being squeezed into the opening of the central channel, while making the vase. "Making the vase" entails lifting the abdominal floor, pressing down the abdominal ceiling to make compression, and then holding the breath. Once the energy drops enter the central channel, the energy starts to churn (like boiling water), and then heat develops. After holding the breath a bit, the practitioner exhales the air slowly while simultaneously visualizing the energy drops becoming separated and reconstituting themselves just above the top of each side channel on each side of the crown protuberance. The visualization is repeated a number of times to churn the energy. The practitioner then ends by looking directly into the field of awareness to recognize the lucidity. Although this practice generally develops a lot of bliss, the bliss is best seen as a side effect and possibly a distraction. The main objective is always to look into the lucid nature of the field of awareness. Even bliss is none other than the liveliness of primordial wisdom's awakened awareness.

Various kinds of inner fire practice differ in the degree of force used. The more force, the quicker the effect; but the more force, the greater the risk. It is absolutely critical to have full control over the movement and direction of energy flow in the central channel. If this is not done with full control, the energy can rise too forcefully and irregularly, with serious side effects. It is generally advised to keep the energy below the navel chakra until proper mastery and control have been learned; and only then slowly learn to raise the energy in the central channel. As mentioned, it is best done under the guidance of a qualified teacher.

## Liveliness and the Clear-Light Body

Once the practitioner has developed awakened awareness as the stable basis of operation in meditation, and in everyday life off the meditation stool, emphasis naturally turns to what is known as the "appearance aspect" of awakening. At this point, the practitioner views whatever arises moment-by-moment—all thoughts, emotions, sights, sounds, tastes, smells, and bodily sensations—as none other than the liveliness of primordial wisdom's awakened awareness. With familiarity, the practitioner develops skill in recognizing whatever arises every moment as a continuous flow of liveliness (Sonam Gurang and Brown, in press) or as "the ups and downs of *dharmakaya*" (Palden Sherab and Tsewang Dongyal, 1998). At some point, the process begins to continue by itself and becomes automatic.

What is the experience of the body like at this level of practice? This level of practice entails what is called "the King of Samadhi" (Thrangu Rinpoche, 1994). With awakened awareness as the stable basis of operation—i.e., operating out of *being* the unbounded wholeness of empty awareness-space—the practitioner puts the intention into viewing the body. With nothing other than the simplest intention, perfect, pinpointed concentration immediately arises, against the backdrop of unbounded wholeness. There is no contradiction whatsoever between simultaneously holding the view of unbounded wholeness and also pinpoint focus. The difference between the King of Samadhi and ordinary concentration is the basis of operation—i.e., where the concentration comes from: awakened Dharmakaya space as compared to ordinary mind and the ordinary sense of self. King of Samadhi practice is said to be like a great bird of prey, like an eagle or the mythical bird, the Garuda. Such a bird flew with a vast, limitless view of the horizon, simultaneously being able to pinpoint its focus on its prey. For the Garuda practitioner, the body hangs within limitless empty awareness-space, like an empty glass bottle filled with light—an energy body vividly shining forth without any substantiality. With familiarity, the body is experienced as light, a manifestation of wisdom energy. With familiarity, within the domain of this clear-light body, all the energy channels and the flow of the energy currents are vividly illuminated. The energy pathways define themselves to themselves, and energy courses through this system with blazing splendor.

In the Bön Six Lamps practice (Brown, in process), the central channel is said to be the ideal locus for a direct experience of the liveliness of primordial wisdom at its most refined level. After setting up the view of the clear-light body and the energy channels, from the perspective of the King of Samadhi, the skilled practitioner puts their intention into locating consciousness within the central channel and, from that perspective, lets that consciousness directly observe the moment-by-moment "play" (*rol ba*) of energy drops coming into existence and then manifesting as the display of increasing organized visions. Herein, the practitioner has the direct realization of the five wisdom energies. Using a secret channel system with familiarity, four levels of "visions" (*snang ba*) emerge, including the magical-display Buddha fields and realms, until the realization of the one great sphere of energy within which all phenomena within the entire display are interconnected by filaments of loving energy, and the entire display is realized simultaneously. Here, the enlightened bodies of a Buddha emerge, and the practitioner locks into the very structure of being.

## The Enlightened Body

In closing, some comment is needed regarding how the body is perceived at the highest levels of realization. In early Mahayana Buddhism, as exemplified in the Lalitavistara Sutra, the depth of enlightenment was described in terms of the thirty-two major marks and the eighty minor marks (Dharmachakra Translation Committee, 2013). As fantastic as this may seem to a Western scientific audience, serious discussion was given to changes in the very structure of the body as a consequence of enlightenment. For example, the size of the ears grew as a consequence of listening to enlightened Truth; the length of the tongue grew from teaching the eloquent speech of the dharma for others' benefit. In the Bön *A Khrid* system (Sonam Gurang and Brown, in press), an enlightened Buddha body is a body of light, and one of the consequences is "no outflows" (*zag med*). In other words, enlightened beings don't need to go to the bathroom; they don't sweat or sneeze. However, they can intentionally produce tears, an endless flow of tears for the suffering of others. Both within the Nyingma Buddhist and the Bön Great Completion Meditation, the ultimate attainment, with respect to the body, is the "rainbow body." Through special practices, the most advanced practitioners can transform the very elemental energies of their body into light. At the moment of death, the body transforms into rainbow light and fades into the sky. Only the inanimate substance of the body, the hair and nails, are left behind. There is no dead body to dispose of. The achievement of "rainbow body" is considered the ultimate sign of accomplishment, the highest form of enlightenment. In other words, full transformation of the body is the hardest and most precious of Yogic feats.

Not so long ago, Westerners believed that the structure of the body remained relatively constant. However, within neuroscience, a new view of the brain has emerged. According to neuroplasticity theory, areas of the brain and the related neurocircuitry change in volume and structure according to usage. For example, the area of the brain associated with concentration, the anterior cingulate cortex increases in size, and also shows changes in white and gray matter, after intensive concentration training. If Western neuroscience has shown that at least the brain changes structure under certain conditions, then maybe the Buddhist and Bön claims that the body can also change structure as a function of the degree of enlightenment is not completely far-fetched.

## References

Brown, D. P. (in process). *The Six Lamps according to the Bon Zhang Zhung oral transmission lineage of great completion.* Translation into English of the root text by Tapihritsa, the ornament of sun-light commentary by Au ri, and the intention and ultimate meaning commentary by Bru sGom rGyal bag Yung Drung.

Gendun Lodro, G. (1998). *Calm-abiding and special insight: Achieving spiritual transformation through meditation.* Ithaca, NY: Snow Lion.

Hopkins, J. (1996). *Meditations on emptiness.* Somerville, MA: Wisdom.

Dharmachakra Translation Committee. (2013). *The play in full* [Lalitavistara Sutra]. Boudhanath, Nepal: Dharmachakra Translation Committee.

Palden Sherab Rinpoche, K., & Tsewang Dongyal Rinpoche, K. (1998). *Lion's gaze* (J. Kaye & S. Harding, Trans.). Boca Raton, FL: Sky Dancer Press.

Sonam Gurang, G., & Brown, D. (in press). *The stages of meditation in the A Khrid Bon Great Completion Meditation.* Somerville, MA: Wisdom.

Tenzin Wangyal Rinpoche. (2011). *Awakening the sacred body: The Tibetan Yoga of breath and movement.* Carlsbad, CA: Hay House.

Thrangu Rinpoche, K. (1994). *Samadhiraja Sutra* [*King of Samadhi*]. Kathmandu, Nepal: Rangjung Yeshe Publications.

Thupten Yeshe, L., & Courtin, R. (1998). *The bliss of inner fire: Heart practice of the Six Yogas of Naropa*. Somerville, MA: Wisdom.

Tsong-kha-pa & Mullin, G. C. (1996). *The six Yogas of Naropa: Tsong Kha pa'a commentary entitled A book of three inspirations: A treatise on the stages of training in the profound path of Naropa's Six Dharmas*. Ithaca, NY: Snow Lion.

# INDEX OF NAMES

Aalberse, M., 173, 458, 464, 465, 680
Abbey, E., 265
Abraham, K., 51, 104fig.9.2, 109fig.9.6, 199, 756
Adler, A., 105fig.9.3
Adler, J., 44, 86n17, 103, 103fig.9.1, 119, 120–21, 123, 616, 852
Adorno, T. W., 392
Aguilera, T. N., 546
Ahissar, M., 133
Aikin, P., 211
Ainsworth, M., 306, 308, 369, 371
Aktar, S., 265
Alexander, F. G., 64, 142
Alexander, F. M., 107, 111fig.9.7, 211, 328, 874–75, 876, 881
Alexander, G., 105fig.9.3, 106fig.9.4, 107, 108fig.9.5, 132, 159, 393, 423, 456
Almaas, A. H., 47, 104fig.9.2, 105fig.9.3, 185, 583, 901
Amati, D., 880
Anagnostopoulou, L., 27, 598, 684–90
Andersen, H., 106fig.9.4, 108fig.9.5
Andriello, B., 31
Antonovsky, A., 891
Anzieu, D., 212, 471
Aposhyan, S., 276, 356–64, 846
Aristotle, 130
Aron, L., 407, 421, 471
Asay, D., 27
Atwood, G., 181, 183, 185, 479
Aucouturier, B., 106fig.9.4, 108fig.9.5, 110, 276, 381, 790–91
Aurobindo, 178fig.
Avicenna, 892
Ayres, A. J., 787–88

Baars, B. J., 415
Bachar, E., 732–33
Bach-y-Rita, P., 131, 142
Baker, E., 26, 103fig.9.1, 104fig.9.2, 110, 274, 445, 450, 554, 658–60, 662, 694
Balint, E., 89
Balint, M., 27, 64, 89, 91, 109fig.9.6, 159, 210, 481, 520, 576, 591, 592, 676
Ball, A., 502
Banse, R., 546
Barbera, M. R., 185
Barratt, B., 503, 775, 834–39
Bartholomew, K., 372
Bartlett, F. C., 322
Bassal, N., 21, 25, 62–68, 71
Bateson, G., 63, 115, 150n27, 177, 179, 186, 257
Bauer, J., 126, 129, 137
Baumann, S., 239
Beck, H., 707
Becker, R. O., 601
Beebe, B., 305, 306, 307, 663
Belz-Knöferl, A., 598, 675–83
Benedetti, G., 245
Bennett-Levy, J., 313
Benor, D., 601
Ben-Shahar, A. R., 702
Bentzen, M., 274, 277–97, 277n33
Berendt, J. E., 880
Berger, H., 72
Bergson, H., 103fig.9.1, 104fig.9.2, 150
Bernard, C., 62–63
Bernfeld, S., 55, 98
Bernstein, N. A., 106fig.9.4, 108fig.9.5
Bertherat, T., 687n67
Beutel, M., 126, 134, 143
Bhat, D., 597, 615–28
Binswanger, L., 103fig.9.1, 109fig.9.6, 913
Bion, W. R., 109fig.9.6, 816, 822
Blankenburg, W., 30

Blasbend, R., 104fig.9.2
Blau, T., 223
Bleuler, P. E., 86, 109fig.9.6, 616
Bloch, S., 546
Blumenthal, B., 103fig.9.1, 104fig.9.2, 110
Boadella, D., 21, 25, 26, 31, 51, 57, 68, 71, 73, 75, 86, 91, 95, 103fig.9.1, 104fig.9.2, 109fig.9.6, 110, 152, 163, 165, 171, 195, 197–203, 224, 274, 275, 326, 456, 458, 465, 481, 484, 495, 497, 509, 554, 558, 572–73, 582, 592, 596, 598, 616, 626, 645–46, 648, 649, 676, 678, 684, 686–87, 696, 741
Boadella, S. S., 197, 684
Bobath, B., 24
Bock, W., 869
Bois, S., 404
Bollas, C., 210, 212, 463, 464–65, 698
Bonnier, P., 238
Borges, J. L., 653
Boss, M., 103fig.9.1, 109fig.9.6, 230
Bourdieu, P., 156, 196
Bower, G. H., 131
Bowlby, J., 202, 276, 369–71, 546, 621, 756, 776
Boyden-Pesso, D., 436
Boyesen, E., 26, 66, 580–86
Boyesen, G., 25, 63, 65n11, 66, 67–68, 103fig.9.1, 104fig.9.2, 109fig.9.6, 137, 170, 497, 531, 545, 580, 582, 583, 585, 617, 624, 625, 650, 676, 740–41, 820
Boyesen, M. L., 63
Boyesen, P., 104fig.9.2
Braatøy, T., 26, 64, 65–67, 104fig.9.2, 110
Brandchaft, B., 91, 183
Bräuer, U. C., 276, 380–86, 497
Brazelton, T. B., 756

929

Brennan, B. A., 601
Breuer, J., 27, 88, 96, 109fig.9.6, 399, 495, 591
Breyer, D., 44
Briere, J., 221
Britt, J. M., 901, 903–11
Brodén, M, 281, 282, 284
Bromberg, P. M., 183, 766
Brooks, C., 40, 43, 44, 876
Brown, C., 601
Brown, D., 901, 921–26
Brown, K., 675, 676
Brown, M., 25, 26, 29, 30, 47, 103fig.9.1, 104fig.9.2, 109fig.9.6, 111fig.9.7, 178, 497, 502, 598, 675, 676
Brown, N., 445
Bruch, H., 242
Bruha, J., 732
Bruner, J., 347
Bruyere, R., 601
Buber, M., 29, 103fig.9.1, 455, 496, 868
Bucci, W., 729, 774, 794, 797, 798–99, 800
Buch, H. J., 21
Bühler, C., 29, 103fig.9.1, 111fig.9.7, 258
Böhme, G., 95
Bülow-Hansen, A., 25–26, 65–67, 68, 104fig.9.2, 110
Bunkan, B., 66, 67
Büntig, W., 21, 23, 47–60, 71–81, 104fig.9.2, 105fig.9.3, 106fig.9.4, 108fig.9.5, 111fig.9.7
Burnham, D., 181
Burrow, T., 45
Burton, L. A., 288

Cacioppo, J. T., 211
Caldwell, C., 184, 391, 426–34, 497, 500, 501, 846
Callahan, R., 167, 764
Campbell, J., 556
Cannon, W. B., 63, 65, 65n11, 67, 68, 617

Carleton, J., 597, 615–28, 702, 724–35
Carter, S., 44, 106fig.9.4, 108fig.9.5
Casals, P., 880
Casriel, D., 27
Cassidy, J., 309
Castellino, R., 335
Castillo, A., 270
Chace, M., 28, 103fig.9.1, 105fig.9.3, 713, 853–54, 855
Chaiklin, S., 854
Chamberlain, D., 334, 336
Charcot, J-M., 86, 88, 616
Chartrand, T. L., 211
Cheek, D., 334
Cho, G. E., 265
Chodorow, J., 44, 105fig.9.3, 798, 849, 852
Clarke, L., 270
Clarkson, P., 454–56, 483
Clynes, M., 547, 879
Cohen, B. B., 24, 121–22, 123, 276, 318, 361, 610, 846
Cohn, R., 24, 109fig.9.6, 111fig.9.7
Comte, A., 178fig.
Conger, J., 591, 650
Connerton, P., 266–67
Conrad, K., 238–39
Cornell, W., 211
Cornell, W. F., 459, 461–69, 598–99, 663, 692–99
Corwin, A., 265
Cott, A., 104fig.9.2
Cozolino, L., 219
Craig, G., 167
Cremerius, J., 89
Crick, E., 134
Crugnola, C. R., 306
Curcuruto, P., 104fig.9.2

Dalai Lama XIV, 922–23
Dalcroze, J., 105fig.9.3, 106fig.9.4, 108fig.9.5
Damasio, A., 83, 127–28, 129, 134–36, 142, 157, 213, 220, 261, 277, 284, 421, 544, 555, 690, 878, 885–86
D'Andrade, R., 265

Darwin, C., 154, 194, 258, 413n41, 545, 662
Davidson, R., 405
Davies, H., 163
Davis, M., 539
Davis, W., 163, 164, 170, 661
de Ajuriaguerra, J., 106fig.9.4, 108fig.9.5, 239–40
Deblinger, E., 318
de Hennezel, M., 650
Delamont, S., 265
Delsarte, F., 106fig.9.4, 108fig.9.5
DeMeo, J., 80
De M'Uzan, M., 794
DePaulo, B. M., 211
Descartes, R., 83, 194, 206, 509, 609, 878
Deutsch, H., 64
Dilthey, W., 152, 152n29, 178fig.
Dimen, M., 698
Dinnerstein, D., 696, 698
Dmochowski, S., 702, 724–35
Dornes, M., 380, 582
Downing, G., 24, 33, 84, 94, 103fig.9.1, 104fig.9.2, 106fig.9.4, 108fig.9.5, 156, 159, 213–14, 261–62, 275, 305–18, 322, 326, 329, 370, 373, 374, 381, 382, 396, 397, 398, 458, 487, 540, 543–44, 554, 555, 557, 565, 575, 578, 663, 708, 741, 796, 829
Dreitzel, H. P., 393n37
Duncan, I., 23, 105fig.9.3, 118, 120, 121, 850–51
Dürckheim, K., 47, 107
Durham, E. H., 42
Dychtwald, K., 532, 535

Ebert, T. C., 211
Ecker, B., 184
Eckert, P., 265
Ehrenfried, L., 24, 103, 106fig.9.4, 108fig.9.5, 111fig.9.7
Eigen, M., 31, 448, 471
Einstein, A., 75, 232, 874
Eissler, K., 900

## Index of Names

Eitingon, M., 98
Ekman, P., 135–36, 212, 535
Ellenberger, H., 84–85
Emde, R., 696
Emerson, W., 32, 109fig.9.6, 335
Engels, F., 55
Engler, J., 921
Epstein, M., 405
Erickson, M., 47, 51, 104fig.9.2, 580
Erikson, E., 181, 294, 297, 893
Espenak, L., 28, 105fig.9.3, 109fig.9.6, 854–55
Evan, B., 729
Ewen, S., 267

Fahrion, S. E., 601
Fairbairn, W. R., 91
Falmagne, R. J., 265
Farrant, G., 334
Fay, T., 358, 361
Fechner, G., 163
Federn, P., 104fig.9.2, 239
Feher, L., 335
Fehr, T., 297
Feldenkrais, M., 43, 105fig.9.3, 106fig.9.4, 107, 108fig.9.5, 393, 666, 687n67, 727, 847, 872, 876–77
Feldman, R., 307
Feldman Barrett, L., 547
Fenichel, C. N., 24, 41, 51, 64, 65, 103, 110
Fenichel, O., 24, 41, 63–64, 65–66, 67, 98, 103, 104fig.9.2, 109fig.9.6, 110
Ferenczi, S., 22–23, 27, 32, 89, 90, 91, 103, 103fig.9.1, 104fig.9.2, 107, 109fig.9.6, 110, 494–95, 544, 576
Fich, S., 534
Fiedler, P., 244
Field, J. (Milner, M.), 210, 215
Field, T., 514, 589
Fisher, R., 458, 774–75, 802–10
Fliess, W., 131
Fodor, N., 109fig.9.6, 334
Fogal, A., 308
Fonagy, P., 240, 308, 315

Ford, C., 503
Fosha, D., 366
Fosshage, J. L., 179
Foucault, M., 83
Foulkes, S. H., 266, 816
Frank, F., 213–14
Frank, R., 211, 870
Frankl, V., 98, 900, 913
French, T. M., 132, 142
Freud, A., 57, 91, 93, 97, 109fig.9.6
Freud, S., 22–23, 25, 27, 41, 47–55, 57, 63, 64, 84–85, 86n17, 87–90, 95–96, 97, 103, 103fig.9.1, 104fig.9.2, 109fig.9.6, 117, 131, 148–49, 151–52, 163–64, 178fig., 186, 194–95, 201, 206, 210, 216, 219–20, 224, 239, 255, 256–57, 336, 392, 399, 433, 444, 448, 471, 479, 480–81, 486, 491, 494–95, 572–74, 577, 581–82, 586, 591, 600, 616, 634, 688, 738, 763, 838, 900
Freudl, P., 26, 531, 580–86
Frey, S., 458
Friedman, H. S., 211, 297, 749
Friesen, W. V., 135–36
Frijda, N., 309
Fromm, E., 24, 43, 57, 64, 65, 98, 104fig.9.2, 111fig.9.7, 394, 866, 901, 913
Fromm-Reichmann, F., 28, 854
Fuchs, M., 24–25, 103fig.9.1, 106fig.9.4, 107, 274, 393, 704
Fuller, B., 879

Gabbard, G., 500
Gäbler, N., 774, 787–92
Gadamer, H. G., 178fig., 259
Gaddini, E., 214
Gaensbauer, T. J., 288
Gallagher, S., 323
Gallo, F., 167
Gariaev, P., 166
Gasanov, 137
Gautama Buddha, 178fig.
Gazzaniga, , 127

Gebauer, R., 80
Gebser, J., 178fig.
Geddes, G., 65
Gedo, J., 179
Geissler, C., 557, 567
Geissler, P., 29, 312, 329, 531, 557, 567, 571–78, 741
Gendlin, E., 31, 111fig.9.7, 118–19, 121, 123, 184, 195, 248–54, 417n47, 472, 544, 623, 837
Gergely, G., 308
Geuter, U., 20, 22–33, 102–11, 530, 543–50, 740
Ghent, E., 698
Gibb, R., 211
Gilbert, P., 313
Gill, M., 471
Gilligan, S., 727
Gindler, E., 20–21, 23–24, 29, 40–45, 58, 64–65, 66, 106fig.9.4, 107, 108fig.9.5, 110, 111fig.9.7, 393–94, 395, 402–3, 532, 866–67, 875–76
Ginsburg, C., 408
Glaser, V., 106fig.9.4, 108fig.9.5, 167
Glazer, R., 297
Glenn, M., 275, 332–41
Glover, E., 64
Glover, J., 64
Goethe, J. W. v., 150
Goldberg, M., 24, 42, 106fig.9.4, 108fig.9.5
Goldenberg, B., 659
Goldstein, K., 64, 65, 65n11, 103fig.9.1, 111fig.9.7, 864–65
Goleman, D., 405, 414
Goodheart, R., 167
Goodman, P., 74, 104fig.9.2, 111fig.9.7, 159, 392–93, 828, 847, 870
Goodrich-Dunn, B., 31, 178
Gottwald, C., 126–44
Graber, G., 275
Graf Dürckheim, K., 103fig.9.1, 105fig.9.3, 106fig.9.4, 108fig.9.5, 109fig.9.6, 230
Graham, M., 32, 105fig.9.3, 852, 853

Grand, I. J., 195, 196, 209–17, 264–70
Gratier, M., 214
Grawe, K., 132, 168, 322, 323, 327, 420
Gray, W., 603
Greenberg, G., 91
Greenberg, J., 471
Greenberg, L., 313, 419–21
Greene, E., 31, 178
Gregory, S., 44
Grepmair, L., 408
Griggers, C., 847, 872–81
Groddeck, G., 22, 87, 103fig.9.1, 107, 109fig.9.6, 544
Grof, S., 30–31, 32, 226, 334
Grohmann, P., 398, 399
Gruen, A., 380, 386
Guilliams, J., 270
Günther, D., 105fig.9.3, 106fig.9.4, 108fig.9.5
Guntrip, H, 91, 109fig.9.6
Gurwitsch, A., 166
Gutheil, T., 500
Guths-Muths, J. C. F., 106fig.9.4, 108fig.9.5

Habermas, J., 148, 151–52, 158, 178
Hackmann, A., 313
Hahnemann, S., 150
Hall, E. T., 266
Hall, R., 104fig.9.2, 105fig.9.3, 106fig.9.4, 108fig.9.5, 111fig.9.7
Hanisch, O., 106fig.9.4, 108fig.9.5
Hanson, J., 265
Harlow, H., 139, 369
Harms, T., 774, 776–84
Harrer, M., 195, 255–62
Harrison, A., 309
Hart, S., 277
Hartmann, M., 164, 238–39
Havrevold, O., 104fig.9.2
Hawkins, E., 121
Hayek, F., 323
Haynal, V., 66
Head, H., 238–39, 324, 381

Hebb, D., 323
Hebenstreit, G., 80
Heckhausen, H., 887
Heckler, R. A., 459, 471–77
Heckler, R. S., 184
Hefferline, R., 392
Heidegger, M., 103fig.9.1, 120, 120n22
Heisterkamp, G., 29, 32, 109fig.9.6, 328
Heller, G., 24, 42, 71, 73, 106fig.9.4, 108fig.9.5, 110, 309, 623
Heller, M. C., 21, 25, 62–68, 458
Hendricks-Gendlin, M. N., 195, 248–54
Hengstenberg, E., 24, 40, 43, 105fig.9.3, 106fig.9.4, 108fig.9.5
Herder, J. G., 150
Herman, J., 766
Hesse, E., 372
Heyer, G. R., 24, 44, 103fig.9.1, 106fig.9.4, 107, 108fig.9.5, 109fig.9.6, 110
Heyer, L., 44, 105fig.9.3, 106fig.9.4, 109fig.9.6, 110
Hilton, R., 458
Hitschmann, E., 51
Hjortso, E. M., 136
Hodann, M., 104fig.9.2
Hoffman, E., 694
Holifield, B., 647
Holland, J., 420
Holmes, A., 313
Hoppe, W., 77
Hopper, E., 266
Horkheimer, M., 392
Horner, A. J., 180, 181, 183
Horney, K., 57, 64, 104fig.9.2, 109fig.9.6, 111fig.9.7
Horowitz, L. M., 372
Houston, G., 820–21
Hulley, L., 184
Hunt, V., 429–30, 601
Hunter, M., 497
Hüther, G., 126, 130, 138–39, 142

IIjine, V. N., 109fig.9.6
Insel, T., 138
Ito, H., 44
Izard, C., 134, 135–36

Jacobs, T., 327
Jacobson, E., 64, 65, 65n11, 98, 211
Jacoby, H., 24, 41, 43, 103fig.9.1, 106fig.9.4, 108fig.9.5, 875–76
Jacomini, V., 717
Jaffe, J., 213
Jahn, F. L., 106fig.9.4, 108fig.9.5
James, W., 65n11, 104fig.9.2, 137, 180, 236, 399, 447
Janet, P., 20, 85–87, 86n17, 107, 109fig.9.6, 163, 367, 395, 494–95, 600, 615, 616, 617, 763
Janov, A., 27, 335, 588, 591
Jantsch, E., 257
Janus, L., 109fig.9.6, 385
Jarlnaes, E., 459, 509–15
Johanson, G. J., 115, 176–87, 459, 471–77, 837
Johnsen, L., 26, 66, 110, 280, 283–84
Johnson, D. H., 21, 104fig.9.2, 106fig.9.4, 108fig.9.5, 111fig.9.7, 115, 117–24, 178, 209, 741
Johnson, L., 104fig.9.2, 869
Johnson, S., 91, 186
Johnson, V. E., 51
Jones, E., 27, 57, 495
Joraschky, P., 239, 537
Joseph, R., 336
Jung, C. G., 28, 30, 86n17, 87, 96, 103fig.9.1, 105fig.9.3, 109fig.9.6, 178fig., 399, 616, 852

Kabat-Zinn, J., 133–34, 405–6
Kagan, J., 288
Kallmeyer, H., 40, 106fig.9.4, 108fig.9.5
Kandel, E. R., 212, 219, 221
Kant, I., 95, 150, 194
Keane, B. W., 43
Kegan, R., 889

Keith-Speigel, P., 500
Keleman, S., 29, 44, 47, 97, 103fig.9.1, 104fig.9.2, 106fig.9.4, 107, 108fig.9.5, 109fig.9.6, 171, 195, 209, 230–36, 275, 301, 302tab.28.2, 312, 373, 397–98, 458, 545, 554, 555, 556, 561, 566, 567, 568, 591, 597, 598, 620, 645–46, 652–57, 675, 676, 678, 680, 684, 688, 694, 734, 741, 758, 798
Kelley, C., 26, 104fig.9.2, 178, 597, 658–60, 662, 694, 794, 796, 799
Kepner, J. I., 111fig.9.7, 184, 497, 597, 600–614, 847, 868–69
Kernberg, O., 30, 92, 97, 109fig.9.6, 199, 484, 546, 738
Kestenberg, J., 372, 853, 858
Kiener, F., 239
Kierkegaard, S., 180
Kinsey, A., 51
Kiphard, E., 382, 383
Klein, M., 64, 91, 109fig.9.6, 202
Koemeda-Lutz, M., 775, 836
Koestler, A., 177, 257
Kofler, L., 106fig.9.4, 107, 108fig.9.5
Kogan, G., 863, 868
Kohut, H., 109fig.9.6, 157, 183, 199, 663, 738, 798, 912
Kolb, B., 211
Kolb, L. C., 239
Korzybski, A., 878
Kraus, F., 58, 72, 164
Krause, R., 546
Krauss-Kogan, W., 847, 863–70
Kretschmer, E., 24, 107
Krieger, D., 601
Krier, L., 901, 903–11
Kris, A. O., 181
Kristeller, L., 106fig.9.4, 108fig.9.5
Kronfeld, A., 51
Krüger, A., 741
Kuhl, J., 163, 168–69, 172, 329
Kuhn, T., 178fig.
Kurtz, R., 30, 103fig.9.1, 104fig.9.2, 105fig.9.3, 106fig.9.4, 108fig.9.5, 111fig.9.7, 159, 176, 178, 180, 184, 221, 274, 279, 312, 391, 405, 408, 411–17, 422, 650, 741

Laban, R., 23, 43, 64, 105fig.9.3, 110, 241, 429, 532, 539, 676, 858
Laborit, H., 63, 200, 202
Lacan, J., 109fig.9.6
Lachmann, F. M., 179
Laing, R. D., 109fig.9.6
Lake, F., 32, 109fig.9.6, 275, 283, 334, 676
Lakin, J. L., 211
Lalich, J., 591
Lane, K., 270
Langer, E., 405
Langer, S., 179
Langfeld, H., 21, 102–11
Lausberg, H., 539
Lawrence, D. H., 450
Lazarus, A., 884
Leboyer, F., 678, 679
LeDoux, J., 126, 132, 134, 284
Leibowitz, J., 879
Leites, A., 464
Lemeignan, M., 546
Lenski, G., 178fig.
LeShan, L., 177
Levine, P., 44, 90, 104fig.9.2, 106fig.9.4, 108fig.9.5, 167, 301, 588, 597, 620, 621, 627–28, 634–35, 703, 763, 764, 765n71
Levy, J., 288
Levy, R., 728
Lewis, R., 373
Lewis, T., 219, 224, 417n45
Lewis Bernstein, P., 853
Lichtenberg, J. D., 94, 103fig.9.1, 109fig.9.6, 177, 179, 275, 329, 368, 370
Lindenberg, E., 23, 24, 41, 56–57, 58, 64, 65, 68, 71, 73, 74, 104fig.9.2, 105fig.9.3, 106fig.9.4, 108fig.9.5, 110
Linehan, M., 406, 886

Ling, P. H., 63
Liss, J., 31, 676
Loevinger, J., 181
Loewald, H., 210
Loftus, E., 256
Lorenz, K., 369
Lorenzer, A., 154
Lowen, A., 26–27, 29, 33, 44, 47, 51–52, 91–93, 95, 103fig.9.1, 104fig.9.2, 110, 153, 156, 170, 195, 205–8, 214, 222, 226, 255, 258, 274, 276, 293, 301, 310, 312, 446, 487, 535, 545, 546, 554, 560, 561, 568, 571, 574–75, 582, 597, 598, 625, 634, 635, 644–48, 650, 658–60, 662, 666, 676, 684, 685, 694, 730, 738, 739–40, 741, 745, 757, 759–60, 799
Ludwig, M., 276, 366–76
Lurija, A. R., 106fig.9.4, 108fig.9.5
Lyons-Ruth, K., 309

Maaz, H. J., 396, 741
Mace, C., 406
Macho, T., 157
MacKaye, S., 106fig.9.4, 108fig.9.5
MacLean, P. D., 616, 765, 878
Macnaughton, I., 597, 633–43
Mahler, M., 109fig.9.6, 201, 288, 573, 738, 741, 856
Mahoney, M. J., 180
Malinowski, B., 55, 104fig.9.2
Malsburg, v. d., 323
Mann, W., 694
Mannarino, A. P., 318
Marcel, G., 30, 83, 396, 396n38
Marcher, L., 26, 66, 68, 90, 211, 280, 459, 509–15, 534, 676, 684, 688
Marcuse, H., 57
Margraf, J., 884
Marlock, G., 20–21, 83–98, 102–11, 114–16, 148–61, 194–96, 215, 274–76, 390–91, 392–400, 454–59, 464, 530–31, 596–99, 663, 702–3, 741, 774–75, 846–47, 900–901

Maron, M., 519
Marshak, M., 468
Martin, L. L., 544
Marvin, R., 309
Marx, K., 178fig.
Maslow, A., 103fig.9.1, 111fig.9.7, 450, 666, 900–901
Masson, J., 89
Masters, W. H., 51
Maurer, Y., 30
Mauss, M., 264, 267
May, J., 503, 597, 774, 794–800
May, P. R. A., 712–13
May, R., 103fig.9.1, 109fig.9.6, 111fig.9.7, 563, 663, 666, 913
McCarty, W., 335
McDougall, J., 693
McKenzie, N., 597, 658–64
McLaughlin, J., 465
Mead, M., 893
Meermann, R., 238–39
Meltzoff, A., 214
Mensendieck, B., 106fig.9.4, 108fig.9.5
Merker, B., 336
Merleau-Ponty, M., 30, 83, 103fig.9.1
Mesmer, F. A., 20, 84–85, 84n14, 109fig.9.6, 163, 616
Meyer, R., 31, 104fig.9.2
Mezirow, J., 275
Mhé, M., 106fig.9.4, 108fig.9.5, 109fig.9.6
Middendorf, I., 106fig.9.4, 107, 108fig.9.5
Miller, A., 89
Milner, M. (Field, J.), 210, 215
Miltner, W. H. R., 260
Mindell, A., 221, 648–49
Minton, K., 588, 702, 763–69
Mitchell, J or S. A., 91, 210
Mitchell, S., 471
Moberg, U., 513
Monsen, J. T., 544
Monsen, K., 26, 544
Moore, M. K., 214
Moreno, J., 28, 105fig.9.3, 111fig.9.7, 744, 853

Morgan, M., 195, 219–28
Morse, B. K., 598, 666–74
Moser, T., 32, 109fig.9.6, 459, 518–28, 741
Mott, F., 109fig.9.6, 275, 334
Mrazek, D., 288
Müller, L. R., 164, 617
Münster, K., 459, 509–15
Murphy, M., 178
Müschenich, S., 80
Myers, F., 399

Nadis, S., 880
Nagler, N., 96
Naranjo, C., 45, 403
Nathanson, C., 41, 64
Navarro, F., 25, 26, 31, 103fig.9.1, 104fig.9.2, 748–49
Neill, A. S., 65, 78, 103fig.9.1, 104fig.9.2, 105fig.9.3
Neisser, U., 322
Nelson, A., 749
Nettheim, N., 547
Neumann, E., 210, 215, 852
Niedenthal, P. M., 134
Nietzsche, , 392
Nietzsche, F., 195
Nijenhuis, E. R. S., 765n71
Nitsun, M., 705
Nunberg, H., 52
Nörenberg, R., 41–42

Ogden, P., 90, 184, 312, 471, 588–89, 616, 702, 703, 763–69
O'Keeffe, G., 232
Olds, J., 138, 176
Olesen, J., 648
Ollendorf, E., 74
Orff, C., 106fig.9.4, 108fig.9.5
Orgass, B., 238
Orr, L., 591
Oschman, J. L., 166, 172, 515

Painter, J., 590
Panksepp, J., 172, 173, 284, 696
Papousek, H., 545

Papousek, M., 545
Parnas, J., 243
Parsons, T., 178fig.
Pasini, W., 66
Paykel, E. S., 706
Payne, H., 372
Perls, F., 24, 29–30, 43–44, 64, 65, 98, 103fig.9.1, 104fig.9.2, 110, 111fig.9.7, 132, 153, 155, 158, 159, 209, 224, 258, 392–93, 394, 397, 399–400, 404, 455, 563, 666, 824–25, 847, 863–67, 870, 872, 879
Perls, L., 24, 43, 64, 110, 111fig.9.7, 863–67, 869, 872, 879
Perry, B., 223, 275, 278, 281, 311, 345–54
Pert, C., 129, 219, 224, 430, 512, 515
Peseschkian, N., 847, 891–96
Pesso, A., 32, 94, 103fig.9.1, 105fig.9.3, 109fig.9.6, 133, 135, 141, 143, 158–59, 178, 184, 312, 407, 436–43, 520, 526, 563, 568, 846
Pestalozzi, J. H., 108fig.9.5
Peterfreund, E., 177, 184, 471
Petzold, H., 24, 33, 89, 94, 103fig.9.1, 105fig.9.3, 106fig.9.4, 107, 108fig.9.5, 109fig.9.6, 111fig.9.7, 154–55, 159, 259–60, 396n38, 421, 521, 536, 540, 556, 703, 763
Philipson, T., 51, 56–57, 78
Phillips, M., 167, 173
Piaget, J., 63, 109fig.9.6, 178fig., 180, 186, 256, 322, 323, 326, 381, 399, 616, 884–85, 888–89
Pierrakos, E., 104fig.9.2
Pierrakos, J., 26, 92, 95, 103fig.9.1, 104fig.9.2, 110, 163, 170, 178, 184, 205, 274, 276, 446, 533, 560, 582, 598, 625, 648, 648n64, 666, 676, 741
Pikler, E., 24, 43, 106fig.9.4, 108fig.9.5, 276, 383–85
Pincus, L., 42
Pitzal, W., 663
Plassman, R., 240

Plato, 194, 903
Plessner, H., 83
Plotinus, 178fig.
Poeck, K., 238–39
Polster, E., 111fig.9.7
Poortman, J. J., 166
Pope, K. S., 500
Porges, S., 126, 280–81, 413n43, 555, 620, 634, 677, 765n71, 778, 829, 838
Posner, M., 134
Priebe, S., 243, 537, 705
Proskauer, M., 24, 106fig.9.4, 108fig.9.5, 109fig.9.6
Puységur, M. d., 84–85, 109fig.9.6

Racker, H., 480, 491
Radó, S., 64, 104fig.9.2
Raknes, O., 25, 26, 31, 64, 65, 66, 67, 103fig.9.1, 104fig.9.2, 110, 197, 580, 740
Raleigh, M. J., 139
Ramachandran, V., 130, 136
Rand, M., 27, 44, 184
Randall, R., 823
Randolph, M., 391, 444–50
Rank, O., 23, 91, 94, 103, 103fig.9.1, 109fig.9.6, 111fig.9.7, 275, 334
Ray, S., 591
Razi, 896
Reich, A., 41, 64, 65, 98
Reich, E., 40, 41, 63, 104fig.9.2, 622, 650, 774, 775, 777, 784, 811–14
Reich, P., 74
Reich, W., 20–21, 23, 25, 26–27, 28, 29, 30, 41, 43, 47 58, 62 63, 64, 65–66, 67–68, 71–81, 86, 87–88, 90–91, 92, 96, 97–98, 103, 103fig.9.1, 104fig.9.2, 107, 109fig.9.6, 110, 111fig.9.7, 115, 117, 120–21, 123, 126, 149–50, 150nn27–28, 152, 153, 158, 164–65, 166, 170, 171, 178, 195, 196, 198–99, 201, 202, 205, 210–11, 214, 222, 274, 275, 276, 278, 279, 282, 293, 301, 312, 367, 370, 374, 393, 394, 445–46, 448, 457–58, 463, 464–65, 480–81, 483, 483n48, 485, 485n49, 486, 487, 494–95, 532, 534, 535, 544–45, 546, 554, 555, 558, 560, 562, 580, 581–82, 584–85, 589–90, 596, 597, 598, 600, 601, 615, 616, 617–18, 625, 633–35, 637, 644, 645, 658–60, 668, 669, 671, 673, 678, 680, 693, 694, 695–96, 698, 720, 739, 745, 748, 751, 758, 774, 776–78, 794, 796, 798, 799, 823–24, 847, 863–64, 865, 867, 878, 900, 912
Reichelt, F., 851
Rellensmann, D., 21, 102–11
Reynolds, J., 138
Rhumber, L., 164
Richter, A., 398–99
Ricoeur, P., 151–52
Riemann, F., 913
Rispoli, L., 31, 104fig.9.2, 109fig.9.6, 110
Ritter, P., 103fig.9.1, 104fig.9.2
Rittmeister, J., 107
Rizzolatti, G., 140
Robinson, T. E., 211
Roche, M. A., 45
Rogers, C., 29, 91, 105fig.9.3, 111fig.9.7, 119, 248, 421, 455, 666, 798, 912
Rogoff, B., 265, 266
Rolef Ben-Shahar, A., 724–35
Rolf, I., 105fig.9.3, 106fig.9.4, 108fig.9.5, 111fig.9.7, 666, 687n67, 847, 870, 873–74, 876
Rolland, R., 900
Romanyshyn, R., 463
Roosevelt, E., 232
Rosen, J., 591
Rosen, M., 44–45
Rosenberg, J. L., 27, 104fig.9.2, 105fig.9.3, 111fig.9.7, 567, 598, 666–74
Rosenblatt, A., 177
Ross, C., 733
Rossi, E., 684

Roth, G., 126, 127, 130, 256, 261, 725
Rothschild, B., 90, 588, 703, 764
Rousseau, J., 264
Rubenfeld, I., 178, 184, 502, 626, 847, 872–81
Rudolf, G., 150
Rüegg, J. C., 128, 136, 137
Röhricht, F., 237–45, 313, 503, 530, 532–40, 702, 704–14, 775
Rushforth, W., 684
Russell, J. A., 547
Rywerant, Y., 876

Sachse, R., 328, 741
Sameroff, A., 177
Samuels, A., 480
Sander, L., 369
Sándor, P., 31–32
Sartory, A., 274, 301–3
Sartre, J. P., 103fig.9.1
Sass, L. A., 243
Satir, V., 807
Schacter, D., 130–31
Scharfetter, C., 30, 245, 712
Scheid, V., 382, 383
Schelling, F., 150
Scherer, K. R., 546
Schilder, P., 104fig.9.2, 105fig.9.3, 107, 109fig.9.6, 195, 238–39, 381, 856
Schilling, F., 382
Schlaffhorst, C., 106fig.9.4, 108fig.9.5
Schlimme, J. E., 704
Schmidt, V., 78
Schmidt-Zimmermann, I., 270, 530, 553–69
Schmitt, L., 106fig.9.4, 108fig.9.5
Schneider, S., 884
Schoop, T., 28, 105fig.9.3, 851
Schopenhauer, A., 83, 195
Schore, A., 126, 171, 172, 202, 219, 222, 227, 293, 369, 408, 446, 487, 616, 663, 829, 917
Schrauth, N., 26, 530, 543–50, 740
Schroeter, V., 374
Schultz, J. H., 106fig.9.4, 107, 108fig.9.5

Schutz, W., 111fig.9.7
Schwartz, R., 180, 183, 184, 185, 407
Scott, J., 706
Sechehaye, M., 591
Seewald, J., 383
Segal, Z., 313
Seligman, S., 366
Selver, C., 24, 40, 41, 43–44, 65, 103, 106fig.9.4, 108fig.9.5, 110, 111fig.9.7, 393–94, 402–3, 404, 867, 872, 875–76, 881
Serrano Hortelano, X., 702, 748–54
Shahar-Levy, Y., 858
Shapiro, F., 90, 659, 764
Sharaf, M., 21, 73
Sheldrake, R., 166, 197
Sherrington, C., 622
Shontz, F. C., 239
Sibler, C., 65
Siegel, D., 219, 414, 487n53, 667
Siegel, E., 32, 103fig.9.1, 105fig.9.3, 109fig.9.6, 849, 854–57
Sifneos, P., 794
Simmel, E., 98
Simmons, B., 104fig.9.2
Sinatra, S., 645, 647
Singer, M., 591
Skinner, B. F., 178fig.
Slade, A., 369
Slater, V. E., 601
Sloterdijk, P., 275, 380
Smith, D., 676
Smith, E., 497, 847, 868
Smith, L. B., 382
Smith, S., 591
Solms, M., 220–21
Sørensen, L., 286
Soth, M., 214, 459, 479–92, 733, 775, 816–31
Speads, C., 24, 44, 103, 106fig.9.4, 108fig.9.5, 110
Spielrein, S., 96
Spinoza, B., 202, 487n52
Spitz, R., 369, 756, 776

Spitzer, M., 134, 141
Staemmler, F., 869
Stark, M., 184, 185, 454–55, 466, 473, 483
Stattman, J., 30, 103fig.9.1, 104fig.9.2, 105fig.9.3, 106fig.9.4, 108fig.9.5, 109fig.9.6, 111fig.9.7, 458, 556, 575, 592, 818
Staunton-Jones, K., 244
Stebbins, G., 106fig.9.4, 108fig.9.5
Steele, C. M., 266
Steiner, R., 866
Stephens, N., 265
Stepper, S., 544
Stern, D., 94, 109fig.9.6, 129, 153, 201, 202, 210, 221, 222, 224, 227, 275, 285, 286, 287, 305, 307, 309, 325, 327–28, 369, 370, 374, 381, 383, 447, 471, 545, 546, 577, 663, 695–96, 741–42, 756, 823, 829, 851, 913
Stevens, B., 111fig.9.7
Stolorow, R., 181, 183, 185, 479
Stolze, H., 24, 42, 95, 103fig.9.1, 106fig.9.4, 108fig.9.5, 109fig.9.6, 393
Strack, F., 544
Strauss, C., 265
Strean, H. S., 480
Struve, J., 497
Sullivan, H. S., 28, 43, 105fig.9.3, 854
Sulz, S., 847, 883–89
Sun Ra, 468
Suzuki, D. T., 403
Suzuki, S., 901
Szent-Györgyi, A., 164

Tabachnick, B. G., 500
Talge, N. M., 337
Tardos, A., 383
Target, M., 240
Tart, C., 405
Teasdale, J., 313
Tenzin Wangyal Rinpoche, 924

Tharner, A., 621
Thelen, E., 180, 382
Theweleit, K., 196
Thich Nhat Hanh, 393
Thickstun, J., 177
Thielen, M., 702, 737–45
Thompson, C., 43, 537
Tonella, G., 702, 717–22, 756–62
Torres de Beā, E., 239
Totton, N., 588, 624, 798
Traue, H., 27
Trautmann-Voigt, S., 32, 741, 846, 849–59
Trevarthen, C., 829
Tronick, E. Z., 210, 275, 305, 307–8, 309, 345–54, 369, 663
Tropp, S. J., 104fig.9.2
Trümpy, B., 105fig.9.3, 106fig.9.4, 108fig.9.5
Trungpa, C., 901
Tulkin, S. R., 288
Turnbull, , 220–21

Uexküll, T., 30, 274–75
Ukhtomsky, A. A., 106fig.9.4, 108fig.9.5
Ungerer, D., 239

van der Kolk, B. A., 86, 89, 126, 167, 399, 557, 588, 616, 703, 767
Vaughan, F., 405
Vaughan, S., 219
Veening, C., 106fig.9.4, 108fig.9.5
Velzeboer, J., 104fig.9.2
Ventling, C., 374, 731
Verny, T., 334
Vissing, S. F., 136
Voigt, B., 32
Volkas, A., 270
von Bertalanffy, L., 367
Vygotsky, L., 31, 63

Waal, N., 26, 64, 65, 68, 104fig.9.2, 110, 777

Wagner-Jauregg, J., 104fig.9.2
Waldstein, S. R., 211
Wallace, B. A., 406
Wallbott, H., 545–46
Wallock, S., 849
Wallon, H., 106fig.9.4, 108fig.9.5, 109fig.9.6, 110, 381
Walsh, R., 405
Walter, C., 877
Warnecke, T., 500
Warzlawick, P., 184
Waterston, J., 502
Watson, J., 178fig.
Watts, A., 43, 393, 394, 404, 901
Watzawick, P., 185
Weaver, J., 20–21, 40–45, 775, 811–14
Weber, M., 178fig.
Weber, R., 496
Wehowsky, A., 115, 163–73, 275, 322–29

Weinberg, M. K., 663
Weiss, H., 20–21, 102–11, 114–16, 194–96, 255–62, 274–76, 402–9, 419–24, 454–59, 464, 530–31, 596–99, 663, 702–3, 774–75, 846–47, 900–901, 912–19
Weizsäcker, V. v., 24, 107
Welch, M., 335
Welldon, E., 109fig.9.6, 818
Wenger, J., 137
Westland, G., 459, 494–504
Whitehouse, M., 28, 44, 103fig.9.1, 105fig.9.3, 119, 121, 852, 854
Whitmont, E., 43
Wiegmann, M., 103
Wigman, M., 23, 28, 43, 44, 103, 105fig.9.3, 851, 852
Wilber, K., 115, 163, 165, 166, 167, 173, 176, 177–78, 257, 405, 765, 829, 921

Williams, J., 313
Winnicott, D., 26, 27, 91, 94, 103fig.9.1, 109fig.9.6, 181, 199, 210, 215, 260, 274, 369, 383, 421, 463, 465, 467–68, 471, 482, 585, 591, 658, 688, 788, 820, 859
Witten, E., 880
Wolfe, T., 52, 73
Wolkenstein, E., 104fig.9.2
Wortham, S., 265
Wygotsky, L. S., 106fig.9.4, 108fig.9.5

Yalom, I., 818, 913
Yau, S-T., 880
Young, C., 21, 31, 47, 71–81, 459, 531, 587–93, 597, 644–50
Yuasa, Y., 123

Zinker, J., 868

# SUBJECT INDEX

Abdominal segment, 669, 672–73
Abortion, 336–38, 341
Abstinence, 22, 28, 76, 96, 183, 201, 205–8, 495, 500
Abuse, 89, 223, 311, 431, 500, 503, 519, 587, 606, 620, 673, 695, 725, 766
Abusive touch, 589
Accommodation, 180, 322, 323, 360, 885
Actions, 3, 361–62, 549fig.53.1, 549fig.53.2
Activation, 546–47, 640–41
Acupressure, 511, 513
Acupuncture, 512, 513, 601, 645
Adaptation, 57, 368, 371, 385, 446, 752
  body-mind, 91
  character, 607
  coping, 621, 655
  creative, 865
  defensive, 766, 767, 820
  environmental, 885
  global, 324
  hysteria, 282
  mechanisms, 637, 718–20, 778
  neurotic, 600
  social, 839
  stress, 619, 622
Adaptive assimilation, 719
Adolescence, 341, 698
Adrenaline reaction, 59
Adult attachment, 372
Adult movements, 361–62
Adynamic conditions, 707–8
Affect, 134–35
Affect cycle, 740
Affect discharge. *See* catharsis
Affect motor schemas, 2, 12, 156–58, 160
Affect regulation, 33, 115, 210, 244, 278, 290, 369, 446, 498, 532, 537, 547, 622, 727, 728, 886
Affective arousal, 2
Affective cycle, 548–50, 549fig.53.1-53.2, 568, 740
Affective domain, 2, 239
Affective expression, 328
Affective-motor schemas, 33, 94, 156–58, 160, 275, 322–29, 884–85
Afferent modulations, 353, 353fig.32.2
Aggression, 467–68, 561
Aging, 233–34
Agitated/aggrieved conditions, 708–9
Aikido, 105fig.9.3, 589
Alcoholism, 759
Alexander technique, 10–11, 44, 117, 874–75
Ambivalence, 372–73
Analytic social psychology, 111fig.9.7
Analytical body psychotherapy, 32, 109fig.9.6
Analytical dance and movement therapy, 32
Analytical psychology, 109fig.9.6
Analytic/insight orientation, 14–15
Anesthesia, 339
Anger, 72, 635, 636, 645, 648, 660, 662, 670, 671, 673, 708–10, 731
Anguish, 449
Animalistic magnetism, 84, 84n14
Anorexia nervosa, 242, 267, 270, 536, 724, 726, 727, 728, 729, 730
Anxiety, 72, 93, 883–84
Anxiety disorders, 76, 242, 709–11
Applications
  Child Somatic Psychotherapy, 787–92
  Couples Therapy, 802–10
  Emotional First aid, 811–14
  Group Therapy, 816–31
  overview, 773–75
  Parent-Child Body Psychotherapy, 776–84
  Research, 834–40
  subsymbolic processing, 794–800
Arbeit am menschen. *See* Gindler work
Archetypes, 30, 199, 556
Armoring, 78
  Character armoring, 26, 45, 53, 635–36
  Muscular armoring, 29, 57–59
Arousal, 59, 546–48, 567, 588, 610, 612, 618–22, 624, 627
Arrested development, 15, 93
Artificial intelligence, 63
Artificiality, 518–28
Assessments, 532–40
Assimilation, 158, 180, 185–86, 322, 323, 719, 885
Association, 348–52, 398–99, 449, 495, 538, 574, 598
Attachment, 305, 308–9, 621–22, 778–79
Attachment bonds, 781–82
Attachment relationship, 373
Attachment style, 370–72, 375–76
Attachment theory, 2, 222–23, 366–76
Attention, 133–34, 402, 781
Attunement. *See* Mirroring
Authentic movement, 5, 44, 103fig.9.1, 105fig.9.3, 117, 119–21
Authenticity, 918
Autogenic training, 106fig.9.4
Autonomic nervous system (ans), 15, 59, 68, 72, 280–83, 610–11, 612fig.59.9, 615–28
Autonomy, 2, 5–6, 170, 178, 183, 288, 325, 326, 372, 380–86, 400, 446, 489, 499, 561, 567–68, 573, 598, 675, 680, 684, 687, 688, 712, 789, 790, 913

939

Autonomy structure, 288, 288n35, 613, 613n62
Aversion, 72, 149, 158, 212, 323, 325, 329, 368, 500, 559, 721, 756
Avoidant, 225, 227, 242, 281, 284, 312, 371, 372, 373, 545, 711
Awakened body, 909–10
Awareness, 3, 14, 24, 402–8, 622–23, 922–23. *See also* mindfulness; Sensory Awareness
Awareness, embodied, 600–609
Awareness through movement, 43, 876–77

Babies. *See* Infants
Basic being experience, 609–10
Behaviorism, 178fig.15.1, 380
Being, 15, 395–96, 610, 908
Belonging, 733–35
Biochemistry, 178fig.15.1
Biodynamic psychology, 26, 66, 67–68
Biodynamic psychotherapy, 32, 66, 625–26
Biodynamics, 31, 103fig.9.1, 104fig.9.2
Bioelectrics, 72
Bioenergetic analysis, 26, 31, 104fig.9.2, 109fig.9.6, 110, 279, 625, 730–31
Bioenergetics, 13, 27, 31, 60, 103fig.9.1, 303tab.28.3, 685
Bioenergy, 14, 25, 165
Bions, 73–74, 76
Bio-psycho-social model, 30
Biosynthesis, 7, 26, 31, 103fig.9.1, 104fig.9.2, 115, 626
Biosystemics, 31
Bipolar disorder, 706
Birth reflex, 66
Blockages, bioenergy, 14
Bode gymnastik, 43
Bodily awareness, 780–81
Bodily dialogue, 32
Bodily experience, 237–45, 411–17
Body culture movement, 23, 103, 106fig.9.4, 108fig.9.5

Body dysmorphic disorders, 97
Body expression, 258–59
Body fantasy, 857
Body image, 97, 130, 237–45, 324, 856–57
Body knowledge, 260–61
Body language, 258–59
Body organizing, 309–10, 313–16
Body points, 32
Body psychotherapy, 104fig.9.2. *See also* Psychology; Psychotherapy; Therapy
  acceptance of, 7
  contraindications, 714
  defined, 11
  erotic field, 698–99
  evolution of, 6–8
  field of, 2–3
  foundational structures, 13
  graphic overview, 102–10
  historical development of, 3–5
  influences, 102, 103fig.9.1
  interventions, 553–69
  metapsychology, 5
  models, 312–13
  polarities, 13–16
  practice, 5, 385–86, 553–69
  and psychotherapy, 11–13
  reformulations, 613–14
  roots of, 103fig.9.1
  schools of, 9–10
  spectrum of, 8–9
  term use, 17
Body psychotherapy field, 5–6, 16, 177–79
Body regression, 575–76
Body schema, 97, 237–45, 324
Body segments, 669–74
Body structure, 258–59
Body therapies, 106fig.9.4, 108fig.9.5
Body therapy, 10–11, 20, 103fig.9.1, 107
Body therapy movement, 110
Body unconscious, 219–28
Body-centered psychotherapy, 692–99
Body-culture movement, 23–25

Body-focused therapy, 316–18
Body-language dialogue, 32
Body-mind centering, 24, 117, 121–22
Body-mind experience. *See also* felt sense
Body-mind fragment, 488–89
Body-mind relationship, 88, 96
Body-mind relationship model, 206fig.18.1
Body-mind resources, 15
Body-mind-spirit unity, 128–29
Bodynamic psychotherapy, 303tab.28.3
Bodynamics, 26, 66, 68, 104fig.9.2, 109fig.9.6, 280
Body-oriented psychotherapies, 264–70
Body-oriented psychotherapy, 30, 45. *See also* Body Psychotherapy
Body-oriented work, 556–69, 863–64, 867–70
Body-related processes, 532–40
Body-self experience, 23–25
Bodywork methods, 10–11, 30. *See also* Massage
Bohr effect, 363–64
Bonding, 781–84
Bonding therapy, 27
Borderline disorder, 23, 30
Bottom-up processes, 95
Boundaries, 562
Boundary setting, 561
Brain, 66n12, 128, 129–30, 511–12, 609–10, 886–89
Breath, 107, 633–43
Breath block, 58
Breath education, 11
Breath healing, 106fig.9.4, 108fig.9.5
Breath techniques, 107
Breath therapy, 11, 106fig.9.4
Breath work, 106fig.9.4, 108fig.9.5
Breathing, 31, 41, 59, 64
Breathing awareness, 641
Breathing patterns, 23, 86
Breathing practice, 557–58

Breathing stool, 559–60
Breathing techniques, 44
Breathing therapy, 24
Breathing wave, 59
Breathwork, 24–25, 31, 636, 638–40
Buddhism, 30, 43, 105fig.9.3
Budo, 105fig.9.3
Bülow-Hansen-institute, 104fig.9.2
Bön meditation, 921

Calibration, 423
Cancer, 73, 75–78, 80
Cannon's model, 68
Catharsis, 16, 27, 58, 84–85, 783–84
Catharsis affect, 90
Cathartic method, 86, 88
Cellular metabolism, 76
Centering, 26, 562–63, 733–35, 760–61
Cephalalgia, 749–51
Cervical segment, 669, 671
Cesarean section, 339
Chace circle, 853–54
Change, 315–16
    Change Process, 414–17
    Meaning-making, 351
    Windows of Opportunities for, 225–28
Character, 155–60. *See also* Character structure
Character, understanding, 464–65
Character analysis, 52–53, 72, 92
Character armoring, 26, 45, 53, 635–36
Character development, 296–97
Character formation, 93, 278–79
Character resistance patterns, 53
Character structure, 12, 23, 27, 52–53, 636, 638–40
    anal, 277, 291, 535
    compulsive-dominant/submissive polarity, 649
    hysteric, 283–84, 288, 302tab.28.1
    impulsive, 52, 53
    masochistic, 53, 280, 290–93, 302tab.28.1, 303tab.28.3, 636, 638, 659
    and muscle tone, 686–87
    narcissistic borderline, 92, 225
    neurotic, 53, 55, 66, 86, 88
    ocular segment, 283, 659–60
    oral, 280, 286–87, 303tab.28.3, 636, 638, 639, 659
    oral-compensation, 303tab.28.3
    phallic-narcissistic, 53, 302tab.28.1
    phallic-rigid, 280, 294–96
    psychopathic, 280, 289–90, 303tab.28.3, 636, 638, 659
    rigid, 280, 294–96, 303tab.28.3, 636, 638, 659
    rigid-hysteric, 280, 303tab.28.3
    sadistic, 292–93
    schizoid, 635, 638, 639, 642, 659, 713–14, 730, 916
    schizoid, 93, 183–84, 227, 280, 281, 282, 283–84, 303tab.28.3, 635
    schizoid-hysteric, 282
    schizoid-hysteric, 280, 649
Character structure model, 30
Character structure theory, 91–92
Character styles, 827–28
Character themes, 912–19
Character theory, 301–3, 303tab.28.3, 914–15
Character theory (Keleman's), 302tab.28.2
Character theory (Reich's), 302tab.28.1
Character types, 913–14. *See also* Character structure
Character-analytic vegetotherapy, 57–59, 65, 73, 87, 110
Character-analytic work, 6
Character-analytical technique, 59
Character-analytical theory, 25, 153–55
Characteristics, 310–11
Child development, 33, 92, 311–12, 741–43. *See also* infant development
Child somatic psychotherapy, 787–92. *See also* Parent-Child Body Psychotherapy

Child therapy, 31
Childhood attachment theory, 369–70
Children, 776–84
Choline reaction, 59
Chronic defense structures, 23
Chronic expression, 550
Clear-light body, 925–26
Client-centered psychotherapy, 31, 111fig.9.7
Clinical assessment, 338–39, 530–31
Clinical formulation, 532–40
Clinical implications, 140–44, 313
Clinical practice, 244–45
Cognition limitations, 127
Cognitions, 31
Cognitive assessments, 33
Cognitive behavioral therapy, 3, 8, 12, 114, 883–89
Cognitive theory, 95
Cognitive-affective consciousness, 30
Coherencies, 426–28
Cohesions, 426–28
Collapsed structure, 302tab.28.2
Collective/individual polarity, 817–18
Communism, 7, 56, 74, 80, 97
Complementarity, 171–72
Compression, 63
Compulsive character, 53, 302tab.28.1
Concentrative movement therapy, 24, 42
Concept formation, 237–45
Conceptual systems, 122–24
Conflict, 23, 25–28, 757, 893
Conflict resolution, 53
Conflict-oriented work, 27, 563–65, 893
Consciousness, 2, 5, 16, 133–34, 165–66, 223, 336, 402–8, 904–5
Consciousness psychology, 48
Contact/contactlessness, 394–95
Containment, 562, 662
Contingency. *See* Mirroring
Continuum, 117, 426–28
Conventional energies, 166–68
Coping, 893
Core affects, 547–48

Core energetics, 26, 103fig.9.1, 104fig.9.2, 303tab.28.3
Core organizers, 180
Core self, 610–11
Corrective emotional experience, 14, 16
Corrective experiences, 436–43
Cortisol, 514
Counterpoint, 448
Countertransference, 29, 456, 479–92
Couples therapy, 802–10
Creative unconscious processes, 215
Creativity, 857
Crises, 84n14, 708–9
Critical social theory, 57
Cultural values, 178fig.15.1, 264–70, 628, 891–96
Cybernetics, 63

Dance, 2, 23, 42, 65, 103fig.9.1, 106fig.9.4, 107, 108fig.9.5
Dance movement therapy, 11, 28, 849–59
Dance psychotherapy, 65
Dance therapy, 31, 32, 64, 68, 103, 103fig.9.1, 105fig.9.3
  aim, 850
  Body Image, 856–57
  East Coast approach, 853–55
  German Expressionist, 850–51
  Movement Analysis, 858–59
  overview, 849–50
  resources, 857
  Rhythmic-Dynamic Active Dialogue, 857–58
  West Coast approach, 851–53
Deadly orgone radiation, 79–80
Death wish, 52, 53, 96
Defense, 23, 52, 53, 214–15, 396–98, 589–91. *See also* Character structures; repression
Defense function, 23
Defense mechanism, 16, 97, 718–19
Defense processes, 23, 543–50
Defensive character formations, 92, 93

Denials, somatic, 214–15
Dense structure, 302tab.28.2
Depression, 241, 285–87, 290, 335, 337, 498, 514, 537, 619, 626, 695, 705, 706–7, 724, 725, 731–32, 739, 894, 895
  oral, 756–62
Depressive (dependent) personality structure, 707–8
Depressive disorders, 706–9
Depressive process, 756–57
Depth psychology, 3, 7, 83–98, 104fig.9.2, 148–61
Depth therapy, 103fig.9.1
Development, 663–64
  arrested, 15, 93
  changes, 351
  character, 296–97
  child, 33, 92, 311–12, 741–43. *See also* infant development
  disorders, 91
  early childhood, 222, 741–43
  early motor, 356–64
  embryonic, 359–60
  free motoric, 383–85
  functional-developmental orientation, 14–15
  infant, 2, 78, 91, 129
  neonatal, 280–83
  neuroaffective, 2, 277–80, 285, 294, 296, 298, 346–47
  Normal, 912–13
  Pathological Development, 912–13
  prenatal, 280–83
  psychology of, 32–33, 94–95, 274–76, 277–97, 346–47
  psycho-sexual, 91
  research, 33
  somatic self-development, 230–36, 279–80, 788–90
  spiritual development, 903–11
  themes, 915–16
Developmental changes, 351
Developmental disorders, 91
Developmental psychology, 32–33, 94–95, 274–76, 277–97, 346–47

Developmental themes, 915–16
Developmentally needed (reparative) modality, 456
Developmental-psychological perspective, 346–47
Diagnosis, 197–99
Diagnostic parameters, 556
Diagnostics, 240–41, 532–40
Dialogic body model, 32
Dialogic relationships, 15
Diaphragm block, 86
Diaphragmatic segment, 669, 672
DIDE diagnosis, 749–51
Dimensions of resonance, 201–3
Discharge cycle, 590
Disindentification, 406–8
Dismissive, 372
Disorders, 33, 895–96
  eating, 724–35
  mental, 704–14
  overview, 702–3
  Psychosomatic Disorders, 748–54, 895–96
Disruption, 699
Dissociation, 87, 88, 214–15, 398–99
Disturbances, 788–90
DOR experiments, 79–80
Dreams, 30, 31, 43, 652–57
Drive, 581
Drive theory, 91
Dyadic regulation, 730, 732–33
Dyadic resonance, 829–30
Dynamic model, 94, 367–68, 539
Dysmorphobia, 97
Dysregulation, 766–67

Early childhood development, 32, 130, 222, 280–83, 305–18, 351, 356–64, 380–82, 741–43
East coast approach, 853–55
Eastern philosophies, 12, 30, 103fig.9.1, 105fig.9.3, 123
Eating disorders, 33, 97, 242, 724–35
Echoing. *See* Mirroring
Ecological movement, 6
Efferent distribution, 350, 350fig

Effleurage, 63
Effort, voluntary, 231–32
Ego, 30, 32, 52, 127–28, 489–90, 687, 757, 907–8
Ego psychology, 23, 49
Élan vital, 104fig.9.2
Electro-dermograph, 72
Electroencephalographs, 72
Electro-physiology, 59, 72
Embedded thinking, 90
Embodied attunement, 829–30
Embodied awareness, 600–609
Embodied experiences, 234–36
Embodied human needs, 368–69
Embodied interpersonal patterns, 827–28
Embodied knowledge, 14
Embodied mind, 209–17
Embodied self, 609–13
Embodied thinking, 90
Embodied unconscious, 209–17
Embodiment, 3, 12, 14, 32, 88, 97, 209–17, 315–16, 366–76, 600–614, 837–38, 910–11
Embryology, 336, 677–78
EMDR (eye movement desensitization and reprocessing), 90, 729
Emergence, 826–29
Emigration, 850–51
Emotion, 134–35, 544
Emotion formation, 135–36
Emotional attunement, 88
Emotional balance, 624
Emotional cycle, 3, 397, 550, 625
Emotional defense processes, 543–50
Emotional energy, 49
Emotional experience, 6, 29
Emotional expression, 3
Emotional first aid, 811–14
Emotional flooding, 637
Emotional injuries, 88–90
Emotional plague, 78–79
Emotional process, 877–78, 880–81
Emotional regulation, 88, 625
Emotional states, 88
Emotional theory, 543–50

Emotions, 31, 32, 53, 88, 155–60, 877–81
Emotions, basic, 546–47
Empathy. See mindfulness, 224–25
Empiricism, 178fig.15.1
Emptiness, 923
Enactments, 327–28
Encounter, 111fig.9.7, 327–28
Encounter group movement, 27
Endorphins, 513–14
Energetic body, 13–14
Energetic monism, 152–53
Energy, 49, 201–3, 600–609, 758
Energy concept, 115, 163–73, 824–26
  Multilevel Model, 172
Energy model, 14
Energy paradigms, 170–71
Energy system, 600–614
Energy-monism, 165–66
Engrams, 32
Enlightened body, 926
Enlightenment, 95
Epigenetics, 335–36
Equality, 818–19
Eros, 95–97
Eroticism, 692–99
Esalen institute, 28, 44, 66, 106fig.9.4, 108fig.9.5, 110
Ethics of touch, 500–504, 589
Eutony, 106fig.9.4, 108fig.9.5, 117
Evidence base, 836
Evidence experience, 259–60
Evolution, 62–63
Excitation, 550, 697fig.68.1
Existentialism, 109fig.9.6
Existentialism, 30, 104fig.9.2, 109fig.9.6, 111fig.9.7, 609–10, 900–901, 912–19
Expanding, 15
Experience, 28–31, 90–94, 129, 130, 176–87, 234–36, 347–48, 419–24, 790–91, 905–6, 909–10
Experiential work, 117–24, 557–58
Expression, 28, 88, 129, 549fig.53.1, 549fig.53.2, 550, 658–64, 760–61
Expressional dance, 31, 105fig.9.3

Expressionist dance, 23, 28
Expressive movements, 14, 28, 545–46
Expressiveness, 88, 559
External-objective perspective, 257–58
Eye movement desensitization and reprocessing. See EMDR
Eyes, Centering, 563

Facial expression, 808–9
Facing, 658–64
Family systems, 55, 67
Fantasy, 662–63, 857
Fascism, 54, 56, 57, 97, 103, 107
Fear, 49, 50–51, 59, 66n12, 66nas, 72, 77
Fear system, 138–39
Feedback loops, 95
Feeling, 7, 544, 757–58
Feelings, 134–35, 877–78
Feldenkrais-method, 10, 43, 117
Felt sense, 5, 7, 14, 31, 90, 248–54
Feminism, 6
Ferenczian psychoanalysis, 30, 32
First-person perspective, 258
Flooding, 140
Flow, 809–10, 826–29
Focused movement therapy, 11
Focusing, 13, 31, 111fig.9.7, 117, 118–19
Forceps delivery, 339
Forgetting. See repression
Formative psychology, 93, 103fig.9.1, 104fig.9.2, 107, 110
Free association, 52, 85, 131, 223, 402, 431, 495, 565, 583, 853
Free motoric development, 383–85
Freedom, 97, 917–18
Freeze response, 620
Freudian theory, 49, 51, 63, 87, 89
Friction, 63
Frustration, 53
Function relaxation, 103fig.9.1
Functional approach, 660–62
Functional body psychotherapy, 31, 104fig.9.2

Functional capacity, 15
Functional integration. *See* Feldenkrais-Method, 876–77
Functional perspectives, 596–614
Functional relaxation, 11, 24–25, 26
Functional-developmental orientation, 14–15
Functionalism, 92, 115
Fundamental actions, 361–62
Fundamental perspectives, 111fig.9.7, 114–16

Gastrointestinal ulcers, 751–53
Genetics, 129
Genital character, 53
Genital sensory maturation, 293–94
German expressionist dance, 850–51
Gestalt circle theory, 24
Gestalt therapy, 3, 4, 11, 16, 24, 29, 30, 44, 64–65, 97, 105fig.9.3, 110, 111fig.9.7, 114, 863–70
Gestalt tradition, 88, 94
Gesture, 5, 463–64, 559, 809
"Get off my back" practice, 561
Gindler work, 40–45, 64–65
Global organismal regulation systems, 67
Global physiological regulation systems, 67
Golden age of body psychotherapy, 62, 65–68, 71–74
Gratifications, 215–16
Grief work, 760
Grounding, 26, 27, 128, 561, 568, 733–35
  horizontal, 675–83
  vertical, 684–90
Group energy, 823–24
Group therapy, 111fig.9.7, 816–31
Groupwork. *See* Group therapy
Growth, 446, 787–88
Gut brain, 128, 136–37
Gymnastics, 23–25, 63, 106fig.9.4, 107, 108fig.9.5
  harmonious, 40–41

Gymnastics pedagogy, 106fig.9.4, 108fig.9.5

Habitual forms, psychosomatic, 729–30
Hakomi method, 13, 30, 103fig.9.1, 104fig.9.2, 115, 279–80, 303tab.28.3
Hands-on approaches, 872–82
Harmonische gymnastik, 40–41
*Having a body*, 395–96
Headaches, 64, 749–51
Heart, 644–50
Hebb's axiom, 130
Hellerwork, 11
Helplessness, 759
Here-and-now psychotherapy, 91
Hierarchy, 185–86
Hippie movement, 57
Holding patterns, 566–68, 666–74
Holes, personality, 399–400
Holistic perspective, 487, 892–93
Holistic psycho-physiology, 65
Holotropic breathwork, 31
Homeostasis, 63, 65, 67, 68
Horizontal grounding, 675–83
Hostility, 52
Human interaction models, 63
Human potential movement, 6, 28, 97
Humanistic perspective, 28–31, 91, 817
Humanistic psychology, 6, 21, 29, 57, 78, 97, 103fig.9.1, 110, 111fig.9.7
Humanistic psychotherapy, 12, 28, 30
Hypertonia, 67, 110
Hyperventilation, 637–39
Hypnosis, 84, 85
Hypnotherapy, 104fig.9.2
Hypotonia, 67
Hypoventilation, 639–40
Hysteria, 49, 63, 79, 85, 88, 96
Hysterical character, 53, 280, 302tab.28.1

Illusions, 757
Imagery, 662–63
Imagination, 30, 782–83
Immediacy, 471–77
Implicit memory, 2, 14
Implicit relational knowing, 90, 129
Imprints, 336, 338–39
Impulses, 23
Impulsive characters, 53
Inappropriate (or malign) regression, 591–92
Individual/collective polarity, 817–18
Induction, 340
Infant development, 2, 78, 91, 129
Infant meaning-making systems, 349–50
Infant research, 94, 104fig.9.2, 109fig.9.6, 857–58
Infantile roots of sexuality, 696–98
Infants, 380, 776–84, 891–96
  Behavioral Competence, 380
  development, 2, 78, 91, 129
  Early infant Contact Disturbances, 280–83
  meaning-making systems, 349–50
  Orgonomic Infant Research Center, 78
  Parent-Infant Body Psychology, 780–84
  research, 32, 94, 104fig.9.2, 109fig.9.6, 857–58
  sexuality, 696–98
Information theory, 14
Inhibited conditions, 707–8
Inhibition, 14, 88
Inhibitory regulation, 290–93
Initiatic somatic therapy, 103fig.9.1
Inner fire practice, 923–25
Inner nature, 908–9
Inner representations, 287–89
Insecure attachment, 374–75
Insensitivity, 707–8
Insides experience, 610–11
Insight blockage, 550
Integrated breath therapy, 104fig.9.2

Integrated respiration therapy, 66
Integration, 628, 820, 854, 893–94
Integrative body psychotherapy, 44, 104fig.9.2, 115
Integrative body therapy, 9, 30, 89, 103fig.9.1
Intentional aspects, 178fig.15.1
Interaction analysis, 857–58
Interactions, 305–18, 361–62, 576
Interindividual regulation, 67
Internalizations, 370–72
Internal-subjective perspective, 258
Interpersonal theory, 33, 92, 105fig.9.3, 827–28
Interpretations, 255
Intersubjectivity, 91, 721–22
Interventions, 32, 553–69
Intimacy, 471–77
Intrapsychic conflict, 88
Involuntary movement, 121–22
I-Thou modality, 29, 455

Jacoby-Gindler work, 41
Jellyfish, 560–61
Judo, 105fig.9.3
Jungian analysis, 32, 43, 44, 122

KBT (Konzentrative Bewegungstherapie). See Concentrative Movement Therapy (CMT)
Kindling, 140
Kinesthetic awareness, 7
Knowing, 7, 260–61
Knowing body, 13–14, 260–61
Knowledge, 83, 260–61

Latent doubt, 52
Learnable facility, 408
Learning, 13, 130, 131–32
Lebensreform (life reform) movement. See Life Reform movement, 103
Lebens-schule (school of life), 42–43
Lethargy, 707–8
Liberation, 25–28
Libido, 25–28, 48, 76, 163–65, 580–86

Libido theory, 30, 49
Life against death, 445–46
Life energy, 77
Life philosophy, 104fig.9.2
Life Reform movement, 5, 10, 20, 21, 23, 24, 95–96, 97, 103
Life teaching, 106fig.9.4
Life themes, 916–19
Life-deprived, partially, 445
Limbic system, 2, 127–29, 284–87
Lingering, 15
Live experience, 803–4
Lived body, 382–83
Liveliness, 925–26
Living systems approach, 176–77
Location, 609–10
Lodzy home, 106fig.9.4, 108fig.9.5
Lomi school, 104fig.9.2, 111fig.9.7
Looking, 26
Loss, sense of, 760
Loss of contact, 399–400
Love, lack of, 73
Lust, 49–50, 59

Maieutics, 160–61
Malign (or inappropriate) regression, 591–92
Mania, 242, 706
Manic-depressive dynamic, 758–59
Marxism, 25, 54, 55, 56–57
Masculine-aggressive woman, 53
Masochistic character structure, 53, 280, 290–93, 302tab.28.1, 303tab.28.3
Massage, 11, 13, 14, 26, 44, 58, 63, 66, 68, 86, 107, 110
Matching, 305–8. See also Mirroring
Matter, 903–4
Maturation, 16, 230–36, 293–94
Mature body, 230–33
Mature shape, 232–33
Mazdaznan, 106fig.9.4, 108fig.9.5
Meaning, 151–52, 422–23, 797
Meaning-making, 345–54
Meaning-making systems, 348–50

Medical-model conception, 485–86
Meditation, 921–26
Memory, 2, 23, 49, 52, 130–32, 255–57
Mental disorders, 704–14
Methodological foundations, overview, 390–91
Micro-tracking, 438–43
Middendorf breath work, 117
Migraines, 64
Mind/body dichotomy, 2
Mind-body psychotherapy, 633–43
Mindfulness, 2, 3, 28–31, 402–8, 731–32, 805–6
Mirror neurons, 140
Mirroring, 305, 798. See also Matching
Mistrust, 52
Mobility, 559
Modalities, 625
Moments of meeting, 797
Montessori school, 106fig.9.4, 108fig.9.5
Mood disorders
  depression, 241
  mania, 242
Morality, 79
Morpho-dynamics, 199–201
Mother-infant research, 94
Motivation, 366–76
Motivational systems, 91, 94, 329, 368–69
Motor patterns, 66
Motoric ego, 64
Motoric therapy, 68
Movable equilibrium, 24
Movement, 5, 28, 31, 361–62, 426–34, 790–91, 806–7
Movement analysis, 64, 106fig.9.4, 429–31, 539, 858–59
Movement in depth. See Authentic Movement
Movement observation, 429–31
Movement therapy, 24, 30, 428–29, 431–34

Moving cycles, 426, 431, 432
Muscle tone, 15, 686–87
Muscular armoring, 29, 57–59
Mutual regulation, 733–35
Mycoplasmas (t-bacilli), 75

Narcissism, 95–97, 737–45
Negative experience, 129
Neglect, 223, 725–27
Neonatal development, 280–83
Neo-Reichian tradition, 11, 25–26, 29, 30, 31, 88
Nervous system, 600–614
Neuroaffective development, 277–80, 285, 294, 296, 298
Neurobiology, 2, 93, 106fig.9.4, 126–44, 178fig.15.1, 346–47, 361–62, 613, 857–58
Neuroplasticity, 129–30, 223, 352
Neuropsychology, 3
Neuroscience, 71, 88, 106fig.9.4, 219–28, 277–97, 621–22, 838–39
Neurotic character structures, 53, 205–8
Neurotransmitters, 514
Neurovegetative reactions, 2, 31
New Age movement, 11
New counseling, 44
New identity group process, 27
New learning, 215–16
Nonverbal processes, 5, 15, 804–5
Norwegian tradition, 21, 26, 31, 47, 62–68
Nuclear radiation, 79

Object relations tradition, 2, 91, 93
Object relationship theory, 32–33, 90–94, 109fig.9.6
Ocular segment, 658–64, 669, 670–71
Oedipus complex, 55, 739
One-and-a-half-person psychology, 455–56, 483–85
One-person psychology, 13, 29, 455
Oral character structure, 27, 280, 303tab.28.3, 707–8

Oral depression, 756–62
Oral segment, 669, 671
Oral somatic pattern, 287
Oral-compensated, 303tab.28.3
Oral-depressive structures, 284–87
Oral-paranoid structures, 284–87
Orbitofrontal elation, 287–89
Organismic energy, 77
Organismic psychotherapy, 26, 103fig.9.1, 104fig.9.2
Organismic regulation, 624
Organismic relaxation, 25
Organismic rhythms, 78
Organismic theory, 111fig.9.7
Organization paradigms, 170–71
Organization revealed, 182
Organizational failure, 185–86
Organizing experience, 179–80
"Organizing in", 181
"Organizing out", 182–83
Organizing transference, 181–82
Orgasm function, 49
Orgasm reflex, 59
Orgasm theory, 50–52
Orgasmic cycle, 823
Orgiastic reflex, 66, 584–85
Orgiastic impotence, 697fig.68.1
Orgiastic potency, 50, 59, 63, 697fig.68.1
Orgon therapy, 104fig.9.2
Orgone box, 73
Orgone energy, 26, 71, 75–76, 77–78, 79, 80, 163–65
Orgone energy accumulator, 75, 76, 77–78, 79, 80
Orgone radiation, 76
Orgone therapy, 26, 77, 103fig.9.1, 104fig.9.2, 110
Orgonon research institute, 78, 79, 80
Osteopathy, 106fig.9.4, 108fig.9.5
Oxytocin, 512–13

Pace, 806–7
Paradoxical breathing, 86

Parasympathetic nervous system, 68, 611–12, 619–20
Parent-child body psychotherapy, 32–33, 776–78, 779–80, 834–40
Parent-child relationship, 32, 55, 94
Parent-infant body psychology, 780–84
Parents, 776–84
Passive-feminine man, 53
Pathology, 328–29
Patterns, 130, 199–201, 340, 356–64, 827–28
Patterns, defense, 52, 53
Patterns, psychomotor, 26
Patterns, resistance. *See* character structures
Patterns, segmental holding, 666–74
Peekaboo, 347–48
Pelvic segment, 669, 673–74
Penetration experience type, 697fig.68.1
Perception, 5, 95, 128, 133–34, 548–50
Perinatal care, 78
Perinatal psychology, 2, 109fig.9.6, 332–41, 679
Perinatal traumatization, 32
Peristaltic movements, 67, 68
Personality, 86–87, 97
Personality disorders, 90, 243, 713–14
Personality psychology, 168–69
Personality systems, 329
Person-centered therapy, 91
Personhood, 93, 472–73
Petrissage, 63
Phallic
  phallic-narcissistic character, 53, 302tab.28.1
  rigid-hysteric, 280
  rigid-phallic, 280, 294–96, 303tab.28.3
Phallic-narcissistic character, 53, 302tab.28.1
Phallic-narcissistic, 53, 302tab.28.1
Phallic-rigid, 280, 294–96

Phenomenology, 7, 13, 30, 96, 111fig.9.7, 148–61, 609–13, 916–19
Philanthropism, 106fig.9.4, 108fig.9.5
Philosophy, 30, 83, 95, 103, 103fig.9.1, 109fig.9.6, 496
Physical defensive responses, 765–66
Physical re-education, 44
Physiology, 59
Physiotherapy, 65, 67
Piaget's intelligence theory, 63
Pikler model, 383–85
Plasticity, 129–30, 223, 352, 356–64
Play, 790–91, 857
Pleasure, 66n12, 97
Pleasure arousal, 59, 72
Polarizations, 12, 649–50
    Individual/Collective polarity, 817–18
    power differential/equality, 818–19
    structured groupwork/unstructured space polarity, 819–20
Positive body management, 891–96
Positive experiences, 129
Postmodernism, 97, 114
Postnatal psychology, 679–80
Post-traumatic stress disorders, 139–40
Postural integrative psychotherapy, 11
Postures, 5, 23, 31, 58, 544, 807
Power differential, 818–19
Practices, 553–69
Prenatal care, 78
Prenatal development, 280–83
Prenatal psychology, 2, 109fig.9.6, 332–41, 678
Prenatal therapy, 109fig.9.6
Prenatal traumatization, 32
Preoccupation, 372–73
Preparatory practices, 557
Presence, 658–64
Present-time experience, 132–33
Pressure points, 58
Presymbolic space, 261–62
Pre-verbal domains, 2, 5
Pre-verbal experiences, 94

Pre-verbal phases, 88
Pre-verbal space, 261–62
Primal therapy, 27, 89
Primary needs, 53
Primary regulatory networks, 353, 353fig.32.2
Procedural memory, 2, 14, 640–41
Process flow, 809–10
Process oriented psychotherapy, 13, 31, 563–65
Projection, 826–27
Proprioceptive sense, 25
Proto-self, 12
Pruning, 130
Psyche and soma, overview, 194–96
Psychoanalysis, 22–23, 30, 31, 32–33, 41, 42, 47–49, 52, 53, 54–55, 56, 57, 63, 66, 84–85, 86, 87–88, 89, 91, 92, 93, 95, 97, 103fig.9.1, 105fig.9.3, 109fig.9.6, 110
Psychodrama, 3, 7, 28, 29, 111fig.9.7
Psychodynamic psychology, 3–4, 7, 21, 33, 83–84, 87, 94–95, 96–97, 837–38
Psychodynamic unconscious, 219–28
Psycho-motor retardation, 707–8
Psycho-motor therapy, 26, 30, 32
Psycho-motoric education, 31, 67
Psychomotricité, 106fig.9.4, 108fig.9.5, 110
Psychoneuroendocrinology, 510–14
Psycho-neurotic fear, 50
Psycho-organic analysis, 9, 104fig.9.2
Psychopathic, 280
Psychopathic 1, 303tab.28.3
Psychopathic 2, 303tab.28.3
Psychopathic somatic structure, 289–90
Psychopathic structure, 287–89
Psychopathology, 65
Psychopaths, 53
Psycho-peristalsis, 67, 68
Psycho-physical functions, 31
Psycho-physical structure formation, 720–21

Psycho-physiology, 63, 65
Psycho-sexual development stages, 91
Psychosis, 717–22
Psychosomatic disorders, 77, 748–54, 895–96
Psychosomatic functional systems, 15
    autonomic nervous system, 15
    flexibility, bodily, 15
    muscle tone, 15
    respiration, 15
    sexual potency, 15
    sexual sensitivity, 15
    vision, 15
Psychosomatic habitual forms, 729–30
Psychosomatics, 106fig.9.4
Psychotherapeutic field, 88
Psychotherapists, 489–90
Psychotherapy
    and body psychotherapy, 11–13
    defined, 11
    Experience in, 419–20
Psychotonics, 106fig.9.4, 108fig.9.5

Radix emotional work, 26
Rating systems, 137–39
Reality, 97, 128, 129, 760–61
Reassimilation, 93, 151
Rebirthing, 27
Reciprocal inspirations, 103fig.9.1
Recollection, 130–31
Reform pedagogy, 103fig.9.1
Refusals, somatic, 214–15
Regeneration blockage, 550
Regression, 15–16, 571–78, 591–92, 828–29
Regulation, 33, 67, 94, 730
    dysregulation, 766–67
Regulation, dyadic, 732–33
Regulation, mutual, 733–35
Regulation, self. *See* self-regulation
Rehabilitation, 89
Reichian tradition, 11, 13, 14, 26, 30, 47–60, 67, 71–81, 88, 107, 206fig.18.1, 625

Reimportation, 850–51
Reinforcement, 129
Rejection, 73
Relating, 457, 465–67, 838
Relational approach, 461–69, 539–40, 660–62
Relational modalities, 456–57, 479–83
Relational psychoanalysis, 91
Relational trauma, 91
Relationships, 28–31, 171–72, 201–3, 791–92
Relationships, therapeutic, 224–25, 454–59, 471–77
Relaxation, 25, 32, 41, 65n11, 67, 68, 550, 620, 697fig.68.1, 781
Reorganization, 183–85, 729–30
Reparative (developmentally needed) modality, 456
Representations, 324–26
Representations of interactions (RIPs), 94
Repression, 14, 23, 27, 52, 63, 67, 87, 760–61. *See also* Defense
Research, 33, 834–39
   Applications, 834–40
   Attachment styles, 375–76
   biological, 72
   bion research work, 73
   Bodily Experience, 243–44
   Body Regression, 575–76, 577–78
   brain, 886–89
   coding systems, 68
   developmental-psychological, 33
   early trauma, 341
   Energy Concept, 172–73
   infant, 32, 94
   infants, 32, 94, 104fig.9.2, 109fig.9.6, 857–58
   Integration, 628
   Psychosis, 722
   Scientific, 837–39
   Touch therapies, 503, 515
Residues, 216
Resignation, 76
Resistance, 23, 30, 52, 58

Resistance analysis, 29
Resonance dimensions, 201–3
Respiration, 15, 781–82
Retraumatization, 587–89
Revelations, 471–72
Reward system, 137–39
Rhythmic gymnastics, 105fig.9.3, 106fig.9.4, 108fig.9.5
Rhythmic-dynamic active dialogue, 857–58
Rigid structure, 302tab.28.2
Rigid structures, 293–94
Rigid-hysteric, 280, 303tab.28.3
Rigid-phallic, 280, 303tab.28.3
Rigid-phallic somatic pattern, 294–96
RIGs (representations of interactions), 94
Risks, 587–93
   retraumatization, 587–89
Rolfing, 106fig.9.4, 108fig.9.5, 117
Rosen method, 44
Rotenburger breath school, 106fig.9.4, 108fig.9.5
Rubenfeld synergy method, 626, 878–81

Sadness, 707–8
Safe context, 472–73
Safe holding environment, 26
Salutogenic model, 891–96
Scenarios, 155–60
Schema, 324–26
Schema concept, 322–24
Schizoid (hysteric), 280
Schizoid somatic pattern, 283–84, 303tab.28.3
Schizoid-hysteric traits, 280–84
Schizophrenic character structure, 73
Schizophrenic disorders, 86, 711–13
Schizophreniform disorders, 243
Secondary drive, 53
Second-person perspective, 258
Security, 782, 916
Seduction theory, 88–89
Segmental holding patterns, 666–74

Segments, 749–54
Self, 127–28, 613, 687–89, 787–88, 906–7
Self psychology, 91, 109fig.9.6, 857–58
Self-actualization, 29, 78, 111fig.9.7
Self-assertion, 561
Self-awareness, 128, 556–57, 622–23
Self-conscious ego, 205–8
Self-degradation crises, 708–9
Self-determination, 13, 97
Self-development, somatic, 788–90
Self-discovery, 557–58
Self-efficacy, 380, 383–85
Self-esteem crises, 708–9
Self-exploration, therapeutic, 3, 4–5
Self-expression, 97, 559, 757–58
Self-forming, 231–32
Self-healing, 107
Self-image, 130, 856–57
Self-organization, 179–80
Self-perception, 259–60, 560
Self-psychology, 97
Self-realization, 78
Self-realization, free, 78–79
Self-regulation, 13, 25, 59, 63, 68, 78, 79, 128, 583–84, 623–24, 730, 733–35
Sense-ability, 560
Senses, 130
Sensing, 7, 15, 43
Sensing the self, 560
Sensorimotor psychotherapy, 626–27
Sensory awareness, 11, 24, 43, 44, 106fig.9.4, 108fig.9.5
Sensory awareness foundation, 45, 117
Sensory awareness method, 875–76
Sensory self-reflexivity, 392–400
Sensory-motor organization, 66
Sensory-motor processing, 763–69
Sensory-motor systems, 66
Seventh sense, 518–19
Severe mental disorders, 704–14
Sex hormones, 293–94
Sex-economy theory, 49, 50–51, 53, 72

Sexology, 63, 66
Sexual abuse, 89
Sexual movements, 697fig.68.1
Sexual politics, 25, 104fig.9.2
Sexual potency, 15
Sexual repression, 23, 25
Sexual science of berlin, 104fig.9.2
Sexual sensitivity, 15
Sexual stasis, 76
Sexuality, 27, 48, 50, 55–56, 59, 63, 72, 76, 87, 96, 97, 692–99, 760–61
Sexual-political movement, 55–56
Situational body, 249–51
Social hysteria, 79
Social nervous system, 620–22
Social parameters, 97
Social repression, 89
Social structures, 178fig.15.1
Socialism, 54, 56, 57, 65, 110
Sociology, 54, 792
Soma semantics, 197–203
Somatic analytic approaches, 210–11
Somatic attunement, 29
Somatic authenticity, 449
Somatic character structure, 277–97
Somatic defenses, 214–15, 544–45
Somatic developmental character structure, 279–80
Somatic dimension, 274–76, 471–77
Somatic education, 20, 115
Somatic emotional co-regulation, 94
Somatic emotional release work, 872–82
Somatic experience, 12, 44, 627–28
Somatic exploration, 5
Somatic interventions, 802–10
Somatic patterns, 14
Somatic psychology, 17, 40, 45, 122–24
Somatic psychotherapy, 44
Somatic reclaiming, 40, 44
Somatic representations, 212–13
Somatic residues, 216
Somatic resonance, 29
Somatic schemas, 884–85

Somatic self-development, 230–36, 788–90
Somatic subjectivity, 232
Somatic theories, 457
Somatic transference dynamics, 732–33
Somatic unconscious identity, 213–14
Somatics, 104fig.9.2, 509–15
Somatoanalysis, 31, 104fig.9.2
Somtaform disorders, 33
Space, 382–83, 467–69, 819–20
Spirit, 903–4
Spiritual consciousness, 904–5
Spiritual development, 903–11
Spiritual dimension, 900–901, 903–11
Spiritual realization, 907–8
Spiritual traditions, 30, 105fig.9.3
Spiritual work, 905
Stalinism, 56
Startle reflex, 66
Stasis anxiety, 51
Stimulation, 130
Strategies of power, 83
Stress, 76, 328–29
Stress exploration, 780–81
Stress positions, 14
Stress response, 619–20
Stress system, 138–39
Stretching, 15
Structural analysis, 534–36
Structural disorders, 95
Structural integration, 873–74
Structural levels, 328–29
Structure, 396–98
Stutter-step attunement, 448–49
Subjective anatomy theory, 91
Subjective awareness, 15
Subjective experience, 169–70
Subsymbolic processing, 794–800
Sufism, 105fig.9.3
Suicide, 759–60
Summerhill school, 65, 104fig.9.2
Supervision, 479–92
Support, 916–17
Suppression, 53, 58, 76, 89, 129

Surrender, 583–85, 695–96, 698–99
Swedish massage, 63, 117
Swollen structure, 302tab.28.2
Symbolization, 422–23. *See also* object relations
Sympathetic nervous system, 59, 68, 612–13, 619–20
Symptomatology, 759
Synchronicity, 130
Synchronization. *See* Mirroring
Systemic synthesis, 186–87
Systems theory, 30, 31, 178fig.15.1

Talk limitations, 127
Taoism, 30, 105fig.9.3, 149, 165, 166, 633
Tapotement, 63
*Tasten* (sensing the way), 41
T-bacilli (mycoplasmas), 75
Tension, 49–50, 58–59, 807
Tension-charge formula, 50, 72
Terror, 72, 73, 784
Thalamus, 66n12
Theater, 103fig.9.1, 106fig.9.4, 108fig.9.5
Theme-centered interaction, 24, 111fig.9.7
Theory divergence, 556
Theory formation, 33
Therapeutic action, 392–400
Therapeutic practice, 743–45
Therapeutic process, 720–22, 760–61
Therapeutic relatedness, 457, 465–67
Therapeutic relationships, 32, 454–59, 471–77, 761–62
Therapeutic reorganization, 183–85
Therapeutic space, 467–69
Therapeutic technique, 52
Therapeutic transformation, 90
Third-person perspective, 257–58
Thoracic segment, 669, 671–72
Tibetan Buddhist mediations, 921–26
Titration, 640–41
Tolerance, window of, 766–67
Toques sutis (fine touching), 31–32

Touch, 26, 27–28, 63, 66, 68, 86, 96, 130, 494–504, 509–15, 782
Touch, abusive, 28, 589
Touch, fine (toques sutis), 31–32
Touch benefits, 498
Touch debate, 494–96
Touch therapies, 45
Touch types, 496–98
Touch/no touch polarity, 15, 23
Trajectories, 446–47
Transcultural perspective, 891–96
Transference, 29, 52, 67, 93, 224–25, 479–92, 828–29
Transference dynamics, 728–29
Transference modality, 456
Transformation, 96
Transforming experience, 423–24
Transmarginal stress, 91
Trauma, 52, 85–86, 223, 339, 341, 719–20
Trauma, relational, 91
Trauma recovery, 763–69
Trauma therapy, 16, 33, 44, 90, 91, 104fig.9.2, 107, 689–90
Traumatic experiences, 2, 15, 88–90, 518–28
Traumatic stress, 619–20
Traumatic symbolization, 729
Traumatization, 89, 519
   prenatal and perinatal, 32
   Retraumatization, 587–89
Treatment concepts, 13, 705–14
Treatment effectiveness, 834–36

Treatment methodologies, 727–28
Treatment modality, 455
Treatment orientation, 13
Trobriand islanders, 55
Truth, 83, 255–62
Two-person psychology, 455

Umbilical-cord trauma, 339
Unconscious, 5, 32, 581–82
Unconscious, embodied, 209–17, 219–28
Unconscious conflict, 23
Unconscious processes, 2, 485
Unconventional energies, 166–68
Unethical practices, 500–501
Unitive psychology, 30, 103fig.9.1, 104fig.9.2, 109fig.9.6, 115
Unwanted, 336–38

Vacuum-extraction delivery, 339
Vagal experience, 611
Vaginismus, 753–54
Validation, 130
Vasomotoric cycles, 26, 625
Vegetative affects, 546–47
Vegetative arousal, 2
Vegetative domain, 2
Vegetative reactions, 549fig.53.1-53.2
Vegetotherapy, 23, 25–26, 31, 59, 64, 65, 68, 76, 86, 103fig.9.1, 104fig.9.2, 748–54. *See also* Functional Body Psychotherapy

Vertebral movement organization, 357–58
Vertical grounding, 684–90
Vibration, 63, 562
Visual contact, 658–64
Vitality, 27, 444–50, 558
Vitality affects, 88
Vitality contours, 153, 447
Vitality psychology, 169–70
Voluntary effort, 231–32
Voluntary movement, 121

Wanted, 336–38
West coast approach, 851–53
Wilhelm Reich archives, 81
Window of tolerance, 766–67
Withdrawal, 76
Work democracy, 73, 124
Working alliance, 456
Working through processes, 16, 23, 88, 94
World knot, 83
Worth, 918–19
Wounding, 91, 93, 94, 490–93

Yielding, 357
Yoga, 105fig.9.3, 106fig.9.4, 731–32

Zeitgeist, 48, 87, 95, 96, 97
Zen Buddhism, 43, 105fig.9.3